THE ANNOTATED™
Shakespeare

THE ANNOTATED™
Shakespeare

VOLUME III

The Tragedies and Romances

*Edited, with Introductions, Notes,
and Bibliography by*

A. L. ROWSE

Clarkson N. Potter, Inc./Publishers New York
DISTRIBUTED BY CROWN PUBLISHERS, INC.

Annotated, illustrated and designed by
Octavian Books Limited
Copyright © 1978 Orbis Publishing Limited

Published simultaneously in Great Britain by
Orbis Publishing Limited, 20–22 Bedfordbury,
London WC2

FIRST EDITION

Printed in the U.S.A.

Library of Congress Cataloging in Publication Data
Shakespeare, William, 1546–1616.
    The annotated Shakespeare
    Bibliography: p.
    CONTENTS: v. 1. Comedies.—v. 2. Histories.—
v. 3. Tragedies and romances.
    I. Rowse, Alfred Leslie 1903–   II. Title.
PR2754.R67   822.3'3   78-12271
ISBN 0-517-53509-2 ISBN 0-517-535084 (v. 3.)

Annotation and introduction text composed by
SX Composing Ltd., Rayleigh, Essex

The Shakespeare text used in this edition is that of the
Globe Edition (edited by William George Clark and
William Aldis Wright), Macmillan, 1900

CONTENTS

Shakespeare's Tragedies & Romances

EACH AGE FLATTERS ITSELF that it understands the past better than its predecessors have done. But I think that we in our time do understand the Elizabethan age better than the Victorians did, for not the best of reasons. The Victorians enjoyed a blissful period of security, exceptional in human history, such as the Elizabethans did not have and we can never hope to enjoy.

Our very insecurity, the sense of contingency upon which all life hangs, the clouds hanging over humanity in our time, the nuclear threat to life on the planet, give us better – or, rather, worse – reason for understanding the tragic depiction of life in Shakespeare's greatest works.

For it is as a tragic dramatist that he is most highly appreciated – or at least, since he shines equally in comedy, history and romance, it is the great tragedies that are regarded as his highest achievement.

It is all the more remarkable since his first gift seems to have been for comedy – a euphoric, merry spirit. His earliest attempt at tragedy, *Titus Andronicus*, was visibly not natural to him and went rather against the grain. The author was not involved by its blood-curdling horrors – he was merely engaged in going one better than his model, Thomas Kyd. And yet, as with all the early work, one glimpses the elastic potentialities of finer things to come with maturity.

Experience deepened, and certainly darkened, his view of life and the character of mankind, until we reach the despairing depiction of *King Lear* and the disillusionment of *Timon of Athens*. From the time of *Julius Caesar* and *Hamlet* there are no illusions; after *Timon* there was nothing for it but to turn to the consoling world of fantasy and romance.

We come to a more specific reason for our understanding his tragedies better. With our remarkable advances in modern psychology – though experience could have told us – we no longer expect consistency or much reason from human beings. Shakespeare has often been criticised for improbability or inconsistency – and Bradley, in a celebrated monument to dead Victorian rationalism, struggled in vain, like a good man struggling with sin, to reduce Shakespearean tragedy to a system of ethics.

Let us be quite clear: there is a firm moral background to Shakespeare's thought, but

Opposite:
Frontispiece to the Tragedies volume The Complete Works of Shakespeare, *edited by J. O. Halliwell, 1853*

it is that of the Elizabethans, not the Victorians. And he was not one to challenge the accepted code, the norms and beliefs, of the age – unlike Marlowe, and *he* died young. Shakespeare was a maturer spirit, with a vein of scepticism, like Montaigne, who also conformed. It is sometimes the subtler spirit who conforms.

On the superficial question of probability or improbability, of course it is true – as the American critic, Edgar Stoll, never tired of enforcing – that the Elizabethans did not go to the theatre to see what was probable: they preferred the improbable, the exciting and sensational, the truly dramatic. There *are*, however, murderers, like Richard III or Macbeth; psychotics like Leontes; evil men like Iago, who hate others' happiness; or foolish old men like Lear, who give away all they have and then expect gratitude. There are even such women as Goneril and Regan. Oddly enough, a case of their kind happened about the time of the play. Sir William Harvey married Cordelia, the youngest daughter of Sir Brian Annesley, an old gentleman Pensioner (body-guard) of Queen Elizabeth. His two elder daughters had sought to have him 'agnominated' a lunatic to get his property.[1]

But we must dig deeper, for Shakespeare moves along deeper levels of the human spirit in his tragedies.

He strains his situations to the utmost limit, not only for the purpose of achieving sensation in the theatre – though there is no doubt as to the effectiveness of that: nothing in the history of drama is more thrilling or more dire than the ominous developments of *Macbeth*, *Othello*, or *Hamlet*. We derive a clue from the observation of a short-story writer of genius, Flannery O'Connor, that it is at moments of emergency, of extreme tension, that people reveal their true character. Thus it is that we recognise in the theatre, and carry away from it, the essential *truth* of the characters – that this is the way Macbeth or Lady Macbeth would have behaved, when Shakespeare has heightened and exaggerated the tension beyond the historical fact or even what was necessary to account for it.

Robert Bridges perceived that: 'his success depends on the power and skill with which this character is chosen and enforced upon the audience; for it is when their minds are preoccupied with his personality that the actions follow as unquestionable realities, and, in *Macbeth*, even preordained and prophesied'. Bridges, as a Victorian, was shocked by the lengths to which Shakespeare would go (his own classic closet-dramas are utterly dead).

For Shakespeare, with his unparalleled observation of human nature, intuited the workings of the subconscious and unconscious, and is closely corroborated by the findings of modern psychology. And he prefigures these in his dramatic art, above all in the tragedies. People have been accustomed till recently to think that moral character was all of a piece, simple and integrated. 'But in life, as we know, perhaps every personality is in some degree dissociated; and this fact of universal significance, which is given gross expression in certain pathological states, often finds a species of covert (and perhaps obscurely cathartic or therapeutic) release in art.'[2]

In everyone there are these recesses, these dark forces, ready to spring out, given the circumstances. A time which has witnessed the horrors of Belsen and Auschwitz, the mass-murders of Communist Russia or China, let alone of darkest Africa, need have no difficulty in recognising the truth of Shakespeare's revelation of what lurks beneath the surface, smiling or unsmiling. A Jewish critic observes perceptively that we all have a touch of paranoia in us. We are all (or almost all) capable of anything, when the bonds of customary civilised behaviour are broken. Iago is not at all incredible, as so many good people have said. Othello already has the grounds of suspicion in him, as he himself owns pathetically: he is black, declined in the vale of years, and made a marriage

1. cf. my
*Shakespeare's
Southampton*

2. J. I. M.
Stewart,
*Character and
Motive in
Shakespeare*, 90.

which was contrary to the mores of Venice. Macbeth already had the murder in him: the evil spirits corroborated and confirmed his unconscious desires.

Most of these characters are unaware of the workings of their unconscious; certainly Othello and, pitifully, King Lear. Interestingly, Iago may very well have been self-aware – he was of the stuff of which such are made: a reason for his closing up at the end, with

> From this time forth I never will speak word.

Hamlet too was extremely self-aware: another reason why he speaks to us today more than any of Shakespeare's tragic heroes, or above any other of his characters. He is almost a symbol of modern man caught in his tragic fate and in his awareness of it.

Similarly Shakespeare reached down to profound archetypal situations: Hamlet's sexual revulsion from his mother; Leontes' sexual jealousy of his wife; Othello's killer-reaction to suspected infidelity. And the dramatist reaped the rewards of trusting to his intuitions. When Desdemona receives the shock of learning what Othello suspects, and answers Emilia's inquiry, 'Faith, half asleep', it is not insensibility but the numbness a woman feels from shock. When Coriolanus wants to fire the beloved city that has rejected him, his reaction is well known to contemporary psycho-analysis.

Above: Henry Irving as King Lear, Lyceum Theatre, London, 1892. Portrait by Sir Bernard Partridge (1861–1945)

Above left: Laurence Olivier as Macbeth, Old Vic Theatre, London, 1937

9

'Come Unto These Yellow Sands', The Tempest; *painting by Robert Huskisson* c. *1847*

Hence the universality of the appeal: the world bears witness to the truth to human nature of these depictions by the writer who knew it best and observed its operations most closely and intuitively. The setting and the trappings may be realistic enough, for his declared object was to hold the mirror up to nature; then he went further and deeper, always ready to follow his intuitions and clothe them with the splendour and terrors of his imagination.

As to the effect, there is no shadow of doubt. It reaches so deeply into such depths of our conscience, our sense of regret and remorse, guilt and grief, that sometimes one can hardly bear to look or hear the searching words that are being spoken. The tender heart of the great bully, Dr. Johnson, could not bear to think of the last scene of *Lear* with the old man carrying the dead body of Cordelia. Here we see the *ne plus ultra* of Shakespeare: all other versions of the story end happily; it was out of the rigour of his imaginative understanding that he saw that it could all end only thus.

This is why, as a writer, he has meant so much to the world, and to each one of us. And has no equal.

The Romances. We have observed how effectively, and how subtly, the very practical and successful man of the theatre responded to its demands, often with something new; but also how this most sensitive register of the age picked up what was in the air and being talked about. Thirdly, there are his own personal circumstances to consider, as with any writer, his inner development and inflexion, his own affections and choices that give a man's writing its individuality and character.

All these come together to form a last phase which it is convenient to subsume as 'the Romances'. We have seen that all through – at least since he matured and found his own style – Shakespeare broke the rules and transcended the boundaries. Indeed, in *Hamlet*, he specifically expressed disrespect for the rigid categories beloved of dull, prosaic people, Poloniuses. *Richard III*, for example, is melodramatic but also has elements of tragedy; some of the comedies tremble on the edge of the tragic, others are farces; some of the history plays are tragedies. Plays like *All's Well* and *Measure for Measure* all critics have been hard put to it to define, let alone categorise. The truth is, it is impossible to circumscribe him.

Now, in this last phase, he achieves something new – and again different. Though these four plays end happily enough, they have much that is melancholy and wistful, backward-looking and nostalgic, some tragedy mixed with comedy, some brutal realism with the pathos and sentiment, much poetry and music. Above all, these last plays are atmospherical; it is the atmosphere, touched with magic, that they have in common.

Externally, and dramaturgically, the old master was responding to the new demands of the Blackfriars theatre: new stage-conditions, indoors, more scenery and music, a more select audience demanding surprise, sentiment, fantasy, the improbable and unreal. This must have chimed with his own nature and aptitude, which had always leaned to the romantic (with his first mentors, Spenser and Sidney), not with Jonsonian realism and satire. Now, for the Blackfriars audience, he found kindred spirits among the younger generation to take up this side of his own more catholic and multifarious work: Beaumont and Fletcher, Massinger.

From the life of the time something came too: these plays are full of the sea, of sea-ventures and voyages, of losses and wrecks at sea, of travellers and movement – as were those years with the founding of Virginia (with which Blackfriars was closely in touch, through William Strachey), the colonies being sent out, the incursion in strength into the Mediterranean, the new voyages via the Cape to India.

These plays are full of findings as well as losses, lost children and wives found again, reconciliation and forgiveness, at the end perhaps farewell to his art. We are hardly at liberty to speculate from what depths in his personal life these things came, or to what they spoke in his own ambivalent experience. But the historian may point out that they coincide with his return to family life at Stratford, with which he had never lost touch, whatever had been his *égarements* in London. There, at home, life was being renewed for him in the birth of a little daughter (named Elizabeth, with what memories!) to his own daughter, Susanna, who took after him; and there was his faithful, silent wife waiting:

Ubera, tu mater, tu lac vitamque dedisti.

Titus Andronicus

1590-1

THIS PLAY IS SHAKESPEARE'S FIRST TRAGEDY, very much based on his school reading of Ovid and Seneca, filled with classical references and Latin tags, to show that, though not a university wit, he too was sufficiently learned. It is already strongly marked by Shakespearean characteristics: the masterly plotting, the use of rare impressive words – accite, affy, palliament; the vigorous attack, the rhetoric; in particular, the mingling of classical oratory with numerous country images. It is a countryman writing. The horrors, in which the newcomer strove to outdo Kyd – and succeeded – themselves come from classical sources: the story of Tereus and Philomela, the fearful banquet from Seneca's *Thyestes*. These things make the play repellent to modern taste, though it much appealed to Elizabethan. Shakespeare wrote them up from a distance, himself not engaged emotionally. But, after all, they are not much removed from the horrors of Belsen and Auschwitz in our own enlightened time. We must however view the play in its proper Elizabethan perspective.

Stage. It belongs to the early Elizabethan stage, which was dominated by Marlowe's *Tamburlaine* and *The Jew of Malta*, and by Kyd's *Jeronimo, or the Spanish Tragedy*, with the last two of which *Titus* has strong affinities. The most striking character in the piece, the villain Aaron the Moor, is suggested by Marlowe's Barabas. It is significant that, where Barabas has no love-interest, Shakespeare's Aaron is the lover of the Empress Tamora, who has a base black child by him. (The play has even a topical racialist interest today.) The feigned madness of *Titus* was suggested by Kyd's *Jeronimo*, which Shakespeare succeeded in equalling in popularity, to Ben Jonson's grumpy disapprobation from the superior vantage-ground of a quarter of a century later.

The play was good theatre – if to us horrid, with its murders on stage, the chaste Lavinia raped, tongue torn out and hands cut off so that she could neither tell nor write her tale; let alone the cannibal banquet *pour comble de tout*. The public wanted to read the play too: three quartos were printed in Shakespeare's lifetime – the first discovered only in ours. (So that we need not be surprised at discovering something new about Shakespeare.) From these imprints we learn that the play had been performed by the following Companies – Pembroke's (which was broken by the plague in 1593); Derby's (active between September 1593 and April 1594, though earlier as Lord Strange's); Sussex's; and the Lord Chamberlain's from the formation in the summer of 1594. This gives us some idea of the Companies Shakespeare was connected with, or writing for, before he betook himself and his plays to his permanent partnership with the Chamberlain's men.

Among the plays which were originally Pembroke's were *2* and *3 Henry VI*, which chime with *Titus*: there are verbal echoes, and both the third part of *Henry VI* and *Titus* are Revenge plays. In the last the wicked Empress Tamora – the Queen of the Goths whom the gulled Emperor Saturninus had married – appears disguised as Revenge, with her sons as Rape and Murder on either side. Shakespeare seems to have picked up the story from some chapbook, which got it from Italy, though the outlines were familiar enough. He garnished it from his classical schoolbooks, naïvely citing them and their tags on the stage:

> Titus: Lucius, what book is that she tosseth so?
> Boy: Grandsire, 'tis Ovid's Metamorphoses.

Again:

> Demetrius: What's here? a scroll, and written round about,
>   Let's see:
>   Integer vitae, scelerisque purus,
>   Non eget Mauri iaculis, nec arcu.
> Chiron: O, 'tis a verse in Horace; I know it well:
>   I read it in the Grammar long ago.

This is very much early Shakespeare – school was not far away as usher. There are many such classical clichés all the way through – no play has so many. Several times situations in the action remind us of Coriolanus: the election by the Romans of Titus, their general, for his good service against the Goths; he makes way for Saturninus as Emperor. Then, for all the wrongs put upon him, he goes over to the Goths against Rome:

> Who threats in course of this revenge, to do
> As much as ever Coriolanus did.

In fact, this play of a novice already foreshadows so much: Titus is a kind of Coriolanus; Aaron, the villain who is pure evil incarnate, looks forward to Iago; the racial theme to *The Merchant of Venice*; the ruthless Tamora to Lady Macbeth. And, if the stage ends up littered with dead bodies, so it does in *Hamlet*. The difference is that the tragedy in *Hamlet*, as in all the great tragedies, is *innerlich* and is borne home deeply to the emotions, where the impact of *Titus* is external. We may, however, suffer from shock: when performed in London, not long after the war and the revelations of Belsen, people went· out sick.

The Shakespearean Mixture. On his classical ground-work and the pseudo-classical basis of the story the actor-dramatist worked in his own Gothic enrichment, his recognisable imagery, phrasing and background. An extraordinary feature of the play, considering its nature, is the depiction of countryside, country sports and aspects

The black
American actor,
Ira Aldridge, as
Aaron in Titus
Andronicus,
Britannia Theatre,
1852

it contains. Had it been written at Stratford and brought up in the playing-fardel Greene gibed at? Tamora, somewhat improbably, waxes eloquent about countryside:

> The birds chant melody on every bush,
> The snake lies rollèd in the cheerful sun,
> The green leaves quiver with the cooling wind,
> And make a chequered shadow on the ground.

Nothing like that in Marlowe. And it is a prelude to a fond description of a deer-hunt, on which the countryman had a perfect fixation in all his early work. Nothing of that in the urban (but not urbane) Marlowe either.

> The hunt is up, the morn is bright and grey,
> The fields are fragrant and the woods are green.
> Uncouple here and let us make a bay.

Not only is the country everywhere in the background of this improbable play, but the countryman turned author betrays himself:

> What, hast thou not full often struck a doe,
> And borne her cleanly by the keeper's nose?

He seems to be on familiar terms with the operation. But he also knows, what we do not, things about country lore – that a surfeit of clover can be fatal to sheep. Red clover was known as 'honeysuckle' in Warwickshire, and we find that feeding 'honey-stalks' to sheep could end in their being 'rotted with delicious feed'. Or, rustic enmities could

> Make poor men's cattle break their necks;
> Set fire on barns and haystacks in the night.

Not much bawdy appears – in which he was to become such a virtuoso; but Lavinia does hail Tamora:

> Under your patience, gentle empress,
> 'Tis thought you have a goodly gift in horning,
> And to be doubted that the Moor and you
> Are singled forth to try experiments.
> Jove shield your husband from his hounds today!
> 'Tis pity they should take him for a stag –

i.e. with cuckold's horns. This was indeed to ask for trouble at Tamora's hands, though the come-uppance Lavinia received proved rather severe.

Background. Some touches of contemporary life appèar in this play loaded down with the classics. When Tamora's dreadful sons 'enter braving', Aaron cries,

> Clubs, clubs! these lovers will not keep the peace.

This was the regular cry at a street-brawl of the time to call the watch. And he reproaches them:

The first illustration to Shakespeare : Titus Andronicus *in performance* c. *1595. Drawing by Henry Peacham*

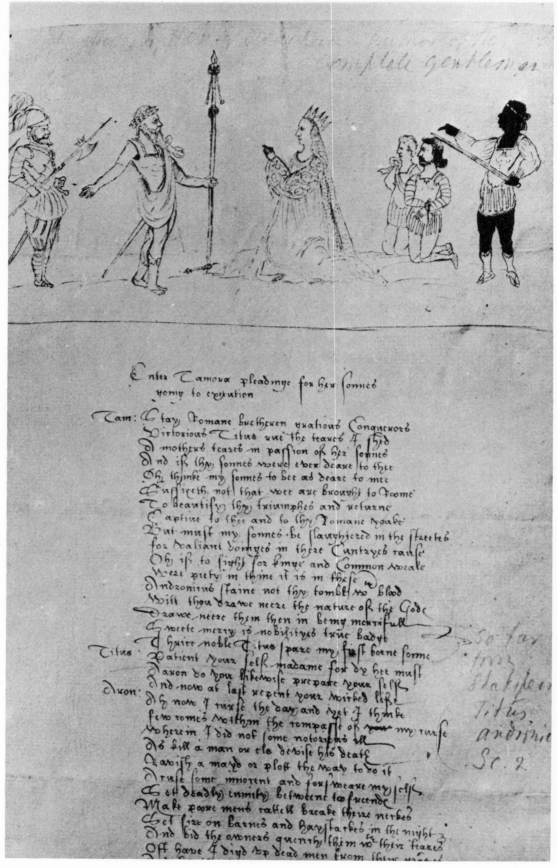

> So near the emperor's palace dare ye draw,
> And maintain such a quarrel openly!

It was a special offence to quarrel and draw swords within what was known as the verge of the Court. The base black child of Tamora and the Moor is incongruously thus found by a Goth:

> Renowned Lucius, from our troops I strayed
> To gaze upon a ruinous monastery . . .

Shakespeare must have seen many such as he toured the post-Dissolution countryside, with its wreckage – 'bare ruined choirs'; he had an eye for such things, overthrown monuments and ripped up brasses, 'slave to mortal rage'.

The Text of the play offers no problems, even that of the quartos. The stage-directions are full and 'suggest an author's hand', according to E. K. Chambers. The Folio printing was set up from the latest quarto of 1611, with the addition of a whole scene.

The first illustration of a Shakespeare play is of a scene from this one, in which Tamora kneels to Titus to spare her sons from execution, with speeches reproduced beneath. It is signed and dated by Henry Peacham, 1594 or 5. 'Who this Peacham was', says the Arden editor, 'we do not know'. On the contrary, he was the well known author of a standard book, *The Compleat Gentleman*, and is the subject of a full biography in the *Dictionary of National Biography*. In addition to writing much, 'he could paint, draw, and engrave portraits and landscapes', and he wrote a treatise on pen-drawing and limning in water-colours, published during Shakespeare's career, in 1606. There is no reason whatever why the depiction of the scene should not be authentic: misplaced scepticism is as absurd as superfluous conjectures.

TITUS ANDRONICUS.

DRAMATIS PERSONÆ.

SATURNINUS, son to the late Emperor of Rome, and afterwards declared Emperor.
BASSIANUS, brother to Saturninus; in love with Lavinia.
TITUS ANDRONICUS, a noble Roman, general against the Goths.
MARCUS ANDRONICUS, tribune of the people, and brother to Titus.
LUCIUS,
QUINTUS,
MARTIUS, } sons to Titus Andronicus.
MUTIUS,
YOUNG LUCIUS, a boy, son to Lucius.

PUBLIUS, son to Marcus the Tribune.
SEMPRONIUS,
CAIUS, } kinsmen to Titus.
VALENTINE,

ÆMILIUS, a noble Roman.
ALARBUS,
DEMETRIUS, } sons to Tamora.
CHIRON,
AARON, a Moor, beloved by Tamora.
A Captain, Tribune, Messenger, and Clown; Romans.
Goths and Romans.

TAMORA, Queen of the Goths.
LAVINIA, daughter to Titus Andronicus.
A Nurse.

Senators, Tribunes, Officers, Soldiers, and Attendants.

SCENE: *Rome, and the country near it.*

● *A bullet beside a text line indicates an annotation in the opposite column.*

ACT I.

SCENE I. *Rome. Before the Capitol.*

The Tomb of the ANDRONICI *appearing; the* Tribunes *and* Senators *aloft. Enter, below, from one side,* SATURNINUS *and his* Followers; *and, from the other side,* BASSIANUS *and his* Followers; *with drum and colours.*

Sat. Noble patricians, patrons of my right,
Defend the justice of my cause with arms,
And, countrymen, my loving followers,
Plead my successive title with your swords:
I am his first-born son, that was the last
That wore the imperial diadem of Rome;

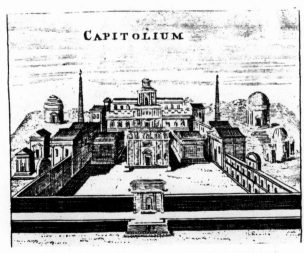

The Capitol. Engraving from Basil Kennett's *Romae Antiquae Notitia*, 1769

Opposite: Aaron defends his child. Painting by Thomas Kirk (1765–1797)

11 *gracious*. Readily accepted.

15 *continence*. Self-control.

19 *empery*. Empire.

27 *accited*. Summoned.

42 *pretend*. Claim.

Laurence Olivier as Titus Andronicus, Stratford-upon-Avon, 1955

47 *affy*. Trust.

61 *confident*. Trusting.

Then let my father's honours live in me,
Nor wrong mine age with this indignity.
   Bas.   Romans, friends, followers, favourers of
    my right,
If ever Bassianus, Cæsar's son,   10
●Were gracious in the eyes of royal Rome,
Keep then this passage to the Capitol
And suffer not dishonour to approach
The imperial seat, to virtue consecrate,
●To justice, continence and nobility;
But let desert in pure election shine,
And, Romans, fight for freedom in your choice.

   Enter MARCUS ANDRONICUS, *aloft, with the*
       crown.

   Marc.   Princes, that strive by factions and by
    friends
●Ambitiously for rule and empery,
Know that the people of Rome, for whom we
    stand   20
A special party, have, by common voice,
In election for the Roman empery,
Chosen Andronicus, surnamed Pius
For many good and great deserts to Rome:
A nobler man, a braver warrior,
Lives not this day within the city walls:
●He by the senate is accited home
From weary wars against the barbarous Goths;
That, with his sons, a terror to our foes,
Hath yoked a nation strong, train'd up in arms.
Ten years are spent since first he undertook   31
This cause of Rome and chastised with arms
Our enemies' pride: five times he hath return'd
Bleeding to Rome, bearing his valiant sons
In coffins from the field;
And now at last, laden with honour's spoils,
Returns the good Andronicus to Rome,
Renowned Titus, flourishing in arms.
Let us entreat, by honour of his name,
Whom worthily you would have now succeed, 40
And in the Capitol and senate's right,
●Whom you pretend to honour and adore,
That you withdraw you and abate your strength;
Dismiss your followers and, as suitors should,
Plead your deserts in peace and humbleness.
   Sat.   How fair the tribune speaks to calm my
    thoughts!
● *Bas.*   Marcus Andronicus, so I do affy
In thy uprightness and integrity,
And so I love and honour thee and thine,
Thy noble brother Titus and his sons,   50
And her to whom my thoughts are humbled all,
Gracious Lavinia, Rome's rich ornament,
That I will here dismiss my loving friends,
And to my fortunes and the people's favour
Commit my cause in balance to be weigh'd.
       [*Exeunt the Followers of Bassianus.*
   Sat.   Friends, that have been thus forward in
    my right,
I thank you all and here dismiss you all,
And to the love and favour of my country
Commit myself, my person and the cause.
       [*Exeunt the Followers of Saturninus.*
Rome, be as just and gracious unto me   60
●As I am confident and kind to thee.
Open the gates, and let me in.
   Bas.   Tribunes, and me, a poor competitor.
      [*Flourish.   Saturninus and Bassianus go
          up into the Capitol.*

Enter a Captain.

Cap.   Romans, make way: the good Andro-
nicus,
Patron of virtue, Rome's best champion,
Successful in the battles that he fights,
With honour and with fortune is return'd
From where he circumscribed with his sword,
And brought to yoke, the enemies of Rome.

Drums and trumpets sounded.   Enter MAR-
TIUS *and* MUTIUS; *after them, two* Men
bearing a coffin covered with black; then
LUCIUS *and* QUINTUS.   *After them,* TITUS
ANDRONICUS; *and then* TAMORA, *with* ALAR-
BUS, DEMETRIUS, CHIRON, AARON, *and other*
Goths, *prisoners;* Soldiers *and* People *follow-
ing.   The* Bearers *set down the coffin, and*
TITUS *speaks.*

Tit.   Hail, Rome, victorious in thy mourning
weeks!   70
● Lo, as the bark, that hath discharged her fraught,
Returns with precious lading to the bay
From whence at first she weigh'd her anchorage,
Cometh Andronicus, bound with laurel boughs,
To re-salute his country with his tears,
Tears of true joy for his return to Rome.
Thou great defender of this Capitol,
Stand gracious to the rites that we intend!
Romans, of five and twenty valiant sons,
● Half of the number that King Priam had,   80
Behold the poor remains, alive and dead!
These that survive let Rome reward with love;
These that I bring unto their latest home,
With burial amongst their ancestors:
Here Goths have given me leave to sheathe my
sword.
Titus, unkind and careless of thine own,
Why suffer'st thou thy sons, unburied yet,
● To hover on the dreadful shore of Styx?
Make way to lay them by their brethren.
                        [*The tomb is opened.*
There greet in silence, as the dead are wont, 90
And sleep in peace, slain in your country's wars!
O sacred receptacle of my joys,
Sweet cell of virtue and nobility,
How many sons of mine hast thou in store,
That thou wilt never render to me more!
Luc.   Give us the proudest prisoner of the
Goths,
That we may hew his limbs, and on a pile
● Ad manes fratrum sacrifice his flesh,
Before this earthy prison of their bones;
That so the shadows be not unappeased,   100
Nor we disturb'd with prodigies on earth.
Tit.   I give him you, the noblest that survives,
The eldest son of this distressed queen.
Tam.   Stay, Roman brethren!   Gracious con-
queror,
Victorious Titus, rue the tears I shed,
A mother's tears in passion for her son:
And if thy sons were ever dear to thee,
O, think my son to be as dear to me!
Sufficeth not that we are brought to Rome,
To beautify thy triumphs and return,   110
Captive to thee and to thy Roman yoke,
But must my sons be slaughter'd in the streets,
For valiant doings in their country's cause?
O, if to fight for king and commonweal

71 *fraught.* Load.

80 *King Priam.* Said to be the father of fifty sons.

Gothic captives. Nineteenth century engraving from the
Constantinople Column

88 *Styx.* The legendary river surrounding hell.

98 *Ad manes fratrum.* i.e. to the ghosts of our brothers.

Tamora: 'Sweet mercy is nobility's true badge: Thrice noble Titus, spare my first-born son.' Maxine Audley as Tamora and Laurence Olivier as Titus, Stratford-upon-Avon, 1955

131 *Scythia*. South-East Russia.

138 *Thracian tyrant*. i.e. Polymestor, who had killed the son of Hecuba, Queen of Troy.

141 *quit*. Pay back.

147 *'larums*. Rousing fanfares.

159 *tributary*. i.e. in tribute.

Were piety in thine, it is in these.
Andronicus, stain not thy tomb with blood:
Wilt thou draw near the nature of the gods?
Draw near them then in being merciful:
Sweet mercy is nobility's true badge:
Thrice noble Titus, spare my first-born son.   120
   Tit. Patient yourself, madam, and pardon me.
These are their brethren, whom you Goths beheld
Alive and dead, and for their brethren slain
Religiously they ask a sacrifice:
To this your son is mark'd, and die he must,
To appease their groaning shadows that are gone.
   Luc. Away with him! and make a fire straight;
And with our swords, upon a pile of wood,
Let's hew his limbs till they be clean consumed.
   [*Exeunt Lucius, Quintus, Martius, and*
     Mutius, with Alarbus.
   Tam.   O cruel, irreligious piety!   130
   Chi. Was ever Scythia half so barbarous?
   Dem. Oppose not Scythia to ambitious Rome.
Alarbus goes to rest; and we survive
To tremble under Titus' threatening looks.
Then, madam, stand resolved, but hope withal
The self-same gods that arm'd the Queen of Troy
With opportunity of sharp revenge
Upon the Thracian tyrant in his tent,
May favour Tamora, the Queen of Goths—
When Goths were Goths and Tamora was queen—
To quit the bloody wrongs upon her foes.   141

Re-enter Lucius, Quintus, Martius, *and*
   Mutius, *with their swords bloody.*

   Luc.   See, lord and father, how we have perform'd
Our Roman rites: Alarbus' limbs are lopp'd,
And entrails feed the sacrificing fire,
Whose smoke, like incense, doth perfume the sky.
Remaineth nought, but to inter our brethren,
And with loud 'larums welcome them to Rome.
   Tit.   Let it be so; and let Andronicus
Make this his latest farewell to their souls.
   [*Trumpets sounded, and the coffin laid in*
     the tomb.
In peace and honour rest you here, my sons;   150
Rome's readiest champions, repose you here in rest,
Secure from worldly chances and mishaps!
Here lurks no treason, here no envy swells,
Here grow no damned grudges; here are no storms,
No noise, but silence and eternal sleep:
In peace and honour rest you here, my sons!

Enter Lavinia.

   Lav.   In peace and honour live Lord Titus long;
My noble lord and father, live in fame!
Lo, at this tomb my tributary tears
I render, for my brethren's obsequies;   160
And at thy feet I kneel, with tears of joy,
Shed on the earth, for thy return to Rome:
O, bless me here with thy victorious hand,
Whose fortunes Rome's best citizens applaud!
   Tit.   Kind Rome, that hast thus lovingly reserved
The cordial of mine age to glad my heart!
Lavinia, live; outlive thy father's days,
And fame's eternal date, for virtue's praise!

Enter, below, MARCUS ANDRONICUS *and* Tribunes; *re-enter* SATURNINUS *and* BASSIANUS, *attended.*

Marc. Long live Lord Titus, my beloved brother,
Gracious triumpher in the eyes of Rome! 170
   Tit. Thanks, gentle tribune, noble brother Marcus.
   Marc. And welcome, nephews, from successful wars,
You that survive, and you that sleep in fame!
Fair lords, your fortunes are alike in all,
That in your country's service drew your swords:
But safer triumph is this funeral pomp,
•That hath aspired to Solon's happiness
And triumphs over chance in honour's bed.
Titus Andronicus, the people of Rome,
Whose friend in justice thou hast ever been, 180
Send thee by me, their tribune and their trust,
•This palliament of white and spotless hue;
And name thee in election for the empire,
With these our late-deceased emperor's sons:
Be candidatus then, and put it on,
And help to set a head on headless Rome.
   Tit. A better head her glorious body fits
Than his that shakes for age and feebleness:
What should I don this robe, and trouble you?
Be chosen with proclamations to-day, 190
To-morrow yield up rule, resign my life,
And set abroad new business for you all?
Rome, I have been thy soldier forty years,
And led my country's strength successfully,
And buried one and twenty valiant sons,
Knighted in field, slain manfully in arms,
In right and service of their noble country:
Give me a staff of honour for mine age,
But not a sceptre to control the world:
Upright he held it, lords, that held it last. 200
• *Marc.* Titus, thou shalt obtain and ask the empery.
   Sat. Proud and ambitious tribune, canst thou tell?
   Tit. Patience, Prince Saturninus.
   Sat.   Romans, do me right:
Patricians, draw your swords, and sheathe them not
Till Saturninus be Rome's emperor.
Andronicus, would thou wert shipp'd to hell,
Rather than rob me of the people's hearts!
   Luc. Proud Saturnine, interrupter of the good
That noble-minded Titus means to thee!
   Tit. Content thee, prince; I will restore to thee 210
The people's hearts, and wean them from themselves.
   Bas. Andronicus, I do not flatter thee,
But honour thee, and will do till I die:
My faction if thou strengthen with thy friends,
I will most thankful be; and thanks to men
Of noble minds is honourable meed.
   Tit. People of Rome, and people's tribunes here,
I ask your voices and your suffrages:
Will you bestow them friendly on Andronicus?
   Tribunes. To gratify the good Andronicus, 220
And gratulate his safe return to Rome,
The people will accept whom he admits.

177 *Solon.* Greek legislator attributed with saying 'Call no man happy till he is dead'; hence Solon's happiness equals death.

Solon announcing his reforms to the Athenians. Engraving by Bartolomeo Pinelli, 1821

182 *palliament.* Candidate's gown.

201 *obtain and ask.* i.e. obtain if you request.

226 *Titan.* God of the sun.

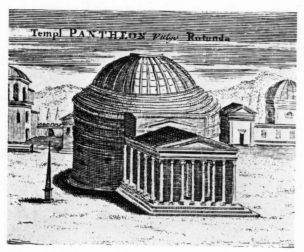

The Pantheon. Engraving from Basil Kennett's *Romae Antiquae Notitia*, 1769

257 *fealty.* Loyalty.

271 *sith.* Since.

Tit.   Tribunes, I thank you: and this suit I make,
That you create your emperor's eldest son,
Lord Saturnine; whose virtues will, I hope,
● Reflect on Rome as Titan's rays on earth,
And ripen justice in this commonweal:
Then, if you will elect by my advice,
Crown him, and say ' Long live our emperor!' 229
   Marc. With voices and applause of every sort,
Patricians and plebeians, we create
Lord Saturninus Rome's great emperor,
And say ' Long live our Emperor Saturnine!'
          [*A long flourish till they come down.*
   Sat.   Titus Andronicus, for thy favours done
To us in our election this day,
I give thee thanks in part of thy deserts,
And will with deeds requite thy gentleness:
And, for an onset, Titus, to advance
Thy name and honourable family,
Lavinia will I make my empress,   240
Rome's royal mistress, mistress of my heart,
And in the sacred Pantheon her espouse:
Tell me, Andronicus, doth this motion please thee?
   Tit.   It doth, my worthy lord; and in this match
I hold me highly honour'd of your grace:
And here in sight of Rome to Saturnine,
King and commander of our commonweal,
The wide world's emperor, do I consecrate
My sword, my chariot and my prisoners;
Presents well worthy Rome's imperial lord: 250
Receive them then, the tribute that I owe,
Mine honour's ensigns humbled at thy feet.
   Sat.   Thanks, noble Titus, father of my life!
How proud I am of thee and of thy gifts
Rome shall record, and when I do forget
The least of these unspeakable deserts,
● Romans, forget your fealty to me.
   Tit.   [*To Tamora*] Now, madam, are you
          prisoner to an emperor;
To him that, for your honour and your state,
Will use you nobly and your followers.   260
   Sat.   A goodly lady, trust me; of the hue
That I would choose, were I to choose anew.
Clear up, fair queen, that cloudy countenance:
Though chance of war hath wrought this change
          of cheer,
Thou comest not to be made a scorn in Rome:
Princely shall be thy usage every way.
Rest on my word, and let not discontent
Daunt all your hopes: madam, he comforts you
Can make you greater than the Queen of Goths.
Lavinia, you are not displeased with this?   270
● *Lav.*   Not I, my lord; sith true nobility
Warrants these words in princely courtesy.
   Sat.   Thanks, sweet Lavinia. Romans, let
          us go:
Ransomless here we set our prisoners free:
Proclaim our honours, lords, with trump and
          drum.
          [*Flourish.   Saturninus courts Tamora
                              in dumb show.*
   Bas.   Lord Titus, by your leave, this maid is
          mine.   [*Seizing Lavinia.*
   Tit.   How, sir! are you in earnest then, my
          lord?
   Bas.   Ay, noble Titus; and resolved withal
To do myself this reason and this right.   279

● *Marc*. 'Suum cuique' is our Roman justice:
This prince in justice seizeth but his own.
  Luc. And that he will, and shall, if Lucius live.
● *Tit*. Traitors, avaunt! Where is the empe-
    ror's guard?
Treason, my lord! Lavinia is surprised!
  Sat. Surprised! by whom?
  Bas.   By him that justly may
Bear his betroth'd from all the world away.
  [*Exeunt Bassianus and Marcus with Lavinia*.
  Mut. Brothers, help to convey her hence away,
And with my sword I'll keep this door safe.
        [*Exeunt Lucius, Quintus, and Martius*.
  Tit. Follow, my lord, and I'll soon bring her
    back.
  Mut. My lord, you pass not here.
  Tit.   What, villain boy! 290
Barr'st me my way in Rome? [*Stabbing Mutius*.
  Mut. Help, Lucius, help! [*Dies*.
    [*During the fray, Saturninus, Tamora,
      Demetrius, Chiron and Aaron go out
      and re-enter, above*.

        Re-enter LUCIUS.

  Luc. My lord, you are unjust, and, more
    than so,
In wrongful quarrel you have slain your son.
  Tit. Nor thou, nor he, are any sons of mine;
My sons would never so dishonour me:
Traitor, restore Lavinia to the emperor.
  Luc. Dead, if you will; but not to be
    his wife,
That is another's lawful promised love. [*Exit*.
  Sat. No, Titus, no; the emperor needs her
    not,
Nor her, nor thee, nor any of thy stock: 300
I'll trust, by leisure, him that mocks me once;
Thee never, nor thy traitorous haughty sons,
Confederates all thus to dishonour me.
● Was there none else in Rome to make a stale,
But Saturnine? Full well, Andronicus,
Agree these deeds with that proud brag of thine,
That said'st I begg'd the empire at thy hands.
  Tit. O monstrous! what reproachful words
    are these?
● *Sat*. But go thy ways; go, give that chang-
    ing piece   309
To him that flourish'd for her with his sword:
A valiant son-in-law thou shalt enjoy;
● One fit to bandy with thy lawless sons,
● To ruffle in the commonwealth of Rome.
  Tit. These words are razors to my wounded
    heart.
  Sat. And therefore, lovely Tamora, queen of
    Goths,
● That like the stately Phœbe 'mongst her nymphs
Dost overshine the gallant'st dames of Rome,
If thou be pleased with this my sudden choice,
Behold, I choose thee, Tamora, for my bride,
And will create thee empress of Rome.   320
Speak, Queen of Goths, dost thou applaud my
    choice?
And here I swear by all the Roman gods,
Sith priest and holy water are so near
And tapers burn so bright and every thing
● In readiness for Hymenæus stand,
I will not re-salute the streets of Rome,
Or climb my palace, till from forth this place
I lead espoused my bride along with me.

280 *'Suum cuique'*. To each his own.

283 *avaunt*. Away!

304 *stale*. Laughing stock.

309 *changing piece*. Fickle wench.

312 *bandy*. Brawl.

313 *ruffle*. Swagger.

316 *Phœbe*. i.e. Diana, goddess of the moon.

325 *Hymenæus*. God of marriage.

Costume design for Mutius by Desmond Heeley,
Stratford-upon-Avon, 1955

Saturninus: 'There shall we consummate our spousal rites.' Woodcut from *The Roxburghe Ballads*, 17th century

---

340 *challenged*. Accused.

Tam. And here, in sight of heaven, to Rome
  I swear,
If Saturnine advance the Queen of Goths,   330
She will a handmaid be to his desires,
A loving nurse, a mother to his youth.
  Sat. Ascend, fair queen, Pantheon. Lords,
  accompany
Your noble emperor and his lovely bride,
Sent by the heavens for Prince Saturnine,
Whose wisdom hath her fortune conquered:
There shall we consummate our spousal rites.
              [*Exeunt all but Titus.*
  Tit. I am not bid to wait upon this bride.
Titus, when wert thou wont to walk alone,
● Dishonour'd thus, and challenged of wrongs? 340

  Re-enter MARCUS, LUCIUS, QUINTUS, *and*
        MARTIUS.

  Marc. O Titus, see, O, see what thou hast
  done!
In a bad quarrel slain a virtuous son.
  Tit. No, foolish tribune, no; no son of mine,
Nor thou, nor these, confederates in the deed
That hath dishonour'd all our family;
Unworthy brother, and unworthy sons!
  Luc. But let us give him burial, as becomes;
Give Mutius burial with our brethren.
  Tit. Traitors, away! he rests not in this
  tomb:
This monument five hundred years hath stood,
Which I have sumptuously re-edified:
Here none but soldiers and Rome's servitors
Repose in fame; none basely slain in brawls:
Bury him where you can; he comes not here.
  Marc. My lord, this is impiety in you:
My nephew Mutius' deeds do plead for him;
He must be buried with his brethren.
  Quin. ⎱ And shall, or him we will accom-
  Mart. ⎰   pany.
  Tit. 'And shall!' what villain was it spake
  that word?
  Quin. He that would vouch it in any place
  but here.   360
  Tit. What, would you bury him in my
  despite?
  Marc. No, noble Titus, but entreat of thee
To pardon Mutius and to bury him.
  Tit. Marcus, even thou hast struck upon
  my crest,
And, with these boys, mine honour thou hast
  wounded:
My foes I do repute you every one;
So, trouble me no more, but get you gone.
  Mart. He is not with himself; let us with-
  draw.
  Quin. Not I, till Mutius' bones be buried.
        [*Marcus and the Sons of Titus kneel.*
  Marc. Brother, for in that name doth nature
  plead,—   370
  Quin. Father, and in that name doth nature
  speak,—
  Tit. Speak thou no more, if all the rest will
  speed.
  Marc. Renowned Titus, more than half my
  soul,—
  Luc. Dear father, soul and substance of
  us all,—
  Marc. Suffer thy brother Marcus to inter
His noble nephew here in virtue's nest,

That died in honour and Lavinia's cause.
Thou art a Roman; be not barbarous:
The Greeks upon advice did bury Ajax
● That slew himself; and wise Laertes' son   380
Did graciously plead for his funerals:
Let not young Mutius, then, that was thy joy,
Be barr'd his entrance here.
 Tit.   Rise, Marcus, rise.
The dismall'st day is this that e'er I saw,
To be dishonour'd by my sons in Rome!
Well, bury him, and bury me the next.
     [*Mutius is put into the tomb.*
 Luc. There lie thy bones, sweet Mutius, with
  thy friends,
Till we with trophies do adorn thy tomb.
 All. [*Kneeling*] No man shed tears for noble
  Mutius;
He lives in fame that died in virtue's cause. 390
● *Marc.* My lord, to step out of these dreary
  dumps,
How comes it that the subtle Queen of Goths
Is of a sudden thus advanced in Rome?
 Tit. I know not, Marcus; but I know it is:
Whether by device or no, the heavens can tell:
Is she not then beholding to the man
That brought her for this high good turn so far?
Yes, and will nobly him remunerate.

Flourish. Re-enter, from one side, SATURNINUS
attended, TAMORA, DEMETRIUS, CHIRON, *and*
AARON; *from the other,* BASSIANUS, LAVINIA,
and others.

 Sat. So, Bassianus, you have play'd your prize:
God give you joy, sir, of your gallant bride! 400
 Bas. And you of yours, my lord! I say no
  more,
Nor wish no less; and so, I take my leave.
 Sat. Traitor, if Rome have law or we have
  power,
Thou and thy faction shall repent this rape.
 Bas. Rape, call you it, my lord, to seize my own,
My true-betrothed love and now my wife?
But let the laws of Rome determine all;
Meanwhile I am possess'd of that is mine.
 Sat. 'Tis good, sir: you are very short with us;
But, if we live, we'll be as sharp with you. 410
 Bas. My lord, what I have done, as best I may,
Answer I must and shall do with my life.
Only thus much I give your grace to know:
By all the duties that I owe to Rome,
This noble gentleman, Lord Titus here,
Is in opinion and in honour wrong'd;
That in the rescue of Lavinia
With his own hand did slay his youngest son,
In zeal to you and highly moved to wrath
● To be controll'd in that he frankly gave: 420
Receive him, then, to favour, Saturnine,
That hath express'd himself in all his deeds
A father and a friend to thee and Rome.
 Tit. Prince Bassianus, leave to plead my deeds:
'Tis thou and those that have dishonour'd me.
Rome and the righteous heavens be my judge,
How I have loved and honour'd Saturnine!
 Tam. My worthy lord, if ever Tamora
Were gracious in those princely eyes of thine,
Then hear me speak indifferently for all; 430
And at my suit, sweet, pardon what is past.
 Sat. What, madam! be dishonour'd openly,
And basely put it up without revenge?

380 *Laertes' son.* i.e. Ulysses.

391 *these dreary dumps.* Melancholy.

420 *controll'd.* Thwarted. *frankly.* Unreservedly.

449 *at entreats.* To entreaty.

Titus: 'Tomorrow . . . To hunt the panther and the hart.'
Woodcut from George Turberville's *The Noble Art of
Venerie or Hunting*, 1611

495 *gramercy.* Thanks.

Tam.   Not so, my lord; the gods of Rome
    forfend
I should be author to dishonour you!
But on mine honour dare I undertake
For good Lord Titus' innocence in all;
Whose fury not dissembled speaks his griefs:
Then, at my suit, look graciously on him;
Lose not so noble a friend on vain suppose,   440
Nor with sour looks afflict his gentle heart.
[*Aside to Sat.*] My lord, be ruled by me, be won
    at last;
Dissemble all your griefs and discontents:
You are but newly planted in your throne;
Lest, then, the people, and patricians too,
Upon a just survey, take Titus' part,
And so supplant you for ingratitude,
Which Rome reputes to be a heinous sin,
Yield at entreats; and then let me alone:
I'll find a day to massacre them all   450
And raze their faction and their family,
The cruel father and his traitorous sons,
To whom I sued for my dear son's life,
And make them know what 'tis to let a queen
Kneel in the streets and beg for grace in vain.

Come, come, sweet emperor; come, Andronicus;
Take up this good old man, and cheer the heart
That dies in tempest of thy angry frown.
    Sat.   Rise, Titus, rise; my empress hath pre-
    vail'd.   459
    Tit.   I thank your majesty, and her, my lord:
These words, these looks, infuse new life in me.
    Tam.   Titus, I am incorporate in Rome,
A Roman now adopted happily,
And must advise the emperor for his good.
This day all quarrels die, Andronicus;
And let it be mine honour, good my lord,
That I have reconciled your friends and you.
For you, Prince Bassianus, I have pass'd
My word and promise to the emperor,
That you will be more mild and tractable.   470
And fear not, lords, and you, Lavinia;
By my advice, all humbled on your knees,
You shall ask pardon of his majesty.
    Luc.   We do, and vow to heaven and to his
    highness,
That what we did was mildly as we might,
Tendering our sister's honour and our own.
    Marc.   That, on mine honour, here I do protest.
    Sat.   Away, and talk not; trouble us no more.
    Tam.   Nay, nay, sweet emperor, we must all
    be friends: 479
The tribune and his nephews kneel for grace;
I will not be denied: sweet heart, look back.
    Sat.   Marcus, for thy sake and thy brother's here,
And at my lovely Tamora's entreats,
I do remit these young men's heinous faults:
Stand up.
Lavinia, though you left me like a churl,
I found a friend, and sure as death I swore
I would not part a bachelor from the priest.
Come, if the emperor's court can feast two brides,
You are my guest, Lavinia, and your friends.   490
This day shall be a love-day, Tamora.
    Tit.   To-morrow, an it please your majesty
To hunt the panther and the hart with me,
With horn and hound we'll give your grace bonjour.
    Sat.   Be it so, Titus, and gramercy too.
    [*Flourish.   Exeunt.*

ACT II.

SCENE I. *Rome. Before the palace.*

Enter AARON.

● *Aar.* Now climbeth Tamora Olympus' top,
Safe out of fortune's shot; and sits aloft,
Secure of thunder's crack or lightning flash;
Advanced above pale envy's threatening reach.
As when the golden sun salutes the morn,
And, having gilt the ocean with his beams,
Gallops the zodiac in his glistering coach,
And overlooks the highest-peering hills;
So Tamora:
● Upon her wit doth earthly honour wait,   10
And virtue stoops and trembles at her frown.
Then, Aaron, arm thy heart, and fit thy thoughts,
To mount aloft with thy imperial mistress,
And mount her pitch, whom thou in triumph long
Hast prisoner held, fetter'd in amorous chains
And faster bound to Aaron's charming eyes
● Than is Prometheus tied to Caucasus.
Away with slavish weeds and servile thoughts!
I will be bright, and shine in pearl and gold,
To wait upon this new-made empress.   20
To wait, said I? to wanton with this queen,
● This goddess, this Semiramis, this nymph,
This siren, that will charm Rome's Saturnine,
And see his shipwreck and his commonweal's.
Holloa! what storm is this?

Enter DEMETRIUS *and* CHIRON, *braving.*

Dem. Chiron, thy years want wit, thy wit
wants edge,
And manners, to intrude where I am graced;
● And may, for aught thou know'st, affected be.
Chi. Demetrius, thou dost over-ween in all;
● And so in this, to bear me down with braves.   30
'Tis not the difference of a year or two
Makes me less gracious or thee more fortunate:
I am as able and as fit as thou
To serve, and to deserve my mistress' grace;
● And that my sword upon thee shall approve,
And plead my passions for Lavinia's love.
● *Aar.* [*Aside*] Clubs, clubs! these lovers will
not keep the peace.
Dem. Why, boy, although our mother, un-
advised,
Gave you a dancing-rapier by your side,
Are you so desperate grown, to threat your friends?
● Go to; have your lath glued within your sheath 41
Till you know better how to handle it.
Chi. Meanwhile, sir, with the little skill I have,
Full well shalt thou perceive how much I dare.
Dem. Ay, boy, grow ye so brave? [*They draw.*
Aar. [*Coming forward*] Why, how now, lords!
● So near the emperor's palace dare you draw,
And maintain such a quarrel openly?
Full well I wot the ground of all this grudge:
I would not for a million of gold
The cause were known to them it most concerns;
Nor would your noble mother for much more   51
Be so dishonour'd in the court of Rome.
For shame, put up.
Dem.   Not I, till I have sheathed
My rapier in his bosom and withal
Thrust these reproachful speeches down his throat
That he hath breathed in my dishonour here.
Chi. For that I am prepared and full resolved.

1 *Olympus.* Mountain home of the gods.

Aaron: 'As when the golden sun salutes the morn . . .'
Engraving from a painting by Dominiquin, 1803

10 *wit.* Whim.

17 *Prometheus.* In mythology, chained to Mount Caucasus in punishment for stealing fire from heaven.

22 *Semiramis.* Legendary queen of great beauty and sensuality.

28 *affected.* Loved.

30 *braves.* Threats.

35 *approve.* Prove.

37 *Clubs . . . peace.* See introduction.

41 *lath.* Toy sword.

46-47 *So near . . . openly.* See introduction.

62 *brabble.* Quarrel.

64 *jet.* Encroach.

87 *shive.* Slice.

89 *Vulcan.* Legendary god of fire whose wife Venus was unfaithful, hence Vulcan's badge is the sign of a cuckold.

Vulcan. From a 19th century engraving

100 *square.* Squabble.

103 *join for that you jar.* Unite to obtain what you are arguing over.

104 *policy.* Craftiness.

Foul-spoken coward, that thunder'st with thy
    tongue,
And with thy weapon nothing darest perform!
  Aar. Away, I say!   60
Now, by the gods that warlike Goths adore,
●This petty brabble will undo us all.
Why, lords, and think you not how dangerous
●It is to jet upon a prince's right?
What, is Lavinia then become so loose,
Or Bassianus so degenerate,
That for her love such quarrels may be broach'd
Without controlment, justice, or revenge?
Young lords, beware! an should the empress know
This discord's ground, the music would not please.
  Chi. I care not, I, knew she and all the world:
I love Lavinia more than all the world.
  Dem. Youngling, learn thou to make some
    meaner choice:
Lavinia is thine elder brother's hope.
    Aar. Why, are ye mad? or know ye not, in
    Rome
How furious and impatient they be,
And cannot brook competitors in love?
I tell you, lords, you do but plot your deaths
By this device.
    Chi.   Aaron, a thousand deaths
Would I propose to achieve her whom I love. 80
    Aar. To achieve her! how?
    Dem.   Why makest thou it so strange?
She is a woman, therefore may be woo'd;
She is a woman, therefore may be won;
She is Lavinia, therefore must be loved.
What, man! more water glideth by the mill
Than wots the miller of; and easy it is
●Of a cut loaf to steal a shive, we know:
Though Bassianus be the emperor's brother,
●Better than he have worn Vulcan's badge.
    Aar. [*Aside*] Ay, and as good as Saturninus
    may.   90
    Dem. Then why should he despair that knows
    to court it
With words, fair looks and liberality?
What, hast not thou full often struck a doe,
And borne her cleanly by the keeper's nose?
    Aar. Why, then, it seems, some certain snatch
    or so
Would serve your turns.
    Chi.   Ay, so the turn were served.
    Dem. Aaron, thou hast hit it.
    Aar.   Would you had hit it too!
Then should not we be tired with this ado.
Why, hark ye, hark ye! and are you such fools
●To square for this? would it offend you, then, 100
That both should speed?
    Chi. Faith, not me.
    Dem.   Nor me, so I were one.
●   *Aar.* For shame, be friends, and join for that
    you jar:
●'Tis policy and stratagem must do
That you affect; and so must you resolve,
That what you cannot as you would achieve,
You must perforce accomplish as you may.
Take this of me: Lucrece was not more chaste
Than this Lavinia, Bassianus' love.
A speedier course than lingering languishment
Must we pursue, and I have found the path. 111
My lords, a solemn hunting is in hand;
There will the lovely Roman ladies troop:
The forest walks are wide and spacious;

And many unfrequented plots there are
Fitted by kind for rape and villany:
Single you thither then this dainty doe,
And strike her home by force, if not by words:
This way, or not at all, stand you in hope.
Come, come, our empress, with her sacred wit
To villany and vengeance consecrate,   121
Will we acquaint with all that we intend;
● And she shall file our engines with advice,
That will not suffer you to square yourselves,
But to your wishes' height advance you both.
The emperor's court is like the house of Fame,
The palace full of tongues, of eyes, and ears:
The woods are ruthless, dreadful, deaf, and dull;
There speak, and strike, brave boys, and take
　　your turns;
There serve your lusts, shadow'd from heaven's
　　eye,   130
And revel in Lavinia's treasury.
　　Chi. Thy counsel, lad, smells of no cowardice,
● *Dem.* Sit fas aut nefas, till I find the stream
To cool this heat, a charm to calm these fits,
● Per Styga, per manes vehor.   [*Exeunt.*

SCENE II. *A forest near Rome. Horns and
　　　　cry of hounds heard.*

Enter TITUS ANDRONICUS, *with* Hunters, &c.,
MARCUS, LUCIUS, QUINTUS, *and* MARTIUS.

● *Tit.* The hunt is up, the morn is bright and
　　grey,
The fields are fragrant and the woods are green:
● Uncouple here and let us make a bay
And wake the emperor and his lovely bride
And rouse the prince and ring a hunter's peal,
That all the court may echo with the noise.
Sons, let it be your charge, as it is ours,
To attend the emperor's person carefully:
I have been troubled in my sleep this night,
But dawning day new comfort hath inspired.   10

A cry of hounds, and horns winded in a peal.
　　Enter SATURNINUS, TAMORA, BASSIANUS, LA-
VINIA, DEMETRIUS, CHIRON, *and* Attendants.

Many good morrows to your majesty;
Madam, to you as many and as good:
I promised your grace a hunter's peal.
　　Sat. And you have rung it lustily, my lord;
Somewhat too early for new-married ladies.
　　Bas. Lavinia, how say you?
　　Lav.　　　　　　　I say, no;
I have been broad awake two hours and more.
　　Sat. Come on, then; horse and chariots let
　　us have,
And to our sport. [*To Tamora*] Madam, now
　　shall ye see
Our Roman hunting.
　　Marc.　　　　I have dogs, my lord,   20
Will rouse the proudest panther in the chase,
And climb the highest promontory top.
　　Tit. And I have horse will follow where the
　　game
Makes way, and run like swallows o'er the plain.
　　Dem. Chiron, we hunt not, we, with horse
　　nor hound,
But hope to pluck a dainty doe to ground.
　　　　　　　　　　　　　　[*Exeunt.*

123 *file our engines.* Sharpen our minds.

133 *Sit fas aut nefas.* Be it right or wrong.

135 *Per Styga, per manes vehor.* I am borne through the Stygian regions (i.e. to the shores of the Styx).

1–3 *The hunt . . . bay.* See introduction.

3 *bay.* Prolonged barking.

Lavinia: 'I have been broad awake two hours and more.'
Mrs P. Hopkins, the 18th century actress, as Lavinia.
Engraving from Bell's edition of Shakespeare's works,
1776

12-15 *The birds . . . the ground.* See introduction.

22 *The wandering prince.* Aeneas, legendary hero of Troy. *Dido.* His lover, Queen of Carthage.

30 *Venus.* Legendary goddess of love.

Venus accompanied by a Cupid. Engraving from a painting by Raphael, 1811

31 *Saturn.* i.e. moroseness.

37 *venereal.* Amorous.

43 *Philomel.* In mythology, ravished by Tereus, who cut out her tongue to prevent her naming the crime.

53 *Be cross.* Start an argument.

SCENE III.   *A lonely part of the forest.*

Enter AARON, *with a bag of gold.*

Aar.   He that had wit would think that I had none,
To bury so much gold under a tree,
And never after to inherit it.
Let him that thinks of me so abjectly
Know that this gold must coin a stratagem,
Which, cunningly effected, will beget
A very excellent piece of villany:
And so repose, sweet gold, for their unrest
                                        [*Hides the gold.*
That have their alms out of the empress' chest.

Enter TAMORA.

Tam.   My lovely Aaron, wherefore look'st thou sad,   10
When every thing doth make a gleeful boast?
●The birds chant melody on every bush,
The snake lies rolled in the cheerful sun,
The green leaves quiver with the cooling wind
And make a chequer'd shadow on the ground:
Under their sweet shade, Aaron, let us sit,
And, whilst the babbling echo mocks the hounds,
Replying shrilly to the well-tuned horns,
As if a double hunt were heard at once,
Let us sit down and mark their yelping noise; 20
And, after conflict such as was supposed
●The wandering prince and Dido once enjoy'd,
When with a happy storm they were surprised
And curtain'd with a counsel-keeping cave,
We may, each wreathed in the other's arms,
Our pastimes done, possess a golden slumber;
Whiles hounds and horns and sweet melodious birds
Be unto us as is a nurse's song
Of lullaby to bring her babe asleep.
●   *Aar.*   Madam, though Venus govern your desires,   30
●Saturn is dominator over mine:
What signifies my deadly-standing eye,
My silence and my cloudy melancholy,
My fleece of woolly hair that now uncurls
Even as an adder when she doth unroll
To do some fatal execution?
●No, madam, these are no venereal signs:
Vengeance is in my heart, death in my hand,
Blood and revenge are hammering in my head.
Hark, Tamora, the empress of my soul,   40
Which never hopes more heaven than rests in thee,
This is the day of doom for Bassianus:
●His Philomel must lose her tongue to-day,
Thy sons make pillage of her chastity
And wash their hands in Bassianus' blood.
Seest thou this letter? take it up, I pray thee,
And give the king this fatal-plotted scroll.
Now question me no more; we are espied;
Here comes a parcel of our hopeful booty,
Which dreads not yet their lives' destruction. 50
     Tam.   Ah, my sweet Moor, sweeter to me than life!
     Aar.   No more, great empress; Bassianus comes:
●Be cross with him; and I'll go fetch thy sons
To back thy quarrels, whatsoe'er they be. [*Exit.*

Enter BASSIANUS *and* LAVINIA.

 Bas.   Who have we here? Rome's royal empress,
Unfurnish'd of her well-beseeming troop?
● Or is it Dian, habited like her,
Who hath abandoned her holy groves
To see the general hunting in this forest?
● *Tam.*   Saucy controller of our private steps!
Had I the power that some say Dian had,   61
Thy temples should be planted presently
● With horns, as was Actæon's; and the hounds
Should drive upon thy new-transformed limbs,
Unmannerly intruder as thou art!
● *Lav.*   Under your patience, gentle empress,
'Tis thought you have a goodly gift in horning;
● And to be doubted that your Moor and you
Are singled forth to try experiments:
Jove shield your husband from his hounds to-day!
'Tis pity they should take him for a stag.   71
● *Bas.*   Believe me, queen, your swarth Cimmerian
Doth make your honour of his body's hue,
Spotted, detested, and abominable.
Why are you sequester'd from all your train,
Dismounted from your snow-white goodly steed,
And wander'd hither to an obscure plot,
Accompanied but with a barbarous Moor,
If foul desire had not conducted you?
 Lav.   And, being intercepted in your sport,   80
● Great reason that my noble lord be rated
For sauciness.   I pray you, let us hence,
And let her joy her raven-colour'd love;
This valley fits the purpose passing well.
 Bas.   The king my brother shall have note of
       this.
 Lav.   Ay, for these slips have made him noted
       long:
Good king, to be so mightily abused!
 Tam.   Why have I patience to endure all this?

Enter DEMETRIUS *and* CHIRON.

 Dem.   How now, dear sovereign, and our
       gracious mother!
Why doth your highness look so pale and wan?
 Tam.   Have I not reason, think you, to look
       pale?   91
These two have 'ticed me hither to this place:
A barren detested vale, you see it is;
The trees, though summer, yet forlorn and lean,
O'ercome with moss and baleful mistletoe:
Here never shines the sun; here nothing breeds,
● Unless the nightly owl or fatal raven:
And when they show'd me this abhorred pit,
They told me, here, at dead time of the night,
A thousand fiends, a thousand hissing snakes,   100
● Ten thousand swelling toads, as many urchins,
Would make such fearful and confused cries
As any mortal body hearing it
Should straight fall mad, or else die suddenly.
No sooner had they told this hellish tale,
But straight they told me they would bind me
       here
Unto the body of a dismal yew,
And leave me to this miserable death:
And then they call'd me foul adulteress,
Lascivious Goth, and all the bitterest terms   110
That ever ear did hear to such effect:
And, had you not by wondrous fortune come,

57 *Dian.* Diana, goddess of the moon and of the hunt.

60 *Saucy controller.* Impertinent critic. *steps.* Actions.

63 *Actæon.* Hunter who was turned into a stag by Diana for watching her bathing, and was then torn in pieces by his hounds.

Actaeon torn apart by his own dogs. Woodcut from the 16th century

66–71 *Under your . . . stag.* See introduction.

68 *to be doubted.* i.e. it is suspected.

72 *Cimmerian.* According to myth, a race of people living in a land of perpetual darkness.

81 *rated.* Scolded.

97 *fatal.* Ominous.

101 *urchins.* Hedgehogs.

124 *stood upon.* Made much of.

126 *painted.* Feigned.

135 *nice-preserved.* Carefully guarded. *honesty.* Chastity.

This vengeance on me had they executed.
Revenge it, as you love your mother's life,
Or be ye not henceforth call'd my children.
   Dem.   This is a witness that I am thy son.
                        [*Stabs Bassianus.*
   Chi.   And this for me, struck home to show my
     strength. [*Also stabs Bassianus, who dies.*
   Lav.   Ay, come, Semiramis, nay, barbarous
     Tamora,
For no name fits thy nature but thy own!
   Tam.   Give me thy poniard; you shall know,
     my boys,   120
Your mother's hand shall right your mother's
     wrong.
   Dem.   Stay, madam; here is more belongs to
     her;
First thrash the corn, then after burn the straw:
• This minion stood upon her chastity,
Upon her nuptial vow, her loyalty,
• †And with that painted hope braves your mighti-
     ness:
And shall she carry this unto her grave?
   Chi.   An if she do, I would I were an eunuch.
Drag hence her husband to some secret hole,
And make his dead trunk pillow to our lust. 130
   Tam.   But when ye have the honey ye desire,
Let not this wasp outlive, us both to sting.
   Chi.   I warrant you, madam, we will make
     that sure.
Come, mistress, now perforce we will enjoy
• That nice-preserved honesty of yours.
   Lav.   O Tamora! thou bear'st a woman's
     face,—
   Tam.   I will not hear her speak; away with
     her!
   Lav.   Sweet lords, entreat her hear me but a
     word.
   Dem.   Listen, fair madam: let it be your glory
To see her tears; but be your heart to them 140
As unrelenting flint to drops of rain.
   Lav.   When did the tiger's young ones teach
     the dam?
O, do not learn her wrath; she taught it thee:
The milk thou suck'dst from her did turn to
     marble;
Even at thy teat thou hadst thy tyranny.
Yet every mother breeds not sons alike:
[*To Chiron*] Do thou entreat her show a woman
     pity.
   Chi.   What, wouldst thou have me prove my-
     self a bastard?
   Lav.   'Tis true; the raven doth not hatch a
     lark:
Yet have I heard,—O, could I find it now!— 150
The lion moved with pity did endure
To have his princely paws pared all away:
Some say that ravens foster forlorn children,
The whilst their own birds famish in their nests:
O, be to me, though thy hard heart say no,
Nothing so kind, but something pitiful!
   Tam.   I know not what it means; away with
     her!
   Lav.   O, let me teach thee! for my father's
     sake,
That gave thee life, when well he might have
     slain thee,
Be not obdurate, open thy deaf ears. 160
   Tam.   Hadst thou in person ne'er offended me,
Even for his sake am I pitiless.

Opposite: Tamora: 'I will not hear her speak; away with her!' Painting by Samuel Woodforde (1763–1817)

173 *present.* Immediate.

Lavinia: ''Tis present death I beg; and one thing more
That womanhood denies my tongue to tell:' Engraving
by J. K. Sherwin (1751–90)

183 *our general name.* Our generic name, i.e. womankind.

191 *trull.* Slut.

Remember, boys, I pour'd forth tears in vain,
To save your brother from the sacrifice;
But fierce Andronicus would not relent:
Therefore, away with her, and use her as you will,
The worse to her, the better loved of me.
   Lav.   O Tamora, be call'd a gentle queen,
And with thine own hands kill me in this place!
For 'tis not life that I have begg'd so long;   170
Poor I was slain when Bassianus died.
   Tam.   What begg'st thou, then? fond woman,
     let me go.
   Lav.   'Tis present death I beg; and one thing
     more
That womanhood denies my tongue to tell:
O, keep me from their worse than killing lust,
And tumble me into some loathsome pit,
Where never man's eye may behold my body:
Do this, and be a charitable murderer.
   Tam.   So should I rob my sweet sons of their
     fee:
No, let them satisfy their lust on thee.   180
   Dem.   Away! for thou hast stay'd us here too
     long.
   Lav.   No grace? no womanhood? Ah, beastly
     creature!
The blot and enemy to our general name!
Confusion fall—
   Chi.   Nay, then I'll stop your mouth.   Bring
     thou her husband:
This is the hole where Aaron bid us hide him.
     [*Demetrius throws the body of Bassianus into
       the pit; then exeunt Demetrius and Chi-
       ron, dragging off Lavinia.*
   Tam.   Farewell, my sons: see that you make
     her sure.
Ne'er let my heart know merry cheer indeed,
Till all the Andronici be made away.
Now will I hence to seek my lovely Moor,   190
And let my spleenful sons this trull deflour.
                   [*Exit.*

Re-enter AARON, *with* QUINTUS *and* MARTIUS.

   Aar.   Come on, my lords, the better foot be-
     fore:
Straight will I bring you to the loathsome pit
Where I espied the panther fast asleep.
   Quin.   My sight is very dull, whate'er it bodes.
   Mart.   And mine, I promise you; were't not
     for shame,
Well could I leave our sport to sleep awhile.
              [*Falls into the pit.*
   Quin.   What, art thou fall'n? What subtle
     hole is this,
Whose mouth is cover'd with rude-growing briers,
Upon whose leaves are drops of new-shed blood
As fresh as morning dew distill'd on flowers?
A very fatal place it seems to me.
Speak, brother, hast thou hurt thee with the fall?
   Mart.   O brother, with the dismall'st object
     hurt
That ever eye with sight made heart lament!
   Aar.   [*Aside*] Now will I fetch the king to find
     them here,
That he thereby may give a likely guess
How these were they that made away his bro-
     ther.   [*Exit.*
   Mart.   Why dost not comfort me, and help
     me out   209
From this unhallowed and blood-stained hole?

Quin. I am surprised with an uncouth fear:
A chilling sweat o'er-runs my trembling joints:
My heart suspects more than mine eye can see.
   Mart. To prove thou hast a true-divining
      heart,
Aaron and thou look down into this den,
And see a fearful sight of blood and death.
   Quin. Aaron is gone; and my compassionate
      heart
Will not permit mine eyes once to behold
The thing whereat it trembles by surmise:
O, tell me how it is; for ne'er till now   220
Was I a child to fear I know not what.
   Mart. Lord Bassianus lies embrewed here,
All on a heap, like to a slaughter'd lamb,
In this detested, dark, blood-drinking pit.
   Quin. If it be dark, how dost thou know 'tis he?
   Mart. Upon his bloody finger he doth wear
A precious ring, that lightens all the hole,
Which, like a taper in some monument,
Doth shine upon the dead man's earthy cheeks,
And shows the ragged entrails of the pit: 230
So pale did shine the moon on Pyramus
When he by night lay bathed in maiden blood.
O brother, help me with thy fainting hand—
If fear hath made thee faint, as me it hath—
Out of this fell devouring receptacle,
As hateful as Cocytus' misty mouth.
   Quin. Reach me thy hand, that I may help
      thee out;
Or, wanting strength to do thee so much good,
I may be pluck'd into the swallowing womb
Of this deep pit, poor Bassianus' grave.   240
I have no strength to pluck thee to the brink.
   Mart. Nor I no strength to climb without thy
      help.
   Quin. Thy hand once more; I will not loose
      again,
Till thou art here aloft, or I below:
Thou canst not come to me: I come to thee.
                      [Falls in.

    Enter SATURNINUS *with* AARON.

   Sat. Along with me: I'll see what hole is here,
And what he is that now is leap'd into it.
Say, who art thou that lately didst descend.
Into this gaping hollow of the earth?
   Mart. The unhappy son of old Andronicus;
Brought hither in a most unlucky hour,   251
To find thy brother Bassianus dead.
   Sat. My brother dead! I know thou dost
      but jest:
He and his lady both are at the lodge
Upon the north side of this pleasant chase;
'Tis not an hour since I left him there.
   Mart. We know not where you left him all
      alive;
But, out, alas! here have we found him dead.

   Re-enter TAMORA, *with* Attendants; TITUS
      ANDRONICUS, *and* LUCIUS.

   Tam. Where is my lord the king?
   Sat. Here, Tamora, though grieved with kill-
      ing grief.   260
   Tam. Where is thy brother Bassianus?
   Sat. Now to the bottom dost thou search my
      wound:
Poor Bassianus here lies murdered.
   Tam. Then all too late I bring this fatal writ,

Martius: 'Lord Bassianus lies embrewed here, All on a heap, like to a slaughter'd lamb.' Engraving by H. Fuseli (1741–1825)

---

222 *embrewed.* Bloodstained.

230 *ragged entrails.* i.e. rugged interior.

231 *Pyramus.* Who killed himself thinking his beloved Thisbe was dead.

236 *Cocytus.* Legendary river in Hell.

265 *complot.* Plot. *timeless.* Ill-timed.

298 *their suspicion.* i.e. that of which they are suspected.

Costume design for Titus Andronicus by Desmond
Heeley, Stratford-upon-Avon, 1955

3 *bewray.* Reveal.

5 *scrowl.* Scrawl.

The complot of this timeless tragedy;
And wonder greatly that man's face can fold
In pleasing smiles such murderous tyranny.
      [*She giveth Saturnine a letter.*
   Sat. [*Reads*] 'An if we miss to meet him
      handsomely—
Sweet huntsman, Bassianus 'tis we mean—
Do thou so much as dig the grave for him: 270
Thou know'st our meaning. Look for thy reward
Among the nettles at the elder-tree
Which overshades the mouth of that same pit
Where we decreed to bury Bassianus.
Do this, and purchase us thy lasting friends.'
O Tamora! was ever heard the like?
This is the pit, and this the elder-tree.
Look, sirs, if you can find the huntsman ou
That should have murder'd Bassianus here.
   Aar. My gracious lord, here is the bag of
      gold.   280
   Sat. [*To Titus*] Two of thy whelps, fell curs
      of bloody kind,
Have here bereft my brother of his life.
Sirs, drag them from the pit unto the prison:
There let them bide until we have devised
Some never-heard-of torturing pain for them.
   Tam. What, are they in this pit? O won-
      drous thing!
How easily murder is discovered!
   Tit. High emperor, upon my feeble knee
I beg this boon, with tears not lightly shed,
That this fell fault of my accursed sons,   290
Accursed, if the fault be proved in them,—
   Sat. If it be proved! you see it is apparent.
Who found this letter? Tamora, was it you?
   Tam. Andronicus himself did take it up.
   Tit. I did, my lord: yet let me be their bail;
For, by my father's reverend tomb, I vow
They shall be ready at your highness' will
To answer their suspicion with their lives.
   Sat. Thou shalt not bail them: see thou fol-
      low me.
Some bring the murder'd body, some the mur-
      derers: 300
Let them not speak a word; the guilt is plain;
For, by my soul, were there worse end than death,
That end upon them should be executed.
   Tam. Andronicus, I will entreat the king:
Fear not thy sons; they shall do well enough.
   Tit. Come, Lucius, come; stay not to talk
      with them.   [*Exeunt.*

SCENE IV.   *Another part of the forest.*

Enter DEMETRIUS *and* CHIRON, *with* LAVINIA,
*ravished; her hands cut off, and her tongue
cut out.*

   Dem. So, now go tell, an if thy tongue can
      speak,
Who 'twas that cut thy tongue and ravish'd thee.
   Chi. Write down thy mind, bewray thy mean-
      ing so,
An if thy stumps will let thee play the scribe.
   Dem. See, how with signs and tokens she can
      scrowl.
   Chi. Go home, call for sweet water, wash
      thy hands.
   Dem. She hath no tongue to call, nor hands
      to wash;
And so let's leave her to her silent walks.

Chi. An 'twere my case, I should go hang
    myself.
Dem. If thou hadst hands to help thee knit
    the cord. [*Exeunt Demetrius and Chiron.*

       Enter MARCUS.

Mar. Who is this? my niece, that flies away
    so fast!   11
Cousin, a word; where is your husband?
If I do dream, would all my wealth would wake
    me!
If I wake, some planet strike me down,
That I may slumber in eternal sleep!
Speak, gentle niece, what stern ungentle hands
Have lopp'd and hew'd and made thy body bare
Of her two branches, those sweet ornaments,
Whose circling shadows kings have sought to
    sleep in,
And might not gain so great a happiness   20
As have thy love? Why dost not speak to me?
Alas, a crimson river of warm blood,
Like to a bubbling fountain stirr'd with wind,
Doth rise and fall between thy rosed lips,
Coming and going with thy honey breath.
But, sure, some Tereus hath deflowered thee,
And, lest thou shouldst detect him, cut thy tongue.
Ah, now thou turn'st away thy face for shame!
And, notwithstanding all this loss of blood,
As from a conduit with three issuing spouts, 30
• Yet do thy cheeks look red as Titan's face
Blushing to be encounter'd with a cloud.
Shall I speak for thee? shall I say 'tis so?
O, that I knew thy heart; and knew the beast,
That I might rail at him, to ease my mind!
Sorrow concealed, like an oven stopp'd,
Doth burn the heart to cinders where it is.
Fair Philomela, she but lost her tongue,
And in a tedious sampler sew'd her mind:
But, lovely niece, that mean is cut from thee; 40
A craftier Tereus, cousin, hast thou met,
And he hath cut those pretty fingers off,
That could have better sew'd than Philomel.
O, had the monster seen those lily hands
Tremble, like aspen-leaves, upon a lute,
And make the silken strings delight to kiss them,
He would not then have touch'd them for his life!
Or, had he heard the heavenly harmony
Which that sweet tongue hath made,
He would have dropp'd his knife, and fell asleep
• As Cerberus at the Thracian poet's feet. 51
Come, let us go, and make thy father blind;
For such a sight will blind a father's eye:
One hour's storm will drown the fragrant meads;
What will whole months of tears thy father's eyes?
Do not draw back, for we will mourn with thee:
O, could our mourning ease thy misery!
                   [*Exeunt.*

ACT III.

SCENE I. *Rome. A street.*

Enter Judges, Senators *and* Tribunes, *with*
MARTIUS *and* QUINTUS, *bound, passing on to
the place of execution;* TITUS *going before,
pleading.*

Tit. Hear me, grave fathers! noble tribunes,
    stay!
For pity of mine age, whose youth was spent
In dangerous wars, whilst you securely slept;

31 *Titan.* i.e. Hyperion, the sun.

51 *Cerberus.* Three-headed dog-like monster which
guarded the gates of Hell. *Thracian poet.* Orpheus, who
lulled Cerberus to sleep with music.

Hercules leading Cerberus from Hell. Engraving from
Discours de la Religion des Anciens Romains, 1567

Titus: 'O earth, I will befriend thee more with rain ...'
Engraving from John Speed's *A Prospect of the Most
Famous Parts of the World*, 1631

For all my blood in Rome's great quarrel shed;
For all the frosty nights that I have watch'd;
And for these bitter tears, which now you see
Filling the aged wrinkles in my cheeks;
Be pitiful to my condemned sons,
Whose souls are not corrupted as 'tis thought.
For two and twenty sons I never wept,   10
Because they died in honour's lofty bed.
  [*Lieth down; the Judges, &c. pass by
      him, and Exeunt.*
For these, these, tribunes, in the dust I write
My heart's deep languor and my soul's sad tears:
Let my tears stanch the earth's dry appetite;
My sons' sweet blood will make it shame and
  blush.
O earth, I will befriend thee more with rain,
That shall distil from these two ancient urns,
Than youthful April shall with all his showers:
In summer's drought I'll drop upon thee still;
In winter with warm tears I'll melt the snow,   20
And keep eternal spring-time on thy face,
So thou refuse to drink my dear sons' blood.

  Enter LUCIUS, *with his sword drawn.*

O reverend tribunes! O gentle, aged men!
Unbind my sons, reverse the doom of death;
And let me say, that never wept before,
My tears are now prevailing orators.
  Luc. O noble father, you lament in vain:
The tribunes hear you not; no man is by;
And you recount your sorrows to a stone.
  Tit. Ah, Lucius, for thy brothers let me plead.
Grave tribunes, once more I entreat of you,— 31
  Luc. My gracious lord, no tribune hears you
  speak.
  Tit. Why, 'tis no matter, man: if they did
  hear,
They would not mark me, or if they did mark,
They would not pity me, yet plead I must;
†And bootless unto them.................
Therefore I tell my sorrows to the stones;
Who, though they cannot answer my distress,
Yet in some sort they are better than the tribunes,
For that they will not intercept my tale: 40
When I do weep, they humbly at my feet
Receive my tears and seem to weep with me;
And, were they but attired in grave weeds,
Rome could afford no tribune like to these.
A stone is soft as wax,—tribunes more hard than
  stones;
A stone is silent, and offendeth not,
And tribunes with their tongues doom men to
  death.   [*Rises.*
But wherefore stand'st thou with thy weapon
  drawn?
  Luc. To rescue my two brothers from their
  death:
For which attempt the judges have pronounced
My everlasting doom of banishment.   51
  Tit. O happy man! they have befriended thee.
Why, foolish Lucius, dost thou not perceive
That Rome is but a wilderness of tigers?
Tigers must prey, and Rome affords no prey
But me and mine: how happy art thou, then,
From these devourers to be banished!
But who comes with our brother Marcus here?

  Enter MARCUS *and* LAVINIA.

  Marc. Titus, prepare thy aged eyes to weep;

Or, if not so, thy noble heart to break: 60
I bring consuming sorrow to thine age.
 Tit. Will it consume me? let me see it, then.
 Marc. This was thy daughter.
 Tit.   Why, Marcus, so she is.
• *Luc.* Ay me, this object kills me!
 Tit. Faint-hearted boy, arise, and look upon
  her.
Speak, Lavinia, what accursed hand
Hath made thee handless in thy father's sight?
What fool hath added water to the sea,
Or brought a faggot to bright-burning Troy?
My grief was at the height before thou camest,
•And now, like Nilus, it disdaineth bounds.   71
Give me a sword, I'll chop off my hands too;
For they have fought for Rome, and all in vain;
And they have nursed this woe, in feeding life;
In bootless prayer have they been held up,
And they have served me to effectless use:
Now all the service I require of them
Is that the one will help to cut the other.
'Tis well, Lavinia, that thou hast no hands;
For hands, to do Rome service, are but vain.   80
 Luc. Speak, gentle sister, who hath martyr'd
  thee?
• *Marc.* O, that delightful engine of her thoughts,
That blabb'd them with such pleasing eloquence,
Is torn from forth that pretty hollow cage,
Where, like a sweet melodious bird, it sung
Sweet varied notes, enchanting every ear!
 Luc. O, say thou for her, who hath done this
  deed?
 Marc. O, thus I found her, straying in the
  park,
Seeking to hide herself, as doth the deer
•That hath received some unrecuring wound.   90
 Tit. It was my deer; and he that wounded her
Hath hurt me more than had he kill'd me dead:
For now I stand as one upon a rock
Environ'd with a wilderness of sea,
Who marks the waxing tide grow wave by wave,
•Expecting ever when some envious surge
Will in his brinish bowels swallow him.
This way to death my wretched sons are gone;
Here stands my other son, a banish'd man,
And here my brother, weeping at my woes: 100
•But that which gives my soul the greatest spurn,
Is dear Lavinia, dearer than my soul.
Had I but seen thy picture in this plight,
It would have madded me: what shall I do
Now I behold thy lively body so?
Thou hast no hands, to wipe away thy tears;
Nor tongue, to tell me who hath martyr'd thee:
Thy husband he is dead; and for his death
Thy brothers are condemn'd, and dead by this.
Look, Marcus! ah, son Lucius, look on her!   110
When I did name her brothers, then fresh tears
Stood on her cheeks, as doth the honey-dew
Upon a gather'd lily almost wither'd.
 Marc. Perchance she weeps because they
  kill'd her husband;
Perchance because she knows them innocent.
 Tit. If they did kill thy husband, then be
  joyful,
Because the law hath ta'en revenge on them.
No, no, they would not do so foul a deed;
Witness the sorrow that their sister makes.
Gentle Lavinia, let me kiss thy lips;   120
Or make some sign how I may do thee ease:

64 *object.* Sight.

71 *Nilus.* The river Nile.

Costume design for Lavinia by Desmond Heeley,
Stratford-upon-Avon, 1955

82 *engine.* Instrument.

90 *unrecuring.* Incurable.

96 *envious.* Malevolent.

101 *spurn.* Thrust.

128 *clearness.* i.e. clear pool.

149 *Limbo.* The border of Hell.

Hell or Hades. Engraving from a vase painting of the 3rd century B.C.

Shall thy good uncle, and thy brother Lucius,
And thou, and I, sit round about some fountain,
Looking all downwards, to behold our cheeks
How they are stain'd, as meadows, yet not dry,
With miry slime left on them by a flood?
And in the fountain shall we gaze so long
●Till the fresh taste be taken from that clearness,
And made a brine-pit with our bitter tears?
Or shall we cut away our hands, like thine?   130
Or shall we bite our tongues, and in dumb shows
Pass the remainder of our hateful days?
What shall we do? let us, that have our tongues,
Plot some device of further misery,
To make us wonder'd at in time to come.
   Luc.   Sweet father, cease your tears; for, at
     your grief,
See how my wretched sister sobs and weeps.
   Marc.   Patience, dear niece. Good Titus, dry
     thine eyes.
   Tit.   Ah, Marcus, Marcus! brother, well I wot
Thy napkin cannot drink a tear of mine,   140
For thou, poor man, hast drown'd it with thine
     own.
   Luc.   Ah, my Lavinia, I will wipe thy cheeks.
   Tit.   Mark, Marcus, mark! I understand her
     signs:
Had she a tongue to speak, now would she say
That to her brother which I said to thee:
His napkin, with his true tears all bewet,
Can do no service on her sorrowful cheeks.
O, what a sympathy of woe is this,
●As far from help as Limbo is from bliss!   149

       Enter AARON.

   Aar.   Titus Andronicus, my lord the emperor
Sends thee this word,—that, if thou love thy sons,
Let Marcus, Lucius, or thyself, old Titus,
Or any one of you, chop off your hand,
And send it to the king: he for the same
Will send thee hither both thy sons alive;
And that shall be the ransom for their fault.
   Tit.   O gracious emperor! O gentle Aaron!
Did ever raven sing so like a lark,
That gives sweet tidings of the sun's uprise?
With all my heart, I'll send the emperor   160
My hand:
Good Aaron, wilt thou help to chop it off?
   Luc.   Stay, father! for that noble hand of thine,
That hath thrown down so many enemies,
Shall not be sent: my hand will serve the turn:
My youth can better spare my blood than you;
And therefore mine shall save my brothers' lives.
   Marc.   Which of your hands hath not defended
     Rome,
And rear'd aloft the bloody battle-axe,
Writing destruction on the enemy's castle?   170
O, none of both but are of high desert:
My hand hath been but idle; let it serve
To ransom my two nephews from their death;
Then have I kept it to a worthy end.
   Aar.   Nay, come, agree whose hand shall go
     along,
For fear they die before their pardon come.
   Marc.   My hand shall go.
   Luc.   By heaven, it shall not go!
   Tit.   Sirs, strive no more: such wither'd herbs
     as these
Are meet for plucking up, and therefore mine.

Luc. Sweet father, if I shall be thought thy son,   180
Let me redeem my brothers both from death.
  Marc. And, for our father's sake and mother's care,
Now let me show a brother's love to thee.
  Tit. Agree between you; I will spare my hand.
  Luc. Then I'll go fetch an axe.
  Marc. But I will use the axe.
                    [*Exeunt Lucius and Marcus.*
  Tit. Come hither, Aaron; I'll deceive them both:
Lend me thy hand, and I will give thee mine.
  Aar. [*Aside*] If that be call'd deceit, I will be honest,
And never, whilst I live, deceive men so: 190
But I'll deceive you in another sort,
And that you'll say, ere half an hour pass.
                    [*Cuts off Titus's hand.*

Re-enter LUCIUS *and* MARCUS.

  Tit. Now stay your strife: what shall be is dispatch'd.
Good Aaron, give his majesty my hand:
Tell him it was a hand that warded him
From thousand dangers; bid him bury it;
More hath it merited; that let it have.
As for my sons, say I account of them
As jewels purchased at an easy price;   199
And yet dear too, because I bought mine own.
  Aar. I go, Andronicus: and for thy hand
Look by and by to have thy sons with thee.
[*Aside*] Their heads, I mean. O, how this villany
Doth fat me with the very thoughts of it!
Let fools do good, and fair men call for grace,
Aaron will have his soul black like his face. [*Exit.*
  Tit. O, here I lift this one hand up to heaven,
And bow this feeble ruin to the earth:
If any power pities wretched tears,
To that I call! [*To Lav.*] What, wilt thou kneel with me?   210
Do, then, dear heart; for heaven shall hear our prayers;
Or with our sighs we'll breathe the welkin dim,
And stain the sun with fog, as sometime clouds
When they do hug him in their melting bosoms.
  Marc. O brother, speak with possibilities,
And do not break into these deep extremes.
  Tit. Is not my sorrow deep, having no bottom?
Then be my passions bottomless with them.
  Marc. But yet let reason govern thy lament.
  Tit. If there were reason for these miseries,
Then into limits could I bind my woes: 221
When heaven doth weep, doth not the earth o'erflow?
If the winds rage, doth not the sea wax mad,
Threatening the welkin with his big-swoln face?
● And wilt thou have a reason for this coil?
I am the sea; hark, how her sighs do blow!
She is the weeping welkin, I the earth:
Then must my sea be moved with her sighs;
Then must my earth with her continual tears
Become a deluge, overflow'd and drown'd;   230
For why my bowels cannot hide her woes,
But like a drunkard must I vomit them.
Then give me leave, for losers will have leave
To ease their stomachs with their bitter tongues.

Titus: 'Lend me thy hand, and I will give thee mine.'
Derek Godfrey as Titus and Keith Michell as Aaron,
Old Vic, 1957

225 *coil.* To-do.

Messenger: 'Here are the heads of thy two noble sons . . .'
Woodcut attributed to Albrecht Dürer (1471–1528)

253 *fearful slumber*. i.e. nightmare.

257 *dear*. Grievous.

270 *tributary*. In tribute.

Enter a Messenger, *with two heads and a hand.*

Mess. Worthy Andronicus, ill art thou repaid
For that good hand thou sent'st the emperor.
Here are the heads of thy two noble sons;
And here's thy hand, in scorn to thee sent back;
Thy griefs their sports, thy resolution mock'd;
That woe is me to think upon thy woes   240
More than remembrance of my father's death.
                                    [*Exit.*
Marc. Now let hot Ætna cool in Sicily,
And be my heart an ever-burning hell!
These miseries are more than may be borne.
To weep with them that weep doth ease some
    deal;
But sorrow flouted at is double death.
Luc. Ah, that this sight should make so deep
    a wound,
And yet detested life not shrink thereat!
That ever death should let life bear his name, 249
Where life hath no more interest but to breathe!
                        [*Lavinia kisses Titus.*
Marc. Alas, poor heart, that kiss is com-
    fortless
As frozen water to a starved snake.
• *Tit.* When will this fearful slumber have
    an end?
Marc. Now, farewell, flattery: die, Andro-
    nicus;
Thou dost not slumber: see, thy two sons' heads,
Thy warlike hand, thy mangled daughter here;
•Thy other banish'd son, with this dear sight
Struck pale and bloodless; and thy brother, I,
Even like a stony image, cold and numb.
Ah, now no more will I control thy griefs: 260
Rend off thy silver hair, thy other hand
Gnawing with thy teeth; and be this dismal sight
The closing up of our most wretched eyes:
Now is a time to storm; why art thou still?
Tit. Ha, ha, ha!
Marc. Why dost thou laugh? it fits not with
    this hour.
Tit. Why, I have not another tear to shed:
Besides, this sorrow is an enemy,
And would usurp upon my watery eyes,
•And make them blind with tributary tears: 270
Then which way shall I find Revenge's cave?
For these two heads do seem to speak to me,
And threat me I shall never come to bliss
Till all these mischiefs be return'd again
Even in their throats that have committed them.
Come, let me see what task I have to do.
You heavy people, circle me about,
That I may turn me to each one of you,
And swear unto my soul to right your wrongs.
The vow is made. Come, brother, take a head;
And in this hand the other will I bear.   281
Lavinia, thou shalt be employ'd: these arms!
Bear thou my hand, sweet wench, between thy
    teeth.
As for thee, boy, go get thee from my sight:
Thou art an exile, and thou must not stay:
Hie to the Goths, and raise an army there:
And, if you love me, as I think you do,
Let's kiss and part, for we have much to do.
            [*Exeunt Titus, Marcus, and Lavinia.*
Luc. Farewell, Andronicus, my noble father,
The wofull'st man that ever lived in Rome: 290

Farewell, proud Rome; till Lucius come again,
He leaves his pledges dearer than his life:
Farewell, Lavinia, my noble sister;
O, would thou wert as thou tofore hast been!
But now nor Lucius nor Lavinia lives
But in oblivion and hateful griefs.
If Lucius live, he will requite your wrongs;
And make proud Saturnine and his empress
● Beg at the gates, like Tarquin and his queen.
Now will I to the Goths, and raise a power,   300
To be revenged on Rome and Saturnine. [*Exit.*

SCENE II. *A room in Titus's house. A
banquet set out.*

Enter TITUS, MARCUS, LAVINIA, *and young*
LUCIUS, *a* BOY.

Tit. So, so; now sit: and look you eat no more
Than will preserve just so much strength in us
As will revenge these bitter woes of ours.
● Marcus, unknit that sorrow-wreathen knot:
Thy niece and I, poor creatures, want our hands,
● And cannot passionate our tenfold grief
With folded arms. This poor right hand of mine
Is left to tyrannize upon my breast;
Who, when my heart, all mad with misery,
Beats in this hollow prison of my flesh,   10
Then thus I thump it down.
[*To Lavinia.*] Thou map of woe, that thus dost
talk in signs!
When thy poor heart beats with outrageous
beating,
Thou canst not strike it thus to make it still.
Wound it with sighing, girl, kill it with groans;
Or get some little knife between thy teeth,
And just against thy heart make thou a hole;
That all the tears that thy poor eyes let fall
May run into that sink, and soaking in
Drown the lamenting fool in sea-salt tears.   20
Marc. Fie, brother, fie! teach her not thus
to lay
Such violent hands upon her tender life.
Tit. How now! has sorrow made thee dote
already?
Why, Marcus, no man should be mad but I.
What violent hands can she lay on her life?
Ah, wherefore dost thou urge the name of hands;
To bid Æneas tell the tale twice o'er,
How Troy was burnt and he made miserable?
O, handle not the theme, to talk of hands,
Lest we remember still that we have none.   30
Fie, fie, how franticly I square my talk,
As if we should forget we had no hands,
If Marcus did not name the word of hands!
Come, let's fall to; and, gentle girl, eat this:
Here is no drink! Hark, Marcus, what she says;
I can interpret all her martyr'd signs;
She says she drinks no other drink but tears,
Brew'd with her sorrow, mesh'd upon her
cheeks:
Speechless complainer, I will learn thy thought;
In thy dumb action will I be as perfect   40
As begging hermits in their holy prayers:
Thou shalt not sigh, nor hold thy stumps to
heaven,
● Nor wink, nor nod, nor kneel, nor make a sign,
But I of these will wrest an alphabet
● And by still practice learn to know thy meaning.

299 *Tarquin.* Lucius Tarquinius Superbus, King of
Rome, expelled because his son had committed rape on
Lucretia.

The rape of Lucretia. Engraving by Bartolomeo Pinelli,
1821

4 *unknit that sorrow-wreathen knot.* i.e. uncross your
arms.

6 *passionate.* Express with feeling.

43 *wink.* Close the eyes.

45 *still.* Constant.

Costume design for young Lucius by Desmond Heeley,
Stratford-upon-Avon, 1955

Boy. Good grandsire, leave these bitter deep
   laments:
Make my aunt merry with some pleasing tale.
   Marc. Alas, the tender boy, in passion moved,
Doth weep to see his grandsire's heaviness.
   Tit. Peace, tender sapling; thou art made
   of tears,   50
And tears will quickly melt thy life away.
    [*Marcus strikes the dish with a knife*
What dost thou strike at, Marcus, with thy knife?
   Marc. At that that I have kill'd, my lord;
   a fly.
   Tit. Out on thee, murderer! thou kill'st my
   heart;
Mine eyes are cloy'd with view of tyranny:
A deed of death done on the innocent
Becomes not Titus' brother: get thee gone;
I see thou art not for my company.
   Marc. Alas, my lord, I have but kill'd a fly.
   Tit. But how, if that fly had a father and
   mother?   60
How would he hang his slender gilded wings,
And buzz lamenting doings in the air!
Poor harmless fly,
That, with his pretty buzzing melody,
Came here to make us merry! and thou hast
   kill'd him.
   Marc. Pardon me, sir; it was a black ill-
   favour'd fly,
Like to the empress' Moor; therefore I kill'd him.
   Tit. O, O, O,
Then pardon me for reprehending thee,
For thou hast done a charitable deed.   70
Give me thy knife, I will insult on him;
Flattering myself, as if it were the Moor
Come hither purposely to poison me.—
There's for thyself, and that's for Tamora
Ah, sirrah!
Yet, I think, we are not brought so low,
But that between us we can kill a fly
That comes in likeness of a coal-black Moor.
   Marc. Alas, poor man! grief has so wrought
   on him,
He takes false shadows for true substances.   80
   Tit. Come, take away. Lavinia, go with me:
I'll to thy closet; and go read with thee
Sad stories chanced in the times of old.
Come, boy, and go with me: thy sight is young,
And thou shalt read when mine begin to dazzle.
     [*Exeunt.*

ACT IV.

SCENE I. *Rome. Titus's garden.*

Enter young LUCIUS, *and* LAVINIA *running
after him, and the boy flies from her, with
books under his arm. Then enter* TITUS *and*
MARCUS.

   Young Luc. Help, grandsire, help! my aunt
   Lavinia
Follows me every where, I know not why:
Good uncle Marcus, see how swift she comes.
Alas, sweet aunt, I know not what you mean
   Marc. Stand by me, Lucius; do not fear
   thine aunt.
   Tit. She loves thee, boy, too well to do thee
   harm.
   Young Luc. Ay, when my father was in Rome
   she did.

Marc. What means my niece Lavinia by these signs?

Tit. Fear her not, Lucius: somewhat doth she mean:
See, Lucius, see how much she makes of thee: 10
Somewhither would she have thee go with her.
• Ah, boy, Cornelia never with more care
Read to her sons than she hath read to thee
• Sweet poetry and Tully's Orator.

Marc. Canst thou not guess wherefore she plies thee thus?

Young Luc. My lord, I know not, I, nor can I guess,
Unless some fit or frenzy do possess her:
For I have heard my grandsire say full oft,
Extremity of griefs would make men mad;
And I have read that Hecuba of Troy 20
Ran mad for sorrow : that made me to fear;
Although, my lord, I know my noble aunt
Loves me as dear as e'er my mother did,
• And would not, but in fury, fright my youth:
Which made me down to throw my books, and fly,—
Causeless, perhaps. But pardon me, sweet aunt:
And, madam, if my uncle Marcus go,
I will most willingly attend your ladyship.

Marc. Lucius, I will.

[*Lavinia turns over with her stumps the books which Lucius has let fall.*

Tit. How now, Lavinia! Marcus, what means this? 30
Some book there is that she desires to see.
Which is it, girl, of these? Open them, boy.
But thou art deeper read, and better skill'd:
Come, and take choice of all my library,
And so beguile thy sorrow, till the heavens
Reveal the damn'd contriver of this deed.
Why lifts she up her arms in sequence thus?

Marc. I think she means that there was more than one
Confederate in the fact: ay, more there was;
Or else to heaven she heaves them for revenge. 40

• *Tit.* Lucius, what book is that she tosseth so?

Young Luc. Grandsire, 'tis Ovid's Metamorphoses;
My mother gave it me.

Marc. For love of her that's gone,
Perhaps she cull'd it from among the rest.

Tit. Soft! see how busily she turns the leaves! [*Helping her.*
What would she find? Lavinia, shall I read?
This is the tragic tale of Philomel,
And treats of Tereus' treason and his rape;
And rape, I fear, was root of thine annoy.

• *Marc.* See, brother, see; note how she quotes the leaves. 50

Tit. Lavinia, wert thou thus surprised, sweet girl,
Ravish'd and wrong'd, as Philomela was,
Forced in the ruthless, vast, and gloomy woods?
See, see!
Ay, such a place there is, where we did hunt—
O, had we never, never hunted there !—
• Pattern'd by that the poet here describes,
By nature made for murders and for rapes.

Marc. O, why should nature build so foul a den,
Unless the gods delight in tragedies? 60

Tit. Give signs, sweet girl, for here are none but friends,

12 *Cornelia.* Mother of two famous orators.

Cornelia with her two sons Tiberius and Caius, to whose education she devoted her life. Engraving by Bartolomeo Pinelli, 1821

14 *Tully's Orator.* Cicero's *De Oratore.*

24 *fury.* Madness.

41 *tosseth.* i.e. flicks through.

50 *quotes.* Examines.

57 *Pattern'd by.* In the manner of.

63 *erst.* First.

72 *shift.* Contrivance.

Titus: 'O, do ye read, my lord, what she hath writ?'
Derek Godfrey as Titus and Ingrid Hafner as Lavinia,
Old Vic, 1957

78 *Stuprum.* Rape.

81–82 *Magni . . . vides?* Ruler of the great heavens, are
you so slow to hear and see crimes?

86 *exclaims.* Protests.

89 *fere.* Spouse.

97 *wind.* Catch scent of.

103 *gad.* Spike.

105 *Sibyl.* Prophetess who wrote her predictions in
verses upon leaves which were scattered about on the
wind.

What Roman lord it was durst do the deed:
● Or slunk not Saturnine, as Tarquin erst,
That left the camp to sin in Lucrece' bed?
   Marc. Sit down, sweet niece: brother, sit
     down by me.
Apollo, Pallas, Jove, or Mercury,
Inspire me, that I may this treason find!
My lord, look here: look here, Lavinia:
This sandy plot is plain; guide, if thou canst,
This after me, when I have writ my name   70
Without the help of any hand at all.
   [*He writes his name with his staff, and guides
         it with feet and mouth.*
● Cursed be that heart that forced us to this shift!
Write thou, good niece; and here display, at last,
What God will have discover'd for revenge:
Heaven guide thy pen to print thy sorrows plain,
That we may know the traitors and the truth!
   [*She takes the staff in her mouth, and guides
         it with her stumps, and writes.*
   Tit. O, do ye read, my lord, what she hath
     writ?
● 'Stuprum. Chiron. Demetrius.'
   Marc. What, what! the lustful sons of Tamora
Performers of this heinous, bloody deed?   80
●   *Tit.* Magni Dominator poli,
Tam lentus audis scelera? tam lentus vides?
   Marc. O, calm thee, gentle lord; although I
     know
There is enough written upon this earth
To stir a mutiny in the mildest thoughts
● And arm the minds of infants to exclaims.
My lord, kneel down with me; Lavinia, kneel;
And kneel, sweet boy, the Roman Hector's hope;
● And swear with me, as, with the woful fere
And father of that chaste dishonour'd dame,   90
Lord Junius Brutus sware for Lucrece' rape,
That we will prosecute by good advice
Mortal revenge upon these traitorous Goths,
And see their blood, or die with this reproach.
   Tit. 'Tis sure enough, an you knew how.
But if you hunt these bear-whelps, then beware:
● The dam will wake; and, if she wind you once,
She's with the lion deeply still in league,
And lulls him whilst she playeth on her back,
And when he sleeps will she do what she list.   100
You are a young huntsman, Marcus; let it alone;
And, come, I will go get a leaf of brass,
● And with a gad of steel will write these words,
And lay it by: the angry northern wind
● Will blow these sands, like Sibyl's leaves, abroad,
And where's your lesson, then? Boy, what say
   you?
   Young Luc. I say, my lord, that if I were a man,
Their mother's bed-chamber should not be safe
For these bad bondmen to the yoke of Rome.
   Marc. Ay, that's my boy! thy father hath
     full oft   110
For his ungrateful country done the like.
   Young Luc. And, uncle, so will I, an if I live.
   Tit. Come, go with me into mine armoury;
Lucius, I'll fit thee; and withal, my boy,
Shalt carry from me to the empress' sons
Presents that I intend to send them both:
Come, come; thou'lt do thy message, wilt thou not?
   Young Luc. Ay, with my dagger in their
     bosoms, grandsire.
   Tit. No, boy, not so; I'll teach thee another
     course.

Lavinia, come.   Marcus, look to my house: 120
● Lucius and I'll go brave it at the court:
Ay, marry, will we, sir; and we'll be waited on.
   [*Exeunt Titus, Lavinia, and Young Luc.*
   Marc. O heavens, can you hear a good man
         groan,
And not relent, or not compassion him?
● Marcus, attend him in his ecstasy,
That hath more scars of sorrow in his heart
Than foemen's marks upon his batter'd shield;
But yet so just that he will not revenge.
Revenge, ye heavens, for old Andronicus! [*Exit.*

SCENE II.   *The same.   A room in the palace.*

Enter, from one side, AARON, DEMETRIUS, *and*
   CHIRON; *from the other side, young* LUCIUS,
   and an Attendant, *with a bundle of weapons,*
   and verses writ upon them.

   Chi. Demetrius, here's the son of Lucius;
He hath some message to deliver us.
   Aar. Ay, some mad message from his mad
         grandfather.
   Young Luc. My lords, with all the humbleness
         I may,
I greet your honours from Andronicus.
[*Aside*] And pray the Roman gods confound you
         both!
   Dem. Gramercy, lovely Lucius: what's the
         news?
   Young Luc. [*Aside*] That you are both de-
         cipher'd, that's the news,
For villains mark'd with rape.—May it please you,
● My grandsire, well advised, hath sent by me   10
The goodliest weapons of his armoury
To gratify your honourable youth,
The hope of Rome; for so he bade me say;
And so I do, and with his gifts present
Your lordships, that, whenever you have need,
You may be armed and appointed well:
And so I leave you both: [*Aside*] like bloody
         villains.
         [*Exeunt young Lucius and Attendant.*
●   *Dem.* What's here? A scroll; and written
         round about?
Let's see:
● [*Reads*] 'Integer vitæ, scelerisque purus,   20
         Non eget Mauri jaculis, nec arcu.'
   Chi. O, 'tis a verse in Horace; I know it well:
I read it in the grammar long ago.
   Aar. Ay, just; a verse in Horace; right, you
         have it.
[*Aside*] Now, what a thing it is to be an ass!
Here's no sound jest! the old man hath found
         their guilt;
And sends them weapons wrapp'd about with lines,
That wound, beyond their feeling, to the quick.
● But were our witty empress well afoot,
● She would applaud Andronicus' conceit: 30
But let her rest in her unrest awhile.

And now, young lords, was't not a happy star
Led us to Rome, strangers, and more than so,
Captives, to be advanced to this height?
It did me good, before the palace gate
To brave the tribune in his brother's hearing.
   Dem. But me more good, to see so great a lord
● Basely insinuate and send us gifts.
   Aar. Had he not reason, Lord Demetrius?

121 *brave it.* Challenge.

125 *ecstasy.* Fit of madness.

10 *well advised.* In his right mind.

18-23 *What's here . . . long ago.* See introduction.

20-21 '*Integer . . . arcu*'. The man who is upright in life and free from crime has no need of the javelins or bow of the Moor.

29 *witty.* Clever.

30 *conceit.* Device.

38 *insinuate.* Try to gain favour.

42 *At such a bay*. i.e. in such a tight corner.

72 *blowse*. Fat serving-woman.

85 *broach*. Impale.

Did you not use his daughter very friendly?   40
   Dem. I would we had a thousand Roman dames
• At such a bay, by turn to serve our lust.
   Chi. A charitable wish and full of love.
   Aar. Here lacks but your mother for to say
     amen.
   Chi. And that would she for twenty thousand
     more.
   Dem. Come, let us go; and pray to all the gods
For our beloved mother in her pains.
   Aar. [*Aside*] Pray to the devils; the gods
     have given us over.
             [*Trumpets sound within.*
   Dem. Why do the emperor's trumpets flourish
     thus?
   Chi. Belike, for joy the emperor hath a son. 50
   Dem. Soft! who comes here?

Enter a Nurse, *with a blackamoor* Child *in her
arms.*

   Nur.   Good morrow, lords:
O, tell me, did you see Aaron the Moor?
   Aar. Well, more or less, or ne'er a whit at all,
Here Aaron is; and what with Aaron now?
   Nur. O gentle Aaron, we are all undone!
Now help, or woe betide thee evermore!
   Aar. Why, what a caterwauling dost thou keep!
What dost thou wrap and fumble in thine arms?
   Nur. O, that which I would hide from heaven's
     eye,   59
Our empress' shame, and stately Rome's disgrace!
She is deliver'd, lords; she is deliver'd.
   Aar. To whom?
   Nur.   I mean, she is brought a-bed.
   Aar. Well, God give her good rest! What
     hath he sent her?
   Nur. A devil.
   Aar. Why, then she is the devil's dam; a
     joyful issue.
   Nur. A joyless, dismal, black, and sorrowful
     issue:
Here is the babe, as loathsome as a toad
Amongst the fairest breeders of our clime:
The empress sends it thee, thy stamp, thy seal,
And bids thee christen it with thy dagger's point.
   Aar. 'Zounds, ye whore! is black so base a hue?
• Sweet blowse, you are a beauteous blossom, sure.
   Dem. Villain, what hast thou done?
   Aar. That which thou canst not undo.
   Chi. Thou hast undone our mother.
   Aar. Villain, I have done thy mother.
   Dem. And therein, hellish dog, thou hast un-
     done.
Woe to her chance, and damn'd her loathed choice!
Accursed the offspring of so foul a fiend!
   Chi. It shall not live.   80
   Aar. It shall not die.
   Nur. Aaron, it must; the mother wills it so.
   Aar. What, must it, nurse? then let no man but I
Do execution on my flesh and blood.
•   *Dem.* I'll broach the tadpole on my rapier's
     point:
Nurse, give it me; my sword shall soon dispatch it.
   Aar. Sooner this sword shall plough thy bowels
     up.
           [*Takes the Child from the Nurse,
                 and draws.*
Stay, murderous villains! will you kill your
   brother?

Now, by the burning tapers of the sky,
●That shone so brightly when this boy was got, 90
He dies upon my scimitar's sharp point
That touches this my first-born son and heir!
●I tell you, younglings, not Enceladus,
●With all his threatening band of Typhon's brood,
●Nor great Alcides, nor the god of war,
Shall seize this prey out of his father's hands.
●What, what, ye sanguine, shallow-hearted boys!
Ye white-limed walls! ye alehouse painted signs!
Coal-black is better than another hue,
In that it scorns to bear another hue;   100
For all the water in the ocean
Can never turn the swan's black legs to white,
Although she lave them hourly in the flood.
Tell the empress from me, I am of age
To keep mine own, excuse it how she can.
  Dem. Wilt thou betray thy noble mistress thus?
  Aar. My mistress is my mistress; this myself,
The vigour and the picture of my youth:
This before all the world do I prefer;
●This maugre all the world will I keep safe,   110
Or some of you shall smoke for it in Rome.
  Dem. By this our mother is for ever shamed.
● *Chi.* Rome will despise her for this foul escape.
  Nur. The emperor, in his rage, will doom her
    death.
  Chi. I blush to think upon this ignomy.
  Aar. Why, there's the privilege your beauty
    bears:
Fie, treacherous hue, that will betray with blushing
●The close enacts and counsels of the heart!
●Here's a young lad framed of another leer:
Look, how the black slave smiles upon the father,
As who should say 'Old lad, I am thine own.' 121
●He is your brother, lords, sensibly fed
Of that self-blood that first gave life to you,
And from that womb where you imprison'd were
He is enfranchised and come to light:
●Nay, he is your brother by the surer side,
Although my seal be stamped in his face.
  Nur. Aaron, what shall I say unto the empress?
  Dem. Advise thee, Aaron, what is to be done,
And we will all subscribe to thy advice: 130
Save thou the child, so we may all be safe.
  Aar. Then sit we down, and let us all consult.
My son and I will have the wind of you:
Keep there: now talk at pleasure of your safety.
                                    [*They sit.*
  Dem. How many women saw this child of his?
  Aar. Why, so, brave lords! when we join in
    league,
I am a lamb: but if you brave the Moor,
The chafed boar, the mountain lioness,
The ocean swells not so as Aaron storms.
But say, again, how many saw the child?   140
  Nur. Cornelia the midwife and myself;
And no one else but the deliver'd empress.
  Aar. The empress, the midwife, and yourself:
Two may keep counsel when the third's away:
Go to the empress, tell her this I said.
                              [*He kills the nurse.*
●Weke, weke! so cries a pig prepared to the spit.
  Dem. What mean'st thou, Aaron? wherefore
    didst thou this?
● *Aar.* O Lord, sir, 'tis a deed of policy:
Shall she live to betray this guilt of ours,
A long-tongued babbling gossip? no, lords, no:
And now be it known to you my full intent. 151

90 *got.* Begat.

93 *Enceladus.* Son of Typhon who fought against the gods.

94 *Typhon.* Monster with a hundred heads.

95 *Alcides.* Hercules.

Hercules resting after one of his labours. Engraving from a painting by Raphael, 1811

97 *sanguine.* Pink-faced.

110 *maugre.* In spite of.

113 *escape.* Misbehaviour.

118 *close enacts.* Secret purposes.

119 *another leer.* A different complexion.

122 *sensibly.* i.e. clearly.

126 *surer.* i.e. mother's.

146 *Weke.* Squeal.

148 *policy.* Contrivance.

155 *pack*. Make compact.

163 *bestow*. i.e. arrange.

176 *puts us to our shifts*. i.e. causes so much trouble.

179 *cabin*. Shelter.

3 *draw home enough*. i.e. pull back to the fullest extent.

4 *Terras Astræa reliquit*. The goddess of justice has left the Earth.

The symbolic figure of Justice. Engraving from a painting by Raphael, 1811

13 *Pluto's region*. i.e. Hell.

19 *suffrages*. Votes, choice.

Not far, one Muli lives, my countryman;
His wife but yesternight was brought to bed;
His child is like to her, fair as you are:
● Go pack with him, and give the mother gold,
And tell them both the circumstance of all;
And how by this their child shall be advanced,
And be received for the emperor's heir,
And substituted in the place of mine,
To calm this tempest whirling in the court;   160
And let the emperor dandle him for his own.
Hark ye, lords; ye see I have given her physic,
[*Pointing to the nurse.*
● And you must needs bestow her funeral;
The fields are near, and you are gallant grooms:
This done, see that you take no longer days,
But send the midwife presently to me.
The midwife and the nurse well made away,
Then let the ladies tattle what they please.
   Chi.   Aaron, I see thou wilt not trust the air
With secrets.
   Dem.   For this care of Tamora,   170
Herself and hers are highly bound to thee.
   [*Exeunt Dem. and Chi. bearing off the
                           Nurse's body.*
   Aar.   Now to the Goths, as swift as swallow
      flies;
There to dispose this treasure in mine arms,
And secretly to greet the empress' friends.
Come on, you thick-lipp'd slave, I'll bear you
      hence;
● For it is you that puts us to our shifts:
I'll make you feed on berries and on roots,
And †feed on curds and whey, and suck the goat,
● And cabin in a cave, and bring you up   179
To be a warrior, and command a camp. [*Exit.*

SCENE III.   *The same.   A public place.*

Enter Titus, *bearing arrows with letters at
   the ends of them; with him,* Marcus, *young*
   Lucius, Publius, Sempronius, Caius, *and
   other* Gentlemen, *with bows.*

   Tit.   Come, Marcus; come, kinsmen; this is
      the way.
Sir boy, now let me see your archery;
● Look ye draw home enough, and 'tis there
      straight.
● Terras Astræa reliquit:
Be you remember'd, Marcus, she's gone, she's fled.
Sirs, take you to your tools.   You, cousins, shall
Go sound the ocean, and cast your nets;
Happily you may catch her in the sea;
Yet there's as little justice as at land:
No; Publius and Sempronius, you must do it; 10
'Tis you must dig with mattock and with spade,
And pierce the inmost centre of the earth:
● Then, when you come to Pluto's region,
I pray you, deliver him this petition;
Tell him, it is for justice and for aid,
And that it comes from old Andronicus,
Shaken with sorrows in ungrateful Rome.
Ah, Rome!   Well, well; I made thee miserable
● What time I threw the people's suffrages
On him that thus doth tyrannize o'er me.   20
Go, get you gone; and pray be careful all,
And leave you not a man-of-war unsearch'd:
This wicked emperor may have shipp'd her hence;
And, kinsmen, then we may go pipe for justice.
   Marc.   O Publius, is not this a heavy case,

To see thy noble uncle thus distract?
   Pub. Therefore, my lord, it highly us con-
     cerns
By day and night to attend him carefully,
● And feed his humour kindly as we may,
Till time beget some careful remedy.   30
   Marc. Kinsmen, his sorrows are past remedy.
Join with the Goths; and with revengeful war
Take wreak on Rome for this ingratitude,
And vengeance on the traitor Saturnine.
   Tit. Publius, how now! how now, my masters!
What, have you met with her?
   Pub. No, my good lord; but Pluto sends you
     word,
If you will have Revenge from hell, you shall:
Marry, for Justice, she is so employ'd,
He thinks, with Jove in heaven, or somewhere
     else,   40
So that perforce you must needs stay a time.
   Tit. He doth me wrong to feed me with delays.
I'll dive into the burning lake below,
● And pull her out of Acheron by the heels.
Marcus, we are but shrubs, no cedars we,
● No big-boned men framed of the Cyclops' size;
But metal, Marcus, steel to the very back,
Yet wrung with wrongs more than our backs can
     bear:
And, sith there's no justice in earth nor hell,
We will solicit heaven and move the gods   50
To send down Justice for to wreak our wrongs.
● Come, to this gear. You are a good archer,
     Marcus;   [*He gives them the arrows.*
'Ad Jovem,' that's for you: here, 'Ad Apolli-
     nem:'
'Ad Martem,' that's for myself:
Here, boy, to Pallas: here, to Mercury:
To Saturn, Caius, not to Saturnine;
You were as good to shoot against the wind.
To it, boy! Marcus, loose when I bid.
Of my word, I have written to effect;
There's not a god left unsolicited.   60
   Marc. Kinsmen, shoot all your shafts into the
     court:
We will afflict the emperor in his pride.
   Tit. Now, masters, draw. [*They shoot.*] O,
     well said, Lucius!
Good boy, in Virgo's lap; give it Pallas.
   Marc. My lord, I aim a mile beyond the moon;
Your letter is with Jupiter by this.
   Tit. Ha, ha!
Publius, Publius, what hast thou done?
See, see, thou hast shot off one of Taurus' horns.
   Marc. This was the sport, my lord: when
     Publius shot,   70
The Bull, being gall'd, gave Aries such a knock
That down fell both the Ram's horns in the court;
● And who should find them but the empress' vil-
     lain?
She laugh'd, and told the Moor he should not
     choose
But give them to his master for a present.
   Tit. Why, there it goes: God give his lord-
     ship joy!

Enter a Clown, *with a basket, and two pigeons
in it.*

News, news from heaven! Marcus, the post is
     come.
Sirrah, what tidings? have you any letters?

29 *humour.* Disposition.

44 *Acheron.* River in Hell.

46 *Cyclops.* Fabled monster.

52 *gear.* Business.

Astrological chart of the heavens. Woodcut by Albrecht
Dürer (1471–1528)

73 *villain.* Minion.

92 *tribunal plebs.* Tribune of the people.

94 *emperial's.* Emperor's.

Saturninus: 'was ever seen An emperor in Rome thus overborne, Troubled, confronted thus.' John Wood as Saturninus, Royal Shakespeare Co. 1972

---

3 *extent.* Extending.

4 *egal.* Equal.

8 *even.* In keeping.

11 *wreaks.* Vindictive actions.

Shall I have justice? what says Jupiter?   79
  Clo. O, the gibbet-maker! he says that he
hath taken them down again, for the man must
not be hanged till the next week.
  Tit. But what says Jupiter, I ask thee?
  Clo. Alas, sir, I know not Jupiter; I never
drank with him in all my life.
  Tit. Why, villain, art not thou the carrier?
  Clo. Ay, of my pigeons, sir; nothing else.
  Tit. Why, didst thou not come from heaven?
  Clo. From heaven! alas, sir, I never came
there: God forbid I should be so bold to press to
heaven in my young days. Why, I am going
with my pigeons to the tribunal plebs, to take up
a matter of brawl betwixt my uncle and one of
the emperial's men.
  Marc. Why, sir, that is as fit as can be to
serve for your oration; and let him deliver the
pigeons to the emperor from you.
  Tit. Tell me, can you deliver an oration to
the emperor with a grace?
  Clo. Nay, truly, sir, I could never say grace
in all my life.   101
  Tit. Sirrah, come hither: make no more ado,
But give your pigeons to the emperor:
By me thou shalt have justice at his hands.
Hold, hold; meanwhile here's money for thy
    charges.
Give me pen and ink. Sirrah, can you with a
grace deliver a supplication?
  Clo. Ay, sir.
  Tit. Then here is a supplication for you.
And when you come to him, at the first approach
you must kneel, then kiss his foot, then deliver
up your pigeons, and then look for your reward.
I'll be at hand, sir; see you do it bravely.
  Clo. I warrant you, sir, let me alone.
  Tit. Sirrah, hast thou a knife? come, let me
    see it.
Here, Marcus, fold it in the oration;
For thou hast made it like an humble suppliant.
And when thou hast given it the emperor,
Knock at my door, and tell me what he says.
  Clo. God be with you, sir; I will,   120
  Tit. Come, Marcus, let us go. Publius, fol-
    low me.   [*Exeunt.*

SCENE IV. *The same. Before the palace.*

Enter SATURNINUS, TAMORA, DEMETRIUS,
CHIRON, Lords, *and others;* SATURNINUS
with the arrows in his hand that TITUS *shot.*

  Sat. Why, lords, what wrongs are these! was
    ever seen
An emperor in Rome thus overborne,
Troubled, confronted thus; and, for the extent
Of egal justice, used in such contempt?
My lords, you know, as know the mightful gods,
However these disturbers of our peace
Buz in the people's ears, there nought hath pass'd,
But even with law, against the wilful sons
Of old Andronicus. And what an if
His sorrows have so overwhelm'd his wits,   10
Shall we be thus afflicted in his wreaks,
His fits, his frenzy, and his bitterness?
And now he writes to heaven for his redress:
See, here's to Jove, and this to Mercury;
This to Apollo; this to the god of war;
Sweet scrolls to fly about the streets of Rome!

What's this but libelling against the senate,
● And blazoning our injustice every where?
A goodly humour, is it not, my lords?
As who would say, in Rome no justice were.   20
● But if I live, his feigned ecstasies
Shall be no shelter to these outrages:
But he and his shall know that justice lives
In Saturninus' health, whom, if she sleep,
He'll so awake as she in fury shall
Cut off the proud'st conspirator that lives.
   Tam. My gracious lord, my lovely Saturnine,
Lord of my life, commander of my thoughts,
Calm thee, and bear the faults of Titus' age,
The effects of sorrow for his valiant sons,   30
Whose loss hath pierced him deep and scarr'd his
     heart;
And rather comfort his distressed plight
Than prosecute the meanest or the best
For these contempts.   [*Aside*] Why, thus it shall
     become
● High-witted Tamora to gloze with all:
But, Titus, I have touch'd thee to the quick,
Thy life-blood out: if Aaron now be wise,
Then is all safe, the anchor's in the port.

     Enter Clown.

How now, good fellow! wouldst thou speak
     with us?
   Clo. Yea, forsooth, an your mistership be
     emperial.   40
   Tam. Empress I am, but yonder sits the
     emperor.
   Clo. 'Tis he.   God and Saint Stephen give
● you good den: I have brought you a letter and a
couple of pigeons here.
     [*Saturninus reads the letter.*
   Sat. Go, take him away, and hang him pre-
     sently.
   Clo. How much money must I have?
   Tam. Come, sirrah, you must be hanged.
   Clo. Hanged! by'r lady, then I have brought
up a neck to a fair end.   [*Exit, guarded.*
●   *Sat.* Despiteful and intolerable wrongs!   50
Shall I endure this monstrous villany?
I know from whence this same device proceeds:
May this be borne?—as if his traitorous sons,
That died by law for murder of our brother,
Have by my means been butcher'd wrongfully!
Go, drag the villain hither by the hair;
● Nor age nor honour shall shape privilege:
For this proud mock I'll be thy slaughter-man;
Sly frantic wretch, that holp'st to make me great,
In hope thyself should govern Rome and me.   60

     Enter ÆMILIUS.

What news with thee, Æmilius?
   Æmil. Arm, arm, my lord;—Rome never had
     more cause.
● The Goths have gather'd head; and with a power
Of high-resolved men, bent to the spoil,
They hither march amain, under conduct
Of Lucius, son to old Andronicus;
Who threats, in course of this revenge, to do
As much as ever Coriolanus did.
   Sat. Is warlike Lucius general of the Goths?
These tidings nip me, and I hang the head   70
As flowers with frost or grass beat down with
     storms:
Ay, now begin our sorrows to approach:

18 *blazoning*. Proclaiming.

21 *feigned ecstasies*. Pretended fits of madness.

35 *gloze*. Speak speciously.

Roman clown. From a fresco at Herculaneum

43 *den*. Evening.

50 *Despiteful*. i.e. despicable.

57 *shape privilege*. Arrange immunity.

63 *head*. An army.

86 *stint*. Halt.

91 *honey-stalks*. Clover.

96 *smooth*. Flatter.

105 *stand*. Insist.

SATURNINUS

Costume design for Saturninus by Desmond Heeley,
Stratford-upon-Avon, 1955

---

1 *Approved*. Tried.

7 *scath*. Harm.

'Tis he the common people love so much;
Myself hath often over-heard them say,
When I have walked like a private man,
That Lucius' banishment was wrongfully,
And they have wish'd that Lucius were their
   emperor.
  Tam.   Why should you fear? is not your city
   strong?
  Sat.   Ay, but the citizens favour Lucius,
And will revolt from me to succour him.   80
  Tam.   King, be thy thoughts imperious, like
   thy name.
Is the sun dimm'd, that gnats do fly in it?
The eagle suffers little birds to sing,
And is not careful what they mean thereby,
Knowing that with the shadow of his wings
• He can at pleasure stint their melody:
Even so mayst thou the giddy men of Rome.
Then cheer thy spirit: for know, thou emperor,
I will enchant the old Andronicus
With words more sweet, and yet more dangerous,
• Than baits to fish, or honey-stalks to sheep, 91
When as the one is wounded with the bait,
The other rotted with delicious feed.
  Sat.   But he will not entreat his son for us.
  Tam.   If Tamora entreat him, then he will:
• For I can smooth and fill his aged ear
With golden promises; that, were his heart
Almost impregnable, his old ears deaf,
Yet should both ear and heart obey my tongue.
[*To Æmilius*] Go thou before, be our ambas-
   sador: 100
Say that the emperor requests a parley
Of warlike Lucius, and appoint the meeting
Even at his father's house, the old Andronicus.
  Sat.   Æmilius, do this message honourably:
• And if he stand on hostage for his safety,
Bid him demand what pledge will please him best.
  Æmil.   Your bidding shall I do effectually.
                   [*Exit*.
  Tam.   Now will I to that old Andronicus,
And temper him with all the art I have,
To pluck proud Lucius from the warlike Goths.
And now, sweet emperor, be blithe again,   111
And bury all thy fear in my devices.
  Sat.   Then go successantly, and plead to him.
                  [*Exeunt*.

ACT V.

Scene I.   *Plains near Rome.*

Enter Lucius *with an army of* Goths, *with
drum and colours.*

•   *Luc.*   Approved warriors, and my faithful
   friends,
I have received letters from great Rome,
Which signify what hate they bear their emperor
And how desirous of our sight they are.
Therefore, great lords, be, as your titles witness,
Imperious and impatient of your wrongs,
• And wherein Rome hath done you any scath,
Let him make treble satisfaction.
  First Goth.   Brave slip, sprung from the great
   Andronicus,
Whose name was once our terror, now our com-
   fort;   10
Whose high exploits and honourable deeds
Ingrateful Rome requites with foul contempt,

●Be bold in us: we'll follow where thou lead'st,
Like stinging bees in hottest summer's day
Led by their master to the flowered fields,
And be avenged on cursed Tamora.
　　All the Goths.   And as he saith, so say we all
　　with him.
　　Luc.   I humbly thank him, and I thank you
　　all.
But who comes here, led by a lusty Goth?

Enter a Goth, *leading* AARON *with his Child
in his arms.*

　　Sec. Goth.   Renowned Lucius, from our troops
　　I stray'd　　　　　　　　　　　　　　　20
To gaze upon a ruinous monastery;
And, as I earnestly did fix mine eye
Upon the wasted building, suddenly
I heard a child cry underneath a wall.
I made unto the noise; when soon I heard
The crying babe controll'd with this discourse:
'Peace, tawny slave, half me and half thy dam!
●Did not thy hue bewray whose brat thou art,
Had nature lent thee but thy mother's look,
Villain, thou mightst have been an emperor:　30
But where the bull and cow are both milk-white,
They never do beget a coal-black calf.
●Peace, villain, peace!—even thus he rates the
　　babe,—
'For I must bear thee to a trusty Goth;
Who, when he knows thou art the empress' babe,
Will hold thee dearly for thy mother's sake.'
With this, my weapon drawn, I rush'd upon him,
Surprised him suddenly, and brought him hither,
●To use as you think needful of the man.
　　Luc.   O worthy Goth, this is the incarnate
　　devil　　　　　　　　　　　　　　　40
That robb'd Andronicus of his good hand;
This is the pearl that pleased your empress' eye,
And here's the base fruit of his burning lust.
●Say, wall-eyed slave, whither wouldst thou convey
This growing image of thy fiend-like face?
Why dost not speak? what, deaf? not a word?
A halter, soldiers! hang him on this tree,
And by his side his fruit of bastardy.
　　Aar.   Touch not the boy; he is of royal
　　blood.
　　Luc.   Too like the sire for ever being good. 50
First hang the child, that he may see it sprawl;
A sight to vex the father's soul withal.
Get me a ladder.
　　　　　[*A ladder brought, which Aaron is
　　　　　　　made to ascend.*
　　Aar.　　　　Lucius, save the child,
And bear it from me to the empress.
If thou do this, I'll show thee wondrous things,
That highly may advantage thee to hear:
If thou wilt not, befall what may befall,
I'll speak no more but 'Vengeance rot you all!'
　　Luc.   Say on: an if it please me which thou
　　speak'st,
Thy child shall live, and I will see it nourish'd.60
　　Aar.   An if it please thee! why, assure thee,
　　Lucius,
'Twill vex thy soul to hear what I shall speak;
For I must talk of murders, rapes and massacres,
Acts of black night, abominable deeds,
Complots of mischief, treason, villanies
●Ruthful to hear, yet piteously perform'd:
And this shall all be buried by my death,

First Goth: 'we'll follow where thou lead'st . . .' Roman
general leading barbarian troops. Nineteenth century
engraving from a bas-relief on the Column of Trajan

---

13 *Be bold.* Have confidence.

28 *bewray.* Demonstrate.

33 *rates.* Berates.

39 *To use . . . man.* i.e. to treat him as you think he
deserves.

44 *wall-eyed.* Staring.

66 *Ruthful.* Sad.

88 *luxurious*. Lustful.

99 *codding*. Highly-sexed.

100 *set*. Game.

102 *at head*. Head on.

104 *train'd*. Enticed.

111 *cheater*. Escheator; man in charge of property which is forfeited to a king.

Costume design for Aaron by Desmond Heeley, Stratford-upon-Avon, 1955

Unless thou **swear** to me my child shall live.
  Luc. Tell on thy mind; I say thy child shall live.
  Aar. Swear that he shall, and then I will begin.   *70*
  Luc. Who should I swear by? thou believest no god:
That granted, how canst thou believe an oath?
  Aar. What if I do not? as, indeed, I do not;
Yet, for I know thou art religious
And hast a thing within thee called conscience,
With twenty popish tricks and ceremonies,
Which I have seen thee careful to observe,
Therefore I urge thy oath; for that I know
An idiot holds his bauble for a god   *79*
And keeps the oath which by that god he swears,
To that I'll urge him: therefore thou shalt vow
By that same god, what god soe'er it be,
That thou adorest and hast in reverence,
To save my boy, to nourish and bring him up;
Or else I will discover nought to thee.
  Luc. Even by my god I swear to thee I will.
  Aar. First know thou, I begot him on the empress.
●   *Luc.* O most insatiate and luxurious woman!
  Aar. Tut, Lucius, this was but a deed of charity
To that which thou shalt hear of me anon.   *90*
'Twas her two sons that murder'd Bassianus;
They cut thy sister's tongue and ravish'd her
And cut her hands and trimm'd her as thou saw'st.
  Luc. O detestable villain! call'st thou that trimming?
  Aar. Why, she was wash'd and cut and trimm'd, and 'twas
Trim sport for them that had the doing of it.
  Luc. O barbarous, beastly villains, like thyself!
  Aar. Indeed, I was their tutor to instruct them:
● That codding spirit had they from their mother,
● As sure a card as ever won the set;   *100*
That bloody mind, I think, they learn'd of me,
● As true a dog as ever fought at head.
Well, let my deeds be witness of my worth.
● I train'd thy brethren to that guileful hole
Where the dead corpse of Bassianus lay:
I wrote the letter that thy father found
And hid the gold within the letter mention'd,
Confederate with the queen and her two sons:
And what not done, that thou hast cause to rue,
Wherein I had no stroke of mischief in it?   *110*
● I play'd the cheater for thy father's hand,
And, when I had it, drew myself apart
And almost broke my heart with extreme laughter:
I pry'd me through the crevice of a wall
When, for his hand, he had his two sons' heads;
Beheld his tears, and laugh'd so heartily,
That both mine eyes were rainy like to his:
And when I told the empress of this sport,
She swooned almost at my pleasing tale,
And for my tidings gave me twenty kisses.   *120*
  First Goth. What, canst thou say all this, and never blush?
  Aar. Ay, like a black dog, as the saying is.
  Luc. Art thou not sorry for these heinous deeds?
  Aar. Ay, that I had not done a thousand more.

Even now I curse the day—and yet, I think,
Few come within the compass of my curse—
Wherein I did not some notorious ill,
As kill a man, or else devise his death,
Ravish a maid, or plot the way to do it,
● Accuse some innocent and forswear myself,   130
Set deadly enmity between two friends,
†Make poor men's cattle break their necks;
Set fire on barns and hay-stacks in the night,
And bid the owners quench them with their tears.
Oft have I digg'd up dead men from their graves,
And set them upright at their dear friends' doors,
Even when their sorrows almost were forgot;
And on their skins, as on the bark of trees,
Have with my knife carved in Roman letters,
'Let not your sorrow die, though I am dead.'140
Tut, I have done a thousand dreadful things
As willingly as one would kill a fly,
● And nothing grieves me heartily indeed
But that I cannot do ten thousand more.
   Luc.   Bring down the devil; for he must not die
So sweet a death as hanging presently.
   Aar.   If there be devils, would I were a devil,
To live and burn in everlasting fire,
So I might have your company in hell,
But to torment you with my bitter tongue!   150
   Luc.   Sirs, stop his mouth, and let him speak
no more.

Enter a Goth.

Third Goth.   My lord, there is a messenger
from Rome
Desires to be admitted to your presence.
   Luc.   Let him come near.

Enter ÆMILIUS.

Welcome, Æmilius: what's the news from Rome?
   Æmil.   Lord Lucius, and you princes of the
Goths,
The Roman emperor greets you all by me;
And, for he understands you are in arms,
He craves a parley at your father's house,
Willing you to demand your hostages,   160
And they shall be immediately deliver'd.
   First Goth.   What says our general?
   Luc.   Æmilius, let the emperor give his
pledges
Unto my father and my uncle Marcus,
And we will come.   March away.   [*Exeunt.*

SCENE II.   *Rome.   Before Titus's house.*

Enter TAMORA, DEMETRIUS, *and* CHIRON, *disguised.*

●   *Tam.*   Thus, in this strange and sad habiliment,
I will encounter with Andronicus,
And say I am Revenge, sent from below
To join with him and right his heinous wrongs.
Knock at his study, where, they say, he keeps,
To ruminate strange plots of dire revenge;
Tell him Revenge is come to join with him,
● And work confusion on his enemies.
                  [*They knock.*

Enter TITUS, *above.*

   Tit.   Who doth molest my contemplation?
Is it your trick to make me ope the door,   10
That so my sad decrees may fly away,
And all my study be to no effect?

130 *forswear.* Perjure.

143 *heartily.* To my heart.

Aaron: 'If there be devils, would I were a devil, to live
and burn in everlasting fire ...' Engraving from an 11th
century manuscript

---

1 *sad habiliment.* Dismal clothing.

8 *work confusion on.* Arrange the destruction of.

19 *odds*. Better.

38 *couch*. Lie concealed.

46 *surance*. i.e. evidence in proof.

50 *proper palfreys*. Good horses.

56 *Hyperion*. The sun god.

Costume design for Demetrius by Desmond Heeley,
Stratford-upon-Avon, 1955

59 *Rapine*. Rape.

70 *closing*. Agreeing.

You are deceived : for what I mean to do
See here in bloody lines I have set down ;
And what is written shall be executed.
   Tam.   Titus, I am come to talk with thee.
   Tit.   No, not a word ; how can I grace my
     talk,
Wanting a hand to give it action ?
●Thou hast the odds of me ; therefore no more.
   Tam.   If thou didst know me, thou wouldest
     talk with me.   20
   Tit.   I am not mad ; I know thee well enough :
Witness this wretched stump, witness these crim-
     son lines ;
Witness these trenches made by grief and care ;
Witness the tiring day and heavy night ;
Witness all sorrow, that I know thee well
For our proud empress, mighty Tamora :
Is not thy coming for my other hand ?
   Tam.   Know, thou sad man, I am not Tamora ;
She is thy enemy, and I thy friend :
I am Revenge : sent from the infernal kingdom, 30
To ease the gnawing vulture of thy mind,
By working wreakful vengeance on thy foes.
Come down, and welcome me to this world's light ;
Confer with me of murder and of death :
There's not a hollow cave or lurking-place,
No vast obscurity or misty vale,
Where bloody murder or detested rape
●Can couch for fear, but I will find them out ;
And in their ears tell them my dreadful name,
Revenge, which makes the foul offender quake.
   Tit.   Art thou Revenge ? and art thou sent
     to me,   41
To be a torment to mine enemies ?
   Tam.   I am ; therefore come down, and wel-
     come me
   Tit.   Do me some service, ere I come to thee.
Lo, by thy side where Rape and Murder stands ;
●Now give some surance that thou art Revenge,
Stab them, or tear them on thy chariot-wheels ;
And then I'll come and be thy waggoner,
And whirl along with thee about the globe.
●Provide thee two proper palfreys, black as jet, 50
To hale thy vengeful waggon swift away,
And find out murderers in their guilty caves :
And when thy car is loaden with their heads,
I will dismount, and by the waggon-wheel
Trot, like a servile footman, all day long,
●Even from Hyperion's rising in the east
Until his very downfall in the sea :
And day by day I'll do this heavy task,
●So thou destroy Rapine and Murder there.
   Tam.   These are my ministers, and come with
     me.   60
   Tit.   Are these thy ministers ? what are they
     call'd ?
   Tam.   Rapine and Murder ; therefore called so,
Cause they take vengeance of such kind of men.
   Tit.   Good Lord, how like the empress' sons
     they are !
And you, the empress ! but we worldly men
Have miserable, mad, mistaking eyes.
O sweet Revenge, now do I come to thee ;
And, if one arm's embracement will content thee,
I will embrace thee in it by and by. [*Exit above.*
● *Tam.*   This closing with him fits his lunacy :
Whate'er I forge to feed his brain-sick fits, 71
Do you uphold and maintain in your speeches,
For now he firmly takes me for Revenge ;

And, being credulous in this mad thought,
I'll make him send for Lucius his son;
And, whilst I at a banquet hold him sure,
● I'll find some cunning practice out of hand,
To scatter and disperse the giddy Goths,
Or, at the least, make them his enemies.
See, here he comes, and I must ply my theme.

Enter TITUS *below.*

Tit.   Long have I been forlorn, and all for
        thee :   81
Welcome, dread Fury, to my woful house :
Rapine and Murder, you are welcome too.
How like the empress and her sons you are!
Well are you fitted, had you but a Moor :
Could not all hell afford you such a devil?
● For well I wot the empress never wags
But in her company there is a Moor;
And, would you represent our queen aright,
It were convenient you had such a devil :   90
But welcome, as you are.   What shall we do?
    Tam.   What wouldst thou have us do, Andro-
        nicus?
    Dem.   Show me a murderer, I'll deal with him.
    Chi.   Show me a villain that hath done a rape,
And I am sent to be revenged on him.
    Tam.   Show me a thousand that have done
        thee wrong,
And I will be revenged on them all.
    Tit.   Look round about the wicked streets of
        Rome ;
And when thou find'st a man that's like thyself,
Good Murder, stab him; he's a murderer.   100
Go thou with him; and when it is thy hap
To find another that is like to thee,
Good Rapine, stab him; he's a ravisher.
Go thou with them; and in the emperor's court
There is a queen, attended by a Moor;
Well mayst thou know her by thy own propor-
        tion,
For up and down she doth resemble thee :
I pray thee, do on them some violent death ;
They have been violent to me and mine.
    Tam.   Well hast thou lesson'd us ; this shall
        we do.   110
But would it please thee, good Andronicus,
To send for Lucius, thy thrice-valiant son,
Who leads towards Rome a band of warlike Goths,
And bid him come and banquet at thy house ;
When he is here, even at thy solemn feast,
I will bring in the empress and her sons,
The emperor himself and all thy foes ;
And at thy mercy shall they stoop and kneel,
And on them shalt thou ease thy angry heart.
What says Andronicus to this device?   120
    Tit.   Marcus, my brother ! 'tis sad Titus calls.

Enter MARCUS.

Go, gentle Marcus, to thy nephew Lucius ;
Thou shalt inquire him out among the Goths :
Bid him repair to me, and bring with him
Some of the chiefest princes of the Goths ;
Bid him encamp his soldiers where they are :
Tell him the emperor and the empress too
Feast at my house, and he shall feast with them.
This do thou for my love ; and so let him,
As he regards his aged father's life.   130
    Marc.   This will I do, and soon return again.
                                        [*Exit.*

A Fury, who punished the crimes of those who escaped justice. From a 19th century engraving

61

Tam.   Now will I hence about thy business,
And take my ministers along with me.
 Tit.   Nay, nay, let Rape and Murder stay
  with me;
Or else I'll call my brother back again,
And cleave to no revenge but Lucius.
 Tam. [*Aside to her sons*] What say you, boys?
  will you bide with him,
Whiles I go tell my lord the emperor
How I have govern'd our determined jest?
Yield to his humour, smooth and speak him fair,
And tarry with him till I turn again.   141
 Tit.   [*Aside*] I know them all, though they
  suppose me mad,
And will o'erreach them in their own devices:
A pair of cursed hell-hounds and their dam!
 Dem.   Madam, depart at pleasure; leave us
  here.
 Tam.   Farewell, Andronicus: Revenge now
  goes
To lay a complot to betray thy foes.
 Tit.   I know thou dost; and, sweet Revenge,
  farewell.   [*Exit Tamora.*
 Chi.   Tell us, old man, how shall we be em-
  ploy'd?
 Tit.   Tut, I have work enough for you to do.
Publius, come hither, Caius, and Valentine!   151

    Enter PUBLIUS *and others.*

 Pub.   What is your will?
 Tit.   Know you these two?
 Pub.   The empress' sons, I take them, Chiron
and Demetrius.
 Tit.   Fie, Publius, fie! thou art too much de-
  ceived;
The one is Murder, Rape is the other's name;
And therefore bind them, gentle Publius.
Caius and Valentine, lay hands on them.
Oft have you heard me wish for such an hour, 160
And now I find it; therefore bind them sure,
And stop their mouths, if they begin to cry. [*Exit.*
    [*Publius, &c. lay hold on Chiron and
      Demetrius.*
 Chi.   Villains, forbear! we are the empress'
  sons.
 Pub.   And therefore do we what we are com-
  manded.
Stop close their mouths, let them not speak a
  word.
Is he sure bound? look that you bind them fast.

 Re-enter TITUS, *with* LAVINIA; *he bearing a
    knife, and she a basin.*

 Tit.   Come, come, Lavinia; look, thy foes are
  bound.
Sirs, stop their mouths, let them not speak to me;
But let them hear what fearful words I utter.
O villains, Chiron and Demetrius!   170
Here stands the spring whom you have stain'd
  with mud,
This goodly summer with your winter mix'd.
You kill'd her husband, and for that vile fault
Two of her brothers were condemn'd to death,
My hand cut off and made a merry jest;
Both her sweet hands, her tongue, and that more
  dear
Than hands or tongue, her spotless chastity,
Inhuman traitors, you constrain'd and forced.

What would you say, if I should let you speak?
Villains, for shame you could not beg for grace.
Hark, wretches! how I mean to martyr you. 181
This one hand yet is left to cut your throats,
Whilst that Lavinia 'tween her stumps doth hold
The basin that receives your guilty blood.
You know your mother means to feast with me,
And calls herself Revenge, and thinks me mad:
Hark, villains! I will grind your bones to dust
And with your blood and it I'll make a paste,
●And of the paste a coffin I will rear
And make two pasties of your shameful heads, 190
And bid that strumpet, your unhallow'd dam,
Like to the earth swallow her own increase.
This is the feast that I have bid her to,
And this the banquet she shall surfeit on:
For worse than Philomel you used my daughter,
●And worse than Progne I will be revenged:
And now prepare your throats.   Lavinia, come,
                              [*He cuts their throats.*
Receive the blood: and when that they are dead,
Let me go grind their bones to powder small
●And with this hateful liquor temper it;   200
And in that paste let their vile heads be baked.
●Come, come, be every one officious
To make this banquet; which I wish may prove
●More stern and bloody than the Centaurs' feast.
So, now bring them in, for I'll play the cook,
And see them ready 'gainst their mother comes.
                    [*Exeunt, bearing the dead bodies.*

SCENE III. *Court of Titus's house.   A banquet
set out.*

Enter LUCIUS, MARCUS, *and* Goths, *with*
AARON *prisoner.*

Luc. Uncle Marcus, since it is my father's mind
That I repair to Rome, I am content.
    First Goth.   And ours with thine, befall what
        fortune will.
    Luc.   Good uncle, take you in this barbarous
        Moor,
This ravenous tiger, this accursed devil;
Let him receive no sustenance, fetter him,
Till he be brought unto the empress' face,
For testimony of her foul proceedings:
And see the ambush of our friends be strong;
I fear the emperor means no good to us.   10
    Aar.   Some devil whisper curses in mine ear,
And prompt me, that my tongue may utter forth
The venomous malice of my swelling heart!
    Luc.   Away, inhuman dog! unhallow'd slave!
Sirs, help our uncle to convey him in.
[*Exeunt Goths, with Aaron. Flourish within.*
The trumpets show the emperor is at hand.

Enter SATURNINUS *and* TAMORA, *with* ÆMI-
LIUS, Tribunes, Senators, *and others.*

    Sat.   What, hath the firmament more suns than
        one?
    Luc.   What boots it thee to call thyself a sun?
●   *Marc.*   Rome's emperor, and nephew, break
        the parle;
These quarrels must be quietly debated.   20
●The feast is ready, which the careful Titus
Hath ordain'd to an honourable end,
For peace, for love, for league, and good to Rome:

189 *coffin.* Pie-crust.

196 *Progne.* Sister of Philomel and wife of Tereus.
When her husband raped her sister she killed their son
and served him as a meal.

200 *temper.* Mix.

202 *officious.* Busy.

204 *Centaurs' feast.* The Centaurs were invited to a
wedding banquet by the Lapiths, who then engaged
them in battle.

The Battle between the Lapiths and the Centaurs.
Detail of a painting by Piero di Cosimo (1462–1521?)

19 *break the parle.* i.e. stop this arguing.

21 *careful.* Full of care.

38 *enforced.* i.e. raped.

Virginius killed his daughter Virginia to wipe out the dishonour of her rape. Engraving by Bartolomeo Pinelli, 1821

Please you, therefore, draw nigh, and take your
    places.
   Sat. Marcus, we will.
   [*Hautboys sound. The Company sit down at*
                    table.

Enter TITUS *dressed like a Cook,* LAVINIA *veiled,*
young LUCIUS, *and others.* TITUS *places the*
dishes on the table.

   Tit. Welcome, my gracious lord; welcome,
    dread queen;
Welcome, ye warlike Goths; welcome, Lucius;
And welcome, all: although the cheer be poor,
'Twill fill your stomachs; please you eat of it. 29
   Sat. Why art thou thus attired, Andronicus?
   Tit. Because I would be sure to have all well,
To entertain your highness and your empress.
   Tam. We are beholding to you, good Andro-
    nicus.
   Tit. An if your highness knew my heart, you
    were.
My lord the emperor, resolve me this:
Was it well done of rash Virginius
To slay his daughter with his own right hand,
● Because she was enforced, stain'd, and deflower'd?
   Sat. It was, Andronicus.
   Tit. Your reason, mighty lord?   40
   Sat. Because the girl should not survive her
    shame,
And by her presence still renew his sorrows.
   Tit. A reason mighty, strong, and effectual;
A pattern, precedent, and lively warrant,
For me, most wretched, to perform the like.
Die, die, Lavinia, and thy shame with thee:
                 [*Kills Lavinia.*
And, with thy shame, thy father's sorrow die!
   Sat. What hast thou done, unnatural and un-
    kind?
   Tit. Kill'd her, for whom my tears have made
    me blind.
I am as woful as Virginius was,   50
And have a thousand times more cause than he
To do this outrage: and it now is done.
   Sat. What, was she ravish'd? tell who did the
    deed.
   Tit. Will't please you eat? will't please your
    highness feed?
   Tam. Why hast thou slain thine only daughter
    thus?
   Tit. Not I; 'twas Chiron and Demetrius:
They ravish'd her, and cut away her tongue;
And they, 'twas they, that did her all this wrong.
   Sat. Go fetch them hither to us presently.
   Tit. Why, there they are both, baked in that
    pie;   60
Whereof their mother daintily hath fed,
Eating the flesh that she herself hath bred.
'Tis true, 'tis true; witness my knife's sharp point.
                 [*Kills Tamora.*
   Sat. Die, frantic wretch, for this accursed deed!
                 [*Kills Titus.*
   Luc. Can the son's eye behold his father bleed?
There's meed for meed, death for a deadly deed!
        [*Kills Saturninus. A great tumult.*
         Lucius, Marcus, and others go up
         into the balcony.
   Marc. You sad-faced men, people and sons of
    Rome,
By uproar sever'd, like a flight of fowl

Scatter'd by winds and high tempestuous gusts,
O, let me teach you how to knit again   70
This scatter'd corn into one mutual sheaf,
These broken limbs again into one body;
● Lest Rome herself be bane unto herself,
And she whom mighty kingdoms court'sy to,
Like a forlorn and desperate castaway,
Do shameful execution on herself.
● But if my frosty signs and chaps of age,
Grave witnesses of true experience,
Cannot induce you to attend my words,
●[*To Lucius*] Speak, Rome's dear friend, as erst
                    our ancestor,   80
When with his solemn tongue he did discourse
To love-sick Dido's sad attending ear
The story of that baleful burning night
When subtle Greeks surprised King Priam's Troy,
● Tell us what Sinon hath bewitch'd our ears,
Or who hath brought the fatal engine in
That gives our Troy, our Rome, the civil wound.
My heart is not compact of flint nor steel;
Nor can I utter all our bitter grief,
But floods of tears will drown my oratory,   90
And break my utterance, even in the time
When it should move you to attend me most,
Lending your kind commiseration.
Here is a captain, let him tell the tale;
Your hearts will throb and weep to hear him speak.
    Luc. Then, noble auditory, be it known to you,
That cursed Chiron and Demetrius
Were they that murdered our emperor's brother;
And they it were that ravished our sister: 99
● For their fell faults our brothers were beheaded;
● Our father's tears despised, and basely cozen'd
Of that true hand that fought Rome's quarrel out,
And sent her enemies unto the grave.
Lastly, myself unkindly banished,
The gates shut on me, and turn'd weeping out,
To beg relief among Rome's enemies;
Who drown'd their enmity in my true tears,
And oped their arms to embrace me as a friend.
I am the turned forth, be it known to you,
That have preserved her welfare in my blood;   110
And from her bosom took the enemy's point,
Sheathing the steel in my adventurous body.
● Alas, you know I am no vaunter, I;
My scars can witness, dumb although they are,
That my report is just and full of truth.
But, soft! methinks I do digress too much,
Citing my worthless praise: O, pardon me;
For when no friends are by, men praise themselves.
    Marc. Now is my turn to speak.   Behold this
        child:
            [*Pointing to the Child in the arms of an
                                Attendant.*
Of this was Tamora delivered;   120
The issue of an irreligious Moor,
Chief architect and plotter of these woes:
The villain is alive in Titus' house,
†And as he is, to witness this is true.
Now judge what cause had Titus to revenge
These wrongs, unspeakable, past patience,
Or more than any living man could bear.
Now you have heard the truth, what say you,
        Romans?
Have we done aught amiss,—show us wherein,
And, from the place where you behold us now,
The poor remainder of Andronici   131
Will, hand in hand, all headlong cast us down,

73 *bane*. Destructive.

77 *chaps*. Cracks.

80 *ancestor*. i.e. Aeneas.

Aeneas. Engraving from a Sicilian vase

85 *Sinon*. Whose false information induced the Trojans to admit the wooden horse into Troy.

100 *fell faults*. Savage crimes.

101 *cozen'd*. Cheated.

113 *vaunter*. Bragger.

134 *mutual closure.* i.e. simultaneous end.

149 *give me aim.* i.e. guide me.

The goddess Roma. Nineteenth century engraving from
the Arch of Constantine

182 *doom.* Sentence.

And on the ragged stones beat forth our brains,
And make a mutual closure of our house.
Speak, Romans, speak; and if you say we shall,
Lo, hand in hand, Lucius and I will fall.
 Æmil. Come, come, thou reverend man of
  Rome,
And bring our emperor gently in thy hand,
Lucius our emperor; for well I know
The common voice do cry it shall be so. 140
 All. Lucius, all hail, Rome's royal emperor!
 Marc. Go, go into old Titus' sorrowful house,
          [To Attendants.
And hither hale that misbelieving Moor,
To be adjudged some direful slaughtering death,
As punishment for his most wicked life.
        [Exeunt Attendants.

LUCIUS, MARCUS, *and the others descend.*

 All. Lucius, all hail, Rome's gracious governor!
 Luc. Thanks, gentle Romans: may I govern so,
To heal Rome's harms, and wipe away her woe!
But, gentle people, give me aim awhile,
For nature puts me to a heavy task: 150
Stand all aloof: but, uncle, draw you near,
To shed obsequious tears upon this trunk.
O, take this warm kiss on thy pale cold lips,
         [Kissing Titus.
These sorrowful drops upon thy blood-stain'd face,
The last true duties of thy noble son!
 Marc. Tear for tear, and loving kiss for kiss,
Thy brother Marcus tenders on thy lips:
O, were the sum of these that I should pay
Countless and infinite, yet would I pay them!
 Luc. Come hither, boy; come, come, and learn
  of us 160
To melt in showers: thy grandsire loved thee well:
Many a time he danced thee on his knee,
Sung thee asleep, his loving breast thy pillow;
Many a matter hath he told to thee,
Meet and agreeing with thine infancy;
In that respect, then, like a loving child,
Shed yet some small drops from thy tender spring,
Because kind nature doth require it so:
Friends should associate friends in grief and woe:
Bid him farewell; commit him to the grave; 170
Do him that kindness, and take leave of him.
 Young Luc. O grandsire, grandsire! even with
  all my heart
Would I were dead, so you did live again!
O Lord, I cannot speak to him for weeping;
My tears will choke me, if I ope my mouth.

Re-enter Attendants *with* AARON.

 Æm. You sad Andronici, have done with woes:
Give sentence on this execrable wretch,
That hath been breeder of these dire events.
 Luc. Set him breast-deep in earth, and famish
  him; 179
There let him stand, and rave, and cry for food:
If any one relieves or pities him,
For the offence he dies. This is our doom:
Some stay to see him fasten'd in the earth.
 Aar. O, why should wrath be mute, and fury
  dumb?
I am no baby, I, that with base prayers
I should repent the evils I have done:
Ten thousand worse than ever yet I did
Would I perform, if I might have my will:

If one good deed in all my life I did,
I do repent it from my very soul.   190
   Luc.   Some loving friends convey the emperor
        hence,
And give him burial in his father's grave:
My father and Lavinia shall forthwith
Be closed in our household's monument.
As for that heinous tiger, Tamora,
No funeral rite, nor man in mourning weeds,
No mournful bell shall ring her burial;
But throw her forth to beasts and birds of prey:
Her life was beast-like, and devoid of pity;
And, being so, shall have like want of pity.   200
See justice done on Aaron, that damn'd Moor,
By whom our heavy haps had their beginning:
Then, afterwards, to order well the state,
That like events may ne'er it ruinate.   [*Exeunt.*

Imperial funeral rites. Engraving from Basil Kennetts
Romae Antiquae Notitia, 1769

Romeo and Juliet

1594-5

WITH ROMEO AND JULIET we come to the most ever-popular of the plays, along with *Hamlet* and *Richard III*, and it has been a never-ending source of inspiration for the sister arts of painting and music. In our time it has been the direct source of inspiration for a remarkable musical, *West Side Story*, which may be regarded as a modern version of the play in American idiom.

It visibly belongs to the period of the later Sonnets, of which it has several echoes; no less than three sonnets are incorporated in the play, and there is a good deal of rhyme – one whole scene being in rhyme, as in *Richard II*, to which it is also close. Both are lyrical tragedies, with Shakespeare's characteristic mixture of artificial – or, as Elizabethans would say, 'conceited' – language, along with simple. Indeed, he gives us a pointer to his use of 'conceits':

> Conceit, more rich in matter than in words,
> Brags of his substance, not of ornament –

i.e. the idea behind it is more important than the expression, it is not mere decoration. And that goes too for the verbal play, the punning, to which he was so much given.

The plague of 1592 and 1593, that had such decisive effects on his career, is in the immediate background. Friar John and a brother friar were visiting the sick, when

> the searchers of the town,
> Suspecting that we both were in a house
> Where the infectious pestilence did reign,
> Sealed up the doors, and would not let us forth.

This was the regulation in plague-time. Juliet's Nurse, a marvellous down-to-earth old crone, gives us a corroboration of date:

> On Lammas-eve at night shall she be fourteen . . .
> 'Tis since the earthquake now eleven years.

The first meeting of Romeo and Juliet. Engraving from an 18th century painting by William Miller

This would be 31 July, and in the summer of 1583 there was an earthquake in Dorset which opened a large cavity in the vale of Blackmore, according to Camden.

Love and Family Feud. Everyone knows that the story is one of young love, 'star-crossed' by the deadly feud between the families of Montagu and Capulet: Romeo is a Montagu, Juliet is a Capulet. They are victims of the feud; so are Romeo's friend, Mercutio, and Juliet's cousin, Tybalt. Her mother, Lady Capulet, drives forward her revenge for her nephew against Romeo. The whole love-story is placed against the background of feuding and duelling. Though a modern mind may find it adolescent, and some critics speak of it as 'idiotic', it was utterly true to the age. Marlowe was involved in several such affrays, and had recently been stabbed to death in a tavern-brawl; Ben Jonson killed the quarrelsome actor, Gabriel Spencer. Marlowe's friend, the poet and musician Thomas Watson, came to Marlowe's aid in his affray with William Bradley and killed him.

Mercutio says of his friend Benvolio, 'and there were two such, we should have none shortly, for one would kill the other. Thou! why, thou wilt quarrel with a man that hath a hair more, or a hair less in his beard, than thou hast.' Actually, Mercutio is describing himself, much quicker on the draw. He describes Tybalt, the leading Capulet swordsman: 'he fights as you sing prick-song, keeps time, distance, and proportion, rests me his minim rest, one, two, and the third in your bosom; the very butcher of a silk button, a duellist, a duellist'. Tybalt kills Mercutio; then Romeo kills Tybalt: this is fatal to his love for Juliet, for the Capulets, egged on by Lady Capulet, are determined on revenge.

One theatre-person who never involved himself in this kind of thing was the prudent dramatist. What suggested to his mind the placing of his next love-story in the background of fatal family-feuding? The suggestion came from close at hand.

Southampton's Friends. Down at Titchfield Southampton was close friends with his Wiltshire neighbours, two young swordsmen, Sir Charles and Sir Henry Danvers. The Danvers family were engaged in a bitter feud with another county family, the Longs of Wraxall. Sir John Danvers the father was a quiet man, but his wife, Lady Danvers, drove her sons on. John Aubrey, who knew them, describes her as 'Italian' – he probably means in temperament; for he goes on, 'a great politician [i.e. schemer], great wit and spirit, but revengeful'.

On 4 October 1599 the two Danvers brothers with their following broke into the house at Corsham where the Long party were, and Henry Danvers – Southampton's particular friend – killed Henry Long, son and heir of his house. The brothers fled and took refuge in a lodge in Southampton's park at Titchfield, where he fed them and enabled them to make their get-away across the Channel to Henri IV. When the sheriff was leading the hue-and-cry after them over Itchen Ferry, a couple of the Earl's servants threatened to throw him overboard: one of them was 'Signor Florio, an Italian.'

The two young swordsmen remained in the service of the former Henri of Navarre. Their scheming mother procured their return, Aubrey tells us how. The father was 'of a mild and peaceable nature [just like old Capulet in the play], and his sons' sad accident brake his heart.' Thereupon, his spirited widow 'to obtain pardon for her sons married Sir Edmund Carey, cousin-german to Queen Elizabeth.' This is correct: Carey was the sixth son of the philoprogenitive Lord Chamberlain Hunsdon, and this marriage provided for him, though 'she kept him to hard meat.' We see how these things come together – when we know enough about them in detail to interpret them.

The Play. Shakespeare found what he wanted to ignite his play ready to hand in the story of Romeo and Juliet, and the feuding of Montagus and Capulets. He read it up in Arthur Brooke's poem, *The Tragical History of Romeus and Juliet*, and in the prose story in Painter's *Palace of Pleasure*. He adhered fairly closely to the poem, speeding it up and telescoping events; the play moves at tremendous speed, making all the more impact – we are swept off our feet, as Romeo and Juliet were, by the inspired upthrust and onrush of the play, as if composed at high pressure in one musical movement.

Shakespeare's chief addition is the character of Mercutio, Romeo's devoted friend. Some people have thought to see Marlowe in the quarrelling, poetic Mercutio, given to fantasy and friendship. This is mere conjecture; but there is nothing against it: we can never know. What is for it is that the love of women is not for Mercutio; he rallies Romeo on it and goes in for a gay combat of wits with him. And, 'is not this better now than groaning for love? Now art thou sociable; now art thou Romeo. Now art thou what thou art, by art as well as by nature.'

When Romeo goes off wenching, 'stabbed with a white wench's black eye,' Mercutio takes to his single 'truckle-bed'. But he is given the most magical poetry in the play, the wonderful evocation of Queen Mab – which looks as if it had been left over from *A Midsummer Night's Dream*. But these dreams

> . . . are the children of an idle brain,
> Begot of nothing but vain fantasy,
> Which is as thin of substance as the air,
> And more inconstant than the wind.

Is 'Mercutio' intended to suggest 'mercurial'? We remember Drayton's tribute to Marlowe: 'his raptures were all air and fire.'

It is Lady Capulet who drives forward revenge upon Romeo for Tybalt's death: she would send to one in Mantua to give him a dram that would make him soon join Tybalt.

The citation of Petrarch – the only one in Shakespeare – he would easily have got from the company of Florio, of whom he would have seen a good deal in Southampton's household at this time. Mercutio says of Romeo in love: 'Now is he for the numbers

John Gielgud and Peggy Ashcroft as Romeo and Juliet, New Theatre, London, 1935

Petrarch flowed in. Laura, to his lady, was but a kitchen-wench – marry, she had a better love to be-rhyme her; Dido a dowdy, Cleopatra a gipsy, Helen and Hero hildings [sluts] and harlots. Thisbe a grey eye or so, but not to the purpose. Signor Romeo, *bon jour*.' This passage has many reverberations: all of these ladies were celebrated one way or another, either by Marlowe or by Shakespeare.

Juliet's excited speech beginning,

> Gallop apace, you fiery-footed steeds,
> Towards Phoebus' lodging –

echoes a speech from Marlowe's *Edward II*, as Lady Capulet's lament over Juliet, when she thinks her dead, is an echo from Kyd. No work of Shakespeare is without a reference to his profession: on the young Montagus entering masked for the party at the Capulets, we find Benvolio saying,

> We'll have no Cupid hoodwinked with a scarf,
> Bearing a Tartar's painted bow of lath . . .
> Nor no without-book prologue, faintly spoke
> After the prompter, for our entrance.

Personal. We note Shakespeare's personal idiom in the phrase to 'groan' for love, which occurs contemporaneously in the Sonnets:

> Thy face hath not the power to make love groan.

And we observe his increased familiarity with the *train-de-vie* of a great house: he would know Southampton's house in Holborn, and Titchfield in the country. Here we have the serving-men preparing the Capulets' banquet:

> Sampson: You are looked for and called for, asked for, and sought for, in the great chamber.

That would be the great presence-chamber, upstairs, as at Hardwick or Hatfield. And Potpan replies:

> We cannot be here and there too.

How authentic! how often one has heard that in the days when there were servants. Lady Capulet herself keeps the keys of the spice-cupboard, and

> They call for dates and quinces in the pastry –

i.e. the pastry-kitchen.

Shakespeare reveals himself in his knowledge of cheveril, the first of several times he mentions it: the glover's son knew the softest doeskin, of which gloves were made. Rather than marry Count Paris Juliet says:

> Or hide me nightly in a charnel-house,
> O'er-covered quite with dead men's rattling bones
> With reeky shanks, and yellow, chapless skulls.

In Shakespeare's day there was such a charnel-house along the churchyard path to the parish church. The little page who accompanies Paris to the Capulets' monument, treading the hollow churchyard path, says charmingly:

> I am almost afraid to stand alone
> Here in the churchyard; yet I will venture.

Folk customs and beliefs appear; for example, in 'did'st thou not fall out with a tailor for wearing his new doublet before Easter?' Again, in:

> Some say the lark and loathèd toad change eyes.

And in the belief that mandrakes – a forked earth-plant with two hairy roots – shriek when torn out of the earth and 'living mortals, hearing them, run mad.' Evidently, a piece of sympathetic magic.

Music. *Romeo and Juliet* is notable for much greater use of music and references to music, contemporary songs and ballads, than any play so far. Several occasions are made for music, of which indications remain in one or other of the quartos. When Juliet sees Romeo down from her window at dawn, after the night they had spent together, and questioning whether they would ever meet again, she speaks words that echo a haunting Elizabethan air, 'Fortune, my foe', and may have sung a verse of it to herself after he has gone. A whole scene is given to the musicians who had been engaged for her wedding-feast to Count Paris. Peter the Clown bids them play the famous tune 'Heart's ease, Heart's ease', while his own heart plays 'My heart is full of woe'. In the end he sings the early Elizabethan song, 'When griping grief the heart doth wound', written by Richard Edwards, Master of the Children of the Chapel and producer of their plays.

Why is there a marked increase of musical interest in this play?

We have noticed something of the immense amount Shakespeare learned from the prolonged association with Southampton, the introduction into a cultivated aristocratic circle with sophisticated taste in painting, etc. It is not to be supposed that he learned nothing from his exposure to the charms of the musical dark lady, daughter and wife of royal musicians, one of whose spells was the touch of her fingers upon the virginals.

Perhaps we should also notice a marked increase of bawdy and suggestive talk.

The Text is a fair one. An unauthorised quarto of so popular a play was put out in 1597, a reported version, which was also cut, though it preserves some useful readings which do not appear in the authorised quarto of 1599, as 'newly corrected, augmented, and amended'. The first quarto had some descriptive notes as to stage-business evidently from some actors; the second quarto also contains errors, but was printed from the author's manuscript, whose stage-directions reveal him when he says at one point, 'Enter Will Kemp' for 'Enter Peter.' Peter, the Clown's, is not a large part for a star; I dare say he doubled it with another part. The Folio text was based on a reprint in 1609 of the 1599 quarto. Editors have had fun conflating and supplementing to arrive at a sufficiently satisfactory text.

ROMEO AND JULIET.

DRAMATIS PERSONÆ.

ESCALUS, prince of Verona.
PARIS, a young nobleman, kinsman to the prince.
MONTAGUE, } heads of two houses at variance
CAPULET, } with each other.
An old man, cousin to Capulet.
ROMEO, son to Montague.
MERCUTIO, kinsman to the prince, and friend to Romeo.
BENVOLIO, nephew to Montague, and friend to Romeo.
TYBALT, nephew to Lady Capulet.
FRIAR LAURENCE, } Franciscans.
FRIAR JOHN, }
BALTHASAR, servant to Romeo.
SAMPSON, } servants to Capulet.
GREGORY, }

PETER, servant to Juliet's nurse.
ABRAHAM, servant to Montague.
An Apothecary.
Three Musicians.
Page to Paris; another Page; an Officer.

LADY MONTAGUE, wife to Montague
LADY CAPULET, wife to Capulet.
JULIET, daughter to Capulet.
Nurse to Juliet.

Citizens of Verona; several Men and Women, relations to both houses; Maskers, Guards, Watchmen, and Attendants.

Chorus.

SCENE: *Verona: Mantua.*

● *A bullet beside a text line indicates an annotation in the opposite column*

PROLOGUE.

Two households, both alike in dignity,
    In fair Verona, where we lay our scene,
● From ancient grudge break to new mutiny,
    Where civil blood makes civil hands unclean.
From forth the fatal loins of these two foes
    A pair of star-cross'd lovers take their life;
Whose misadventured piteous overthrows
    Do with their death bury their parents' strife.
● The fearful passage of their death-mark'd love,
    And the continuance of their parents' rage,   10
Which, but their children's end, nought could

Set design for the opening scene by Jean Hugo for Jean Cocteau's production, Paris, 1924

---

3 *break*. Break out into. *mutiny*. Violence.

9 *passage*. Course.

Opposite: Juliet on the balcony. Painting by W. Hatherell (1855–1928)

14 *What here shall miss.* i.e. shall be missing. *toil.* i.e. performance.

1-2 *carry coals.* Perform menial duties, i.e. put up with insults.

4 *draw.* Draw swords.

7 *moved.* Aroused.

15 *take the wall.* Pass on the inside of.

37 *poor John.* Cheap dried fish. *tool.* Weapon.

44 *of.* On.

48-49 *bite my thumb.* An insulting gesture.

remove,
Is now the two hours' traffic of our stage;
The which if you with patient ears attend,
● What here shall miss, our toil shall strive to
mend.

ACT I.

SCENE I.   *Verona.   A public place.*

Enter SAMPSON *and* GREGORY, *of the house of
Capulet, armed with swords and bucklers.*

● *Sam.*   Gregory, o' my word, we'll not carry
coals.
   Gre.   No, for then we should be colliers.
● *Sam.*   I mean, an we be in choler, we'll draw.
   Gre.   Ay, while you live, draw your neck out
o' the collar.
● *Sam.*   I strike quickly, being moved.
   Gre.   But thou art not quickly moved to strike.
   Sam.   A dog of the house of Montague
moves me.   10
   Gre.   To move is to stir; and to be valiant is
to stand: therefore, if thou art moved, thou
runn'st away.
   Sam.   A dog of that house shall move me to
● stand: I will take the wall of any man or maid
of Montague's.
   Gre.   That shows thee a weak slave; for the
weakest goes to the wall.
   Sam.   True; and therefore women, being the
weaker vessels, are ever thrust to the wall: therefore I will push Montague's men from the wall,
and thrust his maids to the wall.
   Gre.   The quarrel is between our masters and
us their men.
   Sam.   'Tis all one, I will show myself a
tyrant: when I have fought with the men, I
will be cruel with the maids, and cut off their
heads.
   Gre.   The heads of the maids?   29
   Sam.   Ay, the heads of the maids, or their
maidenheads; take it in what sense thou wilt.
   Gre.   They must take it in sense that feel it.
   Sam.   Me they shall feel while I am able
to stand: and 'tis known I am a pretty piece
of flesh.
   Gre.   'Tis well thou art not fish; if thou hadst,
● thou hadst been poor John. Draw thy tool; here
comes two of the house of the Montagues.
   Sam.   My naked weapon is out: quarrel, I
will back thee.   40
   Gre.   How! turn thy back and run?
   Sam.   Fear me not.
   Gre.   No, marry; I fear thee!
● *Sam.*   Let us take the law of our sides; let
them begin.
   Gre.   I will frown as I pass by, and let them
take it as they list.
● *Sam.*   Nay, as they dare. I will bite my
thumb at them; which is a disgrace to them, if
they bear it.   50

Enter ABRAHAM *and* BALTHASAR.

   Abr.   Do you bite your thumb at us, sir?
   Sam.   I do bite my thumb, sir.
   Abr.   Do you bite your thumb at us, sir?
   Sam.   [*Aside to Gre.*] Is the law of our side,
if I say ay?

Gre.   No.

Sam.   No, sir, I do not bite my thumb at you, sir, but I bite my thumb, sir.

Gre.   Do you quarrel, sir?

Abr.   Quarrel, sir! no, sir.   60

Sam.   If you do, sir, I am for you: I serve as good a man as you.

Abr.   No better.

Sam.   Well, sir.

Gre.   Say 'better:' here comes one of my master's kinsmen.

Sam.   Yes, better, sir.

Abr.   You lie.

Sam.   Draw, if you be men. Gregory, remember thy swashing blow.   [*They fight.*   70

> *Enter* BENVOLIO.

Ben.   Part, fools!
Put up your swords; you know not what you do.
                              [*Beats down their swords.*

> *Enter* TYBALT.

Tyb.   What, art thou drawn among these heartless hinds?
Turn thee, Benvolio, look upon thy death.

Ben.   I do but keep the peace: put up thy sword,
Or manage it to **part** these men with me.

Tyb.   What, drawn, and talk of peace! I hate the word,
As I hate hell, all Montagues, and thee:
Have at thee, coward!   [*They fight.*

> *Enter several of both houses, who join the fray; then enter* Citizens, *with clubs.*

First Cit.   Clubs, bills, and partisans! strike! beat them down!   80
Down with the Capulets! down with the Montagues!

> *Enter* CAPULET *in his gown, and* LADY CAPULET.

Cap.   What noise is this? Give me my long sword, ho!

La. Cap.   A crutch, a crutch! why call you for a sword?

Cap.   My sword, I say! Old Montague is come,
And flourishes his blade in spite of me.

> *Enter* MONTAGUE *and* LADY MONTAGUE.

Mon.   Thou villain Capulet,—Hold me not, let me go.

La. Mon.   Thou shalt not stir a foot to seek a foe.

> *Enter* PRINCE, *with* Attendants.

Prin.   Rebellious subjects, enemies to peace,
Profaners of this neighbour-stained steel,—
Will they not hear? What, ho! you men, you beasts,   90
That quench the fire of your pernicious rage
With purple fountains issuing from your veins,
On pain of torture, from those bloody hands
Throw your mistemper'd weapons to the ground,
And hear the sentence of your moved prince.
Three civil brawls, bred of an airy word,
By thee, old Capulet, and Montague,
Have thrice disturb'd the quiet of our streets,

70 *swashing.* Slashing.

73 *heartless hinds.* Cowardly lot.

80 *bills.* Pikes with curved blades. *partisans.* Pikes with doubled edged blades.

Costume design for Capulet by Jean Hugo for Jean Cocteau's production, Paris, 1924

85 *in spite of.* To defy.

89 *neighbour-stained.* Stained with the blood of neighbours.

94 *mistemper'd.* i.e. misused.

100 *beseeming ornaments.* Proper clothes.

102 *canker'd.* Rusty.

Prince: 'If ever you disturb our streets again, Your lives shall pay the forfeit of the peace'. Illustration by Ludovic Marchetti from an edition of *Shakespeare*, 1892

109 *Free-town.* i.e. Villafranca, the Capulets' residence.

111 *set . . . new abroach.* Reopened.

121 *part and part.* Some on one side, some on the other.

127 *drave.* Drove.

142 *Aurora.* Goddess of dawn.

156 *sounding.* Discreet inquiry.

And made Verona's ancient citizens
● Cast by their grave beseeming ornaments,   100
 To wield old partisans, in hands as old,
● Canker'd with peace, to part your canker'd hate:
 If ever you disturb our streets again,
 Your lives shall pay the forfeit of the peace.
 For this time, all the rest depart away:
 You, Capulet, shall go along with me:
 And, Montague, come you this afternoon,
 To know our further pleasure in this case,
● To old Free-town, our common judgement-place.
 Once more, on pain of death, all men depart.   110
　　　[*Exeunt all but Montague, Lady Mon-*
　　　　　　tague, and Benvolio.
● *Mon.* Who set this ancient quarrel new
 abroach?
 Speak, nephew, were you by when it began?
　Ben. Here were the servants of your adversary,
 And yours, close fighting ere I did approach:
 I drew to part them: in the instant came
 The fiery Tybalt, with his sword prepared,
 Which, as he breathed defiance to my ears,
 He swung about his head and cut the winds,
 Who nothing hurt withal hiss'd him in scorn: 119
 While we were interchanging thrusts and blows,
● Came more and more and fought on part and part,
 Till the prince came, who parted either part.
　La. Mon. O, where is Romeo? saw you him
 to-day?
 Right glad I am he was not at this fray.
　Ben. Madam, an hour before the worshipp'd sun
 Peer'd forth the golden window of the east,
● A troubled mind drave me to walk abroad;
 Where, underneath the grove of sycamore
 That westward rooteth from the city's side,
 So early walking did I see your son: 130
 Towards him I made, but he was ware of me
 And stole into the covert of the wood:
 I, measuring his affections by my own,
 That most are busied when they're most alone,
 Pursued my humour not pursuing his,
 And gladly shunn'd who gladly fled from me.
　Mon. Many a morning hath he there been
 seen,
 With tears augmenting the fresh morning's dew,
 Adding to clouds more clouds with his deep sighs;
 But all so soon as the all-cheering sun   140
 Should in the furthest east begin to draw
● The shady curtains from Aurora's bed,
 Away from light steals home my heavy son,
 And private in his chamber pens himself,
 Shuts up his windows, locks fair daylight out
 And makes himself an artificial night:
 Black and portentous must this humour prove,
 Unless good counsel may the cause remove.
　Ben. My noble uncle, do you know the cause?
　Mon. I neither know it nor can learn of him.
　Ben. Have you importuned him by any means?
　Mon. Both by myself and many other friends:
 But he, his own affections' counsellor,
 Is to himself—I will not say how true—
 But to himself so secret and so close,
● So far from sounding and discovery,
 As is the bud bit with an envious worm,
 Ere he can spread his sweet leaves to the air,
 Or dedicate his beauty to the sun.
 Could we but learn from whence his sorrows
 grow,   160
 We would as willingly give cure as know.

Enter ROMEO.

Ben. ·See, where he comes: so please you,
    step aside;
I'll know his grievance, or be much denied.
    Mon. I would thou wert so happy by thy stay,
●To hear true shrift.   Come, madam, let's away.
              [*Exeunt Montague and Lady*.
    Ben.   Good morrow, cousin.
    Rom.   Is the day so young?
    Ben.   But new struck nine.
    Rom.   Ay me! sad hours seem long.
Was that my father that went hence so fast?
    Ben. It was. What sadness lengthens Romeo's
    hours?
    Rom.   Not having that, which, having, makes
    them short.   170
    Ben.   In love?
    Rom.   Out—
    Ben.   Of love?
    Rom.   Out of her favour, where I am in love.
    Ben.   Alas, that love, so gentle in his view,
Should be so tyrannous and rough in proof!
    Rom.   Alas, that love, whose view is muffled
    still,
Should, without eyes, see pathways to his will!
Where shall we dine? O me! What fray was
    here?
Yet tell me not, for I have heard it all.   180
Here's much to do with hate, but more with love.
Why, then, O brawling love! O loving hate!
O any thing, of nothing first create!
O heavy lightness! serious vanity!
Mis-shapen chaos of well-seeming forms!
Feather of lead, bright smoke, cold fire, sick
    health!
Still-waking sleep, that is not what it is!
This love feel I, that feel no love in this.
Dost thou not laugh?
    Ben.   No, coz, I rather weep. 189
    Rom.   Good heart, at what?
    Ben.   At thy good heart's oppression.
    Rom.   Why, such is love's transgression.
Griefs of mine own lie heavy in my breast,
●Which thou wilt propagate, to have it prest
With more of thine: this love that thou hast
    shown
Doth add more grief to too much of mine own.
Love is a smoke raised with the fume of sighs;
Being purged, a fire sparkling in lovers' eyes;
Being vex'd, a sea nourish'd with lovers' tears:
What is it else? a madness most discreet,
A choking gall and a preserving sweet.   200
Farewell, my coz.
    Ben.   Soft! I will go along;
An if you leave me so, you do me wrong.
    Rom. Tut, I have lost myself; I am not here;
This is not Romeo, he's some other where.
    Ben. Tell me in sadness, who is that you love.
    Rom. What, shall I groan and tell thee?
    Ben.   Groan! why, no;
But sadly tell me who.
    Rom. Bid a sick man in sadness make his will:
Ah, word ill urged to one that is so ill!
In sadness, cousin, I do love a woman.   210
    Ben.   I aim'd so near, when I supposed you
    loved.
    Rom.   A right good mark-man! And she's
    fair I love.

Matheson Lang, English Edwardian actor, as Romeo,
Lyceum Theatre, London, 1908

---

165 *shrift.* Confession.

193 *prest.* Oppressed.

215 *Dian.* Diana, goddess of chastity. *Wit.* Inclination.

216 *proof.* Armour.

Romeo: '. . . she'll not be hit with Cupid's arrow'.
Painting 'The Combat of Love and Chastity' from
Florentine School, 15th century

244 *pay that doctrine.* i.e. convince you that you can
forget.

Ben. A right fair mark, fair coz, is soonest hit.
Rom. Well, in that hit you miss : she'll not be
hit
● With Cupid's arrow; she hath Dian's wit;
● And, in strong proof of chastity well arm'd,
From love's weak childish bow she lives unharm'd.
She will not stay the siege of loving terms,
Nor bide the encounter of assailing eyes,
Nor ope her lap to saint-seducing gold: 220
O, she is rich in beauty, only poor,
That when she dies with beauty dies her store.
Ben. Then she hath sworn that she will still
live chaste?
Rom. She hath, and in that sparing makes
huge waste,
For beauty starved with her severity
Cuts beauty off from all posterity.
She is too fair, too wise, wisely too fair,
To merit bliss by making me despair :
She hath forsworn to love, and in that vow
Do I live dead that live to tell it now.   230
Ben. Be ruled by me, forget to think of her.
Rom. O, teach me how I should forget to
think.
Ben. By giving liberty unto thine eyes;
Examine other beauties.
Rom.   'Tis the way
To call hers exquisite, in question more :
These happy masks that kiss fair ladies' brows
Being black put us in mind they hide the fair ;
He that is strucken blind cannot forget
The precious treasure of his eyesight lost :
Show me a mistress that is passing fair,   240
What doth her beauty serve, but as a note
Where I may read who pass'd that passing fair?
Farewell : thou canst not teach me to forget.
● *Ben.* I'll pay that doctrine, or else die in debt.
[*Exeunt.*

SCENE II.   *A street.*

Enter CAPULET, PARIS, *and* Servant.

Cap. But Montague is bound as well as I,
In penalty alike ; and 'tis not hard, I think,
For men so old as we to keep the peace.
Par. Of honourable reckoning are you both ;
And pity 'tis you lived at odds so long.
But now, my lord, what say you to my suit?
Cap. But saying o'er what I have said before :
My child is yet a stranger in the world ;
She hath not seen the change of fourteen years ;
Let two more summers wither in their pride,   10
Ere we may think her ripe to be a bride.
Par. Younger than she are happy mothers
made.
Cap. And too soon marr'd are those so early
made.
The earth hath swallow'd all my hopes but she,
She is the hopeful lady of my earth :
But woo her, gentle Paris, get her heart,
My will to her consent is but a part ;
An she agree, within her scope of choice
Lies my consent and fair according voice.
This night I hold an old accustom'd feast,   20
Whereto I have invited many a guest,
Such as I love ; and you, among the store,
One more, most welcome, makes my number
more.
At my poor house look to behold this night

Earth-treading stars that make dark heaven
    light:
Such comfort as do lusty young men feel
When well-apparell'd April on the heel
Of limping winter treads, even such delight
Among fresh female buds shall you this night
• Inherit at my house; hear all, all see,   30
And like her most whose merit most shall be:
† Which on more view, of many mine being one
May stand in number, though in reckoning none.
Come, go with me. [*To Serv., giving a paper.*]
    Go, sirrah, trudge about
Through fair Verona; find those persons out
Whose names are written there, and to them say,
My house and welcome on their pleasure stay.
    [*Exeunt Capulet and Paris.*
  Serv. Find them out whose names are written
here! It is written, that the shoemaker should
meddle with his yard, and the tailor with his last,
the fisher with his pencil, and the painter with his
nets; but I am sent to find those persons whose
names are here writ, and can never find what
names the writing person hath here writ. I
• must to the learned.—In good time.

    Enter BENVOLIO *and* ROMEO.

  Ben. Tut, man, one fire burns out another's
    burning,
One pain is lessen'd by another's anguish;
• Turn giddy, and be holp by backward turning;
  One desperate grief cures with another's lan-
    guish:
Take thou some new infection to thy eye,   50
And the rank poison of the old will die.
  Rom. Your plaintain-leaf is excellent for that.
  Ben. For what, I pray thee?
  Rom.   For your broken shin.
  Ben. Why, Romeo, art thou mad?
  Rom. Not mad, but bound more than a mad-
    man is;
Shut up in prison, kept without my food,
• Whipp'd and tormented and—God-den, good
    fellow.
  Serv. God gi' god-den. I pray, sir, can you
read?
  Rom. Ay, mine own fortune in my misery. 60
  Serv. Perhaps you have learned it without
book: but, I pray, can you read any thing you
see?
  Rom. Ay, if I know the letters and the lan-
    guage.
  Serv. Ye say honestly: rest you merry!
  Rom. Stay, fellow; I can read.   [*Reads.*
'Signior Martino and his wife and daughters;
• County Anselme and his beauteous sisters; the
lady widow of Vitruvio; Signior Placentio and
his lovely nieces; Mercutio and his brother Valen-
tine; mine uncle Capulet, his wife, and daugh-
ters; my fair niece Rosaline; Livia; Signior Va-
lentio and his cousin Tybalt; Lucio and the lively
Helena.'
A fair assembly: whither should they come?
  Serv. Up.
  Rom. Whither?
  Serv. To supper; to our house.
  Rom. Whose house?
  Serv. My master's.   80
  Rom. Indeed, I should have ask'd you that
before.

30 *Inherit.* Enjoy.

45 *In good time.* i.e. 'you have arrived at a good moment'.

48 *holp.* Helped.

Costume design for Romeo by Randolf Schwabe, Lyric Theatre, London, 1919.

57 *God-den.* Good evening.

68 *County.* i.e. the Count of.

90 *unattainted.* Unprejudiced.

104 *scant.* Scarcely.

13 *teen.* Grief.

15 *Lammas-tide.* August 1st. *odd.* A few.

21–23 *On Lammas . . . years.* See introduction.

26 *laid . . . dug.* i.e. giving the nipple a bitter taste, to wean the child.

Costume design for Lady Capulet by Jean Hugo for Jean Cocteau's production, Paris, 1924

Serv. Now I'll tell you without asking: my master is the great rich Capulet; and if you be not of the house of Montagues, I pray, come and crush a cup of wine.   Rest you merry!   [*Exit.*
   Ben.   At this same ancient feast of Capulet's
Sups the fair Rosaline whom thou so lovest,
With all the admired beauties of Verona:
●Go thither; and, with unattainted eye,   90
Compare her face with some that I shall show,
And I will make thee think thy swan a crow.
   Rom.   When the devout religion of mine eye
   Maintains such falsehood, then turn tears to fires;
And these, who often drown'd could never die,
   Transparent heretics, be burnt for liars!
One fairer than my love! the all-seeing sun
Ne'er saw her match since first the world begun.
   Ben.   Tut, you saw her fair, none else being by,
Herself poised with herself in either eye: 100
But in that crystal scales let there be weigh'd
Your lady's love against some other maid
That I will show you shining at this feast,
●And she shall scant show well that now shows best.
   Rom.   I'll go along, no such sight to be shown,
But to rejoice in splendour of mine own.
                   [*Exeunt.*

SCENE III.   *A room in Capulet's house.*

Enter LADY CAPULET *and* Nurse.

   La. Cap.   Nurse, where's my daughter? call her forth to me.
   Nurse.   Now, by my maidenhead, at twelve year old,
I bade her come.   What, lamb! what, lady-bird!
God forbid!   Where's this girl?   What, Juliet!

Enter JULIET.

   Jul.   How now! who calls?
   Nurse.   Your mother.
   Jul.   Madam, I am here.
What is your will?
   La. Cap.   This is the matter:—Nurse, give leave awhile,
We must talk in secret:—nurse, come back again;
I have remember'd me, thou's hear our counsel.
Thou know'st my daughter's of a pretty age.   10
   Nurse.   Faith, I can tell her age unto an hour.
   La. Cap.   She's not fourteen.
   Nurse.   I'll lay fourteen of my teeth,—
●And yet, to my teen be it spoken, I have but four,—
She is not fourteen.   How long is it now
●To Lammas-tide?
   La. Cap.   A fortnight and odd days.
   Nurse.   Even or odd, of all days in the year,
Come Lammas-eve at night shall she be fourteen.
Susan and she—God rest all Christian souls!—
Were of an age: well, Susan is with God;
She was too good for me: but, as I said,   20
●On Lammas-eve at night shall she be fourteen;
That shall she, marry; I remember it well.
'Tis since the earthquake now eleven years;
And she was wean'd,—I never shall forget it,—
Of all the days of the year, upon that day:
●For I had then laid wormwood to my dug,
Sitting in the sun under the dove-house wall;
My lord and you were then at Mantua:—

• Nay, I do bear a brain:—but, as I said,
When it did taste the wormwood on the nipple 30
• Of my dug and felt it bitter, pretty fool,
• To see it tetchy and fall out with the dug!
• 'Shake' quoth the dove-house: 'twas no need, I trow,
To bid me trudge:
And since that time it is eleven years;
• For then she could stand alone; nay, by the rood,
She could have run and waddled all about;
• For even the day before, she broke her brow:
And then my husband—God be with his soul!
A' was a merry man—took up the child: 40
'Yea,' quoth he, 'dost thou fall upon thy face?
Thou wilt fall backward when thou hast more wit;
• Wilt thou not, Jule?' and, by my holidame,
The pretty wretch left crying and said 'Ay.'
To see, now, how a jest shall come about!
I warrant, an I should live a thousand years,
I never should forget it: 'Wilt thou not, Jule?' quoth he;
• And, pretty fool, it stinted and said 'Ay.'
    La. Cap.   Enough of this; I pray thee, hold thy peace.
    Nurse.   Yes, madam: yet I cannot choose but laugh, 50
To think it should leave crying and say 'Ay.'
And yet, I warrant, it had upon its brow
• A bump as big as a young cockerel's stone;
• A parlous knock; and it cried bitterly:
'Yea,' quoth my husband, 'fall'st upon thy face?
Thou wilt fall backward when thou comest to age;
Wilt thou not, Jule?' it stinted and said 'Ay.'
    Jul.   And stint thou too, I pray thee, nurse, say I.
    Nurse.   Peace, I have done.   God mark thee to his grace!
Thou wast the prettiest babe that e'er I nursed:
An I might live to see thee married once, 61
I have my wish.
    La. Cap.   Marry, that 'marry' is the very theme
I came to talk of.   Tell me, daughter Juliet,
How stands your disposition to be married?
    Jul.   It is an honour that I dream not of.
    Nurse.   An honour! were not I thine only nurse,
I would say thou hadst suck'd wisdom from thy teat.
    La. Cap.   Well, think of marriage now; younger than you,
Here in Verona, ladies of esteem, 70
Are made already mothers: by my count,
• I was your mother much upon these years
That you are now a maid.   Thus then in brief:
The valiant Paris seeks you for his love.
    Nurse.   A man, young lady! lady, such a man
• As all the world—why, he's a man of wax.
    La. Cap.   Verona's summer hath not such a flower.
    Nurse.   Nay, he's a flower; in faith, a very flower.
    La. Cap.   What say you? can you love the gentleman?
This night you shall behold him at our feast; 80
Read o'er the volume of young Paris' face
And find delight writ there with beauty's pen;
• Examine every married lineament
And see how one another lends content,

29 *I do bear a brain.* I have a good memory.

31 *felt.* Tasted.

32 *tetchy.* Fretful.

33 *'Shake' quoth the dove-house.* i.e. the earthquake caused the dove house to shake. *trow.* Am certain.

36 *rood.* Cross.

38 *broke her brow.* Cut her forehead.

43 *holidame.* Mild oath, by Our Lady.

Edith Evans as the Nurse, Stratford-upon-Avon, 1961

48 *stinted.* Stopped.

53 *stone.* Testicle.

54 *parlous.* Serious.

72 *much upon these years.* i.e. when I was about this age.

76 *man of wax.* i.e. a very model of a man.

83 *married.* Harmonious. *lineament.* Feature.

87 *unbound.* Unmarried.

98 *endart.* Shoot as a dart.

102 *cursed.* Cursed for her absence.

Costume design for Mercutio by Randolf Schwabe, Lyric Theatre, London, 1919

---

3 *The date is out of.* It is no longer in fashion.

4-8 *We'll . . . entrance.* See introduction.

6 *crow-keeper.* Scarecrow.

10 *measure.* Dance.

12 *heavy.* Sad.

28 *Prick love for pricking.* i.e. diminish lust by satisfying.

29 *case.* Mask. *visage.* Face.

And what obscured in this fair volume lies
Find written in the margent of his eyes.
• This precious book of love, this unbound lover,
To beautify him, only lacks a cover:
The fish lives in the sea, and 'tis much pride
For fair without the fair within to hide: 90
That book in many's eyes doth share the glory,
That in gold clasps locks in the golden story;
So shall you share all that he doth possess,
By having him, making yourself no less.
   Nurse. No less! nay, bigger; women grow
      by men.
   La. Cap. Speak briefly, can you like of Paris'
      love?
   Jul. I'll look to like, if looking liking move:
• But no more deep will I endart mine eye
Than your consent gives strength to make it fly.

                Enter a Servant.

   Serv. Madam, the guests are come, supper
served up, you called, my young lady asked for,
• the nurse cursed in the pantry, and every thing in
extremity. I must hence to wait; I beseech you,
follow straight.
   La. Cap. We follow thee. [*Exit Servant.*]
      Juliet, the county stays.
   Nurse. Go, girl, seek happy nights to happy
      days.   [*Exeunt.*

            SCENE IV.   *A street.*

Enter ROMEO, MERCUTIO, BENVOLIO, *with five
   or six* Maskers, Torch-bearers, *and others.*

   Rom. What, shall this speech be spoke for our
      excuse?
Or shall we on without apology?
•   *Ben.* The date is out of such prolixity:
• We'll have no Cupid hoodwink'd with a scarf,
Bearing a Tartar's painted bow of lath,
• Scaring the ladies like a crow-keeper;
Nor no without-book prologue, faintly spoke
After the prompter, for our entrance:
But let them measure us by what they will;
• We'll measure them a measure, and be gone.   10
   Rom. Give me a torch: I am not for this
      ambling;
• Being but heavy, I will bear the light.
   Mer. Nay, gentle Romeo, we must have you
      dance.
   Rom. Not I, believe me: you have dancing
      shoes
With nimble soles: I have a soul of lead
So stakes me to the ground I cannot move.
   Mer. You are a lover; borrow Cupid's wings,
And soar with them above a common bound.
   Rom. I am too sore enpierced with his shaft
To soar with his light feathers, and so bound,   20
I cannot bound a pitch above dull woe:
Under love's heavy burden do I sink.
   Mer. And, to sink in it, should you burden
      love;
Too great oppression for a tender thing.
   Rom. Is love a tender thing? it is too rough,
Too rude, too boisterous, and it pricks like thorn.
   Mer. If love be rough with you, be rough with
      love;
• Prick love for pricking, and you beat love down.
• Give me a case to put my visage in:
A visor for a visor! what care I   30

What curious eye doth quote deformities?
Here are the beetle brows shall blush for me.
  Ben. Come, knock and enter; and no sooner in,
But every man betake him to his legs.
  Rom. A torch for me: let wantons light of
    heart
Tickle the senseless rushes with their heels,
For I am proverb'd with a grandsire phrase;
I'll be a candle-holder, and look on.
The game was ne'er so fair, and I am done.
  Mer. Tut, dun's the mouse, the constable's
    own word: 40
If thou art dun, we'll draw thee from the mire
Of this sir-reverence love, wherein thou stick'st
Up to the ears. Come, we burn daylight, ho!
  Rom. Nay, that's not so.
  Mer.   I mean, sir, in delay
We waste our lights in vain, like lamps by day.
Take our good meaning, for our judgement sits
Five times in that ere once in our five wits.
  Rom. And we mean well in going to this mask;
But 'tis no wit to go.
  Mer.   Why, may one ask?
  Rom. I dream'd a dream to-night.
  Mer.   And so did I. 50
  Rom. Well, what was yours?
  Mer.   That dreamers often lie.
  Rom. In bed asleep, while they do dream
    things true.
  Mer. O, then, I see Queen Mab hath been
    with you.
She is the fairies' midwife, and she comes
In shape no bigger than an agate-stone
On the fore-finger of an alderman,
Drawn with a team of little atomies
Athwart men's noses as they lie asleep;
Her waggon-spokes made of long spinners' legs,
The cover of the wings of grasshoppers, 60
The traces of the smallest spider's web,
The collars of the moonshine's watery beams,
Her whip of cricket's bone, the lash of film,
Her waggoner a small grey-coated gnat,
Not half so big as a round little worm
Prick'd from the lazy finger of a maid;
Her chariot is an empty hazel-nut
Made by the joiner squirrel or old grub,
Time out o' mind the fairies' coachmakers.
And in this state she gallops night by night 70
Through lovers' brains, and then they dream of
    love;
O'er courtiers' knees, that dream on court'sies
    straight,
O'er lawyers' fingers, who straight dream on fees,
O'er ladies' lips, who straight on kisses dream,
Which oft the angry Mab with blisters plagues,
Because their breaths with sweetmeats tainted
    are:
Sometime she gallops o'er a courtier's nose,
And then dreams he of smelling out a suit;
And sometime comes she with a tithe-pig's tail
Tickling a parson's nose as a' lies asleep, 80
Then dreams he of another benefice:
Sometime she driveth o'er a soldier's neck,
And then dreams he of cutting foreign throats,
Of breaches, ambuscadoes, Spanish blades,
Of healths five-fathom deep; and then anon
Drums in his ear, at which he starts and wakes,
And being thus frighted swears a prayer or two
And sleeps again. This is that very Mab

31 *quote.* Notice.

32 *Here.* i.e. here on the mask.

37 *I am proverb'd . . . grandsire.* I am provided with an old proverb.

38 *candle-holder.* i.e. spectator.

Johnston Forbes Robertson as Romeo, Lyceum Theatre, London, 1895

40 *dun's.* Be as quiet as.

41 *dun . . . mire.* Alluding to a game where a 'dun', a large log, was pulled out of a marsh.

42 *sir-reverence.* Irreverent.

43 *daylight.* i.e. waste our effort.

53 *Queen Mab.* Fairy Queen.

57 *atomies.* Small creatures.

59 *spinners.* Spiders.

79 *tithe-pig.* A pig paid as a tithe to a parson by a parishioner.

84 *ambuscadoes.* Ambushes.

85 *healths.* i.e. drinks.

90 *bakes the elf-locks.* Mats the tangled hairs.

92 *hag.* Nightmare.

97–100 *are the . . . the wind.* See introduction.

109 *expire.* Bring to an end.

Set design for a room in Capulet's house by Jean Hugo for Jean Cocteau's production, Paris, 1924

2 *trencher.* Wooden plate.

7 *joint-stools.* Stools made by a joiner.

8 *court-cupboard.* Sideboard. *plate.* Cutlery.

9 *marchpane.* Marzipan.

19 *bout.* Dance.

That plats the manes of horses in the night,
● And bakes the elf-locks in foul sluttish hairs,   90
Which once untangled much misfortune bodes:
● This is the hag, when maids lie on their backs,
That presses them and learns them first to bear,
Making them women of good carriage:
This is she—
   Rom.   Peace, peace, Mercutio, peace!
Thou talk'st of nothing.
   Mer.   True, I talk of dreams,
● Which are the children of an idle brain,
Begot of nothing but vain fantasy,
Which is as thin of substance as the air
And more inconstant than the wind, who wooes
Even now the frozen bosom of the north,   101
And, being anger'd, puffs away from thence,
Turning his face to the dew-dropping south.
   Ben.   This wind, you talk of, blows us from
      ourselves;
Supper is done, and we shall come too late.
   Rom.   I fear, too early: for my mind misgives
Some consequence yet hanging in the stars
Shall bitterly begin his fearful date
● With this night's revels and expire the term
Of a despised life closed in my breast   110
By some vile forfeit of untimely death.
But He, that hath the steerage of my course,
Direct my sail! On, lusty gentlemen.
   Ben.   Strike, drum.   [*Exeunt.*

SCENE V.   *A hall in Capulet's house.*

Musicians *waiting.   Enter* Servingmen, *with
napkins.*

   First Serv.   Where's Potpan, that he helps
● not to take away? He shift a trencher? he scrape
a trencher!
   Sec. Serv.   When good manners shall lie all in
one or two men's hands and they unwashed too,
'tis a foul thing.
●   *First Serv.*   Away with the joint-stools, re-
● move the court-cupboard, look to the plate. Good
● thou, save me a piece of marchpane; and, as thou
lovest me, let the porter let in Susan Grindstone
and Nell. Antony, and Potpan!   11
   Sec. Serv.   Ay, boy, ready.
   First Serv.   You are looked for and called for,
asked for and sought for, in the great chamber.
   Sec. Serv.   We cannot be here and there too.
Cheerly, boys; be brisk awhile, and the longer
liver take all.

Enter CAPULET, *with* JULIET *and others of his
house, meeting the* Guests *and* Maskers.

   Cap.   Welcome, gentlemen! ladies that have
      their toes
● Unplagued with corns will have a bout with you.
Ah ha, my mistresses! which of you all   20
Will now deny to dance? she that makes dainty,
She, I'll swear, hath corns; am I come near ye
      now?
Welcome, gentlemen! I have seen the day
That I have worn a visor and could tell
A whispering tale in a fair lady's ear,
Such as would please: 'tis gone, 'tis gone, 'tis
      gone:
You are welcome, gentlemen! Come, musicians,
      play.

● A hall, a hall! give room! and foot it, girls.
     [*Music plays, and they dance.*
More light, you knaves; and turn the tables up,
And quench the fire, the room is grown too hot.
Ah, sirrah, this unlook'd-for sport comes well. 31
Nay, sit, nay, sit, good cousin Capulet;
For you and I are past our dancing days:
How long is't now since last yourself and I
Were in a mask?
 Sec. Cap. By'r lady, thirty years.
 Cap. What, man! 'tis not so much, 'tis not so
   much:
'Tis since the nuptial of Lucentio,
● Come pentecost as quickly as it will,
Some five and twenty years; and then we mask'd.
 Sec. Cap. 'Tis more, 'tis more: his son is elder,
   sir;   40
His son is thirty.
 Cap.   Will you tell me that?
His son was but a ward two years ago.
 Rom. [*To a Servingman*] What lady is that,
   which doth enrich the hand
Of yonder knight?
 Serv. I know not, sir.
 Rom. O, she doth teach the torches to burn
   bright!
It seems she hangs upon the cheek of night
● Like a rich jewel in an Ethiope's ear;
Beauty too rich for use, for earth too dear!
So shows a snowy dove trooping with crows, 50
As yonder lady o'er her fellows shows.
The measure done, I'll watch her place of stand,
And, touching hers, make blessed my rude hand.
Did my heart love till now? forswear it, sight!
For I ne'er saw true beauty till this night.
 Tyb. This, by his voice, should be a Montague.
Fetch me my rapier, boy. What dares the slave
● Come hither, cover'd with an antic face,
● To fleer and scorn at our solemnity?
Now, by the stock and honour of my kin, 60
To strike him dead I hold it not a sin.
 Cap. Why, how now, kinsman! wherefore
   storm you so?
 Tyb. Uncle, this is a Montague, our foe,
A villain that is hither come in spite,
To scorn at our solemnity this night.
 Cap. Young Romeo is it?
 Tyb.   'Tis he, that villain Romeo.
 Cap. Content thee, gentle coz, let him alone;
He bears him like a portly gentleman;
And, to say truth, Verona brags of him
To be a virtuous and well govern'd youth: 70
I would not for the wealth of all the town
Here in my house do him disparagement:
Therefore be patient, take no note of him:
It is my will, the which if thou respect,
Show a fair presence and put off these frowns,
An ill-beseeming semblance for a feast.
 Tyb. It fits, when such a villain is a guest:
I'll not endure him.
 Cap.   He shall be endured:
What, goodman boy! I say, he shall: go to;
Am I the master here, or you? go to. 80
You'll not endure him! God shall mend my
   soul!
You'll make a mutiny among my guests!
● You will set cock-a-hoop! you'll be the man!
 Tyb. Why, uncle, 'tis a shame.
 Cap.   Go to, go to;

28 *A hall.* Clear a way.

The ball scene. Design by Hawes Craven for the production at the Lyceum Theatre, London, 1895

---

38 *pentecost.* Whitsuntide.

48 *Ethiope.* Black African.

58 *antic face.* Comic mask.

59 *fleer.* Sneer. *solemnity.* Dignity.

83 *set cock-a-hoop.* Cause trouble. *be the man.* Play the big man.

86 *trick.* Behaviour. *scathe.* Damage. *what.* What I say.

88 *princox.* Insolent youth.

The Capulet ball. Drawing by Anthony Walker (1726–1765)

102 *palmers.* Pilgrims.

119 *chinks.* Coins.

128 *fay.* Faith.

You are a saucy boy: is't so, indeed?
● This trick may chance to scathe you, I know what:
You must contrary me! marry, 'tis time.
● Well said, my hearts! You are a princox; go:
Be quiet, or—More light, more light! For shame!
I'll make you quiet. What, cheerly, my hearts!
    Tyb. Patience perforce with wilful choler meeting   91
Makes my flesh tremble in their different greeting.
I will withdraw: but this intrusion shall
Now seeming sweet convert to bitter gall. [*Exit.*
Rom. [*To Juliet*] If I profane with my unworthiest hand
    This holy shrine, the gentle fine is this:
My lips, two blushing pilgrims, ready stand
    To smooth that rough touch with a tender kiss.
    Jul. Good pilgrim, you do wrong your hand too much,
    Which mannerly devotion shows in this;   100
For saints have hands that pilgrims' hands do touch,
●   And palm to palm is holy palmers' kiss.
    Rom. Have not saints lips, and holy palmers too?
    Jul. Ay, pilgrim, lips that they must use in prayer.
    Rom. O, then, dear saint, let lips do what hands do;
They pray, grant thou, lest faith turn to despair.
    Jul. Saints do not move, though grant for prayers' sake.
    Rom. Then move not, while my prayer's effect I take.
Thus from my lips, by yours, my sin is purged.
    Jul. Then have my lips the sin that they have took.   110
    Rom. Sin from my lips? O trespass sweetly urged!
Give me my sin again.
    Jul.   You kiss by the book.
    Nurse. Madam, your mother craves a word with you.
    Rom. What is her mother?
    Nurse.   Marry, bachelor,
Her mother is the lady of the house,
And a good lady, and a wise and virtuous:
I nursed her daughter, that you talk'd withal;
I tell you, he that can lay hold of her
● Shall have the chinks.
    Rom.   Is she a Capulet?
O dear account! my life is my foe's debt.   120
    Ben. Away, be gone; the sport is at the best.
    Rom. Ay, so I fear; the more is my unrest.
    Cap. Nay, gentlemen, prepare not to be gone;
We have a trifling foolish banquet towards.
Is it e'en so? why, then, I thank you all;
I thank you, honest gentlemen; good night.
More torches here! Come on then, let's to bed.
● Ah, sirrah, by my fay, it waxes late:
I'll to my rest.
            [*Exeunt all but Juliet and Nurse.*
    Jul. Come hither, nurse. What is yond gentleman?   130
    Nurse. The son and heir of old Tiberio.
    Jul. What's he that now is going out of door?
    Nurse. Marry, that, I think, be young Petrucio.
    Jul. What's he that follows there, that would not dance?
    Nurse. I know not.

Jul. Go, ask his name: if he be married,
My grave is like to be my wedding bed.
   Nurse. His name is Romeo, and a Montague;
The only son of your great enemy.
   Jul. My only love sprung from my only hate!
Too early seen unknown, and known too late! 141
Prodigious birth of love it is to me,
That I must love a loathed enemy.
   Nurse. What's this? what's this?
   Jul.   A rhyme I learn'd even now
Of one I danced withal. [*One calls within* 'Juliet.'
   Nurse.   Anon, anon!
Come, let's away; the strangers all are gone.
                         [*Exeunt.*

ACT II.

PROLOGUE.

Enter Chorus.

Chor. Now old desire doth in his death-bed lie,
   And young affection gapes to be his heir;
That fair for which love groan'd for and would
     die,
   With tender Juliet match'd, is now not fair.
Now Romeo is beloved and loves again,
   Alike bewitched by the charm of looks,
But to his foe supposed he must complain,
   And she steal love's sweet bait from fearful
     hooks:
Being held a foe, he may not have access
   To breathe such vows as lovers use to swear;
And she as much in love, her means much less 11
   To meet her new-beloved any where:
But passion lends them power, time means, to
     meet,
Tempering extremities with extreme sweet. [*Exit.*

SCENE I. *A lane by the wall of Capulet's*
orchard.

Enter ROMEO.

   Rom. Can I go forward when my heart is
     here?
• Turn back, dull earth, and find thy centre out.
   [*He climbs the wall, and leaps down within it.*

Enter BENVOLIO *and* MERCUTIO.

   Ben. Romeo! my cousin Romeo!
   Mer.   He is wise;
And, on my life, hath stol'n him home to bed.
   Ben. He ran this way, and leap'd this orchard
     wall:
• Call, good Mercutio.
   Mer.   Nay, I'll conjure too.
• Romeo! humours! madman! passion! lover!
Appear thou in the likeness of a sigh:
Speak but one rhyme, and I am satisfied;
Cry but 'Ay me!' pronounce but 'love' and
   'dove;'   10
Speak to my gossip Venus one fair word,
• One nick-name for her purblind son and heir,
Young Adam Cupid, he that shot so trim,
• When King Cophetua loved the beggar-maid!
He heareth not, he stirreth not, he moveth not;
The ape is dead, and I must conjure him.
I conjure thee by Rosaline's bright eyes,
By her high forehead and her scarlet lip,
By her fine foot, straight leg and quivering thigh

Costume design for Juliet by Randolf Schwabe, Lyric
Theatre, London, 1919

---

2 *earth.* Body. *find.* Reveal. *centre.* Heart.

6 *conjure.* Summon spirits.

7 *humours.* Whims.

12 *purblind.* Blindfolded; strictly speaking, partly blind,
even (originally) completely blind.

14 *Cophetua . . . maid.* From an Elizabethan ballad, a
favourite with Shakespeare.

20 *demesnes.* Domains.

24 *circle.* Magic circle, circle of legs (pun).

38 *poperin.* Poperinghe, in Flanders, whence this variety of pear (with bawdy innuendo).

39 *truckle-bed.* Small bed, pushed under a larger.

Costume design for Romeo (Christopher Hassall) by Motley, Oxford University Dramatic Society production, 1933

---

8 *vestal.* Virginal. *green.* Anaemic.

● And the demesnes that there adjacent lie,   20
That in thy likeness thou appear to us!
   Ben.   An if he hear thee, thou wilt anger him.
   Mer.   This cannot anger him: 'twould anger
     him
● To raise a spirit in his mistress' circle
Of some strange nature, letting it there stand
Till she had laid it and conjured it down;
That were some spite: my invocation
Is fair and honest, and in his mistress' name
I conjure only but to raise up him.
   Ben.   Come, he hath hid himself among these
     trees,   30
To be consorted with the humorous night:
Blind is his love and best befits the dark.
   Mer.   If love be blind, love cannot hit the
     mark.
Now will he sit under a medlar tree,
And wish his mistress were that kind of fruit
As maids call medlars, when they laugh alone.
O, Romeo, that she were, O, that she were
● An open et cætera, thou a poperin pear!
● Romeo, good night: I'll to my truckle-bed;
This field-bed is too cold for me to sleep: 40
Come, shall we go?
   Ben.   Go, then; for 'tis in vain
To seek him here that means not to be found.
                  [Exeunt.

Scene II.   *Capulet's orchard.*

Enter Romeo.

   Rom.   He jests at scars that never felt a
     wound.
        [Juliet appears above at a window.
But, soft! what light through yonder window
     breaks?
It is the east, and Juliet is the sun.
Arise, fair sun, and kill the envious moon,
Who is already sick and pale with grief,
That thou her maid art far more fair than she:
Be not her maid, since she is envious;
● Her vestal livery is but sick and green
And none but fools do wear it; cast it off.
It is my lady, O, it is my love!   10
O, that she knew she were!
She speaks, yet she says nothing: what of that?
Her eye discourses; I will answer it.
I am too bold, 'tis not to me she speaks:
Two of the fairest stars in all the heaven,
Having some business, do entreat her eyes
To twinkle in their spheres till they return.
What if her eyes were there, they in her head?
The brightness of her cheek would shame those
     stars,
As daylight doth a lamp; her eyes in heaven   20
Would through the airy region stream so bright
That birds would sing and think it were not night.
See, how she leans her cheek upon her hand!
O, that I were a glove upon that hand,
That I might touch that cheek!
   Jul.   Ay me!
   Rom.   She speaks:
O, speak again, bright angel! for thou art
As glorious to this night, being o'er my head,
As is a winged messenger of heaven
Unto the white-upturned wondering eyes
Of mortals that fall back to gaze on him   30
When he bestrides the lazy-pacing clouds

And sails upon the bosom of the air.

Jul. O Romeo, Romeo! wherefore art thou
    Romeo?
Deny thy father and refuse thy name;
Or, if thou wilt not, be but sworn my love,
And I'll no longer be a Capulet.

    Rom. [*Aside*] Shall I hear more, or shall I
    speak at this?

    Jul. 'Tis but thy name that is my enemy;
Thou art thyself, though not a Montague.
What's Montague? it is nor hand, nor foot,   40
Nor arm, nor face, nor any other part
Belonging to a man.   O, be some other name!
What's in a name? that which we call a rose
By any other name would smell as sweet;
So Romeo would, were he not Romeo call'd,
● Retain that dear perfection which he owes
Without that title.   Romeo, doff thy name,
And for that name which is no part of thee
Take all myself.

    Rom.   I take thee at thy word:
Call me but love, and I'll be new baptized;   50
Henceforth I never will be Romeo.

    Jul. What man art thou that thus bescreen'd
    in night
So stumblest on my counsel?

    Rom.   By a name
I know not how to tell thee who I am:
My name, dear saint, is hateful to myself,
Because it is an enemy to thee;
Had I it written, I would tear the word.

    Jul. My ears have not yet drunk a hundred
    words
Of that tongue's utterance, yet I know the sound:
Art thou not Romeo and a Montague?   60

    Rom. Neither, fair saint, if either thee dislike.

    Jul. How camest thou hither, tell me, and
    wherefore?
The orchard walls are high and hard to climb,
And the place death, considering who thou art,
If any of my kinsmen find thee here.

●   *Rom.* With love's light wings did I o'er-perch
    these walls;
For stony limits cannot hold love out,
And what love can do that dares love attempt;
Therefore thy kinsmen are no let to me.

    Jul. If they do see thee, they will murder
    thee.   70

    Rom. Alack, there lies more peril in thine eye
Than twenty of their swords: look thou but sweet,
● And I am proof against their enmity.

    Jul. I would not for the world they saw thee
    here.

    Rom. I have night's cloak to hide me from
    their sight;
And but thou love me, let them find me here:
My life were better ended by their hate,
Than death prorogued, wanting of thy love.

    Jul. By whose direction found'st thou out
    this place?

    Rom. By love, who first did prompt me to
    inquire;   80
He lent me counsel and I lent him eyes.
I am no pilot; yet, wert thou as far
As that vast shore wash'd with the farthest sea,
I would adventure for such merchandise.

    Jul. Thou know'st the mask of night is on
    my face,
Else would a maiden blush bepaint my cheek

46 *owes.* Owns.

Spranger Barry as Romeo and Mrs Rossiter as Juliet,
Covent Garden Theatre, London 1753.

66 *o'er-perch.* Leap over.

73 *proof.* Armoured.

For that which thou hast heard me speak to-night.
● Fain would I dwell on form, fain, fain deny
What I have spoke: but farewell compliment! 89
Dost thou love me?   I know thou wilt say 'Ay,'
And I will take thy word: yet, if thou swear'st,
Thou mayst prove false; at lovers' perjuries,
They say, Jove laughs.   O gentle Romeo,
If thou dost love, pronounce it faithfully:
Or if thou think'st I am too quickly won,
I'll frown and be perverse and say thee nay,
So thou wilt woo; but else, not for the world.
● In truth, fair Montague, I am too fond,
And therefore thou mayst think my 'haviour light:
But trust me, gentleman, I'll prove more true 100
● Than those that have more cunning to be strange.
I should have been more strange, I must confess,
But that thou overheard'st, ere I was ware,
My true love's passion: therefore pardon me,
And not impute this yielding to light love,
Which the dark night hath so discovered.
  Rom. Lady, by yonder blessed moon I swear
That tips with silver all these fruit-tree tops—
  Jul. O, swear not by the moon, the inconstant moon,
That monthly changes in her circled orb,   110
Lest that thy love prove likewise variable.
  Rom. What shall I swear by?
  Jul.   Do not swear at all;
Or, if thou wilt, swear by thy gracious self,
Which is the god of my idolatry,
And I'll believe thee.
  Rom.   If my heart's dear love—
  Jul. Well, do not swear: although I joy in thee,
I have no joy of this contract to-night:
It is too rash, too unadvised, too sudden;
Too like the lightning, which doth cease to be
Ere one can say 'It lightens.'   Sweet, good night!
This bud of love, by summer's ripening breath, 121
May prove a beauteous flower when next we meet.
Good night, good night! as sweet repose and rest
Come to thy heart as that within my breast!
  Rom. O, wilt thou leave me so unsatisfied?
  Jul. What satisfaction canst thou have tonight?
  Rom. The exchange of thy love's faithful vow for mine.
  Jul. I gave thee mine before thou didst request it:
And yet I would it were to give again.
  Rom. Wouldst thou withdraw it? for what purpose, love?   130
  Jul. But to be frank, and give it thee again.
And yet I wish but for the thing I have:
My bounty is as boundless as the sea,
My love as deep; the more I give to thee,
The more I have, for both are infinite.
                              [*Nurse calls within.*
I hear some noise within; dear love, adieu!
Anon, good nurse!   Sweet Montague, be true.
Stay but a little, I will come again. [*Exit, above.*
  Rom. O blessed, blessed night! I am afeard,
Being in night, all this is but a dream,   140
Too flattering-sweet to be substantial.

Re-enter JULIET, above.

  Jul. Three words, dear Romeo, and good night indeed.

88 *Fain.* Gladly.

98 *fond.* Foolish.

101 *cunning.* Ability. *strange.* Distant.

Juliet: 'My bounty is as boundless as the sea, My love as deep . . .' Engraving from a painting by John Francis Rigaud (1742–1810)

Opposite: The balcony scene. Drawing by Francis Philip Stephanoff (1790?–1860)

Juliet: 'Hist, Romeo, hist!' Drawing by Anthony Walker
(1726–1765)

---

160 *tassel-gentle.* Male falcon.

178 *wanton.* Spoiled child.

180 *gyves.* Shackles.

190 *dear hap.* Good fortune.

If that thy bent of love be honourable,
Thy purpose marriage, send me word to-morrow,
By one that I'll procure to come to thee,
Where and what time thou wilt perform the
    rite;
And all my fortunes at thy foot I'll lay
And follow thee my lord throughout the world.
    Nurse. [*Within*] Madam!
    Jul. I come, anon.—But if thou mean'st not
    well,   150
I do beseech thee—
    Nurse. [*Within*] Madam!
    Jul.   By and by, I come:—
To cease thy suit, and leave me to my grief:
To-morrow will I send.
    Rom.   So thrive my soul—
    Jul. A thousand times good night!
        [*Exit, above.*
    Rom. A thousand times the worse, to want
    thy light.
Love goes toward love, as schoolboys from their
    books,
But love from love, toward school with heavy
    looks.   [*Retiring.*

Re-enter JULIET, *above.*

    Jul. Hist! Romeo, hist! O, for a falconer's
    voice,
To lure this tassel-gentle back again!   160
Bondage is hoarse, and may not speak aloud;
Else would I tear the cave where Echo lies,
And make her airy tongue more hoarse than mine,
With repetition of my Romeo's name.
    Rom. It is my soul that calls upon my name:
How silver-sweet sound lovers' tongues by night,
Like softest music to attending ears!
    Jul. Romeo!
    Rom.   My dear?
    Jul.   At what o'clock to-morrow
Shall I send to thee?
    Rom.   At the hour of nine.   169
    Jul. I will not fail: 'tis twenty years till then.
I have forgot why I did call thee back.
    Rom. Let me stand here till thou remember it.
    Jul. I shall forget, to have thee still stand
    there,
Remembering how I love thy company.
    Rom. And I'll still stay, to have thee still forget,
Forgetting any other home but this.
    Jul. 'Tis almost morning; I would have thee
    gone:
And yet no further than a wanton's bird;
Who lets it hop a little from her hand,
Like a poor prisoner in his twisted gyves,   180
And with a silk thread plucks it back again,
So loving-jealous of his liberty.
    Rom. I would I were thy bird.
    Jul.   Sweet, so would I:
Yet I should kill thee with much cherishing.
Good night, good night! parting is such sweet
    sorrow,
That I shall say good night till it be morrow.
        [*Exit above.*
    Rom. Sleep dwell upon thine eyes, peace in
    thy breast!
Would I were sleep and peace, so sweet to rest!
Hence will I to my ghostly father's cell,   189
His help to crave, and my dear hap to tell. [*Exit.*

SCENE III.   *Friar Laurence's cell.*

Enter FRIAR LAURENCE, *with a basket.*

Fri. L. The grey-eyed morn smiles on the
    frowning night,
Chequering the eastern clouds with streaks of
    light,
And flecked darkness like a drunkard reels
● From forth day's path and Titan's fiery wheels:
Now, ere the sun advance his burning eye,
The day to cheer and night's dank dew to dry,
● I must up-fill this osier cage of ours
With baleful weeds and precious-juiced flowers.
The earth that's nature's mother is her tomb;
What is her burying grave that is her womb,   10
And from her womb children of divers kind
We sucking on her natural bosom find,
Many for many virtues excellent,
None but for some and yet all different.
● O, mickle is the powerful grace that lies
In herbs, plants, stones, and their true qualities:
For nought so vile that on the earth doth live
But to the earth some special good doth give,
Nor aught so good but strain'd from that fair use
Revolts from true birth, stumbling on abuse: 20
Virtue itself turns vice, being misapplied;
And vice sometimes by action dignified.
Within the infant rind of this small flower
Poison hath residence and medicine power:
For this, being smelt, with that part cheers each
    part;
Being tasted, slays all senses with the heart.
Two such opposed kings encamp them still
In man as well as herbs, grace and rude will;
And where the worser is predominant,
Full soon the canker death eats up that plant. 30

Enter ROMEO.

● *Rom.* Good morrow, father.
    Fri. L.   Benedicite!
What early tongue so sweet saluteth me?
Young son, it argues a distemper'd head
So soon to bid good morrow to thy bed:
Care keeps his watch in every old man's eye,
And where care lodges, sleep will never lie;
But where unbruised youth with unstuff'd brain
Doth couch his limbs, there golden sleep doth
    reign:
Therefore thy earliness doth me assure
Thou art up-roused by some distemperature;   40
Or if not so, then here I hit it right,
Our Romeo hath not been in bed to-night.
    Rom. That last is true; the sweeter rest was
    mine.
    Fri. L. God pardon sin! wast thou with Rosa-
    line?
    Rom. With Rosaline, my ghostly father? no;
I have forgot that name, and that name's woe.
    Fri. L. That's my good son: but where hast
    thou been, then?
    Rom. I'll tell thee, ere thou ask it me again.
I have been feasting with mine enemy,
Where on a sudden one hath wounded me,   50
That's by me wounded: both our remedies
Within thy help and holy physic lies:
I bear no hatred, blessed man, for, lo,
My intercession likewise steads my foe.

Set design for Friar Laurence's cell by Jean Hugo for
Jean Cocteau's production, Paris, 1924

4 *Titan.* Hyperion, the sun.

7 *osier cage.* Willow basket.

15 *mickle.* Great.

31 *Benedicite.* Bless you.

55 *homely*. Straightforward. *drift*. Story.

56 *shrift*. Absolution.

Friar Laurence: 'Holy Saint Francis, what a change is here!' Romeo (Richard Johnson) and Friar (Cyril Luckham), Stratford-upon-Avon, 1958

---

80 *strength*. Constancy.

86 *grace*. Favour.

● *Fri. L.*   Be plain, good son, and homely in thy drift;
● Riddling confession finds but riddling shrift.
   Rom. Then plainly know my heart's dear love is set
On the fair daughter of rich Capulet:
As mine on hers, so hers is set on mine;   59
And all combined, save what thou must combine
By holy marriage: when and where and how
We met, we woo'd and made exchange of vow,
I'll tell thee as we pass; but this I pray,
That thou consent to marry us to-day.
   Fri. L. Holy Saint Francis, what a change is here!
Is Rosaline, whom thou didst love so dear,
So soon forsaken? young men's love then lies
Not truly in their hearts, but in their eyes.
Jesu Maria, what a deal of brine
Hath wash'd thy sallow cheeks for Rosaline!   70
How much salt water thrown away in waste,
To season love, that of it doth not taste!
The sun not yet thy sighs from heaven clears,
Thy old groans ring yet in my ancient ears;
Lo, here upon thy cheek the stain doth sit
Of an old tear that is not wash'd off yet:
If e'er thou wast thyself and these woes thine,
Thou and these woes were all for Rosaline:
And art thou changed? pronounce this sentence then,   79
● Women may fall, when there's no strength in men.
   Rom. Thou chid'st me oft for loving Rosaline.
   Fri. L. For doting, not for loving, pupil mine.
   Rom. And bad'st me bury love.
   Fri. L.   Not in a grave,
To lay one in, another out to have.
   Rom. I pray thee, chide not: she whom I love now
● Doth grace for grace and love for love allow;
The other did not so.
   Fri L.   O, she knew well
Thy love did read by rote and could not spell.
But come, young waverer, come, go with me,
In one respect I'll thy assistant be;   90
For this alliance may so happy prove,
To turn your households' rancour to pure love.
   Rom. O, let us hence; I stand on sudden haste.
   Fri. L. Wisely and slow; they stumble that run fast.   [*Exeunt.*

SCENE IV.   *A street.*

Enter BENVOLIO *and* MERCUTIO.

   Mer. Where the devil should this Romeo be?
Came he not home to-night?
   Ben. Not to his father's; I spoke with his man.
   Mer. Ah, that same pale hard-hearted wench, that Rosaline,
Torments him so, that he will sure run mad.
   Ben. Tybalt, the kinsman of old Capulet,
Hath sent a letter to his father's house.
   Mer. A challenge, on my life.
   Ben. Romeo will answer it.
   Mer. Any man that can write may answer a letter.   10
   Ben. Nay, he will answer the letter's master, how he dares, being dared.
   Mer. Alas, poor Romeo! he is already dead; stabbed with a white wench's black eye; shot thorough the ear with a love-song; the very pin

of his heart cleft with the blind bow-boy's butt-shaft: and is he a man to encounter Tybalt?

Ben. Why, what is Tybalt?

Mer. More than prince of cats, I can tell you. O, he is the courageous captain of complements.
● He fights as you sing prick-song, keeps time, distance, and proportion; rests me his minim rest, one, two, and the third in your bosom : the very butcher of a silk button, a duellist, a duel-list; a gentleman of the very first house, of the
● first and second cause : ah, the immortal passado !
● the punto reverso ! the hai !

Ben. The what ?

Mer. The pox of such antic, lisping, affecting fantasticoes ; these new tuners of accents ! 'By Jesu, a very good blade ! a very tall man ! a very good whore !' Why, is not this a lament-able thing, grandsire, that we should be thus afflicted with these strange flies, these fashion-
● mongers, these perdona-mi's, who stand so much on the new form, that they cannot sit at ease on the old bench ? O, their bones, their bones !

Enter ROMEO.

Ben. Here comes Romeo, here comes Romeo.

Mer. Without his roe, like a dried herring:
● O flesh, flesh, how art thou fishified ! Now is he for the numbers that Petrarch flowed in : Laura to his lady was but a kitchen-wench; marry, she had a better love to be-rhyme her ; Dido a dowdy ;
● Cleopatra a gipsy; Helen and Hero hildings and harlots; Thisbe a grey eye or so, but not to the purpose. Signior Romeo, bon jour ! there's a
● French salutation to your French slop. You gave
● us the counterfeit fairly last night.

Rom. Good morrow to you both. What coun-terfeit did I give you?   50

● *Mer.* The slip, sir, the slip; can you not con-ceive ?

Rom. Pardon, good Mercutio, my business was great ; and in such a case as mine a man may strain courtesy.

Mer. That's as much as to say, such a case as
● yours constrains a man to bow in the hams.

Rom. Meaning, to court'sy.

Mer. Thou hast most kindly hit it.

Rom. A most courteous exposition.   60

Mer. Nay, I am the very pink of courtesy.

Rom. Pink for flower.

Mer. Right.

Rom. Why, then is my pump well flowered.

Mer. Well said : follow me this jest now till thou hast worn out thy pump, that when the single sole of it is worn, the jest may remain after the wearing sole singular.

Rom. O single-soled jest, solely singular for the singleness !   70

Mer. Come between us, good Benvolio; my wits faint.

Rom. Switch and spurs, switch and spurs; or
● I'll cry a match.

Mer. Nay, if thy wits run the wild-goose chase, I have done, for thou hast more of the wild-goose in one of thy wits than, I am sure, I have in my whole five : was I with you there for the goose?

Rom. Thou wast never with me for any thing
● when thou wast not there for the goose.   80

Mer. I will bite thee by the ear for that jest.

Rom. Nay, good goose, bite not.

James William Dod as Mercutio. Engraving from Bell's edition of *Shakespeare*, 1775

21-25 *He fights . . . duellist.* See introduction.

21 *prick-song.* Printed music. i.e. to the book.

26 *passado.* Lunge.

27 *punto reverso.* Backhand stroke. *hai.* Thrust.

35 *perdona-mi's.* Sticklers for etiquette. *stand.* Insist.

40-46 *Now is . . . bon jour.* See introduction.

44 *hildings.* Worthless women.

47 *slop.* Loosely-cut trousers.

48 *fairly.* Effectively.

51 *slip.* Counterfeit, evasion.

57 *hams.* Hips.

74 *a match.* A victory.

80 *goose.* Prostitute.

87 *cheveril.* Soft deerskin, favoured for gloves.

88 *ell.* Forty-five inches.

100 *the hair.* i.e. my will.

115 *morrow.* Morning.

117 *good den.* Good afternoon.

Nurse: 'Out upon you! what a man are you!' Illustration by Ludovic Marchetti from an edition of *Shakespeare*, 1892

135 *indite.* Invite.

146 *hoars.* Goes mouldy.

Mer. Thy wit is a very bitter sweeting; it is a most sharp sauce.

Rom. And is it not well served in to a sweet goose?

● *Mer.* O, here's a wit of cheveril, that stretches
● from an inch narrow to an ell broad!

Rom. I stretch it out for that word 'broad;' which added to the goose, proves thee far and wide a broad goose.   91

Mer. Why, is not this better now than groaning for love? now art thou sociable, now art thou Romeo; now art thou what thou art, by art as well as by nature: for this drivelling love is like a great natural, that runs lolling up and down to hide his bauble in a hole.

Ben. Stop there, stop there.

● *Mer.* Thou desirest me to stop in my tale against the hair.   100

Ben. Thou wouldst else have made thy tale large.

Mer. O, thou art deceived; I would have made it short: for I was come to the whole depth of my tale; and meant, indeed, to occupy the argument no longer.

Rom. Here's goodly gear!

Enter Nurse *and* PETER.

Mer. A sail, a sail!

Ben. Two, two; a shirt and a smock.

Nurse. Peter!   110

Peter. Anon!

Nurse. My fan, Peter.

Mer. Good Peter, to hide her face; for her fan's the fairer face.

● *Nurse.* God ye good morrow, gentlemen.

Mer. God ye good den, fair gentlewoman.

● *Nurse.* Is it good den?

Mer. 'Tis no less, I tell you, for the bawdy hand of the dial is now upon the prick of noon. 119

Nurse. Out upon you! what a man are you!

Rom. One, gentlewoman, that God hath made for himself to mar.

Nurse. By my troth, it is well said; 'for himself to mar,' quoth a'? Gentlemen, can any of you tell me where I may find the young Romeo?

Rom. I can tell you; but young Romeo will be older when you have found him than he was when you sought him: I am the youngest of that name, for fault of a worse.

Nurse. You say well.   130

Mer. Yea, is the worst well? very well took, i' faith; wisely, wisely.

Nurse. If you be he, sir, I desire some confidence with you.

● *Ben.* She will indite him to some supper.

Mer. A bawd, a bawd, a bawd! So ho!

Rom. What hast thou found?

Mer. No hare, sir; unless a hare, sir, in a lenten pie, that is something stale and hoar ere it be spent   [*Sings.* 140

      An old hare hoar,
      And an old hare hoar,
   Is very good meat in lent:
     But a hare that is hoar
     Is too much for a score,
●   When it hoars ere it be spent.

Romeo, will you come to your father's? we'll to dinner, thither.

Rom. I will follow you.

Mer. Farewell, ancient lady; farewell, [*singing*] 'lady, lady, lady.'   151
                [*Exeunt Mercutio and Benvolio.*
Nurse. Marry, farewell! I pray you, sir, what saucy merchant was this, that was so full of his ropery?

Rom. A gentleman, nurse, that loves to hear himself talk, and will speak more in a minute than he will stand to in a month.

Nurse. An a' speak any thing against me, I 'll take him down, an a' were lustier than he is, and twenty such Jacks; and if I cannot, I 'll find those that shall. Scurvy knave! I am none of his flirt-gills; I am none of his skains-mates. And thou must stand by too, and suffer every knave to use me at his pleasure?

Peter. I saw no man use you at his pleasure; if I had, my weapon should quickly have been out, I warrant you: I dare draw as soon as another man, if I see occasion in a good quarrel, and the law on my side.   169

Nurse. Now, afore God, I am so vexed, that every part about me quivers. Scurvy knave! Pray you, sir, a word: and as I told you, my young lady bade me inquire you out; what she bade me say, I will keep to myself: but first let me tell ye, if ye should lead her into a fool's paradise, as they say, it were a very gross kind of behaviour, as they say: for the gentlewoman is young; and, therefore, if you should deal double with her, truly it were an ill thing to be offered to any gentlewoman, and very weak dealing.   181

Rom. Nurse, commend me to thy lady and mistress. I protest unto thee—

Nurse. Good heart, and, i' faith, I will tell her as much: Lord, Lord, she will be a joyful woman.

Rom. What wilt thou tell her, nurse? thou dost not mark me.

Nurse. I will tell her, sir, that you do protest; which, as I take it, is a gentlemanlike offer.

Rom. Bid her devise   191
Some means to come to shrift this afternoon;
And there she shall at Friar Laurence' cell
Be shrived and married. Here is for thy pains.

Nurse. No, truly, sir; not a penny.

Rom. Go to; I say you shall.

Nurse. This afternoon, sir? well, she shall be there.

Rom. And stay, good nurse, behind the abbey wall:
Within this hour my man shall be with thee, 200
And bring thee cords made like a tackled stair;
Which to the high top-gallant of my joy
Must be my convoy in the secret night.
Farewell; be trusty, and I 'll quit thy pains:
Farewell; commend me to thy mistress.

Nurse. Now God in heaven bless thee! Hark you, sir.

Rom. What say'st thou, my dear nurse?

Nurse. Is your man secret? Did you ne'er hear say,
Two may keep counsel, putting one away?

Rom. I warrant thee, my man's as true as steel.   210

Nurse. Well, sir; my mistress is the sweetest lady—Lord, Lord! when 'twas a little prating thing:—O, there is a nobleman in town, one

154 *ropery*. Roguery.

162 *flirt-gills*. Giddy girls. *skains-mates*. Cut-throat companions.

201 *tackled stair*. Rope ladder.

202 *top-gallant*. Ship's rigging higher than the topmast, i.e. summit.

203 *convoy*. Conveyance.

212 *prating*. Prattling.

214 *lay knife aboard*. Possess her.

215 *as lief*. As soon.

218 *clout*. Cloth.

219 *versal world*. Universe.

225 *sententious*. Sentences.

Peggy Ashcroft as Juliet, London, 1935. Portrait by Ethel Gabain (1883–1950)

14 *bandy*. Volley.

● Paris, that would fain lay knife aboard; but she,
● good soul, had as lief see a toad, a very toad,
as see him.   I anger her sometimes and tell her
that Paris is the properer man; but, I'll warrant
● you, when I say so, she looks as pale as any clout
● in the versal world.   Doth not rosemary and
Romesary and Romeo begin both with a letter?   220
Rom. Ay, nurse; what of that? both with
an R.
Nurse. Ah, mocker! that's the dog's name; R
is for the— No; I know it begins with some other
● letter:—and she hath the prettiest sententious of
it, of you and rosemary, that it would do you
good to hear it.
Rom. Commend me to thy lady.
Nurse. Ay, a thousand times. [*Exit Romeo.*]
Peter!   230
Pet. Anon!
Nurse. Peter, take my fan, and go before, and
apace.   [*Exeunt.*

SCENE V. *Capulet's orchard.*

Enter JULIET.

Jul. The clock struck nine when I did send
the nurse;
In half an hour she promised to return.
Perchance she cannot meet him: that's not so.
O, she is lame! love's heralds should be thoughts,
Which ten times faster glide than the sun's beams,
Driving back shadows over louring hills:
Therefore do nimble-pinion'd doves draw love,
And therefore hath the wind-swift Cupid wings.
Now is the sun upon the highmost hill
Of this day's journey, and from nine till twelve 10
Is three long hours, yet she is not come.
Had she affections and warm youthful blood,
She would be as swift in motion as a ball:
● My words would bandy her to my sweet love,
And his to me:
† But old folks, many feign as they were dead;
Unwieldy, slow, heavy and pale as lead.
O God, she comes!

Enter Nurse *and* PETER.

            O honey nurse, what news?
Hast thou met with him? Send thy man away.
Nurse. Peter, stay at the gate. [*Exit Peter.*
Jul. Now, good sweet nurse,—O Lord, why
look'st thou sad?   21
Though news be sad, yet tell them merrily;
If good, thou shamest the music of sweet news
By playing it to me with so sour a face.
Nurse. I am a-weary, give me leave awhile:
Fie, how my bones ache! what a jaunt have
I had!
Jul. I would thou hadst my bones, and I
thy news.
Nay, come, I pray thee, speak; good, good
nurse, speak.
Nurse. Jesu, what haste? can you not stay
awhile?
Do you not see that I am out of breath?   30
Jul. How art thou out of breath, when thou
hast breath
To say to me that thou art out of breath?
The excuse that thou dost make in this delay
Is longer than the tale thou dost excuse.
Is thy news good, or bad? answer to that;

Say either, and I'll stay the circumstance:
Let me be satisfied, is't good or bad?
  Nurse.   Well, you have made a simple choice;
you know not how to choose a man: Romeo! no,
not he; though his face be better than any man's,
yet his leg excels all men's; and for a hand, and
a foot, and a body, though they be not to be
talked on, yet they are past compare: he is not
the flower of courtesy, but, I'll warrant him, as
gentle as a lamb.   Go thy ways, wench; serve
God.   What, have you dined at home?
  Jul.   No, no: but all this did I know before.
What says he of our marriage? what of that?
  Nurse.   Lord, how my head aches! what a
    head have I!
It beats as it would fall in twenty pieces.   50
My back o' t' other side,—O, my back, my
    back!
● Beshrew your heart for sending me about,
To catch my death with jaunting up and down!
  Jul.   I' faith, I am sorry that thou art not well.
Sweet, sweet, sweet nurse, tell me, what says
    my love?
  Nurse.   Your love says, like an honest gentle-
man, and a courteous, and a kind, and a hand-
some, and, I warrant, a virtuous,—Where is your
mother?
  Jul.   Where is my mother! why, she is
    within;   60
Where should she be?   How oddly thou repliest!
'Your love says, like an honest gentleman,
Where is your mother?'
  Nurse.   O God's lady dear!
● Are you so hot? marry, come up, I trow;
Is this the poultice for my aching bones?
Henceforward do your messages yourself.
●   *Jul.*   Here's such a coil! come, what says
    Romeo?
  Nurse.   Have you got leave to go to shrift
    to-day?
  Jul.   I have.
  Nurse.   Then hie you hence to Friar Lau-
    rence' cell;   70
There stays a husband to make you a wife:
Now comes the wanton blood up in your cheeks,
They'll be in scarlet straight at any news.
Hie you to church; I must another way,
To fetch a ladder, by the which your love
Must climb a bird's nest soon when it is dark:
I am the drudge and toil in your delight,
But you shall bear the burden soon at night.
Go; I'll to dinner: hie you to the cell.
  Jul   Hie to high fortune!   Honest nurse,
    farewell.   [*Exeunt.* 80

SCENE VI.   *Friar Laurence's cell.*

Enter FRIAR LAURENCE *and* ROMEO.

  Fri. L.   So smile the heavens upon this
    holy act,
That after hours with sorrow chide us not!
  Rom.   Amen, amen! but come what sorrow can,
● It cannot countervail the exchange of joy
That one short minute gives me in her sight:
Do thou but close our hands with holy words,
Then love-devouring death do what he dare;
It is enough I may but call her mine.
  Fri. L.   These violent delights have violent
    ends

52 *Beshrew.* Shame upon.

64 *hot.* Eager. *trow.* Trust.

67 *coil.* Fuss.

Juliet: '. . . come, what says Romeo?' Drawing by John
Haytes of Fanny Kemble as Juliet, with the Nurse,
Covent Garden Theatre, London, 1829

4 *countervail.* Overbalance.

18 *gossamer.* Spiders' webs.

26 *blazon.* Demonstrate.

30 *Conceit.* Imagination.

Friar Laurence: 'Come, come with me, and we will make short work'. Painting of Friar, Romeo and Juliet by Mather Brown (mid-18th century–1831)

8 *operation.* Influence.

9 *draws.* Draws his sword. *drawer.* Waiter.

And in their triumph die, like fire and powder, 10
Which as they kiss consume: the sweetest honey
Is loathsome in his own deliciousness
And in the taste confounds the appetite:
Therefore love moderately; long love doth so;
Too swift arrives as tardy as too slow.

Enter JULIET.

Here comes the lady: O, so light a foot
Will ne'er wear out the everlasting flint:
●A lover may bestride the gossamer
That idles in the wanton summer air,
And yet not fall; so light is vanity.   20
   Jul. Good even to my ghostly confessor.
   Fri. L. Romeo shall thank thee, daughter,
     for us both.
   Jul. As much to him, else is his thanks too
     much.
   Rom. Ah, Juliet, if the measure of thy joy
Be heap'd like mine and that thy skill be more
●To blazon it, then sweeten with thy breath
This neighbour air, and let rich music's tongue
Unfold the imagined happiness that both
Receive in either by this dear encounter.
  ● *Jul.* Conceit, more rich in matter than in
     words,   30
Brags of his substance, not of ornament:
They are but beggars that can count their worth;
But my true love is grown to such excess
I cannot sum up sum of half my wealth.
   Fri. L. Come, come with me, and we will
     make short work;
For, by your leaves, you shall not stay alone
Till holy church incorporate two in one.
                   [Exeunt.

ACT III.

SCENE I. *A public place.*

Enter MERCUTIO, BENVOLIO, Page, *and*
Servants.

   Ben. I pray thee, good Mercutio, let's retire:
The day is hot, the Capulets abroad,
And, if we meet, we shall not scape a brawl;
For now, these hot days, is the mad blood
     stirring.
   Mer. Thou art like one of those fellows that
when he enters the confines of a tavern claps me
his sword upon the table and says 'God send me
●no need of thee!' and by the operation of the
●second cup draws it on the drawer, when indeed
there is no need.   10
   Ben. Am I like such a fellow?
   Mer. Come, come, thou art as hot a Jack in
thy mood as any in Italy; and as soon moved
to be moody, and as soon moody to be moved.
   Ben. And what to?
   Mer. Nay, an there were two such, we should
have none shortly, for one would kill the other.
Thou! why, thou wilt quarrel with a man that
hath a hair more, or a hair less, in his beard,
than thou hast: thou wilt quarrel with a man for
cracking nuts, having no other reason but because thou hast hazel eyes: what eye but such
an eye would spy out such a quarrel? Thy
head is as full of quarrels as an egg is full of
meat, and yet thy head hath been beaten as
addle as an egg for quarrelling: thou hast quar-

relled with a man for coughing in the street, because he hath wakened thy dog that hath lain asleep in the sun: didst thou not fall out with a
● tailor for wearing his new doublet before Easter? with another, for tying his new shoes with old riband? and yet thou wilt tutor me from quarrelling!

   Ben. An I were so apt to quarrel as thou art,
● any man should buy the fee-simple of my life for an hour and a quarter.

   Mer. The fee-simple! O simple!

   Ben. By my head, here come the Capulets.

   Mer. By my heel, I care not.   39

Enter TYBALT *and others.*

   Tyb. Follow me close, for I will speak to them. Gentlemen, good den: a word with one of you.

   Mer. And but one word with one of us? couple it with something; make it a word and a blow.

   Tyb. You shall find me apt enough to that, sir, an you will give me occasion.

   Mer. Could you not take some occasion without giving?

   Tyb. Mercutio, thou consort'st with Romeo,—

   Mer. Consort! what, dost thou make us minstrels? an thou make minstrels of us, look to hear nothing but discords: here's my fiddlestick; here's that shall make you dance. 'Zounds, consort!

   Ben. We talk here in the public haunt of men:
Either withdraw unto some private place,
And reason coldly of your grievances,
Or else depart; here all eyes gaze on us.

   Mer. Men's eyes were made to look, and let them gaze;
I will not budge for no man's pleasure, I.

Enter ROMEO.

   Tyb. Well, peace be with you, sir: here comes my man.

   Mer. But I'll be hang'd, sir, if he wear your livery: 60
Marry, go before to field, he'll be your follower;
Your worship in that sense may call him 'man.'

   Tyb. Romeo, the hate I bear thee can afford
No better term than this,—thou art a villain.

   Rom. Tybalt, the reason that I have to love thee
Doth much excuse the appertaining rage
To such a greeting: villain am I none;
Therefore farewell; I see thou know'st me not.

   Tyb. Boy, this shall not excuse the injuries
That thou hast done me; therefore turn and draw.

   Rom. I do protest, I never injured thee,   71
But love thee better than thou canst devise,
Till thou shalt know the reason of my love:
And so, good Capulet,—which name I tender
As dearly as my own,—be satisfied.

   Mer. O calm, dishonourable, vile submission!
● *Alla stoccata* carries it away.   [*Draws.*
Tybalt, you rat-catcher, will you walk?

   Tyb. What wouldst thou have with me?   79

   Mer. Good king of cats, nothing but one of your nine lives; that I mean to make bold withal,
● and, as you shall use me hereafter, dry-beat the rest of the eight. Will you pluck your sword out
● of his pilcher by the ears? make haste, lest mine be about your ears ere it be out.

   Tyb. I am for you.   [*Drawing.*

   Rom. Gentle Mercutio, put thy rapier up.

30 *doublet.* Jacket.

35 *fee-simple.* Property.

77 *Alla stoccata.* To the thrust! *carries it away.* Will triumph.

Costume design for Tybalt by Jean Hugo for Jean Cocteau's production, Paris, 1924

82 *dry-beat.* Thrash.

84 *pilcher.* Scabbard.

88 *passado*. Lunge.

92 *bandying*. Fighting.

Romeo: 'Hold Tybalt! good Mercutio!' Mercutio (Ian Bannen) Romeo (Brian Murray) and Tybalt (Peter McEnery), Stratford-upon-Avon, 1961

94 *sped*. Mortally wounded.

102 *peppered*. Done for.

106 *book of arithmetic*. Timing of strokes: 'one, two, and the third in your bosom'.

122 *aspired*. Reached.

128 *respective lenity*. Careful behaviour.

● *Mer.* Come, sir, your passado.   [*They fight.*
   Rom. Draw, Benvolio; beat down their weapons.
Gentlemen, for shame, forbear this outrage!   90
Tybalt, Mercutio, the prince expressly hath
● Forbidden bandying in Verona streets:
   Hold, Tybalt! good Mercutio!
     [*Tybalt under Romeo's arm stabs Mercutio,
              and flies with his followers.*
   Mer.   I am hurt.
● A plague o' both your houses!   I am sped.
   Is he gone, and hath nothing?
   Ben.   What, art thou hurt?
   Mer. Ay, ay, a scratch, a scratch; marry,
   'tis enough.
Where is my page?   Go, villain, fetch a surgeon.
                    [*Exit Page.*
   Rom. Courage, man; the hurt cannot be much.
   Mer. No, 'tis not so deep as a well, nor so
wide as a church-door; but 'tis enough, 'twill
serve: ask for me to-morrow, and you shall find
● me a grave man.   I am peppered, I warrant, for
this world.   A plague o' both your houses!
'Zounds, a dog, a rat, a mouse, a cat, to scratch
a man to death! a braggart, a rogue, a villain,
● that fights by the book of arithmetic!   Why the
devil came you between us?   I was hurt under
your arm.
   Rom. I thought all for the best.   109
   Mer. Help me into some house, Benvolio,
Or I shall faint.   A plague o' both your houses!
They have made worms' meat of me: I have it,
And soundly too: your houses!
          [*Exeunt Mercutio and Benvolio.*
   Rom. This gentleman, the prince's near ally,
My very friend, hath got his mortal hurt
In my behalf; my reputation stain'd
With Tybalt's slander,—Tybalt, that an hour
Hath been my kinsman!   O sweet Juliet,
Thy beauty hath made me effeminate
And in my temper soften'd valour's steel!   120

     Re-enter BENVOLIO.

   Ben. O Romeo, Romeo, brave Mercutio's dead!
● That gallant spirit hath aspired the clouds,
Which too untimely here did scorn the earth.
   Rom. This day's black fate on more days doth
      depend;
This but begins the woe others must end.
   Ben. Here comes the furious Tybalt back
     again.
   Rom. Alive, in triumph! and Mercutio slain!
● Away to heaven, respective lenity,
And fire-eyed fury be my conduct now!

     Re-enter TYBALT.

Now, Tybalt, take the villain back again,   130
That late thou gavest me; for Mercutio's soul
Is but a little way above our heads,
Staying for thine to keep him company:
Either thou, or I, or both, must go with him.
   Tyb. Thou, wretched boy, that didst consort
     him here,
Shalt with him hence.
   Rom.   This shall determine that.
             [*They fight; Tybalt falls.*
   Ben. **Romeo** away, be gone!
The citizens are up, and Tybalt slain.

- Stand not amazed: the prince will doom thee death,
If thou art taken: hence, be gone, away!   140
    Rom.   O, I am fortune's fool!
    Ben.   Why dost thou stay?
                            [*Exit Romeo.*

Enter Citizens, &c.

    First Cit.   Which way ran he that kill'd Mercutio?
Tybalt, that murderer, which way ran he?
    Ben.   There lies that Tybalt.
    First Cit.   Up, sir, go with me;
I charge thee in the prince's name, obey.

Enter Prince, *attended;* MONTAGUE, CAPULET,
        their Wives, *and others.*

    Prin.   Where are the vile beginners of this fray?
    Ben.   O noble prince, I can discover all
- The unlucky manage of this fatal brawl:
There lies the man, slain by young Romeo,
That slew thy kinsman, brave Mercutio.   150
    La. Cap.   Tybalt, my cousin! O my brother's child!
O prince! O cousin! husband! O, the blood is spilt
Of my dear kinsman! Prince, as thou art true,
For blood of ours, shed blood of Montague.
O cousin, cousin!
    Prin.   Benvolio, who began this bloody fray?
    Ben.   Tybalt, here slain, whom Romeo's hand did slay;
Romeo that spoke him fair, bade him bethink
- How nice the quarrel was, and urged withal
Your high displeasure: all this uttered   160
With gentle breath, calm look, knees humbly bow'd,
Could not take truce with the unruly spleen
Of Tybalt deaf to peace, but that he tilts
With piercing steel at bold Mercutio's breast,
Who, all as hot, turns deadly point to point,
And, with a martial scorn, with one hand beats
Cold death aside, and with the other sends
It back to Tybalt, whose dexterity
Retorts it: Romeo he cries aloud,
'Hold, friends! friends, part!' and, swifter than his tongue,   170
His agile arm beats down their fatal points,
And 'twixt them rushes; underneath whose arm
- An envious thrust from Tybalt hit the life
Of stout Mercutio, and then Tybalt fled;
But by and by comes back to Romeo,
Who had but newly entertain'd revenge,
And to't they go like lightning, for, ere I
Could draw to part them, was stout Tybalt slain,
And, as he fell, did Romeo turn and fly.
This is the truth, or let Benvolio die.   180
    La. Cap.   He is a kinsman to the Montague;
Affection makes him false; he speaks not true:
Some twenty of them fought in this black strife,
And all those twenty could but kill one life.
I beg for justice, which thou, prince, must give;
Romeo slew Tybalt, Romeo must not live.
    Prin.   Romeo slew him, he slew Mercutio;
Who now the price of his dear blood doth owe?
    Mon.   Not Romeo, prince, he was Mercutio's friend;   189
His fault concludes but what the law should end,

139 *doom thee.* Sentence you to.

Prince: 'Where are the vile beginners of this fray?'
Scene illustration by Hawes Craven for the production
at the Lyceum Theatre, London, 1895

148 *manage.* Course.

159 *nice.* Trivial.

173 *envious.* Spiteful.

195 *amerce.* Punish.

Ellen Terry as Juliet, Lyceum Theatre, London, 1882

2 *Phœbus' lodging.* i.e. towards the west.

3 *Phaethon.* Phoebus' son who drove the horses, pulling the sun near to Earth.

6 *wink.* Close.

14 *unmann'd.* Uncontrolled. *bating.* Fluttering.

The life of Tybalt.
   Prin.   And for that offence
Immediately we do exile him hence:
I have an interest in your hate's proceeding,
My blood for your rude brawls doth lie a-bleed-
    ing;
● But I 'll amerce you with so strong a fine
That you shall all repent the loss of mine:
I will be deaf to pleading and excuses;
Nor tears nor prayers shall purchase out abuses:
Therefore use none: let Romeo hence in haste,
Else, when he 's found, that hour is his last.   200
Bear hence this body and attend our will:
Mercy but murders, pardoning those that kill.
                       [*Exeunt.*

SCENE II. *Capulet's orchard.*

Enter JULIET.

   Jul. Gallop apace, you fiery-footed steeds,
● Towards Phœbus' lodging: such a waggoner
● As Phaethon would whip you to the west,
And bring in cloudy night immediately.
Spread thy close curtain, love-performing night,
● That runaways' eyes may wink, and Romeo
Leap to these arms, untalk'd of and unseen.
Lovers can see to do their amorous rites
By their own beauties; or, if love be blind,
It best agrees with night. Come, civil night, 10
Thou sober-suited matron, all in black,
And learn me how to lose a winning match,
Play'd for a pair of stainless maidenhoods:
● Hood my unmann'd blood, bating in my cheeks,
With thy black mantle; till strange love, grown
    bold,
Think true love acted simple modesty.
Come, night; come, Romeo; come, thou day in
    night;
For thou wilt lie upon the wings of night
Whiter than new snow on a raven's back.
Come, gentle night, come, loving, black-brow'd
    night,   20
Give me my Romeo; and, when he shall die,
Take him and cut him out in little stars,
And he will make the face of heaven so fine
That all the world will be in love with night
And pay no worship to the garish sun.
O, I have bought the mansion of a love,
But not possess'd it, and, though I am sold,
Not yet enjoy'd: so tedious is this day
As is the night before some festival
To an impatient child that hath new robes   30
And may not wear them. O, here comes my
    nurse,
And she brings news; and every tongue that
    speaks
But Romeo's name speaks heavenly eloquence.

Enter Nurse, *with cords.*

Now, nurse, what news? What hast thou there?
    the cords
That Romeo bid thee fetch?
   Nurse.   Ay, ay, the cords.
                 [*Throws them down.*
   Jul. Ay me! what news? why dost thou
    wring thy hands?
   Nurse. Ah, well-a-day! he 's dead, he 's dead,
    he 's dead!

We are undone, lady, we are undone!
Alack the day! he's gone, he's kill'd, he's dead!
 Jul. Can heaven be so envious?
 Nurse.   Romeo can, 40
Though heaven cannot: O Romeo, Romeo!
Who ever would have thought it? Romeo!
 Jul. What devil art thou, that dost torment
  me thus?
This torture should be roar'd in dismal hell.
Hath Romeo slain himself? say thou but 'I,'
And that bare vowel 'I' shall poison more
● Than the death-darting eye of cockatrice:
I am not I, if there be such an I;
Or those eyes shut, that make thee answer 'I.'
If he be slain, say 'I'; or if not, no: 50
Brief sounds determine of my weal or woe.
 Nurse. I saw the wound, I saw it with mine
  eyes,—
God save the mark!—here on his manly breast:
● A piteous corse, a bloody piteous corse;
Pale, pale as ashes, all bedaub'd in blood,
● All in gore-blood; I swounded at the sight.
 Jul. O, break, my heart! poor bankrupt,
  break at once!
To prison, eyes, ne'er look on liberty!
Vile earth, to earth resign; end motion here;
And thou and Romeo press one heavy bier! 60
 Nurse. O Tybalt, Tybalt, the best friend I
  had!
O courteous Tybalt! honest gentleman!
That ever I should live to see thee dead!
 Jul. What storm is this that blows so con-
  trary?
Is Romeo slaughter'd, and is Tybalt dead?
My dear-loved cousin, and my dearer lord?
Then, dreadful trumpet, sound the general doom!
For who is living, if those two are gone?
 Nurse. Tybalt is gone, and Romeo banished;
Romeo that kill'd him, he is banished. 70
 Jul. O God! did Romeo's hand shed Tybalt's
  blood?
 Nurse. It did, it did; alas the day, it did!
 Jul. O serpent heart, hid with a flowering
  face!
Did ever dragon keep so fair a cave?
Beautiful tyrant! fiend angelical!
Dove-feather'd raven! wolvish-ravening lamb!
Despised substance of divinest show!
Just opposite to what thou justly seem'st,
A damned saint, an honourable villain!
O nature, what hadst thou to do in hell, 80
● When thou didst bower the spirit of a fiend
In mortal paradise of such sweet flesh?
Was ever book containing such vile matter
So fairly bound? O, that deceit should dwell
In such a gorgeous palace!
 Nurse.   There's no trust,
No faith, no honesty in men; all perjured,
All forsworn, all naught, all dissemblers.
● Ah, where's my man? give me some aqua vitæ:
These griefs, these woes, these sorrows make me
  old.
Shame come to Romeo!
 Jul.   Blister'd be thy tongue 90
For such a wish! he was not born to shame:
Upon his brow shame is ashamed to sit;
For 'tis a throne where honour may be crown'd
Sole monarch of the universal earth.
O, what a beast was I to chide at him!

47 *cockatrice.* The basilisk, the legendary serpent which could kill with a glance.

Nurse: 'I saw the wound, I saw it with mine eyes'. Painting of Juliet with the Nurse by Robert Smirke (1752–1845)

54 *corse.* Corpse.

56 *swounded.* Fainted.

81 *bower.* Enclose.

88 *aqua vitæ.* Strong spirit.

98 *smooth*. Flatter.

120 *modern*. Conventional.

Set design for the Friar's cell by Gordon Craig, 1891

Nurse. Will you speak well of him that kill'd your cousin?

Jul. Shall I speak ill of him that is my husband?

● Ah, poor my lord, what tongue shall smooth thy name,
When I, thy three-hours wife, have mangled it?
But, wherefore, villain, didst thou kill my cousin?   100
That villain cousin would have kill'd my husband:
Back, foolish tears, back to your native spring;
Your tributary drops belong to woe,
Which you, mistaking, offer up to joy.
My husband lives, that Tybalt would have slain;
And Tybalt's dead, that would have slain my husband:
All this is comfort; wherefore weep I then?
Some word there was, worser than Tybalt's death,
That murder'd me: I would forget it fain;
But, O, it presses to my memory,   110
Like damned guilty deeds to sinners' minds:
'Tybalt is dead, and Romeo—banished;'
That 'banished,' that one word 'banished,'
Hath slain ten thousand Tybalts. Tybalt's death
Was woe enough, if it had ended there:
Or, if sour woe delights in fellowship
And needly will be rank'd with other griefs,
Why follow'd not, when she said 'Tybalt's dead,'
Thy father, or thy mother, nay, or both,   119
● Which modern lamentation might have moved?
But with a rearward following Tybalt's death,
'Romeo is banished,' to speak that word,
Is father, mother, Tybalt, Romeo, Juliet,
All slain, all dead. 'Romeo is banished!'
There is no end, no limit, measure, bound,
In that word's death; no words can that woe sound.
Where is my father, and my mother, nurse?

Nurse. Weeping and wailing over Tybalt's corse:
Will you go to them? I will bring you thither.

Jul. Wash they his wounds with tears: mine shall be spent,   130
When theirs are dry, for Romeo's banishment.
Take up those cords: poor ropes, you are beguiled,
Both you and I; for Romeo is exiled:
He made you for a highway to my bed;
But I, a maid, die maiden-widowed.
Come, cords, come, nurse; I'll to my wedding-bed;
And death, not Romeo, take my maidenhead!

Nurse. Hie to your chamber: I'll find Romeo
To comfort you: I wot well where he is.
Hark ye, your Romeo will be here at night: 140
I'll to him; he is hid at Laurence' cell.

Jul. O, find him! give this ring to my true knight,
And bid him come to take his last farewell.

[*Exeunt.*

SCENE III. *Friar Laurence's cell.*

Enter FRIAR LAURENCE

Fri. L. Romeo, come forth; come forth, thou fearful man:
Affliction is enamour'd of thy parts,
And thou art wedded to calamity.

Enter ROMEO.

Rom. Father, what news? what is the prince's
doom?
What sorrow craves acquaintance at my hand,
That I yet know not?
Fri. L.   Too familiar
Is my dear son with such sour company:
I bring thee tidings of the prince's doom.
Rom. What less than dooms-day is the prince's
doom?
Fri. L. A gentler judgement vanish'd from
his lips,   10
Not body's death, but body's banishment.
Rom. Ha, banishment! be merciful, say
'death;'
For exile hath more terror in his look,
Much more than death: do not say 'banishment.'
Fri. L. Hence from Verona art thou banished:
Be patient, for the world is broad and wide.
Rom. There is no world without Verona walls,
But purgatory, torture, hell itself.
Hence-banished is banish'd from the world,
And world's exile is death: then banished,   20
Is death mis-term'd: calling death banishment,
Thou cutt'st my head off with a golden axe,
And smilest upon the stroke that murders me.
Fri. L. O deadly sin! O rude unthankful-
ness!
Thy fault our law calls death; but the kind prince,
Taking thy part, hath rush'd aside the law,
And turn'd that black word death to banishment:
This is dear mercy, and thou seest it not.
Rom. 'Tis torture, and not mercy: heaven is
here,
Where Juliet lives; and every cat and dog   30
And little mouse, every unworthy thing,
Live here in heaven and may look on her;
• But Romeo may not: more validity,
• More honourable state, more courtship lives
In carrion-flies than Romeo: they may seize
On the white wonder of dear Juliet's hand
And steal immortal blessing from her lips,
Who, even in pure and vestal modesty,
Still blush, as thinking their own kisses sin;
But Romeo may not; he is banished: 40
Flies may do this, but I from this must fly:
They are free men, but I am banished.
And say'st thou yet that exile is not death?
Hadst thou no poison mix'd, no sharp-ground
knife,
No sudden mean of death, though ne'er so mean,
But 'banished' to kill me?—'banished'?
O friar, the damned use that word in hell;
Howlings attend it: how hast thou the heart,
Being a divine, a ghostly confessor,
A sin-absolver, and my friend profess'd,   50
To mangle me with that word 'banished'?
Fri. L. Thou fond mad man, hear me but
speak a word.
Rom. O, thou wilt speak again of banishment.
Fri. L. I'll give thee armour to keep off that
word;
Adversity's sweet milk, philosophy,
To comfort thee, though thou art banished.
Rom. Yet 'banished'? Hang up philosophy!
Unless philosophy can make a Juliet,
Displant a town, reverse a prince's doom,
It helps not, it prevails not: talk no more.   60

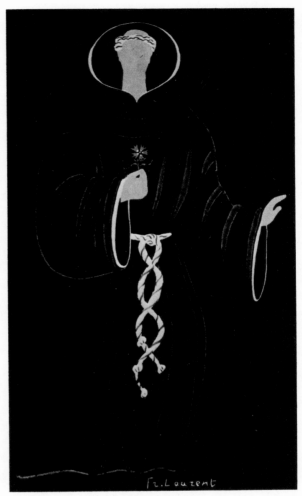

Costume design for Friar Laurence by Jean Hugo for
Jean Cocteau's production, Paris, 1924

33 *validity.* Value.

34 *courtship.* i.e. courtly behaviour.

63 *dispute.* Discuss. *estate.* Position.

Romeo: 'Thou canst not speak of that thou dost not feel'. Romeo (Ian Holm) and Friar Laurence (Sebastian Shaw), Royal Shakespeare Co, 1967

90 *an O.* Groan.

Fri. L. O, then I see that madmen have no ears.
Rom.   How should they, when that wise men have no eyes?
● *Fri. L.* Let me dispute with thee of thy estate.
Rom.   Thou canst not speak of that thou dost not feel:
Wert thou as young as I, Juliet thy love,
An hour but married, Tybalt murdered,
Doting like me and like me banished,
Then mightst thou speak, then mightst thou tear thy hair,
And fall upon the ground, as I do now,
Taking the measure of an unmade grave.   70
                    [*Knocking within.*
Fri. L. Arise; one knocks; good Romeo, hide thyself.
Rom.   Not I; unless the breath of heart-sick groans,
Mist-like, infold me from the search of eyes.
                    [*Knocking.*
Fri. L. Hark, how they knock! Who's there? Romeo, arise;
Thou wilt be taken. Stay awhile! Stand up;
                    [*Knocking.*
Run to my study. By and by! God's will,
What simpleness is this! I come, I come!
                    [*Knocking.*
Who knocks so hard? whence come you? what's your will?
Nurse. [*Within*] Let me come in, and you shall know my errand;
I come from Lady Juliet.
Fri. L.   Welcome, then.   80

Enter Nurse.

Nurse. O holy friar, O, tell me, holy friar,
Where is my lady's lord, where's Romeo?
Fri. L. There on the ground, with his own tears made drunk.
Nurse. O, he is even in my mistress' case,
Just in her case! O woful sympathy!
Piteous predicament! Even so lies she,
Blubbering and weeping, weeping and blubbering.
Stand up, stand up; stand, an you be a man:
For Juliet's sake, for her sake, rise and stand;
● Why should you fall into so deep an O?   90
Rom.   Nurse!
Nurse. Ah sir! ah sir! Well, death's the end of all.
Rom.   Spakest thou of Juliet? how is it with her?
Doth she not think me an old murderer,
Now I have stain'd the childhood of our joy
With blood removed but little from her own?
Where is she? and how doth she? and what says
My conceal'd lady to our cancell'd love?
Nurse. O, she says nothing, sir, but weeps and weeps;
And now falls on her bed; and then starts up,   100
And Tybalt calls; and then on Romeo cries,
And then down falls again.
Rom.   As if that name,
Shot from the deadly level of a gun,
Did murder her; as that name's cursed hand
Murder'd her kinsman. O, tell me, friar, tell me,
In what vile part of this anatomy
Doth my name lodge? tell me, that I may sack
The hateful mansion.   [*Drawing his sword.*
Fri. L.   Hold thy desperate hand:

Art thou a man? thy form cries out thou art:
Thy tears are womanish; thy wild acts denote
The unreasonable fury of a beast: 111
Unseemly woman in a seeming man!
Or ill-beseeming beast in seeming both!
Thou hast amazed me: by my holy order,
I thought thy disposition better temper'd.
Hast thou slain Tybalt? wilt thou slay thyself?
And slay thy lady too that lives in thee,
By doing damned hate upon thyself?
Why rail'st thou on thy birth, the heaven, and
    earth?
Since birth, and heaven, and earth, all three do
    meet   120
In thee at once; which thou at once wouldst lose.
Fie, fie, thou shamest thy shape, thy love, thy
    wit;
Which, like a usurer, abound'st in all,
And usest none in that true use indeed
• Which should bedeck thy shape, thy love, thy wit:
Thy noble shape is but a form of wax,
Digressing from the valour of a man;
Thy dear love sworn but hollow perjury,
Killing that love which thou hast vow'd to cherish;
Thy wit, that ornament to shape and love,   130
Mis-shapen in the conduct of them both,
Like powder in a skilless soldier's flask,
Is set a-fire by thine own ignorance,
• And thou dismember'd with thine own defence.
What, rouse thee, man! thy Juliet is alive,
For whose dear sake thou wast but lately dead;
There art thou happy: Tybalt would kill thee,
But thou slew'st Tybalt; there art thou happy too:
The law that threaten'd death becomes thy friend
And turns it to exile; there art thou happy: 140
A pack of blessings lights upon thy back;
Happiness courts thee in her best array;
But, like a misbehaved and sullen wench,
Thou pout'st upon thy fortune and thy love:
Take heed, take heed, for such die miserable.
Go, get thee to thy love, as was decreed,
Ascend her chamber, hence and comfort her:
But look thou stay not till the watch be set,
For then thou canst not pass to Mantua;
Where thou shalt live, till we can find a time 150
To blaze your marriage, reconcile your friends,
Beg pardon of the prince, and call thee back
With twenty hundred thousand times more joy
Than thou went'st forth in lamentation.
Go before, nurse: commend me to thy lady;
And bid her hasten all the house to bed,
Which heavy sorrow makes them apt unto:
Romeo is coming.
    Nurse. O Lord, I could have stay'd here all
        the night
To hear good counsel: O, what learning is! 160
My lord, I'll tell my lady you will come.
    Rom. Do so, and bid my sweet prepare to
        chide.
    Nurse. Here, sir, a ring she bid me give you,
        sir:
Hie you, make haste, for it grows very late.
                                        [*Exit.*
    Rom. How well my comfort is revived by this!
• *Fri. L.* Go hence; good night; and here
        stands all your state:
Either be gone before the watch be set,
Or by the break of day disguised from hence:
Sojourn in Mantua; I'll find out your man,

Max Adrian as the Friar, Stratford-upon-Avon, 1961

---

125 *wit.* Intelligence.

134 *defence.* i.e. means of defence, fencing.

166 *stands.* Depends. *state.* Fortune.

2 *move.* Speak to.

11 *mew'd up.* Enclosed. *heaviness.* Grief.

12 *desperate.* Bold. *tender.* Approach.

Juliet: 'Wilt thou be gone? it is not yet near day'. John Gielgud as Romeo and Gwen Ffrangcon Davies as Juliet, Regent's Theatre, London, 1924

And he shall signify from time to time   170
Every good hap to you that chances here:
Give me thy hand; 'tis late: farewell; good night.
 Rom.   But that a joy past joy calls out on me,
It were a grief, so brief to part with thee:
Farewell.   [*Exeunt.*

SCENE IV.   *A room in Capulet's house.*

Enter CAPULET, LADY CAPULET, *and* PARIS.

 Cap.   Things have fall'n out, sir, so unluckily,
• That we have had no time to move our daughter:
Look you, she loved her kinsman Tybalt dearly,
And so did I:—Well, we were born to die.
'Tis very late, she'll not come down to-night:
I promise you, but for your company,
I would have been a-bed an hour ago.
 Par.   These times of woe afford no time to
    woo.
Madam, good night: commend me to your
    daughter.
 La. Cap.   I will, and know her mind early to-
    morrow;   10
• To-night she is mew'd up to her heaviness.
• *Cap.*   Sir Paris, I will make a desperate tender
Of my child's love: I think she will be ruled
In all respects by me; nay, more, I doubt it not.
Wife, go you to her ere you go to bed;
Acquaint her here of my son Paris' love;
And bid her, mark you me, on Wednesday next—
But, soft! what day is this?
 Par.   Monday, my lord.
 Cap.   Monday! ha, ha!   Well, Wednesday is
    too soon,
O' Thursday let it be: o' Thursday, tell her,   20
She shall be married to this noble earl.
Will you be ready? do you like this haste?
We'll keep no great ado,—a friend or two;
For, hark you, Tybalt being slain so late,
It may be thought we held him carelessly,
Being our kinsman, if we revel much:
Therefore we'll have some half a dozen friends,
And there an end.   But what say you to Thurs-
    day?
 Par.   My lord, I would that Thursday were
    to-morrow.
 Cap.   Well, get you gone: o' Thursday be it,
    then.   30
Go you to Juliet ere you go to bed,
Prepare her, wife, against this wedding-day.
Farewell, my lord.   Light to my chamber, ho!
Afore me! it is so very very late,
That we may call it early by and by.
Good night.   [*Exeunt.*

SCENE V.   *Capulet's orchard.*

Enter ROMEO *and* JULIET *above, at the
    window.*

 Jul.   Wilt thou be gone? it is not yet near day:
It was the nightingale, and not the lark,
That pierced the fearful hollow of thine ear;
Nightly she sings on yon pomegranate-tree:
Believe me, love, it was the nightingale.
 Rom.   It was the lark, the herald of the morn,
No nightingale: look, love, what envious streaks
Do lace the severing clouds in yonder east:
Night's candles are burnt out, and jocund day
Stands tiptoe on the misty mountain tops.   10

I must be gone and live, or stay and die.
    Jul.   Yon light is not day-light, I know it, I:
It is some meteor that the sun exhales,
To be to thee this night a torch-bearer,
And light thee on thy way to Mantua:
Therefore stay yet; thou need'st not to be gone.
    Rom.   Let me be ta'en, let me be put to death;
I am content, so thou wilt have it so.
I'll say yon grey is not the morning's eye,
●'Tis but the pale reflex of Cynthia's brow;   20
Nor that is not the lark, whose notes do beat
The vaulty heaven so high above our heads:
I have more care to stay than will to go:
Come, death, and welcome! Juliet wills it so.
How is't, my soul? let's talk; it is not day.
    Jul.   It is, it is: hie hence, be gone, away!
It is the lark that sings so out of tune,
Straining harsh discords and unpleasing sharps.
●Some say the lark makes sweet division;
This doth not so, for she divideth us: 30
Some say the lark and loathed toad change eyes;
O, now I would they had changed voices too!
●Since arm from arm that voice doth us affray,
Hunting thee hence with hunt's-up to the day.
O, now be gone; more light and light it grows.
    Rom.   More light and light; more dark and
    dark our woes!

       Enter Nurse, *to the chamber.*

Nurse.   Madam!
Jul.   Nurse?
Nurse.   Your lady mother is coming to your
    chamber:
The day is broke; be wary, look about. [*Exit.* 40
    Jul.   Then, window, let day in, and let life
    out.
    Rom.   Farewell, farewell! one kiss, and I'll
    descend.   [*He goeth down.*
    Jul.   Art thou gone so? love, lord, ay, hus-
    band, friend!
I must hear from thee every day in the hour,
For in a minute there are many days:
O, by this count I shall be much in years
Ere I again behold my Romeo!
    Rom.   Farewell!
I will omit no opportunity
That may convey my greetings, love, to thee. 50
    Jul.   O, think'st thou we shall ever meet
    again?
    Rom.   I doubt it not; and all these woes shall
    serve
For sweet discourses in our time to come.
●   *Jul.*   O God, I have an ill-divining soul!
Methinks I see thee, now thou art below,
As one dead in the bottom of a tomb:
Either my eyesight fails, or thou look'st pale.
    Rom.   And trust me, love, in my eye so do you:
Dry sorrow drinks our blood.   Adieu, adieu!
              [*Exit.*
    Jul.   O fortune, fortune! all men call thee
    fickle: 60
If thou art fickle, what dost thou with him
That is renown'd for faith?   Be fickle, fortune;
For then, I hope, thou wilt not keep him long,
But send him back.
    La. Cap. [*Within*] Ho, daughter! are you up?
    Jul.   Who is't that calls? is it my lady mother?
●Is she not down so late, or up so early?
What unaccustom'd cause procures her hither?

20 *Cynthia.* i.e. the moon.

29 *division.* Run of notes.

33 *affray.* Separate in fear.

Juliet: 'O, think'st thou we shall ever meet again?'
Illustration by Frank Dicksee, 1916

54 *ill-divining.* Prophetic of evil.

67 *down.* In bed.

Mrs Patrick Campbell as Juliet, Lyceum Theatre, London, 1896

---

90 *runagate.* Vagabond.

110 *sorted.* Selected. *sudden.* Immediate.

Enter LADY CAPULET

La. Cap. Why, how now, Juliet!
Jul.   Madam, I am not well.
La. Cap. Evermore weeping for your cousin's
death?   70
What, wilt thou wash him from his grave with
tears?
An if thou couldst, thou couldst not make him
live;
Therefore, have done: some grief shows much of
love;
But much of grief shows still some want of wit.
Jul. Yet let me weep for such a feeling loss.
La. Cap. So shall you feel the loss, but not
the friend
Which you weep for.
Jul.   Feeling so the loss,
I cannot choose but ever weep the friend.
La. Cap. Well, girl, thou weep'st not so much
for his death,
As that the villain lives which slaughter'd him. 80
Jul. What villain, madam?
La. Cap.   That same villain, Romeo.
Jul. [*Aside*] Villain and he be many miles
asunder.—
God pardon him! I do, with all my heart;
And yet no man like he doth grieve my heart.
La. Cap. That is, because the traitor murderer
lives.
Jul. Ay, madam, from the reach of these my
hands:
Would none but I might venge my cousin's death!
La. Cap. We will have vengeance for it, fear
thou not:
Then weep no more. I'll send to one in Man-
tua,
● Where that same banish'd runagate doth live,
Shall give him such an unaccustom'd dram,   91
That he shall soon keep Tybalt company:
And then, I hope, thou wilt be satisfied.
Jul. Indeed, I never shall be satisfied
With Romeo, till I behold him—dead—
Is my poor heart so for a kinsman vex'd:
Madam, if you could find out but a man
To bear a poison, I would temper it;
That Romeo should, upon receipt thereof,
Soon sleep in quiet. O, how my heart abhors 100
To hear him named, and cannot come to him,
To wreak the love I bore my cousin
Upon his body that hath slaughter'd him!
La. Cap. Find thou the means, and I'll find
such a man.
But now I'll tell thee joyful tidings, girl.
Jul. And joy comes well in such a needy time:
What are they, I beseech your ladyship?
La. Cap. Well, well, thou hast a careful
father, child;
One who, to put thee from thy heaviness,
● Hath sorted out a sudden day of joy,   110
That thou expect'st not nor I look'd not for.
Jul. Madam, in happy time, what day is that?
La. Cap. Marry, my child, early next Thurs-
day morn,
The gallant, young and noble gentleman,
The County Paris, at Saint Peter's Church,
Shall happily make thee there a joyful bride.
Jul. Now, by Saint Peter's Church and Peter
too,

He shall not make me there a joyful bride.
I wonder at this haste; that I must wed
Ere he, that should be husband, comes to woo.
I pray you, tell my lord and father, madam,   121
I will not marry yet; and, when I do, I swear,
It shall be Romeo, whom you know I hate,
Rather than Paris.   These are news indeed!
   La. Cap.   Here comes your father; tell him
    so yourself,
And see how he will take it at your hands.

     Enter CAPULET *and* Nurse.

   Cap.   When the sun sets, the air doth drizzle
    dew;
But for the sunset of my brother's son
It rains downright.
• How now! a conduit, girl? what, still in tears?
Evermore showering?   In one little body   131
Thou counterfeit'st a bark, a sea, a wind;
For still thy eyes, which I may call the sea,
Do ebb and flow with tears; the bark thy body is,
Sailing in this salt flood; the winds, thy sighs;
Who, raging with thy tears, and they with them,
Without a sudden calm, will overset
Thy tempest-tossed body.   How now, wife!
Have you deliver'd to her our decree?
   La. Cap.   Ay, sir; but she will none, she gives
    you thanks.   140
I would the fool were married to her grave!
   Cap.   Soft! take me with you, take me with
    you, wife.
How! will she none? doth she not give us thanks?
Is she not proud? doth she not count her blest,
Unworthy as she is, that we have wrought
So worthy a gentleman to be her bridegroom?
   Jul.   Not proud, you have; but thankful, that
    you have:
Proud can I never be of what I hate;
But thankful even for hate, that is meant love.
   Cap.   How now, how now, chop-logic!   What
    is this?   150
'Proud,' and 'I thank you,' and 'I thank you
    not;'
And yet 'not proud:' mistress minion, you,
Thank me no thankings, nor proud me no prouds,
• But fettle your fine joints 'gainst Thursday next,
To go with Paris to Saint Peter's Church,
Or I will drag thee on a hurdle thither.
Out, you green-sickness carrion! out, you bag-
    gage!
You tallow-face!
   La. Cap.   Fie, fie! what, are you mad?
   Jul.   Good father, I beseech you on my knees,
Hear me with patience but to speak a word.   160
   Cap.   Hang thee, young baggage! disobedient
    wretch!
I tell thee what: get thee to church o' Thursday,
Or never after look me in the face:
Speak not, reply not, do not answer me;
My fingers itch.   Wife, we scarce thought us
    blest
That God had lent us but this only child;
But now I see this one is one too much,
And that we have a curse in having her:
Out on her, hilding!
   Nurse.   God in heaven bless her!
• You are to blame, my lord, to rate her so.   170
   Cap.   And why, my lady wisdom? hold your
    tongue,

130 *conduit.* Fountain.

154 *fettle.* Prepare.

Mrs H. Marston as the Nurse, Haymarket Theatre, London, 1846

170 *rate.* Berate.

172 *smatter*. Chatter.

185 *puling*. Whimpering.

186 *mammet*. Doll. *fortune's tender*. Fortunate offer.

192 *advise*. Take note.

197 *forsworn*. Let down, i.e. break my word.

211 *practise stratagems*. Contrive deception.

Juliet: 'Speakest thou from thy heart?' Ellen Terry as Juliet and Mrs Stirling as the Nurse, Lyceum Theatre, London, 1882

● Good prudence; smatter with your gossips, go.
  Nurse.   I speak no treason.
  Cap.   O, God ye god-den.
  Nurse.   May not one speak?
  Cap.   Peace, you mumbling fool!
Utter your gravity o'er a gossip's bowl;
For here we need it not.
  La. Cap.   You are too hot.
  Cap.   †God's bread! it makes me mad:
†Day, night, hour, tide, time, work, play,
Alone, in company, still my care hath been   179
To have her match'd: and having now provided
A gentleman of noble parentage,
Of fair demesnes, youthful, and nobly train'd,
Stuff'd, as they say, with honourable parts,
Proportion'd as one's thought would wish a man;
● And then to have a wretched puling fool,
● A whining mammet, in her fortune's tender,
To answer 'I'll not wed; I cannot love,
I am too young; I pray you, pardon me.'
But, an you will not wed, I'll pardon you:
Graze where you will, you shall not house with
    me: 190
Look to't, think on't, I do not use to jest.
● Thursday is near; lay hand on heart, advise:
An you be mine, I'll give you to my friend;
An you be not, hang, beg, starve, die in the
    streets,
For, by my soul, I'll ne'er acknowledge thee,
Nor what is mine shall never do thee good:
● Trust to't, bethink you; I'll not be forsworn.
                         [*Exit.*
  Jul.   Is there no pity sitting in the clouds,
That sees into the bottom of my grief?
O, sweet my mother, cast me not away!   200
Delay this marriage for a month, a week;
Or, if you do not, make the bridal bed
In that dim monument where Tybalt lies.
  La. Cap.   Talk not to me, for I'll not speak a
    word:
Do as thou wilt, for I have done with thee. [*Exit.*
  Jul.   O God!—O nurse, how shall this be pre-
    vented?
My husband is on earth, my faith in heaven;
How shall that faith return again to earth,
Unless that husband send it me from heaven
By leaving earth? comfort me, counsel me.   210
● Alack, alack, that heaven should practise strata-
    gems
Upon so soft a subject as myself!
What say'st thou? hast thou not a word of joy?
Some comfort, nurse.
  Nurse.   Faith, here it is.
Romeo is banish'd; and all the world to nothing,
That he dares ne'er come back to challenge you;
Or, if he do, it needs must be by stealth.
Then, since the case so stands as now it doth,
I think it best you married with the county.
O, he's a lovely gentleman!   220
Romeo's a dishclout to him: an eagle, madam,
Hath not so green, so quick, so fair an eye
As Paris hath. Beshrew my very heart,
I think you are happy in this second match,
For it excels your first: or if it did not,
Your first is dead; or 'twere as good he were,
As living here and you no use of him.
  Jul.   Speakest thou from thy heart?
  Nurse.   And from my soul too;
Or else beshrew them both.

Jul.   Amen !
Nurse.   What ?
Jul.   Well, thou hast comforted me marvel-
lous much.   230
Go in ; and tell my lady I am gone,
Having displeased my father, to Laurence' cell,
To make confession and to be absolved.
Nurse.   Marry, I will ; and this is wisely done.
[*Exit.*

Jul.   Ancient damnation ! O most wicked fiend !
Is it more sin to wish me thus forsworn,
Or to dispraise my lord with that same tongue
Which she hath praised him with above compare
So many thousand times ?   Go, counsellor ;   239
Thou and my bosom henceforth shall be twain.
I 'll to the friar, to know his remedy :
If all else fail, myself have power to die.   [*Exit.*

ACT IV.

SCENE I.   *Friar Laurence's cell.*

Enter FRIAR LAURENCE *and* PARIS.

Fri. L.   On Thursday, sir ? the time is very
short.
Par.   My father Capulet will have it so ;
And I am nothing slow to slack his haste.
Fri. L.   You say you do not know the lady's
mind :
Uneven is the course, I like it not.
Par.   Immoderately she weeps for Tybalt's
death,
And therefore have I little talk'd of love ;
For Venus smiles not in a house of tears.
Now, sir, her father counts it dangerous
That she doth give her sorrow so much sway,   10
And in his wisdom hastes our marriage,
To stop the inundation of her tears ;
Which, too much minded by herself alone,
• May be put from her by society :
Now do you know the reason of this haste.
Fri. L.   [*Aside*]   I would I knew not why it
should be slow'd.
Look, sir, here comes the lady towards my cell.

Enter JULIET.

Par.   Happily met, my lady and my wife !
Jul.   That may be, sir, when I may be a wife.
Par.   That may be must be, love, on Thursday
next.   20
Jul.   What must be shall be.
Fri. L.   That's a certain text.
Par.   Come you to make confession to this father ?
Jul.   To answer that, I should confess to you.
Par.   Do not deny to him that you love me.
Jul.   I will confess to you that I love him.
Par.   So will ye, I am sure, that you love me.
• *Jul.*   If I do so, it will be of more price,
Being spoke behind your back, than to your face.
Par.   Poor soul, thy face is much abused with
tears.
Jul.   The tears have got small victory by that ;
For it was bad enough before their spite.   31
Par.   Thou wrong'st it, more than tears, with
that report.
Jul.   That is no slander, sir, which is a truth ;
And what I spake, I spake it to my face.
Par.   Thy face is mine, and thou hast slan-
der'd it.

Costume design for Paris by Jean Hugo for Jean
Cocteau's production, Paris, 1924

---

14 *society.* Others.

27 *price.* Value.

41 *shield.* Prevent.

Juliet in Friar Laurence's cell. Engraving from a painting by E. M. Ward (1816–1879)

61 *present.* Immediate.

64 *commission.* Authority.

81 *charnel-house.* Small building where bones of the dead were placed.

83 *chapless.* Jawless.

96 *humour.* Moisture.

97 *native.* Natural. *surcease.* Cease.

Jul. It may be so, for it is not mine own.
Are you at leisure, holy father, now;
Or shall I come to you at evening mass?
   Fri. L. My leisure serves me, pensive daughter, now.
My lord, we must entreat the time alone.   40
   Par. God shield I should disturb devotion!
Juliet, on Thursday early will I rouse ye:
Till then, adieu; and keep this holy kiss. [*Exit.*
   Jul. O, shut the door! and when thou hast done so,
Come weep with me; past hope, past cure, past help!
   Fri. L. Ah, Juliet, I already know thy grief;
It strains me past the compass of my wits:
I hear thou must, and nothing may prorogue it,
On Thursday next be married to this county.
   Jul. Tell me not, friar, that thou hear'st of this,
Unless thou tell me how I may prevent it: 51
If, in thy wisdom, thou canst give no help,
Do thou but call my resolution wise,
And with this knife I'll help it presently.
God join'd my heart and Romeo's, thou our hands;
And ere this hand, by thee to Romeo seal'd,
Shall be the label to another deed,
Or my true heart with treacherous revolt
Turn to another, this shall slay them both:
Therefore, out of thy long-experienced time,   60
Give me some present counsel, or, behold,
'Twixt my extremes and me this bloody knife
Shall play the umpire, arbitrating that
Which the commission of thy years and art
Could to no issue of true honour bring.
Be not so long to speak; I long to die,
If what thou speak'st speak not of remedy.
   Fri. L. Hold, daughter: I do spy a kind of hope,
Which craves as desperate an execution
As that is desperate which we would prevent. 70
If, rather than to marry County Paris,
Thou hast the strength of will to slay thyself,
Then is it likely thou wilt undertake
A thing like death to chide away this shame,
That copest with death himself to scape from it;
And, if thou darest, I'll give thee remedy.
   Jul. O, bid me leap, rather than marry Paris,
From off the battlements of yonder tower;
Or walk in thievish ways; or bid me lurk
Where serpents are; chain me with roaring bears;
Or shut me nightly in a charnel-house,   81
O'er-cover'd quite with dead men's rattling bones,
With reeky shanks and yellow chapless skulls;
Or bid me go into a new-made grave
And hide me with a dead man in his shroud;
Things that, to hear them told, have made me tremble;
And I will do it without fear or doubt,
To live an unstain'd wife to my sweet love.
   Fri. L. Hold, then; go home, be merry, give consent
To marry Paris: Wednesday is to-morrow: 90
To-morrow night look that thou lie alone;
Let not thy nurse lie with thee in thy chamber:
Take thou this vial, being then in bed,
And this distilled liquor drink thou off;
When presently through all thy veins shall run
A cold and drowsy humour, for no pulse
Shall keep his native progress, but surcease:

No warmth, no breath, shall testify thou livest;
The roses in thy lips and cheeks shall fade
To paly ashes, thy eyes' windows fall,   100
Like death, when he shuts up the day of life;
● Each part, deprived of supple government,
Shall, stiff and stark and cold, appear like death:
And in this borrow'd likeness of shrunk death
Thou shalt continue two and forty hours,
And then awake as from a pleasant sleep.
Now, when the bridegroom in the morning comes
To rouse thee from thy bed, there art thou dead:
Then, as the manner of our country is,
In thy best robes uncover'd on the bier   110
Thou shalt be borne to that same ancient vault
Where all the kindred of the Capulets lie.
In the mean time, against thou shalt awake,
Shall Romeo by my letters know our drift,
And hither shall he come: and he and I
Will watch thy waking, and that very night
Shall Romeo bear thee hence to Mantua.
And this shall free thee from this present shame;
● If no inconstant toy, nor womanish fear,
Abate thy valour in the acting it.   120
   Jul. Give me, give me! O, tell not me of fear!
   Fri. L. Hold; get you gone, be strong and
     prosperous
In this resolve: I'll send a friar with speed
To Mantua, with my letters to thy lord.
   Jul. Love give me strength! and strength shall
     help afford.
Farewell, dear father!   [*Exeunt.*

   SCENE II.   *Hall in Capulet's house.*

Enter CAPULET, LADY CAPULET, Nurse, *and*
     two Servingmen.

   Cap. So many guests invite as here are writ.
          [*Exit First Servant.*
Sirrah, go hire me twenty cunning cooks.
   Sec. Serv. You shall have none ill, sir; for I'll
try if they can lick their fingers.
   Cap. How canst thou try them so?
   Sec. Serv. Marry, sir, 'tis an ill cook that
cannot lick his own fingers: therefore he that
cannot lick his fingers goes not with me.
   Cap. Go, be gone.   [*Exit Sec. Servant.*
● We shall be much unfurnish'd for this time.   10
What, is my daughter gone to Friar Laurence?
   Nurse. Ay, forsooth.
   Cap. Well, he may chance to do some good on
     her:
● A peevish self-will'd harlotry it is.
   Nurse. See where she comes from shrift with
     merry look.

     Enter JULIET.

   Cap. How now, my headstrong! where have
     you been gadding?
   Jul. Where I have learn'd me to repent the sin
Of disobedient opposition
To you and your behests, and am enjoin'd
By holy Laurence to fall prostrate here,   20
And beg your pardon: pardon, I beseech you!
Henceforward I am ever ruled by you.
   Cap. Send for the county; go tell him of this:
I'll have this knot knit up to-morrow morning.
   Jul. I met the youthful lord at Laurence' cell;
● And gave him what becomed love I might,
Not stepping o'er the bounds of modesty.

102 *supple government.* Muscular control.

Peggy Ashcroft as Juliet and Morland Graham as Friar
Laurence, Old Vic Theatre, London, 1933

119 *toy.* Caprice.

10 *unfurnish'd.* Inadequately prepared.

14 *harlotry.* Wench.

26 *becomed.* Suitable.

The Nurse. Engraving from a painting by H. Briggs (1791?–1846)

---

3 *orisons*. Prayers.

8 *state*. i.e. wedding.

Cap. Why, I am glad on't; this is well: stand up:
This is as 't should be. Let me see the county;
Ay, marry, go, I say, and fetch him hither.   30
Now, afore God! this reverend holy friar,
All our whole city is much bound to him.
   Jul. Nurse, will you go with me into my closet,
To help me sort such needful ornaments
As you think fit to furnish me to-morrow?
   La. Cap. No, not till Thursday; there is time
      enough.
   Cap. Go, nurse, go with her: we'll to church
      to-morrow.   [*Exeunt Juliet and Nurse.*
   La. Cap. We shall be short in our provision:
'Tis now near night.
   Cap.   Tush, I will stir about,
And all things shall be well, I warrant thee, wife:
Go thou to Juliet, help to deck up her;   41
I'll not to bed to-night; let me alone;
I'll play the housewife for this once.   What, ho!
They are all forth.   Well, I will walk myself
To County Paris, to prepare him up
Against to-morrow: my heart is wondrous light,
Since this same wayward girl is so reclaim'd.
                                    [*Exeunt.*

SCENE III.   *Juliet's chamber.*

Enter JULIET *and* Nurse.

   Jul. Ay, those attires are best: but, gentle
      nurse,
I pray thee, leave me to myself to-night;
For I have need of many orisons
To move the heavens to smile upon my state,
Which, well thou know'st, is cross and full of sin.

Enter LADY CAPULET.

   La. Cap. What, are you busy, ho? need you
      my help?
   Jul. No, madam; we have cull'd such neces-
      saries
As are behoveful for our state to-morrow:
So please you, let me now be left alone,
And let the nurse this night sit up with you;   10
For, I am sure, you have your hands full all,
In this so sudden business.
   La. Cap.   Good night:
Get thee to bed, and rest; for thou hast need.
               [*Exeunt Lady Capulet and Nurse.*
   Jul. Farewell! God knows when we shall
      meet again.
I have a faint cold fear thrills through my veins,
That almost freezes up the heat of life:
I'll call them back again to comfort me:
Nurse!   What should she do here?
My dismal scene I needs must act alone.
Come, vial.   20
What if this mixture do not work at all?
Shall I be married then to-morrow morning?
No, no: this shall forbid it: lie thou there.
               [*Laying down her dagger.*
What if it be a poison, which the friar
Subtly hath minister'd to have me dead,
Lest in this marriage he should be dishonour'd,
Because he married me before to Romeo?
I fear it is: and yet, methinks, it should not,
For he hath still been tried a holy man.
How if, when I am laid into the tomb,   30
I wake before the time that Romeo
Come to redeem me? there's a fearful point!

Opposite: Juliet: 'How if, when I am laid into the tomb, I wake before the time . . .' Estelle Kohler as Juliet, Royal Shakespeare Co, 1973

47 *mandrakes*. Forked roots like human limbs.

Margaret Halston, the English Edwardian actress as Juliet

---

6 *cot-quean*. Man playing housewife.

11 *mouse-hunt*. A man who seeks women by night.

13 *jealous-hood*. Jealousy.

19 *whoreson*. Rascal, bastard.

Shall I not, then, be stifled in the vault,
To whose foul mouth no healthsome air breathes in,
And there die strangled ere my Romeo comes?
Or, if I live, is it not very like,
The horrible conceit of death and night,
Together with the terror of the place,—
As in a vault, an ancient receptacle,
Where, for these many hundred years, the bones
Of all my buried ancestors are pack'd: 41
Where bloody Tybalt, yet but green in earth,
Lies festering in his shroud; where, as they say,
At some hours in the night spirits resort;—
Alack, alack, is it not like that I,
So early waking, what with loathsome smells,
● And shrieks like mandrakes' torn out of the earth,
That living mortals, hearing them, run mad:—
O, if I wake, shall I not be distraught,
Environed with all these hideous fears?   50
And madly play with my forefathers' joints?
And pluck the mangled Tybalt from his shroud?
And, in this rage, with some great kinsman's bone,
As with a club, dash out my desperate brains?
O, look! methinks I see my cousin's ghost
Seeking out Romeo, that did spit his body
Upon a rapier's point: stay, Tybalt, stay!
Romeo, I come! this do I drink to thee.
　　　[*She falls upon her bed, within the curtains.*

SCENE IV. *Hall in Capulet's house.*

Enter LADY CAPULET *and* Nurse.

La. Cap. Hold, take these keys, and fetch
　　more spices, nurse.
Nurse. They call for dates and quinces in the
　　pastry.
　　　　　Enter CAPULET.
Cap. Come, stir, stir, stir! the second cock hath
　　crow'd,
The curfew-bell hath rung, 'tis three o'clock:
Look to the baked meats, good Angelica:
Spare not for cost.
● *Nurse.*　　　　Go, you cot-quean, go,
Get you to bed; faith, you'll be sick to-morrow
For this night's watching.
　Cap. No, not a whit: what! I have watch'd ere
　　now
All night for lesser cause, and ne'er been sick. 10
● *La. Cap.* Ay, you have been a mouse-hunt in
　　your time;
But I will watch you from such watching now.
　　　　　[*Exeunt Lady Capulet and Nurse.*
● *Cap.* A jealous-hood, a jealous-hood!

Enter three or four Servingmen, *with spits, logs,
　　　　and baskets.*
　　　　　　　　　Now, fellow,
What's there?
　First Serv. Things for the cook, sir; but I
　　know not what.
　Cap. Make haste, make haste. [*Exit First
　　Serv.*] Sirrah, fetch drier logs:
Call Peter, he will show thee where they are.
　Sec. Serv. I have a head, sir, that will find out
　　logs,
And never trouble Peter for the matter. [*Exit.*
● *Cap.* Mass, and well said; a merry whoreson, ha!
Thou shalt be logger-head. Good faith, 'tis day:
The county will be here with music straight, 21

For so he said he would: I hear him near.
[*Music within.*
Nurse! Wife! What, ho! What, nurse, I say!

Re-enter Nurse.

● Go waken Juliet, go and trim her up;
I 'll go and chat with Paris: hie, make haste,
Make haste; the bridegroom he is come already:
Make haste, I say.   [*Exeunt.*

SCENE V.   *Juliet's chamber.*

Enter Nurse.

● *Nurse.* Mistress! what, mistress! Juliet! fast,
I warrant her, she:
● Why, lamb! why, lady! fie, you slug-a-bed!
Why, love, I say! madam! sweet-heart! why,
bride!
● What, not a word? you take your pennyworths
now;
Sleep for a week; for the next night, I warrant,
● The County Paris hath set up his rest,
That you shall rest but little.   God forgive me,
Marry, and amen, how sound is she asleep!
I must needs wake her. Madam, madam, madam!
Ay, let the county take you in your bed;   10
He 'll fright you up, i' faith.   Will it not be?
[*Undraws the curtains.*
What, dress'd! and in your clothes! and down
again!
I must needs wake you: Lady! lady! lady!
Alas, alas! Help, help! my lady's dead!
O, well-a-day, that ever I was born!
Some aqua vitæ, ho! My lord! my lady!

Enter LADY CAPULET.

La. Cap. What noise is here?
Nurse.   O lamentable day!
La. Cap. What is the matter?
Nurse.   Look, look! O heavy day!
La. Cap. O me, O me! My child, my only life,
Revive, look up, or I will die with thee!   20
Help, help! Call help.

Enter CAPULET.

Cap. For shame, bring Juliet forth; her lord
is come.
Nurse. She's dead, deceased, she's dead;
alack the day!
La. Cap. Alack the day, she's dead, she's dead,
she's dead!
Cap. Ha! let me see her: out, alas! she's
cold;
● Her blood is settled, and her joints are stiff;
Life and these lips have long been separated:
Death lies on her like an untimely frost
Upon the sweetest flower of all the field.
Nurse. O lamentable day!
La. Cap.   O woful time!   30
Cap. Death, that hath ta'en her hence to make
me wail,
Ties up my tongue, and will not let me speak.

Enter FRIAR LAURENCE *and* PARIS, *with* Musicians.

Fri. L. Come, is the bride ready to go to church?
Cap. Ready to go, but never to return.
O son! the night before thy wedding-day
Hath Death lain with thy wife. There she lies,

24 *trim her up.* Prepare her.

1 *fast.* Fast asleep.

2 *slug-a-bed.* Lie-a-bed.

4 *pennyworths.* Catnaps.

6 *set up his rest.* i.e. decided.

Lady Capulet: 'O me, O me! My child, my only life . . .'
Brenda Bruce as Lady Capulet and Estelle Kohler as
Juliet, Royal Shakespeare Co, 1973

26 *settled.* Congealed.

41 *thought long.* Longed for.

69 *Your part.* i.e. her life.

Flower as she was, deflowered by him.
Death is my son-in-law, Death is my heir ;
My daughter he hath wedded: I will die,
And leave him all; life, living, all is Death's. 40
   ● *Par.* Have I thought long to see this morning's face,
And doth it give me such a sight as this?
   La. Cap. Accursed, unhappy, wretched, hateful day !
Most miserable hour that e'er time saw
In lasting labour of his pilgrimage !
But one, poor one, one poor and loving child,
But one thing to rejoice and solace in,
And cruel death hath catch'd it from my sight !
   Nurse. O woe ! O woful, woful, woful day !
Most lamentable day, most woful day,   50
That ever, ever, I did yet behold !
O day ! O day ! O day ! O hateful day !
Never was seen so black a day as this :
O woful day, O woful day !
   Par. Beguiled, divorced, wronged, spited, slain !
Most detestable death, by thee beguiled,
By cruel cruel thee quite overthrown !
O love ! O life ! not life, but love in death !
   Cap. Despised, distressed, hated, martyr'd, kill'd !
Uncomfortable time, why camest thou now   60
To murder, murder our solemnity?
O child ! O child ! my soul, and not my child !
Dead art thou ! Alack ! my child is dead ;
And with my child my joys are buried.
   Fri. L. Peace, ho, for shame ! confusion's cure lives not
In these confusions.   Heaven and yourself
Had part in this fair maid ; now heaven hath all,
And all the better is it for the maid :
  ●Your part in her you could not keep from death,
But heaven keeps his part in eternal life.   70
The most you sought was her promotion ;
For 'twas your heaven she should be advanced :
And weep ye now, seeing she is advanced
Above the clouds, as high as heaven itself?
O, in this love, you love your child so ill,
That you run mad, seeing that she is well :
She's not well married that lives married long ;
But she's best married that dies married young.
Dry up your tears, and stick your rosemary
On this fair corse ; and, as the custom is,   80
In all her best array bear her to church :
For though fond nature bids us all lament,
Yet nature's tears are reason's merriment.
   Cap. All things that we ordained festival,
Turn from their office to black funeral ;
Our instruments to melancholy bells,
Our wedding cheer to a sad burial feast,
Our solemn hymns to sullen dirges change,
Our bridal flowers serve for a buried corse,
And all things change them to the contrary.   90
   Fri. L. Sir, go you in ; and, madam, go with him ;
And go, Sir Paris ; every one prepare
To follow this fair corse unto her grave :
The heavens do lour upon you for some ill ;
Move them no more by crossing their high will.
         [*Exeunt Capulet, Lady Capulet,
               Paris, and Friar.*
   First Mus. Faith, we may put up our pipes, and be gone.

Nurse. Honest goodfellows, ah, put up, put up;
For, well you know, this is a pitiful case. [*Exit.*
First Mus. Ay, by my troth, the case may
be amended.   101

Enter PETER.

Pet. Musicians, O, musicians, 'Heart's ease,
Heart's ease:' O, an you will have me live, play
'Heart's ease.'
First Mus. Why 'Heart's ease'?
Pet. O, musicians, because my heart itself
plays 'My heart is full of woe:' O, play me some
merry dump, to comfort me.
First Mus. Not a dump we; 'tis no time to
play now.   110
Pet. You will not, then?
First Mus. No.
Pet. I will then give it you soundly.
First Mus. What will you give us?
Pet. No money, on my faith, but the gleek; I
will give you the minstrel.
First Mus. Then will I give you the serving-
creature.
Pet. Then will I lay the serving-creature's
dagger on your pate. I will carry no crotchets:
I'll re you, I'll fa you; do you note me?   121
First Mus. An you re us and fa us, you note us.
Sec. Mus. Pray you, put up your dagger, and
put out your wit.
Pet. Then have at you with my wit! I will
dry-beat you with an iron wit, and put up my iron
dagger. Answer me like men:
   'When griping grief the heart doth wound,
      And doleful dumps the mind oppress,
   Then music with her silver sound'—   130
why 'silver sound'? why 'music with her silver
sound'? What say you, Simon Catling?
First Mus. Marry, sir, because silver hath a
sweet sound.
Pet. Pretty! What say you, Hugh Rebeck?
Sec. Mus. I say 'silver sound,' because musi-
cians sound for silver.
Pet. Pretty too! What say you, James Sound-
post?   139
Third Mus. Faith, I know not what to say.
Pet. O, I cry you mercy; you are the singer:
I will say for you. It is 'music with her silver
sound,' because musicians have no gold for sound-
ing:
   'Then music with her silver sound
      With speedy help doth lend redress.' [*Exit.*
First Mus. What a pestilent knave is this
same!
Sec. Mus. Hang him, Jack! Come, we'll in
here; tarry for the mourners, and stay dinner.
                                      [*Exeunt.*

ACT V.

SCENE I. *Mantua. A street.*

Enter ROMEO.

Rom. If I may trust the flattering truth of
   sleep,
My dreams presage some joyful news at hand:
My bosom's lord sits lightly in his throne;
And all this day an unaccustom'd spirit
Lifts me above the ground with cheerful thoughts.
I dreamt my lady came and found me dead—

108 *dump.* Sad melody.

115 *gleek.* Jeer.

Peter: "'Then music with her silver sound'". Painting
'A Concert' by Lorenzo Costa (1459/60–1535)

132 *Catling.* Lute string.

135 *Rebeck.* Three-stringed violin.

138-139 *Soundpost.* Sounding-peg in a violin.

3 *bosom's lord.* i.e. heart.

18 *Capel.* Capulet.

21 *took post.* Hired fast horses.

40 *simples.* Herbs.

52 *caitiff wretch.* Miserable creature.

60 *soon-speeding gear.* Fast-working stuff.

Romeo with the Apothecary. Engraving from Bell's edition of *Shakespeare*, 1773

Strange dream, that gives a dead man leave to
    think !—
And breathed such life with kisses in my lips,
That I revived, and was an emperor.
Ah me ! how sweet is love itself possess'd,   10
When but love's shadows are so rich in joy !

Enter BALTHASAR, *booted.*

News from Verona !—How now, Balthasar !
Dost thou not bring me letters from the friar?
How doth my lady?   Is my father well?
How fares my Juliet? that I ask again ;
For nothing can be ill, if she be well.
   Bal.   Then she is well, and nothing can be ill :
Her body sleeps in Capel's monument,
And her immortal part with angels lives.
I saw her laid low in her kindred's vault,   20
And presently took post to tell it you :
O, pardon me for bringing these ill news,
Since you did leave it for my office, sir.
   Rom.   Is it even so? then I defy you, stars !
Thou know'st my lodging : get me ink and paper,
And hire post-horses ; I will hence to-night.
   Bal.   I do beseech you, sir, have patience :
Your looks are pale and wild, and do import
Some misadventure.
   Rom.   Tush, thou art deceived :
Leave me, and do the thing I bid thee do.   30
Hast thou no letters to me from the friar?
   Bal.   No, my good lord.
   Rom.   No matter : get thee gone,
And hire those horses ; I 'll be with thee straight.
                       [Exit Balthasar.
Well, Juliet, I will lie with thee to-night.
Let's see for means : O mischief, thou art swift
To enter in the thoughts of desperate men !
I do remember an apothecary,—
And hereabouts he dwells,—which late I noted
In tatter'd weeds, with overwhelming brows,
Culling of simples ; meagre were his looks,   40
Sharp misery had worn him to the bones :
And in his needy shop a tortoise hung,
An alligator stuff'd, and other skins
Of ill-shaped fishes ; and about his shelves
A beggarly account of empty boxes,
Green earthen pots, bladders and musty seeds,
Remnants of packthread and old cakes of roses,
Were thinly scatter'd, to make up a show.
Noting this penury, to myself I said
'An if a man did need a poison now,   50
Whose sale is present death in Mantua,
Here lives a caitiff wretch would sell it him.'
O, this same thought did but forerun my need ;
And this same needy man must sell it me.
As I remember, this should be the house.
Being holiday, the beggar's shop is shut.
What, ho ! apothecary !

Enter Apothecary.

   Ap.   Who calls so loud?
   Rom.   Come hither, man.   I see that thou art
    poor :
Hold, there is forty ducats : let me have
A dram of poison, such soon-speeding gear   60
As will disperse itself through all the veins
That the life-weary taker may fall dead
And that the trunk may be discharged of breath

As violently as hasty powder fired
Doth hurry from the fatal cannon's womb.
    Ap.   Such mortal drugs I have; but Mantua's
      law
• Is death to any he that utters them.
    Rom.   Art thou so bare and full of wretched-
      ness,
And fear'st to die? famine is in thy cheeks,
Need and oppression starveth in thine eyes,   70
Contempt and beggary hangs upon thy back;
The world is not thy friend nor the world's law;
The world affords no law to make thee rich;
Then be not poor, but break it, and take this.
    Ap.   My poverty, but not my will, consents.
    Rom.   I pay thy poverty, and not thy will.
    Ap.   Put this in any liquid thing you will,
And drink it off; and, if you had the strength
Of twenty men, it would dispatch you straight.
    Rom.   There is thy gold, worse poison to men's
      souls,   80
Doing more murders in this loathsome world,
Than these poor compounds that thou mayst not
      sell.
I sell thee poison; thou hast sold me none.
Farewell: buy food, and get thyself in flesh.
Come, cordial and not poison, go with me
To Juliet's grave; for there must I use thee.
                          [*Exeunt.*

SCENE II. *Friar Laurence's cell.*

Enter FRIAR JOHN.

    Fri. J.   Holy Franciscan friar! brother, ho!

Enter FRIAR LAURENCE.

    Fri. L.   This same should be the voice of
      Friar John.
Welcome from Mantua: what says Romeo?
Or, if his mind be writ, give me his letter.
    Fri. J.   Going to find a bare-foot brother out,
One of our order, to associate me,
Here in this city visiting the sick,
And finding him, the searchers of the town,
Suspecting that we both were in a house
Where the infectious pestilence did reign,   10
Seal'd up the doors, and would not let us forth;
So that my speed to Mantua there was stay'd.
    Fri. L.   Who bare my letter, then, to Romeo?
    Fri. J.   I could not send it,—here it is again,—
Nor get a messenger to bring it thee,
So fearful were they of infection.
    Fri. L.   Unhappy fortune! by my brother-
      hood,
• The letter was not nice but full of charge
Of dear import, and the neglecting it
May do much danger. Friar John, go hence;   20
Get me an iron crow, and bring it straight
Unto my cell.
    Fri. J.   Brother, I'll go and bring it thee.
                          [*Exit.*
    Fri. L.   Now must I to the monument alone;
Within this three hours will fair Juliet wake:
She will beshrew me much that Romeo
Hath had no notice of these accidents;
But I will write again to Mantua,
And keep her at my cell till Romeo come;
Poor living corse, closed in a dead man's tomb!
                          [*Exit.*

67 *utters.* Issues.

18 *charge.* Instructions.

Friar Laurence: 'Now must I go to the monument alone'. Detail from a drawing by Anthony Walker (1726–1765)

Set design for the Churchyard with tomb by Jean Hugo for Jean Cocteau's production, Paris, 1924

___

33 *jealous.* Curious.

SCENE III.   *A churchyard; in it a tomb belonging to the Capulets.*

Enter PARIS, *and his* Page *bearing flowers and a torch.*

Par.   Give me thy torch, boy: hence, and stand aloof:
Yet put it out, for I would not be seen.
Under yond yew-trees lay thee all along,
Holding thine ear close to the hollow ground;
So shall no foot upon the churchyard tread,
Being loose, unfirm, with digging up of graves,
But thou shalt hear it: whistle then to me,
As signal that thou hear'st something approach.
Give me those flowers.   Do as I bid thee, go.
  Page. [*Aside*] I am almost afraid to stand alone   10
Here in the churchyard; yet I will adventure.
                                                    [*Retires.*
  Par.   Sweet flower, with flowers thy bridal bed I strew,—
    O woe! thy canopy is dust and stones;—
    Which with sweet water nightly I will dew,
      Or, wanting that, with tears distill'd by moans:
    The obsequies that I for thee will keep
Nightly shall be to strew thy grave and weep.
                                        [*The Page whistles.*
The boy gives warning something doth approach.
What cursed foot wanders this way to-night,
To cross my obsequies and true love's rite?   20
What, with a torch! muffle me, night, awhile.
                                                    [*Retires.*

Enter ROMEO *and* BALTHASAR, *with a torch, mattock, &c.*

  Rom.   Give me that mattock and the wrenching iron.
Hold, take this letter; early in the morning
See thou deliver it to my lord and father.
Give me the light: upon thy life, I charge thee,
Whate'er thou hear'st or seest, stand all aloof,
And do not interrupt me in my course.
Why I descend into this bed of death,
Is partly to behold my lady's face;   29
But chiefly to take thence from her dead finger
A precious ring, a ring that I must use
In dear employment: therefore hence, be gone:
•But if thou, jealous, dost return to pry
In what I further shall intend to do,
By heaven, I will tear thee joint by joint
And strew this hungry churchyard with thy limbs:
The time and my intents are savage-wild,
More fierce and more inexorable far
Than empty tigers or the roaring sea.   39
  Bal.   I will be gone, sir, and not trouble you.
  Rom.   So shalt thou show me friendship. Take thou that:
Live, and be prosperous: and farewell, good fellow.
  Bal. [*Aside*] For all this same, I'll hide me hereabout:
His looks I fear, and his intents I doubt.
                                                    [*Retires.*
  Rom.   Thou detestable maw, thou womb of death,
Gorged with the dearest morsel of the earth,
Thus I enforce thy rotten jaws to open,

And, in despite, I'll cram thee with more food!
                                    [*Opens the tomb.*
  Par. This is that banish'd haughty Mon-
    tague,   49
That murder'd my love's cousin, with which grief,
It is supposed, the fair creature died;
And here is come to do some villanous shame
To the dead bodies: I will apprehend him.
                                    [*Comes forward.*
Stop thy unhallow'd toil, vile Montague!
Can vengeance be pursued further than death?
Condemned villain, I do apprehend thee:
Obey, and go with me; for thou must die.
  Rom. I must indeed; and therefore came I
    hither.
Good gentle youth, tempt not a desperate man;
Fly hence, and leave me: think upon these gone;
Let them affright thee. I beseech thee, youth,
Put not another sin upon my head,
By urging me to fury: O, be gone!
By heaven, I love thee better than myself;
For I come hither arm'd against myself:
Stay not, be gone; live, and hereafter say,
A madman's mercy bade thee run away.
  Par. I do defy thy conjurations,
And apprehend thee for a felon here.
  Rom. Wilt thou provoke me? then have at
    thee, boy!   [*They fight.* 70
  Page. O Lord, they fight! I will go call the
    watch.   [*Exit.*
  Par. O, I am slain! [*Falls.*] If thou be mer-
    ciful,
Open the tomb, lay me with Juliet.   [*Dies.*
  Rom. In faith, I will. Let me peruse this
    face.
Mercutio's kinsman, noble County Paris!
What said my man, when my betossed soul
Did not attend him as we rode? I think
He told me Paris should have married Juliet:
Said he not so? or did I dream it so?
Or am I mad, hearing him talk of Juliet,   80
To think it was so? O, give me thy hand,
One writ with me in sour misfortune's book!
I'll bury thee in a triumphant grave;
A grave? O, no! a lantern, slaughter'd youth,
For here lies Juliet, and her beauty makes
This vault a feasting presence full of light.
Death, lie thou there, by a dead man interr'd.
                    [*Laying Paris in the tomb.*
How oft when men are at the point of death
Have they been merry! which their keepers call
A lightning before death: O, how may I   90
Call this a lightning? O my love! my wife!
Death, that hath suck'd the honey of thy breath,
Hath had no power yet upon thy beauty:
Thou art not conquer'd; beauty's ensign yet
Is crimson in thy lips and in thy cheeks,
And death's pale flag is not advanced there.
Tybalt, liest thou there in thy bloody sheet?
O, what more favour can I do to thee,
Than with that hand that cut thy youth in twain
To sunder his that was thine enemy?   100
Forgive me, cousin! Ah, dear Juliet,
Why art thou yet so fair? shall I believe
That unsubstantial death is amorous,
And that the lean abhorred monster keeps
Thee here in dark to be his paramour?
For fear of that, I still will stay with thee:
And never from this palace of dim night

Romeo: 'Ah, dear Juliet, Why art thou yet so fair?'
David Garrick as Romeo in the tomb scene, Theatre
Royal, Drury Lane, London, 1750

115 *engrossing.* Embracing.

116 *conduct.* Transport, i.e. poison.

117 *pilot.* i.e. soul.

118 *bark.* i.e. body.

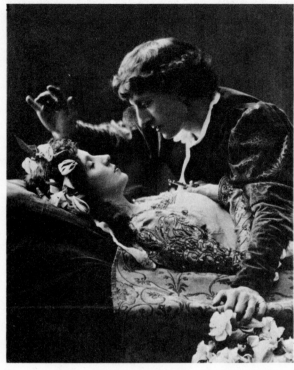

Romeo: 'Thus with a kiss I die'. Mrs Patrick Campbell as Juliet with Johnston Forbes Robertson as Romeo, Lyceum Theatre, London, 1895

148 *comfortable.* Comforting.

Depart again: here, here will I remain
With worms that are thy chamber-maids; O, here
Will I set up my everlasting rest,   110
And shake the yoke of inauspicious stars
From this world-wearied flesh.   Eyes, look your
    last!
Arms, take your last embrace! and, lips, O you
The doors of breath, seal with a righteous kiss
● A dateless bargain to engrossing death!
● Come, bitter conduct, come, unsavoury guide!
● Thou desperate pilot, now at once run on
● The dashing rocks thy sea-sick weary bark!
Here's to my love! [*Drinks.*] O true apothe-
    cary!
Thy drugs are quick.   Thus with a kiss I die. 120
                                                      [*Dies.*

Enter, at the other end of the churchyard, FRIAR
    LAURENCE, *with a lantern, crow, and spade.*
    Fri. L.   Saint Francis be my speed! how oft
        to-night
Have my old feet stumbled at graves!   Who's
    there?
    Bal.   Here's one, a friend, and one that knows
        you well.
    Fri. L.   Bliss be upon you!   Tell me, good
        my friend,
What torch is yond, that vainly lends his light
To grubs and eyeless skulls? as I discern,
It burneth in the Capels' monument.
    Bal.   It doth so, holy sir; and there's my
        master,
One that you love.
    Fri. L.   Who is it?
    Bal.   Romeo.
    Fri. L.   How long hath he been there?
    Bal.   Full half an hour. 130
    Fri. L.   Go with me to the vault.
    Bal.   I dare not, sir:
My master knows not but I am gone hence;
And fearfully did menace me with death,
If I did stay to look on his intents.
    Fri. L.   Stay, then; I'll go alone.   Fear comes
        upon me:
O, much I fear some ill unlucky thing.
    Bal.   As I did sleep under this yew-tree here,
I dreamt my master and another fought,
And that my master slew him.
    Fri. L.   Romeo!
                                                  [*Advances.*
Alack, alack, what blood is this, which stains 140
The stony entrance of this sepulchre?
What mean these masterless and gory swords
To lie discolour'd by this place of peace?
                                              [*Enters the tomb.*
Romeo! O, pale!   Who else? what, Paris too?
And steep'd in blood?   Ah, what an unkind hour
Is guilty of this lamentable chance!
The lady stirs.   [*Juliet wakes.*
● *Jul.*   O comfortable friar! where is my lord?
I do remember well where I should be,
And there I am.   Where is my Romeo?   150
                                              [*Noise within.*
    Fri. L.   I hear some noise.   Lady, come from
        that nest
Of death, contagion, and unnatural sleep:
A greater power than we can contradict
Hath thwarted our intents.   Come, come away.
Thy husband in thy bosom there lies dead;

And Paris too.   Come, I'll dispose of thee
Among a sisterhood of holy nuns :
Stay not to question, for the watch is coming ;
Come, go, good Juliet [*Noise again*], I dare no
    longer stay.   159
    Jul. Go, get thee hence, for I will not away.
                      [*Exit Fri. L.*
What's here? a cup, closed in my true love's
    hand?
● Poison, I see, hath been his timeless end :
O churl! drunk all, and left no friendly drop
To help me after? I will kiss thy lips ;
Haply some poison yet doth hang on them,
● To make me die with a restorative. [*Kisses him.*
Thy lips are warm.
    First Watch. [*Within*] Lead, boy : which way?
    Jul. Yea, noise? then I'll be brief. O happy
    dagger!   [*Snatching Romeo's dagger.*
This is thy sheath [*Stabs herself*]; there rust,
    and let me die.   170
        [*Falls on Romeo's body, and dies.*

    Enter Watch, *with the* Page *of* PARIS.

    Page. This is the place ; there, where the
    torch doth burn.
    First Watch. The ground is bloody ; search
    about the churchyard :
● Go, some of you, whoe'er you find attach.
Pitiful sight! here lies the county slain ;
And Juliet bleeding, warm, and newly dead,
Who here hath lain these two days buried.
Go, tell the prince : run to the Capulets :
Raise up the Montagues : some others search :
We see the ground whereon these woes do lie ;
But the true ground of all these piteous woes 180
We cannot without circumstance descry.

    Re-enter some of the Watch, *with* BALTHASAR.

    Sec. Watch. Here's Romeo's man ; we found
    him in the churchyard.
    First Watch. Hold him in safety, till the
    prince come hither.

    Re-enter others of the Watch, *with* FRIAR
                LAURENCE.

    Third Watch. Here is a friar, that trembles,
    sighs, and weeps :
We took this mattock and this spade from him,
As he was coming from this churchyard side.
    First Watch. A great suspicion : stay the
    friar too.

    Enter the PRINCE *and* Attendants.
    Prince. What misadventure is so early up,
That calls our person from our morning's rest?

    Enter CAPULET, LADY CAPULET, *and others.*
    Cap. What should it be, that they so shriek
    abroad?   190
    La. Cap. The people in the street cry Romeo,
Some Juliet, and some Paris ; and all run,
With open outcry, toward our monument.
    Prince. What fear is this which startles in
    our ears?
    First Watch. Sovereign, here lies the County
    Paris slain ;
And Romeo dead ; and Juliet, dead before,
Warm and new kill'd.

Juliet finds Romeo dead on the steps of her bier. Painting
by Ferdinand Piloty (1828–1895)

---

162 *timeless.* Ill-timed.

166 *restorative.* An action bringing us together again.

173 *attach.* Arrest.

Capulet: 'O heavens! O wife, look how our daughter bleeds!' Detail from a painting by Lord Frederick Leighton, 1806

---

203 *mista'en.* Been removed. *house.* i.e. wound.

214 *untaught.* Ill-mannered.

226 *impeach.* i.e. accuse. *purge.* i.e. exonerate.

229 *date of breath.* Expectation of life.

237 *siege.* Seat.

248 *borrow'd.* Temporary.

Prince. Search, seek, and know how this foul murder comes.
First Watch. Here is a friar, and slaughter'd Romeo's man;
With instruments upon them, fit to open   200
These dead men's tombs.
  Cap. O heavens! O wife, look how our daughter bleeds!
This dagger hath mista'en,—for, lo, his house
Is empty on the back of Montague,—
And it mis-sheathed in my daughter's bosom!
  La. Cap. O me! this sight of death is as a bell,
That warns my old age to a sepulchre.

Enter MONTAGUE *and others.*

Prince. Come, Montague; for thou art early up,
To see thy son and heir more early down.   209
  Mon. Alas, my liege, my wife is dead to-night;
Grief of my son's exile hath stopp'd her breath:
What further woe conspires against mine age?
  Prince. Look, and thou shalt see.
  Mon. O thou untaught! what manners is in this,
To press before thy father to a grave?
  Prince. Seal up the mouth of outrage for a while,
Till we can clear these ambiguities,
And know their spring, their head, their true descent;
And then will I be general of your woes,   219
And lead you even to death: meantime forbear,
And let mischance be slave to patience.
Bring forth the parties of suspicion.
  Fri. L. I am the greatest, able to do least,
Yet most suspected, as the time and place
Doth make against me, of this direful murder;
And here I stand, both to impeach and purge
Myself condemned and myself excused.
  Prince. Then say at once what thou dost know in this.
  Fri. L. I will be brief, for my short date of breath
Is not so long as is a tedious tale.   230
Romeo, there dead, was husband to that Juliet;
And she, there dead, that Romeo's faithful wife:
I married them; and their stol'n marriage-day
Was Tybalt's dooms-day, whose untimely death
Banish'd the new-made bridegroom from this city,
For whom, and not for Tybalt, Juliet pined.
You, to remove that siege of grief from her,
Betroth'd and would have married her perforce
To County Paris: then comes she to me,   239
And, with wild looks, bid me devise some mean
To rid her from this second marriage,
Or in my cell there would she kill herself.
Then gave I her, so tutor'd by my art,
A sleeping potion; which so took effect
As I intended, for it wrought on her
The form of death: meantime I writ to Romeo,
That he should hither come as this dire night,
To help to take her from her borrow'd grave,
Being the time the potion's force should cease.
But he which bore my letter, Friar John,   250
Was stay'd by accident, and yesternight
Return'd my letter back.   Then all alone
At the prefixed hour of her waking,
Came I to take her from her kindred's vault;

Meaning to keep her closely at my cell,
Till I conveniently could send to Romeo:
But when I came, some minute ere the time
Of her awaking, here untimely lay
The noble Paris and true Romeo dead.
She wakes; and I entreated her come forth, 260
And bear this work of heaven with patience:
But then a noise did scare me from the tomb;
And she, too desperate, would not go with me,
But, as it seems, did violence on herself.
All this I know; and to the marriage
Her nurse is privy: and, if aught in this
Miscarried by my fault, let my old life
Be sacrificed, some hour before his time,
Unto the rigour of severest law.
    Prince.   We still have known thee for a
      holy man.   270
Where's Romeo's man? what can he say in this?
    Bal.   I brought my master news of Juliet's
      death;
And then in post he came from Mantua
To this same place, to this same monument.
This letter he early bid me give his father,
And threaten'd me with death, going in the
    vault,
If I departed not and left him there.
    Prince. Give me the letter; I will look on it.
Where is the county's page, that raised the
    watch?
Sirrah, what made your master in this place? 280
    Page.   He came with flowers to strew his
      lady's grave;
And bid me stand aloof, and so I did:
Anon comes one with light to ope the tomb;
And by and by my master drew on him;
And then I ran away to call the watch.
    Prince. This letter doth make good the friar's
      words,
Their course of love, the tidings of her death:
And here he writes that he did buy a poison
Of a poor 'pothecary, and therewithal
Came to this vault to die, and lie with Juliet. 290
Where be these enemies? Capulet! Monta-
    gue!
See, what a scourge is laid upon your hate,
That heaven finds means to kill your joys with
    love.
And I for winking at your discords too
Have lost a brace of kinsmen: all are punish'd.
    Cap. O brother Montague, give me thy hand:
• This is my daughter's jointure, for no more
Can I demand.
    Mon.   But I can give thee more:
For I will raise her statue in pure gold;
That while Verona by that name is known, 300
There shall no figure at such rate be set
As that of true and faithful Juliet.
    Cap. As rich shall Romeo's by his lady's lie;
Poor sacrifices of our enmity!
    Prince. A glooming peace this morning with
      it brings;
The sun, for sorrow, will not show his head:
Go hence, to have more talk of these sad things;
    Some shall be pardon'd, and some punished:
For never was a story of more woe
Than this of Juliet and her Romeo. [*Exeunt.* 310

Reconciliation of the Montagues and the Capulets,
Stratford-upon-Avon, 1961

297 *jointure.* Wedding settlement.

Julius Caesar

1599

JULIUS CAESAR is, along with *Coriolanus*, the most classic of Shakespeare's plays, as if to show the world – and in particular Ben Jonson, who was at this time writing for the Chamberlain's Men – that he knew quite well what classic decorum demanded, though it was not in keeping with his richer, romantic nature. Paradoxically, it was precisely because of this that the Augustan Dr. Johnson was not much drawn to the play: he preferred Shakespeare's characteristic mixture, the more coloured texture, the richer variousness – and perhaps this betrays a latent romanticism in the soul of the great Augustan.

Nothing of this impeded the success of the play in the dramatist's own age, more catholic in its tastes and with no inhibitions. John Weever tells us:

> The many-headed multitude were drawn
> By Brutus' speech that Caesar was ambitious:
> When eloquent Mark Antony had shown
> His virtues, who but Brutus then was vicious?

It is significant that this was the moral that people drew from the play in the year of its performance. Years later Leonard Digges testified to the response of the audience:

> So have I seen when Caesar would appear,
> And on the stage at half-sword parley were
> Brutus and Cassius – O how the audience
> Were ravished! with what wonder they went thence!

This is contrasted with the failure of Ben Jonson's 'tedious, though well-laboured' classic plays. Shakespeare's sense of the theatre was infallible, whether tragedy or comedy, romantic (though even those plays are full of classical allusions, from his education) or even classic in the more specialised sense of the word.

Though classic work, the dramatic onrush is irresistible – as a perceptive producer, Granville-Barker, emphasises, and as all audiences find. The play is short, swift and stream-lined, with little decoration; no sub-plot, hardly a comic touch or even a sentence that is bawdy (a rarity), but it is immensely exciting, even haunting, full of famous lines that go on and on in the mind and have entered into the consciousness of all who speak the tongue.

Date. The dramatist already had *Julius Caesar* in mind before finishing *Henry V*. In the Prologue to the last act of that he had described the city's expectation of a welcome to conquering Essex on his return from Ireland. Now, in the very first scene of *Julius Caesar* we find:

> Many a time and oft
> Have you climbed up to walls and battlements,
> To towers and windows, yea, to chimney-tops,
> Your infants in your arms, and there have sat
> The live-long day with patient expectation
> To see great Pompey pass the streets of Rome;
> And when you saw his chariot but appear,
> Have you not made an universal shout . . .

Windows and chimney-tops . . . this is not ancient Rome, but the London mob giving Essex the send-off from which he returned so abortively. We see how quickly Shakespeare worked. In this same year the young Swiss tourist, Thomas Platter, reports 'after dinner on 21 September, about 2 o'clock, I went with my companions across the water, and in the straw-thatched house saw the tragedy of the first emperor, Julius Caesar, excellently performed by some fifteen persons.' The play has a much larger number of characters, so some parts were, as usual, doubled. It was followed by a jig, danced by two actors as men and two – in the ambivalent fashion of the Elizabethan stage – as women.

Reading. Much as Shakespeare had depended upon Hall and Holinshed for his English history, he had even more congenial reading for his classical plays in Sir Thomas North's translation of Plutarch. Plutarch's interest in character was as lively and perceptive as his own; moreover, where Holinshed was a rustic *bourgeois*, North was a cultivated aristocrat who wrote the language like a gentleman. Whole passages of fine prose could be rendered in as fine, or finer, blank verse with the greatest of ease. (Much of Elizabethan prose communication goes readily into blank verse – as indeed is the case with the speeches of Abraham Lincoln, whose style was formed by the Bible and Shakespeare.)[1]

The quick reading man not only wrote with North's Plutarch open beside him, but we can tell that he was reading Sir John Davies' philosophic poem, *Nosce Teipsum*, and the congenial Daniel's *Musophilus* contemporaneously. At the assassination of Caesar, Cassius says,

> How many ages hence
> Shall this our lofty scene be acted over
> In states unborn and accents yet unknown!

Shakespeare had been struck, as we all are, by the fine imaginative passage of Daniel:

1. As I found when putting his farewell speech to his Illinois neighbours in my blank-verse poem 'Abraham Lincoln at Springfield' in *Poems Partly American.*

And who in time knows whither we may vent
The treasure of our tongue, to what strange shores
This gain of our best glory shall be sent,
To enrich unknowing nations with our stores?
What worlds in the yet unformèd Occident
May come refined with th'accents that are ours?

But, observe, where Daniel is reflective, Shakespeare instinctively turns the lines into theatre, 'our lofty scene . . . acted over'.

The Tragedy of Brutus. The criticism that the play falls into two halves, with Caesar disappearing in the middle, is imperceptive, for the subject is described, in so many words, as 'the spirit of Caesar': his spirit dominates the whole play, as his assassination did the historical event. But it might alternatively be described as the tragedy of Brutus, who has a far larger part and whose character is much more fully delineated.

It is recognised that the dramatist wrote Caesar down in the interests of dramatic balance, and wrote Brutus up, better than he deserved, to give him a chance – for, after all, he was an assassin. We are assured that Brutus was an honest, indeed the one honourable, man in the conspiracy against Caesar: he was the only one moved by what he considered to be the public interest, as against the others, who were moved by envy or spleen or personal resentment. And, after all, Brutus had personal reason to be grateful to Caesar, who was attached to him. (William Shakespeare hated ingratitude, of all things.)

He makes Caesar deaf, for which there is no evidence; he gives Cassius a long speech enumerating Caesar's weaknesses, even timorousness for which there was no warrant, for he was a man of indomitable courage and resolution. He was also a supreme opportunist, who was very clear-eyed about the way things were going and ready to take advantage of them. He saw that antiquated republican institutions were breaking down, and personal rule was inevitable, to take their place. Like Bolingbroke, who *had* to take the crown for sheer self-preservation, apart from anything else, Caesar had to cross the Rubicon and march on Rome or his enemies would have destroyed him; then civil war would have broken out anyway. His assassination made this inevitable.

Once more Shakespeare shows his regular concern for social order, and the horror of its breakdown.

However, for the balance of his play, the dramatist holds the scales in favour of Brutus (historically, he was not such a noble character). Everybody looks up to him as *sans peur et sans reproche*; Caesar might never have been assassinated if Brutus had not lent himself to the conspiracy. Like such men who are generally admired for their nobility, he is morally self-complacent, even conceited, for ever congratulating himself on the purity of his motives:

For I am armed so strong in honesty
That they [threats] pass by me as the idle wind
Which I respect not.

He is an idealist and, like all idealists, shows bad judgment throughout. After murdering Caesar he insists on sparing Mark Antony against the judgment of his fellow-assassins – and he proceeded to turn the tables on them and destroy them. In the quarrel with Cassius before Philippi it is Brutus who shows himself unreasonable; and he urges on an immediate battle – against Cassius' more experienced judgment – in circumstances

Death of Julius Caesar. Nineteenth century engraving from a painting by J. L. Gérôme (1824–1904)

which brought disaster upon them. Indeed, the assassination of Caesar itself was a mistake, apart from the crime: it caused civil war, and did not save the republic, which was the only excuse for it.

Brutus is an idealist, i.e. an idealogue: Napoleon knew their worth in society and in great events – after all, he had been one himself when young and ignorant. But he learned; Brutus was one of those who never learn from experience. It cannot be supposed that William Shakespeare's sympathies were with such a type; but he does his best for him and writes him an epitaph, which people have taken literally, though placed in Antony's mouth:

> This was the noblest Roman of them all:
> All the conspirators save only he
> Did that they did in envy of great Caesar;
> He only, in a general honest thought
> And common good to all, made one of them.

He assassinated in the cause of liberty and for the good of the people. We are shown by the dramatist what that was worth; nor did Shakespeare bother much about consistency, any more than there is in life.

The People as a Character. We see all through Shakespeare's plays what his, and the Elizabethans', view of the people was; in this play and in *Coriolanus* they constitute a character in the action.

The tribunes of the people, in the very first scene, have nothing but contempt for them, for their ingratitude and changeability, basely transferring their worship of Pompey to his enemy, Caesar. (What else are poor people to do, but fall in with the winning side?) Casca, one of the conspirators on behalf of liberty of the people, describes their servility to Caesar at the offer of the crown: 'the rabble hooted and clapped their chapped hands and threw up their sweaty nightcaps and uttered such a deal of stinking breath . . . that it had almost choked Caesar.' The detail of the 'nightcaps' reveals the contemporary scene, and indeed an Elizabethan crowd must have smelt horribly.

After the assassination it is to the wisdom of the people that Brutus, so true to type, appeals: 'censure me in your wisdom, and awake your senses, that you may the better judge.' If he has offended, 'if any, speak: for him I have offended. I pause for a reply.' The response of the rational people to this appeal to their reason is:

> Let him be Caesar!
>   Caesar's better parts
> Shall be crowned in Brutus –

i.e. make Brutus king. He should have been shocked at such a response.

Mark Antony is described by Cassius as 'a masker and a reveller'; but he knows what the people are, and has no difficulty in twisting them round his little finger, assuring them the while that Brutus and his fellow-assassins are 'honourable men'. He goes on assuring them, while gradually bringing home the enormity of the crime and Caesar's good intentions towards them, his generosity and bequests to them in his will, so that in the end the appeal to their emotions makes them weep, and the irony of the insistence upon the honourable men who had done the deed drives them wild:

> All: Revenge! About! Seek! Burn! Fire! Kill!
>   Slay! Let not a traitor live . . .
> 1 Plebeian: We'll burn his [Caesar's] body in the holy place,
>   And with the brands fire the traitors' houses.
> 2 Plebeian: Go, fetch fire.
> 3 Plebeian: Pluck down benches.
> 4 Plebeian: Pluck down forms, windows, anything.

William Shakespeare knew his people, ordinary humanity, very well.

The Age. His own time thus reveals itself. The conspirators are depicted as all muffled up, just as we see them in Gunpowder Plot engravings a few years later. Cassius boasts,

> So often shall the knot of us be called
> The men that gave their country liberty –

'knot' was the regular word for conspirators at the time. Caesar was quite right, by the way, in his judgment of Cassius' type:

> Such men as he be never at heart's ease
> While they behold a greater than themselves.

The play is full of dreams and omens, and, though they are authenticated in the sources, they are so much in keeping with the beliefs of the time as to have added much to the dramatic effect. The appearance of Caesar's ghost to Brutus before Philippi not only keeps his spirit before us, but is thrilling in the theatre, and it reminds us of the ghosts that appeared to Richard III before Bosworth. The soothsayer – of whom Caesar, in his generous over-confidence, will take no notice – was frequently to be met with in

Elizabethan life: everybody believed in omens, dreams, and foretellings.

We catch another of Shakespeare's regular references to his profession, that appear in every play; at the offer of the crown to Caesar: 'if the tag-rag people did not clap him and hiss him according as he pleased and displeased them, as they use [i.e. are accustomed] to do the players in the theatre, I am no true man.'

A few personal reflections reveal the man behind the dramatist:

> But when I tell him he hates flatterers,
> He says he does, being then most flattered.

And what are we to think of the sadness in:

> When love begins to sicken and decay,
> It useth an enforcèd ceremony.

Text. No problems. E. K. Chambers describes it as 'one of the best printed of the Folio additions' – since there are no quartos; 'a few abrupt short lines may be evidence of cuts.' Ben Jonson made fun of a couple of passages: Shakespeare, writing hurriedly as usual, had made Caesar say, 'Caesar never did wrong but with just cause', which Ben considered 'ridiculous'. He must have told Shakespeare as much, for in the Folio text it is rectified to –

> Know, Caesar doth not wrong, nor without cause
> Will he be satisfied.

Ben made fun, too, of another passage:

> O judgment! thou art fled to brutish beasts,
> And men have lost their reason.

Immediately after, in *Every Man out of his Humour*, Jonson takes this up:

> Reason long since is fled to animals, you know.

These are but amusing exchanges between fellows writing for the same Company; it is heavy-footed to speak of Ben's twitting the Master, to whom he was indebted for his introduction to the Company, as showing 'animosity' (Dover-Wilson). Such exchanges alerted performers and audience, and provided fun.

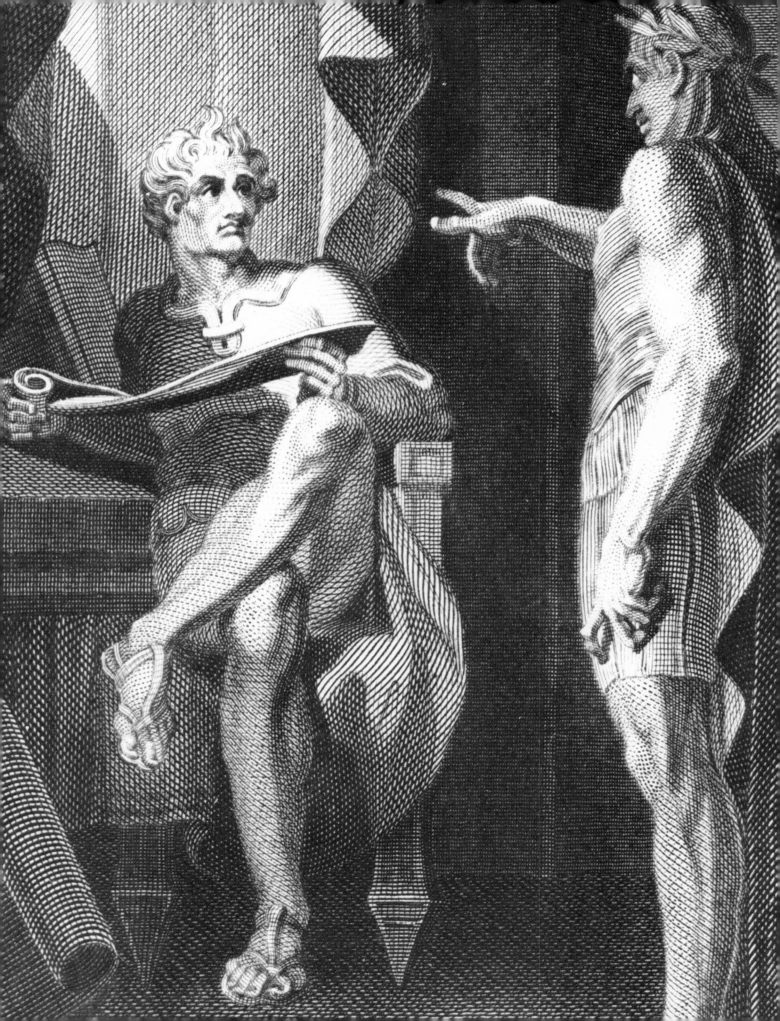

JULIUS CÆSAR.

DRAMATIS PERSONÆ.

JULIUS CÆSAR.
OCTAVIUS CÆSAR, } triumvirs after the
MARCUS ANTONIUS,   death of Julius
M. ÆMILIUS LEPIDUS, } Cæsar.
CICERO,
PUBLIUS, } senators.
POPILIUS LENA, }
MARCUS BRUTUS,
CASSIUS,
CASCA,
TREBONIUS,   } conspirators against
LIGARIUS,   Julius Cæsar.
DECIUS BRUTUS,
METELLUS CIMBER,
CINNA,
FLAVIUS and MARULLUS, tribunes.
ARTEMIDORUS of Cnidos, a teacher of Rhe-
toric.
A Soothsayer.
CINNA, a poet.   Another Poet.

LUCILIUS,
TITINIUS,
MESSALA,   } friends to Brutus and
Young CATO,   Cassius.
VOLUMNIUS,
VARRO,
CLITUS,
CLAUDIUS,   } servants to Brutus.
STRATO,
LUCIUS,
DARDANIUS,
PINDARUS, servant to Cassius.

CALPURNIA, wife to Cæsar.
PORTIA, wife to Brutus.

Senators, Citizens, Guards, Attendants, &c.

SCENE: *Rome: the neighbourhood of Sardis:
the neighbourhood of Philippi.*

ACT I.

SCENE I. *Rome. A street.*

Enter FLAVIUS, MARULLUS, *and certain*
Commoners.

Flav.   Hence! home, you idle creatures, get
you home:
Is this a holiday? what! know you not,
● Being mechanical, you ought not walk
Upon a labouring day without the sign
Of your profession? Speak, what trade art thou?
First Com.   Why, sir, a carpenter.
Mar.   Where is thy leather apron and thy
rule?
What dost thou with thy best apparel on?
You, sir, what trade are you?
Sec. Com.   Truly, sir, in respect of a fine work-
man, I am but, as you would say, a cobbler.   11
Mar.   But what trade art thou? answer me
directly.
Sec. Com.   A trade, sir, that, I hope, I may
use with a safe conscience; which is, indeed, sir,
a mender of bad soles.
Mar.   What trade, thou knave? thou naughty
knave, what trade?
Sec. Com.   Nay, I beseech you, sir, be not
out with me: yet, if you be out, sir, I can mend
you.
Mar.   What meanest thou by that? mend me,
thou saucy fellow!   21
Sec. Com.   Why, sir, cobble you.
Flav.   Thou art a cobbler, art thou?
Sec. Com.   Truly, sir, all that I live by is with
the awl: I meddle with no tradesman's matters,
nor women's matters, but with awl. I am, indeed, sir, a surgeon to old shoes; when they are
in great danger, I recover them. As proper men

● *A bullet beside a textline indicates an annotation in the
opposite column*

Dramatis Personae. *triumvirs*. A commission of three
rulers of the state of Rome.

3 *mechanical*. A working man.

Opposite : Brutus with the ghost of Caesar. Engraving
by Henry Fuseli (1741–1825)

Second Commoner: '... we make holiday, to see Caesar and to rejoice in his triumph.' Painting 'The Triumph of Caesar' by Andrea Mantegna (c. 1430/1–1506)

38 *tributaries.* Captives.

42–49 *Many a time ... shout.* See introduction.

Triumph of Pompey. Engraving from P. J. Mariette's *Traité des Pierres Gravées*, 1769

51 *replication.* Echo.

54 *cull.* Choose.

as ever trod upon neat's leather have gone upon my handiwork.   30

Flav.   But wherefore art not in thy shop to-day?

Why dost thou lead these men about the streets?

Sec. Com.   Truly, sir, to wear out their shoes, to get myself into more work.   But, indeed, sir, we make holiday, to see Cæsar and to rejoice in his triumph.

Mar.   Wherefore rejoice?   What conquest brings he home?

• What tributaries follow him to Rome,
To grace in captive bonds his chariot-wheels?
You blocks, you stones, you worse than sense-
less things!   40
O you hard hearts, you cruel men of Rome,
• Knew you not Pompey?   Many a time and oft
Have you climb'd up to walls and battlements,
To towers and windows, yea, to chimney-tops,
Your infants in your arms, and there have sat
The live-long day, with patient expectation,
To see great Pompey pass the streets of Rome:
And when you saw his chariot but appear,
Have you not made an universal shout,
That Tiber trembled underneath her banks,   50
• To hear the replication of your sounds
Made in her concave shores?
And do you now put on your best attire?
• And do you now cull out a holiday?
And do you now strew flowers in his way
That comes in triumph over Pompey's blood?
Be gone!
Run to your houses, fall upon your knees,
Pray to the gods to intermit the plague
That needs must light on this ingratitude.   60

Flav.   Go, go, good countrymen, and, for this fault,
Assemble all the poor men of your sort;

Draw them to Tiber banks, and weep your tears
Into the channel, till the lowest stream
Do kiss the most exalted shores of all.
      [*Exeunt all the Commoners.*
See, whether their basest metal be not moved;
They vanish tongue-tied in their guiltiness.
Go you down that way towards the Capitol;
This way will I: disrobe the images,
● If you do find them deck'd with ceremonies. 70
 Mar. May we do so?
● You know it is the feast of Lupercal.
 Flav. It is no matter; let no images
Be hung with Cæsar's trophies.   I'll about,
And drive away the vulgar from the streets:
So do you too, where you perceive them thick.
These growing feathers pluck'd from Cæsar's
  wing
Will make him fly an ordinary pitch,
Who else would soar above the view of men 79
And keep us all in servile fearfulness. [*Exeunt.*

SCENE II. *A public place.*

Flourish.   Enter Cæsar; Antony, *for the
 course;* Calpurnia, Portia, Decius, Cicero,
 Brutus, Cassius, *and* Casca; *a great crowd
 following, among them a* Soothsayer.

 Cæs. Calpurnia!
 Casca.   Peace, ho! Cæsar speaks.
 Cæs.   Calpurnia!
 Cal. Here, my lord.
 Cæs. Stand you directly in Antonius' way,
When he doth run his course.   Antonius!
 Ant. Cæsar, my lord?
 Cæs. Forget not, in your speed, Antonius,
To touch Calpurnia; for our elders say,
The barren, touched in this holy chase,
Shake off their sterile curse.
 Ant.   I shall remember:
When Cæsar says 'do this,' it is perform'd. 10
 Cæs. Set on; and leave no ceremony out.
          [*Flourish.*

 Sooth. Cæsar!
 Cæs. Ha! who calls?
 Casca. Bid every noise be still: peace yet
  again!
 Cæs. Who is it in the press that calls on me?
I hear a tongue, shriller than all the music,
Cry 'Cæsar!' Speak; Cæsar is turn'd to hear.
● *Sooth.* Beware the ides of March.
 Cæs.   What man is that?
 Bru. A soothsayer bids you beware the ides
  of March.   19
 Cæs. Set him before me; let me see his face.
 Cas. Fellow, come from the throng; look upon
  Cæsar.
 Cæs. What say'st thou to me now? speak
  once again.
 Sooth. Beware the ides of March.
 Cæs. He is a dreamer; let us leave him: pass.
     [*Sennet.   Exeunt all except
        Brutus and Cassius.*

 Cas. Will you go see the order of the course?
 Bru. Not I.
 Cas. I pray you, do.
 Bru. I am not gamesome: I do lack some
  part
Of that quick spirit that is in Antony.
Let me not hinder, Cassius, your desires; 30

70 *ceremonies.* Offerings.

72 *feast of Lupercal.* 15th February.

18 *ides.* 15th day of the month in March, May July, October (but the 13th day in the other months).

HE·IS·A·DREAMER·LET
VS·LEAVE·HIM⸱PASS

Caesar replies to the Soothsayer. Illustration by Byam Shaw, *The Chiswick Shakespeare*, 1900

SD [*Sennet*]. Flourish of trumpets.

42 *soil.* Taint.

71 *jealous on.* Suspicious of.

78 *the rout.* The common herd.

91 *favour.* Appearance.

Cassius: 'I know that virtue to be in you, Brutus, As well as I do know your outward favour'. Engraving by Kenny Meadows from Barry Cornwall's *Works of Shakspere*, 1846

I 'll leave you.
   Cas. Brutus, I do observe you now of late:
I have not from your eyes that gentleness
And show of love as I was wont to have:
You bear too stubborn and too strange a hand
Over your friend that loves you.
   Bru.   Cassius,
Be not deceived: if I have veil'd my look,
I turn the trouble of my countenance
Merely upon myself.   Vexed I am
Of late with passions of some difference,   40
Conceptions only proper to myself,
● Which give some soil perhaps to my behaviours;
But let not therefore my good friends be grieved—
Among which number, Cassius, be you one—
Nor construe any further my neglect,
Than that poor Brutus, with himself at war,
Forgets the shows of love to other men.
   Cas. Then, Brutus, I have much mistook your
       passion;
By means whereof this breast of mine hath buried
Thoughts of great value, worthy cogitations. 50
Tell me, good Brutus, can you see your face?
   Bru. No, Cassius; for the eye sees not itself,
But by reflection, by some other things.
   Cas. 'Tis just:
And it is very much lamented, Brutus,
That you have no such mirrors as will turn
Your hidden worthiness into your eye,
That you might see your shadow.   I have heard,
Where many of the best respect in Rome,
Except immortal Cæsar, speaking of Brutus 60
And groaning underneath this age's yoke,
Have wish'd that noble Brutus had his eyes.
   Bru. Into what dangers would you lead me,
       Cassius,
That you would have me seek into myself
For that which is not in me?
   Cas. Therefore, good Brutus, be prepared to
       hear:
And since you know you cannot see yourself
So well as by reflection, I, your glass,
Will modestly discover to yourself
That of yourself which you yet know not of. 70
● And be not jealous on me, gentle Brutus:
Were I a common laugher, or did use
To stale with ordinary oaths my love
To every new protester; if you know
That I do fawn on men and hug them hard
And after scandal them, or if you know
That I profess myself in banqueting
● To all the rout, then hold me dangerous.
                     [Flourish, and shout.
   Bru. What means this shouting? I do fear,
       the people
Choose Cæsar for their king.
   Cas.   Ay, do you fear it? 80
Then must I think you would not have it so.
   Bru. I would not, Cassius; yet I love him
       well.
But wherefore do you hold me here so long?
What is it that you would impart to me?
If it be aught toward the general good,
Set honour in one eye and death i' the other,
And I will look on both indifferently:
For let the gods so speed me as I love
The name of honour more than I fear death. 89
   Cas. I know that virtue to be in you, Brutus,
● As well as I do know your outward favour.

Well, honour is the subject of my story.
I cannot tell what you and other men
Think of this life; but, for my single self,
●I had as lief not be as live to be
In awe of such a thing as I myself.
I was born free as Cæsar; so were you:
We both have fed as well, and we can both
Endure the winter's cold as well as he:
For once, upon a raw and gusty day,   100
The troubled Tiber chafing with her shores,
Cæsar said to me 'Darest thou, Cassius, now
Leap in with me into this angry flood,
And swim to yonder point?' Upon the word,
●Accoutred as I was, I plunged in
And bade him follow; so indeed he did.
The torrent roar'd, and we did buffet it
With lusty sinews, throwing it aside
●And stemming it with hearts of controversy;
But ere we could arrive the point proposed,   110
Cæsar cried 'Help me, Cassius, or I sink!'
●I, as Æneas, our great ancestor,
Did from the flames of Troy upon his shoulder
The old Anchises bear, so from the waves of
        Tiber
Did I the tired Cæsar.   And this man
Is now become a god, and Cassius is
A wretched creature and must bend his body,
If Cæsar carelessly but nod on him.
He had a fever when he was in Spain,
And when the fit was on him, I did mark   120
How he did shake: 'tis true, this god did shake:
His coward lips did from their colour fly,
And that same eye whose bend doth awe the
        world
Did lose his lustre: I did hear him groan:
Ay, and that tongue of his that bade the Romans
Mark him and write his speeches in their books,
Alas, it cried 'Give me some drink, Titinius,'
As a sick girl.   Ye gods, it doth amaze me
A man of such a feeble temper should
●So get the start of the majestic world   130
And bear the palm alone.   [_Shout. Flourish._
      Bru. Another general shout!
I do believe that these applauses are
For some new honours that are heap'd on Cæsar.
      Cas. Why, man, he doth bestride the narrow
        world
Like a Colossus, and we petty men
Walk under his huge legs and peep about
To find ourselves dishonourable graves.
Men at some time are masters of their fates:
The fault, dear Brutus, is not in our stars,   140
But in ourselves, that we are underlings.
Brutus and Cæsar: what should be in that 'Cæsar'?
Why should that name be sounded more than
        yours?
Write them together, yours is as fair a name;
Sound them, it doth become the mouth as well;
Weigh them, it is as heavy; conjure with 'em,
Brutus will start a spirit as soon as Cæsar.
Now, in the names of all the gods at once,
Upon what meat doth this our Cæsar feed,   149
That he is grown so great? Age, thou art shamed!
Rome, thou hast lost the breed of noble bloods!
When went there by an age, since the great flood,
But it was famed with more than with one man?
When could they say till now, that talk'd of Rome,
That her wide walls encompass'd but one man?
Now is it Rome indeed and room enough,

95 _lief._ Soon.

105 _Accoutred._ Dressed up.

109 _stemming._ Overcoming. _controversy._ Determination.

112-14 _Aeneas . . . Anchises._ From Virgil's _Aeneid._

130 _get the start of._ Take first place.

159 *brook'd*. Allowed.

162 *I am nothing jealous*. I do not doubt.

163 *aim*. Notion.

184 *chidden*. Rebuked.

Caesar: 'Yond Cassius has a lean and hungry look'.
Cassius (John Gielgud) with Brutus (James Mason),
film directed by J. L. Mankiewicz, USA, 1953

197 *given*. Disposed.

When there is in it but one only man.
O, you and I have heard our fathers say,
● There was a Brutus once that would have brook'd
The eternal devil to keep his state in Rome   160
As easily as a king.
●   *Bru.* That you do love me, I am nothing jealous;
● What you would work me to, I have some aim:
How I have thought of this and of these times,
I shall recount hereafter; for this present,
I would not, so with love I might entreat you,
Be any further moved.   What you have said
I will consider; what you have to say
I will with patience hear, and find a time   169
Both meet to hear and answer such high things.
Till then, my noble friend, chew upon this:
Brutus had rather be a villager
Than to repute himself a son of Rome
Under these hard conditions as this time
Is like to lay upon us.
   Cas.   I am glad that my weak words
Have struck but thus much show of fire from
   Brutus.
   Bru.   The games are done and Cæsar is re-
turning.
   Cas.   As they pass by, pluck Casca by the sleeve;
And he will, after his sour fashion, tell you   180
What hath proceeded worthy note to-day.

      Re-enter CÆSAR *and his Train.*

   Bru.   I will do so.   But, look you, Cassius,
The angry spot doth glow on Cæsar's brow,
● And all the rest look like a chidden train:
Calpurnia's cheek is pale; and Cicero
Looks with such ferret and such fiery eyes
As we have seen him in the Capitol,
Being cross'd in conference by some senators.
   Cas.   Casca will tell us what the matter is.
   Cæs.   Antonius!   190
   Ant.   Cæsar?
   Cæs.   Let me have men about me that are fat:
Sleek-headed men and such as sleep o'nights:
Yond Cassius has a lean and hungry look;
He thinks too much: such men are dangerous.
   Ant.   Fear him not, Cæsar; he's not dangerous;
● He is a noble Roman and well given.
   Cæs.   Would he were fatter! But I fear him
not:
Yet if my name were liable to fear,
I do not know the man I should avoid   200
So soon as that spare Cassius. He reads much;
He is a great observer and he looks
Quite through the deeds of men; he loves no plays,
As thou dost, Antony; he hears no music;
Seldom he smiles, and smiles in such a sort
As if he mock'd himself and scorn'd his spirit
That could be moved to smile at any thing.
Such men as he be never at heart's ease
Whiles they behold a greater than themselves,
And therefore are they very dangerous.   210
I rather tell thee what is to be fear'd
Than what I fear; for always I am Cæsar.
Come on my right hand, for this ear is deaf,
And tell me truly what thou think'st of him.
      [*Sennet.   Exeunt Cæsar and all his
            Train, but Casca.*
   Casca.   You pull'd me by the cloak; would you
   speak with me?
   Bru.   Ay, Casca; tell us what hath chanced
   to-day,

That Cæsar looks so sad.

Casca. Why, you were with him, were you not?

Bru. I should not then ask Casca what had chanced. 219

Casca. Why, there was a crown offered him: and being offered him, he put it by with the back of his hand, thus; and then the people fell a-shouting.

Bru. What was the second noise for?

Casca. Why, for that too.

Cas. They shouted thrice: what was the last cry for?

Casca. Why, for that too.

Bru. Was the crown offered him thrice?

Casca. Ay, marry, was't, and he put it by thrice, every time gentler than other, and at every putting-by mine honest neighbours shouted.

Cas. Who offered him the crown?

Casca. Why, Antony.

Bru. Tell us the manner of it, gentle Casca.

Casca. I can as well be hanged as tell the manner of it: it was mere foolery; I did not mark it. I saw Mark Antony offer him a crown;—yet 'twas not a crown neither, 'twas one of these coronets;—and, as I told you, he put it by once: but,
• for all that, to my thinking, he would fain have had it. Then he offered it to him again; then he put it by again: but, to my thinking, he was very loath to lay his fingers off it. And then he offered it the third time; he put it the third time by: and still as he refused it, the rabblement hooted and
• clapped their chopped hands and threw up their sweaty night-caps and uttered such a deal of stinking breath because Cæsar refused the crown
• that it had almost choked Cæsar; for he swounded and fell down at it: and for mine own part, I durst not laugh, for fear of opening my lips and receiving the bad air.

Cas. But, soft, I pray you: what, did Cæsar swound?

Casca. He fell down in the market-place, and foamed at mouth, and was speechless.

• *Bru.* 'Tis very like: he hath the falling sickness.

Cas. No, Cæsar hath it not; but you and I And honest Casca, we have the falling sickness.

Casca. I know not what you mean by that;
• but, I am sure, Cæsar fell down. If the tag-rag people did not clap him and hiss him, according as he pleased and displeased them, as they use to do the players in the theatre, I am no true man.

Bru. What said he when he came unto himself?

Casca. Marry, before he fell down, when he perceived the common herd was glad he refused the crown, he plucked me ope his doublet and offered them his throat to cut. An I had been a man of any occupation, if I would not have taken him at a word, I would I might go to hell among the rogues. And so he fell. When he came to himself again, he said, If he had done or said any thing amiss, he desired their worships to think it was his infirmity. Three or four wenches, where I stood, cried 'Alas, good soul!' and forgave him with all their hearts: but there's no heed to be taken of them; if Cæsar had stabbed their mothers, they would have done no less.

Bru. And after that, he came, thus sad, away?

Casca. Ay. 280

Cas. Did Cicero say any thing?

Casca. Ay, he spoke Greek.

Costume design for Brutus by John Bury, Royal Shakespeare Co, 1963

---

240 *fain.* Gladly.

246 *chopped.* Chapped.

249 *swounded.* Fainted.

256 *falling sickness.* Epilepsy.

260–263 *If the tag-rag ... true man.* See introduction.

317 *bear me hard.* i.e. can scarcely bear me.

Casca: 'Are not you moved, when all the sway of earth Shakes like a thing unfirm?' Engraving of Casca and Cicero by Kenny Meadows from Barry Cornwall's *Works of Shakspere*, 1846

---

6 *rived.* Split.

Cas. To what effect?

Casca. Nay, an I tell you that, I'll ne'er look you i' the face again: but those that understood him smiled at one another and shook their heads; but, for mine own part, it was Greek to me. I could tell you more news too: Marullus and Flavius, for pulling scarfs off Cæsar's images, are put to silence. Fare you well. There was more foolery yet, if I could remember it.   291

Cas. Will you sup with me to-night, Casca?

Casca. No, I am promised forth.

Cas. Will you dine with me to-morrow?

Casca. Ay, if I be alive and your mind hold and your dinner worth the eating.

Cas. Good: I will expect you.

Casca. Do so. Farewell, both.   [*Exit.*

Bru. What a blunt fellow is this grown to be! He was quick mettle when he went to school. 300

Cas. So is he now in execution
Of any bold or noble enterprise,
However he puts on this tardy form.
This rudeness is a sauce to his good wit,
Which gives men stomach to digest his words
With better appetite.

Bru. And so it is. For this time I will leave you:
To-morrow, if you please to speak with me,
I will come home to you; or, if you will,
Come home to me, and I will wait for you.   310

Cas. I will do so: till then, think of the world.
      [*Exit Brutus.*
Well, Brutus, thou art noble; yet, I see,
Thy honourable metal may be wrought
From that it is disposed: therefore it is meet
That noble minds keep ever with their likes;
For who so firm that cannot be seduced?
•Cæsar doth bear me hard; but he loves Brutus:
If I were Brutus now and he were Cassius,
He should not humour me. I will this night,
In several hands, in at his windows throw,   320
As if they came from several citizens,
Writings all tending to the great opinion
That Rome holds of his name; wherein obscurely
Cæsar's ambition shall be glanced at:
And after this let Cæsar seat him sure;
For we will shake him, or worse days endure.
      [*Exit.*

SCENE III. *The same. A street.*

Thunder and lightning. Enter, from opposite sides, CASCA, *with his sword drawn,* and CICERO.

Cic. Good even, Casca: brought you Cæsar home?
Why are you breathless? and why stare you so?

Casca. Are not you moved, when all the sway of earth
Shakes like a thing unfirm? O Cicero,
I have seen tempests, when the scolding winds
•Have rived the knotty oaks, and I have seen
The ambitious ocean swell and rage and foam,
To be exalted with the threatening clouds:
But never till to-night, never till now,
Did I go through a tempest dropping fire.   10
Either there is a civil strife in heaven,
Or else the world, too saucy with the gods,
Incenses them to send destruction.

Cic. Why, saw you any thing more wonderful?

Casca. A common slave—you know him well by sight—

Held up his left hand, which did flame and burn
Like twenty torches join'd, and yet his hand,
Not sensible of fire, remain'd unscorch'd.
Besides—I ha' not since put up my sword—
Against the Capitol I met a lion,   20
Who glared upon me, and went surly by,
Without annoying me : and there were drawn
Upon a heap a hundred ghastly women,
Transformed with their fear ; who swore they saw
Men all in fire walk up and down the streets.
●And yesterday the bird of night did sit
Even at noon-day upon the market-place,
Hooting and shrieking.   When these prodigies
Do so conjointly meet, let not men say
'These are their reasons ; they are natural ;'   30
For, I believe, they are portentous things
●Unto the climate that they point upon.
    Cic.   Indeed, it is a strange-disposed time :
But men may construe things after their fashion,
Clean from the purpose of the things themselves.
Comes Cæsar to the Capitol to-morrow?
    Casca.   He doth ; for he did bid Antonius
Send word to you he would be there to-morrow.
    Cic.   Good night then, Casca : this disturbed
       sky
Is not to walk in.
    Casca.   Farewell, Cicero. [*Exit Cicero.* 40

            Enter CASSIUS.

    Cas.   Who's there?
    Casca.   A Roman.
    Cas.   Casca, by your voice.
    Casca.   Your ear is good.   Cassius, what night
       is this !
    Cas.   A very pleasing night to honest men.
    Casca.   Who ever knew the heavens menace so?
    Cas.   Those that have known the earth so full
       of faults.
For my part, I have walk'd about the streets,
Submitting me unto the perilous night,
And, thus unbraced, Casca, as you see,
Have bared my bosom to the thunder-stone ;
And when the cross blue lightning seem'd to open
The breast of heaven, I did present myself   51
Even in the aim and very flash of it.
    Casca.   But wherefore did you so much tempt
       the heavens?
It is the part of men to fear and tremble,
When the most mighty gods by tokens send
Such dreadful heralds to astonish us.
    Cas.   You are dull, Casca, and those sparks
       of life
That should be in a Roman you do want,
Or else you use not.   You look pale and gaze
And put on fear and cast yourself in wonder,   60
To see the strange impatience of the heavens :
But if you would consider the true cause
Why all these fires, why all these gliding ghosts,
Why birds and beasts from quality and kind,
●Why old men fool and children calculate,
●Why all these things change from their ordinance
Their natures and preformed faculties
To monstrous quality,—why, you shall find
That heaven hath infused them with these spirits,
To make them instruments of fear and warning 70
Unto some monstrous state.
Now could I, Casca, name to thee a man
Most like this dreadful night,

26 *the bird of night.* i.e. owl.

32 *climate.* Situation.

65 *calculate.* Prophesy.

66 *ordinance.* Normal pattern.

77 *prodigious*. Portentous.

81 *thews*. Sinews.

117 *fleering*. Sneering.

118 *factious*. Active.

129 *favour*. Appearance.

That thunders, lightens, opens graves, and roars
As doth the lion in the Capitol,
A man no mightier than thyself or me
● In personal action, yet prodigious grown
And fearful, as these strange eruptions are.
   Casca. 'Tis Cæsar that you mean; is it not,
     Cassius?
   Cas. Let it be who it is: for Romans now 80
● Have thews and limbs like to their ancestors;
But, woe the while! our fathers' minds are dead,
And we are govern'd with our mothers' spirits;
Our yoke and sufferance show us womanish.
   Casca. Indeed, they say the senators to-mor-
     row
Mean to establish Cæsar as a king;
And he shall wear his crown by sea and land,
In every place, save here in Italy.
   Cas. I know where I will wear this dagger
     then;
Cassius from bondage will deliver Cassius: 90
Therein, ye gods, you make the weak most strong;
Therein, ye gods, you tyrants do defeat:
Nor stony tower, nor walls of beaten brass,
Nor airless dungeon, nor strong links of iron,
Can be retentive to the strength of spirit;
But life, being weary of these worldly bars,
Never lacks power to dismiss itself.
If I know this, know all the world besides,
That part of tyranny that I do bear
I can shake off at pleasure.   [*Thunder still.*
   Casca.   So can I: 100
So every bondman in his own hand bears
The power to cancel his captivity.
   Cas. And why should Cæsar be a tyrant then?
Poor man! I know he would not be a wolf,
But that he sees the Romans are but sheep:
He were no lion, were not Romans hinds.
Those that with haste will make a mighty fire
Begin it with weak straws: what trash is Rome,
What rubbish and what offal, when it serves
For the base matter to illuminate 110
So vile a thing as Cæsar! But, O grief,
Where hast thou led me? I perhaps speak this
Before a willing bondman; then I know
My answer must be made. But I am arm'd,
And dangers are to me indifferent.
   Casca. You speak to Casca, and to such a man
● That is no fleering tell-tale. Hold, my hand:
● Be factious for redress of all these griefs,
And I will set this foot of mine as far
As who goes farthest.
   Cas.   There's a bargain made. 120
Now know you, Casca, I have moved already
Some certain of the noblest-minded Romans
To undergo with me an enterprise
Of honourable-dangerous consequence;
And I do know, by this, they stay for me
In Pompey's porch: for now, this fearful night,
There is no stir or walking in the streets;
And the complexion of the element
● In favour's like the work we have in hand,
Most bloody, fiery, and most terrible. 130
   Casca. Stand close awhile, for here comes one
     in haste.
   Cas. 'Tis Cinna; I do know him by his gait.
He is a friend.

       Enter CINNA.
Cinna, where haste you so?

Cin. To find out you.   Who's that? Metellus
        Cimber?
● *Cas.* No, it is Casca; one incorporate
To our attempts.   Am I not stay'd for, Cinna?
        Cin. I am glad on't.   What a fearful night is
        this!
There's two or three of us have seen strange
        sights.
        Cas. Am I not stay'd for? tell me.
        Cin.   Yes, you are.
O Cassius, if you could   140
But win the noble Brutus to our party—
        Cas. Be you content: good Cinna, take this
        paper,
●And look you lay it in the prætor's chair,
Where Brutus may but find it: and throw this
In at his window; set this up with wax
Upon old Brutus' statue: all this done,
Repair to Pompey's porch, where you shall find us.
Is Decius Brutus and Trebonius there?
        Cin. All but Metellus Cimber; and he's gone
●To seek you at your house.   Well, I will hie, 150
And so bestow these papers as you bade me.
        Cas. That done, repair to Pompey's theatre.
                                                [*Exit Cinna.*
Come, Casca, you and I will yet ere day
See Brutus at his house: three parts of him
Is ours already, and the man entire
Upon the next encounter yields him ours.
        Casca. O, he sits high in all the people's
        hearts:
And that which would appear offence in us,
His countenance, like richest alchemy,
Will change to virtue and to worthiness.   160
        Cas. Him and his worth and our great need
        of him
●You have right well conceited.   Let us go,
For it is after midnight; and ere day
We will awake him and be sure of him. [*Exeunt.*

ACT II.

SCENE I. *Rome.   Brutus's orchard.*

Enter BRUTUS.

Bru. What, Lucius, ho!
I cannot, by the progress of the stars,
Give guess how near to day.   Lucius, I say!
I would it were my fault to sleep so soundly.
When, Lucius, when? awake, I say! what,
        Lucius!

Enter LUCIUS.

Luc. Call'd you, my lord?
Bru. Get me a taper in my study, Lucius:
When it is lighted, come and call me here.
        Luc. I will, my lord.   [*Exit.*
        Bru. It must be by his death: and for my part,
I know no personal cause to spurn at him,   11
●But for the general.   He would be crown'd:
How that might change his nature, there's the
        question.
It is the bright day that brings forth the adder;
●And that craves wary walking.   Crown him?—
        that;—
And then, I grant, we put a sting in him,
That at his will he may do danger with.
The abuse of greatness is, when it disjoins

135–136 *incorporate To.* Involved in.

143 *praetor's.* Magistrate's.

150 *hie.* Hasten.

162 *conceited.* Judged.

Brutus: 'It must be by his death'. Thomas Sheridan as
Brutus. Engraving from Bell's edition of *Shakespeare*,
1778

12 *general.* Commonweal.

15 *craves.* Requires.

Basil Gill as Brutus, St James's Theatre, London, 1920

21 *proof.* Experience.

24 *round.* Rung.

26 *base degrees.* Lower steps.

29 *bear no colour.* Not excuse.

30 *Fashion.* Put.

54 *Tarquin.* Last king of Rome, and father of the Tarquin (Sextus) who raped Lucrece. This event resulted in the expulsion of the Tarquins and the overthrow of the monarchy, a movement led by Brutus's ancestor, Lucius Junius Brutus.

66 *mortal instruments.* The powers of the body.

Remorse from power: and, to speak truth of Cæsar,
I have not known when his affections sway'd 20
● More than his reason.   But 'tis a common proof,
That lowliness is young ambition's ladder,
Whereto the climber-upward turns his face;
● But when he once attains the upmost round,
He then unto the ladder turns his back,
● Looks in the clouds, scorning the base degrees
By which he did ascend.   So Cæsar may.
Then, lest he may, prevent.   And, since the quarrel
● Will bear no colour for the thing he is,
● Fashion it thus; that what he is, augmented, 30
Would run to these and these extremities:
And therefore think him as a serpent's egg
Which, hatch'd, would, as his kind, grow mischievous,
And kill him in the shell.

Re-enter LUCIUS.

Luc.   The taper burneth in your closet, sir.
Searching the window for a flint, I found
This paper, thus seal'd up; and, I am sure,
It did not lie there when I went to bed.
[*Gives him the letter*
Bru.   Get you to bed again; it is not day.
Is not to-morrow, boy, the ides of March? 40
Luc.   I know not, sir.
Bru.   Look in the calendar, and bring me word.
Luc.   I will, sir. [*Exit.*
Bru.   The exhalations whizzing in the air
Give so much light that I may read by them.
[*Opens the letter and reads.*
'Brutus, thou sleep'st: awake, and see thyself.
Shall Rome, &c.   Speak, strike, redress!
Brutus, thou sleep'st: awake!'
Such instigations have been often dropp'd
Where I have took them up. 50
'Shall Rome, &c.'   Thus must I piece it out:
Shall Rome stand under one man's awe?   What, Rome?
My ancestors did from the streets of Rome
● The Tarquin drive, when he was call'd a king.
'Speak, strike, redress!'   Am I entreated
To speak and strike?   O Rome, I make thee promise;
If the redress will follow, thou receivest
Thy full petition at the hand of Brutus!

Re-enter LUCIUS.

Luc.   Sir, March is wasted fourteen days.
[*Knocking within.*
Bru.   'Tis good.   Go to the gate; somebody knocks. [*Exit Lucius.* 60
Since Cassius first did whet me against Cæsar,
I have not slept.
Between the acting of a dreadful thing
And the first motion, all the interim is
Like a phantasma, or a hideous dream:
● The Genius and the mortal instruments
Are then in council; and the state of man,
Like to a little kingdom, suffers then
The nature of an insurrection.

Re-enter LUCIUS.

Luc.   Sir, 'tis your brother Cassius at the door,
Who doth desire to see you.
Bru.   Is he alone? 71

Luc.   No, sir, there are moe with him.
Bru.   Do you know them?
Luc.   No, sir; their hats are pluck'd about
their ears,
And half their faces buried in their cloaks,
That by no means I may discover them
By any mark of favour.
Bru.   Let 'em enter. [*Exit Lucius.*
They are the faction. O conspiracy,
Shamest thou to show thy dangerous brow by
night,
When evils are most free? O, then by day
Where wilt thou find a cavern dark enough   80
To mask thy monstrous visage? Seek none, con-
spiracy;
Hide it in smiles and affability:
For if thou path, thy native semblance on,
Not Erebus itself were dim enough
To hide thee from prevention.

Enter the conspirators, CASSIUS, CASCA, DECIUS,
CINNA, METELLUS CIMBER, *and* TREBONIUS.

Cas.   I think we are too bold upon your rest:
Good morrow, Brutus; do we trouble you?
Bru.   I have been up this hour, awake all
night.
Know I these men that come along with you?
Cas.   Yes, every man of them, and no man
here   90
But honours you; and every one doth wish
You had but that opinion of yourself
Which every noble Roman bears of you.
This is Trebonius.
Bru.   He is welcome hither.
Cas.   This, Decius Brutus.
Bru.   He is welcome too.
Cas.   This, Casca; this, Cinna; and this, Me-
tellus Cimber.
Bru.   They are all welcome.
What watchful cares do interpose themselves
Betwixt your eyes and night?
Cas.   Shall I entreat a word?   100
        [*Brutus and Cassius whisper.*
Dec.   Here lies the east: doth not the day
break here?
Casca.   No.
Cin.   O, pardon, sir, it doth; and yon gray
lines
That fret the clouds are messengers of day.
Casca.   You shall confess that you are both
deceived.
Here, as I point my sword, the sun arises,
Which is a great way growing on the south,
Weighing the youthful season of the year.
Some two months hence up higher toward the
north
He first presents his fire; and the high east   110
Stands, as the Capitol, directly here.
Bru.   Give me your hands all over, one by one.
Cas.   And let us swear our resolution.
Bru.   No, not an oath: if not the face of men,
The sufferance of our souls, the time's abuse,—
If these be motives weak, break off betimes,
And every man hence to his idle bed;
So let high-sighted tyranny range on,
Till each man drop by lottery. But if these,
As I am sure they do, bear fire enough   120
To kindle cowards and to steel with valour
The melting spirits of women, then, countrymen,

72 *moe.* More.

73 *pluck'd.* Pulled down.

76 *mark of favour.* External feature.

83 *path.* Go about. *thy native semblance on.* Showing
yourself as you are.

84 *Erebus.* Mythical dark area beneath the earth on the
way to hell.

85 *prevention.* Detection.

Brutus: 'Know I these men that come along with you?'
Engraving of Brutus with the conspirators by Kenny
Meadows from Barry Cornwall's *Works of Shakspere,*
1846

Cassius and Brutus with the conspirators. Illustration by Byam Shaw, *The Chiswick Shakespeare*, 1900

126 *palter*. Shuffle.

129 *cautelous*. Crafty.

133 *even*. Solid.

138 *several bastardy*. Particular baseness.

What need we any spur but our own cause,
To prick us to redress? what other bond
Than secret Romans, that have spoke the word,
● And will not palter? and what other oath
Than honesty to honesty engaged,
That this shall be, or we will fall for it?
● Swear priests and cowards and men cautelous,
Old feeble carrions and such suffering souls   130
That welcome wrongs; unto bad causes swear
Such creatures as men doubt; but do not stain
● The even virtue of our enterprise,
Nor the insuppressive mettle of our spirits,
To think that or our cause or our performance
Did need an oath; when every drop of blood
That every Roman bears, and nobly bears,
● Is guilty of a several bastardy,
If he do break the smallest particle
Of any promise that hath pass'd from him.   140
  Cas.   But what of Cicero? shall we sound him?
I think he will stand very strong with us.
  Casca.   Let us not leave him out.
  Cin.   No, by no means.
  Met.   O, let us have him, for his silver hairs
Will purchase us a good opinion
And buy men's voices to commend our deeds:
It shall be said, his judgement ruled our hands;
Our youths and wildness shall no whit appear,
But all be buried in his gravity.
  Bru.   O, name him not: let us not break with
        him;   150
For he will never follow any thing
That other men begin.
  Cas.   Then leave him out.
  Casca.   Indeed he is not fit.
  Dec.   Shall no man else be touch'd but only
        Cæsar?
  Cas.   Decius, well urged: I think it is not
        meet,
Mark Antony, so well beloved of Cæsar,
Should outlive Cæsar: we shall find of him
A shrewd contriver; and, you know, his means,
If he improve them, may well stretch so far
As to annoy us all: which to prevent,   160
Let Antony and Cæsar fall together.
  Bru.   Our course will seem too bloody, Caius
        Cassius,
To cut the head off and then hack the limbs,
Like wrath in death and envy afterwards;
For Antony is but a limb of Cæsar:
Let us be sacrificers, but not butchers, Caius.
We all stand up against the spirit of Cæsar;
And in the spirit of men there is no blood:
O, that we then could come by Cæsar's spirit,
And not dismember Cæsar! But, alas,   170
Cæsar must bleed for it! And, gentle friends,
Let's kill him boldly, but not wrathfully;
Let's carve him as a dish fit for the gods,
Not hew him as a carcass fit for hounds:
And let our hearts, as subtle masters do,
Stir up their servants to an act of rage,
And after seem to chide 'em. This shall make
Our purpose necessary and not envious:
Which so appearing to the common eyes,
We shall be call'd purgers, not murderers.   180
And for Mark Antony, think not of him;
For he can do no more than Cæsar's arm
When Cæsar's head is off.
  Cas.   Yet I fear him;
For in the ingrafted love he bears to Cæsar—

Bru. Alas, good Cassius, do not think of him:
If he love Cæsar, all that he can do
Is to himself, take thought and die for Cæsar:
And that were much he should; for he is given
To sports, to wildness and much company.
  Treb. There is no fear in him; let him not die;
For he will live, and laugh at this hereafter. 191
                              [*Clock strikes.*
  Bru. Peace! count the clock.
  Cas.   The clock hath stricken three.
  Treb. 'Tis time to part.
  Cas.   But it is doubtful yet,
Whether Cæsar will come forth to-day, or no;
For he is superstitious grown of late,
Quite from the main opinion he held once
Of fantasy, of dreams and ceremonies:
It may be, these apparent prodigies,
The unaccustom'd terror of this night,
And the persuasion of his augurers, 200
May hold him from the Capitol to-day.
  Dec. Never fear that: if he be so resolved,
I can o'ersway him; for he loves to hear
That unicorns may be betray'd with trees,
And bears with glasses, elephants with holes,
●Lions with toils and men with flatterers;
●But when I tell him he hates flatterers,
He says he does, being then most flattered.
Let me work;
●For I can give his humour the true bent, 210
And I will bring him to the Capitol.
  Cas. Nay, we will all of us be there to fetch
    him.
  Bru. By the eighth hour: is that the utter-
    most?
  Cin. Be that the uttermost, and fail not then.
  Met. Caius Ligarius doth bear Cæsar hard,
Who rated him for speaking well of Pompey:
I wonder none of you have thought of him.
  Bru. Now, good Metellus, go along by him:
He loves me well, and I have given him reasons;
Send him but hither, and I'll fashion him. 220
  Cas. The morning comes upon 's: we'll leave
    you, Brutus.
And, friends, disperse yourselves; but all re-
    member
What you have said, and show yourselves true
    Romans.
  Bru. Good gentlemen, look fresh and merrily:
Let not our looks put on our purposes,
But bear it as our Roman actors do,
With untired spirits and formal constancy:
And so good morrow to you every one.
                    [*Exeunt all but Brutus.*
Boy! Lucius! Fast asleep? It is no matter;
Enjoy the honey-heavy dew of slumber: 230
●Thou hast no figures nor no fantasies,
Which busy care draws in the brains of men;
Therefore thou sleep'st so sound.

              Enter PORTIA.

  Por.   Brutus, my lord!
  Bru. Portia, what mean you? wherefore rise
    you now?
It is not for your health thus to commit
Your weak condition to the raw cold morning.
  Por. Nor for yours neither. You've ungently,
    Brutus,
Stole from my bed: and yesternight, at supper,
You suddenly arose, and walk'd about,

206 *toils.* Snares.

207–208 *But when . . . flattered.* See introduction.

210 *I can give his humour the true bent.* i.e. I can make
him incline his mind.

231 *figures nor no fantasies.* Dreams and imaginings.

Portia: 'You've ungently, Brutus, Stole from my bed:'
Alec Clunes as Brutus and Joan Miller as Portia,
Stratford-upon-Avon, 1957

246 *wafture.* Waving.

253 *shape.* Appearance.

254 *condition.* Mind.

259 *come by it.* Recover.

261 *physical.* Healthy.

271 *charm.* Entreat.

Brutus: 'Kneel not, gentle Portia.' Drawing of Portia and Brutus by J. M. Wright (1777–1866)

295 *Cato.* A famous Roman statesman, much honoured for uprightness.

Musing and sighing, with your arms across,   240
And when I ask'd you what the matter was,
You stared upon me with ungentle looks;
I urged you further; then you scratch'd your
   head,
And too impatiently stamp'd with your foot;
Yet I insisted, yet you answer'd not,
● But, with an angry wafture of your hand,
Gave sign for me to leave you: so I did;
Fearing to strengthen that impatience
Which seem'd too much enkindled, and withal
Hoping it was but an effect of humour,   250
Which sometime hath his hour with every man.
It will not let you eat, nor talk, nor sleep,
● And could it work so much upon your shape
● As it hath much prevail'd on your condition,
I should not know you, Brutus.   Dear my lord,
Make me acquainted with your cause of grief.
   Bru.   I am not well in health, and that is all.
   Por.   Brutus is wise, and, were he not in
      health,
● He would embrace the means to come by it.
   Bru.   Why, so I do.   Good Portia, go to bed.
● *Por.*   Is Brutus sick? and is it physical   261
To walk unbraced and suck up the humours
Of the dank morning?   What, is Brutus sick,
And will he steal out of his wholesome bed,
To dare the vile contagion of the night
And tempt the rheumy and unpurged air
To add unto his sickness?   No, my Brutus;
You have some sick offence within your mind,
Which, by the right and virtue of my place,
I ought to know of: and, upon my knees,   270
● I charm you, by my once-commended beauty,
By all your vows of love and that great vow
Which did incorporate and make us one,
That you unfold to me, yourself, your half,
Why you are heavy, and what men to-night
Have had resort to you: for here have been
Some six or seven, who did hide their faces
Even from darkness.
   Bru.   Kneel not, gentle Portia.
   Por.   I should not need, if you were gentle
      Brutus.
Within the bond of marriage, tell me, Brutus,   280
Is it excepted I should know no secrets
That appertain to you?   Am I yourself
But, as it were, in sort or limitation,
To keep with you at meals, comfort your bed,
And talk to you sometimes?   Dwell I but in the
      suburbs
Of your good pleasure?   If it be no more,
Portia is Brutus' harlot, not his wife.
   Bru.   You are my true and honourable wife,
As dear to me as are the ruddy drops
That visit my sad heart.   290
   Por.   If this were true, then should I know
      this secret.
I grant I am a woman; but withal
A woman that Lord Brutus took to wife:
I grant I am a woman; but withal
● A woman well-reputed, Cato's daughter.
Think you I am no stronger than my sex,
Being so father'd and so husbanded?
Tell me your counsels, I will not disclose 'em:
I have made strong proof of my constancy,
Giving myself a voluntary wound   300
Here, in the thigh: can I bear that with patience,
And not my husband's secrets?

Bru.   O ye gods,
Render me worthy of this noble wife!
                    [*Knocking within.*
Hark, hark! one knocks: Portia, go in awhile;
And by and by thy bosom shall partake
The secrets of my heart.
● All my engagements I will construe to thee,
● All the charactery of my sad brows:
Leave me with haste. [*Exit Portia.*] Lucius,
        who's that knocks?

        Re-enter LUCIUS *with* LIGARIUS.

    Luc. Here is a sick man that would speak
        with you.   310
    Bru. Caius Ligarius, that Metellus spake of.
Boy, stand aside. Caius Ligarius! how?
● *Lig.* Vouchsafe good morrow from a feeble
        tongue.
    Bru. O, what a time have you chose out,
        brave Caius,
To wear a kerchief! Would you were not sick!
    Lig. I am not sick, if Brutus have in hand
Any exploit worthy the name of honour.
    Bru. Such an exploit have I in hand, Ligarius,
Had you a healthful ear to hear of it.
    Lig. By all the gods that Romans bow before,
I here discard my sickness! Soul of Rome! 321
Brave son, derived from honourable loins!
Thou, like an exorcist, hast conjured up
My mortified spirit. Now bid me run,
And I will strive with things impossible;
Yea, get the better of them. What's to do?
    Bru. A piece of work that will make sick
        men whole.
    Lig. But are not some whole that we must
        make sick?
    Bru. That must we also. What it is, my
        Caius,
I shall unfold to thee, as we are going   330
To whom it must be done.
    Lig.   Set on your foot,
And with a heart new-fired I follow you,
To do I know not what: but it sufficeth
That Brutus leads me on.
    Bru.   Follow me, then. [*Exeunt.*

        SCENE II. *Cæsar's house.*

Thunder and lightning. Enter CÆSAR, *in
        his night-gown.*

    Cæs. Nor heaven nor earth have been at
        peace to-night:
Thrice hath Calpurnia in her sleep cried out,
'Help, ho! they murder Cæsar!' Who's within?

        Enter a Servant.

    Serv. My lord?
    Cæs. Go bid the priests do present sacrifice
And bring me their opinions of success.
    Serv. I will, my lord.   [*Exit.*

        Enter CALPURNIA.

    Cal. What mean you, Cæsar? think you to
        walk forth?
You shall not stir out of your house to-day.
    Cæs. Cæsar shall forth: the things that
        threaten'd me   10
Ne'er look'd but on my back; when they shall see
The face of Cæsar, they are vanished.

307 *construe.* Explain.

308 *charactery.* Expression.

313 *Vouchsafe.* Accept.

NOR·HEAVEN·NOR·EARTH
HAVE·BEEN·AT·PEACE·Tonight

Caesar in his nightgown. Illustration by Byam Shaw,
The Chiswick Shakespeare, 1900

13 *stood on ceremonies.* Attached importance to omens.

25 *use.* Normality.

Caesar with Calpurnia. Drawing by J. H. Ramberg (1763–1840)

49 *consumed in confidence.* i.e. blinded by over-confidence.

56 *humour.* Whim.

● *Cal.*   Cæsar, I never stood on ceremonies,
Yet now they fright me.   There is one within,
Besides the things that we have heard and seen,
Recounts most horrid sights seen by the watch.
A lioness hath whelped in the streets;
And graves have yawn'd, and yielded up their dead;
Fierce fiery warriors fought upon the clouds,
In ranks and squadrons and right form of war, 20
Which drizzled blood upon the Capitol;
The noise of battle hurtled in the air,
Horses did neigh, and dying men did groan,
And ghosts did shriek and squeal about the streets.
●O Cæsar! these things are beyond all use,
And I do fear them.
   Cæs.   What can be avoided
Whose end is purposed by the mighty gods?
Yet Cæsar shall go forth; for these predictions
Are to the world in general as to Cæsar.
   Cal.   When beggars die, there are no comets seen;   30
The heavens themselves blaze forth the death of princes.
   Cæs.   Cowards die many times before their deaths;
The valiant never taste of death but once.
Of all the wonders that I yet have heard,
It seems to me most strange that men should fear;
Seeing that death, a necessary end,
Will come when it will come.

Re-enter Servant.

                                What say the augurers?
   Serv.   They would not have you to stir forth to-day.
Plucking the entrails of an offering forth,
They could not find a heart within the beast.   40
   Cæs.   The gods do this in shame of cowardice:
Cæsar should be a beast without a heart,
If he should stay at home to-day for fear.
No, Cæsar shall not: danger knows full well
That Cæsar is more dangerous than he:
We are two lions litter'd in one day,
And I the elder and more terrible:
And Cæsar shall go forth.
   Cal.   Alas, my lord,
●Your wisdom is consumed in confidence.
Do not go forth to-day: call it my fear   50
That keeps you in the house, and not your own.
We'll send Mark Antony to the senate-house;
And he shall say you are not well to-day:
Let me, upon my knee, prevail in this.
   Cæs.   Mark Antony shall say I am not well;
●And, for thy humour, I will stay at home.

Enter Decius.

Here's Decius Brutus, he shall tell them so.
   Dec.   Cæsar, all hail! good morrow, worthy Cæsar:
I come to fetch you to the senate-house.
   Cæs.   And you are come in very happy time, 60
To bear my greeting to the senators
And tell them that I will not come to-day:
Cannot, is false, and that I dare not, falser:
I will not come to-day: tell them so, Decius.
   Cal.   Say he is sick.
   Cæs.   Shall Cæsar send a lie?
Have I in conquest stretch'd mine arm so far,

To be afeard to tell graybeards the truth?
Decius, go tell them Cæsar will not come.
   Dec. Most mighty Cæsar, let me know some cause,
Lest I be laugh'd at when I tell them so.   70
   Cæs. The cause is in my will: I will not come;
That is enough to satisfy the senate.
But for your private satisfaction,
Because I love you, I will let you know:
Calpurnia here, my wife, stays me at home:
• She dreamt to-night she saw my statua,
Which, like a fountain with an hundred spouts,
Did run pure blood; and many lusty Romans
Came smiling, and did bathe their hands in it:
And these does she apply for warnings, and portents,   80
And evils imminent; and on her knee
Hath begg'd that I will stay at home to-day.
   Dec. This dream is all amiss interpreted;
It was a vision fair and fortunate:
Your statue spouting blood in many pipes,
In which so many smiling Romans bathed,
Signifies that from you great Rome shall suck
Reviving blood, and that great men shall press
For tinctures, stains, relics and cognizance.
This by Calpurnia's dream is signified.   90
   Cæs. And this way have you well expounded it.
   Dec. I have, when you have heard what I can say:
And know it now: the senate have concluded
To give this day a crown to mighty Cæsar.
If you shall send them word you will not come,
• Their minds may change. Besides, it were a mock
Apt to be render'd, for some one to say
' Break up the senate till another time,
When Cæsar's wife shall meet with better dreams.'
If Cæsar hide himself, shall they not whisper 100
' Lo, Cæsar is afraid'?
Pardon me, Cæsar; for my dear dear love
• To your proceeding bids me tell you this;
And reason to my love is liable.
   Cæs. How foolish do your fears seem now, Calpurnia!
I am ashamed I did yield to them.
Give me my robe, for I will go.

Enter PUBLIUS, BRUTUS, LIGARIUS, METELLUS,
   CASCA, TREBONIUS, *and* CINNA.

And look where Publius is come to fetch me.
   Pub. Good morrow, Cæsar.
   Cæs.   Welcome, Publius.
What, Brutus, are you stirr'd so early too?   110
Good morrow, Casca. Caius Ligarius,
Cæsar was ne'er so much your enemy
As that same ague which hath made you lean.
What is 't o'clock?
   Bru.   Cæsar, 'tis strucken eight.
   Cæs. I thank you for your pains and courtesy.

Enter ANTONY.

See! Antony, that revels long o' nights,
Is notwithstanding up. Good morrow, Antony.
   Ant. So to most noble Cæsar.
   Cæs.   Bid them prepare within:

76 *statua.* Statue.

96 *mock.* Taunt.

103 *To your proceeding.* For your future.

Wendy Hiller as Calpurnia, Old Vic Theatre, London, 1955

Julius Caesar. Engraving from a Roman medal in
G. du Choul's *Discours de la Religion des Anciens
Romains*, 1567

---

14 *Out of the teeth of emulation.* i.e. beyond the reach of
envy.

18 *rumour.* Noise.

I am to blame to be thus waited for.
Now, Cinna : now, Metellus : what, Trebonius !
I have an hour's talk in store for you ;
Remember that you call on me to-day :
Be near me, that I may remember you.
 Treb. Cæsar, I will : [*Aside*] and so near
  will I be,
That your best friends shall wish I had been
 further.
 Cæs. Good friends, go in, and taste some wine
  with me ;
And we, like friends, will straightway go to-
 gether.
 Bru. [*Aside*] That every like is not the same,
  O Cæsar,
The heart of Brutus yearns to think upon !
           [*Exeunt.*

   SCENE III.   *A street near the Capitol.*

  Enter ARTEMIDORUS, *reading a paper.*

 Art. 'Cæsar, beware of Brutus ; take heed
of Cassius ; come not near Casca ; have an eye
to Cinna ; trust not Trebonius ; mark well Metellus Cimber : Decius Brutus loves thee not :
thou hast wronged Caius Ligarius. There is
but one mind in all these men, and it is bent
against Cæsar.   If thou beest not immortal, look
about you : security gives way to conspiracy.
The mighty gods defend thee !   Thy lover,
       'ARTEMIDORUS.'
Here will I stand till Cæsar pass along,   11
And as a suitor will I give him this.
My heart laments that virtue cannot live
Out of the teeth of emulation.
If thou read this, O Cæsar, thou mayst live ;
If not, the Fates with traitors do contrive. [*Exit.*

  SCENE IV.   *Another part of the same street,
    before the house of Brutus.*

   Enter PORTIA *and* LUCIUS.

 Por.   I prithee, boy, run to the senate-house ;
Stay not to answer me, but get thee gone :
Why dost thou stay ?
 Luc.   To know my errand, madam.
 Por.   I would have had thee there, and here
  again,
Ere I can tell thee what thou shouldst do there.
O constancy, be strong upon my side,
Set a huge mountain 'tween my heart and tongue !
I have a man's mind, but a woman's might.
How hard it is for women to keep counsel !
Art thou here yet ?
 Luc.   Madam, what should I do ? 10
Run to the Capitol, and nothing else ?
And so return to you, and nothing else ?
 Por.   Yes, bring me word, boy, if thy lord look
  well,
For he went sickly forth : and take good note
What Cæsar doth, what suitors press to him.
Hark, boy ! what noise is that ?
 Luc.   I hear none, madam.
 Por.   Prithee, listen well ;
I heard a bustling rumour, like a fray,
And the wind brings it from the Capitol.
 Luc.   Sooth, madam, I hear nothing.   20

Enter the Soothsayer.

SD *Flourish.* Fanfare.

Por. Come hither, fellow: which way hast thou been?

Sooth. At mine own house, good lady.

Por. What is't o'clock?

Sooth.   About the ninth hour, lady.

Por. Is Cæsar yet gone to the Capitol?

Sooth. Madam, not yet: I go to take my stand,

To see him pass on to the Capitol.

Por. Thou hast some suit to Cæsar, hast thou not?

Sooth. That I have, lady: if it will please Cæsar

To be so good to Cæsar as to hear me,

I shall beseech him to befriend himself.   30

Por. Why, know'st thou any harm's intended towards him?

Sooth. None that I know will be, much that I fear may chance.

Good morrow to you. Here the street is narrow:

The throng that follows Cæsar at the heels,

Of senators, of prætors, common suitors,

Will crowd a feeble man almost to death:

I'll get me to a place more void, and there

Speak to great Cæsar as he comes along. [*Exit.*

Por. I must go in. Ay me, how weak a thing

The heart of woman is! O Brutus,   40

The heavens speed thee in thine enterprise!

Sure, the boy heard me: Brutus hath a suit

That Cæsar will not grant. O, I grow faint.

Run, Lucius, and commend me to my lord;

Say I am merry: come to me again,

And bring me word what he doth say to thee.

[*Exeunt severally.*

ACT III.

SCENE I.   *Rome.   Before the Capitol; the Senate sitting above.*

A crowd of people; among them ARTEMIDORUS *and the* Soothsayer. *Flourish. Enter* CÆSAR, BRUTUS, CASSIUS, CASCA, DECIUS, METELLUS, TREBONIUS, CINNA, ANTONY, LEPIDUS, POPILIUS, PUBLIUS, *and others.*

Cæs. [*To the Soothsayer*] The ides of March are come.

Sooth. Ay, Cæsar; but not gone.

Art. Hail, Cæsar! read this schedule.

Dec. Trebonius doth desire you to o'er-read,

At your best leisure, this his humble suit.

Art. O Cæsar, read mine first; for mine's a suit

That touches Cæsar nearer: read it, great Cæsar.

Cæs. What touches us ourself shall be last served.

Art. Delay not, Cæsar; read it instantly.

Cæs. What, is the fellow mad?

Pub.   Sirrah, give place. 10

Cas. What, urge you your petitions in the street?

Come to the Capitol.

CÆSAR *goes up to the Senate-House, the rest following.*

Pop. I wish your enterprise to-day may thrive.

Cas. What enterprise, Popilius?

Costume design for Julius Caesar by John Bury, Royal Shakespeare Co, 1963

33 *puissant.* Powerful.

36 *These couchings.* This bowing.

38–39 *And turn . . . of children.* i.e. and make common precedent and established law seem childish practice.

Pop.   Fare you well.
                          [*Advances to Cæsar.*
Bru.   What said Popilius Lena?
Cas.   He wish'd to-day our enterprise might
      thrive.
I fear our purpose is discovered.
Bru.   Look, how he makes to Cæsar: mark him.
Cas.   Casca, be sudden, for we fear prevention.
Brutus, what shall be done? If this be known,   20
Cassius or Cæsar never shall turn back,
For I will slay myself.
Bru.   Cassius, be constant:
Popilius Lena speaks not of our purposes;
For, look, he smiles, and Cæsar doth not change.
Cas.   Trebonius knows his time; for, look you,
      Brutus,
He draws Mark Antony out of the way.
                  [*Exeunt Antony and Trebonius.*
Dec.   Where is Metellus Cimber? Let him go,
And presently prefer his suit to Cæsar.
Bru.   He is address'd: press near and second
      him.
Cin.   Casca, you are the first that rears your
      hand.   30
Cæs.   Are we all ready? What is now amiss
That Cæsar and his senate must redress?
● *Met.*   Most high, most mighty, and most puis-
      sant Cæsar,
Metellus Cimber throws before thy seat
An humble heart,—   [*Kneeling.*
Cæs.   I must prevent thee, Cimber.
●These couchings and these lowly courtesies
Might fire the blood of ordinary men,
●And turn pre-ordinance and first decree
Into the law of children.   Be not fond,
To think that Cæsar bears such rebel blood   40
That will be thaw'd from the true quality
With that which melteth fools; I mean, sweet
      words,
Low-crooked court'sies and base spaniel-fawning
Thy brother by decree is banished:
If thou dost bend and pray and fawn for him,
I spurn thee like a cur out of my way.
Know, Cæsar doth not wrong, nor without cause
Will he be satisfied.
Met.   Is there no voice more worthy than my
      own,
To sound more sweetly in great Cæsar's ear   50
For the repealing of my banish'd brother?
Bru.   I kiss thy hand, but not in flattery,
      Cæsar;
Desiring thee that Publius Cimber may
Have an immediate freedom of repeal.
Cæs.   What, Brutus!
Cas.   Pardon, Cæsar; Cæsar, pardon:
As low as to thy foot doth Cassius fall,
To beg enfranchisement for Publius Cimber.
Cæs.   I could be well moved, if I were as you:
If I could pray to move, prayers would move me:
But I am constant as the northern star,   60
Of whose true-fix'd and resting quality
There is no fellow in the firmament.
The skies are painted with unnumber'd sparks,
They are all fire and every one doth shine,
But there's but one in all doth hold his place:
So in the world; 'tis furnish'd well with men,
And men are flesh and blood, and apprehensive:
Yet in the number I do know but one
That unassailable holds on his rank,

Unshaked of motion: and that I am he,   70
Let me a little show it, even in this;
That I was constant Cimber should be banish'd,
And constant do remain to keep him so.
 Cin. O Cæsar,—
 Cæs.   Hence! wilt thou lift up Olympus?
 Dec. Great Cæsar,—
 Cæs.   Doth not Brutus bootless kneel?
 Casca. Speak, hands, for me!
  [*Casca first, then the other Conspirators and*
     Marcus Brutus stab Cæsar.
 Cæs. Et tu, Brute! Then fall, Cæsar! [*Dies.*
 Cin. Liberty! Freedom! Tyranny is dead!
Run hence, proclaim, cry it about the streets.
 Cas. Some to the common pulpits, and cry out
'Liberty, freedom, and enfranchisement!'   81
 Bru. People and senators, be not affrighted;
Fly not; stand still: ambition's debt is paid.
 Casca. Go to the pulpit, Brutus.
 Dec.   And Cassius too.
 Bru. Where's Publius?
 Cin. Here, quite confounded with this mutiny.
 Met. Stand fast together, lest some friend of
  Cæsar's
Should chance—
 Bru. Talk not of standing. Publius, good
  cheer;
There is no harm intended to your person,   90
Nor to no Roman else: so tell them, Publius.
 Cas. And leave us, Publius; lest that the
  people,
Rushing on us, should do your age some mischief.
• *Bru.* Do so: and let no man abide this deed,
But we the doers.

   Re-enter TREBONIUS.

 Cas.   Where is Antony?
 Tre. Fled to his house amazed:
Men, wives and children stare, cry out and run
As it were doomsday.
 Bru.   Fates, we will know your pleasures:
That we shall die, we know; 'tis but the time
And drawing days out, that men stand upon. 100
 Cas. Why, he that cuts off twenty years of
  life
Cuts off so many years of fearing death.
 Bru. Grant that, and then is death a benefit:
So are we Cæsar's friends, that have abridged
His time of fearing death. Stoop, Romans, stoop,
And let us bathe our hands in Cæsar's blood
Up to the elbows, and besmear our swords:
Then walk we forth, even to the market-place,
And, waving our red weapons o'er our heads,
Let's all cry 'Peace, freedom and liberty!' 110
• *Cas.* Stoop, then, and wash. How many ages
  hence
Shall this our lofty scene be acted over
In states unborn and accents yet unknown!
 Bru. How many times shall Cæsar bleed in
  sport,
•That now on Pompey's basis lies along
No worthier than the dust!
 Cas.   So oft as that shall be,
•So often shall the knot of us be call'd
The men that gave their country liberty.
 Dec. What, shall we forth?
 Cas.   Ay, every man away:
Brutus shall lead; and we will grace his heels 120
With the most boldest and best hearts of Rome.

The death of Julius Caesar. Engraving by Bartolomeo
Pinelli, 1821

94 *abide.* Pay the penalty for.

111–113 *How many . . . yet unknown.* See introduction.

115 *That now . . . lies along.* That now lies at the foot of
Pompey's statue.

117 *knot.* Group of men.

131 *resolved.* Satisfied.

136 *untrod state.* i.e. new state of affairs.

161 *mean.* Means.

175 *Of brothers' temper.* i.e. of brotherly affection.

Brutus: 'Only be patient ...' Painting of the murder scene by George Clint (1770–1854)

Enter a Servant.

Bru. Soft! who comes here? A friend of Antony's.
Serv. Thus, Brutus, did my master bid me kneel;
Thus did Mark Antony bid me fall down;
And, being prostrate, thus he bade me say:
Brutus is noble, wise, valiant, and honest;
Cæsar was mighty, bold, royal, and loving:
Say I love Brutus, and I honour him;
Say I fear'd Cæsar, honour'd him and loved him.
If Brutus will vouchsafe that Antony   130
● May safely come to him, and be resolved
How Cæsar hath deserved to lie in death,
Mark Antony shall not love Cæsar dead
So well as Brutus living; but will follow
The fortunes and affairs of noble Brutus
● Thorough the hazards of this untrod state
With all true faith.   So says my master Antony.
Bru. Thy master is a wise and valiant Roman;
I never thought him worse.
Tell him, so please him come unto this place, 140
He shall be satisfied; and, by my honour,
Depart untouch'd.
Serv.   I'll fetch him presently. [*Exit.*
Bru. I know that we shall have him well to friend.
Cas. I wish we may: but yet have I a mind
That fears him much; and my misgiving still
Falls shrewdly to the purpose.
Bru.   But here comes Antony.

Re-enter ANTONY.

          Welcome, Mark Antony.
Ant. O mighty Cæsar! dost thou lie so low?
Are all thy conquests, glories, triumphs, spoils,
Shrunk to this little measure?   Fare thee well.
I know not, gentlemen, what you intend,   151
Who else must be let blood, who else is rank:
If I myself, there is no hour so fit
As Cæsar's death's hour, nor no instrument
Of half that worth as those your swords, made rich
With the most noble blood of all this world.
I do beseech ye, if you bear me hard,
Now, whilst your purpled hands do reek and smoke,
Fulfil your pleasure.   Live a thousand years,
I shall not find myself so apt to die: 160
● No place will please me so, no mean of death,
As here by Cæsar, and by you cut off,
The choice and master spirits of this age.
Bru. O Antony, beg not your death of us.
Though now we must appear bloody and cruel,
As, by our hands and this our present act,
You see we do, yet see you but our hands
And this the bleeding business they have done:
Our hearts you see not; they are pitiful;
And pity to the general wrong of Rome—   170
As fire drives out fire, so pity pity—
Hath done this deed on Cæsar.   For your part,
To you our swords have leaden points, Mark Antony:
†Our arms, in strength of malice, and our hearts
● Of brothers' temper, do receive you in
With all kind love, good thoughts, and reverence.
Cas. Your voice shall be as strong as any man's
In the disposing of new dignities.
Bru. Only be patient till we have appeased

The multitude, beside themselves with fear,   180
And then we will deliver you the cause,
Why I, that did love Cæsar when I struck him,
Have thus proceeded.
  Ant.   I doubt not of your wisdom.
Let each man render me his bloody hand:
First, Marcus Brutus, will I shake with you;
Next, Caius Cassius, do I take your hand;
Now, Decius Brutus, yours; now yours, Me-
  tellus;
Yours, Cinna; and, my valiant Casca, yours;
Though last, not least in love, yours, good Tre-
  bonius.
Gentlemen all,—alas, what shall I say?   190
My credit now stands on such slippery ground,
That one of two bad ways you must conceit me,
Either a coward or a flatterer.
That I did love thee, Cæsar, O, 'tis true:
If then thy spirit look upon us now,
Shall it not grieve thee dearer than thy death,
To see thy Antony making his peace,
Shaking the bloody fingers of thy foes,
Most noble! in the presence of thy corse?
Had I as many eyes as thou hast wounds,   200
Weeping as fast as they stream forth thy blood,
It would become me better than to close
In terms of friendship with thine enemies.
Pardon me, Julius! Here wast thou bay'd, brave
  hart;
Here didst thou fall; and here thy hunters stand,
Sign'd in thy spoil, and crimson'd in thy lethe.
O world, thou wast the forest to this hart;
And this, indeed, O world, the heart of thee.
How like a deer, strucken by many princes,
Dost thou here lie!   210
  Cas. Mark Antony,—
  Ant.   Pardon me, Caius Cassius:
The enemies of Cæsar shall say this;
Then, in a friend, it is cold modesty.
  Cas. I blame you not for praising Cæsar so;
But what compact mean you to have with us?
•Will you be prick'd in number of our friends;
Or shall we on, and not depend on you?
  Ant. Therefore I took your hands, but was,
  indeed,
Sway'd from the point, by looking down on Cæsar.
Friends am I with you all and love you all,   220
Upon this hope, that you shall give me reasons
Why and wherein Cæsar was dangerous.
  Bru. Or else were this a savage spectacle:
Our reasons are so full of good regard
That were you, Antony, the son of Cæsar,
You should be satisfied.
  Ant.   That's all I seek:
And am moreover suitor that I may
Produce his body to the market-place;
And in the pulpit, as becomes a friend,
Speak in the order of his funeral.   230
  Bru. You shall, Mark Antony.
  Cas.   Brutus, a word with you.
[*Aside to Bru.*] You know not what you do: do
  not consent
That Antony speak in his funeral:
Know you how much the people may be moved
By that which he will utter?
  Bru.   By your pardon;
I will myself into the pulpit first,
And show the reason of our Cæsar's death:
What Antony shall speak, I will protest

216 *prick'd.* Included.

Antony: '. . . you shall give me reasons Why and wherein Cæsar was dangerous'. Decius Brutus (John Hoyt), Cassius (John Gielgud), Brutus (James Mason) and Mark Antony (Marlon Brando), film directed by J. L. Mankiewicz, USA, 1953

Antony: 'O, pardon me, thou bleeding piece of earth,
That I am meek and gentle with these butchers!'
Engraving from a painting by Richard Westall (1765–1836)

264 *cumber*. Harass.

269 *fell*. Fierce.

271 *Ate*. Goddess of destruction in classical mythology.

273 *let slip*. Unleash.

He speaks by leave and by permission,
And that we are contented Cæsar shall   240
Have all true rites and lawful ceremonies.
It shall advantage more than do us wrong.
    Cas.   I know not what may fall; I like it not.
    Bru.   Mark Antony, here, take you Cæsar's body.
You shall not in your funeral speech blame us,
But speak all good you can devise of Cæsar,
And say you do 't by our permission;
Else shall you not have any hand at all
About his funeral: and you shall speak
In the same pulpit whereto I am going,   250
After my speech is ended.
    Ant.   Be it so;
I do desire no more.
    Bru.   Prepare the body then, and follow us.
                              [*Exeunt all but Antony.*
    Ant.   O, pardon me, thou bleeding piece of earth,
That I am meek and gentle with these butchers!
Thou art the ruins of the noblest man
That ever lived in the tide of times.
Woe to the hand that shed this costly blood!
Over thy wounds now do I prophesy,—   259
Which, like dumb mouths, do ope their ruby lips,
To beg the voice and utterance of my tongue—
A curse shall light upon the † limbs of men;
Domestic fury and fierce civil strife
• Shall cumber all the parts of Italy;
Blood and destruction shall be so in use
And dreadful objects so familiar
That mothers shall but smile when they behold
Their infants quarter'd with the hands of war;
• All pity choked with custom of fell deeds:
And Cæsar's spirit, ranging for revenge,   270
• With Ate by his side come hot from hell,
Shall in these confines with a monarch's voice
• Cry ' Havoc,' and let slip the dogs of war;
That this foul deed shall smell above the earth
With carrion men, groaning for burial.

Enter a Servant.

You serve Octavius Cæsar, do you not?
    Serv.   I do, Mark Antony.
    Ant.   Cæsar did write for him to come to Rome.
    Serv.   He did receive his letters, and is coming;
And bid me say to you by word of mouth—   280
O Cæsar!—   [*Seeing the body.*
    Ant.   Thy heart is big, get thee apart and weep.
Passion, I see, is catching; for mine eyes,
Seeing those beads of sorrow stand in thine,
Began to water.   Is thy master coming?
    Serv.   He lies to-night within seven leagues of Rome.
    Ant.   Post back with speed, and tell him what hath chanced:
Here is a mourning Rome, a dangerous Rome,
No Rome of safety for Octavius yet;   289
Hie hence, and tell him so.   Yet, stay awhile;
Thou shalt not back till I have borne this corse
Into the market-place: there shall I try,
In my oration, how the people take
The cruel issue of these bloody men;
According to the which, thou shalt discourse
To young Octavius of the state of things.
Lend me your hand.   [*Exeunt with Cæsar's body.*

SCENE II. *The Forum.*

Enter BRUTUS *and* CASSIUS, *and a throng of* Citizens.

Citizens. We will be satisfied; let us be satisfied.
Bru. Then follow me, and give me audience, friends.
Cassius, go you into the other street,
And part the numbers.
Those that will hear me speak, let 'em stay here;
Those that will follow Cassius, go with him;
And public reasons shall be rendered
Of Cæsar's death.
First Cit.   I will hear Brutus speak.
Sec. Cit. I will hear Cassius; and compare their reasons,
●When severally we hear them rendered.   10
    [*Exit Cassius, with some of the Citizens.*
                Brutus goes into the pulpit.
Third Cit. The noble Brutus is ascended: silence!
Bru. Be patient till the last.
Romans, countrymen, and lovers! hear me for my cause, and be silent, that you may hear: believe me for mine honour, and have respect to mine honour, that you may believe: censure me in your wisdom, and awake your senses, that you may the better judge. If there be any in this assembly, any dear friend of Cæsar's, to him I say, that Brutus' love to Cæsar was no less than his. If then that friend demand why Brutus rose against Cæsar, this is my answer:—Not that I loved Cæsar less, but that I loved Rome more. Had you rather Cæsar were living and die all slaves, than that Cæsar were dead, to live all free men? As Cæsar loved me, I weep for him; as he was fortunate, I rejoice at it; as he was valiant, I honour him: but, as he was ambitious, I slew him. There is tears for his love; joy for his fortune; honour for his valour; and death for his ambition. Who is here so base that would be a bondman? If any, speak; for him have I offended. Who is here so rude that would not be a Roman? If any, speak; for him have I offended. Who is here so vile that will not love his country? If any, speak; for him have I offended. I pause for a reply.
All. None, Brutus, none.
Bru. Then none have I offended. I have done no more to Cæsar than you shall do to Brutus. The question of his death is enrolled in the Capitol; his glory not extenuated, wherein he was worthy, nor his offences enforced, for which he suffered death.

Enter ANTONY *and others, with* CÆSAR's *body.*

Here comes his body, mourned by Mark Antony: who, though he had no hand in his death, shall receive the benefit of his dying, a place in the commonwealth; as which of you shall not? With this I depart,—that, as I slew my best lover for the good of Rome, I have the same dagger for myself, when it shall please my country to need my death.
All. Live, Brutus! live, live!
First Cit. Bring him with triumph home unto his house.
Sec. Cit. Give him a statue with his ancestors.

10 *severally.* Separately.

Brutus: '. . . hear me for my cause, and be silent, that you may hear:' Engraving by Bartolomeo Pinelli, 1821

56–57 *Let him ... Brutus.* See introduction.

100 *Lupercal.* i.e. 15th February.

The Feast of Lupercal commemorated the suckling of Rome's founders, Romulus and Remus, by a wolf. Engraving from a Roman medal in G. du Choul's *Discours de la Religion des Anciens Romains*, 1567

Third Cit.   Let him be Cæsar.
Fourth Cit.   Cæsar's better parts
Shall be crown'd in Brutus.
First Cit.   We'll bring him to his house
With shouts and clamours.
Bru.   My countrymen,—
Sec. Cit.   Peace, silence! Brutus speaks.
First Cit.   Peace, ho!
Bru.   Good countrymen, let me depart alone,
And, for my sake, stay here with Antony: 61
Do grace to Cæsar's corpse, and grace his speech
Tending to Cæsar's glories; which Mark Antony,
By our permission, is allow'd to make.
I do entreat you, not a man depart,
Save I alone, till Antony have spoke.   [*Exit.*
First Cit.   Stay, ho! and let us hear Mark
      Antony.
Third Cit.   Let him go up into the public
      chair;
We'll hear him.   Noble Antony, go up.
Ant.   For Brutus' sake, I am beholding to
      you.   [*Goes into the pulpit.* 70
Fourth Cit.   What does he say of Brutus?
Third Cit.   He says, for Brutus' sake,
He finds himself beholding to us all.
Fourth Cit.   'Twere best he speak no harm of
      Brutus here.
First Cit.   This Cæsar was a tyrant.
Third Cit.   Nay, that's certain:
We are blest that Rome is rid of him.
Sec. Cit.   Peace! let us hear what Antony
      can say.
Ant.   You gentle Romans,—
Citizens.   Peace, ho! let us hear him.
Ant.   Friends, Romans, countrymen, lend me
      your ears;
I come to bury Cæsar, not to praise him.
The evil that men do lives after them;   80
The good is oft interred with their bones;
So let it be with Cæsar.   The noble Brutus
Hath told you Cæsar was ambitious:
If it were so, it was a grievous fault,
And grievously hath Cæsar answer'd it.
Here, under leave of Brutus and the rest—
For Brutus is an honourable man;
So are they all, all honourable men—
Come I to speak in Cæsar's funeral.
He was my friend, faithful and just to me: 90
But Brutus says he was ambitious;
And Brutus is an honourable man.
He hath brought many captives home to Rome,
Whose ransoms did the general coffers fill:
Did this in Cæsar seem ambitious?
When that the poor have cried, Cæsar hath wept:
Ambition should be made of sterner stuff:
Yet Brutus says he was ambitious;
And Brutus is an honourable man.
You all did see that on the Lupercal   100
I thrice presented him a kingly crown,
Which he did thrice refuse: was this ambition?
Yet Brutus says he was ambitious;
And, sure, he is an honourable man.
I speak not to disprove what Brutus spoke,
But here I am to speak what I do know.
You all did love him once, not without cause:
What cause withholds you then, to mourn for
      him?
O judgement! thou art fled to brutish beasts, 109
And men have lost their reason.   Bear with me:

My heart is in the coffin there with Cæsar,
And I must pause till it come back to me.
    First Cit. Methinks there is much reason in
      his sayings.
    Sec. Cit. If thou consider rightly of the matter,
Cæsar has had great wrong.
    Third Cit.   Has he, masters?
I fear there will a worse come in his place.
    Fourth Cit. Mark'd ye his words? He would
      not take the crown;
Therefore 'tis certain he was not ambitious.
 • *First Cit.* If it be found so, some will dear
      abide it.
    Sec. Cit. Poor soul! his eyes are red as fire
      with weeping.   120
    Third Cit. There's not a nobler man in Rome
      than Antony.
    Fourth Cit. Now mark him, he begins again
      to speak.
    Ant. But yesterday the word of Cæsar might
Have stood against the world; now lies he there,
And none so poor to do him reverence.
O masters, if I were disposed to stir
Your hearts and minds to mutiny and rage,
I should do Brutus wrong, and Cassius wrong,
Who, you all know, are honourable men:
I will not do them wrong; I rather choose   130
To wrong the dead, to wrong myself and you,
Than I will wrong such honourable men.
But here's a parchment with the seal of Cæsar;
I found it in his closet, 'tis his will:
Let but the commons hear this testament—
Which, pardon me, I do not mean to read—
And they would go and kiss dead Cæsar's wounds
And dip their napkins in his sacred blood,
Yea, beg a hair of him for memory,
And, dying, mention it within their wills,   140
Bequeathing it as a rich legacy
Unto their issue.
    Fourth Cit. We'll hear the will: read it,
      Mark Antony.
    All. The will, the will! we will hear Cæsar's
      will.
    Ant. Have patience, gentle friends, I must
      not read it;
It is not meet you know how Cæsar loved you.
You are not wood, you are not stones, but men;
And, being men, hearing the will of Cæsar,
It will inflame you, it will make you mad: 149
'Tis good you know not that you are his heirs;
For, if you should, O, what would come of it!
    Fourth Cit. Read the will; we'll hear it,
      Antony;
You shall read us the will, Cæsar's will.
    Ant. Will you be patient? will you stay
      awhile?
I have o'ershot myself to tell you of it:
I fear I wrong the honourable men
Whose daggers have stabb'd Cæsar; I do fear it.
    Fourth Cit. They were traitors: honourable
      men!
    All. The will! the testament!
    Sec. Cit. They were villains, murderers: the
will! read the will.   160
    Ant. You will compel me, then, to read the
      will?
Then make a ring about the corpse of Cæsar,
And let me show you him that made the will.
Shall I descend? and will you give me leave?

119 *abide.* Pay for.

Mark Antony (Herbert Beerbohm Tree) addressing the citizens, His Majesty's Theatre, London, 1910

177 *Nervii.* Warriors (conquered in the Gallic wars).

198 *dint.* Mark.

Antony: 'Kind souls, what, weep you when you but behold Our Caesar's vesture wounded?' Engraving from A. Pope's edition of *Works ... 1728*

208–209 *Revenge ... live.* See introduction.

Several Cit.   Come down.
Sec. Cit.   Descend.
Third Cit.   You shall have leave.
                                    [*Antony comes down.*
Fourth Cit.   A ring; stand round.
First Cit.   Stand from the hearse, stand from the body.   169
Sec. Cit.   Room for Antony, most noble Antony.
Ant.   Nay, press not so upon me; stand far off.
Several Cit.   Stand back; room; bear back.
Ant.   If you have tears, prepare to shed them now.
You all do know this mantle: I remember
The first time ever Cæsar put it on;
'Twas on a summer's evening, in his tent,
●That day he overcame the Nervii:
Look, in this place ran Cassius' dagger through:
See what a rent the envious Casca made:
Through this the well-beloved Brutus stabb'd;
And as he pluck'd his cursed steel away,   181
Mark how the blood of Cæsar follow'd it,
As rushing out of doors, to be resolved
If Brutus so unkindly knock'd, or no;
For Brutus, as you know, was Cæsar's angel:
Judge, O you gods, how dearly Cæsar loved him!
This was the most unkindest cut of all;
For when the noble Cæsar saw him stab,
Ingratitude, more strong than traitors' arms,
Quite vanquish'd him: then burst his mighty heart;   190
And, in his mantle muffling up his face,
Even at the base of Pompey's statua,
Which all the while ran blood, great Cæsar fell.
O, what a fall was there, my countrymen!
Then I, and you, and all of us fell down,
Whilst bloody treason flourish'd over us.
O, now you weep; and, I perceive, you feel
●The dint of pity: these are gracious drops.
Kind souls, what, weep you when you but behold
Our Cæsar's vesture wounded?   Look you here,
Here is himself, marr'd, as you see, with traitors.
First Cit.   O piteous spectacle!
Sec. Cit.   O noble Cæsar!
Third Cit.   O woful day!
Fourth Cit.   O traitors, villains!
First Cit.   O most bloody sight!
Sec. Cit.   We will be revenged.
●*All.*   Revenge! About! Seek! Burn! Fire!
Kill! Slay! Let not a traitor live!
Ant.   Stay, countrymen.   210
First Cit.   Peace there! hear the noble Antony.
Sec. Cit.   We'll hear him, we'll follow him, we'll die with him.
Ant.   Good friends, sweet friends, let me not stir you up
To such a sudden flood of mutiny.
They that have done this deed are honourable:
What private griefs they have, alas, I know not,
That made them do it: they are wise and honourable,
And will, no doubt, with reasons answer you.
I come not, friends, to steal away your hearts:
I am no orator, as Brutus is;   221
But, as you know me all, a plain blunt man,
That love my friend; and that they know full well
That gave me public leave to speak of him:
For I have neither wit, nor words, nor worth,
Action, nor utterance, nor the power of speech,

To stir men's blood: I only speak right on:
I tell you that which you yourselves do know;
Show you sweet Cæsar's wounds, poor poor dumb
    mouths,   229
And bid them speak for me: but were I Brutus,
And Brutus Antony, there were an Antony
Would ruffle up your spirits and put a tongue
In every wound of Cæsar that should move
The stones of Rome to rise and mutiny.
    All. We'll mutiny.
    First Cit. We'll burn the house of Brutus.
    Third Cit. Away, then! come, seek the con-
    spirators.
    Ant. Yet hear me, countrymen; yet hear me
    speak.
    All. Peace, ho! Hear Antony. Most noble
    Antony!
    Ant. Why, friends, you go to do you know
    not what: 240
Wherein hath Cæsar thus deserved your loves?
Alas, you know not: I must tell you, then:
You have forgot the will I told you of.
    All. Most true. The will! Let's stay and
    hear the will.
    Ant. Here is the will, and under Cæsar's seal.
To every Roman citizen he gives,
To every several man, seventy five drachmas.
    Sec. Cit. Most noble Cæsar! We'll revenge
    his death.
    Third Cit. O royal Cæsar!
    Ant. Hear me with patience.   250
    All. Peace, ho!
    Ant. Moreover, he hath left you all his walks,
His private arbours and new-planted orchards,
On this side Tiber; he hath left them you,
● And to your heirs for ever, common pleasures,
To walk abroad, and recreate yourselves.
Here was a Cæsar! when comes such another?
    First Cit. Never, never. Come, away, away!
● We'll burn his body in the holy place,
And with the brands fire the traitors' houses. 260
Take up the body.
    Sec. Cit. Go fetch fire.
    Third Cit. Pluck down benches.
    Fourth Cit. Pluck down forms, windows, any
    thing.   [*Exeunt Citizens with the body.*
    Ant. Now let it work. Mischief, thou art afoot,
Take thou what course thou wilt!

        Enter a Servant.

                  How now, fellow!
    Serv. Sir, Octavius is already come to Rome.
    Ant. Where is he?
    Serv. He and Lepidus are at Cæsar's house.
    Ant. And thither will I straight to visit him:
● He comes upon a wish. Fortune is merry, 271
And in this mood will give us any thing.
    Serv. I heard him say, Brutus and Cassius
● Are rid like madmen through the gates of Rome.
    Ant. Belike they had some notice of the
    people,
How I had moved them. Bring me to Octavius.
                        [*Exeunt.*

      SCENE III. *A street.*

      Enter CINNA *the poet.*

    Cin. I dreamt to-night that I did feast with
    Cæsar,

255 *common pleasures.* Public areas for recreation.

259–264 *We'll burn ... anything.* See introduction.

First Citizen: 'We'll burn his body in the holy place'. The Forum, near which were the sacred temples. From a 19th century engraving

271 *upon a wish.* Exactly when I wish.

274 *Are rid.* Have ridden.

20 *bear me a bang.* Take a blow.

Antony, Octavius and Lepidus. Engraving by Kenny Meadows from Barry Cornwall's *Works of Shakspere,* 1846

---

1 *prick'd.* Listed.

9 *cut off some charge in legacies.* i.e. reduce Caesar's legacies.

And things unluckily charge my fantasy:
I have no will to wander forth of doors,
Yet something leads me forth.

Enter Citizens.

First Cit.   What is your name?
Sec. Cit.   Whither are you going?
Third Cit.   Where do you dwell?
Fourth Cit.   Are you a married man or a bachelor?
Sec. Cit.   Answer every man directly.   10
First Cit.   Ay, and briefly.
Fourth Cit.   Ay, and wisely.
Third Cit.   Ay, and truly, you were best.
Cin.   What is my name? Whither am I going? Where do I dwell? Am I a married man or a bachelor? Then, to answer every man directly and briefly, wisely and truly: wisely I say, I am a bachelor.
Sec. Cit.   That's as much as to say, they are fools that marry: you'll bear me a bang for that, I fear.   Proceed; directly.   21
Cin.   Directly, I am going to Cæsar's funeral.
First Cit.   As a friend or an enemy?
Cin.   As a friend.
Sec. Cit.   That matter is answered directly.
Fourth Cit.   For your dwelling,—briefly.
Cin.   Briefly, I dwell by the Capitol.
Third Cit.   Your name, sir, truly.
Cin.   Truly, my name is Cinna.
First Cit.   Tear him to pieces; he's a conspirator.   31
Cin.   I am Cinna the poet, I am Cinna the poet.
Fourth Cit.   Tear him for his bad verses, tear him for his bad verses.
Cin.   I am not Cinna the conspirator.
Fourth Cit.   It is no matter, his name's Cinna; pluck but his name out of his heart, and turn him going.
Third Cit.   Tear him, tear him! Come, brands, ho! fire-brands: to Brutus', to Cassius'; burn all: some to Decius' house, and some to Casca's; some to Ligarius': away, go!
                                          [*Exeunt.*

ACT IV.

Scene I.   *A house in Rome.*

Antony, Octavius, *and* Lepidus, *seated at a table.*

Ant.   These many, then, shall die; their names are prick'd.
Oct.   Your brother too must die; consent you, Lepidus?
Lep.   I do consent,—
Oct.   Prick him down, Antony.
Lep.   Upon condition Publius shall not live,
Who is your sister's son, Mark Antony.
Ant.   He shall not live; look, with a spot I damn him.
But, Lepidus, go you to Cæsar's house;
Fetch the will hither, and we shall determine
How to cut off some charge in legacies.
Lep.   What, shall I find you here?   10
Oct.   Or here, or at the Capitol.
                                 [*Exit Lepidus.*
Ant.   This is a slight unmeritable man,

Meet to be sent on errands: is it fit,
●The three-fold world divided, he should stand
●One of the three to share it?
    Oct.   So you thought him;
And took his voice who should be prick'd to die,
In our black sentence and proscription.
    Ant. Octavius, I have seen more days than
        you:
And though we lay these honours on this man,
To ease ourselves of divers slanderous loads,   20
He shall but bear them as the ass bears gold,
To groan and sweat under the business,
Either led or driven, as we point the way;
And having brought our treasure where we will,
Then take we down his load, and turn him off,
Like to the empty ass, to shake his ears,
And graze in commons.
    Oct.   You may do your will;
But he's a tried and valiant soldier.
    Ant. So is my horse, Octavius; and for that
I do appoint him store of provender: 30
It is a creature that I teach to fight,
●To wind, to stop, to run directly on,
His corporal motion govern'd by my spirit.
●And, in some taste, is Lepidus but so;
He must be taught and train'd and bid go forth;
A barren-spirited fellow; one that feeds
●On abjects, orts and imitations,
Which, out of use and staled by other men,
●Begin his fashion: do not talk of him,
●But as a property. And now, Octavius,   40
Listen great things:—Brutus and Cassius
●Are levying powers: we must straight make head:
Therefore let our alliance be combined,
†Our best friends made, our means stretch'd;
And let us presently go sit in council,
How covert matters may be best disclosed,
And open perils surest answered.
    Oct. Let us do so: for we are at the stake,
And bay'd about with many enemies;   49
And some that smile have in their hearts, I fear,
Millions of mischiefs.   [*Exeunt.*

SCENE II. *Camp near Sardis. Before Brutus's*
tent.

Drum. Enter BRUTUS, LUCILIUS, LUCIUS, *and*
Soldiers; TITINIUS *and* PINDARUS *meeting*
them.

    Bru. Stand, ho!
    Lucil. Give the word, ho! and stand.
    Bru. What now, Lucilius! is Cassius near?
    Lucil. He is at hand; and Pindarus is come
To do you salutation from his master.
    Bru. He greets me well. Your master, Pin-
        darus,
●In his own change, or by ill officers,
Hath given me some worthy cause to wish
Things done, undone: but, if he be at hand,
I shall be satisfied.
    Pin.   I do not doubt   10
But that my noble master will appear
Such as he is, full of regard and honour.
    Bru. He is not doubted. A word, Lucilius;
How he received you, let me be resolved.
    Lucil. With courtesy and with respect enough;
But not with such familiar instances,
Nor with such free and friendly conference,
As he hath used of old.

14 *three-fold world.* Europe, Africa, Asia.

15 *One of the three.* i.e. one of the triumvirs.

32 *wind.* Turn.

34 *taste.* Extent.

37 *abjects.* Castoffs. *orts.* Scraps.

39 *Begin his fashion.* Start his interest.

40 *property.* A mere thing.

42 *make head.* Raise a force.

Octavius, later the Emperor Augustus (63B.C–14A.D).
Engraving from a Roman medal in G. Du Choul's
Discours de la Religion des Anciens Romains, 1567

7 *In his own change.* Because of a change of mind. *by ill*
officers. Because he has been badly advised.

23 *hot at hand.* Brave-looking when they are led on show.

26 *fall.* Drop.

8 *nice.* Trivial. *bear.* Require.

15 *honours this corruption.* i.e. excuses this offence.

Lewis Waller as Brutus, Her Majesty's Theatre, London 1898

Bru.   Thou hast described
A hot friend cooling: ever note, Lucilius,
When love begins to sicken and decay,   20
It useth an enforced ceremony.
There are no tricks in plain and simple faith:
● But hollow men, like horses hot at hand,
Make galiant show and promise of their mettle;
But when they should endure the bloody spur,
● They fall their crests, and, like deceitful jades,
Sink in the trial. Comes his army on?
Lucil.   They mean this night in Sardis to be
          quarter'd;
The greater part, the horse in general,
Are come with Cassius.
Bru.   Hark! he is arrived.   30
                    [*Low march within.*
March gently on to meet him.

          Enter CASSIUS *and his powers.*

Cas.   Stand, ho!
Bru.   Stand, ho! Speak the word along.
First Sol. Stand!
Sec. Sol. Stand!
Third Sol. Stand!
Cas.   Most noble brother, you have done me
          wrong.
Bru.   Judge me, you gods! wrong I mine
          enemies?
And, if not so, how should I wrong a brother?
Cas.   Brutus, this sober form of yours hides
          wrongs;   40
And when you do them—
Bru.   Cassius, be content:
Speak your griefs softly: I do know you well.
Before the eyes of both our armies here,
Which should perceive nothing but love from us,
Let us not wrangle: bid them move away;
Then in my tent, Cassius, enlarge your griefs,
And I will give you audience.
Cas.   Pindarus,
Bid our commanders lead their charges off
A little from this ground.
Bru.   Lucilius, do you the like; and let no
          man   50
Come to our tent till we have done our conference.
Let Lucius and Titinius guard our door. [*Exeunt.*

          SCENE III.   *Brutus's tent.*

          Enter BRUTUS *and* CASSIUS.

Cas.   That you have wrong'd me doth appear
          in this:
You have condemn'd and noted Lucius Pella
For taking bribes here of the Sardians;
Wherein my letters, praying on his side,
Because I knew the man, were slighted off.
Bru.   You wrong'd yourself to write in such a
          case.
Cas.   In such a time as this it is not meet
● That every nice offence should bear his comment.
Bru.   Let me tell you, Cassius, you yourself
Are much condemn'd to have an itching palm; 10
To sell and mart your offices for gold
To undeservers.
Cas.   I an itching palm!
You know that you are Brutus that speak this,
Or, by the gods, this speech were else your last.
● *Bru.*   The name of Cassius honours this cor-
          ruption,

And chastisement doth therefore hide his head.
    Cas.   Chastisement!
    Bru.   Remember March, the ides of March
    remember:
Did not great Julius bleed for justice' sake?
What villain touch'd his body, that did stab,   20
And not for justice? What, shall one of us,
That struck the foremost man of all this world
But for supporting robbers, shall we now
Contaminate our fingers with base bribes,
And sell the mighty space of our large honours
For so much trash as may be grasped thus?
I had rather be a dog, and bay the moon,
Than such a Roman.
    Cas.   Brutus, bay not me;
I'll not endure it: you forget yourself,
To hedge me in; I am a soldier, I,   30
●Older in practice, abler than yourself
To make conditions.
    Bru.   Go to; you are not, Cassius.
    Cas.   I am.
    Bru.   I say you are not.
    Cas.   Urge me no more, I shall forget myself;
●Have mind upon your health, tempt me no farther.
    Bru.   Away, slight man!
    Cas.   Is't possible?
    Bru.   Hear me, for I will speak.
●Must I give way and room to your rash choler?
Shall I be frighted when a madman stares?   40
    Cas.   O ye gods, ye gods! must I endure all
    this?
    Bru.   All this! ay, more: fret till your proud
    heart break;
Go show your slaves how choleric you are,
And make your bondmen tremble. Must I
    budge?
Must I observe you? must I stand and crouch
Under your testy humour? By the gods,
You shall digest the venom of your spleen,
Though it do split you; for, from this day forth,
I'll use you for my mirth, yea, for my laughter,
When you are waspish.
    Cas.   Is it come to this?   50
    Bru.   You say you are a better soldier:
●Let it appear so; make your vaunting true,
And it shall please me well: for mine own part,
I shall be glad to learn of noble men.
    Cas.   You wrong me every way; you wrong
    me, Brutus;
I said, an elder soldier, not a better:
Did I say 'better'?
    Bru.   If you did, I care not.
    Cas.   When Cæsar lived, he durst not thus have
    moved me.
    Bru.   Peace, peace! you durst not so have
    tempted him.
    Cas.   I durst not!   60
    Bru.   No.
    Cas.   What, durst not tempt him!
    Bru.   For your life you durst not.
    Cas.   Do not presume too much upon my love;
I may do that I shall be sorry for.
    Bru.   You have done that you should be sorry for.
There is no terror, Cassius, in your threats,
For I am arm'd so strong in honesty
That they pass by me as the idle wind,
Which I respect not. I did send to you
For certain sums of gold, which you denied me:
For I can raise no money by vile means: 71

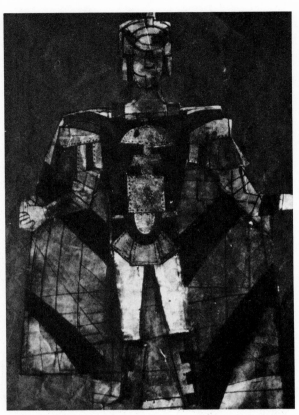

Costume design for Cassius by Nicholas Georgiadis, Old Vic Theatre, London, 1962

---

31 *Older in practice.* i.e. longer in service.

36 *Have mind upon.* Be careful of your well-being.

39 *choler.* Temper.

52 *vaunting.* i.e. boasting.

80 *lock.* Withhold. *rascal counters.* Miserable coins.

102 *Plutus.* Pluto, considered by the Romans to be the richest of the gods.

109 *humour.* A caprice.

120 *humour.* Disposition.

Brutus: 'When you are over-earnest with your Brutus, He'll think your mother chides ...' Engraving by Kenny Meadows from Barry Cornwall's *Works of Shakspere,* 1846

By heaven, I had rather coin my heart,
And drop my blood for drachmas, than to wring
From the hard hands of peasants their vile trash
By any indirection : I did send
To you for gold to pay my legions,
Which you denied me : was that done like Cassius?
Should I have answer'd Caius Cassius so?
When Marcus Brutus grows so covetous,
● To lock such rascal counters from his friends,   80
Be ready, gods, with all your thunderbolts;
Dash him to pieces!
   Cas.   I denied you not.
   Bru. You did.
   Cas. I did not: he was but a fool that brought
My answer back.   Brutus hath rived my heart:
A friend should bear his friend's infirmities,
But Brutus makes mine greater than they are.
   Bru. I do not, till you practise them on me.
   Cas. You love me not.
   Bru.   I do not like your faults.
   Cas. A friendly eye could never see such faults.
   Bru. A flatterer's would not, though they do appear   91
As huge as high Olympus.
   Cas. Come, Antony, and young Octavius, come,
Revenge yourselves alone on Cassius,
For Cassius is aweary of the world;
Hated by one he loves; braved by his brother;
Check'd like a bondman; all his faults observed,
Set in a note-book, learn'd, and conn'd by rote,
To cast into my teeth.   O, I could weep
My spirit from mine eyes!   There is my dagger,
And here my naked breast; within, a heart   101
● Dearer than Plutus' mine, richer than gold:
If that thou be'st a Roman, take it forth;
I, that denied thee gold, will give my heart:
Strike, as thou didst at Cæsar; for, I know,
When thou didst hate him worst, thou lovedst him better
Than ever thou lovedst Cassius.
   Bru.   Sheathe your dagger:
Be angry when you will, it shall have scope;
● Do what you will, dishonour shall be humour.
O Cassius, you are yoked with a lamb   110
That carries anger as the flint bears fire;
Who, much enforced, shows a hasty spark,
And straight is cold again.
   Cas.   Hath Cassius lived
To be but mirth and laughter to his Brutus,
When grief, and blood ill-temper'd, vexeth him?
   Bru. When I spoke that, I was ill-temper'd too.
   Cas. Do you confess so much? Give me your hand.
   Bru. And my heart too.
   Cas.   O Brutus!
   Bru.   What's the matter?
   Cas. Have not you love enough to bear with me,
● When that rash humour which my mother gave me
Makes me forgetful?
   Bru.   Yes, Cassius; and, from henceforth,
When you are over-earnest with your Brutus,
He'll think your mother chides, and leave you so.
   Poet. [*Within*] Let me go in to see the generals;
There is some grudge between 'em, 'tis not meet
They be alone.
   Lucil. [*Within*] You shall not come to them.
   Poet. [*Within*] Nothing but death shall stay me.

Enter Poet, *followed by* LUCILIUS, TITINIUS,
and LUCIUS.

Cas.   How now! what's the matter?
Poet.   For shame, you generals! what do you
    mean?   130
Love, and be friends, as two such men should be;
For I have seen more years, I'm sure, than ye.
Cas.   Ha, ha! how vilely doth this cynic rhyme!
Bru.   Get you hence, sirrah; saucy fellow,
    hence!
Cas.   Bear with him, Brutus; 'tis his fashion.
Bru.   I'll know his humour, when he knows
    his time:
● What should the wars do with these jigging fools?
Companion, hence!
    Cas.   Away, away, be gone!
                        [Exit Poet.
Bru.   Lucilius and Titinius, bid the commanders
Prepare to lodge their companies to-night.   140
Cas.   And come yourselves, and bring Messala
    with you
Immediately to us.
          [Exeunt Lucilius and Titinius.
Bru.   Lucius, a bowl of wine! *[Exit Lucius.*
Cas.   I did not think you could have been so
    angry.
Bru.   O Cassius, I am sick of many griefs.
Cas.   Of your philosophy you make no use,
If you give place to accidental evils.
Bru.   No man bears sorrow better.   Portia is
    dead.
Cas.   Ha! Portia!
Bru.   She is dead.
Cas.   How 'scaped I killing when I cross'd you so?
O insupportable and touching loss!   151
Upon what sickness?
    Bru.   Impatient of my absence,
And grief that young Octavius with Mark Antony
Have made themselves so strong:—for with her
    death
That tidings came;—with this she fell distract,
And, her attendants absent, swallow'd fire.
Cas.   And died so?
Bru.   Even so.
Cas.   O ye immortal gods!

Re-enter LUCIUS, *with wine and taper.*

Bru.   Speak no more of her.   Give me a bowl
    of wine.
In this I bury all unkindness, Cassius.
Cas.   My heart is thirsty for that noble pledge.
Fill, Lucius, till the wine o'erswell the cup;   161
I cannot drink too much of Brutus' love.
Bru.   Come in, Titinius!   *[Exit Lucius.*

Re-enter TITINIUS, *with* MESSALA.

                 Welcome, good Messala.
Now sit we close about this taper here,
● And call in question our necessities.
    Cas.   Portia, art thou gone?
    Bru.   No more, I pray you.
Messala, I have here received letters,
That young Octavius and Mark Antony
Come down upon us with a mighty power,
Bending their expedition toward Philippi.   170
    Mes.   Myself have letters of the selfsame tenour.
    Bru.   With what addition?
● *Mes.*   That by proscription and bills of outlawry,

Brutus, Cassius and Lucius. Illustration by Byam Shaw,
The Chiswick Shakespeare, 1900

165 *call in question.* Examine. *necessities.* Needs.

173 *proscription.* Denunciation.

194 *in art.* Theoretically.

201 *offence.* Harm.

228 *niggard.* Be sparing.

Octavius, Antony, and Lepidus,
Have put to death an hundred senators.
Bru. Therein our letters do not well agree;
Mine speak of seventy senators that died
By their proscriptions, Cicero being one.
Cas. Cicero one!
Mes.   Cicero is dead,
And by that order of proscription.   180
Had you your letters from your wife, my lord?
Bru. No, Messala.
Mes. Nor nothing in your letters writ of her?
Bru. Nothing, Messala.
Mes.   That, methinks, is strange.
Bru. Why ask you? hear you aught of her in
          yours?
Mes. No, my lord.
Bru. Now, as you are a Roman, tell me true.
Mes. Then like a Roman bear the truth I tell:
For certain she is dead, and by strange manner.
Bru. Why, farewell, Portia. We must die,
          Messala: 190
With meditating that she must die once,
I have the patience to endure it now.
Mes. Even so great men great losses should
          endure.
● *Cas.* I have as much of this in art as you,
But yet my nature could not bear it so.
Bru. Well, to our work alive. What do you think
Of marching to Philippi presently?
Cas. I do not think it good.
Bru.   Your reason?
Cas.   This it is:
'Tis better that the enemy seek us: 199
So shall he waste his means, weary his soldiers,
●Doing himself offence; whilst we, lying still,
Are full of rest, defence, and nimbleness.
Bru. Good reasons must, of force, give place
          to better.
The people 'twixt Philippi and this ground
Do stand but in a forced affection;
For they have grudged us contribution:
The enemy, marching along by them,
By them shall make a fuller number up,
Come on refresh'd, new-added, and encouraged;
From which advantage shall we cut him off,   210
If at Philippi we do face him there,
These people at our back.
Cas.   Hear me, good brother.
Bru. Under your pardon. You must note
          beside,
That we have tried the utmost of our friends,
Our legions are brim-full, our cause is ripe:
The enemy increaseth every day;
We, at the height, are ready to decline.
There is a tide in the affairs of men,
Which, taken at the flood, leads on to fortune:
Omitted, all the voyage of their life   220
Is bound in shallows and in miseries.
On such a full sea are we now afloat;
And we must take the current when it serves,
Or lose our ventures.
Cas.   Then, with your will, go on;
We'll along ourselves, and meet them at Philippi.
Bru. The deep of night is crept upon our talk,
And nature must obey necessity;
●Which we will niggard with a little rest.
There is no more to say?
Cas.   No more. Good night:
Early to-morrow will we rise, and hence.   230

Bru. Lucius! [*Enter Lucius.*] My gown.
    [*Exit Lucius.*] Farewell, good Messala:
Good night, Titinius. Noble, noble Cassius,
Good night, and good repose.
    Cas.   O my dear brother!
This was an ill beginning of the night:
Never come such division 'tween our souls!
Let it not, Brutus.
    Bru.   Every thing is well.
    Cas. Good night, my lord.
    Bru.   Good night, good brother.
    Tit. Mes.   Good night, Lord Brutus.
    Bru.   Farewell, every one.
               [*Exeunt all but Brutus.*

     Re-enter Lucius, *with the gown.*

Give me the gown. Where is thy instrument?
    Luc. Here in the tent.
    Bru.   What, thou speak'st drowsily? 240
Poor knave, I blame thee not; thou art o'er-
    watch'd.
Call Claudius and some other of my men;
I'll have them sleep on cushions in my tent.
    Luc. Varro and Claudius!

    Enter Varro *and* Claudius.

    Var. Calls my lord?
    Bru. I pray you, sirs, lie in my tent and sleep;
It may be I shall raise you by and by
On business to my brother Cassius.
    Var. So please you, we will stand and watch
    your pleasure.
    Bru. I will not have it so: lie down, good
    sirs;   250
It may be I shall otherwise bethink me.
Look, Lucius, here's the book I sought for so;
I put it in the pocket of my gown.
               [*Var. and Clau. lie down.*
    Luc. I was sure your lordship did not give
    it me.
    Bru. Bear with me, good boy, I am much
    forgetful.
Canst thou hold up thy heavy eyes awhile,
And touch thy instrument a strain or two?
    Luc. Ay, my lord, an't please you.
    Bru.   It does, my boy:
I trouble thee too much, but thou art willing.
    Luc. It is my duty, sir.   260
    Bru. I should not urge thy duty past thy
    might;
I know young bloods look for a time of rest.
    Luc. I have slept, my lord, already.
    Bru. It was well done; and thou shalt sleep
    again;
I will not hold thee long: if I do live,
I will be good to thee.   [*Music, and a song.*
This is a sleepy tune. O murderous slumber,
Lay'st thou thy leaden mace upon my boy,
That plays thee music? Gentle knave, good
    night;   269
I will not do thee so much wrong to wake thee:
If thou dost nod, thou break'st thy instrument;
I'll take it from thee; and, good boy, good night.
Let me see, let me see; is not the leaf turn'd
    down
Where I left reading? Here it is, I think.

    Enter the Ghost of Cæsar.

How ill this taper burns! Ha! who comes here?

Brutus: 'Canst thou hold up thy heavy eyes awhile, And touch thy instrument a strain or two?' Leo Genn as Brutus. Old Vic Theatre, London, 1935

280 *stare.* i.e. stand on end.

Brutus: 'Speak to me what thou art.' Brutus with the ghost of Caesar. Engraving from a painting by Richard Westall (1765–1836)

292 *false.* Out of tune.

308 *betimes before.* As early as possible.

5 *warn.* Prevent.

I think it is the weakness of mine eyes
That shapes this monstrous apparition.
It comes upon me.   Art thou any thing?
Art thou some god, some angel, or some devil,
● That makest my blood cold and my hair to stare?
Speak to me what thou art.   281
   Ghost.   Thy evil spirit, Brutus.
   Bru.   Why comest thou?
   Ghost.   To tell thee thou shalt see me at
     Philippi.
   Bru.   Well; then I shall see thee again?
   Ghost.   Ay, at Philippi.
   Bru.   Why, I will see thee at Philippi, then.
                           [*Exit Ghost.*
Now I have taken heart thou vanishest:
Ill spirit, I would hold more talk with thee.
Boy, Lucius! Varro! Claudius! Sirs, awake!
Claudius!   291
●   *Luc.*   The strings, my lord, are false.
   Bru.   He thinks he still is at his instrument.
Lucius, awake!
   Luc.   My lord?
   Bru.   Didst thou dream, Lucius, that thou so
     criedst out?
   Luc.   My lord, I do not know that I did cry.
   Bru.   Yes, that thou didst: didst thou see any
     thing?
   Luc.   Nothing, my lord.
   Bru.   Sleep again, Lucius.   Sirrah Claudius!
To Var.] Fellow thou, awake!   301
   Var.   My lord?
   Clau.   My lord?
   Bru.   Why did you so cry out, sirs, in your
     sleep?
   Var. Clau.   Did we, my lord?
   Bru.   Ay: saw you any thing?
   Var.   No, my lord, I saw nothing.
   Clau.   Nor I, my lord.
   Bru.   Go and commend me to my brother
     Cassius;
● Bid him set on his powers betimes before,
And we will follow.
   Var. Clau.   It shall be done, my lord. 309
                          [*Exeunt.*

ACT V.

SCENE I.   *The plains of Philippi.*

Enter OCTAVIUS, ANTONY, *and their* army.

   Oct.   Now, Antony, our hopes are answered:
You said the enemy would not come down,
But keep the hills and upper regions:
It proves not so: their battles are at hand;
● They mean to warn us at Philippi here,
Answering before we do demand of them.
   Ant.   Tut, I am in their bosoms, and I know
Wherefore they do it: they could be content
To visit other places; and come down
With fearful bravery, thinking by this face   10
To fasten in our thoughts that they have courage;
But 'tis not so.

Enter a Messenger.

   Mess.   Prepare you, generals:
The enemy comes on in gallant show;
Their bloody sign of battle is hung out,
And something to be done immediately.

Ant.   Octavius, lead your battle softly on,
Upon the left hand of the even field.
   Oct.   Upon the right hand I; keep thou the
     left.
● *Ant.*   Why do you cross me in this exigent?
   Oct.   I do not cross you; but I will do so.   20
                            [*March.*

Drum.   Enter BRUTUS, CASSIUS, *and their*
Army; LUCILIUS, TITINIUS, MESSALA, *and
others.*

   Bru.   They stand, and would have parley.
   Cas.   Stand fast, Titinius: we must out and
     talk.
   Oct.   Mark Antony, shall we give sign of battle?
● *Ant.*   No, Cæsar, we will answer on their
     charge.
Make forth; the generals would have some words.
   Oct.   Stir not until the signal.
   Bru.   Words before blows: is it so, country-
     men?
   Oct.   Not that we love words better, as you do.
   Bru.   Good words are better than bad strokes,
     Octavius.
   Ant.   In your bad strokes, Brutus, you give
     good words: 30
Witness the hole you made in Cæsar's heart,
Crying 'Long live! hail, Cæsar!'
   Cas.   Antony,
●The posture of your blows are yet unknown;
●But for your words, they rob the Hybla bees,
And leave them honeyless.
   Ant.   Not stingless too.
   Bru.   O, yes, and soundless too;
For you have stol'n their buzzing, Antony,
And very wisely threat before you sting.
   Ant.   Villains, you did not so, when your vile
     daggers
Hack'd one another in the sides of Cæsar: 40
You show'd your teeth like apes, and fawn'd like
     hounds,
And bow'd like bondmen, kissing Cæsar's feet;
Whilst damned Casca, like a cur, behind
Struck Cæsar on the neck.   O you flatterers!
   Cas.   Flatterers!   Now, Brutus, thank your-
     self:
This tongue had not offended so to-day,
If Cassius might have ruled.
   Oct.   Come, come, the cause: if arguing make
     us sweat,
The proof of it will turn to redder drops.
Look;   50
I draw a sword against conspirators;
When think you that the sword goes up again?
Never, till Cæsar's three and thirty wounds
Be well avenged; or till another Cæsar
Have added slaughter to the sword of traitors.
   Bru.   Cæsar, thou canst not die by traitors'
     hands,
Unless thou bring'st them with thee.
   Oct.   So I hope;
I was not born to die on Brutus' sword.
   Bru.   O, if thou wert the noblest of thy strain,
Young man, thou couldst not die more honour-
     able.   60
   Cas.   A peevish schoolboy, worthless of such
     honour,
Join'd with a masker and a reveller!
   Ant.   Old Cassius still!

Antony: 'Octavius, lead your battle softly on ...' Engraving by Bartolomeo Pinelli, 1821

19 *exigent.* Emergency.

24 *answer on.* Meet.

33 *posture.* i.e. efficacy.

34 *Hybla.* Area of Sicily famous for honey.

75 *set.* i.e. risk.

77 *Epicurus.* A philosopher who gave no credit to omens.

79 *presage.* Portend.

83 *consorted.* Escorted.

105 *prevent.* i.e. shorten.

Oct.   Come, Antony, away!
Defiance, traitors, hurl we in your teeth:
If you dare fight to-day, come to the field;
If not, when you have stomachs.
        [*Exeunt Octavius, Antony, and their army.*
        Cas.   Why, now, blow wind, swell billow and
            swim bark!
The storm is up, and all is on the hazard.
        Bru.   Ho, Lucilius! hark, a word with you.
        Lucil.   [*Standing forth*] My lord?
            [*Brutus and Lucilius converse apart.*
        Cas.   Messala!
        Mes. [*Standing forth*] What says my general?
        Cas.   Messala,   71
This is my birth-day; as this very day
Was Cassius born.   Give me thy hand, Messala:
Be thou my witness that against my will,
● As Pompey was, am I compell'd to set
Upon one battle all our liberties.
● You know that I held Epicurus strong
And his opinion: now I change my mind,
● And partly credit things that do presage.
Coming from Sardis, on our former ensign   80
Two mighty eagles fell, and there they perch'd,
Gorging and feeding from our soldiers' hands;
● Who to Philippi here consorted us:
This morning are they fled away and gone;
And in their steads do ravens, crows and kites,
Fly o'er our heads and downward look on us,
As we were sickly prey: their shadows seem
A canopy most fatal, under which
Our army lies, ready to give up the ghost.
        Mes.   Believe not so.
        Cas.   I but believe it partly; 90
For I am fresh of spirit and resolved
To meet all perils very constantly.
        Bru.   Even so, Lucilius.
        Cas.   Now, most noble Brutus,
The gods to-day stand friendly, that we may,
Lovers in peace, lead on our days to age!
But since the affairs of men rest still incertain,
Let's reason with the worst that may befall.
If we do lose this battle, then is this
The very last time we shall speak together:
What are you then determined to do?   100
        Bru.   Even by the rule of that philosophy
By which I did blame Cato for the death
Which he did give himself, I know not how,
But I do find it cowardly and vile,
● For fear of what might fall, so to prevent
The time of life: arming myself with patience
To stay the providence of some high powers
That govern us below.
        Cas.   Then, if we lose this battle,
You are contented to be led in triumph
Thorough the streets of Rome?   110
        Bru.   No, Cassius, no: think not, thou noble
            Roman,
That ever Brutus will go bound to Rome;
He bears too great a mind.   But this same day
Must end that work the ides of March begun;
And whether we shall meet again I know not.
Therefore our everlasting farewell take:
For ever, and for ever, farewell, Cassius!
If we do meet again, why, we shall smile;
If not, why then, this parting was well made.
        Cas.   For ever, and for ever, farewell, Brutus!
If we do meet again, we'll smile indeed;   121
If not, 'tis true this parting was well made.

Bru. Why, then, lead on.   O, that a man might know
The end of this day's business ere it come!
But it sufficeth that the day will end,
And then the end is known.   Come, ho! away!
[*Exeunt.*

SCENE II.   *The same.   The field of battle.*

Alarum.   Enter BRUTUS *and* MESSALA.

● *Bru.* Ride, ride, Messala, ride, and give these bills
Unto the legions on the other side. [*Loud alarum.*
Let them set on at once; for I perceive
● But cold demeanour in Octavius' wing,
And sudden push gives them the overthrow.
Ride, ride, Messala: let them all come down.
[*Exeunt.*

SCENE III.   *Another part of the field.*

Alarums.   Enter CASSIUS *and* TITINIUS.

Cas. O, look, Titinius, look, the villains fly!
Myself have to mine own turn'd enemy:
This ensign here of mine was turning back;
I slew the coward, and did take it from him.
Tit. O Cassius, Brutus gave the word too early:
Who, having some advantage on Octavius,
Took it too eagerly: his soldiers fell to spoil,
Whilst we by Antony are all enclosed.

Enter PINDARUS.

Pin. Fly further off, my lord, fly further off;
Mark Antony is in your tents, my lord: 10
Fly, therefore, noble Cassius, fly far off.
Cas. This hill is far enough.   Look, look, Titinius;
Are those my tents where I perceive the fire?
Tit. They are, my lord.
Cas.   Titinius, if thou lovest me,
Mount thou my horse, and hide thy spurs in him,
Till he have brought thee up to yonder troops,
And here again; that I may rest assured
Whether yond troops are friend or enemy.
Tit. I will be here again, even with a thought.
[*Exit.*
Cas. Go, Pindarus, get higher on that hill;   20
My sight was ever thick; regard Titinius,
And tell me what thou notest about the field.
[*Pindarus ascends the hill.*
This day I breathed first: time is come round,
And where I did begin, there shall I end;
My life is run his compass.   Sirrah, what news?
Pin. [*Above*] O my lord!
Cas. What news?
Pin. [*Above*] Titinius is enclosed round about
With horsemen, that make to him on the spur;
Yet he spurs on.   Now they are almost on him.
● Now, Titinius! Now some light.   O, he lights too.   31
He's ta'en. [*Shout.*] And, hark! they shout for joy.
Cas. Come down, behold no more.
O, coward that I am, to live so long,
To see my best friend ta'en before my face!

PINDARUS *descends.*

Come hither, sirrah:

Set design for the field of battle by William Armstrong, Stratford-upon-Avon, 1950

1 *bills.* Written orders.

4 *cold demeanour.* Lack of spirit.

31 *lights.* Alights.

Cassius: 'Come down, behold no more.' Engraving by Kenny Meadows from Barry Cornwall's *Works of Shakspere,* 1846

43 *Stand*. Delay.

51 *change*. Exchange.

68 *apt*. Ready, willing.

88 *regarded*. Respected.

In Parthia did I take thee prisoner;
And then I swore thee, saving of thy life,
That whatsoever I did bid thee do,
Thou shouldst attempt it.   Come now, keep thine
    oath;   40
Now be a freeman: and with this good sword,
That ran through Cæsar's bowels, search this
    bosom.
 ● Stand not to answer: here, take thou the hilts;
And, when my face is cover'd, as 'tis now,
Guide thou the sword.   [*Pindarus stabs him.*]
    Cæsar, thou art revenged,
Even with the sword that kill'd thee.   [*Dies.*
    Pin. So, I am free; yet would not so have been,
Durst I have done my will.   O Cassius,
Far from this country Pindarus shall run,
Where never Roman shall take note of him.   50
                            [*Exit.*

Re-enter TITINIUS *with* MESSALA.

 ● *Mes.*   It is but change, Titinius; for Octavius
Is overthrown by noble Brutus' power,
As Cassius' legions are by Antony.
    Tit.   These tidings will well comfort Cassius.
    Mes.   Where did you leave him?
    Tit.   All disconsolate,
With Pindarus his bondman, on this hill.
    Mes.   Is not that he that lies upon the ground?
    Tit.   He lies not like the living.   O my heart!
    Mes.   Is not that he?
    Tit.   No, this was he, Messala,
But Cassius is no more.   O setting sun,   60
As in thy red rays thou dost sink to night,
So in his red blood Cassius' day is set;
The sun of Rome is set!   Our day is gone;
Clouds, dews, and dangers come; our deeds are
    done!
Mistrust of my success hath done this deed.
    Mes.   Mistrust of good success hath done this
    deed.
O hateful error, melancholy's child,
 ● Why dost thou show to the apt thoughts of men
The things that are not?   O error, soon con-
    ceived,
Thou never comest unto a happy birth,   70
But kill'st the mother that engender'd thee!
    Tit.   What, Pindarus! where art thou, Pin-
    darus?
    Mes.   Seek him, Titinius, whilst I go to meet
The noble Brutus, thrusting this report
Into his ears; I may say, thrusting it;
For piercing steel and darts envenomed
Shall be as welcome to the ears of Brutus
As tidings of this sight.
    Tit.   Hie you, Messala,
And I will seek for Pindarus the while.
                     [*Exit Messala.*
Why didst thou send me forth, brave Cassius? 80
Did I not meet thy friends? and did not they
Put on my brows this wreath of victory,
And bid me give it thee?   Didst thou not hear
    their shouts?
Alas, thou hast misconstrued every thing!
But, hold thee, take this garland on thy brow;
Thy Brutus bid me give it thee, and I
Will do his bidding.   Brutus, come apace,
 ● And see how I regarded Caius Cassius.
By your leave, gods:—this is a Roman's part: 89

Come, Cassius' sword, and find Titinius' heart.
[*Kills himself.*

Alarum. Re-enter MESSALA, *with* BRUTUS,
young CATO, STRATO, VOLUMNIUS, *and* LU-
CILIUS.

Bru. Where, where, Messala, doth his body lie?
Mes. Lo, yonder, and Titinius mourning it.
Bru. Titinius' face is upward.
Cato.   He is slain.
Bru. O Julius Cæsar, thou art mighty yet!
Thy spirit walks abroad, and turns our swords
In our own proper entrails.   [*Low alarums.*
Cato.   Brave Titinius!
Look, whether he have not crown'd dead Cas-
sius!
Bru. Are yet two Romans living such as these?
The last of all the Romans, fare thee well!
It is impossible that ever Rome   100
● Should breed thy fellow. Friends, I owe more
tears
To this dead man than you shall see me pay.
I shall find time, Cassius, I shall find time.
Come, therefore, and to Thasos send his body:
His funerals shall not be in our camp,
Lest it discomfort us. Lucilius, come;
And come, young Cato; let us to the field.
Labeo and Flavius, set our battles on:
'Tis three o'clock; and, Romans, yet ere night
We shall try fortune in a second fight. [*Exeunt.*

SCENE IV. *Another part of the field.*

Alarum. Enter fighting, Soldiers *of both
armies; then* BRUTUS, *young* CATO, LU-
CILIUS, *and others.*

Bru. Yet, countrymen, O, yet hold up your
heads!
Cato. What bastard doth not? Who will go
with me?
I will proclaim my name about the field:
I am the son of Marcus Cato, ho!
A foe to tyrants, and my country's friend;
I am the son of Marcus Cato, ho!
Bru. And I am Brutus, Marcus Brutus, I;
Brutus, my country's friend; know me for
Brutus!   [*Exit.*
Lucil. O young and noble Cato, art thou
down?
Why, now thou diest as bravely as Titinius;   10
And mayst be honour'd, being Cato's son.
First Sold. Yield, or thou diest.
Lucil.   Only I yield to die:
There is so much that thou wilt kill me straight;
[*Offering money.*
Kill Brutus, and be honour'd in his death.
First Sold. We must not. A noble prisoner!
Sec. Sold. Room, ho! Tell Antony, Brutus
is ta'en.
First Sold. I'll tell the news. Here comes
the general.

Enter ANTONY.

Brutus is ta'en, Brutus is ta'en, my lord.
Ant. Where is he?
Lucil. Safe, Antony; Brutus is safe enough:
I dare assure thee that no enemy   21
Shall ever take alive the noble Brutus:
The gods defend him from so great a shame!

101 *fellow.* Equal.

Roman battle scene. Engraving by Bartolomeo Pinelli,
1821

Brutus: 'And I am Brutus, Marcus Brutus, I;' Detail
from a drawing by J. Coghlan (early 19th century)

18 *several.* Separate.

Brutus: 'So fare you well at once.' Engraving by Bartolomeo Pinelli, 1821

When you do find him, or alive or dead,
He will be found like Brutus, like himself.
    Ant.   This is not Brutus, friend; but, I
      assure you,
A prize no less in worth: keep this man safe;
Give him all kindness: I had rather have
Such men my friends than enemies.   Go on,
And see whether Brutus be alive or dead;   30
And bring us word unto Octavius' tent
How every thing is chanced.   [*Exeunt.*

    SCENE V.   *Another part of the field.*

Enter BRUTUS, DARDANIUS, CLITUS, STRATO,
    and VOLUMNIUS.

    Bru.   Come, poor remains of friends, rest on
      this rock.
    Cli.   Statilius show'd the torch-light, but, my
      lord,
He came not back: he is or ta'en or slain.
    Bru.   Sit thee down, Clitus: slaying is the
      word;
It is a deed in fashion.   Hark thee, Clitus.
                      [*Whispers.*
    Cli.   What, I, my lord?   No, not for all the
      world.
    Bru.   Peace then! no words.
    Cli.   I'll rather kill myself.
    Bru.   Hark thee, Dardanius.   [*Whispers.*
    Dar.   Shall I do such a deed?
    Cli.   O Dardanius!
    Dar.   O Clitus!   10
    Cli.   What ill request did Brutus make to thee?
    Dar.   To kill him, Clitus.   Look, he meditates.
    Cli.   Now is that noble vessel full of grief,
That it runs over even at his eyes.
    Bru.   Come hither, good Volumnius; list a
      word.
    Vol.   What says my lord?
    Bru.   Why, this, Volumnius:
The ghost of Cæsar hath appear'd to me
Two several times by night; at Sardis once,
And, this last night, here in Philippi fields:
I know my hour is come.
    Vol.   Not so, my lord.   20
    Bru.   Nay, I am sure it is, Volumnius.
Thou seest the world, Volumnius, how it goes;
Our enemies have beat us to the pit:
                [*Low alarums.*
It is more worthy to leap in ourselves,
Than tarry till they push us.   Good Volumnius,
Thou know'st that we two went to school to-
    gether:
Even for that our love of old, I prithee,
Hold thou my sword-hilts, whilst I run on it.
    Vol.   That's not an office for a friend, my
      lord.   [*Alarum still.*
    Cli.   Fly, fly, my lord; there is no tarrying
      here.   30
    Bru.   Farewell to you; and you; and you,
    Volumnius.
Strato, thou hast been all this while asleep;
Farewell to thee too, Strato.   Countrymen,
My heart doth joy that yet in all my life
I found no man but he was true to me.
I shall have glory by this losing day
More than Octavius and Mark Antony
By this vile conquest shall attain unto.
So fare you well at once; for Brutus' tongue

Hath almost ended his life's history: 40
Night hangs upon mine eyes; my bones would
    rest,
That have but labour'd to attain this hour.
       [*Alarum. Cry within, ' Fly, fly, fly !'*
Cli. Fly, my lord, fly.
Bru.   Hence! I will follow.
    [*Exeunt Clitus, Dardanius, and Volumnius.*
I prithee, Strato, stay thou by thy lord:
Thou art a fellow of a good respect;
Thy life hath had some smatch of honour in it:
Hold then my sword, and turn away thy face,
While I do run upon it.   Wilt thou, Strato?
   Stra. Give me your hand first.   Fare you
    well, my lord.
   Bru. Farewell, good Strato. [*Runs on his*
    sword.] Cæsar, now be still: 50
I kill'd not thee with half so good a will. [*Dies.*

Alarum. Retreat. Enter OCTAVIUS, ANTONY,
   MESSALA, LUCILIUS, *and the army.*

   Oct. What man is that?
   Mes. My master's man.   Strato, where is thy
    master?
   Stra. Free from the bondage you are in,
    Messala:
The conquerors can but make a fire of him;
For Brutus only overcame himself,
And no man else hath honour by his death.
   Lucil. So Brutus should be found.   I thank
    thee, Brutus,
That thou hast proved Lucilius' saying true.
   Oct. All that served Brutus, I will entertain
    them.   60
Fellow, wilt thou bestow thy time with me?
   Stra. Ay, if Messala will prefer me to you.
   Oct. Do so, good Messala.
   Mes. How died my master, Strato?
   Stra. I held the sword, and he did run on it.
   Mes. Octavius, then take him to follow thee,
That did the latest service to my master.
   Ant. This was the noblest Roman of them all:
All the conspirators save only he
Did that they did in envy of great Cæsar;   70
He only, in a general honest thought
And common good to all, made one of them.
His life was gentle, and the elements
So mix'd in him that Nature might stand up
And say to all the world 'This was a man !'
   Oct. According to his virtue let us use him,
With all respect and rites of burial.
Within my tent his bones to-night shall lie,
Most like a soldier, order'd honourably.
So call the field to rest; and let's away,   80
To part the glories of this happy day. [*Exeunt.*

46 *smatch.* Taste.

62 *prefer me.* i.e. speak well of me.

68-72 *This was . . . of them.* See introduction.

Antony: 'This was the noblest Roman of them all ...'
Mark Antony (Marlon Brando) with the dead body of
Brutus (James Mason), film directed by J. L. Mankiewicz,
USA, 1953

Hamlet

1600-1

HAMLET is the most wonderful play ever written, to judge from the fascination it has generally exerted and the amount of discussion to which it has given rise, as Bradley observes. Most of this has been devoted to moralising about Hamlet's character. Here we must be careful to keep an Elizabethan perspective and remind ourselves that Shakespeare was writing a play, not a text for ethical disquisition. And of course there are inconsistencies and loose ends – as in life.

There is also general agreement that the play has a strong reference to its topical background. Dover-Wilson regards it as 'the most topical play in the whole corpus'; but he goes on, 'the main trouble with "historical" critics is their ignorance of history and their lack of historical curiosity.' So this is where the historian can be of use, indeed is necessary. The true historian is a cautious animal: we must be careful not to make crude and simple identifications. A creative writer takes hints and suggestions from his real environment and then does what he likes with them.

What an Elizabethan historian knows is that the political scene in these very years, 1600–1, was dominated by the question of the succession to the throne and by the personality of Essex, near to the throne yet tottering unsteadily, hesitantly, to his fall. Then again the character of Polonius is very important. These three elements were very much at the back of Shakespeare's mind as he wrote. Though not now close to Southampton as he had been earlier, Shakespeare could not but be concerned when his former patron, to whom he had been so close, was Essex's right-hand man. Hamlet is provided with a noble and true-hearted friend in Horatio; and both Verity and Dover-Wilson have seen a personal allusion in the passage (IV.7.80 foll.) devoted to a gallant horseman in Normandy, 'which does not arise naturally out of the context, in which the accomplishment dwelt on is fencing, not horsemanship.' Dover-Wilson points out that Southampton was in command of the horse under Essex in Ireland (as Lieutenant-General, by the way, not Master, a different office).

The contemporary siege of Ostend appears, and there is a lot about the War of the Theatres at the time, the stage and the state of acting.

No doubt *Hamlet is* a highly topical play. As we have seen with *Romeo and Juliet,* Shakespeare resorted to a story which expressed what was working in his mind. He had known the Hamlet story all along from the days of Kyd and Marlowe, from whom there are echoes. But, significantly, we have no forward references to Hamlet in Shakespeare's earlier plays, as there are to Troy and Priam and Cressida, to Julius Caesar and the story of Lucrece. Something brought the story of Hamlet to mind, and urged it on, as was his instinctive way.

The Story. This early Teutonic story goes right back to Saxo Grammaticus at least, and was known to Shakespeare from Kyd. He refreshed his memory for details by looking it up in Belleforest's *Histoires Tragiques*. Practically all the elements are there. Brother-murder is an archetypal theme – one of the reasons why the play is so gripping. Cain's crime is referred to, but it also occurs among Shakespeare's most frequent echoes from the Bible.

Claudius murders his brother, Hamlet's father, to take his throne and his wife. So Hamlet's complex about his mother – revulsion from love – is another powerfully archetypal theme. In it Shakespeare intuited the whole findings of psycho-analysis with regard to the Oedipus complex. Hamlet undoubtedly felt that the throne was his by right. It has not been noticed that he reports that he is 'dreadfully attended': this means in Elizabethan parlance that he is not being given due honour. He is regally Hamlet the Dane; after his death Fortinbras pays tribute:

> For he was likely, had he been put on,
> To have proved most royal.

I cannot refrain from adding, what is insufficiently regarded, the sheer intellectual brilliance he displays, the scintillation of his wit at all times, both naturally and when he feigns madness.

The Danish background was familiar to the Elizabethans, ever since Leicester's players had visited Elsinore in 1587. The finest of lutenists and song-writers, John Dowland, had his career at the Danish Court. English actors frequently visited North Germany; Robert Browne, whose family was wiped out in the plague of 1592–3, had most of his career there.

We do not need to discuss the character of Hamlet, or describe the events of the play – let it speak for itself; merely to illuminate the real background and what it suggested to Shakespeare's mind, where we can.

The Character of Polonius. We have several times had reason to notice the increasing faction-fighting at Court between the Cecils and Essex with his following. There is nothing original in pointing out that Polonius is clearly based on old Lord Burghley – merely in showing how close the resemblance is in detail. Lord Treasurer and the Queen's leading minister, he had been Southampton's guardian, whose grand-daughter the young Earl would not marry and had been made to pay for it.[1] All the Essex faction detested the politic old man, who was irremovable until his death in 1598; after that it was safe to portray him as Polonius.

Hamlet describes Polonius to his face: 'old men have grey beards, their faces are wrinkled, their eyes purging thick amber and plumtree gum . . . together with most weak hams.' Those who are familiar with Burghley's letters in his last years will know that they are full of his querulous complaints about his health, the weakness of his limbs, his gout, his running eyes: 'I am but as a monoculus' (one-eyed), he writes.

One clue to Burghley's hold on power was his remarkable intelligence system. This is clearly rendered in Polonius' interview with Reynaldo, setting him to spy on his son's

1. cf. my
*Shakespeare's
Southampton,*
c. iii.

doings in Paris and report on them. Burghley's elder son, Thomas, had had an unsatis-factory record in France and been similarly reported on. Burghley's famous Precepts, however, were for his clever younger son, Robert – Essex's enemy: Polonius has a similar set for his son, while his perpetual moralising is Burghley all over – it drove the young men mad, all the more because the old man was all-powerful and wise, though prosy and pedestrian.

Essex. Burghley, indeed, warned Essex as to the dizziness of his course; but he was led astray by ambition and popularity – he was always beloved of the people. As there were flecks of this in Bolingbroke, so there are here:

> The courtier's, soldier's, scholar's, eye, tongue, sword,
> Th' expectancy and rose of the fair state,
> The glass of fashion, and the mould of form,
> Th' observed of all observers . . .

Claudius, the king, gives as a reason for dealing secretly with the threat from Hamlet that he is 'loved of the distracted multitude'.

Contemporaneously, Essex was staggering to his downfall, already foreshadowed, but he could not make up his mind to his final throw. Essex himself hesitated, until it was Southampton who propelled him with: 'Shall we then resolve on nothing?' Dover-Wilson describes Hamlet's 'sense of frustration, of infirmity of purpose, of character inhibited from meeting the demands of destiny, of the futility of life in general and action in particular. His melancholy and his procrastination are all of a piece.' Historians know that this perfectly describes Essex at this time: he was quite as psychotic as Hamlet.

The Theatre. *Hamlet* contains Shakespeare's extensive treatment of the contemporary theatre and his view of his profession and of acting – all fascinating. These years 1600–1 were enlivened by the theatre-war set going by the row between Ben Jonson and Marston, brought to the fore in Ben's plays, *Cynthia's Revels* and *Poetaster*, performed by the Children of the Chapel; against Dekker and Marston's *Satiromastix*, played by Shakespeare's Company. All this was no doubt good box-office, as Shakespeare hints; so we must not take it too seriously, any more than he did.

He himself never wrote for the Boys' Companies; nor did he go in for their comical satires. But he reflects on the situation. 'There is an eyrie of children, little eyases [a bawdy pun], that cry out on the top of the question, and are most tyrannically clapped for't: these are now the fashion, and so berattle the common stages, so they call them, that many wearing rapiers are afraid of goose-quills, and dare scarce come thither.' Hamlet comments: 'What, are they children? Who maintains 'em? . . . Will they pursue the quality no longer than they can sing? Will they not say afterwards, if they should grow themselves to common players – as it is like most will if their means are not better – their writers [i.e. Jonson, who had left off writing for Shakespeare's Company] do them wrong, to make them exclaim against their own succession', i.e. professional prospects.

This was pretty plain speaking, and in keeping with his practical common sense. What would be the boy-actors' future when their voices had broken, but as 'common players . . . if their means are not better'? A touch of his own hard experience was there, his old reproach in the Sonnets against the luck

> That did not better for my life provide
> Than public means which public manners breeds.

The public spurred on the controversy. 'There was, for a while, no money bid for argument, unless the Poet and the Player went to cuffs in the question.' For the time, the Boys' Companies carried it off, 'Hercules and his load too', i.e. against the Globe, whose sign that was.

Acting. We cannot go in detail into all that he instructs us about acting: here is the *locus classicus*, two whole scenes devoted to the subject, in which he tells us all that is in his mind, a summing-up of years of experience. He had already put into Polonius' mouth, to show that he had no use for it, the too precise classification of plays, laughing at it – 'the tragical-comical-historical-pastoral', etc. His own, like all living works of genius, transcended the categories.

Shakespeare's convictions about acting are given at length in Hamlet's instructions to the players: speak the speech trippingly on the tongue, not mouth it; do not saw the air with clumsy gestures, but use all gently, show temperance and smoothness even in the moment of passion – in a word, control. He inveighs against the prating he had observed in tragic parts, the gags which clowns would insert at the expense of some necessary part of the action. It is all summed up in his message that 'the purpose of playing . . . was, and is, to hold as 'twere the mirror up to nature, to show . . the very age and body of the time.'

This was evidently what he himself stood for and had learned to practise, as actor and producer, in the transition from the crude early Elizabethan stage to the mature dramaturgy of which he was the foremost and most successful exponent. With artistic and professional success had come at length reconciliation to the necessity he had been under to earn his living the hard way, by public means: let the players be well used, 'for they are the abstracts and brief chronicles of the time; after your death you were better have a bad epitaph than their ill report while you live.' Next follows the marvellous soliloquy of Hamlet, reflecting on the mystery of the actor's art, by which he can produce effects more moving and real than life itself. And this is inset within an inset, a kind of double-mirror. Shakespeare owed it to art as well as nature that his mind moved in double-track; Dover-Wilson says well, 'when he used a word, all possible meanings of it were commonly present to his mind.' Hence, too, all the word-play and punning he was given to, and in which Hamlet is such a virtuoso.

The Age. More evidences of the time remain in this rich, deep, inexhaustible mine. During these years and for some time to come the struggle continued for Ostend, between Spaniards and the Dutch with English aid, costing thousands of lives:

> We go to gain a little patch of ground
> That hath in it no profit but the name.
> To pay five ducats, five, I would not farm it.

The contest had become a matter of prestige. Hamlet comments:

> to my shame I see
> The imminent death of twenty thousand men,
> That for a fantasy and trick of fame
> Go to their graves like beds, fight for a plot
> Whereon the numbers cannot try the cause,
> Which is not tomb enough and continent
> To hide the slain.

We cannot doubt that Hamlet expressed William Shakespeare's view of the matter: he never was one of the fighting fools, he observed them and put them in his plays.

Indeed, Hamlet meditating in the grave-yard gives a fine opportunity for bitter reflections on the time, the great age gone sour. Here's the skull of a lawyer: 'where be his quiddities now, his quillities, his cases, his tenures, and his tricks?' Another might have been a grand buyer of land in his time, 'with his statutes, his recognisances, his fines, his double vouchers, his recoveries. Is this the fine of his fines, and the recovery of his recoveries, to have his fine pate full of fine dirt?' 'That skull had a tongue in it, and could sing once! . . . This might be the pate of a politician, which this ass now o'er-reaches – one that would circumvent God, might it not?'

The time itself was enough to induce bitterness, the kind of bitterness that went into *Troilus and Cressida*, when one's own friends showed what fools they were: 'fools on both sides', he called them.

Personal. Many touches of him occur in this most personal play. We cannot tell whether he had Tarleton in mind in Yorick's skull: 'where be your gibes now? Your gambols, your songs, your flashes of merriment, that were wont to set the table on a roar?' Some think that the reflection on clowns who insist on gagging to the detriment of the play may refer to Will Kemp, who had left the Company the year before.

The quip against 'equivocation' is directed against the unpopular casuistry of the Jesuits. He would be familiar with the many Catholic terms in this, as in other plays, through frequenting Southampton House, which the priests were constantly in and out of – though Southampton's Catholicism was not political, unlike his father's.[1]

The whole episode of Osric, his affected manner, his inflated, sycophantic speech – all contemptuously held up to ridicule by Hamlet – is a sharp reflection on Court manners, at this moment when Essex and his friends had been driven from it. The depiction of the Court of Denmark shows Shakespeare out of sympathy with it: to him it was rotten. The last years of Elizabeth's reign were indeed disheartening.

One need say nothing of all the heart-break in this most moving of all plays: the unbearable reproaches of Hamlet against his mother –

1. cf. my *Shakespeare's Southampton,* c. ii.

A churchyard, Hamlet, Horatio and Clown. Watercolour by Sir John Millais, 1871

> Refrain tonight,
> And that shall lend a kind of easiness
> To the next abstinence, the next more easy.

He knew that well enough from experience. Bitterest of all are Hamlet's words to Ophelia: he is riven with suspicion, torn in two by his situation – and knowledge of psychology tells one of the desire to mortify what one loves. Such unbelievable imperceptiveness has been shown in critical comment on this – with no excuse, for Hamlet himself says,

> I loved Ophelia, forty thousand brothers
> Could not with all their quantity of love
> Make up my sum.

Ophelia's madness is so heart-rending, it is like Cordelia's death or Lady Macbeth's ritual washing of her hands; such is Shakespeare's unparalleled force of impact, that one can hardly bear to see or hear what is going on, he so searches the human heart, and all its crevices of guilt and fear, remorse and grief.

> O, from what power has thou this powerful might?

A Katharine Hamlet was drowned in the Avon in December 1579; an inquest took place at Stratford early in 1580, when he was rising sixteen. It is unlikely that he would forget that, and with it her name; it was uncertain whether the girl had not drowned herself. It suggested Ophelia's end – which has inspired other artists in turn.

We detect him, as always, in his love of rare words ending in 'ive' – conjunctive, splenetive. He never forgot anything; he is still remembering Marlowe's words: 'the whiff and wind of his fell sword' is a reminiscence from *Dido, Queen of Carthage*; the hebona with which Hamlet's father was poisoned comes from *The Jew of Malta*. Reading, as usual, while writing his play Shakespeare derived some psychological suggestions from Bright's *Treatise of Melancholy*, and more from Florio's *Montaigne*.

The play is full of scraps of ballads, songs and contemporary lore – about ghosts, for example. It is not likely that an Elizabethan like Shakespeare would not have believed in ghosts. Eclipses come into this play full of foreboding and suspicion – and the years 1598 to 1601 were marked by several, both of sun and moon.

The Text offers some difficulties. That of the quarto put out in 1604 is by far the fullest, though it omits some 85 lines to be found in the Folio version. E. K. Chambers considers that this quarto 'substantially represents the original text of the play . . . It is a fair text, with little mislineation, light punctuation, and a good many abnormal spellings, and may very possibly be from the author's manuscript; but, if so, numerous misprints suggest that this was not very legible.' This is very likely: we know that Shakespeare wrote rapidly and in old English script, not our modern Italian hand (as Robert Cecil did).

A first quarto, of 1603, mentioned the play as having been performed in the city of London, as well as in the two universities of Oxford and Cambridge, but this would mean merely the university towns. An early tradition has it that Shakespeare acted the part of the Ghost of Hamlet's father – it was 'a kingly part'. An endearing performance was that by the crew on board the East Indiaman *Dragon*, at Sierra Leone for Portuguese and English guests in 1607–8.

HAMLET, PRINCE OF DENMARK.

DRAMATIS PERSONÆ.

CLAUDIUS, king of Denmark.
HAMLET, son to the late, and nephew to the present king.
POLONIUS, lord chamberlain.
HORATIO, friend to Hamlet.
LAERTES, son to Polonius.
VOLTIMAND,
CORNELIUS,
ROSENCRANTZ,
GUILDENSTERN, } courtiers.
OSRIC,
A Gentleman,
A Priest.
MARCELLUS, } officers.
BERNARDO, }
FRANCISCO, a soldier.

REYNALDO, servant to Polonius.
Players.
Two Clowns, grave-diggers.
FORTINBRAS, prince of Norway.
A Captain.
English Ambassadors.

GERTRUDE, queen of Denmark, and mother to Hamlet.
OPHELIA, daughter to Polonius.

Lords, Ladies, Officers, Soldiers, Sailors, Messengers, and other Attendants.

Ghost of Hamlet's Father.

SCENE: *Denmark.*

● *A bullet beside a text line indicates an annotation in the opposite column*

ACT I.

SCENE I. *Elsinore. A platform before the castle.*

FRANCISCO *at his post. Enter to him* BERNARDO.

Ber. Who's there?
Fran. Nay, answer me: stand, and unfold yourself.
Ber. Long live the king!
Fran. Bernardo?
Ber. He.
Fran. You come most carefully upon your hour.

Set design for the platform before the castle at Elsinore by J. O'Connor, 1879

Opposite: Portrait of John Philip Kemble as Hamlet by Sir Thomas Lawrence (1769–1830)

13 *rivals.* Companions. *watch.* Guard.

15 *liegemen.* Subjects. *the Dane.* The king of Denmark.

29 *approve.* Confirm.

35 *Last night of all.* Only last night.

46 *usurps't.* Intrudes upon.

48 *buried Denmark.* i.e. the buried king of Denmark, Hamlet's father.

Costume design for Horatio by Ann Curtis, Royal Shakespeare Co, 1965

Ber. 'Tis now struck twelve; get thee to bed, Francisco.
Fran. For this relief much thanks: 'tis bitter cold,
And I am sick at heart.
Ber. Have you had quiet guard?
Fran.   Not a mouse stirring. 10
Ber. Well, good night.
If you do meet Horatio and Marcellus,
●The rivals of my watch, bid them make haste.
Fran. I think I hear them. Stand, ho! Who's there?

Enter HORATIO *and* MARCELLUS.

● *Hor.* Friends to this ground.
Mar.   And liegemen to the Dane.
Fran. Give you good night.
Mar.   O, farewell, honest soldier:
Who hath relieved you?
Fran.   Bernardo has my place.
Give you good night.   [*Exit.*
Mar.   Holla! Bernardo!
Ber.   Say,
What, is Horatio there?
Hor.   A piece of him.
Ber. Welcome, Horatio: welcome, good Mar-
cellus.   20
Mar. What, has this thing appear'd again to-
night?
Ber. I have seen nothing.
Mar. Horatio says 'tis but our fantasy,
And will not let belief take hold of him
Touching this dreaded sight, twice seen of us:
Therefore I have entreated him along
With us to watch the minutes of this night;
That if again this apparition come,
●He may approve our eyes and speak to it.
Hor. Tush, tush, 'twill not appear.
Ber.   Sit down awhile; 30
And let us once again assail your ears,
That are so fortified against our story
What we have two nights seen.
Hor.   Well, sit we down,
And let us hear Bernardo speak of this.
● *Ber.* Last night of all,
When yond same star that's westward from the pole
Had made his course to illume that part of heaven
Where now it burns, Marcellus and myself,
The bell then beating one,—

Enter Ghost.

Mar. Peace, break thee off; look, where it comes again!   40
Ber. In the same figure, like the king that's dead.
Mar. Thou art a scholar; speak to it, Horatio.
Ber. Looks it not like the king? mark it, Horatio.
Hor. Most like: it harrows me with fear and wonder.
Ber. It would be spoke to.
Mar.   Question it, Horatio.
● *Hor.* What art thou that usurp'st this time of night,
Together with that fair and warlike form
●In which the majesty of buried Denmark

Did sometimes march? by heaven I charge thee,
    speak!
Mar.   It is offended.
Ber.   See, it stalks away!   50
Hor.   Stay! speak, speak! I charge thee,
    speak!   [*Exit Ghost.*
Mar.   'Tis gone, and will not answer.
Ber.   How now, Horatio! you tremble and
    look pale:
Is not this something more than fantasy?
What think you on't?
    Hor.   Before my God, I might not this believe
● Without the sensible and true avouch
Of mine own eyes.
    Mar.   Is it not like the king?
    Hor.   As thou art to thyself:
Such was the very armour he had on   60
● When he the ambitious Norway combated;
● So frown'd he once, when, in an angry parle,
● He smote the sledded Polacks on the ice.
'Tis strange.
●   *Mar.*   Thus twice before, and jump at this
    dead hour,
● With martial stalk hath he gone by our watch.
    Hor.   In what particular thought to work I
    know not;
● But in the gross and scope of my opinion,
This bodes some strange eruption to our state.
    Mar.   Good now, sit down, and tell me, he
    that knows,   70
Why this same strict and most observant watch
So nightly toils the subject of the land,
And why such daily cast of brazen cannon,
And foreign mart for implements of war;
Why such impress of shipwrights, whose sore task
Does not divide the Sunday from the week;
What might be toward, that this sweaty haste
Doth make the night joint-labourer with the day:
Who is't that can inform me?
    Hor.   That can I;
At least, the whisper goes so.   Our last king, 80
Whose image even but now appear'd to us,
Was, as you know, by Fortinbras of Norway,
● Thereto prick'd on by a most emulate pride,
Dared to the combat; in which our valiant Ham-
    let—
For so this side of our known world esteem'd
    him—
Did slay this Fortinbras; who, by a seal'd com-
    pact,
● Well ratified by law and heraldry,
Did forfeit, with his life, all those his lands
Which he stood seized of, to the conqueror:
● Against the which, a moiety competent   90
Was gaged by our king; which had return'd
To the inheritance of Fortinbras,
● Had he been vanquisher; as, by the same coven-
    ant,
And carriage of the article design'd,
His fell to Hamlet.   Now, sir, young Fortinbras,
Of unimproved mettle hot and full,
● Hath in the skirts of Norway here and there
● Shark'd up a list of lawless resolutes,
For food and diet, to some enterprise
● That hath a stomach in't; which is no other—
As it doth well appear unto our state—   101
But to recover of us, by strong hand
And terms compulsatory, those foresaid lands
So by his father lost: and this, I take it,

57 *sensible.* Actual. *avouch.* Witness.

61 *Norway.* The king of Norway.

62 *parle.* Conference.

63 *the sledded Polacks.* The Poles in sledges.

Horatio: 'He smote the sledded Polacks on the ice'.
Engraving from Sigmund Herberstein's *Rerum Mosco-
vitacarum Commentarii*, 1549

65 *jump.* Exactly.

66 *martial stalk.* Military bearing.

68 *gross and scope.* Overall view.

83 *prick'd.* Spurred. *emulate.* Rivalling.

87 *law and heraldry.* i.e. law and right.

90 *moiety competent.* A sufficient share.

93-94 *covenant And carriage.* Conditions and terms.

97 *skirts.* Outlying regions.

98 *Shark'd up.* Gathered together. *resolutes.* Despera-
does.

100 *hath a stomach.* Has promise.

106 *chief head*. Main reason.

107 *romage*. Turmoil.

109 *sort*. Transpire.

118 *moist star*. Moon.

121 *like precurse*. Similar forewarnings.

125 *climatures*. Regions.

Horatio: 'Stay, illusion! . . . Speak to me.' Engraving by Kenny Meadows from Barry Cornwall's *Works of Shakspere*, 1846

140 *partisan*. Pike.

154 *extravagant and erring*. Wandering.

162 *strike*. Work evil influences.

Is the main motive of our preparations,
●The source of this our watch and the chief head
●Of this post-haste and romage in the land.
   Ber. I think it be no other but e'en so:
●Well may it sort that this portentous figure
Comes armed through our watch; so like the
    king   110
That was and is the question of these wars.
   Hor. A mote it is to trouble the mind's eye.
In the most high and palmy state of Rome,
A little ere the mightiest Julius fell,
The graves stood tenantless and the sheeted dead
Did squeak and gibber in the Roman streets:
†As stars with trains of fire and dews of blood,
●Disasters in the sun; and the moist star
Upon whose influence Neptune's empire stands
Was sick almost to doomsday with eclipse: 120
●And even the like precurse of fierce events,
As harbingers preceding still the fates
And prologue to the omen coming on,
Have heaven and earth together demonstrated
●Unto our climatures and countrymen.—
But soft, behold! lo, where it comes again!

         Re-enter Ghost.

I'll cross it, though it blast me. Stay, illusion!
If thou hast any sound, or use of voice,
Speak to me:
If there be any good thing to be done,   130
That may to thee do ease and grace to me,
Speak to me: [*Cock crows.*
If thou art privy to thy country's fate,
Which, happily, foreknowing may avoid,
O, speak!
Or if thou hast uphoarded in thy life
Extorted treasure in the womb of earth,
For which, they say, you spirits oft walk in death,
Speak of it: stay, and speak! Stop it, Marcellus.
● *Mar.* Shall I strike at it with my partisan?
   Hor. Do, if it will not stand.   141
   Ber.   'Tis here!
   Hor.   'Tis here!
   Mar. 'Tis gone!   [*Exit Ghost.*
We do it wrong, being so majestical,
To offer it the show of violence;
For it is, as the air, invulnerable,
And our vain blows malicious mockery.
   Ber. It was about to speak, when the cock
    crew.
   Hor. And then it started like a guilty thing
Upon a fearful summons. I have heard,
The cock, that is the trumpet to the morn, 150
Doth with his lofty and shrill-sounding throat
Awake the god of day; and, at his warning,
Whether in sea or fire, in earth or air,
●The extravagant and erring spirit hies
To his confine: and of the truth herein
This present object made probation.
   Mar. It faded on the crowing of the cock.
Some say that ever 'gainst that season comes
Wherein our Saviour's birth is celebrated,
The bird of dawning singeth all night long: 160
And then, they say, no spirit dare stir abroad;
●The nights are wholesome; then no planets strike,
No fairy takes, nor witch hath power to charm,
So hallow'd and so gracious is the time.
   Hor. So have I heard and do in part believe it.
But, look, the morn, in russet mantle clad,
Walks o'er the dew of yon high eastward hill:

Break we our watch up; and by my advice,
Let us impart what we have seen to-night
Unto young Hamlet; for, upon my life,   170
This spirit, dumb to us, will speak to him.
Do you consent we shall acquaint him with it,
As needful in our loves, fitting our duty?
    Mar.   Let's do't, I pray; and I this morning
         know
Where we shall find him most conveniently.
                                        [*Exeunt.*

SCENE II.   *A room of state in the castle.*

Enter the KING, QUEEN, HAMLET, POLONIUS,
LAERTES, VOLTIMAND, CORNELIUS, Lords,
and Attendants.

    King.   Though yet of Hamlet our dear bro-
         ther's death
The memory be green, and that it us befitted
To bear our hearts in grief and our whole kingdom
• To be contracted in one brow of woe,
Yet so far hath discretion fought with nature
That we with wisest sorrow think on him,
Together with remembrance of ourselves.
Therefore our sometime sister, now our queen,
• The imperial jointress to this warlike state,
Have we, as 'twere with a defeated joy,—   10
With an auspicious and a dropping eye,
With mirth in funeral and with dirge in marriage,
• In equal scale weighing delight and dole,—
Taken to wife: nor have we herein barr'd
Your better wisdoms, which have freely gone
With this affair along.   For all, our thanks.
Now follows, that you know, young Fortinbras,
Holding a weak supposal of our worth,
Or thinking by our late dear brother's death
Our state to be disjoint and out of frame,   20
Colleagued with the dream of his advantage,
He hath not fail'd to pester us with message,
Importing the surrender of those lands
Lost by his father, with all bonds of law,
To our most valiant brother.   So much for him.
Now for ourself and for this time of meeting:
Thus much the business is: we have here writ
To Norway, uncle of young Fortinbras,—
Who, impotent and bed-rid, scarcely hears
Of this his nephew's purpose,—to suppress   30
• His further gait herein; in that the levies,
• The lists and full proportions, are all made
Out of his subject: and we here dispatch
You, good Cornelius, and you, Voltimand,
For bearers of this greeting to old Norway;
Giving to you no further personal power
To business with the king, more than the scope
• Of these delated articles allow.
Farewell, and let your haste commend your duty.
    Cor.} In that and all things will we show our
    Vol.}   duty.   40
    King.   We doubt it nothing: heartily farewell.
              [*Exeunt Voltimand and Cornelius.*
And now, Laertes, what's the news with you?
You told us of some suit; what is't, Laertes?
You cannot speak of reason to the Dane,
• And lose your voice: what wouldst thou beg,
         Laertes,
• That shall not be my offer, not thy asking?
The head is not more native to the heart,
The hand more instrumental to the mouth,
Than is the throne of Denmark to thy father.

4 *contracted in one brow.* Drawn together in a frown.

9 *jointress.* A widow who inherits her husband's entire estate for her life-time.

13 *dole.* Sorrow.

31 *gait.* Course.

32 *full proportions.* Entire establishment.

38 *delated.* Explanatory.

Costume design for Claudius by Ann Curtis, Royal Shakespeare Co, 1965

45 *lose your voice.* Speak in vain.

46 *That . . . asking.* i.e. that I would give you, even without your asking.

60 *hard*. Hard-earned.

64 *cousin*. i.e. nephew.

65 *A . . . kind*. Rather more than a kinsman, yet not of the same nature (with a pun on 'kind').

67 *sun*. Hamlet plays on the word 'son'.

Queen: 'Good Hamlet, cast thy nighted colour off. . .'
Lithograph of Queen, Hamlet and the King by Eugene Delacroix, 1834

---

74 *common*. i.e. 'natural' and 'base'.

79 *suspiration*. Respiration.

92 *obsequious*. Funereal. *persever*. Persist.

105 *corse*. Corpse.

107 *unprevailing*. Profitless.

What wouldst thou have, Laertes?
  Laer.   My dread lord, 50
Your leave and favour to return to France;
From whence though willingly I came to Denmark,
To show my duty in your coronation,
Yet now, I must confess, that duty done,
My thoughts and wishes bend again toward France
And bow them to your gracious leave and pardon.
  King.   Have you your father's leave?   What says Polonius?
  Pol.   He hath, my lord, wrung from me my slow leave
By laboursome petition, and at last
• Upon his will I seal'd my hard consent :   60
I do beseech you, give him leave to go.
  King.   Take thy fair hour, Laertes; time be thine,
And thy best graces spend it at thy will!
• But now, my cousin Hamlet, and my son,—
• *Ham.* [*Aside*]   A little more than kin, and less than kind.
  King.   How is it that the clouds still hang on you?
  Ham.   Not so, my lord; I am too much i' the
• sun.
  Queen. Good Hamlet, cast thy nighted colour off,
And let thine eye look like a friend on Denmark.
Do not for ever with thy vailed lids   70
Seek for thy noble father in the dust :
Thou know'st 'tis common; all that lives must die,
Passing through nature to eternity.
• *Ham.*   Ay, madam, it is common.
  Queen.   If it be,
Why seems it so particular with thee?
  Ham.   Seems, madam! nay, it is; I know not 'seems.'
'Tis not alone my inky cloak, good mother,
Nor customary suits of solemn black,
• Nor windy suspiration of forced breath,
No, nor the fruitful river in the eye,   80
Nor the dejected 'haviour of the visage,
Together with all forms, moods, shapes of grief,
That can denote me truly : these indeed seem,
For they are actions that a man might play :
But I have that within which passeth show;
These but the trappings and the suits of woe.
  King.   'Tis sweet and commendable in your nature, Hamlet,
To give these mourning duties to your father :
But, you must know, your father lost a father;
That father lost, lost his, and the survivor bound
In filial obligation for some term   91
• To do obsequious sorrow : but to persever
In obstinate condolement is a course
Of impious stubbornness; 'tis unmanly grief;
It shows a will most incorrect to heaven,
A heart unfortified, a mind impatient,
An understanding simple and unschool'd :
For what we know must be and is as common
As any the most vulgar thing to sense,
Why should we in our peevish opposition   100
Take it to heart?   Fie! 'tis a fault to heaven,
A fault against the dead, a fault to nature,
To reason most absurd : whose common theme
Is death of fathers, and who still hath cried,
• From the first corse till he that died to-day,
'This must be so.'   We pray you, throw to earth
• This unprevailing woe, and think of us

As of a father: for let the world take note,
●You are the most immediate to our throne;
And with no less nobility of love   110
Than that which dearest father bears his son,
Do I impart toward you. For your intent
●In going back to school in Wittenberg,
It is most retrograde to our desire:
And we beseech you, bend you to remain
Here, in the cheer and comfort of our eye,
Our chiefest courtier, cousin, and our son.
● *Queen.* Let not thy mother lose her prayers,
    Hamlet:
I pray thee, stay with us; go not to Wittenberg.
    Ham. I shall in all my best obey you, madam.
    King. Why, 'tis a loving and a fair reply: 121
Be as ourself in Denmark. Madam, come;
This gentle and unforced accord of Hamlet
Sits smiling to my heart: in grace whereof,
No jocund health that Denmark drinks to-day,
But the great cannon to the clouds shall tell,
●And the king's rouse the heavens shall bruit again,
Re-speaking earthly thunder. Come away.
                    [*Exeunt all but Hamlet.*
    Ham. O, that this too too solid flesh would
        melt,
Thaw and resolve itself into a dew!   130
Or that the Everlasting had not fix'd
●His canon 'gainst self-slaughter! O God! God!
How weary, stale, flat and unprofitable,
Seem to me all the uses of this world!
Fie on't! ah fie! 'tis an unweeded garden,
That grows to seed; things rank and gross in
    nature
●Possess it merely. That it should come to this!
But two months dead: nay, not so much, not two:
So excellent a king; that was, to this,
●Hyperion to a satyr; so loving to my mother 140
●That he might not beteem the winds of heaven
Visit her face too roughly. Heaven and earth!
Must I remember? why, she would hang on him,
As if increase of appetite had grown
By what it fed on: and yet, within a month—
Let me not think on't—Frailty, thy name is
        woman!—
A little month, or ere those shoes were old
With which she follow'd my poor father's body,
●Like Niobe, all tears:—why she, even she— 149
O God! a beast, that wants discourse of reason,
Would have mourn'd longer—married with my
        uncle,
My father's brother, but no more like my father
●Than I to Hercules: within a month:
Ere yet the salt of most unrighteous tears
●Had left the flushing in her galled eyes,
She married. O, most wicked speed, to post
●With such dexterity to incestuous sheets!
It is not nor it cannot come to good:
But break, my heart; for I must hold my tongue.

Enter HORATIO, MARCELLUS, *and* BERNARDO.

    Hor. Hail to your lordship!
    Ham.   I am glad to see you well: 160
Horatio,—or I do forget myself.
    Hor. The same, my lord, and your poor servant
        ever.
    Ham. Sir, my good friend; I'll change that
        name with you:
And what make you from Wittenberg, Horatio?
Marcellus?

109 *most immediate.* i.e. next in line.

113 *Wittenberg.* University town in Germany.

118 *lose.* Waste.

127 *rouse.* Revel. *bruit again.* Echo.

132 *canon.* Law.

137 *merely.* Entirely.

140 *Hyperion.* Legendary sun-god. *satyr.* Mythical
creature, half-man, half-goat, a symbol of lust.

141 *beteem.* Permit.

149 *Niobe.* Zeus turned her into a rock which wept
continually.

153 *Hercules.* Legendary Greek hero of great strength.

155 *galled.* Sore.

157 *incestuous.* It was thought so to marry a close relation of a previous partner.

Johnston Forbes Robertson as Hamlet, Lyceum Theatre,
London, 1897

172 *make it truster of.* Entrust it with.

182 *dearest.* Greatest.

192 *Season your admiration.* Control your amazement.

200 *at point.* Completely. *cap-a-pe.* From head to foot.

Horatio: '. . . A figure like your father, Armed at point exactly'. Ghost of Hamlet's father. Engraving from a painting by H. Fuseli (1741–1825)

204 *distill'd.* Turned.

209 *in time.* At the same time.

Mar. My good lord—
Ham. I am very glad to see you. Good even, sir.
But what, in faith, make you from Wittenberg?
Hor. A truant disposition, good my lord.
Ham. I would not hear your enemy say so,
Nor shall you do mine ear that violence,   171
● To make it truster of your own report
Against yourself: I know you are no truant.
But what is your affair in Elsinore?
We'll teach you to drink deep ere you depart.
Hor. My lord, I came to see your father's funeral.
Ham. I pray thee, do not mock me, fellow-student;
I think it was to see my mother's wedding.
Hor. Indeed, my lord, it follow'd hard upon.
Ham. Thrift, thrift, Horatio! the funeral baked meats   180
Did coldly furnish forth the marriage tables.
● Would I had met my dearest foe in heaven
Or ever I had seen that day, Horatio!
My father!—methinks I see my father.
Hor. Where, my lord?
Ham.   In my mind's eye, Horatio.
Hor. I saw him once; he was a goodly king.
Ham. He was a man, take him for all in all,
I shall not look upon his like again.
Hor. My lord, I think I saw him yesternight.
Ham. Saw? who?   190
Hor. My lord, the king your father.
Ham.   The king my father!
● *Hor.* Season your admiration for a while
With an attent ear, till I may deliver,
Upon the witness of these gentlemen,
This marvel to you.
Ham.   For God's love, let me hear.
Hor. Two nights together had these gentlemen,
Marcellus and Bernardo, on their watch,
In the dead vast and middle of the night,
Been thus encounter'd. A figure like your father,
● Armed at point exactly, cap-a-pe,   200
Appears before them, and with solemn march
Goes slow and stately by them: thrice he walk'd
By their oppress'd and fear-surprised eyes,
● Within his truncheon's length; whilst they, dis-till'd
Almost to jelly with the act of fear,
Stand dumb and speak not to him. This to me
In dreadful secrecy impart they did;
And I with them the third night kept the watch:
● Where, as they had deliver'd, both in time,
Form of the thing, each word made true and good,
The apparition comes: I knew your father;   211
These hands are not more like.
Ham.   But where was this?
Mar. My lord, upon the platform where we watch'd.
Ham. Did you not speak to it?
Hor.   My lord, I did;
But answer made it none: yet once methought
It lifted up it head and did address
Itself to motion, like as it would speak;
But even then the morning cock crew loud,
And at the sound it shrunk in haste away,
And vanish'd from our sight.
Ham.   'Tis very strange. 220
Hor. As I do live, my honour'd lord, 'tis true;
And we did think it writ down in our duty

To let you know of it.

Ham. Indeed, indeed, sirs, but this troubles me.
Hold you the watch to-night?

Mar.⎰
Ber.⎱   We do, my lord.

Ham. Arm'd, say you?

Mar.⎰
Ber.⎱ Arm'd, my lord.

Ham. From top to toe?

Mar.⎰
Ber.⎱   My lord, from head to foot.

Ham. Then saw you not his face?

Hor. O, yes, my lord; he wore his beaver up.

Ham. What, look'd he frowningly?   231

Hor. A countenance more in sorrow than in
anger.

Ham. Pale or red?

Hor. Nay, very pale.

Ham.   And fix'd his eyes upon you?

Hor. Most constantly.

Ham.   I would I had been there.

Hor. It would have much amazed you.

Ham. Very like, very like.   Stay'd it long?

Hor. While one with moderate haste might
tell a hundred.

Mar.⎰
Ber.⎱ Longer, longer.

Hor. Not when I saw't.

Ham.   His beard was grizzled,—no? 240

Hor. It was, as I have seen it in his life,
A sable silver'd.

Ham.   I will watch to-night;
Perchance 'twill walk again.

Hor.   I warrant it will.

Ham. If it assume my noble father's person,
I'll speak to it, though hell itself should gape
And bid me hold my peace.   I pray you all,
If you have hitherto conceal'd this sight,
Let it be tenable in your silence still;
And whatsoever else shall hap to-night,
Give it an understanding, but no tongue: 250
I will requite your loves.   So, fare you well:
Upon the platform, 'twixt eleven and twelve,
I'll visit you.

All.   Our duty to your honour.

Ham. Your loves, as mine to you: farewell.
                    [*Exeunt all but Hamlet.*
My father's spirit in arms! all is not well;
I doubt some foul play: would the night were
come!
Till then sit still, my soul: foul deeds will rise,
Though all the earth o'erwhelm them, to men's
eyes.   [*Exit*

SCENE III. *A room in Polonius' house.*

Enter LAERTES *and* OPHELIA.

Laer. My necessaries are embark'd: farewell:
And, sister, as the winds give benefit
And convoy is assistant, do not sleep,
But let me hear from you.

Oph.   Do you doubt that?

Laer. For Hamlet and the trifling of his favour,
Hold it a fashion and a toy in blood,
A violet in the youth of primy nature,
Forward, not permanent, sweet, not lasting,
The perfume and suppliance of a minute;
No more.

Oph. No more but so?

230 *beaver*. Face-guard on helmet.

Hamlet: '. . . though hell itself should gape'. The mouth
of hell. Engraving from a medieval manuscript

248 *tenable*. Kept. *still*. Always.

7 *primy*. Springtime.

9 *suppliance*. Diversion.

11 *crescent.* Growing.

12 *thews.* Strength. *temple.* Body.

15 *cautel.* Deception.

17 *greatness weigh'd.* High position considered.

30 *credent.* Believing.

39 *canker.* Swelling disease. *galls.* Harms.

40 *buttons.* i.e. buds.

51 *recks.* Considers. *rede.* Advice.

59 *character.* Inscribe.

Ophelia (Estelle Kohler), Laertes (Michael Jayston) and
Polonius (Tony Church), Royal Shakespeare Co, 1966

Laer.   Think it no more: **10**
● For nature, crescent, does not grow alone
● In thews and bulk, but, as this temple waxes,
The inward service of the mind and soul
Grows wide withal.   Perhaps he loves you now,
● And now no soil nor cautel doth besmirch
The virtue of his will: but you must fear,
● His greatness weigh'd, his will is not his own;
For he himself is subject to his birth:
He may not, as unvalued persons do,
Carve for himself; for on his choice depends   **20**
The safety and health of this whole state;
And therefore must his choice be circumscribed
Unto the voice and yielding of that body
Whereof he is the head.   Then if he says he loves
   you,
It fits your wisdom so far to believe it
As he in his particular act and place
May give his saying deed; which is no further
Than the main voice of Denmark goes withal.
Then weigh what loss your honour may sustain,
● If with too credent ear you list his songs,   **30**
Or lose your heart, or your chaste treasure open
To his unmaster'd importunity.
Fear it, Ophelia, fear it, my dear sister,
And keep you in the rear of your affection,
Out of the shot and danger of desire.
The chariest maid is prodigal enough,
If she unmask her beauty to the moon:
Virtue itself 'scapes not calumnious strokes:
● The canker galls the infants of the spring,
● Too oft before their buttons be disclosed,   **40**
And in the morn and liquid dew of youth
Contagious blastments are most imminent.
Be wary then; best safety lies in fear:
Youth to itself rebels, though none else near.
   Oph. I shall the effect of this good lesson keep,
As watchman to my heart.   But, good my brother,
Do not, as some ungracious pastors do,
Show me the steep and thorny way to heaven;
Whiles, like a puff'd and reckless libertine,
Himself the primrose path of dalliance treads,   **50**
● And recks not his own rede.
   Laer.   O, fear me not.
I stay too long: but here my father comes.

Enter POLONIUS.

A double blessing is a double grace;
Occasion smiles upon a second leave.
   Pol.   Yet here, Laertes! aboard, aboard, for
      shame!
The wind sits in the shoulder of your sail,
And you are stay'd for.   There; my blessing with
      thee!
And these few precepts in thy memory
● See thou character.   Give thy thoughts no tongue,
Nor any unproportion'd thought his act.   **60**
Be thou familiar, but by no means vulgar.
Those friends thou hast, and their adoption tried,
Grapple them to thy soul with hoops of steel;
But do not dull thy palm with entertainment
Of each new-hatch'd, unfledged comrade.   Be-
      ware
Of entrance to a quarrel, but being in,
Bear't that the opposed may beware of thee.
Give every man thy ear, but few thy voice;
Take each man's censure, but reserve thy judge-
      ment.
Costly thy habit as thy purse can buy,   **70**

But not express'd in fancy; rich, not gaudy;
For the apparel oft proclaims the man,
And they in France of the best rank and station
†Are of a most select and generous chief in that.
Neither a borrower nor a lender be;
For loan oft loses both itself and friend,
And borrowing dulls the edge of husbandry.
This above all: to thine own self be true,
And it must follow, as the night the day,
Thou canst not then be false to any man.   80
Farewell: my blessing season this in thee!
   Laer.   Most humbly do I take my leave, my
    lord.
● *Pol.*   The time invites you; go; your servants
    tend.
   Laer.   Farewell, Ophelia; and remember well
What I have said to you.
   Oph.   'Tis in my memory lock'd,
And you yourself shall keep the key of it.
   Laer.   Farewell.   [*Exit.*
   Pol.   What is't, Ophelia, he hath said to you?
   Oph.   So please you, something touching the
    Lord Hamlet.
● *Pol.*   Marry, well bethought: 90
'Tis told me, he hath very oft of late
Given private time to you; and you yourself
Have of your audience been most free and boun-
    teous:
If it be so, as so 'tis put on me,
And that in way of caution, I must tell you,
You do not understand yourself so clearly
As it behoves my daughter and your honour.
What is between you? give me up the truth.
● *Oph.*   He hath, my lord, of late made many
    tenders
Of his affection to me.   100
   Pol.   Affection! pooh! you speak like a green
    girl,
Unsifted in such perilous circumstance.
Do you believe his tenders, as you call them?
   Oph.   I do not know, my lord, what I should
    think.
   Pol.   Marry, I'll teach you: think yourself a
    baby;
That you have ta'en these tenders for true pay,
Which are not sterling. Tender yourself more
    dearly;
Or—not to crack the wind of the poor phrase,
Running it thus—you'll tender me a fool.
   Oph.   My lord, he hath importuned me with
    love   110
In honourable fashion.
   Pol.   Ay, fashion you may call it; go to, go to.
   Oph.   And hath given countenance to his
    speech, my lord,
With almost all the holy vows of heaven.
● *Pol.*   Ay, springes to catch woodcocks. I do
    know,
When the blood burns, how prodigal the soul
Lends the tongue vows: these blazes, daughter,
Giving more light than heat, extinct in both,
Even in their promise, as it is a-making,
You must not take for fire. From this time   120
●Be somewhat scanter of your maiden presence;
●Set your entreatments at a higher rate
●Than a command to parley. For Lord Hamlet,
Believe so much in him, that he is young,
And with a larger tether may he walk
Than may be given you: in few, Ophelia,

83 *tend.* Wait.

90 *Marry.* By the Virgin Mary!

99 *tenders.* Offers.

Mrs Patrick Campbell as Ophelia, Lyceum Theatre,
London, 1897

115 *springes.* Spring traps.

121 *scanter.* Less prodigal.

122 *entreatments.* Negotiations.

123 *parley.* Merely confer.

129 *implorators*. Those who solicit.

8 *wake*. Stay up. *rouse*. Revels.

9 *wassail*. Drinking of toasts. *up-spring*. German dance.

12 *triumph*. Fulfilment.

18 *traduced and tax'd*. Criticised and censured.

19 *clepe*. Call.

20 *addition*. Title, i.e. good name.

22 *pith and marrow*. i.e. substance. *attribute*. Good name.

24 *mole*. Blemish.

27 *complexion*. Characteristic.

28 *pales and forts*. Boundaries and defences.

29 *too much o'er-leavens*. i.e. predominates.

30 *plausive*. Acceptable.

35 *censure*. Criticism.

36 *dram of eale*. Smallest amount of evil.

37-38 *of . . . scandal*. i.e. implant doubt against even the natural feelings of the man.

40 *health*. Good. *goblin*. Fiend.

Hamlet: 'Be thy intents wicked or charitable. . .'
Illustration of Henry Irving as Hamlet, Lyceum Theatre, London, 1874

Do not believe his vows; for they are brokers,
Not of that dye which their investments show,
● But mere implorators of unholy suits,
Breathing like sanctified and pious bawds,   130
The better to beguile.   This is for all:
I would not, in plain terms, from this time forth,
Have you so slander any moment leisure,
As to give words or talk with the Lord Hamlet.
Look to 't, I charge you : come your ways.
    Oph.   I shall obey, my lord.   [*Exeunt.*

SCENE IV.   *The platform.*

Enter HAMLET, HORATIO, *and* MARCELLUS.

Ham.   The air bites shrewdly ; it is very cold.
Hor.   It is a nipping and an eager air.
Ham.   What hour now?
Hor.   I think it lacks of twelve.
Mar.   No, it is struck.
Hor.   Indeed?   I heard it not : then it draws
    near the season
Wherein the spirit held his wont to walk.
    [*A flourish of trumpets, and ordnance
        shot off, within.*
What does this mean, my lord?
● *Ham.*   The king doth wake to-night and takes
    his rouse,
●Keeps wassail, and the swaggering up-spring
    reels ;
And, as he drains his draughts of Rhenish down,
The kettle-drum and trumpet thus bray out   11
●The triumph of his pledge.
    Hor.   Is it a custom?
    Ham.   Ay, marry, is 't :
But to my mind, though I am native here
And to the manner born, it is a custom
More honour'd in the breach than the observance.
This heavy-headed revel east and west
●Makes us traduced and tax'd of other nations :
●They clepe us drunkards, and with swinish phrase
●Soil our addition ; and indeed it takes   20
From our achievements, though perform'd at
    height,
●The pith and marrow of our attribute.
So, oft it chances in particular men,
●That for some vicious mole of nature in them,
As, in their birth—wherein they are not guilty,
Since nature cannot choose his origin—
●By the o'ergrowth of some complexion,
●Oft breaking down the pales and forts of reason,
●Or by some habit that too much o'er-leavens
●The form of plausive manners, that these men, 30
Carrying, I say, the stamp of one defect,
Being nature's livery, or fortune's star,—
Their virtues else—be they as pure as grace,
As infinite as man may undergo—
●Shall in the general censure take corruption
●From that particular fault : the dram of ┼eale
●Doth all the noble substance ┼ of a doubt
To his own scandal.
    Hor.   Look, my lord, it comes !

Enter Ghost.

Ham.   Angels and ministers of grace defend
    us !
●Be thou a spirit of health or goblin damn'd,   40
Bring with thee airs from heaven or blasts from
    hell,
Be thy intents wicked or charitable,

Thou comest in such a questionable shape
That I will speak to thee: I'll call thee Hamlet,
King, father, royal Dane: O, answer me!
Let me not burst in ignorance; but tell
● Why thy canonized bones, hearsed in death,
● Have burst their cerements; why the sepulchre,
Wherein we saw thee quietly inurn'd,
Hath oped his ponderous and marble jaws,   50
To cast thee up again.   What may this mean,
● That thou, dead corse, again in complete steel
Revisit'st thus the glimpses of the moon,
Making night hideous; and we fools of nature
So horridly to shake our disposition
With thoughts beyond the reaches of our souls?
Say, why is this? wherefore? what should we
    do?   [*Ghost beckons Hamlet.*
    Hor.   It beckons you to go away with it,
● As if it some impartment did desire
To you alone.
    Mar.   Look, with what courteous action 60
It waves you to a more removed ground:
But do not go with it.
    Hor.   No, by no means.
    Ham.   It will not speak; then I will follow it.
    Hor.   Do not, my lord.
    Ham.   Why, what should be the fear?
● I do not set my life at a pin's fee;
And for my soul, what can it do to that,
Being a thing immortal as itself?
It waves me forth again: I'll follow it.
    Hor.   What if it tempt you toward the flood,
        my lord,
Or to the dreadful summit of the cliff   70
That beetles o'er his base into the sea,
And there assume some other horrible form,
Which might deprive your sovereignty of reason
And draw you into madness? think of it:
● The very place puts toys of desperation,
Without more motive, into every brain
That looks so many fathoms to the sea
And hears it roar beneath.
    Ham.   It waves me still.
Go on; I'll follow thee.
    Mar.   You shall not go, my lord.
    Ham.   Hold off your hands.   80
    Hor.   Be ruled; you shall not go.
    Ham.   My fate cries out,
And makes each petty artery in this body
● As hardy as the Nemean lion's nerve.
Still am I call'd.   Unhand me, gentlemen.
● By heaven, I'll make a ghost of him that lets me!
I say, away!   Go on; I'll follow thee.
            [*Exeunt Ghost and Hamlet.*
    Hor.   He waxes desperate with imagination.
    Mar.   Let's follow; 'tis not fit thus to obey
        him.
    Hor.   Have after.   To what issue will this
        come?
    Mar.   Something is rotten in the state of
        Denmark.   90
    Hor.   Heaven will direct it.
    Mar.   Nay, let's follow him. [*Exeunt.*

SCENE V.   *Another part of the platform.*

    Enter GHOST *and* HAMLET.

Ham.   Where wilt thou lead me? speak; I'll
    go no further.
Ghost.   Mark me.

47 *canonized.* i.e. blest. *hearsed.* Coffined.

48 *cerements.* Shroud.

52 *corse.* Corpse. *complete.* A suit of.

59 *impartment.* Communication.

65 *pin's fee.* The value of a pin.

75 *toys of desperation.* i.e. thoughts of destruction.

Hamlet: 'Hold off your hands'. Engraving by Kenny Meadows from Barry Cornwall's *Works of Shakspere*, 1846

83 *Nemean lion.* A legendary large, fierce lion which Hercules had to strangle. *nerve.* Sinews.

85 *lets.* Hinders.

Ghost: 'I am thy father's spirit. . .' Lithograph by Eugene Delacroix, 1835

---

12 *nature.* Living.

20 *porpentine.* Porcupine.

32-33 *the fat . . . wharf.* The succulent weed that flourishes on the banks of the Lethe. *Lethe.* Legendary river on the borders of hell, the waters of which induced forgetfulness.

42 *wit.* Intelligence.

54 *a shape of heaven.* Angel.

56 *sate.* Satisfy.

Ham.   I will.
Ghost.   My hour is almost come,
When I to sulphurous and tormenting flames
Must render up myself.
Ham.   Alas, poor ghost!
Ghost.   Pity me not, but lend thy serious hearing
To what I shall unfold.
Ham.   Speak; I am bound to hear.
Ghost.   So art thou to revenge, when thou shalt hear.
Ham.   What?
Ghost.   I am thy father's spirit,
Doom'd for a certain term to walk the night,   10
And for the day confined to fast in fires,
●Till the foul crimes done in my days of nature
Are burnt and purged away.   But that I am forbid
To tell the secrets of my prison-house,
I could a tale unfold whose lightest word
Would harrow up thy soul, freeze thy young blood,
Make thy two eyes, like stars, start from their spheres,
Thy knotted and combined locks to part
And each particular hair to stand an end,
●Like quills upon the fretful porpentine: 20
But this eternal blazon must not be
To ears of flesh and blood.   List, list, O, list!
If thou didst ever thy dear father love—
Ham.   O God!
Ghost.   Revenge his foul and most unnatural murder.
Ham.   Murder!
Ghost.   Murder most foul, as in the best it is;
But this most foul, strange and unnatural.
Ham.   Haste me to know't, that I, with wings as swift
As meditation or the thoughts of love,   30
May sweep to my revenge.
Ghost.   I find thee apt;
●And duller shouldst thou be than the fat weed
●That roots itself in ease on Lethe wharf,
Wouldst thou not stir in this.   Now, Hamlet, hear:
'Tis given out that, sleeping in my orchard,
A serpent stung me; so the whole ear of Denmark
Is by a forged process of my death
Rankly abused: but know, thou noble youth,
The serpent that did sting thy father's life
Now wears his crown.
Ham.   O my prophetic soul!   40
My uncle!
Ghost.   Ay, that incestuous, that adulterate beast,
●With witchcraft of his wit, with traitorous gifts,—
O wicked wit and gifts, that have the power
So to seduce!—won to his shameful lust
The will of my most seeming-virtuous queen:
O Hamlet, what a falling-off was there!
From me, whose love was of that dignity
That it went hand in hand even with the vow
I made to her in marriage, and to decline   50
Upon a wretch whose natural gifts were poor
To those of mine!
But virtue, as it never will be moved,
●Though lewdness court it in a shape of heaven,
So lust, though to a radiant angel link'd,
●Will sate itself in a celestial bed,
And prey on garbage.

But, soft ! methinks I scent the morning air;
Brief let me be.   Sleeping within my orchard,
My custom always of the afternoon,   60
Upon my secure hour thy uncle stole,
●With juice of cursed hebenon in a vial,
●And in the porches of my ears did pour
The leperous distilment; whose effect
Holds such an enmity with blood of man
That swift as quicksilver it courses through
The natural gates and alleys of the body,
●And with a sudden vigour it doth posset
●And curd, like eager droppings into milk,
The thin and wholesome blood: so did it mine; 70
●And a most instant tetter bark'd about,
●Most lazar-like, with vile and loathsome crust,
All my smooth body.
Thus was I, sleeping, by a brother's hand
Of life, of crown, of queen, at once dispatch'd:
Cut off even in the blossoms of my sin,
●Unhousel'd, disappointed, unaneled,
No reckoning made, but sent to my account
With all my imperfections on my head:
O, horrible! O, horrible! most horrible!   80
If thou hast nature in thee, bear it not:
Let not the royal bed of Denmark be
A couch for luxury and damned incest.
But, howsoever thou pursuest this act,
Taint not thy mind, nor let thy soul contrive
Against thy mother aught: leave her to heaven
And to those thorns that in her bosom lodge,
To prick and sting her.   Fare thee well at once !
The glow-worm shows the matin to be near,
And 'gins to pale his uneffectual fire: 90
Adieu, adieu! Hamlet, remember me. [*Exit.*
    Ham.   O all you host of heaven!   O earth!
        what else?
●And shall I couple hell? O, fie!   Hold, hold,
        my heart;
And you, my sinews, grow not instant old,
●But bear me stiffly up.   Remember thee !
Ay, thou poor ghost, while memory holds a seat
●In this distracted globe.   Remember thee !
Yea, from the table of my memory
I'll wipe away all trivial fond records,
●All saws of books, all forms, all pressures past,
That youth and observation copied there;   101
And thy commandment all alone shall live
Within the book and volume of my brain,
Unmix'd with baser matter: yes, by heaven !
O most pernicious woman !
O villain, villain, smiling, damned villain !
●My tables,—meet it is I set it down,
That one may smile, and smile, and be a villain ;
At least I'm sure it may be so in Denmark:
                [*Writing.*
●So, uncle, there you are.   Now to my word;
It is 'Adieu, adieu! remember me.' ·   111
I have sworn 't.
    Mar.⎫ [*Within*] My lord, my lord,—
    Hor.⎭
    Mar.   [*Within*] Lord Hamlet,—
    Hor.   [*Within*] Heaven secure him !
    Ham.   So be it !
    Hor. [*Within*] Hillo, ho, ho, my lord !
    Ham.   Hillo, ho, ho, boy ! come, bird, come.

    Enter HORATIO *and* MARCELLUS.

    Mar.   How is't, my noble lord?
    Hor.   What news, my lord?

62 *hebenon*. Poisonous distillation of a herb, possibly henbane.

63 *porches*. Openings.

68 *posset*. Curdle.

69 *eager*. Acid.

71 *tetter*. Rash.

72 *lazar-like*. Leprous.

77 *Unhousel'd*. Not having taken the sacrament. *disappointed*. Unprepared. *unaneled*. Unanointed.

93 *couple*. Include.

95 *stiffly*. Strongly.

97 *distracted globe*. i.e. 'crazy world' and 'my mad mind'.

100 *saws*. Wise sayings. *forms*. Images. *pressures*. Impressions.

107 *tables*. Tablets for taking notes.

110 *word*. Promise.

127 *circumstance.* Formality.

135–136 *offence.* Crime. *Saint Patrick.* Patron of Purgatory.

Hamlet: 'Never make known what you have seen to-night'. David Garrick as Hamlet, Theatre Royal, Drury Lane, London, 1754

150 *truepenny.* Honest person.

151 *cellarage.* i.e. 'cellar' and 'underworld'.

156 *Hic et ubique.* Here and everywhere.

163 *pioner.* Miner.

Ham.   O, wonderful!
Hor.   Good my lord, tell it.
Ham.   No; you'll reveal it.
Hor.   Not I, my lord, by heaven.
Mar.   Nor I, my lord.   120
Ham.   How say you, then; would heart of
man once think it?
But you'll be secret?
Hor. }
Mar. }   Ay, by heaven, my lord.
Ham.   There's ne'er a villain dwelling in all
Denmark
But he's an arrant knave.
Hor.   There needs no ghost, my lord, come
from the grave
To tell us this.
Ham.   Why, right; you are i' the right;
●And so, without more circumstance at all,
I hold it fit that we shake hands and part:
You, as your business and desire shall point you:
For every man has business and desire,   130
Such as it is; and for mine own poor part,
Look you, I'll go pray.
Hor.   These are but wild and whirling words,
my lord.
Ham.   I'm sorry they offend you, heartily;
●Yes, 'faith, heartily.
Hor.   There's no offence, my lord.
Ham.   Yes, by Saint Patrick, but there is,
Horatio,
And much offence too. Touching this vision here,
It is an honest ghost, that let me tell you:
For your desire to know what is between us,
O'ermaster 't as you may. And now, good friends,
As you are friends, scholars and soldiers,   141
Give me one poor request.
Hor.   What is 't, my lord? we will.
Ham.   Never make known what you have
seen to-night.
Hor. }
Mar. } My lord, we will not.
Ham.   Nay, but swear 't.
Hor.   In faith,
My lord, not I.
Mar.   Nor I, my lord, in faith.
Ham.   Upon my sword.
Mar.   We have sworn, my lord, already.
Ham.   Indeed, upon my sword, indeed.
Ghost.   [*Beneath*] Swear.
●   *Ham.*   Ah, ha, boy! say'st thou so? art thou
there, truepenny?   150
●Come on—you hear this fellow in the cellarage—
Consent to swear.
Hor.   Propose the oath, my lord.
Ham.   Never to speak of this that you have
seen,
Swear by my sword.
Ghost.   [*Beneath*] Swear.
●   *Ham.*   Hic et ubique? then we'll shift our
ground.
Come hither, gentlemen,
And lay your hands again upon my sword:
Never to speak of this that you have heard,
Swear by my sword.   160
Ghost.   [*Beneath*] Swear.
Ham.   Well said, old mole! canst work i' the
earth so fast?
●A worthy pioner!   Once more remove, good
friends.

Hor. O day and night, but this is wondrous strange!

Ham. And therefore as a stranger give it welcome.
There are more things in heaven and earth, Horatio,
Than are dreamt of in your philosophy.
But come;
Here, as before, never, so help you mercy,
How strange or odd soe'er I bear myself,   170
As I perchance hereafter shall think meet
● To put an antic disposition on,
That you, at such times seeing me, never shall,
● With arms encumber'd thus, or this head-shake,
Or by pronouncing of some doubtful phrase,
As 'Well, well, we know,' or 'We could, an if we would,'
● Or 'If we list to speak,' or 'There be, an if they might,'
Or such ambiguous giving out, to note
● That you know aught of me: this not to do,
So grace and mercy at your most need help you,
Swear.   181

Ghost. [*Beneath*] Swear.

Ham. Rest, rest, perturbed spirit! [*They swear.*] So, gentlemen,
With all my love I do commend me to you:
And what so poor a man as Hamlet is
May do, to express his love and friending to you,
God willing, shall not lack. Let us go in together;
And still your fingers on your lips, I pray.
The time is out of joint: O cursed spite,
That ever I was born to set it right!   190
Nay, come, let's go together.   [*Exeunt.*

ACT II.

SCENE I. *A room in Polonius' house.*

Enter POLONIUS *and* REYNALDO.

Pol. Give him this money and these notes, Reynaldo.

Rey. I will, my lord.

Pol. You shall do marvellous wisely, good Reynaldo,
Before you visit him, to make inquire
Of his behaviour.

Rey.   My lord, I did intend it.

Pol. Marry, well said; very well said. Look you, sir,
● Inquire me first what Danskers are in Paris;
● And how, and who, what means, and where they keep,
What company, at what expense; and finding
● By this encompassment and drift of question   10
That they do know my son, come you more nearer
Than your particular demands will touch it:
Take you, as 'twere, some distant knowledge of him;
As thus, 'I know his father and his friends,
And in part him:' do you mark this, Reynaldo?

Rey. Ay, very well, my lord.

Pol. 'And in part him; but' you may say 'not well:
But, if 't be he I mean, he's very wild;
Addicted so and so:' and there put on him   19
● What forgeries you please; marry, none so rank
As may dishonour him; take heed of that;

172 *antic disposition.* Fantastic behaviour.

174 *encumber'd.* Folded.

177 *list.* Wish.

179–181 *this not to do ... Swear.* Promise not to do these things.

Horatio and Marcellus swear never to speak of the night's events. Engraving by Kenny Meadows from Barry Cornwall's *Works of Shakspere*, 1846

7 *Danskers.* Danes.

8 *keep.* Stay.

10 *encompassment and drift.* Indirect manner.

20 *forgeries.* False attributes.

26 *Drabbing.* Associating with sluts.

31 *quaintly.* Cleverly.

34 *unreclaimed.* Inexperienced.

35 *general assault.* Common affliction.

38 *fetch.* Effort.

45 *in this consequence.* In this manner.

Quando pila et Sphæræ flectuntur corporis artus,   Go oft ich thue den Ballen schlägn/
Corpus erit levius, pectus erit levius.   Erfrisch ich mir hertz.tragen vnd magn

Polonius: 'There falling out at tennis ...' The game of tennis in Shakespeare's time. Engraving from *Le centre de l'amour c.*1600

60 *house of sale.* i.e. brothel.

61 *Videlicet.* That is to say.

65 *assays of bias.* i.e. tests of inclination.

73 *ply his music.* i.e. go his own way.

But, sir, such wanton, wild and usual slips
As are companions noted and most known
To youth and liberty.
 Rey.   As gaming, my lord.
 Pol. Ay, or drinking, fencing, swearing, quar-
  relling,
Drabbing: you may go so far.
 Rey.   My lord, that would dishonour him.
 Pol. 'Faith, no; as you may season it in the
  charge.
You must not put another scandal on him,
That he is open to incontinency;   30
That's not my meaning: but breathe his faults so
  quaintly
That they may seem the taints of liberty,
The flash and outbreak of a fiery mind,
A savageness in unreclaimed blood,
Of general assault.
 Rey.   But, my good lord,—
 Pol. Wherefore should you do this?
 Rey.   Ay, my lord,
I would know that.
 Pol.   Marry, sir, here's my drift;
And, I believe, it is a fetch of wit:
You laying these slight sullies on my son,
As 'twere a thing a little soil'd i' the working, 40
Mark you,
Your party in converse, him you would sound,
Having ever seen in the prenominate crimes
The youth you breathe of guilty, be assured
He closes with you in this consequence;
'Good sir,' or so, or 'friend,' or 'gentleman,'
According to the phrase or the addition
Of man and country.
 Rey.   Very good, my lord.
 Pol. And then, sir, does he this—he does—
what was I about to say? By the mass, I was
about to say something: where did I leave?   51
 Rey. At 'closes in the consequence,' at 'friend
or so,' and 'gentleman.'
 Pol. At 'closes in the consequence,' ay, marry;
He closes thus: 'I know the gentleman;
I saw him yesterday, or t'other day,
Or then, or then; with such, or such; and, as you
  say,
There was a' gaming; there o'ertook in 's rouse;
There falling out at tennis:' or perchance,
'I saw him enter such a house of sale,'   60
Videlicet, a brothel, or so forth.
See you now;
Your bait of falsehood takes this carp of truth:
And thus do we of wisdom and of reach,
With windlasses and with assays of bias,
By indirections find directions out:
So by my former lecture and advice,
Shall you my son. You have me, have you not?
 Rey. My lord, I have.
 Pol.   God be wi' you; fare you well.
 Rey. Good my lord!   70
 Pol. Observe his inclination in yourself.
 Rey. I shall, my lord.
 Pol. And let him ply his music.
 Rey.   Well, my lord.
 Pol. Farewell!   [*Exit Reynaldo.*

       Enter OPHELIA.

       How now, Ophelia! what's the matter?
 Oph. O, my lord, my lord, I have been so affrighted!

Pol. With what, i' the name of God?

Oph. My lord, as I was sewing in my closet,
Lord Hamlet, with his doublet all unbraced;
No hat upon his head; his stockings foul'd,
● Ungarter'd, and down-gyved to his ancle;   80
Pale as his shirt; his knees knocking each other;
And with a look so piteous in purport
As if he had been loosed out of hell
To speak of horrors,—he comes before me.

Pol. Mad for thy love?

Oph.   My lord, I do not know;
But truly, I do fear it.

Pol.   What said he?

Oph. He took me by the wrist and held me hard;
Then goes he to the length of all his arm;
And, with his other hand thus o'er his brow,
He falls to such perusal of my face   90
As he would draw it.   Long stay'd he so;
At last, a little shaking of mine arm
And thrice his head thus waving up and down,
He raised a sigh so piteous and profound
As it did seem to shatter all his bulk
And end his being: that done, he lets me go:
And, with his head over his shoulder turn'd,
He seem'd to find his way without his eyes;
For out o' doors he went without their helps,
And, to the last, bended their light on me.   100

Pol. Come, go with me: I will go seek the
    king.
● This is the very ecstasy of love,
● Whose violent property fordoes itself
And leads the will to desperate undertakings
As oft as any passion under heaven
That does afflict our natures.   I am sorry.
What, have you given him any hard words of late?

Oph. No, my good lord, but, as you did com-
    mand,
I did repel his letters and denied
His access to me.

Pol.   That hath made him mad.   110
I am sorry that with better heed and judgement
● I had not quoted him: I fear'd he did but trifle,
And meant to wreck thee; but, beshrew my jea-
    lousy!
By heaven, it is as proper to our age
To cast beyond ourselves in our opinions
As it is common for the younger sort
To lack discretion.   Come, go we to the king:
● This must be known; which, being kept close,
    might move
More grief to hide than hate to utter love.
                                        [*Exeunt.*

SCENE II. *A room in the castle.*

Enter KING, QUEEN, ROSENCRANTZ, GUILDEN-
    STERN, *and* Attendants.

King. Welcome, dear Rosencrantz and Guild-
    enstern!
Moreover that we much did long to see you,
The need we have to use you did provoke
Our hasty sending.   Something have you heard
Of Hamlet's transformation; so call it,
● Sith nor the exterior nor the inward man
Resembles that it was.   What it should be,
More than his father's death, that thus hath put
    him
So much from the understanding of himself,
I cannot dream of: I entreat you both,   10

Ophelia: 'He took me by the wrist and held me hard'.
Drawing of Polonius and Ophelia by William Nelson
Gardiner (1766–1814)

102 *ecstasy.* Madness.

103 *fordoes.* Ruins.

112 *quoted.* Watched upon.

118 *move.* i.e. give movement to.

6 *Sith.* Since.

11 *of so young days.* From early childhood.

13 *vouchsafe your rest.* Agree to spend some time.

22 *gentry.* Courtesy.

38 *practices.* Actions.

47 *policy.* i.e. 'insight' and 'deviousness'.

King: 'Welcome, my good friends!' The ambassadors from Norway before the King and Queen. Engraving by Kenny Meadows from Barry Cornwall's *Works of Shakspere,* 1846

●That, being of so young days brought up with him,
And sith so neighbour'd to his youth and haviour,
●That you vouchsafe your rest here in our court
Some little time : so by your companies
To draw him on to pleasures, and to gather,
So much as from occasion you may glean,
Whether aught, to us unknown, afflicts him thus,
That, open'd, lies within our remedy.
    Queen.   Good gentlemen, he hath much talk'd of you;
And sure I am two men there are not living   20
To whom he more adheres.   If it will please you
●To show us so much gentry and good will
As to expend your time with us awhile,
For the supply and profit of our hope,
Your visitation shall receive such thanks
As fits a king's remembrance.
    Ros.   Both your majesties
Might, by the sovereign power you have of us,
Put your dread pleasures more into command
Than to entreaty.
    Guil.   But we both obey,
And here give up ourselves, in the full bent   30
To lay our service freely at your feet,
To be commanded.
    King.   Thanks, Rosencrantz and gentle Guildenstern.
    Queen.   Thanks, Guildenstern and gentle Rosencrantz:
And I beseech you instantly to visit
My too much changed son.   Go, some of you,
And bring these gentlemen where Hamlet is.
●   *Guil.*   Heavens make our presence and our practices
Pleasant and helpful to him !
    Queen.   Ay, amen !
        [*Exeunt Rosencrantz, Guildenstern, and
                some Attendants.*

Enter POLONIUS.

    Pol.   The ambassadors from Norway, my good lord,
Are joyfully return'd.   40
    King.   Thou still hast been the father of good news.
    Pol.   Have I, my lord?   I assure my good liege,
I hold my duty, as I hold my soul,
Both to my God and to my gracious king :
And I do think, or else this brain of mine
●Hunts not the trail of policy so sure
As it hath used to do, that I have found
The very cause of Hamlet's lunacy.   49
    King.   O, speak of that; that do I long to hear.
    Pol.   Give first admittance to the ambassadors;
My news shall be the fruit to that great feast.
    King.   Thyself do grace to them, and bring them in.   [*Exit Polonius.*
He tells me, my dear Gertrude, he hath found
The head and source of all your son's distemper.
    Queen.   I doubt it is no other but the main ;
His father's death, and our o'erhasty marriage.
    King.   Well, we shall sift him.

Re-enter POLONIUS, *with* VOLTIMAND *and*
CORNELIUS.

                    Welcome, my good friends !
Say, Voltimand, what from our brother Norway?
    Volt.   Most fair return of greetings and desires.

● Upon our first, he sent out to suppress 61
His nephew's levies; which to him appear'd
To be a preparation 'gainst the Polack;
But, better look'd into, he truly found
It was against your highness: whereat grieved,
That so his sickness, age and impotence
● Was falsely borne in hand, sends out arrests
On Fortinbras; which he, in brief, obeys;
Receives rebuke from Norway, and in fine
Makes vow before his uncle never more 70
● To give the assay of arms against your majesty.
Whereon old Norway, overcome with joy,
Gives him three thousand crowns in annual fee,
And his commission to employ those soldiers,
So levied as before, against the Polack:
With an entreaty, herein further shown,
                         [*Giving a paper.*
That it might please you to give quiet pass
Through your dominions for this enterprise,
● On such regards of safety and allowance
As therein are set down.
          King.   It likes us well; 80
And at our more consider'd time we'll read,
Answer, and think upon this business.
Meantime we thank you for your well-took
          labour:
Go to your rest; at night we'll feast together:
Most welcome home!
                    [*Exeunt Voltimand and Cornelius.*
     Pol.   This business is well ended.
My liege, and madam, to expostulate
What majesty should be, what duty is,
Why day is day, night night, and time is
          time,
Were nothing but to waste night, day and time.
Therefore, since brevity is the soul of wit, 90
And tediousness the limbs and outward flourishes,
I will be brief: your noble son is mad:
Mad call I it; for, to define true madness,
What is't but to be nothing else but mad?
● But let that go.
     Queen.   More matter, with less art.
     Pol. Madam, I swear I use no art at all.
That he is mad, 'tis true: 'tis true 'tis pity;
And pity 'tis 'tis true: a foolish figure;
But farewell it, for I will use no art.
Mad let us grant him, then: and now remains
That we find out the cause of this effect, 101
Or rather say, the cause of this defect,
For this effect defective comes by cause:
Thus it remains, and the remainder thus.
● Perpend.
I have a daughter—have while she is mine—
Who, in her duty and obedience, mark,
Hath given me this: now gather, and surmise.
                              [*Reads.*
'To the celestial and my soul's idol, the most
beautified Ophelia,'— 110
That's an ill phrase, a vile phrase; 'beautified' is
a vile phrase: but you shall hear. Thus: [*Reads.*
'In her excellent white bosom, these, &c.'
     Queen. Came this from Hamlet to her?
     Pol. Good madam, stay awhile; I will be
          faithful.   [*Reads.*
     'Doubt thou the stars are fire;
          Doubt that the sun doth move;
       Doubt truth to be a liar;
          But never doubt I love. 119
'O dear Ophelia, I am ill at these numbers; I

61 *Upon our first.* When he first heard what we reported.

67–68 *arrests On.* Countermanding orders to.

71 *assay.* Attempt.

79 *regards.* Stipulations.

95 *art.* i.e. 'artificiality' and 'rhetoric'.

105 *Perpend.* Consider.

Costume design for the Queen by Ann Curtis, Royal Shakespeare Co, 1965

124 *machine*. Body.

137 *a winking*. Blind.

139 *round*. Openly.

142 *prescripts*. Orders.

163 *arras*. Tapestry hanging.

170 *board*. Accost. *presently*. Straight away.

Hamlet reading. Sarah Bernhardt as Hamlet, Adelphi Theatre, London, 1899

have not art to reckon my groans: but that I love thee best, O most best, believe it.   Adieu.

•   'Thine evermore, most dear lady, whilst this
                machine is to him, HAMLET.'
This, in obedience, hath my daughter shown me,
And more above, hath his solicitings,
As they fell out by time, by means and place,
All given to mine ear.
    King.   But how hath she
Received his love?
    Pol.   What do you think of me?
    King. As of a man faithful and honourable.
    Pol. I would fain prove so.   But what might
        you think,   131
When I had seen this hot love on the wing—
As I perceived it, I must tell you that,
Before my daughter told me—what might you,
Or my dear majesty your queen here, think,
If I had play'd the desk or table-book,
• Or given my heart a winking, mute and dumb,
Or look'd upon this love with idle sight;
• What might you think? No, I went round to work,
And my young mistress thus I did bespeak: 140
'Lord Hamlet is a prince, out of thy star;
• This must not be:' and then I prescripts gave her,
That she should lock herself from his resort,
Admit no messengers, receive no tokens.
Which done, she took the fruits of my advice;
And he, repulsed—a short tale to make—
Fell into a sadness, then into a fast,
Thence to a watch, thence into a weakness,
Thence to a lightness, and, by this declension,
Into the madness wherein now he raves,   150
And all we mourn for.
    King.   Do you think 'tis this?
    Queen. It may be, very likely.
    Pol. Hath there been such a time—I'd fain
        know that—
That I have positively said ''Tis so,'
When it proved otherwise?
    King.   Not that I know.
    Pol. [*Pointing to his head and shoulder*] Take
        this from this, if this be otherwise:
If circumstances lead me, I will find
Where truth is hid, though it were hid indeed
Within the centre.
    King.   How may we try it further?
    Pol. You know, sometimes he walks four hours
        together   160
Here in the lobby.
    Queen.   So he does indeed.
    Pol. At such a time I'll loose my daughter to
        him:
• Be you and I behind an arras then;
Mark the encounter: if he love her not
And be not from his reason fall'n thereon,
Let me be no assistant for a state,
But keep a farm and carters.
    King.   We will try it.
    Queen. But, look, where sadly the poor wretch
        comes reading.
    Pol. Away, I do beseech you, both away:
• I'll board him presently.
       [*Exeunt King, Queen, and Attendants*.

      Enter HAMLET, *reading*.

              O, give me leave: 170
How does my good Lord Hamlet?
    Ham. Well, God-a-mercy.

Pol. Do you know me, my lord?

Ham. Excellent well; you are a fishmonger.

Pol. Not I, my lord.

Ham. Then I would you were so honest a man.

Pol. Honest, my lord!

Ham. Ay, sir; to be honest, as this world goes, is to be one man picked out of ten thousand.

Pol. That's very true, my lord. 180

Ham. For if the sun breed maggots in a dead dog, being a god kissing carrion,—Have you a daughter?

Pol. I have, my lord.

Ham. Let her not walk i' the sun: conception is a blessing: but not as your daughter may conceive. Friend, look to 't.

Pol. [*Aside*] How say you by that? Still harping on my daughter: yet he knew me not at first; he said I was a fishmonger: he is far gone, far gone: and truly in my youth I suffered much extremity for love; very near this. I'll speak to him again. What do you read, my lord?

Ham. Words, words, words.

Pol. What is the matter, my lord?

Ham. Between who?

Pol. I mean, the matter that you read, my lord.

Ham. Slanders, sir: for the satirical rogue says here that old men have grey beards, that their faces are wrinkled, their eyes purging thick amber and plum-tree gum and that they have a plentiful lack of wit, together with most weak hams: all which, sir, though I most powerfully and potently believe, yet I hold it not honesty to have it thus set down, for yourself, sir, should be old as I am, if like a crab you could go backward.

Pol. [*Aside*] Though this be madness, yet there is method in 't. Will you walk out of the air, my lord?

Ham. Into my grave. 210

Pol. Indeed, that is out o' the air. [*Aside*] How pregnant sometimes his replies are! a happiness that often madness hits on, which reason and sanity could not so prosperously be delivered of. I will leave him, and suddenly contrive the means of meeting between him and my daughter.—My honourable lord, I will most humbly take my leave of you.

Ham. You cannot, sir, take from me any thing that I will more willingly part withal: except my life, except my life, except my life. 221

Pol. Fare you well, my lord.

Ham. These tedious old fools!

Enter ROSENCRANTZ *and* GUILDENSTERN.

Pol. You go to seek the Lord Hamlet; there he is.

Ros. [*To Polonius*] God save you, sir!
                                [*Exit Polonius.*

Guil. My honoured lord!

Ros. My most dear lord!

Ham. My excellent good friends! How dost thou, Guildenstern? Ah, Rosencrantz! Good lads, how do ye both? 230

Ros. As the indifferent children of the earth.

Guil. Happy, in that we are not over-happy; On fortune's cap we are not the very button.

Ham. Nor the soles of her shoe?

Ros. Neither, my lord.

Ham. Then you live about her waist, or in the middle of her favours?

174 *fishmonger.* i.e. 'man who sells fish' and 'pimp'.

182 *god.* Good. *kissing carrion.* Flesh to kiss.

185 *conception.* i.e. 'understanding' and 'reproduction'.

Polonius: 'What do you read, my lord?' Lithograph of Polonius with Hamlet by Eugene Delacroix (1798–1863)

200 *purging.* Discharging.

201 *amber and plum-tree gum.* Images of heavy mucus.

213 *happiness.* Appropriateness.

231 *indifferent.* Ordinary.

238 *privates*. i.e. 'intimate friends' and 'genitals'.

271 *fay*. Faith.

274 *sort*. Associate.

276 *dreadfully*. i.e. 'poorly' and 'fearfully'.

290 *colour*. Disguise.

294 *conjure*. Prevail upon.

295 *consonancy*. i.e. closeness.

301 *I have an eye of*. I am watching.

Guil. 'Faith, her privates we.

Ham. In the secret parts of fortune? O, most true; she is a strumpet. What's the news? 240

Ros. None, my lord, but that the world's grown honest.

Ham. Then is doomsday near: but your news is not true. Let me question more in particular: what have you, my good friends, deserved at the hands of fortune, that she sends you to prison hither?

Guil. Prison, my lord!

Ham. Denmark's a prison.

Ros. Then is the world one. 250

Ham. A goodly one; in which there are many confines, wards and dungeons, Denmark being one o' the worst.

Ros. We think not so, my lord.

Ham. Why, then, 'tis none to you; for there is nothing either good or bad, but thinking makes it so: to me it is a prison.

Ros. Why then, your ambition makes it one; 'tis too narrow for your mind. 259

Ham. O God, I could be bounded in a nut-shell and count myself a king of infinite space, were it not that I have bad dreams.

Guil. Which dreams indeed are ambition, for the very substance of the ambitious is merely the shadow of a dream.

Ham. A dream itself is but a shadow.

Ros. Truly, and I hold ambition of so airy and light a quality that it is but a shadow's shadow.

Ham. Then are our beggars bodies, and our monarchs and outstretched heroes the beggars' shadows. Shall we to the court? for, by my fay, I cannot reason.

Ros. ⎱
Guil. ⎰ We'll wait upon you.

Ham. No such matter: I will not sort you with the rest of my servants, for, to speak to you like an honest man, I am most dreadfully attended. But, in the beaten way of friendship, what make you at Elsinore?

Ros. To visit you, my lord; no other occasion.

Ham. Beggar that I am, I am even poor in thanks; but I thank you: and sure, dear friends, my thanks are too dear a halfpenny. Were you not sent for? Is it your own inclining? Is it a free visitation? Come, deal justly with me: come, come; nay, speak.

Guil. What should we say, my lord?

Ham. Why, any thing, but to the purpose. You were sent for; and there is a kind of confession in your looks which your modesties have not craft enough to colour: I know the good king and queen have sent for you. 291

Ros. To what end, my lord?

Ham. That you must teach me. But let me conjure you, by the rights of our fellowship, by the consonancy of our youth, by the obligation of our ever-preserved love, and by what more dear a better proposer could charge you withal, be even and direct with me, whether you were sent for, or no?

Ros. [*Aside to Guil.*] What say you? 300

Ham. [*Aside*] Nay, then, I have an eye of you.—If you love me, hold not off.

Guil. My lord, we were sent for.

Ham. I will tell you why; so shall my anticipation prevent your discovery, and your secrecy to the king and queen moult no feather. I have of late—but wherefore I know not—lost all my mirth, forgone all custom of exercises; and indeed it goes so heavily with my disposition that this goodly frame, the earth, seems to me a sterile promontory, this most excellent canopy, the air, look you, this brave o'erhanging firmament, this majestical roof fretted with golden fire, why, it appears no other thing to me than a foul and pestilent congregation of vapours. What a piece of work is a man! how noble in reason! how infinite in faculty! in form and moving how express and admirable! in action how like an angel! in apprehension how like a god! the beauty of the world! the paragon of animals! And yet, to me, what is this quintessence of dust? man delights not me: no, nor woman neither, though by your smiling you seem to say so.

Ros. My lord, there was no such stuff in my thoughts.

Ham. Why did you laugh then, when I said 'man delights not me'?

Ros. To think, my lord, if you delight not in man, what lenten entertainment the players shall receive from you: we coted them on the way; and hither are they coming, to offer you service.

Ham. He that plays the king shall be welcome; his majesty shall have tribute of me; the adventurous knight shall use his foil and target; the lover shall not sigh gratis; the humorous man shall end his part in peace; the clown shall make those laugh whose lungs are tickle o' the sere; and the lady shall say her mind freely, or the blank verse shall halt for't. What players are they? 340

Ros. Even those you were wont to take delight in, the tragedians of the city.

Ham. How chances it they travel? their residence, both in reputation and profit, was better both ways.

Ros. I think their inhibition comes by the means of the late innovation.

Ham. Do they hold the same estimation they did when I was in the city? are they so followed? 350

Ros. No, indeed, are they not.

Ham. How comes it? do they grow rusty?

Ros. Nay, their endeavour keeps in the wonted pace: but there is, sir, an aery of children, little eyases, that cry out on the top of question, and are most tyrannically clapped for't: these are now the fashion, and so berattle the common stages—so they call them—that many wearing rapiers are afraid of goose-quills and dare scarce come thither. 360

Ham. What, are they children? who maintains 'em? how are they escoted? Will they pursue the quality no longer than they can sing? will they not say afterwards, if they should grow themselves to common players—as it is most like, if their means are no better—their writers do them wrong, to make them exclaim against their own succession?

Ros. 'Faith, there has been much to do on both sides; and the nation holds it no sin to tarre them to controversy: there was, for a while, no money bid for argument, unless the poet and the player went to cuffs in the question.

Ham. Is't possible?

317 *faculty.* Ability. *express.* Expressive.

319 *apprehension.* Understanding.

Hamlet: 'And yet, to me, what is this quintessence of dust?' John Barrymore as Hamlet, Haymarket Theatre, London, 1925

329 *lenten.* i.e. simple, abstemious.

330 *coted.* Passed.

337 *are tickle o' the sere.* i.e. will laugh at the slightest thing.

346 *inhibition.* i.e. prohibition from being allowed to act in the town.

347 *innovation.* Perhaps a reference to Essex's rebellion.

354 *wonted.* Accustomed. *aery.* Brood.

355–356 *cry ... question.* Whose shrill voices are too much in evidence.

359 *goose-quills.* i.e. pens or satirists.

362 *escoted.* Maintained, paid.

363 *than ... sing.* i.e. until their voices break.

367 *exclaim.* i.e. abuse.

368 *succession.* Future career.

370 *tarre.* Provoke.

376 *brains.* Opinions.

378–379 *Hercules . . . load.* Alluding to the legend when Hercules carries the world while Atlas is elsewhere.

381 *make mows.* Pull faces.

384 *little.* Miniature.

Guildenstern: 'There are the players'. Travelling players in the 18th century. Detail from an engraving by William Hogarth (1697–1764)

388 *appurtenance.* Accessory.

389 *fashion.* Demonstration.

390 *garb.* i.e. manner. *extent.* Display of friendliness.

397 *handsaw.* Heron.

401 *swaddling-clouts.* Clothes wrapped around babies.

410 *Roscius.* A famous Roman actor in Cicero's time.

419 *Seneca.* Roman tragedian.

420 *Plautus.* Early Roman comedy writer.

422 *Jephthah.* Biblical figure who sacrificed his daughter.

437 *row.* Verse. *chanson.* Song.

438 *my abridgement.* Interruption.

Guil. O, there has been much throwing about of brains.

Ham. Do the boys carry it away?

Ros. Ay, that they do, my lord; Hercules and his load too.   379

Ham. It is not very strange; for mine uncle is king of Denmark, and those that would make mows at him while my father lived, give twenty, forty, fifty, an hundred ducats a-piece for his picture in little. 'Sblood, there is something in this more than natural, if philosophy could find it out.

[*Flourish of trumpets within.*

Guil. There are the players.

Ham. Gentlemen, you are welcome to Elsinore. Your hands, come then: the appurtenance of welcome is fashion and ceremony: let me comply with you in this garb, lest my extent to the players, which, I tell you, must show fairly outward, should more appear like entertainment than yours. You are welcome: but my uncle-father and aunt-mother are deceived.

Guil. In what, my dear lord?

Ham. I am but mad north-north-west: when the wind is southerly I know a hawk from a handsaw.

Re-enter POLONIUS.

Pol. Well be with you, gentlemen!

Ham. Hark you, Guildenstern; and you too: at each ear a hearer: that great baby you see there is not yet out of his swaddling-clouts.

Ros. Happily he's the second time come to them; for they say an old man is twice a child.

Ham. I will prophesy he comes to tell me of the players; mark it. You say right, sir: o' Monday morning; 'twas so indeed.

Pol. My lord, I have news to tell you.

Ham. My lord, I have news to tell you. When Roscius was an actor in Rome,—   410

Pol. The actors are come hither, my lord.

Ham. Buz, buz!

Pol. Upon mine honour,—

Ham. Then came each actor on his ass,—

Pol. The best actors in the world, either for tragedy, comedy, history, pastoral, pastoral-comical, historical-pastoral, tragical-historical, tragical-comical-historical-pastoral, scene individable, or poem unlimited: Seneca cannot be too heavy, nor Plautus too light. For the law of writ and the liberty, these are the only men.   421

Ham. O Jephthah, judge of Israel, what a treasure hadst thou!

Pol. What a treasure had he, my lord?

Ham. Why,

'One fair daughter, and no more,
    The which he loved passing well.'

Pol. [*Aside*] Still on my daughter.

Ham. Am I not i' the right, old Jephthah?

Pol. If you call me Jephthah, my lord, I have a daughter that I love passing well.   431

Ham. Nay, that follows not.

Pol. What follows, then, my lord?

Ham. Why,

'As by lot, God wot,'

and then, you know,

'It came to pass, as most like it was,'—

the first row of the pious chanson will show you more; for look, where my abridgement comes.

Enter four or five Players.

You are welcome, masters; welcome, all. I am glad to see thee well. Welcome, good friends. O, my old friend! thy face is valanced since I saw thee last: comest thou to beard me in Denmark? What, my young lady and mistress! By'r lady, your ladyship is nearer to heaven than when I saw you last, by the altitude of a chopine. Pray God, your voice, like a piece of uncurrent gold, be not cracked within the ring. Masters, you are all welcome. We'll e'en to't like French falconers, fly at any thing we see: we'll have a speech straight: come, give us a taste of your quality: come, a passionate speech.

First Play. What speech, my lord?

Ham. I heard thee speak me a speech once, but it was never acted; or, if it was, not above once; for the play, I remember, pleased not the million; 'twas caviare to the general: but it was —as I received it, and others, whose judgements in such matters cried in the top of mine—an excellent play, well digested in the scenes, set down with as much modesty as cunning. I remember, one said there were no sallets in the lines to make the matter savoury, nor no matter in the phrase that might indict the author of affectation; but called it an honest method, as wholesome as sweet, and by very much more handsome than fine. One speech in it I chiefly loved: 'twas Æneas' tale to Dido; and thereabout of it especially, where he speaks of Priam's slaughter: if it live in your memory, begin at this line: let me see, let me see—   471

'The rugged Pyrrhus, like the Hyrcanian beast,'— it is not so:—it begins with Pyrrhus:—

'The rugged Pyrrhus, he whose sable arms,
Black as his purpose, did the night resemble
When he lay couched in the ominous horse,
Hath now this dread and black complexion smear'd
With heraldry more dismal; head to foot
Now is he total gules; horridly trick'd
With blood of fathers, mothers, daughters, sons,
Baked and impasted with the parching streets,
That lend a tyrannous and damned light
To their lord's murder: roasted in wrath and fire,
And thus o'er-sized with coagulate gore,
With eyes like carbuncles, the hellish Pyrrhus
Old grandsire Priam seeks.'

So, proceed you.

Pol. 'Fore God, my lord, well spoken, with good accent and good discretion.

First Play.   'Anon he finds him
Striking too short at Greeks; his antique sword,
Rebellious to his arm, lies where it falls,
Repugnant to command: unequal match'd,
Pyrrhus at Priam drives; in rage strikes wide;
But with the whiff and wind of his fell sword
The unnerved father falls. Then senseless Ilium,
Seeming to feel this blow, with flaming top
Stoops to his base, and with a hideous crash
Takes prisoner Pyrrhus' ear: for, lo! his sword,
Which was declining on the milky head   500
Of reverend Priam, seem'd i' the air to stick:
So, as a painted tyrant, Pyrrhus stood,
And like a neutral to his will and matter,

441 *valanced.* Fringed (with a beard).

446 *chopine.* High-heeled shoe.

Man wearing chopines. Engraving from a medieval woodcut by F. W. Fairholt from J. O. Halliwell's edition of Shakespeare's works, 1853–1865

447 *uncurrent.* i.e. defaced.

457 *received.* Understood.

458 *cried . . . mine.* Bettered.

461 *sallets.* Savoury morsels.

472 *Hyrcanian beast.* Legendary tiger.

476 *horse.* i.e. the wooden horse inside which the Greeks entered Troy.

479 *gules.* Red. *trick'd.* Marked.

481 *impasted.* Encrusted.

484 *o'er-sized.* Plastered over.

495 *fell.* Fierce.

496 *senseless.* Unfeeling. *Ilium.* Troy.

511 *Cyclops.* Legendary one-eyed giants.

512 *Mars.* God of war.

517 *fellies.* Rims of wheels.

518 *nave.* Hub.

523 *Hecuba.* Wife of King Priam.

525 *mobled.* Veiled.

529 *bisson.* Blind. *rheum.* Tears.

531 *o'er-teemed.* Worn out with delivering children.

540 *milch.* Flow (with tears).

Costume design for the First Player by Mariano Andreu, New Theatre, London, 1951

548 *used.* Treated. *abstract.* Account.

554 *God's bodykins.* By God's little body!

Did nothing.
But, as we often see, against some storm,
A silence in the heavens, the rack stand still,
The bold winds speechless and the orb below
As hush as death, anon the dreadful thunder
Doth rend the region, so, after Pyrrhus' pause,
Aroused vengeance sets him new a-work;   510
● And never did the Cyclops' hammers fall
● On Mars's armour forged for proof eterne
With less remorse than Pyrrhus' bleeding sword
Now falls on Priam.
Out, out, thou strumpet, Fortune! All you gods,
In general synod, take away her power;
● Break all the spokes and fellies from her wheel,
● And bowl the round nave down the hill of heaven,
As low as to the fiends!'
Pol.   This is too long.   520
Ham.   It shall to the barber's, with your beard.
Prithee, say on: he's for a jig or a tale of bawdry,
● or he sleeps: say on: come to Hecuba.
First Play.   'But who, O, who had seen the
● mobled queen—'
Ham.   'The mobled queen?'
Pol.   That's good; 'mobled queen' is good.
First Play.   'Run barefoot up and down,
threatening the flames
● With bisson rheum; a clout upon that head
Where late the diadem stood, and for a robe,
● About her lank and all o'er-teemed loins,   531
A blanket, in the alarm of fear caught up;
Who this had seen, with tongue in venom steep'd,
'Gainst Fortune's state would treason have pronounced:
But if the gods themselves did see her then
When she saw Pyrrhus make malicious sport
In mincing with his sword her husband's limbs,
The instant burst of clamour that she made,
Unless things mortal move them not at all,
● Would have made milch the burning eyes of heaven,   540
And passion in the gods.'
Pol.   Look, whether he has not turned his colour and has tears in's eyes. Pray you, no more.
Ham.   'Tis well; I'll have thee speak out the rest soon.   Good my lord, will you see the players well bestowed?   Do you hear, let them
● be well used; for they are the abstract and brief chronicles of the time: after your death you were better have a bad epitaph than their ill report while you live.   551
Pol.   My lord, I will use them according to their desert.
● *Ham.*   God's bodykins, man, much better: use every man after his desert, and who should 'scape whipping?   Use them after your own honour and dignity: the less they deserve, the more merit is in your bounty.   Take them in.
Pol.   Come, sirs.   559
Ham.   Follow him, friends: we'll hear a play to-morrow. [*Exit Polonius with all the Players but the First.*] Dost thou hear me, old friend; can you play the Murder of Gonzago?
First Play.   Ay, my lord.
Ham.   We'll ha't to-morrow night.   You could, for a need, study a speech of some dozen

or sixteen lines, which I would set down and
insert in't, could you not?
    First Play. Ay, my lord.   569
    Ham. Very well. Follow that lord; and look
you mock him not. [*Exit First Player.*] My
good friends, I'll leave you till night: you are
welcome to Elsinore.
    Ros. Good my lord!
    Ham. Ay, so, God be wi' ye; [*Exeunt
Rosencrantz and Guildenstern.*] Now I am
    alone.
O, what a rogue and peasant slave am I!
Is it not monstrous that this player here,
But in a fiction, in a dream of passion,
● Could force his soul so to his own conceit
● That from her working all his visage wann'd, 580
Tears in his eyes, distraction in's aspect,
● A broken voice, and his whole function suiting
With forms to his conceit? and all for nothing!
For Hecuba!
What's Hecuba to him, or he to Hecuba,
That he should weep for her? What would he do,
Had he the motive and the cue for passion
That I have? He would drown the stage with
    tears
And cleave the general ear with horrid speech,
● Make mad the guilty and appal the free,   590
Confound the ignorant, and amaze indeed
The very faculties of eyes and ears.
Yet I,
● A dull and muddy-mettled rascal, peak,
Like John-a-dreams, unpregnant of my cause,
And can say nothing; no, not for a king,
Upon whose property and most dear life
A damn'd defeat was made. Am I a coward?
Who calls me villain? breaks my pate across?
Plucks off my beard, and blows it in my face?
Tweaks me by the nose? gives me the lie i' the
    throat,   601
As deep as to the lungs? who does me this?
Ha!
● 'Swounds, I should take it: for it cannot be
● But I am pigeon-liver'd and lack gall
To make oppression bitter, or ere this
● I should have fatted all the region kites
With this slave's offal: bloody, bawdy villain!
Remorseless, treacherous, lecherous, kindless vil-
    lain!
O, vengeance!   610
Why, what an ass am I! This is most brave,
That I, the son of a dear father murder'd,
Prompted to my revenge by heaven and hell,
Must, like a whore, unpack my heart with words,
And fall a-cursing, like a very drab,
A scullion!
Fie upon't! foh! About, my brain! I have
    heard
That guilty creatures sitting at a play
Have by the very cunning of the scene
Been struck so to the soul that presently   620
They have proclaim'd their malefactions;
For murder, though it have no tongue, will speak
With most miraculous organ. I'll have these
    players
Play something like the murder of my father
Before mine uncle: I'll observe his looks;
● I'll tent him to the quick: if he but blench,
I know my course. The spirit that I have seen
May be the devil: and the devil hath power

579 *conceit.* Imagination.

580 *working.* i.e. deriving. *wann'd.* Turned pale.

583 *suiting with forms.* i.e. appropriate.

590 *free.* Innocent.

594 *muddy-mettled.* Thick-witted. *peak.* Mope.

604 *'Swounds.* God's wounds!

605 *pigeon-liver'd.* i.e. gentle.

607 *region.* Of the air.

626 *tent.* Probe. *quick.* Most sensitive area of the body.
blench. Flinch.

Hamlet: 'I know my course'. Laurence Olivier as
Hamlet, Old Vic Theatre, London, 1937

Costume design for the King by Motley, Stratford-upon-Avon, 1958

---

633 *relative*. Conclusive.

1 *drift of circumstance*. Roundabout conversation.

3 *Grating*. Upsetting.

13 *Niggard of question*. Asking few questions.

14-15 *assay . . . pastime*. Test his interest in any amusement.

17 *o'er-raught*. Overtook.

26 *a further edge*. More incitement.

To assume a pleasing shape; yea, and perhaps
Out of my weakness and my melancholy,   630
As he is very potent with such spirits,
Abuses me to damn me: I'll have grounds
● More relative than this: the play's the thing
Wherein I'll catch the conscience of the king.
                                    [*Exit.*

ACT III.

SCENE I.   *A room in the castle.*

Enter KING, QUEEN, POLONIUS, OPHELIA,
     ROSENCRANTZ, *and* GUILDENSTERN.

● *King.* And can you, by no drift of circum-
          stance,
Get from him why he puts on this confusion,
● Grating so harshly all his days of quiet
With turbulent and dangerous lunacy?
     Ros. He does confess he feels himself dis-
          tracted;
But from what cause he will by no means speak.
     Guil. Nor do we find him forward to be
          sounded,
But, with a crafty madness, keeps aloof,
When we would bring him on to some confession
Of his true state.
     Queen.   Did he receive you well?   10
     Ros. Most like a gentleman.
     Guil. But with much forcing of his dispos-
          ition.
● *Ros.* Niggard of question; but, of our demands,
Most free in his reply.
● *Queen.*   Did you assay him
To any pastime?
     Ros. Madam, it so fell out, that certain players
● We o'er-raught on the way: of these we told him;
And there did seem in him a kind of joy
To hear of it: they are about the court,
And, as I think, they have already order   20
This night to play before him.
     Pol.   'Tis most true:
And he beseech'd me to entreat your majesties
To hear and see the matter.
     King. With all my heart; and it doth much
          content me
To hear him so inclined.
● Good gentlemen, give him a further edge,
And drive his purpose on to these delights.
     Ros. We shall, my lord.
          [*Exeunt Rosencrantz and Guildenstern.*
     King.   Sweet Gertrude, leave us too;
For we have closely sent for Hamlet hither,
That he, as 'twere by accident, may here   30
Affront Ophelia:
Her father and myself, lawful espials,
Will so bestow ourselves that, seeing, unseen,
We may of their encounter frankly judge,
And gather by him, as he is behaved,
If 't be the affliction of his love or no
That thus he suffers for.
     Queen.   I shall obey you.
And for your part, Ophelia, I do wish
That your good beauties be the happy cause
Of Hamlet's wildness: so shall I hope your
          virtues   40
Will bring him to his wonted way again,
To both your honours.
     Oph. Madam, I wish it may. [*Exit Queen.*

Pol. Ophelia, walk you here. Gracious, so
please you,
We will bestow ourselves. [*To Ophelia*] Read
on this book;
●That show of such an exercise may colour
Your loneliness. We are oft to blame in this,—
'Tis too much proved—that with devotion's visage
And pious action we do sugar o'er
The devil himself.
King. [*Aside*] O, 'tis too true!
How smart a lash that speech doth give my
conscience!   50
The harlot's cheek, beautied with plastering art,
Is not more ugly to the thing that helps it
Than is my deed to my most painted word:
O heavy burthen!
Pol. I hear him coming: let's withdraw, my
lord.   [*Exeunt King and Polonius.*

Enter HAMLET.

Ham. To be, or not to be: that is the question:
Whether 'tis nobler in the mind to suffer
The slings and arrows of outrageous fortune,
Or to take arms against a sea of troubles,
And by opposing end them? To die: to sleep; 60
No more; and by a sleep to say we end
The heart-ache and the thousand natural shocks
That flesh is heir to, 'tis a consummation
Devoutly to be wish'd. To die, to sleep;
●To sleep: perchance to dream: ay, there's the
rub;
For in that sleep of death what dreams may come
●When we have shuffled off this mortal coil,
●Must give us pause: there's the respect
That makes calamity of so long life;
For who would bear the whips and scorns of
time,   70
●The oppressor's wrong, the proud man's con-
tumely,
The pangs of despised love, the law's delay,
The insolence of office and the spurns
That patient merit of the unworthy takes,
●When he himself might his quietus make
●With a bare bodkin? who would fardels bear,
To grunt and sweat under a weary life,
But that the dread of something after death,
●The undiscover'd country from whose bourn
No traveller returns, puzzles the will   80
And makes us rather bear those ills we have
Than fly to others that we know not of?
Thus conscience does make cowards of us all;
●And thus the native hue of resolution
Is sicklied o'er with the pale cast of thought,
And enterprises of great pitch and moment
With this regard their currents turn awry,
And lose the name of action.—Soft you now!
●The fair Ophelia! Nymph, in thy orisons
Be all my sins remember'd.
Oph.   Good my lord,   90
How does your honour for this many a day?
Ham. I humbly thank you; well, well, well.
Oph. My lord, I have remembrances of yours,
That I have longed long to re-deliver;
I pray you, now receive them.
Ham.   No, not I;
I never gave you aught.
Oph. My honour'd lord, you know right well
you did;

45 *colour*. Disguise.

65 *rub*. Obstacle.

67 *mortal coil*. Stress of life.

68 *respect*. Consideration.

71 *contumely*. Insolence.

75 *quietus*. Final release.

76 *bodkin*. Dagger. *fardels*. Burdens.

79 *bourn*. Boundaries.

84 *native*. Natural.

89 *orisons*. Prayers.

John Neville as Hamlet and Judi Dench as Ophelia, Old
Vic Theatre, London, 1957

105 *fair.* i.e. 'beautiful' and 'honest'.

108 *discourse.* Discussion.

110 *commerce.* Close dealings.

113 *bawd.* Slut.

Hamlet: 'Get thee to a nunnery: why wouldst thou be a breeder of sinners?' Lithograph of Hamlet and Ophelia by Eugene Delacroix (1798–1863)

131 *arrant.* Notorious, downright.

148 *paintings.* Use of cosmetics.

155 *all but one.* i.e. Claudius.

160 *expectancy.* Hope.

And, with them, words of so sweet breath composed
As made the things more rich : their perfume lost,
Take these again ; for to the noble mind   100
Rich gifts wax poor when givers prove unkind.
There, my lord.
   Ham.   Ha, ha ! are you honest ?
   Oph.   My lord ?
   Ham.   Are you fair ?
   Oph.   What means your lordship ?
   Ham.   That if you be honest and fair, your honesty should admit no discourse to your beauty.
   Oph.   Could beauty, my lord, have better commerce than with honesty ?   110
   Ham.   Ay, truly ; for the power of beauty will sooner transform honesty from what it is to a bawd than the force of honesty can translate beauty into his likeness : this was sometime a paradox, but now the time gives it proof.   I did love you once.
   Oph.   Indeed, my lord, you made me believe so.
   Ham.   You should not have believed me ; for virtue cannot so inoculate our old stock but we shall relish of it : I loved you not.   120
   Oph.   I was the more deceived.
   Ham.   Get thee to a nunnery : why wouldst thou be a breeder of sinners ?   I am myself indifferent honest ; but yet I could accuse me of such things that it were better my mother had not borne me : I am very proud, revengeful, ambitious, with more offences at my beck than I have thoughts to put them in, imagination to give them shape, or time to act them in.   What should such fellows as I do crawling between earth and heaven ?   We are arrant knaves, all ; believe none of us.   Go thy ways to a nunnery.   Where's your father ?
   Oph.   At home, my lord.
   Ham.   Let the doors be shut upon him, that he may play the fool no where but in 's own house.   Farewell.
   Oph.   O, help him, you sweet heavens !
   Ham.   If thou dost marry, I 'll give thee this plague for thy dowry : be thou as chaste as ice, as pure as snow, thou shalt not escape calumny. Get thee to a nunnery, go : farewell.   Or, if thou wilt needs marry, marry a fool ; for wise men know well enough what monsters you make of them.   To a nunnery, go, and quickly too. Farewell.
   Oph.   O heavenly powers, restore him !
   Ham.   I have heard of your paintings too, well enough ; God has given you one face, and you make yourselves another : you jig, you amble, and you lisp, and nick-name God's creatures, and make your wantonness your ignorance. Go to, I 'll no more on 't ; it hath made me mad. I say, we will have no more marriages : those that are married already, all but one, shall live ; the rest shall keep as they are.   To a nunnery, go.   [*Exit.*
   Oph.   O, what a noble mind is here o'erthrown !
The courtier's, soldier's, scholar's, eye, tongue, sword ;
The expectancy and rose of the fair state,   160
The glass of fashion and the mould of form,
The observed of all observers, quite, quite down !
And I, of ladies most deject and wretched,
That suck'd the honey of his music vows,

Now see that noble and most sovereign reason,
Like sweet bells jangled, out of tune and harsh;
●That unmatch'd form and feature of blown
    youth
●Blasted with ecstasy: O, woe is me,
To have seen what I have seen, see what I see!

Re-enter KING *and* POLONIUS.

King.   Love! his affections do not that way
    tend;   170
Nor what he spake, though it lack'd form a little,
Was not like madness.   There's something in
    his soul,
O'er which his melancholy sits on brood;
●And I do doubt the hatch and the disclose
Will be some danger: which for to prevent,
I have in quick determination
Thus set it down: he shall with speed to England,
For the demand of our neglected tribute:
Haply the seas and countries different
With variable objects shall expel   180
This something-settled matter in his heart,
Whereon his brains still beating puts him thus
●From fashion of himself.   What think you on't?
    Pol.   It shall do well: but yet do I believe
The origin and commencement of his grief
Sprung from neglected love.   How now, Ophelia!
You need not tell us what Lord Hamlet said;
We heard it all.   My lord, do as you please;
But, if you hold it fit, after the play
Let his queen mother all alone entreat him   190
To show his grief: let her be round with him;
●And I'll be placed, so please you, in the ear
●Of all their conference.   If she find him not,
To England send him, or confine him where
Your wisdom best shall think.
    King.   It shall be so:
Madness in great ones must not unwatch'd go.
                                        [*Exeunt.*

SCENE II.   *A hall in the castle.*

Enter HAMLET *and* Players.

Ham.   Speak the speech, I pray you, as I
pronounced it to you, trippingly on the tongue:
but if you mouth it, as many of your players do,
●I had as lief the town-crier spoke my lines.   Nor
●do not saw the air too much with your hand,
thus, but use all gently; for in the very torrent,
tempest, and, as I may say, the whirlwind of
passion, you must acquire and beget a temperance that may give it smoothness.   O, it offends
me to the soul to hear a robustious periwig-pated
fellow tear a passion to tatters, to very rags, to
●split the ears of the groundlings, who for the most
part are capable of nothing but inexplicable
dumb-shows and noise: I would have such a
●fellow whipped for o'erdoing Termagant; it out-
herods Herod: pray you, avoid it.
    First Play.   I warrant your honour.
    Ham.   Be not too tame neither, but let your
own discretion be your tutor: suit the action to
the word, the word to the action; with this special observance, that you o'erstep not the modesty
of nature: for any thing so overdone is from the
purpose of playing, whose end, both at the first
and now, was and is, to hold, as 'twere, the mirror
up to nature; to show virtue her own feature,
scorn her own image, and the very age and body

167 *blown.* In full bloom.

168 *ecstasy.* Madness.

174 *doubt.* Fear. *hatch.* Hatching. *disclose.* Outcome.

183 *From . . . himself.* So unlike his real self.

192 *in the ear.* In earshot.

193 *find.* i.e. discovers the answer.

4 *as lief.* As soon.

5 *saw.* i.e. cut.

12 *groundlings.* People in the cheapest standing room of
a theatre.

15–16 *Termagant . . . Herod.* Tyrants' parts in medieval
plays.

Actors performing in a playhouse. Woodcut from
Comenius, *Orbis Sensualium Pictus,* 1689

27 *pressure.* Impression.

28 *come tardy off.* Badly timed.

37 *journeymen.* Unskilled labourers.

41 *indifferently.* To some extent.

Hamlet: '... And let those that play your clowns speak no more than is set down for them'. King with a jester. Engraving from an early 15th century manuscript

46 *barren.* Stupid.

47 *question.* Matter.

63 *revenue.* Income.

66 *crook.* Bend. *pregnant.* Ready.

67 *thrift.* Advantage.

69 *election.* Choice.

of the time his form and pressure. Now this overdone, or come tardy off, though it make the unskilful laugh, cannot but make the judicious grieve; the censure of the which one must in your allowance o'erweigh a whole theatre of others. O, there be players that I have seen play, and heard others praise, and that highly, not to speak it profanely, that, neither having the accent of Christians nor the gait of Christian, pagan, nor man, have so strutted and bellowed that I have thought some of nature's journeymen had made men and not made them well, they imitated humanity so abominably.

First Play. I hope we have reformed that indifferently with us, sir.   41

Ham. O, reform it altogether. And let those that play your clowns speak no more than is set down for them; for there be of them that will themselves laugh, to set on some quantity of barren spectators to laugh too; though, in the mean time, some necessary question of the play be then to be considered: that's villanous, and shows a most pitiful ambition in the fool that uses it. Go, make you ready. [*Exeunt Players.*

Enter POLONIUS, ROSENCRANTZ, *and* GUILD-
ENSTERN.

How now, my lord! will the king hear this piece of work?

Pol. And the queen too, and that presently.

Ham. Bid the players make haste. [*Exit Polonius.*] Will you two help to hasten them?

Ros. } We will, my lord.
Guil. }

[*Exeunt Rosencrantz and Guildenstern.*
Ham. What ho! Horatio!

Enter HORATIO.

Hor. Here, sweet lord, at your service.

Ham. Horatio, thou art e'en as just a man
As e'er my conversation coped withal.   60

Hor. O, my dear lord,—

Ham.   Nay, do not think I flatter;
For what advancement may I hope from thee
That no revenue hast but thy good spirits,
To feed and clothe thee? Why should the poor be flatter'd?
No, let the candied tongue lick absurd pomp,
And crook the pregnant hinges of the knee
Where thrift may follow fawning. Dost thou hear?
Since my dear soul was mistress of her choice
And could of men distinguish, her election
Hath seal'd thee for herself; for thou hast been
As one, in suffering all, that suffers nothing,   71
A man that fortune's buffets and rewards
Hast ta'en with equal thanks: and blest are those
Whose blood and judgement are so well comming-
led,
That they are not a pipe for fortune's finger
To sound what stop she please. Give me that man
That is not passion's slave, and I will wear him
In my heart's core, ay, in my heart of heart,
As I do thee.—Something too much of this.—
There is a play to-night before the king;   80.
One scene of it comes near the circumstance
Which I have told thee of my father's death:

I prithee, when thou seest that act afoot,
Even with the very comment of thy soul
● Observe mine uncle : if his occulted guilt
● Do not itself unkennel in one speech,
It is a damned ghost that we have seen,
And my imaginations are as foul
● As Vulcan's stithy. Give him heedful note ;
For I mine eyes will rivet to his face,   90
And after we will both our judgements join
● In censure of his seeming.
　　　Hor.　　　　　　　　Well, my lord :
If he steal aught the whilst this play is playing,
And 'scape detecting, I will pay the theft.
　　　Ham. They are coming to the play ; I must
　　　　be idle :
Get you a place.

Danish march. A flourish. Enter KING, QUEEN,
POLONIUS, OPHELIA, ROSENCRANTZ, GUILD-
ENSTERN, *and others.*

　　　King. How fares our cousin Hamlet ?
●　*Ham.* Excellent, i' faith ; of the chameleon's
dish : I eat the air, promise-crammed : you cannot feed capons so.   100
　　　King. I have nothing with this answer, Ham-
● let ; these words are not mine.
　　　Ham. No, nor mine now. [*To Polonius*] My
lord, you played once i' the university, you say ?
　　　Pol. That did I, my lord ; and was accounted
a good actor.
　　　Ham. What did you enact ?
　　　Pol. I did enact Julius Cæsar : I was killed
i' the Capitol ; Brutus killed me.
●　*Ham.* It was a brute part of him to kill so
capital a calf there. Be the players ready ? 111
　　　Ros. Ay, my lord ; they stay upon your pa-
tience.
　　　Queen. Come hither, my dear Hamlet, sit by
me.
●　*Ham.* No, good mother, here's metal more
attractive.
　　　Pol. [*To the King*] O, ho ! do you mark that ?
●　*Ham.* Lady, shall I lie in your lap ?
　　　　　　　　[*Lying down at Ophelia's feet.*
　　　Oph. No, my lord.   120
　　　Ham. I mean, my head upon your lap ?
　　　Oph. Ay, my lord.
●　*Ham.* Do you think I meant country matters ?
　　　Oph. I think nothing, my lord.
　　　Ham. That's a fair thought to lie between
maids' legs.
　　　Oph. What is, my lord ?
　　　Ham. Nothing.
　　　Oph. You are merry, my lord.
　　　Ham. Who, I ?   130
　　　Oph. Ay, my lord.
●　*Ham.* O God, your only jig-maker. What
should a man do but be merry ? for, look you,
how cheerfully my mother looks, and my father
died within these two hours.
　　　Oph. Nay, 'tis twice two months, my lord.
　　　Ham. So long ? Nay then, let the devil wear
black, for I'll have a suit of sables. O heavens !
die two months ago, and not forgotten yet ?
Then there's hope a great man's memory may
outlive his life half a year : but, by'r lady, he
must build churches, then ; or else shall he suffer
not thinking on, with the hobby-horse, whose

85 *occulted.* Hidden.

86 *unkennel.* Reveal.

89 *Vulcan.* Roman god of fire. *stithy.* Forge.

92 *censure.* Judging. *seeming.* Conduct.

98 *chameleon.* It was believed that this small lizard lived
on air.

102 *not mine.* i.e. have no relevance to my question.

110 *brute.* Brutal – pun on 'Brutus'.

116 *metal.* Material.

119 *lie.* i.e. 'tell lies' and 'lie down'.

123 *country matters.* Simple things ; also sexual innuendo – lying together out in the country.

132 *jig-maker.* Clown.

Hamlet (John Barrymore) with Ophelia (Fay Compton),
Haymarket Theatre, London, 1925

SD *Hautboys*. Oboes.

147 *miching mallecho*. i.e. sneaky crime.

162 *posy*. Motto engraved on the inside of a ring.

165 *Phœbus' cart*. Phoebus, sun-god of the Greeks, drove the sun across the sky each day in a chariot.

166 *Neptune*. Roman sea god. *Tellus*. Goddess of the Earth.

169 *Hymen*. God of marriage.

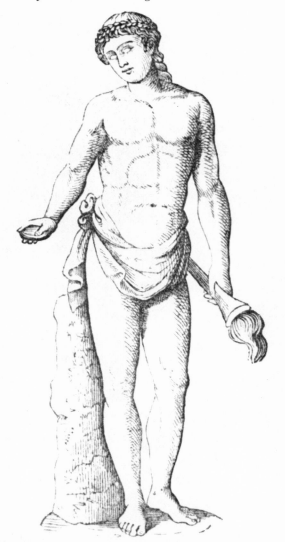

Hymen, the god of marriage in classical mythology. From a 19th century engraving

170 *commutual*. Reciprocally.

177 *holds quantity*. Keep proportion.

180 *sized*. Of a size.

184 *leave*. Cease.

epitaph is 'For, O, for, O, the hobby-horse is forgot.'

●   *Hautboys play.   The dumb-show enters.*

Enter a King *and a* Queen *very lovingly; the* Queen *embracing him, and he her. She kneels, and makes show of protestation unto him. He takes her up, and declines his head upon her neck: lays him down upon a bank of flowers: she, seeing him asleep, leaves him. Anon comes in a fellow, takes off his crown, kisses it, and pours poison in the* King's *ears, and exit. The* Queen *returns; finds the* King *dead, and makes passionate action. The* Poisoner, *with some two or three* Mutes, *comes in again, seeming to lament with her. The dead body is carried away. The* Poisoner *wooes the* Queen *with gifts: she seems loath and unwilling awhile, but in the end accepts his love.*   [*Exeunt.*

Oph.   What means this, my lord?
● *Ham.*   Marry, this is miching mallecho; it means mischief.
Oph.   Belike this show imports the argument of the play.   150

Enter Prologue.

Ham.   We shall know by this fellow: the players cannot keep counsel; they'll tell all.
Oph.   Will he tell us what this show meant?
Ham.   Ay, or any show that you'll show him: be not you ashamed to show, he'll not shame to tell you what it means.
Oph.   You are naught, you are naught: I'll mark the play.
Pro.   For us, and for our tragedy,
    Here stooping to your clemency,   160
    We beg your hearing patiently. [*Exit.*
● *Ham.*   Is this a prologue, or the posy of a ring?
Oph.   'Tis brief, my lord.
Ham.   As woman's love.

Enter two Players, King *and* Queen.

● *P. King.*   Full thirty times hath Phœbus' cart gone round
● Neptune's salt wash and Tellus' orbed ground,
And thirty dozen moons with borrow'd sheen
About the world have times twelve thirties been.
● Since love our hearts and Hymen did our hands
● Unite commutual in most sacred bands.   170
P. Queen.   So many journeys may the sun and moon
Make us again count o'er ere love be done!
But, woe is me, you are so sick of late,
So far from cheer and from your former state,
That I distrust you. Yet, though I distrust,
Discomfort you, my lord, it nothing must:
● For women's fear and love holds quantity;
In neither aught, or in extremity.
Now, what my love is, proof hath made you know;
● And as my love is sized, my fear is so: 180
Where love is great, the littlest doubts are fear;
Where little fears grow great, great love grows there.
P. King.   'Faith, I must leave thee, love, and shortly too;
● My operant powers their functions leave to do:

And thou shalt live in this fair world behind,
Honour'd, beloved ; and haply one as kind
For husband shalt thou—
    P. Queen.   O, confound the rest !
Such love must needs be treason in my breast :
In second husband let me be accurst !   189
None wed the second but who kill'd the first.
• *Ham.* [*Aside*] Wormwood, wormwood.
    P. Queen. The instances that second marriage move
• Are base respects of thrift, but none of love :
A second time I kill my husband dead,
When second husband kisses me in bed.
    P. King. I do believe you think what now you speak ;
But what we do determine oft we break.
Purpose is but the slave to memory,
• Of violent birth, but poor validity :   199
Which now, like fruit unripe, sticks on the tree ;
But fall, unshaken, when they mellow be.
Most necessary 'tis that we forget
To pay ourselves what to ourselves is debt :
What to ourselves in passion we propose,
The passion ending, doth the purpose lose.
The violence of either grief or joy
• Their own enactures with themselves destroy :
Where joy most revels, grief doth most lament ;
Grief joys, joy grieves, on slender accident.
This world is not for aye, nor 'tis not strange
That even our loves should with our fortunes change ;
For 'tis a question left us yet to prove,
Whether love lead fortune, or else fortune love.
The great man down, you mark his favourite flies ;
The poor advanced makes friends of enemies.
And hitherto doth love on fortune tend ;
For who not needs shall never lack a friend,
And who in want a hollow friend doth try,
Directly seasons him his enemy.
• But, orderly to end where I begun,   220
Our wills and fates do so contrary run
That our devices still are overthrown ;
Our thoughts are ours, their ends none of our own :
So think thou wilt no second husband wed ;
But die thy thoughts when thy first lord is dead.
    P. Queen. Nor earth to me give food, nor heaven light !
Sport and repose lock from me day and night !
To desperation turn my trust and hope !
• An anchor's cheer in prison be my scope !
• Each opposite that blanks the face of joy   230
Meet what I would have well and it destroy !
Both here and hence pursue me lasting strife,
If, once a widow, ever I be wife !
Ham. If she should break it now !
    P. King. 'Tis deeply sworn. Sweet, leave me here awhile ;
My spirits grow dull, and fain I would beguile
The tedious day with sleep.   [*Sleeps.*
    P. Queen.   Sleep rock thy brain ;
And never come mischance between us twain !
                    [*Exit.*
Ham. Madam, how like you this play ?   239
Queen. The lady doth protest too much, me-
Ham. O, but she'll keep her word. [thinks.
King. Have you heard the argument ? Is there no offence in 't ?

191 *Wormwood.* Bitter herb.

193 *respects of thrift.* Considerations of gain.

199 *validity.* Strength.

207 *enactures.* Doings.

220 *orderly.* In order.

229 *anchor.* Hermit. *scope.* Outcome.

230 *blanks.* Pales.

Hamlet: 'Madam, how like you this play ?' Watercolour of the play scene by John Faed (1819–1902)

247-8 *Tropically.* Figuratively.

253 *galled jade.* Broken down horse rubbed sore. *withers.* Highest part of horse's back. *unwrung.* Not wrenched.

260 *edge.* Desire.

267 *Confederate season.* Propitious moment.

269 *Hecate.* Goddess of black magic.

Hamlet: 'What, frighted with false fire!' Herbert Beerbohm Tree as Hamlet, Haymarket Theatre, 1892

---

286 *forest of feathers.* Reference to feathers worn by actors.

287 *turn Turk.* i.e. turn against.

288 *Provincial.* i.e. from Provence. *razed.* Slashed.

289 *cry.* Crowd.

292 *Damon.* Alluding to a legend where Damon was a true friend.

295 *pajock.* Peacock.

The play scene, Theatre Royal, Drury Lane, London, 1730. Engraving from *Universal Magazine*

Ham. No, no, they do but jest, poison in jest; no offence i' the world.

King. What do you call the play?

Ham. The Mouse-trap. Marry, how? Tropically. This play is the image of a murder done in Vienna: Gonzago is the duke's name; his wife, Baptista: you shall see anon; 'tis a knavish piece of work: but what o' that? your majesty and we that have free souls, it touches us not: let the galled jade wince, our withers are unwrung.

Enter LUCIANUS.

This is one Lucianus, nephew to the king.

Oph. You are as good as a chorus, my lord.

Ham. I could interpret between you and your love, if I could see the puppets dallying.

Oph. You are keen, my lord, you are keen.

Ham. It would cost you a groaning to take off my edge.   260

Oph. Still better, and worse.

Ham. So you must take your husbands. Begin, murderer; pox, leave thy damnable faces, and begin. Come: 'the croaking raven doth bellow for revenge.'

Luc. Thoughts black, hands apt, drugs fit, and time agreeing;
Confederate season, else no creature seeing;
Thou mixture rank, of midnight weeds collected,
With Hecate's ban thrice blasted, thrice infected,
Thy natural magic and dire property,   270
On wholesome life usurp immediately.

[Pours the poison into the sleeper's ears.

Ham. He poisons him i' the garden for's estate. His name's Gonzago: the story is extant, and writ in choice Italian: you shall see anon how the murderer gets the love of Gonzago's wife.

Oph. The king rises.

Ham. What, frighted with false fire!

Queen. How fares my lord?

Pol. Give o'er the play.

King. Give me some light: away!   280

All. Lights, lights, lights!

[Exeunt all but Hamlet and Horatio.

Ham. Why, let the stricken deer go weep,
The hart ungalled play;
For some must watch, while some must sleep:
So runs the world away.
Would not this, sir, and a forest of feathers—if the rest of my fortunes turn Turk with me—with two Provincial roses on my razed shoes, get me a fellowship in a cry of players, sir?

Hor. Half a share.   290

Ham. A whole one, I.
For thou dost know, O Damon dear,
This realm dismantled was
Of Jove himself; and now reigns here
A very, very—pajock.

Hor. You might have rhymed.

Ham. O good Horatio, I'll take the ghost's word for a thousand pound. Didst perceive?

Hor. Very well, my lord.

Ham. Upon the talk of the poisoning?   300

Hor. I did very well note him.

Ham. Ah, ha! Come, some music! come, the recorders!
For if the king like not the comedy,
Why then, belike, he likes it not, perdy.
Come, some music!

315 *choler.* Anger.

339 *admiration.* Astonishment.

346 *trade.* Business.

348–349 *pickers and stealers.* i.e. hands.

361–362 *go about.* A pun upon a sailing manoeuvre. *to recover the wind of me.* Trying to get the advantage of me; getting up-wind of one's enemy was an essential tactic in a battle at sea. *toil.* Net.

Hamlet: 'Will you play upon this pipe?' Lithograph of Hamlet with Rosencrantz and Guildenstern by Eugene Delacroix (1798–1863)

Re-enter ROSENCRANTZ *and* GUILDENSTERN.

Guil. Good my lord, vouchsafe me a word with you.

Ham. Sir, a whole history.

Guil. The king, sir,—   310

Ham. Ay, sir, what of him?

Guil. Is in his retirement marvellous distempered.

Ham. With drink, sir?

Guil. No, my lord, rather with choler.

Ham. Your wisdom should show itself more richer to signify this to his doctor; for, for me to put him to his purgation would perhaps plunge him into far more choler.   319

Guil. Good my lord, put your discourse into some frame and start not so wildly from my affair.

Ham. I am tame, sir: pronounce.

Guil. The queen, your mother, in most great affliction of spirit, hath sent me to you.

Ham. You are welcome.

Guil. Nay, good my lord, this courtesy is not of the right breed. If it shall please you to make me a wholesome answer, I will do your mother's commandment: if not, your pardon and my return shall be the end of my business.   330

Ham. Sir, I cannot.

Guil. What, my lord?

Ham. Make you a wholesome answer; my wit's diseased: but, sir, such answer as I can make, you shall command; or, rather, as you say, my mother: therefore no more, but to the matter: my mother, you say,—

Ros. Then thus she says; your behaviour hath struck her into amazement and admiration.   339

Ham. O wonderful son, that can so astonish a mother! But is there no sequel at the heels of this mother's admiration? Impart.

Ros. She desires to speak with you in her closet, ere you go to bed.

Ham. We shall obey, were she ten times our mother. Have you any further trade with us?

Ros. My lord, you once did love me.

Ham. So I do still, by these pickers and stealers.   349

Ros. Good my lord, what is your cause of distemper? you do, surely, bar the door upon your own liberty, if you deny your griefs to your friend.

Ham. Sir, I lack advancement.

Ros. How can that be, when you have the voice of the king himself for your succession in Denmark?

Ham. Ay, sir but, 'While the grass grows,'— the proverb is something musty.   359

Re-enter Players *with recorders.*

O, the recorders! let me see one. To withdraw with you:—why do you go about to recover the wind of me, as if you would drive me into a toil?

Guil. O, my lord, if my duty be too bold, my love is too unmannerly.

Ham. I do not well understand that. Will you play upon this pipe?

Guil. My lord, I cannot.

Ham. I pray you.

Guil. Believe me, I cannot.

Ham. I do beseech you.   370

Guil. I know no touch of it, my lord.

Ham. 'Tis as easy as lying: govern these ventages with your fingers and thumb, give it breath with your mouth, and it will discourse most eloquent music. Look you, these are the stops.

Guil. But these cannot I command to any utterance of harmony; I have not the skill.

Ham. Why, look you now, how unworthy a thing you make of me! You would play upon me; you would seem to know my stops; you would pluck out the heart of my mystery; you would sound me from my lowest note to the top of my compass: and there is much music, excellent voice, in this little organ; yet cannot you make it speak. 'Sblood, do you think I am easier to be played on than a pipe? Call me what instrument you will, though you can fret me, yet you cannot play upon me.

Enter POLONIUS.

God bless you, sir!   390

Pol. My lord, the queen would speak with you, and presently.

Ham. Do you see yonder cloud that's almost in shape of a camel?

Pol. By the mass, and 'tis like a camel, indeed.

Ham. Methinks it is like a weasel.

Pol. It is backed like a weasel.

Ham. Or like a whale?

Pol. Very like a whale.   399

Ham. Then I will come to my mother by and by. They fool me to the top of my bent. I will come by and by.

Pol. I will say so.

Ham. By and by is easily said. [*Exit Polonius.*] Leave me, friends.

[*Exeunt all but Hamlet.*

'Tis now the very witching time of night,
When churchyards yawn and hell itself breathes out
Contagion to this world: now could I drink hot blood,
And do such bitter business as the day
Would quake to look on. Soft! now to my mother.   410
O heart, lose not thy nature; let not ever
The soul of Nero enter this firm bosom:
Let me be cruel, not unnatural:
I will speak daggers to her, but use none;
My tongue and soul in this be hypocrites;
How in my words soever she be shent,
To give them seals never, my soul, consent!

[*Exit.*

SCENE III.   *A room in the castle.*

Enter KING, ROSENCRANTZ, *and*
GUILDENSTERN.

King. I like him not, nor stands it safe with us
To let his madness range. Therefore prepare you;
I your commission will forthwith dispatch,
And he to England shall along with you:
The terms of our estate may not endure
Hazard so near us as doth hourly grow
Out of his lunacies.

Guil.   We will ourselves provide:
Most holy and religious fear it is
To keep those many many bodies safe

373 *ventages.* Finger holes.

388 *fret me.* i.e. 'finger me' and 'anger me'.

412 *Nero.* Emperor of Rome who gave instructions for the murder of his mother.

416 *shent.* Humiliated.

Edwin Booth as Hamlet, New York, 1870

11 *peculiar*. Private.

13 *noyance*. Harm.

15 *cease*. Death. *majesty*. The king.

24 *Arm*. Prepare.

33 *of vantage*. In addition.

37 *primal eldest curse*. Fratricide, the story of Cain and Abel.

41 *double business*. i.e. two things at once.

61 *shuffling*. Trickery.

68 *limed*. Trapped, as a bird in bird-lime.

King: 'O wretched state! O bosom black as death! O limed soul. . .' Detail from a lithograph by Eugene Delacroix, 1843

That live and feed upon your majesty.   10
●   *Ros.*   The single and peculiar life is bound,
With all the strength and armour of the mind,
●To keep itself from noyance; but much more
That spirit upon whose weal depend and rest
●The lives of many.   The cease of majesty
Dies not alone; but, like a gulf, doth draw
What's near it with it: it is a massy wheel,
Fix'd on the summit of the highest mount,
To whose huge spokes ten thousand lesser things
Are mortised and adjoin'd; which, when it falls,
Each small annexment, petty consequence,   21
Attends the boisterous ruin.   Never alone
Did the king sigh, but with a general groan.
●   *King.*   Arm you, I pray you, to this speedy
            voyage;
For we will fetters put upon this fear,
Which now goes too free-footed.
      Ros. }
      Guil. }   We will haste us.
            [*Exeunt Rosencrantz and Guildenstern.*

            Enter POLONIUS.

      Pol.   My lord, he's going to his mother's closet:
Behind the arras I'll convey myself,
To hear the process; I'll warrant she'll tax him
            home:
And, as you said, and wisely was it said,   30
'Tis meet that some more audience than a mother,
Since nature makes them partial, should o'erhear
●The speech, of vantage.   Fare you well, my liege:
I'll call upon you ere you go to bed,
And tell you what I know.
      King.   Thanks, dear my lord.
            [*Exit Polonius.*
O, my offence is rank, it smells to heaven;
●It hath the primal eldest curse upon't,
A brother's murder.   Pray can I not,
Though inclination be as sharp as will:
My stronger guilt defeats my strong intent;   40
●And, like a man to double business bound,
I stand in pause where I shall first begin,
And both neglect.   What if this cursed hand
Were thicker than itself with brother's blood,
Is there not rain enough in the sweet heavens
To wash it white as snow?   Whereto serves mercy
But to confront the visage of offence?
And what's in prayer but this two-fold force,
To be forestalled ere we come to fall,
Or pardon'd being down?   Then I'll look up; 50
My fault is past.   But, O, what form of prayer
Can serve my turn?   'Forgive me my foul mur-
            der'?
That cannot be; since I am still possess'd
Of those effects for which I did the murder,
My crown, mine own ambition and my queen.
May one be pardon'd and retain the offence?
In the corrupted currents of this world
Offence's gilded hand may shove by justice,
And oft 'tis seen the wicked prize itself
Buys out the law: but 'tis not so above;   60
●There is no shuffling, there the action lies
In his true nature; and we ourselves compell'd,
Even to the teeth and forehead of our faults,
To give in evidence.   What then? what rests?
Try what repentance can: what can it not?
Yet what can it when one can not repent?
O wretched state!   O bosom black as death!
●O limed soul, that, struggling to be free,

Art more engaged ! Help, angels ! Make assay !
Bow, stubborn knees ; and, heart with strings of
    steel,   70
Be soft as sinews of the new-born babe !
All may be well.   *[Retires and kneels.*

Enter HAMLET.

Ham. Now might I do it pat, now he is
    praying ;
And now I'll do 't. And so he goes to heaven ;
●And so am I revenged. That would be scann'd :
A villain kills my father ; and for that,
I, his sole son, do this same villain send
To heaven.
●O, this is hire and salary, not revenge.
He took my father grossly, full of bread ;   80
●With all his crimes broad blown, as flush as May ;
And how his audit stands who knows save heaven ?
But in our circumstance and course of thought,
'Tis heavy with him : and am I then revenged,
To take him in the purging of his soul,
When he is fit and season'd for his passage ?
No !
●Up, sword ; and know thou a more horrid hent :
When he is drunk asleep, or in his rage,
Or in the incestuous pleasure of his bed ;   90
At gaming, swearing, or about some act
That has no relish of salvation in 't ;
Then trip him, that his heels may kick at heaven,
And that his soul may be as damn'd and black
As hell, whereto it goes. My mother stays :
This physic but prolongs thy sickly days. *[Exit.*
    King. *[Rising]* My words fly up, my thoughts
    remain below :
Words without thoughts never to heaven go.
    [Exit.

SCENE IV. *The Queen's closet.*

Enter QUEEN *and* POLONIUS.

Pol. He will come straight. Look you lay
    home to him :
Tell him his pranks have been too broad to bear
    with,
And that your grace hath screen'd and stood be-
    tween
●Much heat and him. I'll sconce me even here.
Pray you, be round with him.
    Ham. *[Within]* Mother, mother, mother !
    Queen.   I'll warrant you,
Fear me not : withdraw, I hear him coming.
    [Polonius hides behind the arras.

Enter HAMLET.

Ham. Now, mother, what's the matter ?
Queen. Hamlet, thou hast thy father much
    offended.
Ham. Mother, you have my father much
    offended.   10
Queen. Come, come, you answer with an idle
    tongue.
Ham. Go, go, you question with a wicked
    tongue.
Queen. Why, how now, Hamlet !
Ham.   What's the matter now ?
Queen. Have you forgot me ?
● *Ham.*   No, by the rood, not so :
You are the queen, your husband's brother's wife ;
And—would it were not so !—you are my mother.

75 *scann'd.* Considered.

79 *hire and salary.* i.e. being hired for reward.

81 *broad blown.* In full blossom.

88 *Up.* i.e. be sheathed. *hent.* Seizing.

Hamlet : 'Up, sword ; and know thou a more horrid hent.'
Richard Burton as Hamlet and Lawrence Harvey as
Claudius, Old Vic Theatre, London, 1953

4 *sconce.* Hide.

14 *rood.* Cross.

23 *ducat.* Gold coin.

Hamlet: 'How now! a rat? Dead, for a ducat, dead!'
Lithograph of Hamlet and the Queen before the arras by
Eugene Delacroix (1798–1863)

37 *custom.* Familiarity. *brass'd.* i.e. hardened.

38 *proof.* Armoured. *bulwark.* Fortified. *sense.* Feeling.

46 *contraction.* Law of contract.

50 *tristful.* Sorry. *doom.* Judgement.

56 *Hyperion.* Legendary son of earth and heaven. *front.*
Forehead.

58 *Mercury.* Messenger of the gods.

67 *moor.* Wasteland.

Queen.   Nay, then, I'll set those to you that
can speak.
Ham.   Come, come, and sit you down; you
shall not budge;
You go not till I set you up a glass
Where you may see the inmost part of you.   20
Queen.   What wilt thou do? thou wilt not mur-
der me?
Help, help, ho!
Pol.   [*Behind*] What, ho! help, help, help!
● *Ham.*   [*Drawing*] How now! a rat? Dead,
for a ducat, dead!
       [*Makes a pass through the arras.*
Pol.   [*Behind*] O, I am slain! [*Falls and dies.*
Queen.   O me, what hast thou done?
Ham.   Nay, I know not:
Is it the king?
Queen.   O, what a rash and bloody deed is this!
Ham.   A bloody deed! almost as bad, good
mother,
As kill a king, and marry with his brother.
Queen.   As kill a king!
Ham.   Ay, lady, 'twas my word.   30
   [*Lifts up the arras and discovers Polonius.*
Thou wretched, rash, intruding fool, farewell!
I took thee for thy better: take thy fortune;
Thou find'st to be too busy is some danger.
Leave wringing of your hands: peace! sit you
down,
And let me wring your heart; for so I shall,
If it be made of penetrable stuff,
●If damned custom have not brass'd it so
●That it be proof and bulwark against sense.
Queen.   What have I done, that thou darest wag
thy tongue
In noise so rude against me?
Ham.   Such an act   40
That blurs the grace and blush of modesty,
Calls virtue hypocrite, takes off the rose
From the fair forehead of an innocent love
And sets a blister there, makes marriage-vows
As false as dicers' oaths: O, such a deed
●As from the body of contraction plucks
The very soul, and sweet religion makes
A rhapsody of words: heaven's face doth glow;
Yea, this solidity and compound mass,
●With tristful visage, as against the doom,   50
Is thought-sick at the act.
Queen.   Ay me, what act,
That roars so loud, and thunders in the index?
Ham.   Look here, upon this picture, and on
this,
The counterfeit presentment of two brothers.
See, what a grace was seated on this brow;
●Hyperion's curls; the front of Jove himself;
An eye like Mars, to threaten and command;
●A station like the herald Mercury
New-lighted on a heaven-kissing hill;
A combination and a form indeed,   60
Where every god did seem to set his seal,
To give the world assurance of a man:
This was your husband.   Look you now, what
follows:
Here is your husband; like a mildew'd ear,
Blasting his wholesome brother.   Have you eyes?
Could you on this fair mountain leave to feed,
●And batten on this moor?   Ha! have you eyes?
You cannot call it love; for at your age
The hey-day in the blood is tame, it's humble,

And waits upon the judgement: and what judge-
ment   70
Would step from this to this?   Sense, sure, you
have,
Else could you not have motion; but sure, that
sense
Is apoplex'd; for madness would not err,
Nor sense to ecstasy was ne'er so thrall'd
But it reserved some quantity of choice,
To serve in such a difference.   What devil was't
●That thus hath cozen'd you at hoodman-blind?
Eyes without feeling, feeling without sight,
Ears without hands or eyes, smelling sans all,
Or but a sickly part of one true sense   80
●Could not so mope.
O shame! where is thy blush?   Rebellious hell,
●If thou canst mutine in a matron's bones,
To flaming youth let virtue be as wax,
And melt in her own fire: proclaim no shame
When the compulsive ardour gives the charge,
Since frost itself as actively doth burn
And reason pandars will.
      Queen.   O Hamlet, speak no more:
Thou turn'st mine eyes into my very soul;
And there I see such black and grained spots 90
●As will not leave their tinct.
      Ham.   Nay, but to live
●In the rank sweat of an enseamed bed,
Stew'd in corruption, honeying and making love
Over the nasty sty,—
      Queen.   O, speak to me no more;
These words, like daggers, enter in mine ears;
No more, sweet Hamlet!
      Ham.   A murderer and a villain;
●A slave that is not twentieth part the tithe
Of your precedent lord; a vice of kings;
A cutpurse of the empire and the rule,
That from a shelf the precious diadem stole, 100
And put it in his pocket!
      Queen.   No more!
      Ham.   A king of shreds and patches,—

Enter Ghost.

Save me, and hover o'er me with your wings,
You heavenly guards!   What would your gracious
figure?
      Queen.   Alas, he's mad!
      Ham.   Do you not come your tardy son to
chide,
That, lapsed in time and passion, lets go by
The important acting of your dread command?
O, say!
      Ghost.   Do not forget: this visitation   110
Is but to whet thy almost blunted purpose.
But, look, amazement on thy mother sits:
O, step between her and her fighting soul:
Conceit in weakest bodies strongest works:
Speak to her, Hamlet.
      Ham.   How is it with you, lady?
      Queen.   Alas, how is't with you,
That you do bend your eye on vacancy
And with the incorporal air do hold discourse?
Forth at your eyes your spirits wildly peep;
And, as the sleeping soldiers in the alarm,   120
●Your bedded hair, like life in excrements,
Start up, and stand an end.   O gentle son,
Upon the heat and flame of thy distemper
Sprinkle cool patience.   Whereon do you look?

77 *cozen'd.* Cheated. *hoodman-blind.* Blind-man's buff.

81 *mope.* Act foolishly.

83 *mutine.* Rebel. *matron.* Mother.

91 *leave.* Lose. *tinct.* Colour.

92 *enseamed.* Sweat stained.

Queen: 'These words, like daggers, enter in mine ears.'
Lithograph of Hamlet and the Queen by Eugene
Delacroix (1798–1863)

97 *tithe.* One-tenth.

121 *bedded.* Layered. *like.* As if there were. *excrements.*
i.e. outgrowths.

127 *capable*. Able to understand.

129 *effects*. Intentions.

Hamlet: 'Why, look you there! ... My father, in his habit as he lived!' Engraving from Rowe's edition of *Shakespeare*, 1709

137 *coinage*. Invention.

139 *cunning*. Skilful.

153 *fatness*. Slackness. *pursy*. Shortwinded, i.e. sick.

162 *habits devil*. i.e. the evil of becoming accustomed to anything.

169 *And . . . out*. i.e. master the devil or exorcise him.

175 *scourge*. Whip. *minister*. Instrument.

176 *bestow*. Dispose of. *answer*. Excuse.

183 *Pinch wanton*. Colour with desire. *mouse*. Term of affection.

184 *reechy*. Filthy.

Ham.   On him, on him! Look you, how pale he glares!
His form and cause conjoin'd, preaching to stones,
● Would make them capable. Do not look upon me;
Lest with this piteous action you convert
● My stern effects: then what I have to do   129
Will want true colour; tears perchance for blood.
    Queen.   To whom do you speak this?
    Ham.   Do you see nothing there?
    Queen.   Nothing at all; yet all that is I see.
    Ham.   Nor did you nothing hear?
    Queen.   No, nothing but ourselves.
    Ham.   Why, look you there! look, how it steals away!
My father, in his habit as he lived!
Look, where he goes, even now, out at the portal!
                                   [*Exit Ghost.*
●   *Queen.*   This is the very coinage of your brain:
This bodiless creation ecstasy
● Is very cunning in.
    Ham.   Ecstasy!   139
My pulse, as yours, doth temperately keep time,
And makes as healthful music: it is not madness
That I have utter'd: bring me to the test,
And I the matter will re-word; which madness
Would gambol from.   Mother, for love of grace,
Lay not that flattering unction to your soul,
That not your trespass, but my madness speaks:
It will but skin and film the ulcerous place,
Whiles rank corruption, mining all within,
Infects unseen.   Confess yourself to heaven;
Repent what's past; avoid what is to come;   150
And do not spread the compost on the weeds,
To make them ranker.   Forgive me this my virtue;
● For in the fatness of these pursy times
Virtue itself of vice must pardon beg,
Yea, curb and woo for leave to do him good.
    Queen.   O Hamlet, thou hast cleft my heart in twain.
    Ham.   O, throw away the worser part of it,
And live the purer with the other half.
Good night: but go not to mine uncle's bed;
Assume a virtue, if you have it not.   160
That monster, custom, who all sense doth eat,
● Of habits devil, is angel yet in this,
That to the use of actions fair and good
He likewise gives a frock or livery,
That aptly is put on.   Refrain to-night,
And that shall lend a kind of easiness
To the next abstinence: the next more easy;
For use almost can change the stamp of nature,
●† And either . . . . the devil, or throw him out 169
With wondrous potency.   Once more, good night:
And when you are desirous to be bless'd,
I'll blessing beg of you.   For this same lord,
                              [*Pointing to Polonius.*
I do repent: but heaven hath pleased it so,
To punish me with this and this with me,
● That I must be their scourge and minister.
● I will bestow him, and will answer well
The death I gave him.   So, again, good night.
I must be cruel, only to be kind:
Thus bad begins and worse remains behind.
One word more, good lady.
    Queen.   What shall I do?   180
    Ham.   Not this, by no means, that I bid you do:
Let the bloat king tempt you again to bed;
● Pinch wanton on your cheek; call you his mouse;
● And let him, for a pair of reechy kisses,

240

Or paddling in your neck with his damn'd fingers,
Make you to ravel all this matter out,
That I essentially am not in madness,
But mad in craft. 'Twere good you let him know;
For who, that's but a queen, fair, sober, wise, 189
Would from a paddock, from a bat, a gib,
Such dear concernings hide? who would do so?
No, in despite of sense and secrecy,
Unpeg the basket on the house's top,
Let the birds fly, and, like the famous ape,
To try conclusions, in the basket creep,
And break your own neck down.
  Queen. Be thou assured, if words be made of
   breath,
And breath of life, I have no life to breathe
What thou hast said to me.
  Ham. I must to England; you know that?
  Queen.   Alack, 200
I had forgot: 'tis so concluded on.
  Ham. There's letters seal'd: and my two
   schoolfellows,
Whom I will trust as I will adders fang'd,
They bear the mandate; they must sweep my
  way,
And marshal me to knavery. Let it work;
For 'tis the sport to have the enginer
Hoist with his own petar: and 't shall go hard
But I will delve one yard below their mines,
And blow them at the moon: O, 'tis most
  sweet,
When in one line two crafts directly meet. 210
This man shall set me packing:
I'll lug the guts into the neighbour room.
Mother, good night. Indeed this counsellor
Is now most still, most secret and most grave,
Who was in life a foolish prating knave.
Come, sir, to draw toward an end with you.
Good night, mother.
    [*Exeunt severally; Hamlet dragging
        in Polonius.*

ACT IV.

Scene I. *A room in the castle.*

Enter King, Queen, Rosencrantz, *and*
  Guildenstern.

  King. There's matter in these sighs, these
   profound heaves:
You must translate: 'tis fit we understand them.
Where is your son?
  Queen. Bestow this place on us a little while.
    [*Exeunt Rosencrantz and Guildenstern.*
Ah, mine own lord, what have I seen to-night!
  King. What, Gertrude? How does Hamlet?
  Queen. Mad as the sea and wind, when both
   contend
Which is the mightier: in his lawless fit,
Behind the arras hearing something stir,
Whips out his rapier, cries, 'A rat, a rat!' 10
And, in this brainish apprehension, kills
The unseen good old man.
  King.   O heavy deed!
It had been so with us, had we been there:
His liberty is full of threats to all;
To you yourself, to us, to every one.
Alas, how shall this bloody deed be answer'd?
It will be laid to us, whose providence

186 *ravel . . . out.* Untangle.

190 *paddock.* Toad. *gib.* Cat.

193–196 Hamlet alludes to a fable. *try conclusions.* Experiment. *down.* i.e. by jumping out.

205 *marshal . . . knavery.* Mislead me into danger.

206 *enginer.* Engineer.

207 *Hoist.* Blown up. *petar.* Bomb.

A petard, a small war machine. Woodcut from Robert Ward's *Animadversions of War*, 1639

210 *crafts.* i.e. 'ships' and 'plots'.

11 *brainish.* Imagined. *apprehension.* Fear.

Costume design for the Queen by Leslie Hurry, Royal Shakespeare Co, 1961

---

18 *short.* i.e. on a short lead. *haunt.* Society.

22 *divulging.* Being known.

25 *ore.* Gold.

42 *level.* Straight. *blank.* Target.

1 *Safely stowed.* The body is safely hidden.

12 *demanded of.* Interrogated by.

● Should have kept short, restrain'd and out of
    haunt,
This mad young man: but so much was our love,
We would not understand what was most fit;   20
But, like the owner of a foul disease,
● To keep it from divulging, let it feed
Even on the pith of life.   Where is he gone?
   Queen. To draw apart the body he hath kill'd:
● O'er whom his very madness, like some ore
Among a mineral of metals base,
Shows itself pure; he weeps for what is done.
   King.   O Gertrude, come away!
The sun no sooner shall the mountains touch,
But we will ship him hence: and this vile deed 30
We must, with all our majesty and skill,
Both countenance and excuse.   Ho, Guildenstern!

Re-enter ROSENCRANTZ *and* GUILDENSTERN.

Friends both, go join you with some further aid:
Hamlet in madness hath Polonius slain,
And from his mother's closet hath he dragg'd him:
Go seek him out; speak fair, and bring the body
Into the chapel.   I pray you, haste in this.
   [*Exeunt Rosencrantz and Guildenstern.*
Come, Gertrude, we'll call up our wisest friends;
And let them know, both what we mean to do,
† And what's untimely done.........   40
Whose whisper o'er the world's diameter,
● As level as the cannon to his blank,
Transports his poison'd shot, may miss our name,
And hit the woundless air.   O, come away!
My soul is full of discord and dismay.   [*Exeunt.*

SCENE II.   *Another room in the castle.*

Enter HAMLET.

● *Ham.*   Safely stowed.
  Ros. } [*Within*] Hamlet! Lord Hamlet!
  Guil. }
  Ham.   But soft, what noise? who calls on
Hamlet? O, here they come.

Enter ROSENCRANTZ *and* GUILDENSTERN.

  Ros.   What have you done, my lord, with the
dead body?
  Ham.   Compounded it with dust, whereto
'tis kin.
  Ros.   Tell us where 'tis, that we may take it
thence
And bear it to the chapel.
  Ham.   Do not believe it.
  Ros.   Believe what?   10
  Ham.   That I can keep your counsel and not
● mine own. Besides, to be demanded of a sponge!
what replication should be made by the son of
a king?
  Ros.   Take you me for a sponge, my lord?
  Ham.   Ay, sir, that soaks up the king's countenance, his rewards, his authorities.   But such
officers do the king best service in the end: he
keeps them, like an ape, in the corner of his
jaw; first mouthed, to be last swallowed: when
he needs what you have gleaned, it is but
squeezing you. and, sponge, you shall be dry
again.
  Ros.   I understand you not, my lord.
  Ham. I am glad of it: a knavish speech sleeps
in a foolish ear.

Ros. My lord, you must tell us where the body is, and go with us to the king.

● *Ham.* The body is with the king, but the ●king is not with the body. The king is a thing—

Guil. A thing, my lord! 31

Ham. Of nothing: bring me to him. Hide fox, and all after. [*Exeunt*.

SCENE III. *Another room in the castle.*

Enter KING, *attended.*

King. I have sent to seek him, and to find the body.
How dangerous is it that this man goes loose!
Yet must not we put the strong law on him:
He's loved of the distracted multitude,
Who like not in their judgement, but their eyes;
And where 'tis so, the offender's scourge is weigh'd,
But never the offence. To bear all smooth and even,
This sudden sending him away must seem
Deliberate pause: diseases desperate grown
By desperate appliance are relieved, 10
Or not at all.

Enter ROSENCRANTZ.

How now! what hath befall'n?

Ros. Where the dead body is bestow'd, my lord,
We cannot get from him.

King. But where is he?

Ros. Without, my lord; guarded, to know your pleasure.

King. Bring him before us.

Ros. Ho, Guildenstern! bring in my lord.

Enter HAMLET *and* GUILDENSTERN.

King. Now, Hamlet, where's Polonius?

Ham. At supper.

King. At supper! where? 19

Ham. Not where he eats, but where he is
●eaten: a certain convocation of politic worms are e'en at him. Your worm is your only emperor for diet: we fat all creatures else to fat us, and we fat ourselves for maggots: your fat king and your lean beggar is but variable service, two dishes, but to one table: that's the end.

King. Alas, alas!

Ham. A man may fish with the worm that hath eat of a king, and eat of the fish that hath fed of that worm. 30

King. What dost thou mean by this?

Ham. Nothing but to show you how a king
●may go a progress through the guts of a beggar.

King. Where is Polonius?

Ham. In heaven; send thither to see: if your messenger find him not there, seek him i' the other place yourself. But indeed, if you find him not within this month, you shall nose him as you go up the stairs into the lobby.

King. Go seek him there. 40
[*To some Attendants.*

Ham. He will stay till you come.
[*Exeunt Attendants.*

King. Hamlet, this deed, for thine especial safety,—
●Which we do tender, as we dearly grieve

Costume design for Hamlet by Audrey Cruddas, Old Vic Theatre, London, 1957

29 *king.* i.e. king of heaven.

30 *king.* i.e. Claudius.

21 *politic.* Shrewd.

33 *progress.* Royal visit.

43 *tender.* Have regard for.

47 *The associates tend.* Your travelling companions await.

Hamlet: 'For England!' Hamlet (Alan Howard) with Rosencrantz (Phillip Manikum), and Guildenstern (John Kane), Royal Shakespeare Co, 1970

56 *at foot.* On his heels.

59 *else leans on.* Otherwise affects.

64 *set.* Estimate.

65 *process.* Course.

66 *congruing.* Concurring.

67 *present.* Immediate.

68 *hectic.* Fever.

70 *Howe'er my haps.* Whatever chance may bring me.

15 *main.* Main part.

22 *ranker.* Higher. *in fee.* Freehold.

For that which thou hast done,—must send thee hence
With fiery quickness: therefore prepare thyself;
The bark is ready, and the wind at help,
● The associates tend, and every thing is bent
For England.
   Ham.   For England!
   King.   Ay, Hamlet.
   Ham.   Good.
   King.   So is it, if thou knew'st our purposes.
   Ham.   I see a cherub that sees them.   But,
come; for England!   Farewell, dear mother. 51
   King.   Thy loving father, Hamlet.
   Ham.   My mother: father and mother is man
and wife; man and wife is one flesh; and so, my
mother.   Come, for England!   *[Exit.*
●   *King.*   Follow him at foot; tempt him with
    speed aboard;
Delay it not; I'll have him hence to-night:
Away! for every thing is seal'd and done
● That else leans on the affair: pray you, make haste.
    [Exeunt Rosencrantz and Guildenstern.
And, England, if my love thou hold'st at aught—
As my great power thereof may give thee sense,
Since yet thy cicatrice looks raw and red
After the Danish sword, and thy free awe
● Pays homage to us—thou mayst not coldly set
● Our sovereign process; which imports at full,
● By letters conguing to that effect,
● The present death of Hamlet.   Do it, England;
● For like the hectic in my blood he rages,
And thou must cure me: till I know 'tis done,
● Howe'er my haps, my joys were ne'er begun. 70
                            [Exit.

SCENE IV.   *A plain in Denmark.*

Enter FORTINBRAS, *a* Captain, *and* Soldiers,
marching.

   For.   Go, captain, from me greet the Danish
    king;
Tell him that, by his license, Fortinbras
Craves the conveyance of a promised march
Over his kingdom.   You know the rendezvous.
If that his majesty would aught with us,
We shall express our duty in his eye;
And let him know so.
   Cap.   I will do't, my lord.
   For.   Go softly on.
       [Exeunt Fortinbras and Soldiers.

Enter HAMLET, ROSENCRANTZ, GUILDENSTERN,
and others.

   Ham.   Good sir, whose powers are these?
   Cap.   They are of Norway, sir.   10
   Ham.   How purposed, sir, I pray you?
   Cap.   Against some part of Poland.
   Ham.   Who commands them, sir?
   Cap.   The nephew to old Norway, Fortinbras.
●   *Ham.*   Goes it against the main of Poland, sir,
Or for some frontier?
   Cap.   Truly to speak, and with no addition,
We go to gain a little patch of ground
That hath in it no profit but the name.
To pay five ducats, five, I would not farm it; 20
Nor will it yield to Norway or the Pole
● A ranker rate, should it be sold in fee.
   Ham.   Why, then the Polack never will
    defend it.

Cap. Yes, it is already garrison'd.
Ham. Two thousand souls and twenty thousand
  ducats
Will not debate the question of this straw :
● This is the imposthume of much wealth and peace,
That inward breaks, and shows no cause without
Why the man dies. I humbly thank you, sir.
  Cap. God be wi' you, sir.   [*Exit.*
  Ros.   Will 't please you go, my lord? 30
  Ham. I'll be with you straight. Go a little
    before.   [*Exeunt all except Hamlet.*
How all occasions do inform against me,
And spur my dull revenge ! What is a man,
● If his chief good and market of his time
Be but to sleep and feed ? a beast, no more.
Sure, he that made us with such large discourse,
Looking before and after, gave us not
That capability and god-like reason
● To fust in us unused. Now, whether it be
Bestial oblivion, or some craven scruple   40
Of thinking too precisely on the event,
A thought which, quarter'd, hath but one part
    wisdom
And ever three parts coward, I do not know
Why yet I live to say 'This thing's to do ; '
Sith I have cause and will and strength and means
To do 't.   Examples gross as earth exhort me :
● Witness this army of such mass and charge
Led by a delicate and tender prince,
Whose spirit with divine ambition puff'd
Makes mouths at the invisible event,   50
Exposing what is mortal and unsure
To all that fortune, death and danger dare,
Even for an egg-shell. Rightly to be great
Is not to stir without great argument,
But greatly to find quarrel in a straw
When honour's at the stake. How stand I then,
That have a father kill'd, a mother stain'd,
Excitements of my reason and my blood,
And let all sleep ? while, to my shame, I see
The imminent death of twenty thousand men, 60
● That, for a fantasy and trick of fame,
Go to their graves like beds, fight for a plot
● Whereon the numbers cannot try the cause,
● Which is not tomb enough and continent
To hide the slain ? O, from this time forth,
My thoughts be bloody, or be nothing worth !
                                        [*Exit.*

SCENE V. *Elsinore.   A room in the castle.*

Enter QUEEN, HORATIO, *and a* Gentleman.

Queen. I will not speak with her.
Gent. She is importunate, indeed distract :
Her mood will needs be pitied.
  Queen.   What would she have ?
  Gent. She speaks much of her father ; says
    she hears
● There's tricks i' the world ; and hems, and beats
    her heart ;
● Spurns enviously at straws ; speaks things in doubt,
That carry but half sense : her speech is nothing,
Yet the unshaped use of it doth move
● The hearers to collection ; they aim at it,
● And botch the words up fit to their own thoughts ;
Which, as her winks, and nods, and gestures yield
    them,   11
Indeed would make one think there might be
    thought,

27 *imposthume.* Abscess.

34 *market.* i.e. most profitable use.

39 *fust.* Grow mouldy.

47 *mass and charge.* Size and cost.

61 *fantasy.* Whim. *trick.* hint.

63 *Whereon . . . cause.* i.e. which is too small to accommodate the armies which have gathered to fight over it.

64 *and continent.* i.e. or a large enough container.

5 *hems.* Splutters.

6 *Spurns.* Kicks. *enviously.* In anger. *straws.* Trifling matters.

9 *collection.* Put the words together. *aim.* Guess.

10 *botch.* Patch together.

Ophelia. Engraving from a 19th century painting by Arthur Hughes (1830–1915)

15 *ill-breeding*. i.e. malevolent.

18 *toy*. Trifle.

19 *artless*. Uncontrolled.

25 *cockle hat*. Hat worn with a cockleshell to indicate that the wearer had travelled as a pilgrim to the shrine of St James at Compostella.

Ophelia: 'How should I your true love know ...' Helen M. Holte as Ophelia in Poel's production, 1881

26 *shoon*. Shoes.

27 *imports*. Means.

37 *Larded*. Bedecked.

41 *'ild*. Shield.

45 *Conceit upon*. i.e. she's thinking about.

53 *dupp'd*. Opened.

59 *Gis*. Jesus.

62 *cock*. i.e. 'God' and 'male genitals'.

Though nothing sure, yet much unhappily.
   Hor. 'Twere good she were spoken with; for she may strew
● Dangerous conjectures in ill-breeding minds.
   Queen. Let her come in.　　[*Exit Horatio*.
To my sick soul, as sin's true nature is,
● Each toy seems prologue to some great amiss:
● So full of artless jealousy is guilt,
It spills itself in fearing to be spilt.　　20

   Re-enter HORATIO, *with* OPHELIA.

   Oph. Where is the beauteous majesty of Denmark?
   Queen. How now, Ophelia!
   Oph. [*Sings*] How should I your true love know
         From another one?
●   By his cockle hat and staff,
●   And his sandal shoon.
● *Queen*. Alas, sweet lady, what imports this song?
   Oph. Say you? nay, pray you, mark.
[*Sings*]　　He is dead and gone, lady,
         He is dead and gone;　　30
         At his head a grass-green turf,
         At his heels a stone.
   Queen. Nay, but, Ophelia,—
   Oph. Pray you, mark.
[*Sings*] White his shroud as the mountain snow,—

   Enter KING.

   Queen. Alas, look here, my lord.
● *Oph*. [*Sings*] Larded with sweet flowers;
         Which bewept to the grave did go
         With true-love showers.
   King. How do you, pretty lady?　　40
● *Oph*. Well, God 'ild you! They say the owl was a baker's daughter. Lord, we know what we are, but know not what we may be. God be at your table!
● *King*. Conceit upon her father.
   Oph. Pray you, let's have no words of this; but when they ask you what it means, say you this:
[*Sings*.] To-morrow is Saint Valentine's day,
         All in the morning betime,
        And I a maid at your window,　　50
         To be your Valentine.
       Then up he rose, and donn'd his clothes,
●   And dupp'd the chamber-door;
       Let in the maid, that out a maid
         Never departed more.
   King. Pretty Ophelia!
   Oph. Indeed, la, without an oath, I'll make an end on't:
● [*Sings*] By Gis and by Saint Charity,
         Alack, and fie for shame!　　60
       Young men will do't, if they come to't;
●   By cock, they are to blame.
       Quoth she, before you tumbled me,
         You promised me to wed.
       So would I ha' done, by yonder sun,
         An thou hadst not come to my bed.
   King. How long hath she been thus?
   Oph. I hope all will be well. We must be patient: but I cannot choose but weep, to think they should lay him i' the cold ground. My brother shall know of it: and so I thank you for your good counsel. Come, my coach! Good night, ladies; good night, sweet ladies; good night, good night.　　　　　　　[*Exit*.

King. Follow her close; give her good watch,
I pray you.   [*Exit Horatio.*
O, this is the poison of deep grief; it springs
All from her father's death. O Gertrude, Gertrude,
● When sorrows come, they come not single spies,
But in battalions.   First, her father slain :
Next, your son gone ; and he most violent author
● Of his own just remove : the people muddied, 81
Thick and unwholesome in their thoughts and
    whispers,
● For good Polonius' death ; and we have done but
    greenly,
● In hugger-mugger to inter him : poor Ophelia
Divided from herself and her fair judgement,
Without the which we are pictures, or mere beasts :
Last, and as much containing as all these,
Her brother is in secret come from France ;
Feeds on his wonder, keeps himself in clouds,
● And wants not buzzers to infect his ear   90
With pestilent speeches of his father's death ;
● Wherein necessity, of matter beggar'd,
● Will nothing stick our person to arraign
In ear and ear.   O my dear Gertrude, this,
● Like to a murdering-piece, in many places
Gives me superfluous death.   [*A noise within.*
    Queen.   Alack, what noise is this ?
● *King.* Where are my Switzers? Let them
    guard the door.

Enter another Gentleman.

What is the matter?
    Gent.   Save yourself, my lord :
● The ocean, overpeering of his list,
Eats not the flats with more impetuous haste 100
● Than young Laertes, in a riotous head,
O'erbears your officers.   The rabble call him
    lord ;
And, as the world were now but to begin,
● Antiquity forgot, custom not known,
● The ratifiers and props of every word,
They cry 'Choose we : Laertes shall be king :'
Caps, hands, and tongues, applaud it to the
    clouds :
'Laertes shall be king, Laertes king !'
    Queen. How cheerfully on the false trail they
    cry !
O, this is counter, you false Danish dogs !   110
    King. The doors are broke. [*Noise within.*

Enter LAERTES, *armed*; Danes *following.*

Laer. Where is this king? Sirs, stand you
    all without.
Danes. No, let's come in.
Laer.   I pray you, give me leave.
Danes. We will, we will.
                    [*They retire without the door.*
Laer. I thank you: keep the door.   O thou
    vile king,
Give me my father !
    Queen.   Calmly, good Laertes.
Laer. That drop of blood that's calm pro-
    claims me bastard,
Cries cuckold to my father, brands the harlot
● Even here, between the chaste unsmirched brow
Of my true mother.
    King.   What is the cause, Laertes, 120
That thy rebellion looks so giant-like?
Let him go, Gertrude; do not fear our person :
● There's such divinity doth hedge a king,

78 *single spies.* i.e. alone.

81 *just remove.* Justified removal. *muddied.* Stirred up.

83 *greenly.* Recently.

84 *hugger-mugger.* Secret.

90 *buzzers.* Tattlers.

92 *beggar'd.* Lacking.

93 *nothing stick.* Stop at nothing.

95 *murdering-piece.* Small cannon which fired shrapnel.

97 *Switzers.* Swiss body guards.

99 *overpeering of his list.* Exceeding its highest tide.

101 *in a riotous head.* With a hostile army.

104 *Antiquity.* Tradition.

105 *ratifiers and props.* Confirmation and support.

119 *unsmirched.* Unbranded.

123 *hedge.* Protect.

Costume design for Laertes by Motley for Byam Shaw's
production, New Theatre, London, 1934

124 *but peep.* Only glimpse.

142 *swoopstake.* All at one time.

146 *pelican.* Pelicans were thought to feed their young with their own blood.

151 *level.* i.e. readily.

160 *mortal.* Frail.

•That treason can but peep to what it would,
Acts little of his will.   Tell me, Laertes,
Why thou art thus incensed.   Let him go, Gertrude.
Speak, man.
   Laer.   Where is my father?
   King.   Dead.
   Queen.   But not by him.
   King.   Let him demand his fill.
   Laer.   How came he dead?   I'll not be juggled with: 130
To hell, allegiance! vows, to the blackest devil!
Conscience and grace, to the profoundest pit!
I dare damnation.   To this point I stand,
That both the worlds I give to negligence,
Let come what comes; only I'll be revenged
Most throughly for my father.
   King.   Who shall stay you?
   Laer.   My will, not all the world:
And for my means, I'll husband them so well,
They shall go far with little.
   King.   Good Laertes,
If you desire to know the certainty   140
Of your dear father's death, is't writ in your revenge,
•That, swoopstake, you will draw both friend and foe,
Winner and loser?
   Laer.   None but his enemies.
   King.   Will you know them then?
   Laer.   To his good friends thus wide I'll ope my arms;
•And like the kind life-rendering pelican,
Repast them with my blood.
   King.   Why, now you speak
Like a good child and a true gentleman.
That I am guiltless of your father's death,
And am most sensibly in grief for it,   150
•It shall as level to your judgement pierce
As day does to your eye.
   Danes.   [*Within*]   Let her come in.
   Laer.   How now! what noise is that?

Re-enter OPHELIA.

O heat, dry up my brains! tears seven times salt,
Burn out the sense and virtue of mine eye!
By heaven, thy madness shall be paid with weight,
Till our scale turn the beam.   O rose of May!
Dear maid, kind sister, sweet Ophelia!
O heavens! is't possible, a young maid's wits
•Should be as mortal as an old man's life?   160
Nature is fine in love, and where 'tis fine,
It sends some precious instance of itself
After the thing it loves.
   Oph. [*Sings*]
     They bore him barefaced on the bier;
     Hey non nonny, nonny, hey nonny;
     And in his grave rain'd many a tear:—
Fare you well, my dove!
   Laer.   Hadst thou thy wits, and didst persuade revenge,
It could not move thus.
   Oph. [*Sings*] You must sing a-down a-down,
     An you call him a-down-a.   171
O, how the wheel becomes it!   It is the false
steward, that stole his master's daughter.
   Laer.   This nothing's more than matter.
   Oph.   There's rosemary, that's for remem-

brance; pray, love, remember: and there is pansies, that's for thoughts.

Laer.   A document in madness, thoughts and remembrance fitted.   179

Oph.   There's fennel for you, and columbines: there's rue for you; and here's some for me: we may call it herb-grace o' Sundays: O, you must wear your rue with a difference.   There's a daisy: I would give you some violets, but they withered all when my father died: they say he made a good end,—

[*Sings*]   For bonny sweet Robin is all my joy.

Laer.   Thought and affliction, passion, hell itself,
She turns to favour and to prettiness.

Oph. [*Sings*] And will he not come again?
And will he not come again?
No, no, he is dead:
Go to thy death-bed:
He never will come again.

His beard was as white as snow,
All flaxen was his poll:
He is gone, he is gone,
And we cast away moan:
God ha' mercy on his soul!

And of all Christian souls, I pray God.   God be
wi' ye.   [*Exit.* 200

Laer.   Do you see this, O God?

King.   Laertes, I must commune with your grief,
Or you deny me right.   Go but apart,
Make choice of whom your wisest friends you
will,
And they shall hear and judge 'twixt you and me:
If by direct or by collateral hand
They find us touch'd, we will our kingdom give,
Our crown, our life, and all that we call ours,
To you in satisfaction; but if not,
Be you content to lend your patience to us,   210
And we shall jointly labour with your soul
To give it due content.

Laer.   Let this be so;
His means of death, his obscure funeral—
No trophy, sword, nor hatchment o'er his bones,
No noble rite nor formal ostentation—
Cry to be heard, as 'twere from heaven to earth,
That I must call 't in question.

King.   So you shall;
And where the offence is let the great axe fall.
I pray you, go with me.   [*Exeunt.*

SCENE VI.   *Another room in the castle.*

Enter HORATIO *and a* Servant.

Hor.   What are they that would speak with
me?

Serv.   Sailors, sir: they say they have letters
for you.

Hor.   Let them come in.   [*Exit Servant.*
I do not know from what part of the world
I should be greeted, if not from lord Hamlet.

Enter Sailors.

First Sail.   God bless you, sir.

Hor.   Let him bless thee too.

First Sail.   He shall, sir, an't please him.
There's a letter for you, sir: it comes from the

178 *document.* Lesson, example.

Ophelia: 'There's fennel for you, and columbines . . .'
Jane Lessingham as Ophelia. Engraving from Bell's
edition of *Shakespeare,* 1778

206 *collateral.* Indirect. *hand.* i.e. action.

207 *touch'd.* Implicated.

214 *hatchment.* Funeral coat of arms.

249

First Sailor: '. . . if your name be Horatio'. Engraving by Kenny Meadows from Barry Cornwall's *Works of Shakspere*, 1846

3 *Sith.* Since.

6 *feats.* Deeds.

14 *conjunctive.* Close.

17 *count.* Trial.

18 *general gender.* Common people.

21 *gyves.* Shackles.

22 *Too slightly timber'd.* Made of too light a wood.

26 *terms.* Conditions.

28 *on mount.* Above. *age.* Generation.

ambassador that was bound for England; if your name be Horatio, as I am let to know it is. 11

Hor. [*Reads*] 'Horatio, when thou shalt have overlooked this, give these fellows some means to the king: they have letters for him. Ere we were two days old at sea, a pirate of very warlike appointment gave us chase. Finding ourselves too slow of sail, we put on a compelled valour, and in the grapple I boarded them: on the instant they got clear of our ship; so I alone became their prisoner. They have dealt with me like thieves of mercy: but they knew what they did; I am to do a good turn for them. Let the king have the letters I have sent; and repair thou to me with as much speed as thou wouldst fly death. I have words to speak in thine ear will make thee dumb; yet are they much too light for the bore of the matter. These good fellows will bring thee where I am. Rosencrantz and Guildenstern hold their course for England: of them I have much to tell thee. Farewell. 30
     'He that thou knowest thine, HAMLET.'
Come, I will make you way for these your letters;
And do't the speedier, that you may direct me
To him from whom you brought them. [*Exeunt.*

SCENE VII. *Another room in the castle.*

Enter KING *and* LAERTES.

King. Now must your conscience my acquit-
          tance seal,
And you must put me in your heart for friend,
●Sith you have heard, and with a knowing ear,
That he which hath your noble father slain
Pursued my life.
     Laer.   It well appears: but tell me
●Why you proceeded not against these feats,
So crimeful and so capital in nature,
As by your safety, wisdom, all things else,
You mainly were stirr'd up.
     King.   O, for two special reasons;
Which may to you, perhaps, seem much unsinew'd,
But yet to me they are strong. The queen his
          mother   11
Lives almost by his looks; and for myself—
My virtue or my plague, be it either which—
●She's so conjunctive to my life and soul,
That, as the star moves not but in his sphere,
I could not but by her. The other motive,
●Why to a public count I might not go,
●Is the great love the general gender bear him;
Who, dipping all his faults in their affection,
Would, like the spring that turneth wood to stone,
●Convert his gyves to graces; so that my arrows,
●Too slightly timber'd for so loud a wind,
Would have reverted to my bow again,
And not where I had aim'd them.
     Laer. And so have I a noble father lost;
●A sister driven into desperate terms,
Whose worth, if praises may go back again,
●Stood challenger on mount of all the age
For her perfections: but my revenge will come.
     King. Break not your sleeps for that: you
          must not think   30
That we are made of stuff so flat and dull
That we can let our beard be shook with danger
And think it pastime. You shortly shall hear
          more:

I loved your father, and we love ourself;
And that, I hope, will teach you to imagine—

Enter a Messenger.

How now! what news?
   Mess.   Letters, my lord, from Hamlet:
This to your majesty; this to the queen.
   King.   From Hamlet! who brought them?
   Mess.   Sailors, my lord, they say; I saw them
      not:
They were given me by Claudio; he received
      them   40
Of him that brought them.
   King.   Laertes, you shall hear them.
Leave us.   [*Exit Messenger.*
   [*Reads*] 'High and mighty, You shall know I
am set naked on your kingdom. To-morrow
shall I beg leave to see your kingly eyes: when
I shall, first asking your pardon thereunto, re-
count the occasion of my sudden and more
strange return.
                              'HAMLET.'
What should this mean? Are all the rest come
      back?   50
● Or is it some abuse, and no such thing?
   Laer.   Know you the hand?
   King.   'Tis Hamlet's character. 'Naked!'
And in a postscript here, he says 'alone.'
Can you advise me?
   Laer.   I'm lost in it, my lord. But let him
      come;
It warms the very sickness in my heart,
That I shall live and tell him to his teeth,
'Thus didest thou.'
   King.   If it be so, Laertes—
As how should it be so? how otherwise?—
Will you be ruled by me?
   Laer.   Ay, my lord;   60
So you will not o'errule me to a peace.
   King.   To thine own peace. If he be now
      return'd,
● As checking at his voyage, and that he means
No more to undertake it, I will work him
● To an exploit, now ripe in my device,
Under the which he shall not choose but fall:
And for his death no wind of blame shall breathe,
● But even his mother shall uncharge the practice
And call it accident.
   Laer.   My lord, I will be ruled;
The rather, if you could devise it so   70
That I might be the organ.
   King.   It falls right.
You have been talk'd of since your travel much,
And that in Hamlet's hearing, for a quality
Wherein, they say, you shine: your sum of parts
Did not together pluck such envy from him
As did that one, and that, in my regard,
● Of the unworthiest siege.
   Laer.   What part is that, my lord?
●   *King.*   A very riband in the cap of youth,
Yet needful too; for youth no less becomes
The light and careless livery that it wears   80
Than settled age his sables and his weeds,
Importing health and graveness. Two months
      since,
Here was a gentleman of Normandy:—
I've seen myself, and served against, the French,
And they can well on horseback: but this gallant
● Had witchcraft in't; he grew unto his seat;

51 *abuse.* Deception.

63 *checking at.* Objecting to.

65 *ripe in my device.* i.e. ready in my thoughts.

68 *uncharge the practice.* Not suspect a trick.

77 *siege.* Category.

78 *very riband.* Mere decoration.

86 *grew unto his seat.* i.e. seemed to be rooted to his saddle.

88 *incorpsed.* United in one body.

90–91 *in ... did.* In my imagination I could not have invented such things as he could actually do.

101 *scrimers.* Fencers.

106 *play.* Fight.

117 *at a like goodness still.* Always of such high quality.

118 *plurisy.* Excess.

124 *quick.* Centre.

128 *sanctuarize.* Preclude (as in a sanctuary).

138 *shuffling.* Muddled selecting.

139 *unbated.* Without a button on its point.

140 *Requite.* Pay him back for.

And to such wondrous doing brought his horse,
●As had he been incorpsed and demi-natured
With the brave beast: so far he topp'd my thought,
●That I, in forgery of shapes and tricks,   90
Come short of what he did.
   Laer.   A Norman was't?
   King. A Norman.
   Laer. Upon my life, Lamond.
   King.   The very same.
   Laer. I know him well: he is the brooch indeed
And gem of all the nation.
   King. He made confession of you,
And gave you such a masterly report
For art and exercise in your defence
And for your rapier most especial,
That he cried out, 'twould be a sight indeed,   100
●If one could match you: the scrimers of their nation,
He swore, had neither motion, guard, nor eye,
If you opposed them.   Sir, this report of his
Did Hamlet so envenom with his envy
That he could nothing do but wish and beg
●Your sudden coming o'er, to play with him.
Now, out of this,—
   Laer.   What out of this, my lord?
   King. Laertes, was your father dear to you?
Or are you like the painting of a sorrow,
A face without a heart?
   Laer.   Why ask you this?   110
   King. Not that I think you did not love your father;
But that I know love is begun by time;
And that I see, in passages of proof,
Time qualifies the spark and fire of it.
There lives within the very flame of love
A kind of wick or snuff that will abate it;
●And nothing is at a like goodness still;
●For goodness, growing to a plurisy,
Dies in his own too much: that we would do,
We should do when we would; for this 'would' changes   120
And hath abatements and delays as many
As there are tongues, are hands, are accidents;
And then this 'should' is like a spendthrift sigh,
●That hurts by easing.   But, to the quick o' the ulcer:—
Hamlet comes back: what would you undertake,
To show yourself your father's son in deed
More than in words?
   Laer.   To cut his throat i' the church.
● *King.* No place, indeed, should murder sanctuarize;
Revenge should have no bounds.   But, good Laertes,   129
Will you do this, keep close within your chamber.
Hamlet return'd shall know you are come home:
We'll put on those shall praise your excellence
And set a double varnish on the fame
The Frenchman gave you, bring you in fine together
And wager on your heads: he, being remiss,
Most generous and free from all contriving,
Will not peruse the foils; so that, with ease,
●Or with a little shuffling, you may choose
●A sword unbated, and in a pass of practice
●Requite him for your father.
   Laer.   I will do 't: 140

And, for that purpose, I'll anoint my sword.
I bought an unction of a mountebank,
●So mortal that, but dip a knife in it,
●Where it draws blood no cataplasm so rare,
●Collected from all simples that have virtue
Under the moon, can save the thing from death
That is but scratch'd withal : I'll touch my point
●With this contagion, that, if I gall him slightly,
It may be death.
    King.   Let's further think of this;   149
Weigh what convenience both of time and means
●May fit us to our shape : if this should fail,
And that our drift look through our bad performance,
'Twere better not assay'd : therefore this project
Should have a back or second, that might hold,
If this should blast in proof. Soft ! let me see :
We'll make a solemn wager on your cunnings :
I ha't :
When in your motion you are hot and dry—
As make your bouts more violent to that end—
And that he calls for drink, I'll have prepared
him   160
●A chalice for the nonce, whereon but sipping,
If he by chance escape your venom'd stuck,
Our purpose may hold there.

        Enter QUEEN.

                How now, sweet queen !
  Queen. One woe doth tread upon another's heel,
So fast they follow : your sister's drown'd, Laertes.
   Laer. Drown'd ! O, where?
   Queen. There is a willow grows aslant a brook,
That shows his hoar leaves in the glassy stream ;
There with fantastic garlands did she come   169
Of crow-flowers, nettles, daisies, and long purples
●That liberal shepherds give a grosser name,
But our cold maids do dead men's fingers call them :
There, on the pendent boughs her coronet weeds
Clambering to hang, an envious sliver broke ;
When down her weedy trophies and herself
Fell in the weeping brook. Her clothes spread wide ;
And, mermaid-like, awhile they bore her up :
Which time she chanted snatches of old tunes ;
As one incapable of her own distress,
Or like a creature native and indued   180
Unto that element : but long it could not be
Till that her garments, heavy with their drink,
Pull'd the poor wretch from her melodious lay
To muddy death.
   Laer.   Alas, then, she is drown'd?
   Queen. Drown'd, drown'd.
   Laer.   Too much of water hast thou, poor Ophelia,
And therefore I forbid my tears : but yet
It is our trick ; nature her custom holds,
Let shame say what it will : when these are gone,
The woman will be out. Adieu, my lord :   190
I have a speech of fire, that fain would blaze,
●But that this folly douts it.   [*Exit.*
   King.   Let's follow, Gertrude :
How much I had to do to calm his rage !
Now fear I this will give it start again ;
Therefore let's follow.   [*Exeunt.*

143 *mortal.* Deadly.

144 *cataplasm.* Dressing.

145 *simples.* Medicinal herbs. *virtue.* Power.

148 *contagion.* Poison. *gall.* Graze.

151 *shape.* Purpose.

161 *nonce.* Moment.

171 *liberal.* Frank.

Death of Ophelia. Detail from a painting by Sir John Millais (1829–1896)

192 *douts.* Douses.

ACT V.

Scene I. *A churchyard.*

Enter two Clowns, *with spades, &c.*

First Clo. Is she to be buried in Christian burial that wilfully seeks her own salvation?

Sec. Clo. I tell thee she is; and therefore make her grave straight: the crowner hath sat on her, and finds it Christian burial.

First Clo. How can that be, unless she drowned herself in her own defence?

Sec. Clo. Why, 'tis found so.

First Clo. It must be ' se offendendo;' it cannot be else. For here lies the point: if I drown myself wittingly, it argues an act: and an act hath three branches; it is, to act, to do, and to perform: argal, she drowned herself wittingly.

Sec. Clo. Nay, but hear you, goodman delver,—

First Clo. Give me leave. Here lies the water; good: here stands the man; good: if the man go to this water, and drown himself, it is, will he, nill he, he goes,—mark you that; but if the water come to him and drown him, he drowns not himself: argal, he that is not guilty of his own death shortens not his own life.

Sec. Clo. But is this law?

First Clo. Ay, marry, is't; crowner's quest law.

Sec. Clo. Will you ha' the truth on't? If this had not been a gentlewoman, she should have been buried out o' Christian burial.

First Clo. Why, there thou say'st: and the more pity that great folk should have countenance in this world to drown or hang themselves, more than their even Christian. Come, my spade. There is no ancient gentlemen but gardeners, ditchers, and grave-makers: they hold up Adam's profession.

Sec. Clo. Was he a gentleman?

First Clo. A' was the first that ever bore arms.

Sec. Clo. Why, he had none.   39

First Clo. What, art a heathen? How dost thou understand the Scripture? The Scripture says 'Adam digged:' could he dig without arms? I'll put another question to thee: if thou answerest me not to the purpose, confess thyself—

Sec. Clo. Go to.

First Clo. What is he that builds stronger than either the mason, the shipwright, or the carpenter?

Sec. Clo. The gallows-maker; for that frame outlives a thousand tenants.   50

First Clo. I like thy wit well, in good faith: the gallows does well; but how does it well? it does well to those that do ill: now thou dost ill to say the gallows is built stronger than the church: argal, the gallows may do well to thee. To 't again, come.

Sec. Clo. 'Who builds stronger than a mason, a shipwright, or a carpenter?'

First Clo. Ay, tell me that, and unyoke.

Sec. Clo. Marry, now I can tell.   60

First Clo. To 't.

Sec. Clo. Mass, I cannot tell.

The two clowns with spades. Engraving by Kenny Meadows from Barry Cornwall's *Works of Shakspere,* 1846

4 *crowner.* Coroner.

13 *argal.* 'Ergo' – therefore.

15 *delver.* Digger.

19 *will . . . he.* Like it or not.

24 *crowner's quest.* Coroner's inquest.

30–31 *countenance.* Permission.

35 *Adam's profession.* i.e. gardener.

37–38 *bore arms.* Pun on 'arms' and 'coat of arms'.

45 *Go to.* Get away with you!

Opposite: First Clown: '. . .she drowned herself wittingly'. Painting of Ophelia by Ferdinand Piloty (1828–1895)

Set design for the Churchyard by J. O'Connor, 1879

---

68 *Yaughan.* Johann, presumably a publican. *stoup* Cup.

84 *jowls.* Throws.

97-8 *mazzard.* Head.

100 *loggats.* Skittles.

107-108 *quiddities ... quillets.* Subtleties and verbal niceties.

110 *sconce.* Head.

111 *action of battery.* Breaking the law by assault.

113 *recognizances.* Legal form recognising indebtedness on properties.

114 *double vouchers.* Legal statements from two people as to rights of a tenant. *recoveries.* Deeds of recovery.

119 *pair of indentures.* Two parts of an agreement along a torn or cut line.

Enter HAMLET *and* HORATIO, *at a distance.*

First Clo. Cudgel thy brains no more about it, for your dull ass will not mend his pace with beating; and, when you are asked this question next, say 'a grave-maker:' the houses that he makes last till doomsday. Go, get thee to ●†Yaughan: fetch me a stoup of liquor.

[Exit Sec. Clown.
[He digs, and sings.

In youth, when I did love, did love,
    Methought it was very sweet,   70
To contract, O, the time, for, ah, my behove,
    O, methought, there was nothing meet.

Ham. Has this fellow no feeling of his business, that he sings at grave-making?

Hor. Custom hath made it in him a property of easiness.

Ham. 'Tis e'en so: the hand of little employment hath the daintier sense.

First Clo. *[Sings]*
But age, with his stealing steps,
    Hath claw'd me in his clutch,   80
And hath shipped me intil the land,
    As if I had never been such.

[Throws up a skull.

Ham. That skull had a tongue in it, and could ●sing once: how the knave jowls it to the ground, as if it were Cain's jaw-bone, that did the first murder! It might be the pate of a politician, which this ass now o'er-reaches; one that would circumvent God, might it not?

Hor. It might, my lord.   89

Ham. Or of a courtier; which could say 'Good morrow, sweet lord! How dost thou, good lord?' This might be my lord such-a-one, that praised my lord such-a-one's horse, when he meant to beg it; might it not?

Hor. Ay, my lord.

Ham. Why, e'en so: and now my Lady ●Worm's; chapless, and knocked about the mazzard with a sexton's spade: here's fine revolution, an we had the trick to see't. Did these bones ●cost no more the breeding, but to play at loggats with 'em? mine ache to think on't.   101

First Clo. *[Sings]*
A pick-axe, and a spade, a spade,
    For and a shrouding sheet:
O, a pit of clay for to be made
    For such a guest is meet.

[Throws up another skull.

Ham. There's another: why may not that ●be the skull of a lawyer? Where be his quiddities now, his quillets, his cases, his tenures, and his tricks? why does he suffer this rude knave now ●to knock him about the sconce with a dirty shovel, ●and will not tell him of his action of battery? Hum! This fellow might be in's time a great ●buyer of land, with his statutes, his recognizances, ●his fines, his double vouchers, his recoveries: is this the fine of his fines, and the recovery of his recoveries, to have his fine pate full of fine dirt? will his vouchers vouch him no more of his purchases, and double ones too, than the length and ●breadth of a pair of indentures? The very conveyances of his lands will hardly lie in this box; and must the inheritor himself have no more, ha?

Hor. Not a jot more, my lord.

Ham. Is not parchment made of sheep-skins?

Hor. Ay, my lord, and of calf-skins too.

Ham. They are sheep and calves which seek out assurance in that. I will speak to this fellow. Whose grave's this, sirrah?

First Clo. Mine, sir.

[*Sings*] O, a pit of clay for to be made
For such a guest is meet. 130

Ham. I think it be thine, indeed; for thou liest in't.

First Clo. You lie out on't, sir, and therefore it is not yours: for my part, I do not lie in't, and yet it is mine.

Ham. Thou dost lie in't, to be in't and say it is thine: 'tis for the dead, not for the quick; therefore thou liest.

First Clo. 'Tis a quick lie, sir; 'twill away again, from me to you. 140

Ham. What man dost thou dig it for?

First Clo. For no man, sir.

Ham. What woman, then?

First Clo. For none, neither.

Ham. Who is to be buried in't?

First Clo. One that was a woman, sir; but, rest her soul, she's dead.

Ham. How absolute the knave is! we must speak by the card, or equivocation will undo us. By the Lord, Horatio, these three years I have taken note of it; the age is grown so picked that the toe of the peasant comes so near the heel of the courtier, he galls his kibe. How long hast thou been a grave-maker?

First Clo. Of all the days i' the year, I came to't that day that our last king Hamlet overcame Fortinbras.

Ham. How long is that since?

First Clo. Cannot you tell that? every fool can tell that: it was the very day that young Hamlet was born; he that is mad, and sent into England.

Ham. Ay, marry, why was he sent into England?

First Clo. Why, because he was mad: he shall recover his wits there; or, if he do not, it's no great matter there.

Ham. Why?

First Clo. 'Twill not be seen in him there; there the men are as mad as he. 170

Ham. How came he mad?

First Clo. Very strangely, they say.

Ham. How strangely?

First Clo. Faith, e'en with losing his wits.

Ham. Upon what ground?

First Clo. Why, here in Denmark: I have been sexton here, man and boy, thirty years.

Ham. How long will a man lie i' the earth ere he rot? 179

First Clo. I' faith, if he be not rotten before he die—as we have many pocky corses now-a-days, that will scarce hold the laying in—he will last you some eight year or nine year: a tanner will last you nine year.

Ham. Why he more than another?

First Clo. Why, sir, his hide is so tanned with his trade, that he will keep out water a great while; and your water is a sore decayer of your whoreson dead body. Here's a skull now; this skull has lain in the earth three and twenty years. 191

Ham. Whose was it?

149 *by the card.* Precisely.

151 *picked.* Refined.

153 *galls his kibe.* Grazes the chilblain on his heel.

175 *what ground.* i.e. 'what reasons' and 'which country'.

181 *pocky.* Rotten.

182 *hold.* Keep whole for.

189 *whoreson.* Bastard.

Costume design for Hamlet by Motley for Byam Shaw's production, Stratford-upon-Avon, 1958

Hamlet: 'Alas, poor Yorick!' Stacy Keach as Hamlet, Joseph Papp's New York Shakespeare Festival production, 1972

---

212 *chap-fallen*. Dispirited; also 'jaw hanging open'.

214 *favour*. Appearance.

218 *Alexander*. i.e. Alexander the Great.

242 *maimed rites*. Curtailed ceremony.

244 *Fordo*. Take. *estate*. High rank.

245 *Couch*. Hide.

250 *warranty*. Authority.

251 *great ... order*. i.e. the king had over-ridden the custom.

First Clo.   A whoreson mad fellow's it was: whose do you think it was?
Ham.   Nay, I know not.
First Clo.   A pestilence on him for a mad rogue! a' poured a flagon of Rhenish on my head once. This same skull, sir, was Yorick's skull, the king's jester.
Ham.   This?   200
First Clo.   E'en that.
Ham.   Let me see.   [*Takes the skull.*] Alas, poor Yorick! I knew him, Horatio: a fellow of infinite jest, of most excellent fancy: he hath borne me on his back a thousand times; and now, how abhorred in my imagination it is! my gorge rises at it. Here hung those lips that I have kissed I know not how oft. Where be your gibes now? your gambols? your songs? your flashes of merriment, that were wont to set the table on a roar? Not one now, to mock your own grinning? quite chap-fallen? Now get you to my lady's chamber, and tell her, let her paint an inch thick, to this favour she must come; make her laugh at that. Prithee, Horatio, tell me one thing.
Hor.   What's that, my lord?
Ham.   Dost thou think Alexander looked o' this fashion i' the earth?
Hor.   E'en so.   220
Ham.   And smelt so? pah!
                              [*Puts down the skull.*
Hor.   E'en so, my lord.
Ham.   To what base uses we may return, Horatio! Why may not imagination trace the noble dust of Alexander, till he find it stopping a bung-hole?
Hor.   'Twere to consider too curiously, to consider so.
Ham.   No, faith, not a jot; but to follow him thither with modesty enough, and likelihood to lead it: as thus: Alexander died, Alexander was buried, Alexander returneth into dust; the dust is earth; of earth we make loam; and why of that loam, whereto he was converted, might they not stop a beer-barrel?
Imperious Cæsar, dead and turn'd to clay,
Might stop a hole to keep the wind away:
O, that that earth, which kept the world in awe,
Should patch a wall to expel the winter's flaw!
But soft! but soft! aside: here comes the king,

Enter Priests, *&c. in procession; the Corpse of* OPHELIA, LAERTES *and* Mourners *following;* KING, QUEEN, *their trains, &c.*

The queen, the courtiers: who is this they follow?
And with such maimed rites? This doth betoken
The corse they follow did with desperate hand
Fordo it own life: 'twas of some estate.
Couch we awhile, and mark.
                              [*Retiring with Horatio.*
Laer.   What ceremony else?
Ham.   That is Laertes,
A very noble youth: mark.
Laer.   What ceremony else?
First Priest.   Her obsequies have been as
                              far enlarged   249
As we have warranty: her death was doubtful;
And, but that great command o'ersways the order,
She should in ground unsanctified have lodged
Till the last trumpet; for charitable prayers,

Shards, flints and pebbles should be thrown on her:
● Yet here she is allow'd her virgin crants,
Her maiden strewments and the bringing home
Of bell and burial.
    Laer. Must there no more be done?
    First Priest.   No more be done:
We should profane the service of the dead
To sing a requiem and such rest to her   260
As to peace-parted souls.
    Laer.   Lay her i' the earth:
And from her fair and unpolluted flesh
May violets spring! I tell thee, churlish priest,
A ministering angel shall my sister be,
When thou liest howling.
    Ham.   What, the fair Ophelia!
    Queen. Sweets to the sweet: farewell!
                           [Scattering flowers.
I hoped thou shouldst have been my Hamlet's wife;
I thought thy bride-bed to have deck'd, sweet maid,
And not have strew'd thy grave.
    Laer.   O, treble woe
Fall ten times treble on that cursed head,   270
● Whose wicked deed thy most ingenious sense
Deprived thee of! Hold off the earth awhile,
Till I have caught her once more in mine arms:
                           [Leaps into the grave.
Now pile your dust upon the quick and dead,
Till of this flat a mountain you have made,
● To o'ertop old Pelion, or the skyish head
Of blue Olympus.
    Ham. [*Advancing*] What is he whose grief
Bears such an emphasis? whose phrase of sorrow
Conjures the wandering stars, and makes them stand
● Like wonder-wounded hearers? This is I,   280
Hamlet the Dane.   *[Leaps into the grave.*
    Laer.   The devil take thy soul!
                        [Grappling with him.
    Ham. Thou pray'st not well.
I prithee, take thy fingers from my throat;
For, though I am not splenitive and rash,
Yet have I something in me dangerous,
Which let thy wiseness fear: hold off thy hand.
    King. Pluck them asunder.
    Queen.   Hamlet, Hamlet!
    All. Gentlemen,—
    Hor.   Good my lord, be quiet.
        *[The Attendants part them, and they
                come out of the grave.*
    Ham. Why, I will fight with him upon this theme
Until my eyelids will no longer wag.   290
    Queen. O my son, what theme?
    Ham. I loved Ophelia: forty thousand brothers
Could not, with all their quantity of love,
Make up my sum. What wilt thou do for her?
    King. O, he is mad, Laertes.
●   *Queen.* For love of God, forbear him.
    Ham. 'Swounds, show me what thou'lt do:
Woo't weep? woo't fight? woo't fast? woo't tear thyself?
● Woo't drink up eisel? eat a crocodile?
I'll do't. Dost thou come here to whine?   300
To outface me with leaping in her grave?
Be buried quick with her, and so will I:

Hamlet: 'What, the fair Ophelia!' Painting of Hamlet and Horatio watching Ophelia's funeral by Victor Müller (1830–1871)

271 *ingenious sense.* Lively intelligence.

276–277 *Pelion . . . Olympus.* The Titans tried to pile up mountains in the Pelion range to get up to the heavens.

280 *wounded.* Struck.

296 *forbear him.* Let him be.

299 *eisel.* Vinegar.

305 *burning zone.* i.e. the sun.

306 *Ossa.* Legendary high mountain.

310 *couplets.* Twin chicks. *disclosed.* Hatched.

318 *present push.* Immediate trial.

6 *mutines in the bilboes.* Mutineers in their shackles.

15 *Finger'd.* Stole. *packet.* i.e. documents.

20 *Larded.* Garnished.

22 *bugs.* Bugbears.

23 *supervise.* First reading. *no leisure bated.* No time spared.

33 *statists.* Statesmen.

And, if thou prate of mountains, let them throw
Millions of acres on us, till our ground,
● Singeing his pate against the burning zone,
● Make Ossa like a wart! Nay, an thou'lt mouth,
I'll rant as well as thou.
 Queen.   This is mere madness:
And thus awhile the fit will work on him;
Anon, as patient as the female dove,
● When that her golden couplets are disclosed, 310
His silence will sit drooping.
 Ham.   Hear you, sir;
What is the reason that you use me thus?
I loved you ever: but it is no matter;
Let Hercules himself do what he may,
The cat will mew and dog will have his day. [*Exit.*
  King. I pray you, good Horatio, wait upon
    him.   [*Exit Horatio.*
[*To Laertes*] Strengthen your patience in our
   last night's speech;
● We'll put the matter to the present push.
Good Gertrude, set some watch over your son.
This grave shall have a living monument: 320
An hour of quiet shortly shall we see;
Till then, in patience our proceeding be. [*Exeunt.*

SCENE II.   *A hall in the castle.*

Enter HAMLET *and* HORATIO.

 Ham. So much for this, sir: now shall you
   see the other;
You do remember all the circumstance?
 Hor.   Remember it, my lord!
 Ham.   Sir, in my heart there was a kind of
   fighting,
That would not let me sleep: methought I lay
● Worse than the mutines in the bilboes. Rashly,
And praised be rashness for it, let us know,
Our indiscretion sometimes serves us well,
When our deep plots do pall: and that should
   teach us
There's a divinity that shapes our ends,   10
Rough-hew them how we will,—
 Hor.   That is most certain.
 Ham. Up from my cabin,
My sea-gown scarf'd about me, in the dark
Groped I to find out them; had my desire,
● Finger'd their packet, and in fine withdrew
To mine own room again; making so bold,
My fears forgetting manners, to unseal
Their grand commission; where I found, Ho-
   ratio,—
O royal knavery!—an exact command,
● Larded with many several sorts of reasons   20
Importing Denmark's health and England's too,
● With, ho! such bugs and goblins in my life,
● That, on the supervise, no leisure bated,
No, not to stay the grinding of the axe,
My head should be struck off.
 Hor.   Is't possible?
 Ham. Here's the commission: read it at more
   leisure.
But wilt thou hear me how I did proceed?
 Hor. I beseech you.
 Ham. Being thus be-netted round with vil-
   lanies,—
Ere I could make a prologue to my brains,   30
They had begun the play—I sat me down,
Devised a new commission, wrote it fair:
● I once did hold it, as our statists do,

A baseness to write fair and labour'd much
How to forget that learning, but, sir, now
● It did me yeoman's service: wilt thou know
The effect of what I wrote?
    Hor.   Ay, good my lord.
    Ham. An earnest conjuration from the king,
As England was his faithful tributary,
As love between them like the palm might flou-
    rish,   40
As peace should still her wheaten garland wear
● And stand a comma 'tween their amities,
And many such-like 'As'es of great charge,
That, on the view and knowing of these contents,
Without debatement further, more or less,
He should the bearers put to sudden death,
● Not shriving-time allow'd.
    Hor.   How was this seal'd?
    Ham. Why, even in that was heaven ordinant.
I had my father's signet in my purse,
Which was the model of that Danish seal;   50
Folded the writ up in form of the other,
● Subscribed it, gave't the impression, placed it
    safely,
The changeling never known. Now, the next day
Was our sea-fight; and what to this was sequent
Thou know'st already.
    Hor. So Guildenstern and Rosencrantz go to't.
    Ham. Why, man, they did make love to this
    employment;
They are not near my conscience; their defeat
● Does by their own insinuation grow:
'Tis dangerous when the baser nature comes 60
Between the pass and fell incensed points
Of mighty opposites.
    Hor.   Why, what a king is this!
    Ham. Does it not, thinks't thee, stand me
    now upon—
He that hath kill'd my king and whored my
    mother,
Popp'd in between the election and my hopes,
Thrown out his angle for my proper life,
● And with such cozenage—is't not perfect con-
    science,
● To quit him with this arm? and is't not to be
    damn'd,
To let this canker of our nature come
In further evil?   70
    Hor. It must be shortly known to him from
    England
What is the issue of the business there.
    Ham. It will be short: the interim is mine;
And a man's life's no more than to say 'One.'
But I am very sorry, good Horatio,
That to Laertes I forgot myself;
For, by the image of my cause, I see
The portraiture of his: I'll court his favours:
But, sure, the bravery of his grief did put me
Into a towering passion.
    Hor.   Peace! who comes here? 80

         Enter OSRIC.

    Osr. Your lordship is right welcome back to
Denmark.
    Ham. I humbly thank you, sir. Dost know
● this water-fly?
    Hor. No, my good lord.
    Ham. Thy state is the more gracious; for 'tis
a vice to know him. He hath much land, and
● fertile: let a beast be lord of beasts, and his crib

36 *yeoman's.* i.e. faithful.

42 *comma.* In rhetoric, a short connecting group of words.

47 *shriving-time.* Confession.

52 *gave't the impression.* Sealed it.

59 *insinuation.* Involvement.

67 *cozenage.* Trickery.

68 *quit.* Take revenge on.

84 *water-fly.* i.e. busy insect.

88 *crib.* Trough.

Osric before Hamlet and Horatio. Engraving by Kenny Meadows from Barry Cornwall's *Works of Shakspere*, 1846

261

89 *mess.* Table. *chough.* A chattering crow.

112 *differences.* Characteristics. *soft.* Gentlemanly.

113 *showing.* Appearance.

114 *card or calendar.* Guide or directory.

115 *continent.* Complete version.

117 *definement.* Definition. *perdition.* Loss.

120 *yaw.* Fall behind.

122 *infusion.* Innate characteristics.

123 *dearth.* Scarcity. *diction.* Report.

124 *his semblable.* His like.

128 *concernancy.* Meaning.

149 *meed.* Merit.

Duelling with rapiers. Engraving from Girard Thibaust's *Academie de l'Epee*, 1628

155-156 *Barbary horses.* Fine horses from North Africa. *imponed.* Wagered.

shall stand at the king's mess: 'tis a chough; but, as I say, spacious in the possession of dirt.   90

Osr.   Sweet lord, if your lordship were at leisure, I should impart a thing to you from his majesty.

Ham.   I will receive it, sir, with all diligence of spirit.   Put your bonnet to his right use; 'tis for the head.

Osr.   I thank your lordship, it is very hot.

Ham.   No, believe me, 'tis very cold; the wind is northerly.   99

Osr.   It is indifferent cold, my lord, indeed.

Ham.   But yet methinks it is very sultry and hot for my complexion.

Osr.   Exceedingly, my lord; it is very sultry,—as 'twere,—I cannot tell how.   But, my lord, his majesty bade me signify to you that he has laid a great wager on your head: sir, this is the matter,—

Ham.   I beseech you, remember—

   [*Hamlet moves him to put on his hat.*

Osr.   Nay, good my lord; for mine ease, in good faith.   Sir, here is newly come to court Laertes; believe me, an absolute gentleman, full of most excellent differences, of very soft society and great showing: indeed, to speak feelingly of him, he is the card or calendar of gentry, for you shall find in him the continent of what part a gentleman would see.

Ham.   Sir, his definement suffers no perdition in you; though, I know, to divide him inventorially would dizzy the arithmetic of memory, †and yet but yaw neither, in respect of his quick sail. But, in the verity of extolment, I take him to be a soul of great article; and his infusion of such dearth and rareness, as, to make true diction of him, his semblable is his mirror; and who else would trace him, his umbrage, nothing more.

Osr.   Your lordship speaks most infallibly of him.

Ham.   The concernancy, sir? why do we wrap the gentleman in our more rawer breath?

Osr.   Sir?   130

Hor.   Is't not possible to understand in another tongue?   You will do't, sir, really.

Ham.   What imports the nomination of this gentleman?

Osr.   Of Laertes?

Hor.   His purse is empty already; all's golden words are spent.

Ham.   Of him, sir.

Osr.   I know you are not ignorant—

Ham.   I would you did, sir; yet, in faith, if you did, it would not much approve me.   Well, sir?

Osr.   You are not ignorant of what excellence Laertes is—

Ham.   I dare not confess that, lest I should compare with him in excellence; but, to know a man well, were to know himself.

Osr.   I mean, sir, for his weapon; but in the imputation laid on him by them, in his meed he's unfellowed.   150

Ham.   What's his weapon?

Osr.   Rapier and dagger.

Ham.   That's two of his weapons: but, well.

Osr.   The king, sir, hath wagered with him six Barbary horses: against the which he has imponed, as I take it, six French rapiers and poniards, with their assigns, as girdle, hangers, and so: three of the carriages, in faith, are very dear to fancy, very responsive to the hilts, most delicate carriages, and of very liberal conceit.

Ham. What call you the carriages?

Hor. I knew you must be edified by the margent ere you had done.

Osr. The carriages, sir, are the hangers.

Ham. The phrase would be more german to the matter, if we could carry cannon by our sides: I would it might be hangers till then. But, on: six Barbary horses against six French swords, their assigns, and three liberal-conceited carriages; that's the French bet against the Danish. Why is this 'imponed,' as you call it?   171

Osr. The king, sir, hath laid, that in a dozen passes between yourself and him, he shall not exceed you three hits: he hath laid on twelve for nine; and it would come to immediate trial, if your lordship would vouchsafe the answer.

Ham. How if I answer 'no'?

Osr. I mean, my lord, the opposition of your person in trial.   179

Ham. Sir, I will walk here in the hall: if it please his majesty, 'tis the breathing time of day with me; let the foils be brought, the gentleman willing, and the king hold his purpose, I will win for him an I can; if not, I will gain nothing but my shame and the odd hits.

Osr. Shall I re-deliver you e'en so?

Ham. To this effect, sir; after what flourish your nature will.

Osr. I commend my duty to your lordship.

Ham. Yours, yours. [*Exit Osric.*] He does well to commend it himself; there are no tongues else for's turn.

Hor. This lapwing runs away with the shell on his head.

Ham. He did comply with his dug, before he sucked it. Thus has he—and many more of the same breed that I know the drossy age dotes on—only got the tune of the time and outward habit of encounter; a kind of yesty collection, which carries them through and through the most †fond and winnowed opinions; and do but blow them to their trial, the bubbles are out.

Enter a Lord.

Lord. My lord, his majesty commended him to you by young Osric, who brings back to him, that you attend him in the hall: he sends to know if your pleasure hold to play with Laertes, or that you will take longer time.

Ham. I am constant to my purposes; they follow the king's pleasure: if his fitness speaks, mine is ready; now or whensoever, provided I be so able as now.   211

Lord. The king and queen and all are coming down.

Ham. In happy time.

Lord. The queen desires you to use some gentle entertainment to Laertes before you fall to play.

Ham. She well instructs me.   [*Exit Lord.*

Hor. You will lose this wager, my lord.

Ham. I do not think so; since he went into France, I have been in continual practice; I shall win at the odds. But thou wouldst not think how ill all's here about my heart: but it is no matter.

157 *poniards.* Daggers. *assigns.* Accessories.

159 *dear to fancy.* Fancy. *responsive.* Matching.

160 *liberal conceit.* Tasteful design.

162–163 *margent.* Margin (i.e. explanatory notes).

181 *breathing.* Leisure.

195 *comply.* Act courteously. *his dug.* His mother's teat.

199 *yesty.* Frothy.

202 *to their trial.* To test them. *out.* Burst.

209 *his fitness speaks.* He says he is ready.

Costume design for Hamlet by Motley for Byam Shaw's production, Stratford-upon-Avon, 1958

226 *gain-giving.* Misgiving.

230 *augury.* Reading the future from the behaviour of birds.

242 *exception.* Outstanding qualities.

255 *in nature.* i.e. within myself.

258 *aloof.* Apart.

261 *ungored.* Uninjured.

268 *Stick fiery off.* Stand out.

276 *a length.* An equal length.

Herbert Beerbohm Tree as Hamlet, Haymarket Theatre, London, 1892

Hor.   Nay, good my lord,—
Ham.   It is but foolery; but it is such a kind of
●gain-giving, as would perhaps trouble a woman.
   Hor.   If your mind dislike any thing, obey it:
I will forestal their repair hither, and say you are
not fit.   229
● *Ham.*   Not a whit, we defy augury: there's a
special providence in the fall of a sparrow. If it
be now, 'tis not to come; if it be not to come, it
will be now; if it be not now, yet it will come:
the readiness is all: since no man has aught of
what he leaves, what is 't to leave betimes?

Enter KING, QUEEN, LAERTES, Lords, OSRIC,
   and Attendants *with foils, &c.*

   King.   Come, Hamlet, come, and take this
      hand from me.
[*The King puts Laertes' hand into Hamlet's.*
   Ham.   Give me your pardon, sir: I've done
      you wrong;
But pardon 't, as you are a gentleman.
This presence knows,
And you must needs have heard, how I am pun-
   ish'd   240
With sore distraction.   What I have done,
●That might your nature, honour and exception
Roughly awake, I here proclaim was madness.
Was 't Hamlet wrong'd Laertes? Never Hamlet:
If Hamlet from himself be ta'en away,
And when he's not himself does wrong Laertes,
Then Hamlet does it not, Hamlet denies it.
Who does it, then? His madness: if 't be so,
Hamlet is of the faction that is wrong'd;
His madness is poor Hamlet's enemy.   250
Sir, in this audience,
Let my disclaiming from a purposed evil
Free me so far in your most generous thoughts,
That I have shot mine arrow o'er the house,
●And hurt my brother.
   Laer.   I am satisfied in nature,
Whose motive, in this case, should stir me most
To my revenge: but in my terms of honour
●I stand aloof; and will no reconcilement,
Till by some elder masters, of known honour,
I have a voice and precedent of peace,   260
●To keep my name ungored.   But till that time,
I do receive your offer'd love like love,
And will not wrong it.
   Ham.   I embrace it freely;
And will this brother's wager frankly play.
Give us the foils.   Come on.
   Laer.   Come, one for me.
   Ham.   I'll be your foil, Laertes: in mine ig-
      norance
Your skill shall, like a star i' the darkest night,
●Stick fiery off indeed.
   Laer.   You mock me, sir.
   Ham.   No, by this hand.
   King.   Give them the foils, young Osric. Cousin
      Hamlet,   270
You know the wager?
   Ham.   Very well, my lord;
Your grace hath laid the odds o' the weaker side.
   King.   I do not fear it; I have seen you both:
But since he is better'd, we have therefore odds.
   Laer.   This is too heavy, let me see another.
● *Ham.*   This likes me well.   These foils have
      all a length?   [*They prepare to play.*
   Osr.   Ay, my good lord.

King. Set me the stoups of wine upon that table.
If Hamlet give the first or second hit,
Or quit in answer of the third exchange, 280
Let all the battlements their ordnance fire;
The king shall drink to Hamlet's better breath;
●And in the cup an union shall he throw,
Richer than that which four successive kings
In Denmark's crown have worn. Give me the cups;
●And let the kettle to the trumpet speak,
The trumpet to the cannoneer without,
The cannons to the heavens, the heavens to earth,
'Now the king drinks to Hamlet.' Come, begin:
And you, the judges, bear a wary eye. 290
    Ham. Come on, sir.
    Laer.   Come, my lord. [*They play.*
    Ham.   One.
    Laer.   No.
    Ham.   Judgement.
    Osr. A hit, a very palpable hit.
    Laer.   Well; again.
    King. Stay; give me drink. Hamlet, this pearl is thine;
Here's to thy health.
    [*Trumpets sound, and cannon shot off within.*
                Give him the cup.
    Ham. I'll play this bout first; set it by awhile.
Come. [*They play.*] Another hit; what say you?
    Laer A touch, a touch, I do confess.
    King. Our son shall win.
    Queen.   He's fat, and scant of breath.
Here, Hamlet, take my napkin, rub thy brows:
The queen carouses to thy fortune, Hamlet. 300
    Ham. Good madam!
    King.   Gertrude, do not drink.
    Queen. I will, my lord; I pray you, pardon me.
    King. [*Aside*] It is the poison'd cup: it is too late.
    Ham. I dare not drink yet, madam; by and by.
    Queen. Come, let me wipe thy face.
    Laer. My lord, I'll hit him now.
    King.   I do not think 't.
    Laer. [*Aside*] And yet 'tis almost 'gainst my conscience.
    Ham. Come, for the third, Laertes: you but dally;
I pray you, pass with your best violence;
●I am afeard you make a wanton of me. 310
    Laer. Say you so? come on. [*They play.*
    Osr. Nothing, neither way.
    Laer. Have at you now!
    [*Laertes wounds Hamlet; then, in scuffling, they change rapiers, and Hamlet wounds Laertes.*
    King.   Part them; they are incensed.
    Ham. Nay, come, again. [*The Queen falls.*
    Osr.   Look to the queen there, ho!
    Hor. They bleed on both sides. How is it, my lord?
    Osr. How is't, Laertes?
● *Laer.* Why, as a woodcock to mine own springe, Osric;
I am justly kill'd with mine own treachery.
    Ham. How does the queen?
● *King.*   She swounds to see them bleed.
    Queen. No, no, the drink, the drink,—O my dear Hamlet,— 320
The drink, the drink! I am poison'd. [*Dies.*

283 *union.* Pearl.

286 *kettle.* Drum.

Hamlet: 'Another hit; what say you?' Hamlet (Laurence Olivier) and Laertes (Owen Jones), Old Vic, 1936

310 *wanton.* Weakling.

317 *woodcock.* Bird used as a decoy to trap other birds. *springe.* Trap.

319 *swounds.* Faints.

328 *practice.* Trick.

339 *temper'd.* Prepared.

364 *o'er-crows.* Overcomes.

366 *lights.* Alights.

369 *have solicited.* Led me to this.

Death of Hamlet. Lithograph by Eugene Delacroix,
1843

Ham. O villany! Ho! let the door be lock'd:
Treachery! Seek it out.
    Laer. It is here, Hamlet: Hamlet, thou art
    slain;
No medicine in the world can do thee good;
In thee there is not half an hour of life;
The treacherous instrument is in thy hand,
● Unbated and envenom'd: the foul practice
Hath turn'd itself on me; lo, here I lie,   329
Never to rise again: thy mother's poison'd:
I can no more: the king, the king's to blame.
    Ham. The point envenom'd too!
Then, venom, to thy work.   [*Stabs the King.*
    All. Treason! treason!
    King. O, yet defend me, friends; I am but
    hurt.
    Ham. Here, thou incestuous, murderous,
    damned Dane,
Drink off this potion. Is thy union here?
Follow my mother.   [*King dies.*
    Laer.   He is justly served;
● It is a poison temper'd by himself.   339
Exchange forgiveness with me, noble Hamlet:
Mine and my father's death come not upon thee,
Nor thine on me!   [*Dies.*
    Ham. Heaven make thee free of it! I follow
    thee.
I am dead, Horatio. Wretched queen, adieu!
You that look pale and tremble at this chance,
That are but mutes or audience to this act,
Had I but time—as this fell sergeant, death,
Is strict in his arrest—O, I could tell you—
But let it be. Horatio, I am dead;
Thou livest; report me and my cause aright
To the unsatisfied.
    Hor.   Never believe it: 351
I am more an antique Roman than a Dane:
Here's yet some liquor left.
    Ham.   As thou'rt a man,
Give me the cup: let go; by heaven, I'll have't.
O good Horatio, what a wounded name,
Things standing thus unknown, shall live behind
    me!
If thou didst ever hold me in thy heart,
Absent thee from felicity awhile,
And in this harsh world draw thy breath in pain,
To tell my story.
    [*March afar off, and shot within.*
    What warlike noise is this?   360
    Osr. Young Fortinbras, with conquest come
    from Poland,
To the ambassadors of England gives
This warlike volley.
    Ham.   O, I die, Horatio;
● The potent poison quite o'er-crows my spirit:
I cannot live to hear the news from England;
● But I do prophesy the election lights
On Fortinbras: he has my dying voice;
So tell him, with the occurrents, more and less,
● Which have solicited. The rest is silence. [*Dies.*
    Hor. Now cracks a noble heart. Good night,
    sweet prince;   370
And flights of angels sing thee to thy rest!
Why does the drum come hither?
    [*March within.*

Enter FORTINBRAS, *the* English Ambassadors,
and others.

    Fort. Where is this sight?

Hor.   What is it ye would see?
If aught of woe or wonder, cease your search.
● *Fort.* This quarry cries on havoc.   O proud
     death,
What feast is toward in thine eternal cell,
That thou so many princes at a shot
So bloodily hast struck?
     First Amb.   The sight is dismal;
And our affairs from England come too late:
The ears are senseless that should give us hearing,
To tell him his commandment is fulfill'd,   381
That Rosencrantz and Guildenstern are dead:
Where should we have our thanks?
     Hor.   Not from his mouth,
Had it the ability of life to thank you:
He never gave commandment for their death.
● But since, so jump upon this bloody question,
You from the Polack wars, and you from Eng-
     land,
Are here arrived, give order that these bodies
High on a stage be placed to the view;   389
And let me speak to the yet unknowing world
How these things came about: so shall you hear
Of carnal, bloody, and unnatural acts,
Of accidental judgements, casual slaughters,
Of deaths put on by cunning and forced cause,
And, in this upshot, purposes mistook
Fall'n on the inventors' heads: all this can I
Truly deliver.
     Fort.   Let us haste to hear it,
And call the noblest to the audience.
For me, with sorrow I embrace my fortune:
● I have some rights of memory in this kingdom,
Which now to claim my vantage doth invite me.
     Hor. Of that I shall have also cause to speak,
And from his mouth whose voice will draw on
     more:
But let this same be presently perform'd,
Even while men's minds are wild; lest more mis-
     chance,
On plots and errors, happen.
     Fort.   Let four captains
Bear Hamlet, like a soldier, to the stage;
For he was likely, had he been put on,
To have proved most royally: and, for his pas-
     sage,
The soldiers' music and the rites of war   410
Speak loudly for him.
Take up the bodies: such a sight as this
Becomes the field, but here shows much amiss.
Go, bid the soldiers shoot.
          [*A dead march. Exeunt, bearing off the
               dead bodies; after which a peal of ord-
               nance is shot off.*

375 *quarry.* Pile of corpses.

386 *jump.* Precisely.

400 *rights of memory.* Rights of long-standing.

Fortinbras: 'For he was likely, had he been put on, To have proved most royally...' Final scene, Lyceum Theatre, London, 1897

Othello

1604

OTHELLO offers a marked contrast to *Hamlet*; where that has a large cast and much variety of action, this has few characters, with most of the action concentrated on three alone – Othello, Desdemona and Iago. Hardly anything distracts from the main theme, which advances at headlong speed with tremendous, purely tragic impact. It is like an opera; in that, and in its speed, analogous to *Romeo and Juliet* – both, by the way, made subjects of opera.

Shakespeare took his theme straight from a 'mediocre' story of Cinthio, as Bentley describes it. And see what an unforgettable play Shakespeare made of it! It shows how unimportant 'sources' and all the fuss about them are.

The Character of Iago. The tragedy of the heroic but simple Othello and the charming but innocent Desdemona has haunted the world's imagination ever since. But Iago is the most complex and interesting psychological study in the play; it is not surprising that this part has chiefly attracted the ambition of actors – it is such a challenge. In a way, Iago is a psychotic, as Hamlet was; it forms another aspect of the universality of Shakespeare's genius that he should have had such an intuitive understanding of the operations of psychosis, and foreshadowed many of the findings of modern psycho-analysis.

It is often said that Iago, whose villainy causes the whole tragedy, is an incarnation of pure evil, without motivation. This is not true: he has several motives for what he does. He is suspicious by nature, and he thinks that the Moor has colted his wife, Emilia. At one point he suspects Cassio also with his wife. Iago is a Venetian; but Othello has promoted the Florentine Cassio to be his lieutenant over his head, and relegated him, Iago, to be Cassio's ancient, or ensign. So Iago has his reasons for resentment, and he hates the Moor.

But his hatred is more generalised and more interesting psychologically. It has usually been found inexplicable; but though rare, it is understandable. He is one of those beings, not unknown, who hate the sight of other people's happiness. He is not happy himself, he is not happily married: he gives a hint that he suffers the lash of Emilia's tongue. He is not interested in sex, and is envious of the pleasure it gives others. Desdemona's bridal night with her magnificent, and very male, black lover is described thus by Iago to her father:

> Even now, now, very now, an old black ram
> Is tupping your white ewe.

He regularly describes Cassio's light o'love as a strumpet, and

> it is a creature
> That dotes on Cassio, as 'tis the strumpet's plague
> To beguile many, and be beguiled by one.

Cassio rubs salt in his wound – for Iago's is a wounded nature – when talking of hoping 'to be saved', by saying, 'the lieutenant is to be saved before the ancient.'

There is no love in Iago; he hates humans for being the fools they are; 'thus credulous fools are caught', he says – and they all are caught by their various forms of human foolery. Othello is caught by his jealousy and gullibility; Desdemona by her precious innocence; Roderigo is just an ass, and Iago takes his money and jewels off him; Cassio is caught by his weakness for drink. Iago was not a fool about drink, as so many are.

He has complete contempt for humans – a Swiftian character. And what is so interesting psychologically is that he carries it so far as to sail right into the wind. He actually warns Othello against jealousy:

> O, beware, my lord, of jealousy.
> It is the green-eyed monster, which doth mock
> The meat it feeds on.

Why? Because he knows that to tell people the truth is an effective way of putting them off the scent. Hitler knew this, and practised it to devastating effect: 'the German people have no idea how they have to be gulled in order to be led', was the epigraph of *Mein Kampf*, which told everybody exactly what he meant to do – and they wouldn't believe it.

'Men should be what they seem', Iago assures Othello brazenly. He even speaks a word to him in favour of Cassio, 'an honest man' – sailing right into the wind again, which makes Othello the readier to believe Iago's insinuations about Cassio and Desdemona. Iago's very cynicism is beguiling. He eggs on Roderigo with, 'Virtue? A fig! 'Tis in ourselves that we are thus and thus!' And he has a very Swiftian image in his assurance: 'Ere I would say I would drown myself for the love of a guinea hen, I would change my humanity with a baboon.' His argument to Roderigo again and again is to look after his money, 'Put money in thy purse' – just when he is taking it off him.

And so with his consoling Cassio, when he has disgraced himself with the General:

> Cassio: I have lost the immortal part of myself . . . my reputation, Iago, my
>   reputation.
> Iago: As I am an honest man, I thought you had received some bodily wound.
>   There is more sense in that than in reputation. Reputation is an idle and
>   most false imposition: oft got without merit and lost without deserving.

There is always something to be said for what Iago says; nothing for what he does. On the pros and cons of morality he is an able and plausible reasoner – notably in the remarkable scene with Othello in which he sows suspicions against Desdemona. One

*William Haviland,
19th century
English actor, as
Iago*

might suppose that Iago was more rational than other men, as certainly he considered himself, besides being much less of a fool. But such is Shakespeare's intuitive, as well as conscious, knowledge of human nature that Iago, too, is as much in the clutch of his complex as Othello is in his. Othello is driven mad by suspicion and jealousy; perhaps Iago is already mad – he is certainly not sane – with envy, hatred and contempt.

He and Othello stand out as the two protagonists in this simple, haunting tragedy, Desdemona their sacrificial victim.

Race. Again it is so like Shakespeare's universality to have prefigured a prime issue of today. As in *The Merchant of Venice* the crux of the action is that Shylock is a Jew, so now the crux is that Othello is a black. At the crucial moment of his persuasion by Iago of his wife's unfaithfulness, he says, with great pathos, for the trouble it has brought: 'for I am black . . . declined into the vale of years'. This in itself is a source of insecurity, already inclined to suspicion, and makes him think that it was a mistake to have thought that he could hold Desdemona's love.

Her love, too, had been rash, like Juliet's. In 16th century terms it was a grievous fault to have married without her father's knowledge or approval – so that she too had some responsibility for the tragedy that was provoked. Iago further inflames her father with, 'you'll have your daughter covered with a Barbary horse; you'll have your nephews [Elizabethan for grandsons] neigh to you.'

The Age. Her father indeed thinks that the only explanation for such infatuation –

> To fall in love with what she feared to look on! –

was witchcraft, love-philtres, charms:

> She is abused, stolen from me, and corrupted
> By spells and medicines bought of mountebanks.

This was very cogent to Elizabethans, as we know from Simon Forman's practice for these very purposes. In a year or two he would be supplying love-philtres and charms to Frances Howard, Countess of Essex, to compel the love of James I's boy-friend, Robert Carr. Forman was already well known; it is by no means improbable that Shakespeare thought him a 'mountebank'. Even the handkerchief that did such damage to Desdemona would be recognised for its magic potency by Forman:

> There's magic in the web of it –

it had been given to Othello's mother by an Egyptian, a charmer;

> The worms were hallowed that did breed the silk,
> And it was dyed in mummy –

which Forman, by the way, dealt in.

He also treated people for venereal disease, to which there is a reference *à propos* of Naples. Forman had a good record for treating people during plague, when the doctors fled. Severe plague is again in the background of 1603–4:

> As doth the raven o'er the infected house
> Boding to all.

Iago has a candid passage on servants at the time:

> Who, trimmed in forms and visages of duty,
> Keep yet their hearts attending on themselves;
> And, throwing but shows of service on their lords,
> Do well thrive by them, and when they have lined their coats,
> Do themselves homage.

An historian recognises how true that was to the age.

Iago describes Othello's marriage:

> Faith, he tonight hath boarded a land carrack,
> If it prove lawful prize, he's made for ever.

Portuguese carracks were the treasure-ships from the Indies, several of which the Elizabethans boarded and made prizes of. The voyages, as recounted in Hakluyt, are present behind Othello's account of his experiences:

> And of the Cannibals that each other eat,
> The Anthropophagi, and men whose heads
> Do grow beneath their shoulders.

The description of the Pontic Sea and the Hellespont comes straight out of our reading man's looking into Philemon Holland's translation of Pliny.

Personal. No references to the stage, after the extended treatment of the subject in *Hamlet*, except for the regular use of the word 'cue'. The play itself suggests, in part, a reversion to the old Morality, with Iago as the stage-villain informing the audience of his intended villainies. There is a good deal of rhyme, too, with regular *sententiae* at one point in couplets, presenting Shakespeare's own conclusions:

> When remedies are past, the griefs are ended
> By seeing the worst, which late on hopes depended
> To mourn a mischief that is past and gone
> Is the next way to draw new mischief on –

very Shakespearean thoughts in their cautious prudence.

Above all, one notices the increasing idiosyncrasy of the vocabulary, the oblique words and phrases, the extraordinary expressions. We find 'conjunctive' again from *Hamlet*; phrases like 'sequent messengers' are very characteristic, words like 'indign', 'sequestration' for divorce, 'segregation' of the Turkish fleet for scattering, 'equinox' for equivalent, 'exsufflicate', 'iterance' for repetition. Who but Shakespeare would say 'fortitude' for fortification; or write,

> My speculative and officed instruments?

Equally characteristic is the conjunction of grand words with simple and colloquial: a tempest had so 'banged' the Turks that the 'sufferance' of it could be seen in the fleet. Or, if drink did not rock Cassio's cradle, he'd watch the 'horologe' round.

What it all testifies to is Shakespeare's unparalleled linguistic range, which constitutes a difficulty for modern and foreign readers alike.

Text. Two versions have come down to us, both good ones: a quarto of 1622, and the Folio of 1623. Each helps to complement and correct the other, and are thought to rest on the same original manuscript. The Folio is fuller, by some 160 lines; it has the spelling Æmilia for Emilia, the form Emilia Lanier used in publishing her poem.

The play was performed in the old banqueting hall at Whitehall on All Saints' Day (November 1) 1604, and other Court performances are recorded.

Othello and Desdemona. Drawing by Henry Singleton (1766–1839)

273

M.ʳ KEAN ᴀꜱ OTHELLO,

Published by M.&.M.SKELT 11.Swan S.ᵗ Minories London.

OTHELLO,
THE MOOR OF VENICE.

DRAMATIS PERSONÆ.

DUKE OF VENICE.
BRABANTIO, a senator.
Other Senators.
GRATIANO, brother to Brabantio.
LODOVICO, kinsman to Brabantio.
OTHELLO, a noble Moor in the service of the
    Venetian state.
CASSIO, his lieutenant.
IAGO, his ancient.
RODERIGO, a Venetian gentleman.
MONTANO, Othello's predecessor in the go-
    vernment of Cyprus.

Clown, servant to Othello.

DESDEMONA, daughter to Brabantio and wife
    to Othello.
EMILIA, wife to Iago.
BIANCA, mistress to Cassio.

Sailor, Messenger, Herald, Officers, Gentlemen,
    Musicians, and Attendants.

SCENE: *Venice: a Sea-port in Cyprus.*

● *A bullet beside a text line indicates an annotation in
the opposite column*

ACT I.

SCENE I. *Venice. A street.*

Enter RODERIGO *and* IAGO.

Rod. Tush! never tell me; I take it much
    unkindly
That thou, Iago, who hast had my purse
As if the strings were thine, shouldst know of this.
● *Iago.* 'Sblood, but you will not hear me:
If ever I did dream of such a matter,
Abhor me.
    Rod. Thou told'st me thou didst hold him in
        thy hate.
    Iago. Despise me, if I do not. Three great
        ones of the city,
In personal suit to make me his lieutenant,

Porta della Carta, Venice. From a contemporary
engraving

4 *'Sblood.* God's blood.

Opposite: Edmund Kean as Othello, Theatre Royal,
Drury Lane, London, 1837

13 *a bombast circumstance.* Boastful talk.

16 *Nonsuits.* Rejects. *'Certes'.* Certainly.

24 *theoric.* Theory.

25 *toged.* Wearing togas.

30 *be-lee'd.* Caught in the lee, that is, unable to sail because out of the wind.

31 *counter-caster.* One who can count only by counters.

33 *ancient.* Ensign, the lowest rank of officer.

37 *old gradation.* Strict promotion.

39 *affined.* Bound.

50-54 *Who, trimm'd . . . homage.* See introduction.

62 *native act.* Natural motion. *figure.* Make.

63 *compliment extern.* Outward appearance.

65 *daws.* Jackdaws.

66 *owe.* Possess.

Off-capp'd to him : and, by the faith of man,   10
I know my price, I am worth no worse a place :
But he, as loving his own pride and purposes,
●Evades them, with a bombast circumstance
Horribly stuff'd with epithets of war ;
And, in conclusion,
●Nonsuits my mediators ; for, 'Certes,' says he,
' I have already chose my officer.'
And what was he ?
Forsooth, a great arithmetician,
One Michael Cassio, a Florentine,   20
†A fellow almost damn'd in a fair wife ;
That never set a squadron in the field,
Nor the division of a battle knows
●More than a spinster ; unless the bookish theoric,
●Wherein the toged consuls can propose
As masterly as he : mere prattle, without practice,
Is all his soldiership. But he, sir, had the election :
And I, of whom his eyes had seen the proof
At Rhodes, at Cyprus and on other grounds
●Christian and heathen, must be be-lee'd and calm'd   30
●By debitor and creditor : this counter-caster,
He, in good time, must his lieutenant be,
●And I—God bless the mark !—his Moorship's ancient.
   Rod. By heaven, I rather would have been his hangman.'
   Iago. Why, there's no remedy ; 'tis the curse of service,
Preferment goes by letter and affection,
●And not by old gradation, where each second
Stood heir to the first.   Now, sir, be judge yourself,
●Whether I in any just term am affined
To love the Moor.
   Rod.   I would not follow him then. 40
   Iago. O, sir, content you :
I follow him to serve my turn upon him :
We cannot all be masters, nor all masters
Cannot be truly follow'd.   You shall mark
Many a duteous and knee-crooking knave,
That, doting on his own obsequious bondage,
Wears out his time, much like his master's ass,
For nought but provender, and when he's old, cashier'd :
Whip me such honest knaves.   Others there are
●Who, trimm'd in forms and visages of duty,   50
Keep yet their hearts attending on themselves,
And, throwing but shows of service on their lords,
Do well thrive by them and when they have lined their coats
Do themselves homage : these fellows have some soul :
And such a one do I profess myself.   For, sir,
It is as sure as you are Roderigo,
Were I the Moor, I would not be Iago :
In following him, I follow but myself ;
Heaven is my judge, not I for love and duty,
But seeming so, for my peculiar end :   60
For when my outward action doth demonstrate
●The native act and figure of my heart
●In compliment extern, 'tis not long after
But I will wear my heart upon my sleeve
●For daws to peck at : I am not what I am.
●   *Rod.* What a full fortune does the thick-lips owe,
If he can carry 't thus !
   Iago.   Call up her father,

Rouse him: make after him, poison his delight,
Proclaim him in the streets; incense her kinsmen,
And, though he in a fertile climate dwell,   70
Plague him with flies: though that his joy be joy,
Yet throw such changes of vexation on't,
As it may lose some colour.
  Rod. Here is her father's house; I'll call
    aloud.
  Iago. Do, with like timorous accent and dire
    yell
As when, by night and negligence, the fire
Is spied in populous cities.
  Rod. What, ho, Brabantio! Signior Brabantio,
    ho!
  Iago. Awake! what, ho, Brabantio! thieves!
    thieves! thieves!
Look to your house, your daughter and your bags!
Thieves! thieves!   81

BRABANTIO *appears above, at a window.*

  Bra. What is the reason of this terrible sum-
    mons?
What is the matter there?
  Rod. Signior, is all your family within?
  Iago. Are your doors lock'd?
  Bra.   Why, wherefore ask you this?
  Iago. 'Zounds, sir, you're robb'd; for shame,
    put on your gown;
Your heart is burst, you have lost half your soul;
Even now, now, very now, an old black ram
• Is tupping your white ewe. Arise, arise;
• Awake the snorting citizens with the bell,   90
Or else the devil will make a grandsire of you:
Arise, I say.
  Bra.   What, have you lost your wits?
  Rod. Most reverend signior, do you know my
    voice?
  Bra. Not I: what are you?
  Rod. My name is Roderigo.
  Bra.   The worser welcome:
I have charged thee not to haunt about my doors:
In honest plainness thou hast heard me say
My daughter is not for thee; and now, in mad-
    ness,
• Being full of supper and distempering draughts,
Upon malicious bravery, dost thou come   100
• To start my quiet.
  Rod. Sir, sir, sir,—
  Bra.   But thou must needs be sure
My spirit and my place have in them power
To make this bitter to thee.
  Rod.   Patience, good sir.
  Bra. What tell'st thou me of robbing? this is
    Venice;
• My house is not a grange.
  Rod.   Most grave Brabantio,
In simple and pure soul I come to you.
  Iago. 'Zounds, sir, you are one of those that
will not serve God, if the devil bid you. Because
we come to do you service and you think we are
• ruffians, you'll have your daughter covered with
• a Barbary horse; you'll have your nephews neigh
• to you; you'll have coursers for cousins and gen-
• nets for germans.
  Bra. What profane wretch art thou?
  Iago. I am one, sir, that comes to tell you your
• daughter and the Moor are now making the beast
with two backs.
  Bra. Thou art a villain.

Costume design for Brabantio by Carleton Smyth, New
Theatre, London, 1920

89 *tupping.* Mating with.

90 *snorting.* Snoring.

99 *distempering draughts.* Intoxicating drinks.

101 *start.* Disturb.

106 *grange.* Country house with barns.

111-113 *you'll have . . . to you.* See introduction.

112 *Barbary.* North African, Arab.

113-114 *gennets.* Small horse of Spanish breeding.

114 *germans.* Close relatives.

117-118 *making the beast with two backs.* Copulating.

124 *odd-even.* Late night – early morning.

128 *allowance.* With your consent.

137 *extravagant and wheeling.* Wandering.

152 *stand in act.* Are in progress.

153 *fathom.* Ability.

159 *the Sagittary.* The name of the house or inn where his daughter is staying.

Iago.   You are—a senator.
Bra. This thou shalt answer; I know thee,
     Roderigo.   120
Rod. Sir, I will answer any thing. But, I be-
     seech you,
If 't be your pleasure and most wise consent,
As partly I find it is, that your fair daughter,
●At this odd-even and dull watch o' the night,
Transported, with no worse nor better guard
But with a knave of common hire, a gondolier,
To the gross clasps of a lascivious Moor,—
●If this be known to you and your allowance,
We then have done you bold and saucy wrongs;
But if you know not this, my manners tell me 130
We have your wrong rebuke.   Do not believe
That, from the sense of all civility,
I thus would play and trifle with your reverence:
Your daughter, if you have not given her leave,
I say again, hath made a gross revolt;
Tying her duty, beauty, wit and fortunes
●In an extravagant and wheeling stranger
Of here and every where.   Straight satisfy your-
     self:
If she be in her chamber or your house,
Let loose on me the justice of the state   140
For thus deluding you.
Bra.   Strike on the tinder, ho!
Give me a taper! call up all my people!
This accident is not unlike my dream:
Belief of it oppresses me already.
Light, I say! light!   [*Exit above.*
Iago.   Farewell; for I must leave you:
It seems not meet, nor wholesome to my place,
To be produced—as, if I stay, I shall—
Against the Moor: for, I do know, the state,
However this may gall him with some check,
Cannot with safety cast him, for he's embark'd
With such loud reason to the Cyprus wars,   151
●Which even now stand in act, that, for their souls,
●Another of his fathom they have none,
To lead their business: in which regard,
Though I do hate him as I do hell-pains,
Yet, for necessity of present life,
I must show out a flag and sign of love,
Which is indeed but sign.   That you shall surely
     find him,
●Lead to the Sagittary the raised search;
And there will I be with him.   So, farewell. 160
                                              [*Exit.*

Enter, below, BRABANTIO, *and* Servants *with
     torches.*

Bra. It is too true an evil: gone she is;
And what's to come of my despised time
Is nought but bitterness.   Now, Roderigo,
Where didst thou see her? O unhappy girl!
With the Moor, say'st thou? Who would be a
     father!
How didst thou know 'twas she? O, she deceives
     me
Past thought! What said she to you? Get more
     tapers:
Raise all my kindred.   Are they married, think
     you?
Rod. Truly, I think they are.
Bra. O heaven! How got she out? O treason
     of the blood!   170
Fathers, from hence trust not your daughters'
     minds

By what you see them act.   Is there not charms
By which the property of youth and maidhood
May be abused?   Have you not read, Roderigo,
Of some such thing?
   Rod.   Yes, sir, I have indeed.
   Bra.   Call up my brother.   O, would you had
      had her !
Some one way, some another.   Do you know
Where we may apprehend her and the Moor?
   Rod.   I think I can discover him, if you please
To get good guard and go along with me.   180
   Bra.   Pray you, lead on.   At every house I'll
     call;
I may command at most.   Get weapons, ho !
And raise some special officers of night.
•On, good Roderigo : I'll deserve your pains.
                             [*Exeunt.*

     SCENE II.   *Another street.*

 Enter OTHELLO, IAGO, *and* Attendants *with*
     torches.

   Iago.   Though in the trade of war I have slain
     men,
Yet do I hold it very stuff o' the conscience
To do no contrived murder : I lack iniquity
•Sometimes to do me service : nine or ten times
•I had thought to have yerk'd him here under the
     ribs.
   Oth.   'Tis better as it is.
   Iago.   Nay, but he prated,
And spoke such scurvy and provoking terms
Against your honour
That, with the little godliness I have,
I did full hard forbear him. But, I pray you, sir,
Are you fast married?   Be assured of this,   11
•That the magnifico is much beloved,
And hath in his effect a voice potential
As double as the duke's : he will divorce you ;
Or put upon you what restraint and grievance
The law, with all his might to enforce it on,
•Will give him cable.
   Oth.   Let him do his spite :
•My services which I have done the signiory
Shall out-tongue his complaints.   'Tis yet to
     know,—
Which, when I know that boasting is an honour,
I shall promulgate—I fetch my life and being   21
•From men of royal siege, and my demerits
•May speak unbonneted to as proud a fortune
As this that I have reach'd : for know, Iago,
But that I love the gentle Desdemona,
•I would not my unhoused free condition
Put into circumscription and confine
For the sea's worth. But, look ! what lights come
     yond?
   Iago.   Those are the raised father and his
     friends :
You were best go in.
   Oth.   Not I : I must be found :   30
My parts, my title and my perfect soul
Shall manifest me rightly.   Is it they?
• *Iago.*   By Janus, I think no.

 Enter CASSIO, *and certain* Officers *with torches.*

   Oth.   The servants of the duke, and my lieu-
     tenant.
The goodness of the night upon you, friends !
What is the news?

184 *deserve.* Reward.

A street in Venice. From a 16th century engraving

4 *to do me service.* i.e. for my own good.

5 *yerk'd.* Stabbed.

12 *magnifico.* Venetian lord, referring to Brabantio.

17 *give him cable.* Allow him.

18 *signiory.* The government of Venice.

22 *siege.* Standing.

23 *unbonneted.* Openly.

26 *unhoused.* Unrestricted.

33 *Janus.* Roman god with two faces.

37 *haste-post-haste.* Immediate.

Ira Aldridge, the 19th century black actor, as Othello

50-51 *'Faith, he . . . for ever.* See introduction.

53 *Marry.* The Virgin Mary.

59 *Keep up.* Keep them in their scabbards.

70 *guardage.* My guardianship of her.

72 *gross in sense.* Clearly true.

79 *out of warrant.* Unlawful.

Cas.　　　The duke does greet you, general,
And he requires your haste-post-haste appearance,
Even on the instant.
　Oth.　　　　　What is the matter, think you?
　Cas. Something from Cyprus, as I may divine:
It is a business of some heat: the galleys　　40
Have sent a dozen sequent messengers
This very night at one another's heels,
And many of the consuls, raised and met,
Are at the duke's already: you have been hotly
　　　call'd for;
When, being not at your lodging to be found,
The senate hath sent about three several quests
To search you out.
　Oth.　　　　　'Tis well I am found by you.
I will but spend a word here in the house,
And go with you.　　　　　　　[*Exit.*
　Cas.　　　　Ancient, what makes he here?
　Iago. 'Faith, he to-night hath boarded a land
　　　carack:　　　　　　　　　　50
If it prove lawful prize, he's made for ever.
　Cas. I do not understand.
　Iago.　　　　　　He's married.
　Cas.　　　　　　　　To who?

Re-enter OTHELLO.

　Iago. Marry, to—Come, captain, will you go?
　Oth.　　　　　　Have with you.
　Cas. Here comes another troop to seek for you.
　Iago. It is Brabantio. General, be advised;
He comes to bad intent.

Enter BRABANTIO, RODERIGO, *and* Officers *with
torches and weapons.*

　Oth.　　　　Holla! stand there!
　Rod. Signior, it is the Moor.
　Bra.　　　　Down with him, thief!
　　　　　[*They draw on both sides.*
　Iago. You, Roderigo! come, sir, I am for you.
　Oth. Keep up your bright swords, for the dew
　　　will rust them.
Good signior, you shall more command with years
Than with your weapons.　　　　61
　Bra. O thou foul thief, where hast thou stow'd
　　　my daughter?
Damn'd as thou art, thou hast enchanted her;
For I'll refer me to all things of sense,
If she in chains of magic were not bound,
Whether a maid so tender, fair and happy,
So opposite to marriage that she shunn'd
The wealthy curled darlings of our nation,
Would ever have, to incur a general mock,
Run from her guardage to the sooty bosom　70
Of such a thing as thou, to fear, not to delight.
Judge me the world, if 'tis not gross in sense
That thou hast practised on her with foul charms,
Abused her delicate youth with drugs or minerals
That weaken motion: I'll have 't disputed on;
'Tis probable and palpable to thinking.
I therefore apprehend and do attach thee
For an abuser of the world, a practiser
Of arts inhibited and out of warrant.
Lay hold upon him: if he do resist,　　　80
Subdue him at his peril.
　Oth.　　　　Hold your hands,
Both you of my inclining, and the rest:
Were it my cue to fight, I should have known it
Without a prompter. Where will you that I go
To answer this your charge?

Bra.   To prison, till fit time
●Of law and course of direct session
Call thee to answer.
        Oth.   What if I do obey?
How may the duke be therewith satisfied,
Whose messengers are here about my side,
Upon some present business of the state   90
To bring me to him?
        First Off.   'Tis true, most worthy signior;
The duke's in council, and your noble self,
I am sure, is sent for.
        Bra.   How! the duke in council!
In this time of the night!   Bring him away:
Mine 's not an idle cause: the duke himself,
Or any of my brothers of the state,
Cannot but feel this wrong as 'twere their own;
For if such actions may have passage free,
Bond-slaves and pagans shall our statesmen be.
                                [*Exeunt.*

SCENE III. *A council-chamber.*

The DUKE *and* Senators *sitting at a table;*
Officers *attending.*

● *Duke.*   There is no composition in these news
That gives them credit.
        First Sen.   Indeed, they are disproportion'd;
My letters say a hundred and seven galleys.
        Duke.   And mine, a hundred and forty.
        Sec. Sen.   And mine, two hundred:
●But though they jump not on a just account,—
As in these cases, where the aim reports,
'Tis oft with difference—yet do they all confirm
A Turkish fleet, and bearing up to Cyprus.
        Duke.   Nay, it is possible enough to judgement:
I do not so secure me in the error,   10
●But the main article I do approve
In fearful sense.
        Sailor. [*Within*] What, ho! what, ho! what, ho!
        First Off.   A messenger from the galleys.

Enter a Sailor.

Duke.   Now, what's the business?
Sail.   The Turkish preparation makes for
        Rhodes;
So was I bid report here to the state
By Signior Angelo.
        Duke.   How say you by this change?
        First Sen.   This cannot be,
By no assay of reason: 'tis a pageant,
●To keep us in false gaze.   When we consider
The importancy of Cyprus to the Turk,   20
And let ourselves again but understand,
That as it more concerns the Turk than Rhodes,
So may he with more facile question bear it,
●For that it stands not in such warlike brace,
But altogether lacks the abilities
●That Rhodes is dress'd in: if we make thought
        of this,
We must not think the Turk is so unskilful
To leave that latest which concerns him first,
Neglecting an attempt of ease and gain,
To wake and wage a danger profitless.   30
        Duke.   Nay, in all confidence, he's not for
        Rhodes.
        First Off.   Here is more news.

86 *course of direct session.* Normal course of justice.

1 *composition.* Consistency.

5 *jump not on a just account.* Do not exactly tally.

11 *approve.* Accept.

Costume design for a Sailor by Tanya Moiseiwitch,
Stratford-upon-Avon, 1952

19 *in false gaze.* Looking the wrong way.

24 *warlike brace.* Prepared for war.

26 *dress'd in.* Possesses.

The Empire of the Turk. Map from Abraham Ortelius, *Epitome to the theatre of the world*, 1598

---

33 *Ottomites.* Turks, of the Ottoman Empire.

35 *injointed.* United. *after.* Second.

37 *re-stem.* Retrace.

57 *engluts.* Overwhelms.

61 *bought of mountebanks.* Purchased from 'quacks'.

64 *Sans.* Without.

69–70 *though our . . . your action.* Even if it were my own son who is the accused.

Enter a Messenger.

● *Mess.*   The Ottomites, reverend and gracious,
Steering with due course towards the isle of Rhodes,
● Have there injointed them with an after fleet.
First Sen.   Ay, so I thought.   How many, as you guess?
● *Mess.*   Of thirty sail: and now they do re-stem
Their backward course, bearing with frank appearance
Their purposes toward Cyprus.   Signior Montano,
Your trusty and most valiant servitor,   40
With his free duty recommends you thus,
And prays you to believe him.
Duke.   'Tis certain, then, for Cyprus.
Marcus Luccicos, is not he in town?
First Sen.   He's now in Florence.
Duke.   Write from us to him; post-post-haste dispatch.
First Sen.   Here comes Brabantio and the valiant Moor.

Enter BRABANTIO, OTHELLO, IAGO,
RODERIGO, *and* Officers.

Duke.   Valiant Othello, we must straight employ you
Against the general enemy Ottoman.
[*To Brabantio*] I did not see you; welcome, gentle signior;   50
We lack'd your counsel and your help to-night.
Bra.   So did I yours.   Good your grace, pardon me;
Neither my place nor aught I heard of business
Hath raised me from my bed, nor doth the general care
Take hold on me, for my particular grief
Is of so flood-gate and o'erbearing nature
● That it engluts and swallows other sorrows
And it is still itself.
Duke.   Why, what's the matter?
Bra.   My daughter! O, my daughter!
Duke and Sen.   Dead?
Bra.   Ay, to me;
She is abused, stol'n from me, and corrupted   60
● By spells and medicines bought of mountebanks;
For nature so preposterously to err,
Being not deficient, blind, or lame of sense,
● Sans witchcraft could not.
Duke.   Whoe'er he be that in this foul proceeding
Hath thus beguiled your daughter of herself
And you of her, the bloody book of law
You shall yourself read in the bitter letter
● After your own sense, yea, though our proper son
Stood in your action.
Bra.   Humbly I thank your grace.   70
Here is the man, this Moor, whom now, it seems,
Your special mandate for the state-affairs
Hath hither brought.
Duke and Sen.   We are very sorry for't.
Duke.   [*To Othello*] What, in your own part, can you say to this?
Bra.   Nothing, but this is so.
Oth.   Most potent, grave, and reverend signiors,
My very noble and approved good masters,
That I have ta'en away this old man's daughter,
It is most true; true, I have married her:

The very head and front of my offending   80
Hath this extent, no more.   Rude am I in my
      speech,
And little bless'd with the soft phrase of peace.
• For since these arms of mine had seven years' pith,
Till now some nine moons wasted, they have used
Their dearest action in the tented field,
And little of this great world can I speak,
More than pertains to feats of broil and battle,
And therefore little shall I grace my cause
In speaking for myself.   Yet, by your gracious
      patience,
• I will a round unvarnish'd tale deliver   90
Of my whole course of love; what drugs, what
      charms,
What conjuration and what mighty magic,
For such proceeding I am charged withal,
I won his daughter.
      Bra.   A maiden never bold;
Of spirit so still and quiet, that her motion
Blush'd at herself; and she, in spite of nature,
Of years, of country, credit, every thing,
To fall in love with what she fear'd to look on!
It is a judgement maim'd and most imperfect
That will confess perfection so could err   100
Against all rules of nature, and must be driven
To find out practices of cunning hell,
Why this should be.   I therefore vouch again
That with some mixtures powerful o'er the blood,
Or with some dram conjured to this effect,
He wrought upon her.
      Duke.   To vouch this, is no proof,
Without more wider and more overt test
• Than these thin habits and poor likelihoods
• Of modern seeming do prefer against him.
      First Sen.   But, Othello, speak: 110
Did you by indirect and forced courses
Subdue and poison this young maid's affections?
• Or came it by request and such fair question
As soul to soul affordeth?
      Oth.   I do beseech you,
Send for the lady to the Sagittary,
And let her speak of me before her father:
If you do find me foul in her report,
The trust, the office I do hold of you,
Not only take away, but let your sentence
Even fall upon my life.
      Duke.   Fetch Desdemona hither. 120
      Oth.   Ancient, conduct them: you best know
      the place.   [*Exeunt Iago and Attendants.*
And, till she come, as truly as to heaven
I do confess the vices of my blood,
So justly to your grave ears I'll present
How I did thrive in this fair lady's love,
And she in mine.
      Duke.   Say it, Othello.
      Oth.   Her father loved me; oft invited me;
Still question'd me the story of my life,   129
From year to year, the battles, sieges, fortunes,
That I have pass'd.
I ran it through, even from my boyish days,
To the very moment that he bade me tell it;
Wherein I spake of most disastrous chances
Of moving accidents by flood and field,
Of hair-breadth scapes i' the imminent deadly
      breach,
Of being taken by the insolent foe
And sold to slavery, of my redemption thence
• And portance in my travels' history:

Doge of Venice, Niccolo Marcello, 1474. Painting after
Gentile Bellini (d. 1507)

83 *seven years' pith.* The strength of a boy of seven.

90 *round unvarnish'd.* Blunt and unembellished.

108 *thin habits.* Faint indications.

109 *modern seeming.* Ordinary appearance.

113 *question.* Conversation.

139 *portance.* Carriage, bearing.

Othello relating the story of his life to Desdemona.
Painting by Henri Joseph Fradelle (1778–1865)

140 *antres.* Caves.

144 *Anthropophagi.* Tribe of cannibals.

Othello: '. . . and men whose heads Do grow beneath their shoulders'. Engraving from Michael Drayton's *Polyolbion*, 1612

153 *dilate.* Relate.

Desdemona: '. . . but here's my husband'. Othello (Paul Robeson), Desdemona (Mary Ure) and Brabantio (Paul Hardwick), Stratford-upon-Avon, 1959

191 *get.* Beget.

197 *escape.* Elopement.

●Wherein of antres vast and deserts idle,   140
Rough quarries, rocks and hills whose heads touch heaven,
It was my hint to speak,—such was the process:
And of the Cannibals that each other eat,
●The Anthropophagi and men whose heads
Do grow beneath their shoulders.   This to hear
Would Desdemona seriously incline:
But still the house-affairs would draw her thence:
Which ever as she could with haste dispatch,
She'ld come again, and with a greedy ear
Devour up my discourse: which I observing,   150
Took once a pliant hour, and found good means
To draw from her a prayer of earnest heart
●That I would all my pilgrimage dilate,
Whereof by parcels she had something heard,
But not intentively: I did consent,
And often did beguile her of her tears,
When I did speak of some distressful stroke
That my youth suffer'd.   My story being done,
She gave me for my pains a world of sighs:
She swore, in faith, 'twas strange, 'twas passing strange,   160
'Twas pitiful, 'twas wondrous pitiful:
She wish'd she had not heard it, yet she wish'd
That heaven had made her such a man: she thank'd me,
And bade me, if I had a friend that loved her,
I should but teach him how to tell my story,
And that would woo her.   Upon this hint I spake:
She loved me for the dangers I had pass'd,
And I loved her that she did pity them.
This only is the witchcraft I have used:
Here comes the lady; let her witness it.   170

Enter DESDEMONA, IAGO, *and* Attendants.

Duke.   I think this tale would win my daughter too.
Good Brabantio,
Take up this mangled matter at the best:
Men do their broken weapons rather use
Than their bare hands.
Bra.   I pray you, hear her speak:
If she confess that she was half the wooer,
Destruction on my head, if my bad blame
Light on the man! Come hither, gentle mistress:
Do you perceive in all this noble company
Where most you owe obedience?
Des.   My noble father,   180
I do perceive here a divided duty:
To you I am bound for life and education;
My life and education both do learn me
How to respect you; you are the lord of duty;
I am hitherto your daughter: but here's my husband,
And so much duty as my mother show'd
To you, preferring you before her father,
So much I challenge that I may profess
Due to the Moor my lord.
Bra.   God be wi' you! I have done.
Please it your grace, on to the state-affairs: 190
●I had rather to adopt a child than get it.
Come hither, Moor:
I here do give thee that with all my heart
Which, but thou hast already, with all my heart
I would keep from thee.   For your sake, jewel,
I am glad at soul I have no other child:
●For thy escape would teach me tyranny,

To hang clogs on them. I have done, my lord.
Duke. Let me speak like yourself, and lay a sentence, 199
●Which, as a grise or step, may help these lovers
Into your favour.
When remedies are past, the griefs are ended
By seeing the worst, which late on hopes depended.
To mourn a mischief that is past and gone
Is the next way to draw new mischief on.
What cannot be preserved when fortune takes
Patience her injury a mockery makes.
The robb'd that smiles steals something from the thief;
●He robs himself that spends a bootless grief. 209
Bra. So let the Turk of Cyprus us beguile;
We lose it not, so long as we can smile.
He bears the sentence well that nothing bears
But the free comfort which from thence he hears,
But he bears both the sentence and the sorrow
That, to pay grief, must of poor patience borrow.
●These sentences, to sugar, or to gall,
Being strong on both sides, are equivocal:
But words are words; I never yet did hear
That the bruised heart was pierced through the ear.
I humbly beseech you, proceed to the affairs of state. 220
Duke. The Turk with a most mighty preparation makes for Cyprus. Othello, the fortitude of the place is best known to you; and though we have there a substitute of most allowed sufficiency, yet opinion, a sovereign mistress of effects, throws a more safer voice on you: you must
●therefore be content to slubber the gloss of your new fortunes with this more stubborn and boisterous expedition. 229
Oth. The tyrant custom, most grave senators,
Hath made the flinty and steel couch of war
●My thrice-driven bed of down: I do agnize
A natural and prompt alacrity
I find in hardness, and do undertake
These present wars against the Ottomites.
Most humbly therefore bending to your state,
●I crave fit disposition for my wife,
Due reference of place and exhibition,
●With such accommodation and besort
As levels with her breeding.
Duke. If you please, 240
Be 't at her father's.
Bra. I 'll not have it so.
Oth. Nor I.
Des. Nor I; I would not there reside,
To put my father in impatient thoughts
By being in his eye. Most gracious duke,
To my unfolding lend your prosperous ear;
●And let me find a charter in your voice,
To assist my simpleness.
Duke. What would you, Desdemona?
Des. That I did love the Moor to live with him, 249
My downright violence and storm of fortunes
May trumpet to the world: my heart's subdued
Even to the very quality of my lord:
I saw Othello's visage in his mind,
And to his honours and his valiant parts
Did I my soul and fortunes consecrate.
So that, dear lords, if I be left behind,
A moth of peace, and he go to the war,

200 *grise.* Step.

209 *bootless.* Pointless.

216 *to sugar, or to gall.* To sweeten or to sour.

227 *slubber.* Smear.

Desdemona, Brabantio and Othello. Engraving from a painting by C. W. Cope (1811–1890)

232 *agnize.* Acknowledge.

237 *fit disposition.* Suitable arrangements.

239 *besort.* Attention.

246 *a charter.* Inclination.

270 *seel*. Blind.

271 *speculative and officed instruments*. Thoughts and senses.

272 *disports*. Carnal enjoyments.

273 *skillet*. Cooking pot.

274 *indign*. Unworthy.

284 *import*. Concern.

306 *incontinently*. Immediately.

The rites for which I love him are bereft me,
And I a heavy interim shall support
By his dear absence.   Let me go with him.   260
   Oth.   Let her have your voices
Vouch with me, heaven, I therefore beg it not,
To please the palate of my appetite,
Nor to comply with heat—the young affects
In me defunct—and proper satisfaction,
But to be free and bounteous to her mind:
And heaven defend your good souls, that you
    think
I will your serious and great business scant
For she is with me: no, when light-wing'd toys
•Of feather'd Cupid seel with wanton dullness   270
•My speculative and officed instruments,
•That my disports corrupt and taint my business,
•Let housewives make a skillet of my helm,
•And all indign and base adversities
Make head against my estimation!
   Duke.   Be it as you shall privately determine,
Either for her stay or going: the affair cries
    haste,
And speed must answer it.
   First Sen.   You must away to-night.
   Oth.   With all my heart.
   Duke.   At nine i' the morning here we 'll meet
    again.   280
Othello, leave some officer behind,
And he shall our commission bring to you;
With such things else of quality and respect
•As doth import you.
   Oth.   So please your grace, my ancient;
A man he is of honesty and trust:
To his conveyance I assign my wife,
With what else needful your good grace shall
    think
To be sent after me.
   Duke   Let it be so.
Good night to every one. [*To Brab.*] And, noble
    signior,
If virtue no delighted beauty lack,   290
Your son-in-law is far more fair than black.
   First Sen.   Adieu, brave Moor; use Desde-
    mona well
   Bra.   Look to her, Moor, if thou hast eyes
    to see:
She has deceived her father, and may thee.
   [*Exeunt Duke, Senators, Officers, &c.*
   Oth.   My life upon her faith! Honest Iago,
My Desdemona must I leave to thee:
I prithee, let thy wife attend on her:
And bring them after in the best advantage.
Come, Desdemona: I have but an hour
Of love, of worldly matters and direction,   300
To spend with thee: we must obey the time.
   [*Exeunt Othello and Desdemona.*
   Rod.   Iago,—
   Iago.   What say'st thou, noble heart?
   Rod.   What will I do, thinkest thou?
   Iago.   Why, go to bed, and sleep.
• *Rod.*   I will incontinently drown myself.
   Iago.   If thou dost, I shall never love thee
after.   Why, thou silly gentleman!
   Rod.   It is silliness to live when to live is tor-
ment; and then have we a prescription to die
when death is our physician   311
   Iago.   O villanous! I have looked upon the
world for four times seven years; and since I
could distinguish betwixt a benefit and an injury,

I never found man that knew how to love himself.
Ere I would say, I would drown myself for the
● love of a guinea-hen, I would change my humanity with a baboon.

Rod. What should I do? I confess it is my
● shame to be so fond; but it is not in my virtue to
amend it.   321

Iago. Virtue! a fig! 'tis in ourselves that we
are thus or thus. Our bodies are our gardens, to
the which our wills are gardeners; so that if we
● will plant nettles, or sow lettuce, set hyssop and
weed up thyme, supply it with one gender of
herbs, or distract it with many, either to have it
sterile with idleness, or manured with industry,
why, the power and corrigible authority of this
lies in our wills. If the balance of our lives had
not one scale of reason to poise another of sensuality, the blood and baseness of our natures
would conduct us to most preposterous conclusions: but we have reason to cool our raging
● motions, our carnal stings, our unbitted lusts,
● whereof I take this that you call love to be a sect
or scion.

Rod. It cannot be.

Iago. It is merely a lust of the blood and a
permission of the will. Come, be a man. Drown
thyself! drown cats and blind puppies. I have
professed me thy friend and I confess me knit to
● thy deserving with cables of perdurable tough-
● ness; I could never better stead thee than now.
Put money in thy purse; follow thou the wars;
● defeat thy favour with an usurped beard; I say,
put money in thy purse. It cannot be that Desdemona should long continue her love to the
Moor,—put money in thy purse,—nor he his to
her: it was a violent commencement, and thou
● shalt see an answerable sequestration:—put but
money in thy purse. These Moors are changeable in their wills:—fill thy purse with money:—
the food that to him now is as luscious as locusts,
● shall be to him shortly as bitter as coloquintida.
She must change for youth: when she is sated
with his body, she will find the error of her
choice: she must have change, she must: therefore put money in thy purse. If thou wilt needs
damn thyself, do it a more delicate way than
drowning. Make all the money thou canst: if
sanctimony and a frail vow betwixt an erring
barbarian and a supersubtle Venetian be not too
hard for my wits and all the tribe of hell, thou
shalt enjoy her; therefore make money. A pox
of drowning thyself! it is clean out of the way:
seek thou rather to be hanged in compassing thy
joy than to be drowned and go without her.

● *Rod.* Wilt thou be fast to my hopes, if I depend on the issue?   370

Iago. Thou art sure of me:—go, make money:
—I have told thee often, and I re-tell thee again
and again, I hate the Moor: my cause is hearted;
thine hath no less reason. Let us be conjunctive
in our revenge against him; if thou canst cuckold
him, thou dost thyself a pleasure, me a sport.
There are many events in the womb of time which
● will be delivered. Traverse! go, provide thy
money. We will have more of this to-morrow.
Adieu.   380

Rod. Where shall we meet i' the morning?

Iago. At my lodging.

Rod. I'll be with thee betimes.

317 *guinea-hen.* Promiscuous female.

320 *fond.* Infatuated, foolish.

325 *set.* Sow. *hyssop.* A herb.

335 *unbitted.* Unbridled.

Costume design for Iago by Carleton Smyth, New Theatre, London, 1920

336-337 *sect or scion.* Cutting or offshoot.

343 *perdurable.* Enduring.

344 *stead.* Aid.

346 *usurped.* False.

351 *sequestration.* Sequel.

355 *coloquintida.* Purgative.

369 *fast.* Loyal.

378 *Traverse!* Turn around!

The port of Cyprus. Stage design by William Telbin, the Elder (1813–1873) for the Princess's Theatre, London, 1860

---

396 *as if for surety.* As if it were fact.

398 *proper.* Handsome.

399 *plume up my will.* Sharpen my design.

409 *engender'd.* Conceived.

12 *chidden.* Chiding.

14 *burning bear.* The constellation of the little Bear.

17 *enchafed.* Angry.

23 *sufferance.* Damage.

Iago.   Go to; farewell.   Do you hear, Roderigo?
Rod.   What say you?
Iago.   No more of drowning, do you hear?
Rod.   I am changed: I'll go sell all my land.
                                                    [*Exit.*
Iago.   Thus do I ever make my fool my purse;
For I mine own gain'd knowledge should profane,
If I would time expend with such a snipe,
But for my sport and profit.   I hate the Moor;
And it is thought abroad, that 'twixt my sheets
He has done my office: I know not if 't be true;
But I, for mere suspicion in that kind,
● Will do as if for surety.   He holds me well;
The better shall my purpose work on him.
● Cassio's a proper man: let me see now:
● To get his place and to plume up my will   399
In double knavery—How, how?—Let's see:—
After some time, to abuse Othello's ear
That he is too familiar with his wife.
He hath a person and a smooth dispose
To be suspected, framed to make women false.
The Moor is of a free and open nature,
That thinks men honest that but seem to be so,
And will as tenderly be led by the nose
As asses are.
● I have't.   It is engender'd.   Hell and night
Must bring this monstrous birth to the world's
            light.   [*Exit.* 410

ACT II.

SCENE I.   *A Sea-port in Cyprus.   An open place near the quay.*

Enter MONTANO *and two* Gentlemen.

Mon.   What from the cape can you discern at sea?
First Gent.   Nothing at all: it is a high-wrought flood;
I cannot, 'twixt the heaven and the main,
Descry a sail.
Mon.   Methinks the wind hath spoke aloud at land;
A fuller blast ne'er shook our battlements:
If it hath ruffian'd so upon the sea,
What ribs of oak, when mountains melt on them,
Can hold the mortise?   What shall we hear of this?
Sec. Gent.   A segregation of the Turkish fleet:
For do but stand upon the foaming shore,   11
● The chidden billow seems to pelt the clouds;
The wind-shaked surge, with high and monstrous mane,
● Seems to cast water on the burning bear,
And quench the guards of the ever-fixed pole:
I never did like molestation view
● On the enchafed flood.
Mon.   If that the Turkish fleet
Be not enshelter'd and embay'd, they are drown'd;
It is impossible they bear it out.   19

Enter a third Gentleman.

Third Gent.   News, lads! our wars are done.
The desperate tempest hath so bang'd the Turks,
That their designment halts: a noble ship of Venice
● Hath seen a grievous wreck and sufferance
On most part of their fleet

Mon.   How! is this true?
Third Gent.   The ship is here put in,
A Veronesa; Michael Cassio,
Lieutenant to the warlike Moor Othello,
Is come on shore: the Moor himself at sea,
And is in full commission here for Cyprus.   29
   Mon.   I am glad on't; 'tis a worthy governor.
   Third Gent.   But this same Cassio, though he
      speak of comfort
Touching the Turkish loss, yet he looks sadly,
And prays the Moor be safe: for they were parted
With foul and violent tempest.
   Mon.   Pray heavens he be;
For I have served him, and the man commands
Like a full soldier.   Let's to the seaside, ho!
As well to see the vessel that's come in
As to throw out our eyes for brave Othello,
Even till we make the main and the aerial blue
An indistinct regard.
   Third Gent.   Come, let's do so: 40
For every minute is expectancy
Of more arrivance.

Enter CASSIO.

   Cas.   Thanks, you the valiant of this warlike
      isle,
That so approve the Moor!   O, let the heavens
Give him defence against the elements,
For I have lost him on a dangerous sea.
   Mon.   Is he well shipp'd?
   Cas.   His bark is stoutly timber'd, and his
      pilot
Of very expert and approved allowance;
Therefore my hopes, not surfeited to death,   50
Stand in bold cure.
      [*A cry within* 'A sail, a sail, a sail!'

Enter a fourth Gentleman.

   Cas.   What noise?
   Fourth Gent.   The town is empty; on the
      brow o' the sea
Stand ranks of people, and they cry 'A sail!'
   Cas.   My hopes do shape him for the governor.
      [*Guns heard.*
   Sec. Gent.   They do discharge their shot of
      courtesy:
Our friends at least.
   Cas.   I pray you, sir, go forth,
And give us truth who 'tis that is arrived.
   Sec. Gent.   I shall.   [*Exit.*
   Mon.   But, good lieutenant, is your general
      wived?   60
   Cas.   Most fortunately: he hath achieved a
      maid
That paragons description and wild fame;
One that excels the quirks of blazoning pens,
And in the essential vesture of creation
Does tire the ingener.

Re-enter second Gentleman.

                  How now! who has put in?
   Sec. Gent.   'Tis one Iago, ancient to the general.
   Cas.   Has had most favourable and happy
      speed:
Tempests themselves, high seas and howling
      winds,
The gutter'd rocks and congregated sands,—
Traitors ensteep'd to clog the guiltless keel,—
As having sense of beauty, do omit   71

26   *A Veronesa.* A boat belonging to Verona.

39   *the main and the aerial blue.* The sea and the sky.

49   *approved allowance.* Established reputation.

50-51   *not surfeited . . . bold cure.* Not over pessimistic,
are ready to be reassured.

Costume design for Cassio by Carleton Smyth, New
Theatre, London, 1920

62   *paragons.* Surpasses.

65   *ingener.* Maker, designer.

77 *A se'nnight's speed.* By a week.

81 *extincted.* Extinguished.

Desdemona. Drawing by D. G. Rossetti (1828–1882)

87 *Enwheel thee round.* Surround you.

108 *chides with thinking.* Scolds only in her mind.

121 *assay.* Try.

Their mortal natures, letting go safely by
The divine Desdemona.
   Mon.   **What is she?**
   Cas.   She that I spake of, our great captain's
    captain,
Left in the conduct of the bold Iago,
Whose footing here anticipates our thoughts
● A se'nnight's speed.   Great Jove, Othello guard,
And swell his sail with thine own powerful breath,
That he may bless this bay with his tall ship,   79
Make love's quick pants in Desdemona's arms,
● Give renew'd fire to our extincted spirits,
And bring all Cyprus comfort!

Enter DESDEMONA, EMILIA, IAGO, RODERIGO,
    and Attendants.

                       O, behold,
The riches of the ship is come on shore!
Ye men of Cyprus, let her have your knees.
Hail to thee, lady! and the grace of heaven,
Before, behind thee and on every hand,
● Enwheel thee round!
   Des.   I thank you, valiant Cassio.
What tidings can you tell me of my lord?
   Cas.   He is not yet arrived: nor know I aught
But that he's well and will be shortly here.   90
   Des.   O, but I fear—How lost you company?
   Cas.   The great contention of the sea and skies
Parted our fellowship—But, hark! a sail.
        [*Within* 'A sail, a sail!' *Guns heard.*
   Sec. Gent.   They give their greeting to the
    citadel:
This likewise is a friend.
   Cas.   See for the news. [*Exit Gentleman*
Good ancient, you are welcome.   [*To Emilia*]
    Welcome, mistress:
Let it not gall your patience, good Iago,
That I extend my manners; 'tis my breeding
That gives me this bold show of courtesy.   100
                   [*Kissing her.*
   Iago.   Sir, would she give you so much of her
    lips
As of her tongue she oft bestows on me,
You'ld have enough.
   Des.   Alas, she has no speech.
   Iago.   In faith, too much;
I find it still, when I have list to sleep:
Marry, before your ladyship, I grant,
She puts her tongue a little in her heart,
● And chides with thinking.
   Emil.   You have little cause to say so.
   Iago.   Come on, come on; you are pictures
    out of doors,   110
Bells in your parlours, wild-cats in your kitchens,
Saints in your injuries, devils being offended,
Players in your housewifery, and housewives in
    your beds.
   Des.   O, fie upon thee, slanderer!
   Iago.   Nay, it is true, or else I am a Turk:
You rise to play and go to bed to work.
   Emil.   You shall not write my praise.
   Iago.   No, let me not.
   Des.   What wouldst thou write of me, if thou
    shouldst praise me?
   Iago.   O gentle lady, do not put me to't;
For I am nothing, if not critical.   120
●   *Des.*   Come on, assay.   There's one gone to
    the harbour?
   Iago.   Ay, madam.

Des. I am not merry; but I do beguile
The thing I am, by seeming otherwise.
Come, how wouldst thou praise me?
   Iago. I am about it; but indeed my invention
●Comes from my pate as birdlime does from frize;
It plucks out brains and all: but my Muse labours,
And thus she is deliver'd.
If she be fair and wise, fairness and wit,   130
The one's for use, the other useth it.
   Des. Well praised! How if she be black and
      witty?
   Iago. If she be black, and thereto have a wit,
She'll find a white that shall her blackness fit.
   Des. Worse and worse.
   Emil. How if fair and foolish?
   Iago. She never yet was foolish that was fair;
For even her folly help'd her to an heir.
●   *Des.* These are old fond paradoxes to make
fools laugh i' the alehouse. What miserable praise
hast thou for her that's foul and foolish?   141
   Iago. There's none so foul and foolish thereunto,
But does foul pranks which fair and wise ones do.
   Des. O heavy ignorance! thou praisest the
worst best. But what praise couldst thou bestow
on a deserving woman indeed, one that, in the
●authority of her merit, did justly put on the vouch
of very malice itself?
   Iago. She that was ever fair and never proud,
Had tongue at will and yet was never loud,   150
Never lack'd gold and yet went never gay,
Fled from her wish and yet said 'Now I may,'
She that being anger'd, her revenge being nigh,
Bade her wrong stay and her displeasure fly,
She that in wisdom never was so frail
To change the cod's head for the salmon's tail,
She that could think and ne'er disclose her mind,
See suitors following and not look behind,
She was a wight, if ever such wight were,—
   Des. To do what?   160
   Iago. To suckle fools and chronicle small beer.
   Des. O most lame and impotent conclusion!
Do not learn of him, Emilia, though he be thy
husband. How say you, Cassio? is he not a
most profane and liberal counsellor?
●   *Cas.* He speaks home, madam: you may relish
him more in the soldier than in the scholar.
   Iago. [*Aside*] He takes her by the palm: ay,
well said, whisper: with as little a web as this
will I ensnare as great a fly as Cassio. Ay, smile
●upon her, do; I will gyve thee in thine own courtship. You say true; 'tis so, indeed: if such tricks
as these strip you out of your lieutenantry, it had
been better you had not kissed your three fingers
so oft, which now again you are most apt to play
the sir in. Very good; well kissed! an excellent
courtesy! 'tis so, indeed. Yet again your fingers
●to your lips? would they were clyster-pipes for
your sake! [*Trumpet within.*] The Moor! I
know his trumpet.   180
   Cas. 'Tis truly so.
   Des. Let's meet him and receive him.
   Cas. Lo, where he comes!

     Enter OTHELLO *and* Attendants.

   Oth. O my fair warrior!
   Des.   My dear Othello!
   Oth. It gives me wonder great as my content
To see you here before me. O my soul's joy!
If after every tempest come such calms,

Costume design for Emilia by Carleton Smyth, New
Theatre, London, 1920

---

127 *frize*. Coarse muslin.

139 *fond*. Foolish.

147-148 *put on the vouch of*. Attest to.

166 *home*. To the point. *relish*. Appreciate.

171 *gyve*. Fetter.

178 *clyster-pipes*. Surgical douches.

190 *Olympus.* Mountain home of Greek gods.

The return of Othello, Cyprus. Detail from a painting by Thomas Stothard (1755–1834)

203 *set down the pegs.* i.e. untune the strings.

208 *prattle out of fashion.* Gabble irrelevantly.

May the winds blow till they have waken'd death!
And let the labouring bark climb hills of seas
Olympus-high and duck again as low   190
As hell's from heaven!   If it were now to die,
'Twere now to be most happy; for, I fear,
My soul hath her content so absolute
That not another comfort like to this
Succeeds in unknown fate.
   Des.   The heavens forbid
But that our loves and comforts should increase,
Even as our days do grow!
   Oth.   Amen to that, sweet powers!
I cannot speak enough of this content;
It stops me here; it is too much of joy:
And this, and this, the greatest discords be   200
                          [*Kissing her.*
That e'er our hearts shall make!
   Iago. [*Aside*] O, you are well tuned now!
But I'll set down the pegs that make this music,
As honest as I am.
   Oth.   Come, let us to the castle.
News, friends; our wars are done, the Turks are
     drown'd.
How does my old acquaintance of this isle?
Honey, you shall be well desired in Cyprus:
I have found great love amongst them.   O my
     sweet,
I prattle out of fashion, and I dote
In mine own comforts.   I prithee, good Iago,
Go to the bay and disembark my coffers: 210
Bring thou the master to the citadel;
He is a good one, and his worthiness
Does challenge much respect.   Come, Desde-
     mona,
Once more, well met at Cyprus.
[*Exeunt Othello, Desdemona, and Attendants.*
   Iago.   Do thou meet me presently at the har-
bour.   Come hither.   If thou be'st valiant,—as,
they say, base men being in love have then a
nobility in their natures more than is native to
them,—list me.   The lieutenant to-night watches
on the court of guard:—first, I must tell thee this
—Desdemona is directly in love with him.   221
   Rod.   With him! why, 'tis not possible.
   Iago.   Lay thy finger thus, and let thy soul be
instructed.   Mark me with what violence she
first loved the Moor, but for bragging and telling
her fantastical lies: and will she love him still for
prating? let not thy discreet heart think it.   Her
eye must be fed; and what delight shall she have
to look on the devil?   When the blood is made
dull with the act of sport, there should be, again
to inflame it and to give satiety a fresh appetite,
loveliness in favour, sympathy in years, manners
and beauties; all which the Moor is defective in:
now, for want of these required conveniences,
her delicate tenderness will find itself abused,
begin to heave the gorge, disrelish and abhor the
Moor; very nature will instruct her in it and
compel her to some second choice.   Now, sir,
this granted,—as it is a most pregnant and unforced position—who stands so eminent in the
degree of this fortune as Cassio does? a knave
very voluble; no further conscionable than in
putting on the mere form of civil and humane
seeming, for the better compassing of his salt and
most hidden loose affection?   why, none; why,
none: a slipper and subtle knave, a finder of occasions, that has an eye can stamp and counter-

feit advantages, though true advantage never present itself; a devilish knave. Besides, the knave is handsome, young, and hath all those requisites in him that folly and green minds look after: a pestilent complete knave; and the woman hath found him already.

Rod. I cannot believe that in her; she's full of most blessed condition.

Iago. Blessed fig's-end! the wine she drinks is made of grapes: if she had been blessed, she would never have loved the Moor. Blessed pudding!
● Didst thou not see her paddle with the palm of his hand? didst not mark that?   260

Rod. Yes, that I did; but that was but courtesy.

Iago. Lechery, by this hand; an index and obscure prologue to the history of lust and foul thoughts. They met so near with their lips that their breaths embraced together. Villanous thoughts, Roderigo! when these mutualities so marshal the way, hard at hand comes the master and main exercise, the incorporate conclusion, Pish! But, sir, be you ruled by me: I have brought you from Venice. Watch you to-night; for the command, I'll lay't upon you. Cassio knows you not. I'll not be far from you: do you find some occasion to anger Cassio, either by speaking too loud, or tainting his discipline; or from what other course you please, which the time shall more favourably minister.

Rod. Well.

● *Iago.* Sir, he is rash and very sudden in choler, and haply may strike at you: provoke him, that he may; for even out of that will I cause these of Cyprus to mutiny; whose qualification shall come into no true taste again but by the displanting of Cassio. So shall you have a shorter journey to your desires by the means I shall then have to prefer them; and the impediment most profitably removed, without the which there were no expectation of our prosperity.

Rod. I will do this, if I can bring it to any opportunity.   290

Iago. I warrant thee. Meet me by and by at the citadel: I must fetch his necessaries ashore. Farewell.

Rod. Adieu.   [*Exit.*

Iago. That Cassio loves her, I do well believe it;
That she loves him, 'tis apt and of great credit:
The Moor, howbeit that I endure him not,
Is of a constant, loving, noble nature,
And I dare think he'll prove to Desdemona   299
A most dear husband. Now, I do love her too;
● Not out of absolute lust, though peradventure
I stand accountant for as great a sin,
But partly led to diet my revenge,
For that I do suspect the lusty Moor
● Hath leap'd into my seat; the thought whereof
Doth, like a poisonous mineral, gnaw my inwards;
And nothing can or shall content my soul
Till I am even'd with him, wife for wife,
Or failing so, yet that I put the Moor
At least into a jealousy so strong   310
That judgement cannot cure. Which thing to do,
If this poor trash of Venice, whom I trash
● For his quick hunting, stand the putting on,
I'll have our Michael Cassio on the hip,
● Abuse him to the Moor in the rank garb—

Costume design for Roderigo by Carleton Smyth, New Theatre, London, 1920

259 *paddle.* Tickle with a finger.

279 *choler.* Temper.

301 *peradventure.* Perhaps.

305 *leap'd into my seat.* i.e. committed adultery with my wife.

313 *stand the putting on.* Withstand the incitement.

315 *rank garb.* Gross fashion.

9 *offices.* Facilities.

7 *with your earliest.* As early as you can.

23 *sounds a parley of.* Arouses.

27 *alarum.* Signal.

30 *stoup.* Quart jug.

For I fear Cassio with my night-cap too—
Make the Moor thank me, love me and reward
   me,
For making him egregiously an ass
And practising upon his peace and quiet   319
Even to madness. 'Tis here, but yet confused:
Knavery's plain face is never seen till used. [*Exit.*

SCENE II.   *A street.*

Enter a Herald *with a proclamation;* People
following.

Her. It is Othello's pleasure, our noble and
valiant general, that, upon certain tidings now
arrived, importing the mere perdition of the
Turkish fleet, every man put himself into triumph;
some to dance, some to make bonfires, each man
to what sport and revels his addiction leads him:
for, besides these beneficial news, it is the celebration of his nuptial. So much was his pleasure
should be proclaimed. All offices are open, and
there is full liberty of feasting from this present
hour of five till the bell have told eleven. Heaven
bless the isle of Cyprus and our noble general
Othello!   [*Exeunt.*

SCENE III.   *A hall in the castle.*

Enter OTHELLO, DESDEMONA, CASSIO, *and*
Attendants.

Oth. Good Michael, look you to the guard to-
   night:
Let's teach ourselves that honourable stop,
Not to outsport discretion.
Cas. Iago hath direction what to do;
But, notwithstanding, with my personal eye
Will I look to 't.
Oth.   Iago is most honest.
Michael, good night: to-morrow with your ear-
   liest
Let me have speech with you. [*To Desdemona*]
      Come, my dear love,
The purchase made, the fruits are to ensue;
That profit's yet to come 'tween me and you. 10
Good night.
[*Exeunt Othello, Desdemona, and Attendants.*

Enter IAGO.

Cas. Welcome, Iago; we must to the watch.
Iago. Not this hour, lieutenant; 'tis not yet
ten o' the clock. Our general cast us thus early
for the love of his Desdemona; who let us not
therefore blame: he hath not yet made wanton
the night with her; and she is sport for Jove.
Cas. She's a most exquisite lady.
Iago. And, I'll warrant her, full of game.
Cas. Indeed, she's a most fresh and delicate
creature.   21
Iago. What an eye she has! methinks it
sounds a parley of provocation.
Cas. An inviting eye; and yet methinks right
modest.
Iago. And when she speaks, is it not an
alarum to love?
Cas. She is indeed perfection.
Iago. Well, happiness to their sheets! Come,
lieutenant, I have a stoup of wine; and here
without are a brace of Cyprus gallants that

would fain have a measure to the health of black Othello.

Cas. Not to-night, good Iago: I have very poor and unhappy brains for drinking: I could well wish courtesy would invent some other custom of entertainment.

Iago. O, they are our friends; but one cup: I'll drink for you.   39

Cas. I have drunk but one cup to-night, and
● that was craftily qualified too, and, behold, what innovation it makes here: I am unfortunate in
● the infirmity, and dare not task my weakness with any more.

Iago. What, man! 'tis a night of revels: the gallants desire it.

Cas. Where are they?

Iago. Here at the door; I pray you, call them in.

Cas. I'll do't; but it dislikes me.   [*Exit.*

Iago. If I can fasten but one cup upon him, 50
With that which he hath drunk to-night already,
He'll be as full of quarrel and offence
As my young mistress' dog.   Now, my sick fool Roderigo,
Whom love hath turn'd almost the wrong side out,
To Desdemona hath to-night caroused
● Potations pottle-deep; and he's to watch:
Three lads of Cyprus, noble swelling spirits,
That hold their honours in a wary distance,
The very elements of this warlike isle,
Have I to-night fluster'd with flowing cups, 60
And they watch too.   Now, 'mongst this flock of drunkards,
Am I to put our Cassio in some action
That may offend the isle.—But here they come:
If consequence do but approve my dream,
My boat sails freely, both with wind and stream.

Re-enter CASSIO; *with him* MONTANO *and* Gentlemen; *Servants following with wine.*

● *Cas.* 'Fore God, they have given me a rouse already.

Mon. Good faith, a little one; not past a pint, as I am a soldier.

Iago. Some wine, ho!   70
● [*Sings*] And let me the canakin clink, clink;
         And let me the canakin clink:
              A soldier's a man;
              A life's but a span;
         Why, then, let a soldier drink.
Some wine, boys!

Cas. 'Fore God, an excellent song.

Iago. I learned it in England, where, indeed,
● they are most potent in potting: your Dane, your German, and your swag-bellied Hollander—
Drink, ho!—are nothing to your English.   81

Cas. Is your Englishman so expert in his drinking?

Iago. Why, he drinks you, with facility, your Dane dead drunk; he sweats not to overthrow
● your Almain; he gives your Hollander a vomit, ere the next pottle can be filled.

Cas. To the health of our general!

Mon. I am for it, lieutenant; and I'll do you justice.   90

Iago. O sweet England!
         King Stephen was a worthy peer,
              His breeches cost him but a crown;
         He held them sixpence all too dear,
● With that he call'd the tailor lown.

41 *craftily qualified.* Well diluted.

43 *task.* Press.

56 *pottle-deep.* Down to the bottom of a tankard.

66 *rouse.* Large measure of drink.

Iago: 'Some wine, ho!' Iago (Ralph Richardson) with Cassio, Montano and Gentlemen, Old Vic Theatre, London, 1932

71 *canakin.* Small can.

79 *potent in potting.* i.e. able at drinking.

86 *Almain.* German.

95 *lown.* A lout.

96 *wight.* Man.

125 *set the watch.* Mount the guard.

129 *equinox.* i.e. an exact and opposite amount.

135 *horologe.* Clock. *a double set.* Twice round.

144 *second.* Lieutenant.

145 *ingraft.* Ingrained.

152 *twiggen.* Wicker.

Cassio: 'I'll beat the knave into a twiggen bottle.' Leo Genn as Cassio, Old Vic Theatre, London, 1935

          He was a wight of high renown,
      And thou art but of low degree:
      'Tis pride that pulls the country down;
      Then take thine auld cloak about thee.
Some wine, ho! **100**
  Cas. Why, this is a more exquisite song than the other.
  Iago. Will you hear 't again?
  Cas. No; for I hold him to be unworthy of his place that does those things. Well, God's above all; and there be souls must be saved, and there be souls must not be saved.
  Iago. It's true, good lieutenant.
  Cas. For mine own part,—no offence to the general, nor any man of quality,—I hope to be saved. **111**
  Iago. And so do I too, lieutenant.
  Cas. Ay, but, by your leave, not before me; the lieutenant is to be saved before the ancient. Let's have no more of this; let's to our affairs.— Forgive us our sins!—Gentlemen, let's look to our business. Do not think, gentlemen, I am drunk: this is my ancient; this is my right hand, and this is my left: I am not drunk now; I can stand well enough, and speak well enough. **120**
  All. Excellent well.
  Cas. Why, very well then; you must not think then that I am drunk. [*Exit.*
  Mon. To the platform, masters; come, let's set the watch.
  Iago. You see this fellow that is gone before;
He is a soldier fit to stand by Cæsar
And give direction: and do but see his vice;
'Tis to his virtue a just equinox,
The one as long as the other: 'tis pity of him. **130**
I fear the trust Othello puts him in,
On some odd time of his infirmity,
Will shake this island.
  Mon.   But is he often thus?
  Iago. 'Tis evermore the prologue to his sleep:
He'll watch the horologe a double set,
If drink rock not his cradle.
  Mon.   It were well
The general were put in mind of it.
Perhaps he sees it not; or his good nature
Prizes the virtue that appears in Cassio,
And looks not on his evils: is not this true? **140**

          Enter RODERIGO.

  Iago. [*Aside to him*] How now, Roderigo!
I pray you, after the lieutenant; go.
              [*Exit Roderigo.*
  Mon. And 'tis great pity that the noble Moor
Should hazard such a place as his own second
With one of an ingraft infirmity:
It were an honest action to say
So to the Moor.
  Iago.   Not I, for this fair island:
I do love Cassio well; and would do much
To cure him of this evil—But, hark! what noise?
          [*Cry within:* 'Help! help!']

    Re-enter CASSIO, *driving in* RODERIGO.

  Cas. You rogue! you rascal!
  Mon.   What's the matter, lieutenant?
  Cas. A knave teach me my duty! **151**
I'll beat the knave into a twiggen bottle.
  Rod. Beat me!

Cas.   Dost thou prate, rogue?
                    [*Striking Roderigo.*
Mon.   Nay, good lieutenant;
                    [*Staying him.*
I pray you, sir, hold your hand.
Cas.   Let me go, sir,
●Or I'll knock you o'er the mazzard.
Mon.   Come, come, you're drunk.
Cas.   Drunk!   [*They fight.*
Iago. [*Aside to Roderigo*] Away, I say; go
    out, and cry a mutiny.   [*Exit Roderigo.*
Nay, good lieutenant,—alas, gentlemen;—
Help, ho!—Lieutenant,—sir,—Montano,—sir;—
Help, masters!—Here's a goodly watch indeed!
                    [*Bell rings.*
●Who's that which rings the bell?—Diablo, ho!
The town will rise: God's will, lieutenant, hold!
You will be shamed for ever.

        Re-enter Othello *and* Attendants.

Oth.   What is the matter here?
Mon. 'Zounds, I bleed still; I am hurt to the
    death.   [*Faints.*
Oth.   Hold, for your lives!
Iago. Hold, ho! Lieutenant,—sir,—Montano,
    —gentlemen,—
Have you forgot all sense of place and duty?
Hold! the general speaks to you; hold, hold, for
    shame!
Oth.   Why, how now, ho! from whence ariseth
    this?
Are we turn'd Turks, and to ourselves do that
Which heaven hath forbid the Ottomites?   171
For Christian shame, put by this barbarous brawl:
He that stirs next to carve for his own rage
●Holds his soul light; he dies upon his motion.
Silence that dreadful bell: it frights the isle
From her propriety. What is the matter, masters?
Honest Iago, that look'st dead with grieving,
Speak, who began this? on thy love, I charge
    thee.
Iago. I do not know: friends all but now, even
    now,
●In quarter, and in terms like bride and groom
Devesting them for bed; and then, but now— 181
As if some planet had unwitted men—
Swords out, and tilting one at other's breast,
In opposition bloody.   I cannot speak
●Any beginning to this peevish odds;
And would in action glorious I had lost
Those legs that brought me to a part of it!
Oth.   How comes it, Michael, you are thus
    forgot?
Cas.   I pray you, pardon me; I cannot speak.
Oth.   Worthy Montano, you were wont be
    civil;   190
The gravity and stillness of your youth
The world hath noted, and your name is great
In mouths of wisest censure: what's the matter,
That you unlace your reputation thus
And spend your rich opinion for the name
Of a night-brawler? give me answer to it.
Mon.   Worthy Othello, I am hurt to danger:
Your officer, Iago, can inform you,—
While I spare speech, which something now
    offends me,—
Of all that I do know: nor know I aught   200
By me that's said or done amiss this night;
Unless self-charity be sometimes a vice,

156 *mazzard.* Head.

161 *Diablo.* The Devil.

Othello: 'Hold, for your lives!' Illustration by F. B. Dicksee (1853–1928)

174 *Holds . . . light.* Places small value on.

180 *quarter.* Relations with each other.

185 *peevish odds.* Petulant quarrel.

206 *collied.* Obscured.

212 *Though he . . . a birth.* i.e. even if he were my twin brother.

246 *pass.* Support.

247 *mince.* Dilute, colour.

248 *light.* Favourable.

Othello: 'Lead him off.' Engraving by Kenny Meadows from Barry Cornwall's *Works of Shakspere*, 1846

And to defend ourselves it be a sin
When violence assails us.
  Oth.   Now, by heaven,
My blood begins my safer guides to rule;
● And passion, having my best judgement collied,
Assays to lead the way: if I once stir,
Or do but lift this arm, the best of you
Shall sink in my rebuke.   Give me to know
How this foul rout began, who set it on;   210
And he that is approved in this offence,
● Though he had twinn'd with me, both at a birth,
Shall lose me.   What! in a town of war,
Yet wild, the people's hearts brimful of fear,
To manage private and domestic quarrel,
In night, and on the court and guard of safety!
'Tis monstrous.   Iago, who began 't?
  Mon.   If partially affined, or leagued in office,
Thou dost deliver more or less than truth,
Thou art no soldier.
  Iago.   Touch me not so near: 220
I had rather have this tongue cut from my mouth
Than it should do offence to Michael Cassio;
Yet, I persuade myself, to speak the truth
Shall nothing wrong him.   Thus it is, general.
Montano and myself being in speech,
There comes a fellow crying out for help:
And Cassio following him with determined sword,
To execute upon him.   Sir, this gentleman
Steps in to Cassio, and entreats his pause:
Myself the crying fellow did pursue,   230
Lest by his clamour—as it so fell out—
The town might fall in fright: he, swift of foot,
Outran my purpose; and I return'd the rather
For that I heard the clink and fall of swords,
And Cassio high in oath; which till to-night
I ne'er might say before.   When I came back—
For this was brief—I found them close together,
At blow and thrust; even as again they were
When you yourself did part them.
More of this matter cannot I report: 240
But men are men; the best sometimes forget:
Though Cassio did some little wrong to him,
As men in rage strike those that wish them best,
Yet surely Cassio, I believe, received
From him that fled some strange indignity,
● Which patience could not pass.
  Oth.   I know, Iago,
● Thy honesty and love doth mince this matter,
● Making it light to Cassio.   Cassio, I love thee;
But never more be officer of mine.

        Re-enter DESDEMONA, *attended.*

Look, if my gentle love be not raised up!   250
I'll make thee an example.
  Des.   What's the matter?
  Oth.   All's well now, sweeting; come away
        to bed.
Sir, for your hurts, myself will be your surgeon:
Lead him off.   [*To Montano, who is led off.*
Iago, look with care about the town,
And silence those whom this vile brawl distracted.
Come, Desdemona: 'tis the soldiers' life
To have their balmy slumbers waked with strife.
        [*Exeunt all but Iago and Cassio.*
  Iago.   What, are you hurt, lieutenant?
  Cas.   Ay, past all surgery.   260
  Iago.   Marry, heaven forbid!
  Cas.   Reputation, reputation, reputation! O,
I have lost my reputation! I have lost the im-

mortal part of myself, and what remains is bestial.
My reputation, Iago, my reputation!

Iago. As I am an honest man, I thought you had received some bodily wound; there is more sense in that than in reputation. Reputation is an idle and most false imposition: oft got without merit, and lost without deserving: you have lost no reputation at all, unless you repute yourself such a loser. What, man! there are ways to recover the general again: you are but now cast in his mood, a punishment more in policy than in malice; even so as one would beat his offenceless dog to affright an imperious lion: sue to him again, and he's yours.

Cas. I will rather sue to be despised than to deceive so good a commander with so slight, so drunken, and so indiscreet an officer. Drunk? and speak parrot? and squabble? swagger? swear? and discourse fustian with one's own shadow? O thou invisible spirit of wine, if thou hast no name to be known by, let us call thee devil!

Iago. What was he that you followed with your sword? What had he done to you?

Cas. I know not.

Iago. Is 't possible?

Cas. I remember a mass of things, but nothing distinctly; a quarrel, but nothing wherefore. O God, that men should put an enemy in their mouths to steal away their brains! that we should, with joy, pleasance, revel and applause, transform ourselves into beasts!

Iago. Why, but you are now well enough: how came you thus recovered?

Cas. It hath pleased the devil drunkenness to give place to the devil wrath: one unperfectness shows me another, to make me frankly despise myself. 300

Iago. Come, you are too severe a moraler: as the time, the place, and the condition of this country stands, I could heartily wish this had not befallen; but, since it is as it is, mend it for your own good.

Cas. I will ask him for my place again; he shall tell me I am a drunkard! Had I as many mouths as Hydra, such an answer would stop them all. To be now a sensible man, by and by a fool, and presently a beast! O strange! Every inordinate cup is unblessed and the ingredient is a devil.

Iago. Come, come, good wine is a good familiar creature, if it be well used: exclaim no more against it. And, good lieutenant, I think you think I love you.

Cas. I have well approved it, sir. I drunk!

Iago. You or any man living may be drunk at a time, man. I'll tell you what you shall do. Our general's wife is now the general: I may say so in this respect, for that he hath devoted and given up himself to the contemplation, mark, and denotement of her parts and graces: confess yourself freely to her; importune her help to put you in your place again: she is of so free, so kind, so apt, so blessed a disposition, she holds it a vice in her goodness not to do more than she is requested: this broken joint between you and her husband entreat her to splinter; and, my fortunes against any lay worth naming, this crack of your love shall grow stronger than it was before. 331

Cas. You advise me well.

265–270 *My reputation . . . without deserving.* See introduction.

274 *in policy.* As an example, on principle.

282 *fustian.* Bombastic nonsense.

Cassio: '. . . we should with joy, pleasance, revel and applause, transform ourselves into beasts!' Drunkards as beasts. Woodcut from the title page of T. Heywood's *Philocothonista*, 1635

301 *moraler.* Moraliser.

308 *Hydra.* Legendary many-headed serpent.

323 *denotement.* Devotion.

329 *splinter.* Bind with splints.

330 *lay.* Bet.

344 *Probal to thinking.* Reasoned.

Costume design for Iago by Le Cette, Lyric Theatre, London, 1902

351 *enfetter'd.* Bound.

352 *list.* Wishes.

363 *repeals.* Calls to mind.

390 *set her on.* Get her at it.

Iago. I protest, in the sincerity of love and honest kindness.

Cas. I think it freely; and betimes in the morning I will beseech the virtuous Desdemona to undertake for me: I am desperate of my fortunes if they check me here.

Iago. You are in the right. Good night, lieutenant; I must to the watch.   340

Cas. Good night, honest Iago.   [*Exit.*

Iago. And what's he then that says I play the villain?
When this advice is free I give and honest,
• Probal to thinking and indeed the course
To win the Moor again? For 'tis most easy
The inclining Desdemona to subdue
In any honest suit: she's framed as fruitful
As the free elements. And then for her
To win the Moor—were't to renounce his baptism,
All seals and symbols of redeemed sin,   350
• His soul is so enfetter'd to her love,
• That she may make, unmake, do what she list,
Even as her appetite shall play the god
With his weak function. How am I then a villain
To counsel Cassio to this parallel course,
Directly to his good? Divinity of hell!
When devils will the blackest sins put on,
They do suggest at first with heavenly shows,
As I do now: for whiles this honest fool
Plies Desdemona to repair his fortunes   360
And she for him pleads strongly to the Moor,
I'll pour this pestilence into his ear,
• That she repeals him for her body's lust;
And by how much she strives to do him good,
She shall undo her credit with the Moor.
So will I turn her virtue into pitch,
And out of her own goodness make the **net**
That shall enmesh them all.

Re-enter RODERIGO.

How now, Roderigo!

Rod. I do follow here in the chase, not like a hound that hunts, but one that fills up the cry. My money is almost spent; I have been to-night exceedingly well cudgelled; and I think the issue will be, I shall have so much experience for my pains, and so, with no money at all and a little more wit, return again to Venice.

Iago. How poor are they that have not patience!
What wound did ever heal but by degrees?
Thou know'st we work by wit, and not by witchcraft;
And wit depends on dilatory time.
Does't not go well? Cassio hath beaten thee,
And thou, by that small hurt, hast cashier'd Cassio: 381
Though other things grow fair against the sun,
Yet fruits that blossom first will first be ripe:
Content thyself awhile. By the mass, 'tis morning;
Pleasure and action make the hours seem short.
Retire thee; go where thou art billeted:
Away, I say; thou shalt know more hereafter:
Nay, get thee gone. [*Exit Roderigo.*] Two things are to be done:
My wife must move for Cassio to her mistress;
• I'll set her on;   390
Myself the while to draw the Moor apart,

And bring him jump when he may Cassio find
Soliciting his wife: ay, that's the way:
Dull not device by coldness and delay.   [*Exit*.

ACT III.

Scene I. *Before the castle.*

Enter Cassio *and some* Musicians.

Cas. Masters, play here; I will content your
    pains;
Something that's brief; and bid 'Good morrow,
    general.'   [*Music*.

Enter Clown.

Clo. Why, masters, have your instruments
been in Naples, that they speak i' the nose thus?
First Mus. How, sir, how!
Clo. Are these, I pray you, wind-instruments?
First Mus. Ay, marry, are they, sir.
Clo. O, thereby hangs a tail.
First Mus. Whereby hangs a tale, sir?   9
Clo. Marry, sir, by many a wind-instrument
that I know. But, masters, here's money for
you: and the general so likes your music, that he
desires you, for love's sake, to make no more noise
with it.
First Mus. Well, sir, we will not.
Clo. If you have any music that may not be
heard, to 't again: but, as they say, to hear music
the general does not greatly care.
First Mus. We have none such, sir.
Clo. Then put up your pipes in your bag, for
I 'll away: go; vanish into air; away!   21
    [*Exeunt Musicians*.
Cas. Dost thou hear, my honest friend?
Clo. No, I hear not your honest friend; I
hear you.
Cas. Prithee, keep up thy quillets. There's
a poor piece of gold for thee: if the gentlewoman
that attends the general's wife be stirring, tell her
there's one Cassio entreats her a little favour of
speech: wilt thou do this?
Clo. She is stirring, sir: if she will stir hither,
I shall seem to notify unto her.   31
Cas. Do, good my friend.   [*Exit Clown*.

Enter Iago.

                In happy time, Iago.
Iago. You have not been a-bed, then?
Cas. Why, no; the day had broke
Before we parted. I have made bold, Iago,
To send in to your wife: my suit to her
Is, that she will to virtuous Desdemona
Procure me some access.
Iago.   I 'll send her to you presently;
And I 'll devise a mean to draw the Moor
Out of the way, that your converse and business
May be more free.   41
Cas. I humbly thank you for 't. [*Exit Iago*.]
    I never knew
A Florentine more kind and honest.

Enter Emilia.

Emil. Good morrow, good lieutenant: I am
    sorry
For your displeasure; but all will sure be well.
The general and his wife are talking of it;
And she speaks for you stoutly: the Moor replies,

392 *jump*. Exactly at the time.

Group of musicians. From a Venetian woodcut, 1510

4 *speak i' the nose*. Smell (innuendo as to syphilis).

25 *quillets*. Quibbling.

49 *great affinity.* Allied to important people.

52 *front.* Forelock.

Gustavus Vaughan Brooke, English Victorian actor, as Iago.

13 *politic.* Careful.

15 *nice.* Trivial.

23 *watch him tame.* i.e. keep him awake.

24 *shrift.* Confessional.

That he you hurt is of great fame in Cyprus
● And great affinity and that in wholesome wisdom
He might not but refuse you, but he protests he
loves you   50
And needs no other suitor but his likings
● To take the safest occasion by the front
To bring you in again.
   Cas.   Yet, I beseech you,
If you think fit, or that it may be done,
Give me advantage of some brief discourse
With Desdemona alone.
   Emil.   Pray you, come in:
I will bestow you where you shall have time
To speak your bosom freely.
   Cas.   I am much bound to you. [*Exeunt.*

SCENE II.   *A room in the castle.*

Enter OTHELLO, IAGO, *and* Gentlemen.

   Oth.   These letters give, Iago, to the pilot;
And by him do my duties to the senate:
That done, I will be walking on the works;
Repair there to me.
   Iago.   Well, my good lord, I'll do't.
   Oth.   This fortification, gentlemen, shall we
see 't?
   Gent.   We'll wait upon your lordship.
                     [*Exeunt.*

SCENE III.   *The garden of the castle.*

Enter DESDEMONA, CASSIO, *and* EMILIA.

   Des.   Be thou assured, good Cassio, I will do
All my abilities in thy behalf.
   Emil.   Good madam, do: I warrant it grieves
my husband,
As if the case were his.
   Des. O, that's an honest fellow. Do not doubt,
Cassio,
But I will have my lord and you again
As friendly as you were.
   Cas.   Bounteous madam,
Whatever shall become of Michael Cassio,
He's never any thing but your true servant.
   Des. I know't; I thank you. You do love my
lord: 10
You have known him long; and be you well as-
sured
He shall in strangeness stand no further off
● Than in a politic distance.
   Cas.   Ay, but, lady,
That policy may either last so long,
● Or feed upon such nice and waterish diet,
Or breed itself so out of circumstance,
That, I being absent and my place supplied,
My general will forget my love and service.
   Des. Do not doubt that; before Emilia here
I give thee warrant of thy place: assure **thee,** 20
If I do vow a friendship, I'll perform it
To the last article: my lord shall never rest;
● I'll watch him tame and talk him out of patience;
● His bed shall seem a school, his board a shrift;
I'll intermingle every thing he does
With Cassio's suit: therefore be merry, Cassio;
For thy solicitor shall rather die
Than give thy cause away.
   Emil. Madam, here comes my lord.
   Cas. Madam, I'll take my leave.   30
   Des. Why, stay, and hear me speak.

Cas.   Madam, not now: I am very ill at ease,
Unfit for mine own purposes.
Des.   Well, do your discretion. [*Exit Cassio.*

Enter OTHELLO *and* IAGO.

Iago.   Ha! I like not that.
Oth.   What dost thou say?
Iago.   Nothing, my lord: or if—I know not
what.
Oth.   Was not that Cassio parted from my wife?
Iago.   Cassio, my lord! No, sure, I cannot
think it,
That he would steal away so guilty-like,
Seeing you coming.
Oth.   I do believe 'twas he.   40
Des.   How now, my lord!
I have been talking with a suitor here,
A man that languishes in your displeasure.
Oth.   Who is't you mean?
Des.   Why, your lieutenant, Cassio.   Good my
lord,
If I have any grace or power to move you,
His present reconciliation take;
For if he be not one that truly loves you,
That errs in ignorance and not in cunning,
I have no judgement in an honest face: 50
I prithee, call him back.
Oth.   Went he hence now?
Des.   Ay, sooth; so humbled
That he hath left part of his grief with me,
To suffer with him.   Good love, call him back.
Oth.   Not now, sweet Desdemona; some other
time.
Des.   But shall't be shortly?
Oth.   The sooner, sweet, for you.
Des.   Shall't be to-night at supper?
Oth.   No, not to-night.
Des.   To-morrow dinner, then?
Oth.   I shall not dine at home;
I meet the captains at the citadel.
Des.   Why, then, to-morrow night; or Tuesday
morn;   60
On Tuesday noon, or night; on Wednesday morn:
I prithee, name the time, but let it not
Exceed three days: in faith, he's penitent;
And yet his trespass, in our common reason—
Save that, they say, the wars must make exam-
ples
Out of their best—is not almost a fault
To incur a private check.   When shall he come?
Tell me, Othello: I wonder in my soul,
What you would ask me, that I should deny,
• Or stand so mammering on.   What! Michael
Cassio,   70
That came a-wooing with you, and so many a
time,
When I have spoke of you dispraisingly,
Hath ta'en your part; to have so much to do
To bring him in! Trust me, I could do much,—
Oth.   Prithee, no more: let him come when he
will;
I will deny thee nothing.
Des.   Why, this is not a boon;
'Tis as I should entreat you wear your gloves,
Or feed on nourishing dishes, or keep you warm,
Or sue to you to do a peculiar profit
To your own person: nay, when I have a suit 80
Wherein I mean to touch your love indeed,
It shall be full of poise and difficult weight

70 *mammering on.* Hesitating.

Othello: 'I will deny thee nothing'. The Edwardian
actors, Hubert Carter as Othello and Tita Brand as
Desdemona, Shaftesbury Theatre, London, 1905

88 *your fancies teach you.* You feel.

90 *wretch.* Used affectionately.

Othello: 'Thou dost mean something . . .' Othello with
Iago. Engraving from Bell's edition of *Shakespeare*, 1773

115 *conceit.* Conception.

120 *stops.* Breaks in speech.

122 *of custom.* Customary.

123 *close delations.* Natural hesitancy.

And fearful to be granted.
   Oth.   I will deny thee nothing:
Whereon, I do beseech thee, grant me this,
To leave me but a little to myself.
   Des.   Shall I deny you? no : farewell, my lord.
   Oth.   Farewell, my Desdemona : I'll come to
      thee straight.
   Des.   Emilia, come.   Be as your fancies teach
      you ;
Whate'er you be, I am obedient.
                [*Exeunt Desdemona and Emilia.*
   Oth.   Excellent wretch !   Perdition catch my
      soul,   90
But I do love thee ! and when I love thee not,
Chaos is come again.
   Iago.   My noble lord,—
   Oth.   What dost thou say, Iago?
   Iago.   Did Michael Cassio, when you woo'd
      my lady,
Know of your love?
   Oth.   He did, from first to last : why dost
      thou ask?
   Iago.   But for a satisfaction of my thought ;
No further harm.
   Oth.   Why of thy thought, Iago?
   Iago.   I did not think he had been acquainted
      with her.
   Oth.   O, yes ; and went between us very oft.
   Iago.   Indeed !   101
   Oth.   Indeed ! ay, indeed : discern'st thou
      aught in that?
Is he not honest?
   Iago.   Honest, my lord !
   Oth.   Honest ! ay, honest.
   Iago.   My lord, for aught I know.
   Oth.   What dost thou think?
   Iago.   Think, my lord !
   Oth.   Think, my lord !
By heaven, he echoes me,
As if there were some monster in his thought
Too hideous to be shown.   Thou dost mean some-
      thing :
I heard thee say even now, thou likedst not that,
When Cassio left my wife : what didst not like?
And when I told thee he was of my counsel   111
In my whole course of wooing, thou criedst
      'Indeed !'
And didst contract and purse thy brow together,
As if thou then hadst shut up in thy brain
Some horrible conceit : if thou dost love me,
Show me thy thought.
   Iago.   My lord, you know I love you.
   Oth.   I think thou dost ;
And, for I know thou 'rt full of love and honesty,
And weigh'st thy words before thou givest them
      breath,
Therefore these stops of thine fright me the more :
For such things in a false disloyal knave   121
Are tricks of custom, but in a man that's just
They are close delations, working from the heart
That passion cannot rule.
   Iago.   For Michael Cassio,
I dare be sworn I think that he is honest.
   Oth.   I think so too.
   Iago.   Men should be what they seem ;
Or those that be not, would they might seem none !
   Oth.   Certain, men should be what they seem.
   Iago.   Why, then, I think Cassio's an honest
      man.

Oth. Nay, yet there's more in this: 130
I prithee, speak to me as to thy thinkings,
As thou dost ruminate, and give thy worst of
    thoughts
The worst of words.
    Iago. Good my lord, pardon me:
Though I am bound to every act of duty,
I am not bound to that all slaves are free to.
Utter my thoughts? Why, say they are vile and
    false;
As where's that palace whereinto foul things
Sometimes intrude not? who has a breast so pure,
But some uncleanly apprehensions
● Keep leets and law-days and in session sit 140
With meditations lawful?
    Oth. Thou dost conspire against thy friend,
    Iago,
If thou but think'st him wrong'd and makest his ear
A stranger to thy thoughts.
    Iago. I do beseech you—
Though I perchance am vicious in my guess,
As, I confess, it is my nature's plague
To spy into abuses, and oft my jealousy
Shapes faults that are not—that your wisdom yet,
● From one that so imperfectly conceits,
Would take no notice, nor build yourself a trouble
● Out of his scattering and unsure observance. 151
It were not for your quiet nor your good,
Nor for my manhood, honesty, or wisdom,
To let you know my thoughts.
    Oth. What dost thou mean?
    Iago. Good name in man and woman, dear my
    lord,
Is the immediate jewel of their souls:
Who steals my purse steals trash; 'tis something,
    nothing;
'Twas mine, 'tis his, and has been slave to thou-
    sands;
But he that filches from me my good name
Robs me of that which not enriches him 160
And makes me poor indeed.
    Oth. By heaven, I'll know thy thoughts.
    Iago. You cannot, if my heart were in your
    hand;
Nor shall not, whilst 'tis in my custody.
    Oth. Ha!
    Iago. O, beware, my lord, of jealousy;
It is the green-eyed monster which doth mock
The meat it feeds on: that cuckold lives in bliss
Who, certain of his fate, loves not his wronger;
But, O, what damned minutes tells he o'er
Who dotes, yet doubts, suspects, yet strongly
    loves! 170
    Oth. O misery!
    Iago. Poor and content is rich and rich enough,
● But riches fineless is as poor as winter
To him that ever fears he shall be poor.
Good heaven, the souls of all my tribe defend
From jealousy!
    Oth. Why, why is this?
Think'st thou I'ld make a life of jealousy,
To follow still the changes of the moon
With fresh suspicions? No; to be once in doubt
Is once to be resolved: exchange me for a goat,
When I shall turn the business of my soul 181
● To such exsufflicate and blown surmises,
    Matching thy inference. 'Tis not to make me
    jealous
To say my wife is fair, feeds well, loves company,

140 *leets.* Courts.

149 *conceits.* Conceives.

151 *scattering.* Haphazard.

Iago: 'O beware, my lord, of jealousy'. Robert Bensley as Iago. Engraving from Bell's edition of *Shakespeare*, 1773

173 *fineless.* Limitless.

182 *exsufflicate.* Extravagant. *blown.* Inflated.

200 *self-bounty.* Generosity.

210 *seel.* Blind.

Iago: 'I see this hath a little dash'd your spirits'. Drawing of Iago and Othello by Isaac Taylor (1730–1807)

229 *affect.* Incline to.

234 *position.* Definitely.

237 *match.* Answer. *country forms.* i.e. Venetian manners, loose morality.

Is free of speech, sings, plays and dances well;
Where virtue is, these are more virtuous:
Nor from mine own weak merits will I draw
The smallest fear or doubt of her revolt;
For she had eyes, and chose me.   No, Iago;
I'll see before I doubt; when I doubt, prove: 190
And on the proof, there is no more but this,—
Away at once with love or jealousy!
 Iago.   I am glad of it; for now I shall have reason
To show the love and duty that I bear you
With franker spirit: therefore, as I am bound,
Receive it from me.   I speak not yet of proof.
Look to your wife; observe her well with Cassio;
Wear your eye thus, not jealous nor secure:
I would not have your free and noble nature,
● Out of self-bounty, be abused; look to't: 200
I know our country disposition well;
In Venice they do let heaven see the pranks
They dare not show their husbands; their best conscience
Is not to leave't undone, but keep't unknown.
 Oth.   Dost thou say so?
 Iago.   She did deceive her father, marrying you;
And when she seem'd to shake and fear your looks,
She loved them most.
 Oth.   And so she did.
 Iago.   Why, go to then;
She that, so young, could give out such a seeming,
● To seel her father's eyes up close as oak— 210
He thought 'twas witchcraft—but I am much to blame;
I humbly do beseech you of your pardon
For too much loving you.
 Oth.   I am bound to thee for ever.
 Iago.   I see this hath a little dash'd your spirits.
 Oth.   Not a jot, not a jot.
 Iago.   I' faith, I fear it has.
I hope you will consider what is spoke
Comes from my love.   But I do see you're moved:
I am to pray you not to strain my speech
To grosser issues nor to larger reach
Than to suspicion.   220
 Oth.   I will not.
 Iago.   Should you do so, my lord,
My speech should fall into such vile success
As my thoughts aim not at.   Cassio's my worthy friend—
My lord, I see you're moved.
 Oth.   No, not much moved:
I do not think but Desdemona's honest.
 Iago.   Long live she so! and long live you to think so!
 Oth.   And yet, how nature erring from itself,—
 Iago.   Ay, there's the point: as—to be bold with you—
● Not to affect many proposed matches
Of her own clime, complexion, and degree, 230
Whereto we see in all things nature tends—
Foh! one may smell in such a will most rank,
Foul disproportion, thoughts unnatural.
● But pardon me; I do not in position
Distinctly speak of her; though I may fear
Her will, recoiling to her better judgement,
● May fall to match you with her country forms
And happily repent.
 Oth.   Farewell, farewell:

If more thou dost perceive, let me know more;
Set on thy wife to observe: leave me, Iago.   240
   Iago. [*Going*] My lord, I take my leave.
   Oth. Why did I marry? This honest creature doubtless
Sees and knows more, much more, than he unfolds.
   Iago. [*Returning*] My lord, I would I might entreat your honour
To scan this thing no further; leave it to time:
Though it be fit that Cassio have his place,
For, sure, he fills it up with great ability,
Yet, if you please to hold him off awhile,
•You shall by that perceive him and his means:
•Note, if your lady strain his entertainment   250
With any strong or vehement importunity;
Much will be seen in that. In the mean time,
Let me be thought too busy in my fears—
As worthy cause I have to fear I am—
And hold her free, I do beseech your honour.
   Oth. Fear not my government.
   Iago. I once more take my leave.   [*Exit.*
   Oth. This fellow's of exceeding honesty,
And knows all qualities, with a learned spirit, 259
•Of human dealings. If I do prove her haggard,
•Though that her jesses were my dear heart-strings,
I'ld whistle her off and let her down the wind,
•To prey at fortune. Haply, for I am black
And have not those soft parts of conversation
•That chamberers have, or for I am declined
Into the vale of years,—yet that's not much—
She's gone. I am abused; and my relief
Must be to loathe her. O curse of marriage,
That we can call these delicate creatures ours,
And not their appetites! I had rather be a toad,
And live upon the vapour of a dungeon,   271
Than keep a corner in the thing I love
For others' uses. Yet, 'tis the plague of great ones;
Prerogatived are they less than the base;
'Tis destiny unshunnable, like death:
•Even then this forked plague is fated to us
•When we do quicken. Desdemona comes.

   Re-enter DESDEMONA *and* EMILIA.

If she be false, O, then heaven mocks itself!
I'll not believe 't.
   Des.   How now, my dear Othello!
Your dinner, and the generous islanders   280
By you invited, do attend your presence.
   Oth. I am to blame.
   Des.   Why do you speak so faintly?
Are you not well?
   Oth. I have a pain upon my forehead here.
   Des. 'Faith, that's with watching; 'twill away again:
Let me but bind it hard, within this hour
It will be well.
   Oth.   Your napkin is too little:
   [*He puts the handkerchief from him; and it drops.*
Let it alone. Come, I'll go in with you.
   Des. I am very sorry that you are not well.
        [*Exeunt Othello and Desdemona.*
   Emil. I am glad I have found this napkin: 290
This was her first remembrance from the Moor:
My wayward husband hath a hundred times
Woo'd me to steal it; but she so loves the token,
•For he conjured her she should ever keep it,
That she reserves it evermore about her

---

249 *his means*. What he intends.

250 *strain*. Urge. *entertainment*. Support.

260 *haggard*. Wild hawk.

261 *jesses*. Straps that held a hawk's legs.

263 *To prey at fortune*. To fend for herself.

265 *chamberers*. Gallants.

276 *forked*. Horned. i.e. cuckolded.

277 *do quicken*. Are born.

Desdemona: 'Let me but bind it hard . . .' Gertrude Elliot, English Edwardian actress, as Desdemona, Lyric Theatre, London, 1902

---

294 *conjured her*. Impressed upon her.

299 *nothing.* i.e. do nothing.

319 *Be not acknown on 't.* i.e. do not discuss the matter.

333 *owedst.* Possessed.

346 *Pioners.* Diggers, sappers.

Oscar Asche as Othello, His Majesty's Theatre, London, 1907

To kiss and talk to.   I 'll have the work ta'en out,
And give 't Iago : what he will do with it
Heaven knows, not I ;
●I nothing but to please his fantasy.

Re-enter IAGO.

Iago.   How now ! what do you here alone? 300
Emil.   Do not you chide ; I have a thing for
      you.
Iago.   A thing for me? it is a common thing—
Emil.   Ha !
Iago.   To have a foolish wife.
Emil.   O, is that all? What will you give me now
For that same handkerchief?
Iago.   What handkerchief?
Emil.   What handkerchief !
Why, that the Moor first gave to Desdemona ;
That which so often you did bid me steal.
Iago.   Hast stol'n it from her?   310
Emil.   No, 'faith ; she let it drop by negligence,
And, to the advantage, I, being here, took 't up.
Look, here it is.
Iago.   A good wench ; give it me.
Emil.   What will you do with 't, that you have
      been so earnest
To have me filch it?
Iago.   [*Snatching it*] Why, what's that to you?
Emil.   If it be not for some purpose of import,
Give 't me again : poor lady, she 'll run mad
When she shall lack it.
●*Iago.*   Be not acknown on 't ; I have use for it.
Go, leave me.   [*Exit Emilia.* 320
I will in Cassio's lodging lose this napkin,
And let him find it.   Trifles light as air
Are to the jealous confirmations strong
As proofs of holy writ : this may do something.
The Moor already changes with my poison :
Dangerous conceits are, in their natures, poisons,
Which at the first are scarce found to distaste,
But with a little act upon the blood,
Burn like the mines of sulphur.   I did say so :
Look, where he comes !

Re-enter OTHELLO.

                    Not poppy, nor mandragora, 330
Nor all the drowsy syrups of the world,
Shall ever medicine thee to that sweet sleep
●Which thou owedst yesterday.
Oth.   Ha ! ha ! false to me?
Iago.   Why, how now, general ! no more of that.
Oth.   Avaunt ! be gone ! thou hast set me on
      the rack :
I swear 'tis better to be much abused
Than but to know 't a little.
Iago.   How now, my lord !
Oth.   What sense had I of her stol'n hours of
      lust?
I saw 't not, thought it not, it harm'd not me :
I slept the next night well, was free and merry ;
I found not Cassio's kisses on her lips :   341
He that is robb'd, not wanting what is stol'n,
Let him not know 't, and he's not robb'd at all.
Iago.   I am sorry to hear this.
Oth.   I had been happy, if the general camp,
●Pioners and all, had tasted her sweet body,
So I had nothing known.   O, now, for ever
Farewell the tranquil mind ! farewell content !
Farewell the plumed troop, and the big wars,
That make ambition virtue ! O, farewell !   350

Farewell the neighing steed, and the shrill trump,
The spirit-stirring drum, the ear-piercing fife,
The royal banner, and all quality,
Pride, pomp and circumstance of glorious war!
And, O you mortal engines, whose rude throats
●The immortal Jove's dread clamours counterfeit,
Farewell! Othello's occupation's gone!
   Iago. Is't possible, my lord?
   Oth. Villain, be sure thou prove my love a
     whore,
Be sure of it; give me the ocular proof;   360
Or, by the worth of man's eternal soul,
Thou hadst been better have been born a dog
Than answer my waked wrath!
   Iago.   Is't come to this?
   Oth. Make me to see't; or, at the least, so
     prove it,
That the probation bear no hinge nor loop
To hang a doubt on; or woe upon thy life!
   Iago. My noble lord,—
   Oth. If thou dost slander her and torture me,
Never pray more; abandon all remorse;
On horror's head horrors accumulate;   370
Do deeds to make heaven weep, all earth amazed;
For nothing canst thou to damnation add
Greater than that.
   Iago.   O grace! O heaven forgive me!
Are you a man? have you a soul or sense?
God be wi' you; take mine office. O wretched fool,
That livest to make thine honesty a vice!
O monstrous world! Take note, take note, O
   world,
To be direct and honest is not safe.
I thank you for this profit; and from hence
●I'll love no friend, sith love breeds such offence.
   Oth. Nay, stay: thou shouldst be honest. 381
   Iago. I should be wise, for honesty's a fool
And loses that it works for.
   Oth.   By the world,
I think my wife be honest and think she is not;
I think that thou art just and think thou art not.
I'll have some proof. Her name, that was as
   fresh
●As Dian's visage, is now begrimed and black
As mine own face. If there be cords, or knives,
Poison, or fire, or suffocating streams,
I'll not endure it. Would I were satisfied!   390
   Iago. I see, sir, you are eaten up with passion:
I do repent me that I put it to you.
You would be satisfied?
   Oth.   Would! nay, I will.
   Iago. And may: but, how? how satisfied, my
     lord?
Would you, the supervisor, grossly gape on—
Behold her topp'd?
   Oth.   Death and damnation! O!
   Iago. It were a tedious difficulty, I think,
●To bring them to that prospect: damn them
   then,
●If ever mortal eyes do see them bolster
More than their own! What then? how then?
What shall I say? Where's satisfaction?   401
It is impossible you should see this,
Were they as prime as goats, as hot as monkeys,
●As salt as wolves in pride, and fools as gross
As ignorance made drunk. But yet, I say,
If imputation and strong circumstances,
Which lead directly to the door of truth,
Will give you satisfaction, you may have 't.

356 *Jove's dread clamours.* i.e. thunderbolts.

Othello: 'Villain, be sure thou prove my love a whore...'
Iago (Richard Burton) and Othello (John Neville), Old
Vic Theatre, London, 1955

380 *sith.* Since.

387 *Dian.* Diana, goddess of virginity.

398 *prospect.* Position.

399 *bolster.* Share a pillow.

404 *salt.* Full of lust.

416 *loose of soul*. Open.

430 *thicken*. Substantiate.

Iago: '. . . but such a handkerchief – I am sure it was your wife's . . .' John Henderson as Iago. Engraving from Bell's edition of *Shakespeare*, 1773

450 *aspics'*. Asps.

453 *Pontic sea*. Black Sea.

456 *Propontic*. Sea of Marmora. *Hellespont*. The Dardanelles.

Oth.   Give me a living reason she's disloyal.
Iago.   I do not like the office: 410
But, sith I am enter'd in this cause so far,
Prick'd to 't by foolish honesty and love,
I will go on.   I lay with Cassio lately;
And, being troubled with a raging tooth,
I could not sleep.
• There are a kind of men so loose of soul,
That in their sleeps will mutter their affairs:
One of this kind is Cassio:
In sleep I heard him say 'Sweet Desdemona,
Let us be wary, let us hide our loves;'   420
And then, sir, would he gripe and wring my hand,
Cry 'O sweet creature!' and then kiss me hard,
As if he pluck'd up kisses by the roots
That grew upon my lips: then laid his leg
Over my thigh, and sigh'd, and kiss'd; and then
Cried 'Cursed fate that gave thee to the Moor!'
   Oth.   O monstrous! monstrous!
   Iago.   Nay, this was but his dream.
   Oth.   But this denoted a foregone conclusion:
'Tis a shrewd doubt, though it be but a dream.
•   *Iago.*   And this may help to thicken other proofs   430
That do demonstrate thinly.
   Oth.   I'll tear her all to pieces.
   Iago.   Nay, but be wise: yet we see nothing done;
She may be honest yet.   Tell me but this,
Have you not sometimes seen a handkerchief
Spotted with strawberries in your wife's hand?
   Oth.   I gave her such a one; 'twas my first gift.
   Iago.   I know not that: but such a handkerchief—
I am sure it was your wife's—did I to-day
See Cassio wipe his beard with.
   Oth.   If it be that,—
   Iago.   If it be that, or any that was hers,   440
It speaks against her with the other proofs.
   Oth.   O, that the slave had forty thousand lives!
One is too poor, too weak for my revenge.
Now do I see 'tis true.   Look here, Iago;
All my fond love thus do I blow to heaven.
'Tis gone.
Arise, black vengeance, from thy hollow cell!
Yield up, O love, thy crown and hearted throne
To tyrannous hate!   Swell, bosom, with thy fraught,
• For 'tis of aspics' tongues!
   Iago.   Yet be content.   450
   Oth.   O, blood, blood, blood!
   Iago.   Patience, I say; your mind perhaps may change.
•   *Oth.*   Never, Iago.   Like to the Pontic sea,
Whose icy current and compulsive course
Ne'er feels retiring ebb, but keeps due on
• To the Propontic and the Hellespont,
Even so my bloody thoughts, with violent pace,
Shall ne'er look back, ne'er ebb to humble love,
Till that a capable and wide revenge
Swallow them up.   Now, by yond marble heaven,   460
[*Kneels*] In the due reverence of a sacred vow
I here engage my words.
   Iago.   Do not rise yet.
[*Kneels*] Witness, you ever-burning lights above,

You elements that clip us round about,
Witness that here Iago doth give up
The execution of his wit, hands, heart,
To wrong'd Othello's service! Let him command,
And to obey shall be in me remorse,
What bloody business ever.   [*They rise.*
    Oth.   I greet thy love,
Not with vain thanks, but with acceptance bounteous,   470
And will upon the instant put thee to 't:
Within these three days let me hear thee say
That Cassio's not alive.
    Iago. My friend is dead; 'tis done at your request:
But let her live.
    Oth.   Damn her, lewd minx! O, damn her!
Come, go with me apart; I will withdraw,
To furnish me with some swift means of death
For the fair devil.   Now art thou my lieutenant.
    Iago. I am your own for ever.   [*Exeunt.*

SCENE IV. *Before the castle.*

Enter DESDEMONA, EMILIA, *and* Clown.

    Des. Do you know, sirrah, where Lieutenan
Cassio lies?
    Clo. I dare not say he lies any where.
    Des. Why, man?
    Clo. He's a soldier, and for one to say a
soldier lies, is stabbing.
    Des. Go to: where lodges he?
    Clo. To tell you where he lodges, is to tell
you where I lie.
    Des. Can any thing be made of this?   10
    Clo. I know not where he lodges, and for me
to devise a lodging and say he lies here or he
lies there, were to lie in mine own throat.
    Des. Can you inquire him out, and be edified
by report?
    Clo. I will catechize the world for him; that
is, make questions, and by them answer.
    Des. Seek him, bid him come hither: tell
him I have moved my lord on his behalf, and
hope all will be well.   20
    Clo. To do this is within the compass of man's
wit; and therefore I will attempt the doing it.
                              [*Exit.*
    Des. Where should I lose that handkerchief,
Emilia?
    Emil. I know not, madam.
    Des. Believe me, I had rather have lost my
purse
Full of crusadoes: and, but my noble Moor
Is true of mind and made of no such baseness
As jealous creatures are, it were enough
To put him to ill thinking.
    Emil.   Is he not jealous?
    Des. Who, he? I think the sun where he was
born   30
Drew all such humours from him.
    Emil.   Look, where he comes.
    Des. I will not leave him now till Cassio
Be call'd to him.

Enter OTHELLO.

              How is 't with you, my lord?
    Oth. Well, my good lady. [*Aside*] O, hardness to dissemble!—

Lily Brayton as Desdemona, His Majesty's Theatre, London, 1907

1 *sirrah.* Sir.

26 *crusadoes.* Gold coins.

31 *humours.* Feelings.

51 *salt and sorry rheum.* A streaming cold.

Othello: 'I have a salt . . . Lend me thy handkerchief'.
Brewster Mason as Othello and Lisa Harrow as Desdemona, Royal Shakespeare Co, 1971

55-74 *That handkerchief . . . mummy.* See introduction.

69 *web.* Weave.

70 *sibyl.* Prophetess.

74 *mummy.* A preparation from embalmed bodies.

How do you, Desdemona?
  Des.   Well, my good lord.
  Oth. Give me your hand: this hand is **moist**,
    my lady.
  Des. It yet hath felt no age nor known **no**
    sorrow.
  Oth. This argues fruitfulness and liberal
    heart:
Hot, hot, and moist: this hand of **yours** requires
A sequester from liberty, fasting and prayer,   40
Much castigation, exercise devout;
For here's a young and sweating devil here,
That commonly rebels. 'Tis a good hand,
A frank one.
  Des.   You may, indeed, say so;
For 'twas that hand that gave away my heart.
  Oth. A liberal hand: the hearts of old gave
    hands;
But our new heraldry is hands, not hearts.
  Des. I cannot speak of this. Come **now**, your
    promise.
  Oth. What promise, chuck?
  Des. I have sent to bid Cassio come speak
    with you.   50
● *Oth.* I have a salt and sorry rheum offends me;
Lend me thy handkerchief.
  Des.   Here, my lord.
  Oth. That which I gave you.
  Des.   I have it not **about** me.
  Oth. Not?
  Des.   No, indeed, my lord.
  Oth.   That is a fault.
●That handkerchief
Did an Egyptian to my mother give;
She was a charmer, and could almost read
The thoughts of people: she told her, while she
    kept it,
'Twould make her amiable and subdue my **father**
Entirely to her love, but if she lost it   60
Or made a gift of it, my father's eye
Should hold her loathed and his spirits should
    hunt
After new fancies: she, dying, gave it me;
And bid me, when my fate would have me wive,
To give it her. I did so: and take heed on 't;
Make it a darling like your precious eye;
To lose 't or give 't away were such perdition
As nothing else could match.
  Des.   Is't possible?
● *Oth.* 'Tis true: there's magic in the web of it:
●A sibyl, that had number'd in the world   70
The sun to course two hundred compasses,
In her prophetic fury sew'd the work;
The worms were hallow'd that did breed the silk;
●And it was dyed in mummy which the skilful
Conserved of maidens' hearts.
  Des.   Indeed! is't true?
  Oth. Most veritable; therefore look to 't well.
  Des. Then would to God that I had never
    seen 't!
  Oth. Ha! wherefore?
  Des. Why do you speak so startingly and rash?
  Oth. Is't lost? is't gone? speak, is it out o'
    the way?   80
  Des. Heaven bless us!
  Oth. Say you?
  Des. It is not lost; but what an if it were?
  Oth. How!
  Des. I say, it is not lost.

Oth.   Fetch 't, let me see 't.
Des.   Why, so I can, sir, but I will not now.
This is a trick to put me from my suit:
Pray you, let Cassio be received again.
Oth.   Fetch me the handkerchief: my mind
   misgives.
Des.   Come, come;   90
You 'll never meet a more sufficient man.
Oth.   The handkerchief!
Des.   I pray, talk me of Cassio.
Oth.   The handkerchief!
Des.   A man that all his time
Hath founded his good fortunes on your love,
Shared dangers with you,—
Oth.   The handkerchief!
Des.   In sooth, you are to blame.
Oth. Away!   [*Exit.*
Emil.   Is not this man jealous?
Des.   I ne'er saw this before.   100
Sure, there 's some wonder in this handkerchief:
I am most unhappy in the loss of it.
Emil.   'Tis not a year or two shows us a man:
They are all but stomachs, and we all but food;
They eat us hungerly, and when they are full,
They belch us.   Look you, Cassio and my hus-
   band!

Enter CASSIO *and* IAGO.

Iago.   There is no other way; 'tis she must do 't:
And, lo, the happiness! go, and importune her.
Des.   How now, good Cassio! what 's the news
   with you?
Cas.   Madam, my former suit: I do beseech you
That by your virtuous means I may again   111
Exist, and be a member of his love
Whom I with all the office of my heart
Entirely honour: I would not be delay'd.
If my offence be of such mortal kind
That nor my service past, nor present sorrows,
Nor purposed merit in futurity,
Can ransom me into his love again,
But to know so must be my benefit;
So shall I clothe me in a forced content,   120
And shut myself up in some other course,
To fortune's alms.
Des.   Alas, thrice-gentle Cassio!
My advocation is not now in tune;
My lord is not my lord; nor should I know him,
Were he in favour as in humour alter'd.
So help me every spirit sanctified,
As I have spoken for you all my best
•And stood within the blank of his displeasure
For my free speech! you must awhile be patient:
What I can do I will; and more I will   130
Than for myself I dare: let that suffice you.
Iago.   Is my lord angry?
Emil.   He went hence but now,
And certainly in strange unquietness.
Iago.   Can he be angry?   I have seen the
   cannon,
When it hath blown his ranks into the air,
And, like the devil, from his very arm
Puff'd his own brother:—and can he be angry?
Something of moment then: I will go meet him:
There 's matter in't indeed, if he be angry.
Des.   I prithee, do so.   [*Exit Iago.*
   Something, sure, of state,   140
•Either from Venice, or some unhatch'd practice
Made demonstrable here in Cyprus to him,

Desdemona: 'My advocation is not now in tune.' Cassio (David Calder), Desdemona (Lisa Harrow) and Iago (Emrys James) Royal Shakespeare Co, 1971

---

128 *blank.* Target.

141 *unhatch'd practice.* Unconcluded plan.

Costume design for Desdemona by Le Cette, Lyric Theatre, London, 1902

143 *puddled.* Muddied.

146 *indues.* Encourages.

178 *continuate.* Convenient.

●Hath puddled his clear spirit; and in such cases
Men's natures wrangle with inferior things,
Though great ones are their object. 'Tis even so;
●For let our finger ache, and it indues
Our other healthful members even to that sense
Of pain: nay, we must think men are not gods,
Nor of them look for such observances
As fit the bridal   Beshrew me much, Emilia, 150
I was, unhandsome warrior as I am,
Arraigning his unkindness with my soul;
But now I find I had suborn'd the witness,
And he's indicted falsely.
   Emil.   Pray heaven it be state-matters, as you
     think,
And no conception nor no jealous toy
Concerning you.
   Des.   Alas the day! I never gave him cause.
   Emil.   But jealous souls will not be answer'd so;
They are not ever jealous for the cause,   160
But jealous for they are jealous: 'tis a monster
Begot upon itself, born on itself.
   Des.   Heaven keep that monster from Othello's
     mind!
   Emil.   Lady, amen.
   Des.   I will go seek him.   Cassio, walk here-
     about:
If I do find him fit, I'll move your suit
And seek to effect it to my uttermost.
   Cas.   I humbly thank your ladyship.
          [*Exeunt Desdemona and Emilia.*

     Enter BIANCA.

   Bian.   Save you, friend Cassio!
   Cas.   What make you from home?
How is it with you, my most fair Bianca?   170
I' faith, sweet love, I was coming to your house.
   Bian.   And I was going to your lodging, Cassio.
What, keep a week away? seven days and nights?
Eight score eight hours? and lovers' absent hours,
More tedious than the dial eight score times?
O weary reckoning!
   Cas.   Pardon me, Bianca:
I have this while with leaden thoughts been
     press'd;
●But I shall, in a more continuate time,
Strike off this score of absence.   Sweet Bianca,
    [*Giving her Desdemona's handkerchief.*
Take me this work out.
   Bian.   O Cassio, whence came this? 180
This is some token from a newer friend:
To the felt absence now I feel a cause:
Is't come to this?   Well, well.
   Cas.   Go to, woman!
Throw your vile guesses in the devil's teeth,
From whence you have them.   You are jealous
     now
That this is from some mistress, some remem-
     brance:
No, in good troth, Bianca.
   Bian.   Why, whose is it?
   Cas.   I know not, sweet: I found it in my
     chamber.
I like the work well: ere it be demanded—
As like enough it will—I 'ld have it copied: 190
Take it, and do't; and leave me for this time.
   Bian.   Leave you! wherefore?
   Cas.   I do attend here on the general;
And think it no addition, nor my wish,
To have him see me woman'd.

Bian.   Why, I pray you?
Cas. Not that I love you not.
Bian.   But that you do not love me.
I pray you, bring me on the way a little,
And say if I shall see you soon at night.
Cas. 'Tis but a little way that I can bring you;
For I attend here: but I'll see you soon.   200
• Bian. 'Tis very good; I must be circumstanced.
                              [Exeunt.

ACT IV.

SCENE I. Cyprus. Before the castle.

Enter OTHELLO and IAGO.

Iago. Will you think so?
Oth.   Think so, Iago!
Iago.   What,
To kiss in private?
Oth.   An unauthorized kiss.
Iago. Or to be naked with her friend in bed
An hour or more, not meaning any harm?
Oth. Naked in bed, Iago, and not mean harm!
It is hypocrisy against the devil:
They that mean virtuously, and yet do so,
The devil their virtue tempts, and they tempt
heaven.
Iago. So they do nothing, 'tis a venial slip:
But if I give my wife a handkerchief,—   10
Oth. What then?
Iago. Why, then, 'tis hers, my lord; and,
being hers,
She may, I think, bestow't on any man.
Oth. She is protectress of her honour too:
May she give that?
Iago. Her honour is an essence that's not seen;
They have it very oft that have it not:
But, for the handkerchief,—
Oth. By heaven, I would most gladly have
forgot it.
Thou said'st—O, it comes o'er my memory,   20
As doth the raven o'er the infected house,
Boding to all—he had my handkerchief.
Iago. Ay, what of that?
Oth.   That's not so good now.
Iago.   What,
If I had said I had seen him do you wrong?
Or heard him say,—as knaves be such abroad,
Who having, by their own importunate suit,
Or voluntary dotage of some mistress,
Convinced or supplied them, cannot choose
But they must blab—
Oth.   Hath he said any thing?
Iago. He hath, my lord; but be you well
assured,   30
No more than he'll unswear.
Oth.   What hath he said?
Iago. 'Faith, that he did—I know not what he
did.
Oth. What? what?
Iago. Lie—
Oth.   With her?
Iago.   With her, on her; what you will.
Oth. Lie with her! lie on her! We say lie on
her, when they belie her. Lie with her! that's
fulsome.—Handkerchief—confessions—handker-
chief!—To confess, and be hanged for his labour;
—first, to be hanged, and then to confess.—I
tremble at it. Nature would not invest herself in

Charles Dillon, the Victorian actor, as Othello, Theatre
Royal, Drury Lane, London, 1869

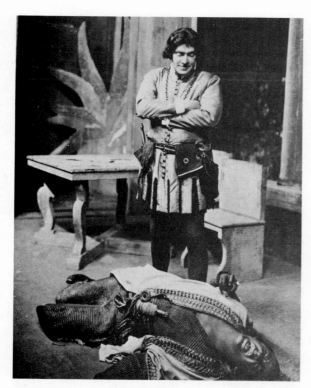

Iago: 'Work on, My medicine, work! . . .' Othello falls into a trance. Arthur Bouchier as Iago and Matheson Lang as Othello, New Theatre, London, 1920

70 *peculiar.* Only their own.

76 *in a patient list.* Patiently.

80 *ecstasy.* Rage.

83 *fleers.* Jeers.

87 *cope.* Top.

such shadowing passion without some instruction. It is not words that shake me thus. Pish! Noses, ears, and lips.—Is't possible?—Confess—hand-kerchief!—O devil!   [*Falls in a trance.*
Iago.   Work on,
My medicine, work! Thus credulous fools are caught;
And many worthy and chaste dames even thus,
All guiltless, meet reproach. What, ho! my lord!
My lord, I say! Othello!

Enter CASSIO.

                    How now, Cassio!
Cas.   What's the matter?   50
Iago.   My lord is fall'n into an epilepsy:
This is his second fit; he had one yesterday.
Cas.   Rub him about the temples.
Iago.   No, forbear;
The lethargy must have his quiet course:
If not, he foams at mouth and by and by
Breaks out to savage madness.   Look, he stirs:
Do you withdraw yourself a little while,
He will recover straight: when he is gone,
I would on great occasion speak with you.   59
                    [*Exit Cassio.*
How is it, general? have you not hurt your head?
Oth.   Dost thou mock me?
Iago.   I mock you! no, by heaven.
Would you would bear your fortune like a man!
Oth.   A horned man's a monster and a beast.
Iago.   There's many a beast then in a populous city,
And many a civil monster.
Oth.   Did he confess it?
Iago.   Good sir, be a man;
Think every bearded fellow that's but yoked
May draw with you: there's millions now alive
That nightly lie in those unproper beds
●Which they dare swear peculiar: your case is better.   70
O, 'tis the spite of hell, the fiend's arch-mock,
To lip a wanton in a secure couch,
And to suppose her chaste!   No, let me know;
And knowing what I am, I know what she shall be.
Oth.   O, thou art wise; 'tis certain.
Iago.   Stand you awhile apart;
●Confine yourself but in a patient list.
Whilst you were here o'erwhelmed with your grief—
A passion most unsuiting such a man—
Cassio came hither: I shifted him away,
●And laid good 'scuse upon your ecstasy,   80
Bade him anon return and here speak with me;
The which he promised.   Do but encave yourself,
●And mark the fleers, the gibes, and notable scorns,
That dwell in every region of his face;
For I will make him tell the tale anew,
Where, how, how oft, how long ago, and when
●He hath, and is again to cope your wife:
I say, but mark his gesture.   Marry, patience;
Or I shall say you are all in all in spleen,
And nothing of a man.
Oth.   Dost thou hear, Iago?   90
I will be found most cunning in my patience;
But—dost thou hear?—most bloody.
Iago.   That's not amiss;
But yet keep time in all.   Will you withdraw?
                    [*Othello retires.*

Now will I question Cassio of Bianca,
A housewife that by selling her desires
Buys herself bread and clothes: it is a creature
That dotes on Cassio; as 'tis the strumpet's plague
To beguile many and be beguiled by one:
He, when he hears of her, cannot refrain 99
From the excess of laughter. Here he comes:

Re-enter CASSIO.

As he shall smile, Othello shall go mad;
And his unbookish jealousy must construe
Poor Cassio's smiles, gestures and light behaviour,
Quite in the wrong. How do you now, lieutenant?
● *Cas.* The worser that you give me the addition
Whose want even kills me.
Iago. Ply Desdemona well, and you are sure
on 't.
[*Speaking lower*] Now, if this suit lay in Bianca's
power,
●How quickly should you speed!
Cas. Alas, poor caitiff!
Oth. Look, how he laughs already! 110
Iago. I never knew woman love man so.
Cas. Alas, poor rogue! I think, i' faith, she
loves me.
Oth. Now he denies it faintly, and laughs it
out.
Iago. Do you hear, Cassio?
Oth. Now he importunes him
To tell it o'er: go to; well said, well said.
Iago. She gives it out that you shall marry
her:
Do you intend it?
Cas. Ha, ha, ha! 120
Oth. Do you triumph, Roman? do you tri-
umph?
● *Cas.* I marry her! what? a customer! Pri-
thee, bear some charity to my wit; do not think
it so unwholesome. Ha, ha, ha!
Oth. So, so, so, so: they laugh that win.
Iago. 'Faith, the cry goes that you shall marry
her.
Cas. Prithee, say true.
Iago. I am a very villain else.
Oth. Have you scored me? Well. 130
Cas. This is the monkey's own giving out:
she is persuaded I will marry her, out of her own
love and flattery, not out of my promise.
Oth. Iago beckons me; now he begins the
story.
Cas. She was here even now; she haunts me
in every place. I was the other day talking on
the sea-bank with certain Venetians; and thither
comes the bauble, and, by this hand, she falls me
thus about my neck— 140
Oth. Crying 'O dear Cassio!' as it were:
his gesture imports it.
Cas. So hangs, and lolls, and weeps upon me;
●so hales, and pulls me: ha, ha, ha!
Oth. Now he tells how she plucked him to
my chamber. O, I see that nose of yours, but
not that dog I shall throw it to.
Cas. Well, I must leave her company.
Iago. Before me! look, where she comes.
● *Cas.* 'Tis such another fitchew! marry, a perfumed one. 151

Enter BIANCA.

What do you mean by this haunting of me?

105 *addition*. i.e. title of lieutenant.

109 *caitiff*. Wretch.

Othello: 'Look, how he laughs already!' Engraving by
Kenny Meadows from Barry Cornwall's *Works of
Shakspere*, 1846

122 *customer*. One who takes trade. i.e. prostitute.

144 *hales*. Drags.

150 *fitchew*. Polecat, whore.

153 *dam.* Mate.

160 *hobby-horse.* Whore.

188 *nine years a-killing.* Take nine years to kill.

209 *patent.* Licence.

211 *messes.* Pieces of meat.

218 *unprovide.* Sway.

● *Bian.* Let the devil and his dam haunt you! What did you mean by that same handkerchief you gave me even now? I was a fine fool to take it. I must take out the work?—A likely piece of work, that you should find it in your chamber, and not know who left it there! This is some minx's token, and I must take out the work?
●There; give it your hobby-horse: wheresoever you had it, I'll take out no work on 't.   161
   Cas. How now, my sweet Bianca! how now! how now!
   Oth. By heaven, that should be my hand-kerchief!
   Bian. An you'll come to supper to-night, you may; an you will not, come when you are next prepared for.   [*Exit.*
   Iago. After her, after her.
   Cas. 'Faith, I must; she'll rail in the street else.   171
   Iago. Will you sup there?
   Cas. 'Faith, I intend so.
   Iago. Well, I may chance to see you: for I would very fain speak with you.
   Cas. Prithee, come; will you?
   Iago. Go to; say no more.   [*Exit Cassio.*
   Oth. [*Advancing*] How shall I murder him, Iago?
   Iago. Did you perceive how he laughed at his vice?   181
   Oth. O Iago!
   Iago. And did you see the handkerchief?
   Oth. Was that mine?
   Iago. Yours, by this hand: and to see how he prizes the foolish woman your wife! she gave it him, and he hath given it his whore.
● *Oth.* I would have him nine years a-killing. A fine woman! a fair woman! a sweet woman!
   Iago. Nay, you must forget that.   190
   Oth. Ay, let her rot, and perish, and be damned to-night; for she shall not live: no, my heart is turned to stone; I strike it, and it hurts my hand. O, the world hath not a sweeter crea-ture: she might lie by an emperor's side and command him tasks.
   Iago. Nay, that's not your way.
   Oth. Hang her! I do but say what she is: so delicate with her needle: an admirable musician: O! she will sing the savageness out of a bear: of so high and plenteous wit and invention:— 201
   Iago. She's the worse for all this.
   Oth. O, a thousand thousand times: and then, of so gentle a condition!
   Iago. Ay, too gentle.
   Oth. Nay, that's certain: but yet the pity of it, Iago! O Iago, the pity of it, Iago!
   Iago. If you are so fond over her iniquity,
●give her patent to offend; for, if it touch not you, it comes near nobody.   210
● *Oth.* I will chop her into messes: cuckold me!
   Iago. O, 'tis foul in her.
   Oth. With mine officer!
   Iago. That's fouler.
   Oth. Get me some poison, Iago; this night: I'll not expostulate with her, lest her body and
●beauty unprovide my mind again: this night, Iago.   219
   Iago. Do it not with poison, strangle her in her bed, even the bed she hath contaminated.

Oth. Good, good: the justice of it pleases: very good.

Iago. And for Cassio, let me be his undertaker: you shall hear more by midnight.

Oth. Excellent good. [*A trumpet within.*] What trumpet is that same?

Iago. Something from Venice, sure. 'Tis Lodovico
Come from the duke: and, see, your wife is with him.

Enter LODOVICO, DESDEMONA, *and* Attendants.

Lod. Save you, worthy general!

Oth.   With all my heart, sir.

Lod. The duke and senators of Venice greet you.   [*Gives him a letter.*

Oth. I kiss the instrument of their pleasures.
                    [*Opens the letter, and reads.*

Des. And what's the news, good cousin Lodovico?

Iago. I am very glad to see you, signior;
Welcome to Cyprus.

Lod. I thank you. How does Lieutenant Cassio?

Iago. Lives, sir.

Des. Cousin, there's fall'n between him and my lord
An unkind breach: but you shall make all well.

Oth. Are you sure of that?

Des. My lord?

Oth. [*Reads*] 'This fail you not to do, as you will—'   240

Lod. He did not call; he's busy in the paper.
Is there division 'twixt my lord and Cassio?

Des. A most unhappy one: I would do much
To atone them, for the love I bear to Cassio.

Oth. Fire and brimstone!

Des.   My lord?

Oth.   Are you wise?

Des. What, is he angry?

Lod.   May be the letter moved him;
For, as I think, they do command him home,
Deputing Cassio in his government.

Des. Trust me, I am glad on't.

Oth.   Indeed!

Des.   My lord?

Oth. I am glad to see you mad.

Des.   Why, sweet Othello,—   250

Oth. [*Striking her*] Devil!

Des. I have not deserved this.

Lod. My lord, this would not be believed in Venice,
Though I should swear I saw't: 'tis very much:
Make her amends; she weeps.

Oth.   O devil, devil!
If that the earth could teem with woman's tears,
●Each drop she falls would prove a crocodile.
Out of my sight!

Des.   I will not stay to offend you. [*Going.*

Lod. Truly, an obedient lady:
I do beseech·your lordship, call her back.   260

Oth. Mistress!

Des.   My lord?

Oth.   What would you with her, sir?

Lod. Who, I, my lord?

Oth. Ay; you did wish that I would make her turn:
Sir, she can turn, and turn, and yet go on,

F. R. Benson, the Edwardian actor, as Othello, Globe Theatre, London, 1890

257 *falls.* Lets fall.

271 *avaunt.* Away.

Costume design for Lodovico by Carleton Smyth, New Theatre, London, 1920

12 *durst.* Dare.

And turn again; and she can weep, sir, weep;
And she's obedient, as you say, obedient,
Very obedient.   Proceed you in your tears.
Concerning this, sir,—O well-painted passion!—
I am commanded home.   Get you away;   269
I'll send for you anon.   Sir, I obey the mandate,
● And will return to Venice.   Hence, avaunt!
                              [*Exit Desdemona.*
Cassio shall have my place.   And, sir, to-night,
I do entreat that we may sup together:
You are welcome, sir, to Cyprus.—Goats and
          monkeys!   [*Exit.*
  Lod.   Is this the noble Moor whom our full
          senate
Call all in all sufficient?   Is this the nature
Whom passion could not shake? whose solid
          virtue
The shot of accident, nor dart of chance,
Could neither graze nor pierce?
  Iago.   He is much changed.
  Lod.   Are his wits safe? is he not light of
          brain?   280
  Iago.   He's that he is: I may not breathe my
          censure
What he might be: if what he might he is not,
I would to heaven he were!
  Lod.   What, strike his wife!
  Iago.   'Faith, that was not so well; yet would
          I knew
That stroke would prove the worst!
  Lod.   Is it his use?
Or did the letters work upon his blood,
And new-create this fault?
  Iago.   Alas, alas!
It is not honesty in me to speak
What I have seen and known.   You shall observe
          him,
And his own courses will denote him so   290
That I may save my speech: do but go after,
And mark how he continues.
  Lod.   I am sorry that I am deceived in him.
                              [*Exeunt.*

Scene II.   *A room in the castle.*

Enter Othello *and* Emilia.

  Oth.   You have seen nothing then?
  Emil.   Nor ever heard, nor ever did suspect.
  Oth.   Yes, you have seen Cassio and she
          together.
  Emil.   But then I saw no harm, and then I
          heard
Each syllable that breath made up between them.
  Oth.   What, did they never whisper?
  Emil.   Never, my lord.
  Oth.   Nor send you out o' the way?
  Emil.   Never.
  Oth.   To fetch her fan, her gloves, her mask,
          nor nothing?
  Emil.   Never, my lord.   10
  Oth.   That's strange.
● *Emil.*   I durst, my lord, to wager she is honest,
Lay down my soul at stake: if you think other,
Remove your thought; it doth abuse your bosom.
If any wretch have put this in your head,
Let heaven requite it with the serpent's curse!
For, if she be not honest, chaste, and true,
There's no man happy; the purest of their wives
Is foul as slander.

Oth.   Bid her come hither: go.
                [Exit Emilia.
She says enough; yet she's a simple bawd   20
That cannot say as much. This is a subtle whore,
● A closet lock and key of villanous secrets:
And yet she'll kneel and pray; I have seen
    her do't.

    Enter DESDEMONA *with* EMILIA.

Des. My lord, what is your will?
Oth.   Pray, chuck, come hither.
Des. What is your pleasure?
Oth.   Let me see your eyes;
Look in my face.
Des.   What horrible fancy's this?
Oth. [*To Emilia*] Some of your function,
    mistress;
Leave procreants alone and shut the door;
Cough, or cry 'hem,' if any body come:
Your mystery, your mystery: nay, dispatch.   30
                [Exit Emilia.
● *Des.* Upon my knees, what doth your speech
    import?
I understand a fury in your words,
But not the words.
Oth. Why, what art thou?
Des.   Your wife, my lord; your true
And loyal wife.
Oth.   Come, swear it, damn thyself;
Lest, being like one of heaven, the devils them-
    selves
Should fear to seize thee: therefore be double
    damn'd:
Swear thou art honest.
Des.   Heaven doth truly know it.
Oth. Heaven truly knows that thou art false
    as hell.
Des. To whom, my lord? with whom? how
    am I false?   40
Oth. O Desdemona! away! away! away!
Des. Alas the heavy day! Why do you weep?
Am I the motive of these tears, my lord?
If haply you my father do suspect
An instrument of this your calling back,
Lay not your blame on me: if you have lost him,
Why, I have lost him too.
Oth.   Had it pleased heaven
To try me with affliction; had they rain'd
All kinds of sores and shames on my bare head,
Steep'd me in poverty to the very lips,   50
Given to captivity me and my utmost hopes,
I should have found in some place of my soul
A drop of patience: but, alas, to make me
A fixed figure for the time of scorn
To point his slow unmoving finger at!
Yet could I bear that too; well, very well:
But there, where I have garner'd up my heart,
Where either I must live, or bear no life;
The fountain from the which my current runs,
Or else dries up; to be discarded thence!   60
Or keep it as a cistern for foul toads
● To knot and gender in! Turn thy complexion
    there,
Patience, thou young and rose-lipp'd cherubin,—
Ay, there, look grim as hell!
Des. I hope my noble lord esteems me honest.
● *Oth.* O, ay; as summer flies are in the sham-
    bles,
● That quicken even with blowing. O thou weed,

22 *closet lock and key.* Secure hiding place.

31 *import.* Mean.

Othello: 'Come, swear it, damn thyself . . . Swear thou art honest.' Othello (Laurence Olivier) and Desdemona (Billie Whitelaw), National Theatre, London, 1964

62 *knot and gender.* Couple and reproduce.

66 *shambles.* Slaughter house.

67 *quicken.* Live.

70 *ignorant.* Unknown.

73 *commoner.* Prostitute.

83 *vessel.* Body.

Othello: 'What, not a whore?' Othello (Brewster Mason) and Desdemona (Lisa Harrow), Royal Shakespeare Co, 1971

94 *keep our counsel.* Keep quiet.

104 *what should go by water.* What good will tears be.

Who art so lovely fair and smell'st so sweet
That the sense aches at thee, would thou hadst
  ne'er been born!
    Des. Alas, what ignorant sin have I com-
      mitted?   70
    Oth. Was this fair paper, this most goodly
      book,
Made to write 'whore' upon?   What committed!
Committed!   O thou public commoner!
I should make very forges of my cheeks,
That would to cinders burn up modesty,
Did I but speak thy deeds.   What committed!
Heaven stops the nose at it and the moon winks,
The bawdy wind that kisses all it meets
Is hush'd within the hollow mine of earth,
And will not hear it.   What committed!   80
Impudent strumpet!
    Des.   By heaven, you do me wrong.
    Oth. Are not you a strumpet?
    Des.   No, as I am a Christian:
If to preserve this vessel for my lord
From any other foul unlawful touch
Be not to be a strumpet, I am none.
    Oth. What, not a whore?
    Des.   No, as I shall be saved.
    Oth. Is't possible?
    Des. O, heaven forgive us!
    Oth.   I cry you mercy, then:
I took you for that cunning whore of Venice
That married with Othello.   [*Raising his voice*]
      You, mistress,   90
That have the office opposite to Saint Peter,
And keep the gate of hell!

        Re-enter EMILIA.

                 You, you, ay, you!
We have done our course; there's money for
  your pains:
I pray you, turn the key and keep our counsel.
                     [*Exit.*
    Emil. Alas, what does this gentleman con-
      ceive?
How do you, madam? how do you, my good
  lady?
    Des. 'Faith, half asleep.
    Emil. Good madam, what's the matter with
      my lord?
    Des. With who?
    Emil. Why, with my lord, madam.   100
    Des. Who is thy lord?
    Emil.   He that is yours, sweet lady.
    Des. I have none: do not talk to me, Emilia;
I cannot weep; nor answer have I none,
But what should go by water.   Prithee, to-night
Lay on my bed my wedding sheets: remember;
And call thy husband hither.
    Emil.   Here's a change indeed! [*Exit.*
    Des. 'Tis meet I should be used so, very meet.
How have I been behaved, that he might stick
The small'st opinion on my least misuse?

      Re-enter EMILIA *with* IAGO.

    Iago. What is your pleasure, madam?   How
    is't with you?   110
    Des. I cannot tell.   Those that do teach
    young babes
Do it with gentle means and easy tasks:
He might have chid me so; for, in good faith,
I am a child to chiding.

Iago.   What's the matter, lady?
Emil. Alas, Iago, my lord hath so bewhored
          her,
Thrown such despite and heavy terms upon her,
As true hearts cannot bear.
     Des. Am I that name, Iago?
     Iago.   What name, fair lady?
     Des. Such as she says my lord did say I was.
     Emil. He call'd her whore: a beggar in his
          drink   120
● Could not have laid such terms upon his callet.
     Iago. Why did he so?
     Des. I do not know; I am sure I am none
          such.
     Iago. Do not weep, do not weep. Alas the
          day!
     Emil. Hath she forsook so many noble matches,
Her father and her country and her friends,
To be call'd whore? would it not make one weep?
     Des. It is my wretched fortune.
     Iago.   Beshrew him for't!
How comes this trick upon him?
     Des.   Nay, heaven doth know.
     Emil. I will be hang'd, if some eternal villain,
Some busy and insinuating rogue,   131
● Some cogging, cozening slave, to get some office,
Have not devised this slander; I'll be hang'd
          else.
     Iago. Fie, there is no such man; it is impos-
          sible.
     Des. If any such there be, heaven pardon him!
● *Emil.* A halter pardon him! and hell gnaw
          his bones!
Why should he call her whore? who keeps her
          company?
What place? what time? what form? what likeli-
          hood?
The Moor's abused by some most villanous knave,
Some base notorious knave, some scurvy fellow.
O heaven, that such companions thou'ldst unfold,
And put in every honest hand a whip
To lash the rascals naked through the world
Even from the east to the west!
     Iago.   Speak within door.
     Emil. O, fie upon them! Some such squire
          he was
That turn'd your wit the seamy side without,
And made you to suspect me with the Moor.
     Iago. You are a fool; go to.
     Des.   O good Iago,
What shall I do to win my lord again?
Good friend, go to him; for, by this light of
          heaven,   150
I know not how I lost him. Here I kneel:
If e'er my will did trespass 'gainst his love,
● Either in discourse of thought or actual deed,
Or that mine eyes, mine ears, or any sense,
Delighted them in any other form;
Or that I do not yet, and ever did,
And ever will—though he do shake me off
To beggarly divorcement—love him dearly,
Comfort forswear me! Unkindness may do much;
And his unkindness may defeat my life,   160
But never taint my love. I cannot say 'whore:'
It doth abhor me now I speak the word;
To do the act that might the addition earn
Not the world's mass of vanity could make me.
     Iago. I pray you, be content; 'tis but his
          humour:

121 *callet.* Whore.

Costume design for Iago by Henry Irving, 1881

---

132 *cogging.* Deceiving. *cozening.* Cheating.

136 *halter.* Hanging rope.

153 *discourse.* Course.

166 *does him offence.* Has offended him.

176 *daffest.* Defer.

177 *device.* Excuse.

185 *no kin together.* Not related.

190 *votarist.* Nun.

197 *fopped.* Deceived.

207 *mettle.* Spirit, courage.

221 *engines for.* Schemes against.

The business of the state does him offence,
And he does chide with you.
 Des. If 'twere no other,—
 Iago.   'Tis but so, I warrant.
            [Trumpets within.
Hark, how these instruments summon to supper!
The messengers of Venice stay the meat: 170
Go in, and weep not; all things shall be well.
     [Exeunt Desdemona and Emilia.

    Enter RODERIGO.
How now, Roderigo!
 Rod. I do not find that thou dealest justly
with me.
 Iago. What in the contrary?
 Rod. Every day thou daffest me with some
device, Iago; and rather, as it seems to me now,
keepest from me all conveniency than suppliest
me with the least advantage of hope. I will
indeed no longer endure it, nor am I yet persuaded
to put up in peace what already I have foolishly
suffered.
 Iago. Will you hear me, Roderigo?
 Rod. 'Faith, I have heard too much, for your
words and performances are no kin together.
 Iago. You charge me most unjustly.
 Rod. With nought but truth. I have wasted
myself out of my means. The jewels you have
had from me to deliver to Desdemona would half
have corrupted a votarist: you have told me she
hath received them and returned me expectations
and comforts of sudden respect and acquaintance,
but I find none.
 Iago. Well; go to; very well.
 Rod. Very well! go to! I cannot go to, man;
nor 'tis not very well: nay, I think it is scurvy,
and begin to find myself fopped in it.
 Iago. Very well.
 Rod. I tell you 'tis not very well. I will
make myself known to Desdemona: if she will
return me my jewels, I will give over my suit
and repent my unlawful solicitation; if not, assure
yourself I will seek satisfaction of you.
 Iago. You have said now.
 Rod. Ay, and said nothing but what I protest
intendment of doing.
 Iago. Why, now I see there's mettle in thee,
and even from this instant do build on thee a better opinion than ever before. Give me thy hand,
Roderigo: thou hast taken against me a most
just exception; but yet, I protest, I have dealt
most directly in thy affair.
 Rod. It hath not appeared.
 Iago. I grant indeed it hath not appeared,
and your suspicion is not without wit and judgement. But, Roderigo, if thou hast that in thee
indeed, which I have greater reason to believe
now than ever, I mean purpose, courage and
valour, this night show it: if thou the next night
following enjoy not Desdemona, take me from
this world with treachery and devise engines for
my life.
 Rod. Well, what is it? is it within reason and
compass?
 Iago. Sir, there is especial commission come
from Venice to depute Cassio in Othello's place.
 Rod. Is that true? why, then Othello and
Desdemona return again to Venice.
 Iago. O, no; he goes into Mauritania and

takes away with him the fair Desdemona, unless his abode be lingered here by some accident:
● wherein none can be so determinate as the removing of Cassio.

Rod. How do you mean, removing of him?

Iago. Why, by making him uncapable of Othello's place; knocking out his brains.

Rod. And that you would have me to do?

Iago. Ay, if you dare do yourself a profit and
● a right. He sups to-night with a harlotry, and thither will I go to him: he knows not yet of his honourable fortune. If you will watch his going thence, which I will fashion to fall out between twelve and one, you may take him at your pleasure: I will be near to second your attempt, and he shall fall between us. Come, stand not amazed at it, but go along with me; I will show you such a necessity in his death that you shall think yourself bound to put it on him. It is now high supper-time, and the night grows to waste: about it.   250

Rod. I will hear further reason for this.

Iago. And you shall be satisfied.   [*Exeunt.*

SCENE III. *Another room in the castle.*

Enter OTHELLO, LODOVICO, DESDEMONA, EMILIA, *and* Attendants.

Lod. I do beseech you, sir, trouble yourself no further.

Oth. O, pardon me; 'twill do me good to walk.

Lod. Madam, good night; I humbly thank your ladyship.

Des. Your honour is most welcome.

Oth.   Will you walk, sir?
O,—Desdemona,—

Des. My lord?

Oth. Get you to bed on the instant; I will be returned forthwith: dismiss your attendant there: look it be done.

Des. I will, my lord.   10
[*Exeunt Othello, Lodovico, and Attendants.*

Emil. How goes it now? he looks gentler than he did.

● *Des.* He says he will return incontinent:
He hath commanded me to go to bed,
And bade me to dismiss you.

Emil.   Dismiss me!

Des. It was his bidding; therefore, good Emilia,
● Give me my nightly wearing, and adieu:
We must not now displease him.

Emil. I would you had never seen him!

Des. So would not I: my love doth so approve him,
That even his stubbornness, his checks, his frowns,—   20
Prithee, unpin me,—have grace and favour in them.

Emil. I have laid those sheets you bade me on the bed.

Des. All's one. Good faith, how foolish are our minds!
If I do die before thee, prithee, shroud me
In one of those same sheets.

Emil.   Come, come, you talk.

Des. My mother had a maid call'd Barbara:
She was in love, and he she loved proved mad
And did forsake her: she had a song of 'willow;'

232 *determinate.* Effective.

239 *harlotry.* Whore.

Set design for Desdemona's bedchamber by R. Atkins, 1939

12 *incontinent.* Straight away.

16 *nightly wearing.* Bed clothes.

57 *moe.* More.

73 *joint-ring.* Ring in two pieces. *measures of lawn.* Lengths of linen.

75 *exhibition.* Present.

An old thing 'twas, but it express'd her fortune,
And she died singing it: that song to-night   30
Will not go from my mind; I have much to do,
But to go hang my head all at one side,
And sing it like poor Barbara.   Prithee, dispatch.
   Emil. Shall I go fetch your night-gown?
   Des.   No, unpin me here.
This Lodovico is a proper man.
   Emil. A very handsome man.
   Des. He speaks well.
   Emil. I know a lady in Venice would have·
walked barefoot to Palestine for a touch of his
nether lip.   40
   Des. [*Singing*] The poor soul sat sighing by a
     sycamore tree,
   Sing all a green willow;
   Her hand on her bosom, her head on her knee,
   Sing willow, willow, willow:
   The fresh streams ran by her, and murmur'd
     her moans;
   Sing willow, willow, willow;
   Her salt tears fell from her, and soften'd the
     stones;—
Lay by these:—
[*Singing*] Sing willow, willow, willow;
Prithee, hie thee; he'll come anon:—   50
[*Singing*] Sing all a green willow must be my
     garland.
   Let nobody blame him; his scorn I approve,—
Nay, that's not next.—Hark! who is't that
     knocks?
   Emil. It's the wind.
   Des. [*Singing*] I call'd my love false love;
     but what said he then?
         Sing willow, willow, willow:
  If I court moe women, you'll couch with moe
     men.—
So, get thee gone; good night. Mine eyes do itch;
Doth that bode weeping?
   Emil.   'Tis neither here nor there.
   Des. I have heard it said so. O, these men,
     these men!   60
Dost thou in conscience think,—tell me, Emilia,—
That there be women do abuse their husbands
In such gross kind?
   Emil.   There be some such, no question.
   Des. Wouldst thou do such a deed for all the
     world?
   Emil. Why, would not you?
   Des.   No, by this heavenly light!
   Emil. Nor I neither by this heavenly light;
I might do't as well i' the dark.
   Des. Wouldst thou do such a deed for all the
     world?
   Emil. The world's a huge thing: it is a great
     price
For a small vice.
   Des.   In troth, I think thou wouldst not. 70
   Emil. In troth, I think I should; and undo't
when I had done. Marry, I would not do such a
thing for a joint-ring, nor for measures of lawn,
nor for gowns, petticoats, nor caps, nor any petty
exhibition; but, for the whole world,—why, who
would not make her husband a cuckold to make
him a monarch? I should venture purgatory for't.
   Des. Beshrew me, if I would do such a wrong
For the whole world.   79
   Emil. Why, the wrong is but a wrong i' the
world; and having the world for your labour, 'tis

a wrong in your own world, and you might quickly make it right.

Des. I do not think there is any such woman.

Emil. Yes, a dozen; and as many to the vantage as would store the world they played for.
But I do think it is their husbands' faults
If wives do fall: say that they slack their duties,
And pour our treasures into foreign laps,
Or else break out in peevish jealousies,   90
Throwing restraint upon us; or say they strike us,
Or scant our former having in despite;
Why, we have galls, and though we have some grace,
Yet have we some revenge.   Let husbands know
Their wives have sense like them: they see and smell
And have their palates both for sweet and sour,
As husbands have.   What is it that they do
When they change us for others?   Is it sport?
I think it is: and doth affection breed it?
I think it doth: is't frailty that thus errs?   100
It is so too: and have not we affections,
Desires for sport, and frailty, as men have?
Then let them use us well: else let them know,
The ills we do, their ills instruct us so.

Des. Good night, good night: heaven me such uses send,
Not to pick bad from bad, but by bad mend!

[*Exeunt.*

ACT V.

SCENE I. *Cyprus. A street.*

Enter IAGO *and* RODERIGO.

Iago. Here, stand behind this bulk; straight will he come:
Wear thy good rapier bare, and put it home:
Quick, quick; fear nothing; I'll be at thy elbow:
It makes us, or it mars us; think on that,
And fix most firm thy resolution.

Rod. Be near at hand; I may miscarry in't.

Iago. Here, at thy hand: be bold, and take thy stand.   [*Retires.*

Rod. I have no great devotion to the deed;
And yet he hath given me satisfying reasons: 9
'Tis but a man gone.   Forth, my sword: he dies.

Iago. I have rubb'd this young quat almost to the sense,
And he grows angry.   Now, whether he kill Cassio,
Or Cassio him, or each do kill the other,
Every way makes my gain: live Roderigo,
He calls me to a restitution large
Of gold and jewels that I bobb'd from him,
As gifts to Desdemona;
It must not be: if Cassio do remain,
He hath a daily beauty in his life
That makes me ugly; and, besides, the Moor   20
May unfold me to him; there stand I in much peril:
No, he must die.   But so: I hear him coming.

Enter CASSIO.

Rod. I know his gait, 'tis he.—Villain, thou diest!   [*Makes a pass at Cassio.*

Cas. That thrust had been mine enemy indeed,
But that my coat is better than thou know'st:

85-86 *to the vantage.* In addition.

93 *galls.* Bad tempers.

105 *uses.* Habit.

1 *bulk.* Pillar.

2 *bare.* Unsheathed.

Iago: 'Quick, quick; fear nothing; I'll be at thy elbow.'
Edwin Booth as Iago, Lyceum Theatre, London, 1881

---

11 *quat.* Ass. *to the sense.* Till it hurt.

16 *bobb'd.* Swindled.

26 *make proof.* Test.

● I will make proof of thine.
                    [*Draws, and wounds Roderigo.*
Rod.   O, I am slain!
[*Iago from behind wounds Cassio in the
                         leg, and exit.*
Cas.   I am maim'd for ever.   Help, ho! mur-
     der! murder!   [*Falls.*

Enter OTHELLO.

Oth.   The voice of Cassio: Iago keeps his
     word.
Rod.   O, villain that I am!
Oth.   It is even so.
Cas.   O, help, ho! light! a surgeon!   30
Oth.   'Tis he:—O brave Iago, honest and just,
That hast such noble sense of thy friend's wrong!
Thou teachest me.   Minion, your dear lies dead,
And your unblest fate hies: strumpet, I come.
Forth of my heart those charms, thine eyes, are
     blotted;
Thy bed, lust-stain'd, shall with lust's blood be
     spotted.   [*Exit.*

Enter LODOVICO *and* GRATIANO.

Cas.   What, ho! no watch? no passage? mur-
     der! murder!
Gra.   'Tis some mischance; the cry is very
     direful.
Cas.   O, help!
Lod.   Hark!   40
Rod.   O wretched villain!
Lod.   Two or three groan: it is a heavy night:
These may be counterfeits: let's think't unsafe
To come in to the cry without more help.
Rod.   Nobody come? then shall I bleed to
     death.
Lod.   Hark!

Re-enter IAGO, *with a light.*

Gra.   Here's one comes in his shirt, with light
     and weapons.
Iago.   Who's there? whose noise is this that
     cries on murder?
Lod.   We do not know.
Iago.   Did not you hear a cry?
Cas.   Here, here! for heaven's sake, help me!
Iago.   What's the matter?   50
Gra.   This is Othello's ancient, as I take it.
Lod.   The same indeed; a very valiant fellow.
Iago.   What are you here that cry so griev-
     ously?
Cas.   Iago? O, I am spoil'd, undone by villains!
Give me some help.
Iago.   O me, lieutenant! what villains have
     done this?
Cas.   I think that one of them is hereabout,
And cannot make away.
Iago.   O treacherous villains!
What are you there? come in, and give some
     help.   [*To Lodovico and Gratiano.*
Rod.   O, help me here!   60
Cas.   That's one of them.
Iago.   O murderous slave! O villain!
                    [*Stabs Roderigo.*
Rod.   O damn'd Iago! O inhuman dog!
Iago.   Kill men i' the dark!—Where be these
     bloody thieves?—
How silent is this town!—Ho! murder! murder!—

What may you be? are you of good or evil?
Lod.   As you shall prove us, praise us.
Iago.   Signior Lodovico?
Lod.   He, sir.
Iago.   I cry you mercy.   Here's Cassio hurt
   by villains.
Gra.   Cassio!   70
Iago.   How is't, brother!
Cas.   My leg is cut in two.
Iago.   Marry, heaven forbid!
Light, gentlemen: I'll bind it with my shirt.

Enter BIANCA.

Bian.   What is the matter, ho? who is't that
   cried?
Iago.   Who is't that cried!
Bian.   O my dear Cassio! my sweet Cassio!
O Cassio, Cassio, Cassio!
Iago.   O notable strumpet!   Cassio, may you
   suspect
Who they should be that have thus mangled you?
Cas.   No.   80
Gra.   I am sorry to find you thus: I have been
   to seek you.
Iago.   Lend me a garter.   So.   O, for a chair,
To bear him easily hence!
Bian.   Alas, he faints!   O Cassio, Cassio,
   Cassio!
Iago.   Gentlemen all, I do suspect this trash
To be a party in this injury.
Patience awhile, good Cassio.   Come, come;
Lend me a light.   Know we this face or no?
Alas, my friend and my dear countryman
Roderigo! no:—yes, sure:—O heaven! Roderigo.
Gra.   What, of Venice?   91
Iago.   Even he, sir: did you know him?
Gra.   Know him! ay.
Iago.   Signior Gratiano?   I cry you gentle
   pardon;
These bloody accidents must excuse my manners,
That so neglected you.
Gra.   I am glad to see you.
Iago.   How do you, Cassio?   O, a chair, a chair!
Gra.   Roderigo!
Iago.   He, he, 'tis he.   [*A chair brought in.*]
   O, that's well said; the chair.
Some good man bear him carefully from hence;
I'll fetch the general's surgeon.   [*To Bianca*]
   For you, mistress,   100
Save you your labour.   He that lies slain here,
   Cassio,
Was my dear friend: what malice was between
   you?
Cas.   None in the world; nor do I know the
   man.
Iago.   [*To Bian.*] What, look you pale?   O,
   bear him out o' the air.
            [*Cassio and Roderigo are borne off.*
Stay you, good gentlemen.   Look you pale, mis-
   tress?
● Do you perceive the gastness of her eye?
Nay, if you stare, we shall hear more anon.
Behold her well; I pray you, look upon her:
Do you see, gentlemen? nay, guiltiness will speak,
Though tongues were out of use.   110

Enter EMILIA.

Emil.   'Las, what's the matter? what's the
   matter, husband?

106 *gastness.* Aghast look.

Charles Fechter, the French actor, as Iago, Princess's Theatre, London, 1861

113 *scaped.* Escaped.

129 *fordoes.* Finishes.

8 *flaming minister.* i.e. torch.

12 *Promethean.* Of Prometheus, prime discoverer of fire.

13 *relume.* Relight.

Bedchamber scene. Desdemona (Peggy Ashcroft) and Othello (Paul Robeson). Sketch from *Punch*, May 1930

Iago. Cassio hath here been set on in the dark
●By Roderigo and fellows that are scaped:
He's almost slain, and Roderigo dead.
    Emil. Alas, good gentleman! alas, good Cassio!
    Iago. This is the fruit of whoring. Prithee, Emilia,
Go know of Cassio where he supp'd to-night.
[*To Bianca*] What, do you shake at that?
    Bian. He supp'd at my house; but I therefore shake not.
    Iago. O, did he so? I charge you, go with me.
    Emil. Fie, fie upon thee, strumpet!   121
    Bian. I am no strumpet; but of life as honest
As you that thus abuse me.
    Emil.   As I! foh! fie upon thee!
    Iago. Kind gentlemen, let's go see poor Cassio dress'd.
Come, mistress, you must tell's another tale.
Emilia, run you to the citadel,
And tell my lord and lady what hath happ'd.
Will you go on? I pray. [*Aside*] This is the night
●That either makes me or fordoes me quite.
                      [*Exeunt.*

SCENE II. *A bedchamber in the castle:* DESDEMONA *in bed asleep; a light burning.*

Enter OTHELLO.

    Oth. It is the cause, it is the cause, my soul,—
Let me not name it to you, you chaste stars!—
It is the cause. Yet I'll not shed her blood;
Nor scar that whiter skin of hers than snow,
And smooth as monumental alabaster.
Yet she must die, else she'll betray more men.
Put out the light, and then put out the light:
●If I quench thee, thou flaming minister,
I can again thy former light restore,
Should I repent me: but once put out thy light,
Thou cunning'st pattern of excelling nature,   11
●I know not where is that Promethean heat
●That can thy light relume. When I have pluck'd the rose,
I cannot give it vital growth again,
It must needs wither: I'll smell it on the tree.
                    [*Kissing her.*
Ah, balmy breath, that dost almost persuade
Justice to break her sword! One more, one more.
Be thus when thou art dead, and I will kill thee,
And love thee after. One more, and this the last:
So sweet was ne'er so fatal. I must weep,   20
But they are cruel tears: this sorrow's heavenly;
It strikes where it doth love. She wakes.
    Des. Who's there? Othello?
    Oth.   Ay, Desdemona.
    Des. Will you come to bed, my lord?
    Oth. Have you pray'd to-night, Desdemona?
    Des.   Ay, my lord.
    Oth. If you bethink yourself of any crime
Unreconciled as yet to heaven and grace,
Solicit for it straight.
    Des. Alas, my lord, what do you mean by that?
    Oth. Well, do it, and be brief; I will walk by:
I would not kill thy unprepared spirit;   31
No; heaven forfend! I would not kill thy soul.
    Des. Talk you of killing?
    Oth.   Ay, I do.
    Des.   Then heaven

Have mercy on me!
  Oth.   Amen, with all my heart!
  Des. If you say so, I hope you will not kill me.
  Oth. Hum!
  Des. And yet I fear you; for you are fatal then
When your eyes roll so: why I should fear I know not,
Since guiltiness I know not; but yet I feel I fear.
  Oth. Think on thy sins.
  Des.   They are loves I bear to you. 40
  Oth. Ay, and for that thou diest.
  Des. That death's unnatural that kills for loving.
Alas, why gnaw you so your nether lip?
Some bloody passion shakes your very frame:
These are portents; but yet I hope, I hope,
They do not point on me.
  Oth.   Peace, and be still!
  Des. I will so. What's the matter?
  Oth. That handkerchief which I so loved and gave thee
Thou gavest to Cassio.
  Des.   No, by my life and soul!
Send for the man, and ask him.
  Oth.   Sweet soul, take heed, 50
Take heed of perjury; thou art on thy death-bed.
  Des. Ay, but not yet to die.
  Oth.   Yes, presently:
Therefore confess thee freely of thy sin;
For to deny each article with oath
Cannot remove nor choke the strong conception
That I do groan withal. Thou art to die.
  Des. Then Lord have mercy on me!
  Oth.   I say, amen.
  Des. And have you mercy too! I never did
Offend you in my life; never loved Cassio
But with such general warranty of heaven   60
As I might love; I never gave him token.
  Oth. By heaven, I saw my handkerchief in's hand.
O perjured woman! thou dost stone my heart,
And makest me call what I intend to do
A murder, which I thought a sacrifice:
I saw the handkerchief.
  Des.   He found it then;
I never gave it him: send for him hither;
Let him confess a truth.
  Oth.   He hath confess'd.
  Des. What, my lord?
  Oth. That he hath used thee.
  Des.   How? unlawfully?
  Oth.   Ay. 70
  Des. He will not say so.
  Oth.   No, his mouth is stopp'd;
Honest Iago hath ta'en order for't.
  Des. O! my fear interprets: what, is he dead?
  Oth. Had all his hairs been lives, my great revenge
Had stomach for them all.
  Des. Alas! he is betray'd and I undone.
  Oth. Out, strumpet! weep'st thou for him to my face?
  Des. O, banish me, my lord, but kill me not!
  Oth. Down, strumpet!
  Des. Kill me to-morrow: let me live to-night!
  Oth. Nay, if you strive,—   81
  Des. But half an hour!
  Oth.   Being done, there is no pause.
  Des. But while I say one prayer!

Desdemona: 'And yet I fear you . . .' Desdemona (Curigwen Lewis) and Othello (Ralph Richardson), Old Vic Theatre, London, 1938

Othello: 'It is too late.' Death of Desdemona. Drawing by H. Gravelot (1699–1773)

_____

101 *yawn at alteration.* Open wide at the great change.

Oth.   It is too late.
                                   [*He stifles her.*
Emil. [*Within*] My lord, my lord! what, ho!
   my lord, my lord!
Oth.   What noise is this?   Not dead? not yet
   quite dead?
I that am cruel am yet merciful;
I would not have thee linger in thy pain:
So, so.
   Emil. [*Within*] What, ho! my lord, my lord!
   Oth.   Who's there?
   Emil.   [*Within*] O, good my lord, I would
      speak a word with you!   90
   Oth.   Yes: 'tis Emilia.   By and by.   She's
      dead.
'Tis like she comes to speak of Cassio's death.—
The noise was here.   Ha! no more moving?
Still as the grave.   Shall she come in? were't
   good?—
I think she stirs again:—no.   What's best to do?
If she come in, she'll sure speak to my wife:
My wife! my wife! what wife? I have no wife.
O, insupportable! O heavy hour!
Methinks it should be now a huge eclipse
Of sun and moon, and that the affrighted globe
•Should yawn at alteration.
   Emil.   [*Within*] I do beseech you   101
That I may speak with you, O, good my lord!
   Oth.   I had forgot thee: O, come in, Emilia:
Soft; by and by.   Let me the curtains draw.
Where art thou?   [*Unlocks the door.*

      Enter EMILIA.

                    What's the matter with thee now?
   Emil.   O, my good lord, yonder's foul mur-
      ders done!
   Oth.   What, now?
   Emil.   But now, my lord.
   Oth.   It is the very error of the moon;
She comes more nearer earth than she was wont,
And makes men mad.   111
   Emil.   Cassio, my lord, hath kill'd a young
      Venetian
Call'd Roderigo.
   Oth.   Roderigo kill'd!
And Cassio kill'd!
   Emil.   No, Cassio is not kill'd.
   Oth.   Not Cassio kill'd! then murder's out of
      tune,
And sweet revenge grows harsh.
   Des.   O, falsely, falsely murder'd!
   Emil.   Alas, what cry is that?
   Oth.   That! what?
   Emil.   Out, and alas! that was my lady's voice.
Help! help, ho! help! O lady, speak again! 120
Sweet Desdemona! O sweet mistress, speak!
   Des.   A guiltless death I die.
   Emil.   O, who hath done this deed?
   Des.   Nobody; I myself.   Farewell:
Commend me to my kind lord: O, farewell! [*Dies.*
   Oth.   Why, how should she be murder'd?
   Emil.   Alas, who knows?
   Oth.   You heard her say herself, it was not I.
   Emil.   She said so: I must needs report the
      truth.
   Oth.   She's, like a liar, gone to burning hell:
'Twas I that kill'd her.
   Emil.   O, the more angel she, 130
And you the blacker devil!

Oth. She turn'd to folly, and she was a whore.

● *Emil.* Thou dost belie her, and thou art a devil.

Oth. She was false as water.

Emil.   Thou art rash as fire, to say
That she was false: O, she was heavenly true!

Oth. Cassio did top her; ask thy husband else.
O, I were damn'd beneath all depth in hell,
But that I did proceed upon just grounds
To this extremity.   Thy husband knew it all.

Emil. My husband!   140

Oth. Thy husband.

Emil. That she was false to wedlock?

Oth. Ay, with Cassio. Nay, had she been true,
If heaven would make me such another world

● Of one entire and perfect chrysolite,
I'ld not have sold her for it.

Emil. My husband!

Oth.   Ay, 'twas he that told me first:
An honest man he is, and hates the slime
That sticks on filthy deeds.

Emil.   My husband!

Oth. What needs this iteration, woman? I
say thy husband.   150

Emil. O mistress, villany hath made mocks
with love!
My husband say that she was false!

Oth.   He, woman;
I say thy husband: dost understand the word?
My friend, thy husband, honest, honest Iago.

Emil. If he say so, may his pernicious soul
Rot half a grain a day! he lies to the heart:
She was too fond of her most filthy bargain.

Oth. Ha!

Emil. Do thy worst:
This deed of thine is no more worthy heaven 160
Than thou wast worthy her.

Oth.   Peace, you were best.

Emil. Thou hast not half that power to do
me harm
As I have to be hurt.   O gull! O dolt!
As ignorant as dirt! thou hast done a deed—
I care not for thy sword: I'll make thee known,
Though I lost twenty lives.—Help! help, ho!
help!
The Moor hath kill'd my mistress! Murder!
murder!

Enter Montano, Gratiano, Iago, *and others.*

Mon. What is the matter? How now, general!

Emil. O, are you come, Iago? you have done
well,
That men must lay their murders on your neck.

Gra. What is the matter?   171

Emil. Disprove this villain, if thou be'st a man:
He says thou told'st him that his wife was false:
I know thou didst not, thou 'rt not such a villain:
Speak, for my heart is full.

Iago. I told him what I thought, and told no
more
Than what he found himself was apt and true.

Emil. But did you ever tell him she was false?

Iago. I did.

Emil. You told a lie; an odious, damned lie;
Upon my soul, a lie, a wicked lie.   181
She false with Cassio!—did you say with Cassio?

● *Iago.* With Cassio, mistress. Go to, charm
your tongue.

133 *belie.* Wrong.

145 *chrysolite.* Semi-precious stone.

Emilia: 'O gull! O dolt! As ignorant as dirt! thou hast done a deed . . .' Emilia (Sybil Thorndike) and Othello (Paul Robeson). Sketch from *Punch*, May 1930

183 *charm your tongue.* Be quiet.

214 *recognizance.* Token.

Emilia: 'Your sword upon a woman?' Iago (Raymond Westwell) threatens Emilia (Joan MacArthur), Stratford-upon-Avon, 1954

Emil.   I will not charm my tongue; I am bound to speak:
My mistress here lies murder'd in her bed,—
All.   O heavens forfend!
Emil.   And your reports have set the murder on.
Oth.   Nay, stare not, masters: it is true, indeed.
Gra.   'Tis a strange truth.
Mon.   O monstrous act!
Emil.   Villany, villany, villany!   190
I think upon 't, I think: I smell 't: O villany!—
I thought so then:—I 'll kill myself for grief:—
O villany, villany!
Iago.   What, are you mad? I charge you, get you home.
Emil.   Good gentlemen, let me have leave to speak:
'Tis proper I obey him, but not now.
Perchance, Iago, I will ne'er go home.
Oth.   O! O! O!   [*He falls on the bed.*
Emil.   Nay, lay thee down and roar;
For thou hast kill'd the sweetest innocent
That e'er did lift up eye.
Oth.   [*Rising*] O, she was foul!   200
I scarce did know you, uncle: there lies your niece,
Whose breath, indeed, these hands have newly stopp'd:
I know this act shows horrible and grim.
Gra.   Poor Desdemona! I am glad thy father's dead:
Thy match was mortal to him, and pure grief
Shore his old thread in twain: did he live now,
This sight would make him do a desperate turn,
Yea, curse his better angel from his side,
And fall to reprobation.
Oth.   'Tis pitiful; but yet Iago knows   210
That she with Cassio hath the act of shame
A thousand times committed; Cassio confess'd it:
And she did gratify his amorous works
•With that recognizance and pledge of love
Which I first gave her; I saw it in his hand:
It was a handkerchief, an antique token
My father gave my mother.
Emil.   O heaven! O heavenly powers!
Iago.   Come, hold your peace.
Emil.   'Twill out, 'twill out: I peace!
No, I will speak as liberal as the north: 220
Let heaven and men and devils, let them all,
All, all, cry shame against me, yet I 'll speak.
Iago.   Be wise, and get you home.
Emil.   I will not.
                      [*Iago offers to stab Emilia.*
Gra.   Fie!
Your sword upon a woman?
Emil.   O thou dull Moor! that handkerchief thou speak'st of
I found by fortune and did give my husband;
For often, with a solemn earnestness,
More than indeed belong'd to such a trifle,
He begg'd of me to steal it.
Iago.   Villanous whore! 229
Emil.   She give it Cassio! no, alas! I found it,
And I did give 't my husband.
Iago.   Filth, thou liest!
Emil.   By heaven, I do not, I do not, gentlemen.
O murderous coxcomb! what should such a fool
Do with so good a woman?
Oth.   Are there no stones in heaven

But what serve for the thunder?—Precious villain!
> [*He runs at Iago: Iago, from behind, stabs*
> *Emilia, and exit.*

Gra. The woman falls; sure, he hath kill'd
   his wife.
Emil. Ay, ay: O, lay me by my mistress'
   side.
Gra. He's gone, but his wife's kill'd.
Mon. 'Tis a notorious villain.   Take you this
   weapon,
Which I have here recover'd from the Moor: 240
Come, guard the door without; let him not pass,
But kill him rather.   I'll after that same villain,
For 'tis a damned slave.
> [*Exeunt Montano and Gratiano.*

Oth.   I am not valiant neither,
• But every puny whipster gets my sword:
But why should honour outlive honesty?
Let it go all.
Emil. What did thy song bode, lady?
Hark, canst thou hear me? I will play the swan,
And die in music. [*Singing*] Willow, willow,
   willow.—
Moor, she was chaste; she loved thee, cruel
   Moor;
So come my soul to bliss, as I speak true;   250
So speaking as I think, I die, I die.   [*Dies.*
Oth. I have another weapon in this chamber;
• It is a sword of Spain, the ice-brook's temper:—
O, here it is.   Uncle, I must come forth.
Gra. [*Within*] If thou attempt it, it will cost
   thee dear:
Thou hast no weapon, and perforce must suffer.
Oth. Look in upon me then and speak with me,
Or, naked as I am, I will assault thee

Re-enter GRATIANO.

Gra. What is the matter?
Oth.   Behold, I have a weapon;
A better never did itself sustain   260
Upon a soldier's thigh: I have seen the day,
That, with this little arm and this good sword,
I have made my way through more impediments
Than twenty times your stop: but, O vain boast!
Who can control his fate? 'tis not so now.
Be not afraid, though you do see me weapon'd;
Here is my journey's end, here is my butt,
• And very sea-mark of my utmost sail.
Do you go back dismay'd? 'tis a lost fear;
Man but a rush against Othello's breast,   270
And he retires.   Where should Othello go?
Now, how dost thou look now? O ill-starr'd
   wench!
• Pale as thy smock! when we shall meet at compt,
This look of thine will hurl my soul from heaven,
And fiends will snatch at it.   Cold, cold, my girl!
Even like thy chastity.   O cursed slave!
Whip me, ye devils,
From the possession of this heavenly sight!
Blow me about in winds! roast me in sulphur!
Wash me in steep-down gulfs of liquid fire!   280
O Desdemona! Desdemona! dead!
Oh! Oh! Oh!

Enter LODOVICO, MONTANO, CASSIO *carried in*
a chair, and Officers *with* IAGO, *prisoner.*

Lod. Where is this rash and most unfortunate
   man?

244 *whipster.* Contemptible type.

253 *ice-brook's temper.* Tempered in iced water.

268 *sea-mark.* Beacon, maritime equivalent to landmark.

273 *at compt.* On Judgment day.

Othello: 'O ill-starr'd wench! Pale as thy smock! . . .
Cold, cold, my girl!' Engraving from Bell's edition of
Shakespeare, 1773

292 *practice*. Plotting.

Iago: 'I bleed, sir; but not kill'd.' Laurence Oliver as Iago, Old Vic Theatre, London, 1938

Oth.   That's he that was Othello: here I am.
Lod.   Where is that viper? bring the villain forth.
Oth.   I look down towards his feet; but that's a fable.
If that thou be'st a devil, I cannot kill thee.
                                        [*Wounds Iago.*
Lod.   Wrench his sword from him.
Iago.   I bleed, sir; but not kill'd.
Oth.   I am not sorry neither: I'ld have thee live;
For, in my sense, 'tis happiness to die.   290
Lod.   O thou Othello, that wert once so good,
● Fall'n in the practice of a damned slave,
What shall be said to thee?
Oth.   Why, any thing:
An honourable murderer, if you will;
For nought I did in hate, but all in honour.
Lod.   This wretch hath part confess'd his villany:
Did you and he consent in Cassio's death?
Oth.   Ay.
Cas.   Dear general, I never gave you cause.
Oth.   I do believe it, and I ask you pardon.
Will you, I pray, demand that demi-devil   301
Why he hath thus ensnared my soul and body?
Iago.   Demand me nothing: what you know, you know:
From this time forth I never will speak word.
Lod.   What, not to pray?
Gra.   Torments will ope your lips.
Oth.   Well, thou dost best.
Lod.   Sir, you shall understand what hath befall'n,
Which, as I think, you know not. Here is a letter
Found in the pocket of the slain Roderigo:
And here another: the one of them imports   310
The death of Cassio to be undertook
By Roderigo.
Oth.   O villain!
Cas.   Most heathenish and most gross!
Lod.   Now here's another discontented paper,
Found in his pocket too; and this, it seems,
Roderigo meant to have sent this damned villain;
But that belike Iago in the interim
Came in and satisfied him.
Oth.   O the pernicious caitiff!
How came you, Cassio, by that handkerchief
That was my wife's?
Cas.   I found it in my chamber: 320
And he himself confess'd but even now
That there he dropp'd it for a special purpose
Which wrought to his desire.
Oth.   O fool! fool! fool!
Cas.   There is besides in Roderigo's letter,
How he upbraids Iago, that he made him
Brave me upon the watch; whereon it came
That I was cast: and even but now he spake,
After long seeming dead, Iago hurt him,
Iago set him on.
Lod.   You must forsake this room, and go with us: 330
Your power and your command is taken off,
And Cassio rules in Cyprus. For this slave,
If there be any cunning cruelty
That can torment him much and hold him long,
It shall be his. You shall close prisoner rest,
Till that the nature of your fault be known
To the Venetian state. Come, bring him away.

Oth.   Soft you; a word or two before you go.
I have done the state some service, and they
    know't.   339
No more of that.   I pray you, in your letters,
When you shall these unlucky deeds relate,
Speak of me as I am; nothing extenuate,
Nor set down aught in malice: then must you
    speak
Of one that loved not wisely but too well;
Of one not easily jealous, but being wrought
Perplex'd in the extreme; of one whose hand,
Like the base Indian, threw a pearl away
Richer than all his tribe; of one whose subdued
    eyes,
Albeit unused to the melting mood,
Drop tears as fast as the Arabian trees   350
Their medicinal gum.   Set you down this;
And say besides, that in Aleppo once,
Where a malignant and a turban'd Turk
Beat a Venetian and traduced the state,
I took by the throat the circumcised dog,
And smote him, thus.   [*Stabs himself.*

  Lod.   O bloody period!
  Gra.   All that's spoke is marr'd.
  Oth.   I kiss'd thee ere I kill'd thee: no way
    but this;
Killing myself, to die upon a kiss.
        [*Falls on the bed, and dies.*

  Cas.   This did I fear, but thought he had no
    weapon;   360
For he was great of heart.
  ● *Lod.*   [*To Iago*] O Spartan dog,
●More fell than anguish, hunger, or the sea!
Look on the tragic loading of this bed;
This is thy work: the object poisons sight;
Let it be hid.   Gratiano, keep the house,
And seize upon the fortunes of the Moor,
For they succeed on you.   To you, lord governor,
●Remains the censure of this hellish villain;
The time, the place, the torture: O, enforce it!
Myself will straight aboard; and to the state 370
This heavy act with heavy heart relate. [*Exeunt.*

Othello: 'I kissed thee ere I kill'd thee: no way but this . . .' Drawing by John Thurston (1744–1822)

361 *Spartan dog.* Bloodhound.

362 *fell.* Fierce.

368 *censure.* Judging.

King Lear

1605-6

THE STORY of King Lear was familiar to Elizabethans, who for the most part did not distinguish between pre-history and history. To them – to Holinshed, for example – the story of King Lear and his daughters had the status of authentic history, and both early quartos of the play describe it as a 'true chronicle history'. Only a critical spirit like Camden knew better. Shakespeare picked up a detail from his popular *Remains*, which came out in 1605 not long before the play was written, which he used for the test put to Cordelia, when she reserved half of her love for her future husband – unlike her sisters who pretended all was for their father.

However, Shakespeare followed Holinshed's account more or less, though still more the old play, *The True Chronicle History of King Lear*, which was also published in 1605. It may be that these two publications inclined him towards the subject. (Llyr is apparently a Celtic name, and Elizabethans derived the name of Leicester from it; they thought that it went back to a Caerleir, i.e. Leir's castrum or ceister.) So the story is a very early one. His instinct told him to prefer the poet Spenser's form of the name Cordelia, and he adapted a story from Sidney's *Arcadia* for his under plot concerning Gloucester and his sons.

The Play. The importance of this underplot marks this play off from the other tragedies. It complicates and enriches, and at the same time counterpoints and enforces, the main plot, with which it is most expertly interwoven. Thus the structure of the play is a complex and Gothic one, as against the classic simplicity of *Julius Caesar* or the romantic unity of *Othello*. Again, the rôle of the Fool in *King Lear*, which the pseudo-classic taste from the Restoration onwards could not tolerate, is also important: as Lear's familiar he brings home to him the truth of his situation and his folly. Wisdom and truth are spoken through the mouth of a Fool, with all the more caustic effect. Once more, Shakespeare's mixing of genres gave him unlimited scope, in keeping with the opulent age in which he lived (compare the effects of Tintoretto or Veronese), as against the restricted taste of the later 17th or 18th century.

Though the cast is not large, the parts are well distributed and several characters are fully delineated in their good or evil qualities. Evil is dispersed throughout the play:

Lear's daughters, Goneril and Regan, Regan's husband, Duke of Cornwall, Gloucester's bastard son, Edmund, are all evil. Indeed, Edmund is of a piece with Iago:

> A credulous father, and a brother noble,
> Whose nature is so far from doing harms
> That he suspects none: on whose foolish honesty
> My practices ride easy!

Gloucester is gullible and suffers for his illusions; the chief sufferer for his illusions is King Lear himself. We may be sure that William Shakespeare suffered from no illusions – in fact, we know it, even at the height of his sexual infatuation.

Exceptionally, after the courtly beginning, the character of the King is fully revealed in the very first scene, rashly giving away his kingdom, exposing himself to the bitterest ingratitude, throwing away the devotion of his youngest daughter and his most loyal supporter, Kent. He gets what he asked for, or, rather more: rash and intemperate by nature, later, from his sufferings his wits are turned. The rest of the play is devoted to drawing the consequences: he at last, through adversity, learns the truth about himself, and others, about life itself. It is the Fool who brings it home to him:

King Lear in the Storm. Painting by John Runciman, 1767

Thou shouldst not have been old till thou hadst been wise.

It might be regarded as the moral of the play in one sentence.

Moral Lessons. Unlike lesser spirits, and contrary to many critics, Shakespeare is never afraid to drive home the moral, or lessons, of what he has exposed – indeed, it would have been un-Elizabethan of him not to do so. These often take the form of sententious rhymed couplets, such as Elizabethans regaled themselves or plastered their houses with. Under the description Shakespeare's 'gnomic verse' this is currently depreciated – again, without imagination or knowledge of the age of which it is very characteristic. As in *Othello* these *sententiae* are given prominence, and evidently speak for the poet himself, tell us what his conclusions were.

It is the Fool who advises Lear (and us):

> Have more than thou showest,
> Speak less than thou knowest,
> Lend less than thou owest,
> Ride more than thou goest (i.e. walk),
> Learn more than thou trowest (i.e. know),
> Set [i.e. stake] less than thou throwest . . .
> And thou shalt have more
> Than two tens to a score.

That evidently spoke for William Shakespeare, and it had certainly stood him in good stead.

> When we our betters see bearing our woes,
> We scarcely think our miseries our foes.
> Who alone suffers suffers most i'the mind,
> Leaving free things and happy shows behind.
> But then the mind much sufferance doth o'erskip,
> When grief hath mates, and bearing fellowship.

Here speaks the sociable Shakespeare, the family man; nor can we doubt that these didactic words of wisdom were much to the taste of an Elizabethan audience.

Personal. Similar touches reveal his thought to us. Gloucester, blinded, says, 'I stumbled when I saw'; there follows a very Shakespearean thought:

> full oft 'tis seen,
> Our means secure us, and our mere defects
> Prove our commodities.

That is, our resources make us feel secure and careless, when our very defects may prove to benefit us. How like his prudence, always keeping a weather-eye open! And there is the consoling reflection, often proved true:

> the worst is not
> So long as we can say, 'This is the worst.'

Left: *Ellen Terry as Cordelia, Lyceum Theatre, London, 1892*

Far left: *Paul Scofield as King Lear, Royal Shakespeare Theatre, Stratford-upon-Avon, 1962*

Or again,

> Striving to better, oft we mar what's well.

His scepticism is like that of Montaigne, a comparable spirit of the time, *divers et ondoyant*. It enables him to make reflections through his characters which are, in a sense, in inverted commas and yet his own – on others, on men in general, and on *la condition humaine*. It is Lear, mad, who tells blinded Gloucester: 'A man may see how this world goes with no eyes. Look with thine ears: see how yon justice rails on yon simple thief. Hark, in thine ear: change places, and – handy-dandy – which is the justice, which is the thief?' In a beggar running from a farmer's dog, you may behold the great image of authority: 'a dog's obeyed in office'. And the conclusion? –

> Get thee glass eyes,
> And, like a scurvy politician, seem
> To see the things thou dost not.

'Politicians' never get a good word in Shakespeare: only good rulers, and good people. It is given to the cynical Edmund to reflect on the foolery of people – at that time, of course – that, when things went wrong with them, often through their own ill conduct, they would impute it to the planets, 'as if we were villains by necessity; fools by heavenly compulsion; knaves, thieves, treachers [i.e. traitors], drunkards, liars and adulterers' through the influence of the stars. Plenty of people thought like that – Shakespeare's message is that they could all be a bit more intelligent and responsible.

The Age. Many indications denote the background. Shakespeare had read Samuel Harsnet's book, *Declaration of Egregious Popish Impostures*, which had come out a couple of years before, in 1603. Professor Harbage[1] calls it an 'excursion into pseudo-demonology'; it is not: it is a fascinating exposure of the claims of contemporary Catholic priests to exorcise demons from women, and as such a revealing psychological investigation of the phenomena of female hysteria and male credulity and imposture.

1. Introduction to the *Pelican* edition of the play, which, the Professor is also able to tell us, 'is a sad play, as all tragedies are sad'!

341

It was this useful reading that suggested to Shakespeare the names of the spirits that haunted the hovel on the heath, according to Edgar, feigning madness, who had taken refuge from the storm there with Lear, Kent and the Fool.

Edgar himself, in this world wheeling round, with madness in the air, Lear's wits becoming unsettled and the elements raging, takes on the folklore character of Tom o'Bedlam – about whom the age produced a mysterious, but marvellous, anonymous poem. Such beggars were a feature of the time:

> The country gives me proof and precedent
> Of Bedlam beggars, who, with roaring voices,
> Strike in their numbed and mortified bare arms
> Pins, wooden pricks, nails, sprigs of rosemary;
> And with this horrible object, from low farms,
> Poor pelting villages, sheepcotes, and mills,
> Sometime with lunatic bans [curses], sometime with prayers,
> Enforce their charity.

And serving-men of the time? Edgar pretends to have been one, 'proud in heart and mind; that curled my hair; wore gloves in my cap . . . swore as many oaths as I spake words, and broke them in the sweet face of heaven; one that slept in the contriving of lust, and waked to it.' He then offers a warning that betrays William Shakespeare himself: 'let not the creaking of shoes nor the rustling of silks betray thy poor heart to woman.' One has known heterosexuals whose senses were as keen to that alert. Perhaps one may see him personally too in the comment:

> Love's not love
> When it is mingled with regards that stand
> Aloof from the entire point.

Many more indications portray the age out of which Shakespeare's creation sprang. We have the stage itself in Edmund speaking of Edgar, 'and pat he comes like the catastrophe of the old comedy: my cue is villainous melancholy, with a sigh like Tom o'Bedlam. O, these eclipses do portend these divisions!' And these years were marked by a number of eclipses, which were regarded as portents at the time. Putting people in the stocks makes an appearance – in the porches of many country churches we used to see the village-stocks, useful to lock delinquents in. It was, however, shocking on the part of Regan's husband to put her father the King's messenger, the Eart of Kent, in the stocks. Gloucester protests:

> Your purposed low correction
> Is such as basest and contemned'st wretches
> For pilferings and most common trespasses
> Are punished with.

An hierarchical society knew what was proper in these matters. And, again, it is given to the Fool to speak common sense about society: 'he's a mad yeoman that sees his son a gentleman before him.'

An interesting piece of information, not usually known, crops up when Gloucester is told by his bastard son, Edgar, that his legitimate brother had intended to murder their father:

> his picture
> I will send far and near, that all the kingdom
> May have due note of him –

as is the habit of the police today with wanted criminals. Kent neatly tripped Goneril's horrid steward, Oswald, by the heels with 'you base football player'. Football was but a low street-game then, not the organised mass-orgies of today which give such opportunities for the civilised masses to express themselves in their behaviour.

The play is filled with snatches of contemporary songs and ballads, bits of folklore and such. One notices, as in so many of the plays, Shakespeare's consciousness of snakes: were the Cotswolds particularly a haunt of them – as Salisbury plain evidently was of geese? The famous description of the tall cliff at Dover now known by his name reminds us that the Chamberlain's Men had been touring there not many years before.

Shakespeare's addiction to grand words is what we notice all along, and it is not just a matter of scansion: a man reveals himself in the words he chooses. Goneril tells King Lear to 'disquantity' his train, i.e. to reduce. Edgar, instead of saying 'a follower of the stars', says 'sectary astronomical', and it comes in a passage of prose. Edmund, suggesting that his brother cautiously retires for a bit, words it 'have a continent forbearance.' We have 'cadent tears', 'festinate' for speedy, 'questrists' for followers. Even the 'catastrophe' of the old play merely meant its end.

The Play. There is no other play like it – one can only call it epical. The elements themselves, storm and rain, heath and hovel, men mad and pretending to be mad, mingle together in a roaring, howling symphony. Madness on the stage is extraordinarily exciting, as Shakespeare learned from Kyd's *Jeronimo*, and as we experience from Hamlet's affected madness. For one thing, it removes all restraint upon the tongue: anything can be said, and with a more cutting edge. For all that we may compare *King Lear* with *Hamlet* as the twin peaks of Shakespeare's achievement in tragedy, the two plays are very different and in some ways at opposite poles. Hamlet is introspective and *innerlich*: there are no bounds to the exploration of that dark interior. King Lear is, in one sense, extrovert; his character is clear from the first, and he brings his tragedy on his own head. Hamlet has his burden imposed upon him from without, through no fault of his own: our sympathies are thus more deeply engaged with him. *King Lear* is intensive too, but far more extensive: it shows us a world afflicted by evil. Because of the sheer scale of the work Charles Lamb has often been cited, with approval, saying that the play is impossible of representation on the stage. But this is absurd: however epical our own imaginations may be, it was written for representation on the stage by the most experienced dramatist we have ever had.

Hazlitt concluded, 'all that we can say must fall far short of the subject, or even what we ourselves conceive of it.' Precisely – the best of reasons for letting the play speak for itself.

The Text has come down to us in two versions, that of the two quartos and that of the Folio; both, E. K. Chambers says, 'substantially derived from the same original.' The Folio is the better text, with 110 lines not in the quartos, while they contain some 300 lines not in the Folio. So editors have the job of conflating the two, and modern editions are happily longer than the originals.

The earliest recorded Court performance was 'before the King's Majesty at Whitehall upon St. Stephen's night in Christmas holidays', i.e. 26 December 1606. One would like to know what King James made of it.

KING LEAR.

DRAMATIS PERSONÆ.

LEAR, king of Britain.
KING OF FRANCE.
DUKE OF BURGUNDY.
DUKE OF CORNWALL.
DUKE OF ALBANY.
EARL OF KENT.
EARL OF GLOUCESTER.
EDGAR, son to Gloucester.
EDMUND, bastard son to Gloucester.
CURAN, a courtier.
Old Man, tenant to Gloucester.
Doctor.
Fool.

OSWALD, steward to Goneril.
A Captain employed by Edmund.
Gentleman attendant on Cordelia.
A Herald.
Servants to Cornwall.

GONERIL,
REGAN,   } daughters to Lear.
CORDELIA,

Knights of Lear's train, Captains, Messengers,
Soldiers, and Attendants.

SCENE: *Britain.*

● *A bullet beside a text line indicates an annotation in the opposite column*

ACT I.

SCENE I. *King Lear's palace.*

Enter KENT, GLOUCESTER, *and* EDMUND.

● *Kent.* I thought the king had more affected the Duke of Albany than Cornwall.

Glou. It did always seem so to us: but now, in the division of the kingdom, it appears not which of the dukes he values most; for equalities
●are so weighed, that curiosity in neither can make
●choice of either's moiety.

Kent. Is not this your son, my lord?

Glou. His breeding, sir, hath been at my charge: I have so often blushed to acknowledge
●him, that now I am brazed to it.   11

Kent. I cannot conceive you.

Glou. Sir, this young fellow's mother could: whereupon she grew round-wombed, and had, indeed, sir, a son for her cradle ere she had a husband for her bed. Do you smell a fault?

Kent. I cannot wish the fault undone, the
●issue of it being so proper.

Set design for King Lear's palace by C. Ricketts, Theatre Royal, London, 1909

---

1 *affected.* Esteemed.

6 *curiosity.* Close scrutiny.

7 *moiety.* Share.

11 *brazed to it.* Hardened to it.

18 *proper.* Handsome.

Opposite: William and Clara Rousby, Theatre Royal, Drury Lane, London, 1873

21 *account.* Estimation.

33 *out.* Abroad.

SD *Sennet.* A trumpet call.

Orson Welles as King Lear, City Center, New York, 1956

39 *fast.* Firm.

45 *several.* Individual.

51 *Interest.* Possession.

54 *nature.* Natural affection.

65 *champains.* Plains.

Glou.   But I have, sir, a son by order of law, some year elder than this, who yet is no dearer in my account: though this knave came something saucily into the world before he was sent for, yet was his mother fair; there was good sport at his making, and the whoreson must be acknowledged. Do you know this noble gentleman, Edmund?

Edm.   No, my lord.

Glou.   My lord of Kent: remember him hereafter as my honourable friend.

Edm.   My services to your lordship.

Kent.   I must love you, and sue to know you better.   31

Edm.   Sir, I shall study deserving.

Glou.   He hath been out nine years, and away he shall again.   The king is coming.

Sennet. Enter KING LEAR, CORNWALL, ALBANY, GONERIL, REGAN, CORDELIA, *and* Attendants.

Lear.   Attend the lords of France and Burgundy, Gloucester.

Glou.   I shall, my liege.
                           [*Exeunt Gloucester and Edmund.*

Lear.   Meantime we shall express our darker purpose.

Give me the map there.   Know that we have divided

In three our kingdom: and 'tis our fast intent

To shake all cares and business from our age;   40

Conferring them on younger strengths, while we

Unburthen'd crawl toward death.   Our son of Cornwall,

And you, our no less loving son of Albany,

We have this hour a constant will to publish

Our daughters' several dowers, that future strife

May be prevented now.   The princes, France and Burgundy,

Great rivals in our youngest daughter's love,

Long in our court have made their amorous sojourn,

And here are to be answer'd.   Tell me, my daughters,—

Since now we will divest us, both of rule,   50

Interest of territory, cares of state,—

Which of you shall we say doth love us most?

That we our largest bounty may extend

Where nature doth with merit challenge.   Goneril,

Our eldest-born, speak first.

Gon.   Sir, I love you more than words can wield the matter;

Dearer than eye-sight, space, and liberty;

Beyond what can be valued, rich or rare;

No less than life, with grace, health, beauty, honour;

As much as child e'er loved, or father found;   60

A love that makes breath poor, and speech unable;

Beyond all manner of so much I love you.

Cor.   [*Aside*] What shall Cordelia do?   Love, and be silent.

Lear.   Of all these bounds, even from this line to this,

With shadowy forests and with champains rich'd,

With plenteous rivers and wide-skirted meads,

We make thee lady: to thine and Albany's issue

Be this perpetual.   What says our second daughter,

Our dearest Regan, wife to Cornwall?   Speak.

Reg.   Sir, I am made   70

Of the self-same metal that my sister is,

And prize me at her worth.   In my true heart

I find she names my very deed of love;
Only she comes too short: that I profess
Myself an enemy to all other joys,
● Which the most precious square of sense possesses;
And find I am alone felicitate
In your dear highness' love.
    Cor.   [*Aside*] Then poor Cordelia!
And yet not so; since, I am sure, my love's
More richer than my tongue.   80
    Lear. To thee and thine hereditary ever
Remain this ample third of our fair kingdom;
No less in space, validity, and pleasure,
Than that conferr'd on Goneril. Now, our joy,
Although the last, not least; to whose young love
The vines of France and milk of Burgundy
Strive to be interess'd; what can you say to draw
A third more opulent than your sisters? Speak.
    Cor. Nothing, my lord.
    Lear. Nothing!   90
    Cor. Nothing.
    Lear. Nothing will come of nothing: speak
    again.
    Cor. Unhappy that I am, I cannot heave
My heart into my mouth: I love your majesty
● According to my bond; nor more nor less.
    Lear. How, how, Cordelia! mend your speech
    a little,
Lest it may mar your fortunes.
    Cor.   Good my lord,
You have begot me, bred me, loved me: I
Return those duties back as are right fit,
Obey you, love you, and most honour you. 100
Why have my sisters husbands, if they say
They love you all? Haply, when I shall wed,
● That lord whose hand must take my plight shall
    carry
Half my love with him, half my care and duty:
Sure, I shall never marry like my sisters,
To love my father all.
    Lear. But goes thy heart with this?
    Cor.   Ay, good my lord
    Lear. So young, and so untender?
    Cor. So young, my lord, and true.
    Lear. Let it be so; thy truth, then, be thy
    dower: 110
For, by the sacred radiance of the sun,
● The mysteries of Hecate, and the night;
● By all the operation of the orbs
From whom we do exist, and cease to be;
Here I disclaim all my paternal care,
Propinquity and property of blood,
And as a stranger to my heart and me
● Hold thee, from this, for ever. The barbarous
    Scythian,
● Or he that makes his generation messes
To gorge his appetite, shall to my bosom 120
Be as well neighbour'd, pitied, and relieved,
As thou my sometime daughter.
    Kent.   Good my liege,—
    Lear. Peace, Kent!
Come not between the dragon and his wrath.
● I loved her most, and thought to set my rest
On her kind nursery. Hence, and avoid my sight!
So be my grave my peace, as here I give
● Her father's heart from her! Call France; who
    stirs?
Call Burgundy. Cornwall and Albany, 129
With my two daughters' dowers digest this third:
Let pride, which she calls plainness, marry her.

76 *the most precious square of sense.* The most precisely sensitive part.

95 *bond.* Duty.

103 *plight.* Troth-plight.

Lear: 'But goes thy heart with this?' Michael Redgrave as Lear and Yvonne Mitchell as Cordelia, Stratford-upon-Avon, 1953

112 *Hecate.* Goddess of witchcraft and sorcery.

113 *operation of the orbs.* Influence of the planets.

118 *Scythian.* Synonymous with barbarism.

119 *makes his generation messes.* Eats his offspring.

125 *set my rest.* 'Stake my all', also suggesting 'rest in retirement'.

128 *who stirs?* Somebody move to obey my command!

145 *make from.* Avoid.

146 *fork.* Barb.

161 *blank.* Centre of the target.

169 *recreant.* Coward or traitor.

Sir Henry Irving as Lear. Drawing by Bernard Partridge, 1892

I do invest you jointly with my power,
Pre-eminence, and all the large effects
That troop with majesty.   Ourself, by monthly
   course,
With reservation of an hundred knights,
By you to be sustain'd, shall our abode
Make with you by due turns.   Only we still retain
The name, and all the additions to a king;
The sway, revenue, execution of the rest,
Beloved sons, be yours: which to confirm,   140
This coronet part betwixt you. [*Giving the crown.*
   Kent.   Royal Lear,
Whom I have ever honour'd as my king,
Loved as my father, as my master follow'd,
As my great patron thought on in my prayers,—
• *Lear.*   The bow is bent and drawn, make from
   the shaft.
• *Kent.*   Let it fall rather, though the fork invade
The region of my heart: be Kent unmannerly,
When Lear is mad.   What wilt thou do, old man?
Think'st thou that duty shall have dread to speak,
When power to flattery bows? To plainness
   honour's bound,   150
When majesty stoops to folly. Reverse thy doom;
And, in thy best consideration, check
This hideous rashness: answer my life my judge-
   ment,
Thy youngest daughter does not love thee least;
Nor are those empty-hearted whose low sound
Reverbs no hollowness.
   Lear.   Kent, on thy life, no more.
   Kent.   My life I never held but as a pawn
To wage against thy enemies; nor fear to lose it,
Thy safety being the motive.
   Lear.   Out of my sight!
   Kent.   See better, Lear; and let me still remain
•The true blank of thine eye.   161
   Lear.   Now, by Apollo,—
   Kent.   Now, by Apollo, king,
Thou swear'st thy gods in vain.
   Lear.   O, vassal! miscreant!
         [*Laying his hand on his sword.*
   Alb. }
   Corn.} Dear sir, forbear.
   Kent.   Do;
Kill thy physician, and the fee bestow
Upon thy foul disease.   Revoke thy doom;
Or, whilst I can vent clamour from my throat,
•I'll tell thee thou dost evil.
   Lear.   Hear me, recreant!
On thine allegiance, hear me!   170
Since thou hast sought to make us break our vow,
Which we durst never yet, and with strain'd
   pride
To come between our sentence and our power,
Which nor our nature nor our place can bear,
Our potency made good, take thy reward.
Five days we do allot thee, for provision
To shield thee from diseases of the world;
And on the sixth to turn thy hated back
Upon our kingdom: if, on the tenth day following,
Thy banish'd trunk be found in our dominions,
The moment is thy death.   Away! by Jupiter,
This shall not be revoked.
   Kent.   Fare thee well, king: sith thus thou wilt
   appear,
Freedom lives hence, and banishment is here.
[*To Cordelia*] The gods to their dear shelter take
   thee, maid,

That justly think'st, and hast most rightly said!
[*To Regan and Goneril*] And your large speeches
may your deeds approve,
That good effects may spring from words of love.
Thus Kent, O princes, bids you all adieu;
He'll shape his old course in a country new. [*Exit.*

Flourish. Re-enter GLOUCESTER, *with* FRANCE,
BURGUNDY, *and* Attendants.

 Glou. Here's France and Burgundy, my noble
  lord.   191
 Lear. My lord of Burgundy,
We first address towards you, who with this
 king
Hath rivall'd for our daughter: what, in the least,
Will you require in present dower with her,
Or cease your quest of love?
 Bur.   Most royal majesty,
I crave no more than what your highness offer'd,
Nor will you tender less.
 Lear.   Right noble Burgundy,
When she was dear to us, we did hold her so;
But now her price is fall'n. Sir, there she stands:
If aught within that little seeming substance, 201
Or all of it, with our displeasure pieced,
And nothing more, may fitly like your grace,
She's there, and she is yours.
 Bur.   I know no answer.
 ● *Lear.* Will you, with those infirmities she
  owes,
Unfriended, new-adopted to our hate,
Dower'd with our curse, and stranger'd with our
 oath,
Take her, or leave her?
 Bur.   Pardon me, royal sir;
● Election makes not up on such conditions.
 Lear. Then leave her, sir; for, by the power
  that made me,   210
I tell you all her wealth. [*To France*] For you,
  great king,
● I would not from your love make such a stray,
To match you where I hate; therefore beseech
 you
To avert your liking a more worthier way
Than on a wretch whom nature is ashamed
Almost to acknowledge hers.
 France.   This is most strange,
That she, that even but now was your best object,
The argument of your praise, balm of your age,
Most best, most dearest, should in this trice of
 time
Commit a thing so monstrous, to dismantle 220
So many folds of favour. Sure, her offence
Must be of such unnatural degree,
That monsters it, or your fore-vouch'd affection
Fall'n into taint: which to believe of her,
Must be a faith that reason without miracle
Could never plant in me.
 Cor.   I yet beseech your majesty,—
If for I want that glib and oily art,
To speak and purpose not; since what I well
 intend,
I'll do't before I speak,—that you make known
It is no vicious blot, murder, or foulness, 230
No unchaste action, or dishonour'd step,
That hath deprived me of your grace and favour;
But even for want of that for which I am richer,
A still-soliciting eye, and such a tongue
As I am glad I have not, though not to have it

205 *owes.* Owns.

209 *Election . . . conditions.* A decision is impossible in
such circumstances.

212 *stray.* Stray so far.

Ellen Terry as Cordelia, Lyceum Theatre, London,
1892

242–243 *with regards ... entire point.* With considerations that are irrelevant to the point (i.e. love).

Costume design for the Duke of Burgundy by Isamu Noguchi, Stratford-upon-Avon, 1955

268 *benison.* Blessing.

Hath lost me in your liking.
  Lear.   Better thou
Hadst not been born than not to have pleased me
    better.
  France. Is it but this,—a tardiness in nature
Which often leaves the history unspoke
That it intends to do? My lord of Burgundy,
What say you to the lady? Love's not love 241
When it is mingled with regards that stand
Aloof from the entire point. Will you have her?
She is herself a dowry.
  Bur.   Royal Lear,
Give but that portion which yourself proposed,
And here I take Cordelia by the hand,
Duchess of Burgundy.
  Lear. Nothing: I have sworn: I am firm.
  Bur. I am sorry, then, you have so lost a
    father
That you must lose a husband.
  Cor.   Peace be with Burgundy! 250
Since that respects of fortune are his love,
I shall not be his wife.
  France. Fairest Cordelia, that art most rich,
    being poor;
Most choice, forsaken; and most loved, despised!
Thee and thy virtues here I seize upon:
Be it lawful I take up what's cast away.
Gods, gods! 'tis strange that from their cold'st
    neglect
My love should kindle to inflamed respect.
Thy dowerless daughter, king, thrown to my
    chance,
Is queen of us, of ours, and our fair France: 260
Not all the dukes of waterish Burgundy
Can buy this unprized precious maid of me.
Bid them farewell, Cordelia, though unkind:
Thou losest here, a better where to find.
  Lear. Thou hast her, France: let her be
    thine; for we
Have no such daughter, nor shall ever see
That face of hers again. Therefore be gone
Without our grace, our love, our benison.
Come, noble Burgundy.
        [*Flourish. Exeunt all but France,
          Goneril, Regan, and Cordelia.*
  France. Bid farewell to your sisters. 270
  Cor. The jewels of our father, with wash'd
    eyes
Cordelia leaves you: I know you what you are;
And like a sister am most loath to call
Your faults as they are named. Use well our
    father:
To your professed bosoms I commit him:
But yet, alas, stood I within his grace,
I would prefer him to a better place.
So, farewell to you both.
  Reg. Prescribe not us our duties.
  Gon.   Let your study 279
Be to content your lord, who hath received you
At fortune's alms. You have obedience scanted,
And well are worth the want that you have
    wanted.
  Cor. Time shall unfold what plaited cunning
    hides:
Who cover faults, at last shame them derides.
Well may you prosper!
  France.   Come, my fair Cordelia.
        [*Exeunt France and Cordelia.*
  Gon. Sister, it is not a little I have to say of

what most nearly appertains to us both.   I think our father will hence to-night.

Reg.   That's most certain, and with you; next month with us.   290

Gon.   You see how full of changes his age is; the observation we have made of it hath not been little: he always loved our sister most; and with what poor judgement he hath now cast her off appears too grossly.

Reg.   'Tis the infirmity of his age: yet he hath ever but slenderly known himself.

Gon.   The best and soundest of his time hath been but rash; then must we look to receive from his age, not alone the imperfections of long-engraffed condition, but therewithal the unruly waywardness that infirm and choleric years bring with them.

● *Reg.*   Such unconstant starts are we like to have from him as this of Kent's banishment.

Gon.   There is further compliment of leave-taking between France and him.   Pray you, let's hit together: if our father carry authority with such dispositions as he bears, this last surrender of his will but offend us.   310

Reg.   We shall further think on't.

Gon.   We must do something, and i' the heat.
                                             [*Exeunt.*

SCENE II.   *The Earl of Gloucester's castle.*

Enter EDMUND, *with a letter.*

Edm.   Thou, nature, art my goddess; to thy law
My services are bound.   Wherefore should I
● Stand in the plague of custom, and permit
● The curiosity of nations to deprive me,
For that I am some twelve or fourteen moon-shines
● Lag of a brother?   Why bastard?   wherefore base?
When my dimensions are as well compact,
My mind as generous, and my shape as true,
● As honest madam's issue?   Why brand they us
With base? with baseness? bastardy? base, base?
Who, in the lusty stealth of nature, take   11
More composition and fierce quality
Than doth, within a dull, stale, tired bed,
Go to the creating a whole tribe of fops,
Got 'tween asleep and wake?   Well, then,
Legitimate Edgar, I must have your land:
Our father's love is to the bastard Edmund
As to the legitimate: fine word,—legitimate!
Well, my legitimate, if this letter speed,
And my invention thrive, Edmund the base   20
Shall top the legitimate.   I grow; I prosper:
Now, gods, stand up for bastards!

Enter GLOUCESTER.

Glou.   Kent banish'd thus! and France in choler parted!
And the king gone to-night! subscribed his power!
Confined to exhibition!   All this done
● Upon the gad!   Edmund, how now! what news?
Edm.   So please your lordship, none.
                          [*Putting up the letter.*
Glou.   Why so earnestly seek you to put up that letter?
Edm.   I know no news, my lord.
Glou.   What paper were you reading?   30

304   *unconstant starts.* Sudden impulses.

3   *Stand . . . custom.* Abide by bothersome convention.

4   *curiosity of nations.* The distinctions of national laws.

6   *Lag of.* Younger than.

9   *honest.* Chaste.

26   *gad.* Spur (of the moment).

Costume design for Regan by Isamu Noguchi, Stratford-upon Avon, 1955

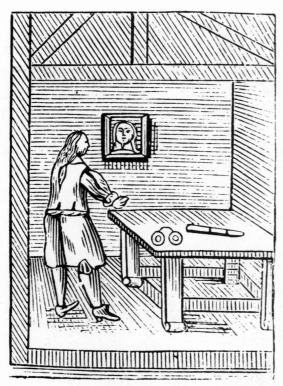

Gloucester: '. . . if it be nothing, I shall not need spectacles.' Woodcut of a spectacle maker from Comenius' *Orbis Sensualium Pictus* 1659

66 *character*. Handwriting.

83 *sirrah*. Sir, a familiar form.

95 *pretence of danger*. Dangerous intention.

Edm. Nothing, my lord

Glou. No? What needed, then, that terrible dispatch of it into your pocket? the quality of nothing hath not such need to hide itself. Let's see: come, if it be nothing, I shall not need spectacles.

Edm. I beseech you, sir, pardon me: it is a letter from my brother, that I have not all o'er-read; and for so much as I have perused, I find it not fit for your o'er-looking.   40

Glou. Give me the letter, sir.

Edm. I shall offend, either to detain or give it. The contents, as in part I understand them, are to blame.

Glou. Let's see, let's see.

Edm. I hope, for my brother's justification, he wrote this but as an essay or taste of my virtue.

Glou. [*Reads*] 'This policy and reverence of age makes the world bitter to the best of our times; keeps our fortunes from us till our oldness cannot relish them. I begin to find an idle and fond bondage in the oppression of aged tyranny; who sways, not as it hath power, but as it is suffered. Come to me, that of this I may speak more. If our father would sleep till I waked him, you should enjoy half his revenue for ever, and live the beloved of your brother,   EDGAR.'
Hum—conspiracy!—'Sleep till I waked him,—you should enjoy half his revenue,'—My son Edgar! Had he a hand to write this? a heart and brain to breed it in?—When came this to you? who brought it?

Edm. It was not brought me, my lord; there's the cunning of it; I found it thrown in at the casement of my closet.

Glou. You know the character to be your brother's?

Edm. If the matter were good, my lord, I durst swear it were his; but, in respect of that, I would fain think it were not.   70

Glou. It is his.

Edm. It is his hand, my lord; but I hope his heart is not in the contents.

Glou. Hath he never heretofore sounded you in this business?

Edm. Never, my lord: but I have heard him oft maintain it to be fit, that, sons at perfect age, and fathers declining, the father should be as ward to the son, and the son manage his revenue.

Glou. O villain, villain! His very opinion in the letter! Abhorred villain! Unnatural, detested, brutish villain! worse than brutish! Go, sirrah, seek him; I'll apprehend him: abominable villain! Where is he?

Edm. I do not well know, my lord. If it shall please you to suspend your indignation against my brother till you can derive from him better testimony of his intent, you shall run a certain course; where, if you violently proceed against him, mistaking his purpose, it would make a great gap in your own honour, and shake in pieces the heart of his obedience. I dare pawn down my life for him, that he hath wrote this to feel my affection to your honour, and to no further pretence of danger.

Glou. Think you so?

Edm. If your honour judge it meet, I will place you where you shall hear us confer of this, and by an auricular assurance have your satisfaction; and that without any further delay than this very evening.   101

Glou. He cannot be such a monster—

Edm. Nor is not, sure.

Glou. To his father, that so tenderly and entirely loves him. Heaven and earth! Edmund, seek him out: wind me into him, I pray you: frame the business after your own wisdom. I would unstate myself, to be in a due resolution.

Edm. I will seek him, sir, presently; convey the business as I shall find means, and acquaint you withal.   111

Glou. These late eclipses in the sun and moon portend no good to us: though the wisdom of nature can reason it thus and thus, yet nature finds itself scourged by the sequent effects: love cools, friendship falls off, brothers divide: in cities, mutinies; in countries, discord; in palaces, treason; and the bond cracked 'twixt son and father. This villain of mine comes under the prediction; there's son against father: the king falls from bias of nature; there's father against child. We have seen the best of our time: machinations, hollowness, treachery, and all ruinous disorders, follow us disquietly to our graves. Find out this villain, Edmund; it shall lose thee nothing; do it carefully. And the noble and true-hearted Kent banished! his offence, honesty! 'Tis strange.

[*Exit.*

Edm. This is the excellent foppery of the world, that, when we are sick in fortune,—often the surfeit of our own behaviour,—we make guilty of our disasters the sun, the moon, and the stars: as if we were villains by necessity; fools by heavenly compulsion; knaves, thieves, and treachers, by spherical predominance; drunkards, liars, and adulterers, by an enforced obedience of planetary influence; and all that we are evil in, by a divine thrusting on: an admirable evasion of whoremaster man, to lay his goatish disposition to the charge of a star! My father compounded with my mother under the dragon's tail; and my nativity was under Ursa major; so that it follows, I am rough and lecherous. Tut, I should have been that I am, had the maidenliest star in the firmament twinkled on my bastardizing. Edgar—

Enter EDGAR.

and pat he comes like the catastrophe of the old comedy: my cue is villanous melancholy, with a sigh like Tom o' Bedlam. O, these eclipses do portend these divisions! fa, sol, la, mi.

Edg. How now, brother Edmund! what serious contemplation are you in?   151

Edm. I am thinking, brother, of a prediction I read this other day, what should follow these eclipses.

Edg. Do you busy yourself about that?

Edm. I promise you, the effects he writes of succeed unhappily; as of unnaturalness between the child and the parent; death, dearth, dissolutions of ancient amities; divisions in state, menaces and maledictions against king and nobles; needless diffidences, banishment of friends, dissipation of cohorts, nuptial breaches, and I know not what.

Edg. How long have you been a sectary astronomical?

106 *wind me into him.* Gain his confidence.

108 *unstate . . . resolution.* Forfeit everything to have my doubts resolved.

109 *presently.* Immediately.

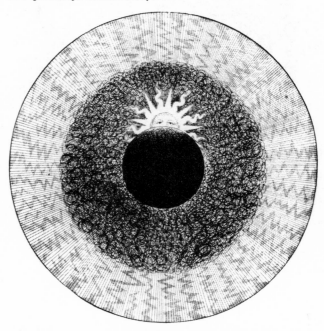

Edmund: '. . . we make guilty of our disasters the sun, the moon, and the stars?' Astronomical diagram. Engraving from Robert Fludd's *Utriusque Cosmi Metaphysica*, 1617

133–134 *treachers, by spherical predominance.* See introduction.

138 *goatish.* Lecherous.

140–141 *dragon's tail . . . Ursa major.* Constellations.

148 *Tom o' Bedlam.* A generic name for beggars who were mad or who claimed to be so.

161 *diffidences.* Suspicions.

164–165 *a sectary astronomical.* An adherent of astrology.

182 *continent forbearance.* Keep away.

198 *practices.* Plots.

Hunting scene. Woodcut from Holinshed's *Chronicles*
1577

20 *checks as flatteries.* Rebukes instead of flattery.

Edm.   Come, come; when saw you my father
last?
Edg.   Why, the night gone by.
Edm.   Spake you with him?
Edg.   Ay, two hours together.   170
Edm.   Parted you in good terms? Found you
no displeasure in him by word or countenance?
Edg.   None at all.
Edm. Bethink yourself wherein you may have
offended him: and at my entreaty forbear his
presence till some little time hath qualified the
heat of his displeasure; which at this instant so
rageth in him, that with the mischief of your
person it would scarcely allay.
Edg.   Some villain hath done me wrong. 180
Edm.   That's my fear. I pray you, have a
continent forbearance till the speed of his rage
goes slower; and, as I say, retire with me to my
lodging, from whence I will fitly bring you to
hear my lord speak: pray ye, go; there's my
key: if you do stir abroad, go armed.
Edg.   Armed, brother!
Edm.   Brother, I advise you to the best; go
armed: I am no honest man if there be any good
meaning towards you: I have told you what I
have seen and heard; but faintly, nothing like
the image and horror of it: pray you, away.
Edg.   Shall I hear from you anon?
Edm.   I do serve you in this business.
                                    [*Exit Edgar.*
A credulous father! and a brother noble,
Whose nature is so far from doing harms,
That he suspects none; on whose foolish honesty
My practices ride easy! I see the business.
Let me, if not by birth, have lands by wit: 199
All with me's meet that I can fashion fit. [*Exit.*

SCENE III.   *The Duke of Albany's palace.*

Enter GONERIL, *and* OSWALD, *her steward.*

Gon.   Did my father strike my gentleman for
       chiding of his fool?
Osw.   Yes, madam.
Gon.   By day and night he wrongs me; every
       hour
He flashes into one gross crime or other,
That sets us all at odds: I'll not endure it:
His knights grow riotous, and himself upbraids us
On every trifle.   When he returns from hunting,
I will not speak with him; say I am sick:
If you come slack of former services,
You shall do well: the fault of it I'll answer.   10
Osw.   He's coming, madam; I hear him.
                                    [*Horns within.*
Gon.   Put on what weary negligence you please,
You and your fellows; I'ld have it come to ques-
       tion:
If he dislike it, let him to our sister,
Whose mind and mine, I know, in that are one,
Not to be over-ruled.   Idle old man,
That still would manage those authorities
That he hath given away!   Now, by my life,
Old fools are babes again; and must be used
With checks as flatteries,—when they are seen
       abused.   20
Remember what I tell you.
Osw.   Well, madam.
Gon.   And let his knights have colder looks
       among you;

What grows of it, no matter; advise your fellows
  so:
● I would breed from hence occasions, and I shall,
That I may speak: I 'll write straight to my sister,
To hold my very course.   Prepare for dinner.
                                    [*Exeunt.*

SCENE IV.   *A hall in the same.*

Enter KENT, *disguised.*

Kent.   If but as well I other accents borrow,
● That can my speech defuse, my good intent
May carry through itself to that full issue
For which I razed my likeness.   Now, banish'd
  Kent,
If thou canst serve where thou dost stand con-
  demn'd,
So may it come, thy master, whom thou lovest,
Shall find thee full of labours.

Horns within.   Enter LEAR, Knights,
  and Attendants.

Lear.   Let me not stay a jot for dinner; go get
it ready.   [*Exit an Attendant.*]   How now!
what art thou?   10
Kent.   A man, sir.
Lear.   What dost thou profess? what wouldst
thou with us?
Kent.   I do profess to be no less than I seem;
to serve him truly that will put me in trust; to
love him that is honest; to converse with him
that is wise, and says little; to fear judgement;
● to fight when I cannot choose; and to eat no fish.
Lear.   What art thou?
Kent.   A very honest-hearted fellow, and as
poor as the king.   21
Lear.   If thou be as poor for a subject as he is
for a king, thou art poor enough.   What wouldst
thou?
Kent.   Service.
Lear.   Who wouldst thou serve?
Kent.   You.
Lear.   Dost thou know me, fellow?
Kent.   No, sir; but you have that in your
countenance which I would fain call master. 30
Lear.   What's that?
Kent.   Authority.
Lear.   What services canst thou do?
Kent.   I can keep honest counsel, ride, run,
● mar a curious tale in telling it, and deliver a plain
message bluntly: that which ordinary men are
fit for, I am qualified in; and the best of me is
diligence.
Lear.   How old art thou?   39
Kent.   Not so young, sir, to love a woman for
singing, nor so old to dote on her for any thing:
I have years on my back forty eight.
Lear.   Follow me; thou shalt serve me: if I
like thee no worse after dinner, I will not part
from thee yet.   Dinner, ho, dinner!   Where's
my knave? my fool?   Go you, and call my fool
hither.   [*Exit an Attendant.*

Enter OSWALD.

You, you, sirrah, where's my daughter?
Osw.   So please you,—   [*Exit.*
Lear.   What says the fellow there?   Call the
● clotpoll back.   [*Exit a Knight.*]   Where's my
fool, ho?   I think the world 's asleep.

24-25 *breed . . . speak.* Use these occasions to take issue and speak out.

John Gielgud as Lear, Old Vic, 1940

2 *defuse.* Disguise.

18 *eat no fish.* Eat solid food.

35 *curious.* Elaborate.

51 *clotpoll.* Blockhead.

75 *jealous curiosity*. Suspicious scrutiny in searching for faults.

Fool: 'Sirrah, you were best take my coxcomb.' Engraving from a medieval manuscript

Re-enter Knight.

How now! where's that mongrel?

Knight. He says, my lord, your daughter is not well.

Lear. Why came not the slave back to me when I called him.

Knight. Sir, he answered me in the roundest manner, he would not.

Lear. He would not!   60

Knight. My lord, I know not what the matter is; but, to my judgement, your highness is not entertained with that ceremonious affection as you were wont; there's a great abatement of kindness appears as well in the general dependants as in the duke himself also and your daughter.

Lear. Ha! sayest thou so?

Knight. I beseech you, pardon me, my lord, if I be mistaken; for my duty cannot be silent when I think your highness wronged.   71

Lear. Thou but rememberest me of mine own conception: I have perceived a most faint neglect of late; which I have rather blamed as mine own jealous curiosity than as a very pretence and purpose of unkindness: I will look further into't. But where's my fool? I have not seen him this two days.

Knight. Since my young lady's going into France, sir, the fool hath much pined away.   80

Lear. No more of that; I have noted it well. Go you, and tell my daughter I would speak with her. [*Exit an Attendant.*] Go you, call hither my fool.   [*Exit an Attendant.*

Re-enter OSWALD.

O, you sir, you, come you hither, sir: who am I, sir?

Osw. My lady's father.

Lear. 'My lady's father'! my lord's knave: you whoreson dog! you slave! you cur!

Osw. I am none of these, my lord; I beseech your pardon.   91

Lear. Do you bandy looks with me, you rascal?   [*Striking him.*

Osw. I'll not be struck, my lord.

Kent. Nor tripped neither, you base foot-ball player.   [*Tripping up his heels.*

Lear. I thank thee, fellow; thou servest me, and I'll love thee.

Kent. Come, sir, arise, away! I'll teach you differences: away, away! If you will measure your lubber's length again, tarry: but away! go to; have you wisdom? so. [*Pushes Oswald out.*

Lear. Now. my friendly knave, I thank thee: there's earnest of thy service.

[*Giving Kent money.*

Enter Fool.

Fool. Let me hire him too: here's my coxcomb.   [*Offering Kent his cap.*

Lear. How now, my pretty knave! how dost thou?

Fool. Sirrah, you were best take my coxcomb.

Kent. Why, fool?   110

Fool. Why, for taking one's part that's out of favour: nay, an thou canst not smile as the wind sits, thou'lt catch cold shortly: there, take my coxcomb: why, this fellow has banished two on's daughters, and did the third a blessing against his will: if thou follow him, thou must needs wear ●my coxcomb.   How now, nuncle!   Would I had two coxcombs and two daughters!

Lear. Why, my boy?   119

Fool. If I gave them all my living, I'ld keep my coxcombs myself.   There's mine; beg another of thy daughters.

Lear. Take heed, sirrah; the whip.

Fool. Truth's a dog must to kennel; he must ●be whipped out, when Lady the brach may stand by the fire and stink.

Lear. A pestilent gall to me!

Fool. Sirrah, I'll teach thee a speech.

Lear. Do.

Fool. Mark it, nuncle: 130
Have more than thou showest,
Speak less than thou knowest,
Lend less than thou owest,
Ride more than thou goest,
Learn more than thou trowest,
Set less than thou throwest;
Leave thy drink and thy whore,
And keep in-a-door,
And thou shalt have more
Than two tens to a score.   140

Kent. This is nothing, fool.

Fool. Then 'tis like the breath of an unfee'd lawyer; you gave me nothing for't.   Can you make no use of nothing, nuncle?

Lear. Why, no, boy; nothing can be made out of nothing.

Fool. [*To Kent*] Prithee, tell him, so much the rent of his land comes to: he will not believe a fool.

Lear. A bitter fool!   150

Fool. Dost thou know the difference, my boy, between a bitter fool and a sweet fool?

Lear. No, lad; teach me.

Fool. That lord that counsell'd thee
To give away thy land,
Come place him here by me,
Do thou for him stand:
The sweet and bitter fool
Will presently appear;
The one in motley here,   160
● The other found out there.

Lear. Dost thou call me fool, boy?

Fool. All thy other titles thou hast given away; that thou wast born with.

Kent. This is not altogether fool, my lord.

● *Fool.* No, faith, lords and great men will not let me: if I had a monopoly out, they would have part on't: and ladies too, they will not let me have all fool to myself; they'll be snatching. Give me an egg, nuncle, and I'll give thee two crowns.   171

Lear. What two crowns shall they be?

Fool. Why, after I have cut the egg i' the middle, and eat up the meat, the two crowns of the egg.   When thou clovest thy crown i' the ●middle, and gavest away both parts, thou borest thy ass on thy back o'er the dirt: thou hadst little wit in thy bald crown, when thou gavest thy golden one away.   If I speak like myself in this, let him be whipped that first finds it so.   180
[*Singing*] Fools had ne'er less wit in a year;
For wise men are grown foppish,

117 *nuncle*. A contraction of 'mine uncle'.

125 *brach*. Bitch hound.

161 *found out there*. i.e. Lear, who has shown himself to be a born fool as opposed to the professional fool.

166–169 *lords . . . to myself*. The fool is not allowed a monopoly of foolishness, because lords and ladies insist on acting stupidly.

176–177 *thou borest . . . dirt*. Lear has reversed the proper order by giving away his lands and titles to his daughters.

Fool: '. . . thou borest thy ass on thy back . . .' Woodcut from the mid-16th century

193 *bo-peep*. Childishly.

197 *An*. If.

Fool: '...and sometimes I am whipped for holding my peace.' Seal of Louth Grammar School. Engraving by F. W. Fairholt from J. O. Halliwell's edition of Shakespeare's works, 1853–65

208 *frontlet*. Frown (literally a headband).

212 *an O without a figure*. Zero.

219 *shealed peascod*. Shelled peaspod.

227–228 *put it ... allowance*. Encourage it by your approval.

230 *in the tender of a wholesome weal*. In the caring of a healthy state.

245 *Jug*. A nickname for Joan.

They know not how their wits to wear,
Their manners are so apish.
Lear. When were you wont to be so full of songs, sirrah?
Fool. I have used it, nuncle, ever since thou madest thy daughters thy mother: for when thou gavest them the rod, and put'st down thine own breeches,   190
[*Singing*] Then they for sudden joy did weep,
And I for sorrow sung,
That such a king should play bo-peep,
And go the fools among.
Prithee, nuncle, keep a schoolmaster that can teach thy fool to lie: I would fain learn to lie.
Lear. An you lie, sirrah, we'll have you whipped.
Fool. I marvel what kin thou and thy daughters are: they'll have me whipped for speaking true, thou'lt have me whipped for lying; and sometimes I am whipped for holding my peace. I had rather be any kind o' thing than a fool: and yet I would not be thee, nuncle; thou hast pared thy wit o' both sides, and left nothing i' the middle: here comes one o' the parings.

Enter GONERIL.

Lear. How now, daughter! what makes that frontlet on? Methinks you are too much of late i' the frown.   209
Fool. Thou wast a pretty fellow when thou hadst no need to care for her frowning; now thou art an O without a figure: I am better than thou art now; I am a fool, thou art nothing. [*To Gon.*] Yes, forsooth, I will hold my tongue; so your face bids me, though you say nothing. Mum, mum,
He that keeps nor crust nor crum,
Weary of all, shall want some.
[*Pointing to Lear*] That's a shealed peascod.
Gon. Not only, sir, this your all-licensed fool,
But other of your insolent retinue   221
Do hourly carp and quarrel; breaking forth
In rank and not-to-be-endured riots.   Sir,
I had thought, by making this well known unto you,
To have found a safe redress; but now grow fearful,
By what yourself too late have spoke and done,
That you protect this course, and put it on
By your allowance; which if you should, the fault
Would not 'scape censure, nor the redresses sleep,
Which, in the tender of a wholesome weal,   230
Might in their working do you that offence,
Which else were shame, that then necessity
Will call discreet proceeding.
Fool. For, you know, nuncle,
The hedge-sparrow fed the cuckoo so long,
That it had it head bit off by it young.
So, out went the candle, and we were left darkling.
Lear. Are you our daughter?
Gon. Come, sir,   239
I would you would make use of that good wisdom,
Whereof I know you are fraught; and put away
These dispositions, that of late transform you
From what you rightly are.
Fool. May not an ass know when the cart draws the horse? Whoop, Jug! I love thee.
Lear. Doth any here know me? This is not Lear:

Doth Lear walk thus? speak thus? Where are
   his eyes?
Either his notion weakens, his discernings
Are lethargied—Ha! waking? 'tis not so.
Who is it that can tell me who I am?   250
   Fool. Lear's shadow.
   Lear. I would learn that; for, by the marks
of sovereignty, knowledge, and reason, I should
be false persuaded I had daughters.
   Fool. Which they will make an obedient
father.
   Lear. Your name, fair gentlewoman?
   Gon. This admiration, sir, is much o' the sa-
vour
Of other your new pranks.   I do beseech you
To understand my purposes aright: 260
As you are old and reverend, you should be wise.
Here do you keep a hundred knights and squires;
Men so disorder'd, so debosh'd and bold,
That this our court, infected with their manners,
Shows like a riotous inn: epicurism and lust
Make it more like a tavern or a brothel
Than a graced palace.   The shame itself doth
   speak
For instant remedy: be then desired
By her, that else will take the thing she begs,
A little to disquantity your train;   270
And the remainder, that shall still depend,
To be such men as may besort your age,
And know themselves and you.
   Lear.   Darkness and devils!
Saddle my horses; call my train together.
Degenerate bastard! I'll not trouble thee:
Yet have I left a daughter.
   Gon. You strike my people; and your dis-
   order'd rabble
Make servants of their betters.

         Enter ALBANY.

   Lear. Woe. that too late repents,—[*To Alb.*]
      O, sir, are you come?
Is it your will?   Speak, sir.   Prepare my horses.
Ingratitude, thou marble-hearted fiend,   281
More hideous when thou show'st thee in a child
Than the sea-monster!
   Alb.   Pray, sir, be patient.
   Lear. [*To Gon.*] Detested kite! thou liest:
My train are men of choice and rarest parts,
That all particulars of duty know,
And in the most exact regard support
The worships of their name.   O most small fault,
How ugly didst thou in Cordelia show!   289
That, like an engine, wrench'd my frame of nature
From the fix'd place; drew from my heart all love,
And added to the gall.   O Lear, Lear, Lear!
Beat at this gate, that let thy folly in,
                           [*Striking his head.*
And thy dear judgement out! Go, go, my people.
   Alb. My lord, I am guiltless, as I am ignorant
Of what hath moved you.
   Lear.   It may be so, my lord.
Hear, nature, hear; dear goddess, hear!
Suspend thy purpose, if thou didst intend
To make this creature fruitful!
Into her womb convey sterility!   300
Dry up in her the organs of increase;
And from her derogate body never spring
A babe to honour her!   If she must teem,
Create her child of spleen; that it may live,

258 *admiration.* Astonishment.

265 *epicurism.* Gluttony.

271 *depend.* Be your dependents.

272 *besort.* Suit.

Lear: 'Beat at this gate, that let thy folly in, And thy
dear judgement out!' Eric Porter as Lear, Royal
Shakespeare Co, 1968

305 *thwart disnatured*. Perverse and unnatural.

322 *untented*. Unprobable. Wounds too deep to be probed.

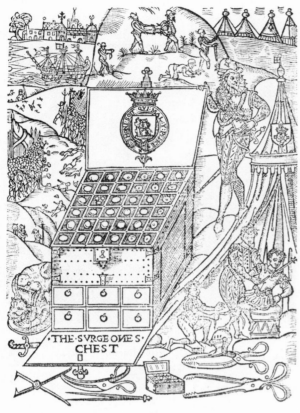

Lear: 'The untented woundings of a father's curse . . .'
A surgeon's chest with various instruments. Woodcut
from William Clowes' *A prooued practise for all young
chirurgians*, 1588

323 *fond*. Foolish.

328 *comfortable*. Comforting.

347 *At point*. Armed for action.

348 *buzz*. Rumour.

•And be a thwart disnatured torment to her!
Let it stamp wrinkles in her brow of youth;
With cadent tears fret channels in her cheeks;
Turn all her mother's pains and benefits
To laughter and contempt; that she may feel
How sharper than a serpent's tooth it is   310
To have a thankless child! Away, away! [*Exit.*
   Alb. Now, gods that we adore, whereof comes
    this?
   Gon. Never afflict yourself to know the cause;
But let his disposition have that scope
That dotage gives it.

       Re-enter LEAR.

   Lear. What, fifty of my followers at a clap!
Within a fortnight!
   Alb.   What's the matter, sir?
   Lear. I'll tell thee: [*To Gon.*] Life and
    death! I am ashamed
That thou hast power to shake my manhood thus;
That these hot tears, which break from me per-
    force,   320
Should make thee worth them.   Blasts and fogs
    upon thee!
•The untented woundings of a father's curse
•Pierce every sense about thee! Old fond eyes,
Beweep this cause again, I'll pluck ye out,
And cast you, with the waters that you lose,
To temper clay. Yea, is it come to this?
Let it be so: yet have I left a daughter,
•Who, I am sure, is kind and comfortable:
When she shall hear this of thee, with her nails
She'll flay thy wolvish visage. Thou shalt find
That I'll resume the shape which thou dost think
I have cast off for ever: thou shalt, I warrant thee.
      [*Exeunt Lear, Kent, and Attendants.*
   Gon. Do you mark that, my lord?
   Alb. I cannot be so partial, Goneril,
To the great love I bear you,—
   Gon. Pray you, content. What, Oswald, ho!
[*To the Fool*] You, sir, more knave than fool,
    after your master.
   Fool. Nuncle Lear, nuncle Lear, tarry and
take the fool with thee.
    A fox, when one has caught her,   340
      And such a daughter,
      Should sure to the slaughter,
      If my cap would buy a halter:
      So the fool follows after.   [*Exit.*
   Gon. This man hath had good counsel:—a
    hundred knights!
'Tis politic and safe to let him keep
•At point a hundred knights: yes, that, on every
    dream,
•Each buzz, each fancy, each complaint, dislike,
He may enguard his dotage with their powers,
And hold our lives in mercy. Oswald, I say!
   Alb. Well, you may fear too far.
   Gon.   Safer than trust too far: 351
Let me still take away the harms I fear,
Not fear still to be taken: I know his heart.
What he hath utter'd I have writ my sister:
If she sustain him and his hundred knights,
When I have show'd the unfitness.—

     Re-enter OSWALD.

                How now, Oswald!
What, have you writ that letter to my sister?
   Osw. Yes, madam.

Gon. Take you some company, and away to
   horse:
Inform her full of my particular fear; 360
And thereto add such reasons of your own
As may compact it more. Get you gone;
And hasten your return. [*Exit Oswald.*] No,
   no, my lord,
This milky gentleness and course of yours
Though I condemn not, yet, under pardon,
You are much more attask'd for want of wisdom
Than praised for harmful mildness.
   Alb. How far your eyes may pierce I cannot
   tell:
Striving to better, oft we mar what's well.
   Gon. Nay, then— 370
   Alb. Well, well; the event. [*Exeunt.*

SCENE V. *Court before the same.*

Enter LEAR, KENT, *and* Fool.

Lear. Go you before to Gloucester with these
letters. Acquaint my daughter no further with
any thing you know than comes from her demand
out of the letter. If your diligence be not speedy,
I shall be there afore you.
   Kent. I will not sleep, my lord, till I have
delivered your letter. [*Exit.*
   Fool. If a man's brains were in's heels, were 't
not in danger of kibes?
   Lear. Ay, boy. 10
   Fool. Then, I prithee, be merry; thy wit shall
ne'er go slip-shod.
   Lear. Ha, ha, ha!
   Fool. Shalt see thy other daughter will use
thee kindly; for though she's as like this as a
crab's like an apple, yet I can tell what I can tell.
   Lear. Why, what canst thou tell, my boy?
   Fool. She will taste as like this as a crab does
to a crab. Thou canst tell why one's nose stands
i' the middle on's face? 20
   Lear. No.
   Fool. Why, to keep one's eyes of either side's
nose; that what a man cannot smell out, he may
spy into.
   Lear. I did her wrong—
   Fool. Canst tell how an oyster makes his
shell?
   Lear. No.
   Fool. Nor I neither; but I can tell why a snail
has a house. 30
   Lear. Why?
   Fool. Why, to put his head in; not to give it
away to his daughters, and leave his horns with-
out a case.
   Lear. I will forget my nature. So kind a
father! Be my horses ready?
   Fool. Thy asses are gone about 'em. The
reason why the seven stars are no more than seven
is a pretty reason.
   Lear. Because they are not eight? 40
   Fool. Yes, indeed: thou wouldst make a good
fool.
   Lear. To take 't again perforce! Monster
ingratitude!
   Fool. If thou wert my fool, nuncle, I 'ld have
thee beaten for being old before thy time.
   Lear. How 's that?
   Fool. Thou shouldst not have been old till
thou hadst been wise.

371 *the event.* We'll wait for the outcome.

Paul Scofield as Lear, Royal Shakespeare Co, 1962

9 *kibes.* Chilblains.

11-12 *thy wit . . . slip-shod.* i.e. because your journey is
witless.

16 *crab.* Crab apple.

Lear: 'O, let me not be mad, not mad, sweet heaven!'
John Gielgud as Lear, Old Vic, 1940

---

19 *of a queasy question*. Requiring sensitive handling.

31 *In cunning*. As a ruse.

Lear.   O, let me not be mad, not mad, sweet
    heaven!   50
Keep me in temper: I would not be mad!

Enter Gentleman.

How now! are the horses ready?
Gent.   Ready, my lord.
Lear.   Come, boy.
Fool.   She that's a maid now, and laughs at
    my departure,
Shall not be a maid long, unless things be cut
    shorter.   [*Exeunt.*

ACT II.

SCENE I.   *The Earl of Gloucester's castle.*

Enter EDMUND, *and* CURAN *meets him.*

Edm.   Save thee, Curan.
Cur.   And you, sir. I have been with your
father, and given him notice that the Duke of
Cornwall and Regan his duchess will be here
with him this night.
Edm.   How comes that?
Cur.   Nay, I know not. You have heard of
the news abroad; I mean the whispered ones,
for they are yet but ear-kissing arguments?
Edm.   Not I: pray you, what are they?   10
Cur.   Have you heard of no likely wars to-
ward, 'twixt the Dukes of Cornwall and Albany?
Edm.   Not a word.
Cur.   You may do, then, in time. Fare you
well, sir.   [*Exit.*
Edm.   The duke be here to-night? The bet-
ter! best!
This weaves itself perforce into my business.
My father hath set guard to take my brother;
●And I have one thing, of a queasy question,
Which I must act: briefness and fortune, work!
Brother, a word; descend: brother, I say!   21

Enter EDGAR.

My father watches: O sir, fly this place;
Intelligence is given where you are hid;
You have now the good advantage of the night:
Have you not spoken 'gainst the Duke of Corn-
    wall?
He's coming hither; now, i' the night, i' the haste,
And Regan with him: have you nothing said
Upon his party 'gainst the Duke of Albany?
Advise yourself.
Edg.   I am sure on't, not a word.
Edm.   I hear my father coming: pardon me;
●In cunning I must draw my sword upon you: 31
Draw; seem to defend yourself; now quit you
    well.
Yield: come before my father. Light, ho, here!
Fly, brother. Torches, torches! So, farewell.
                          [*Exit Edgar.*
Some blood drawn on me would beget opinion
                          [*Wounds his arm.*
Of my more fierce endeavour: I have seen
    drunkards
Do more than this in sport. Father, father!
Stop, stop! No help?

Enter GLOUCESTER, *and* Servants *with torches.*

Glou.   Now, Edmund, where's the villain?

Edm.   Here stood he in the dark, his sharp
          sword out,   40
Mumbling of wicked charms, conjuring the moon
To stand auspicious mistress,—
     Glou.   But where is he?
Edm.   Look, sir, I bleed.
     Glou.   Where is the villain, Edmund?
Edm.   Fled this way, sir. When by no means
          he could—
Glou.   Pursue him, ho! Go after. [*Exeunt
          some Servants.*] By no means what?
     Edm.   Persuade me to the murder of your
          lordship;
But that I told him, the revenging gods
'Gainst parricides did all their thunders bend;
Spoke, with how manifold and strong a bond
The child was bound to the father; sir, in fine, 50
Seeing how loathly opposite I stood
● To his unnatural purpose, in fell motion,
With his prepared sword, he charges home
● My unprovided body, lanced mine arm:
But when he saw my best alarum'd spirits,
Bold in the quarrel's right, roused to the en-
          counter,
● Or whether gasted by the noise I made,
Full suddenly he fled.
     Glou.   Let him fly far:
Not in this land shall he remain uncaught;
And found—dispatch. The noble duke my master,
● My worthy arch and patron, comes to-night: 61
By his authority I will proclaim it,
That he which finds him shall deserve our thanks,
Bringing the murderous coward to the stake;
He that conceals him, death.
     Edm.   When I dissuaded him from his intent,
● And found him pight to do it, with curst speech
I threaten'd to discover him: he replied,
● 'Thou unpossessing bastard! dost thou think,
If I would stand against thee, would the reposal
Of any trust, virtue, or worth in thee   71
Make thy words faith'd? No: what I should
          deny,—
As this I would; ay, though thou didst produce
My very character,—I'ld turn it all
To thy suggestion, plot, and damned practice:
And thou must make a dullard of the world,
If they not thought the profits of my death
Were very pregnant and potential spurs
● To make thee seek it.'
     Glou.   Strong and fasten'd villain!
Would he deny his letter? I never got him. 80
                              [*Tucket within.*
Hark, the duke's trumpets! I know not why he
          comes.
All ports I'll bar; the villain shall not 'scape;
The duke must grant me that: besides, his picture
I will send far and near, that all the kingdom
May have due note of him; and of my land,
Loyal and natural boy, I'll work the means
To make thee capable.

Enter CORNWALL, REGAN, *and* Attendants.

Corn.   How now, my noble friend! since I
          came hither,
Which I can call but now, I have heard strange
          news.
     Reg.   If it be true, all vengeance comes too
          short   90

Edmund: 'Mumbling of wicked charms, conjuring the
moon To stand auspicious mistress.' Woodcut from
Holinshed's *Chronicles*, 1577

52 *fell motion.* Fierce thrust.

54 *unprovided.* Not ready.

57 *gasted.* Aghast, frightened.

61 *arch.* Chief.

67 *pight.* Determined, fixed.

69 *unpossessing.* By law bastards could not inherit land.

79 *fasten'd.* Resolute.

SD   *Tucket.* Flourish on a trumpet.

113–114 *make your ... please.* Carry out your purpose (to capture Edgar) using my authority in whatever way it is most helpful.

122 *poise.* Weight.

Costume design for Gloucester by Leslie Hurry, Stratford-upon-Avon, 1950

Which can pursue the offender.   How dost, my
  lord?
  Glou.   O, madam, my old heart is crack'd,   is
  crack'd!
  Reg.   What, did my father's godson seek your
  life?
He whom my father named? your Edgar?
  Glou.   O, lady, lady, shame would have it hid!
  Reg.   Was he not companion with the riotous
  knights
That tend upon my father?
  Glou.   I know not, madam: 'tis too bad, too
  bad.
  Edm.   Yes, madam, he was of that consort.
  Reg.   No marvel, then, though he were ill af-
  fected: 100
'Tis they have put him on the old man's death,
To have the expense and waste of his revenues.
I have this present evening from my sister
Been well inform'd of them; and with such cau-
  tions,
That if they come to sojourn at my house,
I'll not be there.
  Corn.   Nor I, assure thee, Regan.
Edmund, I hear that you have shown your father
A child-like office.
  Edm.   'Twas my duty, sir.
  Glou.   He did bewray his practice; and re-
  ceived
This hurt you see, striving to apprehend him. 110
  Corn.   Is he pursued?
  Glou.   Ay, my good lord.
  Corn.   If he be taken, he shall never more
● Be fear'd of doing harm: make your own purpose,
How in my strength you please.   For you, Ed-
  mund,
Whose virtue and obedience doth this instant
So much commend itself, you shall be ours:
Natures of such deep trust we shall much need;
You we first seize on.
  Edm.   I shall serve you, sir,
Truly, however else.
  Glou.   For him I thank your grace.
  Corn.   You know not why we came to visit
  you,—   120
  Reg.   Thus out of season, threading dark-eyed
  night:
● Occasions, noble Gloucester, of some poise,
Wherein we must have use of your advice:
Our father he hath writ, so hath our sister,
Of differences, which I least thought it fit
To answer from our home; the several messen-
  gers
From hence attend dispatch.   Our good old friend,
Lay comforts to your bosom; and bestow
Your needful counsel to our business,
Which craves the instant use.
  Glou.   I serve you, madam: 130
Your graces are right welcome.   [*Exeunt.*

    SCENE II.   *Before Gloucester's castle.*

    Enter KENT *and* OSWALD, *severally.*

  Osw.   Good dawning to thee, friend: art of
this house?
  Kent.   Ay.
  Osw.   Where may we set our horses?
  Kent.   I' the mire.
  Osw.   Prithee, if thou lovest me, tell me.

Kent. I love thee not.

Osw. Why, then, I care not for thee.

Kent. If I had thee in Lipsbury pinfold, I would make thee care for me.   10

Osw. Why dost thou use me thus? I know thee not.

Kent. Fellow, I know thee.

Osw. What dost thou know me for?

Kent. A knave; a rascal; an eater of broken meats; a base, proud, shallow, beggarly, three-suited, hundred-pound, filthy, worsted-stocking knave; a lily-livered, action-taking knave, a whoreson, glass-gazing, superserviceable, finical rogue; one-trunk-inheriting slave; one that wouldst be a bawd, in way of good service, and art nothing but the composition of a knave, beggar, coward, pandar, and the son and heir of a mongrel bitch: one whom I will beat into clamorous whining, if thou deniest the least syllable of thy addition.

Osw. Why, what a monstrous fellow art thou, thus to rail on one that is neither known of thee nor knows thee!   29

Kent. What a brazen-faced varlet art thou, to deny thou knowest me! Is it two days ago since I tripped up thy heels, and beat thee before the king? Draw, you rogue: for, though it be night, yet the moon shines; I'll make a sop o' the moonshine of you: draw, you whoreson cullionly barber-monger, draw.

                    [*Drawing his sword.*

Osw. Away! I have nothing to do with thee.

Kent. Draw, you rascal: you come with letters against the king; and take vanity the puppet's part against the royalty of her father: draw, you rogue, or I'll so carbonado your shanks: draw, you rascal: come your ways.

Osw. Help, ho! murder! help!

Kent. Strike, you slave; stand, rogue, stand; you neat slave, strike.   [*Beating him.*

Osw. Help, ho! murder! murder!

Enter EDMUND, *with his rapier drawn*, CORNWALL, REGAN, GLOUCESTER, *and* Servants.

Edm. How now! What's the matter?

Kent. With you, goodman boy, an you please: come, I'll flesh ye; come on, young master.

Glou. Weapons! arms! What's the matter here?   51

Corn. Keep peace, upon your lives: He dies that strikes again. What is the matter?

Reg. The messengers from our sister and the king.

Corn. What is your difference? speak.

Osw. I am scarce in breath, my lord.

Kent. No marvel, you have so bestirred your valour. You cowardly rascal, nature disclaims in thee: a tailor made thee.   60

Corn. Thou art a strange fellow: a tailor make a man?

Kent. Ay, a tailor, sir: a stone-cutter or a painter could not have made him so ill, though he had been but two hours at the trade.

Corn. Speak yet, how grew your quarrel?

Osw. This ancient ruffian, sir, whose life I have spared at suit of his gray beard,—

Kent. Thou whoreson zed! thou unnecessary letter! My lord, if you will give me leave, I will tread this unbolted villain into mortar, and daub

9 *Lipsbury.* Between the teeth. *pinfold.* A pen where stray animals were kept.

15-16 *broken meats.* Left-overs.

16-17 *three-suited.* Servants were given three suits a year.

18 *action-taking.* Resorting to law instead of fighting.

19 *superserviceable, finical.* Obsequious, fussy.

36 *cullionly barber-monger.* Low fop.

41 *carbonado.* Slash, like meat.

49 *flesh ye.* Give you first taste of blood.

Kent: '. . . a tailor made thee.' Engraving by F. W. Fairholt from J. O. Halliwell's edition of Shakespeare's works, 1853–65

69 *zed.* Last and, for the Elizabethans, useless letter.

71 *unbolted.* Unsifted, therefore coarse.

80 *holy cords.* The bonds of natural affection.

84 *halcyon.* Kingfisher; which when suspended by its neck was believed to show which way the wind blew.

89 *Sarum plain.* Salisbury plain.

90 *Camelot.* Legendary capital of King Arthur.

103 *constrains the garb.* Forces the style.

114 *Phœbus' front.* The face of the sun.

130 *fleshment.* Embodiment.

Costume design for Cornwall by Isamu Noguchi, Stratford-upon-Avon, 1955

the walls of a jakes with him.   Spare my gray beard, you wagtail?
   Corn.   Peace, sirrah!
You beastly knave, know you no reverence?
   Kent.   Yes, sir; but anger hath a privilege.
   Corn.   Why art thou angry?
   Kent.   That such a slave as this should wear a
     sword,
Who wears no honesty.   Such smiling rogues as these,
● Like rats, oft bite the holy cords a-twain   80
Which are too intrinse t' unloose; smooth every passion
That in the natures of their lords rebel;
Bring oil to fire, snow to their colder moods;
● Renege, affirm, and turn their halcyon beaks
With every gale and vary of their masters,
Knowing nought, like dogs, but following.
A plague upon your epileptic visage!
Smile you my speeches, as I were a fool?
● Goose, if I had you upon Sarum plain,
● I 'ld drive ye cackling home to Camelot.   90
   Corn.   What, art thou mad, old fellow?
   Glou.   How fell you out? say that.
   Kent.   No contraries hold more antipathy
Than I and such a knave.
   Corn.   Why dost thou call him knave? What's his offence?
   Kent.   His countenance likes me not.
   Corn.   No more, perchance, does mine, nor his, nor hers.
   Kent.   Sir, 'tis my occupation to be plain:
I have seen better faces in my time
Than stands on any shoulder that I see   100
Before me at this instant.
   Corn.   This is some fellow,
Who, having been praised for bluntness, doth affect
● A saucy roughness, and constrains the garb
Quite from his nature: he cannot flatter, he,
An honest mind and plain, he must speak truth!
An they will take it, so; if not, he's plain.
These kind of knaves I know, which in this plainness
Harbour more craft and more corrupter ends
Than twenty silly ducking observants
That stretch their duties nicely.   110
   Kent.   Sir, in good sooth, in sincere verity,
Under the allowance of your great aspect,
Whose influence, like the wreath of radiant fire
● On flickering Phœbus' front,—
   Corn.   What mean'st by this?
   Kent.   To go out of my dialect, which you discommend so much. I know, sir, I am no flatterer: he that beguiled you in a plain accent was a plain knave; which for my part I will not be, though I should win your displeasure to entreat me to 't.   120
   Corn.   What was the offence you gave him?
   Osw.   I never gave him any:
It pleased the king his master very late
To strike at me, upon his misconstruction;
When he, conjunct, and flattering his displeasure,
Tripp'd me behind; being down, insulted, rail'd,
And put upon him such a deal of man,
That worthied him, got praises of the king
For him attempting who was self-subdued;
● And, in the fleshment of this dread exploit,   130
Drew on me here again.

Kent.   None of these rogues and cowards
But Ajax is their fool.
    Corn.   Fetch forth the stocks!
You stubborn ancient knave, you reverend brag-
    gart,
We'll teach you—
    Kent.   Sir, I am too old to learn:
Call not your stocks for me: I serve the king;
On whose employment I was sent to you:
You shall do small respect, show too bold malice
Against the grace and person of my master,
Stocking his messenger.
    Corn. Fetch forth the stocks! As I have life
    and honour,   140
There shall he sit till noon.
    Reg. Till noon! till night, my lord; and all
    night too.
    Kent. Why, madam, if I were your father's dog,
You should not use me so.
    Reg.   Sir, being his knave, I will.
    Corn. This is a fellow of the self-same colour
Our sister speaks of. Come, bring away the
    stocks!   [*Stocks brought out.*
    Glou. Let me beseech your grace not to do so:
His fault is much, and the good king his master
Will check him for't: your purposed low cor-
    rection
Is such as basest and contemned'st wretches 150
For pilferings and most common trespasses
Are punish'd with: the king must take it ill,
That he's so slightly valued in his messenger,
Should have him thus restrain'd.
    Corn.   I'll answer that.
    Reg. My sister may receive it much more
    worse,
To have her gentleman abused, assaulted,
For following her affairs. Put in his legs.
           [*Kent is put in the stocks.*
Come, my good lord, away.
        [*Exeunt all but Gloucester and Kent.*
    Glou. I am sorry for thee, friend; 'tis the
    duke's pleasure,
Whose disposition, all the world well knows, 160
Will not be rubb'd nor stopp'd: I'll entreat for
    thee.
    Kent. Pray, do not, sir: I have watched and
    travell'd hard;
Some time I shall sleep out, the rest I'll whistle.
A good man's fortune may grow out at heels:
Give you good morrow!
    Glou. The duke's to blame in this; 'twill be
    ill taken.   [*Exit.*
    Kent. Good king, that must approve the com-
    mon saw,
Thou out of heaven's benediction comest
To the warm sun!
Approach, thou beacon to this under globe, 170
That by thy comfortable beams I may
Peruse this letter! Nothing almost sees miracles
But misery: I know 'tis from Cordelia,
Who hath most fortunately been inform'd
Of my obscured course; and shall find time
† From this enormous state, seeking to give
Losses their remedies. All weary and o'er-
    watch'd,
Take vantage, heavy eyes, not to behold
This shameful lodging.
Fortune, good night: smile once more; turn thy
    wheel!   [*Sleeps.* 180

132–133 *None . . . fool.* Ajax was a Greek hero, but was brave rather than intelligent. Kent implies that the blustering Oswald thinks himself greater than Ajax, not only in intelligence but in bravery.

161 *rubb'd.* Deflected.

167 *approve the common saw.* Confirm the common saying.

168–169 *Thou out . . . sun.* Go from better to worse.

172–173 *Nothing . . . misery.* Only the most miserable seek for miracles.

Gloucester: 'Fortune, good night: smile once more; turn thy wheel!' Woodcut of the Wheel of Fortune from *Il Ballaino di M. Fabrito Couroso da Sevmonenta,* 1581

5 *attend my taking.* Await my capture.

10 *elf.* Tangle.

Edgar: 'The country gives me proof and precedent Of Bedlam beggars. . .' Engraving of a Tom O'Bedlam by F. W. Fairholt from J. O. Halliwell's edition of Shakespeare's works, 1853–65

11 *nether-stocks.* Stockings.

24 *upon respect.* Upon the person of the king's messenger who merits respect.

SCENE III. *A wood.*

Enter EDGAR.

Edg. I heard myself proclaim'd;
And by the happy hollow of a tree
Escaped the hunt. No port is free; no place,
That guard, and most unusual vigilance,
•Does not attend my taking. Whiles I may 'scape,
I will preserve myself: and am bethought
To take the basest and most poorest shape
That ever penury, in contempt of man,
Brought near to beast: my face I'll grime with filth;
•Blanket my loins; elf all my hair in knots; 10
And with presented nakedness out-face
The winds and persecutions of the sky.
The country gives me proof and precedent
Of Bedlam beggars, who, with roaring voices,
Strike in their numb'd and mortified bare arms
Pins, wooden pricks, nails, sprigs of rosemary;
And with this horrible object, from low farms,
Poor pelting villages, sheep-cotes, and mills,
Sometime with lunatic bans, sometime with prayers,
Enforce their charity. Poor Turlygod! poor Tom! 20
That's something yet: Edgar I nothing am.
[*Exit.*

SCENE IV. *Before Gloucester's castle. Kent in the stocks.*

Enter LEAR, Fool, *and* Gentleman.

Lear. 'Tis strange that they should so depart from home,
And not send back my messenger.
Gent.   As I learn'd,
The night before there was no purpose in them
Of this remove.
Kent.   Hail to thee, noble master!
Lear. Ha!
Makest thou this shame thy pastime?
Kent.   No, my lord.
Fool. Ha, ha! he wears cruel garters. Horses are tied by the heads, dogs and bears by the neck, monkeys by the loins, and men by the legs: when a man's over-lusty at legs, then he wears wooden
•nether-stocks. 11
Lear. What's he that hath so much thy place mistook
To set thee here?
Kent.   It is both he and she;
Your son and daughter.
Lear. No.
Kent. Yes.
Lear. No, I say.
Kent. I say, yea.
Lear. No, no, they would not.
Kent. Yes, they have. 20
Lear. By Jupiter, I swear, no.
Kent. By Juno, I swear, ay.
Lear.   They durst not do't;
They could not, would not do't; 'tis worse than murder,
•To do upon respect such violent outrage:
Resolve me, with all modest haste, which way
Thou mightst deserve, or they impose, this usage,
Coming from us.

Kent.   My lord, when at their home
I did commend your highness' letters to them,
Ere I was risen from the place that show'd
My duty kneeling, came there a reeking post, 30
Stew'd in his haste, half breathless, panting forth
From Goneril his mistress salutations;
Deliver'd letters, spite of intermission,
Which presently they read: on whose contents,
They summon'd up their meiny, straight took
       horse;
Commanded me to follow, and attend
The leisure of their answer; gave me cold looks:
And meeting here the other messenger,
Whose welcome, I perceived, had poison'd mine,—
Being the very fellow that of late   40
Display'd so saucily against your highness,—
Having more man than wit about me, drew:
He raised the house with loud and coward cries.
Your son and daughter found this trespass worth
The shame which here it suffers.
Fool.   Winter's not gone yet, if the wild-geese
fly that way.
          Fathers that wear rags
              Do make their children blind;
          But fathers that bear bags   50
              Shall see their children kind.
          Fortune, that arrant whore,
              Ne'er turns the key to the poor.
But, for all this, thou shalt have as many dolours
for thy daughters as thou canst tell in a year.
Lear.   O, how this mother swells up toward
       my heart!
Hysterica passio, down, thou climbing sorrow,
Thy element's below!   Where is this daughter?
Kent.   With the earl, sir, here within.
Lear.   Follow me not;
Stay here.   [*Exit.* 60
Gent.   Made you no more offence but what
you speak of?
Kent.   None.
How chance the king comes with so small a train?
Fool.   An thou hadst been set i' the stocks for
that question, thou hadst well deserved it.
Kent.   Why, fool?
Fool.   We'll set thee to school to an ant, to
teach thee there's no labouring i' the winter.
All that follow their noses are led by their eyes
but blind men; and there's not a nose among
twenty but can smell him that's stinking.   Let
go thy hold when a great wheel runs down a hill,
lest it break thy neck with following it; but the
great one that goes up the hill, let him draw thee
after.   When a wise man gives thee better counsel, give me mine again: I would have none but
knaves follow it, since a fool gives it.
          That sir which serves and seeks for gain,
              And follows but for form,   80
          Will pack when it begins to rain,
              And leave thee in the storm.
          But I will tarry; the fool will stay,
              And let the wise man fly:
          The knave turns fool that runs away;
              The fool no knave, perdy.
Kent.   Where learned you this, fool?
Fool.   Not i' the stocks, fool.

     Re-enter LEAR, *with* GLOUCESTER.

Lear.   Deny to speak with me?   They are
       sick? they are weary?

35 *meiny.* Attendants.

50 *bags.* i.e. money bags.

56 *mother.* A scummy contamination occurring in the
fermentation of vinegar. There is also a quibble upon
the 'hysterica passio' (hysteria being considered a
woman's ailment) of the following line.

Fool: 'That sir which serves and seeks for gain. . .'
The folly of seeking after material riches and gain.
Woodcut from Alexander Barclay's *The Ship of Fooles*,
1774

90 *fetches.* Tricks.

91 *images.* Signs. *flying off.* Deserting.

Edwin Booth, the American actor, as King Lear, Princess's Theatre, London, 1881

108 *Whereto ... bound.* Which, in health we would perform.

115 *remotion.* Aloofness.

120 *sleep to death.* i.e. murders sleep.

123 *cockney.* City dweller.

125 *knapped.* Rapped.

127–128 *buttered his hay.* Dishonest ostlers used to grease the hay so that the horse would not eat it, but the cockney buttered the hay out of the kindness of his heart.

They have travell'd all the night? Mere fetches;
The images of revolt and flying off. 91
Fetch me a better answer.
    Glou.   My dear lord,
You know the fiery quality of the duke;
How unremoveable and fix'd he is
In his own course.
    Lear.   Vengeance! plague! death! confusion!
Fiery? what quality? Why, Gloucester, Gloucester,
I'ld speak with the Duke of Cornwall and his
    wife.
    Glou. Well, my good lord, I have inform'd
    them so.
    Lear. Inform'd them! Dost thou understand
    me, man?   100
    Glou. Ay, my good lord.
    Lear. The king would speak with Cornwall;
    the dear father
Would with his daughter speak, commands her
    service:
Are they inform'd of this? My breath and blood!
Fiery? the fiery duke? Tell the hot duke that—
No, but not yet: may be he is not well:
Infirmity doth still neglect all office
Whereto our health is bound; we are not our-
    selves
When nature, being oppress'd, commands the
    mind
To suffer with the body: I'll forbear;   110
And am fall'n out with my more headier will,
To take the indisposed and sickly fit
For the sound man.   Death on my state! where-
    fore   [*Looking on Kent.*
Should he sit here? This act persuades me
That this remotion of the duke and her
Is practice only. Give me my servant forth.
Go tell the duke and 's wife I'ld speak with them,
Now, presently: bid them come forth and hear
    me,
Or at their chamber-door I'll beat the drum
Till it cry sleep to death.   120
    Glou. I would have all well betwixt you. [*Exit.*
    Lear. O me, my heart, my rising heart! but,
    down!
    Fool. Cry to it, nuncle, as the cockney did to
the eels when she put 'em i' the paste alive; she
knapped 'em o' the coxcombs with a stick, and
cried 'Down, wantons, down!' 'Twas her brother that, in pure kindness to his horse, buttered
his hay.

Enter CORNWALL, REGAN, GLOUCESTER, *and*
    Servants.

    Lear. Good morrow to you both.
    Corn.   Hail to your grace!
                        [*Kent is set at liberty.*
    Reg. I am glad to see your highness.   130
    Lear. Regan, I think you are; I know what
    reason
I have to think so: if thou shouldst not be glad,
I would divorce me from thy mother's tomb,
Sepulchring an adultress. [*To Kent*] O, are you
    free?
Some other time for that. Beloved Regan,
Thy sister's naught: O Regan, she hath tied
Sharp-tooth'd unkindness, like a vulture, here:
                        [*Points to his heart.*
I can scarce speak to thee; thou'lt not believe

With how depraved a **quality**—O Regan!
Reg.   I pray you, sir, take patience: I have
     hope   140
You less know how to value her desert
Than she to scant her duty.
    Lear.   Say, how is that?
    Reg.   I cannot think my sister in the least
Would fail her obligation: if, sir, perchance
She have restrain'd the riots of your followers,
'Tis on such ground, and to such wholesome end,
As clears her from all blame.
    Lear.   My curses on her!
    Reg.   O, sir, you are old;
● Nature in you stands on the very verge
Of her confine: you should be ruled and led   150
By some discretion, that discerns your state
Better than you yourself. Therefore, I pray you,
That to our sister you do make return;
Say you have wrong'd her, sir.
    Lear.   Ask her forgiveness?
Do you but mark how this becomes the house:
' Dear daughter, I confess that I am old;
                        [*Kneeling.*
Age is unnecessary: on my knees I beg
That you 'll vouchsafe me raiment, bed, and food.'
    Reg.   Good sir, no more; these are unsightly
     tricks:
Return you to my sister.
    Lear.   [*Rising*] Never, Regan: 160
She hath abated me of half my train;
Look'd black upon me; struck me with her
     tongue,
Most serpent-like, upon the very heart:
All the stored vengeances of heaven fall
On her ingrateful top! Strike her young bones,
● You taking airs, with lameness!
    Corn.   Fie, sir, fie!
    Lear.   You nimble lightnings, dart your blind-
     ing flames
Into her scornful eyes! Infect her beauty,
You fen-suck'd fogs, drawn by the powerful sun,
To fall and blast her pride!   170
    Reg.   O the blest gods! so will you wish on
     me,
When the rash mood is on.
    Lear.   No, Regan, thou shalt never have my
     curse:
● Thy tender-hefted nature shall not give
Thee o'er to harshness: her eyes are fierce; but
     thine
Do comfort and not burn. 'Tis not in thee
● To grudge my pleasures, to cut off my train,
● To bandy hasty words, to scant my sizes,
And in conclusion to oppose the bolt
Against my coming in: thou better know'st   180
The offices of nature, bond of childhood,
Effects of courtesy, dues of gratitude;
Thy half o' the kingdom hast thou not forgot,
Wherein I thee endow'd.
    Reg.   Good sir, to the purpose.
    Lear.   Who put my man i' the stocks?
                  [*Tucket within.*
    Corn.   What trumpet's that?
    Reg.   I know't, my sister's: this approves her
     letter,
That she would soon be here.

          Enter OSWALD.

           Is your lady come?

149–150 *very ... confine.* i.e. the end of life.

Costume design for Regan by Leslie Hurry, Stratford-upon-Avon, 1950

166 *taking.* Infectious.

174 *tender-hefted.* Gentle.

177 *cut off my train.* Reduce my followers.

178 *sizes.* Allowances.

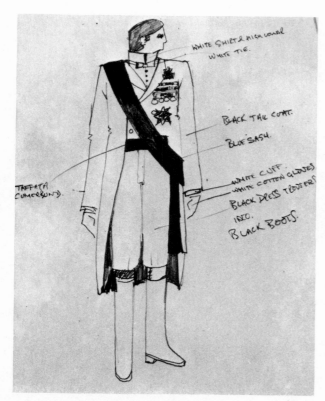

WHITE SHIRT & HIGH COLLAR
WHITE TIE.

BLACK TAIL COAT.

BLUE SASH.

WHITE CUFF
WHITE COTTON GLOVES
BLACK DRESS TROUSERS
INTO.
BLACK BOOTS.

TAFFATA
CUMMERBUND.

Costume design for the Duke of Cornwall by John Napier, Royal Shakespeare Co, 1976

219 *sumpter*. Driver of pack horse.

227 *embossed*. Swollen.

230 *thunder-bearer*. Jupiter.

237 *mingle . . . passion*. Regard your passion reasonably.

Lear. This is a slave, whose easy-borrow'd pride
Dwells in the fickle grace of her he follows.
Out, varlet, from my sight!
   Corn.   What means your grace? 190
   Lear. Who stock'd my servant? Regan, I
      have good hope
Thou didst not know on't. Who comes here?
      O heavens,

Enter GONERIL.

If you do love old men, if your sweet sway
Allow obedience, if yourselves are old,
Make it your cause; send down, and take my
      part!
[*To Gon.*] Art not ashamed to look upon this
      beard?
O Regan, wilt thou take her by the hand?
   Gon. Why not by the hand, sir? How have
      I offended?
All's not offence that indiscretion finds
And dotage terms so.
   Lear.   O sides, you are too tough; 200
Will you yet hold? How came my man i' the
      stocks?
   Corn. I set him there, sir: but his own dis-
      orders
Deserved much less advancement.
   Lear.   You! did you?
   Reg. I pray you, father, being weak, seem so.
If, till the expiration of your month,
You will return and sojourn with my sister,
Dismissing half your train, come then to me:
I am now from home, and out of that provision
Which shall be needful for your entertainment.
   Lear. Return to her, and fifty men dismiss'd?
No, rather I abjure all roofs, and choose   211
To wage against the enmity o' the air;
To be a comrade with the wolf and owl,—
Necessity's sharp pinch! Return with her?
Why, the hot-blooded France, that dowerless took
Our youngest born, I could as well be brought
To knee his throne, and, squire-like, pension beg
To keep base life afoot. Return with her?
● Persuade me rather to be slave and sumpter
To this detested groom. [*Pointing at Oswald.*
   Gon.   At your choice, sir. 220
   Lear. I prithee, daughter, do not make me
      mad:
I will not trouble thee, my child; farewell:
We'll no more meet, no more see one another:
But yet thou art my flesh, my blood, my daughter;
Or rather a disease that's in my flesh,
Which I must needs call mine: thou art a boil,
● A plague-sore, an embossed carbuncle,
In my corrupted blood. But I'll not chide thee:
Let shame come when it will, I do not call it:
● I do not bid the thunder-bearer shoot,   230
Nor tell tales of thee to high-judging Jove:
Mend when thou canst; be better at thy leisure:
I can be patient; I can stay with Regan,
I and my hundred knights.
   Reg.   Not altogether so:
I look'd not for you yet, nor am provided
For your fit welcome. Give ear, sir, to my sister;
● For those that mingle reason with your passion
Must be content to think you old, and so—
But she knows what she does.
   Lear.   Is this well spoken?

Reg. I dare avouch it, sir: what, fifty fol-
lowers?   240
Is it not well? What should you need of more?
Yea, or so many, sith that both charge and danger
Speak 'gainst so great a number? How, in one
house,
Should many people, under two commands,
Hold amity? 'Tis hard; almost impossible.
   Gon. Why might not you, my lord, receive
attendance
From those that she calls servants or from mine?
● *Reg.* Why not, my lord? If then they chanced
to slack you,
We could control them. If you will come to
me,—
For now I spy a danger,—I entreat you   250
To bring but five and twenty: to no more
Will I give place or notice.
   Lear. I gave you all—
   Reg.   And in good time you gave it.
● *Lear.* Made you my guardians, my deposi-
taries;
But kept a reservation to be follow'd
With such a number. What, must I come to you
With five and twenty, Regan? said you so?
   Reg. And speak 't again, my lord; no more
with me.
   Lear. Those wicked creatures yet do look
well-favour'd,
When others are more wicked; not being the
worst   260
Stands in some rank of praise. [*To Gon.*] I'll
go with thee:
Thy fifty yet doth double five-and-twenty,
And thou art twice her love.
   Gon.   Hear me, my lord:
What need you five and twenty, ten, or five,
To follow in a house where twice so many
Have a command to tend you?
   Reg.   What need one?
   Lear. O, reason not the need: our basest
beggars
Are in the poorest thing superfluous:
Allow not nature more than nature needs,
Man's life's as cheap as beast's: thou art a lady;
If only to go warm were gorgeous,   271
Why, nature needs not what thou gorgeous
wear'st,
Which scarcely keeps thee warm. But, for true
need,—
You heavens, give me that patience, patience I
need!
You see me here, you gods, a poor old man,
As full of grief as age; wretched in both!
If it be you that stir these daughters' hearts
Against their father, fool me not so much
To bear it tamely; touch me with noble anger,
And let not women's weapons, water-drops,   280
Stain my man's cheeks! No, you unnatural hags,
I will have such revenges on you both,
That all the world shall—I will do such things,—
What they are, yet I know not; but they shall be
The terrors of the earth. You think I'll weep;
No, I'll not weep:
I have full cause of weeping; but this heart
Shall break into a hundred thousand flaws,
Or ere I'll weep. O fool, I shall go mad!
   [*Exeunt Lear, Gloucester, Kent, and Fool.
Storm and tempest.*

248 *to slack you,* To be slack in their service to you.

254 *depositaries.* Trustees.

Lear: 'Why, nature needs not what thou gorgeous
wear'st, Which scarcely keeps thee warm.' Woodcut of
the fashionably attired Queen Elizabeth from the
Roxburghe Ballads, 17th century

288 *flaws.* Fragments.

295 *particular.* Himself.

6 *main.* Mainland.

12 *cub-drawn.* Sucked dry by cubs.

15 *take all.* Stake all on the last throw.

Charles Kean as King Lear, Princess's Theatre, London, 1858

18 *note.* Knowledge.

Corn. Let us withdraw; 'twill be a storm. 290
Reg. This house is little: the old man and his people
Cannot be well bestow'd.
Gon. 'Tis his own blame; hath put himself from rest,
And must needs taste his folly.
Reg. For his particular, I'll receive him gladly,
But not one follower.
Gon.   So am I purposed.
Where is my lord of Gloucester?
Corn. Follow'd the old man forth: he is return'd.

Re-enter GLOUCESTER.

Glou. The king is in high rage.
Corn.   Whither is he going?
Glou. He calls to horse; but will I know not whither. 300
Corn. 'Tis best to give him way; he leads himself.
Gon. My lord, entreat him by no means to stay.
Glou. Alack, the night comes on, and the bleak winds
Do sorely ruffle; for many miles about
There's scarce a bush.
Reg.   O, sir, to wilful men,
The injuries that they themselves procure
Must be their schoolmasters. Shut up your doors:
He is attended with a desperate train;
And what they may incense him to, being apt
To have his ear abused, wisdom bids fear. 310
Corn. Shut up your doors, my lord; 'tis a wild night:
My Regan counsels well: come out o' the storm.
                                        [*Exeunt.*

ACT III.

SCENE I. *A heath.*

Storm still. Enter KENT *and a* Gentleman, *meeting.*

Kent. Who's there, besides foul weather?
Gent. One minded like the weather, most unquietly.
Kent. I know you. Where's the king?
Gent. Contending with the fretful element;
Bids the wind blow the earth into the sea,
Or swell the curled waters 'bove the main,
That things might change or cease; tears his white hair,
Which the impetuous blasts, with eyeless rage,
Catch in their fury, and make nothing of; .
Strives in his little world of man to out-scorn 10
The to-and-fro-conflicting wind and rain.
This night, wherein the cub-drawn bear would couch,
The lion and the belly-pinched wolf
Keep their fur dry, unbonneted he runs,
And bids what will take all.
Kent.   But who is with him?
Gent. None but the fool; who labours to out-jest
His heart-struck injuries.
Kent.   Sir, I do know you;
And dare, upon the warrant of my note,

Commend a dear thing to you.   There is division,
Although as yet the face of it be cover'd   20
With mutual cunning, 'twixt Albany and Corn-
    wall;
Who have—as who have not, that their great stars
Throned and set high?—servants, who seem no
    less,
• Which are to France the spies and speculations
Intelligent of our state; what hath been seen,
• Either in snuffs and packings of the dukes,
Or the hard rein which both of them have borne
Against the old kind king; or something deeper,
• Whereof perchance these are but furnishings;
• But, true it is, from France there comes a power
• Into this scatter'd kingdom; who already,   31
• Wise in our negligence, have secret feet
In some of our best ports, and are at point
To show their open banner.   Now to you:
If on my credit you dare build so far
To make your speed to Dover, you shall find
Some that will thank you, making just report
Of how unnatural and bemadding sorrow
The king hath cause to plain.
I am a gentleman of blood and breeding;   40
And, from some knowledge and assurance, offer
This office to you.
      Gent.   I will talk further with you.
      Kent.   No, do not.
For confirmation that I am much more
Than my out-wall, open this purse, and take
What it contains.   If you shall see Cordelia,—
As fear not but you shall—show her this ring;
And she will tell you who your fellow is
That yet you do not know.   Fie on this storm!
I will go seek the king.   50
      Gent.   Give me your hand: have you no more
          to say?
      Kent.   Few words, but, to effect, more than
          all yet;
That, when we have found the king,—in which
          your pain
That way, I 'll this,—he that first lights on him
Holla the other.   [*Exeunt severally.*

SCENE II.   *Another part of the heath.   Storm
          still.*

          Enter LEAR *and* Fool.

      Lear.   Blow, winds, and crack your cheeks!
          rage! blow!
You cataracts and hurricanoes, spout
• Till you have drench'd our steeples, drown'd the
          cocks!
You sulphurous and thought-executing fires,
• Vaunt-couriers to oak-cleaving thunderbolts,
Singe my white head! And thou, all-shaking
          thunder,
Smite flat the thick rotundity o' the world!
• Crack nature's moulds, all germens spill at once,
That make ingrateful man!   9
  •   *Fool.*   O nuncle, court holy-water in a dry
house is better than this rain-water out o' door.
Good nuncle, in, and ask thy daughters' blessing:
here's a night pities neither wise man nor fool.
      Lear.   Rumble thy bellyful! Spit, fire!
          spout, rain!
Nor rain, wind, thunder, fire, are my daughters:
I tax not you, you elements, with unkindness;
I never gave you kingdom, call'd you children,

24-25 *speculations Intelligent of our state.* Supplying information of conditions in England.

26 *snuffs and packings.* Quarrels and intrigues.

29 *furnishings.* Pretexts.

30 *power.* Army.

31 *scatter'd.* Divided.

32 *secret feet.* Secret footholds.

Lear: 'Blow, winds, and crack your cheeks!' Engraving by Kenny Meadows from Barry Cornwall's *The Complete Works of Shakspere* (1857–1859)

3 *cocks.* Weathercocks.

5 *Vaunt-couriers.* Fore-runners.

8 *germens.* Seeds.

10 *court holy-water.* Flattery.

●You owe me no subscription: then let fall
Your horrible pleasure; here I stand, your slave,
A poor, infirm, weak, and despised old man: 20
But yet I call you servile ministers,
That have with two pernicious daughters join'd
●Your high engender'd battles 'gainst a head
So old and white as this.   O! O! 'tis foul!
 Fool.   He that has a house to put's head in
has a good head-piece.
● The cod-piece that will house
  Before the head has any,
  The head and he shall louse;
● So beggars marry many.   30
  The man that makes his toe
  What he his heart should make
  Shall of a corn cry woe,
  And turn his sleep to wake.
For there was never yet fair woman but she made
mouths in a glass.
 Lear.   No, I will be the pattern of all patience;
I will say nothing.

   Enter KENT.

 Kent.   Who's there?
 Fool.   Marry, here's grace and a cod-piece;
that's a wise man and a fool.   41
 Kent.   Alas, sir, are you here? things that
love night
Love not such nights as these; the wrathful skies
●Gallow the very wanderers of the dark,
And make them keep their caves: since I was man,
Such sheets of fire, such bursts of horrid thunder,
Such groans of roaring wind and rain, I never
Remember to have heard: man's nature cannot
  carry
The affliction nor the fear.
 Lear.   Let the great gods,
That keep this dreadful pother o'er our heads, 50
Find out their enemies now.   Tremble, thou
  wretch,
That hast within thee undivulged crimes,
Unwhipp'd of justice: hide thee, thou bloody hand;
●Thou perjured, and thou simular man of virtue
●That art incestuous: caitiff, to pieces shake,
That under covert and convenient seeming
●Hast practised on man's life: close pent-up guilts,
●Rive your concealing continents, and cry
These dreadful summoners grace.   I am a man
More sinn'd against than sinning.
 Kent.   Alack, bare-headed! 60
Gracious my lord, hard by here is a hovel;
Some friendship will it lend you 'gainst the
  tempest:
Repose you there; while I to this hard house—
More harder than the stones whereof 'tis raised;
Which even but now, demanding after you,
Denied me to come in—return, and force
Their scanted courtesy.
 Lear.   My wits begin to turn.
Come on, my boy: how dost, my boy? art cold?
I am cold myself.   Where is this straw, my fellow?
The art of our necessities is strange,   70
That can make vile things precious.   Come, your
  hovel.
Poor fool and knave, I have one part in my heart
That's sorry yet for thee.
 Fool.   [*Singing*] He that has and a little tiny
  wit,—
  With hey, ho, the wind and the rain,—

18 *subscription.* Allegiance.

David Garrick as Lear, Theatre Royal, Drury Lane,
London, 1742

23 *high engender'd.* Produced in the heavens.

27 *cod-piece.* Padded covering for the male genitals.

30 *many.* i.e. lice.

44 *Gallow.* Frighten.

54 *simular man of.* Pretender to.

55 *caitiff.* Wretch.

57 *practised on.* Plotted against.

58–59 *cry ... grace.* Ask for mercy. The *summoner* was
an official who arrested offenders for the ecclesiastical
courts.

Opposite: Lear: 'I am a man More sinn'd against than
sinning.' Engraving from Bell's edition, 1773

80 *prophecy.* The lines following start with a parody of a verse that was attributed to Chaucer by Elizabethans.

84 *burn'd.* Pun on venereal disease and its effects.

94 *going . . . feet.* Feet will be used for walking.

95 *Merlin.* Magician in Arthurian legends.

14 *footed.* Landed.

Set design by Thomas Grieve for Charles Kean's production, Princess's Theatre, 1858

Must make content with his fortunes fit,
For the rain it raineth every day.
Lear. True, my good boy. Come, bring us
to this hovel.   [*Exeunt Lear and Kent.*
Fool. This is a brave night to cool a courtezan.
I'll speak a prophecy ere I go: 80
When priests are more in word than matter;
When brewers mar their malt with water;
When nobles are their tailors' tutors;
No heretics burn'd, but wenches' suitors;
When every case in law is right;
No squire in debt, nor no poor knight;
When slanders do not live in tongues;
Nor cutpurses come not to throngs;
When usurers tell their gold i' the field;
And bawds and whores do churches build;   90
Then shall the realm of Albion
Come to great confusion:
Then comes the time, who lives to see't,
That going shall be used with feet.
This prophecy Merlin shall make; for I live
before his time.   [*Exit.*

SCENE III.   *Gloucester's castle.*

Enter GLOUCESTER *and* EDMUND.

Glou. Alack, alack, Edmund, I like not this
unnatural dealing. When I desired their leave
that I might pity him, they took from me the use
of mine own house; charged me, on pain of their
perpetual displeasure, neither to speak of him,
entreat for him, nor any way sustain him.
Edm. Most savage and unnatural!
Glou. Go to; say you nothing. There's a
division betwixt the dukes; and a worse matter
than that: I have received a letter this night:
'tis dangerous to be spoken; I have locked the
letter in my closet: these injuries the king now
bears will be revenged home; there's part of a
power already footed: we must incline to the
king. I will seek him, and privily relieve him:
go you and maintain talk with the duke, that my
charity be not of him perceived: if he ask for me,
I am ill, and gone to bed. Though I die for it,
as no less is threatened me, the king my old master
must be relieved. There is some strange thing
toward, Edmund; pray you, be careful. [*Exit.* 21
Edm. This courtesy, forbid thee, shall the duke
Instantly know; and of that letter too:
This seems a fair deserving, and must draw me
That which my father loses; no less than all:
The younger rises when the old doth fall. [*Exit.*

SCENE IV.   *The heath.   Before a hovel.*

Enter LEAR, KENT, *and* Fool.

Kent. Here is the place, my lord; good my
lord, enter:
The tyranny of the open night's too rough
For nature to endure.   [*Storm still.*
Lear.   Let me alone.
Kent. Good my lord, enter here.
Lear.   Wilt break my heart?
Kent. I had rather break mine own. Good
my lord, enter.
Lear. Thou think'st 'tis much that this con-
tentious storm
Invades us to the skin: so 'tis to thee;
But where the greater malady is fix'd,

The lesser is scarce felt. Thou'ldst shun a bear;
But if thy flight lay toward the raging sea,   10
Thou'ldst meet the bear i' the mouth.   When the
    mind's free,
The body's delicate: the tempest in my mind
Doth from my senses take all feeling else
Save what beats there.   Filial ingratitude!
Is it not as this mouth should tear this hand
For lifting food to't?   But I will punish home:
No, I will weep no more.   In such a night
To shut me out!   Pour on; I will endure.
In such a night as this!   O Regan, Goneril!
Your old kind father, whose frank heart gave all,—
O, that way madness lies; let me shun that;   21
No more of that.
    Kent.   Good my lord, enter here.
    Lear.   Prithee, go in thyself; seek thine own
    ease:
This tempest will not give me leave to ponder
On things would hurt me more.   But I'll go in.
[*To the Fool*]   In, boy; go first.   You houseless
    poverty,—
Nay, get thee in.   I'll pray, and then I'll sleep.
                    [*Fool goes in.*
Poor naked wretches, wheresoe'er you are,
That bide the pelting of this pitiless storm,   29
How shall your houseless heads and unfed sides,
• Your loop'd and window'd raggedness, defend you
From seasons such as these?   O, I have ta'en
Too little care of this!   Take physic, pomp;
Expose thyself to feel what wretches feel,
That thou mayst shake the superflux to them,
And show the heavens more just.
    Edg.   [*Within*] Fathom and half, fathom and
half!   Poor Tom!
          [*The Fool runs out from the hovel.*
    Fool.   Come not in here, nuncle, here's a spirit
Help me, help me!   40
    Kent.   Give me thy hand.   Who's there?
    Fool.   A spirit, a spirit: he says his name's
poor Tom.
    Kent.   What art thou that dost grumble there
i' the straw?   Come forth.

    Enter EDGAR *disguised as a madman.*

    Edg.   Away! the foul fiend follows me!
Through the sharp hawthorn blows the cold wind.
Hum! go to thy cold bed, and warm thee.
    Lear.   Hast thou given all to thy two daughters?
And art thou come to this?   50
    Edg.   Who gives any thing to poor Tom?
whom the foul fiend hath led through fire and
through flame, through ford and whirlipool, o'er
bog and quagmire; that hath laid knives under
his pillow, and halters in his pew; set ratsbane
by his porridge; made him proud of heart,
to ride on a bay trotting-horse over four-inched
bridges, to course his own shadow for a traitor.
Bless thy five wits!   Tom's a-cold,—O, do de,
do de, do de.   Bless thee from whirlwinds, star-
• blasting, and taking!   Do poor Tom some charity,
whom the foul fiend vexes: there could I have
him now,—and there,—and there again, and
there.   [*Storm still.*
    Lear.   What, have his daughters brought him
    to this pass?
Couldst thou save nothing?   Didst thou give them
    all?

Lear: 'Pour on; I will endure.' Engraving from a painting
by Benjamin West (1738–1820)

31 *loop'd and window'd.* Full of holes.

60–61 *star-blasting, and taking.* Evil, influenced by the
stars, and infections.

75 *little . . . flesh.* Torture themselves.

77 *pelican.* The young of pelicans were believed to feed on their parents' blood.

A pelican with her young. Engraving from a seal by F. W. Fairholt from J. O. Halliwell's edition of Shakespeare's works, 1853–65

78 *Pillicock.* Pet-name, defined by Florio as meaning 'darling'; but also with a sexual connotation.

95 *light of ear.* Susceptible to flattery.

100 *plackets.* Slits in petticoats.

104 *sessa.* An exclamation urging speed.

110–111 *sophisticated.* Altered by additions, i.e. clothing.

111–112 *unaccommodated.* Uncared for.

120 *Flibbertigibbet.* A dancing devil mentioned in Samuel Harsnett's *A Declaration of Egregious Popish Impostures*, 1603

121 *first cock.* Cockcrow.

122 *the web and the pin.* Cataract of the eye.

123 *white.* Nearly ripe.

125 *old.* Wold.

126 *night-mare.* Incubus. *nine-fold.* Nine offspring or familiars.

129 *aroint.* Begone.

Fool. Nay, he reserved a blanket, else we had been all shamed.
  Lear. Now, all the plagues that in the pendulous air
Hang fated o'er men's faults light on thy daughters! 70
  Kent. He hath no daughters, sir.
  Lear. Death, traitor! nothing could have subdued nature
To such a lowness but his unkind daughters.
Is it the fashion, that discarded fathers
Should have thus little mercy on their flesh?
Judicious punishment! 'twas this flesh begot
Those pelican daughters.
  Edg. Pillicock sat on Pillicock-hill:
Halloo, halloo, loo, loo!
  Fool. This cold night will turn us all to fools and madmen. 81
  Edg. Take heed o' the foul fiend: obey thy parents; keep thy word justly; swear not; commit not with man's sworn spouse; set not thy sweet heart on proud array. Tom's a-cold.
  Lear. What hast thou been?
  Edg. A serving-man, proud in heart and mind; that curled my hair; wore gloves in my cap; served the lust of my mistress' heart, and did the act of darkness with her; swore as many oaths as I spake words, and broke them in the sweet face of heaven: one that slept in the contriving of lust, and waked to do it: wine loved I deeply, dice dearly; and in woman out-paramoured the Turk: false of heart, light of ear, bloody of hand; hog in sloth, fox in stealth, wolf in greediness, dog in madness, lion in prey. Let not the creaking of shoes nor the rustling of silks betray thy poor heart to woman: keep thy foot out of brothels, thy hand out of plackets, thy pen from lenders' books, and defy the foul fiend. 101
Still through the hawthorn blows the cold wind:
Says suum, mun, ha, no, nonny.
Dolphin my boy, my boy, sessa! let him trot by.
                              [*Storm still.*
  Lear. Why, thou wert better in thy grave than to answer with thy uncovered body this extremity of the skies. Is man no more than this? Consider him well. Thou owest the worm no silk, the beast no hide, the sheep no wool, the cat no perfume. Ha! here's three on 's are sophisticated! Thou art the thing itself: unaccommodated man is no more but such a poor, bare, forked animal as thou art. Off, off, you lendings! come, unbutton here. [*Tearing off his clothes.*
  Fool. Prithee, nuncle, be contented; 'tis a naughty night to swim in. Now a little fire in a wild field were like an old lecher's heart; a small spark, all the rest on 's body cold. Look, here comes a walking fire. 119

Enter GLOUCESTER, *with a torch.*

  Edg. This is the foul fiend Flibbertigibbet: he begins at curfew, and walks till the first cock; he gives the web and the pin, squints the eye, and makes the hare-lip; mildews the white wheat, and hurts the poor creature of earth.
  S. Withold footed thrice the old;
  He met the night-mare, and her nine-fold;
        Bid her alight,
        And her troth plight,
  And, aroint thee, witch, aroint thee!

Kent.   How fares your grace?   130
Lear.   What's he?
Kent.   Who's there?   What is 't you seek?
Glou.   What are you there?   Your names?
Edg.   Poor Tom; that eats the swimming frog,
the toad, the tadpole, the wall-newt and the
● water; that in the fury of his heart, when the
● foul fiend rages, eats cow-dung for sallets; swallows
● the old rat and the ditch-dog; drinks the green
● mantle of the standing pool; who is whipped from
● tithing to tithing, and stock-punished, and im-
prisoned; who hath had three suits to his back,
six shirts to his body, horse to ride, and weapon
to wear;
●   But mice and rats, and such small deer,
    Have been Tom's food for seven long year.
● Beware my follower.   Peace, Smulkin; peace,
    thou fiend!
Glou.   What, hath your grace no better com-
    pany?
Edg.   The prince of darkness is a gentleman:
● Modo he 's call'd, and Mahu.
Glou.   Our flesh and blood is grown so vile,
    my lord,   150
● That it doth hate what gets it.
Edg.   Poor Tom 's a-cold.
Glou.   Go in with me: my duty cannot suffer
To obey in all your daughters' hard commands:
Though their injunction be to bar my doors,
And let this tyrannous night take hold upon you,
Yet have I ventured to come seek you out,
And bring you where both fire and food is ready.
Lear.   First let me talk with this philosopher.
What is the cause of thunder?   160
Kent.   Good my lord, take his offer; go into
    the house.
● *Lear.*   I'll talk a word with this same learned
    Theban.
What is your study?
Edg.   How to prevent the fiend, and to kill
    vermin.
Lear.   Let me ask you one word in private.
Kent.   Importune him once more to go, my
    lord;
His wits begin to unsettle.
Glou.   Canst thou blame him? [*Storm still.*
His daughters seek his death: ah, that good Kent!
He said it would be thus, poor banish'd man!
Thou say'st the king grows mad; I'll tell thee,
    friend,   170
I am almost mad myself: I had a son,
Now outlaw'd from my blood; he sought my life,
But lately, very late: I loved him, friend;
No father his son dearer: truth to tell thee,
The grief hath crazed my wits.   What a night 's
    this!
● I do beseech your grace,—
Lear.   O, cry you mercy, sir.
Noble philosopher, your company.
Edg.   Tom 's a-cold.
Glou.   In, fellow, there, into the hovel: keep
    thee warm.
Lear.   Come, let's in all.
Kent.   This way, my lord.
Lear.   With him; 180
I will keep still with my philosopher.
Kent.   Good my lord, soothe him; let him
    take the fellow.
Glou.   Take him you on.

136 *water.* Water newt.

137 *sallets.* Salads.

138 *ditch-dog.* A dead dog in a ditch.

139 *mantle.* Scum.

140 *tithing.* A district within a parish.

Edgar: '. . . stock-punished, and imprisoned'. Engraving from a 12th century manuscript

144–145 *But mice ... long year.* Taken up from the
medieval romance, *Bevis of Hampton.*

146 *follower ... Smulkin.* Edgar's familiar spirit is
called Smulkin.

149 *Modo . . . Mahu.* The names of two demons in
Harsnett's *Declaration.*

151 *gets.* Begets.

162 *Theban.* Philosopher.

176 *cry you mercy.* Beg your pardon.

185 *Athenian.* Philosopher.

187 *Child Rowland.* The hero of *The Song of Roland.*

188–189 *Fie, foh ... man.* The Giant's refrain from the fairy story *Jack-the-Giant-Killer.*

3 *censured.* Judged.

7 *his.* Gloucester's.

12 *intelligent party.* A spy for.

7 *Frateretto.* Another demon from Harsnett's *Declaration.*

A demon. Woodcut from the Sir John Harington's *Metamorphosis of Ajax*, 1596

Kent. Sirrah, come on; go along with us.
Lear. Come, good Athenian.
Glou. No words, no words: hush.
Edg. Child Rowland to the dark tower came,
His word was still,—Fie, foh, and fum,
I smell the blood of a British man.
[Exeunt.

SCENE V.   *Gloucester's castle.*

Enter CORNWALL *and* EDMUND.

Corn. I will have my revenge ere I depart his house.
Edm. How, my lord, I may be censured, that nature thus gives way to loyalty, something fears me to think of.
Corn. I now perceive, it was not altogether your brother's evil disposition made him seek his death; but a provoking merit, set a-work by a reproveable badness in himself.   9
Edm. How malicious is my fortune, that I must repent to be just! This is the letter he spoke of, which approves him an intelligent party to the advantages of France. O heavens! that this treason were not, or not I the detector!
Corn. Go with me to the duchess.
Edm. If the matter of this paper be certain, you have mighty business in hand.
Corn. True or false, it hath made thee earl of Gloucester. Seek out where thy father is, hat he may be ready for our apprehension.   20
Edm. [*Aside*] If I find h'm comforting the king, it will stuff his suspicion more fully.—I will persevere in my course of loyalty, though the conflict be sore between that and my blood.
Corn. I will lay trust upon thee; and thou shalt find a dearer father in my love. [*Exeunt.*

SCENE VI.   *A chamber in a farmhouse adjoining the castle.*

Enter GLOUCESTER, LEAR, KENT, Fool, *and* EDGAR.

Glou. Here is better than the open air; take it thankfully. I will piece out the comfort with what addition I can: I will not be long from you.
Kent. All the power of his wits have given way to his impatience: the gods reward your kindness!   [*Exit Gloucester.*
Edg. Frateretto calls me; and tells me Nero is an angler in the lake of darkness. Pray, innocent, and beware the foul fiend.
Fool. Prithee, nuncle, tell me whether a madman be a gentleman or a yeoman?   II
Lear. A king, a king!
Fool. No, he's a yeoman that has a gentleman to his son; for he's a mad yeoman that sees his son a gentleman before him.
Lear. To have a thousand with red burning spits
Come hissing in upon 'em,—
Edg. The foul fiend bites my back.
Fool. He's mad that trusts in the tameness of a wolf, a horse's health, a boy's love, or a whore's oath.   21
Lear. It shall be done; I will arraign them straight.
[*To Edgar*] Come, sit thou here, most learned justicer;

[*To the Fool*] Thou, sapient sir, sit here. Now,
 you she foxes!
Edg. Look, where he stands and glares!
Wantest thou eyes at trial, madam?
●   Come o'er the bourn, Bessy, to me,—
● *Fool.* Her boat hath a leak,
         And she must not speak
     Why she dares not come over to thee. 30
Edg. The foul fiend haunts poor Tom in the
●voice of a nightingale. Hopdance cries in Tom's
belly for two white herring. Croak not, black
angel; I have no food for thee.
     Kent. How do you, sir? Stand you not so
         amazed:
Will you lie down and rest upon the cushions?
     Lear. I'll see their trial first. Bring in the
         evidence.
[*To Edgar*] Thou robed man of justice, take thy
         place;
[*To the Fool*] And thou, his yoke-fellow of equity,
●Bench by his side: [*To Kent*] you are o' the
         commission,   40
Sit you too.
     Edg. Let us deal justly.
     Sleepest or wakest thou, jolly shepherd?
         Thy sheep be in the corn;
●   And for one blast of thy minikin mouth,
         Thy sheep shall take no harm.
●Pur! the cat is gray.
     Lear. Arraign her first; 'tis Goneril. I here
take my oath before this honourable assembly,
she kicked the poor king her father.   50
     Fool. Come hither, mistress. Is your name
Goneril?
     Lear. She cannot deny it.
● *Fool.* Cry you mercy, I took you for a joint-
stool.
     Lear. And here's another, whose warp'd looks
         proclaim
What store her heart is made on. Stop her there!
Arms, arms, sword, fire! Corruption in the place!
False justicer, why hast thou let her 'scape?
     Edg. Bless thy five wits!   60
     Kent. O pity! Sir, where is the patience now,
That you so oft have boasted to retain?
     Edg. [*Aside*] My tears begin to take his part
         so much,
They'll mar my counterfeiting.
     Lear. The little dogs and all,
Tray, Blanch, and Sweet-heart, see, they bark
         at me.
     Edg. Tom will throw his head at them.
Avaunt, you curs!
         Be thy mouth or black or white,
         Tooth that poisons if it bite;   70
         Mastiff, greyhound, mongrel grim,
●   Hound or spaniel, brach or lym,
         Or bobtail tike or trundle-tail,
         Tom will make them weep and wail:
         For, with throwing thus my head,
         Dogs leap the hatch, and all are fled.
●Do de, de, de. Sessa! Come, march to wakes
and fairs and market-towns. Poor Tom, thy horn
is dry.   79
     Lear. Then let them anatomize Regan; see
what breeds about her heart. Is there any cause
in nature that makes these hard hearts? [*To Edgar*] You, sir, I entertain for one of my hundred;
only I do not like the fashion of your garments:

27 *bourn.* Brook; Edgar quotes a line from a popular song.

Music for 'Come o'er the bourn . . .' From a 16th century manuscript

28–30 *Her boat . . . thee.* The Fool improvises in a bawdy vein on the song.

32 *voice of a nightingale.* i.e. the Fool's voice. *Hopdance.* The demon Hobberdidance in Harsnett.

40 *commission.* Commissioned as justices of the peace.

45 *minikin.* Small and pretty.

47 *the cat is gray.* Grey cats were thought of as witches' familiars.

54–55 *I took you for a joint-stool.* Colloquial jest for over-looking someone; the joint-stool (one made of pieces joined together) was a common piece of Elizabethan house furniture. See *The Taming of the Shrew*, Act II, Scene I, 199.

72 *brach.* Bitch hound. *lym.* Blood-hound.

77 *Sessa.* Away!

115 *portable*. Bearable.

118 *Mark the high noises.* Listen to the rumours that are high. *bewray*. Reveal.

Michael Pennington as Edgar, Royal Shakespeare Co, 1976

10 *festinate*. Speedy.

you will say they are Persian attire; but let them be changed.
  Kent.   Now, good my lord, lie here and rest awhile.
  Lear.   Make no noise, make no noise; draw the curtains: so, so, so. We'll go to supper i' the morning.   So, so, so.   91
  Fool.   And I'll go to bed at noon.

Re-enter GLOUCESTER.

  Glou.   Come hither, friend: where is the king my master?
  Kent.   Here, sir; but trouble him not, his wits are gone.
  Glou.   Good friend, I prithee, take him in thy arms;
I have o'erheard a plot of death upon him:
There is a litter ready; lay him in't,
And drive towards Dover, friend, where thou shalt meet
Both welcome and protection.   Take up thy master:
If thou shouldst dally half an hour, his life,   100
With thine, and all that offer to defend him,
Stand in assured loss: take up, take up;
And follow me, that will to some provision
Give thee quick conduct.
  Kent.   Oppressed nature sleeps:
This rest might yet have balm'd thy broken sinews,
Which, if convenience will not allow,
Stand in hard cure.   [*To the Fool*] Come, help to bear thy master;
Thou must not stay behind.
  Glou.   Come, come, away.
                          [*Exeunt all but Edgar.*
  Edg.   When we our betters see bearing our woes,
We scarcely think our miseries our foes.   110
Who alone suffers suffers most i' the mind,
Leaving free things and happy shows behind:
But then the mind much sufferance doth o'erskip,
When grief hath mates, and bearing fellowship.
• How light and portable my pain seems now,
When that which makes me bend makes the king bow,
He childed as I father'd!   Tom, away!
• Mark the high noises; and thyself bewray,
When false opinion, whose wrong thought defiles thee,
In thy just proof, repeals and reconciles thee.   120
What will hap more to-night, safe 'scape the king!
Lurk, lurk.   [*Exit.*

SCENE VII.   *Gloucester's castle.*

Enter CORNWALL, REGAN, GONERIL, EDMUND, *and* Servants.

  Corn.   Post speedily to my lord your husband; show him this letter: the army of France is landed.   Seek out the villain Gloucester.
                          [*Exeunt some of the Servants.*
  Reg.   Hang him instantly.
  Gon.   Pluck out his eyes.
  Corn.   Leave him to my displeasure. Edmund, keep you our sister company: the revenges we are bound to take upon your traitorous father are not fit for your beholding. Advise the duke,
• where you are going, to a most festinate prepara-

tion: we are bound to the like. Our posts shall
be swift and intelligent betwixt us. Farewell,
dear sister: farewell, my lord of Gloucester.

Enter OSWALD.

How now! where's the king?
   Osw. My lord of Gloucester hath convey'd
      him hence:
Some five or six and thirty of his knights,
Hot questrists after him, met him at gate;
Who, with some other of the lords dependants,
Are gone with him towards Dover; where they
      boast
To have well-armed friends.
   Corn.   Get horses for your mistress. 20
   Gon. Farewell, sweet lord, and sister.
   Corn. Edmund, farewell.
      [*Exeunt Goneril, Edmund, and Oswald.*
            Go seek the traitor Gloucester,
Pinion him like a thief, bring him before us.
             [*Exeunt other Servants.*
Though well we may not pass upon his life
Without the form of justice, yet our power
Shall do a courtesy to our wrath, which men
May blame, but not control. Who's there? the
      traitor?

Enter GLOUCESTER, *brought in by two or three.*

   Reg. Ingrateful fox! 'tis he.
   Corn. Bind fast his corky arms.
   Glou. What mean your graces? Good my
      friends, consider   30
You are my guests: do me no foul play, friends.
   Corn. Bind him, I say. [*Servants bind him.*
   Reg.   Hard, hard. O filthy traitor!
   Glou. Unmerciful lady as you are, I'm none.
   Corn. To this chair bind him. Villain, thou
      shalt find—   [*Regan plucks his beard.*
   Glou. By the kind gods, 'tis most ignobly done
To pluck me by the beard.
   Reg. So white, and such a traitor!
   Glou.   Naughty lady,
These hairs, which thou dost ravish from my
      chin,
Will quicken, and accuse thee: I am your host:
With robbers' hands my hospitable favours   40
You should not ruffle thus. What will you do?
   Corn. Come, sir, what letters had you late
      from France?
   Reg. Be simple answerer, for we know the
      truth.
   Corn. And what confederacy have you with
      the traitors
Late footed in the kingdom?
   Reg. To whose hands have you sent the luna-
      tic king?
Speak.
   Glou. I have a letter guessingly set down,
Which came from one that's of a neutral heart,
And not from one opposed.
   Corn.   Cunning.
   Reg.   And false.
   Corn. Where hast thou sent the king?   50
   Glou. To Dover.
   Reg. Wherefore to Dover? Wast thou not
      charged at peril—
   Corn. Wherefore to Dover? Let him first
      answer that.

17 *questrists.* Seekers.

24 *pass upon his life.* Pass the death sentence on him.

29 *corky.* Shrivelled.

39 *quicken.* Come alive.

41 *ruffle.* Treat roughly.

54 *course.* The attack of the dogs in bear-baiting.

Bear-baiting. Woodcut from the Loutrell Psalter, *c.* 1340

---

61 *stelled fires.* Fixed stars.

62 *holp.* Helped.

65 *cruels.* Cruel creatures. *subscribed.* Renounced.

78 *villain.* Serf or bondsman.

87 *quit.* Revenge.

89 *overture.* Discovery.

101 *the old course of death.* i.e. a natural death.

● *Glou.* I am tied to the stake, and I must stand
the course.
  Reg.   Wherefore to Dover, sir?
  Glou.   Because I would not see thy cruel nails
Pluck out his poor old eyes; nor thy fierce sister
In his anointed flesh stick boarish fangs.
The sea, with such a storm as his bare head
In hell-black night endured, would have buoy'd up,
●And quench'd the stelled fires: 61
●Yet, poor old heart, he holp the heavens to rain.
If wolves had at thy gate howl'd that stern time,
Thou shouldst have said ' Good porter, turn the
key,'
●All cruels else subscribed: but I shall see
The winged vengeance overtake such children.
  Corn.   See't shalt thou never.   Fellows, hold
the chair.
Upon these eyes of thine I'll set my foot.
  Glou.   He that will think to live till he be old,
Give me some help! O cruel! O you gods!   70
  Reg.   One side will mock another; the other
too.
  Corn.   If you see vengeance,—
  First Serv.   Hold your hand, my lord:
I have served you ever since I was a child;
But better service have I never done you
Than now to bid you hold.
  Reg.   How now, you dog!
  First Serv.   If you did wear a beard upon
your chin,
I'd shake it on this quarrel.   What do you
mean?
● *Corn.*   My villain!   [*They draw and fight.*
  First Serv.   Nay, then, come on, and take the
chance of anger.
  Reg.   Give me thy sword.   A peasant stand
up thus!   80
  [*Takes a sword, and runs at him behind.*
  First Serv.   O, I am slain! My lord, you
have one eye left
To see some mischief on him.   O!   [*Dies.*
  Corn.   Lest it see more, prevent it.   Out, vile
jelly!
Where is thy lustre now?
  Glou.   All dark and comfortless.   Where's my
son Edmund?
Edmund, enkindle all the sparks of nature,
●To quit this horrid act.
  Reg.   Out, treacherous villain!
Thou call'st on him that hates thee: it was he
●That made the overture of thy treasons to us;
Who is too good to pity thee.   90
  Glou.   O my follies! then Edgar was abused.
Kind gods, forgive me that, and prosper him!
  Reg.   Go thrust him out at gates, and let him
smell
His way to Dover.   [*Exit one with Gloucester.*]
How is't, my lord? how look you?
  Corn.   I have received a hurt: follow me, lady.
Turn out that eyeless villain; throw this slave
Upon the dunghill.   Regan, I bleed apace:
Untimely comes this hurt: give me your arm.
            [*Exit Cornwall, led by Regan.*
  Sec. Serv.   I'll never care what wickedness
I do,
If this man come to good.
  Third Serv.   If she live long,   100
●And in the end meet the old course of death,
Women will all turn monsters.

Sec. Serv. Let's follow the old earl, and get the Bedlam
• To lead him where he would: his roguish madness
Allows itself to any thing.
    Third Serv. Go thou: I'll fetch some flax and whites of eggs
To apply to his bleeding face. Now, heaven help him!   [*Exeunt severally.*

ACT IV.

SCENE I. *The heath.*

Enter EDGAR.

Edg. Yet better thus, and known to be contemn'd,
Than still contemn'd and flatter'd. To be worst,
The lowest and most dejected thing of fortune,
• Stands still in esperance, lives not in fear:
The lamentable change is from the best;
• The worst returns to laughter. Welcome, then,
Thou unsubstantial air that I embrace!
The wretch that thou hast blown unto the worst
Owes nothing to thy blasts. But who comes here?

Enter GLOUCESTER, *led by an* Old Man.

My father, poorly led? World, world, O world!
• But that thy strange mutations make us hate thee,
Life would not yield to age.
    Old Man. O, my good lord, I have been your tenant, and your father's tenant, these fourscore years.
    Glou. Away, get thee away; good friend, be gone:
Thy comforts can do me no good at all;
Thee they may hurt.
    Old Man. Alack, sir, you cannot see your way.
    Glou. I have no way, and therefore want no eyes;   20
I stumbled when I saw: full oft 'tis seen,
Our means secure us, and our mere defects
Prove our commodities. O dear son Edgar,
The food of thy abused father's wrath!
Might I but live to see thee in my touch,
I'ld say I had eyes again!
    Old Man.   How now! Who's there?
    Edg. [*Aside*] O gods! Who is't can say 'I am at the worst'?
I am worse than e'er I was.
    Old Man.   'Tis poor mad Tom.
    Edg. [*Aside*] And worse I may be yet: the worst is not
So long as we can say 'This is the worst.'   30
    Old Man. Fellow, where goest?
    Glou.   Is it a beggar-man?
    Old Man. Madman and beggar too.
    Glou. He has some reason, else he could not beg.
I' the last night's storm I such a fellow saw;
Which made me think a man a worm: my son
Came then into my mind; and yet my mind
Was then scarce friends with him: I have heard more since.
• As flies to wanton boys, are we to the gods,
They kill us for their sport.
    Edg.   [*Aside*] How should this be?
Bad is the trade that must play fool to sorrow,   40
Angering itself and others.—Bless thee, master!
    Glou. Is that the naked fellow?
    Old Man.   Ay, my lord.

104–105 *his roguish ... any thing.* Because he is considered mad, he is permitted to do anything.

Samuel Reddish as Edgar. Engraving from Bell's edition, ... 1773

---

4 *esperance.* Hope.

6 *The worst ... laughter.* When your fortune is at its worst any change is for the better.

11-12 *But that ... to age.* We only accept death and old age, because the changes in fortune from good to bad make life unbearable.

38 *wanton.* Playful.

54 *daub it*. Lay it on.

Edgar: '. . . five fiends have been in poor Tom at once'.
Engraving of a fiend. Detail from 'The Temptation of
St Anthony', by Jacques Callot (1593–1636)

70 *superfluous*. Having a superfluity. *lust-dieted*. Whose
desires are sated.

71 *slaves your ordinance*. Subjects the law to his own
ends.

Glou.   Then, prithee, get thee gone: if, for
my sake,
Thou wilt o'ertake us, hence a mile or twain,
I' the way toward Dover, do it for ancient love;
And bring some covering for this naked soul,
Who I'll entreat to lead me.
Old Man.   Alack, sir, he is mad.
Glou.   'Tis the times' plague, when madmen
lead the blind.
Do as I bid thee, or rather do thy pleasure;
Above the rest, be gone.   50
Old Man.   I'll bring him the best 'parel that
I have,
Come on 't what will.   [*Exit.*
Glou.   Sirrah, naked fellow,—
Edg.   Poor Tom's a-cold. [*Aside*] I cannot
daub it further.
Glou.   Come hither, fellow.
Edg. [*Aside*] And yet I must.—Bless thy sweet
eyes, they bleed.
Glou.   Know'st thou the way to Dover?
Edg.   Both stile and gate, horse-way and foot-
path. Poor Tom hath been scared out of his good
wits: bless thee, good man's son, from the foul
fiend! five fiends have been in poor Tom at once;
of lust, as Obidicut; Hobbididance, prince of
dumbness; Mahu, of stealing; Modo, of murder;
Flibbertigibbet, of mopping and mowing, who
since possesses chambermaids and waiting-wo-
men. So, bless thee, master!
Glou.   Here, take this purse, thou whom the
heavens' plagues
Have humbled to all strokes: that I am wretched
Makes thee the happier: heavens, deal so still!
Let the superfluous and lust-dieted man,   70
That slaves your ordinance, that will not see
Because he doth not feel, feel your power quickly;
So distribution should undo excess,
And each man have enough. Dost thou know
Dover?
Edg.   Ay, master.
Glou.   There is a cliff, whose high and bending
head
Looks fearfully in the confined deep:
Bring me but to the very brim of it,
And I'll repair the misery thou dost bear
With something rich about me: from that place
I shall no leading need.
Edg.   Give me thy arm: 81
Poor Tom shall lead thee.   [*Exeunt.*

SCENE II.   *Before the Duke of Albany's palace.*

Enter GONERIL *and* EDMUND.

Gon.   Welcome, my lord: I marvel our mild
husband
Not met us on the way.

Enter OSWALD.

                 Now, where's your master?
Osw.   Madam, within; but never man so
changed.
I told him of the army that was landed;
He smiled at it: I told him you were coming;
His answer was 'The worse:' of Gloucester's
treachery,
And of the loyal service of his son,
When I inform'd him, then he call'd me sot,
And told me I had turn'd the wrong side out:

What most he should dislike seems pleasant to
    him;   10
What like, offensive.
    Gon. [*To Edm.*] Then shall you go no further.
● It is the cowish terror of his spirit,
    That dares not undertake: he'll not feel wrongs
● Which tie him to an answer. Our wishes on
    the way
● May prove effects. Back, Edmund, to my
    brother;
    Hasten his musters and conduct his powers:
● I must change arms at home, and give the distaff
    Into my husband's hands. This trusty servant
    Shall pass between us: ere long you are like
    to hear,
    If you dare venture in your own behalf,   20
    A mistress's command. Wear this; spare speech;
                  [*Giving a favour.*
    Decline your head: this kiss, if it durst speak,
    Would stretch thy spirits up into the air:
    Conceive, and fare thee well.
    Edm.   Yours in the ranks of death.
    Gon.   My most dear Gloucester!
                    [*Exit Edmund.*
O, the difference of man and man!
To thee a woman's services are due:
My fool usurps my body.
    Osw.   Madam, here comes my lord.
                     [*Exit.*

    Enter ALBANY.

●   *Gon.* I have been worth the whistle.
    Alb.   O Goneril!
You are not worth the dust which the rude
    wind   30
Blows in your face. I fear your disposition:
That nature, which contemns it origin,
● Cannot be border'd certain in itself;
● She that herself will sliver and disbranch
● From her material sap, perforce must wither
    And come to deadly use.
    Gon. No more; the text is foolish.
    Alb. Wisdom and goodness to the vile seem
    vile:
Filths savour but themselves. What have you
    done?
Tigers, not daughters, what have you perform'd?
A father, and a gracious aged man,   41
● Whose reverence even the head-lugg'd bear
    would lick,
Most barbarous, most degenerate! have you
    madded.
Could my good brother suffer you to do it?
A man, a prince, by him so benefited!
If that the heavens do not their visible spirits
Send quickly down to tame these vile offences,
It will come,
Humanity must perforce prey on itself,
Like monsters of the deep.
    Gon.   Milk-liver'd man!   50
That bear'st a cheek for blows, a head for
    wrongs:
Who hast not in thy brows an eye discerning
Thine honour from thy suffering; that not know'st
Fools do those villains pity who are punish'd
Ere they have done their mischief. Where's thy
    drum?
● France spreads his banners in our noiseless land,
    With plumed helm thy state begins to threat;

12 *cowish.* Cowardly.

14 *to an answer.* i.e. to retaliate.

15 *prove effects.* Be realised.

17 *change.* Take up. *distaff.* Implement used in spinning:
a symbol of womanishness.

29 *worth the whistle.* Proverbial: It's a poor dog that's
not worth whistling for.

Costume design for Goneril by Isamu Noguchi,
Stratford-upon-Avon, 1955

33 *be border'd certain.* Be kept within bounds.

34 *sliver.* Tear off.

35 *material.* Nourishing.

42 *head-lugg'd.* Dragged by the head.

56 *noiseless.* Unaroused for war.

58 *moral.* Moralising.

60 *Proper.* Appropriate in a devil.

73 *bred.* Brought up.

79 *justicers.* Judges. *nether.* Committed on earth.

86 *building in my fancy.* Dreams.

● Whiles thou, a moral fool, sit'st still, and criest
' Alack, why does he so?'
    Alb.   See thyself, devil!
● Proper deformity seems not in the fiend   60
So horrid as in woman.
    Gon.   O vain fool!
    Alb. Thou changed and self-cover'd thing,
      for shame,
Be-monster not thy feature. Were 't my fitness
To let these hands obey my blood,
They are apt enough to dislocate and tear
Thy flesh and bones: howe'er thou art a fiend,
A woman's shape doth shield thee.
    Gon. Marry, your manhood now—

Enter a Messenger.

    Alb. What news?
    Mess. O, my good lord, the Duke of Corn-
      wall's dead;   70
Slain by his servant, going to put out
The other eye of Gloucester.
    Alb.   Gloucester's eyes!
●   *Mess.* A servant that he bred, thrill'd with
      remorse,
Opposed against the act, bending his sword
To his great master; who, thereat enraged,
Flew on him, and amongst them fell'd him dead;
But not without that harmful stroke, which since
Hath pluck'd him after.
    Alb.   This shows you are above,
● You justicers, that these our nether crimes
So speedily can venge! But, O poor Gloucester!
Lost he his other eye?
    Mess.   Both, both, my lord. 81
This letter, madam, craves a speedy answer;
'Tis from your sister.
    Gon. [*Aside*] One way I like this well;
But being widow, and my Gloucester with her,
● May all the building in my fancy pluck
Upon my hateful life: another way,
The news is not so tart.—I'll read, and answer.
                         [*Exit.*
    Alb. Where was his son when they did take
      his eyes?
    Mess. Come with my lady hither.
    Alb.   He is not here. 90
    Mess. No, my good lord; I met him back
      again.
    Alb. Knows he the wickedness?
    Mess. Ay, my good lord; 'twas he inform'd
      against him;
And quit the house on purpose, that their punish-
      ment
Might have the freer course.
    Alb.   Gloucester, I live
To thank thee for the love thou show'dst the king,
And to revenge thine eyes. Come hither, friend:
Tell me what more thou know'st.   [*Exeunt.*

SCENE III. *The French camp near Dover.*

Enter KENT *and a* Gentleman.

    Kent. Why the King of France is so suddenly
gone back know you the reason?
    Gent. Something he left imperfect in the state,
which since his coming forth is thought of;
which imports to the kingdom so much fear and

Opposite: Costume design for Goneril by Charles
Ricketts, Theatre Royal, London, 1909

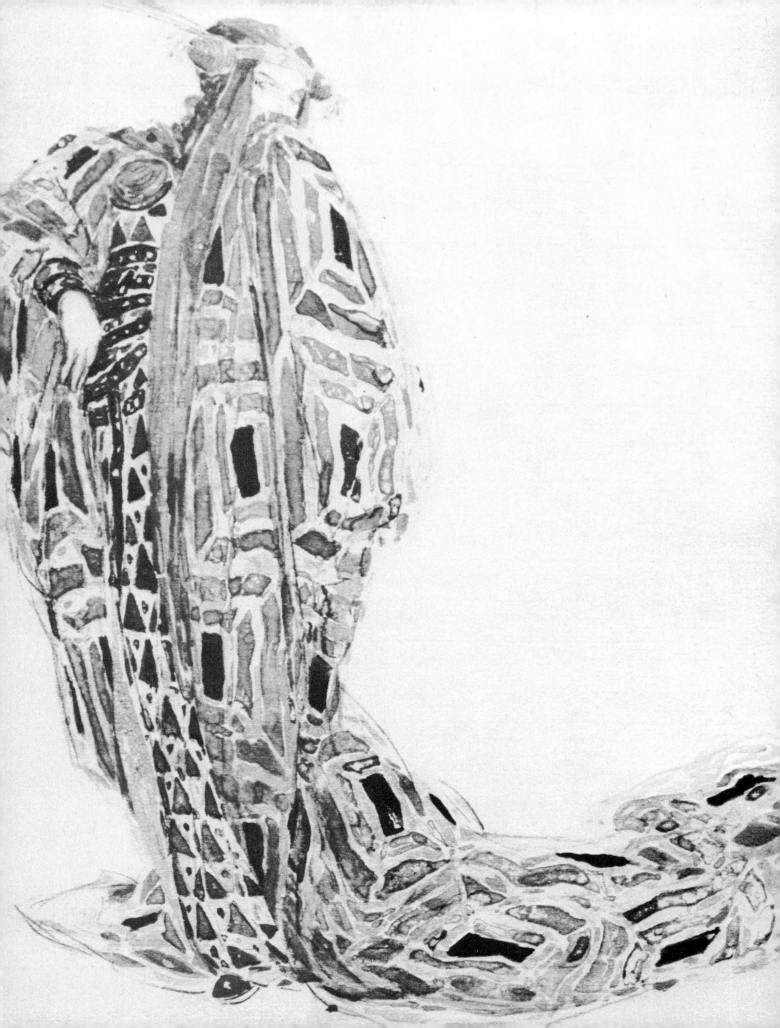

33 *clamour moisten'd.* Tears followed her lamentations.

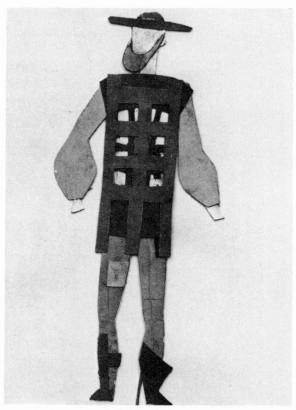

Costume design for Kent by Isamu Noguchi, Stratford-upon-Avon, 1955

36 *one self mate and mate.* One husband and wife.

46 *casualties.* Chances.

danger, that his personal return was most required and necessary.

Kent. Who hath he left behind him general?

Gent. The Marshal of France, Monsieur La Far.   10

Kent. Did your letters pierce the queen to any demonstration of grief?

Gent. Ay, sir; she took them, read them in
   my presence;
And now and then an ample tear trill'd down
Her delicate cheek: it seem'd she was a queen
Over her passion; who, most rebel-like,
Sought to be king o'er her.

Kent.   O, then it moved her.

Gent. Not to a rage: patience and sorrow
   strove
Who should express her goodliest.   You have
   seen
Sunshine and rain at once: her smiles and tears
†Were like a better way: those happy smilets, 21
That play'd on her ripe lip, seem'd not to know
What guests were in her eyes; which parted
   thence,
As pearls from diamonds dropp'd.   In brief,
Sorrow would be a rarity most beloved,
If all could so become it.

Kent.   Made she no verbal question?

Gent. 'Faith, once or twice she heaved the
   name of 'father'
Pantingly forth, as if it press'd her heart;
Cried 'Sisters! sisters! Shame of ladies! sisters!
Kent! father! sisters! What, i' the storm? i'
   the night?   30
Let pity not be believed!'   There she shook
The holy water from her heavenly eyes,
●And clamour moisten'd: then away she started
To deal with grief alone.

Kent.   It is the stars,
The stars above us, govern our conditions;
●Else one self mate and mate could not beget
Such different issues.   You spoke not with her
   since?

Gent. No.

Kent. Was this before the king return'd?

Gent.   No, since.

Kent. Well, sir, the poor distressed Lear's i'
   the town;   40
Who sometime, in his better tune, remembers
What we are come about, and by no means
Will yield to see his daughter.

Gent.   Why, good sir?

Kent. A sovereign shame so elbows him: his
   own unkindness,
That stripp'd her from his benediction, turn'd her
●To foreign casualties, gave her dear rights
To his dog-hearted daughters, these things sting
His mind so venomously, that burning shame
Detains him from Cordelia.

Gent.   Alack, poor gentleman!

Kent. Of Albany's and Cornwall's powers you
   heard not?   50

Gent. 'Tis so, they are afoot.

Kent. Well, sir, I'll bring you to our master
   Lear,
And leave you to attend him: some dear cause
Will in concealment wrap me up awhile;
When I am known aright, you shall not grieve
Lending me this acquaintance.   I pray you, go
Along with me.   [*Exeunt.*

SCENE IV. *The same. A tent.*

Enter, with drum and colours, CORDELIA, *Doctor, and* Soldiers.

Cor. Alack, 'tis he: why, he was met even now
As mad as the vex'd sea; singing aloud;
● Crown'd with rank fumiter and furrow-weeds,
With bur-docks, hemlock, nettles, cuckoo-flowers,
Darnel, and all the idle weeds that grow
● In our sustaining corn. A century send forth;
Search every acre in the high-grown field,
And bring him to our eye. [*Exit an Officer.*]
What can man's wisdom
In the restoring his bereaved sense?
● He that helps him take all my outward worth. 10
Doct. There is means, madam:
Our foster-nurse of nature is repose,
The which he lacks; that to provoke in him,
Are many simples operative, whose power
Will close the eye of anguish.
Cor.   All blest secrets,
All you unpublish'd virtues of the earth,
Spring with my tears! be aidant and remediate
In the good man's distress! Seek, seek for him;
Lest his ungovern'd rage dissolve the life
That wants the means to lead it.

Enter a Messenger.

Mess.   News, madam; 20
The British powers are marching hitherward.
Cor. 'Tis known before; our preparation stands
In expectation of them. O dear father,
It is thy business that I go about;
Therefore great France
My mourning and important tears hath pitied.
No blown ambition doth our arms incite,
But love, dear love, and our aged father's right:
Soon may I hear and see him!   [*Exeunt.*

SCENE V. *Gloucester's castle.*

Enter REGAN *and* OSWALD.

Reg. But are my brother's powers set forth?
Osw.   Ay, madam.
Reg. Himself in person there?
Osw.   Madam, with much ado:
Your sister is the better soldier.
Reg. Lord Edmund spake not with your lord at home?
Osw. No, madam.
Reg. What might import my sister's letter to him?
Osw. I know not, lady.
Reg. 'Faith, he is posted hence on serious matter.
It was great ignorance, Gloucester's eyes being out,
To let him live: where he arrives he moves 10
All hearts against us: Edmund, I think, is gone,
In pity of his misery, to dispatch
His nighted life; moreover, to descry
The strength o' the enemy.
Osw I must needs after him, madam, with my letter.
Reg. Our troops set forth to-morrow: stay with us;
The ways are dangerous.

3 *fumiter*. Fumitory. *Fumaria officinalis*, a herb used as a tonic.

6 *century*. A troop of a hundred soldiers.

10 *helps*. Cures. *outward*. Material.

Costume design for Cordelia by Leslie Hurry, Stratford-upon-Avon, 1950

25 *œillades.* Amorous glances.

26 *of her bosom.* In her confidence.

Costume design for Regan by John Napier, Royal Shakespeare Co, 1976

---

15 *samphire.* A herb used in pickling.

19 *cock.* Cock-boat or dinghy.

Osw.   I may not, madam :
My lady charged my duty in this business.
   Reg. Why should she write to Edmund?
     Might not you
Transport her purposes by word? Belike,   20
Something—I know not what : I'll love thee much,
Let me unseal the letter.
   Osw.   Madam, I had rather—
   Reg. I know your lady does not love her husband ;
I am sure of that : and at her late being here
● She gave strange œillades and most speaking looks
● To noble Edmund. I know you are of her bosom.
   Osw. I, madam ?
   Reg. I speak in understanding; you are, I know't :
Therefore I do advise you, take this note :
My lord is dead ; Edmund and I have talk'd ;   30
And more convenient is he for my hand
Than for your lady's : you may gather more.
If you do find him, pray you, give him this :
And when your mistress hears thus much from you,
I pray, desire her call her wisdom to her.
So, fare you well.
If you do chance to hear of that blind traitor,
Preferment falls on him that cuts him off.
   Osw. Would I could meet him, madam ! I should show
What party I do follow.
   Reg.   Fare thee well. [*Exeunt.* 40

SCENE VI.   *Fields near Dover.*

Enter GLOUCESTER, *and* EDGAR *dressed like a peasant.*

   Glou. When shall we come to the top of that same hill?
   Edg. You do climb up it now : look, how we labour.
   Glou. Methinks the ground is even.
   Edg.   Horrible steep.
Hark, do you hear the sea?
   Glou.   No, truly.
   Edg. Why, then, your other senses grow imperfect
By your eyes' anguish.
   Glou.   So may it be, indeed :
Methinks thy voice is alter'd ; and thou speak'st
In better phrase and matter than thou didst.
   Edg. You're much deceived : in nothing am I changed
But in my garments
   Glou.   Methinks you're better spoken. 10
   Edg. Come on, sir ; here's the place : stand still. How fearful
And dizzy 'tis, to cast one's eyes so low !
The crows and choughs that wing the midway air
Show scarce so gross as beetles : half way down
● Hangs one that gathers samphire, dreadful trade !
Methinks he seems no bigger than his head :
The fishermen, that walk upon the beach,
Appear like mice ; and yond tall anchoring bark,
● Diminish'd to her cock ; her cock, a buoy
Almost too small for sight : the murmuring surge,
That on the unnumber'd idle pebbles chafes,   21
Cannot be heard so high. I'll look no more ;
Lest my brain turn, and the deficient sight

Topple down headlong.
Glou.   Set me where you stand.
Edg.   Give me your hand : you are now within
    a foot
Of the extreme verge : for all beneath the moon
Would I not leap upright.
Glou.   Let go my hand.
Here, friend, 's another purse ; in it a jewel
Well worth a poor man's taking : fairies and gods
Prosper it with thee ! Go thou farther off ;   30
Bid me farewell, and let me hear thee going.
Edg.   Now fare you well, good sir.
Glou.   With all my heart.
Edg.   Why I do trifle thus with his despair
Is done to cure it.
Glou. [Kneeling] O you mighty gods !
This world I do renounce, and, in your sights,
Shake patiently my great affliction off :
If I could bear it longer, and not fall
To quarrel with your great opposeless wills,
My snuff and loathed part of nature should
Burn itself out. If Edgar live, O, bless him ! 40
Now, fellow, fare thee well. [He falls forward.
Edg.   Gone, sir : farewell.
● And yet I know not how conceit may rob
The treasury of life, when life itself
Yields to the theft : had he been where he
    thought,
● By this, had thought been past.   Alive or dead?
Ho, you sir ! friend ! Hear you, sir ! speak !
Thus might he pass indeed : yet he revives.
What are you, sir?
Glou.   Away, and let me die.
Edg.   Hadst thou been aught but gossamer,
    feathers, air,
So many fathom down precipitating,   50
Thou'dst shiver'd like an egg : but thou dost
    breathe ;
Hast heavy substance ; bleed'st not ; speak'st ;
    art sound.
● Ten masts at each make not the altitude
Which thou hast perpendicularly fell :
Thy life's a miracle.   Speak yet again.
Glou. But have I fall'n, or no?
Edg.   From the dread summit of this chalky
    bourn.
● Look up a-height ; the shrill-gorged lark so far
Cannot be seen or heard : do but look up.
Glou. Alack, I have no eyes.   60
's wretchedness deprived that benefit,
To end itself by death? 'Twas yet some comfort,
When misery could beguile the tyrant's rage,
And frustrate his proud will.
Edg.   Give me your arm :
Up : so. How is't? Feel you your legs? You
    stand.
Glou. Too well, too well.
Edg.   This is above all strangeness.
Upon the crown o' the cliff, what thing was that
Which parted from you?
Glou.   A poor unfortunate beggar.
Edg.   As I stood here below, methought his
    eyes
Were two full moons ; he had a thousand noses, 70
● Horns whelk'd and waved like the enridged sea :
It was some fiend ; therefore, thou happy father,
● Think that the clearest gods, who make them
    honours
Of men's impossibilities, have preserved thee.

42 *conceit.* Imagination.

45–48 *Alive or dead? . . . What are you sir?* Edgar now
speaks in a disguised voice.

53 *at each.* End to end.

58 *a-height.* On high.

71 *whelk'd.* Twisted.

Edgar: 'It was some fiend . . .' Engraving of a devil by
F. W. Fairholt from a church statue from J. O. Halliwell's
edition of Shakespeare's works, 1853–65

73–74 *who . . . impossibilities.* Who win honour from men
by doing that which men find impossible.

83 *coining.* Minting coins was a royal prerogative.

87 *press-money.* Money paid to a conscript.

88–89 *clothier's yard.* An arrow a cloth-yard long.

91 *gauntlet.* Glove thrown down as a challenge.

92 *brown bills.* Halberds varnished against rust. *i' the clout.* In the white centre of the target.

93 *word.* Password.

94 *marjoram.* A herb used in treating brain diseases.

119 *luxury.* Lust.

124 *fitchew.* Polecat, also a slang term for prostitute. *soiled.* Well-fed.

126 *Centaurs.* A mythological creature with the body of a horse and the head of a man and synonymous with lechery.

Detail from The Fight between the Lapiths and the Centaurs. by Piero di Cosimo (*c.* 1462–1521 ?)

132 *civet.* Perfume.

Glou. I do remember now: henceforth I 'll bear
Affliction till it do cry out itself
'Enough, enough,' and die. That thing you speak of,
I took it for a man; often 'twould say
'The fiend, the fiend:' he led me to that place.
    Edg. Bear free and patient thoughts. But who comes here?   80

Enter LEAR, *fantastically dressed with wild flowers.*

The safer sense will ne'er accommodate
His master thus.
    Lear. No, they cannot touch me for coining;
I am the king himself.
    Edg. O thou side-piercing sight!
    Lear. Nature's above art in that respect.
There's your press-money. That fellow handles
his bow like a crow-keeper: draw me a clothier's
yard. Look, look, a mouse! Peace, peace; this
piece of toasted cheese will do't There's my
gauntlet; I'll prove it on a giant. Bring up the
brown bills. O, well flown, bird! i' the clout, i'
the clout: hewgh! Give the word.
    Edg. Sweet marjoram.
    Lear. Pass.
    Glou. I know that voice.
    Lear. Ha! Goneril, with a white beard!
They flattered me like a dog; and told me I had
white hairs in my beard ere the black ones were
there. To say 'ay' and 'no' to every thing that
I said!—'Ay' and 'no' too was no good divinity.
When the rain came to wet me once, and the
wind to make me chatter; when the thunder
would not peace at my bidding; there I found
'em, there I smelt 'em out. Go to, they are not
men o' their words: they told me I was every
thing; 'tis a lie, I am not ague-proof.
    Glou. The trick of that voice I do well remember:
Is't not the king?
    Lear.   Ay, every inch a king:
When I do stare, see how the subject quakes. 110
I pardon that man's life. What was thy cause?
Adultery?
Thou shalt not die: die for adultery! No:
The wren goes to't, and the small gilded fly
Does lecher in my sight.
Let copulation thrive; for Gloucester's bastard son
Was kinder to his father than my daughters
Got 'tween the lawful sheets.
To't, luxury, pell-mell! for I lack soldiers.
Behold yond simpering dame,   120
Whose face between her forks presages snow;
That minces virtue, and does shake the head
To hear of pleasure's name;
The fitchew, nor the soiled horse, goes to't
With a more riotous appetite.
Down from the waist they are Centaurs,
Though women all above:
But to the girdle do the gods inherit,
Beneath is all the fiends';
There's hell, there's darkness, there's the sulphurous pit,   130
Burning, scalding, stench, consumption; fie, fie,
fie! pah, pah! Give me an ounce of civet, good

apothecary, to sweeten my imagination: there's money for thee.

Glou.   O, let me kiss that hand!

Lear.   Let me wipe it first; it smells of mortality.

Glou.   O ruin'd piece of nature! This great world
Shall so wear out to nought.   Dost thou know me?

Lear.   I remember thine eyes well enough.
● Dost thou squiny at me?   No, do thy worst, blind Cupid; I 'll not love.   Read thou this challenge; mark but the penning of it.

Glou.   Were all the letters suns, I could not see one.

Edg.   I would not take this from report; it is, And my heart breaks at it.

Lear.   Read.

● *Glou.*   What, with the case of eyes?

Lear.   O, ho, are you there with me?   No eyes in your head, nor no money in your purse? Your eyes are in a heavy case, your purse in a light: yet you see how this world goes.   151

Glou.   I see it feelingly.

Lear.   What, art mad?   A man may see how this world goes with no eyes.   Look with thine ears: see how yond justice rails upon yond simple thief.   Hark, in thine ear: change places; and, handy-dandy, which is the justice, which is the thief?   Thou hast seen a farmer's dog bark at a beggar?

Glou.   Ay, sir.   160

Lear.   And the creature run from the cur? There thou mightst behold the great image of authority: a dog's obeyed in office.
● Thou rascal beadle, hold thy bloody hand! Why dost thou lash that whore?   Strip thine own back;
Thou hotly lust'st to use her in that kind
● For which thou whipp'st her.   The usurer hangs the cozener.
Through tatter'd clothes small vices do appear; Robes and furr'd gowns hide all.   Plate sin with gold,
And the strong lance of justice hurtless breaks; Arm it in rags, a pigmy's straw does pierce it.   171
● None does offend, none, I say, none; I 'll able 'em:
Take that of me, my friend, who have the power
To seal the accuser's lips.   Get thee glass eyes;
And, like a scurvy politician, seem
To see the things thou dost not.   Now, now, now, now:
Pull off my boots: harder, harder: so.

Edg.   O, matter and impertinency mix'd! Reason in madness!

Lear.   If thou wilt weep my fortunes, take my eyes.   180
I know thee well enough; thy name is Gloucester: Thou must be patient; we came crying hither: Thou know'st, the first time that we smell the air, We wawl and cry.   I will preach to thee: mark.

Glou.   Alack, alack the day!

Lear.   When we are born, we cry that we are come
● To this great stage of fools: this' a good block; It were a delicate stratagem, to shoe
A troop of horse with felt: I 'll put 't in proof; And when I have stol'n upon these sons-in-law,

140   *squiny*. Squint.

147   *case*. Sockets.

164   *beadle*. Parish constable.

167   *The usurer hangs the cozener*.   A judge, guilty of usury, sentences the petty cheat to death.

172   *able*. Vouch for.

Lear. 'When we are born, we cry that we are come To this great stage of fools.' Laurence Olivier as Lear, Old Vic, 1946

187   *block*. A block for making felt hats.

198 *seconds.* Supporters.

199 *salt.* Tears.

207 *Sa, sa.* A hunting cry.

Costume design for Lear for Peter Brook's production, RSC, 1962

211 *twain.* i.e. Regan and Goneril.

214 *vulgar.* Common knowledge.

217–218 *the main . . . thought.* Any hour we expect to see the main body of their army.

228 *biding.* Place to stay.

230 *To boot, and boot.* In addition and reward. *proclaim'd prize.* One with a reward on his head.

233 *thyself remember.* Think of your soul.

Then, kill, kill, kill, kill, kill, kill!   191

Enter a Gentleman, *with* Attendants.

Gent. O, here he is: lay hand upon him. Sir,
Your most dear daughter—
Lear. No rescue? What, a prisoner? I am even
The natural fool of fortune. Use me well;
You shall have ransom. Let me have surgeons;
I am cut to the brains.
Gent.   You shall have any thing.
● *Lear.* No seconds? all myself?
● Why, this would make a man a man of salt,
To use his eyes for garden water-pots,   200
Ay, and laying autumn's dust.
Gent.   Good sir,—
Lear. I will die bravely, like a bridegroom. What!
I will be jovial: come, come; I am a king,
My masters, know you that.
Gent. You are a royal one, and we obey you.
Lear. Then there's life in't. Nay, if you get
● it, you shall get it with running. Sa, sa, sa, sa.
                    [*Exit running; Attendants follow.*
Gent. A sight most pitiful in the meanest wretch,
Past speaking of in a king! Thou hast one daughter,
Who redeems nature from the general curse   210
● Which twain have brought her to.
Edg. Hail, gentle sir.
Gent.   Sir, speed you: what's your will?
Edg. Do you hear aught, sir, of a battle toward?
● *Gent.* Most sure and vulgar: every one hears that,
Which can distinguish sound.
Edg.   But, by your favour,
How near's the other army?
● *Gent.* Near and on speedy foot; the main descry
Stands on the hourly thought.
Edg.   I thank you, sir: that's all.
Gent. Though that the queen on special cause is here,
Her army is moved on.
Edg.   I thank you, sir.   220
                    [*Exit Gent.*
Glou. You ever-gentle gods, take my breath from me;
Let not my worser spirit tempt me again
To die before you please!
Edg.   Well pray you, father.
Glou. Now, good sir, what are you?
Edg. A most poor man, made tame to fortune's blows;
Who, by the art of known and feeling sorrows,
Am pregnant to good pity. Give me your hand,
● I'll lead you to some biding.
Glou.   Hearty thanks:
The bounty and the benison of heaven
● To boot, and boot!

Enter OSWALD.

Osw. A proclaim'd prize! Most happy!   230
That eyeless head of thine was first framed flesh
To raise my fortunes. Thou old unhappy traitor,
● Briefly thyself remember: the sword is out

That must destroy thee.
Glou.   Now let thy friendly hand
Put strength enough to't.   [*Edgar interposes.*
Osw.   Wherefore, bold peasant,
Darest thou support a publish'd traitor?   Hence;
Lest that the infection of his fortune take
Like hold on thee.   Let go his arm.
 • *Edg.*   Chill not let go, zir, without vurther
'casion.   240
Osw.   Let go, slave, or thou diest!
Edg.   Good gentleman, go your gait, and let
•poor volk pass.   An chud ha' bin zwaggered out
of my life, 'twould not ha' bin zo long as 'tis by a
vortnight.   Nay, come not near th' old man;
•keep out, che vor ye, or ise try whether your
•costard or my ballow be the harder: chill be
plain with you.
Osw.   Out, dunghill!
Edg.   Chill pick your teeth, zir: come; no
•matter vor your foins.   251
    [*They fight, and Edgar knocks him down.*
Osw.   Slave, thou hast slain me: villain, take
    my purse:
If ever thou wilt thrive, bury my body;
And give the letters which thou find'st about me
To Edmund earl of Gloucester; seek him out
Upon the British party: O, untimely death!
                            [*Dies.*
Edg.   I know thee well: a serviceable villain;
As duteous to the vices of thy mistress
As badness would desire.
Glou.   What, is he dead?
Edg.   Sit you down, father; rest you.   260
Let's see these pockets: the letters that he
    speaks of
May be my friends.   He's dead; I am only sorry
•He had no other death's-man.   Let us see:
Leave, gentle wax: and, manners, blame us not:
To know our enemies' minds, we'ld rip their
    hearts;
Their papers, is more lawful.
    [*Reads*] 'Let our reciprocal vows be remem-
bered.   You have many opportunities to cut him
off: if your will want not, time and place will be
fruitfully offered.   There is nothing done, if he
return the conqueror: then am I the prisoner,
and his bed my gaol; from the loathed warmth
whereof deliver me, and supply the place for your
labour.
    'Your—wife, so I would say—
                'Affectionate servant,
                      'Goneril.'
•O undistinguish'd space of woman's will!
A plot upon her virtuous husband's life;
And the exchange my brother!   Here, in the sands,
Thee I'll rake up, the post unsanctified   281
Of murderous lechers: and in the mature time
With this ungracious paper strike the sight
•Of the death-practised duke: for him 'tis well
That of thy death and business I can tell.
Glou.   The king is mad: how stiff is my vile
    sense,
•That I stand up, and have ingenious feeling
Of my huge sorrows!   Better I were distract:
So should my thoughts be sever'd from my griefs,
And woes by wrong imaginations lose   290
The knowledge of themselves.
    Edg.   Give me your hand:
                    [*Drum afar off.*

239 *Chill.* I will; Edgar assumes a peasant dialect.

243 *An chud.* If I could.

246 *che vor ye.* I warrant you. *ise.* I shall.

247 *costard.* Head. *ballow.* Cudgel.

251 *foins.* Thrusts.

Oswald: 'Slave thou hast slain me'. Woodcut from a
16th century fencing manual.

263 *death's-man.* Executioner.

278 *undistinguish'd.* Unlimited. *will.* Lust.

284 *death-practised.* Whose death is plotted.

287 *ingenious.* Conscious.

6 *clipp'd.* i.e. less. *suited.* Dressed.

7 *weeds.* Clothes.

24 *temperance.* Sanity.

35 *perdu.* A sentry placed in a hopeless position.

36 *thin helm.* A helmet, but in this case hair.

Cordelia watching over the sleeping Lear. Painting by
Ford Madox Brown (1821–1893)

Far off, methinks, I hear the beaten drum:
Come, father, I'll bestow you with a friend.

                            [Exeunt.

SCENE VII. *A tent in the French camp.* LEAR
on a bed asleep, soft music playing; Gentleman, *and others attending.*

    Enter CORDELIA, KENT, *and* Doctor.

  Cor. O thou good Kent, how shall I live and
    work,
To match thy goodness? My life will be too
    short,
And every measure fail me.
  Kent.   To be acknowledged, madam, is o'er-
    paid.
All my reports go with the modest truth;
Nor more nor clipp'd, but so.
  Cor.   Be better suited:
These weeds are memories of those worser hours:
I prithee, put them off.
  Kent.   Pardon me, dear madam;
Yet to be known shortens my made intent:
My boon I make it, that you know me not   10
Till time and I think meet.
  Cor. Then be't so, my good lord. [*To the
    Doctor*] How does the king?
  Doct. Madam, sleeps still.
  Cor. O you kind gods,
Cure this great breach in his abused nature!
The untuned and jarring senses, O, wind up
Of this child-changed father!
  Doct.   So please your majesty
That we may wake the king: he hath slept long.
  Cor. Be govern'd by your knowledge, and
    proceed
I' the sway of your own will. Is he array'd? 20
  Gent. Ay, madam; in the heaviness of his
    sleep
We put fresh garments on him.
  Doct. Be by, good madam, when we do awake
    him;
I doubt not of his temperance.
  Cor.   Very well.
  Doct. Please you, draw near. Louder the
    music there!
  Cor. O my dear father! Restoration hang
Thy medicine on my lips; and let this kiss
Repair those violent harms that my two sisters
Have in thy reverence made!
  Kent.   Kind and dear princess!
  Cor. Had you not been their father, these
    white flakes   30
Had challenged pity of them. Was this a face
To be opposed against the warring winds?
To stand against the deep dread-bolted thunder?
In the most terrible and nimble stroke
Of quick, cross lightning? to watch—poor
    perdu!—
With this thin helm? Mine enemy's dog,
Though he had bit me, should have stood that
    night
Against my fire; and wast thou fain, poor father,
To hovel thee with swine, and rogues forlorn,
In short and musty straw? Alack, alack!   40
'Tis wonder that thy life and wits at once
Had not concluded all. He wakes; speak to
    him.
  Doct. Madam, do you; 'tis fittest.

Cor. How does my royal lord? How fares
   your majesty?
Lear. You do me wrong to take me out o' the
   grave:
Thou art a soul in bliss; but I am bound
Upon a wheel of fire, that mine own tears
Do scald like molten lead.
Cor.   Sir, do you know me?
Lear. You are a spirit, I know: when did
   you die?
Cor. Still, still, far wide!   50
Doct. He's scarce awake: let him alone
   awhile.
Lear. Where have I been? Where am I?
   Fair daylight?
I am mightily abused. I should e'en die with
   pity,
To see another thus. I know not what to say.
I will not swear these are my hands: let's see;
I feel this pin prick. Would I were assured
Of my condition!
Cor.   O, look upon me, sir,
And hold your hands in benediction o'er me:
No, sir, you must not kneel.
Lear.   Pray, do not mock me:
I am a very foolish fond old man,   60
Fourscore and upward, not an hour more nor less;
And, to deal plainly,
I fear I am not in my perfect mind.
Methinks I should know you, and know this man;
Yet I am doubtful: for I am mainly ignorant
What place this is; and all the skill I have
Remembers not these garments; nor I know not
Where I did lodge last night. Do not laugh
   at me;
For, as I am a man, I think this lady
To be my child Cordelia.
Cor.   And so I am, I am.   70
Lear. Be your tears wet? yes, 'faith. I pray,
   weep not:
If you have poison for me, I will drink it.
I know you do not love me; for your sisters
Have, as I do remember, done me wrong:
You have some cause, they have not.
Cor.   No cause, no cause.
Lear. Am I in France?
Kent.   In your own kingdom, sir.
Lear. Do not abuse me.
Doct. Be comforted, good madam: the great
   rage,
You see, is kill'd in him: and yet it is danger
To make him even o'er the time he has lost.   80
Desire him to go in; trouble him no more
Till further settling.
Cor. Will't please your highness walk?
Lear.   You must bear with me:
Pray you now, forget and forgive: I am old and
   foolish.
   [*Exeunt all but Kent and Gentleman.*
Gent. Holds it true, sir, that the Duke of
Cornwall was so slain?
Kent. Most certain, sir.
Gent. Who is conductor of his people?
Kent. As 'tis said, the bastard son of Gloucester.
Gent. They say Edgar, his banished son, is
with the Earl of Kent in Germany.   91
Kent. Report is changeable. 'Tis time to
look about; the powers of the kingdom approach
apace.

Lear: 'You are a spirit, I know:' Painting by George
Romney (1734–1802)

Costume design for the Duke of Albany by John Napier, Royal Shakespeare Co, 1976

---

1 *his last purpose.* i.e. to fight against Cordelia.

4 *constant pleasure.* Firm decision.

11 *forfended.* Forbidden.

30 *particular broils.* Private quarrels.

Gent. The arbitrement is like to be bloody.
Fare you well, sir.   [*Exit.*
Kent. My point and period will be throughly
    wrought,
Or well or ill, as this day's battle's fought.
                                        [*Exit.*

ACT V.

SCENE I. *The British camp, near Dover.*

Enter, with drum and colours, EDMUND,
    REGAN, Gentlemen, *and* Soldiers.

● *Edm.* Know of the duke if his last purpose
    hold,
Or whether since he is advised by aught
To change the course: he's full of alteration
●And self-reproving: bring his constant pleasure.
                    [*To a Gentleman, who goes out.*
Reg. Our sister's man is certainly miscarried.
Edm. 'Tis to be doubted, madam.
Reg.   Now, sweet lord,
You know the goodness I intend upon you:
Tell me—but truly—but then speak the truth,
Do you not love my sister?
Edm.   In honour'd love.
Reg. But have you never found my brother's
    way   10
●To the forfended place?
Edm.   That thought abuses you.
Reg. I am doubtful that you have been con-
    junct
And bosom'd with her, as far as we call hers.
Edm. No, by mine honour, madam.
Reg. I never shall endure her: dear my lord,
Be not familiar with her.
Edm.   Fear me not:
She and the duke her husband!

Enter, with drum and colours, ALBANY,
    GONERIL, *and* Soldiers.

Gon. [*Aside*] I had rather lose the battle than
    that sister
Should loosen him and me.
Alb. Our very loving sister, well be-met.   20
Sir, this I hear; the king is come to his daughter,
With others whom the rigour of our state
Forced to cry out. Where I could not be honest,
I never yet was valiant: for this business,
It toucheth us, as France invades our land,
Not bolds the king, with others, whom, I fear,
Most just and heavy causes make oppose.
Edm. Sir, you speak nobly.
Reg.   Why is this reason'd?
Gon. Combine together 'gainst the enemy;
●For these domestic and particular broils   30
Are not the question here.
Alb.   Let's then determine
With the ancient of war on our proceedings.
Edm. I shall attend you presently at your tent.
Reg. Sister, you'll go with us?
Gon. No.
Reg. 'Tis most convenient; pray you, go
    with us.

Gon. [*Aside*] O, ho, I know the riddle.—I will go.

As they are going out, enter EDGAR *disguised.*

Edg. If e'er your grace had speech with man
    so poor,

Hear me one word.

Alb.   I'll overtake you.   Speak.
          [*Exeunt all but Albany and Edgar.*
Edg.   Before you fight the battle, ope this
          letter.   40
If you have victory, let the trumpet sound
For him that brought it: wretched though I seem,
I can produce a champion that will prove
What is avouched there.   If you miscarry,
Your business of the world hath so an end,
And machination ceases.   Fortune love you!
Alb.   Stay till I have read the letter.
Edg.   I was forbid it.
When time shall serve, let but the herald cry,
And I'll appear again.
Alb.   Why, fare thee well: I will o'erlook thy
          paper.   [*Exit Edgar.* 50

          Re-enter EDMUND.

Edm.   The enemy's in view; draw up your
          powers.
Here is the guess of their true strength and forces
• By diligent discovery; but your haste
Is now urged on you.
Alb.   We will greet the time.   [*Exit.*
Edm.   To both these sisters have I sworn my
          love;
Each jealous of the other, as the stung
Are of the adder.   Which of them shall I take?
Both? one? or neither?   Neither can be enjoy'd,
If both remain alive: to take the widow
Exasperates, makes mad her sister Goneril;   60
And hardly shall I carry out my side,
Her husband being alive.   Now then we'll use
• His countenance for the battle; which being done,
Let her who would be rid of him devise
• His speedy taking off.   As for the mercy
Which he intends to Lear and to Cordelia,
The battle done, and they within our power,
Shall never see his pardon; for my state
Stands on me to defend, not to debate. [*Exit.* 69

SCENE II.   *A field between the two camps.*

Alarum within.   Enter, with drum and colours,
LEAR, CORDELIA, *and* Soldiers, *over the stage;*
and exeunt.

          Enter EDGAR *and* GLOUCESTER.

Edg.   Here, father, take the shadow of this
          tree
For your good host; pray that the right may
          thrive:
If ever I return to you again,
I'll bring you comfort.
Glou.   Grace go with you, sir!
                              [*Exit Edgar.*

Alarum and retreat within.   Re-enter EDGAR.

Edg.   Away, old man; give me thy hand;
          away!
King Lear hath lost, he and his daughter ta'en:
Give me thy hand; come on.
Glou.   No farther, sir; a man may rot even
          here.
Edg.   What, in ill thoughts again?   Men must
          endure   9

53 *discovery.* Spying.

63 *countenance.* Support.

65 *taking off.* Death.

2 *their greater pleasures.* The wishes of those in authority.

3 *censure.* Judge.

Lear and Cordelia in prison. Water colour by William Blake (1757–1827)

24 *good-years.* Undefined malevolent power. *fell.* Skin.

35 *write happy.* Call yourself lucky.

Their going hence, even as their coming hither :
Ripeness is all : come on.
   Glou.   And that's true too. [*Exeunt.*

SCENE III.   *The British camp near Dover.*

Enter, in conquest, with drum and colours,
EDMUND : LEAR *and* CORDELIA, *prisoners;*
Captain, Soldiers, &c.

   Edm.   Some officers take them away : good guard,
● Until their greater pleasures first be known
● That are to censure them.
   Cor.   We are not the first
Who, with best meaning, have incurr'd the worst.
For thee, oppressed king, am I cast down ;
Myself could else out-frown false fortune's frown.
Shall we not see these daughters and these sisters ?
   Lear.   No, no, no, no !   Come, let's away to prison :
We two alone will sing like birds i' the cage :
When thou dost ask me blessing, I'll kneel down,
And ask of thee forgiveness : so we'll live,   11
And pray, and sing, and tell old tales, and laugh
At gilded butterflies, and hear poor rogues
Talk of court news ; and we'll talk with them too,
Who loses and who wins ; who's in, who's out ;
And take upon's the mystery of things,
As if we were God's spies : and we'll wear out,
In a wall'd prison, packs and sects of great ones,
That ebb and flow by the moon.
   Edm.   Take them away.
   Lear.   Upon such sacrifices, my Cordelia, 20
The gods themselves throw incense.   Have I caught thee ?
He that parts us shall bring a brand from heaven,
And fire us hence like foxes.   Wipe thine eyes ;
● The good-years shall devour them, flesh and fell,
Ere they shall make us weep : we'll see 'em starve first.
Come. [*Exeunt Lear and Cordelia, guarded.*
   Edm.   Come hither, captain ; hark.
Take thou this note [*giving a paper*] ; go follow them to prison :
One step I have advanced thee ; if thou dost
As this instructs thee, thou dost make thy way
To noble fortunes : know thou this, that men 30
Are as the time is : to be tender-minded
Does not become a sword : thy great employment
Will not bear question ; either say thou'lt do 't,
Or thrive by other means.
   Capt.   I'll do 't, my lord.
● *Edm.*   About it ; and write happy when thou hast done.
Mark, I say, instantly ; and carry it so
As I have set it down.
   Capt.   I cannot draw a cart, nor eat dried oats ;
If it be man's work, I'll do 't.   [*Exit*

Flourish.   Enter ALBANY, GONERIL, REGAN,
another Captain, *and* Soldiers.

   Alb.   Sir, you have shown to-day your valiant strain,
                         40
And fortune led you well : you have the captives
That were the opposites of this day's strife :
We do require them of you, so to use them
As we shall find their merits and our safety
May equally determine.
   Edm.   Sir, I thought it fit

Opposite : Lear : 'Come, let's away to prison : We two alone will sing like birds i' the cage.' Painting after Thomas Stothard (1755–1834)

61 *list to grace.* Wish to honour.

68 *your addition.* Titles given by you.

76 *the walls are thine.* You have taken the castle.

79 *let-alone.* The prohibition.

83 *in thine attaint.* Arrested with you.

To send the old and miserable king
To some retention and appointed guard;
Whose age has charms in it, whose title more,
To pluck the common bosom on his side,
And turn our impress'd lances in our eyes   50
Which do command them.   With him I sent the
    queen;
My reason all the same; and they are ready
To-morrow, or at further space, to appear
Where you shall hold your session.   At this time
We sweat and bleed; the friend hath lost his
    friend;
And the best quarrels, in the heat, are cursed
By those that feel their sharpness:
The question of Cordelia and her father
Requires a fitter place.
    Alb.   Sir, by your patience,
I hold you but a subject of this war,   60
●Not as a brother.
    Reg.   That's as we list to grace him.
Methinks our pleasure might have been demanded,
Ere you had spoke so far.   He led our powers;
Bore the commission of my place and person;
The which immediacy may well stand up,
And call itself your brother.
    Gon.   Not so hot:
In his own grace he doth exalt himself,
●More than in your addition.
    Reg.   In my rights,
By me invested, he compeers the best.
    Gon.   That were the most, if he should hus-
    band you.   70
    Reg.   Jesters do oft prove prophets.
    Gon.   Holla, holla!
That eye that told you so look'd but a-squint.
    Reg.   Lady, I am not well; else I should
    answer
From a full-flowing stomach.   General,
Take thou my soldiers, prisoners, patrimony;
●Dispose of them, of me; the walls are thine:
Witness the world, that I create thee here
My lord and master.
    Gon.   Mean you to enjoy him?
●   *Alb.*   The let-alone lies not in your good will.
    Edm.   Nor in thine, lord.
    Alb.   Half-blooded fellow, yes. 80
    Reg. [*To Edmund*] Let the drum strike, and
    prove my title thine.
    Alb.   Stay yet; hear reason.   Edmund, I ar-
    rest thee
●On capital treason; and, in thine attaint,
This gilded serpent [*pointing to Gon.*].   For your
    claim, fair sister,
I bar it in the interest of my wife:
'Tis she is sub-contracted to this lord,
And I, her husband, contradict your bans.
If you will marry, make your loves to me,
My lady is bespoke.
    Gon.   An interlude!
    Alb.   Thou art arm'd, Gloucester: let the
    trumpet sound: 90
If none appear to prove upon thy head
Thy heinous, manifest, and many treasons,
There is my pledge [*throwing down a glove*];
    I'll prove it on thy heart,
Ere I taste bread, thou art in nothing less
Than I have here proclaim'd thee.
    Reg.   Sick, O, sick!
    Gon. [*Aside*] If not, I'll ne'er trust medicine.

Edm. There's my exchange [*throwing down
a glove*]: what in the world he is
That names me traitor, villain-like he lies:
Call by thy trumpet: he that dares approach,
On him, on you, who not? I will maintain   100
My truth and honour firmly.
Alb.   A herald, ho!
Edm.   A herald, ho, a herald!
Alb. Trust to thy single virtue; for thy soldiers,
All levied in my name, have in my name
Took their discharge.
Reg.   My sickness grows upon me.
Alb. She is not well; convey her to my tent.
                              [*Exit Regan, led.*

Enter a Herald.

Come hither, herald,—Let the trumpet sound,—
And read out this.
Capt. Sound, trumpet! [*A trumpet sounds.*
Her. [*Reads*] 'If any man of quality or degree
within the lists of the army will maintain upon
Edmund, supposed Earl of Gloucester, that he is
a manifold traitor, let him appear by the third
sound of the trumpet: he is bold in his defence.'
Edm. Sound!   [*First trumpet.*
Her. Again!   [*Second trumpet.*
Her. Again!   [*Third trumpet.*
                 [*Trumpet answers within.*

Enter EDGAR, *at the third sound, armed, with
a trumpet before him.*

Alb. Ask him his purposes, why he appears
Upon this call o' the trumpet.
Her.   What are you? 119
Your name, your quality? and why you answer
This present summons?
Edg.   Know, my name is lost;
●By treason's tooth bare-gnawn and canker-bit:
Yet am I noble as the adversary
I come to cope.
Alb.   Which is that adversary?
Edg. What's he that speaks for Edmund Earl
of Gloucester?
Edm. Himself: what say'st thou to him?
Edg.   Draw thy sword,
That, if my speech offend a noble heart,
Thy arm may do thee justice: here is mine.
Behold, it is the privilege of mine honours,
My oath, and my profession: I protest,   130
●Maugre thy strength, youth, place, and eminence,
Despite thy victor sword and fire-new fortune,
Thy valour and thy heart, thou art a traitor;
False to thy gods, thy brother, and thy father;
Conspirant 'gainst this high-illustrious prince;
And, from the extremest upward of thy head
To the descent and dust below thy foot,
A most toad-spotted traitor. Say thou ' No,'
This sword, this arm, and my best spirits, are bent
To prove upon thy heart, whereto I speak,   140
Thou liest.
Edm. In wisdom I should ask thy name;
But, since thy outside looks so fair and warlike,
And that thy tongue some say of breeding breathes,
What safe and nicely I might well delay
By rule of knighthood, I disdain and spurn:
Back do I toss these treasons to thy head;
With the hell-hated lie o'erwhelm thy heart;
Which, for they yet glance by and scarcely bruise,
This sword of mine shall give them instant way,

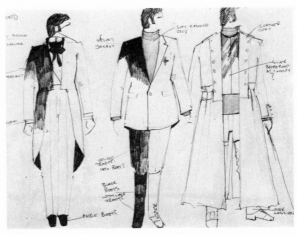

Costume design for Edmund by John Napier, Royal
Shakespeare Co, 1976

122 *canker-bit.* Eaten away.

131 *Maugre.* In spite of (from the French *malgré*).

A fight with rapier and dagger. From a contemporary woodcut

---

151 *practice.* Trickery.

154 *cozen'd.* Cheated.

158 *the laws are mine.* i.e. as ruler.

165 *fortune on.* Victory over.

Where they shall rest for ever. Trumpets, speak!
 [*Alarums. They fight. Edmund falls.*
• *Alb.* Save him, save him!
 Gon.   This is practice, Gloucester: 151
By the law of arms thou wast not bound to answer
An unknown opposite; thou art not vanquish'd,
•But cozen'd and beguiled.
 Alb.   Shut your mouth, dame,
Or with this paper shall I stop it: Hold, sir:
Thou worse than any name, read thine own evil:
No tearing, lady; I perceive you know it.
    [*Gives the letter to Edmund.*
• *Gon.* Say, if I do, the laws are mine, not thine:
Who can arraign me for't?
 Alb.   Most monstrous! oh! 159
Know'st thou this paper?
 Gon.   Ask me not what I know. [*Exit.*
 Alb. Go after her: she's desperate; govern her.
 Edm. What you have charged me with, that
  have I done;
And more, much more; the time will bring it out:
'Tis past, and so am I. But what art thou
•That hast this fortune on me? If thou'rt noble,
I do forgive thee.
 Edg.   Let's exchange charity.
I am no less in blood than thou art, Edmund;
If more, the more thou hast wrong'd me.
My name is Edgar, and thy father's son.
The gods are just, and of our pleasant vices 170
Make instruments to plague us:
The dark and vicious place where thee he got
Cost him his eyes.
 Edm.   Thou hast spoken right, 'tis true;
The wheel is come full circle; I am here.
 Alb. Methought thy very gait did prophesy
A royal nobleness: I must embrace thee:
Let sorrow split my heart, if ever I
Did hate thee or thy father!
 Edg.   Worthy prince, I know't.
 Alb. Where have you hid yourself? 179
How have you known the miseries of your father?
 Edg. By nursing them, my lord. List a brief
  tale;
And when 'tis told, O, that my heart would burst!
The bloody proclamation to escape,
That follow'd me so near,—O, our lives' sweetness!
That we the pain of death would hourly die
Rather than die at once!—taught me to shift
Into a madman's rags; to assume a semblance
That very dogs disdain'd: and in this habit
Met I my father with his bleeding rings, 189
Their precious stones new lost; became his guide,
Led him, begg'd for him, saved him from despair;
Never,—O fault!—reveal'd myself unto him,
Until some half-hour past, when I was arm'd:
Not sure, though hoping, of this good success,
I ask'd his blessing, and from first to last
Told him my pilgrimage: but his flaw'd heart,
Alack, too weak the conflict to support!
'Twixt two extremes of passion, joy and grief,
Burst smilingly.
 Edm. This speech of yours hath moved me,
And shall perchance do good: but speak you on;
You look as you had something more to say. 201
 Alb. If there be more, more woeful, hold it in;
For I am almost ready to dissolve,
Hearing of this.
 Edg.   This would have seem'd a period
To such as love not sorrow; but another,

To amplify too much, would make much more,
And top extremity.
Whilst I was big in clamour came there in a man,
Who, having seen me in my worst estate,   209
Shunn'd my abhorr'd society; but then, finding
Who 'twas that so endured, with his strong arms
He fasten'd on my neck, and bellow'd out
As he'ld burst heaven; threw him on my father;
Told the most piteous tale of Lear and him
That ever ear received; which in recounting
• His grief grew puissant, and the strings of life
Began to crack: twice then the trumpets sounded,
And there I left him tranced.
    Alb.   But who was this?
    Edg.   Kent, sir, the banish'd Kent; who ·in
      disguise
Follow'd his enemy king, and did him service   220
Improper for a slave.

    Enter a Gentleman, *with a bloody knife.*

    Gent.   Help, help, O, help!
    Edg.   What kind of help?
    Alb.   Speak, man.
    Edg.   What means that bloody knife?
    Gent.   'Tis hot, it smokes;
It came even from the heart of—O, she's dead!
    Alb.   Who dead? speak, man.
    Gent.   Your lady, sir, your lady: and her sister
By her is poisoned; she hath confess'd it.
    Edm.   I was contracted to them both: all three
Now marry in an instant.
    Edg.   Here comes Kent.   229
    Alb. Produce their bodies, be they alive or dead:
This judgement of the heavens, that makes us
      tremble,
Touches us not with pity.   [*Exit Gentleman.*

    Enter KENT.·

               O, is this he?
The time will not allow the compliment
Which very manners urges.
    Kent.   I am come
To bid my king and master aye good night:
Is he not here?
    Alb.   Great thing of us forgot!
Speak, Edmund, where's the king? and where's
      Cordelia?
See'st thou this object, Kent?
[*The bodies of Goneril and Regan are brought in.*
    Kent. Alack, why thus?
    Edm.   Yet Edmund was beloved:
The one the other poison'd for my sake,   240
And after slew herself.
    Alb.   Even so. Cover their faces.
    Edm.   I pant for life: some good I mean to do,
Despite of mine own nature. Quickly send,
Be brief in it, to the castle; for my writ
Is on the life of Lear and on Cordelia:
Nay, send in time.
    Alb.   Run, run, O, run!
    Edg.   To who, my lord? Who hath the office?
      send
Thy token of reprieve.
    Edm.   Well thought on: take my sword,   250
Give it the captain.
    Alb.   Haste thee, for thy life. [*Exit Edgar.*
    Edm.   He hath commission from thy wife and me
To hang Cordelia in the prison, and
To lay the blame upon her own despair,

216 *puissant.* Powerful.

Gentleman: 'It came even from the heart of—O, she's dead!' Woodcut from Holinshed's *Chronicles*, 1577

Lear: 'Howl, howl, howl, howl!' Sketch for the Death of Cordelia by Paul F. Poole (1807–1879)

263 *promised end*. The end of the world.

264 *Fall, and cease*. i.e. let the heavens fall and life cease.

276 *falchion*. Small curved sword.

287 *I'll see that straight*. At once.

That she fordid herself.
   Alb. The gods defend her! Bear him hence awhile.   [*Edmund is borne off.*

Re-enter LEAR, *with* CORDELIA *dead in his arms;* EDGAR, Captain, *and others following.*

   Lear. Howl, howl, howl, howl! O, you are men of stones:
Had I your tongues and eyes, I'ld use them so
That heaven's vault should crack. She's gone for ever!   259
I know when one is dead, and when one lives;
She's dead as earth. Lend me a looking-glass;
If that her breath will mist or stain the stone,
Why, then she lives.
   Kent.   Is this the promised end?
   Edg. Or image of that horror?
   Alb.   Fall, and cease!
   Lear. This feather stirs; she lives! if it be so,
It is a chance which does redeem all sorrows
That ever I have felt.
   Kent. [*Kneeling*] O my good master!
   Lear. Prithee, away.
   Edg.   'Tis noble Kent, your friend.
   Lear. A plague upon you, murderers, traitors all!
I might have saved her; now she's gone for ever!
Cordelia, Cordelia! stay a little. Ha!   271
What is't thou say'st? Her voice was ever soft,
Gentle, and low, an excellent thing in woman.
I kill'd the slave that was a-hanging thee.
   Capt. 'Tis true, my lords, he did.
   Lear.   Did I not, fellow?
I have seen the day, with my good biting falchion
I would have made them skip: I am old now,
And these same crosses spoil me. Who are you?
Mine eyes are not o' the best: I'll tell you straight.
   Kent. If fortune brag of two she loved and hated,   280
One of them we behold.
   Lear. This is a dull sight. Are you not Kent?
   Kent.   The same,
Your servant Kent. Where is your servant Caius?
   Lear. He's a good fellow, I can tell you that;
He'll strike, and quickly too: he's dead and rotten.
   Kent. No, my good lord; I am the very man,—
   Lear. I'll see that straight.
   Kent. That, from your first of difference and decay,
Have follow'd your sad steps.
   Lear.   You are welcome hither.
   Kent. Nor no man else: all's cheerless, dark, and deadly.   290
Your eldest daughters have fordone themselves,
And desperately are dead.
   Lear.   Ay, so I think.
   Alb. He knows not what he says: and vain it is
That we present us to him.
   Edg.   Very bootless.

Enter a Captain.

   Capt. Edmund is dead, my lord.
   Alb.   That's but a trifle here.
You lords and noble friends, know our intent.
What comfort to this great decay may come
Shall be applied: for us, we will resign,

During the life of this old majesty,
To him our absolute power: [*To Edgar and
      Kent*] you, to your rights;   300
●With boot, and such addition as your honours
Have more than merited.   All friends shall taste
The wages of their virtue, and all foes
The cup of their deservings.   O, see, see!
●   *Lear.*   And my poor fool is hang'd!   No, no,
      no life!
Why should a dog, a horse, a rat, have life,
And thou no breath at all?   Thou'lt come no more,
Never, never, never, never, never!
Pray you, undo this button: thank you, sir.
Do you see this?   Look on her, look, her lips, 310
Look there, look there!   [*Dies.*
   Edg.   He faints!   My lord, my lord!
   Kent.   Break, heart; I prithee, break!
   Edg.   Look up, my lord.
   Kent.   Vex not his ghost: O, let him pass! he
      hates him much
That would upon the rack of this tough world
Stretch him out longer.
   Edg.   He is gone, indeed.
   Kent.   The wonder is, he hath endured so long:
He but usurp'd his life.
   Alb.   Bear them from hence.   Our present
      business
Is general woe.   [*To Kent and Edgar*] Friends
      of my soul, you twain
Rule in this realm, and the gored state sustain.
   Kent.   I have a journey, sir, shortly to go; 321
My master calls me, I must not say no.
   Alb.   The weight of this sad time we must obey;
Speak what we feel, not what we ought to say.
The oldest hath borne most: we that are young
Shall never see so much, nor live so long.
                  [*Exeunt, with a dead march.*

301 *With boot, and such addition.* With due reward and in addition, such titles. *honours.* Noble deeds.

305 *my poor fool.* Cordelia. 'Fool' was a term of endearment.

King Lear weeping over the dead body of Cordelia. Painting by James Barry (1741–1806)

Macbeth

1606

MACBETH comes immediately after *King Lear*, and there is no problem whatever about its date. It was sparked off by the shattering sensation of the never-to-be-forgotten Gunpowder Plot of 5 November 1605. Nation-wide shock was felt at its carefully handled revelations, and for the first time a genuine movement of sympathy for the new king and his family, whose extirpation would have led to untold confusion. The dramatist, always alert to what was in the air, was moved to cash in on this. He and his Company already had reason to be grateful to King James I, who had doubled the rate of remuneration for Court performances (from £10 to £20), more than doubled the number of performances, and given Shakespeare and his Fellows the status of Grooms of the Chamber.

So the new play was one of Scottish history, in honour to Banquo, the putative ancestor of the Stuarts, with tributes to his 'royalty of nature', the 'dauntless temper of his mind', the 'wisdom that doth guide his valour', while the prophecy is borne home:

> Thou shalt get kings, though thou be none.

Tributes are specifically given to James himself, who was already, with some complacency, exercising the sacramental function of an anointed king of touching for the King's Evil:

> A most miraculous work in this good king,
> Which often, since my here-remain in England,
> I have seen him do. How he solicits heaven,
> Himself best knows; but strangely-visited people,
> All swoll'n and ulcerous, pitiful to the eye,
> The mere despair of surgery, he cures,
> Hanging a golden stamp about their necks,
> Put on with holy prayers. And 'tis spoken,
> To the succeeding royalty he leaves
> The healing benediction.

*Gunpowder Plot:
Guy Fawkes and
his fellow
conspirators 1605*

*James I who, as
James VI of
Scotland,
succeeded to the
English throne in
1603*

This is a description of the rite, which all the Stuarts exercised – Dr. Johnson himself, as a boy, was touched for his scrofula by Queen Anne. The sacrament was discontinued only by the unsacramental Hanoverians, who of course did not claim the prerogative of divine right.

To the King is also imputed 'a heavenly gift of prophecy', and the whole play is, in a way, a compliment to one of his chief intellectual interests, demonology, on which he had written a book. A much better book the dramatist had certainly read – Reginald Scot's *Discovery of Witchcraft*, from which he got some suggestions. Actually the 'Weird Sisters' are of Shakespeare's own conceiving: they are not ordinary witches (though it is convenient to call them such), who were common enough in Jacobean England, and still more so with the growth of the horrid Puritan mentality. We may regard these 'norns' as emanations of evil, the kind of thing the primitive-minded believe in; a modern mind can conceive of them as the hypostatising, or personalising, of the sub-conscious, and their 'prophecies' as projections of Macbeth's unspoken desires. As such, they are still relevant to our minds and may be accepted imaginatively.

Further evidences of the time and what it suggested to Shakespeare's mind as he wrote are to be seen in the specific references to the Jesuit doctrine of equivocation. This made the worst impression at the time and was pressed home at the trial of Henry Garnet, the Jesuit Provincial, who had learned of the Gunpowder Plot under the seal of confession, but had kept quiet about it. Under examination one need not tell the truth, one could always equivocate. Shakespeare was at one with his countrymen on such matters: an equivocator, he says, is one 'that could swear in both scales against either scale, who committed treason enough for God's sake, yet could not equivocate to heaven.' When the young Macduff asks his mother, 'what is a traitor?', she replies, 'why, one that swears and lies. Everyone that does so is a traitor, and must be hanged.'

Shakespeare was never one for going against popular prejudices (unlike Marlowe and Ben Jonson). By this time, Southampton, out of the Tower, had become a Protestant. Shakespeare would certainly have met him again, when the King's Men – as the Chamberlain's had been promoted into being – performed before the King, at Wilton in December 1603, where he was staying to avoid the plague. Both Southampton, and his junior, Pembroke, had been present. It was yet another reason for gratitude to James that he had released Southampton and taken into favour the remnants of Essex' former following.

The Story. So, once more, the dramatist looked up an appropriate story for his play, and found it in the Scottish section of Holinshed's *Chronicles*. He compressed the events of Macbeth's seventeen-year reign into as many weeks. For his purposes he darkened the character of the historic Macbeth and whitened that of Duncan, who was by no means so guileless and good in history as in the play. Again, under the Celtic custom of tanistry,[1] the rule of succession to a throne was uncertain, and left it wide open to murder – as one saw contemporaneously in the succession to tribal chieftainships in Ireland. That, historically speaking, Macbeth had some claim to the throne is not noticed in the play: it would not have been in keeping with Shakespeare's aim, which was always to intensify the horror.

The Play is the only one of the tragedies that is founded on a crime. Its analogy is more with the Histories, in particular with *Richard III*, with whose obsessive and haunted mind Macbeth has something in common, and there are echoes of the earlier play in his remorse and self-reproaches. He is, however, a very different character: nothing noble in Richard III, but a certain gleefulness in doing ill; Macbeth has nothing of that, but

1. The Gaelic and Irish custom by which the succession went, by election, to the 'worthiest' kinsman.

414

*The Weird Sisters.
Painting by Henry
Fuseli
(1741–1825)*

a flawed and ruined nobility – he is the victim of the Weird Sisters' prophecies, or, rather, of the promptings to which their 'prophecies' gave confirmation.

Here Shakespeare speeded up the action to launch the play forward in one grand and simple onrush: nothing of the complex movement of *Hamlet* and *King Lear*. Direct and simple like its neighbour, *Othello*, it yet offers a contrast with it: where that is rich and coloured, *Macbeth* is dark and lurid, full of blood, like the Celtic Northern glooms out of which it comes. Much of the action is by night, torches and guttering candles, knocking at the nocturnally closed gate enough to wake the dead. On the stage this knocking is ominous and thrilling; while the sleep-walking scene of Lady Macbeth is beyond anything, comparable only to the greatest heights of the dramatist's own art, Hamlet's scenes with his mother and Ophelia, Lear with Cordelia at the end of all.

The apparition of the murdered Banquo at Macbeth's feast is hardly less thrilling, and certainly impressed contemporaries. There are two immediate references to it in the very next year, 1607: in *The Puritan* and, more memorably, in *The Knight of the Burning Pestle*:

> When thou art at thy table with thy friends,
> Merry in heart, and filled with swelling wine,
> I'll come in midst of all thy pride and mirth,
> Invisible to all men but thy self . . .
> Shall make thee let the cup fall from thy hand,
> And stand as mute and pale as death itself.

As witchcraft is to the fore in this play so also is the theme of sleep. Immediately after the murder of the King, Macbeth says:

> Methought I heard a voice cry 'Sleep no more!
> Macbeth does murder sleep' – the innocent sleep,
> Sleep that knits up the ravelled sleave of care,
> The death of each day's life, sore labour's bath,
> Balm of hurt minds, great Nature's second course,
> Chief nourisher in life's feast . . .

Shakespeare was recalling the famous apostrophe to sleep of Sir Philip Sidney; but the theme is put to dramatic use, for neither Macbeth nor Lady Macbeth can sleep the sleep of innocence again, and she is driven by her guilt-haunted sleeplessness to suicide.

Short as the play is – and Shakespeare seems to have abridged it for production – it is full of famous lines which have entered into our collective memories:

> After life's fitful fever he sleeps well.

> All the perfumes of Arabia will not sweeten this little hand.

> Nothing in this life became him like the leaving of it.

And one of the most haunting passages relates the action itself to its author's profession:

> Life's but a walking shadow, a poor player
> That struts and frets his hour upon the stage,
> And then is heard no more. It is a tale
> Told by an idiot, full of sound and fury,
> Signifying nothing.

Personal. In so concentrated a play there is little that is not directly relevant. In the 'Hyrcan tiger' we have another fleck from his reading of Pliny's Natural History, like the reference to the Pontic sea in *Othello*. Tarquin is in mind, as so often; once more there are portents in the air, and

> A falcon towering in her pride of place
> Was by a mousing owl hawked at and killed.

Several references to snakes occur. Are we to see him in the reflection:

> And you all know security
> Is mortals' chiefest enemy?

It is a thought characteristic of him.

We have a couple of references to the contemporaneous kerns and gallowglasses, but now these are from the Western Isles – all one Celtic world with Northern Ireland: 'the merciless Macdonald . . . from the Western Isles

> Of kerns and gallowglasses is supplied.

These were much in the news, for the leader of the Ulster resistance, Hugh O'Neill, had

Opening page of
Macbeth *from the*
First Folio of 1623

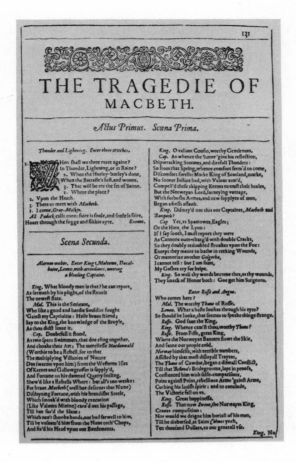

submitted to James I, who was preparing the plantation of Ulster with Scots. There were kern and gallowglass, Macdonalds and MacDonells on either side those narrow waters: to what point their endless scuffling?

The play is true in atmosphere to their dark, lugubrious, bloodstained world.

The Text offers some problems. It has come down to us from the Folio, 'doubtless printed from a prompt-copy', says E. K. Chambers; and this has been cut, perhaps by Shakespeare himself. Greg adds that the stage-directions 'are normal and reveal the hand of the book-keeper, though some probably originated with the author.' For some later performance another hand, probably Middleton, inserted a few things, but not so much as Victorian disintegrators (i.e. of the text) supposed. Dover-Wilson says that 'modern experts are less pessimistic'; the whole drift of scholarship has been in a conservative direction, to substantiate on the whole what has come down to us.

Simon Forman saw a performance at the Globe on 20 April 1611. It is interesting that he refers to the Weird Sisters not as witches but as 'women fairies or nymphs'. He was most impressed by them, the apparition of Banquo's ghost, and Lady Macbeth's sleep-walking.[1]

Macbeth's reference to Banquo:

> under him
> My Genius is rebuked, as it is said
> Mark Antony's was by Caesar –

shows that Shakespeare was already thinking of his next play.

1. cf. my *Simon Forman*, 303–4.

417

MACBETH.

DRAMATIS PERSONÆ.

DUNCAN, king of Scotland.
MALCOLM, } his sons.
DONALBAIN, }
MACBETH, } generals of the king's army.
BANQUO, }
MACDUFF,
LENNOX,
ROSS,
MENTEITH, } noblemen of Scotland.
ANGUS,
CAITHNESS,
FLEANCE, son to Banquo.
SIWARD, Earl of Northumberland, general
of the English forces.
Young SIWARD, his son.
SEYTON, an officer attending on Macbeth.
Boy, son to Macduff.

An English Doctor.
A Scotch Doctor.
A Soldier.
A Porter.
An Old Man.

LADY MACBETH.
LADY MACDUFF.
Gentlewoman attending on Lady Macbeth.

HECATE.
Three Witches.
Apparitions.

Lords, Gentlemen, Officers, Soldiers, Murderers,
Attendants, and Messengers.

SCENE: *Scotland: England.*

Witches with familiars. Woodcut from 17th century, as reproduced in *Book of Days*, 19th century

---

2 *In thunder, lightning, or in rain?* Witches and demons were supposed to be particularly active in turbulent weather, often thought to be caused by their spells.

3 *hurlyburly.* Confusion, turmoil, especially with reference to sedition or insurrection.

9 *Graymalkin.* A grey cat. With the toad the cat was a common 'familiar' or demon-companion of the witch.

10 *Paddock.* A toad.

Opposite: Macbeth and witches. Engraving by Guernier from Pope's *Works of Shakespeare*, 1728

● *A bullet beside a text line indicates an annotation in the opposite column.*

ACT I.

SCENE I. *A desert place.*

Thunder and lightning. Enter three Witches.
  First Witch. When shall we three meet again
● In thunder, lightning, or in rain?
●   *Sec. Witch.* When the hurlyburly's done,
When the battle's lost and won.
  Third Witch. That will be ere the set of sun.
  First Witch. Where the place?
  Sec. Witch.   Upon the heath.
  Third Witch. There to meet with Macbeth.
●   *First Witch.* I come, Graymalkin!
●   *Sec. Witch.* Paddock calls.

12 *Hover.* This implies that the witches depart by flying. They probably left by trapdoor, after vanishing first into a 'fog'. Apparently, such fogs and mists were produced by burning resin and could be used to conceal groups of actors or produce darkness. This kind of stage-effect was used to great advantage by Shakespeare in *A Midsummer Night's Dream.*

9 *The merciless Macdonwald.* One of the leaders of the rebellion against Duncan.

13 *kerns and gallowglasses.* The kern was a light-armed foot-soldier and one of the poorer class of Irish from whom such soldiers were drawn. The gallowglass was a horseman armed with a sharp axe.

19 *minion.* Favourite.

22 *nave to the chaps.* Navel to jaw.

26 *Shipwrecking storms and direful thunders break.* This immediately suggests the witches and informs us from what source the danger threatens. It also relates directly to James's personal experience of witchcraft. In 1589 James went to Oslo to marry Anne, daughter of King Frederick of Denmark, and had a stormy voyage across the North Sea. Soon after he and his bride returned to Scotland a number of women were arrested for witchcraft, one of whom declared that she and others had gone to sea in sieves and had tried to raise a storm to wreck the ship in which James had been sailing to Norway to fetch his queen. James conducted the preliminary examination of the accused himself and it was on this occasion that he was taken aside by one of the accused women, Agnes Sampson, and told the details of a private conversation he had had with his wife on their marriage night. Soon after this case James began work on his *Daemonologie.*

Agnes Sampson and her coven. Woodcut from *Newes from Scotland,* 1591

Third Witch.   Anon.   10
All.   Fair is foul, and foul is fair:
● Hover through the fog and filthy air.   [*Exeunt.*

SCENE II.   *A camp near Forres.*

Alarum within. Enter DUNCAN, MALCOLM, DONALBAIN, LENNOX, *with* Attendants, *meeting a bleeding* Sergeant.

Dun.   What bloody man is that? He can report,
As seemeth by his plight, of the revolt
The newest state.
Mal.   This is the sergeant
Who like a good and hardy soldier fought
'Gainst my captivity.   Hail, brave friend!
Say to the king the knowledge of the broil
As thou didst leave it.
Ser.   Doubtful it stood:
As two spent swimmers, that do cling together
● And choke their art.   The merciless Macdonwald—
Worthy to be a rebel, for to that   10
The multiplying villanies of nature
Do swarm upon him—from the western isles
● Of kerns and gallowglasses is supplied;
And fortune, on his damned quarrel smiling,
Show'd like a rebel's whore: but all's too weak:
For brave Macbeth—well he deserves that name—
Disdaining fortune, with his brandish'd steel,
Which smoked with bloody execution,
● Like valour's minion carved out his passage
Till he faced the slave;   20
†Which ne'er shook hands, nor bade farewell to him,
● Till he unseam'd him from the nave to the chaps,
And fix'd his head upon our battlements.
Dun.   O valiant cousin! worthy gentleman!
Ser.   As whence the sun 'gins his reflection
● Shipwrecking storms and direful thunders break,
So from that spring whence comfort seem'd to come
Discomfort swells.   Mark, king of Scotland, mark:
No sooner justice had with valour arm'd
Compell'd these skipping kerns to trust their heels,
But the Norweyan lord surveying vantage,   31
With furbish'd arms and new supplies of men
Began a fresh assault.
Dun.   Dismay'd not this
Our captains, Macbeth and Banquo?
Ser.   Yes;
As sparrows eagles, or the hare the lion.
If I say sooth, I must report they were
As cannons overcharged with double cracks, so they
Doubly redoubled strokes upon the foe:
Except they meant to bathe in reeking wounds,
Or memorize another Golgotha,   40
I cannot tell.
But I am faint, my gashes cry for help.
Dun.   So well thy words become thee as thy wounds;
They smack of honour both.   Go get him surgeons.   [*Exit Sergeant, attended.*
Who comes here?

Enter ROSS.

Mal. The worthy thane of Ross.
Len. What a haste looks through his eyes!
So should he look
That seems to speak things strange.
Ross. God save the king!
Dun. Whence camest thou, worthy thane?
Ross. From Fife, great king;
Where the Norweyan banners flout the sky
And fan our people cold. Norway himself, 50
With terrible numbers,
Assisted by that most disloyal traitor
● The thane of Cawdor, began a dismal conflict;
● Till that Bellona's bridegroom, lapp'd in proof,
Confronted him with self-comparisons,
Point against point rebellious, arm 'gainst arm,
Curbing his lavish spirit: and, to conclude,
The victory fell on us.
Dun. Great happiness!
Ross. That now
● Sweno, the Norways' king, craves composition;
Nor would we deign him burial of his men 60
● Till he disbursed at Saint Colme's inch
Ten thousand dollars to our general use.
Dun. No more that thane of Cawdor shall
deceive
Our bosom interest: go pronounce his present
death,
And with his former title greet Macbeth.
Ross. I'll see it done.
Dun. What he hath lost noble Macbeth hath
won. [*Exeunt.*

SCENE III. *A heath near Forres.*

Thunder. Enter the three Witches.

First Witch. Where hast thou been, sister?
Sec. Witch. Killing swine.
Third Witch. Sister, where thou?
First Witch. A sailor's wife had chestnuts in
her lap,
And munch'd, and munch'd, and munch'd:—
'Give me,' quoth I:
● 'Aroint thee, witch!' the rump-fed ronyon cries.
Her husband's to Aleppo gone, master o' the
Tiger:
But in a sieve I'll thither sail,
And, like a rat without a tail,
I'll do, I'll do, and I'll do. 10
Sec. Witch. I'll give thee a wind.
First Witch. Thou 'rt kind.
Third Witch. And I another.
First Witch. I myself have all the other,
And the very ports they blow,
All the quarters that they know
I' the shipman's card.
I will drain him dry as hay:
Sleep shall neither night nor day
Hang upon his pent-house lid; 20
He shall live a man forbid:
Weary se'nnights nine times nine
Shall he dwindle, peak and pine:
Though his bark cannot be lost,
Yet it shall be tempest-tost.
Look what I have.
Sec. Witch. Show me, show me.
First Witch. Here I have a pilot's thumb,

53 *thane of Cawdor.* Another rebel, whose title of nobility is later conferred on Macbeth for his exploits in the field.

54 *Bellona's bridegroom.* Macbeth as Mars, the god of war. *lapp'd in proof.* Clad in armour.

59 *Sweno.* A Norwegian king who led an invasion into Scotland, which in history was independent of Macdonwald's rebellion. Shakespeare has united them into one incident. *composition.* Peace terms.

61 *Saint Colme's Inch.* Inchcolm, an island in the Firth of Forth.

SD *Enter the three Witches.* Holinshed describes the witches as august and auspicious figures and in his illustration of their meeting with Macbeth and Banquo they appear as well-dressed gentlewomen.

Macbeth, Banquo and the witches. Woodcut from Holinshed's *Chronicles,* 1577

6 *Aroint thee.* A phrase meaning 'begone'; quite possibly a misprint for 'avaunt' (forward! away). *ronyon.* A term of abuse meaning 'scabby, mangy creature'.

Painting by Francesco Zuccarelli (1702–88)

33 *Posters.* Travellers.

38 *So foul and fair a day I have not seen.* This means 'foul' with regard to the weather and 'fair' with reference to Macbeth's victory.

44 *choppy.* Chapped, rough.

56 *having.* Possession, fortune.

71 *Sinel.* Macbeth's father.

Wreck'd as homeward he did come.
　　　　　　　　　　　　　　　[*Drum within.*
　Third Witch.　A drum, a drum!　　　　30
Macbeth doth come.
　All.　The weird sisters, hand in hand,
Posters of the sea and land,
Thus do go about, about :
Thrice to thine and thrice to mine
And thrice again, to make up nine.
Peace! the charm's wound up.

　　　　Enter MACBETH *and* BANQUO.

　Macb.　So foul and fair a day I have not seen.
　Ban.　How far is 't call'd to Forres?　What are these
So wither'd and so wild in their attire,　　　40
That look not like the inhabitants o' the earth,
And yet are on 't?　Live you? or are you aught
That man may question?　You seem to understand me,
By each at once her choppy finger laying
Upon her skinny lips : you should be women,
And yet your beards forbid me to interpret
That you are so.
　Macb.　　　Speak, if you can : what are you?
　First Witch.　All hail, Macbeth! hail to thee, thane of Glamis!
　Sec. Witch.　All hail, Macbeth! hail to thee, thane of Cawdor!
　Third Witch.　All hail, Macbeth, that shalt be king hereafter!　　　50
　Ban.　Good sir, why do you start ; and seem to fear
Things that do sound so fair?　I' the name of truth,
Are ye fantastical, or that indeed
Which outwardly ye show?　My noble partner
You greet with present grace and great prediction
Of noble having and of royal hope,
That he seems rapt withal : to me you speak not.
If you can look into the seeds of time,
And say which grain will grow and which will not,
Speak then to me, who neither beg nor fear　60
Your favours nor your hate.
　First Witch.　Hail!
　Sec. Witch.　Hail!
　Third Witch.　Hail!
　First Witch.　Lesser than Macbeth, and greater.
　Sec. Witch.　Not so happy, yet much happier.
　Third Witch.　Thou shalt get kings, though thou be none :
So all hail, Macbeth and Banquo!
　First Witch.　Banquo and Macbeth, all hail!
　Macb.　Stay, you imperfect speakers, tell me more :　　　70
By Sinel's death I know I am thane of Glamis ;
But how of Cawdor? the thane of Cawdor lives,
A prosperous gentleman ; and to be king
Stands not within the prospect of belief,
No more than to be Cawdor.　Say from whence
You owe this strange intelligence? or why
Upon this blasted heath you stop our way
With such prophetic greeting?　Speak, I charge
you.　　　　　　　　　　　　[*Witches vanish.*
　Ban.　The earth hath bubbles, as the water has,
And these are of them.　Whither are they vanish'd?　　　80
　Macb.　Into the air ; and what seem'd corporal melted

As breath into the wind. Would they had stay'd!
  Ban. Were such things here as we do speak
    about?
Or have we eaten on the insane root
That takes the reason prisoner?
  Macb. Your children shall be kings.
  Ban.   You shall be king.
  Macb. And thane of Cawdor too: went it
    not so?
  Ban. To the selfsame tune and words. Who's
    here?

        Enter Ross *and* Angus.

  Ross. The king hath happily received, Mac-
    beth,
The news of thy success; and when he reads 90
Thy personal venture in the rebels' fight,
His wonders and his praises do contend
Which should be thine or his: silenced with that,
In viewing o'er the rest o' the selfsame day,
He finds thee in the stout Norweyan ranks,
Nothing afeard of what thyself didst make,
Strange images of death.   As thick as hail
Came post with post; and every one did bear
Thy praises in his kingdom's great defence,
And pour'd them down before him.
  Ang.   We are sent 100
To give thee from our royal master thanks;
Only to herald thee into his sight,
Not pay thee.
  Ross. And, for an earnest of a greater honour,
He bade me, from him, call thee thane of Caw-
    dor:
In which addition, hail, most worthy thane!
For it is thine.
  Ban.   What, can the devil speak true?
  Macb. The thane of Cawdor lives: why do
    you dress me
In borrow'd robes?
  Ang.   Who was the thane lives yet;
But under heavy judgement bears that life 110
Which he deserves to lose.   Whether he was
    combined
With those of Norway, or did line the rebel
With hidden help and vantage, or that with both
He labour'd in his country's wreck, I know not;
But treasons capital, confess'd and proved,
Have overthrown him.
  Macb. [*Aside*] Glamis, and thane of Cawdor!
The greatest is behind.   [*To Ross and Angus*]
    Thanks for your pains.
[*To Ban.*] Do you not hope your children shall
    be kings,
When those that gave the thane of Cawdor
    to me
Promised no less to them?
  Ban.   That trusted home 120
Might yet enkindle you unto the crown,
Besides the thane of Cawdor.   But 'tis strange:
And oftentimes, to win us to our harm,
The instruments of darkness tell us truths,
Win us with honest trifles, to betray 's
In deepest consequence.
Cousins, a word, I pray you.
  Macb.   [*Aside*] Two truths are told,
As happy prologues to the swelling act
Of the imperial theme.—I thank you, gentlemen.
[*Aside*] This supernatural soliciting 130
Cannot be ill, cannot be good: if ill,

84 *insane*. i.e. causing insanity.

92-93 *His wonders . . . . thine or his*. Duncan's speechless admiration contends with his desire to praise Macbeth.

104 *earnest*. Pledge.

112 *line*. Strengthen, support.

120 *home*. Totally.

128 *swelling act*. Magnificent experience.

William Charles Macready as Macbeth, Theatre Royal, Drury Lane, London, 1843

140 *single.* Individual, weak. *function.* The normal operations of the mind.

147 *Time and the hour runs through the roughest day.* Whatever is going to happen will happen inevitably.

The palace at Forres. Engraving by Kenny Meadows, from Cornwall's *Works of Shakspere*, 1846

---

2 *in commission.* Assigned the duty.

9 *had been studied.* Had learnt by heart as for a part in a play.

10 *owed.* Owned.

11 *careless.* Valueless.

11-12 *There's no art . . . the face.* It is impossible to determine the nature of a mind by the outward appearance of the face.

16 *before.* Ahead.

Why hath it given me earnest of success,
Commencing in a truth? I am thane of Cawdor:
If good, why do I yield to that suggestion
Whose horrid image doth unfix my hair
And make my seated heart knock at my ribs,
Against the use of nature?   Present fears
Are less than horrible imaginings:
My thought, whose murder yet is but fantastical,
● Shakes so my single state of man that function
Is smother'd in surmise, and nothing is   141
But what is not.
    Ban.   Look, how our partner's rapt.
    Macb. [*Aside*] If chance will have me king,
      why, chance may crown me,
Without my stir.
    Ban.   New honours come upon him,
Like our strange garments, cleave not to their
    mould
But with the aid of use.
    Macb.   [*Aside*] Come what come may,
● Time and the hour runs through the roughest day.
    Ban. Worthy Macbeth, we stay upon your
    leisure.
    Macb. Give me your favour: my dull brain
    was wrought
With things forgotten.   Kind gentlemen, your
    pains   150
Are register'd where every day I turn
The leaf to read them.   Let us toward the king.
Think upon what hath chanced, and, at more
    time,
The interim having weigh'd it, let us speak
Our free hearts each to other.
    Ban.   Very gladly.
    Macb. Till then, enough.   Come, friends.
                           [*Exeunt.*

SCENE IV.   *Forres.   The palace.*

Flourish.   Enter DUNCAN, MALCOLM, DONAL-
    BAIN, LENNOX, *and* Attendants.

    Dun. Is execution done on Cawdor?   Are not
● Those in commission yet return'd?
    Mal.   My liege,
They are not yet come back.   But I have spoke
With one that saw him die: who did report
That very frankly he confess'd his treasons,
Implored your highness' pardon and set forth
A deep repentance: nothing in his life
Became him like the leaving it; he died
● As one that had been studied in his death
● To throw away the dearest thing he owed,   10
● As 'twere a careless trifle.
    Dun.   There's no art
To find the mind's construction in the face:
He was a gentleman on whom I built
An absolute trust.

    Enter MACBETH, BANQUO, ROSS, *and* ANGUS.
                    O worthiest cousin!
The sin of my ingratitude even now
● Was heavy on me: thou art so far before
That swiftest wing of recompense is slow
To overtake thee.   Would thou hadst less de-
    served,
That the proportion both of thanks and payment
Might have been mine! only I have left to say, 20
More is thy due than more than all can pay.
    Macb. The service and the loyalty I owe,

In doing it, pays itself.   Your highness' part
Is to receive our duties; and our duties
Are to your throne and state children and servants,
Which do but what they should, by doing every
    thing
● Safe toward your love and honour.
    Dun.   Welcome hither:
I have begun to plant thee, and will labour
To make thee full of growing.   Noble Banquo,
That hast no less deserved, nor must be known 30
No less to have done so, let me infold thee
And hold thee to my heart.
    Ban.   There if I grow,
The harvest is your own.
    Dun.   My plenteous joys,
Wanton in fulness, seek to hide themselves
In drops of sorrow.   Sons, kinsmen, thanes,
● And you whose places are the nearest, know
● We will establish our estate upon
Our eldest, Malcolm, whom we name hereafter
● The Prince of Cumberland; which honour must
Not unaccompanied invest him only,   40
But signs of nobleness, like stars, shall shine
● On all deservers.   From hence to Inverness,
And bind us further to you.
    Macb.   The rest is labour, which is not used
    for you:
● I'll be myself the harbinger and make joyful
The hearing of my wife with your approach;
So humbly take my leave.
    Dun.   My worthy Cawdor!
    Macb. [*Aside*] The Prince of Cumberland!
    that is a step
On which I must fall down, or else o'erleap,
For in my way it lies.   Stars, hide your fires; 50
Let not light see my black and deep desires:
● The eye wink at the hand; yet let that be,
Which the eye fears, when it is done, to see.
                                        [*Exit.*

    Dun.   True, worthy Banquo; he is full so
    valiant,
And in his commendations I am fed;
It is a banquet to me.   Let's after him,
Whose care is gone before to bid us welcome:
It is a peerless kinsman.   [*Flourish. Exeunt.*

    SCENE V.   *Inverness.   Macbeth's castle.*

    Enter LADY MACBETH, *reading a letter.*

    Lady M.   'They met me in the day of success:
● and I have learned by the perfectest report, they
have more in them than mortal knowledge.   When
I burned in desire to question them further, they
made themselves air, into which they vanished.
Whiles I stood rapt in the wonder of it, came
● missives from the king, who all-hailed me "Thane
of Cawdor;" by which title, before, these weird
sisters saluted me, and referred me to the coming
on of time, with " Hail, king that shalt be!"
This have I thought good to deliver thee, my
dearest partner of greatness, that thou mightst not
lose the dues of rejoicing, by being ignorant of
what greatness is promised thee.   Lay it to thy
heart, and farewell.'
Glamis thou art, and Cawdor; and shalt be
What thou art promised: yet do I fear thy nature;
It is too full o' the milk of human kindness
● To catch the nearest way: thou wouldst be great;
Art not without ambition, but without   20

27 *Safe toward.* With sure regard to.

36 *And you whose places are the nearest.* Those who might have some claim upon the throne.

37 *establish our estate.* Settle the kingdom.

39 *Prince of Cumberland.* Originally, the crown of Scotland was not inherited. When an heir was chosen during the ruler's life-time, he was sometimes given this title.

42 *Inverness.* Macbeth's castle.

44 *The rest . . . for you.* Inactivity or leisure is labour. In other words, it is wearying to be doing nothing when I could be doing something for you.

45 *harbinger.* The court official who was sent ahead to arrange accommodation for the king.

52 *wink at.* Seem not to see.

2 *perfectest report.* Dr Johnson explains this as 'the best intelligence'.

7 *missives.* Messengers.

19 *To catch the nearest way.* To take the most expedient way (i.e. murder).

Lady Macbeth with letter. Engraving from the painting by Richard Westall. (1765–1836).

21 *illness*. Evil or wickedness.

30 *metaphysical*. Supernatural.

39 *raven*. Believed to be the herald of misfortune.

56 *hereafter*. In the future.

69 *my dispatch*. Lady Macbeth suggests that she will manage the whole affair.

●The illness should attend it: what thou wouldst
     highly,
That wouldst thou holily; wouldst not play false,
And yet wouldst wrongly win: thou'ldst have,
     great Glamis,
That which cries 'Thus thou must do, if thou
     have it;
And that which rather thou dost fear to do
Than wishest should be undone.' Hie thee hither,
That I may pour my spirits in thine ear;
And chastise with the valour of my tongue
All that impedes thee from the golden round,
●Which fate and metaphysical aid doth seem   30
To have thee crown'd withal.

            Enter a Messenger.

                           What is your tidings?
   Mess.   The king comes here to-night.
   Lady M.   Thou'rt mad to say it:
Is not thy master with him? who, were't so,
Would have inform'd for preparation.
   Mess.   So please you, it is true: our thane is
     coming:
One of my fellows had the speed of him,
Who, almost dead for breath, had scarcely more
Than would make up his message.
   Lady M.   Give him tending;
●He brings great news.   [*Exit Messenger.*
                 The raven himself is hoarse
That croaks the fatal entrance of Duncan   40
Under my battlements. Come, you spirits
That tend on mortal thoughts, unsex me here,
And fill me from the crown to the toe top-full
Of direst cruelty! make thick my blood;
Stop up the access and passage to remorse,
That no compunctious visitings of nature
Shake my fell purpose, nor keep peace between
The effect and it! Come to my woman's breasts,
And take my milk for gall, you murdering
     ministers,
Wherever in your sightless substances   50
You wait on nature's mischief! Come, thick night,
And pall thee in the dunnest smoke of hell,
That my keen knife see not the wound it makes,
Nor heaven peep through the blanket of the dark,
To cry 'Hold, hold!'

            Enter MACBETH.

                 Great Glamis! worthy Cawdor!
●Greater than both, by the all-hail hereafter!
Thy letters have transported me beyond
This ignorant present, and I feel now
The future in the instant.
   Macb.   My dearest love,
Duncan comes here to-night.
   Lady M.   And when goes hence? 60
   Macb. To-morrow, as he purposes.
   Lady M.   O, never
Shall sun that morrow see!
Your face, my thane, is as a book where men
May read strange matters. To beguile the time,
Look like the time; bear welcome in your eye,
Your hand, your tongue: look like the innocent
     flower,
But be the serpent under 't. He that's coming
Must be provided for: and you shall put
●This night's great business into my dispatch;
Which shall to all our nights and days to come 70
Give solely sovereign sway and masterdom.

Macb. We will speak further.
Lady M.   Only look up clear;
To alter favour ever is to fear:
Leave all the rest to me.   [*Exeunt.*

SCENE VI. *Before Macbeth's castle.*

Hautboys and torches. Enter DUNCAN, MAL-
COLM, DONALBAIN, BANQUO, LENNOX, MAC-
DUFF, ROSS, ANGUS, *and* Attendants.

Dun. This castle hath a pleasant seat; the air
Nimbly and sweetly recommends itself
Unto our gentle senses.
Ban.   This guest of summer,
The temple-haunting martlet, does approve,
By his loved mansionry, that the heaven's breath
Smells wooingly here: no jutty, frieze,
Buttress, nor coign of vantage, but this bird
Hath made his pendent bed and procreant cradle:
Where they most breed and haunt, I have ob-
          served,
The air is delicate.

Enter LADY MACBETH.

Dun.   See, see, our honour'd hostess! 10
The love that follows us sometime is our trouble,
Which still we thank as love.   Herein I teach you
How you shall bid God 'ild us for your pains,
And thank us for your trouble.
Lady M.   All our service
In every point twice done and then done double
Were poor and single business to contend
Against those honours deep and broad wherewith
Your majesty loads our house: for those of old
And the late dignities heap'd up to them,
We rest your hermits.
Dun.   Where's the thane of Cawdor? 20
We coursed him at the heels, and had a purpose
To be his purveyor: but he rides well;
And his great love, sharp as his spur, hath holp
          him
To his home before us.   Fair and noble hostess,
We are your guest to-night.
Lady M.   Your servants ever
Have theirs, themselves and what is theirs, in
          compt,
To make their audit at your highness' pleasure,
Still to return your own.
Dun.   Give me your hand;
Conduct me to mine host: we love him highly,
And shall continue our graces towards him.   30
By your leave, hostess.   [*Exeunt.*

SCENE VII. *Macbeth's castle.*

Hautboys and torches. Enter a Sewer, *and
divers* Servants *with dishes and service, and
pass over the stage. Then enter* MACBETH.

Macb. If it were done when 'tis done, then
          'twere well
It were done quickly: if the assassination
Could trammel up the consequence, and catch
With his surcease success; that but this blow
Might be the be-all and the end-all here,
But here, upon this bank and shoal of time,
We'ld jump the life to come.   But in these cases
We still have judgement here; that we but teach
Bloody instructions, which, being taught, return
To plague the inventor: this even-handed justice

72–73 *Only look up clear . . . to fear.* Lady Macbeth urges her husband to look undisturbed otherwise people might become suspicious.

4 *temple-haunting martlet.* The house-martin, commonly building its nest in churches.

6 *jutty.* That part of a building which juts out.

7 *coign of vantage.* Advantageous corner.

11–14 *The love that follows us . . . your trouble.* Love is sometimes troublesome; but in such situations we try to think of the love and ignore the trouble. By saying this I have taught you to pray to God for the good of those who trouble you.

16 *contend.* To equal or compete.

20 *We rest your hermits.* We feel bound to pray for you.

26 *in compt.* Subject to account.

SD *Sewer.* From the French *essayeur.* The chief steward who serves at table.

Preparing a banquet. Engraving by Justus Sadeler, after a painting by Antonio Tempesta, 16th century

17 *faculties*. Powers.

18 *clear*. Spotless, free from guilt.

19 *trumpet-tongued*. With voices as clear as trumpet sounds.

23 *sightless couriers of the air*. i.e. the winds.

Portrait of Sarah Siddons, 1784, by Horace Hone (1756–1825)

59 *We fail!* Lady Macbeth's reply is printed as a question in the Folio, but the question mark also served then as an exclamation mark. Mrs Siddons tried 'We fail?' (a scornful echo of his question), then '*We* fail!' and finally 'We fail.' (the acceptance of the possibility of failure and its consequences).

60 *sticking-place*. This was the notch on the crossbow into which the string fitted when sufficiently taut or screwed up.

64 *convince*. Overpower.

67 *limbeck*. A vessel used in distilling alcohol, from alembic.

Commends the ingredients of our poison'd chalice
To our own lips.   He's here in double trust;
First, as I am his kinsman and his subject,
Strong both against the deed; then, as his host,
Who should against his murderer shut the door,
Not bear the knife myself.   Besides, this Duncan
● Hath borne his faculties so meek, hath been
● So clear in his great office, that his virtues
● Will plead like angels, trumpet-tongued, against
The deep damnation of his taking-off;   20
And pity, like a naked new-born babe,
Striding the blast, or heaven's cherubim, horsed
● Upon the sightless couriers of the air,
Shall blow the horrid deed in every eye,
That tears shall drown the wind.   I have no spur
To prick the sides of my intent, but only
Vaulting ambition, which o'erleaps itself
And falls on the other.

Enter LADY MACBETH.

                              How now! what news?
Lady M.   He has almost supp'd: why have
   you left the chamber?
Macb.   Hath he ask'd for me?
Lady M.   Know you not he has? 30
Macb.   We will proceed no further in this
   business:
He hath honour'd me of late; and I have bought
Golden opinions from all sorts of people,
Which would be worn now in their newest gloss,
Not cast aside so soon.
Lady M.   Was the hope drunk
Wherein you dress'd yourself? hath it slept since?
And wakes it now, to look so green and pale
At what it did so freely?   From this time
Such I account thy love.   Art thou afeard
To be the same in thine own act and valour   40
As thou art in desire?   Wouldst thou have that
Which thou esteem'st the ornament of life,
And live a coward in thine own esteem,
Letting 'I dare not' wait upon 'I would,'
Like the poor cat i' the adage?
Macb.   Prithee, peace:
I dare do all that may become a man;
Who dares do more is none.
Lady M.   What beast was't, then,
That made you break this enterprise to me?
When you durst do it, then you were a man;
And, to be more than what you were, you would 50
Be so much more the man.   Nor time nor place
Did then adhere, and yet you would make both:
They have made themselves, and that their fitness now
Does unmake you.   I have given suck, and know
How tender 'tis to love the babe that milks me:
I would, while it was smiling in my face,
Have pluck'd my nipple from his boneless gums,
And dash'd the brains out, had I so sworn as you
Have done to this.
Macb.   If we should fail?
● *Lady M.*   We fail!
● But screw your courage to the sticking-place, 60
And we'll not fail.   When Duncan is asleep—
Whereto the rather shall his day's hard journey
Soundly invite him—his two chamberlains
● Will I with wine and wassail so convince
That memory, the warder of the brain,
Shall be a fume, and the receipt of reason
● A limbeck only: when in swinish sleep

Their drenched natures lie as in a death,
What cannot you and I perform upon
The unguarded Duncan? what not put upon 70
His spongy officers, who shall bear the guilt
Of our great quell?
  Macb.   Bring forth men-children only;
For thy undaunted mettle should compose
Nothing but males. Will it not be received,
When we have mark'd with blood those sleepy two
Of his own chamber and used their very daggers,
That they have done't?
  Lady M.   Who dares receive it other,
As we shall make our griefs and clamour roar
Upon his death?
  Macb.   I am settled, and bend up
Each corporal agent to this terrible feat. 80
Away, and mock the time with fairest show:
False face must hide what the false heart doth
     know.   [*Exeunt.*

ACT II.

SCENE I. *Court of Macbeth's castle.*

Enter BANQUO, *and* FLEANCE *bearing a torch before him.*

  Ban. How goes the night, boy?
  Fle. The moon is down; I have not heard the clock.
  Ban. And she goes down at twelve.
  Fle.   I take't, 'tis later, sir.
  Ban. Hold, take my sword. There's husbandry in heaven;
Their candles are all out. Take thee that too.
A heavy summons lies like lead upon me,
And yet I would not sleep: merciful powers,
Restrain in me the cursed thoughts that nature
Gives way to in repose!

Enter MACBETH, *and a* Servant *with a torch.*

               Give me my sword.
Who's there? 10
  Macb. A friend.
  Ban. What, sir, not yet at rest? The king's a-bed:
He hath been in unusual pleasure, and
Sent forth great largess to your offices.
This diamond he greets your wife withal,
By the name of most kind hostess; and shut up
In measureless content.
  Macb.   Being unprepared,
Our will became the servant to defect;
Which else should free have wrought.
  Ban.   All's well.
I dreamt last night of the three weird sisters: 20
To you they have show'd some truth.
  Macb.   I think not of them:
Yet, when we can entreat an hour to serve,
We would spend it in some words upon that business,
If you would grant the time.
  Ban.   At your kind'st leisure.
  Macb. If you shall cleave to my consent, when 'tis,
It shall make honour for you.
  Ban.   So I lose none
In seeking to augment it, but still keep
My bosom franchised and allegiance clear,

Ellen Terry as Lady Macbeth, 1888. Painting by John Singer Sargent (1856–1925)

4 *husbandry.* Thrift.

14 *offices.* Servants.

18 *defect.* What is lacking.

36-37 *sensible To feeling.* Tangible.

46 *dudgeon.* Handles. *gouts.* Clots.

55 *Tarquin.* Tarquinius Sextus, son of the Roman king, who raped Lucrece.

Lady Macbeth: 'Hark! Peace!' Sarah Siddons as Lady Macbeth, 1802

Lady Macbeth: 'the fatal bellman . . .' Engraving by F. W. Fairholt from a woodcut of 1500, from J. O. Halliwell's edition of Shakespeare's works, 1853–65

6 *charge.* Duty. *possets.* Drink.

I shall be counsell'd.
 Macb.   Good repose the while!
 Ban.   Thanks, sir: the like to you!   30
        [*Exeunt Banquo and Fleance.*
 Macb.   Go bid thy mistress, when my drink is
   ready,
She strike upon the bell.   Get thee to bed.
           [*Exit Servant.*
Is this a dagger which I see before me,
The handle toward my hand?   Come, let me
   clutch thee.
I have thee not, and yet I see thee still.
• Art thou not, fatal vision, sensible
To feeling as to sight? or art thou but
A dagger of the mind, a false creation,
Proceeding from the heat-oppressed brain?
I see thee yet, in form as palpable   40
As this which now I draw.
Thou marshall'st me the way that I was going;
And such an instrument I was to use.
Mine eyes are made the fools o' the other senses,
Or else worth all the rest; I see thee still,
• And on thy blade and dudgeon gouts of blood,
Which was not so before.   There's no such thing:
It is the bloody business which informs
Thus to mine eyes.   Now o'er the one half-world
Nature seems dead, and wicked dreams abuse 50
The curtain'd sleep; witchcraft celebrates
Pale Hecate's offerings, and wither'd murder,
Alarum'd by his sentinel, the wolf,
Whose howl's his watch, thus with his stealthy
   pace,
• With Tarquin's ravishing strides, towards his
   design
Moves like a ghost.   Thou sure and firm-set
   earth,
Hear not my steps, which way they walk, for fear
Thy very stones prate of my whereabout,
And take the present horror from the time,
Which now suits with it.   Whiles I threat, he
   lives: 60
Words to the heat of deeds too cold breath gives.
          [*A bell rings.*
I go, and it is done; the bell invites me.
Hear it not, Duncan; for it is a knell
That summons thee to heaven or to hell. [*Exit.*

SCENE II. *The same.*

Enter LADY MACBETH.

Lady M. That which hath made them drunk
   hath made me bold;
What hath quench'd them hath given me fire.
   Hark! Peace!
It was the owl that shriek'd, the fatal bellman,
Which gives the stern'st good-night.   He is
   about it:
The doors are open; and the surfeited grooms
• Do mock their charge with snores: I have
   drugg'd their possets,
That death and nature do contend about them,
Whether they live or die.
 Macb. [*Within*] Who's there? what, ho!   9
 Lady M. Alack, I am afraid they have awaked,
And 'tis not done.   The attempt and not the deed
Confounds us.   Hark! I laid their daggers ready;
He could not miss 'em.   Had he not resembled
My father as he slept, I had done 't.

Enter MACBETH.

                              My husband!

Macb.   I have done the deed.   Didst thou not
   hear a noise?

Lady M.   I heard the owl scream and the
   crickets cry.

Did not you speak?

Macb.   When?

Lady M.   Now.

Macb.   As I descended?

Lady M.   Ay.

Macb.   Hark!

Who lies i' the second chamber?

Lady M.   Donalbain.   20

Mac.   This is a sorry sight.

                 [*Looking on his hands.*

Lady M.   A foolish thought, to say a sorry sight.

Macb.   There's one did laugh in's sleep, and
   one cried 'Murder!'

That they did wake each other: I stood and heard
   them:

But they did say their prayers, and address'd them

Again to sleep.

Lady M.   There are two lodged together.

Macb.   One cried 'God bless us!' and 'Amen'
   the other;

As they had seen me with these hangman's hands.

Listening their fear, I could not say 'Amen,'

When they did say 'God bless us!'

Lady M.   Consider it not so deeply. 30

Macb.   But wherefore could not I pronounce
   'Amen'?

I had most need of blessing, and 'Amen'

Stuck in my throat.

Lady M.   These deeds must not be thought

After these ways; so, it will make us mad.

Macb.   Methought I heard a voice cry 'Sleep
   no more!

Macbeth does murder sleep', the innocent sleep,

Sleep that knits up the ravell'd sleave of care,

The death of each day's life, sore labour's bath,

Balm of hurt minds, great nature's second course,

Chief nourisher in life's feast,—

Lady M.   What do you mean?

Macb.   Still it cried 'Sleep no more!' to all the
   house: 41

'Glamis hath murder'd sleep, and therefore
   Cawdor

Shall sleep no more; Macbeth shall sleep no more.'

Lady M.   Who was it that thus cried?   Why,
   worthy thane,

You do unbend your noble strength, to think

So brainsickly of things.   Go get some water,

And wash this filthy witness from your hand.

Why did you bring these daggers from the place?

They must lie there: go carry them; and smear

The sleepy grooms with blood.

Macb.   I'll go no more: 50

I am afraid to think what I have done;

Look on 't again I dare not.

Lady M.   Infirm of purpose!

Give me the daggers: the sleeping and the dead

Are but as pictures: 'tis the eye of childhood

That fears a painted devil.   If he do bleed,

I'll gild the faces of the grooms withal;

For it must seem their guilt.

           [*Exit.   Knocking within.*

Macb.   Whence is that knocking?

Macbeth: 'I have done the deed.' Detail from a painting
by George Cattermole (1800–1868)

---

37 *ravell'd sleave.* Tangled tissue.

56 *gild.* Smear.

Lady Macbeth: 'I'll gild the faces of the grooms . . .'
David Garrick as Macbeth and Hannah Pritchard as
Lady Macbeth. Painting by Henry Fuseli, 1812

Lady Macbeth: 'My hands are of your colour . . .'
Judith Anderson as Lady Macbeth and Laurence
Olivier as Macbeth, Michel St Denis production,
Old Vic Theatre, London, 1937

---

68 *constancy*. Resolution.

2 *old*. Sufficient.

Porter: 'If a man were a porter of hell-gate . . .' Patrick
Lynch as the Porter, Stratford-upon-Avon, 1955

How is't with me, when every noise appals me?
What hands are here? ha! they pluck out mine
    eyes.   59
Will all great Neptune's ocean wash this blood
Clean from my hand? No, this my hand will rather
The multitudinous seas incarnadine,
Making the green one red.

Re-enter LADY MACBETH.

Lady M.   My hands are of your colour; but I
    shame
To wear a heart so white.   [*Knocking within.*] I
    hear a knocking
At the south entry: retire we to our chamber:
A little water clears us of this deed:
• How easy is it, then!   Your constancy
Hath left you unattended.   [*Knocking within.*]
    Hark! more knocking.
Get on your nightgown, lest occasion call us,   70
And show us to be watchers.   Be not lost
So poorly in your thoughts.
    Macb.   To know my deed, 'twere best not know
        myself.   [*Knocking within.*
Wake Duncan with thy knocking!   I would thou
    couldst!   [*Exeunt.*

SCENE III.   *The same.*

Knocking within.   Enter a Porter.

Porter.   Here's a knocking indeed!   If a man
• were porter of hell-gate, he should have old turning the key.   [*Knocking within.*] Knock, knock,
knock!   Who's there, i' the name of Beelzebub?
Here's a farmer, that hanged himself on the expectation of plenty: come in time; have napkins
enow about you; here you'll sweat for't.   [*Knocking within.*] Knock, knock!   Who's there, in
the other devil's name?   Faith, here's an equivocator, that could swear in both the scales against
either scale; who committed treason enough for
God's sake, yet could not equivocate to heaven:
O, come in, equivocator.   [*Knocking within.*]
Knock, knock, knock!   Who's there?   Faith,
here's an English tailor come hither, for stealing
out of a French hose: come in, tailor; here you
may roast your goose.   [*Knocking within.*] Knock,
knock; never at quiet!   What are you?   But this
place is too cold for hell.   I'll devil-porter it no
further: I had thought to have let in some of
all professions that go the primrose way to the
everlasting bonfire.   [*Knocking within.*] Anon,
anon!   I pray you, remember the porter.
                                    [*Opens the gate.*

Enter MACDUFF *and* LENNOX.

Macd.   Was it so late, friend, ere you went to bed,
That you do lie so late?
    Port.   'Faith, sir, we were carousing till the
second cock: and drink, sir, is a great provoker
of three things.
    Macd.   What three things does drink especially
provoke?   30
    Port.   Marry, sir, nose-painting, sleep, and
urine.   Lechery, sir, it provokes, and unprovokes;
it provokes the desire, but it takes away the performance: therefore, much drink may be said to
be an equivocator with lechery: it makes him,
and it mars him; it sets him on, and it takes him
off; it persuades him, and disheartens him; makes

him stand to, and not stand to; in conclusion,
equivocates him in a sleep, and, giving him the
lie, leaves him.   40
   Macd. I believe drink gave thee the lie last
night.
   Port. That it did, sir, i' the very throat on me:
but I requited him for his lie; and, I think, being
too strong for him, though he took up my legs
sometime, yet I made a shift to cast him.
   Macd. Is thy master stirring?

       Enter MACBETH.

Our knocking has awaked him; here he comes.
   Len. Good morrow, noble sir.
   Macb.   Good morrow, both.
   Macd. Is the king stirring, worthy thane?
   Macb.   Not yet. 50
   Macd. He did command me to call timely on
  him:
I have almost slipp'd the hour.
   Macb.   I'll bring you to him.
   Macd. I know this is a joyful trouble to you;
But yet 'tis one.
   Macb. The labour we delight in physics pain.
This is the door.
   Macd.   I'll make so bold to call,
For 'tis my limited service.   [*Exit.*
   Len. Goes the king hence to-day?
   Macb.   He does: he did appoint so.
   Len. The night has been unruly: where we lay,
Our chimneys were blown down; and, as they say,
Lamentings heard i' the air; strange screams of
  death,   61
And prophesying with accents terrible
Of dire combustion and confused events
New hatch'd to the woeful time: the obscure bird
Clamour'd the livelong night: some say, the earth
Was feverous and did shake.
   Macb.   'Twas a rough night.
   Len. My young remembrance cannot parallel
A fellow to it.

      Re-enter MACDUFF.

   Macd. O horror, horror, horror! Tongue nor
  heart
Cannot conceive nor name thee!
   Macb. }
   Len. }   What's the matter? 70
   Macd. Confusion now hath made his master-
  piece!
Most sacrilegious murder hath broke ope
The Lord's anointed temple, and stole thence
The life o' the building!
   Macb.   What is't you say? the life?
   Len. Mean you his majesty?
   Macd. Approach the chamber, and destroy
  your sight
With a new Gorgon: do not bid me speak;
See, and then speak yourselves.
     [*Exeunt Macbeth and Lennox.*
              Awake, awake!
Ring the alarum-bell. Murder and treason!
Banquo and Donalbain! Malcolm! awake! 80
Shake off this downy sleep, death's counterfeit,
And look on death itself! up, up, and see
The great doom's image! Malcolm! Banquo!
As from your graves rise up, and walk like sprites,
To countenance this horror! Ring the bell.
                    [*Bell rings.*

46 *made a shift.* Managed. *cast him.* A pun on 'throw' and 'throw up'.

57 *limited.* Appointed.

64 *obscure bird.* Owl.

Lennox: 'the obscure bird Clamour'd . . .' Woodcut from a 12th century Latin bestiary

73 *anointed temple.* i.e. King's body.

Macdonald: '. . . murder hath broke ope The Lord's anointed temple'. Woodcut of Duncan from Holinshed's *Chronicles*, 1577

77 *Gorgon.* Mythical monster, turning one to stone.

Macbeth: 'renown and grace is dead . . .' Charles Kean as Macbeth. Drawing by R. J. Lane from a portrait by Edward Chalon, 1840

100 *the mere lees.* Only the dregs.

117 *pauser.* i.e. giving pause.

122 *breech'd.* Covered.

Lady Macbeth: 'Help me hence, ho!' Sarah Bernhardt as Lady Macbeth, Gaiety Theatre, London, 1884

128 *auger-hole.* Tiny hole.

Enter LADY MACBETH.

Lady M.   What's the business,
That such a hideous trumpet calls to parley
The sleepers of the house? speak, speak!
    Macd.   O gentle lady,
'Tis not for you to hear what I can speak:
The repetition, in a woman's ear,   90
Would murder as it fell.

Enter BANQUO.

                        O Banquo, Banquo,
Our royal master 's murder'd!
    Lady M.   Woe, alas!
What, in our house?
    Ban.   Too cruel any where.
Dear Duff, I prithee, contradict thyself,
And say it is not so.

Re-enter MACBETH *and* LENNOX, *with* ROSS.

    Macb. Had I but died an hour before this chance,
I had lived a blessed time; for, from this instant,
There's nothing serious in mortality:
All is but toys: renown and grace is dead;
●The wine of life is drawn, and the mere lees   100
Is left this vault to brag of.

Enter MALCOLM *and* DONALBAIN.

    Don.   What is amiss?
    Macb.   You are, and do not know 't:
The spring, the head, the fountain of your blood
Is stopp'd; the very source of it is stopp'd.
    Macd.   Your royal father 's murder'd.
    Mal.   O, by whom?
    Len.   Those of his chamber, as it seem'd, had
        done 't:
Their hands and faces were all badged with blood;
So were their daggers, which unwiped we found
Upon their pillows:
They stared, and were distracted; no man's life
Was to be trusted with them.   III
    Macb.   O, yet I do repent me of my fury,
That I did kill them.
    Macd.   Wherefore did you so?
    Macb.   Who can be wise, amazed, temperate
        and furious,
Loyal and neutral, in a moment?   No man:
The expedition of my violent love
●Outrun the pauser, reason.   Here lay Duncan,
His silver skin laced with his golden blood;
And his gash'd stabs look'd like a breach in nature
For ruin's wasteful entrance: there, the murderers,
Steep'd in the colours of their trade, their daggers
●Unmannerly breech'd with gore: who could re-
frain,
That had a heart to love, and in that heart
Courage to make 's love known?
    Lady M.   Help me hence, ho!
    Macd.   Look to the lady.
    Mal. [*Aside to Don.*] Why do we hold our
        tongues,
That most may claim this argument for ours?
    Don. [*Aside to Mal.*] What should be spoken
        here, where our fate,
● Hid in an auger-hole, may rush, and seize us?
Let's away;   129
Our tears are not yet brew'd.
    Mal. [*Aside to Don.*] Nor our strong sorrow
Upon the foot of motion.

Ban.   Look to the lady:
                    [*Lady Macbeth is carried out.*
And when we have our naked frailties hid,
That suffer in exposure, let us meet,
And question this most bloody piece of work,
To know it further. Fears and scruples shake us:
In the great hand of God I stand; and thence
Against the undivulged pretence I fight
Of treasonous malice.
    Macd.   And so do I.
    All.   So all.
    Macb. Let's briefly put on manly readiness,
And meet i' the hall together.
    All.   Well contented.   140
    [*Exeunt all but Malcolm and Donalbain.*
    Mal. What will you do? Let's not consort
        with them:
To show an unfelt sorrow is an office
Which the false man does easy. I'll to England.
    Don. To Ireland, I; our separated fortune
Shall keep us both the safer: where we are,
There's daggers in men's smiles: the near in
        blood,
The nearer bloody.
    Mal.   This murderous shaft that's shot
Hath not yet lighted, and our safest way
Is to avoid the aim. Therefore, to horse;
And let us not be dainty of leave-taking,   150
But shift away: there's warrant in that theft
Which steals itself, when there's no mercy left.
                                    [*Exeunt.*

SCENE IV. *Outside Macbeth's castle.*

Enter Ross *and an* old Man.

Old M. Threescore and ten I can remember
        well:
Within the volume of which time I have seen
Hours dreadful and things strange; but this sore
        night
● Hath trifled former knowings.
    Ross.   Ah, good father,
Thou seest, the heavens, as troubled with man's
        act,
Threaten his bloody stage: by the clock, 'tis day,
● And yet dark night strangles the travelling lamp:
Is't night's predominance, or the day's shame,
That darkness does the face of earth entomb,
When living light should kiss it?
    Old M.   'Tis unnatural,   10
Even like the deed that's done. On Tuesday last,
A falcon, towering in her pride of place,
Was by a mousing owl hawk'd at and kill'd.
    Ross. And Duncan's horses—a thing most
        strange and certain—
● Beauteous and swift, the minions of their race,
Turn'd wild in nature, broke their stalls, flung out,
Contending 'gainst obedience, as they would
        make
War with mankind.
    Old M.   'Tis said they eat each other.
    Ross. They did so, to the amazement of mine
        eyes
That look'd upon't. Here comes the good Mac-
        duff.   20

Enter MACDUFF.

How goes the world, sir, now?
    Macd.   Why, see you not?

4 *trifled.* Reduced to a trifle.

7 *travelling lamp.* Sun.

Ross: '. . . night strangles the travelling lamp.' Engraving
from R. Fludd, *Utriusque Cosmi Metaphysica,* 1617

15 *minions.* Favourites.

Glamis Castle. Engraving from Charles Knight's
Pictorial Edition of the Works of Shakspere, 1839–43

24 *suborn'd.* Bribed.

28 *ravin.* Swallow.

Banquo: 'Thou hast it now: king, Cawdor, Glamis, all.'
Peter Jeffrey as Banquo and Eric Porter as Macbeth,
Stratford-upon-Avon, 1962

Ross. Is't known who did this more than
  bloody deed?
Macd. Those that Macbeth hath slain.
Ross.   Alas, the day!
●What good could they pretend?
Macd.   They were suborn'd:
Malcolm and Donalbain, the king's two sons,
Are stol'n away and fled; which puts upon them
Suspicion of the deed.
Ross.   'Gainst nature still!
●Thriftless ambition, that wilt ravin up
Thine own life's means! Then 'tis most like
The sovereignty will fall upon Macbeth.   30
Macd. He is already named, and gone to
  Scone
To be invested.
Ross.   Where is Duncan's body?
Macd. Carried to Colmekill,
The sacred storehouse of his predecessors,
And guardian of their bones.
Ross.   Will you to Scone?
Macd. No, cousin, I'll to Fife.
Ross.   Well, I will thither.
Macd. Well, may you see things well done
  there: adieu!
Lest our old robes sit easier than our new!
Ross. Farewell, father.
Old M. God's benison go with you; and with
  those   40
That would make good of bad, and friends of
  foes!   [*Exeunt.*

ACT III.

SCENE I. *Forres.   The palace.*

Enter BANQUO.

Ban. Thou hast it now: king, Cawdor,
  Glamis, all,
As the weird women promised, and, I fear,
Thou play'dst most foully for't: yet it was said
It should not stand in thy posterity,
But that myself should be the root and father
Of many kings. If there come truth from them—
As upon thee, Macbeth, their speeches shine—
Why, by the verities on thee made good,
May they not be my oracles as well,
And set me up in hope? But hush! no more. 10

Sennet sounded. Enter MACBETH, *as king,*
LADY MACBETH, *as queen,* LENNOX, ROSS,
Lords, Ladies, *and* Attendants.

Macb. Here's our chief guest.
Lady M.   If he had been forgotten,
It had been as a gap in our great feast,
And all-thing unbecoming.
Macb. To-night we hold a solemn supper, sir,
And I'll request your presence.
Ban.   Let your highness
Command upon me; to the which my duties
Are with a most indissoluble tie
For ever knit.
Macb. Ride you this afternoon?
Ban. Ay, my good lord.   20
Macb. We should have else desired your good
  advice,
Which still hath been both grave and prosperous,
In this day's council; but we'll take to-morrow.
Is't far you ride?

Ban. As far, my lord, as will fill up the time
'Twixt this and supper: go not my horse the better,
I must become a borrower of the night
For a dark hour or twain.
   Macb.   Fail not our feast.
   Ban.   My lord, I will not.
   Macb. We hear, our bloody cousins are bestow'd   30
In England and in Ireland, not confessing
Their cruel parricide, filling their hearers
With strange invention: but of that to-morrow,
When therewithal we shall have cause of state
Craving us jointly. Hie you to horse: adieu,
Till you return at night. Goes Fleance with you?
   Ban. Ay, my good lord: our time does call upon 's.
   Macb. I wish your horses swift and sure of foot;
And so I do commend you to their backs.
Farewell.   [*Exit Banquo.* 40
Let every man be master of his time
Till seven at night: to make society
The sweeter welcome, we will keep ourself
Till supper-time alone: while then, God be with you!
   [*Exeunt all but Macbeth, and an attendant.*
Sirrah, a word with you: attend those men
Our pleasure?
   Atten. They are, my lord, without the palace gate.
   Macb. Bring them before us.
             [*Exit Attendant.*
           To be thus is nothing;
But to be safely thus.—Our fears in Banquo
Stick deep; and in his royalty of nature   50
Reigns that which would be fear'd: 'tis much he dares;
And, to that dauntless temper of his mind,
He hath a wisdom that doth guide his valour
To act in safety. There is none but he
Whose being I do fear: and, under him,
My Genius is rebuked; as, it is said,
Mark Antony's was by Cæsar. He chid the sisters
When first they put the name of king upon me,
And bade them speak to him: then prophet-like
They hail'd him father to a line of kings: 60
Upon my head they placed a fruitless crown,
And put a barren sceptre in my gripe,
Thence to be wrench'd with an unlineal hand,
No son of mine succeeding. If 't be so,
For Banquo's issue have I filed my mind;
For them the gracious Duncan have I murder'd;
Put rancours in the vessel of my peace
Only for them; and mine eternal jewel
Given to the common enemy of man,
To make them kings, the seed of Banquo kings! 70
Rather than so, come fate into the list,
And champion me to the utterance! Who's there?

   Re-enter Attendant, *with two* Murderers.

Now go to the door, and stay there till we call.
           [*Exit Attendant.*
Was it not yesterday we spoke together?
   First Mur. It was, so please your highness.
   Macb.   Well then, now
Have you consider'd of my speeches? Know

65 *filed.* Defiled.

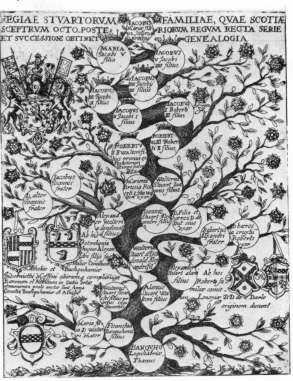

Macbeth: 'For Banquo's issue have I filed my mind.' Genealogical tree tracing James VI of Scotland, I of England, back to Banquo

72 *utterance.* Fight to the death.

94 *Shoughs.* Shaggy dogs. *water-rugs.* Coarse-haired dogs. *clept.* Called.

Macbeth: 'Shoughs, water-rugs and demi-wolves are clept All by the name of dogs.' Water spaniel, from Edward Topsell, *The History of Four-footed Beasts*, 1658

---

100 *addition.* Title. *bill.* List.

112 *tugg'd.* Mauled.

114 *mend.* Improve.

120 *avouch.* Admit.

That it was he in the times past which held you
So under fortune, which you thought had been
Our innocent self: this I made good to you
In our last conference, pass'd in probation with
   you,   80
How you were borne in hand, how cross'd, the
   instruments,
Who wrought with them, and all things else that
   might
To half a soul and to a notion crazed
Say 'Thus did Banquo.'
  First Mur.   You made it known to us.
  Macb. I did so, and went further, which
   is now
Our point of second meeting. Do you find
Your patience so predominant in your nature
That you can let this go? Are you so gospell'd
To pray for this good man and for his issue,
Whose heavy hand hath bow'd you to the grave
And beggar'd yours for ever?
  First Mur.   We are men, my liege. 91
  Macb. Ay, in the catalogue ye go for men;
As hounds and greyhounds, mongrels, spaniels,
   curs,
●Shoughs, water-rugs and demi-wolves are clept
All by the name of dogs: the valued file
Distinguishes the swift, the slow, the subtle,
The housekeeper, the hunter, every one
According to the gift which bounteous nature
Hath in him closed, whereby he does receive
●Particular addition, from the bill   100
That writes them all alike: and so of men.
Now, if you have a station in the file,
Not i' the worst rank of manhood, say 't;
And I will put that business in your bosoms,
Whose execution takes your enemy off,
Grapples you to the heart and love of us,
Who wear our health but sickly in his life,
Which in his death were perfect.
  Sec. Mur.   I am one, my liege,
Whom the vile blows and buffets of the world
Have so incensed that I am reckless what 110
I do to spite the world.
  First Mur.   And I another
●So weary with disasters, tugg'd with fortune,
That I would set my life on any chance,
●To mend it, or be rid on 't.
  Macb.   Both of you
Know Banquo was your enemy.
  Both Mur.   True, my lord.
  Macb. So is he mine; and in such bloody
   distance,
That every minute of his being thrusts
Against my near'st of life: and though I could
With barefaced power sweep him from my sight
●And bid my will avouch it, yet I must not, 120
For certain friends that are both his and mine,
Whose loves I may not drop, but wail his fall
Who I myself struck down; and thence it is,
That I to your assistance do make love,
Masking the business from the common eye
For sundry weighty reasons.
  Sec. Mur.   We shall, my lord,
Perform what you command us.
  First Mur.   Though our lives—
  Macb. Your spirits shine through you. Within
   this hour at most
I will advise you where to plant yourselves;
Acquaint you with the perfect spy o' the time, 130

The moment on't; for't must be done to-night,
And something from the palace; always thought
That I require a clearness: and with him—
To leave no rubs nor botches in the work—
Fleance his son, that keeps him company,
Whose absence is no less material to me
Than is his father's, must embrace the fate
Of that dark hour.   Resolve yourselves apart:
I'll come to you anon.
 Both Mur.   We are resolved, my lord.
 Macb. I'll call upon you straight: abide
  within.   [*Exeunt Murderers.* 140
It is concluded.   Banquo, thy soul's flight,
If it find heaven, must find it out to-night. [*Exit.*

SCENE II.   *The palace.*

Enter LADY MACBETH *and a* Servant.

 Lady M. Is Banquo gone from court?
 Serv. Ay, madam, but returns again to-night.
 Lady M. Say to the king, I would attend his
  leisure
For a few words.
 Serv.   Madam, I will.   [*Exit.*
 Lady M.   Nought's had, all's spent,
Where our desire is got without content:
'Tis safer to be that which we destroy
Than by destruction dwell in doubtful joy.

Enter MACBETH.

How now, my lord! why do you keep alone,
Of sorriest fancies your companions making,
Using those thoughts which should indeed have
 died   10
With them they think on? Things without all
 remedy
Should be without regard: what's done is done.
• *Macb.* We have scotch'd the snake, not kill'd
  it:
She'll close and be herself, whilst our poor malice
Remains in danger of her former tooth.
But let the frame of things disjoint, both the
 worlds suffer,
Ere we will eat our meal in fear and sleep
In the affliction of these terrible dreams
That shake us nightly: better be with the dead,
Whom we, to gain our peace, have sent to peace,
Than on the torture of the mind to lie 21
•In restless ecstasy.   Duncan is in his grave;
After life's fitful fever he sleeps well;
Treason has done his worst: nor steel, nor poison,
•Malice domestic, foreign levy, nothing,
Can touch him further.
 Lady M.   Come on;
Gentle my lord, sleek o'er your rugged looks;
Be bright and jovial among your guests to-night.
 Macb. So shall I, love; and so, I pray, be
  you:
Let your remembrance apply to Banquo; 30
Present him eminence, both with eye and tongue:
†Unsafe the while, that we
•Must lave our honours in these flattering streams,
•And make our faces vizards to our hearts,
Disguising what they are.
 Lady M.   You must leave this.
 Macb. O, full of scorpions is my mind, dear
  wife!
Thou know'st that Banquo, and his Fleance, lives.

13 *scotch'd.* Wounded.

22 *ecstasy.* Madness.

25 *Malice . . . levy.* Civil or foreign wars.

Macbeth: 'Malice domestic . . . nothing, Can touch him further.' Charles Laughton as Macbeth and Flora Robson as Lady Macbeth, Old Vic Theatre, London, 1934

33 *lave.* Wash.

34 *vizards.* Masks.

42 *shard-borne.* Hatched from dung.

46 *seeling.* Blinding.

Second Murderer: 'A light, a light!' Illustration by
Hawes Craven, Lyceum Theatre, London, 1888

Lady M.   But in them nature's copy's not
   eterne.
   Macb.   There's comfort yet; they are assail-
   able;
Then be thou jocund: ere the bat hath flown   40
His cloister'd flight, ere to black Hecate's sum-
   mons
● The shard-borne beetle with his drowsy hums
Hath rung night's yawning peal, there shall be
   done
A deed of dreadful note.
   Lady M.   What's to be done?
   Macb.   Be innocent of the knowledge, dearest
   chuck,
● Till thou applaud the deed. Come, seeling night,
Scarf up the tender eye of pitiful day;
And with thy bloody and invisible hand
Cancel and tear to pieces that great bond
Which keeps me pale!   Light thickens; and the
   crow   50
Makes wing to the rooky wood:
Good things of day begin to droop and drowse;
Whiles night's black agents to their preys do
   rouse.
Thou marvell'st at my words: but hold thee still:
Things bad begun make strong themselves by ill.
So, prithee, go with me.   [*Exeunt.*

   SCENE III.   *A park near the palace.*

      Enter three Murderers.

First Mur. But who did bid thee join with us?
Third Mur.   Macbeth.
Sec. Mur.   He needs not our mistrust, since
   he delivers
Our offices and what we have to do
To the direction just.
   First Mur.   Then stand with us.
The west yet glimmers with some streaks of day:
Now spurs the lated traveller apace
To gain the timely inn; and near approaches
The subject of our watch.
   Third Mur.   Hark! I hear horses.
Ban. [*Within*] Give us a light there, ho!
Sec. Mur.   Then 'tis he: the rest
That are within the note of expectation   10
Already are i' the court.
   First Mur.   His horses go about.
   Third Mur.   Almost a mile: but he does
   usually,
So all men do, from hence to the palace gate
Make it their walk.
   Sec. Mur.   A light, a light!

Enter BANQUO, *and* FLEANCE *with a torch.*

Third Mur.   'Tis he.
First Mur.   Stand to't.
Ban.   It will be rain to-night.
First Mur.   Let it come down.
                     [*They set upon Banquo.*
Ban.   O, treachery! Fly, good Fleance, fly,
   fly, fly!
Thou mayst revenge.   O slave!
                     [*Dies. Fleance escapes.*
Third Mur.   Who did strike out the light?
First Mur.   Was't not the way?
Third Mur.   There's but one down; the son
   is fled.
Sec. Mur.   We have lost   20

Best half of our affair.

First Mur. Well, let's away, and say how much is done. [*Exeunt.*

SCENE IV. *The same. Hall in the palace.*

A banquet prepared. Enter MACBETH, LADY MACBETH, ROSS, LENNOX, Lords, *and* Attendants.

Macb. You know your own degrees; sit down: at first
And last the hearty welcome.

Lords.   Thanks to your majesty.

Macb. Ourself will mingle with society,
And play the humble host.

● Our hostess keeps her state, but in best time
We will require her welcome.

Lady M. Pronounce it for me, sir, to all our friends;
For my heart speaks they are welcome.

First Murderer *appears at the door.*

Macb. See, they encounter thee with their hearts' thanks.
Both sides are even: here I 'll sit i' the midst: 10
Be large in mirth; anon we 'll drink a measure
The table round. [*Approaching the door.*] There's blood upon thy face.

Mur. 'Tis Banquo's then.

Macb. 'Tis better thee without than he within.
Is he dispatch'd?

Mur. My lord, his throat is cut; that I did for him.

Macb. Thou art the best o' the cut-throats: yet he 's good
That did the like for Fleance: if thou didst it,
Thou art the nonpareil.

Mur.   Most royal sir,
Fleance is 'scaped.   20

Macb. Then comes my fit again: I had else been perfect,
Whole as the marble, founded as the rock,
As broad and general as the casing air:
But now I am cabin'd, cribb'd, confined, bound in
● To saucy doubts and fears.   But Banquo's safe?

Mur. Ay, my good lord: safe in a ditch he bides,
With twenty trenched gashes on his head;
The least a death to nature.

Macb.   Thanks for that:
There the grown serpent lies; the worm that's fled
Hath nature that in time will venom breed, 30
No teeth for the present. Get thee gone: to-morrow
We 'll hear, ourselves, again. [*Exit Murderer.*

Lady M.   My royal lord,
You do not give the cheer: the feast is sold
That is not often vouch'd, while 'tis a-making,
'Tis given with welcome: to feed were best at home;
From thence the sauce to meat is ceremony;
Meeting were bare without it.

Macb.   Sweet remembrancer!
Now, good digestion wait on appetite,
And health on both!

Len.   May 't please your highness sit.
[*The Ghost of Banquo enters, and sits in Macbeth's place.*

Banquet scene. Illustration by Hawes Craven, Lyceum Theatre, London, 1888

5 *state.* Throne.

25 *saucy.* Insolent.

Violet Vanbrugh as Lady Macbeth, Garrick Theatre, London, 1906

441

40 *roof'd.* Complete.

60 *O proper stuff!* That's marvellous!

Lady Macbeth: 'O proper stuff!' Margaret Webster as Lady Macbeth and Malcolm Keen as Macbeth, Old Vic Theatre, London, 1932–33.

---

71 *charnel-houses.* Where bones from graveyards were kept.

● *Macb.* Here had we now our country's honour roof'd,   40
Were the graced person of our Banquo present;
Who may I rather challenge for unkindness
Than pity for mischance!
   Ross.   His absence, sir,
Lays blame upon his promise. Please't your highness
To grace us with your royal company.
   Macb. The table's full.
   Len.   Here is a place reserved, sir.
   Macb. Where?
   Len. Here, my good lord. What is't that moves your highness?
   Macb. Which of you have done this?
   Lords.   What, my good lord?
   Macb. Thou canst not say I did it: never shake   50
Thy gory locks at me.
   Ross. Gentlemen, rise; his highness is not well.
   Lady M. Sit, worthy friends: my lord is often thus,
And hath been from his youth: pray you, keep seat;
The fit is momentary; upon a thought
He will again be well: if much you note him,
You shall offend him and extend his passion:
Feed, and regard him not. Are you a man?
   Macb. Ay, and a bold one, that dare look on that
Which might appal the devil.
● *Lady M.*   O proper stuff!   60
This is the very painting of your fear:
This is the air-drawn dagger which, you said,
Led you to Duncan. O, these flaws and starts,
Impostors to true fear, would well become
A woman's story at a winter's fire,
Authorized by her grandam. Shame itself!
Why do you make such faces? When all's done,
You look but on a stool.
   Macb. Prithee, see there! behold! look! lo! how say you?
Why, what care I? If thou canst nod, speak too.
● If charnel-houses and our graves must send   71
Those that we bury back, our monuments
Shall be the maws of kites.   [*Ghost vanishes.*
   Lady M. What, quite unmann'd in folly?
   Macb. If I stand here, I saw him.
   Lady M.   Fie, for shame!
   Macb. Blood hath been shed ere now, i' the olden time,
Ere humane statute purged the gentle weal;
Ay, and since too, murders have been perform'd
Too terrible for the ear: the time has been,
That, when the brains were out, the man would die,
And there an end; but now they rise again,   80
With twenty mortal murders on their crowns,
And push us from our stools: this is more strange
Than such a murder is.
   Lady M.   My worthy lord,
Your noble friends do lack you.
   Macb.   I do forget.
Do not muse at me, my most worthy friends;
I have a strange infirmity, which is nothing
To those that know me. Come, love and health to all;
Then I'll sit down. Give me some wine; fill full.
I drink to the general joy o' the whole table,   89

And to our dear friend Banquo, whom we miss;
Would he were here! to all, and him, we thirst,
And all to all.
    Lords.   Our duties, and the pledge.

                Re-enter Ghost.

● *Macb.*   Avaunt! and quit my sight! let the
        earth hide thee!
Thy bones are marrowless, thy blood is cold;
● Thou hast no speculation in those eyes
Which thou dost glare with!
    Lady M.   Think of this, good peers,
But as a thing of custom: 'tis no other;
Only it spoils the pleasure of the time.
    Macb.   What man dare, I dare:
Approach thou like the rugged Russian bear, 100
● The arm'd rhinoceros, or the Hyrcan tiger;
Take any shape but that, and my firm nerves
Shall never tremble: or be alive again,
And dare me to the desert with thy sword;
† If trembling I inhabit then, protest me
The baby of a girl.   Hence, horrible shadow!
Unreal mockery, hence!   [*Ghost vanishes.*
                Why, so: being gone,
I am a man again.   Pray you, sit still.
    Lady M.   You have displaced the mirth, broke
        the good meeting,
With most admired disorder.
    Macb.   Can such things be, 110
And overcome us like a summer's cloud,
Without our special wonder?   You make me
        strange
Even to the disposition that I owe,
When now I think you can behold such sights,
And keep the natural ruby of your cheeks,
When mine is blanch'd with fear.
    Ross.   What sights, my lord?
    Lady M.   I pray you, speak not; he grows
        worse and worse;
Question enrages him.   At once, good night:
Stand not upon the order of your going,
But go at once.
    Len.   Good night; and better health 120
Attend his majesty!
    Lady M.   A kind good night to all!
        [*Exeunt all but Macbeth and Lady M.*
    Macb.   It will have blood; they say, blood will
        have blood:
Stones have been known to move and trees to
        speak;
Augurs and understood relations have
● By magot-pies and choughs and rooks brought
        forth
The secret'st man of blood.   What is the night?
    Lady M. Almost at odds with morning, which
        is which.
    Macb.   How say'st thou, that Macduff denies
        his person
At our great bidding?
    Lady M.   Did you send to him, sir?
    Macb.   I hear it by the way; but I will send:
There's not a one of them but in his house   131
I keep a servant fee'd.   I will to-morrow,
And betimes I will, to the weird sisters:
More shall they speak; for now I am bent to know,
By the worst means, the worst.   For mine own
        good,
All causes shall give way: I am in blood
Stepp'd in so far that, should I wade no more,

93 *Avaunt.* Away.

95 *speculation.* Sight.

101 *Hyrcan.* Persian.

AT ONCE GOOD NIGHT

Lady Macbeth. Illustration by Byam Shaw, *The Chiswick Shakespeare* 1899

125 *magot-pies.* Magpies. *chough.* Another species of crow.

2 *beldams.* Hags.

15 *Acheron.* River in Hell.

Returning were as tedious as go o'er:
Strange things I have in head, that will to hand;
Which must be acted ere they may be scann'd.
 Lady M. You lack the season of all natures,
  sleep.   141
 Macb. Come, we'll to sleep. My strange and
  self-abuse
Is the initiate fear that wants hard use:
We are yet but young in deed. [*Exeunt.*

SCENE V. *A Heath.*

Thunder. Enter the three Witches,
meeting HECATE.

 First Witch. Why, how now, Hecate! you
  look angerly.
 Hec. Have I not reason, beldams as you are,
Saucy and overbold? How did you dare
To trade and traffic with Macbeth
In riddles and affairs of death;
And I, the mistress of your charms,
The close contriver of all harms,
Was never call'd to bear my part,
Or show the glory of our art?
And, which is worse, all you have done 10
Hath been but for a wayward son,
Spiteful and wrathful, who, as others do,
Loves for his own ends, not for you.
But make amends now: get you gone,
And at the pit of Acheron
Meet me i' the morning: thither he
Will come to know his destiny:
Your vessels and your spells provide,
Your charms and every thing beside.
I am for the air; this night I'll spend 20
Unto a dismal and a fatal end:
Great business must be wrought ere noon:
Upon the corner of the moon
There hangs a vaporous drop profound;
I'll catch it ere it come to ground:
And that distill'd by magic sleights
Shall raise such artificial sprites
As by the strength of their illusion
Shall draw him on to his confusion:
He shall spurn fate, scorn death, and bear 30
His hopes 'bove wisdom, grace and fear:
And you all know, security
Is mortals' chiefest enemy.
  [*Music and a song within:* 'Come away,
      come away,' &c.
Hark! I am call'd; my little spirit, see,
Sits in a foggy cloud, and stays for me. [*Exit.*
 First Witch. Come, let's make haste; she'll
  soon be back again.   [*Exeunt.*

SCENE VI. *Forres. The palace.*

Enter LENNOX *and another* Lord.

 Len. My former speeches have but hit your
  thoughts,
Which can interpret further: only, I say,
Things have been strangely borne. The gracious
  Duncan
Was pitied of Macbeth: marry, he was dead:
And the right-valiant Banquo walk'd too late;
Whom, you may say, if't please you, Fleance
  kill'd,
For Fleance fled: men must not walk too late.
Who cannot want the thought how monstrous

Opposite: The Weird Sisters. Engraving by Richard Westall (1765–1836)

13 *thralls*. In bondage to.

29 *respect*. Reputation.

1 *brinded*. Brindled, i.e. tabby.

2 *hedge-pig*. Hedgehog.

3 *Harpier*. Familiar.

It was for Malcolm and for Donalbain
To kill their gracious father? damned fact!   10
How it did grieve Macbeth! did he not straight
In pious rage the two delinquents tear,
● That were the slaves of drink and thralls of sleep?
Was not that nobly done?   Ay, and wisely too;
For 'twould have anger'd any heart alive
To hear the men deny't.   So that, I say,
He has borne all things well: and I do think
That had he Duncan's sons under his key—
As, an't please heaven, he shall not—they should find
What 'twere to kill a father; so should Fleance. 20
But, peace! for from broad words and 'cause he fail'd
His presence at the tyrant's feast, I hear
Macduff lives in disgrace: sir, can you tell
Where he bestows himself?
   Lord.   The son of Duncan,
From whom this tyrant holds the due of birth,
Lives in the English court, and is received
Of the most pious Edward with such grace
That the malevolence of fortune nothing
● Takes from his high respect: thither Macduff
Is gone to pray the holy king, upon his aid   30
To wake Northumberland and warlike Siward:
That, by the help of these—with Him above
To ratify the work—we may again
Give to our tables meat, sleep to our nights,
Free from our feasts and banquets bloody knives,
Do faithful homage and receive free honours:
All which we pine for now: and this report
Hath so exasperate the king that he
Prepares for some attempt of war.
   Len.   Sent he to Macduff?
   Lord. He did: and with an absolute 'Sir, not I,'   40
The cloudy messenger turns me his back,
And hums, as who should say 'You'll rue the time
That clogs me with this answer.'
   Len.   And that well might
Advise him to a caution, to hold what distance
His wisdom can provide.   Some holy angel
Fly to the court of England and unfold
His message ere he come, that a swift blessing
May soon return to this our suffering country
Under a hand accursed!
   Lord.   I'll send my prayers with him.
                     [*Exeunt.*

ACT IV.

Scene I. *A cavern.   In the middle, a boiling cauldron.*

Thunder.   Enter the three Witches.

● *First Witch.* Thrice the brinded cat hath mew'd.
● *Sec. Witch.* Thrice and once the hedge-pig whined.
● *Third Witch.* Harpier cries 'Tis time, 'tis time.
   First Witch. Round about the cauldron go;
In the poison'd entrails throw.
†Toad, that under cold stone
Days and nights has thirty one
Swelter'd venom sleeping got,
Boil thou first i' the charmed pot.

All. Double, double toil and trouble ; 10
Fire burn, and cauldron bubble.
  Sec. Witch. Fillet of a fenny snake,
In the cauldron boil and bake ;
Eye of newt and toe of frog,
Wool of bat and tongue of dog,
Adder's fork and blind-worm's sting,
• Lizard's leg and howlet's wing,
For a charm of powerful trouble,
Like a hell-broth boil and bubble.
  All. Double, double toil and trouble ; 20
Fire burn and cauldron bubble.
  Third Witch. Scale of dragon, tooth of
    wolf,
Witches' mummy, maw and gulf
• Of the ravin'd salt-sea shark,
Root of hemlock digg'd i' the dark,
Liver of blaspheming Jew,
Gall of goat, and slips of yew
Sliver'd in the moon's eclipse,
Nose of Turk and Tartar's lips,
Finger of birth-strangled babe 30
Ditch-deliver'd by a drab,
Make the gruel thick and slab :
• Add thereto a tiger's chaudron,
For the ingredients of our cauldron.
  All. Double, double toil and trouble ;
Fire burn and cauldron bubble.
  Sec. Witch. Cool it with a baboon's blood,
Then the charm is firm and good.

Enter HECATE *to the other three Witches.*

Hec. O, well done ! I commend your pains ;
And every one shall share i' the gains : 40
And now about the cauldron sing,
Like elves and fairies in a ring,
Enchanting all that you put in.
    [*Music and a song :* 'Black spirits,' &c.
    [*Hecate retires.*
Sec. Witch. By the pricking of my thumbs,
Something wicked this way comes.
    Open, locks,
    Whoever knocks !

Enter MACBETH.

Macb. How now, you secret, black, and mid-
    night hags !
What is't you do ?
  All.   A deed without a name.
  Macb. I conjure you, by that which you pro-
    fess, 50
Howe'er you come to know it, answer me :
Though you untie the winds and let them fight
• Against the churches ; though the yesty waves
Confound and swallow navigation up ;
• Though bladed corn be lodged and trees blown
    down ;
Though castles topple on their warders' heads ;
Though palaces and pyramids do slope
Their heads to their foundations ; though the
    treasure
• Of nature's germens tumble all together,
Even till destruction sicken ; answer me 60
To what I ask you.
  First Witch.   Speak.
  Sec. Witch.   Demand.
  Third Witch.   We'll answer.
  First Witch. Say, if thou'dst rather hear it
    from our mouths,

17 *howlet.* Owl.

24 *ravin'd.* Ravenous.

33 *chaudron.* Entrails.

53 *yesty.* Foaming.

55 *lodged.* Flattened.

59 *germens.* Seeds.

The Witches. Painting by Alexandre Gabriel Decamps
(1803–60)

74 *harp'd.* Struck.

Macbeth: 'What is this That rises like the issue of a king . . .' Engraving from Bell's edition of *Shakespeare*, 1773

91 *chafes.* Becomes angry.

95 *impress.* Conscript.

SD *Hautboys.* Oboes.

Or from our masters?
 Macb.   Call 'em; let me see 'em.
 First Witch. Pour in sow's blood, that hath
  eaten
Her nine farrow; grease that's sweaten
From the murderer's gibbet throw
Into the flame.
 All.   Come, high or low;
Thyself and office deftly show!

Thunder.   First Apparition: an armed Head.

 Macb. Tell me, thou unknown power,—
 First Witch.   He knows thy thought:
Hear his speech, but say thou nought.   70
 First App. ··Macbeth! Macbeth! Macbeth!
  beware Macduff;
Beware the thane of Fife. Dismiss me. Enough.
           [*Descends.*
 Macb. Whate'er thou art, for thy good caution,
  thanks;
• Thou hast harp'd my fear aright: but one word
  more,—
 First Witch. He will not be commanded:
  here's another,
More potent than the first.

Thunder.   Second Apparition: a bloody Child.

 Sec. App. Macbeth! Macbeth! Macbeth!
 Macb. Had I three ears, I'ld hear thee.
 Sec. App. Be bloody, bold, and resolute; laugh
  to scorn
The power of man, for none of woman born 80
Shall harm Macbeth.   [*Descends.*
 Macb. Then live, Macduff: what need I fear
  of thee?
But yet I'll make assurance double sure,
And take a bond of fate: thou shalt not live;
That I may tell pale-hearted fear it lies,
And sleep in spite of thunder.

*Thunder.   Third Apparition: a Child crowned,
    with a tree in his hand.*

        What is this
That rises like the issue of a king,
And wears upon his baby-brow the round
And top of sovereignty?
 All.   Listen, but speak not to 't.
 Third App. Be lion-mettled, proud; and take
  no care   90
• Who chafes, who frets, or where conspirers are:
Macbeth shall never vanquish'd be until
Great Birnam wood to high Dunsinane hill
Shall come against him.   [*Descends.*
 Macb.   That will never be:
• Who can impress the forest, bid the tree
Unfix his earth-bound root? Sweet bodements!
  good!
Rebellion's head, rise never till the wood
Of Birnam rise, and our high-placed Macbeth
Shall live the lease of nature, pay his breath
To time and mortal custom. Yet my heart 100
Throbs to know one thing: tell me, if your art
Can tell so much: shall Banquo's issue ever
Reign in this kingdom?
 All.   Seek to know no more.
 Macb. I will be satisfied: deny me this,
And an eternal curse fall on you! Let me know.
Why sinks that cauldron? and what noise is this?
          [*Hautboys.*

First Witch. Show!
Sec. Witch. Show!
Third Witch. Show!
All. Show his eyes, and grieve his heart; 110
Come like shadows, so depart!

A show of Eight Kings, *the last with a glass in
his hand; Banquo's Ghost following.*

Macb. Thou art too like the spirit of Banquo;
     down!
Thy crown does sear mine eye-balls. And thy
     hair,
Thou other gold-bound brow, is like the first.
A third is like the former. Filthy hags!
Why do you show me this? A fourth! Start, eyes!
What, will the line stretch out to the crack of
     doom?
Another yet! A seventh! I'll see no more:
And yet the eighth appears, who bears a glass
Which shows me many more; and some I see 120
●That two-fold balls and treble sceptres carry:
Horrible sight! Now, I see, 'tis true;
●For the blood-bolter'd Banquo smiles upon me,
And points at them for his. [*Apparitions vanish.*]
     What, is this so?
First Witch. Ay, sir, all this is so: but why
Stands Macbeth thus amazedly?
Come, sisters, cheer we up his sprites,
And show the best of our delights:
I'll charm the air to give a sound,
●While you perform your antic round;   130
That this great king may kindly say,
Our duties did his welcome pay.
     [*Music. The Witches dance, and then
                    vanish, with Hecate.*
Macb. Where are they? Gone? Let this per-
     nicious hour
Stand aye accursed in the calendar!
Come in, without there!

Enter LENNOX.

Len.   What's your grace's will?
Macb. Saw you the weird sisters?
Len.   No, my lord.
Macb. Came they not by you?
Len.   No, indeed, my lord.
Macb. Infected be the air whereon they ride;
And damn'd all those that trust them! I did hear
The galloping of horse: who was't came by? 140
Len. 'Tis two or three, my lord, that bring
     you word
Macduff is fled to England.
Macb.   Fled to England!
Len. Ay, my good lord.
Macb. Time, thou anticipatest my dread ex-
     ploits:
The flighty purpose never is o'ertook
Unless the deed go with it: from this moment
●The very firstlings of my heart shall be
The firstlings of my hand. And even now,
To crown my thoughts with acts, be it thought
     and done:
The castle of Macduff I will surprise;   150
Seize upon Fife; give to the edge o' the sword
His wife, his babes, and all unfortunate souls
That trace him in his line. No boasting like a
     fool:

Macbeth: 'Thou art too like the spirit of Banquo; down!'
Watercolour by Charles Cattermole (1832–1900)

121 *two . . . sceptres.* i.e. orbs and sceptres of Scotland
and England.

123 *bolter'd.* Smeared.

130 *antic.* Fantastic.

147 *firstlings.* First born.

Lady Macduff: 'Father'd he is, and yet he's fatherless.'
Drawing by Henry Singleton (1766–1839)

___

36 *set for.* Sought by trappers.

This deed I'll do before this purpose cool.
But no more sights!—Where are these gentlemen?
Come, bring me where they are.   [*Exeunt.*

SCENE II. *Fife. Macduff's castle.*

Enter LADY MACDUFF, *her* Son, *and* ROSS.

L. Macd. What had he done, to make him fly
the land?
Ross. You must have patience, madam.
L. Macd.   He had none:
His flight was madness: when our actions do not,
Our fears do make us traitors.
Ross.   You know not
Whether it was his wisdom or his fear.
L. Macd. Wisdom! to leave his wife, to leave
his babes,
His mansion and his titles in a place
From whence himself does fly? He loves us not;
He wants the natural touch: for the poor wren,
The most diminutive of birds, will fight,   10
Her young ones in her nest, against the owl.
All is the fear and nothing is the love:
As little is the wisdom, where the flight
So runs against all reason.
Ross.   My dearest coz,
I pray you, school yourself: but for your husband,
He is noble, wise, judicious, and best knows
The fits o' the season. I dare not speak much
further;
But cruel are the times, when we are traitors
And do not know ourselves, when we hold rumour
From what we fear, yet know not what we fear,
But float upon a wild and violent sea   21
Each way and move. I take my leave of you:
Shall not be long but I'll be here again:
Things at the worst will cease, or else climb up-
ward
To what they were before. My pretty cousin,
Blessing upon you!
L. Macd. Father'd he is, and yet he's father-
less.
Ross. I am so much a fool, should I stay longer,
It would be my disgrace and your discomfort:
I take my leave at once.   [*Exit.*
L. Macd.   Sirrah, your father's dead: 30
And what will you do now? How will you live?
Son. As birds do, mother.
L. Macd.   What, with worms and flies?
Son. With what I get, I mean; and so do they.
L. Macd. Poor bird! thou'ldst never fear the
net nor lime,
The pitfall nor the gin.
Son. Why should I, mother? Poor birds they
are not set for.
My father is not dead, for all your saying.
L. Macd. Yes, he is dead: how wilt thou do
for a father?
Son. Nay, how will you do for a husband?
L. Macd. Why, I can buy me twenty at any
market.   40
Son. Then you'll buy 'em to sell again.
L. Macd. Thou speak'st with all thy wit; and
yet, i' faith,
With wit enough for thee.
Son. Was my father a traitor, mother?
L. Macd. Ay, that he was.
Son. What is a traitor?
L. Macd. Why, one that swears and lies.

Son. And be all traitors that do so?
L. Macd. Every one that does so is a traitor,
and must be hanged.   50
Son. And must they all be hanged that swear
and lie?
L. Macd. Every one.
Son. Who must hang them?
L. Macd. Why, the honest men.
Son. Then the liars and swearers are fools,
for there are liars and swearers enow to beat the
honest men and hang up them.
L. Macd. Now, God help thee, poor monkey!
But how wilt thou do for a father?   60
Son. If he were dead, you'ld weep for him:
if you would not, it were a good sign that I should
quickly have a new father.
L. Macd. Poor prattler, how thou talk'st!

Enter a Messenger.

Mess. Bless you, fair dame! I am not to you
known,
Though in your state of honour I am perfect.
I doubt some danger does approach you nearly:
If you will take a homely man's advice,
Be not found here; hence, with your little ones.
To fright you thus, methinks, I am too savage; 70
To do worse to you were fell cruelty,
Which is too nigh your person.   Heaven preserve
you!
I dare abide no longer.   [*Exit.*
L. Macd.   Whither should I fly?
I have done no harm.   But I remember now
I am in this earthly world; where to do harm
Is often laudable, to do good sometime
Accounted dangerous folly: why then, alas,
Do I put up that womanly defence,
To say I have done no harm?

Enter Murderers.

                         What are these faces?
First Mur. Where is your husband?   80
L. Macd. I hope, in no place so unsanctified
Where such as thou mayst find him.
First Mur.   He's a traitor.
Son. Thou liest, thou shag-hair'd villain!
First Mur.   What, you egg!
                         [*Stabbing him.*
Young fry of treachery!
Son.   He has kill'd me, mother:
Run away, I pray you!   [*Dies.*
    [*Exit Lady Macduff, crying* 'Murder!'
        Exeunt Murderers, following her.

SCENE III. *England. Before the King's palace.*

Enter MALCOLM *and* MACDUFF.

Mal. Let us seek out some desolate shade,
and there
Weep our sad bosoms empty.
Macd.   Let us rather
Hold fast the mortal sword, and like good men
Bestride our down-fall'n birthdom: each new morn
New widows howl, new orphans cry, new sorrows
Strike heaven on the face, that it resounds
As if it felt with Scotland and yell'd out
Like syllable of dolour.
Mal.   What I believe I'll wail,
What know believe, and what I can redress,
As I shall find the time to friend, I will.   10

66 *perfect.* Fully aware.

4 *birthdom.* Mother-land.

Murder of Macduff's family. Woodcut from Holinshed's
Chronicles, 1577

34 *affeer'd.* Confirmed.

58 *Luxurious.* Lascivious.

64 *continent.* Chaste.

What you have spoke, it may be so perchance.
This tyrant, whose sole name blisters our tongues,
Was once thought honest: you have loved him
    well.
He hath not touch'd you yet.   I am young; but
    something
You may deserve of him through me, and wisdom
To offer up a weak poor innocent lamb
To appease an angry god.
    Macd.   I am not treacherous.
    Mal.   But Macbeth is.
A good and virtuous nature may recoil
In an imperial charge.   But I shall crave your
    pardon;   20
That which you are my thoughts cannot transpose:
Angels are bright still, though the brightest fell:
Though all things foul would wear the brows of
    grace,
Yet grace must still look so.
    Macd.   I have lost my hopes.
    Mal.   Perchance even there where I did find
    my doubts.
Why in that rawness left you wife and child,
Those precious motives, those strong knots of love,
Without leave-taking?   I pray you,
Let not my jealousies be your dishonours,   29
But mine own safeties.   You may be rightly just,
Whatever I shall think.
    Macd.   Bleed, bleed, poor country!
Great tyranny! lay thou thy basis sure,
For goodness dare not check thee: wear thou thy
    wrongs;
●The title is affeer'd!   Fare thee well, lord:
I would not be the villain that thou think'st
For the whole space that's in the tyrant's grasp,
And the rich East to boot.
    Mal.   Be not offended:
I speak not as in absolute fear of you.
I think our country sinks beneath the yoke;
It weeps, it bleeds; and each new day a gash   40
Is added to her wounds: I think withal
There would be hands uplifted in my right;
And here from gracious England have I offer
Of goodly thousands: but, for all this,
When I shall tread upon the tyrant's head,
Or wear it on my sword, yet my poor country
Shall have more vices than it had before,
More suffer and more sundry ways than ever,
By him that shall succeed.
    Macd.   What should he be?
    Mal.   It is myself I mean: in whom I know 50
All the particulars of vice so grafted
That, when they shall be open'd, black Macbeth
Will seem as pure as snow, and the poor state
Esteem him as a lamb, being compared
With my confineless harms.
    Macd.   Not in the legions
Of horrid hell can come a devil more damn'd
In evils to top Macbeth.
    Mal.   I grant him bloody,
●Luxurious, avaricious, false, deceitful,
Sudden, malicious, smacking of every sin
That has a name: but there's no bottom, none, 60
In my voluptuousness: your wives, your daughters,
Your matrons and your maids, could not fill up
The cistern of my lust, and my desire
●All continent impediments would o'erbear
That did oppose my will: better Macbeth
Than such an one to reign.

Macd.   Boundless intemperance
In nature is a tyranny; it hath been
The untimely emptying of the happy throne
And fall of many kings.   But fear not yet
To take upon you what is yours: you may   70
Convey your pleasures in a spacious plenty,
And yet seem cold, the time you may so hoodwink.
We have willing dames enough; there cannot be
That vulture in you, to devour so many
As will to greatness dedicate themselves,
Finding it so inclined.
    Mal.   With this there grows
In my most ill-composed affection such
●A stanchless avarice that, were I king,
I should cut off the nobles for their lands,
Desire his jewels and this other's house: 80
And my more-having would be as a sauce
To make me hunger more; that I should forge
Quarrels unjust against the good and loyal,
Destroying them for wealth.
    Macd.   This avarice
Sticks deeper, grows with more pernicious root
Than summer-seeming lust, and it hath been
The sword of our slain kings: yet do not fear;
●Scotland hath foisons to fill up your will,
Of your mere own: all these are portable,
With other graces weigh'd.   90
    Mal.   But I have none: the king-becoming
            graces,
As justice, verity, temperance, stableness,
Bounty, perseverance, mercy, lowliness,
Devotion, patience, courage, fortitude,
I have no relish of them, but abound
In the division of each several crime,
Acting it many ways.   Nay, had I power, I should
Pour the sweet milk of concord into hell,
Uproar the universal peace, confound
All unity on earth.
    Macd.   O Scotland, Scotland!   100
    Mal.   If such a one be fit to govern, speak:
I am as I have spoken.
    Macd.   Fit to govern!
No, not to live.   O nation miserable,
With an untitled tyrant bloody-scepter'd,
When shalt thou see thy wholesome days again,
Since that the truest issue of thy throne
●By his own interdiction stands accursed,
And does blaspheme his breed?   Thy royal father
Was a most sainted king: the queen that bore thee,
Oftener upon her knees than on her feet,   110
Died every day she lived.   Fare thee well!
These evils thou repeat'st upon thyself
Have banish'd me from Scotland.   O my breast,
Thy hope ends here!
    Mal.   Macduff, this noble passion,
Child of integrity, hath from my soul
Wiped the black scruples, reconciled my thoughts
To thy good truth and honour.   Devilish Macbeth
By many of these trains hath sought to win me
Into his power, and modest wisdom plucks me
From over-credulous haste: but God above   120
Deal between thee and me! for even now
I put myself to thy direction, and
Unspeak mine own detraction, here abjure
The taints and blames I laid upon myself,
For strangers to my nature.   I am yet
Unknown to woman, never was forsworn,
Scarcely have coveted what was mine own,
At no time broke my faith, would not betray

78 *stanchless.* Insatiable.

88 *foisons.* Plenties.

107 *interdiction.* Accusation.

Macduff: 'These evils . . . Have banished me from Scotland.' Robert Taber as Macduff, Lyceum Theatre, London, 1898

142 *stay*. Await.

170 *modern ecstasy*. Common emotion.

The devil to his fellow and delight
No less in truth than life: my first false speaking
Was this upon myself: what I am truly,   131
Is thine and my poor country's to command:
Whither indeed, before thy here-approach,
Old Siward, with ten thousand warlike men,
Already at a point, was setting forth.
Now we'll together; and the chance of goodness
Be like our warranted quarrel! Why are you
        silent?
    Macd. Such welcome and unwelcome things
        at once
'Tis hard to reconcile.

Enter a Doctor.

    Mal. Well; more anon.—Comes the king forth,
        I pray you?   140
    Doct. Ay, sir; there are a crew of wretched
        souls
That stay his cure: their malady convinces
The great assay of art; but at his touch—
Such sanctity hath heaven given his hand—
They presently amend.
    Mal.   I thank you, doctor. [*Exit Doctor.*
    Macd. What's the disease he means?
    Mal.   'Tis call'd the evil:
A most miraculous work in this good king;
Which often, since my here-remain in England,
I have seen him do. How he solicits heaven,
Himself best knows: but strangely-visited people,
All swoln and ulcerous, pitiful to the eye,   151
The mere despair of surgery, he cures,
Hanging a golden stamp about their necks,
Put on with holy prayers: and 'tis spoken,
To the succeeding royalty he leaves
The healing benediction. With this strange virtue,
He hath a heavenly gift of prophecy,
And sundry blessings hang about his throne,
That speak him full of grace.

Enter Ross.

    Macd.   See, who comes here?
    Mal. My countryman; but yet I know him
        not.   160
    Macd. My ever-gentle cousin, welcome hither.
    Mal. I know him now. Good God, betimes
        remove
The means that makes us strangers!
    Ross.   Sir, amen.
    Macd. Stands Scotland where it did?
    Ross.   Alas, poor country!
Almost afraid to know itself. It cannot
Be call'd our mother, but our grave; where no-
        thing,
But who knows nothing, is once seen to smile;
Where sighs and groans and shrieks that rend the
        air
Are made, not mark'd; where violent sorrow
        seems
A modern ecstasy: the dead man's knell   170
Is there scarce ask'd for who; and good men's
        lives
Expire before the flowers in their caps,
Dying or ere they sicken.
    Macd.   O, relation
Too nice, and yet too true!
    Mal.   What's the newest grief?
    Ross. That of an hour's age doth hiss the
        speaker:

Each minute teems a new one.
   Macd.   How does my wife?
   Ross. Why, well.
   Macd.   And all my children?
   Ross.   Well too.
   Macd. The tyrant has not batter'd at their
     peace?
   Ross. No; they were well at peace when I did
     leave 'em.
   Macd. Be not a niggard of your speech: how
     goes't?   180
   Ross. When I came hither to transport the
     tidings,
Which I have heavily borne, there ran a rumour
Of many worthy fellows that were out;
Which was to my belief witness'd the rather,
For that I saw the tyrant's power a-foot:
Now is the time of help; your eye in Scotland
Would create soldiers, make our women fight,
To doff their dire distresses.
   Mal.   Be't their comfort
We are coming thither: gracious England hath
Lent us good Siward and ten thousand men; 190
An older and a better soldier none
That Christendom gives out.
   Ross.   Would I could answer
This comfort with the like!   But I have words
That would be howl'd out in the desert air,
Where hearing should not latch them.
   Macd.   What concern they?
• The general cause? or is it a fee-grief
Due to some single breast?
   Ross.   No mind that's honest
But in it shares some woe; though the main part
Pertains to you alone.
   Macd.   If it be mine,
Keep it not from me, quickly let me have it. 200
   Ross. Let not your ears despise my tongue for
     ever,
Which shall possess them with the heaviest sound
That ever yet they heard.
   Macd.   Hum! I guess at it.
   Ross. Your castle is surprised; your wife and
     babes
Savagely slaughter'd: to relate the manner,
Were, on the quarry of these murder'd deer,
To add the death of you.
   Mal.   Merciful heaven!
What, man! ne'er pull your hat upon your brows;
Give sorrow words: the grief that does not
     speak
Whispers the o'er-fraught heart and bids it break.
   Macd. My children too?
   Ross.   Wife, children, servants, all 211
That could be found.
   Macd.   And I must be from thence!
My wife kill'd too?
   Ross.   I have said.
   Mal.   Be comforted:
Let's make us medicines of our great revenge,
To cure this deadly grief.
   Macd. He has no children.   All my pretty
     ones?
Did you say all?   O hell-kite!   All?
What, all my pretty chickens and their dam
At one fell swoop?
   Mal. Dispute it like a man.
   Macd.   I shall do so; 220
But I must also feel it as a man:

196 *fee.* Private.

Macduff: '. . . all my pretty chickens and their dam . . .'
Macduff (John Neville) and Malcolm (Paul Daneman),
Old Vic Theatre, London, 1954

232 *intermission.* Delays.

22 *Lo.* Look. *guise.* Manner.

Gentlewoman: 'This is her very guise.' Lady Macbeth.
Drawing by Henry Singleton (1766–1839)

Opposite : Ann Todd as Lady Macbeth, Old Vic Theatre,
London, 1934

I cannot but remember such things were,
That were most precious to me.   Did heaven
    look on,
And would not take their part?   Sinful Macduff,
They were all struck for thee !   naught that I am,
Not for their own demerits, but for mine,
Fell slaughter on their souls.   Heaven rest them
    now !
   Mal.   Be this the whetstone of your sword :
    let grief
Convert to anger ; blunt not the heart, enrage it.
   Macd.   O, I could play the woman with mine
    eyes   230
And braggart with my tongue !   But, gentle
    heavens,
• Cut short all intermission ; front to front
Bring thou this fiend of Scotland and myself ;
Within my sword's length set him ; if he 'scape,
Heaven forgive him too !
   Mal.   This tune goes manly.
Come, go we to the king ; our power is ready ;
Our lack is nothing but our leave : Macbeth
Is ripe for shaking, and the powers above
Put on their instruments.   Receive what cheer
    you may :
The night is long that never finds the day.   240
                              [*Exeunt.*

ACT V.

Scene I. *Dunsinane.   Ante-room in the castle.*

Enter a Doctor of Physic *and a*
Waiting-Gentlewoman.

   Doct.   I have two nights watched with you,
but can perceive no truth in your report.   When
was it she last walked?
   Gent.   Since his majesty went into the field, I
have seen her rise from her bed, throw her nightgown upon her, unlock her closet, take forth
paper, fold it, write upon't, read it, afterwards
seal it, and again return to bed ; yet all this while
in a most fast sleep.   9
   Doct.   A great perturbation in nature, to
receive at once the benefit of sleep, and do the
effects of watching !   In this slumbery agitation,
besides her walking and other actual performances, what, at any time, have you heard her
say ?
   Gent.   That, sir, which I will not report after
her.
   Doct.   You may to me : and 'tis most meet
you should.
   Gent.   Neither to you nor any one ; having no
witness to confirm my speech.   21

Enter Lady Macbeth, *with a taper.*

• Lo you, here she comes ! This is her very guise ;
and, upon my life, fast asleep.   Observe her ;
stand close.
   Doct.   How came she by that light?
   Gent.   Why, it stood by her : she has light by
her continually ; 'tis her command.
   Doct.   You see, her eyes are open.
   Gent.   Ay, but their sense is shut.
   Doct.   What is it she does now?   Look, how
she rubs her hands.   31
   Gent.   It is an accustomed action with her, to

Lady Macbeth: '. . . all the perfumes of Arabia will not sweeten this little hand.' Mrs Patrick Campbell as Lady Macbeth, Lyceum Theatre, London, 1898

---

60 *sorely charged.* Full of grief.

84 *annoyance.* Harm.

seem thus washing her hands: I have known **her** continue in this a quarter of an hour.

Lady M.   Yet here's a spot.

Doct.   Hark! she speaks: I will set down what comes from her, to satisfy my remembrance the more strongly.

Lady M.   Out, damned spot! out, I say!— One: two: why, then 'tis time to do't.—Hell is murky!—Fie, my lord, fie! a soldier, and afeard? What need we fear who knows it, when none can call our power to account?—Yet who would have thought the old man to have had so much blood in him.

Doct.   Do you mark that?

Lady M.   The thane of Fife had a wife: where is she now?—What, will these hands ne'er be clean?—No more o' that, my lord, no more o' that: you mar all with this starting.   50

Doct.   Go to, go to; you have known what you should not.

Gent.   She has spoke what she should not, I am sure of that: heaven knows what she has known.

Lady M.   Here's the smell of the blood still: all the perfumes of Arabia will not sweeten this little hand. Oh, oh, oh!

Doct.   What a sigh is there! The heart is sorely charged.   60

Gent.   I would not have such a heart in my bosom for the dignity of the whole body.

Doct.   Well, well, well,—

Gent.   Pray God it be, sir.

Doct.   This disease is beyond **my** practice: yet I have known those which have walked in their sleep who have died holily in their beds.

Lady M.   Wash your hands, put on your nightgown; look not so pale.—I tell you yet again, Banquo's buried; he cannot come out on's grave.   71

Doct.   Even so?

Lady M.   To bed, to bed! there's knocking at the gate: come, come, come, come, give me your hand. What's done cannot be undone.—To bed, to bed, to bed!   [*Exit.*

Doct.   Will she go now to bed?

Gent.   Directly.

Doct.   Foul whisperings are abroad: unnatural deeds
Do breed unnatural troubles: infected minds   80
To their deaf pillows will discharge their secrets:
More needs she the divine than the physician.
God, God forgive us all! Look after her;
Remove from her the means of all annoyance,
And still keep eyes upon her.   So, good night:
My mind she has mated, and amazed my sight.
I think, but dare not speak.

Gent.   Good night, good doctor.

[*Exeunt.*

Scene II.   *The country near Dunsinane.*

Drum and colours. Enter MENTEITH, CAITH-NESS, ANGUS, LENNOX, *and* Soldiers.

Ment.   The English power is near, led on by Malcolm,
His uncle Siward and the good Macduff:
Revenges burn in them; for their dear causes
Would to the bleeding and the grim alarm

Excite the mortified man.

Ang.   Near Birnam wood
Shall we well meet them; that way are they
        coming.
    Caith.   Who knows if Donalbain be with his
        brother?
    Len.   For certain, sir, he is not: I have a file
Of all the gentry: there is Siward's son,
And many unrough youths that even now   10
Protest their first of manhood.
    Ment.   What does the tyrant?
    Caith.   Great Dunsinane he strongly fortifies:
Some say he's mad; others that lesser hate him
Do call it valiant fury: but, for certain,
He cannot buckle his distemper'd cause
Within the belt of rule.
    Ang.   Now does he feel
His secret murders sticking on his hands;
Now minutely revolts upbraid his faith-breach;
Those he commands move only in command,
Nothing in love: now does he feel his title   20
Hang loose about him, like a giant's robe
Upon a dwarfish thief.
    Ment.   Who then shall blame
His pester'd senses to recoil and start,
When all that is within him does condemn
Itself for being there?
    Caith.   Well, march we on,
To give obedience where 'tis truly owed:
Meet we the medicine of the sickly weal,
And with him pour we in our country's purge
Each drop of us.
    Len.   Or so much as it needs,
To dew the sovereign flower and drown the
        weeds.   30
Make we our march towards Birnam.
                                [*Exeunt, marching.*

SCENE III.   *Dunsinane. A room in the castle.*

Enter MACBETH, Doctor, *and* Attendants.

    Macb.   Bring me no more reports; let them
        fly all:
Till Birnam wood remove to Dunsinane,
I cannot taint with fear. What's the boy
        Malcolm?
Was he not born of woman? The spirits that
        know
All mortal consequences have pronounced me
        thus:
'Fear not, Macbeth; no man that's born of
        woman
Shall e'er have power upon thee.' Then fly,
        false thanes,
And mingle with the English epicures:
The mind I sway by and the heart I bear
Shall never sag with doubt nor shake with fear. 10

Enter a Servant.

The devil damn thee black, thou cream-faced
        loon!
Where got'st thou that goose look?
    Serv.   There is ten thousand—
    Macb.   Geese, villain?
    Serv.   Soldiers, sir.
    Macb.   Go prick thy face, and over-red thy
        fear,

---

5 *mortified.* Dead.

8 *file.* List.

20 *Nothing.* Not at all.

3 *taint.* Tinge.

Macbeth: 'I cannot taint with fear.' H. Beerbohm Tree
as Macbeth, His Majesty's Theatre, London, 1911

459

23 *fall'n . . . sear.* Shrivelled.

35 *moe.* More. *skirr.* Scour.

50-51 *cast The water.* Diagnose the urine.

55 *cyme.* Senna.

59 *bane.* Destruction.

Macbeth: 'Till Birnam forest come to Dunsinane.'
Engraving of Dunsinane from Charles Knight's *Pictorial
Edition of the Works of Shakspere,* 1839–43

Thou lily-liver'd boy.   What soldiers, patch?
Death of thy soul! those linen cheeks of thine
Are counsellors to fear.   What soldiers, whey-
    face?
  Serv.   The English force, so please you.
  Macb.   Take thy face hence. [*Exit Servant.*
              Seyton!—I am sick at heart,
When I behold—Seyton, I say!—This push   20
Will cheer me ever, or disseat me now.
I have lived long enough: my way of life
● Is fall'n into the sear, the yellow leaf;
And that which should accompany old age,
As honour, love, obedience, troops of friends,
I must not look to have; but, in their stead,
Curses, not loud but deep, mouth-honour, breath,
Which the poor heart would fain deny, and dare
    not.
Seyton!

Enter SEYTON.

  Sey.   What is your gracious pleasure?
  Macb.   What news more?   30
  Sey.   All is confirm'd, my lord, which was
    reported.
  Macb.   I'll fight till from my bones my flesh
    be hack'd.
Give me my armour.
  Sey.   'Tis not needed yet.
  Macb.   I'll put it on.
● Send out moe horses; skirr the country round;
Hang those that talk of fear.   Give me mine
    armour.
How does your patient, doctor?
  Doct.   Not so sick, my lord,
As she is troubled with thick-coming fancies,
That keep her from her rest.
  Macb.   Cure her of that.
Canst thou not minister to a mind diseased,   40
Pluck from the memory a rooted sorrow,
Raze out the written troubles of the brain
And with some sweet oblivious antidote
Cleanse the stuff'd bosom of that perilous stuff
Which weighs upon the heart?
  Doct.   Therein the patient
Must minister to himself.
  Macb.   Throw physic to the dogs; I'll none
    of it.
Come, put mine armour on; give me my staff.
Seyton, send out.   Doctor, the thanes fly from
    me.   49
● Come, sir, dispatch.   If thou couldst, doctor, cast
The water of my land, find her disease,
And purge it to a sound and pristine health,
I would applaud thee to the very echo,
That should applaud again.—Pull't off, I say.—
● What rhubarb, †cyme, or what purgative drug,
 Would scour these English hence?   Hear'st thou
    of them?
  Doct.   Ay, my good lord; your royal prepar-
    ation
Makes us hear something.
  Macb.   Bring it after me.
● I will not be afraid of death and bane,
Till Birnam forest come to Dunsinane.   60
  Doct. [*Aside*] Were I from Dunsinane away
    and clear,
Profit again should hardly draw me here.
                  [*Exeunt.*

SCENE IV.   *Country near Birnam wood.*

Drum and colours.   Enter MALCOLM, *old* SI-
WARD *and his* Son, MACDUFF, MENTEITH,
CAITHNESS, ANGUS, LENNOX, ROSS, *and* Sol-
diers, *marching.*

Mal.   Cousins, I hope the days are near at
    hand
That chambers will be safe.
Ment.   We doubt it nothing.
Siw.   What wood is this before us?
Ment.   The wood of Birnam.
Mal.   Let every soldier hew him down a bough
●And bear't before him: thereby shall we shadow
The numbers of our host and make discovery
Err in report of us.
Soldiers.   It shall be done.
Siw.   We learn no other but the confident
    tyrant
Keeps still in Dunsinane, and will endure
Our setting down before 't.
Mal.   'Tis his main hope: 10
For where there is advantage to be given,
Both more and less have given him the revolt,
And none serve with him but constrained things
Whose hearts are absent too.
Macd.   Let our just censures
Attend the true event, and put we on
Industrious soldiership.
Siw.   The time approaches
That will with due decision make us know
What we shall say we have and what we owe.
Thoughts speculative their unsure hopes relate,
But certain issue strokes must arbitrate: 20
Towards which advance the war.
                        [*Exeunt, marching.*

SCENE V.   *Dunsinane.   Within the castle.*

Enter MACBETH, SEYTON, *and* Soldiers, *with
drum and colours.*

Macb.   Hang out our banners on the outward
    walls;
The cry is still 'They come:' our castle's strength
Will laugh a siege to scorn: here let them lie
Till famine and the ague eat them up:
Were they not forced with those that should be
    ours,
We might have met them dareful, beard to beard,
And beat them backward home.
                        [*A cry of women within.*
                        What is that noise?
Sey.   It is the cry of women, my good lord.
                        [*Exit.*
Macb.   I have almost forgot the taste of fears:
The time has been, my senses would have cool'd
●To hear a night-shriek; and my fell of hair   11
Would at a dismal treatise rouse and stir
As life were in 't: I have supp'd full with
    horrors;
Direness, familiar to my slaughterous thoughts,
Cannot once start me.

Re-enter SEYTON.

                        Wherefore was that cry?
Sey.   The queen, my lord, is dead.

5 *shadow.* Cover.

11 *fell of hair.* Scalp.

25 *frets.* Plays.

Macbeth: 'Life's but . . . a poor player that struts and frets his hour . . .' Engraving by F. W. Fairholt from a woodcut of 1570, from J. O. Halliwell's edition of Shakespeare's works, 1853–65

40 *sooth.* True.

10 *harbingers.* Messengers sent ahead to prepare for the coming of an army or a king.

Macb.   She should have died hereafter;
There would have been a time for such a word.
To-morrow, and to-morrow, and to-morrow,
Creeps in this petty pace from day to day   20
To the last syllable of recorded time,
And all our yesterdays have lighted fools
The way to dusty death. Out, out, brief candle!
Life's but a walking shadow, a poor player
●That struts and frets his hour upon the stage
And then is heard no more: it is a tale
Told by an idiot, full of sound and fury,
Signifying nothing.

Enter a Messenger.

Thou comest to use thy tongue; thy story quickly.
    Mess.   Gracious my lord,   30
I should report that which I say I saw,
But know not how to do it.
    Macb.   Well, say, sir.
    Mess.   As I did stand my watch upon the hill,
I look'd toward Birnam, and anon, methought,
The wood began to move.
    Macb.   Liar and slave!
    Mess.   Let me endure your wrath, if't be
        not so:
Within this three mile may you see it coming;
I say, a moving grove.
    Macb.   If thou speak'st false,
Upon the next tree shalt thou hang alive,
●Till famine cling thee: if thy speech be sooth, 40
I care not if thou dost for me as much.
I pull in resolution, and begin
To doubt the equivocation of the fiend
That lies like truth: ' Fear not, till Birnam
        wood
Do come to Dunsinane:' and now a wood
Comes toward Dunsinane. Arm, arm, and out!
If this which he avouches does appear,
There is nor flying hence nor tarrying here.
I gin to be aweary of the sun,
And wish the estate o' the world were now un-
        done.   50
Ring the alarum-bell! Blow, wind! come. wrack!
At least we'll die with harness on our back.
                                        [*Exeunt.*

SCENE VI.   *Dunsinane.   Before the castle.*

Drum and colours.   Enter MALCOLM, *old* SI-
WARD, MACDUFF, *and their* Army, *with
boughs.*

    Mal.   Now near enough: your leavy screens
        throw down,
And show like those you are. You, worthy
        uncle,
Shall, with my cousin, your right-noble son,
Lead our first battle: worthy Macduff and we
Shall take upon 's what else remains to do,
According to our order.
    Siw.   Fare you well.
Do we but find the tyrant's power to-night,
Let us be beaten, if we cannot fight.
    Macd.   Make all our trumpets speak; give
        them all breath,   9
●Those clamorous harbingers of blood and death.
                                        [*Exeunt.*

SCENE VII.   *Another part of the field.*

Alarums.   Enter MACBETH.

Macb.   They have tied me to a stake; I can-
    not fly,
But, bear-like, I must fight the course.   What's he
That was not born of woman?   Such a one
Am I to fear, or none.

Enter young SIWARD.

Yo. Siw.   What is thy name?
Macb.   Thou'lt be afraid to hear it.
Yo. Siw.   No; though thou call'st thyself a
    hotter name
Than any is in hell.
Macb.   My name's Macbeth.
Yo. Siw.   The devil himself could not pro-
    nounce a title
More hateful to mine ear.
Macb.   No, nor more fearful.
Yo. Siw.   Thou liest, abhorred tyrant; with
    my sword   10
I'll prove the lie thou speak'st.
       [They fight and young Siward is slain.
Macb.   Thou wast born of woman.
But swords I smile at, weapons laugh to scorn,
Brandish'd by man that's of a woman born.
                       [Exit.

Alarums.   Enter MACDUFF.

Macd.   That way the noise is.   Tyrant, show
    thy face!
If thou be'st slain and with no stroke of mine,
My wife and children's ghosts will haunt me
    still.
I cannot strike at wretched kerns, whose arms
Are hired to bear their staves: either thou, Mac-
    beth,
Or else my sword with an unbatter'd edge
● I sheathe again undeeded.   There thou shouldst
    be;   20
By this great clatter, one of greatest note
● Seems bruited.   Let me find him, fortune!
And more I beg not.   *[Exit.   Alarums.*

Enter MALCOLM *and old* SIWARD.

● *Siw.*   This way, my lord; the castle's gently
    render'd:
The tyrant's people on both sides do fight;
The noble thanes do bravely in the war;
The day almost itself professes yours,
And little is to do.
Mal.   We have met with foes
That strike beside us.
Siw.   Enter, sir, the castle.
            [Exeunt.   Alarums.

SCENE VIII.   *Another part of the field.*

Enter MACBETH.

Macb.   Why should I play the Roman fool, and
    die
On mine own sword? whiles I see lives, the gashes
Do better upon them.

Macbeth: 'I cannot strike at wretched kerns . . .'
Engraving from John Derrick's *The Image of Ireland*,
1581

20 *undeeded.* Having achieved nothing.

22 *bruited.* Proclaimed.

24 *render'd.* Surrendered.

9 *intrenchant.* Invulnerable.

Macbeth: 'As easy mayst thou the intrenchant air With thy keen sword impress . . .' John Neville as Macduff and Paul Rogers as Macbeth, Old Vic Theatre, London, 1954

20 *palter.* Shuffle, play.

Enter MACDUFF.

Macd.   Turn, hell-hound, turn !
Macb.   Of all men else I have avoided thee :
But get thee back ; my soul is too much charged
With blood of thine already.
Macd.   I have no words :
My voice is in my sword : thou bloodier villain
Than terms can give thee out !   [*They fight.*
Macb.   Thou losest labour :
● As easy mayst thou the intrenchant air
With thy keen sword impress as make me bleed :
Let fall thy blade on vulnerable crests ;   11
I bear a charmed life, which must not yield
To one of woman born.
Macd.   Despair thy charm ;
And let the angel whom thou still hast served
Tell thee, Macduff was from his mother's womb
Untimely ripp'd.
Macb.   Accursed be that tongue that tells me so,
For it hath cow'd my better part of man !
And be these juggling fiends no more believed,
● That palter with us in a double sense ;   20
That keep the word of promise to our ear,
And break it to our hope.   I'll not fight with thee.
Macd.   Then yield thee, coward,
And live to be the show and gaze o' the time :
We'll have thee, as our rarer monsters are,
Painted upon a pole, and underwrit,
'Here may you see the tyrant.'
Macb.   I will not yield,
To kiss the ground before young Malcolm's feet,
And to be baited with the rabble's curse.
Though Birnam wood be come to Dunsinane,   30
And thou opposed, being of no woman born,
Yet I will try the last.   Before my body
I throw my warlike shield.   Lay on, Macduff,
And damn'd be him that first cries 'Hold, e-
      nough !'   [*Exeunt, fighting. Alarums.*

Retreat. Flourish. Enter, with drum and
colours, MALCOLM, *old* SIWARD, ROSS, *the*
other Thanes, *and* Soldiers.

Mal.   I would the friends we miss were safe
      arrived.
Siw.   Some must go off : and yet, by these I see,
So great a day as this is cheaply bought.
Mal.   Macduff is missing, and your noble son.
Ross.   Your son, my lord, has paid a soldier's
      debt :
He only lived but till he was a man ;   40
The which no sooner had his prowess confirm'd
In the unshrinking station where he fought,
But like a man he died.
Siw.   Then he is dead ?
Ross.   Ay, and brought off the field : your
      cause of sorrow
Must not be measured by his worth, for then
It hath no end.
Siw.   Had he his hurts before ?
Ross.   Ay, on the front.
Siw.   Why then, God's soldier be he !
Had I as many sons as I have hairs,
I would not wish them to a fairer death :
And so, his knell is knoll'd.
Mal.   He's worth more sorrow,   50
And that I'll spend for him.
Siw.   He's worth no more :

They say he parted well, and paid his score:
And so, God be with him! Here comes newer
    comfort.

    Re-enter MACDUFF, *with* MACBETH'S *head.*

    Macd.   Hail, king! for so thou art: behold,
    where stands
The usurper's cursed head: the time is free:
I see thee compass'd with thy kingdom's pearl,
That speak my salutation in their minds;
Whose voices I desire aloud with mine:
Hail, King of Scotland!
    All.   Hail, King of Scotland! [*Flourish.*
    Mal. We shall not spend a large expense of
    time   60
Before we reckon with your several loves,
And make us even with you. My thanes and
    kinsmen,
Henceforth be earls, the first that ever Scotland
In such an honour named. What's more to do,
Which would be planted newly with the time,
As calling home our exiled friends abroad
That fled the snares of watchful tyranny;
Producing forth the cruel ministers
Of this dead butcher and his fiend-like queen,
Who, as 'tis thought, by self and violent hands 70
Took off her life; this, and what needful else
That calls upon us, by the grace of Grace,
We will perform in measure, time and place:
So, thanks to all at once and to each one,
Whom we invite to see us crown'd at Scone.
                       [*Flourish. Exeunt.*

Antony
and Cleopatra

1607

THERE COULD HARDLY BE A GREATER CONTRAST than there is between *Macbeth* and *Antony and Cleopatra* – the former dark and smelling of murder, the latter brilliantly lit by all the colours of the Mediterranean and the gorgeous East. Then this play is the only one of the great tragedies to be a love-tragedy; in that it casts the mind back to *Romeo and Juliet*, though neither Antony nor Cleopatra has the excuse of those young and immature lovers. Antony, in fact, has grey hair, and Cleopatra – who had had a child years before by Julius Caesar – is past her youth. The story carries on from *Julius Caesar*, and Antony unexpectedly refers to 'mad' Brutus, showing what he thought of his illusory doctrinairism. But Antony suffers no less from his own dominant illusion, the illusion of love. It seems that Shakespeare by this time had none – at any rate, of sexual love: that theme is not so important again in the plays.

Cleopatra. Shakespeare got his story from Plutarch, who gives us the character of the actual woman in history: her political intelligence and gift for languages, the devouring ambition she derived from her Macedonian-Greek stock. Nothing of this in Shakespeare; and, since we are looking for what reveals him, we should note the characteristics he gives her that are not in Plutarch. With the historic Cleopatra sex was but a means to political power. In the play her aim is simply to exert power over one man, Antony. And well she knows how to do it. When Charmian advises,

> In each thing give him way, cross him in nothing:

Cleopatra replies:

> Thou teachest like a fool: the way to lose him.

So she is contrarious, she holds him on tenter-hooks – as with a recent English king who thought the world well lost for love. But was it? Antony did not think so in the end. Nor apparently did Shakespeare; in a moment of truth Antony admits,

Would I had never seen her!

He himself describes her as one

> Whom everything becomes, to chide, to laugh,
> To weep: whose every passion fully strives
> To make itself in thee.

She uses these as instruments; Antony tells Enobarbus: 'she is cunning past man's thought'. The latter glosses: 'we cannot call her winds and waters sighs and tears; they are greater storms and tempests than almanacs can report.' She was seen once, this queen, to

> Hop forty paces through the public street
> And, having lost her breath, she spoke, and panted,
> That she did make defect perfection,
> And, breathless, power breathe forth.

Shakespeare evidently saw her as a gipsy, exerting a spell over her man by her contrariousness, her changing moods, her tempestuous temperament, her feminine cunning, her passions. (Where have we met all this before? We are surprised only that she was not musical – but that would not have been in keeping with the scheme.)

*Lily Langtry,
English Edwardian
actress, as
Cleopatra,
Princess's Theatre,
London, 1890*

The Play has not the dramatic intensity of the other high tragedies: its action is more dispersed and various, and its interest is almost as much political as it is amorous. Whole scenes are devoted to the political issue between Octavius Caesar and Antony; Antony and Caesar's noble sister, Octavia, loyal and sensible, whom Antony deserts for 'his Egyptian dish'; discussions among the rival followings and battles in the field. It is not until the end that the action speeds into the grand finale; or, rather, there are two of them, Antony's downfall and defeat – his death is postponed for a last meeting with Cleopatra – and then her unique and unparalleled way to death.

Antony. Several strokes reveal the Antony we knew from *Julius Caesar*, where he was described as 'a masker and reveller'. In the later play he revels with Cleopatra in the streets of Alexandria, masquerading as common citizens, night-walkers. What a way for a Triumvir, ruler of one-third of the Roman world to behave! No wonder Octavius Caesar, much younger, but altogether more mature, disapproved. Antony has a weakness for drink and, like such people, eggs on the young Caesar, who, however, says,

> I could well forbear't.
> It's monstrous labour when I wash my brain
> And it grows fouler.

Antony persists:

> Be a child o'the time . . .

But Caesar excuses himself:

> . . . I had rather fast from all, four days,

467

> Than drink so much in one.

Antony goes on

> Till that the conquering wine hath steeped our sense
> In soft and delicate Lethe.

Such men are not made to inherit the earth.

He is, of course, generous, as such types are; but he is a great fool to be led by the nose by a woman, and to follow her flight from the sea-battle at Actium, when he might very well have won. Defeated, he runs mad and rails at her, with the insults such people exchange when things go wrong between them:

> This foul Egyptian hath betrayed me . . .
>   Triple-turned whore, 'tis thou
> Hast sold me to this novice, and my heart
> Makes only wars on thee . . .

Octavius Caesar is no novice, and there is none of this nonsense in him. It is usual for sympathies to run with the lovers, a soft option, and not to appreciate Caesar at his true worth. Critics find him 'unattractive': literary folk find it difficult to understand the true political type with a mind to rule, as with Hazlitt and so many others over Henry V. Octavius is a man in full control of himself, as a ruler must be, and moreover is reasonable, moderate and just. He did not wish the war, or a breach with Antony, and was more than willing to meet him half-way. But Antony fell down on his duty and broke their mutual understanding, while his wife Fulvia and their friends actually attacked Octavius.

He is ready to forgive and forget and, on Fulvia's death, to cement friendship by giving his sister Octavia, whom he much loves, to Antony as wife. Antony of course deserts her, and goes back to Cleopatra. Moreover he is jealous of the younger man, the 'novice'. A soothsayer warns him,

> Near him [Caesar], thy angel
> Becomes afeared, as being overpowered . . .
> If thou dost play with him at any game,
> Thou art sure to lose . . .

Octavius Caesar carries the charisma of the deified Julius: Antony is bound to lose going the way he does. We need not go into the pathetic boasting of what he once was, when he has lost out. Suffice it to say that Caesar is magnanimous; when he hears that Antony is dead, he says:

> The death of Antony
> Is not a single doom, in the name lay
> A moiety of the world.

In pronouncing his panegyric, Octavius laments

> That thou my brother, my competitor,
> In top of all design; my mate in empire,

> Friend and companion in the front of war,
> The arm of mine own body . . .
>   that our stars,
> Unreconcileable, should divide
> Our equalness to this.

Such are the tragedies of high politics, a matter for more mature pity, when all is said, than the misfortunes of elderly lovers, bringing their fate upon themselves.

Their fate gives opportunity for much fine poetry, and I agree with M. R. Ridley – who was sensitive to such things – that 'the peculiar glory of this play is not in its dramatic quality. It is in its poetry.'[1] Many passages of such grandeur are familiar – the description of Cleopatra in her barge upon the river Cydnus, or the too often quoted 'Age cannot wither her'; and Antony's words on being told that Cleopatra had died, with his name on her lips:

> Unarm, Eros, the long day's task is done,
> And we must sleep . . .
> I will o'ertake thee, Cleopatra . . .
> Eros! – I come, my queen. Eros! – Stay for me,
> Where souls do couch on flowers, we'll hand in hand,
> And with our sprightly port make the ghosts gaze:
> Dido and her Aeneas shall want troops,
> And all the haunt be ours.

The master could always fetch up from the depths of his inspiration this magical verbal mastery at such moments, but never more so than in this play. Ridley concludes that here is 'Shakespeare's topmost achievement in dramatic poetry, that kind of poetry which apart from its context is little remarkable, but in its dramatic setting is indefinably moving.' We would merely emend this to say that it is, apart from its context, both remarkable and moving.

Personal. In a play of such Oriental colouring, not many touches of the contemporary background are discernible, but, significantly, more than usual of the personal. A reference to the author's own profession appears in every play; here, along with the ballad makers who, Cleopatra foresees, will make rhymes on her and Antony (they certainly did) –

> the quick comedians
> Extemporally will stage us, and present
> Our Alexandrian revels: Antony
> Shall be brought drunken forth, and I shall see
> Some squeaking Cleopatra boy my greatness
> I' the posture of a whore.

Evidently the boy-actor who played the part of Cleopatra – his inches were fewer than Antony's – had not a squeaking voice; and how professional he must have been to play such a part!

Shakespeare describes the masses in his usual terms. Octavius describes Antony reeling the streets at noon and buffeting with slaves that 'smell of sweat'; Cleopatra foretells that they will be played as puppets in Rome:

1. The Arden edition, Introduction, liv, lv.

> mechanic slaves
> With greasy aprons, rules and hammers shall
> Uplift us to the view. In their thick breaths,
> Rank of gross diet, shall we be enclouded,
> And forced to drink their vapour.

Elizabethan crowds, indeed people in general, were very smelly; grandees at Court, the Queen and Leicester, smothered themselves in scent – and William Shakespeare certainly had a sensitive nose. His consciousness of snakes (whatever Freud would think about that) is naturally more in evidence than ever; two extended passages are devoted to the subject, and Cleopatra's aspics have of course a part to play.

A few lines here and there give us his reflections on what he had observed. We have learned

> That he which is was wished until he were:

this means that the man in power is popular, until he gets there. It is Octavius speaking, and what a penetrating political observation! He goes on,

> And the ebbed man, ne'er loved till ne'er worth love,
> Comes deared, by being lacked.

This is a highly elliptical way of saying that the defeated candidate, never appreciated till he is no longer worth supporting, is all the more popular for being missed. How often we have seen that too!

The dilemma posed to Antony's chief follower, Enobarbus, is fascinating:

> Mine honesty, and I, begin to square [quarrel].
> The loyalty well held to fools does make
> Our faith mere folly.

(That was what Francis Bacon had thought as he watched the folly of Essex's course.) He deserts the falling, foolish Antony – and then finds himself conscience-stricken at his conduct, and repents

> Yet he that can endure
> To follow with allegiance a fallen lord,
> Does conquer him that did his master conquer,
> And earns a place in the story.

In the end Enobarbus did. Everybody remembered Bacon's conduct against Essex; however prudent his action, Shakespeare cannot have regarded it as a matter for commendation.

Again we find, as always, Shakespeare's unsleeping scepticism about the way things will turn out:

> We, ignorant of ourselves,
> Beg often our own harms, which the wise powers
> Deny us for our good: so find we profit
> By losing of our prayers.

Touches of bawdy reappear, naturally in this play in which sex has a decisive role – considering that, there is little enough, and none of the joyous rollicking stuff of earlier plays. People have seen signs of sex-nausea in those from *Hamlet* and *Troilus and Cressida* to *King Lear*, and there is no sex at all in *Macbeth*. Now Cleopatra addresses her eunuch with,

> I take no pleasure
> In aught an eunuch has: 'tis well for thee
> That, being unseminared . . .

perhaps we should spell this, unsemenared. And when it is a question of playing billiards:

> As well a woman with an eunuch played
> As with a woman.

The splendid passages of poetry have often been noticed; here we will call attention only to the extraordinarily oblique and often elliptical language. On hearing unwelcome news from Rome, for 'it offends me: be brief', Antony says: 'Grates me, the sum.' The movement of Shakespeare's mind linguistically is, surely, very odd? When drifting clouds efface a fancied picture, it is simply, but elliptically, 'the rack dislimns'! Dogs die of some disease; here they die of 'languish'. And, within a few lines, Antony imagines Eros 'windowed' in Rome watching her master with 'pleached' arms, bending down

> His corrigible neck, his face subdued
> To penetrative shame.

Extraordinary language – but the clue to it, as always, is that Shakespeare thinks visually.

The Text, from the Folio, is a good one and, both Greg and Dover-Wilson agree, from the author's manuscript. Its mislineation is due to Shakespeare economising space by running on half-lines to fill the rest of the line. Sometimes he punctuated carefully, sometimes not. In 1607 Daniel considerably revised his *Cleopatra* in the light of Shakespeare's play, trying to make it more dramatic. Earlier he had been influenced by *Richard II* in revising his account in the *Civil Wars*, to which Shakespeare in turn was indebted. They would have known each other through Florio, Daniel's brother-in-law. (So the *Parnassus* play's flout at Daniel for 'base imitation' is imperceptive of the real subtlety of the situation.) It is perhaps worth adding that Emilia Lanier knew Daniel through their common patroness, the Countess of Cumberland, to whose daughter, Lady Anne Clifford, he was tutor.

Towards the end of the year Barnes's *Devil's Charter*, 'renewed, corrected and augmented', borrowed Cleopatra's asps for his purposes.

ANTONY AND CLEOPATRA.

DRAMATIS PERSONÆ.

MARK ANTONY,
OCTAVIUS CÆSAR, } triumvirs.
M. ÆMILIUS LEPIDUS,
SEXTUS POMPEIUS.

DOMITIUS ENOBARBUS,
VENTIDIUS,
EROS,
SCARUS, } friends to An-
DERCETAS, tony.
DEMETRIUS,
PHILO,

MECÆNAS,
AGRIPPA,
DOLABELLA, } friends to Cæsar.
PROCULEIUS,
THYREUS,
GALLUS,

MENAS,
MENECRATES, } friends to Pompey.
VARRIUS,

TAURUS, lieutenant-general to Cæsar.
CANIDIUS, lieutenant-general to Antony.
SILIUS, an officer in Ventidius's army.
EUPHRONIUS, an ambassador from Antony to
  Cæsar.
ALEXAS,
MARDIAN, a Eunuch, } attendants on Cleo-
SELEUCUS, patra.
DIOMEDES,
A Soothsayer.
A Clown.

CLEOPATRA, queen of Egypt.
OCTAVIA, sister to Cæsar and wife to Antony.
CHARMIAN, } attendants on Cleopatra.
IRAS,

Officers, Soldiers, Messengers, and other Attendants.

SCENE: *In several parts of the Roman empire.*

• *A bullet beside a text line indicates an annotation in the
opposite column.*

ACT I.

SCENE I. *Alexandria. A room in Cleopatra's
palace.*

Enter DEMETRIUS *and* PHILO.

Phi. Nay, but this dotage of our general's
O'erflows the measure: those his goodly eyes,
That o'er the files and musters of the war

Alexandria. Engraving from John Speed's *A Prospect
of the Most Famous Parts of the World,* 1631

Opposite: Antony and Cleopatra. Painting by Willem
Van Mieris (1662–1747)

473

8 *reneges*. Rejects. *temper*. Restraint.

16 *bourn*. Limit.

18 *Grates me*. It irritates me. *the sum*. Be brief.

28 *process*. Summons.

Antony: 'Let Rome in Tiber melt . . .' Drawing by John Masey Wright (1777–1866)

39 *weet*. Know.

Have glow'd like plated Mars, now bend, now
  turn,
The office and devotion of their view
Upon a tawny front: his captain's heart,
Which in the scuffles of great fights hath burst
• The buckles on his breast, reneges all temper,
And is become the bellows and the fan
To cool a gipsy's lust.

Flourish. Enter ANTONY, CLEOPATRA, *her
Ladies, the Train, with Eunuchs fanning her.*

                         Look, where they come: 10
Take but good note, and you shall see in him
The triple pillar of the world transform'd
Into a strumpet's fool: behold and see.
  Cleo. If it be love indeed, tell me how much.
  Ant. There's beggary in the love that can be
  reckon'd.
• *Cleo.* I'll set a bourn how far to be beloved.
  Ant. Then must thou needs find out new
  heaven, new earth.

          Enter an Attendant.

  Att. News, my good lord, from Rome.
• *Ant.*   Grates me: the sum.
  Cleo. Nay, hear them, Antony:
Fulvia perchance is angry; or, who knows   20
If the scarce-bearded Cæsar have not sent
His powerful mandate to you, 'Do this, or this;
Take in that kingdom, and enfranchise that:
Perform't, or else we damn thee.'
  Ant.   How, my love!
  Cleo. Perchance! nay, and most like:
You must not stay here longer, your dismission
Is come from Cæsar; therefore hear it, Antony.
• Where's Fulvia's process? Cæsar's I would say?
  both?
Call in the messengers. As I am Egypt's queen,
Thou blushest, Antony; and that blood of thine
Is Cæsar's homager: else so thy cheek pays
  shame   31
When shrill-tongued Fulvia scolds. The mes-
  sengers!
  Ant. Let Rome in Tiber melt, and the wide
  arch
Of the ranged empire fall! Here is my space.
Kingdoms are clay: our dungy earth alike
Feeds beast as man: the nobleness of life
Is to do thus; when such a mutual pair
                              [*Embracing.*
And such a twain can do't, in which I bind,
• On pain of punishment, the world to weet
We stand up peerless.
  Cleo.   Excellent falsehood!   40
Why did he marry Fulvia, and not love her?
I'll seem the fool I am not; Antony
Will be himself.
  Ant.   But stirr'd by Cleopatra.
Now, for the love of Love and her soft hours,
Let's not confound the time with conference
  harsh:
There's not a minute of our lives should stretch
Without some pleasure now. What sport to-night?
  Cleo. Hear the ambassadors.
  Ant.   Fie, wrangling queen!
Whom every thing becomes, to chide, to laugh,
To weep; whose every passion fully strives   50
To make itself, in thee, fair and admired!
No messenger, but thine; and all alone

To-night we'll wander through the streets and note
The qualities of people. Come, my queen;
Last night you did desire it: speak not to us.
  [*Exeunt Ant. and Cleo. with their train.*
 Dem. Is Cæsar with Antonius prized so slight?
 Phi. Sir, sometimes, when he is not Antony,
He comes too short of that great property
Which still should go with Antony.
 Dem.   I am full sorry
That he approves the common liar, who   60
Thus speaks of him at Rome: but I will hope
Of better deeds to-morrow. Rest you happy!
         [*Exeunt.*

SCENE II. *The same. Another room.*

Enter CHARMIAN, IRAS, ALEXAS, *and a* Soothsayer.

 Char. Lord Alexas, sweet Alexas, most any thing Alexas, almost most absolute Alexas, where's the soothsayer that you praised so to the queen? O, that I knew this husband, which, you say, must charge his horns with garlands!
 Alex. Soothsayer!
 Sooth. Your will?
 Char. Is this the man? Is't you, sir, that know things?
 Sooth. In nature's infinite book of secrecy A little I can read.
 Alex.   Show him your hand.   10

Enter ENOBARBUS.

 Eno. Bring in the banquet quickly; wine enough
Cleopatra's health to drink.
 Char. Good sir, give me good fortune.
 Sooth. I make not, but foresee.
 Char. Pray, then, foresee me one.
 Sooth. You shall be yet far fairer than you are.
 Char. He means in flesh.
 Iras. No, you shall paint when you are old.
 Char. Wrinkles forbid!
 Alex. Vex not his prescience; be attentive.
 Char. Hush!   21
 Sooth. You shall be more beloving than beloved.
 Char. I had rather heat my liver with drinking.
 Alex. Nay, hear him.
 Char. Good now, some excellent fortune! Let me be married to three kings in a forenoon, and widow them all: let me have a child at fifty, to whom Herod of Jewry may do homage: find me to marry me with Octavius Cæsar, and companion me with my mistress.   30
 Sooth. You shall outlive the lady whom you serve.
 Char. O excellent! I love long life better than figs.
 Sooth. You have seen and proved a fairer former fortune
Than that which is to approach.
 Char. Then belike my children shall have no names: prithee, how many boys and wenches must I have?
 Sooth. If every of your wishes had a womb, And fertile every wish, a million.
 Char. Out, fool! I forgive thee for a witch. 40

58 *property*. Quality.

Soothsayer: 'In nature's infinite book of secrecy A little I can read.' An Egyptian Zodiac, from a 19th century engraving

66 *go*. Walk.

Isis was the most important of the Egyptian goddesses and married her brother Osiris. Illustration from E. A. Wallis Budge's *The Gods of the Egyptians*, 1904

95 *the time's state*. The way things are now.

Alex. You think none but your sheets are privy to your wishes.

Char. Nay, come, tell Iras hers.

Alex. We'll know all our fortunes.

Eno. Mine, and most of our fortunes, to-night, shall be—drunk to bed.

Iras. There's a palm presages chastity, if nothing else.

Char. E'en as the o'erflowing Nilus presageth famine.   50

Iras. Go, you wild bedfellow, you cannot soothsay.

Char. Nay, if an oily palm be not a fruitful prognostication, I cannot scratch mine ear. Prithee, tell her but a worky-day fortune.

Sooth. Your fortunes are alike.

Iras. But how, but how? give me particulars.

Sooth. I have said.

Iras. Am I not an inch of fortune better than she?   60

Char. Well, if you were but an inch of fortune better than I, where would you choose it?

Iras. Not in my husband's nose.

Char. Our worser thoughts heavens mend! Alexas,—come, his fortune, his fortune! O, let him marry a woman that cannot go, sweet Isis, I beseech thee! and let her die too, and give him a worse! and let worse follow worse, till the worst of all follow him laughing to his grave, fifty-fold a cuckold! Good Isis, hear me this prayer, though thou deny me a matter of more weight; good Isis, I beseech thee!

Iras. Amen. Dear goddess, hear that prayer of the people! for, as it is a heart-breaking to see a handsome man loose-wived, so it is a deadly sorrow to behold a foul knave uncuckolded: therefore, dear Isis, keep decorum, and fortune him accordingly!

Char. Amen.   79

Alex. Lo, now, if it lay in their hands to make me a cuckold, they would make themselves whores, but they 'ld do 't!

Eno. Hush! here comes Antony.

Char.   Not he; the queen.

Enter CLEOPATRA.

Cleo. Saw you my lord?

Eno.   No, lady.

Cleo.   Was he not here?

Char. No, madam.

Cleo. He was disposed to mirth; but on the sudden
A Roman thought hath struck him. Enobarbus!

Eno. Madam?

Cleo. Seek him, and bring him hither. Where's Alexas?

Alex. Here, at your service. My lord approaches.   90

Cleo. We will not look upon him: go with us.
                                                                    [*Exeunt.*

Enter ANTONY *with a* Messenger *and* Attendants.

Mess. Fulvia thy wife first came into the field.

Ant. Against my brother Lucius?

Mess. Ay:
But soon that war had end, and the time 's state
Made friends of them, jointing their force 'gainst Cæsar;
Whose better issue in the war, from Italy,

Upon the first encounter, drave them.
Ant.   Well, what worst?
Mess. The nature of bad news infects the
teller.   99
Ant. When it concerns the fool or coward. On:
Things that are past are done with me. 'Tis thus;
Who tells me true, though in his tale lie death,
I hear him as he flatter'd.
Mess.   Labienus—
This is stiff news—hath, with his Parthian force,
• Extended Asia from Euphrates;
His conquering banner shook from Syria
To Lydia and to Ionia;
Whilst—
Ant. Antony, thou wouldst say,—
Mess.   O, my lord!
• *Ant.* Speak to me home, mince not the gene-
ral tongue:
Name Cleopatra as she is call'd in Rome;   110
Rail thou in Fulvia's phrase; and taunt my faults
With such full license as both truth and malice
Have power to utter. O, then we bring forth
weeds,
When our quick minds lie still; and our ills
told us
• Is as our earing. Fare thee well awhile.
Mess. At your noble pleasure.   [*Exit.*
Ant. From Sicyon, ho, the news! Speak
there!
First Att. The man from Sicyon,—is there
such an one?
Sec. Att. He stays upon your will.
Ant.   Let him appear.
These strong Egyptian fetters I must break, 120
Or lose myself in dotage.

Enter another Messenger.

                    What are you?
Sec. Mess. Fulvia thy wife is dead.
Ant.   Where died she?
Sec. Mess. In Sicyon:
Her length of sickness, with what else more
serious
Importeth thee to know, this bears.
                              [*Gives a letter.*
Ant.   Forbear me.
                              [*Exit Sec. Messenger.*
There's a great spirit gone! Thus did I de-
sire it:
What our contempt doth often hurl from us,
We wish it ours again; the present pleasure,
• By revolution lowering, does become   129
The opposite of itself: she's good, being gone;
The hand could pluck her back that shoved
her on.
I must from this enchanting queen break off:
Ten thousand harms, more than the ills I know,
My idleness doth hatch. How now! Enobarbus!

Re-enter ENOBARBUS.

Eno. What's your pleasure, sir?
Ant. I must with haste from hence.
Eno. Why, then, we kill all our women: we
see how mortal an unkindness is to them; if they
suffer our departure, death's the word.
Ant. I must be gone.   140
Eno. Under a compelling occasion, let women
die: it were pity to cast them away for nothing;
though, between them and a great cause, they

105 *Extended.* Seized.

109 *mince ... tongue.* Do not avoid the common
rumours.

115 *earing.* Ploughing.

129 *By ... lowering.* Being lowered on Fortune's wheel.

The Wheel of Fortune. Woodcut from Alexander
Barclay's *The Ship of Fools*, 1774

157 *Jove.* God of heaven.

187 *touches.* Matters.

Cneius Pompeius Magnus, known as Pompey the Great.
From a 19th century engraving

198 *For the main soldier.* As the leading general.

200 *courser.* Horse.

should be esteemed nothing. Cleopatra, catching but the least noise of this, dies instantly; I have seen her die twenty times upon far poorer moment: I do think there is mettle in death, which commits some loving act upon her, she hath such a celerity in dying.

Ant. She is cunning past man's thought. 150

Eno. Alack, sir, no; her passions are made of nothing but the finest part of pure love: we cannot call her winds and waters sighs and tears; they are greater storms and tempests than almanacs can report: this cannot be cunning in her; if it be, she makes a shower of rain as well ●as Jove.

Ant. Would I had never seen her!

Eno. O, sir, you had then left unseen a wonderful piece of work; which not to have been blest withal would have discredited your travel.

Ant. Fulvia is dead.

Eno. Sir?

Ant. Fulvia is dead.

Eno. Fulvia!

Ant. Dead.

Eno. Why, sir, give the gods a thankful sacrifice. When it pleaseth their deities to take the wife of a man from him, it shows to man the tailors of the earth; comforting therein, that when old robes are worn out, there are members to make new. If there were no more women but Fulvia, then had you indeed a cut, and the case to be lamented: this grief is crowned with consolation; your old smock brings forth a new petticoat: and indeed the tears live in an onion that should water this sorrow.

Ant. The business she hath broached in the state
Cannot endure my absence. 179

Eno. And the business you have broached here cannot be without you; especially that of Cleopatra's, which wholly depends on your abode.

Ant. No more light answers. Let our officers
Have notice what we purpose. I shall break
The cause of our expedience to the queen,
And get her leave to part. For not alone
●The death of Fulvia, with more urgent touches,
Do strongly speak to us; but the letters too
Of many our contriving friends in Rome
Petition us at home: Sextus Pompeius 190
Hath given the dare to Cæsar, and commands
The empire of the sea: our slippery people,
Whose love is never link'd to the deserver
Till his deserts are past, begin to throw
Pompey the Great and all his dignities
Upon his son; who, high in name and power,
Higher than both in blood and life, stands up
●For the main soldier: whose quality, going on,
The sides o' the world may danger: much is
    breeding, 199
●Which, like the courser's hair, hath yet but life,
And not a serpent's poison. Say, our pleasure,
To such whose place is under us, requires
Our quick remove from hence.

Eno. I shall do't. [*Exeunt.*

SCENE III. *The same. Another room.*

Enter CLEOPATRA, CHARMIAN, IRAS, *and* ALEXAS.

Cleo. Where is he?

Char.   I did not see him since.

Cleo.   See where he is, who's with him, what
he does:
I did not send you: if you find him sad,
Say I am dancing; if in mirth, report
That I am sudden sick: quick, and return.
                                [*Exit Alexas.*

Char.   Madam, methinks, if you did love him
dearly,
You do not hold the method to enforce
The like from him.

Cleo.   What should I do, I do not?

Char.   In each thing give him way, cross him
in nothing.

Cleo.   Thou teachest like a fool; the way to
lose him.   10

Char.   Tempt him not so too far; I wish,
forbear:
In time we hate that which we often fear.
But here comes Antony.

Enter ANTONY.

Cleo.   I am sick and sullen.

Ant.   I am sorry to give breathing to my
purpose,—

Cleo.   Help me away, dear Charmian; I shall
fall:

● It cannot be thus long, the sides of nature
Will not sustain it.

Ant.   Now, my dearest queen,—

Cleo.   Pray you, stand farther from me.

Ant.   What's the matter?

Cleo.   I know, by that same eye, there's some
good news.
What says the married woman? You may go: 20
Would she had never given you leave to come!
Let her not say 'tis I that keep you here:
I have no power upon you; hers you are.

Ant   The gods best know,—

Cleo.   O, never was there queen
So mightily betray'd! yet at the first
I saw the treasons planted.

Ant.   Cleopatra,—

Cleo.   Why should I think you can be mine
and true,
Though you in swearing shake the throned gods,
Who have been false to Fulvia? Riotous mad-
ness,
To be entangled with those mouth-made vows, 30
Which break themselves in swearing!

Ant.   Most sweet queen,—

Cleo.   Nay, pray you, seek no colour for your
going,
● But bid farewell, and go: when you sued
staying,
Then was the time for words: no going then;
Eternity was in our lips and eyes,
Bliss in our brows' bent; none our parts so poor,
● But was a race of heaven: they are so still,
Or thou, the greatest soldier of the world,
Art turn'd the greatest liar.

Ant.   How now, lady!

Cleo.   I would I had thy inches; thou shouldst
know   40
There were a heart in Egypt.

Ant.   Hear me, queen:
The strong necessity of time commands
Our services awhile; but my full heart
Remains in use with you.   Our Italy

16 *sides of nature.* Human body.

Cleopatra: '. . . seek no colour for your going, But bid farewell, and go:' Ellen Wallis as Cleopatra, Theatre Royal, Drury Lane, London, 1873

33 *sued staying.* Begged to stay with me.

37 *a race of.* i.e. sent from.

Cleopatra. Painting from the Fontainebleau School, 16th century

---

48 *scrupulous*. Over trifles.

61 *garboils*. Brawls.

69 *Nilus*. The Nile.

81 *meetly*. Most suitable.

85 *carriage of his chafe*. The course of his anger.

Shines o'er with civil swords: Sextus Pompeius
Makes his approaches to the port of Rome:
Equality of two domestic powers
●Breed scrupulous faction: the hated, grown to
        strength,
Are newly grown to love: the condemn'd Pompey,
Rich in his father's honour, creeps apace   50
Into the hearts of such as have not thrived
Upon the present state, whose numbers threaten;
And quietness, grown sick of rest, would purge
By any desperate change: my more particular,
And that which most with you should safe my
        going,
Is Fulvia's death.
    Cleo.   Though age from folly could not give
        me freedom,
It does from childishness: can Fulvia die?
    Ant.   She's dead, my queen:
Look here, and at thy sovereign leisure read   60
●The garboils she awaked; at the last, best:
See when and where she died.
    Cleo.   O most false love!
Where be the sacred vials thou shouldst fill
With sorrowful water?   Now I see, I see,
In Fulvia's death, how mine received shall be.
    Ant.   Quarrel no more, but be prepared to
        know
The purposes I bear; which are, or cease,
As you shall give the advice.   By the fire
●That quickens Nilus' slime, I go from hence
Thy soldier, servant; making peace or war   70
As thou affect'st.
    Cleo.   Cut my lace, Charmian, come;
But let it be: I am quickly ill, and well,
So Antony loves.
    Ant.   My precious queen, forbear;
And give true evidence to his love, which stands
An honourable trial.
    Cleo.   So Fulvia told me.
I prithee, turn aside and weep for her;
Then bid adieu to me, and say the tears
Belong to Egypt: good now, play one scene
Of excellent dissembling; and let it look
Like perfect honour.
    Ant.   You'll heat my blood: no more.   80
● *Cleo.* You can do better yet; but this is
        meetly.
    Ant.   Now, by my sword,—
    Cleo.   And target.   Still he mends;
But this is not the best.   Look, prithee, Char-
        mian,
How this Herculean Roman does become
●The carriage of his chafe.
    Ant.   I'll leave you, lady.
    Cleo.   Courteous lord, one word.
Sir, you and I must part, but that's not it:
Sir, you and I have loved, but there's not it;
That you know well: something it is I would,—
O, my oblivion is a very Antony,   90
And I am all forgotten.
    Ant.   But that your royalty
Holds idleness your subject, I should take you
For idleness itself.
    Cleo.   'Tis sweating labour
To bear such idleness so near the heart
As Cleopatra this.   But, sir, forgive me;
Since my becomings kill me, when they do not
Eye well to you: your honour calls you hence;
Therefore be deaf to my unpitied folly,

And all the gods go with you! upon your sword
Sit laurel victory! and smooth success   100
Be strew'd before your feet!
   Ant.   Let us go. Come;
Our separation so abides, and flies,
That thou, residing here, go'st yet with me,
And I, hence fleeting, here remain with thee.
Away!   *[Exeunt.*

   SCENE IV.   *Rome. Cæsar's house.*

  Enter OCTAVIUS CÆSAR, *reading a letter*,
    LEPIDUS, *and their* Train.

  Cæs. You may see, Lepidus, and henceforth
   know,
It is not Cæsar's natural vice to hate
Our great competitor: from Alexandria
This is the news: he fishes, drinks, and wastes
The lamps of night in revel; is not more manlike
Than Cleopatra; nor the queen of Ptolemy
More womanly than he; hardly gave audience, or
Vouchsafed to think he had partners: you shall
   find there
A man who is the abstract of all faults
That all men follow.
  Lep.   I must not think there are   10
Evils enow to darken all his goodness:
His faults in him seem as the spots of heaven,
More fiery by night's blackness; hereditary,
Rather than purchased; what he cannot change,
Than what he chooses.
  Cæs.   You are too indulgent. Let us grant, it
   is not
Amiss to tumble on the bed of Ptolemy;
To give a kingdom for a mirth; to sit
And keep the turn of tippling with a slave;   19
To reel the streets at noon, and stand the buffet
With knaves that smell of sweat: say this becomes
   him,—
As his composure must be rare indeed
Whom these things cannot blemish,—yet must
   Antony
No way excuse his soils, when we do bear
So great weight in his lightness. If he fill'd
His vacancy with his voluptuousness,
Full surfeits, and the dryness of his bones,
Call on him for't: but to confound such time,
That drums him from his sport, and speaks as
   loud
As his own state and ours,—'tis to be chid   30
As we rate boys, who, being mature in know-
   ledge,
Pawn their experience to their present pleasure,
And so rebel to judgement.

      Enter a Messenger.

  Lep.   Here's more news.
  Mess. Thy biddings have been done; and
   every hour,
Most noble Cæsar, shalt thou have report
How 'tis abroad. Pompey is strong at sea;
And it appears he is beloved of those
That only have fear'd Cæsar: to the ports
The discontents repair, and men's reports
Give him much wrong'd.
  Cæs.   I should have known no less.
It hath been taught us from the primal state, 41
That he which is was wish'd until he were;

Cleopatra: 'And all the gods go with you! upon your
sword Sit laurel victory!' Constance Collier as Cleopatra
and H. Beerbohm Tree as Antony, His Majesty's
Theatre, London, 1906

---

6 *queen of Ptolemy*. i.e. Cleopatra.

19 *keep . . . tippling*. Take turns tippling.

20 *stand the buffet*. Exchange blows.

22 *composure*. Character.

28 *confound*. Waste.

30 *state*. Position.

31 *rate*. Scold.

41 *from the primal state*. Since government began.

43 *ebb'd man.* Man left behind by fortune.

45 *flag.* Reed.

46 *lackeying.* Following obsequiously.

49 *ear.* Plough.

62 *stale.* Urine. *gilded.* Golden.

71 *So . . . not.* Did not even become thin.

4 *mandragora.* A narcotic drug.

Cleopatra: 'That I might sleep out this great gap of time My Antony is away.' Lily Langtry as Cleopatra, Princess's Theatre, London, 1890

●And the ebb'd man, ne'er loved till ne'er worth love,
Comes dear'd by being lack'd.   This common body,
●Like to a vagabond flag upon the stream,
●Goes to and back, lackeying the varying tide,
To rot itself with motion.
   Mess.   Cæsar, I bring thee word,
Menecrates and Menas, famous pirates,
●Make the sea serve them, which they ear and wound
With keels of every kind: many hot inroads   50
They make in Italy; the borders maritime
Lack blood to think on't, and flush youth revolt:
No vessel can peep forth, but 'tis as soon
Taken as seen; for Pompey's name strikes more
Than could his war resisted.
   Cæs.   Antony,
Leave thy lascivious wassails.   When thou once
Wast beaten from Modena, where thou slew'st
Hirtius and Pansa, consuls, at thy heel
Did famine follow; whom thou fought'st against,
Though daintily brought up, with patience more
Than savages could suffer: thou didst drink   61
●The stale of horses, and the gilded puddle
Which beasts would cough at: thy palate then did deign
The roughest berry on the rudest hedge;
Yea, like the stag, when snow the pasture sheets,
The barks of trees thou browsed'st; on the Alps
It is reported thou didst eat strange flesh,
Which some did die to look on: and all this—
It wounds thine honour that I speak it now—
Was borne so like a soldier, that thy cheek   70
●So much as lank'd not.
   Lep.   'Tis pity of him.
   Cæs.   Let his shames quickly
Drive him to Rome: 'tis time we twain
Did show ourselves i' the field; and to that end
Assemble we immediate council: Pompey
Thrives in our idleness.
   Lep.   To-morrow, Cæsar,
I shall be furnish'd to inform you rightly
Both what by sea and land I can be able
To front this present time.
   Cæs.   Till which encounter,
It is my business too.   Farewell.   80
   Lep.   Farewell, my lord: what you shall know meantime
Of stirs abroad, I shall beseech you, sir,
To let me be partaker.
   Cæs.   Doubt not, sir;
I knew it for my bond.   [*Exeunt.*

SCENE V.   *Alexandria.   Cleopatra's palace.*

Enter CLEOPATRA, CHARMIAN, IRAS, *and*
MARDIAN.

   Cleo.   Charmian!
   Char.   Madam?
   Cleo.   Ha, ha!
●Give me to drink mandragora.
   Char.   Why, madam?
   Cleo.   That I might sleep out this great gap of time
My Antony is away.
   Char.   You think of him too much.
   Cleo.   O, 'tis treason!
   Char.   Madam, I trust, not so.

Cleo. Thou, eunuch Mardian !

Mar.   What's your highness' pleasure ?

Cleo. Not now to hear thee sing ; I take no pleasure

In aught an eunuch has : 'tis well for thee,   10

● That, being unseminar'd, thy freer thoughts

May not fly forth of Egypt. Hast thou affections ?

Mar. Yes, gracious madam.

Cleo. Indeed !

Mar. Not in deed, madam ; for I can do nothing

But what indeed is honest to be done :

Yet have I fierce affections, and think

What Venus did with Mars.

Cleo.   O Charmian,

Where think'st thou he is now ? Stands he, or sits he ?

Or does he walk ? or is he on his horse ?   20

O happy horse, to bear the weight of Antony !

● Do bravely, horse ! for wot'st thou whom thou movest ?

The demi-Atlas of this earth, the arm

● And burgonet of men. He's speaking now,

Or murmuring 'Where's my serpent of old Nile ?'

For so he calls me : now I feed myself

With most delicious poison. Think on me,

● That am with Phœbus' amorous pinches black,

And wrinkled deep in time ? Broad-fronted Cæsar,

When thou wast here above the ground, I was   30

A morsel for a monarch : and great Pompey

Would stand and make his eyes grow in my brow ;

There would he anchor his aspect and die

With looking on his life.

Enter ALEXAS.

Alex.   Sovereign of Egypt, hail !

Cleo. How much unlike art thou Mark Antony !

Yet, coming from him, that great medicine hath

With his tinct gilded thee.

How goes it with my brave Mark Antony ?

Alex. Last thing he did, dear queen,   39

He kiss'd,—the last of many doubled kisses,—

This orient pearl. His speech sticks in my heart.

Cleo. Mine ear must pluck it thence.

Alex.   'Good friend,' quoth he,

'Say, the firm Roman to great Egypt sends

This treasure of an oyster ; at whose foot,

● To mend the petty present, I will piece

Her opulent throne with kingdoms ; all the east,

Say thou, shall call her mistress.' So he nodded,

● †And soberly did mount an arm-gaunt steed,

Who neigh'd so high, that what I would have spoke

Was beastly dumb'd by him.

Cleo.   What, was he sad or merry ? 50

Alex. Like to the time o' the year between the extremes

Of hot and cold, he was nor sad nor merry.

Cleo. O well-divided disposition ! Note him,

Note him, good Charmian, 'tis the man ; but note him :

He was not sad, for he would shine on those

That make their looks by his ; he was not merry,

Which seem'd to tell them his remembrance lay

In Egypt with his joy ; but between both :

O heavenly mingle ! Be'st thou sad or merry,

The violence of either thee becomes,   60

11 *unseminar'd.* Unsexed.

22 *wot'st.* Knowest.

Atlas holding the heavens on his shoulders. French engraving of the 17th century

24 *burgonet.* Helmet.

28 *Phœbus.* Sun-god.

Russell Waters as Alexas and Mary Newcombe as Cleopatra, Old Vic Theatre, London, 1934

45 *piece.* Decorate.

48 *arm-gaunt.* Stiffly caparisoned.

63 *thick.* Many.

Charmian: 'O that brave Cæsar!' Engraving from a Roman medal from G. du Choul's *Discours de la Religion des Anciens Romains*, 1567

21 *Salt.* Lascivious. *waned.* Faded.

27 *Lethe'd.* i.e. forgetful.

So does it no man else.   Met'st thou my posts?
  Alex. Ay, madam, twenty several messengers:
Why do you send so thick?
  Cleo.   Who's born that day
When I forget to send to Antony,
Shall die a beggar.   Ink and paper, Charmian.
Welcome, my good Alexas.   Did I, Charmian,
Ever love Cæsar so?
  Char.   O that brave Cæsar!
  Cleo. Be choked with such another emphasis!
Say, the brave Antony.
  Char.   The valiant Cæsar!
  Cleo. By Isis, I will give thee bloody teeth,
If thou with Cæsar paragon again   71
My man of men.
  Char.   By your most gracious pardon,
I sing but after you.
  Cleo.   My salad days,
When I was green in judgement: cold in blood,
To say as I said then!   But, come, away;
Get me ink and paper:
He shall have every day a several greeting,
Or I'll unpeople Egypt.   [*Exeunt.*

ACT II.

Scene I. *Messina.   Pompey's house.*

Enter Pompey, Menecrates, *and* Menas,
in warlike manner.

  Pom. If the great gods be just, they shall assist
The deeds of justest men.
  Mene.   Know, worthy Pompey,
That what they do delay, they not deny.
  Pom. Whiles we are suitors to their throne, decays
The thing we sue for.
  Mene.   We, ignorant of ourselves,
Beg often our own harms, which the wise powers
Deny us for our good; so find we profit
By losing of our prayers.
  Pom.   I shall do well:
The people love me, and the sea is mine;
My powers are crescent, and my auguring hope
Says it will come to the full.   Mark Antony   11
In Egypt sits at dinner, and will make
No wars without doors: Cæsar gets money where
He loses hearts: Lepidus flatters both,
Of both is flatter'd; but he neither loves,
Nor either cares for him.
  Men.   Cæsar and Lepidus
Are in the field: a mighty strength they carry.
  Pom. Where have you this? 'tis false.
  Men.   From Silvius, sir.
  Pom. He dreams: I know they are in Rome together,
Looking for Antony.   But all the charms of love,
Salt Cleopatra, soften thy waned lip!   21
Let witchcraft join with beauty, lust with both!
Tie up the libertine in a field of feasts,
Keep his brain fuming; Epicurean cooks
Sharpen with cloyless sauce his appetite;
That sleep and feeding may prorogue his honour
Even till a Lethe'd dulness!

Enter Varrius.

            How now, Varrius!
  Var. This is most certain that I shall deliver:

Mark Antony is every hour in Rome
Expected: since he went from Egypt 'tis   30
A space for further travel.
   Pom.   I could have given less matter
A better ear.   Menas, I did not think
This amorous surfeiter would have donn'd his
   helm
For such a petty war: his soldiership
Is twice the other twain: but let us rear
The higher our opinion, that our stirring
Can from the lap of Egypt's widow pluck
The ne'er-lust-wearied Antony.
   Men.   I cannot hope
Cæsar and Antony shall well greet together:
His wife that's dead did trespasses to Cæsar;
His brother warr'd upon him; although, I think,
Not moved by Antony.
   Pom.   I know not, Menas,
How lesser enmities may give way to greater.
Were't not that we stand up against them all,
'Twere pregnant they should square between
   themselves;
For they have entertained cause enough
To draw their swords: but how the fear of us
May cement their divisions and bind up
The petty difference, we yet not know.
Be't as our gods will have't!   It only stands   50
Our lives upon to use our strongest hands.
Come, Menas.   *[Exeunt.*

   SCENE II.   *Rome.   The house of Lepidus.*

     Enter ENOBARBUS *and* LEPIDUS.

   Lep.   Good Enobarbus, 'tis a worthy deed,
And shall become you well, to entreat your cap-
   tain
To soft and gentle speech.
   Eno.   I shall entreat him
To answer like himself: if Cæsar move him,
Let Antony look over Cæsar's head
And speak as loud as Mars.   By Jupiter,
Were I the wearer of Antonius' beard,
I would not shave't to-day.
   Lep.   'Tis not a time
For private stomaching.
   Eno.   Every time
Serves for the matter that is then born in't.   10
   Lep.   But small to greater matters must give
   way.
   Eno.   Not if the small come first.
   Lep.   Your speech is passion:
But, pray you, stir no embers up.   Here comes
The noble Antony.

     Enter ANTONY *and* VENTIDIUS.

   Eno.   And yonder, Cæsar.

     Enter CÆSAR, MECÆNAS, *and* AGRIPPA.

   Ant.   If we compose well here, to Parthia:
Hark, Ventidius.
   Cæs.   I do not know,
Mecænas; ask Agrippa.
   Lep.   Noble friends,
That which combined us was most great, and let
   not
A leaner action rend us.   What's amiss,
May it be gently heard: when we debate   20
Our trivial difference loud, we do commit
Murder in healing wounds: then, noble partners,
The rather, for I earnestly beseech,

45 *pregnant.* Likely.

4 *move.* Anger.

6 *Mars.* God of war.

Mars. Engraving from a Roman medal from G. du Choul's *Discours de la Religion des Anciens Romains*, 1567

9 *stomaching.* Resentment.

25 *Nor . . . matter.* Nor let ill temper make matters worse.

39 *practise.* Conspire against.

63 *snaffle.* A bridle-bit.

Costume design for Antony by J. Gower Parks, Stratford-upon-Avon, 1945

Touch you the sourest points with sweetest terms,
● Nor curstness grow to the matter.
    Ant.   'Tis spoken well.
Were we before our armies, and to fight,
I should do thus.   [*Flourish.*
    Cæs. Welcome to Rome.
    Ant.   Thank you.
    Cæs.   Sit.
    Ant.   Sit, sir.
    Cæs.   Nay, then.
    Ant. I learn, you take things ill which are
      not so,
Or being, concern you not.
    Cæs.   I must be laugh'd at, 30
If, or for nothing or a little, I
Should say myself offended, and with you
Chiefly i' the world; more laugh'd at, that I
    should
Once name you derogately, when to sound your
    name
It not concern'd me.
    Ant.   My being in Egypt, Cæsar,
What was't to you?
    Cæs. No more than my residing here at Rome
Might be to you in Egypt: yet, if you there
● Did practise on my state, your being in Egypt
Might be my question.
    Ant.   How intend you, practised? 40
    Cæs. You may be pleased to catch at mine
    intent
By what did here befal me. Your wife and bro-
    ther
Made wars upon me; and their contestation
Was theme for you, you were the word of war.
    Ant. You do mistake your business; my bro-
    ther never
Did urge me in his act: I did inquire it;
And have my learning from some true reports,
That drew their swords with you. Did he not
    rather
Discredit my authority with yours;
And make the wars alike against my stomach, 50
Having alike your cause? Of this my letters
Before did satisfy you. If you'll patch a quarrel,
As matter whole you have not to make it with,
It must not be with this.
    Cæs.   You praise yourself
By laying defects of judgement to me; but
You patch'd up your excuses.
    Ant.   Not so, not so;
I know you could not lack, I am certain on't,
Very necessity of this thought, that I,
Your partner in the cause 'gainst which he fought,
Could not with graceful eyes attend those wars 60
Which fronted mine own peace. As for my wife,
I would you had her spirit in such another:
● The third o' the world is yours; which with a
    snaffle
You may pace easy, but not such a wife.
    Eno. Would we had all such wives, that the
men might go to wars with the women!
    Ant. So much uncurbable, her garboils,
    Cæsar,
Made out of her impatience, which not wanted
Shrewdness of policy too, I grieving grant
Did you too much disquiet: for that you must 70
But say, I could not help it.
    Cæs.   I wrote to you
When rioting in Alexandria; you

Did pocket up my letters, and with taunts
● Did gibe my missive out of audience.
 Ant.   Sir,
He fell upon me ere admitted: then
Three kings I had newly feasted, and did want
Of what I was i' the morning: but next day
I told him of myself; which was as much
As to have ask'd him pardon.   Let this fellow
Be nothing of our strife; if we contend,   80
Out of our question wipe him.
 Cæs.   You have broken
The article of your oath; which you shall never
Have tongue to charge me with.
 Lep.   Soft, Cæsar!
 Ant.   No,
Lepidus, let him speak:
The honour is sacred which he talks on now,
Supposing that I lack'd it.   But, on, Cæsar;
The article of my oath.
 Cæs. To lend me arms and aid when I required
    them;
The which you both denied.
 Ant.   Neglected, rather;
And then when poison'd hours had bound me up 90
From mine own knowledge.   As nearly as I may,
I 'll play the penitent to you: but mine honesty
Shall not make poor my greatness, nor my power
Work without it.   Truth is, that Fulvia,
To have me out of Egypt, made wars here,
For which myself, the ignorant motive, do
So far ask pardon as befits mine honour
To stoop in such a case.
 Lep.   'Tis noble spoken.
 Mec. If it might please you, to enforce no
    further
The griefs between ye: to forget them quite 100
Were to remember that the present need
● Speaks to atone you.
 Lep.   Worthily spoken, Mecænas.
 Eno. Or, if you borrow one another's love
for the instant, you may, when you hear no more
words of Pompey, return it again: you shall
have time to wrangle in when you have nothing
else to do.
 Ant. Thou art a soldier only: speak no more.
 Eno. That truth should be silent I had almost
forgot.   110
 Ant. You wrong this presence; therefore
    speak no more.
● *Eno.* Go to, then; your considerate stone.
 Cæs. I do not much dislike the matter, but
The manner of his speech; for't cannot be
We shall remain in friendship, our conditions
So differing in their acts.   Yet, if I knew
What hoop should hold us stanch, from edge to
    edge
O' the world I would pursue it.
 Agr.   Give me leave, Cæsar,—
 Cæs. Speak, Agrippa.
 Agr. Thou hast a sister by the mother's side,
Admired Octavia: great Mark Antony   121
Is now a widower.
 Cæs.   Say not so, Agrippa:
If Cleopatra heard you, your reproof
Were well deserved of rashness.
 Ant. I am not married, Cæsar: let me hear
Agrippa further speak.
 Agr. To hold you in perpetual amity,
To make you brothers, and to knit your hearts

74 *missive.* Messenger.

102 *atone.* Unite.

112 *your . . . stone.* i.e. silent though considering.

Lepidus, a member of the Second Triumvirate with Mark Antony and Octavius, but ousted in 36 B.C. Engraving from P. J. Mariette's *Traité des Pierres Gravées*, 1750

166 *fame.* Report.

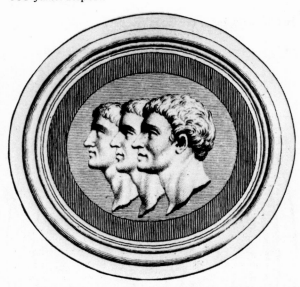

The Second Triumvirate, Mark Antony, Lepidus and Octavius who seized power after the murder of Caesar in 43 BC Engraving from P. J. Mariette's *Traité des Pierres Gravées*, 1750

With an unslipping knot, take Antony
Octavia to his wife; whose beauty claims   130
No worse a husband than the best of men;
Whose virtue and whose general graces speak
That which none else can utter.   By this mar-
     riage,
All little jealousies, which now seem great,
And all great fears, which now import their
     dangers,
Would then be nothing: truths would be tales,
Where now half tales be truths: her love to both
Would, each to other and all loves to both,
Draw after her.   Pardon what I have spoke;
For 'tis a studied, not a present thought,   140
By duty ruminated.
     Ant.   Will Cæsar speak?
     Cæs.   Not till he hears how Antony is touch'd
With what is spoke already.
     Ant.   What power is in Agrippa,
If I would say, 'Agrippa, be it so,'
To make this good?
     Cæs.   The power of Cæsar, and
His power unto Octavia.
     Ant.   May I never
To this good purpose, that so fairly shows,
Dream of impediment!   Let me have thy hand:
Further this act of grace; and from this hour
The heart of brothers govern in our loves   150
And sway our great designs!
     Cæs.   There is my hand.
A sister I bequeath you, whom no brother
Did ever love so dearly: let her live
To join our kingdoms and our hearts; and never
Fly off our loves again!
     Lep.   Happily, amen!
     Ant.   I did not think to draw my sword
     'gainst Pompey;
For he hath laid strange courtesies and great
Of late upon me: I must thank him only,
Lest my remembrance suffer ill report;
At heel of that, defy him.
     Lep.   Time calls upon's: 160
Of us must Pompey presently be sought,
Or else he seeks out us.
     Ant.   Where lies he?
     Cæs.   About the mount Misenum.
     Ant.   What is his strength by land?
     Cæs.   Great and increasing: but by sea
●He is an absolute master.
     Ant   So is the fame.
Would we had spoke together!   Haste we for it:
Yet, ere we put ourselves in arms, dispatch we
The business we have talk'd of.
     Cæs   With most gladness:
And do invite you to my sister's view,   170
Whither straight I'll lead you.
     Ant.   Let us, Lepidus,
Not lack your company.
     Lep.   Noble Antony,
Not sickness should detain me.
               [*Flourish.   Exeunt Cæsar, Antony,
                         and Lepidus.*
     Mec.   Welcome from Egypt, sir.
     Eno.   Half the heart of Cæsar, worthy Mecæ-
nas!   My honourable friend, Agrippa!
     Agr.   Good Enobarbus!
     Mec.   We have cause to be glad that matters
are so well digested.   You stayed well by 't in
Egypt.   180

Eno. Ay, sir; we did sleep day out of countenance, and made the night light with drinking.

Mec. Eight wild-boars roasted whole at a
breakfast, and but twelve persons there; is this
true?

Eno. This was but as a fly by an eagle: we
had much more monstrous matter of feast, which
worthily deserved noting.

Mec. She's a most triumphant lady, if report
be square to her.   190

Eno. When she first met Mark Antony, she
pursed up his heart, upon the river of Cydnus.

Agr. There she appeared indeed; or my reporter devised well for her.

Eno. I will tell you.
The barge she sat in, like a burnish'd throne,
Burn'd on the water: the poop was beaten gold;
Purple the sails, and so perfumed that
The winds were love-sick with them; the oars
          were silver,
Which to the tune of flutes kept stroke, and made
The water which they beat to follow faster,   201
As amorous of their strokes. For her own person,
It beggar'd all description: she did lie
In her pavilion—cloth-of-gold of tissue—
O'er-picturing that Venus where we see
The fancy outwork nature: on each side her
Stood pretty dimpled boys, like smiling Cupids,
With divers-colour'd fans, whose wind did seem
To glow the delicate cheeks which they did cool,
And what they undid did.

Agr.   O, rare for Antony!   210

Eno. Her gentlewomen, like the Nereides,
So many mermaids, tended her i' the eyes,
And made their bends adornings: at the helm
A seeming mermaid steers: the silken tackle
Swell with the touches of those flower-soft hands,
That yarely frame the office.   From the barge
A strange invisible perfume hits the sense
Of the adjacent wharfs.   The city cast
Her people out upon her; and Antony,
Enthroned i' the market-place, did sit alone,   220
Whistling to the air; which, but for vacancy,
Had gone to gaze on Cleopatra too
And made a gap in nature.

Agr.   Rare Egyptian!

Eno. Upon her landing, Antony sent to her,
Invited her to supper: she replied,
It should be better he became her guest;
Which she entreated: our courteous Antony,
Whom ne'er the word of 'No' woman heard
          speak,
Being barber'd ten times o'er, goes to the feast,
And for his ordinary pays his heart   230
For what his eyes eat only.

Agr.   Royal wench!
She made great Cæsar lay his sword to bed:
He plough'd her, and she cropp'd.

Eno.   I saw her once
Hop forty paces through the public street;
And having lost her breath, she spoke, and panted,
That she did make defect perfection,
And, breathless, power breathe forth.

Mec. Now Antony must leave her utterly.

Eno. Never; he will not:
Age cannot wither her, nor custom stale   240
Her infinite variety: other women cloy
The appetites they feed: but she makes hungry
Where most she satisfies: for vilest things

Enobarbus: 'The barge she sat in, like a burnished
throne, Burn'd on the water . . .' Engraving from an
Egyptian tomb painting at Thebes by F. W. Fairholt
from J. O. Halliwell's edition of Shakespeare's works,
1853–1865

211 *Nereides.* Legendary sea nymphs.

216 *yarely.* Nimbly. *frame the office.* Perform their task.

230 *ordinary.* Meal.

233 *cropp'd.* i.e. bore a son.

245 *riggish.* Wanton.

248 *lottery.* Prize.

6 *I . . . square.* I have not always kept to the straight and narrow path.

13 *motion.* Mind.

22 *a fear.* Frightened.

38 *inhoop'd.* Forced to fight.

Antony: 'and his quails ever beat mine . . .' Engraving from a Chinese miniature by F. W. Fairholt from J. O. Halliwell's edition of Shakespeare's works, 1853–1865

Become themselves in her; that the holy priests
●Bless her when she is riggish.
   Mec. If beauty, wisdom, modesty, can settle
The heart of Antony, Octavia is
●A blessed lottery to him.
   Agr.   Let us go.
Good Enobarbus, make yourself my guest   **249**
Whilst you abide here.
   Eno.   Humbly, sir, I thank you. [*Exeunt.*

SCENE III.   *The same.   Cæsar's house.*

Enter ANTONY, CÆSAR, OCTAVIA *between them,
and* Attendants.

   Ant. The world and my great office will some-
      times
Divide me from your bosom.
   Octa.   All which time
Before the gods my knee shall bow my prayers
To them for you.
   Ant.   Good night, sir.   My Octavia,
Read not my blemishes in the world's report:
●I have not kept my square; but that to come
Shall all be done by the rule.   Good night, dear
     lady.
Good night, sir.
   Cæs. Good night.
          [*Exeunt Cæsar and Octavia.*

Enter Soothsayer.

   Ant. Now, sirrah; you do wish yourself in
     Egypt?   **10**
   Sooth. Would I had never come from thence,
     nor you
Thither!
   Ant. If you can, your reason?
   Sooth.   I see it in
●My motion, have it not in my tongue: but yet
Hie you to Egypt again.
   Ant.   Say to me,
Whose fortunes shall rise higher, Cæsar's or mine?
   Sooth. Cæsar's.
Therefore, O Antony, stay not by his side:
Thy demon, that's thy spirit which keeps thee, is
Noble, courageous, high, unmatchable,   **20**
Where Cæsar's is not; but, near him, thy angel
●Becomes a fear, as being o'erpower'd: therefore
Make space enough between you.
   Ant.   Speak this no more.
   Sooth. To none but thee; no more, but when
     to thee.
If thou dost play with him at any game,
Thou art sure to lose; and, of that natural luck,
He beats thee 'gainst the odds: thy lustre
     thickens,
When he shines by: I say again, thy spirit
Is all afraid to govern thee near him;
But, he away, 'tis noble.
   Ant.   Get thee gone: **30**
Say to Ventidius I would speak with him:
          [*Exit Soothsayer.*
He shall to Parthia.   Be it art or hap,
He hath spoken true: the very dice obey him;
And in our sports my better cunning faints
Under his chance: if we draw lots, he speeds;
His cocks do win the battle still of mine,
When it is all to nought; and his quails ever
●Beat mine, inhoop'd, at odds.   I will to Egypt:

And though I make this marriage for my peace,
I' the east my pleasure lies.

Enter VENTIDIUS.

O, come, Ventidius, 40
You must to Parthia: your commission 's ready;
Follow me, and receive 't.   [*Exeunt.*

SCENE IV. *The same. A street.*

Enter LEPIDUS, MECÆNAS, *and* AGRIPPA.

Lep. Trouble yourselves no further: pray you,
    hasten
Your generals after.
    Agr.   Sir, Mark Antony
Will e'en but kiss Octavia, and we 'll follow.
    Lep. Till I shall see you in your soldier's
    dress,
Which will become you both, farewell.
    Mec.   We shall,
As I conceive the journey, be at the Mount
Before you, Lepidus.
    Lep.   Your way is shorter;
My purposes do draw me much about:
You 'll win two days upon me.
    Mec. }
    Agr. }   Sir, good success!
    Lep. Farewell.   [*Exeunt.* 10

SCENE V. *Alexandria. Cleopatra's palace.*

Enter CLEOPATRA, CHARMIAN, IRAS, *and*
    ALEXAS.

Cleo. Give me some music; music, moody food
Of us that trade in love.
    Attend.   The music, ho!

Enter MARDIAN *the Eunuch.*

Cleo. Let it alone; let's to billiards: come,
    Charmian.
    Char. My arm is sore; best play with Mardian.
    Cleo. As well a woman with an eunuch play'd
As with a woman. Come, you 'll play with me,
    sir?
    Mar. As well as I can, madam.
    Cleo. And when good will is show'd, though 't
    come too short,
The actor may plead pardon. I 'll none now:
●Give me mine angle; we 'll to the river: there,
My music playing far off, I will betray   11
Tawny-finn'd fishes; my bended hook shall pierce
Their slimy jaws; and, as I draw them up,
I 'll think them every one an Antony,
And say 'Ah, ha! you 're caught.'
    Char.   'Twas merry when
You wager'd on your angling; when your diver
Did hang a salt-fish on his hook, which he
With fervency drew up.
    Cleo.   That time,—O times!—
I laugh'd him out of patience; and that night
I laugh'd him into patience: and next morn, 20
Ere the ninth hour, I drunk him to his bed;
●Then put my tires and mantles on him, whilst
I wore his sword Philippan.

Enter a Messenger.

O, from Italy!
Ram thou thy fruitful tidings in mine ears,
That long time have been barren.

10 *angle.* Fishing tackle.

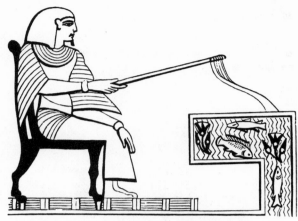

Cleopatra: 'Give me mine angle:' Engraving from a
tomb painting at Thebes by F. W. Fairholt from J. O.
Halliwell's edition of Shakespeare's works, 1853–1865

22 *tires.* Head-dress.

28 *yield.* Admit.

41 *formal.* Ordinary.

50 *allay.* Qualify.

54 *the pack of.* All.

Cleopatra: 'The most infectious pestilence upon thee!'
Engraving by Kenny Meadows from Barry Cornwall's
The Works of Shakspere, 1846

63 *spurn.* Trample.

Mess.   Madam, madam,—
Cleo.   Antonius dead!—If thou say so, villain,
Thou kill'st thy mistress: but well and free,
●If thou so yield him, there is gold, and here
My bluest veins to kiss; a hand that kings
Have lipp'd, and trembled kissing.   30
   Mess.   First, madam, he is well.
   Cleo.   Why, there's more gold.
But, sirrah, mark, we use
To say the dead are well: bring it to that,
The gold I give thee will I melt and pour
Down thy ill-uttering throat.
   Mess.   Good madam, hear me.
   Cleo.   Well, go to, I will;
But there's no goodness in thy face: if Antony
Be free and healthful,—so tart a favour
To trumpet such good tidings! If not well,
Thou shouldst come like a Fury crown'd with
          snakes,   40
●Not like a formal man.
   Mess.   Will 't please you hear me?
   Cleo.   I have a mind to strike thee ere thou
          speak'st:
Yet, if thou say Antony lives, is well,
Or friends with Cæsar, or not captive to him,
I'll set thee in a shower of gold, and hail
Rich pearls upon thee.
   Mess.   Madam, he's well.
   Cleo.   Well said.
   Mess.   And friends with Cæsar.
   Cleo.   Thou'rt an honest man.
   Mess.   Cæsar and he are greater friends than
          ever.
   Cleo.   Make thee a fortune from me.
   Mess.   But yet, madam,—
●   *Cleo.*   I do not like 'But yet,' it does allay 50
The good precedence; fie upon 'But yet'!
'But yet' is as a gaoler to bring forth
Some monstrous malefactor.   Prithee, friend,
●Pour out the pack of matter to mine ear,
The good and bad together: he's friends with
          Cæsar;
In state of health thou say'st; and thou say'st
          free.
   Mess.   Free, madam! no; I made no such
          report:
He's bound unto Octavia.
   Cleo.   For what good turn?
   Mess.   For the best turn i' the bed.
   Cleo.   I am pale, Charmian.
   Mess.   Madam, he's married to Octavia.   60
   Cleo.   The most infectious pestilence upon
          thee!   [*Strikes him down.*
   Mess.   Good madam, patience.
   Cleo.   What say you? Hence,
          [*Strikes him again.*
●Horrible villain! or I'll spurn thine eyes
Like balls before me; I'll unhair thy head:
          [*She hales him up and down.*
Thou shalt be whipp'd with wire, and stew'd in
          brine,
Smarting in lingering pickle.
   Mess.   Gracious madam,
I that do bring the news made not the match.
   Cleo.   Say 'tis not so, a province I will give
          thee,
And make thy fortunes proud: the blow thou
          hadst
Shall make thy peace for moving me to rage; 70

● And I will boot thee with what gift beside
Thy modesty can beg.
    Mess. He's married, madam.
    Cleo. Rogue, thou hast lived too long.
                       [Draws a knife.
    Mess. Nay, then I'll run.
What mean you, madam? I have made no fault.
                             [Exit.
    Char. Good madam, keep yourself within
    yourself:
The man is innocent.
    Cleo. Some innocents 'scape not the thunderbolt.
Melt Egypt into Nile! and kindly creatures
Turn all to serpents! Call the slave again:
Though I am mad, I will not bite him: call.   80
    Char. He is afeard to come.
    Cleo. I will not hurt him.
                    [Exit Charmian.
These hands do lack nobility, that they strike
A meaner than myself; since I myself
Have given myself the cause.

       Re-enter CHARMIAN *and* Messenger.

                   Come hither, sir.
Though it be honest, it is never good
To bring bad news: give to a gracious message
An host of tongues; but let ill tidings tell
Themselves when they be felt.
    Mess. I have done my duty.
    Cleo. Is he married?
I cannot hate thee worser than I do,   90
If thou again say 'Yes.'
    Mess. He's married, madam.
    Cleo. The gods confound thee! dost thou hold
    there still?
    Mess. Should I lie, madam?
    Cleo. O, I would thou didst,
So half my Egypt were submerged and made
A cistern for scaled snakes! Go, get thee hence:
● Hadst thou Narcissus in thy face, to me
Thou wouldst appear most ugly. He is married?
    Mess. I crave your highness' pardon.
    Cleo. He is married?
    Mess. Take no offence that I would not offend
    you:
To punish me for what you make me do   100
Seems much unequal: he's married to Octavia.
    Cleo. O, that his fault should make a knave
    of thee,
That art not what thou'rt sure of! Get thee hence:
The merchandise which thou hast brought from
    Rome
Are all too dear for me: lie they upon thy hand,
And be undone by 'em!   *[Exit Messenger.*
    Char. Good your highness, patience.
    Cleo. In praising Antony, I have dispraised
    Cæsar.
    Char. Many times, madam.
    Cleo. I am paid for't now.
Lead me from hence;
I faint: O Iras, Charmian! 'tis no matter.   110
Go to the fellow, good Alexas; bid him
Report the feature of Octavia, her years,
Her inclination, let him not leave out
The colour of her hair: bring me word quickly.
                     [Exit Alexas.
Let him for ever go:—let him not—Charmian,
● Though he be painted one way like a Gorgon,

71 *boot.* Reward.

96 *Narcissus.* Legendary beautiful youth.

Narcissus fell in love with his own image and was changed into the flower that bears his name. Engraving from a painting by Dominiquin, 1803

116 *Gorgon.* Mythical monster.

27 *oe'r-count.* i.e. 'outnumber' and 'cheat'.

30 *from the present.* Off the point.

39 *targes.* Shields.

Charles Calvert as Mark Antony, Theatre Royal, Drury Lane, London, 1873

The other way's a Mars.   Bid you Alexas
                           [*To Mardian.*
Bring me word how tall she is.   Pity me, Char-
  mian,
But do not speak to me.   Lead me to my chamber.
                              [*Exeunt.*

SCENE VI.   *Near Misenum.*

Flourish. Enter POMPEY *and* MENAS *at one side, with drum and trumpet: at another,* CÆSAR, ANTONY, LEPIDUS, ENOBARBUS, MECÆNAS, *with* Soldiers *marching.*

Pom.   Your hostages I have, so have you
  mine;
And we shall talk before we fight.
  Cæs.   Most meet
That first we come to words; and therefore have we
Our written purposes before us sent;
Which, if thou hast consider'd, let us know
If 'twill tie up thy discontented sword,
And carry back to Sicily much tall youth
That else must perish here.
  Pom.   To you all three,
The senators alone of this great world,
Chief factors for the gods, I do not know   10
Wherefore my father should revengers want,
Having a son and friends; since Julius Cæsar,
Who at Philippi the good Brutus ghosted,
There saw you labouring for him.   What was't
That moved pale Cassius to conspire; and what
Made the all-honour'd, honest Roman, Brutus,
With the arm'd rest, courtiers of beauteous free-
  dom,
To drench the Capitol; but that they would
Have one man but a man?   And that is it   19
Hath made me rig my navy; at whose burthen
The anger'd ocean foams; with which I meant
To scourge the ingratitude that despiteful Rome
Cast on my noble father.
  Cæs.   Take your time.
  Ant.   Thou canst not fear us, Pompey, with
  thy sails;
We'll speak with thee at sea: at land, thou
  know'st
How much we do o'er-count thee.
  Pom.   At land, indeed,
●Thou dost o'er-count me of my father's house:
But, since the cuckoo builds not for himself,
Remain in't as thou mayst.
  Lep.   Be pleased to tell us—
●For this is from the present—how you take   30
The offers we have sent you.
  Cæs.   There's the point.
  Ant.   Which do not be entreated to, but weigh
What it is worth embraced.
  Cæs.   And what may follow,
To try a larger fortune.
  Pom.   You have made me offer
Of Sicily, Sardinia; and I must
Rid all the sea of pirates; then, to send
Measures of wheat to Rome; this 'greed upon,
To part with unhack'd edges, and bear back
●Our targes undinted.
  Cæs. Ant. Lep.   That's our offer.
  Pom.   Know, then, 40
I came before you here a man prepared
To take this offer: but Mark Antony
Put me to some impatience: though I lose

The praise of it by telling, you must know,
When Cæsar and your brother were at blows,
Your mother came to Sicily and did find
Her welcome friendly.
    Ant.   I have heard it, Pompey;
●And am well studied for a liberal thanks
Which I do owe you.
    Pom.   Let me have your hand:
I did not think, sir, to have met you here.   50
    Ant. The beds i' the east are soft; and thanks
        to you,
That call'd me timelier than my purpose hither;
For I have gain'd by't.
    Cæs.   Since I saw you last,
There is a change upon you.
    Pom.   Well, I know not
What counts harsh fortune casts upon my face;
But in my bosom shall she never come,
To make my heart her vassal.
    Lep.   Well met here.
    Pom. I hope so, Lepidus. Thus we are
    agreed:
I crave our composition may be written,
And seal'd between us.
    Cæs.   That's the next to do. 60
    Pom. We'll feast each other ere we part;
    and let's
Draw lots who shall begin.
    Ant.   That will I, Pompey.
    Pom. No, Antony, take the lot: but, first
Or last, your fine Egyptian cookery
Shall have the fame. I have heard that Julius
    Cæsar
Grew fat with feasting there.
    Ant.   You have heard much.
    Pom. I have fair meanings, sir.
    Ant.   And fair words to them.
    Pom. Then so much have I heard:
●And I have heard, Apollodorus carried—
    Eno. No more of that: he did so.
    Pom.   What, I pray you? 70
    Eno. A certain queen to Cæsar in a mattress.
    Pom. I know thee now: how farest thou,
    soldier?
    Eno.   Well;
And well am like to do; for, I perceive,
Four feasts are toward.
    Pom.   Let me shake thy hand;
I never hated thee: I have seen thee fight,
When I have envied thy behaviour.
    Eno.   Sir,
I never loved you much; but I ha' praised ye,
When you have well deserved ten times as much
As I have said you did.
    Pom.   Enjoy thy plainness, 80
It nothing ill becomes thee.
Aboard my galley I invite you all:
Will you lead, lords?
    Cæs. Ant. Lep. Show us the way, sir.
    Pom.   Come.
       [*Exeunt all but Menas and Enobarbus.*
    Men. [*Aside*] Thy father, Pompey, would
ne'er have made this treaty.—You and I have
known, sir.
    Eno. At sea, I think.
    Men. We have, sir.
    Eno. You have done well by water.
    Men. And you by land. 90
    Eno. I will praise any man that will praise

48 *studied.* Prepared.

69 *Apollodorus.* Friend to Cleopatra.

Sextus Pompey, the younger son of Pompey the Great.
He allied himself against Octavius with Antony, but
was betrayed by Antony and put to death in 37 BC

140 *occasion.* Convenience.

5-6 *alms-drink.* i.e. extra.

7 *pinch.* Annoy.

8 *disposition.* Inclination.

me; though it cannot be denied what I have done by land.

Men. Nor what I have done by water.

Eno. Yes, something you can deny for your own safety: you have been a great thief by sea.

Men. And you by land.

Eno. There I deny my land service. But give me your hand, Menas: if our eyes had authority, here they might take two thieves kissing. 101

Men. All men's faces are true, whatsome'er their hands are.

Eno. But there is never a fair woman has a true face.

Men. No slander; they steal hearts.

Eno. We came hither to fight with you.

Men. For my part, I am sorry it is turned to a drinking. Pompey doth this day laugh away his fortune. 110

Eno. If he do, sure, he cannot weep't back again.

Men. You've said, sir. We looked not for Mark Antony here: pray you, is he married to Cleopatra?

Eno. Cæsar's sister is called Octavia.

Men. True, sir; she was the wife of Caius Marcellus.

Eno. But she is now the wife of Marcus Antonius.

Men. Pray ye, sir? 120

Eno. 'Tis true.

Men. Then is Cæsar and he for ever knit together.

Eno. If I were bound to divine of this unity, I would not prophesy so.

Men. I think the policy of that purpose made more in the marriage than the love of the parties.

Eno. I think so too. But you shall find, the band that seems to tie their friendship together will be the very strangler of their amity: Octavia is of a holy, cold, and still conversation. 131

Men. Who would not have his wife so?

Eno. Not he that himself is not so; which is Mark Antony. He will to his Egyptian dish again: then shall the sighs of Octavia blow the fire up in Cæsar; and, as I said before, that which is the strength of their amity shall prove the immediate author of their variance. Antony will use his affection where it is: he married but his occasion here. 140

Men. And thus it may be. Come, sir, will you aboard? I have a health for you.

Eno. I shall take it, sir: we have used our throats in Egypt.

Men. Come, let's away. [*Exeunt.*

SCENE VII. *On board Pompey's galley, off Misenum.*

Music plays. Enter two or three Servants *with a banquet.*

First Serv. Here they'll be, man. Some o' their plants are ill-rooted already; the least wind i' the world will blow them down.

Sec. Serv. Lepidus is high-coloured.

First Serv. They have made him drink alms-drink.

Sec. Serv. As they pinch one another by the disposition, he cries out 'No more;' reconciles them to his entreaty, and himself to the drink.

First Serv. But it raises the greater war between him and his discretion.   11

Sec. Serv. Why, this it is to have a name in great men's fellowship: I had as lief have a reed that will do me no service as a partisan I could not heave.

First Serv. To be called into a huge sphere, and not to be seen to move in't, are the holes where eyes should be, which pitifully disaster the cheeks.

A sennet sounded. Enter Cæsar, Antony, Lepidus, Pompey, Agrippa, Mecænas, Enobarbus, Menas, *with other captains.*

Ant. [*To Cæsar*] Thus do they, sir: they take the flow o' the Nile   20
By certain scales i' the pyramid; they know,
By the height, the lowness, or the mean, if dearth
Or foison follow: the higher Nilus swells,
The more it promises: as it ebbs, the seedsman
Upon the slime and ooze scatters his grain,
And shortly comes to harvest.

Lep. You've strange serpents there.

Ant. Ay, Lepidus.

Lep. Your serpent of Egypt is bred now of your mud by the operation of your sun: so is your crocodile.   31

Ant. They are so.

Pom. Sit,—and some wine! A health to Lepidus!

Lep. I am not so well as I should be, but I'll ne'er out.

Eno. Not till you have slept; I fear me you'll be in till then.

Lep. Nay, certainly, I have heard the Ptolemies' pyramises are very goodly things; without contradiction, I have heard that.   41

Men. [*Aside to Pom.*] Pompey, a word.

Pom.   [*Aside to Men.*] Say in mine ear: what is't?

Men. [*Aside to Pom.*] Forsake thy seat, I do beseech thee, captain,
And hear me speak a word.

Pom. [*Aside to Men.*] Forbear me till anon.
This wine for Lepidus!

Lep. What manner o' thing is your crocodile?

Ant. It is shaped, sir, like itself; and it is as broad as it hath breadth: it is just so high as it is, and moves with it own organs: it lives by that which nourisheth it; and the elements once out of it, it transmigrates.   51

Lep. What colour is it of?

Ant. Of it own colour too.

Lep. 'Tis a strange serpent.

Ant. 'Tis so. And the tears of it are wet.

Cæs. Will this description satisfy him?

Ant. With the health that Pompey gives him, else he is a very epicure.

Pom. [*Aside to Men.*] Go hang, sir, hang! Tell me of that? away!
Do as I bid you. Where's this cup I call'd for?

Men. [*Aside to Pom.*] If for the sake of merit thou wilt hear me,   61
Rise from thy stool.

Pom. [*Aside to Men.*] I think thou'rt mad. The matter?   [*Rises, and walks aside.*

Men. I have ever held my cap off to thy fortunes.

13 *lief.* Soon.

14 *partisan.* Bladed pike.

16 *huge sphere.* Important group.

18 *disaster.* Spoil.

21 *scales.* Graduated marks.

23 *foison.* Plenty.

River gods of the Upper and Lower Nile. Illustration from E. A. W. Budge's *The Gods of the Egyptians*, 1904

35–36 *but . . . out.* But I never give up.

Lepidus: 'What manner o' thing is your crocodile?' Woodcut from Edward Topsell's *History of Serpents*, 1608

69 *entertain it.* Just accept it.

74 *pales.* Surrounds.

88 *pall'd.* Decayed.

103 *Strike.* Open.

110 *Bacchanals.* Dances in honour of Bacchus.

A bacchanalian feast. Engraving from a painting by Nicolas Poussin, 1803

Pom.   Thou hast served me with much faith. What 's else to say?
Be jolly, lords.
Ant.   These quick-sands, Lepidus,
Keep off them, for you sink.
Men.   Wilt thou be lord of all the world?
Pom.   What say'st thou?
Men.   Wilt thou be lord of the whole world?
   That 's twice.
● *Pom.*   How should that be?
Men.   But entertain it, 69
And, though thou think me poor, I am the man
Will give thee all the world.
Pom.   Hast thou drunk well?
Men.   No, Pompey, I have kept me from the
   cup.
Thou art, if thou darest be, the earthly Jove:
●Whate'er the ocean pales, or sky inclips,
Is thine, if thou wilt ha 't.
Pom.   Show me which way.
Men.   These three world-sharers, these com-
   petitors,
Are in thy vessel: let me cut the cable;
And, when we are put off, fall to their throats:
All there is thine.
Pom.   Ah, this thou shouldst have done,
And not have spoke on 't!   In me 'tis villany; 85
In thee 't had been good service.   Thou must
   know,
'Tis not my profit that does lead mine honour;
Mine honour, it.   Repent that e'er thy tongue
Hath so betray'd thine act: being done unknown,
I should have found it afterwards well done;
But must condemn it now.   Desist, and drink.
Men.   [*Aside*] For this,
●I'll never follow thy pall'd fortunes more.
Who seeks, and will not take when once 'tis
   offer'd,
Shall never find it more.
Pom.   This health to Lepidus! 90
Ant.   Bear him ashore.   I'll pledge it for him,
   Pompey.
Eno.   Here's to thee, Menas!
Men.   Enobarbus, welcome!
Pom.   Fill till the cup be hid.
Eno.   There's a strong fellow, Menas.
      [*Pointing to the Attendant who carries
                     off Lepidus.*
Men.   Why?
Eno.   A' bears the third part of the world, man;
see'st not?
Men.   The third part, then, is drunk: would
   it were all,
That it might go on wheels!
Eno.   Drink thou; increase the reels.   100
Men.   Come.
Pom.   This is not yet an Alexandrian feast.
● *Ant.*   It ripens towards it.   Strike the vessels,
   ho!
Here is to Cæsar!
Cæs.   I could well forbear 't.
It 's monstrous labour, when I wash my brain,
And it grows fouler.
Ant.   Be a child o' the time.
Cæs.   Possess it, I'll make answer:
But I had rather fast from all four days
Than drink so much in one.
Eno.   Ha, my brave emperor! [*To Antony.*
●Shall we dance now the Egyptian Bacchanals,

And celebrate our drink?
Pom. Let's ha't, good soldier. 111
Ant. Come, let's all take hands,
Till that the conquering wine hath steep'd our
sense
In soft and delicate Lethe.
Eno. All take hands.
Make battery to our ears with the loud music:
The while I'll place you: then the boy shall sing;
●The holding every man shall bear as loud
As his strong sides can volley.
[*Music plays. Enobarbus places them
hand in hand.*

THE SONG.
Come, thou monarch of the vine, 120
Plumpy Bacchus with pink eyne!
● In thy fats our cares be drown'd,
With thy grapes our hairs be crown'd:
Cup us, till the world go round,
Cup us, till the world go round!

Cæs. What would you more? Pompey, good
night. Good brother,
Let me request you off: our graver business
Frowns at this levity. Gentle lords, let's part;
You see we have burnt our cheeks: strong Eno-
barb
Is weaker than the wine; and mine own tongue
Splits what it speaks: the wild disguise hath
almost 131
●Antick'd us all. What needs more words? Good
night.
Good Antony, your hand.
Pom. I'll try you on the shore.
Ant. And shall, sir: give's your hand.
Pom. O Antony,
You have my father's house,—But, what? we are
friends.
Come, down into the boat.
Eno. Take heed you fall not.
[*Exeunt all but Enobarbus and Menas.*
Menas, I'll not on shore.
Men. No, to my cabin.
These drums! these trumpets, flutes! what!
●Let Neptune hear we bid a loud farewell
To these great fellows: sound and be hang'd,
sound out! [*Sound a flourish, with drums.*
Eno. Ho! says a'. There's my cap. 141
Men. Ho! Noble captain, come. [*Exeunt.*

ACT III.

SCENE I. *A plain in Syria.*

Enter VENTIDIUS *as it were in triumph, with*
SILIUS, *and other* Romans, Officers, *and* Soldiers; *the dead body of* PACORUS *borne before
him.*

Ven. Now, darting Parthia, art thou struck;
and now
Pleased fortune does of Marcus Crassus' death
Make me revenger. Bear the king's son's body
Before our army. Thy Pacorus, Orodes,
Pays this for Marcus Crassus.
Sil. Noble Ventidius,
Whilst yet with Parthian blood thy sword is warm,
The fugitive Parthians follow; spur through
Media,
Mesopotamia, and the shelters whither

117 *holding.* Chorus.

'Come, thou monarch of the vine, Plumpy Bacchus with
pink eyne!' Bacchus with his train. Engraving from a
painting by Raphael, 1811

122 *fats.* Vats.

132 *Antick'd.* Made fools of.

139 *Neptune.* God of the sea.

Parthian soldier. From a 19th century engraving

12 *lower place.* Subordinate.

34 *jaded.* Ridden tired.

6 *green sickness.* i.e. 'girlish anaemia' and 'jealousy'.

12 *Arabian bird.* Legendary phoenix.

The phoenix was supposedly reincarnated from its own ashes every 500 years. From a 17th century engraving

The routed fly: so thy grand captain Antony
Shall set thee on triumphant chariots and   10
Put garlands on thy head.
  Ven.   O Silius, Silius,
●I have done enough; a lower place, note well,
May make too great an act: for learn this, Silius;
Better to leave undone, than by our deed
Acquire too high a fame when him we serve's
    away.
Cæsar and Antony have ever won
More in their officer than person: Sossius,
One of my place in Syria, his lieutenant,
For quick accumulation of renown,   19
Which he achieved by the minute, lost his favour.
Who does i' the wars more than his captain can
Becomes his captain's captain: and ambition,
The soldier's virtue, rather makes choice of loss,
Than gain which darkens him.
I could do more to do Antonius good,
But 'twould offend him; and in his offence
Should my performance perish.
  Sil.   Thou hast, Ventidius, that
Without the which a soldier, and his sword,
Grants scarce distinction. Thou wilt write to
    Antony?
  Ven. I'll humbly signify what in his name, 30
That magical word of war, we have effected;
How, with his banners and his well-paid ranks,
The ne'er-yet-beaten horse of Parthia
●We have jaded out o' the field.
  Sil.   Where is he now?
  Ven. He purposeth to Athens: whither, with
    what haste,
The weight we must convey with 's will permit,
We shall appear before him. On, there; pass
    along!   [*Exeunt.*

SCENE II. *Rome. An ante-chamber in
          Cæsar's house.*

Enter AGRIPPA *at one door,* ENOBARBUS
       at another.

  Agr. What, are the brothers parted?
  Eno. They have dispatch'd with Pompey, he
    is gone;
The other three are sealing. Octavia weeps
To part from Rome; Cæsar is sad; and Lepidus,
Since Pompey's feast, as Menas says, is troubled
●With the green sickness.
  Agr.   'Tis a noble Lepidus.
  Eno. A very fine one: O, how he loves
    Cæsar!
  Agr. Nay, but how dearly he adores Mark
    Antony!
  Eno. Cæsar? Why, he's the Jupiter of men.
  Agr. What's Antony? The god of Jupiter. 10
  Eno. Spake you of Cæsar? How! the non-
    pareil!
  Agr. O Antony! O thou Arabian bird!
  Eno. Would you praise Cæsar, say 'Cæsar:'
    go no further.
  Agr. Indeed, he plied them both with excel-
    lent praises.
  Eno. But he loves Cæsar best; yet he loves
    Antony:
Ho! hearts, tongues, figures, scribes, bards,
    poets, cannot
Think, speak, cast, write, sing, number, ho!
His love to Antony. But as for Cæsar.

Kneel down, kneel down, and wonder.
Agr. Both he loves.
Eno. They are his shards, and he their beetle.
 [*Trumpets within.*] So; 20
This is to horse. Adieu, noble Agrippa.
Agr. Good fortune, worthy soldier; and fare-
 well.

Enter CÆSAR, ANTONY, LEPIDUS, *and* OCTAVIA.

Ant. No further, sir.
Cæs. You take from me a great part of myself;
Use me well in't. Sister, prove such a wife
As my thoughts make thee, and as my farthest
 band
Shall pass on thy approof. Most noble Antony,
Let not the piece of virtue, which is set
Betwixt us as the cement of our love,
To keep it builded, be the ram to batter 30
The fortress of it; for better might we
Have loved without this mean, if on both parts
This be not cherish'd.
Ant. Make me not offended
In your distrust.
Cæs. I have said.
Ant. You shall not find,
Though you be therein curious, the least cause
For what you seem to fear: so, the gods keep you,
And make the hearts of Romans serve your ends!
We will here part.
Cæs. Farewell, my dearest sister, fare thee
 well:
The elements be kind to thee, and make 40
Thy spirits all of comfort! fare thee well.
Oct. My noble brother!
Ant. The April's in her eyes: it is love's
 spring,
And these the showers to bring it on. Be cheerful.
Oct. Sir, look well to my husband's house;
 and—
Cæs. What,
Octavia?
Oct. I'll tell you in your ear.
Ant. Her tongue will not obey her heart,
 nor can
Her heart inform her tongue,—the swan's down-
 feather,
That stands upon the swell at full of tide,
And neither way inclines. 50
Eno. [*Aside to Agr.*] Will Cæsar weep?
Agr. [*Aside to Eno.*] He has a cloud in's face.
Eno. [*Aside to Agr.*] He were the worse for
 that, were he a horse;
So is he, being a man.
Agr. [*Aside to Eno.*] Why, Enobarbus,
When Antony found Julius Cæsar dead,
He cried almost to roaring; and he wept
When at Philippi he found Brutus slain.
Eno. [*Aside to Agr.*] That year, indeed, he
 was troubled with a rheum;
What willingly he did confound he wail'd,
Believe 't, till I wept too.
Cæs. No, sweet Octavia,
You shall hear from me still; the time shall not
Out-go my thinking on you.
Ant. Come, sir, come; 61
I'll wrestle with you in my strength of love:
Look, here I have you; thus I let you go,
And give you to the gods.
Cæs. Adieu; be happy!

20 *shards.* Patches of cow dung.

26–27 *my ... approof.* I would wager my last pound that it will prove to be.

32 *mean.* Means.

35 *curious.* Anxious.

Agrippa: 'When Antony found Julius Caesar dead, He cried ...' Woodcut by Byam Shaw, *The Chiswick Shakespeare*, 1900

57 *rheum.* Streaming cold.

61 *Out-go.* i.e. go faster than.

2 *Go to.* Nonsense!

Cleopatra: 'That's not so good: he cannot like her long.'
Janet Suzman as Cleopatra, Royal Shakespeare Co,
1972

Lep. Let all the number of the stars give light
To thy fair way!
  Cæs.   Farewell, farewell! [*Kisses Octavia.*
  Ant.   Farewell!
        [*Trumpets sound.   Exeunt.*

  Scene III.   *Alexandria.   Cleopatra's
      palace.*

Enter Cleopatra, Charmian, Iras, *and*
     Alexas.

  Cleo. Where is the fellow?
  Alex.   Half afeard to come.
• *Cleo.* Go to, go to.

   Enter the Messenger *as before.*
      Come hither, sir.
  Alex.   Good majesty,
Herod of Jewry dare not look upon you
But when you are well pleased.
  Cleo.   That Herod's head
I'll have: but how, when Antony is gone
Through whom I might command it?   Come
  thou near.
  Mess. Most gracious majesty,—
  Cleo. Didst thou behold Octavia?
  Mess. Ay, dread queen.
  Cleo. Where?   10
  Mess. Madam, in Rome;
I look'd her in the face, and saw her led
Between her brother and Mark Antony.
  Cleo. Is she as tall as me?
  Mess.   She is not, madam.
  Cleo. Didst hear her speak? is she shrill-
  tongued or low?
  Mess. Madam, I heard her speak; she is low-
  voiced.
  Cleo. That's not so good: he cannot like her
  long.
  Char. Like her! O Isis! 'tis impossible.
  Cleo. I think so, Charmian: dull of tongue,
  and dwarfish!
What majesty is in her gait?   Remember, 20
If e'er thou look'dst on majesty.
  Mess.   She creeps:
Her motion and her station are as one;
She shows a body rather than a life,
A statue than a breather.
  Cleo.   Is this certain?
  Mess. Or I have no observance.
  Char.   Three in Egypt
Cannot make better note.
  Cleo.   He's very knowing;
I do perceive 't: there's nothing in her yet:
The fellow has good judgement.
  Char.   Excellent.
  Cleo. Guess at her years, I prithee.
  Mess.   Madam,
She was a widow,—
  Cleo.   Widow! Charmian, hark. 30
  Mess. And I do think she's thirty.
  Cleo. Bear'st thou her face in mind? is't long
  or round?
  Mess. Round even to faultiness.
  Cleo. For the most part, too, they are foolish
  that are so.
Her hair, what colour?
  Mess. Brown, madam: and her forehead
As low as she would wish it.

Cleo.   There 's gold for thee.
Thou must not take my former sharpness ill:
I will employ thee back again; I find thee
Most fit for business: go make thee ready;   40
Our letters are prepared.   *[Exit Messenger.*
   Char.   A proper man.
   Cleo.   Indeed, he is so: I repent me much
That so I harried him. Why, methinks, by him,
This creature's no such thing.
   Char.   Nothing, madam.
   Cleo.   The man hath seen some majesty, and
     should know.
   Char.   Hath he seen majesty? Isis else defend,
And serving you so long!
   Cleo.   I have one thing more to ask him yet,
     good Charmian:
But 'tis no matter; thou shalt bring him to me
Where I will write. All may be well enough. 50
   Char.   I warrant you, madam.   *[Exeunt.*

SCENE IV. *Athens. A room in Antony's house.*

Enter ANTONY *and* OCTAVIA.

   Ant.   Nay, nay, Octavia, not only that,—
That were excusable, that, and thousands more
Of semblable import,—but he hath waged
New wars 'gainst Pompey; made his will, and
     read it
To public ear:
Spoke scantly of me: when perforce he could not
But pay me terms of honour, cold and sickly
He vented them; most narrow measure lent me:
When the best hint was given him, he not took't,
Or did it from his teeth.
   Oct.   O my good lord,   10
Believe not all; or, if you must believe,
Stomach not all. A more unhappy lady,
If this division chance, ne'er stood between,
Praying for both parts:
The good gods will mock me presently,
When I shall pray, 'O, bless my lord and hus-
     band!'
Undo that prayer, by crying out as loud,
'O, bless my brother!' Husband win, win
     brother,
Prays, and destroys the prayer; no midway
'Twixt these extremes at all.
   Ant.   Gentle Octavia,   20
Let your best love draw to that point, which
     seeks
Best to preserve it: if I lose mine honour,
I lose myself: better I were not yours
Than yours so branchless. But, as you re-
     quested,
Yourself shall go between 's: the mean time, lady,
I 'll raise the preparation of a war
Shall stain your brother: make your soonest
     haste;
So your desires are yours.
   Oct.   Thanks to my lord.
The Jove of power make me most weak, most
     weak,
Your reconciler! Wars 'twixt you twain would be
As if the world should cleave, and that slain
     men   31
Should solder up the rift.
   Ant.   When it appears to you where this begins,
Turn your displeasure that way; for our faults
Can never be so equal, that your love

3 *semblable import.* Similar importance.

27 *stain.* Eclipse.

Jove, King of the Gods. Nineteenth century engraving
from a Greek vase

8-9 *rivality*. Equal rights.

13 *up*. Imprisoned. *enlarge*. Free him from.

21 *Domitius*. Enobarbus.

Cleopatra and her son Caesarion sacrificing to the Gods. Engraving from a sculpture in the Great Temple at Dendera, Upper Egypt by F. W. Fairholt from J. O. Halliwell's edition of Shakespeare's works, 1853–1865

17 *habiliments*. Dress.

Can equally move with them.   Provide your
  going;
Choose your own company, and command what
  cost
Your heart has mind to.   [*Exeunt.*

SCENE V.   *The same.   Another room.*

Enter ENOBARBUS *and* EROS, *meeting.*

Eno. How now, friend Eros!
Eros. There's strange news come, sir.
Eno. What, man?
Eros. Cæsar and Lepidus have made wars
upon Pompey.
Eno. This is old: what is the success?
Eros. Cæsar, having made use of him in the
wars 'gainst Pompey, presently denied him rival-
ity; would not let him partake in the glory of the
action: and not resting here, accuses him of
letters he had formerly wrote to Pompey; upon
his own appeal, seizes him: so the poor third is
up, till death enlarge his confine.
Eno. Then, world, thou hast a pair· of chaps,
  no more;
And throw between them all the food thou hast,
They'll grind the one the other.   Where's Antony?
Eros. He's walking in the garden—thus; and
  spurns
The rush that lies before him; cries, 'Fool
  Lepidus!'
And threats the throat of that his officer
That murder'd Pompey.
Eno.   Our great navy's rigg'd.   20
Eros. For Italy and Cæsar.   More, Domitius;
My lord desires you presently: my news
I might have told hereafter.
Eno.   'Twill be naught:
Eut let it be.   Bring me to Antony.
Eros. Come, sir.   [*Exeunt.*

SCENE VI.   *Rome.   Cæsar's house.*

Enter CÆSAR, AGRIPPA, *and* MECÆNAS.

Cæs. Contemning Rome, he has done all this,
  and more,
In Alexandria: here's the manner of't:
I' the market-place, on a tribunal silver'd,
Cleopatra and himself in chairs of gold
Were publicly enthroned: at the feet sat
Cæsarion, whom they call my father's son,
And all the unlawful issue that their lust
Since then hath made between them.   Unto her
He gave the stablishment of Egypt; made her
Of lower Syria, Cyprus, Lydia,   10
Absolute queen.
Mec.   This in the public eye?
Cæs. I' the common show-place, where they
  exercise.
His sons he there proclaim'd the kings of kings:
Great Media, Parthia, and Armenia,
He gave to Alexander; to Ptolemy he assign'd
Syria, Cilicia, and Phœnicia: she
In the habiliments of the goddess Isis
That day appear'd; and oft before gave audience,
As 'tis reported, so.
Mec.   Let Rome be thus
Inform'd.
Agr. Who, queasy with his insolence   20
Already, will their good thoughts call from him.

Cæs.   The people know it; and have now received
His accusations.
   Agr.   Who does he accuse?
   Cæs.   Cæsar: and that, having in Sicily
•Sextus Pompeius spoil'd, we had not rated him
His part o' the isle: then does he say, he lent me
Some shipping unrestored: lastly, he frets
That Lepidus of the triumvirate
Should be deposed; and, being, that we detain
All his revenue.
   Agr.   Sir, this should be answer'd.   30
   Cæs.   'Tis done already, and the messenger gone.
I have told him, Lepidus was grown too cruel;
That he his high authority abused,
And did deserve his change: for what I have
   conquer'd,
I grant him part; but then, in his Armenia,
And other of his conquer'd kingdoms, I
Demand the like.
   Mec.   He'll never yield to that.
   Cæs.   Nor must not then be yielded to in this.

      Enter OCTAVIA *with her train.*

   Oct.   Hail, Cæsar, and my lord! hail, most
     dear Cæsar!   39
   Cæs.   That ever I should call thee castaway!
   Oct.   You have not call'd me so, nor have you
     cause.
   Cæs.   Why have you stol'n upon us thus? You
     come not
Like Cæsar's sister: the wife of Antony
Should have an army for an usher, and
The neighs of horse to tell of her approach
Long ere she did appear; the trees by the way
Should have borne men; and expectation fainted,
Longing for what it had not: nay, the dust
Should have ascended to the roof of heaven,   49
Raised by your populous troops: but you are come
A market-maid to Rome; and have prevented
The ostentation of our love, which, left unshown,
Is often left unloved: we should have met you
By sea and land; supplying every stage
With an augmented greeting.
   Oct.   Good my lord,
To come thus was I not constrain'd, but did it
On my free will.   My lord, Mark Antony,
Hearing that you prepared for war, acquainted
My grieved ear withal; whereon, I begg'd
•His pardon for return.
   Cæs.   Which soon he granted, 60
Being an obstruct 'tween his lust and him.
   Oct.   Do not say so, my lord.
   Cæs.   I have eyes upon him,
And his affairs come to me on the wind.
Where is he now?
   Oct.   My lord, in Athens.
   Cæs.   No, my most wronged sister; Cleopatra
Hath nodded him to her.   He hath given his
     empire
Up to a whore; who now are levying
The kings o' the earth for war: he hath assembled
Bocchus, the king of Libya; Archelaus,
Of Cappadocia; Philadelphos, king   70
Of Paphlagonia; the Thracian king, Adallas;
King Malchus of Arabia; King of Pont;
Herod of Jewry; Mithridates, king
Of Comagene; Polemon and Amyntas,
The kings of Mede and Lycaonia,

25 *spoil'd.* Taken.

60 *pardon.* Consent.

Constance Collier as Cleopatra, His Majesty's Theatre, London, 1906

With a more larger list of sceptres.
Oct.   Ay me, most wretched,
That have my heart parted betwixt two friends
That do afflict each other!
Cæs.   Welcome hither:
Your letters did withhold our breaking forth;   79
Till we perceived, both how you were wrong led,
And we in negligent danger.   Cheer your heart:
Be you not troubled with the time, which drives
O'er your content these strong necessities;
But let determined things to destiny
Hold unbewail'd their way.   Welcome to Rome;
Nothing more dear to me.   You are abused
Beyond the mark of thought: and the high gods,
To do you justice, make them ministers
Of us and those that love you.   Best of comfort;
And ever welcome to us.   90
Agr.   Welcome, lady.
Mec.   Welcome, dear madam.
Each heart in Rome does love and pity you:
Only the adulterous Antony, most large
In his abominations, turns you off;
And gives his potent regiment to a trull,
That noises it against us.
Oct.   Is it so, sir?
Cæs. Most certain. Sister, welcome: pray you,
Be ever known to patience: my dear'st sister!
[*Exeunt.*

SCENE VII.   *Near Actium.   Antony's camp.*

Enter CLEOPATRA *and* ENOBARBUS.

Cleo.   I will be even with thee, doubt it not.
Eno.   But why, why, why?
Cleo.   Thou hast forspoke my being in these wars,
And say'st it is not fit.
Eno.   Well, is it, is it?
Cleo.   If not denounced against us, why should not we
Be there in person?
Eno.   [*Aside*] Well, I could reply:
If we should serve with horse and mares together,
The horse were merely lost; the mares would bear
A soldier and his horse.
Cleo.   What is't you say?   10
Eno. Your presence needs must puzzle Antony;
Take from his heart, take from his brain, from's time,
What should not then be spared.   He is already
Traduced for levity; and 'tis said in Rome
That Photinus an eunuch and your maids
Manage this war.
Cleo.   Sink Rome, and their tongues rot
That speak against us! A charge we bear i' the war,
And, as the president of my kingdom, will
Appear there for a man.   Speak not against it;
I will not stay behind.
Eno.   Nay, I have done.   20
Here comes the emperor.

Enter ANTONY *and* CANIDIUS.

Ant.   Is it not strange, Canidius,
That from Tarentum and Brundusium
He could so quickly cut the Ionian sea,
And take in Toryne? You have heard on't, sweet?
Cleo.   Celerity is never more admired
Than by the negligent.

Ant.   A good rebuke,
Which might have well becomed the best of men,
To taunt at slackness.   Canidius, **we**
Will fight with him by sea.
   Cleo.   By sea! what else?
   Can. Why will my lord do so?
   Ant.   For that he dares us to't. 30
   Eno. So hath my lord dared him to single fight.
   Can. Ay, and to wage this battle at Pharsalia,
Where Cæsar fought with Pompey: but these
     offers,
Which serve not for his vantage, he shakes off;
And so should you.
   Eno.   Your ships are not well mann'd;
● Your mariners are muleters, reapers, people
● Ingross'd by swift impress; in Cæsar's fleet
Are those that often have 'gainst Pompey fought:
● Their ships are yare; yours, heavy: no disgrace
Shall fall you for refusing him at sea,   40
Being prepared for land.
   Ant.   By sea, by **sea.**
   Eno. Most worthy sir, you therein throw away
The absolute soldiership you have by land;
● Distract your army, which doth most consist
Of war-mark'd footmen; leave unexecuted
Your own renowned knowledge; quite forego
The way which promises assurance; and
Give up yourself merely to chance and hazard,
From firm security.
   Ant.   I'll fight at sea.
   Cleo. I have sixty sails, Cæsar none better. 50
   Ant. Our overplus of shipping will we burn;
And, with the rest full-mann'd, from the head of
     Actium
Beat the approaching Cæsar.   But if we fail,
We then can do't at land.

       Enter a Messenger.
             Thy business?
   Mess. The news is true, my lord; he is des-
     cried;
Cæsar has taken Toryne.
   Ant. Can he be there in person? 'tis impos-
     sible;
Strange that his power should be.   Canidius,
Our nineteen legions thou shalt hold by land,
And our twelve thousand horse. We'll to our ship:
● Away, my Thetis!

       Enter a Soldier.
          How now, worthy soldier! 61
   Sold. O noble emperor, do not fight by sea;
Trust not to rotten planks: do you misdoubt
This sword and these my wounds? Let the
     Egyptians
And the Phœnicians go a-ducking: we
Have used to conquer, standing on the earth,
And fighting foot to foot.
   Ant.   Well, well; away!
   [*Exeunt Antony, Cleopatra, and Enobarbus.*
   Sold. By Hercules, I think I am i' the right.
   Can. Soldier, thou art: but his whole action
     grows
Not in the power on't: so our leader's led,   70
And we are women's men.
   Sold.   You keep by land
The legions and the horse whole, do you not?
   Can. Marcus Octavius, Marcus Justeius,
Publicola, and Cælius, are for sea:

36 *muleters.* Mule drivers, muleteers.

37 *Ingross'd.* Conscripted.

39 *yare.* Nimble.

44 *Distract.* Reduce.

Antony: 'I'll fight at sea.' George C. Scott as Antony
and Colleen Dewhurst as Cleopatra in Joseph Papp's
New York Shakespeare Festival Production, 1959

61 *Thetis.* Legendary sea goddess.

77 *distractions.* Detachments.

5 *prescript.* Orders.

6 *jump.* Hazard.

2 *admiral.* Flagship.

6 *cantle.* Portion.

10 *ribaudred nag.* Foul slut.

14 *breese.* Gadfly.

The Battle of Actium. Engraving from a painting attributed to Raphael, 1811

But we keep whole by land. This speed of Cæsar's
Carries beyond belief.
   Sold.   While he was yet in Rome,
• His power went out in such distractions as
Beguiled all spies.
   Can.   Who's his lieutenant, hear you?
   Sold.   They say, one Taurus.
   Can.   Well I know the man.

Enter a Messenger.

   Mess.   The emperor calls Canidius.   80
   Can.   With news the time's with labour, and throes forth,
Each minute, some.   [*Exeunt.*

SCENE VIII.   *A plain near Actium.*

Enter CÆSAR, *and* TAURUS, *with his army, marching.*

   Cæs.   Taurus!
   Taur.   My lord?
   Cæs.   Strike not by land; keep whole: provoke not battle,
Till we have done at sea.   Do not exceed
• The prescript of this scroll: our fortune lies
• Upon this jump.   [*Exeunt.*

SCENE IX.   *Another part of the plain.*

Enter ANTONY *and* ENOBARBUS.

   Ant.   Set we our squadrons on yond side o' the hill,
In eye of Cæsar's battle; from which place
We may the number of the ships behold,
And so proceed accordingly.   {*Exeunt.*

SCENE X.   *Another part of the plain.*

CANIDIUS *marcheth with his land army one way over the stage; and* TAURUS, *the lieutenant of* CÆSAR, *the other way. After their going in, is heard the noise of a sea-fight.*

Alarum.   Enter ENOBARBUS.

   Eno.   Naught, naught, all naught!   I can behold no longer:
• The Antoniad, the Egyptian admiral,
With all their sixty, fly and turn the rudder:
To see't mine eyes are blasted.

Enter SCARUS.

   Scar.   Gods and goddesses,
All the whole synod of them!
   Eno.   What's thy passion?
• *Scar.*   The greater cantle of the world is lost
With very ignorance; we have kiss'd away
Kingdoms and provinces.
   Eno.   How appears the fight?
   Scar.   On our side like the token'd pestilence,
• Where death is sure.   Yon ribaudred nag of Egypt,—   10
Whom leprosy o'ertake!—i' the midst o' the fight,
When vantage like a pair of twins appear'd,
Both as the same, or rather ours the elder,
• The breese upon her, like a cow in June,
Hoists sails and flies.
   Eno.   That I beheld:
Mine eyes did sicken at the sight, and could not

● Endure a further view.

Scar.   She once being loof'd,
The noble ruin of her magic, Antony,
Claps on his sea-wing, and, like a doting mallard,
Leaving the fight in height, flies after her :   21
I never saw an action of such shame;
Experience, manhood, honour, ne'er before
Did violate so itself.

Eno.   Alack, alack!

Enter CANIDIUS.

Can. Our fortune on the sea is out of breath,
And sinks most lamentably.   Had our general
Been what he knew himself, it had gone well :
O, he has given example for our flight,
Most grossly, by his own !

Eno.   Ay, are you thereabouts?
Why, then, good night indeed.   30

Can. Toward Peloponnesus are they fled.

Scar. 'Tis easy to't; and there I will attend
What further comes.

Can.   To Cæsar will I render
My legions and my horse : six kings already
Show me the way of yielding.

Eno.   I 'll yet follow
● The wounded chance of Antony, though my
      reason
Sits in the wind against me.   [*Exeunt*

SCENE XI.   *Alexandria.   Cleopatra's*
                     palace.

Enter ANTONY *with* Attendants.

Ant. Hark ! the land bids me tread no more
      upon't;
It is ashamed to bear me ! Friends, come hither :
● I am so lated in the world, that I
Have lost my way for ever : I have a ship
Laden with gold; take that, divide it; fly,
And make your peace with Cæsar.

All.   Fly ! not we.

Ant. I have fled myself; and have instructed
      cowards
To run and show their shoulders.   Friends, be
      gone;
I have myself resolved upon a course
Which has no need of you; be gone :   10
My treasure's in the harbour, take it.   O,
I follow'd that I blush to look upon :
My very hairs do mutiny; for the white
Reprove the brown for rashness, and they them
● For fear and doting.   Friends, be gone : you
      shall
Have letters from me to some friends that will
Sweep your way for you.   Pray you, look not sad,
Nor make replies of loathness : take the hint
Which my despair proclaims; let that be left
Which leaves itself : to the sea-side straightway :
I will possess you of that ship and treasure.   21
Leave me, I pray, a little : pray you now :
Nay, do so; for, indeed, I have lost command,
Therefore I pray you : I 'll see you by and by.
                              [*Sits down.*

Enter CLEOPATRA *led by* CHARMIAN *and* IRAS;
                  EROS *following.*

Eros. Nay, gentle madam, to him, comfort
      him.

Iras. Do, most dear queen.

18 *loof'd.* Luffed, turned to the wind.

36 *chance.* Fortune.

3 *lated.* Belated, left behind.

15 *doting.* Hesitating.

Eros: 'Nay, gentle madam, to him, comfort him.'
Engraving from a painting by Henry Tresham (1749?–
1814)

509

39 *Dealt on lieutenantry*. Relied on subordinates.

40 *squares*. Squadrons.

44 *unqualitied*. Unmanned.

Cleopatra: 'I little thought You would have follow'd.'
Maria Anne Younge as Cleopatra. Engraving from Bell's
edition of Shakespeare, 1773

63 *palter*. Shuffle.

Char. Do! why: what else?
Cleo. Let me sit down. O Juno!
Ant. No, no, no, no, no.
Eros. See you here, sir?   30
Ant. O fie, fie, fie!
Char. Madam!
Iras. Madam, O good empress!
Eros. Sir, sir,—
Ant. Yes, my lord, yes; he at Philippi kept
His sword e'en like a dancer; while I struck
The lean and wrinkled Cassius; and 'twas I
That the mad Brutus ended: he alone
•Dealt on lieutenantry, and no practice had
•In the brave squares of war: yet now—No matter.
Cleo. Ah, stand by.   41
Eros. The queen, my lord, the queen.
Iras. Go to him, madam, speak to him:
•He is unqualitied with very shame.
Cleo. Well then, sustain me: O!
Eros. Most noble sir, arise; the queen ap-
                                                  proaches:
Her head's declined, and death will seize her, but
Your comfort makes the rescue.
Ant. I have offended reputation,
A most unnoble swerving.
Eros.   Sir, the queen.   50
Ant. O, whither hast thou led me, Egypt?
         See,
How I convey my shame out of thine eyes
By looking back what I have left behind
'Stroy'd in dishonour.
Cleo.   O my lord, my lord,
Forgive my fearful sails! I little thought
You would have follow'd.
Ant.   Egypt, thou knew'st too well
My heart was to thy rudder tied by the strings,
And thou shouldst tow me after: o'er my spirit
Thy full supremacy thou knew'st, and that
Thy beck might from the bidding of the gods 60
Command me.
Cleo.   O, my pardon!
Ant.   Now I must
To the young man send humble treaties, dodge
•And palter in the shifts of lowness; who
With half the bulk o' the world play'd as I
                                                  pleased,
Making and marring fortunes. You did know
How much you were my conqueror; and that
My sword, made weak by my affection, would
Obey it on all cause.
Cleo.   Pardon, pardon!
Ant. Fall not a tear, I say; one of them rates
All that is won and lost: give me a kiss;   70
Even this repays me. We sent our schoolmaster;
Is he come back? Love, I am full of lead.
Some wine, within there, and our viands! For-
                                                  tune knows
We scorn her most when most she offers blows.
                                        [*Exeunt.*

SCENE XII. *Egypt. Cæsar's camp.*

Enter CÆSAR, DOLABELLA, THYREUS, *with
                                  others.*

Cæs. Let him appear that's come from Antony.
Know you him?
Dol.   Cæsar, 'tis his schoolmaster:
An argument that he is pluck'd, when hither
He sends so poor a pinion of his wing,

Which had superfluous kings for messengers
Not many moons gone by.

Enter EUPHRONIUS, *ambassador from Antony.*

Cæs.   Approach, and speak.
Euph.   Such as I am, I come from Antony:
I was of late as petty to his ends
As is the morn-dew on the myrtle-leaf
To his grand sea.
Cæs.   Be't so: declare thine office.   10
Euph.   Lord of his fortunes he salutes thee,
  and
Requires to live in Egypt: which not granted,
He lessens his requests; and to thee sues
To let him breathe between the heavens and
  earth,
A private man in Athens: this for him.
Next, Cleopatra does confess thy greatness;
Submits her to thy might; and of thee craves
The circle of the Ptolemies for her heirs,
Now hazarded to thy grace.
Cæs.   For Antony,
I have no ears to his request.   The queen   20
Of audience nor desire shall fail, so she
From Egypt drive her all-disgraced friend,
Or take his life there: this if she perform,
She shall not sue unheard.   So to them both.
Euph.   Fortune pursue thee!
Cæs.   Bring him through the bands.
                        [*Exit Euphronius.*
[*To Thyreus*]   To try thy eloquence, now 'tis
      time: dispatch;
From Antony win Cleopatra: promise,
And in our name, what she requires; add more,
From thine invention, offers: women are not
In their best fortunes strong; but want will
      perjure   30
The ne'er-touch'd vestal: try thy cunning, Thy-
      reus;
•Make thine own edict for thy pains, which we
Will answer as a law.
Thyr.   Cæsar, I go.
Cæs.   Observe how Antony becomes his flaw,
And what thou think'st his very action speaks
In every power that moves.
Thyr.   Cæsar, I shall. [*Exeunt.*

SCENE XIII.   *Alexandria.   Cleopatra's
                      palace.*

Enter CLEOPATRA, ENOBARBUS, CHARMIAN,
              and IRAS.

Cleo.   What shall we do, Enobarbus?
Eno.   Think, and die.
Cleo.   Is Antony or we in fault for this?
Eno.   Antony only, that would make his will
Lord of his reason.   What though you fled
•From that great face of war, whose several
      ranges
Frighted each other? why should he follow?
The itch of his affection should not then
Have nick'd his captainship; at such a point,
When half to half the world opposed, he being
•The   meered question: 'twas a shame no less   10
Than was his loss, to course your flying flags,
And leave his navy gazing.
Cleo.   Prithee, peace.

32 *Make . . . edict.* Name your own reward.

5 *ranges.* Ranks.

10 *meered.* Only.

Cleopatra's Palace designed by H. Romaine Walker,
His Majesty's Theatre, London, 1898

27 *declined*. In decline.

31 *sworder*. Swordsman.

35 *Knowing all measures*. Being a good judge of all.

41 *square*. Disagree.

Enter ANTONY *with* EUPHRONIUS, *the Ambassador.*

Ant.   Is that his answer?
Euph.   Ay, my lord.
Ant.   The queen shall then have courtesy, so she
Will yield us up.
Euph.   He says so.
Ant.   Let her know 't.
To the boy Cæsar send this grizzled head,
And he will fill thy wishes to the brim
With principalities.
Cleo.   That head, my lord?   19
Ant.   To him again: tell him he wears the rose
Of youth upon him; from which the world should note
Something particular: his coin, ships, legions,
May be a coward's; whose ministers would prevail
Under the service of a child as soon
As i' the command of Cæsar: I dare him therefore
To lay his gay comparisons apart,
●And answer me declined, sword against sword,
Ourselves alone.   I'll write it: follow me.
            [*Exeunt Antony and Euphronius.*
Eno.   [*Aside*] Yes, like enough, high-battled Cæsar will   29
Unstate his happiness, and be staged to the show,
●Against a sworder!   I see men's judgements are
A parcel of their fortunes; and things outward
Do draw the inward quality after them,
To suffer all alike.   That he should dream,
●Knowing all measures, the full Cæsar will
Answer his emptiness!   Cæsar, thou hast subdued
His judgement too.

Enter an Attendant.

Att.   A messenger from Cæsar.
Cleo.   What, no more ceremony?   See, my women!
Against the blown rose may they stop their nose
That kneel'd unto the buds.   Admit him, sir.   40
            [*Exit Attendant.*
● *Eno.*   [*Aside*] Mine honesty and I begin to square.
The loyalty well held to fools does make
Our faith mere folly: yet he that can endure
To follow with allegiance a fall'n lord
Does conquer him that did his master conquer,
And earns a place i' the story.

Enter THYREUS.

Cleo.   Cæsar's will?
Thyr.   Hear it apart.
Cleo.   None but friends: say boldly.
Thyr.   So, haply, are they friends to Antony.
Eno.   He needs as many, sir, as Cæsar has;
Or needs not us.   If Cæsar please, our master   50
Will leap to be his friend: for us, you know
Whose he is we are, and that is, Cæsar's.
Thyr.   So.
Thus then, thou most renown'd: Cæsar entreats,
Not to consider in what case thou stand'st,
Further than he is Cæsar.
Cleo.   Go on: right royal.
Thyr.   He knows that you embrace not Antony
As you did love, but as you fear'd him.
Cleo.   O!

Thyr.   The scars upon your honour, there-
fore, he
Does pity, as constrained blemishes,
Not as deserved.
   Cleo.   He is a god, and knows   60
What is most right: mine honour was not yielded,
But conquer'd merely.
   Eno.   [*Aside*] To be sure of that,
I will ask Antony. Sir, sir, thou art so leaky,
That we must leave thee to thy sinking, for
Thy dearest quit thee.   [*Exit.*
   Thyr.   Shall I say to Cæsar
What you require of him? for he partly begs
To be desired to give. It much would please him,
That of his fortunes you should make a staff
To lean upon: but it would warm his spirits,
To hear from me you had left Antony,   70
†And put yourself under his shrowd,
The universal landlord.
   Cleo.   What's your name?
   Thyr.   My name is Thyreus.
   Cleo.   Most kind messenger,
Say to great Cæsar this: in deputation
I kiss his conquering hand: tell him, I am prompt
To lay my crown at's feet, and there to kneel:
Tell him, from his all-obeying breath I hear
The doom of Egypt.
   Thyr.   'Tis your noblest course.
Wisdom and fortune combating together,
If that the former dare but what it can,   80
No chance may shake it.   Give me grace to lay
My duty on your hand.
   Cleo.   Your Cæsar's father oft,
When he hath mused of taking kingdoms in,
Bestow'd his lips on that unworthy place,
As it rain'd kisses.

    Re-enter ANTONY *and* ENOBARBUS.

   Ant.   Favours, by Jove that thunders!
What art thou, fellow?
   Thyr.   One that but performs
The bidding of the fullest man, and worthiest
To have command obey'd.
   Eno.   [*Aside*] You will be whipp'd.
   Ant.   Approach, there! Ah, you kite! Now,
     gods and devils!
Authority melts from me: of late, when I cried
'Ho!'   90
Like boys unto a muss, kings would start forth,
And cry 'Your will?' Have you no ears? I am
Antony yet.

    Enter Attendants.

        Take hence this Jack, and whip him.
   Eno. [*Aside*] 'Tis better playing with a lion's
     whelp
Than with an old one dying.
   Ant.   Moon and stars!
Whip him. Were't twenty of the greatest tribu-
taries
That do acknowledge Cæsar, should I find them
So saucy with the hand of she here,—what's her
     name,
Since she was Cleopatra? Whip him, fellows,
Till, like a boy, you see him cringe his face,   100
And whine aloud for mercy: take him hence.
   Thyr.   Mark Antony!
   Ant.   Tug him away: being whipp'd,
Bring him again: this Jack of Cæsar's shall

62 *merely.* Totally.

71 *shrowd.* Shelter.

Antony: 'Favours, by Jove that thunders!' Engraving
from Bell's edition, 1773

91 *muss.* Scrum.

109 *feeders*. Menials.

110 *boggler*. Deceiver.

112 *seel*. Blind.

Antony: 'I found you as a morsel cold upon Dead Caesar's trencher:' Drawing by John Masey Wright (1777–1866)

120 *Luxuriously*. Lustfully.

124 *quit*. Requite.

127 *Basan*. A Biblical reference. Basan is a district of Southern Syria frequently referred to in the Old Testament. The 'fat bull of Basan' is cited in *Psalms* xxii, 12; and the hill of Basan in *Psalms* lxviii, 15.

149 *enfranched bondman*. Freed slave.

153 *terrene moon*. Cleopatra.

Bear us an errand to him.
    [Exeunt Attendants with Thyreus.
You were half blasted ere I knew you: ha!
Have I my pillow left unpress'd in Rome,
Forborne the getting of a lawful race,
And by a gem of women, to be abused
By one that looks on feeders?
  Cleo.   Good my lord,—
  Ant. You have been a boggler ever: 110
But when we in our viciousness grow hard—
O misery on 't!—the wise gods seel our eyes;
In our own filth drop our clear judgements; make us
Adore our errors; laugh at 's, while we strut
To our confusion.
  Cleo.   O, is 't come to this?
  Ant. I found you as a morsel cold upon
Dead Cæsar's trencher; nay, you were a fragment
Of Cneius Pompey's; besides what hotter hours,
Unregister'd in vulgar fame, you have
Luxuriously pick'd out: for, I am sure,   120
Though you can guess what temperance should be,
You know not what it is.
  Cleo.   Wherefore is this?
  Ant. To let a fellow that will take rewards
And say 'God quit you!' be familiar with
My playfellow, your hand; this kingly seal
And plighter of high hearts! O, that I were
Upon the hill of Basan, to outroar
The horned herd! for I have savage cause;
And to proclaim it civilly, were like
A halter'd neck which does the hangman thank
For being yare about him.

    Re-enter Attendants *with* THYREUS.

                   Is he whipp'd?   131
  First Att. Soundly, my lord.
  Ant.   Cried he? and begg'd a' pardon?
  First Att. He did ask favour.
  Ant. If that thy father live, let him repent
Thou wast not made his daughter; and be thou sorry
To follow Cæsar in his triumph, since
Thou hast been whipp'd for following him: henceforth
The white hand of a lady fever thee,
Shake thou to look on 't. Get thee back to Cæsar,
Tell him thy entertainment: look, thou say   140
He makes me angry with him; for he seems
Proud and disdainful, harping on what I am,
Not what he knew I was: he makes me angry;
And at this time most easy 'tis to do 't,
When my good stars, that were my former guides,
Have empty left their orbs, and shot their fires
Into the abysm of hell. If he mislike
My speech and what is done, tell him he has
Hipparchus, my enfranched bondman, whom
He may at pleasure whip, or hang, or torture,
As he shall like, to quit me: urge it thou: 151
Hence with thy stripes, begone! *[Exit Thyreus.*
  Cleo. Have you done yet?
  Ant.   Alack, our terrene moon
Is now eclipsed; and it portends alone
The fall of Antony!
  Cleo.   I must stay his time.
  Ant. To flatter Cæsar, would you mingle eyes
With one that ties his points?
  Cleo.   Not know me yet?
  Ant. Cold-hearted toward me?

Cleo.   Ah, dear, if I be so,
From my cold heart let heaven engender hail,
And poison it in the source; and the first stone
Drop in my neck: as it determines, so   161
Dissolve my life! The next Cæsarion smite!
Till by degrees the memory of my womb,
Together with my brave Egyptians all,
● By the discandying of this pelleted storm,
Lie graveless, till the flies and gnats of Nile
Have buried them for prey!
    Ant.   I am satisfied.
Cæsar sits down in Alexandria; where
I will oppose his fate.   Our force by land
Hath nobly held; our sever'd navy too   170
Have knit again, and fleet, threatening most sea-
          like.
Where hast thou been, my heart?   Dost thou
          hear, lady?
If from the field I shall return once more
To kiss these lips, I will appear in blood;
● I and my sword will earn our chronicle:
There's hope in't yet.
    Cleo.   That's my brave lord!
    Ant. I will be treble-sinew'd, hearted, breathed,
And fight maliciously: for when mine hours
Were nice and lucky, men did ransom lives   180
Of me for jests; but now I'll set my teeth,
And send to darkness all that stop me.   Come,
Let's have one other gaudy night: call to me
All my sad captains; fill our bowls once more;
Let's mock the midnight bell.
    Cleo.   It is my birth-day:
I had thought to have held it poor; but, since my
          lord
Is Antony again, I will be Cleopatra.
    Ant.   We will yet do well.
    Cleo.   Call all his noble captains to my lord.
    Ant.   Do so, we'll speak to them; and to-night
          I'll force   190
The wine peep through their scars.   Come on,
          my queen;
There's sap in't yet.   The next time I do fight,
I'll make death love me; for I will contend
Even with his pestilent scythe.
                    [*Exeunt all but Enobarbus.*
    Eno.   Now he'll outstare the lightning.   To
          be furious,
Is to be frighted out of fear; and in that mood
●The dove will peck the estridge; and I see still,
A diminution in our captain's brain
Restores his heart: when valour preys on reason,
It eats the sword it fights with.   I will seek   200
Some way to leave him.   [*Exit.*

ACT IV.

SCENE I. *Before Alexandria. Cæsar's camp.*

Enter CÆSAR, AGRIPPA, *and* MECÆNAS, *with
     his Army;* CÆSAR *reading a letter.*

    Cæs.   He calls me boy; and chides, as he had
          power
To beat me out of Egypt; my messenger
He hath whipp'd with rods; dares me to personal
          combat,
Cæsar to Antony: let the old ruffian know
I have many other ways to die; meantime
Laugh at his challenge.
    Mec.   Cæsar must think,

165 *discandying.* Melting.

175 *chronicle.* Place in history.

197 *estridge.* Ostrich.

The estridge. Woodcut from a 12th century Latin bestiary

9 *boot.* Profit.

The banquet of Cleopatra. Detail of a painting by Giovanni B. Tiepolo (1696–1770)

When one so great begins to rage, he's hunted
Even to falling.   Give him no breath, but now
● Make boot of his distraction: never anger
Made good guard for itself.
   Cæs.   Let our best heads   10
Know, that to-morrow the last of many battles
We mean to fight: within our files there are,
Of those that served Mark Antony but late,
Enough to fetch him in.   See it done:
And feast the army; we have store to do't,
And they have earn'd the waste.   Poor Antony!
                               [*Exeunt.*

SCENE II. *Alexandria.   Cleopatra's palace.*

Enter ANTONY, CLEOPATRA, ENOBARBUS, CHAR-
   MIAN, IRAS, ALEXAS, *with others.*
   Ant.   He will not fight with me, Domitius.
   Eno.   No.
   Ant.   Why should he not?
   Eno.   He thinks, being twenty times of better
     fortune,
He is twenty men to one.
   Ant.   To-morrow, soldier,
By sea and land I'll fight: or I will live,
Or bathe my dying honour in the blood
Shall make it live again.   Woo't thou fight well?
   Eno.   I'll strike, and cry 'Take all.'
   Ant.   Well said; come on.
Call forth my household servants: let's to-night
Be bounteous at our meal.

        Enter three or four Servitors.

                     Give me thy hand,   10
Thou hast been rightly honest;—so hast thou;—
Thou,—and thou,—and thou:—you have served
   me well,
And kings have been your fellows.
   Cleo.   [*Aside to Eno.*] What means this?
   Eno. [*Aside to Cleo.*] 'Tis one of those odd
     tricks which sorrow shoots
Out of the mind.
   Ant.   And thou art honest too.
I wish I could be made so many men,
And all of you clapp'd up together in
An Antony, that I might do you service
So good as you have done.
   All.   The gods forbid!
   Ant.   Well, my good fellows, wait on me to-
     night: 20
Scant not my cups; and make as much of me
As when mine empire was your fellow too,
And suffer'd my command.
   Cleo.   [*Aside to Eno.*] What does he mean?
   Eno. [*Aside to Cleo.*] To make his followers
     weep.
   Ant.   Tend me to-night;
May be it is the period of your duty:
Haply you shall not see me more; or if,
A mangled shadow: perchance to-morrow
You'll serve another master.   I look on you
As one that takes his leave.   Mine honest friends,
I turn you not away; but, like a master   30
Married to your good service, stay till death:
Tend me to-night two hours, I ask no more,
And the gods yield you for't!
   Eno.   What mean you, sir,
To give them this discomfort? Look, they weep;
And I, an ass, am onion-eyed: for shame,

Transform us not to women.
Ant.   Ho, ho, ho!
Now the witch take me, if I meant it thus!
Grace grow where those drops fall! My hearty
    friends,
You take me in too dolorous a sense;
For I spake to you for your comfort; did desire
    you   40
To burn this night with torches: know, my hearts,
I hope well of to-morrow; and will lead you
Where rather I'll expect victorious life
Than death and honour.   Let's to supper, come,
And drown consideration.   [*Exeunt.*

SCENE III.   *The same.   Before the palace.*

Enter two Soldiers *to their guard.*

First Sold.   Brother, good night: to-morrow
    is the day.
Sec. Sold.   It will determine one way: fare
    you well.
Heard you of nothing strange about the streets?
First Sold.   Nothing.   What news?
Sec. Sold.   Belike 'tis but a rumour.   Good
    night to you.
First Sold.   Well, sir, good night.

Enter two other Soldiers.

Sec. Sold.   Soldiers, have careful watch.
Third Sold.   And you.   Good night, good night.
              [*They place themselves in every corner of
                                    the stage.*
● *Fourth Sold.*   Here we: and if to-morrow
Our navy thrive, I have an absolute hope   10
Our landmen will stand up.
    Third Sold.   'Tis a brave army,
And full of purpose.
              [*Music of the hautboys as under the stage.*
Fourth Sold.   Peace! what noise?
First Sold.   List, list!
Sec. Sold.   Hark!
First Sold.   Music i' the air.
Third Sold.   Under the earth.
Fourth Sold.   It signs well, does it not?
Third Sold.   No.
First Sold.   Peace, I say!
What should this mean?
Sec. Sold.   'Tis the god Hercules, whom An-
    tony loved,
Now leaves him.
    First Sold.   Walk; let's see if other watchmen
Do hear what we do.
              [*They advance to another post.*
Sec. Sold.   How now, masters!
All.   [*Speaking together*] How now!
How now! do you hear this?
    First Sold.   Ay; is't not strange? 20
Third Sold.   Do you hear, masters? do you
    hear?
● *First Sold.*   Follow the noise so far as we have
    quarter;
Let's see how it will give off.
    All.   Content. 'Tis strange. [*Exeunt.*

SCENE IV.   *The same.   A room in the palace.*

Enter ANTONY *and* CLEOPATRA, CHARMIAN,
        and others attending.

Ant.   Eros! mine armour, Eros!

9 *Here we.* i.e. place ourselves.

SD *hautboys.* Oboes.

Second Soldier: ''Tis the god Hercules . . .' Hercules,
the son of Jupiter, renowned for his strength. Engraving
from a painting by Raphael, 1811

22 *so . . . quarter.* To the limit of our beat.

Antony: '. . . thou art The armourer of my heart:'
Constance Collier as Cleopatra and H. Beerbohm Tree
as Mark Antony, His Majesty's Theatre, London, 1906

8 *Sooth, la.* Really!

13 *daff't.* Take it off.

22 *riveted trim.* Armour.

23 *port.* Gates.

32 *mechanic.* Formal.

Cleo.   Sleep a little.
Ant. No, my chuck.   Eros, come; mine ar-
    mour, Eros!

Enter EROS *with armour.*

Come, good fellow, put mine iron on:
If fortune be not ours to-day, it is
Because we brave her: come.
Cleo.   Nay, I 'll help too.
What 's this for?
Ant.   Ah, let be, let be! thou art
The armourer of my heart: false, false; this, this.
Cleo. Sooth, la, I 'll help: thus it must be.
Ant.   Well, well;
We shall thrive now. Seest thou, my good fellow?
Go put on thy defences.
Eros.   Briefly, sir.   10
Cleo. Is not this buckled well?
Ant.   Rarely, rarely:
He that unbuckles this, till we do please
To daff't for our repose, shall hear a storm.
Thou fumblest, Eros; and my queen 's a squire
More tight at this than thou: dispatch.   O love,
That thou couldst see my wars to-day, and knew'st
The royal occupation! thou shouldst see
A workman in 't.

Enter an armed Soldier.

                  Good morrow to thee; welcome:
Thou look'st like him that knows a warlike charge:
To business that we love we rise betime,   . 20
And go to 't with delight.
Sold.   A thousand, sir,
Early though 't be, have on their riveted trim,
And at the port expect you.
                        [*Shout. Trumpets flourish.*

Enter Captains *and* Soldiers.

Capt. The morn is fair. Good morrow, general.
All. Good morrow, general.
Ant.   'Tis well blown, lads:
This morning, like the spirit of a youth
That means to be of note, begins betimes.
So, so; come, give me that: this way; well said.
Fare thee well, dame, whate'er becomes of me:
This is a soldier's kiss: rebukeable [*Kisses her.*
And worthy shameful check it were, to stand 31
On more mechanic compliment; I 'll leave thee
Now, like a man of steel.   You that will fight,
Follow me close; I 'll bring you to 't. Adieu.
            [*Exeunt Antony, Eros, Captains, and
                                        Soldiers.*

Char. Please you, retire to your chamber.
Cleo.   Lead me.
He goes forth gallantly. That he and Cæsar might
Determine this great war in single fight!
Then, Antony,—but now—Well, on. [*Exeunt.*

SCENE V. *Alexandria. Antony's camp.*

Trumpets sound.   Enter ANTONY *and* EROS; *a*
    Soldier *meeting them.*

Sold. The gods make this a happy day to
    Antony!
Ant. Would thou and those thy scars had
    once prevail'd
To make me fight at land!
Sold.   Hadst thou done so,
The kings that have revolted, and the soldier

That has this morning left thee, would have still
Follow'd thy heels.
   Ant.   Who's gone this morning?
   Sold.   Who!
One ever near thee: call for Enobarbus,
He shall not hear thee; or from Cæsar's camp
Say ' I am none of thine.'
   Ant.   What say'st thou?
   Sold.   Sir,
He is with Cæsar.
   Eros.   Sir, his chests and treasure   10
He has not with him.
   Ant.   Is he gone?
   Sold.   Most certain.
   Ant. Go, Eros, send his treasure after; do it;
Detain no jot, I charge thee: write to him—
I will subscribe—gentle adieus and greetings;
Say that I wish he never find more cause
To change a master.   O, my fortunes have
Corrupted honest men!   Dispatch.—Enobarbus!
                         [*Exeunt.*

SCENE VI. *Alexandria.   Cæsar's camp.*

Flourish.   Enter CÆSAR, AGRIPPA, *with* ENO-
      BARBUS, *and others.*

   Cæs. Go forth, Agrippa, and begin the fight:
Our will is Antony be took alive;
Make it so known.
   Agr. Cæsar, I shall.   [*Exit.*
   Cæs. The time of universal peace is near:
Prove this a prosperous day, the three-nook'd
    world
Shall bear the olive freely.

        Enter a Messenger.

   Mess.   Antony
Is come into the field.
   Cæs.   Go charge Agrippa
Plant those that have revolted in the van,
That Antony may seem to spend his fury   10
Upon himself.   [*Exeunt all but Enobarbus.*
   Eno. Alexas did revolt; and went to Jewry on
Affairs of Antony; there did persuade
Great Herod to incline himself to Cæsar,
And leave his master Antony: for this pains
Cæsar hath hang'd him.   Canidius and the rest
That fell away have entertainment, but
No honourable trust.   I have done ill:
Of which I do accuse myself so sorely,
That I will joy no more.

      Enter a Soldier *of* CÆSAR'S.

   Sold.   Enobarbus, Antony   20
Hath after thee sent all thy treasure, with
His bounty overplus: the messenger
Came on my guard; and at thy tent is now
Unloading of his mules.
   Eno.   I give it you.
   Sold. Mock not, Enobarbus.
●I tell you true: best you safed the bringer
Out of the host; I must attend mine office,
Or would have done't myself.   Your emperor
Continues still a Jove.   [*Exit.*
   Eno. I am alone the villain of the earth,   30
And feel I am so most.   O Antony,
Thou mine of bounty, how wouldst thou have paid
My better service, when my turpitude

26 *safed.* Gave safe conduct to.

Roman soldiers. From a 19th century engraving

35 *thought*. Grief. *mean*. Means.

9 *bench-holes*. i.e. privy holes.

10 *scotches*. Wounds.

Antony: 'We have beat him to his camp.' Costume design by Motley, Stratford-upon-Avon, 1953

2 *gests*. Actions.

7 *Hector*. Legendary Trojan champion.

Thou dost so crown with gold! This blows my heart:
● If swift thought break it not, a swifter mean
Shall outstrike thought: but thought will do 't, I feel.
I fight against thee! No: I will go seek
Some ditch wherein to die; the foul'st best fits
My latter part of life.   [*Exit.*

SCENE VII.   *Field of battle between the camps.*

Alarum. Drums and trumpets. Enter AGRIPPA *and others.*

Agr.   Retire, we have engaged ourselves too far:
Cæsar himself has work, and our oppression
Exceeds what we expected.   [*Exeunt.*

Alarums.   Enter ANTONY, *and* SCARUS *wounded.*

Scar.   O my brave emperor, this is fought indeed!
Had we done so at first, we had droven them home
With clouts about their heads.
Ant.   Thou bleed'st apace.
Scar.   I had a wound here that was like a T,
But now 'tis made an H.
Ant.   They do retire.
● *Scar.*   We'll beat 'em into bench-holes: I have yet
● Room for six scotches more.   10

Enter EROS.

Eros.   They are beaten, sir; and our advantage serves
For a fair victory.
Scar.   Let us score their backs,
And snatch 'em up, as we take hares, behind:
'Tis sport to maul a runner.
Ant.   I will reward thee
Once for thy spritely comfort, and ten-fold
For thy good valour.   Come thee on.
Scar.   I'll halt after. [*Exeunt.*

SCENE VIII.   *Under the walls of Alexandria.*

Alarum. Enter ANTONY, *in a march;* SCARUS, *with others.*

Ant.   We have beat him to his camp: run one before,
● And let the queen know of our gests. To-morrow,
Before the sun shall see 's, we'll spill the blood
That has to-day escaped.   I thank you all;
For doughty-handed are you, and have fought
Not as you served the cause, but as 't had been
● Each man's like mine; you have shown all Hectors.
Enter the city, clip your wives, your friends,
Tell them your feats; whilst they with joyful tears
Wash the congealment from your wounds, and kiss   10
The honour'd gashes whole.   [*To Scarus*] Give me thy hand;

Enter CLEOPATRA, *attended.*

To this great fairy I'll commend thy acts,
Make her thanks bless thee.   [*To Cleo.*] O thou day o' the world,

Chain mine arm'd neck; leap thou, attire and all,
● Through proof of harness to my heart, and there
Ride on the pants triumphing!
   Cleo.   Lord of lords!
O infinite virtue, comest thou smiling from
The world's great snare uncaught?
   Ant.   My nightingale,
We have beat them to their beds.   What, girl!
   though grey
Do something mingle with our younger brown,
   yet ha' we   20
A brain that nourishes our nerves, and can
Get goal for goal of youth.   Behold this man:
Commend unto his lips thy favouring hand:
Kiss it, my warrior: he hath fought to-day
As if a god, in hate of mankind, had
Destroy'd in such a shape.
   Cleo.   I'll give thee, friend,
An armour all of gold; it was a king's.
●   *Ant.*   He has deserved it, were it carbuncled
Like holy Phœbus' car.   Give me thy hand:
Through Alexandria make a jolly march: 30
● Bear our hack'd targets like the men that owe
   them:
Had our great palace the capacity
To camp this host, we all would sup together,
And drink carouses to the next day's fate,
Which promises royal peril.   Trumpeters,
With brazen din blast you the city's ear;
Make mingle with our rattling tabourines;
That heaven and earth may strike their sounds
   together,
Applauding our approach.   [*Exeunt.* 39

      Scene IX.   *Cæsar's camp.*

     Sentinels *at their post.*

First Sold.   If we be not relieved within this
   hour,
We must return to the court of guard: the night
Is shiny; and they say we shall embattle
By the second hour i' the morn.
   Sec. Sold.   This last day was
● A shrewd one to 's.

    Enter ENOBARBUS.

   Eno.   O, bear me witness, night,—
   Third Sold.   What man is this?
   Sec. Sold.   Stand close, and list him.
   Eno.   Be witness to me, O thou blessed moon,
When men revolted shall upon record
Bear hateful memory, poor Enobarbus did
Before thy face repent!
   First Sold.   Enobarbus!
   Third Sold.   Peace!   10
Hark further.
   Eno.   O sovereign mistress of true melancholy,
● The poisonous damp of night disponge upon me,
That life, a very rebel to my will,
May hang no longer on me: throw my heart
Against the flint and hardness of my fault;
Which, being dried with grief, will break to
   powder,
And finish all foul thoughts.   O Antony,
Nobler than my revolt is infamous,
Forgive me in thine own particular;   20
● But let the world rank me in register
A master-leaver and a fugitive:
O Antony! O Antony!   [*Dies.*

15 *proof of harness.* Strong armour.

28 *carbuncled.* Jeweled.

Charles Coghlan as Antony and Lily Langtry as Cleopatra, Princess's Theatre, London, 1890

31 *targets.* Shields.

5 *shrewd.* Bad.

13 *disponge.* Drip.

21 *register.* History.

Romans in battle. Engraving from a design for a bas-relief by Raphael, 1811

29 *raught*. Reached.

8 *appointment*. Deployment.

1 *But*. Unless, but for.

8 *fretted*. Worn.

Sec. Sold.　　　　　Let's speak
To him.
　First Sold.   Let's hear him, for the things he
　　speaks
May concern Cæsar.
　Third Sold.　　　Let's do so.   But he sleeps.
　First Sold.   Swoons rather; for so bad a prayer
　　as his
Was never yet for sleep.
　Sec. Sold.　　　　　Go we to him.
　Third Sold.   Awake, sir, awake: speak to us.
　Sec. Sold.　　　　　　Hear you, sir?
● *First Sold.*   The hand of death hath raught
　　him. [*Drums afar off.*] Hark! the drums
Demurely wake the sleepers.   Let us bear him 31
To the court of guard; he is of note: our hour
Is fully out.
　Third Sold.   Come on, then;
He may recover yet.　　　[*Exeunt with the body.*

SCENE X.   *Between the two camps.*

Enter ANTONY *and* SCARUS, *with their Army.*

　Ant.   Their preparation is to-day by sea;
We please them not by land.
　Scar.　　　　　　For both, my lord.
　Ant.   I would they 'ld fight i' the fire or i' the
　　air;
We 'ld fight there too.   But this it is; our foot
Upon the hills adjoining to the city
Shall stay with us: order for sea is given;
†They have put forth the haven...
● Where their appointment we may best discover,
And look on their endeavour.　　[*Exeunt.* 9

SCENE XI.   *Another part of the same.*

Enter CÆSAR, *and his Army.*

● *Cæs.*   But being charged, we will be still by
　　land,
Which, as I take 't, we shall; for his best force
Is forth to, man his galleys.   To the vales,
And hold our best advantage.　　[*Exeunt.*

SCENE XII.   *Another part of the same.*

Enter ANTONY *and* SCARUS.

　Ant.   Yet they are not join'd: where yond
　　pine does stand,
I shall discover all: I 'll bring thee word
Straight, how 'tis like to go.　　　[*Exit.*
　Scar.　　　　　Swallows have built
In Cleopatra's sails their nests: the augurers
Say they know not, they cannot tell; look grimly,
And dare not speak their knowledge.   Antony
Is valiant, and dejected; and, by starts,
● His fretted fortunes give him hope, and fear,
Of what he has, and has not.
　　　　　[*Alarum afar off, as at a sea-fight.*

Re-enter ANTONY.

　Ant.　　　　　All is lost;
This foul Egyptian hath betrayed me:　　　10
My fleet hath yielded to the foe; and yonder
They cast their caps up and carouse together
Like friends long lost.   Triple-turn'd whore! 'tis
　　thou
Hast sold me to this novice; and my heart
Makes only wars on thee.   Bid them all fly;

For when I am revenged upon my charm,
I have done all.   Bid them all fly; begone.
                                            [*Exit Scarus.*
O sun, thy uprise shall I see no more:
Fortune and Antony part here; even here
Do we shake hands.   All come to this? The hearts
That spaniel'd me at heels, to whom I gave   21
Their wishes, do discandy, melt their sweets
On blossoming Cæsar; and this pine is bark'd,
That overtopp'd them all.   Betray'd I am:
O this false soul of Egypt! this grave charm,—
Whose eye beck'd forth my wars, and call'd them
        home;
Whose bosom was my crownet, my chief end,—
Like a right gipsy, hath, at fast and loose,
Beguiled me to the very heart of loss.
What, Eros, Eros!

Enter CLEOPATRA.

                        Ah, thou spell!   Avaunt! 30
Cleo. Why is my lord enraged against his love?
Ant. Vanish, or I shall give thee thy deserving,
And blemish Cæsar's triumph.   Let him take thee,
And hoist thee up to the shouting plebeians:
Follow his chariot, like the greatest spot
Of all thy sex; most monster-like, be shown
For poor'st diminutives, for doits; and let
Patient Octavia plough thy visage up
With her prepared nails.
                                    [*Exit Cleopatra.*
                        'Tis well thou'rt gone,
If it be well to live: but better 'twere   40
Thou fell'st into my fury, for one death
Might have prevented many.   Eros, ho!
The shirt of Nessus is upon me: teach me,
Alcides, thou mine ancestor, thy rage:
Let me lodge Lichas on the horns o' the moon;
And with those hands, that grasp'd the heaviest
        club,
Subdue my worthiest self.   The witch shall die:
To the young Roman boy she hath sold me, and
        I fall
Under this plot; she dies for't.   Eros, ho! [*Exit.*

SCENE XIII. *Alexandria.   Cleopatra's*
palace.

Enter CLEOPATRA, CHARMIAN, IRAS, *and*
MARDIAN.

Cleo. Help me, my women! O, he is more mad
Than Telamon for his shield; the boar of Thessaly
Was never so emboss'd.
Char.   To the monument!
There lock yourself, and send him word you are
        dead.
The soul and body rive not more in parting
Than greatness going off.
Cleo.   To the monument!
Mardian, go tell him I have slain myself;
Say, that the last I spoke was 'Antony,'
And word it, prithee, piteously: hence, Mardian,
And bring me how he takes my death.   To the
        monument!   [*Exeunt.* 10

SCENE XIV. *The same.   Another room.*

Enter ANTONY *and* EROS.

Ant. Eros, thou yet behold'st me?
Eros.   Ay, noble lord.

---

22 *discandy*. Dissolve.

37 *doits*. Fractions of a farthing.

Egyptian soldiers. Nineteenth century engraving from a wall painting in an Egyptian tomb

---

43 *of Nessus*. i.e. bloodstained.

44 *Alcides*. Hercules.

2 *Telamon*. Ajax Telamon, who killed himself for failing to win the shield of Achilles for bravery. *boar*. Alludes to the legend that Diana sent a boar to ravage Thessaly.

3 *emboss'd*. Foaming at the mouth.

10 *rack.* Clouds. *dislimns.* Fades away.

14 *knave.* Boy.

Antony: 'Unarm, Eros: the long days' task is done, And we must sleep.' H. Beerbohm Tree as Antony, His Majesty's Theatre, London, 1906

40 *continent.* i.e. body.

Ant.   Sometime we see a cloud that's dragon-
ish;
A vapour sometime like a bear or lion,
A tower'd citadel, a pendent rock,
A forked mountain, or blue promontory
With trees upon't, that nod unto the world,
And mock our eyes with air: thou hast seen these
signs;
They are black vesper's pageants.
  Eros.   Ay, my lord.
  Ant.   That which is now a horse, even with a
thought
The rack dislimns, and makes it indistinct,   10
As water is in water.
  Eros.   It does, my lord.
  Ant.   My good knave Eros, now thy captain is
Even such a body: here I am Antony:
Yet cannot hold this visible shape, my knave.
I made these wars for Egypt: and the queen,—
Whose heart I thought I had, for she had mine;
Which whilst it was mine had annex'd unto't
A million more, now lost,—she, Eros, has
Pack'd cards with Cæsar, and false-play'd my
glory
Unto an enemy's triumph.   20
Nay, weep not, gentle Eros; there is left us
Ourselves to end ourselves.

          Enter MARDIAN.

                    O, thy vile lady!
She has robb'd me of my sword.
  Mar.   No, Antony;
My mistress loved thee, and her fortunes mingled
With thine entirely.
  Ant   Hence, saucy eunuch; peace!
She hath betray'd me and shall die the death.
  Mar.   Death of one person can be paid but once,
And that she has discharged: what thou wouldst do
Is done unto thy hand: the last she spake
Was 'Antony! most noble Antony!'   30
Then in the midst a tearing groan did break
The name of Antony; it was divided
Between her heart and lips: she render'd life,
Thy name so buried in her.
  Ant.   Dead, then?
  Mar.   Dead.
  Ant.   Unarm, Eros: the long day's task is done,
And we must sleep. [*To Mar.*] That thou de-
part'st hence safe,
Does pay thy labour richly; go. [*Exit Mardian.*
                    Off, pluck off:
The seven-fold shield of Ajax cannot keep
The battery from my heart.   O, cleave, my sides!
Heart, once be stronger than thy continent,   40
Crack thy frail case! Apace, Eros, apace.
No more a soldier: bruised pieces, go;
You have been nobly borne.   From me awhile.
                    [*Exit Eros.*
I will o'ertake thee, Cleopatra, and
Weep for my pardon.   So it must be, for now
All length is torture: since the torch is out,
Lie down, and stray no farther: now all labour
Mars what it does; yea, very force entangles
Itself with strength: seal then, and all is done.
Eros!—I come, my queen:—Eros!—Stay for me:
Where souls do couch on flowers, we'll hand in
hand,   51
And with our sprightly port make the ghosts gaze:

• Dido and her Æneas shall want troops,
And all the haunt be ours.   Come, Eros, Eros!

Re-enter EROS.

Eros.   What would my lord?
Ant.   Since Cleopatra died,
I have lived in such dishonour, that the gods
Detest my baseness.   I, that with my sword
Quarter'd the world, and o'er green Neptune's
      back
With ships made cities, condemn myself to lack
The courage of a woman; less noble mind   60
Than she which by her death our Cæsar tells
' I am conqueror of myself.' Thou art sworn, Eros,
• That, when the exigent should come, which now
Is come indeed, when I should see behind me
The inevitable prosecution of
Disgrace and horror, that, on my command,
Thou then wouldst kill me: do't; the time is come:
Thou strikest not me, 'tis Cæsar thou defeat'st.
Put colour in thy cheek.
      Eros.   The gods withhold me!
Shall I do that which all the Parthian darts,   70
Though enemy, lost aim, and could not?
      Ant.   Eros,
Wouldst thou be window'd in great Rome and see
• Thy master thus with pleach'd arms, bending down
His corrigible neck, his face subdued
To penetrative shame, whilst the wheel'd seat
Of fortunate Cæsar, drawn before him, branded
His baseness that ensued?
      Eros.   I would not see't.
Ant.   Come, then; for with a wound I must be
      cured.
Draw that thy honest sword, which thou hast worn
Most useful for thy country.
      Eros.   O, sir, pardon me!   80
Ant.   When I did make thee free, sworest thou
      not then
To do this when I bade thee?   Do it at once;
Or thy precedent services are all
But accidents unpurposed.   Draw, and come.
Eros.   Turn from me, then, that noble count-
      enance,
Wherein the worship of the whole world lies.
Ant.   Lo thee!   [*Turning from him.*
Eros.   My sword is drawn.
Ant.   Then let it do at once
The thing why thou hast drawn it.
      Eros.   My dear master,
My captain, and my emperor, let me say,   90
Before I strike this bloody stroke, farewell.
Ant.   'Tis said, man; and farewell.
Eros.   Farewell, great chief.   Shall I strike now?
Ant.   Now, Eros.
Eros.   Why, there then: thus I do escape the
      sorrow
Of Antony's death.   [*Kills himself.*
      Ant.   Thrice-nobler than myself!
Thou teachest me, O valiant Eros, what
I should, and thou couldst not.   My queen and
      Eros
Have by their brave instruction got upon me
A nobleness in record: but I will be
A bridegroom in my death, and run into't   100
As to a lover's bed.   Come, then; and, Eros,
Thy master dies thy scholar: to do thus
                        [*Falling on his sword.*

53 *Dido and Æneas.* Legendary lovers; the queen of
Carthage and the mythical founder of Rome. *want troops.*
Lack admirers.

Neptune, god of the sea. Engraving from a painting by
Raphael, 1811

---

63 *exigent.* Need.

73 *pleach'd.* Folded.

123 *disposed.* Made terms.

Antony: 'Bear me, good friends, where Cleopatra bides.' Engraving by Kenny Meadows from Barry Cornwall's *The Works of Shakspere*, 1846

I learn'd of thee.   How! not dead? not dead?
The guard, ho! O, dispatch me!

       Enter DERCETAS *and* Guard.

  First Guard.   What's the noise?
  Ant. I have done my work ill, friends: O,
    make an end
Of what I have begun.
  Sec. Guard.   The star is fall'n.
  First Guard. And time is at his period.
  All.   Alas, and woe!
  Ant. Let him that loves me strike me dead.
  First Guard.   Not I.
  Sec. Guard. Nor I.   109
  Third Guard. Nor any one. [*Exeunt Guard.*
  Der. Thy death and fortunes bid thy fol-
    lowers fly.
This sword but shown to Cæsar, with this tidings,
Shall enter me with him.

       Enter DIOMEDES.

  Dio. Where's Antony?
  Der.   There, Diomed, there.
  Dio.   Lives he?
Wilt thou not answer, man?   [*Exit Dercetas.*
  Ant. Art thou there, Diomed? Draw thy
    sword, and give me
Sufficing strokes for death.
  Dio.   Most absolute lord,
My mistress Cleopatra sent me to thee.
  Ant. When did she send thee?
  Dio.   Now, my lord.
  Ant.   Where is she?
  Dio. Lock'd in her monument. She had a
    prophesying fear   120
Of what hath come to pass: for when she saw—
Which never shall be found—you did suspect
•She had disposed with Cæsar, and that your rage
Would not be purged, she sent you word she was
    dead;
But, fearing since how it might work, hath sent
Me to proclaim the truth; and I am come,
I dread, too late.
  Ant. Too late, good Diomed: call my guard,
    I prithee.
  Dio. What, ho, the emperor's guard! The
    guard, what, ho!
Come, your lord calls!   130

    Enter four or five of the Guard *of* ANTONY.

  Ant. Bear me, good friends, where Cleopatra
    bides;
'Tis the last service that I shall command you.
  First Guard. Woe, woe are we, sir, you may
    not live to wear
All your true followers out.
  All.   Most heavy day!
  Ant. Nay, good my fellows, do not please
    sharp fate
To grace it with your sorrows: bid that wel-
    come
Which comes to punish us, and we punish it
Seeming to bear it lightly.   Take me up:
I have led you oft: carry me now, good friends,
And have my thanks for all.   140
        [*Exeunt, bearing Antony.*

SCENE XV. *The same. A monument.*

Enter CLEOPATRA, *and her maids aloft, with* CHARMIAN *and* IRAS.

Cleo. O Charmian, I will never go from hence.
Char. Be comforted, dear madam.
Cleo.   No, I will not:
All strange and terrible events are welcome,
But comforts we despise; our size of sorrow,
Proportion'd to our cause, must be as great
As that which makes it.

Enter, below, DIOMEDES.

                    How now! is he dead?
Dio. His death's upon him, but not dead.
Look out o' the other side your monument;
His guard have brought him thither.

Enter, below, ANTONY, *borne by the* Guard.

Cleo.   O sun,
Burn the great sphere thou movest in! darkling
    stand   10
The varying shore o' the world. O Antony,
Antony, Antony! Help, Charmian, help, Iras,
    help;
Help, friends below; let's draw him hither.
Ant.   Peace!
Not Cæsar's valour hath o'erthrown Antony,
But Antony's hath triumph'd on itself.
Cleo.   So it should be, that none but Antony
Should conquer Antony; but woe 'tis so!
Ant.   I am dying, Egypt, dying; only
I here importune death awhile, until
Of many thousand kisses the poor last   20
I lay upon thy lips.
Cleo.   I dare not, dear,—
Dear my lord, pardon,—I dare not,
Lest I be taken: not the imperious show
Of the full-fortuned Cæsar ever shall
●Be brooch'd with me; if knife, drugs, serpents,
    have
Edge, sting, or operation, I am safe:
Your wife Octavia, with her modest eyes
And still conclusion, shall acquire no honour
●Demuring upon me. But come, come, Antony,—
Help me, my women,—we must draw thee up:
Assist, good friends.   31
Ant.   O, quick, or I am gone.
Cleo. Here's sport indeed! How heavy weighs
    my lord!
Our strength is all gone into heaviness,
That makes the weight: had I great Juno's
    power,
●The strong-wing'd Mercury should fetch thee up,
And set thee by Jove's side. Yet come a little,—
Wishers were ever fools,—O, come, come, come;
    [*They heave Antony aloft to Cleopatra.*
And welcome, welcome! die where thou hast
    lived:
Quicken with kissing: had my lips that power,
Thus would I wear them out.
All.   A heavy sight!   40
Ant. I am dying, Egypt, dying:
Give me some wine, and let me speak a little.
Cleo. No, let me speak; and let me rail so
    high,
That the false housewife Fortune break her wheel,
Provoked by my offence.

Cleopatra: 'Help . . . let's draw him hither.' Engraving by Bartolomeo Pinelli, 1821

25 *brooch'd.* Decorated.

29 *Demuring.* Looking down.

35 *Mercury.* Messenger of gods.

59 *woo't.* Would you.

75 *chares.* Chores.

Costume design for Cleopatra by J. Gower Parks, Stratford-upon-Avon, 1945

Ant.   One word, sweet queen:
Of Cæsar seek your honour, with your safety. O!
  Cleo.   They do not go together.
  Ant.   Gentle, hear me:
None about Cæsar trust but Proculeius.
  Cleo.   My resolution and my hands I'll trust:
None about Cæsar.   50
  Ant.   The miserable change now at my end
Lament nor sorrow at: but please your thoughts
In feeding them with those my former fortunes
Wherein I lived, the greatest prince o' the world,
The noblest; and do now not basely die,
Not cowardly put off my helmet to
My countryman,—a Roman by a Roman
Valiantly vanquish'd.   Now my spirit is going;
• I can no more.
  Cleo.   Noblest of men, woo't die?
Hast thou no care of me? shall I abide   60
In this dull world, which in thy absence is
No better than a sty?   O, see, my women,
                                   [*Antony dies.*
The crown o' the earth doth melt.   My lord!
O, wither'd is the garland of the war,
The soldier's pole is fall'n: young boys and girls
Are level now with men; the odds is gone,
And there is nothing left remarkable
Beneath the visiting moon.   [*Faints.*
  Char.   O, quietness, lady!
  Iras.   She is dead too, our sovereign.
  Char.   Lady!
  Iras.   Madam!
  Char.   O madam, madam, madam!
  Iras.   Royal Egypt, 70
Empress!
  Char.   Peace, peace, Iras!
  Cleo.   No more, but e'en a woman, and commanded
By such poor passion as the maid that milks
• And does the meanest chares.   It were for me
To throw my sceptre at the injurious gods;
To tell them that this world did equal theirs
Till they had stol'n our jewel.   All's but naught;
Patience is sottish, and impatience does
Become a dog that's mad: then is it sin   80
To rush into the secret house of death,
Ere death dare come to us? How do you, women?
What, what! good cheer! Why, how now, Charmian!
My noble girls! Ah, women, women, look,
Our lamp is spent, it's out! Good sirs, take heart:
We'll bury him; and then, what's brave, what's noble,
Let's do it after the high Roman fashion,
And make death proud to take us.   Come, away:
This case of that huge spirit now is cold:
Ah, women, women! come; we have no friend
But resolution, and the briefest end.   91
                    [*Exeunt; those above bearing off
                              Antony's body.*

ACT V.

SCENE I. *Alexandria. Cæsar's camp.*

Enter CÆSAR, AGRIPPA, DOLABELLA, MECÆNAS, GALLUS, PROCULEIUS, *and others, his council of war.*

  Cæs.   Go to him, Dolabella, bid him yield;
Being so frustrate, tell him he mocks

The pauses that he makes.
Dol.   Cæsar, I shall. [*Exit.*

Enter DERCETAS, *with the sword of* ANTONY.

Cæs. Wherefore is that? and what art thou that darest
Appear thus to us?
Der.   I am call'd Dercetas;
Mark Antony I served, who best was worthy
Best to be served: whilst he stood up and spoke,
He was my master; and I wore my life
To spend upon his haters.   If thou please
To take me to thee, as I was to him   10
I'll be to Cæsar; if thou pleasest not,
I yield thee up my life.
Cæs.   What is't thou say'st?
Der. I say, O Cæsar, Antony is dead.
Cæs. The breaking of so great a thing should make
A greater crack: †the round world
Should have shook lions into civil streets,
And citizens to their dens: the death of Antony
Is not a single doom: in the name lay
A moiety of the world.
Der.   He is dead, Cæsar;
Not by a public minister of justice,   20
Nor by a hired knife; but that self hand,
Which writ his honour in the acts it did,
Hath, with the courage which the heart did lend it,
Splitted the heart.   This is his sword;
I robb'd his wound of it; behold it stain'd
With his most noble blood.
Cæs.   Look you sad, friends?
The gods rebuke me, but it is tidings
To wash the eyes of kings.
Agr.   And strange it is,
That nature must compel us to lament
Our most persisted deeds.
Mec.   His taints and honours 30
Waged equal with him.
Agr.   A rarer spirit never
Did steer humanity: but you, gods, will give us
Some faults to make us men.   Cæsar is touch'd.
Mec. When such a spacious mirror's set before him,
He needs must see himself.
Cæs.   O Antony!
I have follow'd thee to this; but we do lance
Diseases in our bodies: I must perforce
Have shown to thee such a declining day,
Or look on thine; we could not stall together
In the whole world: but yet let me lament,   40
With tears as sovereign as the blood of hearts,
That thou, my brother, my competitor
In top of all design, my mate in empire,
Friend and companion in the front of war,
The arm of mine own body, and the heart
Where mine his thoughts did kindle,—that our stars,
Unreconciliable, should divide
Our equalness to this.   Hear me, good friends,—
But I will tell you at some meeter season:

Enter an Egyptian.

The business of this man looks out of him;   50
We'll hear him what he says.   Whence are you?
Egyp. A poor Egyptian yet.   The queen my mistress,
Confined in all she has, her monument,

Octavius Caesar. Engraving from a Roman medal from G. du Choul's *Discours de la Religion des Anciens Romains,* 1567

6 *accidents.* Fortune. *bolts up.* Ends.

23 *Make . . . reference.* Be entirely open.

Jewellery and headdress for Cleopatra designed by Percy Macgnoid, His Majesty's Theatre, London, 1906

Of thy intents desires instruction,
That she preparedly may frame herself
To the way she's forced to.
 Cæs.   Bid her have good heart:
She soon shall know of us, by some of ours,
How honourable and how kindly we
Determine for her; for Cæsar cannot live
To be ungentle.
 Egyp. So the gods preserve thee! [*Exit.* 60
 Cæs. Come hither, Proculeius. Go and say,
We purpose her no shame: give her what comforts
The quality of her passion shall require,
Lest, in her greatness, by some mortal stroke
She do defeat us; for her life in Rome
Would be eternal in our triumph: go,
And with your speediest bring us what she says,
And how you find of her.
 Pro.   Cæsar, I shall. [*Exit.*
 Cæs. Gallus, go you along. [*Exit Gallus.*]
  Where's Dolabella,
To second Proculeius?
 All.   Dolabella!   70
 Cæs. Let him alone, for I remember now
How he's employ'd: he shall in time be ready.
Go with me to my tent; where you shall see
How hardly I was drawn into this war;
How calm and gentle I proceeded still
In all my writings: go with me, and see
What I can show in this.   [*Exeunt.*

SCENE II. *Alexandria. A room in the monument.*

Enter CLEOPATRA, CHARMIAN, *and* IRAS.

 Cleo. My desolation does begin to make
A better life. 'Tis paltry to be Cæsar;
Not being Fortune, he's but Fortune's knave,
A minister of her will: and it is great
To do that thing that ends all other deeds;
⦁Which shackles accidents and bolts up change;
Which sleeps, and never palates more the dug,
The beggar's nurse and Cæsar's.

Enter, to the gates of the monument, PROCULEIUS, GALLUS, *and* Soldiers.

 Pro. Cæsar sends greeting to the Queen of
  Egypt;
And bids thee study on what fair demands 10
Thou mean'st to have him grant thee.
 Cleo.   What's thy name?
 Pro. My name is Proculeius.
 Cleo.   Antony
Did tell me of you, bade me trust you; but
I do not greatly care to be deceived,
That have no use for trusting. If your master
Would have a queen his beggar, you must tell him,
That majesty, to keep decorum, must
No less beg than a kingdom: if he please
To give me conquer'd Egypt for my son,
He gives me so much of mine own, as I 20
Will kneel to him with thanks
 Pro.   Be of good cheer;
You're fall'n into a princely hand, fear nothing:
⦁Make your full reference freely to my lord,
Who is so full of grace, that it flows over
On all that need: let me report to him
Your sweet dependency; and you shall find
A conqueror that will pray in aid for kindness,
Where he for grace is kneel'd to.

Cleo.   Pray you, tell him
I am his fortune's vassal, and I send him
The greatness he has got.   I hourly learn   30
A doctrine of obedience; and would gladly
Look him i' the face.
   Pro.   This I'll report, dear lady.
Have comfort, for I know your plight is pitied
Of him that caused it.
   Gal.   You see how easily she may be surprised:
      [*Here Proculeius and two of the Guard
      ascend the monument by a ladder placed
      against a window, and, having descend-
      ed, come behind Cleopatra.   Some of
      the Guard unbar and open the gates.*
   [*To Proculeius and the Guard*] Guard her till
      Cæsar come.   [*Exit.*
   Iras.   Royal queen!
   Char.   O Cleopatra! thou art taken, queen.
   Cleo.   Quick, quick, good hands.
                     [*Drawing a dagger.*
   Pro.   Hold, worthy lady, hold:
                     [*Seizes and disarms her.*
Do not yourself such wrong, who are in this   40
Relieved, but not betray'd.
   Cleo.   What, of death too,
● That rids our dogs of languish?
   Pro.   Cleopatra,
Do not abuse my master's bounty by
The undoing of yourself: let the world see
His nobleness well acted, which your death
Will never let come forth.
   Cleo.   Where art thou, death?
Come hither, come! come, come, and take a
      queen
Worth many babes and beggars!
   Pro.   O, temperance, lady!
   Cleo.   Sir, I will eat no meat, I'll not drink, sir;
If idle talk will once be necessary,   50
I'll not sleep neither: this mortal house I'll ruin,
Do Cæsar what he can.   Know, sir, that I
Will not wait pinion'd at your master's court;
Nor once be chastised with the sober eye
Of dull Octavia.   Shall they hoist me up
● And show me to the shouting varletry
Of censuring Rome?   Rather a ditch in Egypt
Be gentle grave unto me! rather on Nilus' mud
Lay me stark naked, and let the water-flies
Blow me into abhorring! rather make   60
My country's high pyramides my gibbet,
And hang me up in chains!
   Pro.   You do extend
These thoughts of horror further than you shall
Find cause in Cæsar.

         Enter DOLABELLA.

   Dol.   Proculeius,
What thou hast done thy master Cæsar knows,
And he hath sent for thee: for the queen,
I'll take her to my guard.
   Pro.   So, Dolabella,
It shall content me best: be gentle to her.
[*To Cleo.*] To Cæsar I will speak what you shall
      please,
If you'll employ me to him.
   Cleo.   Say, I would die. 70
            [*Exeunt Proculeius and Soldiers.*
   Dol.   Most noble empress, you have heard of me?
   Cleo.   I cannot tell.
   Dol.   Assuredly you know me.

42 *languish.* Pain.

Cleopatra: 'Know, sir, that I Will not wait pinion'd at
your master's court;' Constance Collier as Cleopatra,
His Majesty's Theatre, London, 1906

56 *varletry.* Common people.

90 *livery.* Service.

Set for Cleopatra's monument designed by Motley,
Stratford-upon-Avon, 1954

Cleo. No matter, sir, what I have heard or
  known.
You laugh when boys or women tell their dreams;
Is't not your trick?
   Dol.   I understand not, madam.
   Cleo. I dream'd there was an Emperor Antony:
O, such another sleep, that I might see
But such another man!
   Dol.   If it might please ye,—
   Cleo. His face was as the heavens; and
   therein stuck
A sun and moon, which kept their course, and
   lighted   80
The little O, the earth.
   Dol.   Most sovereign creature,—
   Cleo. His legs bestrid the ocean: his rear'd arm
Crested the world: his voice was propertied
As all the tuned spheres, and that to friends;
But when he meant to quail and shake the orb,
He was as rattling thunder. For his bounty,
There was no winter in't; an autumn 'twas
That grew the more by reaping: his delights
Were dolphin-like; they show'd his back above
The element they lived in: in his livery   90
Walk'd crowns and crownets; realms and islands
   were
As plates dropp'd from his pocket.
   Dol.   Cleopatra!
   Cleo. Think you there was, or might be, such
   a man
As this I dream'd of?
   Dol.   Gentle madam, no.
   Cleo. You lie, up to the hearing of the gods.
But, if there be, or ever were, one such,
It's past the size of dreaming: nature wants stuff
To vie strange forms with fancy; yet, to imagine
An Antony, were nature's piece 'gainst fancy,
Condemning shadows quite.
   Dol.   Hear me, good madam. 100
Your loss is as yourself, great; and you bear it
As answering to the weight: would I might never
O'ertake pursued success, but I do feel,
By the rebound of yours, a grief that smites
My very heart at root.
   Cleo.   I thank you, sir.
Know you what Cæsar means to do with me?
   Dol. I am loath to tell you what I would you
   knew.
   Cleo. Nay, pray you, sir,—
   Dol.   Though he be honourable,—
   Cleo. He'll lead me, then, in triumph?
   Dol. Madam, he will; I know't.   110
[*Flourish, and shout within,* 'Make way there:
                   Cæsar!'

Enter Cæsar, Gallus, Proculeius, Mecænas, Seleucus, *and others of his Train.*

   Cæs. Which is the Queen of Egypt?
   Dol. It is the emperor, madam.
                 [*Cleopatra kneels.*
   Cæs. Arise, you shall not kneel:
I pray you, rise; rise, Egypt.
   Cleo.   Sir, the gods
Will have it thus; my master and my lord
I must obey.
   Cæs.   Take to you no hard thoughts:
The record of what injuries you did us,
Though written in our flesh, we shall remember
As things but done by chance.

Cleo.   Sole sir o' the world,   120
I cannot project mine own cause so well
To make it clear; but do confess I have
Been laden with like frailties which before
Have often shamed our sex.
    Cæs.   Cleopatra, know,
We will extenuate rather than enforce:
If you apply yourself to our intents,
Which towards you are most gentle, you shall
    find
A benefit in this change; but if you seek
To lay on me a cruelty, by taking
Antony's course, you shall bereave yourself   130
Of my good purposes, and put your children
To that destruction which I'll guard them from,
If thereon you rely.   I'll take my leave.
    Cleo.   And may, through all the world: 'tis
        yours; and we,
● Your scutcheons and your signs of conquest, shall
    Hang in what place you please.   Here, my good
        lord.
    Cæs.   You shall advise me in all for Cleopatra.
●   *Cleo.*   This is the brief of money, plate, and
        jewels,
I am possess'd of: 'tis exactly valued;
Not petty things admitted.   Where's Seleucus?
    Sel.   Here, madam.   141
    Cleo.   This is my treasurer: let him speak,
        my lord,
Upon his peril, that I have reserved
To myself nothing.   Speak the truth, Seleucus.
    Sel.   Madam,
I had rather seal my lips, than, to my peril,
Speak that which is not.
    Cleo.   What have I kept back?
    Sel.   Enough to purchase what you have made
        known.
    Cæs.   Nay, blush not, Cleopatra; I approve
Your wisdom in the deed.
    Cleo.   See, Cæsar! O, behold, 150
How pomp is follow'd! mine will now be yours;
And, should we shift estates, yours would be mine.
The ingratitude of this Seleucus does
Even make me wild: O slave, of no more trust
Than love that's hired!   What, goest thou back?
        thou shalt
Go back, I warrant thee; but I'll catch thine
        eyes,
Though they had wings: slave, soulless villain,
        dog!
O rarely base!
    Cæs.   Good queen, let us entreat you.
    Cleo.   O Cæsar, what a wounding shame is this,
That thou, vouchsafing here to visit me,   160
Doing the honour of thy lordliness
To one so meek, that mine own servant should
Parcel the sum of my disgraces by
Addition of his envy!   Say, good Cæsar,
That I some lady trifles have reserved,
● Immoment toys, things of such dignity
● As we greet modern friends withal; and say,
Some nobler token I have kept apart
For Livia and Octavia, to induce
Their mediation; must I be unfolded   170
With one that I have bred?   The gods! it
        smites me
Beneath the fall I have.   [*To Seleucus*] Prithee,
        go hence;
Or I shall show the cinders of my spirits

Cleopatra and Caesar. Engraving from a painting by
J. Gérôme (1824–1904)

---

135 *scutcheons.* Captured shields.

138 *brief.* List.

166 *Immoment.* Inconsequential.

167 *modern.* Of the day.

191 *words.* Deceives.

209 *mechanic.* Vulgar.

214 *lictors.* Roman officers whose function was to attend the magistrates.

Vivian Leigh as Cleopatra, St James Theatre, London, 1951

Through the ashes of my chance: wert thou a man,
Thou wouldst have mercy on me.
 Cæs.   Forbear, Seleucus.
            [*Exit Seleucus.*
 Cleo. Be it known, that we, the greatest, are misthought
For things that others do; and, when we fall,
We answer others' merits in our name,
Are therefore to be pitied.
 Cæs.   Cleopatra,
Not what you have reserved, nor what acknow-
  ledged,   180
Put we i' the roll of conquest: still be 't yours,
Bestow it at your pleasure; and believe,
Cæsar's no merchant, to make prize with you
Of things that merchants sold. Therefore be cheer'd;
Make not your thoughts your prisons: no, dear queen;
For we intend so to dispose you as
Yourself shall give us counsel. Feed, and sleep:
Our care and pity is so much upon you,
That we remain your friend; and so, adieu.
 Cleo. My master, and my lord!
 Cæs.   Not so. Adieu. 190
   [*Flourish. Exeunt Cæsar and his train.*
 Cleo. He words me, girls, he words me, that I should not
Be noble to myself: but, hark thee, Charmian.
       [*Whispers Charmian.*
 Iras. Finish, good lady; the bright day is done,
And we are for the dark.
 Cleo.   Hie thee again:
I have spoke already, and it is provided;
Go put it to the haste.
 Char.   Madam, I will.

    Re-enter DOLABELLA.

 Dol. Where is the queen?
 Char.   Behold, sir. [*Exit.*
 Cleo.   Dolabella!
 Dol. Madam, as thereto sworn by your com-
  mand,
Which my love makes religion to obey,
I tell you this: Cæsar through Syria 200
Intends his journey; and within three days
You with your children will he send before:
Make your best use of this: I have perform'd
Your pleasure and my promise.
 Cleo.   Dolabella,
I shall remain your debtor.
 Dol.   I your servant.
Adieu, good queen; I must attend on Cæsar.
 Cleo. Farewell, and thanks. [*Exit Dolabella.*
     Now, Iras, what think'st thou?
Thou, an Egyptian puppet, shalt be shown
In Rome, as well as I: mechanic slaves
With greasy aprons, rules, and hammers, shall
Uplift us to the view; in their thick breaths,
Rank of gross diet, shall we be enclouded,
And forced to drink their vapour.
 Iras.   The gods forbid!
 Cleo. Nay, 'tis most certain, Iras: saucy lictors
Will catch at us, like strumpets; and scald rhymers
Ballad us out o' tune: the quick comedians,
Extemporally will stage us, and present

Our Alexandrian revels; Antony
Shall be brought drunken forth, and I shall see
Some squeaking Cleopatra boy my greatness 220
I' the posture of a whore.
    Iras.   O the good gods!
    Cleo. Nay, that's certain.
    Iras. I'll never see't; for, I am sure, my nails
Are stronger than mine eyes.
    Cleo.   Why, that's the way
To fool their preparation, and to conquer
Their most absurd intents.

Re-enter CHARMIAN.

                    Now, Charmian!
Show me, my women, like a queen: go fetch
My best attires: I am again for Cydnus,
To meet Mark Antony: sirrah Iras, go.
Now, noble Charmian, we'll dispatch indeed; 230
And, when thou hast done this chare, I'll give
    thee leave
To play till doomsday. Bring our crown and all.
Wherefore's this noise?
           [*Exit Iras. A noise within.*

Enter a Guardsman.

    Guard.   Here is a rural fellow
That will not be denied your highness' presence:
He brings you figs.
    Cleo. Let him come in. [*Exit Guardsman.*
                What poor an instrument
May do a noble deed! he brings me liberty.
My resolution's placed, and I have nothing
Of woman in me: now from head to foot
I am marble-constant; now the fleeting moon 240
No planet is of mine.

Re-enter Guardsman, *with* Clown *bringing in
a basket.*

    Guard.   This is the man.
    Cleo. Avoid, and leave him.
                 [*Exit Guardsman.*
Hast thou the pretty worm of Nilus there,
That kills and pains not?
    Clown. Truly, I have him: but I would not
be the party that should desire you to touch him,
for his biting is immortal; those that do die of it
do seldom or never recover.
    Cleo. Rememberest thou any that have died
    on't?   249
    Clown. Very many, men and women too. I
heard of one of them no longer than yesterday:
a very honest woman, but something given to
lie: as a woman should not do, but in the way of
honesty: how she died of the biting of it, what
pain she felt: truly, she makes a very good
report o' the worm; but he that will believe all
that they say, shall never be saved by half that
they do: but this is most fallible, the worm's an
odd worm.
    Cleo. Get thee hence; farewell.   260
    Clown. I wish you all joy of the worm.
                [*Setting down his basket.*
    Cleo. Farewell.
    Clown. You must think this, look you, that
the worm will do his kind.
    Cleo. Ay, ay; farewell.
    Clown. Look you, the worm is not to be

231 *chare.* Chore.

242 *Avoid.* Withdraw.

243 *worm.* Snake.

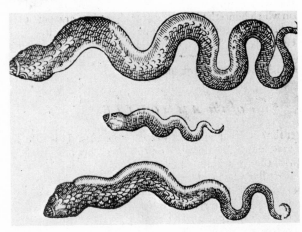

Cleopatra: 'Hast thou the pretty worm of Nilus
there . . .' Woodcut from Edward Topsell's *History of
Serpents*, 1608

286 *Yare.* Quickly.

296 *aspic.* Asp.

Death of Antony and Cleopatra. Engraving by Kenny
Meadows from Barry Cornwall's *The Complete Works
of Shakspere,* (1857–59)

trusted but in the keeping of wise people; for,
indeed, there is no goodness in the worm.
 Cleo. Take thou no care; it shall be heeded.
 Clown. Very good. Give it nothing, I pray
you, for it is not worth the feeding.   271
 Cleo. Will it eat me?
 Clown. You must not think I am so simple
but I know the devil himself will not eat a
woman: I know that a woman is a dish for the
gods, if the devil dress her not. But, truly,
these same whoreson devils' do the gods great
harm in their women; for in every ten that they
make, the devils mar five.
 Cleo. Well, get thee gone; farewell.   280
 Clown. Yes, forsooth: I wish you joy o' the
worm.   [*Exit.*

 Re-enter IRAS *with a robe, crown, &c.*

 Cleo. Give me my robe, put on my crown;
  I have
Immortal longings in me: now no more
The juice of Egypt's grape shall moist this lip:
• Yare, yare, good Iras; quick. Methinks I hear
Antony call; I see him rouse himself
To praise my noble act; I hear him mock
The luck of Cæsar, which the gods give men 289
To excuse their after wrath: husband, I come:
Now to that name my courage prove my title!
I am fire and air; my other elements
I give to baser life. So; have you done?
Come then, and take the last warmth of my lips.
Farewell, kind Charmian; Iras, long farewell.
   [*Kisses them. Iras falls and dies.*
• Have I the aspic in my lips? Dost fall?
If thou and nature can so gently part,
The stroke of death is as a lover's pinch,
Which hurts, and is desired. Dost thou lie still?
If thus thou vanishest, thou tell'st the world 300
It is not worth leave-taking.
 Char. Dissolve, thick cloud, and rain; that I
  may say,
The gods themselves do weep!
 Cleo.   This proves me base:
If she first meet the curled Antony,
He'll make demand of her, and spend that kiss
Which is my heaven to have. Come, thou mor-
  tal wretch,
  [*To an asp, which she applies to her breast.*
With thy sharp teeth this knot intrinsicate
Of life at once untie: poor venomous fool,
Be angry, and dispatch. O, couldst thou speak,
That I might hear thee call great Cæsar ass 310
Unpolicied!
 Char. O eastern star!
 Cleo.   Peace, peace!
Dost thou not see my baby at my breast,
That sucks the nurse asleep?
 Char.   O, break! O, break!
 Cleo. As sweet as balm, as soft as air, as
  gentle,—
O Antony!—Nay, I will take thee too:·
   [*Applying another asp to her arm.*
What should I stay—   [*Dies.*
 Char. In this vile world? So, fare thee well.
Now boast thee, death, in thy possession lies
A lass unparallel'd. Downy windows, close;
And golden Phœbus never be beheld   320
Of eyes again so royal! Your crown's awry;
I'll mend it, and then play.

Opposite: Cleopatra: 'Peace, peace! Dost thou not see
my baby at my breast ...' Engraving from Rowe's
Works ... 1709

First Guard: 'Where is the queen?' Engraving by Henry
Fuseli, 1805

339 *levell'd.* Guessed.

352 *vent.* Stream. *blown.* Swollen.

Enter the Guard, *rushing in.*

First Guard.   Where is the queen?
Char.   Speak softly, wake her not.
First Guard.   Cæsar hath sent—
Char.   Too slow a messenger.
                                        [*Applies an asp.*
O, come apace, dispatch! I partly feel thee.
First Guard.   Approach, ho! All's not well:
       Cæsar's beguiled.
Sec. Guard.   There's Dolabella sent from
       Cæsar; call him.
First Guard.   What work is here! Charmian,
       is this well done?
Char.   It is well done, and fitting for a
       princess
Descended of so many royal kings.   330
Ah, soldier!   [*Dies.*

Re-enter DOLABELLA.

Dol.   How goes it here?
Sec. Guard.   All dead.
Dol.   Cæsar, thy thoughts
Touch their effects in this: thyself art coming
To see perform'd the dreaded act which thou
So sought'st to hinder.
              [*Within* 'A way there, a way for Cæsar!'

Re-enter CÆSAR *and all his train, marching.*

Dol.   O sir, you are too sure an augurer;
That you did fear is done.
Cæs.   Bravest at the last,
• She levell'd at our purposes, and, being royal, 339
Took her own way.   The manner of their deaths?
I do not see them bleed.
Dol.   Who was last with them?
First Guard.   A simple countryman, that
       brought her figs:
This was his basket.
Cæs.   Poison'd, then.
First Guard.   O Cæsar,
This Charmian lived but now; she stood and
       spake:
I found her trimming up the diadem
On her dead mistress; tremblingly she stood
And on the sudden dropp'd.
Cæs.   O noble weakness!
If they had swallow'd poison, 'twould appear
By external swelling: but she looks like sleep,
As she would catch another Antony   350
In her strong toil of grace.
Dol.   Here, on her breast,
• There is a vent of blood and something blown:
The like is on her arm.
First Guard.   This is an aspic's trail: and
       these fig-leaves
Have slime upon them, such as the aspic leaves
Upon the caves of Nile.
Cæs.   Most probable
That so she died; for her physician tells me
She hath pursued conclusions infinite
Of easy ways to die.   Take up her bed;
And bear her women from the monument: 360
She shall be buried by her Antony:
No grave upon the earth shall clip in it
A pair so famous.   High events as these
Strike those that make them; and their story is
No less in pity than his glory which

Brought them to be lamented.   Our army shall
In solemn show attend this funeral;
And then to Rome.   Come, Dolabella, see
High order in this great solemnity.   *[Exeunt.*

Caesar: 'She shall be buried by her Antony: No grave
upon the earth shall clip in it A pair so famous.' Peggy
Ashcroft as Cleopatra, Stratford-upon-Avon, 1953

Coriolanus

1608

THE CONTENT OF CORIOLANUS is almost entirely political, and its interest concentrated upon the character of its chief protagonist. We might say that there are two protagonists in the large cast the play requires – Coriolanus, and the People. The dramatic conflict is essentially between him and them: the varying, changing relationships, reluctant admiration for the man to whom Rome owed so much, his pride and contempt for them, the mistake of submitting himself to them for election while refusing to flatter them and talk the necessary humbug, their turning against him, artfully encouraged by their tribunes – and the whole train of fatal consequences.

What can have turned Shakespeare's mind in this direction? He found his subject in his reading of North's Plutarch, as with *Antony and Cleopatra*, and he used a passage in Camden's *Remains*, that for Menenius' fable of the belly, as he had used another in *King Lear*. But sometimes external events, as we have seen, led him to his subject.

In May there were considerable agrarian disturbances in the Midlands, which affected Warwickshire, where Shakespeare was now a landowner. Most of the trouble was over enclosure; but Shakespeare's friend, William Combe, reported to Cecil, now Lord Salisbury, the widespread complaints at the dearth of corn, 'the prices rising to some height, caused partly by some that are well stored refraining to bring the same to the market out of a covetous conceit that corn will be dearer.' Prices reached their topmost that year.

This is the issue that starts off the very first scene. The citizens are mutinying against the governing class – so here we have a modern theme, that of class-conflict. The First Citizen says: 'What authority surfeits on would relieve us – if they would yield us but the superfluity while it were wholesome . . .' (At this time, at Stratford, the provident dramatist had a considerable store of malt in his big house, New Place.) 'They ne'er cared for us yet . . . and their store-houses crammed with grain; make edicts for usury, to support usurers . . . and provide more piercing statutes daily to chain up and restrain the poor.' This refers to the severe Elizabethan Poor Law statutes of 1598–1601.

The corporate wisdom of the people speaks through the First Citizen; they regard Coriolanus as their chief enemy, 'a very dog to the commonalty . . . Let us kill him, and we'll have corn at our own price.' The Second Citizen suggests that Coriolanus's services to the country be taken into account. The First replies that what won him fame he did to that end: though softies ('soft-conscienced men') said it was for his country, 'he did it to please his mother and to be partly proud, which he is, even to the altitude of his virtue.' Here the people have a point – and it is his pride that proves fatal to him.

The patrician Menenius tries to explain to the plebeians:

> For your wants,
> Your suffering in this dearth, you may as well
> Strike at the heaven with your staves as lift them
> Against the Roman state –

as it might be a bureaucrat in Whitehall explaining that nothing can be done about unemployment. And he expounded to them the function of the belly in the body – the rôle of consumption in the economy.

Coriolanus has rendered supreme service to Rome by saving the state, so he has been prevailed on to stand for consul. The tribunes of the people – in modern terms, the democratic leaders – harp on his pride, instigate the people against him, and manage to entrap and ruin him with them. They are, recognisably, envious of the great man – as an eminent historian said of American democracy, 'their instinct is to lop the tallest'. And Coriolanus is too tall, a very obvious target. The tribune, Junius Brutus, has a contemptuous description of the returning hero's reception – he is no more enamoured of the people than Coriolanus is; but he is not a cynic: they are –

> the kitchen malkin pins
> Her richest lockram 'bout her reechy neck,
> Clambering the walls to eye him. Stalls, bulks, windows
> Are smothered up, leads filled, and ridges horsed
> With variable complexions, all agreeing
> In earnestness to see him.

What contempt is in the terms! – and evidently an Elizabethan, not a Roman, crowd. A messenger makes this even clearer:

> Matrons flung gloves,
> Ladies and maids their scarfs and handkerchers
> Upon him as he passed.

Two officers discuss the prospects of the election. The first: 'That's a brave fellow; but he's vengeance proud, and loves not the common people.' The second replies: 'there hath been many great men that have flattered the people, who ne'er loved them; and there be many that they have loved, they knew not wherefore.' The first puts his finger on Coriolanus' trouble: 'but he seeks their hate with greater devotion than they can render it him, and leaves nothing undone that may fuller discover him their opposite.'

It is an interesting state of mind in the great man, but, that being so, he should never have submitted himself for election by the people he despised. Over-persuaded by the patricians of his order, he reluctantly appears in the garb of humility; but this is what he says when a citizen reproaches him with not loving the common people: 'You should account me the more virtuous that I have not been common in my love. I will, sir, flatter my sworn brother, the people, to earn a dearer estimation of them. 'Tis a condition they account gentle,' i.e. this is what they expect of gentlemen. 'And since the wisdom of their

choice is rather to have my hat than my heart, I will practice the insinuating nod and be
off to them [i.e. take off his hat] most counterfeitly.'

Really! not a very promising election-speech. We can only conclude that, though a
hero, Coriolanus was a bad political candidate:

> Better it is to die, better to starve,
> Than crave the hire which first we do deserve.

Yes, indeed ('er' was always pronounced 'ar', as still with 'serjeant' today).
   The tribunes, who are demagogues – that is their function – have no difficulty in driving such a man into the open, to say what he really thinks of a state of affairs,

> where gentry, title, wisdom,
> Cannot conclude but by the yea and no
> Of general ignorance.

The passionate expression throughout this speech shows that it was what William Shakespeare really thought: such a state of society

> must omit
> Real necessities . . .
> Purpose so barred, it follows,
> Nothing is done to purpose.

This is far-seeing, as we should expect of his extraordinary penetration into human nature and society: long-term interests would be sacrificed for soft options, and nothing done to purpose.

> The multitudinous tongue – let them not lick
> The sweet which is their poison:

that is, do not give way to the people's demands – as it might be for higher wages and less work – against their own well-being in the end, to produce inflation and unemployment. Such democratic weakness, Coriolanus says,

> bereaves the state
> Of that integrity which should become it,
> Not having the power to do the good it would
> For the ill which doth control it.

How true a diagnosis today, and how it brings home once more the universal application of Shakespeare's thought. He understood, too, that

> . . . manhood is called foolery when it stands
> Against a falling fabric.

Today it is called eccentricity, but the fabric breaks down nevertheless. A figure who stands out like a rock against the solvents of society and tells people home-truths they will pay no attention to is already alienated, as Coriolanus was, and may be driven into exile, as again he was. When the people mutinied against him, his reaction is:

> I would they were barbarians – as they are,
> Though in Rome littered: not Romans, as they are not –

not worthy of their country's history.

The Play. So, driven out, he goes over to the enemy, and takes refuge with the Volscians he had saved Rome from. The scene in which, disguised, he enters the house of his great opponent, Aufidius, and is embraced by him, is one of the finest of many fine scenes. We are shown the servingmen there, in realistic prose-dialogue, no other than the populace in Rome, as changeable and as stupid. They look forward to the renewal of war – a contemporary reflection on James I's peace with Spain from 1604. 'This peace is nothing but to rust iron, increase tailors, and breed ballad-makers', says one. 'Let me have war', says another. 'It exceeds peace as far as day does night . . . Peace is a getter of more bastard children than war's a destroyer of men.' 'Ay', says another wiseacre, 'and it makes men hate one another.' Then the popular wisdom scores a point: 'Reason – because they then less need one another.'

This was true of Jacobean society. Elizabethan England had held together in the long struggle against Spain; with peace, it tended to fall apart, the cracks and strains of class- and religious-conflict to come into the open.

Coriolanus, driven into exile, then led the Volscians to victory and had Rome at his mercy. He should have burned the place over their heads, as he meant – again, a penetrating forecast of modern psychology, the frequent reaction of a love–hate complex: the destruction of what one loves.

He is prevented by his love for his mother, Volumnia. Much is made by critics of the beauty of this character and the touching nature of their relationship. She is in fact a stern Roman matron, a kind of female Cato, and is much to blame for the fault in her son – what makes him virtually another of Shakespeare's psychotic characters. She had brought him up harshly, almost savagely, without tenderness; she had urged him to expose himself to the people, and she ruined him by prevailing on him to spare Rome. A solitary soul like Coriolanus should have lived solitary, to himself alone.

Personal. But this would have been contrary to Shakespeare's deep social conviction, his family spirit. In the end, it was not in Coriolanus' nature to

> stand
> As if a man were author of himself
> And knew no other kin.

And in this severe, classic play we come across charming touches that reveal the author:

> O, let me clip ye [embrace you]
> In arms as sound as when I wooed, in heart
> As merry as when our nuptial day was done,
> And tapers burned to bedward!

This must have meant much to the writer when he repeats it later, like a home-coming to Stratford:

> more dances my rapt heart
> Than when I first my wedded mistress saw
> Bestride my threshold.

The more numerous and detailed stage-directions, which, Chambers considered, were from the author's hand, would indicate that some of the play was written in the country. Apart even from the reflection of local circumstances in the inception of the play – the dearth of corn, peasant disturbances, etc. – we find,

> forth he goes,
> Like to a harvest-man that's tasked to mow
> Or all or lose his hire.

Hare-coursing comes in; and we have a noticeable medical reference such as is to become more frequent from now on. 'The most sovereign prescription in Galen is but empiricutic and, to this preservative, of no better report than a horse-drench.' We can tell that, in his later years, he profited from talk with his son-in-law, Dr. John Hall, whom Susanna, his intelligent elder daughter, married this very year, 1607.

A London reference corroborates the date: the 'coal of fire upon the ice' refers to the great frost in the winter of 1607–8, when the Thames was frozen over and fires lighted upon it. It seems to have been a point of honour with him to include a reference to his profession in every play:

> Like a dull actor now,
> I have forgot my part, and I am out,
> Even to a full disgrace.

Style. This is Shakespeare's second classic play, and the style is in keeping – none of the glowing colours of *Antony and Cleopatra*. It is more like *Julius Caesar*, though it has more variety in the colloquial talk of the Roman citizens and the comic exchanges of the serving-men of Aufidius. And the language is the elliptical, overcharged language of the later plays. The blank verse has a considerable proportion of weak, feminine endings. We note the fondness for the rare, rather than the obvious, word: for 'fearless' this writer will say, more visually, 'shunless'. Ben Jonson made fun of one of these odd phrases:

> He lurched all swords of the garland,

meaning, he robbed. In *Epicoene*, next year or so, Ben made somebody say:

> You have lurched your friends of the better half of the garland.

I expect that this gave them both a good laugh; but for us it corroborates the date.

The Text is a fair one, as it appeared first in the Folio, but with many of Shakespeare's mislineations, as in its predecessor, and probably for the same reason – the author saving space over half-lines. We have indications of his idiosyncratic spelling and that the manuscript from which the play was printed was not easy to read. We know from the signatures to his will that Shakespeare's handwriting, like many authors', became rather illegible.

CORIOLANUS.

DRAMATIS PERSONÆ.

CAIUS MARCIUS, afterwards CAIUS MARCIUS
  CORIOLANUS.
TITUS LARTIUS, ⎫ generals against the Vol-
COMINIUS,   ⎭ scians.
MENENIUS AGRIPPA, friend to Coriolanus.
SICINIUS VELUTUS, ⎫ tribunes of the people.
JUNIUS BRUTUS, ⎭
Young MARCIUS, son to Coriolanus.
A Roman Herald.
TULLUS AUFIDIUS, general of the Volscians.
Lieutenant to Aufidius.
Conspirators with Aufidius.
A Citizen of Antium.

Two Volscian Guards.

VOLUMNIA, mother to Coriolanus.
VIRGILIA, wife to Coriolanus.
VALERIA, friend to Virgilia.
Gentlewoman, attending on Virgilia.

Roman and Volscian Senators, Patricians, Ædiles,
  Lictors, Soldiers, Citizens, Messengers, Servants to Aufidius, and other Attendants.

SCENE: *Rome and the neighbourhood; Corioli
  and the neighbourhood; Antium.*

● *A bullet beside a text line indicates an annotation in the
opposite column.*

ACT I.

SCENE I. *Rome. A street.*

*Enter a company of mutinous Citizens, with
    staves, clubs, and other weapons.*

First Cit. Before we proceed any further,
hear me speak.
All. Speak, speak.
First Cit. You are all resolved rather to die
than to famish?
All. Resolved, resolved.
First Cit. First, you know Caius Marcius is
chief enemy to the people.
All. We know't, we know't.
First Cit. Let us kill him, and we'll have
corn at our own price. Is't a verdict?   11
All. No more talking on't; let it be done:
away, away!
Sec. Cit. One word, good citizens.
First Cit. We are accounted poor citizens, the

Opposite: Coriolanus persuaded by his family to spare
Rome. Detail from a painting by Michele da Verona
(*c.*1470–1536/44)

16–18 *What authority . . . wholesome.* See introduction.

49 *Capitol.* Temple of Jupiter, Capitoline Hill.

The Temple of Jupiter. Engraving from G. du Choul's
Discours de la Religion des Anciens Romains, 1567

57 *bats.* Cudgels.

68–71 *For your . . . Roman state.* See introduction.

74 *your impediment.* The obstruction you could cause.

patricians good. What authority surfeits on would relieve us: if they would yield us but the super-fluity, while it were wholesome, we might guess they relieved us humanely; but they think we are too dear: the leanness that afflicts us, the object of our misery, is as an inventory to particularize their abundance; our sufferance is a gain to them. Let us revenge this with our pikes, ere we become rakes: for the gods know I speak this in hunger for bread, not in thirst for revenge.

Sec. Cit. Would you proceed especially against Caius Marcius?

All. Against him first: he's a very dog to the commonalty. 29

Sec. Cit. Consider you what services he has done for his country?

First Cit. Very well; and could be content to give him good report for't, but that he pays him-self with being proud.

Sec. Cit. Nay, but speak not maliciously.

First Cit. I say unto you, what he hath done famously, he did it to that end: though soft-con-scienced men can be content to say it was for his country, he did it to please his mother, and to be partly proud; which he is, even to the altitude of his virtue. 41

Sec. Cit. What he cannot help in his nature, you account a vice in him. You must in no way say he is covetous.

First Cit. If I must not, I need not be barren of accusations; he hath faults, with surplus, to tire in repetition. [*Shouts within.*] What shouts are these? The other side o' the city is risen: why stay we prating here? to the Capitol!

All. Come, come. 50

First Cit. Soft! who comes here?

Enter MENENIUS AGRIPPA.

Sec. Cit. Worthy Menenius Agrippa; one that hath always loved the people.

First Cit. He's one honest enough: would all the rest were so!

Men. What work's, my countrymen, in hand? where go you
With bats and clubs? The matter? speak, I pray you.

First Cit. Our business is not unknown to the senate; they have had inkling this fortnight what we intend to do, which now we'll show 'em in deeds. They say poor suitors have strong breaths: they shall know we have strong arms too.

Men. Why, masters, my good friends, mine honest neighbours,
Will you undo yourselves?

First Cit. We cannot, sir, we are undone already.

Men. I tell you, friends, most charitable care
Have the patricians of you. For your wants,
Your suffering in this dearth, you may as well 69
Strike at the heaven with your staves as lift them
Against the Roman state, whose course will on
The way it takes, cracking ten thousand curbs
Of more strong link asunder than can ever
Appear in your impediment. For the dearth,
The gods, not the patricians, make it, and
Your knees to them, not arms, must help. Alack,
You are transported by calamity
Thither where more attends you, and you slander

●The helms o' the state, who care for you like fathers,
When you curse them as enemies.   80
●   *First Cit.* Care for us! True, indeed! They ne'er cared for us yet: suffer us to famish, and their store-houses crammed with grain; make edicts for usury, to support usurers; repeal daily any wholesome act established against the rich, and provide more piercing statutes daily, to chain up and restrain the poor.   If the wars eat us not up, they will; and there's all the love they bear us.
   Men.   Either you must   90
Confess yourselves wondrous malicious,
Or be accused of folly.   I shall tell you
A pretty tale: it may be you have heard it;
But, since it serves my purpose, I will venture
To stale 't a little more.
   First Cit.   Well, I'll hear it, sir: yet you
●must not think to fob off our disgrace with a tale: but, an 't please you, deliver.
   Men.   There was a time when all the body's members
Rebell'd against the belly, thus accused it: 100
That only like a gulf it did remain
I' the midst o' the body, idle and unactive,
Still cupboarding the viand, never bearing
●Like labour with the rest, where the other instruments
Did see and hear, devise, instruct, walk, feel,
And, mutually participate, did minister
●Unto the appetite and affection common
Of the whole body.   The belly answer'd—
   First Cit.   Well, sir, what answer made the belly?   110
   Men.   Sir, I shall tell you.   With a kind of smile,
Which ne'er came from the lungs, but even thus—
For, look you, I may make the belly smile
As well as speak—it tauntingly replied
To the discontented members, the mutinous parts
●That envied his receipt; even so most fitly
As you malign our senators for that
They are not such as you.
   First Cit.   Your belly's answer?   What!
The kingly-crowned head, the vigilant eye,
The counsellor heart, the arm our soldier,   120
Our steed the leg, the tongue our trumpeter,
●With other muniments and petty helps
In this our fabric, if that they—
   Men.   What then?
'Fore me, this fellow speaks!   What then? what then?
   First Cit.   Should by the cormorant belly be restrain'd,
Who is the sink o' the body,—
   Men.   Well, what then?
   First Cit.   The former agents, if they did complain,
What could the belly answer?
   Men.   I will tell you;
If you'll bestow a small—of what you have little—
Patience awhile, you'll hear the belly's answer.
   First Cit.   Ye're long about it.
   Men.   Note me this, good friend;
●Your most grave belly was deliberate,
Not rash like his accusers, and thus answer'd:

79 *helms.* Heads.

81-87 *They ne'er ... the poor.* See introduction.

97 *disgrace.* Displeasure.

104 *instruments.* Organs.

107 *affection.* Inclination.

116 *his receipt.* i.e. what it received.

122 *muniments.* Supports.

132 *deliberate.* Thoughtful.

141 *cranks.* Windings. *offices.* Organs.

155 *weal o' the common.* Welfare of the people.

167 *bale.* Misfortune.

Marcius: 'Than is the coal of fire upon the ice . . .' Fires were built on the frozen Thames during the Great Frost of 1607–1608, as seen in the foreground of this woodcut from Thomas Dekker's *The Great Frost : Cold doings in London,* 1608

179 *To make him worthy.* To honour that man. *subdues.* i.e. subjects him to the law.

183 *evil.* Illness.

'True is it, my incorporate friends,' quoth he,
'That I receive the general food at first,
Which you do live upon; and fit it is,
Because I am the store-house and the shop
Of the whole body: but, if you do remember,
I send it through the rivers of your blood,
Even to the court, the heart, to the seat o' the
   brain;   140
● And, through the cranks and offices of man,
The strongest nerves and small inferior veins
From me receive that natural competency
Whereby they live: and though that all at once,
You, my good friends,'—this says the belly,
   mark me,—
   First Cit. Ay, sir; well, well.
   Men.   'Though all at once cannot
See what I do deliver out to each,
Yet I can make my audit up, that all
From me do back receive the flour of all,
And leave me but the bran.' What say you to't?
   First Cit. It was an answer: how apply
      you this?   151
   Men. The senators of Rome are this good
      belly,
And you the mutinous members; for examine
Their counsels and their cares, digest things
   rightly
● Touching the weal o' the common, you shall find
No public benefit which you receive
But it proceeds or comes from them to you
And no way from yourselves. What do you
   think,
You, the great toe of this assembly?
   First Cit. I the great toe! why the great toe?
   Men. For that, being one o' the lowest,
      basest, poorest,   161
Of this most wise rebellion, thou go'st foremost:
Thou rascal, that art worst in blood to run,
Lead'st first to win some vantage.
But make you ready your stiff bats and clubs:
Rome and her rats are at the point of battle;
● The one side must have bale.

         Enter CAIUS MARCIUS.

                    Hail, noble Marcius!
   Mar. Thanks. What's the matter, you dis-
      sentious rogues,
That, rubbing the poor itch of your opinion,
Make yourselves scabs?
   First Cit. We have ever your good word. 170
   Mar. He that will give good words to thee
      will flatter
Beneath abhorring. What would you have, you
   curs,
That like nor peace nor war? the one affrights you,
The other makes you proud. He that trusts to
   you,
Where he should find you lions, finds you hares;
Where foxes, geese: you are no surer, no,
Than is the coal of fire upon the ice,
Or hailstone in the sun. Your virtue is
● To make him worthy whose offence subdues him
And curse that justice did it. Who deserves
   greatness   180
Deserves your hate; and your affections are
A sick man's appetite, who desires most that
● Which would increase his evil. He that depends
Upon your favours swims with fins of lead

And hews down oaks with rushes.   Hang ye!
   Trust ye?
With every minute you do change a mind,
And call him noble that was now your hate,
•Him vile that was your garland.   What's the
   matter,
That in these several places of the city
You cry against the noble senate, who,   190
Under the gods, keep you in awe, which else •
Would feed on one another?   What's their
   seeking?
   Men.   For corn at their own rates; whereof,
   they say,
The city is well stored.
   Mar.   Hang 'em!   They say!
They'll sit by the fire, and presume to know
What's done i' the Capitol; who's like to rise,
•Who thrives and who declines; side factions and
   give out
Conjectural marriages; making parties strong
And feebling such as stand not in their liking
Below their cobbled shoes.   They say there's
   grain enough!   200
•Would the nobility lay aside their ruth,
•And let me use my sword, I'ld make a quarry
•With thousands of these quarter'd slaves, as high
•As I could pick my lance.
   Men.   Nay, these are almost thoroughly per-
   suaded;
For though abundantly they lack discretion,
•Yet are they passing cowardly.   But, I beseech
   you,
What says the other troop?
   Mar.   They are dissolved: hang 'em!
They said they were an-hungry; sigh'd forth
   proverbs,
That hunger broke stone walls, that dogs must eat,
That meat was made for mouths, that the gods
   sent not   211
Corn for the rich men only: with these shreds
They vented their complainings; which being
   answer'd,
And a petition granted them, a strange one—
•To break the heart of generosity,
And make bold power look pale—they threw
   their caps
As they would hang them on the horns o' the
   moon,
•Shouting their emulation.
   Men.   What is granted them?
   Mar.   Five tribunes to defend their vulgar
   wisdoms,
Of their own choice: one's Junius Brutus,   220
Sicinius Velutus, and I know not—'Sdeath!
The rabble should have first unroof'd the city,
Ere so prevail'd with me: it will in time
•Win upon power and throw forth greater themes
For insurrection's arguing.
   Men.   This is strange.
   Mar.   Go, get you home, you fragments!

     Enter a Messenger, *hastily.*

   Mess.   Where's Caius Marcius?
   Mar.   Here: what's the matter?
   Mess.   The news is, sir, the Volsces are in
   arms.
•   *Mar.*   I am glad on 't: then we shall ha'
   means to vent
•Our musty superfluity.   See, our best elders.

188 *garland.* Hero.

197 *side.* Take sides with.

201 *ruth.* Pity.

202 *quarry.* Heap of bodies.

203 *quarter'd.* Butchered.

204 *pick.* Pitch.

207 *passing.* Very.

215 *generosity.* Nobility.

218 *their emulation.* i.e. competing in shouting.

224 *Win.* Prevail. *power.* Authority.

229 *vent.* Get rid of.

230 *musty superfluity.* i.e. of people.

245 *stand'st out?* Are you opting out?

251 *priority.* i.e. should lead.

254 *garners.* Granaries.

255 *puts well worth.* Looks well.

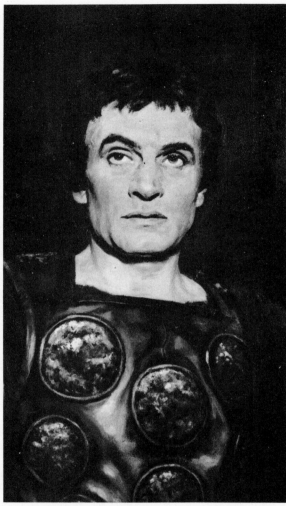

Laurence Olivier as Marcius (later Coriolanus), Stratford-upon-Avon, 1959. Portrait by Clare Duncan

Enter COMINIUS, TITUS LARTIUS, *and other* Senators; JUNIUS BRUTUS *and* SICINIUS VELUTUS.

First Sen.   Marcius, 'tis true that you have lately told us;   231
The Volsces are in arms.
   Mar.   They have a leader,
Tullus Aufidius, that will put you to 't.
I sin in envying his nobility,
And were I any thing but what I am,
I would wish me only he.
   Com.   You have fought together.
   Mar.   Were half to half the world by the ears and he
Upon my party, I'ld revolt, to make
Only my wars with him: he is a lion
That I am proud to hunt.
   First Sen.   Then, worthy Marcius, 240
Attend upon Cominius to these wars.
   Com.   It is your former promise.
   Mar.   Sir, it is;
And I am constant.   Titus Lartius, thou
Shalt see me once more strike at Tullus' face.
● What, art thou stiff? stand'st out?
   Tit.   No, Caius Marcius;
I'll lean upon one crutch and fight with t'other,
Ere stay behind this business.
   Men.   O, true-bred!
   First Sen.   Your company to the Capitol; where, I know,
Our greatest friends attend us.
   Tit.   [*To Com.*] Lead you on.
[*To Mar.*] Follow Cominius; we must follow you;   250
● Right worthy you priority.
   Com.   Noble Marcius!
   First Sen. [*To the Citizens*] Hence to your homes; be gone!
   Mar.   Nay, let them follow:
The Volsces have much corn; take these rats thither
● To gnaw their garners.   Worshipful mutiners,
● Your valour puts well forth: pray, follow.
                [*Citizens steal away.   Exeunt all but
                         Sicinius and Brutus.*
   Sic.   Was ever man so proud as is this Marcius?
   Bru.   He has no equal.
   Sic.   When we were chosen tribunes for the people,—
   Bru.   Mark'd you his lip and eyes?
   Sic.   Nay, but his taunts.
   Bru.   Being moved, he will not spare to gird the gods.   260
   Sic.   Be-mock the modest moon.
   Bru.   The present wars devour him: he is grown
Too proud to be so valiant.
   Sic.   Such a nature,
Tickled with good success, disdains the shadow
Which he treads on at noon: but I do wonder
His insolence can brook to be commanded
Under Cominius.
   Bru.   Fame, at the which he aims,
In whom already he's well graced, can not
Better be held nor more attain'd than by
A place below the first: for what miscarries 270
Shall be the general's fault, though he perform

To the utmost of a man, and giddy censure
Will then cry out of Marcius 'O, if he
Had borne the business!'
  Sic.   Besides, if things go well,
Opinion that so sticks on Marcius shall
Of his demerits rob Cominius.
  Bru.   Come:
Half all Cominius' honours are to Marcius,
Though Marcius earn'd them not, and all his faults
To Marcius shall be honours, though indeed
In aught he merit not.
  Sic.   Let's hence, and hear   280
How the dispatch is made, and in what fashion,
More than his singularity, he goes
Upon this present action.
  Bru.   Let's along.   [*Exeunt.*

SCENE II. *Corioli.   The Senate-house.*

Enter TULLUS AUFIDIUS *and certain* Senators.

  First Sen. So, your opinion is, Aufidius,
That they of Rome are enter'd in our counsels
And know how we proceed.
  Auf.   Is it not yours?
What ever have been thought on in this state,
That could be brought to bodily act ere Rome
Had circumvention? 'Tis not four days gone
Since I heard thence; these are the words: I think
I have the letter here; yes, here it is.
  [*Reads*] 'They have press'd a power, but it is
      not known
Whether for east or west: the dearth is great;   10
The people mutinous; and it is rumour'd,
Cominius, Marcius your old enemy,
Who is of Rome worse hated than of you,
And Titus Lartius, a most valiant Roman,
These three lead on this preparation
Whither 'tis bent: most likely 'tis for you:
Consider of it.'
  First Sen. Our army's in the field:
We never yet made doubt but Rome was ready
To answer us.
  Auf.   Nor did you think it folly
To keep your great pretences veil'd till when   20
They needs must show themselves; which in the
      hatching,
It seem'd, appear'd to Rome. By the discovery
We shall be shorten'd in our aim, which was
To take in many towns ere almost Rome
Should know we were afoot.
  Sec. Sen.   Noble Aufidius,
Take your commission; hie you to your bands:
Let us alone to guard Corioli:
If they set down before 's, for the remove
Bring up your army; but, I think, you'll find
They've not prepared for us.
  Auf.   O, doubt not that;   30
I speak from certainties. Nay, more,
Some parcels of their power are forth already,
And only hitherward.   I leave your honours.
If we and Caius Marcius chance to meet,
'Tis sworn between us we shall ever strike
Till one can do no more.
  All.   The gods assist you!
  Auf. And keep your honours safe!
  First Sen.   Farewell.
  Sec. Sen.   Farewell.
  All. Farewell.   [*Exeunt.*

Aufidius: '[Reads] "They have press'd a power, but it is not known Whether for east or west:"' James Dale as Aufidius, Stratford-upon-Avon, 1939

2 *comfortable sort*. Cheerful fashion.

16 *oak*. Oak leaves; a wreath of oak-leaves was like a wreath of laurel, an honour. It was awarded to a citizen who had saved the life of another.

36 *got*. Conceived.

41 *Jupiter*. Chief of the Roman gods.

43 *Hecuba*. Wife of King Priam of Troy, whose eldest son, Hector, combined wisdom and strength.

48 *fell*. Fierce.

54–55 *manifest house-keepers*. i.e. clearly happy to stay in the house.

Valeria greets Volumnia and Virgilia. Drawing by J. M. Wright (1777–1866)

SCENE III.   *Rome.   A room in Marcius' house.*

Enter VOLUMNIA *and* VIRGILIA: *they set them down on two low stools, and sew.*

Vol.   I pray you, daughter, sing; or express yourself in a more comfortable sort: if my son were my husband, I should freelier rejoice in that absence wherein he won honour than in the embracements of his bed where he would show most love.   When yet he was but tender-bodied and the only son of my womb, when youth with comeliness plucked all gaze his way, when for a day of kings' entreaties a mother should not sell him an hour from her beholding, I, considering how honour would become such a person, that it was no better than picture-like to hang by the wall, if renown made it not stir, was pleased to let him seek danger where he was like to find fame.   To a cruel war I sent him; from whence he returned, his brows bound with oak.   I tell thee, daughter, I sprang not more in joy at first hearing he was a man-child than now in first seeing he had proved himself a man.   19

Vir.   But had he died in the business, madam; how then?

Vol.   Then his good report should have been my son; I therein would have found issue. Hear me profess sincerely: had I a dozen sons, each in my love alike and none less dear than thine and my good Marcius, I had rather had eleven die nobly for their country than one voluptuously surfeit out of action.

Enter a Gentlewoman.

Gent.   Madam, the Lady Valeria is come to visit you.

Vir.   Beseech you, give me leave to retire myself.   30

Vol.   Indeed, you shall not.
Methinks I hear hither your husband's drum,
See him pluck Aufidius down by the hair,
As children from a bear, the Volsces shunning him:
Methinks I see him stamp thus, and call thus:
'Come on, you cowards! you were got in fear,
Though you were born in Rome:' his bloody brow
With his mail'd hand then wiping, forth he goes,
Like to a harvest-man that's task'd to mow
Or all or lose his hire.   40

Vir.   His bloody brow! O Jupiter, no blood!

Vol.   Away, you fool! it more becomes a man
Than gilt his trophy: the breasts of Hecuba,
When she did suckle Hector, look'd not lovelier
Than Hector's forehead when it spit forth blood
At Grecian sword, contemning.   Tell Valeria,
We are fit to bid her welcome.   [*Exit Gent.*

Vir.   Heavens bless my lord from fell Aufidius!

Vol.   He'll beat Aufidius' head below his knee
And tread upon his neck.   50

Enter VALERIA, *with an* Usher *and* Gentlewoman.

Val.   My ladies both, good day to you.

Vol.   Sweet madam.

Vir.   I am glad to see your ladyship.

Val.   How do you both? you are manifest house-keepers.   What are you sewing here?   A fine spot, in good faith. How does your little son?

Vir. I thank your ladyship; well, good madam.

Vol. He had rather see the swords, and hear a drum, than look upon his schoolmaster. 61

Val. O' my word, the father's son: I'll swear, 'tis a very pretty boy. O' my troth, I looked upon him o' Wednesday half an hour together: has such a confirmed countenance. I saw him run after a gilded butterfly; and when he caught it, he let it go again; and after it again; and over and over he comes, and up again; catched it again; or whether his fall enraged him, or how 'twas, he did so set his teeth and tear it; O, I warrant, how he mammocked it! 71

Vol. One on 's father's moods.

Val. Indeed, la, 'tis a noble child.

Vir. A crack, madam.

Val. Come, lay aside your stitchery; I must have you play the idle huswife with me this afternoon.

Vir. No, good madam; I will not out of doors.

Val. Not out of doors!

Vol. She shall, she shall. 80

Vir. Indeed, no, by your patience; I'll not over the threshold till my lord return from the wars.

Val. Fie, you confine yourself most unreasonably: come, you must go visit the good lady that lies in.

Vir. I will wish her speedy strength, and visit her with my prayers; but I cannot go thither.

Vol. Why, I pray you?

Vir. 'Tis not to save labour, nor that I want love. 91

Val. You would be another Penelope: yet, they say, all the yarn she spun in Ulysses' absence did but fill Ithaca full of moths. Come; I would your cambric were sensible as your finger, that you might leave pricking it for pity. Come, you shall go with us.

Vir. No, good madam, pardon me; indeed, I will not forth.

Val. In truth, la, go with me; and I'll tell you excellent news of your husband. 101

Vir. O, good madam, there can be none yet.

Val. Verily, I do not jest with you; there came news from him last night.

Vir. Indeed, madam?

Val. In earnest, it's true; I heard a senator speak it. Thus it is: the Volsces have an army forth; against whom Cominius the general is gone, with one part of our Roman power: your lord and Titus Lartius are set down before their city Corioli; they nothing doubt prevailing and to make it brief wars. This is true, on mine honour; and so, I pray, go with us.

Vir. Give me excuse, good madam; I will obey you in every thing hereafter.

Vol. Let her alone, lady: as she is now, she will but disease our better mirth.

Val. In troth, I think she would. Fare you well, then. Come, good sweet lady. Prithee, Virgilia, turn thy solemness out o' door, and go along with us. 121

Vir. No, at a word, madam; indeed, I must not. I wish you much mirth.

Val. Well, then, farewell. [*Exeunt.*

65 *confirmed countenance.* Determined expression.

68 *over and over.* Head over heels. *comes.* Falls.

71 *mammocked.* Tore into shreds.

74 *crack.* Young rogue.

92 *Penelope.* Wife of Ulysses; weaving by day and unpicking the work at night during her husband's absence, she put off advances from other men.

Penelope weaving. Engraving from a Greek vase painting

95 *cambric.* Fine linen. *sensible.* Sensitive.

111 *nothing doubt prevailing.* Are not in doubt of winning.

112 *make.* i.e. intend to make.

117 *disease.* Spoil.

Roman soldiers. Engraving from H. G. Liddell's *History of Rome*, 1894

Marcius before the gates of Corioli. Engraving by Kenny Meadows from Barry Cornwall's *Works of Shakspere*, 1846

---

4 *spoke*. Encountered.

9 *'larum*. Call to arms.

10 *Mars*. God of war.

17 *pound us up*. Shut us in.

25 *proof*. Armoured.

36 *Pluto*. God of Hell.

SCENE IV. *Before Corioli.*

Enter, with drum and colours, MARCIUS, TITUS LARTIUS, Captains *and* Soldiers. *To them a* Messenger.

Mar. Yonder comes news. A wager they have met.
Lart. My horse to yours, no.
Mar.   'Tis done.
Lart.   Agreed.
Mar. Say, has our general met the enemy?
Mess. They lie in view; but have not spoke as yet.
Lart. So, the good horse is mine.
Mar.   I'll buy him of you.
Lart. No, I'll nor sell nor give him: lend you him I will
For half a hundred years. Summon the town.
Mar. How far off lie these armies?
Mess.   Within this mile and half.
Mar. Then shall we hear their 'larum, and they ours.
Now, Mars, I prithee, make us quick in work, 10
That we with smoking swords may march from hence,
To help our fielded friends! Come, blow thy blast.

They sound a parley. Enter two Senators *with others on the walls.*

Tullus Aufidius, is he within your walls?
First Sen. No, nor a man that fears you less than he,
That's lesser than a little. [*Drums afar off.*]
Hark! our drums
Are bringing forth our youth. We'll break our walls,
Rather than they shall pound us up: our gates,
Which yet seem shut, we have but pinn'd with rushes;
They'll open of themselves. [*Alarum afar off.*]
Hark you, far off!
There is Aufidius; list, what work he makes 20
Amongst your cloven army.
Mar.   O, they are at it!
Lart. Their noise be our instruction. Ladders, ho!

Enter the army of the Volsces.

Mar. They fear us not, but issue forth their city
Now put your shields before your hearts, and fight
With hearts more proof than shields. Advance, brave Titus:
They do disdain us much beyond our thoughts,
Which makes me sweat with wrath. Come on, my fellows:
He that retires, I'll take him for a Volsce,
And he shall feel mine edge.

Alarum.   The Romans *are beat back to their trenches.   Re-enter* MARCIUS, *cursing.*

Mar. All the contagion of the south light on you,
                                                        30
You shames of Rome! you herd of—Boils and plagues
Plaster you o'er, that you may be abhorr'd
Further than seen and one infect another
Against the wind a mile! You souls of geese,
That bear the shapes of men, how have you run
From slaves that apes would beat! Pluto and hell!

All hurt behind; backs red, and faces pale
With flight and agued fear! Mend and charge
    home,
Or, by the fires of heaven, I'll leave the foe   39
And make my wars on you: look to't: come on;
If you'll stand fast, we'll beat them to their wives,
As they us to our trenches followed.

Another alarum. The Volsces *fly, and* MAR-
CIUS *follows them to the gates.*

So, now the gates are ope: now prove good
    seconds:
'Tis for the followers fortune widens them,
Not for the fliers: mark me, and do the like.
                    [*Enters the gates.*
First Sol.   Fool-hardiness; not I.
Sec. Sol.   Nor I.
                    [*Marcius is shut in.*
First Sol.   See, they have shut him in.
● *All.*   To the pot, I warrant him.
                    [*Alarum continues.*

Re-enter TITUS LARTIUS.

Lart.   What is become of Marcius?
All.   Slain, sir, doubtless.
First Sol.   Following the fliers at the very
    heels,
With them he enters; who, upon the sudden,   50
Clapp'd to their gates: he is himself alone,
To answer all the city.
Lart.   O noble fellow!
●Who sensibly outdares his senseless sword,
And, when it bows, stands up. Thou art left,
    Marcius:
●A carbuncle entire, as big as thou art,
Were not so rich a jewel. Thou wast a soldier
●Even to Cato's wish, not fierce and terrible
Only in strokes; but, with thy grim looks and
The thunder-like percussion of thy sounds,   59
Thou madest thine enemies shake, as if the world
Were feverous and did tremble.

Re-enter MARCIUS, *bleeding, assaulted by the
    enemy.*

First Sol.   Look, sir.
Lart.   O, 'tis Marcius!
Let's fetch him off, or make remain alike.
                    [*They fight, and all enter the city.*

SCENE V. *Corioli. A street.*

Enter certain Romans, *with spoils.*

First Rom.   This will I carry to Rome.
Sec. Rom.   And I this.
● *Third Rom.*   A murrain on't! I took this for
silver.   [*Alarum continues still afar off.*

Enter MARCIUS *and* TITUS LARTIUS *with a
    trumpet.*

● *Mar.*   See here these movers that do prize
    their hours
●At a crack'd drachma! Cushions, leaden spoons,
●Irons of a doit, doublets that hangmen would
Bury with those that wore them, these base
    slaves,
Ere yet the fight be done, pack up: down with
    them!
And hark, what noise the general makes! To
    him!   10

47 *pot.* Cooking pot.

53 *sensibly.* i.e. with his life. *senseless.* Unfeeling.

55 *carbuncle entire.* i.e. a whole ruby.

57 *Cato.* i.e. Roman famed for virtue.

Marcus Porcius Cato, the Elder (234–149 BC). Engraving from P. J. Mariette's *Traité des Pierres Gravées*,
1750

Soldiers with spoils. Engraving from Basil Kennett's
Romae Antiquae Notitia, 1769

3 *murrain.* Plague.

4 *movers.* Scavengers.

5 *drachma.* Small coin.

6 *Irons.* Weapons. *of a doit.* Worth half a farthing.
doublets. Jackets.

19 *physical.* Healing.

5 *By interims.* At intervals. *conveying gusts.* i.e. gusts of wind.

17 *confound.* Waste.

25 *tabor.* Small drum played together with the shepherd's pipe.

There is the man of my soul's hate, Aufidius,
Piercing our Romans: then, valiant Titus, take
Convenient numbers to make good the city;
Whilst I, with those that have the spirit, will haste
To help Cominius.
    Lart.   Worthy sir, thou bleed'st;
Thy exercise hath been too violent
For a second course of fight.
    Mar.   Sir, praise me not;
My work hath yet not warm'd me: fare you well:
●The blood I drop is rather physical
Than dangerous to me: to Aufidius thus   20
I will appear, and fight.
    Lart.   Now the fair goddess, Fortune,
Fall deep in love with thee; and her great charms
Misguide thy opposers' swords! Bold gentleman,
Prosperity be thy page!
    Mar.   Thy friend no less
Than those she placeth highest! So, farewell.
    Lart. Thou worthiest Marcius!
                 [*Exit Marcius.*
Go sound thy trumpet in the market-place;
Call thither all the officers o' the town,
Where they shall know our mind: away!
                 [*Exeunt.*

SCENE VI. *Near the camp of Cominius.*

Enter COMINIUS, *as it were in retire, with soldiers.*

    Com. Breathe you, my friends: well fought;
    we are come off
Like Romans, neither foolish in our stands,
Nor cowardly in retire: believe me, sirs,
We shall be charged again. Whiles we have struck,
●By interims and conveying gusts we have heard
The charges of our friends. Ye Roman gods!
Lead their successes as we wish our own,
That both our powers, with smiling fronts encountering,
May give you thankful sacrifice.

Enter a Messenger.

                 Thy news?
    Mess. The citizens of Corioli have issued,   10
And given to Lartius and to Marcius battle:
I saw our party to their trenches driven,
And then I came away.
    Com.   Though thou speak'st truth,
Methinks thou speak'st not well. How long is't since?
    Mess. Above an hour, my lord.
    Com. 'Tis not a mile; briefly we heard their drums:
●How couldst thou in a mile confound an hour,
And bring thy news so late?
    Mess.   Spies of the Volsces
Held me in chase, that I was forced to wheel
Three or four miles about, else had I, sir,   20
Half an hour since brought my report.
    Com.   Who's yonder,
That does appear as he were flay'd? O gods!
He has the stamp of Marcius; and I have
Before-time seen him thus.
    Mar.   [*Within*] Come I too late?
●   *Com.* The shepherd knows not thunder from a tabor

ACT I Scene VI   CORIOLANUS

More than I know the sound of Marcius' tongue
From every meaner man.

Enter MARCIUS.

Mar.   Come I too late?
Com.   Ay, if you come not in the blood of
   others,
● But mantled in your own.
   Mar.   O, let me clip ye
In arms as sound as when I woo'd, in heart   30
As merry as when our nuptial day was done,
And tapers burn'd to bedward!
   Com.   Flower of warriors,
How is't with Titus Lartius?
   Mar.   As with a man busied about decrees:
Condemning some to death, and some to exile;
Ransoming him, or pitying, threatening the other;
Holding Corioli in the name of Rome,
Even like a fawning greyhound in the leash,
To let him slip at will.
   Com.   Where is that slave
Which told me they had beat you to your
   trenches?   40
Where is he? call him hither.
   Mar.   Let him alone;
He did inform the truth: but for our gentlemen,
The common file—a plague! tribunes for them!—
The mouse ne'er shunn'd the cat as they did
   budge
From rascals worse than they.
   Com.   But how prevail'd you?
   Mar.   Will the time serve to tell? I do not
   think.
Where is the enemy? are you lords o' the field?
If not, why cease you till you are so?
   Com.   Marcius,
We have at disadvantage fought and did
Retire to win our purpose.   50
● *Mar.*   How lies their battle? know you on
   which side
They have placed their men of trust?
   Com.   As I guess, Marcius,
● Their bands i' the vaward are the Antiates,
Of their best trust; o'er them Aufidius,
Their very heart of hope.
   Mar.   I do beseech you,
By all the battles wherein we have fought,
By the blood we have shed together, by the vows
We have made to endure friends, that you directly
Set me against Aufidius and his Antiates;
● And that you not delay the present, but,   60
Filling the air with swords advanced and darts,
● We prove this very hour.
   Com.   Though I could wish
You were conducted to a gentle bath
And balms applied to you, yet dare I never
Deny your asking: take your choice of those
That best can aid your action.
   Mar.   Those are they
That most are willing. If any such be here—
As it were sin to doubt—that love this painting
Wherein you see me smear'd; if any fear
Lesser his person than an ill report;   70
If any think brave death outweighs bad life
And that his country's dearer than himself;
Let him alone, or so many so minded,
Wave thus, to express his disposition,
And follow Marcius.
   [*They all shout and wave their swords, take*

51 *battle.* Army; order of battle.

53 *vaward.* Vanguard. *Antiates.* i.e. men from capital of
the Volsces.

Marcius: 'I do beseech you . . . Set me against Aufidius
and his Antiates.' Ian Hogg as Coriolanus, Royal
Shakespeare Co, 1972

60 *the present.* At this time.

62 *prove.* Test.

78 *But is.* Is equal to.

86 *ostentation.* Demonstration.

1 *ports.* Gates.

3 *centuries.* Companies of a hundred men.

Marcius: 'I'll fight with none but thee;' Drawing by
P. J. de Loutherbourg (1740–1812)

---

3 *Afric.* Africa.

*him up in their arms, and cast up their
caps.*
O, me alone !·make you a sword of me?
If these shows be not outward, which of you
●But is four Volsces? none of you but is
Able to bear against the great Aufidius
A shield as hard as his.   A certain number,   80
Though thanks to all, must I select from all : the
rest
Shall bear the business in some other fight,
As cause will be obey'd.   Please you to march ;
†And four shall quickly draw out my command,
Which men are best inclined.
   Com.   March on, my fellows :
●Make good this ostentation, and you shall
Divide in all with us.   [*Exeunt.*

SCENE VII.   *The gates of Corioli.*

TITUS LARTIUS, *having set a guard upon Cori-
oli, going with drum and trumpet toward*
COMINIUS *and* CAIUS MARCIUS, *enters with a*
Lieutenant, *other* Soldiers, *and a* Scout.

●   *Lart.*   So, let the ports be guarded : keep your
    duties,
As I have set them down.   If I do send, dispatch
●Those centuries to our aid : the rest will serve
For a short holding : if we lose the field,
We cannot keep the town.
   Lieu.   Fear not our care, sir.
   Lart.   Hence, and shut your gates upon 's.
Our guider, come ; to the Roman camp conduct
    us.   [*Exeunt.*

SCENE VIII.   *A field of battle.*
Alarum as in battle. Enter, from opposite sides,
MARCIUS *and* AUFIDIUS.

   Mar.   I'll fight with none but thee ; for I do
    hate thee
Worse than a promise-breaker.
   Auf.   We hate alike :
●Not Afric owns a serpent I abhor
More than thy fame and envy.   Fix thy foot.
   Mar.   Let the first budger die the other's slave,
And the gods doom him after !
   Auf.   If I fly, Marcius,
Holloa me like a hare.
   Mar.   Within these three hours, Tullus,
Alone I fought in your Corioli walls,
And made what work I pleased : 'tis not my blood
Wherein thou seest me mask'd ; for thy revenge
Wrench up thy power to the highest.
   Auf.   Wert thou the Hector 11
That was the whip of your bragg'd progeny,
Thou shouldst not scape me here.
      [*They fight, and certain Volsces come in the
        aid of Aufidius. Marcius fights till they
        be driven in breathless.*
Officious, and not valiant, you have shamed me
In your condemned seconds.   [*Exeunt.*

SCENE IX.   *The Roman camp.*
*Flourish. Alarum. A retreat is sounded.
Flourish. Enter, from one side,* COMINIUS
with the Romans ; *from the other side,* MAR-
CIUS, *with his arm in a scarf.*

   Com.   If I should tell thee o'er this thy day's
    work,

Thou'ldst not believe thy deeds : but I'll report it
Where senators shall mingle tears with smiles,
Where great patricians shall attend and shrug,
I' the end admire, where ladies shall be frighted,
And, gladly quaked, hear more ; where the dull
    tribunes,
That, with the fusty plebeians, hate thine honours,
Shall say against their hearts 'We thank the gods
Our Rome hath such a soldier.'
Yet camest thou to a morsel of this feast,   10
Having fully dined before.

    Enter TITUS LARTIUS, *with his power, from
        the pursuit.*

    Lart.   O general,
● Here is the steed, we the caparison :
Hadst thou beheld—
    Mar.   Pray now, no more : my mother,
Who has a charter to extol her blood,
When she does praise me grieves me. I have done
As you have done ; that's what I can ; induced
As you have been ; that's for my country :
He that has but effected his good will
Hath overta'en mine act.
    Com.   You shall not be
The grave of your deserving ; Rome must know
The value of her own : 'twere a concealment   21
● Worse than a theft, no less than a traducement,
To hide your doings ; and to silence that,
Which, to the spire and top of praises vouch'd,
Would seem but modest : therefore, I beseech
    you—
In sign of what you are, not to reward
What you have done—before our army hear me.
    Mar. I have some wounds upon me, and they
    smart
To hear themselves remember'd.
    Com.   Should they not,
Well might they fester 'gainst ingratitude,   30
And tent themselves with death. Of all the
    horses,
Whereof we have ta'en good and good store,
    of all
The treasure in this field achieved and city,
We render you the tenth, to be ta'en forth,
Before the common distribution, at
● Your only choice.
    Mar.   I thank you, general ;
But cannot make my heart consent to take
A bribe to pay my sword : I do refuse it ;
And stand upon my common part with those
That have beheld the doing.   40
    [*A long flourish. They all cry* 'Marcius !
      Marcius !' *cast up their caps and lances :
      Cominius and Lartius stand bare.*
    Mar. May these same instruments, which
    you profane,
Never sound more ! when drums and trumpets
    shall
I' the field prove flatterers, let courts and cities be
Made all of false-faced soothing !
When steel grows soft as the parasite's silk,
Let him be made a coverture for the wars !
No more, I say ! For that I have not wash'd
● My nose that bled, or foil'd some debile wretch,—
Which, without note, here's many else have
    done,—
You shout me forth   50
In acclamations hyperbolical ;

55 *give.* Report.

57 *his proper harm.* His own harm.

Cominius: '. . . be it known, As to us, to all the world, that Caius Marcius Wears this war's garland:' Two of the crowns of honour awarded to Roman generals. The *Corona Triumphalis*, made of wreaths of laurel, was given only to generals who had the honour of a triumph; the *Corona Obsidionalis* for the breaking of a siege. Engravings from Basil Kennett's *Romae Antiquae Notitia*, 1769

62 *trim.* Trappings.

72 *undercrest.* Earn. *addition.* Opinion.

As if I loved my little should be dieted
In praises sauced with lies.
 Com.   Too modest are you;
More cruel to your good report than grateful
To us that give you truly: by your patience,
If 'gainst yourself you be incensed, we'll put you,
Like one that means his proper harm, in manacles,
Then reason safely with you. Therefore, be it known,
As to us, to all the world, that Caius Marcius 59
Wears this war's garland: in token of the which,
My noble steed, known to the camp, I give him,
With all his trim belonging; and from this time,
For what he did before Corioli, call him,
With all the applause and clamour of the host,
CAIUS MARCIUS CORIOLANUS! Bear
The addition nobly ever!
  [*Flourish. Trumpets sound, and drums.*
 All. Caius Marcius Coriolanus!
 Cor. I will go wash;
And when my face is fair, you shall perceive
Whether I blush or no: howbeit, I thank you. 70
I mean to stride your steed, and at all times
To undercrest your good addition
To the fairness of my power.
 Com.   So, to our tent;
Where, ere we do repose us, we will write
To Rome of our success. You, Titus Lartius,
Must to Corioli back: send us to Rome
The best, with whom we may articulate,
For their own good and ours.
 Lart.   I shall, my lord.
 Cor. The gods begin to mock me. I, that now
Refused most princely gifts, am bound to beg 80
Of my lord general.
 Com.   Take't; 'tis yours. What is't?
 Cor. I sometime lay here in Corioli
At a poor man's house; he used me kindly:
He cried to me; I saw him prisoner;
But then Aufidius was within my view,
And wrath o'erwhelm'd my pity: I request you
To give my poor host freedom.
 Com.   O, well begg'd!
Were he the butcher of my son, he should
Be free as is the wind. Deliver him, Titus.
 Lart. Marcius, his name?
 Cor.   By Jupiter! forgot.
I am weary; yea, my memory is tired. 91
Have we no wine here?
 Com.   Go we to our tent:
The blood upon your visage dries; 'tis time
It should be look'd to: come. [*Exeunt.*

SCENE X. *The camp of the Volsces.*

A flourish. Cornets. Enter TULLUS AUFIDIUS,
bloody, with two or three Soldiers.

 Auf. The town is ta'en!
 First Sol. 'Twill be deliver'd back on good condition.
 Auf. Condition!
I would I were a Roman; for I cannot,
Being a Volsce, be that I am. Condition!
What good condition can a treaty find
I' the part that is at mercy? Five times, Marcius,

I have fought with thee: so often hast thou beat
me,
And wouldst do so, I think, should we encounter
As often as we eat. By the elements,   10
If e'er again I meet him beard to beard,
He's mine, or I am his: mine emulation
Hath not that honour in't it had; for where
I thought to crush him in an equal force,
● True sword to sword, I'll potch at him some way
● Or wrath or craft may get him.
    First Sol.   He's the devil.
    Auf. Bolder, though not so subtle. My va-
lour's poison'd
With only suffering stain by him; for him
Shall fly out of itself: nor sleep nor sanctuary,
● Being naked, sick, nor fane nor Capitol,   20
The prayers of priests nor times of sacrifice,
● Embarquements all of fury, shall lift up
Their rotten privilege and custom 'gainst
My hate to Marcius: where I find him, were it
At home, upon my brother's guard, even there,
● Against the hospitable canon, would I
Wash my fierce hand in's heart. Go you to the
city;
Learn how 'tis held; and what they are that
must
Be hostages for Rome.
    First Sol.   Will not you go?
    Auf. I am attended at the cypress grove: I
pray you—   30
'Tis south the city mills—bring me word thither
How the world goes, that to the pace of it
I may spur on my journey.
    First Sol.   I shall, sir.
                           [*Exeunt.*

ACT II.

Scene I. *Rome. A public place.*

Enter Menenius *with the two Tribunes of the
people,* Sicinius *and* Brutus.

● *Men.* The augurer tells me we shall have
news to-night.
    Bru. Good or bad?
    Men. Not according to the prayer of the peo-
ple, for they love not Marcius.
    Sic. Nature teaches beasts to know their
friends.
    Men. Pray you, who does the wolf love?
    Sic. The lamb.
    Men. Ay, to devour him; as the hungry ple-
beians would the noble Marcius.   11
    Bru. He's a lamb indeed, that baes like a
bear.
    Men. He's a bear indeed, that lives like a
lamb. You two are old men: tell me one thing
that I shall ask you.
    Both. Well, sir.
    Men. In what enormity is Marcius poor in,
that you two have not in abundance?
    Bru. He's poor in no one fault, but stored
with all.   21
    Sic. Especially in pride.
    Bru. And topping all others in boasting.
    Men. This is strange now: do you two know
● how you are censured here in the city, I mean of
● us o' the right-hand file? do you?
    Both. Why, how are we censured?

15 *potch.* Poke.

16 *Or wrath or craft.* Either anger or skill.

20 *naked.* Unarmed. *fane.* Temple.

22 *Embarquements.* Impediments, restraints.

26 *hospitable canon.* Laws of hospitality.

A Roman street. From an 18th century Italian engraving

1 *augurer.* Omen-reading priest.

25 *censured.* Thought of.

26 *right-hand file.* The side of honour, i.e. the patricians.

40 *single.* Singular.

51 *humorous.* Capricious.

54-55 *imperfect . . . complaint.* Liable to sympathize.

59 *wealsmen.* Public men.

60 *Lycurguses.* Lycurgus, a legendary wise legislator.

Lycurgus, the Spartan lawgiver. Engraving from P. J. Mariette's *Traité des Pierres Gravées,* 1769

64 *the ass in compound with.* The fool prevalent in.

70 *bisson conspectuities.* Blind wisdoms.

79 *fosset.* Tap. *rejourn.* Adjourn.

84 *bloody flag.* Red flag of war.

92 *bencher.* Senator.

Menenius with Sicinius and Brutus. Engraving by Kenny Meadows from Barry Cornwall's *Works of Shakspere,* 1846

Men. Because you talk of pride now,—will you not be angry?

Both. Well, well, sir, well.   30

Men. Why, 'tis no great matter; for a very little thief of occasion will rob you of a great deal of patience: give your dispositions the reins, and be angry at your pleasures; at the least, if you take it as a pleasure to you in being so. You blame Marcius for being proud?

Bru. We do it not alone, sir.

Men. I know you can do very little alone; for your helps are many, or else your actions would grow wondrous single: your abilities are too infant-like for doing much alone. You talk of pride: O that you could turn your eyes toward the napes of your necks, and make but an interior survey of your good selves! O that you could!

Bru. What then, sir?

Men. Why, then you should discover a brace of unmeriting, proud, violent, testy magistrates, alias fools, as any in Rome.

Sic. Menenius, you are known well enough too.   50

Men. I am known to be a humorous patrician, and one that loves a cup of hot wine with not a drop of allaying Tiber in't; said to be something imperfect in favouring the first complaint; hasty and tinder-like upon too trivial motion; one that converses more with the buttock of the night than with the forehead of the morning: what I think I utter, and spend my malice in my breath. Meeting two such wealsmen as you are—I cannot call you Lycurguses—if the drink you give me touch my palate adversely, I make a crooked face at it. I can't say your worships have delivered the matter well, when I find the ass in compound with the major part of your syllables: and though I must be content to bear with those that say you are reverend grave men, yet they lie deadly that tell you you have good faces. If you see this in the map of my microcosm, follows it that I am known well enough too? what harm can your bisson conspectuities glean out of this character, if I be known well enough too?

Bru. Come, sir, come, we know you well enough.

Men. You know neither me, yourselves, nor any thing. You are ambitious for poor knaves' caps and legs: you wear out a good wholesome forenoon in hearing a cause between an orange-wife and a fosset-seller; and then rejourn the controversy of three pence to a second day of audience. When you are hearing a matter between party and party, if you chance to be pinched with the colic, you make faces like mummers; set up the bloody flag against all patience; and, in roaring for a chamber-pot, dismiss the controversy bleeding, the more entangled by your hearing: all the peace you make in their cause is, calling both the parties knaves. You are a pair of strange ones.   89

Bru. Come, come, you are well understood to be a perfecter giber for the table than a necessary bencher in the Capitol.

Men. Our very priests must become mockers, if they shall encounter such ridiculous subjects as you are. When you speak best unto the purpose, it is not worth the wagging of your beards;

and your beards deserve not so honourable a
grave as to stuff a botcher's cushion, or to be
entombed in an ass's pack-saddle. Yet you must
be saying, Marcius is proud; who, in a cheap
estimation, is worth all your predecessors since
Deucalion, though peradventure some of the best
of 'em were hereditary hangmen. God-den to
your worships: more of your conversation would
infect my brain, being the herdsmen of the beastly
plebeians: I will be bold to take my leave of you.

[*Brutus and Sicinius go aside.*

Enter VOLUMNIA, VIRGILIA, *and* VALERIA.

How now, my as fair as noble ladies,—and the
moon, were she earthly, no nobler,—whither do
you follow your eyes so fast?   109

Vol. Honourable Menenius, my boy Marcius
approaches; for the love of Juno, let's go.

Men. Ha! Marcius coming home!

Vol. Ay, worthy Menenius; and with most
prosperous approbation.

Men. Take my cap, Jupiter, and I thank
thee. Hoo! Marcius coming home!

Vol. Vir. Nay, 'tis true.

Vol. Look, here's a letter from him: the state
hath another, his wife another; and, I think,
there's one at home for you.   120

Men. I will make my very house reel to-
night: a letter for me!

Vir. Yes, certain, there's a letter for you; I
saw't.

Men. A letter for me! it gives me an estate
of seven years' health; in which time I will make
a lip at the physician: the most sovereign prescription in Galen is but empiricutic, and, to this
preservative, of no better report than a horse-
drench. Is he not wounded? he was wont to
come home wounded.   131

Vir. O, no, no, no.

Vol. O, he is wounded; I thank the gods for't.

Men. So do I too, if it be not too much:
brings a' victory in his pocket? the wounds become him.

Vol. On's brows: Menenius, he comes the
third time home with the oaken garland.

Men. Has he disciplined Aufidius soundly?

Vol. Titus Lartius writes, they fought together, but Aufidius got off.   141

Men. And 'twas time for him too, I'll warrant
him that: an he had stayed by him, I would not
have been so fidiused for all the chests in Corioli,
and the gold that's in them. Is the senate possessed of this?

Vol. Good ladies, let's go. Yes, yes, yes:
the senate has letters from the general, wherein
he gives my son the whole name of the war: he
hath in this action outdone his former deeds
doubly.   151

Val. In troth, there's wondrous things spoke
of him.

Men. Wondrous! ay, I warrant you, and not
without his true purchasing.

Vir. The gods grant them true!

Vol. True! pow, wow.

Men. True! I'll be sworn they are true.
Where is he wounded? [*To the Tribunes*] God
save your good worships! Marcius is coming
home: he has more cause to be proud. Where
is he wounded?

98 *botcher.* A patcher of old clothes.

102 *Deucalion.* Noah-figure in Greek legend.

103 *God-den.* Good evening.

125–127 *gives me an estate of.* Endows me with. *make a lip.* Sneer.

128 *Galen.* Famous Greek physician. *empiricutic.* quackery.

144 *fidiused.* i.e. treated like Aufidius.

145–146 *possessed.* Aware.

Edith Evans as Volumnia, Stratford-upon-Avon, 1959.
Portrait by Robert Buhler (b.1916)

166 *repulse of Tarquin.* The battle with Tarquinius Superbus at Rome.

Victarum urbium Imagines

Aurum Argentum æs rude

Signa et Tabulæ

Imperator Triumphans

A triumphal procession into Rome. Engraving from Basil Kennett's *Romae Antiquae Notitia,* 1769

---

205 *crab-trees.* Curmudgeons.

206 *grafted to your relish.* i.e. converted by your success.

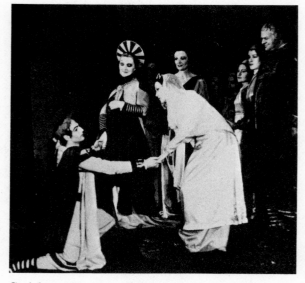

Coriolanus (Laurence Olivier) kneels before Volumnia (Sybil Thorndike) and Virgilia (Vivienne Bennett), Old Vic Theatre, London, 1938

Vol. I' the shoulder and i' the left arm: there will be large cicatrices to show the people, when he shall stand for his place.   He received in the ●repulse of Tarquin seven hurts i' the body.

Men. One i' the neck, and two i' the thigh, —there's nine that I know.

Vol. He had, before this last expedition, twenty-five wounds upon him.   170

Men. Now it's twenty-seven: every gash was an enemy's grave. [*A shout and flourish.*] Hark! the trumpets.

Vol. These are the ushers of Marcius: before him he carries noise, and behind him he leaves tears:
Death, that dark spirit, in's nervy arm doth lie;
Which, being advanced, declines, and then men die.

A sennet. Trumpets sound. Enter COMINIUS *the general, and* TITUS LARTIUS; *between them,* CORIOLANUS, *crowned with an oaken garland; with* Captains *and* Soldiers, *and a* Herald.

Her. Know, Rome, that all alone Marcius did fight
Within Corioli gates: where he hath won,   180
With fame, a name to Caius Marcius; these
In honour follows Coriolanus.
Welcome to Rome, renowned Coriolanus!
                                        [*Flourish.*

All. Welcome to Rome, renowned Coriolanus!

Cor. No more of this; it does offend my heart:
Pray now, no more.

Com.   Look, sir, your mother!

Cor.   O,
You have, I know, petition'd all the gods
For my prosperity!   [*Kneels.*

Vol.   Nay, my good soldier, up;
My gentle Marcius, worthy Caius, and
By deed-achieving honour newly named,—   190
What is it?—Coriolanus must I call thee?—
But, O, thy wife!

Cor.   My gracious silence, hail!
Wouldst thou have laugh'd had I come coffin'd home,
That weep'st to see me triumph? Ah, my dear,
Such eyes the widows in Corioli wear,
And mothers that lack sons.

Men.   Now, the gods crown thee!

Cor. And live you yet? [*To Valeria*] O my sweet lady, pardon.

Vol. I know not where to turn: O, welcome home:
And welcome, general: and ye're welcome all.

Men. A hundred thousand welcomes. I could weep   200
And I could laugh, I am light and heavy. Welcome.
A curse begin at very root on's heart,
That is not glad to see thee! You are three
That Rome should dote on: yet, by the faith of men,
●We have some old crab-trees here at home that will not
●Be grafted to your relish. Yet welcome, warriors:
We call a nettle but a nettle and
The faults of fools but folly.

Com.   Ever right.

Cor. Menenius ever, ever.

Herald. Give way there, and go on!

Cor.   [*To Volumnia and Virgilia*] Your
    hand, and yours: 210
Ere in our own house I do shade my head,
The good patricians must be visited;
From whom I have received not only greetings,
● But with them change of honours.
    Vol.   I have lived
● To see inherited my very wishes
And the buildings of my fancy: only
There's one thing wanting, which I doubt not
    but
Our Rome will cast upon thee.
    Cor.   Know, good mother,
I had rather be their servant in my way,
Than sway with them in theirs.
    Com.   On, to the Capitol! 220
    [*Flourish. Cornets. Exeunt in state, as
    before. Brutus and Sicinius come for-
    ward.*
    Bru. All tongues speak of him, and the bleared
    sights
Are spectacled to see him: your prattling nurse
Into a rapture lets her baby cry
● While she chats him: the kitchen malkin pins
● Her richest lockram 'bout her reechy neck,
● Clambering the walls to eye him: stalls, bulks,
    windows,
Are smother'd up, leads fill'd, and ridges horsed
● With variable complexions, all agreeing
● In earnestness to see him: seld-shown flamens
Do press among the popular throngs and puff 230
● To win a vulgar station: our veil'd dames
Commit the war of white and damask in
● Their nicely-gawded cheeks to the wanton spoil
● Of Phœbus' burning kisses: such a pother
As if that whatsoever god who leads him
Were slily crept into his human powers
And gave him graceful posture.
    Sic.   On the sudden,
I warrant him consul.
    Bru.   Then our office may,
During his power, go sleep.
    Sic. He cannot temperately transport his
    honours   240
From where he should begin and end, but will
Lose those he hath won.
    Bru.   In that there's comfort.
    Sic.   Doubt not
The commoners, for whom we stand, but they
Upon their ancient malice will forget
With the least cause these his new honours, which
That he will give them make I as little question
As he is proud to do 't.
    Bru.   I heard him swear,
Were he to stand for consul, never would he
Appear i' the market-place nor on him put
● The napless vesture of humility;   250
Nor, showing, as the manner is, his wounds
● To the people, beg their stinking breaths.
    Sic.   'Tis right.
    Bru. It was his word: O, he would miss it
    rather
Than carry it but by the suit of the gentry to him
And the desire of the nobles.
    Sic.   I wish no better
Than have him hold that purpose and to put it
In execution.
    Bru.   'Tis most like he will.
    Sic. It shall be to him then as our good wills,

214 *change of.* New.

215 *inherited.* Realised.

Coriolanus: 'Know, good mother, I had rather be their servant in my way, Than sway with them in theirs.' Coriolanus (Laurence Olivier) with Volumnia (Sybil Thorndike), Old Vic Theatre, London, 1938

224–229 *the kitchen . . . see him.* See introduction.

224 *chats.* Chats about. *malkin.* Slut.

225 *lockram.* Coarse linen. *reechy.* Dirty.

226 *bulks.* Frames for stalls.

228 *variable complexions.* All sorts of types.

229 *seld-shown flamens.* Rarely seen priests.

231 *vulgar station.* Place in the crowd.

233 *nicely-gawded.* Carefully made-up.

234 *Phœbus.* Sun god.

250 *napless.* Threadbare.

252 *their . . . breaths.* i.e. their acclaim.

267 *provand.* Provender.

Reconstruction of the Capitoline Hill. From a 19th century engraving

5–7 *That's ... people.* See introduction.

6 *vengeance.* Intensely.

19 *waved.* Wavered. *indifferently.* Impartially.

A sure destruction.
 Bru.   So it must fall out
To him or our authorities. For an end, 260
We must suggest the people in what hatred
He still hath held them; that to's power he would
Have made them mules, silenced their pleaders and
Dispropertied their freedoms, holding them,
In human action and capacity,
Of no more soul nor fitness for the world
Than camels in the war, who have their provand
Only for bearing burdens, and sore blows
For sinking under them.
 Sic.   This, as you say, suggested
At some time when his soaring insolence 270
Shall touch the people,—which time shall not want,
If he be put upon't; and that's as easy
As to set dogs on sheep—will be his fire
To kindle their dry stubble; and their blaze
Shall darken him for ever.

Enter a Messenger.

 Bru.   What's the matter?
 Mess. You are sent for to the Capitol. 'Tis thought
That Marcius shall be consul:
I have seen the dumb men throng to see him and
The blind to hear him speak: matrons flung gloves,
Ladies and maids their scarfs and handkerchers,
Upon him as he pass'd: the nobles bended, 281
As to Jove's statue, and the commons made
A shower and thunder with their caps and shouts:
I never saw the like.
 Bru.   Let's to the Capitol;
And carry with us ears and eyes for the time,
But hearts for the event.
 Sic.   Have with you. [*Exeunt.*

SCENE II. *The same. The Capitol.*

Enter two Officers, *to lay cushions.*

 First Off. Come, come, they are almost here. How many stand for consulships?
 Sec. Off. Three, they say: but 'tis thought of every one Coriolanus will carry it.
 First Off. That's a brave fellow; but he's vengeance proud, and loves not the common people.
 Sec. Off. Faith, there have been many great men that have flattered the people, who ne'er loved them; and there be many that they have loved, they know not wherefore: so that, if they love they know not why, they hate upon no better a ground: therefore, for Coriolanus neither to care whether they love or hate him manifests the true knowledge he has in their disposition; and out of his noble carelessness lets them plainly see't.
 First Off. If he did not care whether he had their love or no, he waved indifferently 'twixt doing them neither good nor harm: but he seeks their hate with greater devotion than they can render it him; and leaves nothing undone that may fully discover him their opposite. Now, to seem to affect the malice and displeasure of the people is as bad as that which he dislikes, to flatter them for their love.

Sec. Off. He hath deserved worthily of his country: and his ascent is not by such easy degrees as those who, having been supple and ● courteous to the people, bonneted, without any further deed to have them at all into their estimation and report: but he hath so planted his honours in their eyes, and his actions in their hearts, that for their tongues to be silent, and not confess so much, were a kind of ingrateful injury; to report otherwise, were a malice, that, giving itself the lie, would pluck reproof and rebuke from every ear that heard it.

First Off. No more of him; he's a worthy man: make way, they are coming. 40

A sennet. Enter, with Lictors *before them,* Cominius *the consul,* Menenius, Coriolanus, Senators, Sicinius *and* Brutus. *The Senators take their places; the Tribunes take their places by themselves.* Coriolanus *stands.*

● *Men.* Having determined of the Volsces and
To send for Titus Lartius, it remains,
As the main point of this our after-meeting,
To gratify his noble service that
Hath thus stood for his country: therefore, please you,
Most reverend and grave elders, to desire
The present consul, and last general
● In our well-found successes, to report
A little of that worthy work perform'd
By Caius Marcius Coriolanus, whom 50
We met here both to thank and to remember
With honours like himself.
    First Sen.   Speak, good Cominius:
Leave nothing out for length, and make us think
Rather our state's defective for requital
Than we to stretch it out. [*To the Tribunes*]
        Masters o' the people,
We do request your kindest ears, and after,
Your loving motion toward the common body,
● To yield what passes here.
    Sic.   We are convented
Upon a pleasing treaty, and have hearts
Inclinable to honour and advance 60
The theme of our assembly.
    Bru.   Which the rather
We shall be blest to do, if he remember
A kinder value of the people than
He hath hereto prized them at.
    Men.   That's off, that's off;
I would you rather had been silent. Please you
To hear Cominius speak?
    Bru.   Most willingly;
But yet my caution was more pertinent
Than the rebuke you give it.
    Men.   He loves your people;
But tie him not to be their bedfellow.
Worthy Cominius, speak. [*Coriolanus offers to go away.*] Nay, keep your place. 70
    First Sen. Sit, Coriolanus; never shame to hear
What you have nobly done.
    Cor.   Your honours' pardon:
I had rather have my wounds to heal again
Than hear say how I got them.
    Bru.   Sir, I hope
● My words disbench'd you not.
    Cor.   No, sir: yet oft,

30 *bonneted.* Hats in hand.

41 *determined of.* Come to a settlement with.

48 *well-found.* Fortunate deserved.

58 *yield.* Accept. *convented.* Met.

First Senator: 'Sit, Coriolanus; never shame to hear What you have nobly done.' Coriolanus (Anthony Quayle) with First Senator (Jack Gwillim), Cominius (Raymond Westwell) and Menenius (Michael Hordern), Stratford-upon-Avon, 1952

75 *disbench'd you not.* Did not unseat you.

77 *soothed.* Flattered.

91 *singly counterpoised.* Equalled by a single person.

92 *made a head for.* Led an army against.

95 *Amazonian.* i.e. beardless (like the legendary female warriors).

Amazon. From a 19th century engraving of a Greek vase

100 *When . . . scene.* i.e. when he could take female parts in plays, with his unbroken voice and beardless face.

105 *lurch'd all swords of the garland.* i.e. stole the show.

111 *stem.* Prow.

115 *mortal.* Fatal.

116 *shunless destiny.* i.e. blood which was destined to be spilled.

120 *ready sense.* Attentive hearing.

131 *misery.* Abject poverty.

When blows have made me stay, I fled from words.
●You soothed not, therefore hurt not: but your people,
I love them as they weigh.
   Men.   Pray now, sit down.
   Cor. I had rather have one scratch my head
     i' the sun
When the alarum were struck than idly sit   80
To hear my nothings monster'd.   [*Exit.*
   Men.   Masters of the people,
Your multiplying spawn how can he flatter—
That's thousand to one good one—when you
    now see
He had rather venture all his limbs for honour
Than one on's ears to hear it? Proceed, Cominius.
   Com. I shall lack voice: the deeds of Coriolanus
Should not be utter'd feebly.   It is held
That valour is the chiefest virtue, and
Most dignifies the haver: if it be,
The man I speak of cannot in the world   90
●Be singly counterpoised.   At sixteen years,
●When Tarquin made a head for Rome, he fought
Beyond the mark of others: our then dictator,
Whom with all praise I point at, saw him fight,
●When with his Amazonian chin he drove
The bristled lips before him: he bestrid
An o'er-press'd Roman and i' the consul's view
Slew three opposers: Tarquin's self he met,
And struck him on his knee: in that day's feats,
●When he might act the woman in the scene,   100
He proved best man i' the field, and for his meed
Was brow-bound with the oak.   His pupil **age**
Man-enter'd thus, he waxed like a sea,
And in the brunt of seventeen battles since
●He lurch'd all swords of the garland.   For this last,
Before and in Corioli, let me say,
I cannot speak him home: he stopp'd the fliers;
And by his rare example made the coward
Turn terror into sport: as weeds before
A vessel under sail, so men obey'd   110
●And fell below his stem: his sword, death's stamp,
Where it did mark, it took; from face to foot
He was a thing of blood, whose every motion
Was timed with dying cries: alone he enter'd
●The mortal gate of the city, which he painted
●With shunless destiny; aidless came off,
And with a sudden re-inforcement struck
Corioli like a planet: now all's his:
When, by and by, the din of war gan pierce   119
●His ready sense; then straight his doubled spirit
Re-quicken'd what in flesh was fatigate,
And to the battle came he; where he did
Run reeking o'er the lives of men, as if
'Twere a perpetual spoil: and till we call'd
Both field and city ours, he never stood
To ease his breast with panting.
   Men.   Worthy **man!**
   First Sen. He cannot but with measure **fit the**
    honours
Which we devise him.
   Com.   Our spoils he kick'd at,
And look'd upon things precious as they were
The common muck of the world: he covets less
●Than misery itself would give; rewards   **131**
His deeds with doing them, and is content
To spend the time to end it.

Men.   He's right noble:
Let him be call'd for.
First Sen.   Call Coriolanus.
Off.   He doth appear.

Re-enter CORIOLANUS.

Men. The senate, Coriolanus, are well pleased
To make thee consul.
Cor.   I do owe them still
My life and services.
Men.   It then remains
That you do speak to the people.
Cor.   I do beseech you,
Let me o'erleap that custom, for I cannot   140
Put on the gown, stand naked and entreat them,
For my wounds' sake, to give their suffrage:
    please you
That I may pass this doing.
Sic.   Sir, the people
Must have their voices; neither will they bate
One jot of ceremony.
Men.   Put them not to't:
Pray you, go fit you to the custom and
Take to you, as your predecessors have,
Your honour with your form.
Cor.   It is a part
That I shall blush in acting, and might well
Be taken from the people.
Bru.   Mark you that?   150
Cor. To brag unto them, thus I did, and thus;
Show them the unaching scars which I should
    hide,
As if I had received them for the hire
Of their breath only!
Men.   Do not stand upon't.
We recommend to you, tribunes of the people,
Our purpose to them: and to our noble consul
Wish we all joy and honour.
Senators. To Coriolanus come all joy and
    honour! [*Flourish of cornets. Exeunt all
                  but Sicinius and Brutus.*
Bru. You see how he intends to use the people.
Sic. May they perceive's intent! He will
    require them,   160
As if he did contemn what he requested
Should be in them to give.
Bru.   Come, we'll inform them
Of our proceedings here: on the market-place,
I know, they do attend us.   [*Exeunt.*

SCENE III. *The same. The Forum.*

Enter seven or eight Citizens.

First Cit. Once, if he do require our voices,
we ought not to deny him.
Sec. Cit. We may, sir, if we will.
Third Cit. We have power in ourselves to do
it, but it is a power that we have no power to do;
for if he show us his wounds and tell us his deeds,
we are to put our tongues into those wounds and
speak for them; so, if he tell us his noble deeds,
we must also tell him our noble acceptance of
them. Ingratitude is monstrous, and for the
multitude to be ingrateful, were to make a monster of the multitude; of the which we being
members, should bring ourselves to be monstrous
members.
First Cit. And to make us no better thought
of, a little help will serve; for once we stood up

148 *your form.* Proper formality.

The Roman Forum. Nineteenth century engraving by
S. Prout

1 *Once.* i.e. once and for all.

48 *by particulars*. One by one.

57 *pace*. Trot.

64 *our divines lose by 'em*. Our priests throw away upon them.

Richard Burton as Coriolanus, Old Vic Theatre, London, 1954

about the corn, he himself stuck not to call us the many-headed multitude.

Third Cit.   We have been called so of many; not that our heads are some brown, some black, some auburn, some bald, but that our wits are so diversely coloured: and truly I think if all our wits were to issue out of one skull, they would fly east, west, north, south, and their consent of one direct way should be at once to all the points o' the compass.

Sec. Cit.   Think you so? Which way do you judge my wit would fly?

Third Cit.   Nay, your wit will not so soon out as another man's will; 'tis strongly wedged up in a block-head, but if it were at liberty, 'twould, sure, southward.

Sec. Cit.   Why that way?

Third Cit.   To lose itself in a fog, where being three parts melted away with rotten dews, the fourth would return for conscience sake, to help to get thee a wife.

Sec. Cit.   You are never without your tricks: you may, you may.   39

Third Cit.   Are you all resolved to give your voices? But that's no matter, the greater part carries it. I say, if he would incline to the people, there was never a worthier man.

Enter CORIOLANUS *in a gown of humility, with* MENENIUS.

Here he comes, and in the gown of humility: mark his behaviour. We are not to stay all together, but to come by him where he stands, by ones, by twos, and by threes. He's to make his requests by particulars; wherein every one of us has a single honour, in giving him our own voices with our own tongues: therefore follow me, and I'll direct you how you shall go by him.

All.   Content, content.   [*Exeunt citizens.*

Men.   O sir, you are not right: have you not known
The worthiest men have done 't?

Cor.   What must I say?
'I pray, sir,'—Plague upon 't! I cannot bring
My tongue to such a pace:—'Look, sir. my wounds!
I got them in my country's service, when
Some certain of your brethren roar'd and ran   59
From the noise of our own drums.'

Men.   O me, the gods!
You must not speak of that: you must desire them
To think upon you.

Cor.   Think upon me! hang 'em!
I would they would forget me, like the virtues
Which our divines lose by 'em.

Men.   You'll mar all:
I'll leave you: pray you, speak to 'em, I pray you,
In wholesome manner.   [*Exit.*

Cor.   Bid them wash their faces
And keep their teeth clean. [*Re-enter two of the Citizens.*] So, here comes a brace. [*Re-enter a third Citizen.*]
You know the cause, sir, of my standing here.

Third Cit.   We do, sir; tell us what hath brought you to 't.   70

Cor.   Mine own desert.

Sec. Cit.   Your own desert!

Cor.   Ay, but not mine own desire.

Third Cit.   How not your own desire?

Cor.   No, sir, 'twas never my desire yet to trouble the poor with begging.

Third Cit.   You must think, if we give you any thing, we hope to gain by you.

Cor.   Well then, I pray, your price o' the consulship?   80

First Cit.   The price is to ask it kindly.

Cor.   Kindly! Sir, I pray, let me ha't: I have wounds to show you, which shall be yours in private.   Your good voice, sir; what say you?

Sec. Cit.   You shall ha't, worthy sir.

● *Cor.*   A match, sir.   There's in all two worthy voices begged.   I have your alms: adieu.

Third Cit.   But this is something odd.

Sec. Cit.   An 'twere to give again,—but 'tis no matter.   [*Exeunt the three Citizens.* 90

Re-enter two other Citizens.

Cor.   Pray you now, if it may stand with the tune of your voices that I may be consul, I have here the customary gown.

Fourth Cit.   You have deserved nobly of your country, and you have not deserved nobly.

Cor.   Your enigma?

Fourth Cit.   You have been a scourge to her enemies, you have been a rod to her friends; you have not indeed loved the common people.   99

● *Cor.*   You should account me the more virtuous that I have not been common in my love. I will, sir, flatter my sworn brother, the people, to earn a dearer estimation of them; 'tis a condition they account gentle: and since the wisdom of their choice is rather to have my hat than my heart, I will practise the insinuating nod and be off to them most counterfeitly; that is, sir, I will counterfeit the bewitchment of some popular man and give it bountiful to the desirers.   Therefore, beseech you, I may be consul.

Fifth Cit.   We hope to find you our friend; and therefore give you our voices heartily.

Fourth Cit.   You have received many wounds for your country.

Cor.   I will not seal your knowledge with showing them.   I will make much of your voices, and so trouble you no further.

Both Cit.   The gods give you joy, sir, heartily!

[*Exeunt.*

Cor.   Most sweet voices!

Better it is to die, better to starve,   120

Than crave the hire which first we do deserve.

● Why in this woolvish toge should I stand here,

● To beg of Hob and Dick, that do appear,

● Their needless vouches? Custom calls me to't:

What custom wills, in all things should we do't,

The dust on antique time would lie unswept,

And mountainous error be too highly heapt

For truth to o'er-peer.   Rather than fool it so,

Let the high office and the honour go

To one that would do thus.   I am half through;

The one part suffer'd, the other will I do.   131

Re-enter three Citizens *more.*

● Here come moe voices.

Your voices: for your voices I have fought;

Watch'd for your voices; for **your** voices bear

Coriolanus: 'I have wounds to show you, which shall be yours in private'. Engraving from Bell's edition of *Shakespeare*, 1773

86 *A match.* Agreed!

100–107 *You should . . . counterfeitly.* See introduction.

122 *woolvish toge.* Wolf-like toga (Roman gown). Perhaps a reference to the saying 'a wolf in sheep's clothing'.

123 *Hob and Dick.* i.e. Tom, Dick or Harry.

124 *vouches.* Votes.

132 *moe.* More.

146 *limitation.* Allotted time.

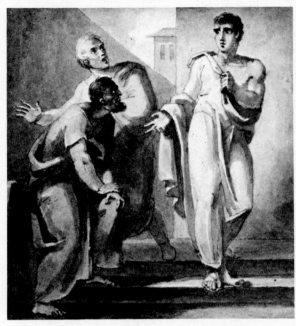

Brutus: 'With a proud heart he wore his humble weeds.'
Brutus and Sicinius with Coriolanus. Drawing by
Henry Tresham (1749?–1814)

Of wounds two dozen odd ; battles thrice six
I have seen and heard of ; for your voices have
Done many things, some less, some more : your
   voices :
Indeed, I would be consul.
   Sixth Cit. He has done nobly, and cannot go
without any honest man's voice.   140
   Seventh Cit. Therefore let him be consul :
the gods give him joy, and make him good friend.
to the people !
   All Cit. Amen, amen. God save thee, noble
   consul !   [*Exeunt.*
   Cor. Worthy voices !

Re-enter MENENIUS, *with* BRUTUS *and* SICINIUS.

   Men. You have stood your limitation ; and
   the tribunes
Endue you with the people's voice : remains
That, in the official marks invested, you
Anon do meet the senate.
   Cor.   Is this done?
   Sic. The custom of request you have dis-
   charged :   150
The people do admit you, and are summon'd
To meet anon, upon your approbation.
   Cor. Where? at the senate-house?
   Sic.   There, Coriolanus.
   Cor. May I change these garments?
   Sic.   You may, sir.
   Cor. That I 'll straight do ; and, knowing
   myself again,
Repair to the senate-house.
   Men. I 'll keep you company. Will you
   along ?
   Bru. We stay here for the people.
   Sic.   Fare you well.
   [*Exeunt Coriolanus and Menenius.*
He has it now, and by his looks methinks
'Tis warm at 's heart.   160
   Bru. With a proud heart he wore his humble
   weeds.
Will you dismiss the people ?

Re-enter Citizens.

   Sic. How now, my masters ! have you chose
   this man ?
   First Cit. He has our voices, sir.
   Bru. We pray the gods he may deserve your
   loves.
   Sec. Cit. Amen, sir : to my poor unworthy
   notice,
He mock'd us when he begg'd our voices.
   Third Cit.   Certainly
He flouted us downright.
   First Cit. No, 'tis his kind of speech : he did
   not mock us.
   Sec. Cit. Not one amongst us, save yourself,
   but says   170
He used us scornfully : he should have show'd us
His marks of merit, wounds received for 's
   country.
   Sic. Why, so he did, I am sure.
   Citizens.   No, no ; no man saw 'em.
   Third Cit. He said he had wounds, which he
   could show in private ;
And with his hat, thus waving it in scorn,
' I would be consul,' says he : 'aged custom,
But by your voices, will not so permit me ;
Your voices therefore.' When we granted that,

Here was ' I thank you for your voices: thank
  you :
Your most sweet voices : now you have left your
  voices,   180
I have no further with you.' Was not this
  mockery?
  Sic. Why either were you ignorant to see 't,
Or, seeing it, of such childish friendliness
To yield your voices?
  Bru.   Could you not have told him
As you were lesson'd, when he had no power,
But was a petty servant to the state,
He was your enemy, ever spake against
Your liberties and the charters that you bear
●I' the body of the weal ; and now, arriving
A place of potency and sway o' the state,   190
If he should still malignantly remain
●Fast foe to the plebeii, your voices might
Be curses to yourselves? You should have said
That as his worthy deeds did claim no less
Than what he stood for, so his gracious nature
Would think upon you for your voices and
Translate his malice towards you into love,
Standing your friendly lord.
  Sic.   Thus to have said,
●As you were fore-advised, had touch'd his spirit
And tried his inclination; from him pluck'd   200
Either his gracious promise, which you might,
As cause had call'd you up, have held him to;
Or else it would have gall'd his surly nature,
●Which easily endures not article
Tying him to aught; so putting him to rage,
You should have ta'en the advantage of his
  choler
And pass'd him unelected.
  Bru.   Did you perceive
●He did solicit you in free contempt
When he did need your loves, and do you think
That his contempt shall not be bruising to you,
When he hath power to crush? Why, had your
  bodies   211
No heart among you? or had you tongues to cry
●Against the rectorship of judgement?
  Sic.   Have you
Ere now denied the asker? and now again
Of him that did not ask, but mock, bestow
Your sued-for tongues?
  Third Cit. He's not confirm'd; we may deny
  him yet.
  Sec. Cit. And will deny him :
I'll have five hundred voices of that sound.
● *First Cit.* I twice five hundred and their
  friends to piece 'em.   220
  Bru. Get you hence instantly, and tell those
  friends,
They have chose a consul that will from them
  take
Their liberties ; make them of no more voice
Than dogs that are as often beat for barking
As therefore kept to do so.
  Sic.   Let them assemble,
And on a safer judgement all revoke
Your ignorant election ; enforce his pride,
And his old hate unto you ; besides, forget not
With what contempt he wore the humble weed,
How in his suit he scorn'd you ; but your loves,
Thinking upon his services, took from you   231
●The apprehension of his present portance,
Which most gibingly, ungravely, he did fashion

189 *body of the weal.* Commonwealth.

192 *plebeii.* Plebeians, the lower class of Roman citizens.

199 *touch'd.* Tested.

204 *article.* Condition.

208 *free.* Undisguised.

213 *rectorship of judgement.* Government of reason.

220 *piece.* Add to.

232 *apprehension.* Perception. *portance.* Behaviour.

247–251 *Numa* ... *Hostilius* ... *Publius* ... *Quintus* ... [*Censorinus*]. Are all famous characters in ancient Rome and are mentioned as ancestors to Coriolanus.

257 *Scaling*. Weighing.

260 *putting on*. Instigation.

268 *vantage of*. Advantage given by.

Citizens rush to the Capitol. Engraving by Kenny Meadows from Barry Cornwall's *Works of Shakspere*, 1846

---

1 *made new head*. Raised another army.

3 *composition*. Agreement of terms.

John Vandenhoff, the Victorian actor, as Coriolanus, Covent Garden Theatre, London, 1834

After the inveterate hate he bears you.
 Bru.   Lay
A fault on us, your tribunes; that we labour'd,
No impediment between, but that you must
Cast your election on him.
 Sic.   Say, you chose him
More after our commandment than as guided
By your own true affections, and that your
  minds,
Pre-occupied with what you rather must do 240
Than what you should, made you against the
  grain
To voice him consul: lay the fault on us.
 Bru. Ay, spare us not.   Say we read lectures
  to you,
How youngly he began to serve his country,
How long continued, and what stock he springs of
The noble house o' the Marcians, from whence
  came
●That Ancus Marcius, Numa's daughter's son,
Who, after great Hostilius, here was king;
Of the same house Publius and Quintus were,
That our best water brought by conduits hither;
And [Censorinus,] nobly named so, 251
Twice being [by the people chosen] censor,
Was his great ancestor.
 Sic.   One thus descended,
That hath beside well in his person wrought
To be set high in place, we did commend
To your remembrances: but you have found,
●Scaling his present bearing with his past,
That he's your fixed enemy, and revoke
Your sudden approbation.
 Bru.   Say, you ne'er had done't—
●Harp on that still—but by our putting on: 260
And presently, when you have drawn your
  number,
Repair to the Capitol.
 All.   We will so: almost all
Repent in their election. [*Exeunt Citizens.*
 Bru.   Let them go on;
This mutiny were better put in hazard,
Than stay, past doubt, for greater:
If, as his nature is, he fall in rage
With their refusal, both observe and answer
●The vantage of his anger.
 Sic.   To the Capitol, come:
We will be there before the stream o' the people;
And this shall seem, as partly 'tis, their own, 270
Which we have goaded onward. [*Exeunt.*

ACT III.

Scene I. *Rome.   A street.*

Cornets.   Enter Coriolanus, Menenius, *all the Gentry,* Cominius, Titus Lartius, *and other* Senators.

● *Cor.* Tullus Aufidius then had made new
  head?
 Lart. He had, my lord; and that it was
  which caused
●Our swifter composition.
 Cor. So then the Volsces stand but as at
  first,
Ready, when time shall prompt them, to make
  road
Upon's again.
 Com.   They are worn, lord consul, so,

●That we shall hardly in our ages see
Their banners wave again.
    Cor.   Saw you Aufidius?
● *Lart.* On safe-guard he came to me; and
    did curse
Against the Volsces, for they had so vilely   10
●Yielded the town: he is retired to Antium.
    Cor. Spoke he of me?
    Lart.   He did, my lord,
    Cor.   How? what?
    Lart. How often he had met you, sword to
    sword;
That of all things upon the earth he hated
Your person most, that he would pawn his
    fortunes
●To hopeless restitution, so he might
Be call'd your vanquisher.
    Cor.   At Antium lives he?
    Lart. At Antium.
    Cor. I wish I had a cause to seek him there,
To oppose his hatred fully. Welcome home. 20

       Enter SICINIUS *and* BRUTUS.

Behold, these are the tribunes of the people,
The tongues o' the common mouth: I do despise
    them;
●For they do prank them in authority,
Against all noble sufferance.
    Sic.   Pass no further.
    Cor. Ha! what is that?
    Bru. It will be dangerous to go on: no further.
    Cor. What makes this change?
    Men. The matter?
    Com. Hath he not pass'd the noble and the
    common?
    Bru. Cominius, no.
    Cor.   Have I had children's voices? 30
    First Sen. Tribunes, give way; he shall to
    the market-place.
    Bru. The people are incensed against him.
    Sic.   Stop,
Or all will fall in broil.
    Cor.   Are these your herd?
Must these have voices, that can yield them now
●And straight disclaim their tongues? What are
    your offices?
You being their mouths, why rule you not their
    teeth?
Have you not set them on?
    Men.   Be calm, be calm.
    Cor. It is a purposed thing, and grows by plot,
To curb the will of the nobility:
Suffer't, and live with such as cannot rule   40
Nor ever will be ruled.
    Bru.   Call't not a plot:
The people cry you mock'd them, and of late,
●When corn was given them gratis, you repined;
Scandal'd the suppliants for the people, call'd
    them
Time-pleasers, flatterers, foes to nobleness.
    Cor. Why, this was known before.
    Bru.   Not to them all.
● *Cor.* Have you inform'd them sithence?
    Bru.   How! I inform them!
    Com. You are like to do such business.
    Bru.   Not unlike,
Each way, to better yours.
    Cor. Why then should I be consul? By yond
    clouds,   50

7 *ages.* Life-times.

9 *On safe-guard.* Under safe-conduct.

11 *Antium.* Capital of the Volsces.

16 *hopeless restitution.* Hopelessly irrecoverable.

23 *prank.* Dress up.

Sicinius: 'Pass no further.' Drawing by J. M. Moreau
le jeune, 1785

35 *straight disclaim.* i.e. immediately take back.

43 *repined.* Grumbled.

47 *sithence.* Since then.

58 *abused.* Deceived. *paltering.* Shallying.

60 *dishonour'd rub.* Dishonourable obstruction.

70 *cockle.* Weed.

78 *measles.* Scabs.

79 *tetter.* Infect.

89 *Triton.* Legendary god of the waves.

90 *from the canon.* Contrary to the law.

93 *Hydra.* Legendary many-headed monster.

96–97 *current . . . his.* i.e. divert your power to his own uses.

98 *vail.* Bow down.

Let me deserve so ill as you, and make me
Your fellow tribune.
   Sic.   You show too much of that
For which the people stir: if you will pass
To where you are bound, you must inquire your way,
Which you are out of, with a gentler spirit,
Or never be so noble as a consul,
Nor yoke with him for tribune.
   Men.   Let's be calm.
• *Com.*   The people are abused; set on. This paltering
Becomes not Rome, nor has Coriolanus
•Deserved this so dishonour'd rub, laid falsely 60
I' the plain way of his merit.
   Cor.   Tell me of corn!
This was my speech, and I will speak't again—
   Men.   Not now, not now.
   First Sen.   Not in this heat, sir, now.
   Cor.   Now, as I live, I will. My nobler friends,
I crave their pardons:
For the mutable, rank-scented many, let them
Regard me as I do not flatter, and
Therein behold themselves: I say again,
In soothing them, we nourish 'gainst our senate
•The cockle of rebellion, insolence, sedition, 70
Which we ourselves have plough'd for, sow'd, and scatter'd,
By mingling them with us, the honour'd number,
Who lack not virtue, no, nor power, but that
Which they have given to beggars.
   Men.   Well, no more.
   First Sen.   No more words, we beseech you.
   Cor.   How! no more!
As for my country I have shed my blood,
Not fearing outward force, so shall my lungs
•Coin words till their decay against those measles,
•Which we disdain should tetter us, yet sought
The very way to catch them.
   Bru.   You speak o' the people, 80
As if you were a god to punish, not
A man of their infirmity.
   Sic.   'Twere well
We let the people know't.
   Men.   What, what? his choler?
   Cor.   Choler!
Were I as patient as the midnight sleep,
By Jove, 'twould be my mind!
   Sic.   It is a mind
That shall remain a poison where it is,
Not poison any further.
   Cor.   Shall remain!
•Hear you this Triton of the minnows? mark you
•His absolute 'shall'?
   Com.   'Twas from the canon.
   Cor.   'Shall'! 90
O good but most unwise patricians! why,
You grave but reckless senators, have you thus
•Given Hydra here to choose an officer,
That with his peremptory 'shall,' being but
The horn and noise o' the monster's, wants not spirit
•To say he'll turn your current in a ditch,
And make your channel his? If he have power,
•Then vail your ignorance; if none, awake
Your dangerous lenity. If you are learn'd,
Be not as common fools; if you are not,   100
Let them have cushions by you. You are plebeians,

If they be senators: and they are no less,
When, both your voices blended, the great'st taste
● Most palates theirs. They choose their magistrate,
And such a one as he, who puts his 'shall,'
His popular 'shall,' against a graver bench
Than ever frown'd in Greece. By Jove himself!
It makes the consuls base: and my soul aches
To know, when two authorities are up,
Neither supreme, how soon confusion   110
May enter 'twixt the gap of both and take
The one by the other.
    Com.   Well, on to the market-place.
    Cor. Whoever gave that counsel, to give forth
The corn o' the storehouse gratis, as 'twas used
Sometime in Greece,—
    Men.   Well, well, no more of that.
    Cor. Though there the people had more absolute power,
I say, they nourish'd disobedience, fed
The ruin of the state.
    Bru.   Why, shall the people give
One that speaks thus their voice?
    Cor.   I 'll give my reasons,
More worthier than their voices. They know the corn   120
Was not our recompense, resting well assured
They ne'er did service for't: being press'd to the war,
Even when the navel of the state was touch'd,
They would not thread the gates. This kind of service
Did not deserve corn gratis. Being i' the war,
Their mutinies and revolts, wherein they show'd
Most valour, spoke not for them: the accusation
Which they have often made against the senate,
All cause unborn, could never be the motive
Of our so frank donation. Well, what then?   130
● How shall this bisson multitude digest
The senate's courtesy? Let deeds express
What's like to be their words: 'We did request it;
We are the greater poll, and in true fear
They gave us our demands.' Thus we debase
The nature of our seats and make the rabble
Call our cares fears; which will in time
Break ope the locks o' the senate and bring in
The crows to peck the eagles.
    Men.   Come, enough.
    Bru. Enough, with over-measure.
    Cor.   No, take more: 140
What may be sworn by, both divine and human,
● Seal what I end withal! This double worship,
Where one part does disdain with cause, the other
Insult without all reason, where gentry, title, wisdom,
Cannot conclude but by the yea and no
Of general ignorance,—it must omit
Real necessities, and give way the while
To unstable slightness: purpose so barr'd, it follows,
Nothing is done to purpose. Therefore, beseech you,—
You that will be less fearful than discreet,   150
That love the fundamental part of state
More than you doubt the change on't, that prefer
A noble life before a long, and wish
● †To jump a body with a dangerous physic

104 *palates.* Agrees with.

John Kemble as Coriolanus, Covent Garden Theatre, London, 1817

131 *bisson.* Blind.

142 *double worship.* Divided authority.

154 *jump.* Risk.

158–161 *bereaves ... control't.* See introduction.

173 *ædiles.* i.e. assistants to the Tribunes.

Menenius: This is the way to kindle, not to quench.'
Menenius (John Moffatt) with Coriolanus (Anthony
Hopkins) and citizens, National Theatre, London, 1971

That's sure of death without it, at once pluck out
The multitudinous tongue ; let them not lick
The sweet which is their poison : your dishonour
• Mangles true judgement and bereaves the state
Of that integrity which should become't,
Not having the power to do the good it would,
For the ill which doth control't.
    Bru.   Has said enough. 161
    Sic. Has spoken like a traitor, and shall answer
As traitors do.
    Cor. Thou wretch, despite o'erwhelm thee !
What should the people do with these bald tri-
    bunes ?
On whom depending, their obedience fails
To the greater bench : in a rebellion,
When what's not meet, but what must be, was law,
Then were they chosen : in a better hour,
Let what is meet be said it must be meet,   170
And throw their power i' the dust.
    Bru. Manifest treason !
    Sic.   This a consul ? no.
•   *Bru.* The ædiles, ho !

             *Enter an Æ*dile.

                     Let him be apprehended.
    Sic. Go, call the people : [*Exit Ædile*] in
    whose name myself
Attach thee as a traitorous innovator,
A foe to the public weal : obey, I charge thee,
And follow to thine answer.
    Cor.   Hence, old goat !
    Senators, &c. We'll surety him.
    Com.   Aged sir, hands off.
    Cor. Hence, rotten thing ! or I shall shake
    thy bones
Out of thy garments.
    Sic.   Help, ye citizens !   180

Enter a rabble of Citizens (*Plebeians*), *with the*
    Ædiles.

    Men. On both sides more respect.
    Sic. Here's he that would take from you all
    your power.
    Bru. Seize him, ædiles !
    Citizens. Down with him ! down with him !
    Senators, &c. Weapons, weapons, weapons !
      [*They all bustle about Coriolanus, crying*
  'Tribunes !' 'Patricians !' 'Citizens !' 'What,
    • ho !'
'Sicinius !' 'Brutus !' 'Coriolanus !' 'Citizens !'
'Peace, peace, peace !' 'Stay, hold, peace !'
    Men. What is about to be ? I am out of
    breath ;
Confusion's near ; I cannot speak. You, tribunes
To the people ! Coriolanus, patience !   191
Speak, good Sicinius.
    Sic.   Hear me, people ; peace !
    Citizens. Let's hear our tribune : peace !
    Speak, speak, speak.
    Sic. You are at point to lose your liberties :
Marcius would have all from you ; Marcius,
Whom late you have named for consul.
    Men.   Fie, fie, fie !
This is the way to kindle, not to quench.
    First Sen. To unbuild the city and to lay all
    flat.
    Sic. What is the city but the people ?
    Citizens.   True,
The people are the city.   200

Bru. By the consent of all, we were establish'd
The people's magistrates.
    Citizens.   You so remain.
    Men. And so are like to do.
    Com. That is the way to lay the city flat;
To bring the roof to the foundation,
• And bury all, which yet distinctly ranges,
In heaps and piles of ruin.
    Sic.   This deserves death.
    Bru. Or let us stand to our authority,
Or let us lose it. We do here pronounce,
Upon the part o' the people, in whose power 210
We were elected theirs, Marcius is worthy
Of present death.
    Sic.   Therefore lay hold of him;
• Bear him to the rock Tarpeian, and from thence
Into destruction cast him.
    Bru.   Ædiles, seize him!
    Citizens. Yield, Marcius, yield!
    Men.   Hear me one word;
Beseech you, tribunes, hear me but a word.
    Æd. Peace, peace!
    Men. [*To Brutus*] Be that you seem, truly
      your country's friend,
And temperately proceed to what you would
Thus violently redress.
    Bru.   Sir, those cold ways, 220
That seem like prudent helps, are very poisonous
Where the disease is violent. Lay hands upon
    him,
And bear him to the rock.
    Cor.   No, I'll die here.
            [*Drawing his sword.*
There's some among you have beheld me fighting:
Come, try upon yourselves what you have seen me.
    Men. Down with that sword! Tribunes, with-
    draw awhile.
    Bru. Lay hands upon him.
    Men.   Help Marcius, help,
You that be noble; help him, young and old!
    Citizens. Down with him, down with him!
    [*In this mutiny, the Tribunes, the Ædiles,
           and the People, are beat in.*
    Men. Go, get you to your house; be gone,
    away!   230
All will be naught else.
    Sec. Sen.   Get you gone.
    Com.   Stand fast;
We have as many friends as enemies.
    Men. Shall it be put to that?
    First Sen.   The gods forbid!
I prithee, noble friend, home to thy house;
Leave us to cure this cause.
    Men.   For 'tis a sore upon us,
• You cannot tent yourself: be gone, beseech you.
    Com. Come, sir, along with us.
    Cor. I would they were barbarians—as they
    are,
Though in Rome litter'd—not Romans—as they
    are not,
Though calved i' the porch o' the Capitol—
    Men.   Be gone; 240
Put not your worthy rage into your tongue;
• One time will owe another.
    Cor.   On fair ground
I could beat forty of them.
    Men.   I could myself
Take up a brace o' the best of them; yea, the
    two tribunes.

206 *distinctly ranges.* Individually stands.

213 *rock Tarpeian.* A high point on the Capitoline Hill in Rome, whence traitors were thrown to death.

Tarpeian rock. From a 19th century engraving by Sir Gardiner Wilkinson

---

236 *tent.* Attend to.

242 *owe.* Compensate for.

248 *tag.* Rabble.

256 *Neptune.* Legendary god of the oceans.

257 *Jove.* i.e. Jupiter, god of heavens, hurler of thunderbolts.

Jupiter. Engraving from P. J. Mariette's *Traité des Pierres Gravées,* 1769

277 *holp.* Helped.

Com. But now 'tis odds beyond arithmetic;
And manhood is call'd foolery, when it stands
Against a falling fabric.   Will you hence,
●Before the tag return? whose rage doth rend
Like interrupted waters and o'erbear
What they are used to bear.
Men.   Pray you, be gone: 250
I'll try whether my old wit be in request
With those that have but little: this must be
    patch'd
With cloth of any colour.
Com.   Nay, come away.
    [*Exeunt Coriolanus, Cominius, and others.*
A Patrician. This man has marr'd his fortune.
Men.   His nature is too noble for the world:
●He would not flatter Neptune for his trident,
●Or Jove for 's power to thunder.   His heart's his
    mouth:
What his breast forges, that his tongue must vent;
And, being angry, does forget that ever   259
He heard the name of death.   [*A noise within.*
Here's goodly work!
Sec. Pat.   I would they were a-bed!
Men.   I would they were in Tiber! What the
    vengeance!
Could he not speak 'em fair?

Re-enter BRUTUS *and* SICINIUS, *with the rabble.*

Sic.   Where is this viper
That would depopulate the city and
Be every man himself?
Men.   You worthy tribunes,—
Sic.   He shall be thrown down the Tarpeian
    rock
With rigorous hands: he hath resisted law,
And therefore law shall scorn him further trial
Than the severity of the public power
Which he so sets at nought.
First Cit.   He shall well know 270
The noble tribunes are the people's mouths,
And we their hands.
Citizens.   He shall, sure on 't.
Men.   Sir, sir,—
Sic.   Peace!
Men.   Do not cry havoc, where you should but
    hunt
With modest warrant.
Sic.   Sir, how comes 't that you
●Have holp to make this rescue?
Men.   Hear me speak:
As I do know the consul's worthiness,
So can I name his faults,—
Sic.   Consul! what consul?
Men.   The consul Coriolanus.
Bru.   He consul! 280
Citizens.   No, no, no, no, no.
Men.   If, by the tribunes' leave, and yours,
    good people,
I may be heard, I would crave a word or two;
The which shall turn you to no further harm
Than so much loss of time.
Sic.   Speak briefly then;
For we are peremptory to dispatch
This viperous traitor: to eject him hence
Were but one danger, and to keep him here
Our certain death: therefore it is decreed
He dies to-night.
Men.   Now the good gods forbid 290
That our renowned Rome, whose gratitude

Towards her deserved children is enroll'd
●In Jove's own book, like an unnatural dam
Should now eat up her own!
    Sic.   He's a disease that must be cut away.
    Men.   O, he's a limb that has but a disease;
Mortal, to cut it off; to cure it, easy.
What has he done to Rome that's worthy death?
Killing our enemies, the blood he hath lost—
Which, I dare vouch, is more than that he hath,
By many an ounce—he dropp'd it for his country;
And what is left, to lose it by his country,
Were to us all, that do't and suffer it,
●A brand to the end o' the world.
    Sic.   This is clean kam.
    Bru.   Merely awry; when he did love his
      country,
It honour'd him.
    Men.   The service of the foot
Being once gangrened, is not then respected
For what before it was.
    Bru.   We'll hear no more.
Pursue him to his house, and pluck him thence;
Lest his infection, being of catching nature,   310
Spread further.
    Men.   One word more, one word.
This tiger-footed rage, when it shall find
●The harm of unscann'd swiftness, will too late
●Tie leaden pounds to's heels.   Proceed by process;
Lest parties, as he is beloved, break out,
And sack great Rome with Romans.
    Bru.   If it were so,—
    Sic.   What do ye talk?
Have we not had a taste of his obedience?
Our ædiles smote? ourselves resisted?   Come.
    Men.   Consider this: he has been bred i' the
      wars   320
Since he could draw a sword, and is ill school'd
●In bolted language; meal and bran together
He throws without distinction.   Give me leave,
I'll go to him, and undertake to bring him
Where he shall answer, by a lawful form,
In peace, to his utmost peril.
    First Sen.   Noble tribunes,
It is the humane way: the other course
Will prove too bloody, and the end of it
Unknown to the beginning.
    Sic.   Noble Menenius,
Be you then as the people's officer.   330
Masters, lay down your weapons.
    Bru.   Go not home.
    Sic.   Meet on the market-place.   We'll attend
      you there:
Where, if you bring not Marcius, we'll proceed
In our first way.
    Men.   I'll bring him to you.
[*To the Senators*] Let me desire your company:
    he must come,
Or what is worst will follow.
    First Sen.   Pray you, let's to him.
                         [*Exeunt.*

SCENE II. *A room in Coriolanus's house.*

Enter CORIOLANUS *with* Patricians.

    Cor.   Let them pull all about mine ears,
    present me
Death on the wheel or at wild horses' heels,
Or pile ten hills on the Tarpeian rock,

---

293 *Jove's own book.* i.e. at the Capitol.

304 *clean kam.* Quite perverse.

313 *unscann'd.* Thoughtless.

314 *process.* Law.

322 *bolted.* Refined.

9 *woollen vassals.* Vassals clad in coarse woollens.

10 *groats.* Coins worth four-pence.

12 *ordinance.* Rank.

Coriolanus: '... would you have me False to my nature?'
Coriolanus (Ian Hogg) and Volumnia (Margaret Tyzack),
Royal Shakespeare Co, 1972

29 *apt.* Compliant.

39 *absolute.* Uncompromising.

42 *policy.* Strategy.

That the precipitation might down stretch
Below the beam of sight, yet will I still
Be thus to them.
  A Patrician. You do the nobler.
  Cor. I muse my mother
Does not approve me further, who was wont
● To call them woollen vassals, things created   9
● To buy and sell with groats, to show bare heads
In congregations, to yawn, be still and wonder,
● When one but of my ordinance stood up
To speak of peace or war.

Enter VOLUMNIA.
       I talk of you:
Why did you wish me milder? would you
  have me
False to my nature? Rather say I play
The man I am.
  Vol.   O, sir, sir, sir,
I would have had you put your power well on,
Before you had worn it out.
  Cor.   Let go.
  Vol. You might have been enough the man
  you are,
With striving less to be so: lesser had been   20
The thwartings of your dispositions, if
You had not show'd them how ye were disposed
Ere they lack'd power to cross you.
  Cor.   Let them hang.
  A Patrician. Ay, and burn too.

Enter MENENIUS *and* Senators.
  Men. Come, come, you have been too rough,
  something too rough;
You must return and mend it.
  First Sen.   There's no remedy;
Unless, by not so doing, our good city
Cleave in the midst, and perish.
  Vol.   Pray, be counsell'd:
● † I have a heart as little apt as yours,
But yet a brain that leads my use of anger   30
To better vantage.
  Men.   Well said, noble woman!
Before he should thus stoop to the herd, but that
The violent fit o' the time craves it as physic
For the whole state, I would put mine armour on,
Which I can scarcely bear.
  Cor.   What must I do?
  Men. Return to the tribunes.
  Cor.   Well, what then? what then?
  Men. Repent what you have spoke.
  Cor. For them! I cannot do it to the gods;
● Must I then do't to them?
  Vol.   You are too absolute;
Though therein you can never be too noble,   40
But when extremities speak. I have heard
  you say,
● Honour and policy, like unsever'd friends,
I' the war do grow together: grant that, and
  tell me,
In peace what each of them by the other lose,
That they combine not there.
  Cor.   Tush, tush!
  Men.   A good demand.
  Vol. If it be honour in your wars to seem
The same you are not, which, for your best ends,
You adopt your policy, how is it less or worse,
That it shall hold companionship in peace
With honour, as in war, since that to both   50

It stands in like request?
    Cor.   Why force you this?
    Vol. Because that now it lies you on to speak
To the people; not by your own instruction,
Nor by the matter which your heart prompts you,
• But with such words that are but roted in
Your tongue, though but bastards and syllables
• Of no allowance to your bosom's truth.
Now, this no more dishonours you at all
Than to take in a town with gentle words,
Which else would put you to your fortune and
The hazard of much blood.   61
I would dissemble with my nature where
My fortunes and my friends at stake required
I should do so in honour: I am in this,
Your wife, your son, these senators, the nobles;
And you will rather show our general louts
How you can frown than spend a fawn upon 'em,
For the inheritance of their loves and safeguard
Of what that want might ruin.
    Men.   Noble lady!
Come, go with us; speak fair: you may salve so,
Not what is dangerous present, but the loss   71
Of what is past.
    Vol.   I prithee now, my son,
Go to them, with this bonnet in thy hand;
And thus far having stretch'd it—here be with them—
• Thy knee bussing the stones—for in such business
Action is eloquence, and the eyes of the ignorant
More learned than the ears—waving thy head,
Which often, thus, correcting thy stout heart,
Now humble as the ripest mulberry
That will not hold the handling: or say to them,
Thou art their soldier, and being bred in broils 81
Hast not the soft way which, thou dost confess,
Were fit for thee to use as they to claim,
In asking their good loves, but thou wilt frame
Thyself, forsooth, hereafter theirs, so far
As thou hast power and person.
    Men.   This but done,
Even as she speaks, why, their hearts were yours;
For they have pardons, being ask'd, as free
As words to little purpose.
    Vol.   Prithee now,
Go, and be ruled: although I know thou hadst rather   90
Follow thine enemy in a fiery gulf
Than flatter him in a bower.   Here is Cominius.

           Enter COMINIUS.

    Com. I have been i' the market-place; and, sir, 'tis fit
You make strong party, or defend yourself
By calmness or by absence: all's in anger.
    Men. Only fair speech.
    Com.   I think 'twill serve, if he
Can thereto frame his spirit.
    Vol.   He must, and will.
Prithee now, say you will, and go about it.
•   *Cor.* Must I go show them my unbarbed sconce?
Must I with base tongue give my noble heart
A lie that it must bear?   Well, I will do't: 101
Yet, were there but this single plot to lose,
This mould of **Marcius, they** to dust should grind it

Dorothy Green as Volumnia, Stratford-upon-Avon, 1939

---

55 *roted in.* Known by heart to.

57 *Of no allowance to.* Unapproved by.

75 *bussing.* Kissing.

99 *unbarbed sconce.* Shaven head.

106 *discharge.* Play.

113 *quired.* Sang together.

121 *surcease.* Cease.

Volumnia: 'At thy choice, then: To beg of thee, it is my more dishonour . . .' Coriolanus (Ian Richardson) and Volumnia (Catherine Lacey), Royal Shakespeare Co, 1967

133 *Cog.* Cheat.

142 *word.* Watchword.

1 *charge him home.* Accuse him.

3 *envy.* Ill will.

And throw't against the wind.   To the market-
        place!
You have put me now to such a part which never
●I shall discharge to the life.
      Com.   Come, come, we'll prompt you.
      Vol.   I prithee now, sweet son, as thou hast
        said
My praises made thee first a soldier, so,
To have my praise for this, perform a part
Thou hast not done before.
      Cor.   Well, I must do't:
Away, my disposition, and possess me   III
Some harlot's spirit! my throat of war be turn'd,
●Which quired with my drum, into a pipe
Small as an eunuch, or the virgin voice
That babies lulls asleep! the smiles of knaves
Tent in my cheeks, and schoolboys' tears take up
The glasses of my sight! a beggar's tongue
Make motion through my lips, and my arm'd
        knees,
Who bow'd but in my stirrup, bend like his
That hath received an alms! I will not do't,   120
●Lest I surcease to honour mine own truth
And by my body's action teach my mind
A most inherent baseness.
      Vol.   At thy choice, then:
To beg of thee, it is my more dishonour
Than thou of them.   Come all to ruin; let
Thy mother rather feel thy pride than fear
Thy dangerous stoutness, for I mock at death
With as big heart as thou.   Do as thou list.
Thy valiantness was mine, thou suck'dst it
        from me,
But owe thy pride thyself.
      Cor.   Pray, be content: 130
Mother, I am going to the market-place;
Chide me no more.   I'll mountebank their loves,
●Cog their hearts from them, and come home
        beloved
Of all the trades in Rome.   Look, I am going:
Commend me to my wife.   I'll return consul;
Or never trust to what my tongue can do
I' the way of flattery further.
      Vol.   Do your will. [*Exit.*
      Com.   Away! the tribunes do attend you:
        arm yourself
To answer mildly; for they are prepared
With accusations, as I hear, more strong   140
Than are upon you yet.
● *Cor.* The word is 'mildly.'   Pray you, let
        us go:
Let them accuse me by invention, I
Will answer in mine honour.
      Men.   Ay, but mildly.
      Cor.   Well, mildly be it then.   Mildly!
                                              [*Exeunt.*

SCENE III.   *The same.   The Forum.*

Enter SICINIUS *and* BRUTUS.

● *Bru.* In this point charge him home, that he
        affects
Tyrannical power: if he evade us there,
●Enforce him with his envy to the people,
And that the spoil got on the Antiates
Was ne'er distributed.

Enter an Ædile.

What, will he come?

Æd.   He's coming.
Bru.   How accompanied?
Æd.   With old Menenius, and those senators
That always favour'd him.
Sic.   Have you a catalogue
Of all the voices that we have procured
Set down by the poll?
Æd.   I have; 'tis ready.   10
Sic.   Have you collected them by tribes?
Æd.   I have.
Sic.   Assemble presently the people hither;
And when they hear me say 'It shall be so
I' the right and strength o' the commons,' be it
     either
For death, for fine, or banishment, then let
     them,
If I say fine, cry 'Fine;' if death, cry 'Death.'
Insisting on the old prerogative
And power i' the truth o' the cause.
Æd.   I shall inform them.
Bru.   And when such time they have begun
     to cry,
Let them not cease, but with a din confused   20
Enforce the present execution
Of what we chance to sentence.
Æd.   Very well.
Sic.   Make them be strong and ready for this
     hint,
When we shall hap to give't them.
Bru.   Go about it. [*Exit Ædile.*
Put him to choler straight: he hath been used
†Ever to conquer, and to have his worth
Of contradiction: being once chafed, he cannot
Be rein'd again to temperance; then he speaks
What's in his heart; and that is there which looks
With us to break his neck.
Sic.   Well, here he comes. 30

Enter CORIOLANUS, MENENIUS, *and* COMINIUS,
     with Senators *and* Patricians.

Men.   Calmly, I do beseech you.
● *Cor.*   Ay, as an ostler, that for the poorest piece
●Will bear the knave by the volume. The ho-
     nour'd gods
Keep Rome in safety, and the chairs of justice
Supplied with worthy men! plant love among 's!
Throng our large temples with the shows of peace,
And not our streets with war!
First Sen.   Amen, amen.
Men.   A noble wish.

          Re-enter Ædile, *with* Citizens.

Sic.   Draw near, ye people.
Æd.   List to your tribunes. Audience! peace,
     I say!   40
Cor.   First, hear me speak.
Both Tri.   Well, say. Peace, ho!
Cor.   Shall I be charged no further than this
     present?
Must all determine here?
Sic.   I do demand,
If you submit you to the people's voices,
Allow their officers and are content
To suffer lawful censure for such faults
As shall be proved upon you?
Cor.   I am content.
Men.   Lo, citizens, he says he is content:
The warlike service he has done, consider; think
Upon the wounds his body bears, which show 50

32 *ostler*. Groom.

33 *bear the*. i.e. bear being called. *by the volume*. i.e. any
number of times.

Coriolanus before the citizens of Rome. Stage design by
W. Bridges-Adams, Stratford-upon-Avon, 1933

57 *envy*. Show malice towards.

Coriolanus: '... being pass'd for consul with full voice, I am so dishonour'd that the very hour You take it off again?' Alec Clunes as Coriolanus, Stratford-upon-Avon, 1939

Like graves i' the holy churchyard.
  Cor.   Scratches with briers,
Scars to move laughter only.
  Men.   Consider further,
That when he speaks not like a citizen,
You find him like a soldier: do not take
His rougher accents for malicious sounds,
But, as I say, such as become a soldier,
●Rather than envy you.
  Com.   Well, well, no more.
  Cor. What is the matter
That being pass'd for consul with full voice,
I am so dishonour'd that the very hour   60
You take it off again?
  Sic.   Answer to us.
  Cor. Say, then: 'tis true, I ought so.
  Sic. We charge you, that you have contrived
    to take
From Rome all season'd office and to wind
Yourself into a power tyrannical;
For which you are a traitor to the people.
  Cor. How! traitor!
  Men.   Nay, temperately; your promise.
  Cor. The fires i' the lowest hell fold-in the
    people!
Call me their traitor! Thou injurious tribune!
Within thine eyes sat twenty thousand deaths, 70
In thy hands clutch'd as many millions, in
Thy lying tongue both numbers, I would say
'Thou liest' unto thee with a voice as free
As I do pray the gods.
  Sic.   Mark you this, people?
  Citizens. To the rock, to the rock with him!
  Sic.   Peace!
We need not put new matter to his charge:
What you have seen him do and heard him speak,
Beating your officers, cursing yourselves,
Opposing laws with strokes and here defying
Those whose great power must try him; even
    this,   80
So criminal and in such capital kind,
Deserves the extremest death.
  Bru.   But since he hath
Served well for Rome,—
  Cor.   What do you prate of service?
  Bru. I talk of that, that know it.
  Cor. You?
  Men. Is this the promise that you made your
    mother?
  Com. Know, I pray you,—
  Cor.   I'll know no further:
Let them pronounce the steep Tarpeian death,
Vagabond exile, flaying, pent to linger
But with a grain a day, I would not buy   90
Their mercy at the price of one fair word;
Nor check my courage for what they can give,
To have't with saying 'Good morrow.'
  Sic.   For that he has,
As much as in him lies, from time to time
Envied against the people, seeking means
To pluck away their power, as now at last
Given hostile strokes, and that not in the presence
Of dreaded justice, but on the ministers
That do distribute it; in the name o' the people
And in the power of us the tribunes, we,   100
Even from this instant, banish him our city,
In peril of precipitation
From off the rock Tarpeian never more
To enter our Rome gates: i' the people's name,

I say it shall be so.
  Citizens. It shall be so, it shall be so; let him away:
He's banish'd, and it shall be so.
  Com. Hear me, my masters, and my common friends,—
  Sic. He's sentenced; no more hearing.
  Com.   Let me speak:
I have been consul, and can show for Rome 110
Her enemies' marks upon me. I do love
My country's good with a respect more tender,
More holy and profound, than mine own life,
My dear wife's estimate, her womb's increase,
And treasure of my loins; then if I would
Speak that,—
  Sic.   We know your drift: speak what?
  Bru. There's no more to be said, but he is banish'd,
As enemy to the people and his country:
It shall be so.
  Citizens. It shall be so, it shall be so.
  Cor. You common cry of curs! whose breath I hate 120
As reek o' the rotten fens, whose loves I prize
As the dead carcasses of unburied men
That do corrupt my air, I banish you;
And here remain with your uncertainty!
Let every feeble rumour shake your hearts!
Your enemies, with nodding of their plumes,
Fan you into despair! Have the power still
To banish your defenders; till at length
Your ignorance, which finds not till it feels,
Making not reservation of yourselves, 130
Still your own foes, deliver you as most
Abated captives to some nation
That won you without blows! Despising,
For you, the city, thus I turn my back:
There is a world elsewhere.
    [Exeunt Coriolanus, Cominius, Menenius, Senators, and Patricians.
  Æd. The people's enemy is gone, is gone!
  Citizens. Our enemy is banish'd! he is gone!
Hoo! hoo! *[Shouting, and throwing up their caps.*
  Sic. Go, see him out at gates, and follow him,
As he hath follow'd you, with all despite;
Give him deserved vexation. Let a guard 140
Attend us through the city.
  Citizens. Come, come; let's see him out at gates; come.
The gods preserve our noble tribunes! Come.
    [Exeunt.

ACT IV.

SCENE I. *Rome. Before a gate of the city.*

Enter CORIOLANUS, VOLUMNIA, VIRGILIA, MENENIUS, COMINIUS, *with the young Nobility of Rome.*

  Cor. Come, leave your tears: a brief farewell: the beast
With many heads butts me away. Nay, mother,
Where is your ancient courage? you were used
To say extremity was the trier of spirits;
That common chances common men could bear;
That when the sea was calm all boats alike
Show'd mastership in floating; fortune's blows,

Coriolanus: 'You common cry of curs!... I banish you.'
Drawing by Henry Singleton (1766–1839)

11 *conn'd.* Studied.

27 *wot.* Know.

33 *cautelous.* Crafty. *practice.* Tricks.

36 *exposture.* Exposure.

Coriolanus taking leave of his family. Engraving by Bartolomeo Pinelli, 1821

When most struck home, being gentle wounded, craves
A noble cunning: you were used to load me
With precepts that would make invincible   10
●The heart that conn'd them.
   Vir. O heavens! O heavens!
   Cor.   Nay, I prithee, woman,—
   Vol. Now the red pestilence strike all trades in Rome,
And occupations perish!
   Cor.   What, what, what!
I shall be loved when I am lack'd. Nay, mother,
Resume that spirit, when you were wont to say,
If you had been the wife of Hercules,
Six of his labours you'ld have done, and saved
Your husband so much sweat. Cominius,   19
Droop not; adieu. Farewell, my wife, my mother:
I'll do well yet. Thou old and true Menenius,
Thy tears are salter than a younger man's,
And venomous to thine eyes. My sometime general,
I have seen thee stern, and thou hast oft beheld
Heart-hardening spectacles; tell these sad women
'Tis fond to wail inevitable strokes,
●As 'tis to laugh at 'em. My mother, you wot well
My hazards still have been your solace: and
Believe't not lightly—though I go alone,
Like to a lonely dragon, that his fen   30
Makes fear'd and talk'd of more than seen—your son
Will or exceed the common or be caught
●With cautelous baits and practice.
   Vol.   My first son,
Whither wilt thou go? Take good Cominius
With thee awhile: determine on some course,
●More than a wild exposture to each chance
That starts i' the way before thee.
   Cor.   O the gods!
   Com. I'll follow thee a month, devise with thee
Where thou shalt rest, that thou mayst hear of us
And we of thee: so if the time thrust forth   40
A cause for thy repeal, we shall not send
O'er the vast world to seek a single man,
And lose advantage, which doth ever cool
I' the absence of the needer.
   Cor.   Fare ye well:
Thou hast years upon thee; and thou art too full
Of the wars' surfeits, to go rove with one
That's yet unbruised: bring me but out at gate.
Come, my sweet wife, my dearest mother, and
My friends of noble touch, when I am forth,
Bid me farewell, and smile. I pray you, come. 50
While I remain above the ground, you shall
Hear from me still, and never of me aught
But what is like me formerly.
   Men.   That's worthily
As any ear can hear. Come, let's not weep.
If I could shake off but one seven years
From these old arms and legs, by the good gods,
I'ld with thee every foot.
   Cor.   Give me thy hand:
Come.   [*Exeunt.*

Scene II.   *The same.   A street near the gate.*

Enter Sicinius, Brutus, *and an Æ*dile.

   Sic. Bid them all home; he's gone, and we'll no further.

The nobility are vex'd, whom we see have sided
In his behalf.
Bru.   Now we have shown our power,
Let us seem humbler after it is done
Than when it was a-doing.
Sic.   Bid them home:
Say their great enemy is gone, and they
Stand in their ancient strength.
Bru.   Dismiss them home. [*Exit Ædile.*
Here comes his mother.
Sic.   Let's not meet her.
Bru.   Why?
Sic. They say she's mad.
Bru. They have ta'en note of us: keep on
     your way.   10

Enter VOLUMNIA, VIRGILIA, *and* MENENIUS.

Vol. O, ye're well met: the hoarded plague
     o' the gods
Requite your love!
Men.   Peace, peace; be not so loud.
Vol. If that I could for weeping, you should
     hear,—
Nay, and you shall hear some. [*To Brutus*]
     Will you be gone?
Vir. [*To Sicinius*] You shall stay too: I
     would I had the power
To say so to my husband.
Sic.   Are you mankind?
Vol. Ay, fool; is that a shame? Note but
     this fool.
• Was not a man my father? Hadst thou foxship
To banish him that struck more blows for Rome
Than thou hast spoken words?
Sic.   O blessed heavens!
Vol. More noble blows than ever thou wise
     words;   21
And for Rome's good. I'll tell thee what;
     yet go:
Nay, but thou shalt stay too: I would my son
Were in Arabia, and thy tribe before him,
His good sword in his hand.
Sic.   What then?
Vir.   What then!
He'ld make an end of thy posterity.
Vol. Bastards and all.
Good man, the wounds that he does bear for
     Rome!
Men. Come, come, peace.
Sic. I would he had continued to his country
As he began, and not unknit himself   31
The noble knot he made.
Bru.   I would he had.
Vol. 'I would he had'! 'Twas you incensed
     the rabble:
Cats, that can judge as fitly of his worth
As I can of those mysteries which heaven
Will not have earth to know.
Bru.   Pray, let us go.
Vol. Now, pray, sir, get you gone:
You have done a brave deed. Ere you go, hear
     this:—
As far as doth the Capitol exceed
The meanest house in Rome, so far my son—   40
This lady's husband here, this, do you see—
Whom you have banish'd, does exceed you all.
Bru. Well, well, we'll leave you.
Sic.   Why stay we to be baited
With one that wants her wits?

Volumnia: '. . . the hoarded plague o' the gods Requite your love!' Drawing by Henry Singleton (1766–1839)

---

18 *foxship.* Foxiness.

52 *puling.* Whining.

53 *Juno-like.* Juno, queen of heaven.

Map showing Rome and its territories (the south being shown to the right). From Abraham Ortelius' *Epitome to the Theatre of the World*, 1598

9 *favour.* Appearance. *approved.* Confirmed.

48 *distinctly.* Separately.

49 *entertainment.* Mobilised.

Vol.   Take my prayers with you.
                                    [*Exeunt Tribunes*.
I would the gods had nothing else to do
But to confirm my curses!   Could I meet 'em
But once a-day, it would unclog my heart
Of what lies heavy to 't.
   Men.   You have told them home;
And, by my troth, you have cause.   You'll sup
      with me?
   Vol. Anger's my meat; I sup upon myself, 50
And so shall starve with feeding.   Come, let's go:
•Leave this faint puling and lament as I do,
•In anger, Juno-like.   Come, come, come.
   Men. Fie, fie, fie!   [*Exeunt*.

SCENE III.   *A highway between Rome
                  and Antium.*

Enter a Roman *and a* Volsce, *meeting.*

   Rom. I know you well, sir, and you know
me: your name, I think, is Adrian.
   Vols. It is so, sir: truly, I have forgot you.
   Rom. I am a Roman; and my services are,
as you are, against 'em: know you me yet?
   Vols. Nicanor? no.
   Rom. The same, sir.
   Vols. You had more beard when I last saw
•you; but your favour is well approved by your
tongue.   What's the news in Rome? I have a
note from the Volscian state, to find you out
there: you have well saved me a day's journey.
   Rom. There hath been in Rome strange in-
surrections; the people against the senators,
patricians, and nobles.
   Vols. Hath been! is it ended, then?   Our
state thinks not so: they are in a most warlike
preparation, and hope to come upon them in the
heat of their division.   19
   Rom. The main blaze of it is past, but a
small thing would make it flame again: for the
nobles receive so to heart the banishment of that
worthy Coriolanus, that they are in a ripe aptness to take all power from the people and to
pluck from them their tribunes for ever.   This
lies glowing, I can tell you, and is almost mature
for the violent breaking out.
   Vols. Coriolanus banished!
   Rom. Banished, sir.   29
   Vols. You will be welcome with this intelligence, Nicanor.
   Rom. The day serves well for them now.
I have heard it said, the fittest time to corrupt
a man's wife is when she's fallen out with her
husband.   Your noble Tullus Aufidius will appear well in these wars, his great opposer,
Coriolanus, being now in no request of his
country.
   Vols. He cannot choose.   I am most fortunate, thus accidentally to encounter you: you
have ended my business, and I will merrily accompany you home.
   Rom. I shall, between this and supper, tell
you most strange things from Rome; all tending
to the good of their adversaries.   Have you an
army ready, say you?
   Vols. A most royal one; the centurions and
•their charges, distinctly billeted, already in the
•entertainment, and to be on foot at an hour's
warning.   50

Rom. I am joyful to hear of their readiness, and am the man, I think, that shall set them in present action. So, sir, heartily well met, and most glad of your company.

Vols. You take my part from me, sir; I have the most cause to be glad of yours.

Rom. Well, let us go together.   [*Exeunt.*

SCENE IV. *Antium. Before Aufidius's house.*

Enter CORIOLANUS *in mean apparel, disguised and muffled.*

Cor. A goodly city is this Antium. City,
'Tis I that made thy widows: many an heir
Of these fair edifices 'fore my wars
Have I heard groan and drop: then know me not,
Lest that thy wives with spits and boys with stones
⚫In puny battle slay me.

Enter a Citizen.

                    Save you, sir.
Cit. And you.
Cor.   Direct me, if it be your will,
Where great Aufidius lies: is he in Antium?
Cit. He is, and feasts the nobles of the state
At his house this night.
Cor.   Which is his house, beseech you?   10
Cit. This, here before you.
Cor.   Thank you, sir: farewell.
                    [*Exit Citizen.*
O world, thy slippery turns! Friends now fast sworn,
Whose double bosoms seem to wear one heart,
Whose hours, whose bed, whose meal, and exercise,
Are still together, who twin, as 'twere, in love
Unseparable, shall within this hour,
⚫On a dissension of a doit, break out
⚫To bitterest enmity: so, fellest foes,
Whose passions and whose plots have broke their sleep
To take the one the other, by some chance,   20
Some trick not worth an egg, shall grow dear friends
⚫And interjoin their issues. So with me:
My birth-place hate I, and my love's upon
This enemy town. I'll enter: if he slay me,
He does fair justice; if he give me way,
I'll do his country service.   [*Exit.*

SCENE V. *The same. A hall in Aufidius's house.*

Music within. Enter a Servingman.

First Serv. Wine, wine, wine! What service is here! I think our fellows are asleep.   [*Exit.*

Enter a second Servingman.

Sec. Serv. Where's Cotus? my master calls for him. Cotus!   [*Exit.*

Enter CORIOLANUS.

Cor. A goodly house: the feast smells well; but I
Appear not like a guest.

6 *puny.* i.e. insignificant.

17 *dissension of a doit.* Trivial dispute.

18 *fellest.* Fiercest.

22 *interjoin their issues.* Intermarry their children.

18 *brave.* Impertinent.

25 *avoid.* Leave.

Aufidius: 'Whence comest thou! what wouldst thou?
thy name?' Engraving of Coriolanus and Aufidius by
Henry Fuseli (1741–1825)

Opposite : Aufidius: '. . . speak, man: what's thy name?'
Engraving by R. Earlham of John Kemble as Coriolanus,
1798

Re-enter the first Servingman.

First Serv. What would you have, friend?
whence are you? Here's no place for you: pray,
go to the door.   [*Exit*.
Cor. I have deserved no better entertainment,
In being Coriolanus.   11

Re-enter second Servingman.

Sec. Serv. Whence are you, sir? Has the
porter his eyes in his head, that he gives entrance
to such companions? Pray, get you out.
Cor. Away!
Sec. Serv. Away! get you away.
Cor. Now thou'rt troublesome.
● *Sec. Serv.* Are you so brave? I'll have you
talked with anon.

Enter a third Servingman. *The first meets him.*

Third Serv. What fellow's this?   20
First Serv. A strange one as ever I looked
on : I cannot get him out o' the house: prithee,
call my master to him.   [*Retires*.
Third Serv. What have you to do here,
●fellow? Pray you, avoid the house.
Cor. Let me but stand; I will not hurt your
hearth.
Third Serv. What are you?
Cor. A gentleman.
Third Serv. A marvellous poor one.   30
Cor. True, so I am.
Third Serv. Pray you, poor gentleman, take
up some other station; here's no place for you;
pray you, avoid: come.
Cor. Follow your function, go, and batten on
cold bits.   [*Pushes him away*.
Third Serv. What, you will not? Prithee,
tell my master what a strange guest he has here.
Sec. Serv. And I shall.   [*Exit*.
Third Serv. Where dwellest thou?   40
Cor. Under the canopy.
Third Serv. Under the canopy!
Cor. Ay.
Third Serv. Where's that?
Cor. I' the city of kites and crows.
Third Serv. I' the city of kites and crows!
What an ass it is! Then thou dwellest with
daws too?
Cor. No, I serve not thy master.
Third Serv. How, sir! do you meddle with
my master?   51
Cor. Ay; 'tis an honester service than to
meddle with thy mistress.
Thou pratest, and pratest; serve with thy trencher,
hence !
[*Beats him away. Exit third Servingman*.

Enter AUFIDIUS *with the second* Servingman.

Auf. Where is this fellow?
Sec. Serv. Here, sir: I'ld have beaten him
like a dog, but for disturbing the lords within.
                                         [*Retires*.
Auf. Whence comest thou? what wouldst
        thou? thy name?
Why speak'st not? speak, man: what's thy name?
Cor. If, Tullus,   [*Unmuffling*. 60
Not yet thou knowest me, and, seeing me,
        dost not
Think me for the man I am, necessity

Aufidius with Coriolanus. Engraving by Kenny Meadows
from Barry Cornwall's *Complete Works of Shakspere*,
1857–59

89 *full quit of.* Fully repaid to.

91 *wreak.* Vengeance.

92 *maims.* Wounds.

115 *clip.* Embrace.

Commands me name myself.
  Auf.   What is thy name?
  Cor. A name unmusical to the Volscians' ears,
And harsh in sound to thine.
  Auf.   Say, what's thy name?
Thou hast a grim appearance, and thy face
Bears a command in 't; though thy tackle's torn,
Thou show'st a noble vessel: what's thy name?
  Cor. Prepare thy brow to frown: know'st
    thou me yet?
  Auf. I know thee not: thy name?   70
  Cor. My name is Caius Marcius, who hath done
To thee particularly and to all the Volsces
Great hurt and mischief; thereto witness may
My surname, Coriolanus: the painful service,
The extreme dangers and the drops of blood
Shed for my thankless country are requited
But with that surname; a good memory,
And witness of the malice and displeasure
Which thou shouldst bear me: only that name
    remains;
The cruelty and envy of the people,   80
Permitted by our dastard nobles, who
Have all forsook me, hath devour'd the rest;
And suffer'd me by the voice of slaves to be
Whoop'd out of Rome.   Now this extremity
Hath brought me to thy hearth; not out of hope—
Mistake me not—to save my life, for if
I had fear'd death, of all the men i' the world
I would have 'voided thee, but in mere spite,
●To be full quit of those my banishers,
Stand I before thee here.   Then if thou hast 90
●A heart of wreak in thee, that wilt revenge
●Thine own particular wrongs and stop those maims
Of shame seen through thy country, speed thee
    straight,
And make my misery serve thy turn: so use it
That my revengeful services may prove
As benefits to thee, for I will fight
Against my canker'd country with the spleen
Of all the under fiends.   But if so be
Thou darest not this and that to prove more for-
    tunes
Thou'rt tired, then, in a word, I also am   100
Longer to live most weary, and present
My throat to thee and to thy ancient malice;
Which not to cut would show thee but a fool,
Since I have ever follow'd thee with hate,
Drawn tuns of blood out of thy country's breast,
And cannot live but to thy shame, unless
It be to do thee service.
  Auf.   O Marcius, Marcius!
Each word thou hast spoke hath weeded from my
    heart
A root of ancient envy.   If Jupiter
Should from yond cloud speak divine things, 110
And say ''Tis true,' I'ld not believe them more
Than thee, all noble Marcius.   Let me twine
Mine arms about that body, where against
My grained ash an hundred times hath broke,
●And scarr'd the moon with splinters: here I clip
The anvil of my sword, and do contest
As hotly and as nobly with thy love
As ever in ambitious strength I did
Contend against thy valour.   Know thou first,
I loved the maid I married; never man   120
Sigh'd truer breath; but that I see thee here,
Thou noble thing! more dances my rapt heart
Than when I first my wedded mistress saw

Bestride my threshold.   Why, thou Mars! I tell
    thee,
We have a power on foot; and I had purpose
●Once more to hew thy target from thy brawn,
Or lose mine arm for't: thou hast beat me out
●Twelve several times, and I have nightly since
Dreamt of encounters 'twixt thyself and me;
We have been down together in my sleep,   130
Unbuckling helms, fisting each other's throat,
And waked half dead with nothing.   Worthy
    Marcius,
Had we no quarrel else to Rome, but that
Thou art thence banish'd, we would muster all
From twelve to seventy, and pouring war
Into the bowels of ungrateful Rome,
Like a bold flood o'er-bear.   O, come, go in,
And take our friendly senators by the hands;
Who now are here, taking their leaves of me,
Who am prepared against your territories, 140
Though not for Rome itself.
   Cor.   You bless me, gods!
● *Auf.* Therefore, most absolute sir, if thou wilt
    have
The leading of thine own revenges, take
●The one half of my commission; and set down—
As best thou art experienced, since thou know'st
Thy country's strength and weakness,—thine
    own ways;
Whether to knock against the gates of Rome,
Or rudely visit them in parts remote,
●To fright them, ere destroy.   But come in:
Let me commend thee first to those that shall 150
Say yea to thy desires.   A thousand welcomes!
And more a friend than e'er an enemy;
Yet, Marcius, that was much.   Your hand: most
    welcome!
      [*Exeunt Coriolanus and Aufidius.   The
              two Servingmen come forward.*
   First Serv.   Here's a strange alteration!
   Sec. Serv.   By my hand, I had thought to
have strucken him with a cudgel; and yet my
●mind gave me his clothes made a false report of
him.
   First Serv.   What an arm he has! he turned
me about with his finger and his thumb, as one
would set up a top.   161
   Sec. Serv.   Nay, I knew by his face that there
was something in him: he had, sir, a kind of face,
methought,—I cannot tell how to term it.
   First Serv.   He had so; looking as it were—
would I were hanged, but I thought there was
more in him than I could think.
   Sec. Serv.   So did I, I'll be sworn: he is simply the rarest man i' the world.
   First Serv.   I think he is: but a greater soldier
than he, you wot one.   171
   Sec. Serv.   Who, my master?
   First Serv.   Nay, it's no matter for that.
   Sec. Serv.   Worth six on him.
   First Serv.   Nay, not so neither: but I take
him to be the greater soldier.
   Sec. Serv.   Faith, look you, one cannot tell
how to say that: for the defence of a town, our
general is excellent.
   First Serv.   Ay, and for an assault too.   180

      Re-enter third Servingman.

   Third Serv.   O slaves, I can tell you news,—
news, you rascals!

126 *target.* Shield. *brawn.* Strong arm.

128 *several.* Separate.

142 *absolute.* Perfect.

144 *commission.* Command. *set down.* Decide.

149 *ere destroy.* Before destroying them.

157 *gave.* Suggested to.

186 *lieve.* Gladly.

198 *troth.* Truth. *scotched.* Slashes.

199 *carbonado.* A piece of grilled meat.

213 *sowl.* Drag.

215 *polled.* Clear.

222 *directitude.* Discredit (malapropism).

226 *conies.* Rabbits.

234–248 *This peace . . . one another.* See introduction.

238 *vent.* Life.

239 *mulled.* Dull.

Third Servingman: 'I hope to see Romans as cheap as Volscians.' Engraving by Kenny Meadows from Barry Cornwall's *Works of Shakspere,* 1846

First and Sec. Serv. What, what, what? let's partake.

Third Serv. I would not be a Roman, of all ●nations; I had as lieve be a condemned man.

First and Sec. Serv. Wherefore? wherefore?

Third Serv. Why, here's he that was wont to thwack our general, Caius Marcius.

First Serv. Why do you say 'thwack our general'? 191

Third Serv. I do not say 'thwack our general;' but he was always good enough for him.

Sec. Serv. Come, we are fellows and friends: he was ever too hard for him; I have heard him say so himself.

First Serv. He was too hard for him directly, ●to say the troth on't: before Corioli he scotched ●him and notched him like a carbonado.

Sec. Serv. An he had been cannibally given, he might have broiled and eaten him too. 201

First Serv. But, more of thy news?

Third Serv. Why, he is so made on here within, as if he were son and heir to Mars; set at upper end o' the table; no question asked him by any of the senators, but they stand bald before him: our general himself makes a mistress of him; sanctifies himself with 's hand and turns up the white o' the eye to his discourse. But the bottom of the news is, our general is cut i' the middle and but one half of what he was yesterday; for the other has half, by the entreaty and grant of the ●whole table. He'll go, he says, and sowl the porter of Rome gates by the ears: he will mow all ●down before him, and leave his passage polled.

Sec. Serv. And he's as like to do't as any man I can imagine.

Third Serv. Do't! he will do't; for, look you, sir, he has as many friends as enemies; which friends, sir, as it were, durst not, look you, sir, show themselves, as we term it, his friends whilst ●he's in directitude.

First Serv. Directitude! what's that?

Third Serv. But when they shall see, sir, his crest up again, and the man in blood, they will ●out of their burrows, like conies after rain, and revel all with him.

First Serv. But when goes this forward?

Third Serv. To-morrow; to-day; presently; you shall have the drum struck up this afternoon: 'tis, as it were, a parcel of their feast, and to be executed ere they wipe their lips.

Sec. Serv. Why, then we shall have a stirring ●world again. This peace is nothing, but to rust iron, increase tailors, and breed ballad-makers.

First Serv. Let me have war, say I; it exceeds peace as far as day does night; it's spritely, ●waking, audible, and full of vent. Peace is a very ●apoplexy, lethargy; mulled, deaf, sleepy, insensible; a getter of more bastard children than war's a destroyer of men. 241

Sec. Serv. 'Tis so: and as war, in some sort, may be said to be a ravisher, so it cannot be denied but peace is a great maker of cuckolds.

First Serv. Ay, and it makes men hate one another.

Third Serv. Reason; because they then less need one another. The wars for my money. I hope to see Romans as cheap as Volscians. They are rising, they are rising. 250

All. In, in, in, in! [*Exeunt.*

SCENE VI. *Rome. A public place.*

Enter SICINIUS *and* BRUTUS.

Sic. We hear not of him, neither need we fear
    him;
His remedies are tame i' the present peace
And quietness of the people, which before
Were in wild hurry. Here do we make his friends
Blush that the world goes well, who rather had,
Though they themselves did suffer by't, behold
Dissentious numbers pestering streets than see
Our tradesmen singing in their shops and going
About their functions friendly.
    Bru. We stood to't in good time. [*Enter*
        Menenius.] Is this Menenius?   10
    Sic. 'Tis he, 'tis he: O, he is grown most kind
        of late.
    Both Tri. Hail, sir!
    Men.   Hail to you both!
    Sic.   Your Coriolanus
Is not much miss'd, but with his friends:
The commonwealth doth stand, and so would do,
Were he more angry at it.
    Men. All's well; and might have been much
        better, if
●He could have temporized.
    Sic.   Where is he, hear you?
    Men. Nay, I hear nothing: his mother and
        his wife
Hear nothing from him.

Enter three or four Citizens.

Citizens. The gods preserve you both!
    Sic.   God-den, our neighbours. 20
    Bru. God-den to you all, god-den to you all.
    First Cit. Ourselves, our wives, and children,
        on our knees,
Are bound to pray for you both.
    Sic.   Live, and thrive!
    Bru. Farewell, kind neighbours: we wish'd
        Coriolanus
Had loved you as we did.
    Citizens.   Now the gods keep you!
    Both Tri. Farewell, farewell.
                [*Exeunt Citizens.*
    Sic. This is a happier and more comely time
Than when these fellows ran about the streets,
Crying confusion.
    Bru.   Caius Marcius was
A worthy officer i' the war; but insolent,   30
O'ercome with pride, ambitious past all thinking,
Self-loving,—
    Sic.   And affecting one sole throne,
●Without assistance.
    Men.   I think not so.
    Sic. We should by this, to all our lamentation,
If he had gone forth consul, found it so.
    Bru. The gods have well prevented it, and
        Rome
Sits safe and still without him.

Enter an Ædile.

    Æd.   Worthy tribunes,
There is a slave, whom we have put in prison,
Reports, the Volsces with two several powers
Are enter'd in the Roman territories,   40
And with the deepest malice of the war
Destroy what lies before 'em.
    Men.   'Tis Aufidius,

Set design for a public place in Rome by Motley,
Stratford-upon-Avon, 1952

17 *temporized.* Compromised.

33 *assistance.* Assistants.

45 *inshell'd*. Drawn in.

60 *raising*. Spreading rumours.

62 *seconded*. i.e. confirmed.

87 *auger's bore*. The small hole made by an auger or bradall.

Menenius: 'Pray now, your news?' Cominius (Paul Hardwick), Sicinius (Robert Hardy), Menenius (Harry Andrews) and Brutus (Peter Woodthorpe), Stratford-upon-Avon, 1959

Who, hearing of our Marcius' banishment,
Thrusts forth his horns again into the world;
●Which were inshell'd when Marcius stood for
    Rome,
And durst not once peep out.
    Sic.   Come, what talk you
Of Marcius?
    Bru.   Go see this rumourer whipp'd.   It cannot be
The Volsces dare break with us.
    Men.   Cannot be!
We have record that very well it can,
And three examples of the like have been   50
Within my age.   But reason with the fellow,
Before you punish him, where he heard this,
Lest you shall chance to whip your information
And beat the messenger who bids beware
Of what is to be dreaded.
    Sic.   Tell not me:
I know this cannot be.
    Bru.   Not possible.

          Enter a Messenger.

    Mess.   The nobles in great earnestness are
    going
All to the senate-house: some news is come
That turns their countenances.
    Sic.   'Tis this slave;— 59
●Go whip him 'fore the people's eyes:—his raising;
Nothing but his report.
    Mess.   Yes, worthy sir,
●The slave's report is seconded; and more,
More fearful, is deliver'd.
    Sic.   What more fearful?
    Mess.   It is spoke freely out of many mouths—
How probable I do not know—that Marcius,
Join'd with Aufidius, leads a power 'gainst Rome,
And vows revenge as spacious as between
The young'st and oldest thing.
    Sic.   This is most likely!
    Bru.   Raised only, that the weaker sort may
    wish
Good Marcius home again.
    Sic.   The very trick on't 70
    Men.   This is unlikely:
He and Aufidius can no more atone
Than violentest contrariety.

       Enter a second Messenger.

    Sec. Mess.   You are sent for to the senate:
A fearful army, led by Caius Marcius
Associated with Aufidius, rages
Upon our territories; and have already
O'erborne their way, consumed with fire, and took
What lay before them.

         Enter COMINIUS.

    Com.   O, you have made good work!
    Men.   What news? what news? 80
    Com.   You have holp to ravish your own daughters and
To melt the city leads upon your pates,
To see your wives dishonour'd to your noses,—
    Men.   What's the news? what's the news?
    Com.   Your temples burned in their cement, and
Your franchises, whereon you stood, confined
●Into an auger's bore.
    Men.   Pray now, your news?

You have made fair work, I fear me.—Pray, your
    news?—
If Marcius should be join'd with Volscians,—
    Com.   If!
He is their god: he leads them like a thing   90
Made by some other deity than nature,
That shapes man better; and they follow him,
Against us brats, with no less confidence
Than boys pursuing summer butterflies,
Or butchers killing flies.
    Men.   You have made good work,
● You and your apron-men; you that stood so much
● Upon the voice of occupation and
The breath of garlic-eaters!
    Com.   He will shake
● Your Rome about your ears.
    Men.   As Hercules
Did shake down mellow fruit. You have made
    fair work!   100
    Bru. But is this true, sir?
    Com.   Ay; and you'll look pale
Before you find it other.   All the regions
Do smilingly revolt; and who resist
Are mock'd for valiant ignorance,
And perish constant fools. Who is't can blame
    him?
Your enemies and his find something in him.
    Men. We are all undone, unless
The noble man have mercy.
    Com.   Who shall ask it?
The tribunes cannot do't for shame; the people
Deserve such pity of him as the wolf   110
Does of the shepherds: for his best friends, if they
Should say 'Be good to Rome,' they charged him
    even
As those should do that had deserved his hate,
And therein show'd like enemies.
    Men.   'Tis true:
If he were putting to my house the brand
That should consume it, I have not the face
● To say 'Beseech you, cease.' You have made
    fair hands,
● You and your crafts! you have crafted fair!
    Com.   You have brought
A trembling upon Rome, such as was never
So incapable of help.
    Both Tri.   Say not we brought it.   120
    Men. How! Was it we? we loved him; but,
    like beasts
And cowardly nobles, gave way unto your clusters,
Who did hoot him out o' the city.
    Com.   But I fear
They'll roar him in again. Tullus Aufidius,
● The second name of men, obeys his points
As if he were his officer: desperation
Is all the policy, strength and defence,
That Rome can make against them.

            Enter a troop of Citizens.

    Men.   Here come the clusters.
And is Aufidius with him? You are they   129
That made the air unwholesome, when you cast
Your stinking greasy caps in hooting at
Coriolanus' exile. Now he's coming;
And not a hair upon a soldier's head
Which will not prove a whip: as many coxcombs
As you threw caps up will he tumble down,
And pay you for your voices. 'Tis no matter;
If he could burn us all into one coal,

96 *apron-men.* Tradesmen. *stood.* Insisted.

97 *voice of occupation.* i.e. the votes of workmen.

99-100 *Hercules . . . fruit.* Hercules' twelfth labour was
to obtain apples from a tree in the Hesperides, guarded
by a dragon.

Hercules in the garden of the Hesperides. Engraving
from P. J. Mariette's *Traité des Pierres Gravées*, 1769

117 *made fair hands.* Done a fine job.

118 *crafted fair.* Acted craftily.

125 *name.* i.e. in fame. *points.* Every point.

148 *cry.* Mob.

161 *buy this for.* i.e. turn this into.

5 *darken'd.* Eclipsed.

13 *particular.* Private concern.

We have deserved it.
 Citizens. Faith, we hear fearful news.
 First Cit.   For mine own part,
When I said, banish him, I said, 'twas pity. 140
 Sec. Cit. And so did I.
 Third Cit. And so did I; and, to say the
truth, so did very many of us: that we did, we
did for the best; and though we willingly consented to his banishment, yet it was against our
will.
 Com. Ye're goodly things, you voices!
 Men.   You have made
•Good work, you and your cry! Shall's to the
  Capitol?
 Com. O, ay, what else?
      [*Exeunt Cominius and Menenius.*
 Sic. Go, masters, get you home; be not dismay'd: 150
These are a side that would be glad to have
This true which they so seem to fear. Go home,
And show no sign of fear.
 First Cit. The gods be good to us! Come,
masters, let's home. I ever said we were i' the
wrong when we banished him.
 Sec. Cit. So did we all. But, come, let's home.
        [*Exeunt Citizens.*
 Bru. I do not like this news.
 Sic. Nor I.
 Bru. Let's to the Capitol. Would half my
  wealth 160
•Would buy this for a lie!
 Sic.   Pray, let us go.
         [*Exeunt.*

 Scene VII. *A camp, at a small distance
     from Rome.*

 Enter Aufidius *and his* Lieutenant.

 Auf. Do they still fly to the Roman?
 Lieu. I do not know what witchcraft's in him,
  but
Your soldiers use him as the grace 'fore meat,
Their talk at table, and their thanks at end;
•And you are darken'd in this action, sir,
Even by your own.
 Auf.   I cannot help it now,
Unless, by using means, I lame the foot
Of our design. He bears himself more proudlier,
Even to my person, than I thought he would
When first I did embrace him: yet his nature 10
In that's no changeling; and I must excuse
What cannot be amended.
 Lieu.   Yet I wish, sir,—
•I mean for your particular,—you had not
Join'd in commission with him; but either
Had borne the action of yourself, or else
To him had left it solely.
 Auf. I understand thee well; and be thou sure,
When he shall come to his account, he knows not
What I can urge against him. Although it seems,
And so he thinks, and is no less apparent 20
To the vulgar eye, that he bears all things fairly,
And shows good husbandry for the Volscian
  state,
Fights dragon-like, and does achieve as soon
As draw his sword; yet he hath left undone
That which shall break his neck or hazard mine,
Whene'er we come to our account.

Lieu. Sir, I beseech you, think you he'll carry
  Rome ?
Auf. All places yield to him ere he sits down;
And the nobility of Rome are his:
The senators and patricians love him too: 30
The tribunes are no soldiers; and their people
Will be as rash in the repeal, as hasty
To expel him thence. I think he'll be to Rome
As is the osprey to the fish, who takes it
By sovereignty of nature. First he was
A noble servant to them; but he could not
Carry his honours even: whether 'twas pride,
Which out of daily fortune ever taints
The happy man; whether defect of judgement,
To fail in the disposing of those chances 40
Which he was lord of; or whether nature,
Not to be other than one thing, not moving
● From the casque to the cushion, but commanding
  peace
● Even with the same austerity and garb
As he controll'd the war; but one of these—
As he hath spices of them all, not all,
For I dare so far free him—made him fear'd,
So hated, and so banish'd: but he has a merit,
To choke it in the utterance. So our virtues
Lie in the interpretation of the time: 50
And power, unto itself most commendable,
● † Hath not a tomb so evident as a chair
To extol what it hath done.
One fire drives out one fire; one nail, one nail;
Rights by rights falter, strengths by strengths do
  fail.
Come, let's away. When, Caius, Rome is thine,
Thou art poor'st of all; then shortly art thou mine.
            [*Exeunt.*

ACT V.

SCENE I. *Rome. A public place.*

Enter MENENIUS, COMINIUS, SICINIUS, BRUTUS,
and others.

Men. No, I'll not go: you hear what he hath
  said
Which was sometime his general; who loved him
● In a most dear particular. He call'd me father:
But what o' that? Go, you that banish'd him;
A mile before his tent fall down, and knee
The way into his mercy: nay, if he coy'd
To hear Cominius speak, I'll keep at home.
Com. He would not seem to know me.
Men.   Do you hear?
Com. Yet one time he did call me by my name:
I urged our old acquaintance, and the drops 10
That we have bled together. Coriolanus
He would not answer to: forbad all names;
He was a kind of nothing, titleless,
Till he had forged himself a name o' the fire
Of burning Rome.
Men. Why, so: you have made good work !
● A pair of tribunes that have rack'd for Rome,
To make coals cheap,—a noble memory !
Com. I minded him how royal 'twas to pardon
When it was less expected: he replied,
It was a bare petition of a state 20
To one whom they had punish'd.
Men.   Very well:
Could he say less?

43 *casque to the cushion.* i.e. battlefield to the Capitol.

44 *garb.* Demeanour.

52 *chair.* i.e. seat at the Capitol.

Set design for a public place in Rome by Boris Aronson,
Stratford-upon-Avon, 1959

3 *particular.* Personal affection.

16 *rack'd.* Striven.

Menenius. Drawing by Henry Singleton (1766–1839)

28 *nose.* Smell. *the offence.* i.e. the noisome chaff.

44 *grief-shot.* Sorrow-stricken.

49 *hum at.* Be hostile to. *unhearts.* Disheartens.

60 *prove.* Try.

Com.   I offer'd to awaken his regard
For's private friends: his answer to me was,
He could not stay to pick them in a pile
Of noisome musty chaff: he said 'twas folly,
For one poor grain or two, to leave unburnt,
●And still to nose the offence.
Men.   For one poor grain or two!
I am one of those; his mother, wife, his child,
And this brave fellow too, we are the grains: 30
You are the musty chaff; and you are smelt
Above the moon: we must be burnt for you.
   Sic.   Nay, pray, be patient: if you refuse your
      aid
In this so never-needed help, yet do not
Upbraid's with our distress.   But, sure, if you
Would be your country's pleader, your good
      tongue,
More than the instant army we can make,
Might stop our countryman.
   Men.   No, I'll not meddle.
   Sic.   Pray you, go to him.
   Men.   What should I do? 39
   Bru.   Only make trial what your love can do
For Rome, towards Marcius.
   Men.   Well, and say that Marcius
Return me, as Cominius is return'd,
Unheard; what then?
●But as a discontented friend, grief-shot
With his unkindness? say't be so?
   Sic.   Yet your good will
Must have that thanks from Rome, after the
      measure
As you intended well.
   Men.   I'll undertake 't:
I think he'll hear me.   Yet, to bite his lip
●And hum at good Cominius, much unhearts me.
He was not taken well; he had not dined: 50
The veins unfill'd, our blood is cold, and then
We pout upon the morning, are unapt
To give or to forgive; but when we have stuff'd
These pipes and these conveyances of our
      blood
With wine and feeding, we have suppler souls
Than in our priest-like fasts: therefore I'll watch
      him
Till he be dieted to my request,
And then I'll set upon him.
   Bru.   You know the very road into his kind-
      ness,
●And cannot lose your way.
   Men.   Good faith, I'll prove him, 60
Speed how it will.   I shall ere long have know-
      ledge
Of my success.   [*Exit.*
   Com.   He'll never hear him.
   Sic.   Not?
   Com.   I tell you, he does sit in gold, his eye
Red as 'twould burn Rome; and his injury
The gaoler to his pity.   I kneel'd before him;
'Twas very faintly he said 'Rise;' dismiss'd me
Thus, with his speechless hand: what he would do,
He sent in writing after me; what he would not,
Bound with an oath to yield to his conditions:
So that all hope is vain,   70
Unless his noble mother, and his wife;
Who, as I hear, mean to solicit him
For mercy to his country.   Therefore, let's hence,
And with our fair entreaties haste them on.
                                [*Exeunt.*

SCENE II. *Entrance of the Volscian camp before Rome. Two* Sentinels *on guard.*

Enter to them, MENENIUS.

First Sen. Stay: whence are you?
Sec. Sen.   Stand, and go back.
Men. You guard like men; 'tis well: but, by your leave,
I am an officer of state, and come
To speak with Coriolanus.
First Sen.   From whence?
Men.   From Rome.
First Sen. You may not pass, you must
    return: our general
Will no more hear from thence.
Sec. Sen. You'll see your Rome embraced
    with fire before
You'll speak with Coriolanus.
Men.   Good my friends,
If you have heard your general talk of Rome,
● And of his friends there, it is lots to blanks,   10
My name hath touch'd your ears: it is Menenius.
First Sen. Be it so; go back: the virtue of
    your name
Is not here passable.
Men.   I tell thee, fellow,
Thy general is my lover: I have been
The book of his good acts, whence men have read
His fame unparallel'd, haply amplified;
For I have ever † verified my friends,
Of whom he's chief, with all the size that verity
Would without lapsing suffer: nay, sometimes,
● Like to a bowl upon a subtle ground,   20
I have tumbled past the throw; and in his praise
● Have almost stamp'd the leasing: therefore,
    fellow,
I must have leave to pass.
First Sen. Faith, sir, if you had told as
many lies in his behalf as you have uttered
words in your own, you should not pass here;
no, though it were as virtuous to lie as to live
chastely. Therefore, go back.
Men. Prithee, fellow, remember my name is
Menenius, always factionary on the party of
your general.   31
Sec. Sen. Howsoever you have been his liar,
as you say you have, I am one that, telling true
under him, must say, you cannot pass. Therefore, go back.
Men. Has he dined, canst thou tell? for I
would not speak with him till after dinner.
First Sen. You are a Roman, are you?
Men. I am, as thy general is.   39
First Sen. Then you should hate Rome, as
he does. Can you, when you have pushed out
your gates the very defender of them, and, in
a violent popular ignorance, given your enemy
your shield, think to front his revenges with
the easy groans of old women, the virginal
palms of your daughters, or with the palsied
● intercession of such a decayed dotant as you
seem to be? Can you think to blow out the
intended fire your city is ready to flame in,
with such weak breath as this? No, you are
deceived; therefore, back to Rome, and prepare
for your execution: you are condemned, our
general has sworn you out of reprieve and
pardon.

Walls of Rome and the Ostian Gate. Engraving from Gibbon's *Decline and Fall of the Roman Empire*, edited by W. Smith, 1862

10 *lots to blanks.* i.e. more likely than not.

20 *subtle.* Tricky.

22 *stamp'd the leasing.* Attested to falsehood.

47 *dotant.* Dotard.

67 *a Jack guardant.* A knave on guard.

68 *office.* i.e. use his authority to separate.

90 *properly.* For myself. *remission.* Power to pardon.

104 *shent.* Scolded.

Men. Sirrah, if thy captain knew I were here, he would use me with estimation.

First Sen. Come, my captain knows you not.

Men. I mean, thy general.

First Sen. My general cares not for you. Back, I say, go; lest I let forth your half-pint of blood; back,—that's the utmost of your having: back.

Men. Nay, but, fellow, fellow,—

Enter CORIOLANUS *and* AUFIDIUS.

Cor. What's the matter?

Men. Now, you companion, I'll say an errand for you: you shall know now that I am in esti-
●mation; you shall perceive that a Jack guardant
●cannot office me from my son Coriolanus: guess, but by my entertainment with him, if thou standest not i' the state of hanging, or of some death more long in spectatorship, and crueller in suffering; behold now presently, and swoon for what's to come upon thee. [*To Cor.*] The glorious gods sit in hourly synod about thy particular prosperity, and love thee no worse than thy old father Menenius does! O my son, my son! thou art preparing fire for us; look thee, here's water to quench it. I was hardly moved to come to thee; but being assured none but myself could move thee, I have been blown out of your gates with sighs; and conjure thee to pardon Rome, and thy petitionary countrymen. The good gods assuage thy wrath, and turn the dregs of it upon this varlet here,—this, who, like a block, hath denied my access to thee.

Cor. Away!

Men. How! away!

Cor. Wife, mother, child, I know not. My affairs
Are servanted to others: though I owe
●My revenge properly, my remission lies   90
In Volscian breasts. That we have been familiar,
Ingrate forgetfulness shall poison, rather
Than pity note how much. Therefore, be gone.
Mine ears against your suits are stronger than
Your gates against my force. Yet, for I loved thee,
Take this along; I writ it for thy sake,
                              [*Gives a letter.*
And would have sent it. Another word, Menenius,
I will not hear thee speak. This man, Aufidius,
Was my beloved in Rome: yet thou behold'st!

Auf. You keep a constant temper.   100
                    [*Exeunt Coriolanus and Aufidius.*

First Sen. Now, sir, is your name Menenius?

Sec. Sen. 'Tis a spell, you see, of much power: you know the way home again.

● *First Sen.* Do you hear how we are shent for keeping your greatness back?

Sec. Sen. What cause, do you think, I have to swoon?

Men. I neither care for the world nor your general: for such things as you, I can scarce think there's any, ye're so slight. He that hath a will to die by himself fears it not from another: let your general do his worst. For you, be that you are, long; and your misery increase with your age! I say to you, as I was said to, Away!
                              [*Exit.*

First Sen. A noble fellow, I warrant him.

Sec. Sen. The worthy fellow is our general:
he's the rock, the oak not to be wind-shaken.

[*Exeunt.*

SCENE III. *The tent of Coriolanus.*

Enter CORIOLANUS, AUFIDIUS, *and others.*

Cor. We will before the walls of Rome to-
    morrow
Set down our host. My partner in this action,
You must report to the Volscian lords, how
    plainly
I have borne this business.
    Auf.   Only their ends
You have respected; stopp'd your ears against
The general suit of Rome; never admitted
A private whisper, no, not with such friends
That thought them sure of you.
    Cor.   This last old man,
Whom with a crack'd heart I have sent to Rome,
Loved me above the measure of a father;   10
• Nay, godded me, indeed. Their latest refuge
Was to send him; for whose old love I have,
Though I show'd sourly to him, once more
    offer'd
The first conditions, which they did refuse
And cannot now accept; to grace him only
That thought he could do more, a very little
I have yielded to: fresh embassies and suits,
Nor from the state nor private friends, hereafter
Will I lend ear to. Ha what shout is this?

[*Shout within.*

Shall I be tempted to infringe my vow   20
In the same time 'tis made? I will not.

Enter, in mourning habits, VIRGILIA, VO-
LUMNIA, *leading young* MARCIUS, VALERIA,
and Attendants.

My wife comes foremost; then the honour'd
    mould
Wherein this trunk was framed, and in her hand
The grandchild to her blood. But, out, affection!
All bond and privilege of nature, break!
Let it be virtuous to be obstinate.
What is that curt'sy worth? or those doves' eyes,
Which can make gods forsworn? I melt, and
    am not
Of stronger earth than others. My mother bows;
• As if Olympus to a molehill should   30
In supplication nod: and my young boy
Hath an aspect of intercession, which
Great nature cries 'Deny not.' Let the Volsces
Plough Rome, and harrow Italy: I'll never
Be such a gosling to obey instinct, but stand,
As if a man were author of himself
And knew no other kin.
    Vir.   My lord and husband!
    Cor. These eyes are not the same I wore
    in Rome.
•   *Vir.* The sorrow that delivers us thus changed
Makes you think so.
    Cor.   Like a dull actor now,   40
I have forgot my part, and I am out,
Even to a full disgrace. Best of my flesh,
Forgive my tyranny; but do not say
For that 'Forgive our Romans.' O, a kiss
Long as my exile, sweet as my revenge!
Now, by the jealous queen of heaven, that kiss
I carried from thee, dear; and my true lip

The family of Coriolanus beg him to spare Rome.
Fresco by Luca Signorelli (1441?–1523)

11 *godded.* Deified.

30 *Olympus.* Legendary mountain-home of the gods.

39 *delivers.* Presents.

48 *virgin'd it.* Kept it intact.

Volumnia: 'I kneel before thee: and unproperly Show duty . . .' Elizabeth Hopkins, 18th century English actress, as Volumnia, 1776

66 *curdied.* Congealed.

67 *Dian.* Diana, goddess of chastity.

68 *epitome.* Miniature.

74 *sea-mark.* Land mark used by seamen for navigation. *flaw.* Gust.

95 *bewray.* Display.

● Hath virgin'd it e'er since.   You gods! I prate,
And the most noble mother of the world
Leave unsaluted: sink, my knee, i' the earth; 50
                                    [*Kneels.*
Of thy deep duty more impression show
Than that of common sons.
  Vol.   O, stand up blest!
Whilst, with no softer cushion than the flint,
I kneel before thee; and unproperly
Show duty, as mistaken all this while
Between the child and parent.   [*Kneels.*
  Cor.   What is this?
Your knees to me? to your corrected son?
Then let the pebbles on the hungry beach
Fillip the stars; then let the mutinous winds
Strike the proud cedars 'gainst the fiery sun; 60
Murdering impossibility, to make
What cannot be, slight work.
  Vol.   Thou art my warrior;
I holp to frame thee.   Do you know this lady?
  Cor.   The noble sister of Publicola,
The moon of Rome, chaste as the icicle
● That's curdied by the frost from purest snow
● And hangs on Dian's temple: dear Valeria!
● *Vol.*   This is a poor epitome of yours,
Which by the interpretation of full time
May show like all yourself.
  Cor.   The god of soldiers, 70
With the consent of supreme Jove, inform
Thy thoughts with nobleness; that thou mayst
      prove
To shame unvulnerable, and stick i' the wars
● Like a great sea-mark, standing every flaw,
And saving those that eye thee!
  Vol.   Your knee, sirrah.
  Cor.   That's my brave boy!
  Vol.   Even he, your wife, this lady, and
      myself,
Are suitors to you.
  Cor.   I beseech you, peace:
Or, if you'ld ask, remember this before:
The thing I have forsworn to grant may never 80
Be held by you denials.   Do not bid me
Dismiss my soldiers, or capitulate
Again with Rome's mechanics: tell me not
Wherein I seem unnatural: desire not
To allay my rages and revenges with
Your colder reasons.
  Vol.   O, no more, no more!
You have said you will not grant us any thing;
For we have nothing else to ask, but that
Which you deny already: yet we will ask;
That, if you fail in our request, the blame   90
May hang upon your hardness: therefore hear us.
  Cor.   Aufidius, and you Volsces, mark; for
      we'll
Hear nought from Rome in private.   Your request?
  Vol.   Should we be silent and not speak, our
      raiment
● And state of bodies would bewray what life
We have led since thy exile.   Think with thyself
How more unfortunate than all living women
Are we come hither: since that thy sight, which
      should
Make our eyes flow with joy, hearts dance with
      comforts,
Constrains them weep and shake with fear and
      sorrow;   100
Making the mother, wife and child to see

The son, the husband and the father tearing
His country's bowels out.   And to poor we
●Thine enmity's most capital: thou barr'st us
Our prayers to the gods, which is a comfort
That all but we enjoy; for how can we,
Alas, how can we for our country pray,
Whereto we are bound, together with thy victory,
Whereto we are bound? alack, or we must lose
The country, our dear nurse, or else thy person,
Our comfort in the country.   We must find   111
An evident calamity, though we had
Our wish, which side should win: for either thou
●Must, as a foreign recreant, be led
With manacles thorough our streets, or else
Triumphantly tread on thy country's ruin,
And bear the palm for having bravely shed
Thy wife and children's blood.   For myself, son,
I purpose not to wait on fortune till
●These wars determine: if I cannot persuade thee
Rather to show a noble grace to both parts   121
Than seek the end of one, thou shalt no sooner
March to assault thy country than to tread—
Trust to't, thou shalt not—on thy mother's womb,
That brought thee to this world.
      Vir.   Ay, and mine,
That brought you forth this boy, to keep your name
Living to time.
      Young Mar.   A' shall not tread on me;
I'll run away till I am bigger, but then I'll fight.
      Cor.   Not of a woman's tenderness to be,
Requires nor child nor woman's face to see.   130
I have sat too long.   [*Rising.*
      Vol.   Nay, go not from us thus.
If it were so that our request did tend
To save the Romans, thereby to destroy
The Volsces whom you serve, you might con-
      demn us,
As poisonous of your honour: no; our suit
Is, that you reconcile them: while the Volsces
May say 'This mercy we have show'd;' the
      Romans,
'This we received;' and each in either side
Give the all-hail to thee, and cry ' Be blest
For making up this peace!' Thou know'st, great
      son,   140
The end of war's uncertain, but this certain,
That, if thou conquer Rome, the benefit
Which thou shalt thereby reap is such a name,
Whose repetition will be dogg'd with curses;
Whose chronicle thus writ: 'The man was noble,
But with his last attempt he wiped it out;
Destroy'd his country, and his name remains
To the ensuing age abhorr'd.' Speak to me, son:
Thou hast affected the fine strains of honour,
To imitate the graces of the gods;   150
To tear with thunder the wide cheeks o' the air,
●And yet to charge thy sulphur with a bolt
That should but rive an oak.   Why dost not
      speak?
Think'st thou it honourable for a noble man
Still to remember wrongs? Daughter, speak you:
He cares not for your weeping. Speak thou, boy:
Perhaps thy childishness will move him more
Than can our reasons.   There's no man in the
      world
More bound to 's mother; yet here he lets me
      prate   159
Like one i' the stocks. Thou hast never in thy life

104 *capital.* Deadly.

114 *recreant.* i.e. traitor.

120 *determine.* Are ended.

Volumnia: 'Nay, go not from us thus.' Engraving of James Quin (1693–1761) as Coriolanus by William Hogarth, 1749

152 *sulphur.* Lightning.

Volumnia: 'Down: an end; This is the last: so we will home to Rome ...' Engraving from a painting by William Hamilton (1751–1801)

---

163 *cluck'd.* i.e. nagged.

1 *coign.* Corner.

Show'd thy dear mother any courtesy,
When she, poor hen, fond of no second brood,
● Has cluck'd thee to the wars and safely home,
Loaden with honour.   Say my request's unjust,
And spurn me back: but if it be not so,
Thou art not honest; and the gods will plague
        thee,
That thou restrain'st from me the duty which
To a mother's part belongs.   He turns away:
Down, ladies; let us shame him with our knees.
To his surname Coriolanus 'longs more pride   170
Than pity to our prayers.   Down: an end;
This is the last: so we will home to Rome,
And die among our neighbours.   Nay, behold 's:
This boy, that cannot tell what he would have,
But kneels and holds up hands for fellowship,
Does reason our petition with more strength
Than thou hast to deny 't.   Come, let us go:
This fellow had a Volscian to his mother;
His wife is in Corioli and his child
Like him by chance.   Yet give us our dispatch:
I am hush'd until our city be afire,   181
And then I'll speak a little. [*He holds her by the
                                    hand, silent.*
  Cor.   O mother, mother!
What have you done?   Behold, the heavens do
        ope,
The gods look down, and this unnatural scene
They laugh at.   O my mother, mother! O!
You have won a happy victory to Rome;
But, for your son,—believe it, O, believe it,
Most dangerously you have with him prevail'd,
If not most mortal to him.   But, let it come.
Aufidius, though I cannot make true wars,   190
I'll frame convenient peace.   Now, good Aufidius,
Were you in my stead, would you have heard
A mother less? or granted less, Aufidius?
  Auf.   I was moved withal.
  Cor.   I dare be sworn you were:
And, sir, it is no little thing to make
Mine eyes to sweat compassion.   But, good sir,
What peace you'll make, advise me: for my part,
I'll not to Rome, I'll back with you; and pray
        you,
Stand to me in this cause.   O mother! wife!
  Auf. [*Aside.*] I am glad thou hast set thy
        mercy and thy honour   200
At difference in thee: out of that I'll work
Myself a former fortune.
        [*The Ladies make signs to Coriolanus.*
  Cor.   Ay, by and by;
        [*To Volumnia, Virgilia, &c.*
But we will drink together; and you shall bear
A better witness back than words, which we,
On like conditions, will have counter-seal'd.
Come, enter with us.   Ladies, you deserve
To have a temple built you: all the swords
In Italy, and her confederate arms,
Could not have made this peace.   [*Exeunt.* 209

SCENE IV.   *Rome.   A public place.*

Enter MENENIUS *and* SICINIUS.

● *Men.* See you yon coign o' the Capitol, yon corner-stone?
  Sic. Why, what of that?
  Men. If it be possible for you to displace it with your little finger, there is some hope the ladies of Rome, especially his mother, may pre-

vail with him.   But I say there is no hope in't:
our throats are sentenced and stay upon execution.
Sic. Is't possible that so short a time can alter
the condition of a man?   10
Men. There is differency between a grub and
a butterfly; yet your butterfly was a grub. This
Marcius is grown from man to dragon: he has
wings; he's more than a creeping thing.
Sic. He loved his mother dearly.
Men. So did he me: and he no more remembers his mother now than an eight-year-old horse.
The tartness of his face sours ripe grapes: when
he walks, he moves like an engine, and the
ground shrinks before his treading: he is able to
● pierce a corslet with his eye; talks like a knell,
● and his hum is a battery. He sits in his state, as
a thing made for Alexander. What he bids be
done is finished with his bidding. He wants nothing of a god but eternity and a heaven to
throne in.
Sic. Yes, mercy, if you report him truly.
Men. I paint him in the character. Mark what
mercy his mother shall bring from him: there is
no more mercy in him than there is milk in a male
tiger; that shall our poor city find: and all this is
long of you.
Sic. The gods be good unto us!
Men. No, in such a case the gods will not be
good unto us. When we banished him, we respected not them; and, he returning to break our
necks, they respect not us.

Enter a Messenger.

Mess. Sir, if you'ld save your life, fly to your
        house:
The plebeians have got your fellow-tribune
And hale him up and down, all swearing, if   40
The Roman ladies bring not comfort home,
They'll give him death by inches.

Enter a second Messenger.

Sic.   What's the news?
Sec. Mess. Good news, good news; the ladies
        have prevail'd,
The Volscians are dislodged, and Marcius gone:
A merrier day did never yet greet Rome,
● No, not the expulsion of the Tarquins.
Sic.   Friend,
Art thou certain this is true? is it most certain?
Sec. Mess. As certain as I know the sun is fire:
Where have you lurk'd, that you make doubt
        of it?   49
Ne'er through an arch so hurried the blown tide,
As the recomforted through the gates. Why,
        hark you! [*Trumpets; hautboys; drums
                        beat; all together.*
● The trumpets, sackbuts, psalteries and fifes,
● Tabors and cymbals and the shouting Romans,
Make the sun dance. Hark you!
                            [*A shout within.*
Men.   This is good news:
I will go meet the ladies. This Volumnia
Is worth of consuls, senators, patricians,
A city full; of tribunes, such as you,
A sea and land full. You have pray'd well to-day:
This morning for ten thousand of your throats 59
● I'ld not have given a doit. Hark, how they joy!
                            [*Music still, with shouts.*

21 *corslet.* Body armour.

22 *hum.* Anger.

46 *expulsion ... Tarquins.* The historical expulsion
from Rome of the family of tyrants.

The expulsion of the Tarquins from Rome. Engraving
by Bartolomeo Pinelli, 1821

52 *sackbuts.* Trombones. *psalteries.* Stringed instruments.

53 *tabors.* Small drums.

60 *doit.* Smallest coin.

6 *ports*. Gates.

14 *parties*. Allies.

Sic. First, the gods bless you for your tidings ; next,
Accept my thankfulness.
  Sec. Mess.   Sir, we have all
Great cause to give great thanks.
  Sic.   They are near the city?
  Sec. Mess. Almost at point to enter.
  Sic.   We will meet them,
And help the joy.   [*Exeunt.*

SCENE V. *The same. A street near the gate.*

Enter two Senators *with* VOLUMNIA, VIRGILIA,
  VALERIA, &c. *passing over the stage, followed
  by Patricians, and others.*

  First Sen. Behold our patroness, the life of
      Rome !
Call all your tribes together, praise the gods,
And make triumphant fires ; strew flowers before
      them :
Unshout the noise that banish'd Marcius,
Repeal him with the welcome of his mother ;
Cry 'Welcome, ladies, welcome !'
  All.   Welcome, ladies,
Welcome ! [*A flourish with drums and trum-
                pets. Exeunt.*

SCENE VI. *Antium. A public place.*

Enter TULLUS AUFIDIUS, *with* Attendants.

  Auf. Go tell the lords o' the city I am here :
Deliver them this paper : having read it,
Bid them repair to the market-place ; where I,
Even in theirs and in the commons' ears,
Will vouch the truth of it. Him I accuse
●The city ports by this hath enter'd and
Intends to appear before the people, hoping
To purge himself with words : dispatch.
                [*Exeunt Attendants.*

Enter three or four Conspirators *of* AUFIDIUS'
  faction.

Most welcome !
  First Con. How is it with our general?
  Auf.   Even so 10
As with a man by his own alms empoison'd,
And with his charity slain.
  Sec. Con.   Most noble sir,
If you do hold the same intent wherein
●You wish'd us parties, we'll deliver you
Of your great danger.
  Auf.   Sir, I cannot tell :
We must proceed as we do find the people.
  Third Con. The people will remain uncertain
      whilst
'Twixt you there's difference ; but the fall of either
Makes the survivor heir of all.
  Auf.   I know it ;
And my pretext to strike at him admits 20
A good construction. I raised him, and I pawn'd
Mine honour for his truth : who being so heighten'd,
He water'd his new plants with dews of flattery,
Seducing so my friends ; and, to this end,
He bow'd his nature, never known before
But to be rough, unswayable and free.
  Third Con. Sir, his stoutness
When he did stand for consul, which he lost
By lack of stooping,—
  Auf.   That I would have spoke of :

Being banish'd for't, he came unto my hearth; 30
Presented to my knife his throat: I took him;
Made him joint-servant with me; gave him way
In all his own desires; nay, let him choose
●Out of my files, his projects to accomplish,
My best and freshest men, served his designments
In mine own person; holp to reap the fame
Which he did end all his; and took some pride
To do myself this wrong: till, at the last,
I seem'd his follower, not partner, and
He waged me with his countenance, as if   40
I had been mercenary.
    First Con.   So he did, my lord:
The army marvell'd at it, and, in the last,
When he had carried Rome and that we look'd
For no less spoil than glory,—
    Auf.   There was it:
For which my sinews shall be stretch'd upon him.
●At a few drops of women's rheum, which are
As cheap as lies, he sold the blood and labour
Of our great action: therefore shall he die,
And I'll renew me in his fall.   But, hark!
      [*Drums and trumpets sound, with great
         . shouts of the People.*
    First Con. Your native town you enter'd like
    a post,   50
And had no welcomes home: but he returns,
Splitting the air with noise.
    Sec. Con.   And patient fools,
Whose children he hath slain, their base throats
    tear
With giving him glory.
    Third Con.   Therefore, at your vantage,
Ere he express himself, or move the people
With what he would say, let him feel your sword,
Which we will second.   When he lies along,
After your way his tale pronounced shall bury
His reasons with his body.
    Auf.   Say no more:
Here come the lords.   60

       Enter the Lords *of the city.*

    All the Lords. You are most welcome home.
    Auf.   I have not deserved it.
But, worthy lords, have you with heed perused
What I have written to you?
    Lords.   We have.
    First Lord.   And grieve to hear't.
What faults he made before the last, I think
●Might have found easy fines: but there to end
Where he was to begin and give away
The benefit of our levies, answering us
With our own charge, making a treaty where
There was a yielding,—this admits no excuse.
    Auf. He approaches: you shall hear him. 70

   Enter CORIOLANUS, *marching with drum and
    colours; Commoners being with him.*

    Cor. Hail, lords! I am return'd your soldier,
No more infected with my country's love
Than when I parted hence, but still subsisting
Under your great command.   You are to know
That prosperously I have attempted and
With bloody passage led your wars even to
The gates of Rome.   Our spoils we have brought
    home
Do more than counterpoise a full third part
The charges of the action.   We have made peace
With no less honour to the Antiates   80

34 *files.* i.e. ranks of troops.

46 *rheum.* Tears.

65 *easy fines.* Light penalties.

Costume design for Coriolanus by Ann Curtis, Royal Shakespeare Co, 1967

84 *compounded.* Agreed.

Coriolanus: 'Measureless liar, thou hast made my heart Too great for what contains it'. Anthony Quayle as Coriolanus, Stratford-upon-Avon, 1952

130 *his tribe.* Of his type.

Than shame to the Romans: and we here deliver,
Subscribed by the consuls and patricians,
Together with the seal o' the senate, what
●We have compounded on.
 Auf.   Read it not, noble lords;
But tell the traitor, in the high'st degree
He hath abused your powers.
 Cor. Traitor! how now!
 Auf.   Ay, traitor, Marcius!
 Cor.   Marcius!
 Auf. Ay, Marcius, Caius Marcius: dost thou
  think
I'll grace thee with that robbery, thy stol'n name
Coriolanus in Corioli?   90
You lords and heads o' the state, perfidiously
He has betray'd your business, and given up,
For certain drops of salt, your city Rome,
I say 'your city,' to his wife and mother;
Breaking his oath and resolution like
A twist of rotten silk, never admitting
Counsel o' the war, but at his nurse's tears
He whined and roar'd away your victory,
That pages blush'd at him and men of heart
Look'd wondering each at other.
 Cor.   Hear'st thou, Mars? 100
 Auf. Name not the god, thou boy of tears!
 Cor.   Ha!
 Auf. No more.
 Cor. Measureless liar, thou hast made my heart
Too great for what contains it. Boy! O slave!
Pardon me, lords, 'tis the first time that ever
I was forced to scold. Your judgements, my
  grave lords,
Must give this cur the lie: and his own notion—
Who wears my stripes impress'd upon him; that
Must bear my beating to his grave—shall join
To thrust the lie unto him.   110
 First Lord. Peace, both, and hear me speak.
 Cor. Cut me to pieces, Volsces; men and lads,
Stain all your edges on me. Boy! false hound!
If you have writ your annals true, 'tis there,
That, like an eagle in a dove-cote, I
Flutter'd your Volscians in Corioli:
Alone I did it. Boy!
 Auf.   Why, noble lords,
Will you be put in mind of his blind fortune,
Which was your shame, by this unholy braggart,
'Fore your own eyes and ears?
 All Consp.   Let him die for't. 120
 All the people. 'Tear him to pieces.' 'Do it
presently.' 'He killed my son.' 'My daughter.'
'He killed my cousin Marcus.' 'He killed my
father.'
 Sec. Lord. Peace, ho! no outrage: peace!
The man is noble and his fame folds-in
This orb o' the earth. His last offences to us
Shall have judicious hearing. Stand, Aufidius,
And trouble not the peace.
 Cor.   O that I had him,
●With six Aufidiuses, or more, his tribe, 130
To use my lawful sword!
 Auf.   Insolent villain!
 All Consp. Kill, kill, kill, kill, kill him!
   [*The Conspirators draw, and kill Corio-*
    lanus: Aufidius stands on his body.
 Lords.   Hold, hold, hold, hold!
 Auf. My noble masters, hear me speak.
 First Lord.   O Tullus,—
 Sec. Lord. Thou hast done a deed whereat

valour will weep.
Third Lord. Tread not upon him. Masters
all, be quiet;
Put up your swords.
Auf. My lords, when you shall know—as in
this rage,
Provoked by him, you cannot—the great danger
Which this man's life did owe you, you'll rejoice
That he is thus cut off. Please it your honours
To call me to your senate, I'll deliver   141
Myself your loyal servant, or endure
Your heaviest censure.
First Lord.   Bear from hence his body;
And mourn you for him: let him be regarded
• As the most noble corse that ever herald
Did follow to his urn.
Sec. Lord.   His own impatience
Takes from Aufidius a great part of blame.
Let's make the best of it.
Auf.   My rage is gone;
And I am struck with sorrow. Take him up. 149
Help, three o' the chiefest soldiers; I'll be one.
Beat thou the drum, that it speak mournfully:
Trail your steel pikes. Though in this city he
Hath widow'd and unchilded many a one,
Which to this hour bewail the injury,
Yet he shall have a noble memory.
Assist.   [*Exeunt, bearing the body of Corio-
lanus. A dead march sounded.*

145 *corse.* Corpse.

Aufidius: 'My rage is gone; And I am struck with
sorrow.' Drawing by Henry Singleton (1766–1839)

Timon of Athens

1608

TIMON followed straight upon the heels of *Coriolanus* with which it has much in common, and it has many indications of the time. In his Plutarch Shakespeare noticed the stories of Timon and Alcibiades, and resolved to combine them for his next play. The situation was repeated from *Coriolanus*: both Timon and Alcibiades were alienated from their native city; Alcibiades was banished and returned to conquer and spare it, Timon banished himself.

The dramatist may also have looked up Lucian's version of Timon's story, perhaps in Latin; certainly not in Greek, for Greek was hardly at all taught in Elizabethan schools, and most of the names in the play are Latin.

The Theme, as with most of the tragedies, is the revelation of his own nature to the protagonist, as with King Lear, whether the self-discovery is adequate and convincing or not. With Timon it is not: he goes from one extreme to another, from prodigality and profuse liberality (Shakespeare may be recalling the old interlude on that theme) to the misanthropy induced by the discovery of the falseness of friends, the undependability of people who will accept one's hospitality and gifts, without giving anything in return, their unwillingness to come to one's help in time of need, the insincerity and hypocrisy of flatterers in one's prosperity, desertion in adversity, ingratitude – a subject on which Shakespeare was peculiarly sensitive (he must have been speaking out of his own experience).

Timon learns all this from bitter experience; he should have known it before, but what he finds suddenly and totally changes him, like a conversion, into a misanthrope. Apemantus, who is another Thersites from *Troilus and Cressida* and a complete cynic about men already, tells Timon the truth about himself: 'the middle of humanity thou never knewest, but the extremity of both ends.' And further:

> If thou didst put this sour cold habit on
> To castigate thy pride, 'twere well; but thou
> Dost it enforcedly.

So Timon's profuseness was a form of pride, and even of patronising others: he gets what is coming to him. On the other hand, he is capable of telling Apemantus the truth about himself too:

> If thou hadst not been born the worst of men
> Thou hadst been a knave and flatterer.

His reviling of men is but the other side of the coin.

So all illusions are exposed in this singularly disillusioned play, the first half of which is devoted to this theme – Timon's illusion (like Lear's).

The Play begins with a strong scene, in which the poet and the painter prepare to present their works to the lordly Timon as patron. This is highly contemporary; Shakespeare could have heard this sort of patter at Southampton's or some other great house. The painter inquires of the poet: 'You are rapt, sir, in some work, some dedication to the great lord.' The poet replies, with the bogus self-depreciation one knows so well,

> A thing slipped idly from me.

The poet commends the painter's work with: 'this comes off well and excellent.' The painter coyly disclaims praise: 'indifferent'. The poet then responds with a piece of outrageous flattery, the interest of which to us is that it tells us what Elizabethans looked for in a portrait – evidently speaking lifelikeness, plus art and grace:

> Admirable! How this grace
> Speaks his own standing! What a mental power
> This eye shoots forth! How big imagination
> Moves in this lip!

The painter is constrained to admit:

> It is a pretty mocking of the life.
> Here is a touch: is't good?

The poet assures him:

> I will say of it
> It tutors nature. Artificial strife
> Lives in these touches livelier than life.

Elizabethans used the word 'artificial' in praise, meaning 'artistic'; these exchanges give us an idea of their aesthetic standards.

This is followed by a banquet at which Timon entertains his lordly friends. We are given a nice parody of Court-flattery, which Shakespeare had had every opportunity of overhearing: 'Might we but have that happiness, my lord, that you would once use our hearts, whereby we might express some part of our zeals, we should think ourselves for ever perfect.'

Apemantus, the cynic, knows perfectly what this is worth and expresses his disbelief in men's assurances, in the *sententiae* of his Grace. Timon is already in debt; his faithful steward is driven to distraction to raise the wherewithal for such bounty, such senseless

Designs by Inigo Jones for Ben Jonson's The Masque of Queens, *February 2, 1609*

extravagance. Bankrupt, Timon tries to cash the assurances of these friends for help to tide him over. Each refuses with a different excuse. Timon invites them to a last banquet, where the covered dishes contain nothing but smoking hot water and stones, with which he pelts them and drives them away. He then departs into the wilderness of solitude and misanthropy.

The Jacobean Age. All this may be seen as a comment on the ostentation and vulgar extravagance, which boomed with the new régime. The financial strain of the war, with Elizabeth and Burghley's watchfulness, had kept things within bounds; with peace and prosperity they passed beyond them all. Neither James I nor his Queen had any idea of money; after Scotland, England was their milch-cow. The magnificent series of Court-masques – for which Ben Jonson was the poet and Inigo Jones the painter – had now begun and cost fortunes. It is interesting that Timon provided a masque with his first banquet.

The costly banquets of James's favourite, James Hay, were notorious; he was popular, too, because – though he got something like £200,000 out of the Exchequer – he ended up, Clarendon says, with not a stitch of land. He had spent it all. Many of his sort were forced to sell their lands to keep up with the improvident Stuarts. Timon is forced to this course: 'Let all my land be sold.' His steward knew the situation too well, but Timon would not listen – and there were many like that:

> His promises fly so beyond his state
> That what he speaks is all in debt: he owes
> For every word. He is so kind that he now
> Pays interest for't: his land's put to their books.

As for promises, the painter is able to tell us, 'Promising is the very air o'the time . . . To promise is most courtly and fashionable; performance . . . argues a great sickness in his judgment that makes it.' One academic critic asks, Why was Timon such a fool? But there were many people like that, and by this time Shakespeare knew that most of humanity were fools, of one sort or another. He puts the knowledge into the mouth of one of these lords, who describes Apemantus as 'opposite to humanity', precisely because he expresses the truth.

Gold and Virginia. In the absence of war people's minds were dominated by money, and religious bickering (that could not be presented on the stage, but we can imagine what Shakespeare thought of it). The first colony went out to Virginia to start Jamestown in 1607, but, instead of cultivating the soil, they gave themselves up to digging for gold, and were shortly starving. The year 1608 saw a gold-craze over there; the report came home, 'no talk, no hope, no work but to dig gold, wash gold, refine gold, load gold.' (In 1609 a large reinforcement was sent out, when the news of the wreck of the flagship on Bermuda provided the subject for *The Tempest*.) Meanwhile, the silly would-be colonists starved, and were forced to dig for roots for sustenance.

Timon digs for roots in the woods by the sea-shore – and finds gold. He has a whole speech on the subject:

> Gold! Yellow, glittering, precious gold!
> . . . Thus much of this will make
> Black white, foul fair, wrong right,
> Base noble, old young, coward valiant . . .
> This yellow slave
> Will knit and break religions, bless th'accursed,
> Make the hoar leprosy adored, place thieves
> And give them title, knee, and approbation
> With senators on the bench.

True enough: money has provided a golden (today, paper) route to the House of Lords. Old Lord Burghley had written in his Precepts that nobility was but ancient riches: he knew well enough, it was his own case.

Plague and Disease. A severe outbreak of plague marked much of 1608–9, and it is no less marked in the background of the play, with several references. When the news gets round that Timon has discovered gold, it brings all the wolves round the door once more, poet and painter, lords and senators, Alcibiades and his whores. To the senators come to greet him, thus Timon:

> I thank them, and would send them back the plague
> Could I but catch it for them.

He launches Alcibiades upon them as their plague, and for his own epitaph leaves:

> Seek not my name. A plague consume you wicked caitiffs left!
> Here lie I, Timon, who alive all living men did hate.

To Alcibiades' whores his wishes are:

> Give them diseases, leaving with thee their lust.
> Make use of thy salt hours. Season the slaves
> For tubs and baths; bring down rose-cheekèd youth
> To the tub – fast and the diet.

Venereal disease was rife in Jacobean London; and anyone who knows Forman's writings will recognise the authentic note in this:

> Be as a planetary plague when Jove
> Will o'er some high-viced city hang his poison
> In the sick air.

The scalpel is quite unsparing:

> Down with the nose –
> Down with it flat; take the bridge quite away.

The dramatist William Davenant, who liked to think that he was an Oxford by-blow of William Shakespeare's – and there was much to be said for it – lost his nose from syphilis.

There is even more of this kind of thing, an exposure of society from top to bottom – even blameless academics come in for a swipe:

> the learned pate
> Ducks to the golden fool –

as it might be Left-wing academics in our time prostituting their services to press-lords.

All this is expressed, as critics have noted, with 'passionate conviction'. What accounts for this, the increasing bitterness – one cannot mistake it – of these plays from *Hamlet* and *Troilus and Cressida*, that is, from 1601 onwards? E. K. Chambers, who enjoyed the liberal illusions of pre-1914 civilisation, was appalled. 'In each alike we find the same readiness of bitter criticism, the same remorseless analysis, probing and dissecting, as with a cruel scalpel, the intimate weaknesses and basenesses of mankind. In each, ideals are shattered, heroes are discrowned and stripped of their heroism, until it is with difficulty', he adds innocently, 'that our sympathies, so essential to the sense of tragedy, are retained.' But are they? It is more important to recognise the truth of the picture.

The Text offers a fascinating problem, as it was inserted in the Folio in the space intended for *Troilus and Cressida*, temporarily held up by copyright difficulties. *Timon* represents the author's rough draft, and from it we can see how he worked – visualising scenes and completing them as he felt inclined. Thus the beginning and end of the play are complete, and contain fine poetry. The middle of the play remains in rough draft, with Shakespeare jotting down his first thoughts sometimes in prose, sometimes in irregular blank verse, at others in rhymed couplets. We know that Ben Jonson wrote his verse first as prose – as his schoolmaster, Camden, had taught him – and then turned it into poetry. This is most unlikely to have been Shakespeare's way. As Heming and Condell, who knew, tell us: 'his mind and hand went together; and what he thought he uttered with easiness' . . . where Ben Jonson was notoriously constipated.

Our leading authority on the printing of the Folio, Charlton Hinman, says that *Timon* represented a 'not yet finally revised text, a version antecedent to "foul papers", as an author's last draft of a play is rather misleadingly called.' I agree: though usual, it is a rather absurd phrase.

HENRY HOLIDAY

TIMON OF ATHENS.

DRAMATIS PERSONÆ.

TIMON, of Athens.
LUCIUS,
LUCULLUS, } flattering lords.
SEMPRONIUS,
VENTIDIUS, one of Timon's false friends.
ALCIBIADES, an Athenian captain.
APEMANTUS, a churlish philosopher.
FLAVIUS, steward to Timon.
Poet, Painter, Jeweller, and Merchant.
An old Athenian.
FLAMINIUS,
LUCILIUS, } servants to Timon.
SERVILIUS,

CAPHIS,
PHILOTUS,
TITUS, } servants to Timon's creditors.
LUCIUS,
HORTENSIUS,
And others,
A Page.   A Fool.   Three Strangers.

PHRYNIA,
TIMANDRA, } mistresses to Alcibiades.

Cupid and Amazons in the mask.
Other Lords, Senators, Officers, Soldiers, Banditti, and Attendants.

SCENE: *Athens, and the neighbouring woods.*

● *A bullet beside a text line indicates an annotation in the opposite column.*

ACT I.

SCENE I.   *Athens.   A hall in Timon's house.*

Enter Poet, Painter, Jeweller, Merchant, *and others, at several doors.*

Poet.   Good day, sir.
Pain.   I am glad you're well.
Poet.   I have not seen you long: how goes the
    world?
Pain.   It wears, sir, as it grows.
Poet.   Ay, that's well known:
But what particular rarity? what strange,
Which manifold record not matches?   See,
Magic of bounty! all these spirits thy power
Hath conjured to attend.   I know the merchant.
Pain.   I know them both; th' other's a jeweller.
Mer.   O, 'tis a worthy lord.
Jew.   Nay, that's most fix'd.

Opposite: Timon, deserted by his friends, denounces them for their ingratitude. Painting by Henry Holiday, 1916

10 *breathed*. Accustomed.

12 *passes*. Excels.

18 *water*. The transparency of a diamond.

Poet: 'Our poesy is as a gum, which oozes From whence 'tis nourish'd.' Nineteenth century engraving from a Greek statue

---

35 *mocking*. Copy.

37 *artificial strife*. Artistic endeavour.

44 *beneath world*. i.e. the Earth.

47 *levell'd*. Aimed.

50 *tract*. Trace.

57 *properties*. Subjects. *tendance*. Attendance.

Mer. A most incomparable man, breathed, as it were,   10
To an untirable and continuate goodness:
He passes.
  Jew. I have a jewel here—
  Mer. O, pray, let's see't: for the Lord Timon, sir?
  Jew. If he will touch the estimate: but, for that—
  Poet. [*Reciting to himself*] 'When we for recompense have praised the vile,
It stains the glory in that happy verse
Which aptly sings the good.'
  Mer.   'Tis a good form.
      [*Looking at the jewel.*
  Jew. And rich: here is a water, look ye.
  Pain. You are rapt, sir, in some work, some dedication
To the great lord.
  Poet.   A thing slipp'd idly from me. 20
Our poesy is as a gum, which oozes
From whence 'tis nourish'd: the fire i' the flint
Shows not till it be struck; our gentle flame
Provokes itself and like the current flies
Each bound it chafes. What have you there?
  Pain. A picture, sir. When comes your book forth?
  Poet. Upon the heels of my presentment, sir.
Let's see your piece.
  Pain.   'Tis a good piece.
  Poet. So 'tis: this comes off well and excellent.
  Pain. Indifferent.
  Poet.   Admirable: how this grace 30
Speaks his own standing! what a mental power
This eye shoots forth! how big imagination
Moves in this lip! to the dumbness of the gesture
One might interpret.
  Pain. It is a pretty mocking of the life.
Here is a touch; is't good?
  Poet.   I will say of it,
It tutors nature: artificial strife
Lives in these touches, livelier than life.

    Enter certain Senators, *and pass over.*
  Pain. How this lord is follow'd!
  Poet. The senators of Athens: happy man!
  Pain. Look, more!   41
  Poet. You see this confluence, this great flood of visitors.
I have, in this rough work, shaped out a man,
Whom this beneath world doth embrace and hug
With amplest entertainment: my free drift
Halts not particularly, but moves itself
In a wide sea of wax: no levell'd malice
Infects one comma in the course I hold;
But flies an eagle flight, bold and forth on,
Leaving no tract behind.   50
  Pain. How shall I understand you?
  Poet.   I will unbolt to you.
You see how all conditions, how all minds,
As well of glib and slippery creatures as
Of grave and austere quality, tender down
Their services to Lord Timon: his large fortune
Upon his good and gracious nature hanging
Subdues and properties to his love and tendance
All sorts of hearts; yea, from the glass-faced flatterer
To Apemantus, that few things loves better
Than to abhor himself: even he drops down 60

The knee before him and returns in peace
Most rich in Timon's nod.
    Pain.   I saw them speak together.
    Poet. Sir, I have upon a high and pleasant
        hill
Feign'd Fortune to be throned: the base o' the
        mount
● Is rank'd with all deserts, all kind of natures,
That labour on the bosom of this sphere
To propagate their states: amongst them all,
Whose eyes are on this sovereign lady fix'd,
One do I personate of Lord Timon's frame,
Whom Fortune with her ivory hand wafts to her;
Whose present grace to present slaves and serv-
        ants   71
● Translates his rivals.
    Pain.   'Tis conceived to scope.
This throne, this Fortune, and this hill, methinks,
With one man beckon'd from the rest below,
Bowing his head against the steepy mount
To climb his happiness, would be well express'd
In our condition.
    Poet.   Nay, sir, but hear me on.
All those which were his fellows but of late,
Some better than his value, on the moment   79
Follow his strides, his lobbies fill with tendance,
Rain sacrificial whisperings in his ear,
Make sacred even his stirrup, and through him
Drink the free air.
    Pain.   Ay, marry, what of these?
    Poet. When Fortune in her shift and change
        of mood
Spurns down her late beloved, all his dependants
Which labour'd after him to the mountain's top
Even on their knees and hands, let him slip down,
Not one accompanying his declining foot.
    Pain. 'Tis common:
A thousand moral paintings I can show   90
That shall demonstrate these quick blows of
        Fortune's
More pregnantly than words. Yet you do well
To show Lord Timon that mean eyes have seen
The foot above the head.

Trumpets sound. Enter LORD TIMON, *address-
ing himself courteously to every suitor; a
Messenger from* VENTIDIUS *talking with him;*
LUCILIUS *and other servants following.*

    Tim.   Imprison'd is he, say you?
● *Mess.* Ay, my good lord: five talents is his
        debt,
His means most short, his creditors most strait:
Your honourable letter he desires
To those have shut him up; which failing,
Periods his comfort.
    Tim.   Noble Ventidius! Well;
I am not of that feather to shake off   100
My friend when he must need me. I do know
        him
A gentleman that well deserves a help:
Which he shall have: I'll pay the debt, and free
        him.
    Mess. Your lordship ever binds him.
    Tim. Commend me to him: I will send his
        ransom;
And being enfranchised, bid him come to me.
'Tis not enough to help the feeble up,
But to support him after. Fare you well.
    Mess. All happiness to your honour! [*Exit.*

65 *rank'd . . . deserts.* Lined with ranks of all kinds.

72 *Translates.* Transfers. *conceived to scope.* Devised to this purpose.

Poet: 'When Fortune in her shift and change of mood
Spurns down her late beloved . . .' Woodcut attributed
to Albrecht Dürer (1471–1528)

95 *five talents.* i.e. a large amount of money.

127 *her resort*. Access to her.

152 *Vouchsafe*. Accept.

Enter an old Athenian.

Old Ath.   Lord Timon, hear me speak.
Tim.   Freely, good father. 110
Old Ath.   Thou hast a servant named Lucilius.
Tim.   I have so: what of him?
Old Ath.   Most noble Timon, call the man
   before thee.
Tim.   Attends he here, or no?   Lucilius!
Luc.   Here, at your lordship's service.
Old Ath.   This fellow here, Lord Timon, this
   thy creature,
By night frequents my house.   I am a man
That from my first have been inclined to thrift:
And my estate deserves an heir more raised
Than one which holds a trencher.
Tim.   Well; what further? 120
Old Ath.   One only daughter have I, no kin
   else,
On whom I may confer what I have got:
The maid is fair, o' the youngest for a bride,
And I have bred her at my dearest cost
In qualities of the best.   This man of thine
Attempts her love: I prithee, noble lord,
●Join with me to forbid him her resort;
Myself have spoke in vain.
Tim.   The man is honest.
Old Ath.   Therefore he will be, Timon:
His honesty rewards him in itself: 130
It must not bear my daughter.
Tim.   Does she love him?
Old Ath.   She is young and apt:
Our own precedent passions do instruct us
What levity's in youth.
Tim.   [*To Lucilius*] Love you the maid?
Luc.   Ay, my good lord, and she accepts of it.
Old Ath.   If in her marriage my consent be
   missing,
I call the gods to witness, I will choose
Mine heir from forth the beggars of the world,
And dispossess her all.
Tim.   How shall she be endow'd,
If she be mated with an equal husband?   140
Old Ath.   Three talents on the present; in
   future, all.
Tim.   This gentleman of mine hath served me
   long:
To build his fortune I will strain a little,
For 'tis a bond in men.   Give him thy daughter:
What you bestow, in him I'll counterpoise,
And make him weigh with her.
Old Ath.   Most noble lord,
Pawn me to this your honour, she is his.
Tim.   My hand to thee; mine honour on my
   promise.
Luc.   Humbly I thank your lordship: never
   may
That state or fortune fall into my keeping,   150
Which is not owed to you!
            [*Exeunt Lucilius and Old Athenian.*
●   *Poet.* Vouchsafe my labour, and long live your
   lordship!
Tim.   I thank you; you shall hear from me
   anon:
Go not away.   What have you there, my friend?
Pain.   A piece of painting, which I do beseech
Your lordship to accept.
Tim.   Painting is welcome.
The painting is almost the natural man;

For since dishonour traffics with man's nature,
He is but outside: these pencill'd figures are
Even such as they give out.   I like your work;
And you shall find I like it: wait attendance   161
Till you hear further from me.
   Pain.   The gods preserve ye!
   Tim.   Well fare you, gentleman: give me your
     hand;
We must needs dine together.   Sir, your jewel
Hath suffer'd under praise.
   Jew.   What, my lord! dispraise?
   Tim.   A mere satiety of commendations.
If I should pay you for 't as 'tis extoll'd,
It would unclew me quite.
   Jew.   My lord, 'tis rated
As those which sell would give: but you well
     know,
Things of like value differing in the owners   170
Are prized by their masters: believe 't, dear lord,
You mend the jewel by the wearing it.
   Tim.   Well mock'd.
   Mer.   No, my good lord; he speaks the com-
     mon tongue,
Which all men speak with him.
   Tim.   Look, who comes here: will you be
     chid?

           Enter APEMANTUS.

   Jew.   We'll bear, with your lordship.
   Mer.   He'll spare none.
   Tim.   Good morrow to thee, gentle Apemantus!
   Apem.   Till I be gentle, stay thou for thy
     good morrow;
When thou art Timon's dog, and these knaves
     honest.   180
   Tim.   Why dost thou call them knaves? thou
     know'st them not.
   Apem.   Are they not Athenians?
   Tim.   Yes.
   Apem.   Then I repent not.
   Jew.   You know me, Apemantus?
   Apem.   Thou know'st I do: I call'd thee by
thy name.
   Tim.   Thou art proud, Apemantus.
   Apem.   Of nothing so much as that I am not
like Timon.   190
   Tim.   Whither art going?
   Apem.   To knock out an honest Athenian's
brains.
   Tim.   That's a deed thou'lt die for.
   Apem.   Right, if doing nothing be death by
the law.
   Tim.   How likest thou this picture, Apeman-
tus?
   Apem.   The best, for the innocence.
   Tim.   Wrought he not well that painted it? 200
   Apem.   He wrought better that made the
painter; and yet he's but a filthy piece of work.
   Pain.   You're a dog.
   Apem.   Thy mother's of my generation: what's
she, if I be a dog?
   Tim.   Wilt dine with me, Apemantus?
   Apem.   No; I eat not lords.
   Tim.   An thou shouldst, thou'ldst anger ladies.
   Apem.   O, they eat lords; so they come by
great bellies.   210
   Tim.   That's a lascivious apprehension.
   Apem.   So thou apprehendest it: take it for
thy labour.

158 *traffics with.* Corrupts.

168 *unclew.* Undo.

172 *mend.* Improve.

173 *mock'd.* Pretended.

Timon: 'How likest thou this picture, Apemantus?'
Engraving by Kenny Meadows from Barry Cornwall's
Works of Shakspere, 1846

211 *apprehension.* Interpretation.

217 *doit*. Coin of little worth.

244 *Traffic*. Trade.

261 *saved my longing*. i.e. prevented me from longing to see you.

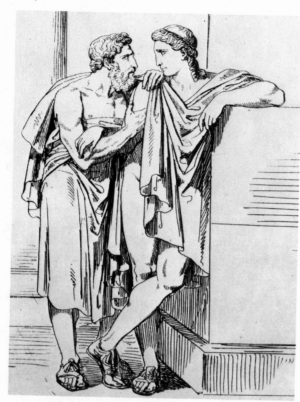

Timon: 'Right welcome, sir! Ere we depart, we'll share a bounteous time In different pleasures.' Engraving by Bartolomeo Pinelli, 1821

Tim. How dost thou like this jewel, Apemantus?

Apem. Not so well as plain-dealing, which will not cost a man a doit.

Tim. What dost thou think 'tis worth?

Apem. Not worth my thinking. How new, poet! 220

Poet. How now, philosopher!

Apem. Thou liest.

Poet. Art not one?

Apem. Yes.

Poet. Then I lie not.

Apem. Art not a poet?

Poet. Yes.

Apem. Then thou liest: look in thy last work, where thou hast feigned him a worthy fellow.

Poet. That's not feigned; he is so. 230

Apem. Yes, he is worthy of thee, and to pay thee for thy labour: he that loves to be flattered is worthy o' the flatterer. Heavens, that I were a lord!

Tim. What wouldst do then, Apemantus?

Apem. E'en as Apemantus does now; hate a lord with my heart.

Tim. What, thyself?

Apem. Ay.

Tim. Wherefore? 240

Apem. †That I had no angry wit to be a lord. Art not thou a merchant?

Mer. Ay, Apemantus.

Apem. Traffic confound thee, if the gods will not!

Mer. If traffic do it, the gods do it.

Apem. Traffic's thy god; and thy god confound thee!

Trumpet sounds.   Enter a Messenger.

Tim. What trumpet's that?

Mess. 'Tis Alcibiades, and some twenty horse, All of companionship. 251

Tim. Pray, entertain them; give them guide to us.   [*Exeunt some Attendants*.
You must needs dine with me: go not you hence Till I have thank'd you: when dinner's done, Show me this piece.   I am joyful of your sights.

Enter ALCIBIADES, *with the rest.*

Most welcome, sir!

Apem.   So, so, there!
Aches contract and starve your supple joints!
That there should be small love 'mongst these sweet knaves,
And all this courtesy!   The strain of man's bred out
Into baboon and monkey. 260

Alcib. Sir, you have saved my longing, and I feed
Most hungerly on your sight.

Tim.   Right welcome, sir!
Ere we depart, we'll share a bounteous time
In different pleasures.   Pray you, let us in.
        [*Exeunt all except Apemantus.*

Enter two Lords.

First Lord. What time o' day is't, Apemantus?

Apem. Time to be honest.

First Lord. That time serves still.

Apem. The more accursed thou, that still omitt'st it.

Sec. Lord. Thou art going to Lord Timon's
feast?   270
  Apem. Ay, to see meat fill knaves and wine
heat fools.
Sec. Lord. Fare thee well, fare thee well.
Apem. Thou art a fool to bid me farewell twice.
Sec. Lord. Why, Apemantus?
Apem. Shouldst have kept one to thyself, for
I mean to give thee none.
  First Lord. Hang thyself!
  Apem. No, I will do nothing at thy bidding:
make thy requests to thy friend.
  Sec. Lord. Away, unpeaceable dog, or I'll
spurn thee hence!   281
  Apem. I will fly, like a dog, the heels o' the
ass.   [*Exit.*
  First Lord. He's opposite to humanity.
    Come, shall we in,
And taste Lord Timon's bounty? he outgoes
The very heart of kindness.
  Sec. Lord. He pours it out; Plutus, the god
    of gold,
•Is but his steward: no meed, but he repays
Sevenfold above itself; no gift to him,
But breeds the giver a return exceeding   290
•All use of quittance.
  First Lord.   The noblest mind he carries
That ever govern'd man.
  Sec. Lord. Long may he live in fortunes!
    Shall we in?
  First Lord. I'll keep you company.
                     [*Exeunt.*

SCENE II. *A banqueting-room in Timon's
           house.*

*Hautboys playing loud music. A great banquet
served in; FLAVIUS and others attending;
then enter LORD TIMON, ALCIBIADES, Lords,
Senators, and VENTIDIUS. Then comes, dropping after all, APEMANTUS, discontentedly,
like himself.*

  Ven. Most honour'd Timon,
It hath pleased the gods to remember my father's
    age,
And call him to long peace.
He is gone happy, and has left me rich:
Then, as in grateful virtue I am bound
To your free heart, I do return those talents,
Doubled with thanks and service, from whose help
I derived liberty.
  Tim.   O, by no means,
Honest Ventidius; you mistake my love:
I gave it freely ever; and there's none   10
Can truly say he gives, if he receives:
If our betters play at that game, we must not dare
To imitate them; faults that are rich are fair.
  Ven. A noble spirit!
  Tim.   Nay, my lords,
  [*They all stand ceremoniously looking
                   on Timon.*
Ceremony was but devised at first
To set a gloss on faint deeds, hollow welcomes,
•Recanting goodness, sorry ere 'tis shown;
But where there is true friendship, there needs
    none.
Pray, sit; more welcome are ye to my fortunes
Than my fortunes to me.   [*They sit.* 20

288 *meed.* Present.

291 *All use of quittance.* All custom of repayment.

A banquet. Engraving from a Greek vase

17 *Recanting goodness.* i.e. favours taken back by the
giver.

26 *humour.* Temperament.

28 *'ira furor brevis est'.* Anger is a brief madness.

32 *apperil.* Peril.

48–49 *pledges . . . draught.* Drinks to his health from the shared cup.

52 *my . . . notes.* i.e. indiscretions.

Apemantus delivers his 'grace'. Engraving by Kenny Meadows from Barry Cornwall's *Complete Works of Shakespere*, 1857–59

63 *pelf.* Reward, possessions.

65 *fond.* Foolish.

73 *dich.* i.e. may it do.

First Lord. My lord, we always have confess'd it.
Apem. Ho, ho, confess'd it! hang'd it, have you not?
Tim. O, Apemantus, you are welcome.
Apem.   No;
You shall not make me welcome:
I come to have thee thrust me out of doors.
● *Tim.* Fie, thou'rt a churl; ye've got a humour there
Does not become a man; 'tis much to blame.
●They say, my lords, 'ira furor brevis est;' but yond man is ever angry.   Go, let him have a table by himself, for he does neither affect company, nor is he fit for't, indeed.   31
● *Apem.* Let me stay at thine apperil, Timon: I come to observe; I give thee warning on't.
Tim. I take no heed of thee; thou'rt an Athenian, therefore welcome: I myself would have no power; prithee, let my meat make thee silent.
Apem. I scorn thy meat; 'twould choke me, for I should ne'er flatter thee.   O you gods, what a number of men eat Timon, and he sees 'em not! It grieves me to see so many dip their meat in one man's blood; and all the madness is, he cheers them up too.
I wonder men dare trust themselves with men: Methinks they should invite them without knives; Good for their meat, and safer for their lives.
There's much example for 't; the fellow that sits
●next him now, parts bread with him, pledges the breath of him in a divided draught, is the readiest man to kill him: 't has been proved.   If I were a huge man, I should fear to drink at meals; 51
●Lest they should spy my windpipe's dangerous notes:
Great men should drink with harness on their throats.
Tim. My lord, in heart; and let the health go round.
Sec. Lord. Let it flow this way, my good lord.
Apem. Flow this way! A brave fellow! he keeps his tides well.   Those healths will make thee and thy state look ill, Timon.   Here's that which is too weak to be a sinner, honest water, which ne'er left man i' the mire: 60
This and my food are equals; there's no odds: Feasts are too proud to give thanks to the gods.

Apemantus' grace.

●   Immortal gods, I crave no pelf;
            I pray for no man but myself:
●   Grant I may never prove so fond,
            To trust man on his oath or bond;
            Or a harlot, for her weeping;
            Or a dog, that seems a-sleeping;
            Or a keeper with my freedom;
            Or my friends, if I should need 'em.   70
        Amen.   So fall to 't:
        Rich men sin, and I eat root.
                            [*Eats and drinks.*
●Much good †dich thy good heart, Apemantus!
Tim. Captain Alcibiades, your heart's in the field now.
Alcib. My heart is ever at your service, my lord.
Tim. You had rather be at a breakfast of enemies than a dinner of friends.   79

●   *Alcib.* So they were bleeding-new, my lord, there's no meat like 'em: I could wish my best friend at such a feast.

Apem. Would all those flatterers were thine enemies then, that then thou mightst kill 'em and bid me to 'em!

First Lord. Might we but have that happi-
●ness, my lord, that you would once use our hearts, whereby we might express some part of our zeals, we should think ourselves for ever perfect.   90

Tim. O, no doubt, my good friends, but the gods themselves have provided that I shall have much help from you: how had you been my friends else? why have you that charitable title from thousands, did not you chiefly belong to my heart? I have told more of you to myself than you can with modesty speak in your own behalf; and thus far I confirm you. O you gods, think I, what need we have any friends, if we should ne'er have need of 'em? they were the most need-less creatures living, should we ne'er have use for 'em, and would most resemble sweet instruments hung up in cases that keep their sounds to them-selves. Why, I have often wished myself poorer, that I might come nearer to you. We are born to do benefits: and what better or properer can we call our own than the riches of our friends? O, what a precious comfort 'tis, to have so many, like brothers, commanding one another's fortunes! O joy, e'en made away ere 't can be born! Mine eyes cannot hold out water, methinks: to forget their faults, I drink to you.

Apem. Thou weepest to make them drink, Timon.

● *Sec. Lord.* Joy had the like conception in our
          eyes
And at that instant like a babe sprung up.

Apem. Ho, ho! I laugh to think that babe a
          bastard.

Third Lord. I promise you, my lord, you
          moved me much.

Apem. Much!   [*Tucket, within.*

Tim. What means that trump?

Enter a Servant.

                                   How now?   120

Serv. Please you, my lord, there are certain ladies most desirous of admittance.

Tim. Ladies! what are their wills?

Serv. There comes with them a forerunner, my lord, which bears that office, to signify their pleasures.

Tim. I pray, let them be admitted.

Enter CUPID.

Cup. Hail to thee, worthy Timon, and to all
That of his bounties taste! The five best senses
Acknowledge thee their patron: and come freely
To gratulate thy plenteous bosom: th' ear,   131
Taste, touch and smell, pleased from thy table
          rise;
They only now come but to feast thine eyes.

Tim. They're welcome all; let 'em have kind
          admittance:
Music, make their welcome!   [*Exit Cupid.*

First Lord. You see, my lord, how ample
          you're beloved.

80 *new.* Afresh.

87–88 *use our hearts.* Test our love.

115 *like conception.* Similar start.

SD [*Tucket*]. Trumpet.

'Enter Cupid' Engraving from a painting by Domini-quin, 1803

137 *Hoy-day*. Well, well! *sweep*. Parade.

140 *oil and root*. i.e. simple diet.

Apemantus: 'We make ourselves fools, to disport ourselves;' Woodcut from Alexander Barclay's *The Ship
of Fools*, 1774

---

176 *advance*. Enhance in value.

Music. Re-enter CUPID, *with a mask of* Ladies
as Amazons, *with lutes in their hands, dancing and playing.*

● *Apem*. Hoy-day, what a sweep of vanity comes
  this way!
They dance! they are mad women.
Like madness is the glory of this life,
● As this pomp shows to a little oil and root. 140
We make ourselves fools, to disport ourselves;
And spend our flatteries, to drink those men
Upon whose age we void it up again,
With poisonous spite and envy.
Who lives that's not depraved or depraves?
Who dies, that bears not one spurn to their graves
Of their friends' gift?
I should fear those that dance before me now
Would one day stamp upon me: 'thas been done;
Men shut their doors against a setting sun. 150

The Lords *rise from table, with much adoring
of* TIMON; *and to show their loves, each singles
out an* Amazon, *and all dance, men with
women, a lofty strain or two to the hautboys,
and cease.*

 Tim. You have done our pleasures much grace,
  fair ladies,
Set a fair fashion on our entertainment,
Which was not half so beautiful and kind;
You have added worth unto 't and lustre,
And entertain'd me with mine own device;
I am to thank you for 't.
 First Lady. My lord, you take us even at the
  best.
 Apem. 'Faith, for the worst is filthy; and
would not hold taking, I doubt me.
 Tim. Ladies, there is an idle banquet attends
  you: 160
Please you to dispose yourselves.
 All Ladies. Most thankfully, my lord.
     [Exeunt Cupid and Ladies.
 Tim. Flavius,
 Flav. My lord?
 Tim.   The little casket bring me hither.
 Flav. Yes, my lord. More jewels yet! *[Aside.*
There is no crossing him in 's humour;
Else I should tell him,—well, i' faith, I should,
When all's spent, he'ld be cross'd then, an he
  could.
'Tis pity bounty had not eyes behind,
That man might ne'er be wretched for his mind.
          [Exit.
 First Lord. Where be our men? 171
 Serv. Here, my lord, in readiness.
 Sec. Lord. Our horses!

 Re-enter FLAVIUS, *with the casket.*

 Tim.   O my friends,
I have one word to say to you: look you, my
  good lord,
I must entreat you, honour me so much
● As to advance this jewel; accept it and wear it,
Kind my lord.
 First Lord. I am so far already in your gifts,—
 All. So are we all.

   Enter a Servant.

 Serv. My lord, there are certain nobles of the
  senate 180

Newly alighted, and come to visit you.
Tim. They are fairly welcome.
Flav.   I beseech your honour,
Vouchsafe me a word; it does concern you near.
Tim. Near! why then, another time I'll hear
   thee:
I prithee, let's be provided to show them enter-
   tainment.
Flav. [*Aside*] I scarce know how.

Enter a second Servant.

Sec. Serv. May it please your honour, Lord
   Lucius,
Out of his free love, hath presented to you
Four milk-white horses, trapp'd in silver.
Tim. I shall accept them fairly; let the presents
Be worthily entertain'd.

Enter a third Servant.

                    How now! what news? 191
Third Serv. Please you, my lord, that honour-
able gentleman, Lord Lucullus, entreats your
company to-morrow to hunt with him, and has sent
your honour two brace of greyhounds.
Tim. I'll hunt with him; and let them be re-
   ceived,
Not without fair reward.
Flav.   [*Aside*] What will this come to?
He commands us to provide, and give great gifts,
And all out of an empty coffer:
Nor will he know his purse, or yield me this, 200
To show him what a beggar his heart is,
Being of no power to make his wishes good:
His promises fly so beyond his state
That what he speaks is all in debt; he owes
For every word: he is so kind that he now
Pays interest for't; his land's put to their books.
Well, would I were gently put out of office
Before I were forced out!
Happier is he that has no friend to feed
Than such that do e'en enemies exceed.   210
I bleed inwardly for my lord.   [*Exit.*
   Tim.   You do yourselves
Much wrong, you bate too much of your own
   merits:
Here, my lord, a trifle of our love.
Sec. Lord. With more than common thanks I
   will receive it.
Third Lord. O, he's the very soul of bounty!
Tim. And now I remember, my lord, you gave
Good words the other day of a bay courser
I rode on: it is yours, because you liked it.
Sec. Lord. O, I beseech you, pardon me, my
   lord, in that.
Tim. You may take my word, my lord; I know,
   no man   220
Can justly praise but what he does affect:
I weigh my friend's affection with mine own;
I'll tell you true. I'll call to you.
All Lords.   O, none so welcome.
Tim. I take all and your several visitations
So kind to heart, 'tis not enough to give;
Methinks, I could deal kingdoms to my friends,
And ne'er be weary. Alcibiades,
Thou art a soldier, therefore seldom rich;
It comes in charity to thee: for all thy living
Is 'mongst the dead, and all the lands thou hast
Lie in a pitch'd field.
   Alcib.   Ay, defiled land, my lord. 231

Third Servant: '... and has sent your honour two brace of greyhounds.' Woodcut from Edward Topsell's *The History of Four-footed Beasts*, 1658

206 *put to their books.* i.e. mortgaged.

212 *bate.* Undervalue.

217 *courser.* Race horse.

221 *affect.* i.e. 'feel' and 'wish for'.

237 *coil.* Fuss.

238 *becks.* Curtsies and bows.

248 *in paper.* i.e. by promissory notes.

Senator: 'steal but a beggar's dog ...' Woodcut from
The Roxburghe Ballads, 17th century

12-13 *no reason ... safety.* i.e. it is unreasonable to
believe his estate can survive.

20 *uses.* Needs.

22 *fracted.* Broken.

26 *turn'd.* Returned.

First Lord.   We are so virtuously bound—
Tim.   And so
Am I to you.
  Sec. Lord.   So infinitely endear'd—
  Tim.   All to you.   Lights, more lights!
  First Lord.   The best of happiness,
Honour and fortunes, keep with you, Lord Timon!
  Tim.   Ready for his friends.
        [*Exeunt all but Apemantus and Timon.*
  Apem.   What a coil's here!
Serving of becks and jutting-out of bums!
I doubt whether their legs be worth the sums
That are given for 'em.   Friendship's full of dregs:
Methinks, false hearts should never have sound
        legs.
Thus honest fools lay out their wealth on court'sies.
  Tim.   Now, Apemantus, if thou wert not sullen,
I would be good to thee.
  Apem.   No, I'll nothing: for if I should be bribed
too, there would be none left to rail upon thee,
and then thou wouldst sin the faster.   Thou givest
so long, Timon, I fear me thou wilt give away
thyself in paper shortly: what need these feasts,
pomps and vain-glories?   249
  Tim.   Nay, an you begin to rail on society
once, I am sworn not to give regard to you.
Farewell; and come with better music.   [*Exit.*
  Apem.   So:
Thou wilt not hear me now; thou shalt not then:
I'll lock thy heaven from thee.
O, that men's ears should be
To counsel deaf, but not to flattery!   [*Exit.*

ACT II.

SCENE I.   *A Senator's house.*

Enter Senator, *with papers in his hand.*

  Sen.   And late, five thousand: to Varro and to
        Isidore
He owes nine thousand; besides my former sum,
Which makes it five and twenty.   Still in motion
Of raging waste?   It cannot hold; it will not.
If I want gold, steal but a beggar's dog,
And give it Timon, why, the dog coins gold.
If I would sell my horse, and buy twenty more
Better than he, why, give my horse to Timon,
Ask nothing, give it him, it foals me, straight,
And able horses.   No porter at his gate,   10
But rather one that smiles and still invites
All that pass by.   It cannot hold; no reason
Can found his state in safety.   Caphis, ho!
Caphis, I say!

Enter CAPHIS.

  Caph.   Here, sir; what is your pleasure?
  Sen.   Get on your cloak, and haste you to Lord
        Timon;
Importune him for my moneys; be not ceased
With slight denial, nor then silenced when—
'Commend me to your master'—and the cap
Plays in the right hand, thus: but tell him,
My uses cry to me, I must serve my turn   20
Out of mine own; his days and times are past
And my reliances on his fracted dates
Have smit my credit: I love and honour him,
But must not break my back to heal his finger;
Immediate are my needs, and my relief
Must not be toss'd and turn'd to me in words,
But find supply immediate.   Get you gone:

Put on a most importunate aspect,
A visage of demand; for, I do fear,
●When every feather sticks in his own wing,   30
Lord Timon will be left a naked gull,
●Which flashes now a phœnix. Get you gone.
 Caph. I go, sir.
 Sen. 'I go, sir!'—Take the bonds along with
 you,
●And have the dates in compt.
 Caph.   I will, sir.
 Sen.   Go. [*Exeunt.*

SCENE II. *The same. A hall in Timon's house.*

Enter FLAVIUS, *with many bills in his hand.*

 Flavius. No care, no stop! so senseless of ex-
  pense,
That he will neither know how to maintain it,
●Nor cease his flow of riot: takes no account
How things go from him, nor resumes no care
Of what is to continue: never mind
Was to be so unwise, to be so kind.
●What shall be done? he will not hear, till feel:
I must be round with him, now he comes from
  hunting.
Fie, fie, fie, fie!

Enter CAPHIS, *and the* Servants *of* ISIDORE
and VARRO.

 Caph. Good even, Varro: what,
You come for money?
 Var. Serv. Is't not your business too? 10
 Caph. It is: and yours too, Isidore?
 Isid. Serv.   It is so.
 Caph. Would we were all discharged!
 Var. Serv.   I fear it.
 Caph. Here comes the lord.

Enter TIMON, ALCIBIADES, *and* Lords, *&c.*

 Tim. So soon as dinner's done, we'll forth
  again,
My Alcibiades. With me? what is your will?
 Caph. My lord, here is a note of certain dues.
 Tim. Dues! Whence are you?
 Caph.   Of Athens here, my lord.
 Tim. Go to my steward.
 Caph. Please it your lordship, he hath put me off
●To the succession of new days this month: 20
●My master is awaked by great occasion
To call upon his own, and humbly prays you
●That with your other noble parts you'll suit
In giving him his right.
 Tim.   Mine honest friend,
I prithee, but repair to me next morning.
 Caph. Nay, good my lord,—
 Tim.   Contain thyself, good friend.
 Var. Serv. One Varro's servant, my good
  lord,—
 Isid Serv.   From Isidore;
He humbly prays your speedy payment.
 Caph. If you did know, my lord, my master's
  wants—
 Var. Serv. 'Twas due on forfeiture, my lord,
  six weeks   30
And past.
 Isid. Serv. Your steward puts me off, my lord;
And I am sent expressly to your lordship.
 Tim. Give me breath.
●I do beseech you, good my lords, keep on;

30 *every feather.* Allusion to fable of the crow which
stole feathers from other birds.

32 *phœnix.* Mythical immortal bird.

The phoenix, which regenerated itself from its own
ashes. Engraving from a painting by Raphael, 1811

---

35 *the dates in compt.* i.e. all the detailed accounts.

3 *riot.* Extravagance.

7 *till feel.* Until he feels it.

20 *succession of new days.* From one day to the next.

21 *awaked.* Forced. *occasion.* Necessity.

23 *suit.* Act accordingly.

34 *keep.* Wait.

61 *bawds.* Go-betweens.

69 *Gramercies.* Many thanks.

73 *Corinth.* Alluding to the licentious reputation of ancient Corinth.

79 *rod.* Stick to chastise you with.

81–82 *superscription.* Addresses.

Apemantus: 'Go; thou wast born a bastard, and thou't die a bawd.' Engraving by Kenny Meadows from Barry Cornwall's *Works of Shakspere*, 1846

I'll wait upon you instantly.
　　　　　[*Exeunt Alcibiades and Lords.*
　　　　　[*To Flav.*] Come hither: pray you,
How goes the world, that I am thus encounter'd
With clamorous demands of date-broke bonds,
And the detention of long-since-due debts,
Against my honour?
　Flav.　　　　　Please you, gentlemen,　40
The time is unagreeable to this business:
Your importunacy cease till after dinner,
That I may make his lordship understand
Wherefore you are not paid.
　Tim.　Do so, my friends.　See them well en-
tertain'd.　　　　　　　　　　[*Exit.*
　Flav.　Pray, draw near.　　　　[*Exit.*

　　　Enter APEMANTUS *and* Fool.

　Caph.　Stay, stay, here comes the fool with
Apemantus: let's ha' some sport with 'em.
　Var. Serv.　Hang him, he'll abuse us.
　Isid. Serv.　A plague upon him, dog!　50
　Var. Serv.　How dost, fool?
　Apem.　Dost dialogue with thy shadow?
　Var. Serv.　I speak not to thee.
　Apem.　No, 'tis to thyself. [*To the Fool*]
Come away.
　Isid. Serv.　There's the fool hangs on your
back already.
　Apem.　No, thou stand'st single, thou'rt not
on him yet.
　Caph.　Where's the fool now?
　Apem.　He last asked the question.　Poor
rogues, and usurers' men! bawds between gold
and want!
　All Serv.　What are we, Apemantus?
　Apem.　Asses.
　All Serv.　Why?
　Apem.　That you ask me what you are, and do
not know yourselves.　Speak to 'em, fool.
　Fool.　How do you, gentlemen?
　All Serv.　Gramercies, good fool: how does
your mistress?　　　　　　　　　70
　Fool.　She's e'en setting on water to scald such
chickens as you are.　Would we could see you at
Corinth!
　Apem.　Good! gramercy.

　　　Enter Page.

　Fool.　Look you, here comes my mistress' page.
　Page. [*To the Fool*] Why, how now, captain!
what do you in this wise company?　How dost
thou, Apemantus?
　Apem.　Would I had a rod in my mouth, that
I might answer thee profitably.　80
　Page.　Prithee, Apemantus, read me the su-
perscription of these letters: I know not which is
which.
　Apem.　Canst not read?
　Page.　No.
　Apem.　There will little learning die then, that
day thou art hanged.　This is to Lord Timon;
this to Alcibiades.　Go; thou wast born a bas-
tard, and thou't die a bawd.　89
　Page.　Thou wast whelped a dog, and thou
shalt famish a dog's death.　Answer not; I am
gone.　　　　　　　　　　　[*Exit.*
　Apem.　E'en so thou outrunnest grace.　Fool,
I will go with you to Lord Timon's.
　Fool.　Will you leave me there?

Apem. If Timon stay at home. You three serve three usurers?

All Serv. Ay; would they served us!

Apem. So would I,—as good a trick as ever hangman served thief.   100

Fool. Are you three usurers' men?

All Serv. Ay, fool.

Fool. I think no usurer but has a fool to his servant: my mistress is one, and I am her fool. When men come to borrow of your masters, they approach sadly, and go away merry; but they enter my mistress' house merrily, and go away sadly: the reason of this?

Var. Serv. I could render one.   109

Apem. Do it then, that we may account thee a whore-master and a knave; which notwithstanding, thou shalt be no less esteemed.

Var. Serv. What is a whoremaster, fool?

Fool. A fool in good clothes, and something like thee. 'Tis a spirit: sometime 't appears like a lord; sometime like a lawyer; sometime like a philosopher, with two stones moe than's artificial one: he is very often like a knight; and, generally, in all shapes that man goes up and down in from fourscore to thirteen, this spirit walks in.   121

Var. Serv. Thou art not altogether a fool.

Fool. Nor thou altogether a wise man: as much foolery as I have, so much wit thou lackest.

Apem. That answer might have become Apemantus.

All Serv. Aside, aside; here comes Lord Timon.

Re-enter TIMON *and* FLAVIUS.

Apem. Come with me, fool, come.

Fool. I do not always follow lover, elder brother and woman; sometime the philosopher. 131

                    [Exeunt Apemantus and Fool.

Flav. Pray you, walk near: I'll speak with you anon.   *[Exeunt Servants.*

Tim. You make me marvel: wherefore ere this time
Had you not fully laid my state before me,
That I might so have rated my expense,
As I had leave of means?

Flav.   You would not hear me,
At many leisures I proposed.

Tim.   Go to:
Perchance some single vantages you took,
When my indisposition put you back:
And that unaptness made your minister,   140
Thus to excuse yourself.

Flav.   O my good lord,
At many times I brought in my accounts,
Laid them before you; you would throw them off,
And say, you found them in mine honesty.
When, for some trifling present, you have bid me
Return so much, I have shook my head and wept;
Yea, 'gainst the authority of manners, pray'd you
To hold your hand more close: I did endure
Not seldom, nor no slight checks, when I have
Prompted you in the ebb of your estate   150
And your great flow of debts. My loved lord,
Though you hear now, too late—yet now's a time—
The greatest of your having lacks a half
To pay your present debts.

Tim.   Let all my land be sold.

117–18 *philosopher...one.* i.e. an alchemist who transformed base metal into gold, by a 'philosopher's stone' (with bawdy innuendo).

Alchemist at work. Detail from an engraving by Peter Bruegel the elder, 1558

137 *leisures.* Occasions when you were free.

138 *single vantages.* Particular occasions.

144 *in mine honesty.* i.e. you trusted that everything was correct because I appeared honest.

149 *Not . . . checks.* i.e. frequent and severe reprimands.

153 *The . . . half.* Everything you own is not even half enough.

160 *Lacedæmon.* i.e. Sparta.

167 *offices.* Quarters. *oppress'd.* Crowded.

171 *wasteful cock.* A wine tap left open in waste.

175 *englutted.* Swallowed down.

181 *flies are couch'd.* Parasites are hidden.

Timon: 'Come, sermon me no further:' Engraving by Kenny Meadows from Barry Cornwall's *The Works of Shakspere*, 1846

189 *Assurance . . . thoughts.* May you be proved right.

Flav. 'Tis all engaged, some forfeited and gone;
And what remains will hardly stop the mouth
Of present dues: the future comes apace:
What shall defend the interim? and at length
How goes our reckoning?
● *Tim.* To Lacedæmon did my land extend. 160
Flav. O my good lord, the world is but a word:
Were it all yours to give it in a breath,
How quickly were it gone!
Tim.   You tell me true.
Flav. If you suspect my husbandry or falsehood,
Call me before the exactest auditors
And set me on the proof.   So the gods bless me,
● When all our offices have been oppress'd
With riotous feeders, when our vaults have wept
With drunken spilth of wine, when every room
Hath blazed with lights and bray'd with minstrelsy, 170
● I have retired me to a wasteful cock,
And set mine eyes at flow.
Tim.   Prithee, no more.
Flav. Heavens, have I said, the bounty of this lord!
How many prodigal bits have slaves and peasants
● This night englutted! Who is not Timon's?
What heart, head, sword, force, means, but is Lord Timon's?
Great Timon, noble, worthy, royal Timon!
Ah, when the means are gone that buy this praise,
The breath is gone whereof this praise is made:
Feast-won, fast-lost; one cloud of winter showers,
● These flies are couch'd.
Tim.   Come, sermon me no further:
No villanous bounty yet hath pass'd my heart;
Unwisely, not ignobly, have I given.
Why dost thou weep? Canst thou the conscience lack,
To think I shall lack friends? Secure thy heart;
If I would broach the vessels of my love,
And try the argument of hearts by borrowing,
Men and men's fortunes could I frankly use
As I can bid thee speak.
● *Flav.*   Assurance bless your thoughts!
Tim. And, in some sort, these wants of mine are crown'd, 190
That I account them blessings; for by these
Shall I try friends: you shall perceive how you
Mistake my fortunes; I am wealthy in my friends.
Within there! Flaminius! Servilius!

Enter FLAMINIUS, SERVILIUS, *and other*
Servants.

Servants. My lord? my lord?
Tim. I will dispatch you severally; you to Lord Lucius; to Lord Lucullus you: I hunted with his honour to-day: you, to Sempronius: commend me to their loves, and, I am proud, say, that my occasions have found time to use 'em toward a supply of money: let the request be fifty talents.
Flam. As you have said, my lord.
Flav. [*Aside*] Lord Lucius and Lucullus? hum!
Tim. Go you, sir, to the senators—
Of whom, even to the state's best health, I have

Deserved this hearing—bid 'em send o' the
    instant
A thousand talents to me.
    Flav.   I have been bold—
For that I knew it the most general way—
• To them to use your signet and your name ;   210
But they do shake their heads, and I am here
No richer in return.
    Tim.   Is't true? can't be?
    Flav. They answer, in a joint and corporate
        voice,
That now they are at fall, want treasure, cannot
Do what they would ; are sorry—you are hon-
    ourable,—
But yet they could have wish'd—they know not—
Something hath been amiss—a noble nature
• May catch a wrench—would all were well—'tis
        pity ;—
And so, intending other serious matters,
• After distasteful looks and these hard fractions,
• With certain half-caps and cold-moving nods
They froze me into silence.
    Tim.   You gods, reward them !
Prithee, man, look cheerly.   These old fellows
Have their ingratitude in them hereditary :
Their blood is caked, 'tis cold, it seldom flows ;
'Tis lack of kindly warmth they are not kind ;
And nature, as it grows again toward earth,
Is fashion'd for the journey, dull and heavy.
[*To a Serv.*] Go to Ventidius.   [*To Flav.*] Pri-
    thee, be not sad,   229
• Thou art true and honest ; ingeniously I speak,
No blame belongs to thee.   [*To Ser.*] Ventidius
    lately
Buried his father ; by whose death he's stepp'd
Into a great estate : when he was poor,
Imprison'd and in scarcity of friends,
I clear'd him with five talents : greet him from
    me ;
• Bid him suppose some good necessity
Touches his friend, which craves to be remem-
    ber'd
With those five talents [*Exit Ser.*].   [*To Flav.*]
    That had, give't these fellows
To whom 'tis instant due.   Ne'er speak, or think,
That Timon's fortunes 'mong his friends can sink.
    Flav. I would I could not think it : that
        thought is bounty's foe ;
Being free itself, it thinks all others so. [*Exeunt.*

ACT III.

Scene I. *A room in Lucullus' house.*

Flaminius *waiting.   Enter a* Servant *to him.*

Serv. I have told my lord of you ; he is coming
    down to you.
Flam. I thank you, sir.

Enter Lucullus.

Serv. Here's my lord.
Lucul. [*Aside*] One of Lord Timon's men? a
gift, I warrant.   Why, this hits right ; I dreamt
of a silver basin and ewer to-night.   Flaminius,
honest Flaminius ; you are very respectively welcome, sir.   Fill me some wine.   [*Exit Servant.*]
And how does that honourable, complete, free-
hearted gentleman of Athens, thy very bountiful
good lord and master?   11

---

210 *signet.* Signet ring.

218 *May . . . wrench.* May be caught out.

220 *fractions.* Fractious remarks.

221 *half-caps.* Half-hearted salutations.

Ralph Richardson as Timon, Old Vic Theatre, London,
1956

---

230 *ingeniously.* Sincerely.

236–237 *good . . . Touches.* Real need affects.

Lucullus: 'Here's to thee.' Engraving from a classical Greek vase

---

45 *solidares*. Shillings.

46 *wink at*. Close your eyes to.

66 *hour*. Last hour.

Flam. His health is well, sir.

Lucul. I am right glad that his health is well, sir: and what hast thou there under thy cloak, pretty Flaminius?

Flam. 'Faith, nothing but an empty box, sir; which, in my lord's behalf, I come to entreat your honour to supply; who, having great and instant occasion to use fifty talents, hath sent to your lordship to furnish him, nothing doubting your present assistance therein. 21

Lucul. La, la, la, la! 'nothing doubting,' says he? Alas, good lord! a noble gentleman 'tis, if he would not keep so good a house. Many a time and often I ha' dined with him, and told him on't, and come again to supper to him, of purpose to have him spend less, and yet he would embrace no counsel, take no warning by my coming. Every man has his fault, and honesty is his: I ha' told him on't, but I could ne'er get him from't. 31

Re-enter Servant, *with wine.*

Serv. Please your lordship, here is the wine.

Lucul. Flaminius, I have noted thee always wise. Here's to thee.

Flam. Your lordship speaks your pleasure.

Lucul. I have observed thee always for a towardly prompt spirit—give thee thy due—and one that knows what belongs to reason; and canst use the time well, if the time use thee well: good parts in thee. [*To Serv.*] Get you gone, sirrah [*Exit Serv.*]. Draw nearer, honest Flaminius. Thy lord's a bountiful gentleman: but thou art wise; and thou knowest well enough, although thou comest to me, that this is no time to lend money, especially upon bare friendship, without security. Here's three solidares for thee: good boy, wink at me, and say thou sawest me not. Fare thee well.

Flam. Is't possible the world should so much differ,
And we alive that lived? Fly, damned baseness,
To him that worships thee! 51
[*Throwing the money back.*

Lucul. Ha! now I see thou art a fool, and fit for thy master. [*Exit.*

Flam. May these add to the number that may scald thee!
Let molten coin be thy damnation,
Thou disease of a friend, and not himself!
Has friendship such a faint and milky heart,
It turns in less than two nights? O you gods,
I feel my master's passion! this slave,
Unto his honour, has my lord's meat in him: 60
Why should it thrive and turn to nutriment,
When he is turn'd to poison?
O, may diseases only work upon't!
And, when he's sick to death, let not that part of nature
Which my lord paid for, be of any power
To expel sickness, but prolong his hour! [*Exit.*

SCENE II. *A public place.*

Enter LUCIUS, *with three* Strangers.

Luc. Who, the Lord Timon? he is my very good friend, and an honourable gentleman.

First Stran. We know him for no less, though we are but strangers to him. But I can tell you one thing, my lord, and which I hear from common rumours: now Lord Timon's happy hours are done and past, and his estate shrinks from him.

Luc. Fie, no, do not believe it; he cannot want for money. 10

Sec. Stran. But believe you this, my lord, that, not long ago, one of his men was with the Lord Lucullus to borrow so many talents, nay, urged extremely for't and showed what necessity belonged to't, and yet was denied.

Luc. How!

Sec. Stran. I tell you, denied, my lord.

Luc. What a strange case was that! now, before the gods, I am ashamed on't. Denied that honourable man! there was very little honour showed in't. For my own part, I must needs confess, I have received some small kindnesses from him, as money, plate, jewels and such-like trifles, nothing comparing to his; yet, had he mistook him and sent to me, I should ne'er have denied his occasion so many talents.

Enter SERVILIUS.

Ser. See, by good hap, yonder's my lord; I have sweat to see his honour. My honoured lord,— [*To Lucius.*

Luc. Servilius! you are kindly met, sir. Fare thee well: commend me to thy honourable virtuous lord, my very exquisite friend.

Ser. May it please your honour, my lord hath sent—

Luc. Ha! what has he sent? I am so much endeared to that lord; he's ever sending: how shall I thank him, thinkest thou? And what has he sent now?

Ser. Has only sent his present occasion now, my lord; requesting your lordship to supply his instant use with so many talents. 41

Luc. I know his lordship is but merry with me;
†He cannot want fifty five hundred talents.

Ser. But in the mean time he wants less, my lord.

●If his occasion were not virtuous,
I should not urge it half so faithfully.

Luc. Dost thou speak seriously, Servilius?

Ser. Upon my soul, 'tis true, sir.

Luc. What a wicked beast was I to disfurnish myself against such a good time, when I might ha' shown myself honourable! how unluckily it happened, that I should purchase the day before
●for a little part, and undo a great deal of honour! Servilius, now, before the gods, I am not able to do,—the more beast, I say:—I was sending to use Lord Timon myself, these gentlemen can witness; but I would not, for the wealth of Athens, I had done't now. Commend me bountifully to his good lordship; and I hope his honour will conceive the fairest of me, because I have no power to be kind: and tell him this from me, I count it one of my greatest afflictions, say, that I cannot pleasure such an honourable gentleman. Good Servilius, will you befriend me so far, as to use mine own words to him?

Ser. Yes, sir, I shall.

Luc. I'll look you out a good turn, Servilius.
[*Exit Servilius.*

True, as you said, Timon is shrunk indeed;

45 *virtuous.* Valid.

53 *for a little part.* i.e. for only a small amount of honour.

Athenian citizens. Nineteenth century engraving from Greek statues

69 *speed*. Succeed.

94 *policy*. Self-interest.

Sempronius: 'Must he needs trouble me in 't ...'
Engraving by Kenny Meadows from Barry Cornwall's
The Works of Shakspere, 1846

6 *touch'd*. Tested. Gold and silver alloys may be identified by use of a touchstone, on which they make different coloured marks.

14 *my place*. i.e. among his friends.

19 *I'll ... last*. I shall be the last to settle with him.

26 *bates*. Undervalues.

● And he that's once denied will hardly speed.
　　　　　　　　　　　　　　　　　　[*Exit*.
First Stran. Do you observe this, Hostilius?
Sec. Stran.　　　　　　Ay, too well. 70
First Stran. Why, this is the world's soul;
　　and just of the same piece
Is every flatterer's spirit. Who can call him
His friend that dips in the same dish? for, in
My knowing, Timon has been this lord's father,
And kept his credit with his purse,
Supported his estate; nay, Timon's money
Has paid his men their wages: he ne'er drinks,
But Timon's silver treads upon his lip;
And yet—O, see the monstrousness of man
When he looks out in an ungrateful shape!— 80
He does deny him, in respect of his,
What charitable men afford to beggars.
　　Third Stran. Religion groans at it.
　　First Stran.　　　　For mine own part,
I never tasted Timon in my life,
Nor came any of his bounties over me,
To mark me for his friend; yet, I protest,
For his right noble mind, illustrious virtue
And honourable carriage,
Had his necessity made use of me,
I would have put my wealth into donation, 90
And the best half should have return'd to him,
So much I love his heart: but, I perceive,
Men must learn now with pity to dispense;
● For policy sits above conscience. [*Exeunt*.

SCENE III. *A room in Sempronius' house.*

Enter SEMPRONIUS, *and a* Servant *of* TIMON'S.

　Sem. Must he needs trouble me in 't,—hum!
　—'bove all others?
He might have tried Lord Lucius or Lucullus;
And now Ventidius is wealthy too,
Whom he redeem'd from prison: all these
Owe their estates unto him.
　Serv.　　　　　　My lord,
● They have all been touch'd and found base metal,
　　for
They have all denied him.
　Sem.　　　　How! have they denied him?
Has Ventidius and Lucullus denied him?
And does he send to me? Three? hum!
It shows but little love or judgement in him: 10
Must I be his last refuge? His friends, like
　　physicians,
†Thrive, give him over: must I take the cure
　　upon me?
Has much disgraced me in 't; I'm angry at him,
● That might have known my place: I see no sense
　　for't,
But his occasions might have woo'd me first;
For, in my conscience, I was the first man
That e'er received gift from him:
And does he think so backwardly of me now,
● That I'll requite it last? No:
So it may prove an argument of laughter 20
To the rest, and 'mongst lords I be thought a fool.
I'ld rather than the worth of thrice the sum,
Had sent to me first, but for my mind's sake;
I'd such a courage to do him good. But now
　　return,
And with their faint reply this answer join;
● Who bates mine honour shall not know my coin.
　　　　　　　　　　　　　　　　　　[*Exit*.

Serv. Excellent! Your lordship's a goodly
villain. The devil knew not what he did when
he made man politic; he crossed himself by 't:
and I cannot think but, in the end, the villanies
of man will set him clear. How fairly this lord
strives to appear foul! takes virtuous copies to be
wicked, like those that under hot ardent zeal
would set whole realms on fire:
Of such a nature is his politic love.
This was my lord's best hope; now all are fled,
Save only the gods: now his friends are dead,
• Doors, that were ne'er acquainted with their wards
Many a bounteous year, must be employ'd
Now to guard sure their master.   40
And this is all a liberal course allows;
Who cannot keep his wealth must keep his house.
                                        [*Exit.*

SCENE IV. *The same. A hall in Timon's house.*

Enter two Servants *of* VARRO, *and the* Servant
of LUCIUS, *meeting* TITUS, HORTENSIUS, *and
other* Servants *of* TIMON'S *creditors, waiting
his coming out.*

First Var. Serv. Well met; good morrow,
    Titus and Hortensius.
Tit. The like to you, kind Varro.
Hor.   Lucius!
What, do we meet together?
Luc. Serv.   Ay, and I think
One business does command us all; for mine
Is money.
Tit. So is theirs and ours.

Enter PHILOTUS.

Luc. Serv.   And Sir Philotus too!
Phi. Good day at once.
Luc. Serv.   Welcome, good brother.
What do you think the hour?
Phi.   Labouring for nine.
Luc. Serv. So much?
Phi.   Is not my lord seen yet?
Luc. Serv.   Not yet.
• *Phi.* I wonder on't; he was wont to shine at
    seven.   10
Luc. Serv. Ay, but the days are wax'd shorter
    with him:
You must consider that a prodigal course
Is like the sun's; but not, like his, recoverable.
I fear 'tis deepest winter in Lord Timon's purse;
That is, one may reach deep enough, and yet
Find little.
Phi. I am of your fear for that.
Tit. I'll show you how to observe a strange
    event.
Your lord sends now for money.
Hor.   Most true, he does.
Tit. And he wears jewels now of Timon's gift,
For which I wait for money.   20
Hor. It is against my heart.
Luc. Serv.   Mark, how strange it shows,
Timon in this should pay more than he owes:
And e'en as if your lord should wear rich jewels,
And send for money for 'em.
Hor. I'm weary of this charge, the gods can
    witness:
I know my lord hath spent of Timon's wealth,
And now ingratitude makes it worse than stealth.

38 *wards.* Locks.

10 *shine.* i.e. rise like the sun.

42 *in a cloud.* i.e. of gloom.

52 *maws.* Stomachs.

70 *take 't of my soul.* Believe me.

First Var. Serv.   Yes, mine's three thousand
  crowns: what's yours?
Luc. Serv.   Five thousand mine.
First Var. Serv.   'Tis much deep: and it
  should seem by the sum,   30
Your master's confidence was above mine;
Else, surely, his had equall'd.

Enter FLAMINIUS.

Tit.   One of Lord Timon's men.
Luc. Serv.   Flaminius! Sir, a word: pray, is
my lord ready to come forth?
Flam.   No, indeed, he is not.
Tit.   We attend his lordship; pray, signify so
much.
Flam.   I need not tell him that; he knows you
are too diligent.   [*Exit.* 40

Enter FLAVIUS *in a cloak, muffled.*

Luc. Serv.   Ha! is not that his steward muf-
  fled so?
●He goes away in a cloud: call him, call him.
Tit.   Do you hear, sir?
Sec. Var. Serv.   By your leave, sir,—
Flav.   What do ye ask of me, my friend?
Tit.   We wait for certain money here, sir.
Flav.   Ay,
If money were as certain as your waiting,
'Twere sure enough.
Why then preferr'd you not your sums and bills,
When your false masters eat of my lord's meat? 50
Then they could smile and fawn upon his debts
●And take down the interest into their gluttonous
  maws.
You do yourselves but wrong to stir me up;
Let me pass quietly:
Believe 't, my lord and I have made an end;
I have no more to reckon, he to spend.
Luc. Serv.   Ay, but this answer will not serve.
Flav.   If 'twill not serve, 'tis not so base as you;
For you serve knaves.   [*Exit.*
First Var. Serv.   How! what does his cash-
  iered worship mutter?   61
Sec. Var. Serv.   No matter what; he's poor,
and that's revenge enough. Who can speak
broader than he that has no house to put his head
in? such may rail against great buildings.

Enter SERVILIUS.

Tit.   O, here's Servilius; now we shall know
some answer.
Ser.   If I might beseech you, gentlemen, to
repair some other hour, I should derive much
●from 't; for, take 't of my soul, my lord leans
wondrously to discontent: his comfortable temper has forsook him; he's much out of health, and
keeps his chamber.
Luc. Serv.   Many do keep their chambers are
  not sick:
And, if it be so far beyond his health,
Methinks he should the sooner pay his debts,
And make a clear way to the gods.
Ser.   Good gods!
Tit.   We cannot take this for answer, sir.
Flam.   [*Within*] Servilius, help! My lord!
  my lord!

644

Enter TIMON, *in a rage;* FLAMINIUS *following.*

Tim. What, are my doors opposed against my
    passage?   80
Have I been ever free, and must my house
• Be my retentive enemy, my gaol?
The place which I have feasted, does it now,
Like all mankind, show me an iron heart?
  Luc. Serv. Put in now, Titus.
  Tit. My lord, here is my bill.
  Luc. Serv. Here's mine.
  Hor. And mine, my lord.
  Both Var. Serv. And ours, my lord.
  Phi. All our bills.   90
  Tim. Knock me down with 'em: cleave me to
    the girdle.
  Luc. Serv. Alas, my lord,—
  Tim. Cut my heart in sums.
  Tit. Mine, fifty talents.
  Tim. Tell out my blood.
  Luc. Serv. Five thousand crowns, my lord.
  Tim. Five thousand drops pays that. What
    yours?—and yours?
  First Var. Serv. My lord,—
  Sec. Var. Serv. My lord,—
  Tim. Tear me, take me, and the gods fall
    upon you!   [*Exit.* 100
• *Hor.* 'Faith, I perceive our masters may throw
their caps at their money: these debts may well
be called desperate ones, for a madman owes 'em.
                [*Exeunt.*

Re-enter TIMON *and* FLAVIUS.

Tim. They have e'en put my breath from me,
    the slaves.
Creditors? devils!
  Flav. My dear lord,—
  Tim. What if it should be so?
  Flav. My lord,—
  Tim. I'll have it so. My steward!
  Flav. Here, my lord.   110
  Tim. So fitly? Go, bid all my friends again,
Lucius, Lucullus, and Sempronius:
All, sirrah, all:
I'll once more feast the rascals.
  Flav.   O my lord,
You only speak from your distracted soul;
There is not so much left, to furnish out
A moderate table.
  Tim.   Be't not in thy care; go,
I charge thee, invite them all: let in the tide
Of knaves once more; my cook and I'll provide.
                [*Exeunt.*

SCENE V. *The same. The senate-house.*

The Senate sitting.

First Sen. My lord, you have my voice to it; the fault's
Bloody; 'tis necessary he should die:
Nothing emboldens sin so much as mercy.
  Sec. Sen. Most true; the law shall bruise him.

Enter ALCIBIADES, *with* Attendants.

  Alcib. Honour, health, and compassion to the
    senate!
  First Sen. Now, captain?
  Alcib. I am an humble suitor to your virtues;
For pity is the virtue of the law,

Timon: 'What, are my doors opposed against my
passage?' Illustration by Gordon Browne for Henry
Irving's *Shakespeare*, 1888

82 *retentive.* Confining.

101–102 *throw ... money.* i.e. give up their money as
lost.

24 *undergo*. Undertake.

27 *form*. Legal process.

34 *prefer . . . heart*. Assume his cries to come from the heart.

45 *repugnancy*. Fighting back.

54 *gust*. i.e. outburst.

60 *Lacedæmon and Byzantium*. Two places; Sparta and Constantinople.

Constantinople. Engraving from John Speed's *A Prospect of the Most Famous Parts of the World, 1631*

And none but tyrants use it cruelly.
It pleases time and fortune to lie heavy   10
Upon a friend of mine, who, in hot blood,
Hath stepp'd into the law, which is past depth
To those that, without heed, do plunge into 't.
He is a man, setting his fate aside,
Of comely virtues:
Nor did he soil the fact with cowardice—
An honour in him which buys out his fault—
But with a noble fury and fair spirit,
Seeing his reputation touch'd to death,
He did oppose his foe: 20
And with such sober and unnoted passion
He did behave his anger, ere 'twas spent,
As if he had but proved an argument.
  First Sen.   You undergo too strict a paradox,
Striving to make an ugly deed look fair:
Your words have took such pains as if they la-
  bour'd
To bring manslaughter into form and set quar-
  relling
Upon the head of valour; which indeed
Is valour misbegot and came into the world
When sects and factions were newly born: 30
He's truly valiant that can wisely suffer
The worst that man can breathe, and make his
  wrongs
His outsides, to wear them like his raiment,
  carelessly,
And ne'er prefer his injuries to his heart,
To bring it into danger.
If wrongs be evils and enforce us kill,
What folly 'tis to hazard life for ill!
  Alcib.   My lord,—
  First Sen.   You cannot make gross sins
  look clear:
To revenge is no valour, but to bear.
  Alcib.   My lords, then, under favour, pardon
  me,   40
If I speak like a captain.
Why do fond men expose themselves to battle,
And not endure all threats? sleep upon 't,
And let the foes quietly cut their throats,
Without repugnancy? If there be
Such valour in the bearing, what make we
Abroad? why then, women are more valiant
That stay at home, if bearing carry it,
And the ass more captain than the lion, the felon
Loaden with irons wiser than the judge,   50
If wisdom be in suffering. O my lords,
As you are great, be pitifully good:
Who cannot condemn rashness in cold blood?
To kill, I grant, is sin's extremest gust;
But, in defence, by mercy, 'tis most just.
To be in anger is impiety;
But who is man that is not angry?
Weigh but the crime with this.
  Sec. Sen.   You breathe in vain.
  Alcib.   In vain! his service done
At Lacedæmon and Byzantium   60
Were a sufficient briber for his life.
  First Sen.   What's that?
  Alcib.   I say, my lords, he has done fair ser-
  vice,
And slain in fight many of your enemies:
How full of valour did he bear himself
In the last conflict, and made plenteous wounds!
  Sec. Sen.   He has made too much plenty with
  'em;

He's a sworn rioter: he has a sin that often
Drowns him, and takes his valour prisoner:
If there were no foes, that were enough   70
To overcome him: in that beastly fury
He has been known to commit outrages,
And cherish factions: 'tis inferr'd to us,
His days are foul and his drink dangerous.
    First Sen. He dies.
    Alcib.   Hard fate! he might have died in war.
My lords, if not for any parts in him—
Though his right arm might purchase his own
    time
And be in debt to none—yet, more to move you,
Take my deserts to his, and join 'em both:
And, for I know your reverend ages love   80
Security, I'll pawn my victories, all
My honours to you, upon his good returns.
If by this crime he owes the law his life,
Why, let the war receive 't in valiant gore;
For law is strict, and war is nothing more.
    First Sen. We are for law: he dies; urge it
    no more,
● On height of our displeasure: friend or brother,
He forfeits his own blood that spills another.
    Alcib. Must it be so? it must not be. My lords,
I do beseech you, know me.   90
    Sec. Sen. How!
    Alcib. Call me to your remembrances.
    Third Sen.   What!
    Alcib. I cannot think but your age has forgot
    me:
It could not else be, I should prove so base,
To sue, and be denied such common grace:
My wounds ache at you.
    First Sen.   Do you dare our anger?
'Tis in few words, but spacious in effect;
We banish thee for ever.
    Alcib.   Banish me!
Banish your dotage; banish usury,
That makes the senate ugly.   100
    First Sen. If, after two days' shine, Athens
    contain thee,
Attend our weightier judgement. And, not to
    swell our spirit,
He shall be executed presently.
                [*Exeunt Senators.*
    Alcib. Now the gods keep you old enough;
    that you may live
Only in bone, that none may look on you!
I'm worse than mad: I have kept back their foes,
While they have told their money and let out
Their coin upon large interest, I myself
Rich only in large hurts. All those for this?
● Is this the balsam that the usuring senate   110
Pours into captains' wounds? Banishment!
It comes not ill; I hate not to be banish'd;
It is a cause worthy my spleen and fury,
That I may strike at Athens. I'll cheer up
● My discontented troops, and lay for hearts.
'Tis honour with most lands to be at odds;
Soldiers should brook as little wrongs as gods.
                  [*Exit.*

SCENE VI. *The same. A banqueting-room in
        Timon's house.*

*Music. Tables set out: Servants attending.
Enter divers Lords, Senators and others, at
several doors.*

    First Lord. The good time of day to you, sir.

87 *On height.* On pain of incurring.

Alcibiades: 'I have kept back their foes …' Engraving
by Bartolomeo Pinelli, 1821

---

110 *balsam.* Balm.

115 *lay for.* Seek to win.

5 *tiring.* Worrying: the word is used to describe how a hawk pulls at its meat.

8-9 *persuasion.* Evidence.

11-12 *earnest.* Pressing. *many my near occasions.* My numerous engagements.

18 *my . . . out.* My money was already on loan.

Timon: 'feast your ears with the music awhile . . .' From a 19th century engraving of Greek musicians

52 *cumber.* Trouble.

Timon: 'Come, bring in all together.' Engraving by Kenny Meadows from Barry Cornwall's *The Works of Shakspere,* 1846

Sec. Lord. I also wish it to you. I think this honourable lord did but try us this other day.

First Lord. Upon that were my thoughts tiring, when we encountered: I hope it is not so low with him as he made it seem in the trial of his several friends.

Sec. Lord. It should not be, by the persuasion of his new feasting.   9

First Lord. I should think so: he hath sent me an earnest inviting, which many my near occasions did urge me to put off; but he hath conjured me beyond them, and I must needs appear.

Sec. Lord. In like manner was I in debt to my importunate business, but he would not hear my excuse. I am sorry, when he sent to borrow of me, that my provision was out.

First Lord. I am sick of that grief too, as I understand how all things go.   20

Sec. Lord. Every man here's so. What would he have borrowed of you?

First Lord. A thousand pieces.

Sec. Lord. A thousand pieces!

First Lord. What of you?

Sec. Lord. He sent to me, sir,—Here he comes.

Enter TIMON *and* Attendants.

Tim. With all my heart, gentlemen both; and how fare you?

First Lord. Ever at the best, hearing well of your lordship.   30

Sec. Lord. The swallow follows not summer more willing than we your lordship.

Tim. [*Aside*] Nor more willingly leaves winter; such summer-birds are men. Gentlemen, our dinner will not recompense this long stay: feast your ears with the music awhile, if they will fare so harshly o' the trumpet's sound; we shall to 't presently.

First Lord. I hope it remains not unkindly with your lordship that I returned you an empty messenger.   41

Tim. O, sir, let it not trouble you.

Sec. Lord. My noble lord,—

Tim. Ah, my good friend, what cheer?

Sec. Lord. My most honourable lord, I am e'en sick of shame, that, when your lordship this other day sent to me, I was so unfortunate a beggar.

Tim. Think not on 't, sir.

Sec. Lord. If you had sent but two hours before,—   51

Tim. Let it not cumber your better remembrance. [*The banquet brought in.*] Come, bring in all together.

Sec. Lord. All covered dishes!

First Lord. Royal cheer, I warrant you.

Third Lord. Doubt not that, if money and the season can yield it.

First Lord. How do you? What's the news?

Third Lord. Alcibiades is banished: hear you of it?   61

First and Sec. Lord. Alcibiades banished!

Third Lord. 'Tis so, be sure of it.

First Lord. How! how!

Sec. Lord. I pray you, upon what?

Tim. My worthy friends, will you draw near?

Third Lord. I'll tell you more anon. Here's a noble feast toward.

Sec. Lord. This is the old man still.
Third Lord. Will 't hold? will 't hold?   70
Sec. Lord. It does: but time will—and so—
Third Lord. I do conceive.
Tim. Each man to his stool, with that spur as he would to the lip of his mistress: your diet shall be in all places alike.   Make not a city feast of it, to let the meat cool ere we can agree
●upon the first place: sit, sit.   The gods require our thanks.

You great benefactors, sprinkle our society with thankfulness.   For your own gifts, make yourselves praised: but reserve still to give, lest your deities be despised.   Lend to each man enough, that one need not lend to another; for, were your godheads to borrow of men, men would forsake the gods.   Make the meat be beloved more than the man that gives it.   Let no assembly of twenty be without a score of villains: if there sit twelve women at the table, let a dozen of them be—as
●they are.   †The rest of your fees, O gods—the senators of Athens, together with the common lag of people—what is amiss in them, you gods, make suitable for destruction.   For these my present friends, as they are to me nothing, so in nothing bless them, and to nothing are they welcome.

Uncover, dogs, and lap.
[*The dishes are uncovered and seen to be full of warm water.*
Some speak. What does his lordship mean?
Some other. I know not.
·*Tim.* May you a better feast never behold,
You knot of mouth-friends! smoke and luke-warm water
●Is your perfection.   This is Timon's last;   100
Who, stuck and spangled with your flatteries,
Washes it off, and sprinkles in your faces
Your reeking villany.
[*Throwing the water in their faces.*
Live loathed and long,
Most smiling, smooth, detested parasites,
Courteous destroyers, affable wolves, meek bears,
You fools of fortune, trencher-friends, time's flies,
●Cap and knee slaves, vapours, and minute-jacks!
Of man and beast the infinite malady
Crust you quite o'er!   What, dost thou go?
Soft! take thy physic first—thou too—and thou;—
Stay, I will lend thee money, borrow none.   111
[*Throws the dishes at them, and drives them out.*
What, all in motion?   Henceforth be no feast,
Whereat a villain's not a welcome guest.
Burn, house! sink, Athens! henceforth hated be
Of Timon man and all humanity!   [*Exit.*

Re-enter the Lords, Senators, *&c.*

First Lord. How now, my lords!
Sec. Lord. Know you the quality of Lord Timon's fury?
Third Lord. Push! did you see my cap?
Fourth Lord. I have lost my gown.   120
First Lord. He's but a mad lord, and nought but humour sways him.   He gave me a jewel th' other day, and now he has beat it out of my hat: did you see my jewel?
Third Lord. Did you see my cap?
Sec. Lord. Here 'tis.
Fourth Lord. Here lies my gown.

Costume design for Timon by Ralph Koltai, Royal Shakespeare Co, 1965

77 *first place.* Who shall sit where.

89 *fees.* Subject creatures.

100 *your perfection.* The perfect image of you. *last.* Final appearance.

107 *minute-jacks.* i.e. fickle folk.

649

Timon: 'Let me look back upon thee.' Engraving by
Henry Fuseli, 1805

3 *incontinent*. Promiscuous.

12 *pill*. Steal.

14 *lined*. Padded.

18 *mysteries*. Professions.

25 *liberty*. Licentiousness.

28 *blains*. Blisters.

First Lord.   Let's make no stay.
Sec. Lord.   Lord Timon's mad.
Third Lord.   I feel 't upon my bones. 130
Fourth Lord.   One day he gives us diamonds,
   next day stones.   [*Exeunt.*

ACT IV.

SCENE I.   *Without the walls of Athens.*

Enter TIMON.

Tim. .Let me look back upon thee.   O thou
   wall,
That girdlest in those wolves, dive in the earth,
●And fence not Athens!   Matrons, turn incontin-
   ent!
Obedience fail in children! slaves and fools,
Pluck the grave wrinkled senate from the bench,
And minister in their steads! to general filths
Convert o' the instant, green virginity,
Do 't in your parents' eyes! bankrupts, hold fast;
Rather than render back, out with your knives,
And cut your trusters' throats! bound servants,
   steal!   10
Large-handed robbers your grave masters are,
●And pill by law.   Maid, to thy master's bed;
Thy mistress is o' the brothel!   Son of sixteen,
●Pluck the lined crutch from thy old limping sire,
With it beat out his brains!   Piety, and fear,
Religion to the gods, peace, justice, truth,
Domestic awe, night-rest, and neighbourhood,
●Instruction, manners, mysteries, and trades,
Degrees, observances, customs, and laws,
Decline to your confounding contraries,   20
And let confusion live!   Plagues, incident to men,
Your potent and infectious fevers heap
On Athens, ripe for stroke!   Thou cold sciatica,
Cripple our senators, that their limbs may halt
●As lamely as their manners!   Lust and liberty
Creep in the minds and marrows of our youth,
That 'gainst the stream of virtue they may strive,
●And drown themselves in riot!   Itches, blains,
Sow all the Athenian bosoms; and their crop
Be general leprosy!   Breath infect breath,   30
That their society, as their friendship, may
Be merely poison!   Nothing I'll bear from thee,
But nakedness, thou detestable town!
Take thou that too, with multiplying bans!
Timon will to the woods; where he shall find
The unkindest beast more kinder than mankind.
The gods confound—hear me, you good gods all—
The Athenians both within and out that wall!
And grant, as Timon grows, his hate may grow
To the whole race of mankind, high and low! 40
Amen.   [*Exit.*

SCENE II.   *Athens.   A room in Timon's house.*

Enter FLAVIUS, *with two or three* Servants.

First Serv.   Hear you, master steward, where's
   our master?
Are we undone? cast off? nothing remaining?
Flav.   Alack, my fellows, what should I say
   to you?
Let me be recorded by the righteous gods,
I am as poor as you.
First Serv.   Such a house broke!
So noble a master fall'n!   All gone! and not
One friend to take his fortune by the arm,

And go along with him!

Sec. Serv.   As we do turn our backs
From our companion thrown into his grave,
● So his familiars to his buried fortunes   10
Slink all away, leave their false vows with him,
Like empty purses pick'd; and his poor self,
A dedicated beggar to the air,
With his disease of all-shunn'd poverty,
Walks, like contempt, alone. More of our fellows.

Enter other Servants.

Flav. All broken implements of a ruin'd house.
Third Serv.   Yet do our hearts wear Timon's
          livery;
That see I by our faces; we are fellows still,
Serving alike in sorrow: leak'd is our bark,
And we, poor mates, stand on the dying deck, 20
Hearing the surges threat: we must all part
Into this sea of air.

Flav.   Good fellows all,
● The latest of my wealth I'll share amongst you.
Wherever we shall meet, for Timon's sake,
Let's yet be fellows; let's shake our heads,
          and say,
As 'twere a knell unto our master's fortunes,
'We have seen better days.' Let each take some;
Nay, put out all your hands.   Not one word
          more:
Thus part we rich in sorrow, parting poor.
          [*Servants embrace, and part several ways.*
O, the fierce wretchedness that glory brings us! 30
Who would not wish to be from wealth exempt,
Since riches point to misery and contempt?
Who would be so mock'd with glory? or to live
But in a dream of friendship?
● To have his pomp and all what state compounds
But only painted, like his varnish'd friends?
Poor honest lord, brought low by his own heart,
Undone by goodness! Strange, unusual blood,
When man's worst sin is, he does too much good!
Who, then, dares to be half so kind again?   40
For bounty, that makes gods, does still mar men.
My dearest lord, bless'd, to be most accursed,
Rich, only to be wretched, thy great fortunes
Are made thy chief afflictions.   Alas, kind lord!
He's flung in rage from this ingrateful seat
Of monstrous friends, nor has he with him to
Supply his life, or that which can command it.
I'll follow and inquire him out:
I'll ever serve his mind with my best will;
Whilst I have gold, I'll be his steward still.   50
                              [*Exit.*

SCENE III. *Woods and cave, near the sea-shore.*

Enter TIMON, *from the cave.*

Tim.   O blessed breeding sun, draw from the
          earth
● Rotten humidity; below thy sister's orb
Infect the air! Twinn'd brothers of one womb,
Whose procreation, residence, and birth,
● Scarce is dividant, touch them with several
          fortunes;
The greater scorns the lesser: not nature,
To whom all sores lay siege, can bear great
          fortune,
But by contempt of nature.
Raise me this beggar, and deny 't that lord;
● The senator shall bear contempt hereditary, 10

10 *familiars.* Friends.

23 *latest.* Very last.

35 *what state compounds.* The splendour of high office
or wealth.

Timon: 'O blessed breeding sun . . .' Engraving of the
sun-god Phoebus and his chariot from a painting by
Raphael, 1811

2 *sister's orb.* The moon's.

5 *dividant.* Different. *touch.* Test. *several.* Separate.

10 *bear contempt hereditary.* Be treated with constant
contempt.

12 *lards.* Fattens. *rother.* Steer.

16 *grise.* A single step or stair.

22 *His semblable.* His like.

23 *fang.* Seize.

Timon: 'Earth, yield me roots!' Engraving from Bell's edition of Shakespeare, 1776

27 *I am no idle votarist.* i.e. my curses are not empty.

38 *wappen'd.* Worn out.

39 *spital-house.* Hospital.

40 *cast the gorge at.* Vomit at the sight of.

41 *To . . . again.* i.e. as fresh as a spring day.

42–43 *odds . . . nations.* Sets the mobs of different nations against each other.

47 *earnest.* Evidence, proof.

59 *gules.* Red.

60 *canons.* Laws.

The beggar native honour.
● It is the pasture lards the rother's sides,
The want that makes him lean. Who dares,
    who dares,
In purity of manhood stand upright,
And say 'This man's a flatterer'? if one be,
● So are they all; for every grise of fortune
Is smooth'd by that below: the learned pate
Ducks to the golden fool: all is oblique;
There's nothing level in our cursed natures,
But direct villany. Therefore, be abhorr'd   20
All feasts, societies, and throngs of men!
● His semblable, yea, himself, Timon disdains:
● Destruction fang mankind! Earth, yield me
    roots!   [*Digging.*
Who seeks for better of thee, sauce his palate
With thy most operant poison! What is here?
Gold? yellow, glittering, precious gold? No, gods,
● I am no idle votarist: roots, you clear heavens!
Thus much of this will make black white, foul
    fair,
Wrong right, base noble, old young, coward
    valiant.
Ha, you gods! why this? what this, you gods?
Why, this   30
Will lug your priests and servants from your
    sides,
Pluck stout men's pillows from below their heads:
This yellow slave
Will knit and break religions, bless the accursed,
Make the hoar leprosy adored, place thieves
And give them title, knee and approbation
With senators on the bench: this is it
● That makes the wappen'd widow wed again;
● She, whom the spital-house and ulcerous sores
● Would cast the gorge at, this embalms and
    spices   40
● To the April day again. Come, damned earth,
● Thou common whore of mankind, that put'st odds
Among the rout of nations, I will make thee
Do thy right nature. [*March afar off.*] Ha!
    a drum? Thou'rt quick,
But yet I'll bury thee: thou'lt go, strong thief,
When gouty keepers of thee cannot stand.
● Nay, stay thou out for earnest.
                          [*Keeping some gold.*

Enter ALCIBIADES, *with drum and fife, in
    warlike manner;* PHRYNIA *and* TIMANDRA.

    Alcib. What art thou there? speak.
    Tim. A beast, as thou art. The canker gnaw
        thy heart,
For showing me again the eyes of man!   50
    Alcib. What is thy name? Is man so hateful
        to thee,
That art thyself a man?
    Tim. I am Misanthropos, and hate mankind.
For thy part, I do wish thou wert a dog,
That I might love thee something.
    Alcib.   I know thee well;
But in thy fortunes am unlearn'd and strange.
    Tim. I know thee too; and more than that I
        know thee,
I not desire to know. Follow thy drum;
● With man's blood paint the ground, gules, gules:
● Religious canons, civil laws are cruel;   60
Then what should war be? This fell whore
    of thine
Hath in her more destruction than thy sword,

For all her cherubin look.
Phry.   Thy lips rot off!
Tim. I will not kiss thee; then the rot returns
To thine own lips again.
   Alcib.   How came the noble Timon to this
     change?
   Tim.   As the moon does, by wanting light
     to give:
But then renew I could not, like the moon;
There were no suns to borrow of.
   Alcib.   Noble Timon,
What friendship may I do thee?
   Tim.   None, but to   70
Maintain my opinion.
   Alcib.   What is it, Timon?
   Tim.   Promise. me friendship, but perform
none: if thou wilt not promise, the gods plague
thee, for thou art a man! if thou dost perform,
confound thee, for thou art a man!
   Alcib.   I have heard in some sort of thy
     miseries.
   Tim.   Thou saw'st them, when I had pros-
     perity.
   Alcib.   I see them now; then was a blessed
     time.
   Tim.   As thine is now, held with a brace of
     harlots.
•   *Timan.*   Is this the Athenian minion, whom
     the world   80
•Voiced so regardfully?
   Tim.   Art thou Timandra?
   Timan.   Yes.
   Tim.   Be a whore still: they love thee not
     that use thee;
Give them diseases, leaving with thee their lust.
•Make use of thy salt hours: season the slaves
•For tubs and baths; bring down rose-cheeked
     youth
To the tub-fast and the diet.
   Timan.   Hang thee, monster!
   Alcib.   Pardon him, sweet Timandra; for
     his wits
Are drown'd and lost in his calamities.
I have but little gold of late, brave Timon,   90
The want whereof doth daily make revolt
In my penurious band: I have heard, and
     grieved,
How cursed Athens, mindless of thy worth,
Forgetting thy great deeds, when neighbour
     states,
But for thy sword and fortune, trod upon them,—
   Tim.   I prithee, beat thy drum, and get
     thee gone.
   Alcib.   I am thy friend, and pity thee, dear
     Timon.
   Tim.   How dost thou pity him whom thou
     dost trouble?
I had rather be alone.
   Alcib.   Why, fare thee well:
Here is some gold for thee.
   Tim.   Keep it, I cannot eat it.   100
   Alcib.   When I have laid proud Athens on
     a heap,—
   Tim.   Warr'st thou 'gainst Athens?
   Alcib.   Ay, Timon, and have cause.
   Tim.   The gods confound them all in thy
     conquest;
And thee after, when thou hast conquer'd!
   Alcib.   Why me, Timon?

80 *minion.* Favourite.

81 *Voiced so regardfully.* Spoke of with such respect.

85 *salt.* Lecherous.

86 *tubs.* Sweating tubs to treat venereal disease.

Costume design for Timandra by Ralph Koltai, Royal Shakespeare Co, 1965

653

116 *window-bars.* i.e. lattice work of a dress.

122 *sans.* Without.

124 *proof.* Armour.

135 *mountant.* Uplifted. *oathable.* Able to take an oath.

139 *conditions.* Nature.

141 *strong in whore.* Good prostitutes.

145 *burthens.* The hair of dead people.

155 *quillets.* Verbal niceties. *Hoar the flamen.* Whiten the priest.

Opposite : Timon: 'Consumption sow In hollow bones of man;' Engraving from A. Pope's edition of *The Works ...* 1728

Tim.   That, by killing of villains,
Thou wast born to conquer my country.
Put up thy gold: go on,—here's gold,—go on ;
Be as a planetary plague, when Jove
Will o'er some high-viced city hang his poison
In the sick air: let not thy sword skip one :   110
Pity not honour'd age for his white beard ;
He is an usurer : strike me the counterfeit
       matron ;
It is her habit only that is honest,
Herself's a bawd : let not the virgin's cheek
Make soft thy trenchant sword ; for those milk-
       paps,
●That through the window-bars bore at men's eyes,
Are not within the leaf of pity writ,
But set them down horrible traitors : spare not
       the babe,
Whose dimpled smiles from fools exhaust their
       mercy ;
Think it a bastard, whom the oracle   120
Hath doubtfully pronounced thy throat shall cut,
●And mince it sans remorse : swear against objects ;
Put armour on thine ears and on thine eyes ;
●Whose proof, nor yells of mothers, maids, nor
       babes,
Nor sight of priests in holy vestments bleeding,
Shall pierce a jot. There's gold to pay thy
       soldiers :
Make large confusion ; and, thy fury spent,
Confounded be thyself ! Speak not, be gone.
       Alcib. Hast thou gold yet ? I'll take the gold
       thou givest me,
Not all thy counsel.   130
       Tim. Dost thou, or dost thou not, heaven's
       curse upon thee !
       Phr. and Timan. Give us some gold, good
       Timon : hast thou more ?
       Tim. Enough to make a whore forswear her
       trade.
And to make whores, a bawd. Hold up, you
       sluts,
●Your aprons mountant : you are not oathable,—
Although, I know, you'll swear, terribly swear
Into strong shudders and to heavenly agues
The immortal gods that hear you,—spare your
       oaths,
●I'll trust to your conditions : be whores still ;
And he whose pious breath seeks to convert you,
●Be strong in whore, allure him, burn him up ; 141
Let your close fire predominate his smoke,
And be no turncoats : yet may your pains, six
       months,
Be quite contrary : and thatch your poor thin
       roofs
●With burthens of the dead ;—some that were
       hang'd,
No matter :—wear them, betray with them : whore
       still ;
Paint till a horse may mire upon your face.
A pox of wrinkles !
       Phr. and Timan. Well, more gold : what
       then ?
Believe 't, that we'll do any thing for gold.   150
       Tim. Consumptions sow
In hollow bones of man ; strike their sharp shins,
And mar men's spurring. Crack the lawyer's
       voice,
That he may never more false title plead,
●Nor sound his quillets shrilly : hoar the flamen,

160 *general weal.* General well-being. *curl'd-pate.* Curly-headed.

Phrynia and Timandra: 'More counsel with more money, bounteous Timon.' Engraving from a painting by John Opie (1761–1807)

184 *Hyperion.* Greek sun-god.

187 *Ensear.* Dry up.

189 *Go great.* Get pregnant.

193 *leas.* Fields.

195 *unctuous.* Rich.

That scolds against the quality of flesh,
And not believes himself: down with the nose,
Down with it flat; take the bridge quite away
Of him that, his particular to foresee,
●Smells from the general weal: make curl'd-pate
   ruffians bald;   160
And let the unscarr'd braggarts of the war
Derive some pain from you: plague all;
That your activity may defeat and quell
The source of all erection.   There's more gold:
Do you damn others, and let this damn you,
And ditches grave you all!
  Phr. and Timan.   More counsel with more
   money, bounteous Timon.
  Tim.   More whore, more mischief first; I have
   given you earnest.
  Alcib.   Strike up the drum towards Athens!
   Farewell, Timon:
If I thrive well, I'll visit thee again.   170
  Tim.   If I hope well, I'll never see thee more.
  Alcib.   I never did thee harm.
  Tim.   Yes, thou spokest well of me.
  Alcib.   Call'st thou that harm?
  Tim.   Men daily find it.   Get thee away, and
   take
Thy beagles with thee.
  Alcib.   We but offend him.   Strike!
    [*Drum beats.   Exeunt Alcibiades,*
         Phrynia, and Timandra.
  Tim.   That nature, being sick of man's un-
   kindness,
Should yet be hungry!   Common mother, thou,
                    [*Digging.*
Whose womb unmeasurable, and infinite breast,
Teems, and feeds all; whose self-same mettle,
Whereof thy proud child, arrogant man, is puff'd,
Engenders the black toad and adder blue,   181
The gilded newt and eyeless venom'd worm,
With all the abhorred births below crisp heaven
●Whereon Hyperion's quickening fire doth shine;
Yield him, who all thy human sons doth hate,
From forth thy plenteous bosom, one poor root!
●Ensear thy fertile and conceptious womb,
Let it no more bring out ingrateful man!
●Go great with tigers, dragons, wolves, and bears;
Teem with new monsters, whom thy upward face
Hath to the marbled mansion all above   191
Never presented!—O, a root,—dear thanks!—
●Dry up thy marrows, vines, and plough-torn leas;
Whereof ingrateful man, with liquorish draughts
●And morsels unctuous, greases his pure mind,
That from it all consideration slips!

       Enter APEMANTUS.

More man? plague, plague!
  Apem.   I was directed hither: men report
Thou dost affect my manners, and dost use them.
  Tim.   'Tis, then, because thou dost not keep
   a dog,   200
Whom I would imitate: consumption catch thee!
  Apem.   This is in thee a nature but infected;
A poor unmanly melancholy sprung
From change of fortune.   Why this spade? this
   place?
This slave-like habit? and these looks of care?
Thy flatterers yet wear silk, drink wine, lie soft;
Hug their diseased perfumes, and have forgot
That ever Timon was.   Shame not these woods,
By putting on the cunning of a carper.

Be thou a flatterer now, and seek to thrive   210
By that which has undone thee: hinge thy knee,
● And let his very breath, whom thou'lt observe,
Blow off thy cap; praise his most vicious strain,
And call it excellent: thou wast told thus;
Thou gavest thine ears like tapsters that bid
    welcome
To knaves and all approachers: 'tis most just
That thou turn rascal; hadst thou wealth again,
Rascals should have 't.   Do not assume my like-
    ness.
    Tim. Were I like thee, I'ld throw away my-
    self.
    Apem. Thou hast cast away thyself, being
    like thyself;   220
A madman so long, now a fool.   What, think'st
● That the bleak air, thy boisterous chamberlain,
Will put thy shirt on warm? will these moss'd
    trees,
That have outlived the eagle, page thy heels,
And skip where thou point'st out? will the cold
    brook,
● Candied with ice, caudle thy morning taste,
To cure thy o'er-night's surfeit? Call the creatures
Whose naked natures live in all the spite
● Of wreakful heaven, whose bare unhoused trunks,
To the conflicting elements exposed,   230
Answer mere nature; bid them flatter thee;
O, thou shalt find—
    Tim.   A fool of thee: depart.
    Apem. I love thee better now than e'er I did.
    Tim. I hate thee worse.
    Apem.   Why?
    Tim.   Thou flatter'st misery.
●   *Apem.* I flatter not; but say thou art a caitiff.
    Tim. Why dost thou seek me out?
    Apem.   To vex thee.
    Tim. Always a villain's office or a fool's.
Dost please thyself in't?
    Apem.   Ay.
    Tim.   What! a knave too?
●   *Apem.* If thou didst put this sour-cold habit on
To castigate thy pride, 'twere well: but thou   240
Dost it enforcedly; thou'ldst courtier be again,
Wert thou not beggar.   Willing misery
Outlives incertain pomp, is crown'd before:
The one is filling still, never complete;
The other, at high wish: best state, contentless,
Hath a distracted and most wretched being,
Worse than the worst, content.
Thou shouldst desire to die, being miserable.
    Tim. Not by his breath that is more miserable.
Thou art a slave, whom Fortune's tender arm   250
With favour never clasp'd; but bred a dog.
● Hadst thou, like us from our first swath, pro-
    ceeded
The sweet degrees that this brief world affords
To such as may the passive drugs of it
Freely command, thou wouldst have plunged
    thyself
In general riot; melted down thy youth
In different beds of lust; and never learn'd
The icy precepts of respect, but follow'd
The sugar'd game before thee.   But myself,
Who had the world as my confectionary,   260
The mouths, the tongues, the eyes and hearts of
    men
● At duty, more than I could frame employment,
That numberless upon me stuck as leaves

212 *observe*. Obsequiously serve.

222 *chamberlain*. Valet.

226 *Candied*. Encrusted. *caudle*. i.e. nurse.

229 *wreakful*. Vengeful. *unhoused*. Uncovered.

235 *caitiff*. Wretch.

239 *habit*. Appearance.

252 *first swath*. Swaddling clothes.

262 *frame*. Provide with.

268 *sufferance.* Suffering.

283 *mend.* Improve.

285 *botch'd.* Patched up.

291 *hired.* By lending or borrowing.

303 *curiosity.* Fastidiousness.

305 *medlar.* Small hard fruit with a harsh flavour, resembling a brown-skinned apple.

Apemantus: 'There's a medlar for thee, eat it.' Engraving from Bell's edition of *Shakespeare*, 1773

312 *after his means.* i.e. when his money had gone.

Do on the oak, have with one winter's brush
Fell from their boughs and left me open, bare
For every storm that blows: I, to bear this,
That never knew but better, is some burden:
●Thy nature did commence in sufferance, time
Hath made thee hard in't.   Why shouldst thou
  hate men?   269
They never flatter'd thee: what hast thou given?
If thou wilt curse, thy father, that poor rag,
Must be thy subject, who in spite put stuff
To some she beggar and compounded thee
Poor rogue hereditary.   Hence, be gone!
If thou hadst not been born the worst of men,
Thou hadst been a knave and flatterer.
    Apem.   Art thou proud yet?
    Tim.   Ay, that I am not thee.
    Apem.   I, that I was
No prodigal.
    Tim.   I, that I am one now:
Were all the wealth I have shut up in thee,
I'ld give thee leave to hang it.   Get thee gone.
That the whole life of Athens were in this!   281
Thus would I eat it.   [*Eating a root.*
    Apem.   Here; I will mend thy feast.
                                [*Offering him a root.*
●   *Tim.*   First mend my company, take away
        thyself.
    Apem.   So I shall mend mine own, by the
        lack of thine.
●   *Tim.*   'Tis not well mended so, it is but botch'd;
If not, I would it were.
    Apem.   What wouldst thou have to Athens?
    Tim.   Thee thither in a whirlwind.   If thou
        wilt,
Tell them there I have gold; look, so I have.
    Apem.   Here is no use for gold.
    Tim.   The best and truest; 290
●For here it sleeps, and does no hired harm.
    Apem.   Where liest o' nights, Timon?
    Tim.   Under that's above me.
Where feed'st thou o' days, Apemantus?
    Apem.   Where my stomach finds meat; or,
rather, where I eat it.
    Tim.   Would poison were obedient and knew
my mind!
    Apem.   Where wouldst thou send it?
    Tim.   To sauce thy dishes.   299
    Apem.   The middle of humanity thou never
knewest, but the extremity of both ends: when
thou wast in thy gilt and thy perfume, they
●mocked thee for too much curiosity; in thy rags
thou knowest none, but art despised for the con-
●trary.   There's a medlar for thee, eat it.
    Tim.   On what I hate I feed not.
    Apem.   Dost hate a medlar?
    Tim.   Ay, though it look like thee.
    Apem.   An thou hadst hated meddlers sooner,
thou shouldst have loved thyself better now.
What man didst thou ever know unthrift that
●was beloved after his means?
    Tim.   Who, without those means thou talkest
of, didst thou ever know beloved?
    Apem.   Myself.
    Tim.   I understand thee; thou hadst some
means to keep a dog.
    Apem.   What things in the world canst thou
nearest compare to thy flatterers?   319
    Tim.   Women nearest; but men, men are the
things themselves.   What wouldst thou do with

the world, Apemantus, if it lay in thy power?

Apem. Give it the beasts, to be rid of the men.

Tim. Wouldst thou have thyself fall in the confusion of men, and remain a beast with the beasts?

Apem. Ay, Timon.

Tim. A beastly ambition, which the gods grant thee t' attain to! If thou wert the lion, the fox would beguile thee : if thou wert the lamb, the fox would eat thee : if thou wert the fox, the lion would suspect thee, when peradventure thou wert accused by the ass : if thou wert the ass, thy dulness would torment thee, and still thou livedst but as a breakfast to the wolf : if thou wert the wolf, thy greediness would afflict thee, and oft thou shouldst hazard thy life for thy dinner : wert thou the unicorn, pride and wrath would confound thee and make thine own self the conquest of thy fury : wert thou a bear, thou wouldst be killed by the horse : wert thou a horse, thou wouldst be seized by the leopard : wert thou a leopard, thou ● wert german to the lion and the spots of thy kindred were jurors on thy life : all thy safety were ● remotion and thy defence absence. What beast couldst thou be, that were not subject to a beast? and what a beast art thou already, that seest not thy loss in transformation!   349

Apem. If thou couldst please me with speaking to me, thou mightst have hit upon it here : the commonwealth of Athens is become a forest of beasts.

Tim. How has the ass broke the wall, that thou art out of the city?

Apem. Yonder comes a poet and a painter : the plague of company light upon thee! I will fear to catch it and give way : when I know not what else to do, I 'll see thee again.   359

Tim. When there is nothing living but thee, thou shalt be welcome. I had rather be a beggar's dog than Apemantus.

Apem. Thou art the cap of all the fools alive.

Tim. Would thou wert clean enough to spit upon!

Apem. A plague on thee! thou art too bad to curse.

Tim. All villains that do stand by thee are pure.

Apem. There is no leprosy but what thou speak'st.

Tim. If I name thee.
I 'll beat thee, but I should infect my hands.

Apem. I would my tongue could rot them off!

Tim. Away, thou issue of a mangy dog!   371
Choler does kill me that thou art alive;
● I swound to see thee.

Apem.   Would thou wouldst burst!

Tim.   Away,
Thou tedious rogue! I am sorry I shall lose
A stone by thee.   [*Throws a stone at him.*

Apem.   Beast!

Tim.   Slave!

Apem.   Toad!

Tim.   Rogue, rogue, rogue!
I am sick of this false world, and will love nought
But even the mere necessities upon 't.
Then, Timon, presently prepare thy grave;
Lie where the light foam of the sea may beat
Thy grave-stone daily : make thine epitaph,   380

Timon: 'wert thou the unicorn, pride and wrath would confound thee...' Woodcut from Edward Topsell's *The History of Four-footed Beasts*, 1658

---

344 *german.* Akin.

346 *remotion.* Keeping apart.

373 *swound.* Faint.

384 *Hymen.* God of marriage. *Mars.* God of war.

387 *Dian.* Goddess of chastity.

Diana bathing with her nymphs. Engraving from a painting by Dominiquin, 1803

397 *quit.* Rid of him.

400–401 *slender . . . remainder.* Tiny portion of his fortune.

428 *con.* i.e. give.

That death in me at others' lives may laugh.
[*To the gold*] O thou sweet king-killer, and dear divorce
'Twixt natural son and sire! thou bright defiler
● Of Hymen's purest bed! thou valiant Mars!
Thou ever young, fresh, loved and delicate wooer,
Whose blush doth thaw the consecrated snow
● That lies on Dian's lap! thou visible god,
That solder'st close impossibilities,
And makest them kiss! that speak'st with every tongue,
To every purpose! O thou touch of hearts!   390
Think, thy slave man rebels, and by thy virtue
Set them into confounding odds, that beasts
May have the world in empire!
   Apem.   Would 'twere so!
But not till I am dead.   I'll say thou'st gold:
Thou wilt be throng'd to shortly.
   Tim.   Throng'd to!
   Apem.   Ay.
   Tim.   Thy back, I prithee.
   Apem.   Live, and love thy misery.
●   *Tim.*   Long live so, and so die. [*Exit Apemantus.*]   I am quit.
Moe things like men!   Eat, Timon, and abhor them.

Enter Banditti.

   First Ban.   Where should he have this gold?
● It is some poor fragment, some slender ort of his remainder: the mere want of gold, and the falling-from of his friends, drove him into this melancholy.
   Sec. Ban.   It is noised he hath a mass of treasure.
   Third Ban.   Let us make the assay upon him: if he care not for't, he will supply us easily; if he covetously reserve it, how shall's get it?
   Sec. Ban.   True; for he bears it not about him, 'tis hid.
   First Ban.   Is not this he?   410
   Banditti.   Where?
   Sec. Ban.   'Tis his description.
   Third Ban.   He; I know him.
   Banditti.   Save thee, Timon.
   Tim.   Now, thieves?
   Banditti.   Soldiers, not thieves.
   Tim.   Both too; and women's sons.
   Banditti.   We are not thieves, but men that much do want.
   Tim.   Your greatest want is, you want much of meat.
Why should you want?   Behold, the earth hath roots;   420
Within this mile break forth a hundred springs;
The oaks bear mast, the briers scarlet hips;
The bounteous housewife, nature, on each bush
Lays her full mess before you.   Want! why want?
   First Ban.   We cannot live on grass, on berries, water,
As beasts and birds and fishes.
   Tim.   Nor on the beasts themselves, the birds, and fishes;
● You must eat men.   Yet thanks I must you con
That you are thieves profess'd, that you work not
In holier shapes: for there is boundless theft   430
In limited professions.   Rascal thieves,

Here's gold. Go, suck the subtle blood o' the
            grape,
●Till the high fever seethe your blood to froth,
And so 'scape hanging: trust not the physician;
His antidotes are poison, and he slays
Moe than you rob: take wealth and lives to-
            gether;
Do villany, do, since you protest to do 't,
Like workmen. I'll example you with thievery:
The sun's a thief, and with his great attraction
Robs the vast sea: the moon's an arrant thief, 440
And her pale fire she snatches from the sun:
The sea's a thief, whose liquid surge resolves
The moon into salt tears: the earth's a thief,
●That feeds and breeds by a composture stolen
From general excrement: each thing's a thief:
The laws, your curb and whip, in their rough
            power
●Have uncheck'd theft. Love not yourselves:
            away,
Rob one another. There's more gold. Cut
            throats:
All that you meet are thieves: to Athens go,
Break open shops; nothing can you steal,   450
But thieves do lose it: steal no less for this
I give you; and gold confound you howsoe'er!
Amen.
    Third Ban. Has almost charmed me from my
profession, by persuading me to it.
    First Ban. 'Tis in the malice of mankind that
he thus advises us; not to have us thrive in our
mystery.
    Sec. Ban. I'll believe him as an enemy, and
give over my trade.   460
    First Ban. Let us first see peace in Athens:
there is no time so miserable but a man may be
true.   [*Exeunt Banditti.*

            Enter FLAVIUS.

    Flav. O you gods!
Is yond despised and ruinous man my lord?
Full of decay and failing? O monument
And wonder of good deeds evilly bestow'd!
What an alteration of honour
Has desperate want made!
What viler thing upon the earth than friends 470
Who can bring noblest minds to basest ends!
●How rarely does it meet with this time's guise,
●When man was wish'd to love his enemies!
Grant I may ever love, and rather woo
Those that would mischief me than those that
            do!
Has caught me in his eye: I will present
My honest grief unto him; and, as my lord,
Still serve him with my life. My dearest master!
    Tim. Away! what art thou?
    Flav.   Have you forgot me, sir?
    Tim. Why dost ask that? I have forgot all
            men;   480
Then, if thou grant'st thou'rt a man, I have
            forgot thee.
    Flav. An honest poor servant of yours.
    Tim. Then I know thee not:
I never had honest man about me, I; all
I kept were knaves, to serve in meat to villains.
    Flav. The gods are witness,
Ne'er did poor steward wear a truer grief
For his undone lord than mine eyes for you.

Illustration of the Bandits by Wyndham Lewis, 1913

---

433 *high fever.* i.e. drunkenness.

444 *composture.* Compost.

447 *uncheck'd theft.* Unrestrained ability to steal.

472 *time's guise.* Way of the world.

473 *wish'd.* Commanded.

Timon: 'Pity's sleeping: Strange times, that weep with laughing, not with weeping!' Watercolour of Pity by William Blake (1757–1827)

---

502 *exceptless*. Making no exceptions.

523 *unmatched*. Unrivalled.

Tim.   What, dost thou weep?   Come nearer.
     Then I love thee,
Because thou art a woman, and disclaim'st   490
Flinty mankind; whose eyes do never give
But thorough lust and laughter. Pity's sleeping:
Strange times, that weep with laughing, not with
     weeping!
   Flav.   I beg of you to know me, good my lord,
To accept my grief and whilst this poor wealth
     lasts
To entertain me as your steward still.
   Tim.   Had I a steward
So true, so just, and now so comfortable?
It almost turns my dangerous nature mild.
Let me behold thy face. Surely, this man   500
Was born of woman.
●Forgive my general and exceptless rashness,
You perpetual-sober gods! I do proclaim
One honest man—mistake me not—but one;
No more, I pray,—and he's a steward.
How fain would I have hated all mankind!
And thou redeem'st thyself: but all, save thee,
I fell with curses.
Methinks thou art more honest now than wise;
For, by oppressing and betraying me,   510
Thou mightst have sooner got another service:
For many so arrive at second masters,
Upon their first lord's neck. But tell me true—
For I must ever doubt, though ne'er so sure—
Is not thy kindness subtle, covetous,
If not a usuring kindness, and, as rich men deal
     gifts,
Expecting in return twenty for one?
   Flav.   No, my most worthy master; in whose
     breast
Doubt and suspect, alas, are placed too late:
You should have fear'd false times when you did
     feast: 520
Suspect still comes where an estate is least.
That which I show, heaven knows, is merely
     love,
●Duty and zeal to your unmatched mind,
Care of your food and living; and, believe it,
My most honour'd lord,
For any benefit that points to me,
Either in hope or present, I'ld exchange
For this one wish, that you had power and wealth
To requite me, by making rich yourself.
   Tim.   Look thee, 'tis so! Thou singly honest
     man,   530
Here, take: the gods out of my misery
Have sent thee treasure. Go, live rich and
     happy;
But thus condition'd: thou shalt build from men:
Hate all, curse all, show charity to none,
But let the famish'd flesh slide from the bone,
Ere thou relieve the beggar; give to dogs
What thou deny'st to men; let prisons swallow
     'em,
Debts wither 'em to nothing; be men like blasted
     woods,
And may diseases lick up their false bloods!
And so farewell and thrive.
   Flav.   O, let me stay,   540
And comfort you, my master.
   Tim.   If thou hatest curses,
Stay not; fly, whilst thou art blest and free:
Ne'er see thou man, and let me ne'er see thee.
     [*Exit Flavius.   Timon retires to his cave.*

12 *a palm.* i.e. flourishing.

25 *air o' the time.* Fashion.

50 *I'll meet you at the turn.* i.e. I'll catch you with your own tricks.

ACT V.

SCENE I. *The woods. Before Timon's cave*

Enter Poet *and* Painter ; TIMON *watching them from his cave.*

Pain. As I took note of the place, it cannot be far where he abides.

Poet. What's to be thought of him? does the rumour hold for true, that he's so full of gold?

Pain. Certain : Alcibiades reports it; Phrynia and Timandra had gold of him: he likewise enriched poor straggling soldiers with great quantity: 'tis said he gave unto his steward a mighty sum.

Poet. Then this breaking of his has been but a try for his friends.   11

Pain. Nothing else: you shall see him a palm in Athens again, and flourish with the highest. Therefore 'tis not amiss we tender our loves to him, in this supposed distress of his: it will show honestly in us; and is very likely to load our purposes with what they travail for, if it be a just and true report that goes of his having.

Poet. What have you now to present unto him?

Pain. Nothing at this time but my visitation: only I will promise him an excellent piece.   21

Poet. I must serve him so too, tell him of an intent that's coming toward him.

Pain. Good as the best. Promising is the very air o' the time: it opens the eyes of expectation: performance is ever the duller for his act; and, but in the plainer and simpler kind of people, the deed of saying is quite out of use. To promise is most courtly and fashionable: performance is a kind of will or testament which argues a great sickness in his judgement that makes it.

[*Timon comes from his cave, behind.*

Tim. [*Aside*] Excellent workman! thou canst not paint a man so bad as is thyself.

Poet. I am thinking what I shall say I have provided for him: it must be a personating of himself; a satire against the softness of prosperity, with a discovery of the infinite flatteries that follow youth and opulency.

Tim. [*Aside*] Must thou needs stand for a villain in thine own work? wilt thou whip thine own faults in other men? Do so, I have gold for thee.

Poet. Nay, let's seek him:
Then do we sin against our own estate,
When we may profit meet, and come too late.

Pain. True;
When the day serves, before black-corner'd night,
Find what thou want'st by free and offer'd light.
Come.

Tim. [*Aside*] I'll meet you at the turn. What a god's gold,   50
That he is worshipp'd in a baser temple
Than where swine feed!
'Tis thou that rigg'st the bark and plough'st the
    foam,
Settlest admired reverence in a slave:
To thee be worship! and thy saints for aye
Be crown'd with plagues that thee alone obey!
Fit I meet them.   [*Coming forward.*

Poet. Hail, worthy Timon!

Pain.   Our late noble master!

Tim. Have I once lived to see two honest men?

663

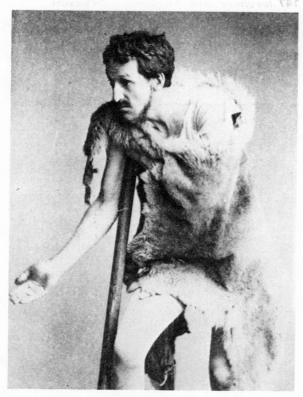

F. R. Benson as Timon, Lyceum Theatre, London, 1882

73 *travail'd.* Laboured.

83–84 *Thou . . . Athens.* You create the best portraits in Athens.

98 *cog.* Cheat.

99 *patchery.* Roguery.

101 *made-up.* Thorough.

Poet. Sir,   60
Having often of your open bounty tasted,
Hearing you were retired, your friends fall'n off,
Whose thankless natures—O abhorred spirits !—
Not all the whips of heaven are large enough :
What ! to you,
Whose star-like nobleness gave life and influence
To their whole being ! I am rapt and cannot cover
The monstrous bulk of this ingratitude
With any size of words.
    Tim. Let it go naked, men may see't the better :
You that are honest, by being what you are,   71
Make them best seen and known.
    Pain.   He and myself
●Have travail'd in the great shower of your gifts,
And sweetly felt it.
    Tim.   Ay, you are honest men.
    Pain. We are hither come to offer you our
        service.
    Tim. Most honest men ! Why, how shall I
        requite you ?
Can you eat roots, and drink cold water ? no.
    Both. What we can do, we'll do, to do you
        service.
    Tim. Ye're honest men : ye've heard that I
        have gold ;
I am sure you have : speak truth ; ye're honest
        men.   80
    Pain. So it is said, my noble lord ; but therefore
Came not my friend nor I.
●   *Tim.*   Good honest men ! Thou draw'st a
        counterfeit
Best in all Athens : thou'rt, indeed, the best ;
Thou counterfeit'st most lively.
    Pain.   So, so, my lord.
    Tim. E'en so, sir, as I say. And, for thy
        fiction,
Why, thy verse swells with stuff so fine and smooth
That thou art even natural in thine art.
But, for all this, my honest-natured friends,
I must needs say you have a little fault :   90
Marry, 'tis not monstrous in you, neither wish I
You take much pains to mend.
    Both.   Beseech your honour
To make it known to us.
    Tim.   You'll take it ill.
    Both. Most thankfully, my lord.
    Tim.   Will you, indeed ?
    Both. Doubt it not, worthy lord.
    Tim. There's never a one of you but trusts a
        knave,
That mightily deceives you.
    Both.   Do we, my lord ?
●   *Tim.* Ay, and you hear him cog, see him dis-
        semble,
●Know his gross patchery, love him, feed him,
Keep in your bosom : yet remain assured   100
●That he's a made-up villain.
    Pain. I know none such, my lord.
    Poet.   Nor I.
    Tim. Look you, I love you well ; I'll give you
        gold,
Rid me these villains from your companies :
Hang them or stab them, drown them in a draught,
Confound them by some course, and come to me,
I'll give you gold enough.
    Both. Name them, my lord, let's know them.
    Tim. You that way and you this, but two in
        company ;

664

Each man apart, all single and alone,   110
Yet an arch-villain keeps him company.
If where thou art two villains shall not be,
Come not near him.   If thou wouldst not reside
But where one villain is, then him abandon.
Hence, pack! there's gold; you came for gold,
        ye slaves:
[*To Painter*] You have work'd for me; there's
        payment for you: hence!
[*To Poet*] You are an alchemist; make gold of
        that.
Out, rascal dogs!   [*Beats them out, and then
                        retires to his cave.*

        Enter FLAVIUS *and two* Senators.

Flav.   It is in vain that you would speak with
        Timon;
For he is set so only to himself   120
That nothing but himself which looks like man
Is friendly with him.
        First Sen.   Bring us to his cave:
It is our part and promise to the Athenians
To speak with Timon.
        Sec. Sen.   At all times alike
Men are not still the same: 'twas time and griefs
That framed him thus: time, with his fairer hand,
Offering the fortunes of his former days,
The former man may make him.   Bring us to him,
And chance it as it may.
        Flav.   Here is his cave.   129
Peace and content be here! Lord Timon! Timon!
Look out, and speak to friends: the Athenians,
By two of their most reverend senate, greet thee:
Speak to them, noble Timon.

        TIMON *comes from his cave.*

Tim.   Thou sun, that comfort'st, burn! Speak,
        and be hang'd:
For each true word, a blister! and each false
Be as a cauterizing to the root o' the tongue,
Consuming it with speaking!
        First Sen.   Worthy Timon,—
Tim.   Of none but such as you, and you of
        Timon.
First Sen.   The senators of Athens greet thee,
        Timon.
Tim.   I thank them; and would send them
        back the plague,   140
Could I but catch it for them.
        First Sen.   O, forget
What we are sorry for ourselves in thee.
The senators with one consent of love
Entreat thee back to Athens; who have thought
On special dignities, which vacant lie
For thy best use and wearing.
        Sec. Sen.   They confess
●Toward thee forgetfulness too general, gross:
Which now the public body, which doth seldom
Play the recanter, feeling in itself
●A lack of Timon's aid, hath sense withal   150
Of it own fail, restraining aid to Timon;
●And send forth us, to make their sorrow'd render,
Together with a recompense more fruitful
Than their offence can weigh down by the dram:
Ay, even such heaps and sums of love and wealth
As shall to thee blot out what wrongs were theirs
●And write in thee the figures of their love,
Ever to read them thine.
        Tim.   You witch me in it;

147 *too general, gross*. Too public and excessive.

150–151 *hath ... fail*. i.e. now sensing its own failings.

152 *sorrow'd render*. Sad confession.

157 *figures*. 'Images' and 'accounts'.

The Athenians appealing to Timon for help. Painting
by Thomas Couture (1815–1879)

165 *Allow'd.* Endowed.

183 *whittle.* Clasp-knife.

Timon: 'Be Alcibiades your plague, you his, And last so long enough!' Engraving by Kenny Meadows from Barry Cornwall's *The Complete Works of Shakspere*, 1857–59

196 *bruit.* Rumour.

206 *prevent.* Anticipate.

Surprise me to the very brink of tears:
Lend me a fool's heart and a woman's eyes,   160
And I'll beweep these comforts, worthy senators.
   First Sen.   Therefore, so please thee to return
    with us
And of our Athens, thine and ours, to take
The captainship, thou shalt be met with thanks,
• Allow'd with absolute power and thy good name
Live with authority: so soon we shall drive back
Of Alcibiades the approaches wild,
Who, like a boar too savage, doth root up
His country's peace.
   Sec. Sen.   And shakes his threatening sword
Against the walls of Athens.
   First Sen.   Therefore, Timon,—   170
   Tim.   Well, sir, I will; therefore, I will, sir;
    thus:
If Alcibiades kill my countrymen,
Let Alcibiades know this of Timon,
That Timon cares not. But if he sack fair
   Athens,
And take our goodly aged men by the beards,
Giving our holy virgins to the stain
Of contumelious, beastly, mad-brain'd war,
Then let him know, and tell him Timon speaks it,
In pity of our aged and our youth,
I cannot choose but tell him, that I care not,   180
And let him take't at worst; for their knives care
   not,
While you have throats to answer: for myself,
• There's not a whittle in the unruly camp
But I do prize it at my love before
The reverend'st throat in Athens. So I leave you
To the protection of the prosperous gods,
As thieves to keepers.
   Flav.   Stay not, all's in vain.
   Tim.   Why, I was writing of my epitaph;
It will be seen to-morrow: my long sickness
Of health and living now begins to mend,   190
And nothing brings me all things. Go, live still;
Be Alcibiades your plague, you his,
And last so long enough!
   First Sen.   We speak in vain.
   Tim.   But yet I love my country, and am not
One that rejoices in the common wreck,
• As common bruit doth put it.
   First Sen.   That's well spoke.
   Tim.   Commend me to my loving country-
    men,—
   First Sen.   These words become your lips as
    they pass thorough them.
   Sec. Sen.   And enter in our ears like great
    triumphers
In their applauding gates.
   Tim.   Commend me to them,   200
And tell them that, to ease them of their griefs,
Their fears of hostile strokes, their aches, losses,
Their pangs of love, with other incident throes
That nature's fragile vessel doth sustain
In life's uncertain voyage, I will some kindness do
   them:
• I'll teach them to prevent wild Alcibiades' wrath.
   First Sen.   I like this well; he will return again.
   Tim.   I have a tree, which grows here in my
    close,
That mine own use invites me to cut down,
And shortly must I fell it: tell my friends,   210
Tell Athens, in the sequence of degree
From high to low throughout, that whoso please

To stop affliction, let him take his haste,
Come hither, ere my tree hath felt the axe,
And hang himself. I pray you, do my greeting.
   Flav. Trouble him no further; thus you still
     shall find him.
   Tim. Come not to me again: but say to Athens,
Timon hath made his everlasting mansion
Upon the beached verge of the salt flood;
Who once a day with his embossed froth   220
The turbulent surge shall cover: thither come,
And let my grave-stone be your oracle.
Lips, let sour words go by and language end:
What is amiss plague and infection mend!
Graves only be men's works and death their gain!
Sun, hide thy beams! Timon hath done his reign.
                [Retires to his cave.
   First Sen. His discontents are unremoveably
Coupled to nature.
   Sec. Sen. Our hope in him is dead: let us return,
And strain what other means is left unto us   230
In our dear peril.
   First Sen.   It requires swift foot. *[Exeunt.*

   SCENE II. *Before the walls of Athens.*

     Enter two Senators *and a* Messenger.

   First Sen. Thou hast painfully discover'd:
     are his files
As full as thy report?
   Mess.   I have spoke the least:
Besides, his expedition promises
Present approach.
   Sec. Sen. We stand much hazard, if they bring
     not Timon.
   Mess. I met a courier, one mine ancient friend;
Whom, though in general part we were opposed,
†Yet our old love made a particular force,
And made us speak like friends: this man was
     riding
From Alcibiades to Timon's cave,   10
With letters of entreaty, which imported
His fellowship i' the cause against your city,
In part for his sake moved.
   First Sen.   Here come our brothers.

     Enter the Senators *from* TIMON.

   Third Sen. No talk of Timon, nothing of him
     expect.
The enemies' drum is heard, and fearful scouring
Doth choke the air with dust: in, and prepare:
Ours is the fall, I fear; our foes the snare.
                    [Exeunt.

   SCENE III. *The woods. Timon's cave, and a*
        rude tomb seen.

     Enter a Soldier, *seeking* TIMON.

   Sold. By all description this should be the place.
Who's here? speak, ho! No answer! What is
     this?
Timon is dead, who hath outstretch'd his span:
Some beast rear'd this; there does not live a man.
Dead, sure; and this his grave. What's on this
     tomb
I cannot read; the character I'll take with wax:
Our captain hath in every figure skill,
An aged interpreter, though young in days:
Before proud Athens he's set down by this,
Whose fall the mark of his ambition is. *[Exit.* 10

Ralph Richardson as Timon, Old Vic Theatre, London,
1956

227–228 *His ... nature.* i.e. this bitterness is of his very
being.

230 *strain.* Consider.

231 *dear.* Grievous.

1 *files.* Ranks.

15 *fearful scouring.* Fearsome scurrying about.

17 *Ours ... snare.* i.e. our part I fear is to fall into their
trap.

6 *character.* Inscription.

Alcibiades: 'Sound to this coward and lascivious town
Our terrible approach.' J. R. Wallack as Alcibiades,
Theatre Royal, Drury Lane, London, 1816

5 *scope.* Aim.

7 *traversed.* Crossed. *breathed.* Spoken.

8 *sufferance.* Suffering. *flush.* Ripe.

9 *crouching marrow.* Latent courage.

14 *conceit.* Idea.

31 *a tithed death.* i.e. the killing of one man in every ten.

34 *by the hazard of the spotted die.* By the throw of a dice.

35 *Let . . . spotted.* May the guilty die.

36 *square.* Just.

43 *cull . . . forth.* Cut out the diseased.

47 *rampired.* Fortified.

SCENE IV.   *Before the walls of Athens.*

Trumpets sound. Enter ALCIBIADES *with his
powers.*

Alcib. Sound to this coward and lascivious town
Our terrible approach.   [*A parley sounded.*

Enter Senators *on the walls.*

Till now you have gone on and fill'd the time
With all licentious measure, making your wills
●The scope of justice; till now myself and such
As slept within the shadow of your power
●Have wander'd with our traversed arms and
          breathed
●Our sufferance vainly: now the time is flush,
●When crouching marrow in the bearer strong
Cries of itself 'No more:' now breathless wrong
Shall sit and pant in your great chairs of ease, 11
And pursy insolence shall break his wind
With fear and horrid flight.
     First Sen.   Noble and young,
●When thy first griefs were but a mere conceit,
Ere thou hadst power or we had cause of fear,
We sent to thee, to give thy rages balm,
To wipe out our ingratitude with loves
Above their quantity.
     Sec. Sen.   So did we woo
Transformed Timon to our city's love
By humble message and by promised means: 20
We were not all unkind, nor all deserve
The common stroke of war.
     First Sen.   These walls of ours
Were not erected by their hands from whom
You have received your griefs; nor are they such
That these great towers, trophies and schools
          should fall
For private faults in them.
     Sec. Sen.   Nor are they living
Who were the motives that you first went out;
Shame that they wanted cunning, in excess
Hath broke their hearts.   March, noble lord,
Into our city with thy banners spread: 30
●By decimation, and a tithed death—
If thy revenges hunger for that food
Which nature loathes—take thou the destined
          tenth,
●And by the hazard of the spotted die
●Let die the spotted.
     First Sen.   All have not offended;
●For those that were, it is not square to take
On those that are, revenges: crimes, like lands,
Are not inherited.   Then, dear countryman,
Bring in thy ranks, but leave without thy rage:
Spare thy Athenian cradle and those kin   40
Which in the bluster of thy wrath must fall
With those that have offended: like a shepherd,
●Approach the fold and cull the infected forth,
But kill not all together.
     Sec. Sen.   What thou wilt,
Thou rather shalt enforce it with thy smile
Than hew to 't with thy sword.
     First Sen.   Set but thy foot
●Against our rampired gates, and they shall ope;
So thou wilt send thy gentle heart before,
To say thou'lt enter friendly.
     Sec. Sen.   Throw thy glove,
Or any token of thine honour else,   50
That thou wilt use the wars as thy redress

And not as our confusion, all thy powers
Shall make their harbour in our town, till we
Have seal'd thy full desire.
 Alcib.   Then there's my glove;
● Descend, and open your uncharged ports:
Those enemies of Timon's and mine own
Whom you yourselves shall set out for reproof
● Fall and no more: and, to atone your fears
With my more noble meaning, not a man
● Shall pass his quarter, or offend the stream 60
Of regular justice in your city's bounds,
But shall be render'd to your public laws
At heaviest answer.
 Both.   'Tis most nobly spoken.
 Alcib. Descend, and keep your words.
  [*The Senators descend, and open the gates.*

Enter Soldier.

 Sold. My noble general, Timon is dead;
Entomb'd upon the very hem o' the sea:
● And on his grave-stone this insculpture, which
With wax I brought away, whose soft impression
Interprets for my poor ignorance.
 Alcib. [*Reads the epitaph*] 'Here lies a wretched
  corse, of wretched soul bereft: 70
Seek not my name: a plague consume you wicked
  caitiffs left!
Here lie I, Timon; who, alive, all living men did
  hate:
● Pass by and curse thy fill, but pass and stay not
  here thy gait.'
● These well express in thee thy latter spirits:
Though thou abhorr'dst in us our human griefs,
Scorn'dst our brain's flow and those our droplets
  which
● From niggard nature fall, yet rich conceit
Taught thee to make vast Neptune weep for aye
On thy low grave, on faults forgiven. Dead
Is noble Timon: of whose memory 80
Hereafter more. Bring me into your city,
● And I will use the olive with my sword,
● Make war breed peace, make peace stint war,
  make each
● Prescribe to other as each other's leech.
Let our drums strike.   [*Exeunt.*

55 *uncharged.* Unassailed. *ports.* Gates.

58 *Fall.* Let them fall.

60 *pass his quarter.* Exceed his duty.

67 *insculpture.* Inscription.

73 *stay . . . gait.* i.e. don't stop here.

74 *These.* These words.

Alcibiades: '. . . to make vast Neptune weep'. Neptune, the god of the sea. From a 17th century engraving

77 *niggard.* Parsimonious.

82 *the olive.* i.e. mercy.

83 *stint.* Stop.

84 *leech.* Physician.

Pericles

1608

AFTER THE ABORTIVENESS OF TIMON OF ATHENS something new was demanded, and Shakespeare certainly produced it with *Pericles*. We must remember that, in spite of the unsatisfactoriness of the text that has come down to us, the play was exceptionally successful: we have plenty of evidence of that. Then, too, we must never forget the bearing of external circumstances upon the mind of a practical dramatist with a strong box-office sense.

John Gower. The subject of Pericles was, as usual with Shakespeare, in the air at the time. Among other publications the story came to mind again with a new edition in 1607 of Lawrence Twine's *The Pattern of Painful Adventures*. Shakespeare took a few touches from this into his play, but far more important to him was the version of the story which he read up in John Gower's *Confessio Amantis*.

We know that Shakespeare, very much a reading man, read his Chaucer; but Chaucer's contemporary, Gower, was visible to the dramatist in the neighbouring church of St. Saviour's, which dominated the whole of Southwark. His youngest brother, Edmund, another actor, was buried in the church in December 1607, with a knell which presumably the prosperous older brother paid for. Within the church a dominating visual image was the splendid monument of the old poet – who had been a benefactor of the church in his time – dating from the reign of Henry IV. There he lies in effigy, full length under a Gothic canopy, his head resting upon his three chief works, one of which is the *Confessio Amantis*, which was Shakespeare's chief reading for his play.

We have seen that, with his unsleeping observancy, he was very conscious of monuments and tombs. In the play Pericles says, on the way to recognising his lost daughter Marina:

> yet thou dost look
> Like Patience gazing on kings' graves –

and it is thought that he had some such sculpted figure in mind. This is very likely, for

Southwark was where the famous monumental workshops were located (whence his own monument at Stratford would come in a few years).

For his play he thought up something new indeed, and gave the whole thing an archaic framework, with John Gower as Chorus, most of his speeches in antique English and octosyllabic couplets like his own. These introduce the first acts; the fifth has Prologue and Epilogue in rhyming pentameter. Very many rhymed couplets occur in the play – the trouble is that an unintelligent reporter, with a pedestrian mind, reported the first two acts. Even here we have recognisable Shakespearean touches, in words and phrases.

The function of Gower's speeches goes back to the Chorus of *Henry V* (with additional propriety, for that was Gower's period), introducing us to the action and leaping over space and time. Altogether the figure of the poet Gower is singularly important to the scheme of the play.

Adventure. The subject of the play is the extraordinary adventures of Pericles – as is the emphasis of Twine's title, *The Pattern of Painful Adventures*: what gave it its appeal. Ben Jonson thought it 'a mouldy tale' – and it certainly was very ancient, going back to Apollonius of Tyre, whom Shakespeare had known about from much earlier. But the public loved it: Pericles fleeing from the Court of Antiochus, after guessing the guilty secret of his incest with his daughter; his travels by sea, in the course of which his daughter, Marina, was born to his wife, Thaisa, whom he had won at the Court of Pentapolis; the wife's presumed death in childbirth, her coffin thrown overboard, which yet arrives on land, with Thaisa awakening out of her trance to become a Vestal at Ephesus; Marina's rescue from pirates, and her more admired rescue from the dangers of the brothel at Mytilene; Pericles meeting with his lost daughter, and the eventual

Above left: *The 14th century poet John Gower, as Chorus in* Pericles. *From the title page of George Wilkins'* The Painful Adventure of Pericles, Prince of Tyre *(1608)*

Above: *Thaisa lifted from her coffin. Frontispiece to Rowe's edition of Shakespeare's Works, 1709*

Above: *A pamphlet adver-tising the advantages of the new Virginia settlement at Jamestown, published in London two years after its foun-dation.*

Above right: *Ralegh, whose second Virginia colony at Roanoke* right *came to a mysterious end after 1587*

Above: *The
dangers and
terrors of the sea,
aptly portrayed by
the younger
Bruegel*

recognition and reunion of all three at Ephesus, with a husband found for Marina in the Governor of Mytilene.

Lost and Found might be a subtitle for the play, and such a farrago of adventures certainly needed a Chorus to fit them all together and tell us where we are – otherwise *we* should be lost.

The sea is everywhere in the play, as again in *The Tempest*, with quite a rôle also in *The Winter's Tale*. The reason is not far to seek. Jacobean London was filled with news of the first English colony, at last, in America and the voyages thither, to New England as well as to Virginia. Hundreds of leading figures subscribed to the Virginia Company (Southampton was to become its Treasurer), i.e. they became 'venturers' in contemporary terms (most of them lost their venture). These later plays of Shakespeare all bear evidences of his reading not only of Hakluyt, as earlier, but of the pamphlets giving news of the voyages and ventures across the Atlantic. Voyages, the sea, storms and tempests, shipwrecks, the sea-shore, pirates, crews – the later plays are full of it all; nor is it at all surprising: the most sensitive register of the time noticed, as Dr. Johnson observed, everything.

Date and Time. Nor is there any difficulty about these: they are obvious. The reprint of Twine's novel came out in 1607; Shakespeare's brother was buried in Gower's church in the same year; the Venetian ambassador saw the play not later than 1608; and in that year George Wilkins cashed in on the success of the play with his novel, *The Painful Adventures of Pericles, Prince of Tyre*. A pamphlet of 1609 bears further witness to the success of the play:

> Amazed I stood to see a crowd
> Of civil throats stretched out so loud . . .
> So that I truly thought all these
> Came to see *Shore* or *Pericles*.

George Wilkins has an interest of his own; for, like Shakespeare, he knew the Montjoies and their house in Silver Street, and gave evidence also in the law-case concerning their daughter and son-in-law. The young couple, whom Master Shakespeare had sponsored, came to lodge in the tavern which Wilkins kept in Turnmill Street.[1] This was frequented by theatre-folk, and he himself tried his hand, with little success, at writing plays as well as this novel.

The more we know about these people the more we see how they relate, and things come together. Common sense and research are what is needed, not academic conjectures.

Turning Point. Everything shows that a turning point was reached, not only in Shakespeare's work but in his life. Even the unimaginative Chambers was 'subjective' enough (his own phrase for it) to posit a possible breakdown for the dramatist at this time. But we do not need to be subjective: consider the objective, external circumstances.

After the successful production of *Pericles*, the theatres were closed on account of plague from July 1608 for eighteen months. One cannot over-estimate the disturbance plague periodically created for contemporary life, but especially for theatre people. With plague raging in London, and the theatres closed, it is pretty certain that Shakespeare retired to the country, and to a full renewal of family life. It is most likely that from these decisive years 1608–9 he was based at Stratford: when he gave evidence in the Montjoie suit in 1612 he had to come up from the country; a second set of interrogatories could not be put to him, for he had gone back there.

At Stratford his mother died in 1608; but a new life was forming around the young couple – the intelligent Susanna and the able doctor, her husband – and Shakespeare's only grandchild, Elizabeth, was born this year.

The intermission of playing gave opportunity for the discussions that took place prior to a further decisive event, the resolution on the part of the Burbages and Shakespeare to take over Blackfriars as an indoor playing-house. This was a step of great importance for the future. Blackfriars had a smaller, more sophisticated upper-class audience, which paid better; it had had, from the Boys' Companies, a tradition of music. Shakespeare now became a part-owner of Blackfriars under the new dispensation; but it also offered a new challenge, and new opportunities, for his writing. It was natural that he, always ready to move with public taste, should experiment, now that he was to write for two audiences, that at the Globe and the other at Blackfriars. This is evident in the plays of his last period.

The Play. The experiment of *Pericles* was a great success, for the public was given everything: not only romantic adventures, and surprising recognitions, but a dumb-show, something like a masque, a dance, a tilt, and a great deal of music: some of it lost, the song Marina sings, for example. Several times music is invoked:

> The still and woeful music that we have,
> Cause it to sound, beseech you.
> The viol once more; how thou stir'st, thou block!
> The music there!

1. cf. Roger Prior, 'The life of George Wilkins', *Shakespeare Survey* 25, 137 foll.

This is to aid in bringing Thaisa back to life, but it is called in at other junctures. Altogether, it was spectacular, as well as new.

For all its newness, much is recognisable. The brothel scenes and characters, the Bawd and Boult, are after the fashion of *Measure for Measure*, and the generous helpings of bawdy would have been another factor making for success. Some of them are commonplace gags, others stamped Shakespearean:

> For your bride goes to that with shame which is her way to go with warrant.
> Faith, some do, and some do not.

> There was a Spaniard's mouth watered, and he went to bed to her very description [Marina's].

We find the phrase, 'the deed of darkness', Shakespeare's word for it before.

Another regular touch we have noticed is Boult's, 'What would you have me do? Go to the wars, would you? where a man may serve seven years for the loss of a leg, and have not money enough in the end to buy him a wooden one?' The name of 'the great pirate Valdez' obviously comes from the Spanish commander whom Drake captured from the Armada of 1588. A touch of the time comes when the knights tilt and King Simonides says to his lords:

> We will withdraw into the gallery.

This was just how Queen Elizabeth viewed the tilts, from her gallery looking down into the tilt-yard below.

Text and Publication. The whole problem of *Pericles* – to which so much discussion has been devoted, mostly beside the point and to little illumination – relates to the text and circumstances of publication. We must keep in mind the hiatus, the upheaval, caused by the plague and Shakespeare's absence from London.

The Company obtained a blocking entry for their very successful play in 1608. But next year a publisher got hold of a text of the play, put together by one or two reporters, and published it, a very poor text, the first two acts badly reported, and much of it badly printed. There was such a demand for it – perhaps all the more on account of the theatres being closed – that another printing was called for the same year; and yet a third in 1611 – six altogether before the horrid Puritans (to whom the play has a reference) closed the theatres altogether.

Heming and Condell did not print the play, for all its success, in the Folio of 1623 – presumably because they had no decent text of it available. The simplest explanation is always best, and the circumstances of 1608–9 make it understandable. All sorts of conjectures have been made, as to divided authorship, unsatisfactory printers, different compositors, etc. Sad as it is, we are grateful for a torso of a play, as with *Timon*, rather than none at all.

PERICLES.

DRAMATIS PERSONÆ.

ANTIOCHUS, king of Antioch.
PERICLES, prince of Tyre.
HELICANUS, } two lords of Tyre.
ESCANES,
SIMONIDES, king of Pentapolis.
CLEON, governor of Tarsus.
LYSIMACHUS, governor of Mytilene.
CERIMON, a lord of Ephesus.
THALIARD, a lord of Antioch.
PHILEMON, servant to Cerimon.
LEONINE, servant to Dionyza.
Marshal.
A Pandar.
BOULT, his servant.

The Daughter of Antiochus.
DIONYZA, wife to Cleon.
THAISA, daughter to Simonides.
MARINA, daughter to Pericles and Thaisa.
LYCHORIDA, nurse to Marina.
A Bawd.

Lords, Knights, Gentlemen, Sailors, Pirates,
Fishermen, and Messengers.

DIANA.

GOWER, as Chorus.

SCENE: *Dispersedly in various countries.*

● *A bullet beside a text line indicates an annotation in the opposite column.*

ACT I.

Enter GOWER.

Before the palace of Antioch.

To sing a song that old was sung,
From ashes ancient Gower is come;
Assuming man's infirmities,
To glad your ear, and please your eyes.
It hath been sung at festivals,
● On ember-eves and holy-ales;
And lords and ladies in their lives
Have read it for restoratives:
The purchase is to make men glorious;
● Et bonum quo antiquius, eo melius.   10
If you, born in these latter times,
When wit's more ripe, accept my rhymes,

6 *ember-eves.* Evenings before fasting days. *holy-ales.* Parish festivals to raise money for the church.

10 *Et . . . melius.* i.e. the older the better.

Opposite: Marina with Pericles. Engraving by Henry Fuseli (1741–1825)

32 *frame*. Journey.

39 *wight*. Man.

1 *at large received*. Fully understood.

7 *Jove*. God of heavens.

8 *Lucina*. Goddess of childbirth.

Pericles: 'See where she comes, apparell'd like the spring ...' Detail from the painting 'Primavera' by Sandro Botticelli (1444–1510)

27 *Hesperides*. Legendary orchard guarded by a dragon.

And that to hear an old man sing
May to your wishes pleasure bring,
I life would wish, and that I might
Waste it for you, like taper-light.
This Antioch, then, Antiochus the Great
Built up, this city, for his chiefest seat;
The fairest in all Syria,
I tell you what mine authors say: 20
This king unto him took a fere,
Who died and left a female heir,
So buxom, blithe, and full of face,
As heaven had lent her all his grace;
With whom the father liking took,
And her to incest did provoke:
Bad child; worse father! to entice his own
To evil should be done by none:
But custom what they did begin
Was with long use account no sin.   30
The beauty of this sinful dame
● Made many princes thither frame,
To seek her as a bed-fellow,
In marriage-pleasures play-fellow:
Which to prevent he made a law,
To keep her still, and men in awe,
That whoso ask'd her for his wife,
His riddle told not, lost his life:
● So for her many a wight did die,
As yon grim looks do testify.   40
What now ensues, to the judgement of your eye
I give, my cause who best can justify.   [*Exit.*

SCENE I.   *Antioch.   A room in the palace.*

Enter ANTIOCHUS, PRINCE PERICLES, *and followers.*

● *Ant.*   Young prince of Tyre, you have at large received
The danger of the task you undertake.
     Per.   I have, Antiochus, and, with a soul
Embolden'd with the glory of her praise,
Think death no hazard in this enterprise.
     Ant.   Bring in our daughter, clothed like a bride,
● For the embracements even of Jove himself;
● At whose conception, till Lucina reign'd,
Nature this dowry gave, to glad her presence,
The senate-house of planets all did sit,   10
To knit in her their best perfections.

Music.   Enter the Daughter of Antiochus.

Per.   See where she comes, apparell'd like the spring,
Graces her subjects, and her thoughts the king
Of every virtue gives renown to men!
Her face the book of praises, where is read
Nothing but curious pleasures, as from thence
Sorrow were ever razed, and testy wrath
Could never be her mild companion.
You gods that made me man, and sway in love,
That have inflamed desire in my breast   20
To taste the fruit of yon celestial tree,
Or die in the adventure, be my helps,
As I am son and servant to your will,
To compass such a boundless happiness!
     Ant.   Prince Pericles,—
     Per.   That would be son to great Antiochus.
● *Ant.*   Before thee stands this fair Hesperides,
With golden fruit, but dangerous to be touch'd;
For death-like dragons here affright thee hard:

Her face, like heaven, enticeth thee to view   30
Her countless glory, which desert must gain;
And which, without desert, because thine eye
• Presumes to reach, all thy whole heap must die.
Yon sometimes famous princes, like thyself,
Drawn by report, adventurous by desire,
Tell thee, with speechless tongues and semblance
    pale,
That without covering, save yon field of stars,
• Here they stand martyrs, slain in Cupid's wars;
And with dead cheeks advise thee to desist
For going on death's net, whom none resist.   40
    Per. Antiochus, I thank thee, who hath taught
My frail mortality to know itself,
And by those fearful objects to prepare
This body, like to them, to what I must;
For death remember'd should be like a mirror,
Who tells us life 's but breath, to trust it error.
I 'll make my will then, and, as sick men do
Who know the world, see heaven, but, feeling woe,
Gripe not at earthly joys as erst they did;
So I bequeath a happy peace to you   50
And all good men, as every prince should do;
My riches to the earth from whence they came;
But my unspotted fire of love to you.
               [To the daughter of Antiochus.
Thus ready for the way of life or death,
I wait the sharpest blow, Antiochus.
    Ant. Scorning advice, read the conclusion,
    then:
Which read and not expounded, 'tis decreed,
As these before thee thou thyself shalt bleed.
•   *Daugh.* Of all say'd yet, mayst thou prove
    prosperous!
Of all say'd yet, I wish thee happiness!   60
•   *Per.* Like a bold champion, I assume the lists,
Nor ask advice of any other thought
But faithfulness and courage.
            He reads the riddle.
     I am no viper, yet I feed
     On mother's flesh which did me breed.
     I sought a husband, in which labour
     I found that kindness in a father:
     He's father, son, and husband mild;
     I mother, wife, and yet his child.
     How they may be, and yet in two,   70
     As you will live, resolve it you.
Sharp physic is the last: but, O you powers
That give heaven countless eyes to view men's
    acts,
Why cloud they not their sights perpetually,
If this be true, which makes me pale to read it?
Fair glass of light, I loved you, and could still,
    [Takes hold of the hand of the Princess.
Were not this glorious casket stored with ill:
But I must tell you, now my thoughts revolt;
For he's no man on whom perfections wait
That, knowing sin within, will touch the gate. 80
You are a fair viol, and your sense the strings;
Who, finger'd to make man his lawful music,
Would draw heaven down, and all the gods, to
    hearken:
But being play'd upon before your time,
Hell only danceth at so harsh a chime.
• Good sooth, I care not for you.
    Ant. Prince Pericles, touch not, upon thy life,
For that's an article within our law,
As dangerous as the rest. Your time's expired:
Either expound now, or receive your sentence. 90

33 *whole heap.* i.e. body.

38 *Cupid.* Attendant on Venus, goddess of love.

59 *say'd.* i.e. assayed, tried.

61 *assume.* Undertake. *lists.* Combat.

86 *Good sooth.* Truly.

101 *Copp'd.* Humped.

110 *gloze.* Use fair words.

Pericles: 'And both like serpents are, who though they feed On sweetest flowers, yet they poison breed.' Emblem 'Latet anguis in herba' from Claude Paradin's *Devises heroiques*, 1557

Per.   Great king,
Few love to hear the sins they love to act;
'Twould braid yourself too near for me to tell it.
Who has a book of all that monarchs do,
He's more secure to keep it shut than shown:
For vice repeated is like the wandering wind,
Blows dust in others' eyes, to spread itself;
And yet the end of all is bought thus dear,
The breath is gone, and the sore eyes see clear
To stop the air would hurt them. The blind mole
    casts   100
●Copp'd hills towards heaven, to tell the earth is
    throng'd
By man's oppression; and the poor worm doth
    die for 't.
Kings are earth's gods; in vice their law 's their
    will;
And if Jove stray, who dares say Jove doth ill?
It is enough you know; and it is fit,
What being more known grows worse, to smo-
    ther it.
All love the womb that their first being bred,
Then give my tongue like leave to love my head.
    Ant.   [*Aside*] Heaven, that I had thy head!
    he has found the meaning:
●But I will gloze with him.—Young prince of Tyre,
Though by the tenour of our strict edict,   111
Your exposition misinterpreting,
We might proceed to cancel of your days;
Yet hope, succeeding from so fair a tree
As your fair self, doth tune us otherwise:
Forty days longer we do respite you:
If by which time our secret be undone,
This mercy shows we'll joy in such a son:
And until then your entertain shall be
As doth befit our honour and your worth.   120
                    [*Exeunt all but Pericles.*
    Per.   How courtesy would seem to cover sin,
When what is done is like an hypocrite,
The which is good in nothing but in sight!
If it be true that I interpret false,
Then were it certain you were not so bad
As with foul incest to abuse your soul;
Where now you 're both a father and a son,
By your untimely claspings with your child,
Which pleasure fits an husband, not a father;
And she an eater of her mother's flesh,   130
By the defiling of her parent's bed;
And both like serpents are, who though they feed
On sweetest flowers, yet they poison breed.
Antioch, farewell! for wisdom sees, those men
Blush not in actions blacker than the night,
Will shun no course to keep them from the light.
One sin, I know, another doth provoke;
Murder's as near to lust as flame to smoke:
Poison and treason are the hands of sin,
Ay, and the targets, to put off the shame: 140
Then, lest my life be cropp'd to keep you clear,
By flight I'll shun the danger which I fear. [*Exit.*

Re-enter ANTIOCHUS.

    Ant.   He hath found the meaning, for which
    we mean
To have his head.
He must not live to trumpet forth my infamy,
Nor tell the world Antiochus doth sin
In such a loathed manner;
And therefore instantly this prince must die;

For by his fall my honour must keep high.
Who attends us there?

Enter THALIARD.

Thal.   Doth your highness call? 150
Ant. Thaliard,
You are of our chamber, and our mind partakes
Her private actions to your secrecy;
And for your faithfulness we will advance you.
Thaliard, behold, here's poison, and here's gold:
We hate the prince of Tyre, and thou must kill
     him:
It fits thee not to ask the reason why,
Because we bid it.   Say, is it done?
     Thal.   My lord,
'Tis done.
Ant. Enough.   160

Enter a Messenger.

●Let your breath cool yourself, telling your haste.
     Mess.   My lord, prince Pericles is fled. [*Exit.*
     Ant.   As thou
Wilt live, fly after: and like an arrow shot
From a well-experienced archer hits the mark
His eye doth level at, so thou ne'er return
Unless thou say 'Prince Pericles is dead.'
     Thal. My lord,
If I can get him within my pistol's length,
I'll make him sure enough: so, farewell to your
     highness.
     Ant. Thaliard, adieu! [*Exit Thal.*] Till
     Pericles be dead,   170
My heart can lend no succour to my head. [*Exit.*

SCENE II.   *Tyre.   A room in the palace.*

Enter PERICLES.

Per. [*To Lords without*]   Let none disturb
     us.—Why should this change of thoughts,
The sad companion, dull-eyed melancholy,
Be my so used a guest as not an hour,
In the day's glorious walk, or peaceful night,
The tomb where grief should sleep, can breed
     me quiet?
Here pleasures court mine eyes, and mine eyes
     shun them,
And danger, which I fear'd, is at Antioch,
Whose arm seems far too short to hit me here:
Yet neither pleasure's art can joy my spirits,
Nor yet the other's distance comfort me.   10
Then it is thus: the passions of the mind,
●That have their first conception by mis-dread,
Have after-nourishment and life by care;
And what was first but fear what might be done,
Grows elder now and cares it be not done.
And so with me: the great Antiochus,
'Gainst whom I am too little to contend,
Since he's so great can make his will his act,
Will think me speaking, though I swear to silence;
●Nor boots it me to say I honour him,   20
If he suspect I may dishonour him:
And what may make him blush in being known,
He'll stop the course by which it might be known;
With hostile forces he'll o'erspread the land,
●And with the ostent of war will look so huge,
Amazement shall drive courage from the state;
Our men be vanquish'd ere they do resist,
And subjects punish'd that ne'er thought offence:
Which care of them, not pity of myself,

Antiochus: 'We hate the prince of Tyre, and thou must kill him'. Engraving from *Le premier Livre d'Amadis de Gaule*, 1555

161 *telling.* While you tell.

12 *mis-dread.* Fear.

20 *boots.* Profits.

25 *ostent.* Display.

Pericles: '. . . as the tops of trees, Which fence the roots they grow by and defend them'. Woodcut from Cesare Ripa's *Iconologia*, 1603

---

44 *Signior Sooth.* i.e. Sir Sweet Tongue.

Who am no more but as the tops of trees,
Which fence the roots they grow by and defend
them,   30
Makes both my body pine and soul to languish,
And punish that before that he would punish.

> *Enter* HELICANUS, *with other* Lords.

First Lord.   Joy and all comfort in your sacred
breast!
Sec. Lord.   And keep your mind, till you
return to us,
Peaceful and comfortable!
Hel.   Peace, peace, and give experience
tongue.
They do abuse the king that flatter him:
For flattery is the bellows blows up sin;
The thing the which is flatter'd, but a spark,   40
To which that blast gives heat and stronger
glowing;
Whereas reproof, obedient and in order,
Fits kings, as they are men, for they may err.
● When Signior Sooth here does proclaim a peace,
He flatters you, makes war upon your life.
Prince, pardon me, or strike me, if you please;
I cannot be much lower than my knees.
Per.   All leave us else; but let your cares
o'erlook
What shipping and what lading's in our haven,
And then return to us. [*Exeunt Lords.*] Heli-
canus, thou   50
Hast moved us: what seest thou in our looks?
Hel.   An angry brow, dread lord.
Per.   If there be such a dart in princes' frowns,
How durst thy tongue move anger to our face?
Hel.   How dare the plants look up to heaven, from whence
They have their nourishment?
Per.   Thou know'st I have power
To take thy life from thee.
Hel. [*Kneeling*]   I have ground the axe my-
self;
Do you but strike the blow.
Per.   Rise, prithee, rise.
Sit down: thou art no flatterer: 60
I thank thee for it; and heaven forbid
That kings should let their ears hear their faults
hid!
Fit counsellor and servant for a prince,
Who by thy wisdom makest a prince thy servant,
What wouldst thou have me do?
Hel.   To bear with patience
Such griefs as you yourself do lay upon yourself.
Per.   Thou speak'st like a physician, Helicanus,
That minister'st a potion unto me
That thou wouldst tremble to receive thyself.
Attend me, then: I went to Antioch,   70
Where as thou know'st, against the face of death,
I sought the purchase of a glorious beauty,
From whence an issue I might propagate,
†Are arms to princes, and bring joys to subjects.
Her face was to mine eye beyond all wonder;
The rest—hark in thine ear—as black as incest:
Which by my knowledge found, the sinful father
Seem'd not to strike, but smooth: but thou
know'st this,
'Tis time to fear when tyrants seem to kiss.
Which fear so grew in me, I hither fled,   80
Under the covering of a careful night,
Who seem'd my good protector; and, being here,

Bethought me what was past, what might succeed.
I knew him tyrannous; and tyrants' fears
Decrease not, but grow faster than the years:
And should he doubt it, as no doubt he doth,
That I should open to the listening air
How many worthy princes' bloods were shed,
To keep his bed of blackness unlaid ope,   89
To lop that doubt, he'll fill this land with arms,
And make pretence of wrong that I have done him;
When all, for mine, if I may call offence,
Must feel war's blow, who spares not innocence:
Which love to all, of which thyself art one,
Who now reprovest me for it,—
  Hel.   Alas, sir!
  Per.   Drew sleep out of mine eyes, blood
    from my cheeks,
Musings into my mind, with thousand doubts
How I might stop this tempest ere it came;
And finding little comfort to relieve them,
I thought it princely charity to grieve them.   100
  Hel.   Well, my lord, since you have given me
    leave to speak,
Freely will I speak.   Antiochus you fear,
And justly too, I think, you fear the tyrant,
Who either by public war or private treason
Will take away your life.
Therefore, my lord, go travel for a while,
Till that his rage and anger be forgot,
Or till the Destinies do cut his thread of life.
Your rule direct to any; if to me,   109
Day serves not light more faithful than I'll be.
  Per.   I do not doubt thy faith;
But should he wrong my liberties in my absence?
  Hel.   We'll mingle our bloods together in the
    earth,
From whence we had our being and our birth.
  Per.   Tyre, I now look from thee then, and to
    Tarsus
Intend my travel, where I'll hear from thee;
And by whose letters I'll dispose myself.
The care I had and have of subjects' good
On thee I lay, whose wisdom's strength can
    bear it.   119
I'll take thy word for faith, not ask thine oath:
Who shuns not to break one will sure crack both:
But in our orbs we'll live so round and safe,
That time of both this truth shall ne'er convince,
Thou show'dst a subject's shine, I a true prince.
                      [*Exeunt.*

SCENE III.   *Tyre.   An ante-chamber in the
      palace.*

Enter THALIARD.

  Thal.   So, this is Tyre, and this the court.
Here must I kill King Pericles; and if I do it
not, I am sure to be hanged at home: 'tis dangerous.   Well, I perceive he was a wise fellow,
and had good discretion, that, being bid to ask
what he would of the king, desired he might
know none of his secrets: now do I see he had
some reason for't; for if a king bid a man be a
villain, he's bound by the indenture of his oath
to be one.   Hush! here come the lords of Tyre.

Enter HELICANUS *and* ESCANES, *with other*
    Lords *of Tyre.*

  Hel.   You shall not need, my fellow peers of
  Tyre,   11

Helicanus: 'Or till the Destinies do cut his thread of life.' Engraving of The Destinies from Vincenzo Cartari's *Imagini de i dei de gli antichi*, 1587

115 *Tarsus.* A city of southern Turkey, famous for its prosperity and beauty in ancient times.

122 *orbs.* Orbits.

Further to question me of your king's departure:
His seal'd commission, left in trust with me,
Doth speak sufficiently he's gone to travel.
 Thal. [*Aside*] How! the king gone!
 Hel. If further yet you will be satisfied,
Why, as it were unlicensed of your loves,
He would depart, I'll give some light unto you.
Being at Antioch——
 Thal. [*Aside*] What from Antioch?
 Hel. Royal Antiochus—on what cause I know
   not—   20
Took some displeasure at him; at least he judged
   so:
And doubting lest that he had err'd or sinn'd,
To show his sorrow, he'ld correct himself;
So puts himself unto the shipman's toil,
With whom each minute threatens life or death.
 Thal. [*Aside*] Well, I perceive
I shall not be hang'd now, although I would;
But since he's gone,† the king's seas must please:
He 'scaped the land, to perish at the sea.
I'll present myself. Peace to the lords of Tyre!
 Hel. Lord Thaliard from Antiochus is wel-
   come.   31
 Thal. From him I come
With message unto princely Pericles;
But since my landing I have understood
Your lord has betook himself to unknown travels,
My message must return from whence it came.
 Hel. We have no reason to desire it,
Commended to our master, not to us:
Yet, ere you shall depart, this we desire,
As friends to Antioch, we may feast in Tyre. 40
             [*Exeunt.*

SCENE IV. *Tarsus. A room in the Governor's
       house.*

Enter CLEON, *the governor of Tarsus, with*
   DIONYZA, *and others.*

 Cle. My Dionyza, shall we rest us here,
And by relating tales of others' griefs,
See if 'twill teach us to forget our own?
 Dio. That were to blow at fire in hope to
   quench it;
For who digs hills because they do aspire
Throws down one mountain to cast up a higher.
O my distressed lord, even such our griefs are:
Here they're but felt, and seen with mischief's
   eyes,
But like to groves, being topp'd, they higher rise.
 Cle. O Dionyza,   1C
Who wanteth food, and will not say he wants it,
Or can conceal his hunger till he famish?
Our tongues and sorrows do sound deep
Our woes into the air; our eyes do weep,
Till tongues fetch breath that may proclaim them
   louder;
That, if heaven slumber while their creatures
   want,
They may awake their helps to comfort them.
I'll then discourse our woes, felt several years,
And wanting breath to speak help me with tears.
 Dio. I'll do my best, sir.   20
 Cle. This Tarsus, o'er which I have the
   government,
A city on whom plenty held full hand,
For riches strew'd herself even in the streets ·

Whose towers bore heads so high they kiss'd the
    clouds,
And strangers ne'er beheld but wonder'd at;
● Whose men and dames so jetted and adorn'd,
Like one another's glass to trim them by:
Their tables were stored full, to glad the sight,
And not so much to feed on as delight;
All poverty was scorn'd, and pride so great,   30
The name of help grew odious to repeat.
    Dio. O, 'tis too true.
    Cle. But see what heaven can do! By this
    our change,
These mouths, who but of late, earth, sea, and air,
Were all too little to content and please,
Although they gave their creatures in abundance,
As houses are defiled for want of use,
They are now starved for want of exercise:
Those palates who, not yet two summers younger,
Must have inventions to delight the taste,   40
Would now be glad of bread, and beg for it:
Those mothers who, to nousle up their babes,
Thought nought too curious, are ready now
To eat those little darlings whom they loved.
So sharp are hunger's teeth, that man and wife
Draw lots who first shall die to lengthen life:
Here stands a lord, and there a lady weeping;
Here many sink, yet those which see them fall
Have scarce strength left to give them burial.
Is not this true?   50
    Dio. Our cheeks and hollow eyes do witness it.
    Cle. O, let those cities that of plenty's cup
And her prosperities so largely taste,
With their superfluous riots, hear these tears!
The misery of Tarsus may be theirs.

        Enter a Lord.

    Lord. Where's the lord governor?
    Cle. Here.
Speak out thy sorrows which thou bring'st in
    haste,
For comfort is too far for us to expect.
    Lord. We have descried, upon our neighbour-
    ing shore,   60
● A portly sail of ships make hitherward.
    Cle. I thought as much.
One sorrow never comes but brings an heir,
That may succeed as his inheritor;
And so in ours: some neighbouring nation,
Taking advantage of our misery,
Hath stuff'd these hollow vessels with their power,
To beat us down, the which are down already;
And make a conquest of unhappy me,
Whereas no glory's got to overcome.   70
    Lord. That's the least fear; for, by the sem-
    blance
Of their white flags display'd, they bring us peace,
And come to us as favourers, not as foes.
    Cle. Thou speak'st like him's untutor'd to
    repeat:
Who makes the fairest show means most deceit.
But bring they what they will and what they can,
What need we fear?
The ground's the lowest, and we are half way
    there.
Go tell their general we attend him here,
To know for what he comes, and whence he comes,
And what he craves.   81
    Lord. I go, my lord.   [*Exit.*

26 *jetted.* Swaggering.

Cleon: 'All poverty was scorn'd . . .' Engraving of the
goddess of Plenty from a Roman medal in G. du Choul's
Discours de la Religion des Anciens Romains, 1567

---

61 *portly sail.* Stately fleet.

83 *consist.* Decide.

Pericles: 'Arise, I pray you, rise:' Pericles (Richard Johnson) with Cleon (Donald Eccles) and Dionyza (Rachel Kempson), Sttatford-upon-Avon, 1958

2 *wis.* Know.

12 *Thinks . . . can.* i.e. believes as the gospel every word he utters.

Cle. Welcome is peace, if he on peace consist;
If wars, we are unable to resist.

Enter PERICLES *with* Attendants.

Per. Lord governor, for so we hear you are,
Let not our ships and number of our men
Be like a beacon fired to amaze your eyes.
We have heard your miseries as far as Tyre,
And seen the desolation of your streets:
Nor come we to add sorrow to your tears,   90
But to relieve them of their heavy load;
And these our ships, you happily may think
Are like the Trojan horse was stuff'd within
With bloody veins, expecting overthrow,
Are stored with corn to make your needy bread,
And give them life whom hunger starved half
      dead.
All. The gods of Greece protect you!
And we'll pray for you.
Per.   Arise, I pray you, rise:
We do not look for reverence, but for love,
And harbourage for ourself, our ships, and men.
Cle. The which when any shall not gratify, 101
Or pay you with unthankfulness in thought,
Be it our wives, our children, or ourselves,
The curse of heaven and men succeed their evils!
Till when,—the which I hope shall ne'er be
      seen,—
Your grace is welcome to our town and us.
Per. Which welcome we'll accept; feast here
      awhile,
Until our stars that frown lend us a smile.
                                          [*Exeunt.*

ACT II.

Enter GOWER.

Gow. Here have you seen a mighty king
His child, I wis, to incest bring;
A better prince and benign lord,
That will prove awful both in deed and word.
Be quiet then as men should be,
Till he hath pass'd necessity.
I'll show you those in troubles reign,
Losing a mite, a mountain gain.
The good in conversation,
To whom I give my benison,   10
Is still at Tarsus, where each man
Thinks all is writ he speken can;
And, to remember what he does,
Build his statue to make him glorious:
But tidings to the contrary
Are brought your eyes; what need speak I?

DUMB SHOW.

Enter at one door PERICLES *talking with*
CLEON; *all the train with them. Enter at
another door a* Gentleman, *with a letter to*
PERICLES; PERICLES *shows the letter to*
CLEON; *gives the* Messenger *a reward, and
knights him. Exit* PERICLES *at one door, and*
CLEON *at another.*

Good Helicane, that stay'd at home,
Not to eat honey like a drone
From others' labours; for though he strive
To killen bad, keep good alive;   20
And to fulfil his prince' desire,
Sends word of all that haps in Tyre:

How Thaliard came full bent with sin
And had intent to murder him;
And that in Tarsus was not best
Longer for him to make his rest.
He, doing so, put forth to seas,
Where when men been, there's seldom ease;
For now the wind begins to blow;
Thunder above and deeps below   30
Make such unquiet, that the ship
Should house him safe is wreck'd and split;
And he, good prince, having all lost,
By waves from coast to coast is tost:

  • All perishen of man, of pelf,
  • Ne aught escapen but himself;
  Till fortune, tired with doing bad,
  • Threw him ashore, to give him glad:
And here he comes.   What shall be next,
Pardon old Gower,—this longs the text.   40
                                    [*Exit.*

SCENE I.   *Pentapolis.   An open place by the
                    sea-side.*

          Enter PERICLES, *wet.*

Per.   Yet cease your ire, you angry stars of
        heaven!
Wind, rain, and thunder, remember, earthly man
Is but a substance that must yield to you;
And I, as fits my nature, do obey you:
Alas, the sea hath cast me on the rocks,
Wash'd me from shore to shore, and left me
        breath
Nothing to think on but ensuing death:
Let it suffice the greatness of your powers
To have bereft a prince of all his fortunes;   9
And having thrown him from your watery grave,
Here to have death in peace is all he'll crave.

          Enter three Fishermen.

  • *First Fish.*   What, ho, Pilch!
  Sec. Fish.   Ha, come and bring away the nets!
  • *First Fish.*   What, Patch-breech, I say!
  Third Fish.   What say you, master?
  First Fish.   Look how thou stirrest now! come
  •away, or I'll fetch thee with a wanion.
  Third Fish.   'Faith, master, I am thinking of
the poor men that were cast away before us even
now.   20
  First Fish.   Alas, poor souls, it grieved my
heart to hear what pitiful cries they made to us to
help them, when, well-a-day, we could scarce
help ourselves.
  Third Fish.   Nay, master, said not I as much
when I saw the porpus how he bounced and
tumbled? they say they're half fish, half flesh:
a plague on them, they ne'er come but I look to
be washed.   Master, I marvel how the fishes live
in the sea.   30
  First Fish.   Why, as men do a-land; the great
ones eat up the little ones: I can compare our
rich misers to nothing so fitly as to a whale; a'
plays and tumbles, driving the poor fry before
him, and at last devours them all at a mouthful:
such whales have I heard on o' the land, who
never leave gaping till they've swallowed the
whole parish, church, steeple, bells, and all.
  Per.   [*Aside*] A pretty moral.   39
  Third Fish.   But, master, if I had been the
sexton, I would have been that day in the belfry.

35 *All . . . man.* All men are perished. *pelf.* Possessions.

36 *Ne aught escapen.* Nothing escapes.

38 *glad.* Gladness.

12 *Pilch.* Leather jacket.

14 *Patch-breech.* Nick-name.

17 *fetch.* Strike. *wanion.* Vengeance.

Third Fisherman: '. . . I saw the porpus how he bounced and tumbled'. Illustration by Byam Shaw, *The Chiswick Shakespeare*, 1902

58-9 *If . . . it.* If you find this pleasant, then let it be struck from the calendar.

82 *quoth-a?* Did he say?

First Fisherman: 'I have a gown here; come, put it on'. Engraving of a fisherman's gown from Pietro Bertelli's *Diversarum nationum habitus,* 1594

97 *beadle.* Parish constable whose duty was to whip offenders.

Sec. Fish.   Why, man?
Third Fish.   Because he should have swallowed me too: and when I had been in his belly, I would have kept such a jangling of the bells, that he should never have left, till he cast bells, steeple, church, and parish, up again.   But if the good King Simonides were of my mind,—
Per. [*Aside*] Simonides!   49
Third Fish.   We would purge the land of these drones, that rob the bee of her honey.
Per. [*Aside*] How from the finny subject of the sea
These fishers tell the infirmities of men;
And from their watery empire recollect
All that may men approve or men detect!
Peace be at your labour, honest fishermen.
Sec. Fish.   Honest! good fellow, what's that?
●If it be a day fits you, †search out of the calendar, and nobody look after it.
Per.   May see the sea hath cast upon your coast.   60
Sec. Fish.   What a drunken knave was the sea to cast thee in our way!
Per.   A man whom both the waters and the wind,
In that vast tennis-court, have made the ball
For them to play upon, entreats you pity him;
He asks of you, that never used to beg.
First Fish.   No, friend, cannot you beg?   Here's them in our country of Greece gets more with begging than we can do with working.
Sec. Fish   Canst thou catch any fishes, then?
Per.   I never practised it.   71
Sec. Fish.   Nay, then thou wilt starve, sure; for here's nothing to be got now-a-days, unless thou canst fish for't.
Per.   What I have been I have forgot to know;
But what I am, want teaches me to think on:
A man throng'd up with cold: my veins are chill,
And have no more of life than may suffice
To give my tongue that heat to ask your help;
Which if you shall refuse, when I am dead,   80
For that I am a man, pray see me buried.
● *First Fish*   Die quoth-a?   Now gods forbid! I have a gown here; come, put it on; keep thee warm.   Now, afore me, a handsome fellow!   Come, thou shalt go home, and we'll have flesh for holidays, fish for fasting-days, and moreo'er puddings and flap-jacks, and thou shalt be welcome.
Per.   I thank you, sir.
Sec. Fish.   Hark you, my friend; you said you could not beg.   90
Per.   I did but crave.
Sec. Fish.   But crave!   Then I'll turn craver too, and so I shall 'scape whipping.
Per.   Why, are all your beggars whipped, then?
Sec. Fish.   O, not all, my friend, not all: for if all your beggars were whipped, I would wish ●no better office than to be beadle.   But, master, I'll go draw up the net.
   [*Exit with Third Fisherman.*
Per. [*Aside*] How well this honest mirth becomes their labour!
First Fish.   Hark you, sir, do you know where ye are?   101
Per.   Not well.
First Fish.   Why, I'll tell you: this is called Pentapolis, and our king the good Simonides.

Per. The good King Simonides, do you call him?

First Fish. Ay, sir; and he deserves so to be called for his peaceable reign and good government.

Per. He is a happy king, since he gains from his subjects the name of good by his government. How far is his court distant from this shore? 111

First Fish. Marry, sir, half a day's journey: and I'll tell you, he hath a fair daughter, and to-morrow is her birth-day; and there are princes and knights come from all parts of the world to just and tourney for her love.

Per. Were my fortunes equal to my desires, I could wish to make one there.

First Fish. O, sir, things must be as they may; and what a man cannot get, he may law-fully deal for—† his wife's soul. 121

Re-enter Second *and* Third Fishermen, *drawing up a net.*

Sec. Fish. Help, master, help! here's a fish hangs in the net, like a poor man's right in the law; 'twill hardly come out. Ha! bots on't, 'tis come at last, and 'tis turned to a rusty armour.

Per. An armour, friends! I pray you, let me see it.
Thanks, fortune, yet, that, after all my crosses,
Thou givest me somewhat to repair myself;
And though it was mine own, part of my heritage,
Which my dead father did bequeath to me, 130
With this strict charge, even as he left his life,
'Keep it, my Pericles; it hath been a shield
'Twixt me and death;'—and pointed to this brace;—
'For that it saved me, keep it; in like necessity—
The which the gods protect thee from!—may defend thee.'
It kept where I kept, I so dearly loved it;
Till the rough seas, that spare not any man,
Took it in rage, though calm'd have given't again:
I thank thee for't: my shipwreck now's no ill,
Since I have here my father's gift in's will. 140

First Fish. What mean you, sir?

Per. To beg of you, kind friends, this coat of worth,
For it was sometime target to a king;
I know it by this mark. He loved me dearly,
And for his sake I wish the having of it;
And that you'ld guide me to your sovereign's court,
Where with it I may appear a gentleman;
And if that ever my low fortune's better,
I'll pay your bounties; till then rest your debtor.

First Fish. Why, wilt thou tourney for the lady?

Per. I'll show the virtue I have borne in arms.

First Fish. Why, do 'e take it, and the gods give thee good on't!

Sec. Fish. Ay, but hark you, my friend; 'twas we that made up this garment through the rough seams of the waters: there are certain condole-ments, certain vails. I hope, sir, if you thrive, you'll remember from whence you had it.

Per. Believe 't, I will.
By your furtherance I am clothed in steel; 160
And, spite of all the rapture of the sea,
This jewel holds his building on my arm:
Unto thy value I will mount myself
Upon a courser, whose delightful steps
Shall make the gazer joy to see him tread.

---

124 *bots on't.* Plague on it! (The botts is an infection of horses with parasitical worms.)

133 *brace.* Armlet.

143 *target.* Shield.

150 *tourney.* Tilt.

156-157 *condolements.* Shares. *vails.* Gratuities.

164 *courser.* Fine horse.

167 *bases.* Breeches.

4 *Return.* Reply.

15 *device.* Crest.

21 '*Lux . . . mihi*'. Your light is life to me.

27 '*Piu . . . fuerza*'. More by gentleness than by force.

The French version of the Second Knight's motto, 'Plus par douceur, que par force' from Giles Corrozet's *Hecatomgraphie*, 1543

30 '*Me . . . apex*'. The crown of triumph has led me on.

33 '*Quod . . . extinguit*'. That which feeds me, extinguishes me.

38 '*Sic . . . fides*'. Thus is faith to be tested.

Only, my friend, I yet am unprovided
● Of a pair of bases.
    Sec. Fish. We'll sure provide: thou shalt have my best gown to make thee a pair; and I'll bring thee to the court myself.   **170**
    Per. Then honour be but a goal to my will,
This day I'll rise, or else add ill to ill. [*Exeunt.*

SCENE II.   *The same. A public way or platform leading to the lists. A pavilion by the side of it for the reception of the King, Princess, Lords, &c.*

Enter SIMONIDES, THAISA, *Lords, and* Attendants.

    Sim. Are the knights ready to begin the triumph?
    First Lord. They are, my liege;
And stay your coming to present themselves.
● *Sim.* Return them, we are ready; and our daughter,
In honour of whose birth these triumphs are,
Sits here, like beauty's child, whom nature gat
For men to see, and seeing wonder at.
               [*Exit a Lord.*
    Thai. It pleaseth you, my royal father, to express
My commendations great, whose merit's less.
    Sim. It's fit it should be so; for princes are 10
A model, which heaven makes like to itself:
As jewels lose their glory if neglected,
So princes their renowns if not respected.
'Tis now your honour, daughter, to explain
● The labour of each knight in his device.
    Thai. Which, to preserve mine honour, I'll perform.

Enter a Knight; *he passes over, and his* Squire *presents his shield to the* Princess.

    Sim. Who is the first that doth prefer himself?
    Thai. A knight of Sparta, my renowned father;
And the device he bears upon his shield
Is a black Ethiope reaching at the sun: **20**
● The word, 'Lux tua vita mihi'.
    Sim. He loves you well that holds his life of you.
      [*The Second Knight passes over.*
Who is the second that presents himself?
    Thai. A prince of Macedon, my royal father;
And the device he bears upon his shield
Is an arm'd knight that's conquer'd by a lady;
● The motto thus, in Spanish, 'Piu por dulzura que por fuerza.'
      [*The Third Knight passes over.*
    Sim. And what's the third?
    Thai.   The third of Antioch;
And his device, a wreath of chivalry;
● The word, 'Me pompæ provexit apex.'   **30**
      [*The Fourth Knight passes over.*
    Sim. What is the fourth?
    Thai. A burning torch that's turned upside down;
● The word, 'Quod me alit, me extinguit.'
    Sim. Which shows that beauty hath his power and will,
Which can as well inflame as it can kill.
      [*The Fifth Knight passes over.*
    Thai. The fifth, an hand environed with clouds,
Holding out gold that's by the touchstone tried:
● The motto thus, 'Sic spectanda fides.'

[*The Sixth Knight, Pericles, passes over.*
Sim.   And what's
The sixth and last, the which the knight himself
With such a graceful courtesy deliver'd?   41
  Thai.   He seems to be a stranger; but his
      present is
A wither'd branch, that's only green at top;
●The motto, 'In hac spe vivo'.
  Sim.   A pretty moral;
From the dejected state wherein he is,
He hopes by you his fortunes yet may flourish.
  First Lord.   He had need mean better than
      his outward show
Can any way speak in his just commend;
For by his rusty outside he appears   50
●To have practised more the whipstock than the
      lance.
  Sec. Lord.   He well may be a stranger, for he
      comes
To an honour'd triumph strangely furnished.
  Third Lord.   And on set purpose let his
      armour rust
Until this day, to scour it in the dust.
  Sim.   Opinion's but a fool, that makes us scan
The outward habit by the inward man.
But stay, the knights are coming: we will with-
      draw
Into the gallery.   [*Exeunt.*
  [*Great shouts within, and all cry* 'The mean
      knight!'

SCENE III.   *The same.   A hall of state: a*
      banquet prepared.

Enter SIMONIDES, THAISA, Lords, Attendants,
      and Knights, *from tilting.*

  Sim.   Knights,
To say you're welcome were superfluous.
To place upon the volume of your deeds,
As in a title-page, your worth in arms,
Were more than you expect, or more than's fit,
Since every worth in show commends itself.
Prepare for mirth, for mirth becomes a feast:
You are princes and my guests.
  Thai.   But you, my knight and guest;
To whom this wreath of victory I give,   10
And crown you king of this day's happiness.
  Per.   'Tis more by fortune, lady, than by merit.
  Sim.   Call it by what you will, the day is yours;
And here, I hope, is none that envies it.
In framing an artist, art hath thus decreed,
To make some good, but others to exceed;
And you are her labour'd scholar.   Come, queen
      o' the feast,—
For, daughter, so you are,—here take your place:
Marshal the rest, as they deserve their grace.
  Knights.   We are honour'd much by good
      Simonides.   20
  Sim.   Your presence glads our days: honour
      we love;
For who hates honour hates the gods above.
  Marshal.   Sir, yonder is your place.
  Per.   Some other is more fit.
  First Knight.   Contend not, sir; for we are
      gentlemen
That neither in our hearts nor outward eyes
Envy the great nor do the low despise.
  Per.   You are right courteous knights.
  Sim.   Sit, sir, sit.

44 '*In . . . vivo*'. In this hope I live.

51 *practised the whipstock.* Used a horse whip i.e. driven
a cart.

A tournament. Woodcut from *Le centre de l'amour,*
c. 1600

29 *cates resist me.* These delicacies are distasteful to me.
she. i.e. Thaisa.

42 *vail.* Lower.

56 *countervail.* Equal.

Per.   By Jove, I wonder, that is king of
  thoughts,
●These cates resist me, she but thought upon.
 Thai.   By Juno, that is queen of marriage, 30
All viands that I eat do seem unsavoury,
Wishing him my meat.   Sure, he's a gallant gen-
  tleman.
 Sim.   He's but a country gentleman;
Has done no more than other knights have done;
Has broken a staff or so; so let it pass.
 Thai.   To me he seems like diamond to glass.
 Per.   Yon king's to me like to my father's
  picture,
Which tells me in that glory once he was;
Had princes sit, like stars, about his throne,
And he the sun, for them to reverence; 40
None that beheld him, but, like lesser lights,
●Did vail their crowns to his supremacy:
Where now his son's like a glow-worm in the
  night,
The which hath fire in darkness, none in light:
Whereby I see that Time's the king of men,
He's both their parent, and he is their grave,
And gives them what he will, not what they crave.
 Sim.   What, are you merry, knights?
 Knights.   Who can be other in this royal pre-
  sence?
 Sim.   Here, with a cup that's stored unto the
  brim,— 50
As you do love, fill to your mistress' lips,—
We drink this health to you.
 Knights.   We thank your grace.
 Sim.   Yet pause awhile:
Yon knight doth sit too melancholy,
As if the entertainment in our court
●Had not a show might countervail his worth.
Note it not you, Thaisa?
 Thai.   What is it
To me, my father?
 Sim.   O, attend, my daughter:
Princes in this should live like gods above,
Who freely give to every one that comes 60
To honour them:
And princes not doing so are like to gnats,
Which make a sound, but kill'd are wonder'd at.
Therefore to make his entrance more sweet,
Here, say we drink this standing-bowl of wine to
  him.
 Thai.   Alas, my father, it befits not me
Unto a stranger knight to be so bold:
He may my proffer take for an offence,
Since men take women's gifts for impudence.
 Sim.   How! 70
Do as I bid you, or you'll move me else.
 Thai.   [*Aside*] Now, by the gods, he could
  not please me better.
 Sim.   And furthermore tell him, we desire to
  know of him,
Of whence he is, his name and parentage.
 Thai.   The king my father, sir, has drunk to you.
 Per.   I thank him.
 Thai.   Wishing it so much blood unto your life.
 Per.   I thank both him and you, and pledge
  him freely.
 Thai.   And further he desires to know of you,
Of whence you are, your name and parentage. 80
 Per.   A gentleman of Tyre; my name, Peri-
  cles;
My education been in arts and arms;

Who, looking for adventures in the world,
Was by the rough seas reft of ships and men,
And after shipwreck driven upon this shore.
 Thai. He thanks your grace; names himself
  Pericles,
A gentleman of Tyre,
Who only by misfortune of the seas
Bereft of ships and men, cast on this shore.
 Sim. Now, by the gods, I pity his misfortune,
And will awake him from his melancholy. 91
Come, gentlemen, we sit too long on trifles,
And waste the time, which looks for other revels.
• Even in your armours, as you are address'd,
Will very well become a soldier's dance.
I will not have excuse, with saying this
Loud music is too harsh for ladies' heads,
Since they love men in arms as well as beds.
       [*The Knights dance.*
So, this was well ask'd, 'twas so well perform'd.
Come, sir;   100
Here is a lady that wants breathing too:
And I have heard, you knights of Tyre
Are excellent in making ladies trip;
And that their measures are as excellent.
 Per. In those that practise them they are, my
  lord.
 Sim. O, that's as much as you would be denied
Of your fair courtesy.
    [*The Knights and Ladies dance.*
    Unclasp, unclasp:
Thanks, gentlemen, to all; all have done well,
[*To Per.*] But you the best. Pages and lights, to
  conduct
These knights unto their several lodgings! [*To
  Per.*] Yours, sir,   110
We have given order to be next our own.
 Per. I am at your grace's pleasure.
 Sim. Princes, it is too late to talk of love;
And that's the mark I know you level at:
Therefore each one betake him to his rest;
To-morrow all for speeding do their best.
          [*Exeunt.*

SCENE IV. *Tyre. A room in the Governor's
    house.*

  Enter HELICANUS *and* ESCANES.

 Hel. No, Escanes, know this of me,
Antiochus from incest lived not free:
For which, the most high gods not minding longer
To withhold the vengeance that they had in store,
Due to this heinous capital offence,
Even in the height and pride of all his glory,
When he was seated in a chariot
Of an inestimable value, and his daughter with him,
A fire from heaven came and shrivell'd up
Their bodies, even to loathing; for they so stunk,
That all those eyes adored them ere their fall 11
Scorn now their hand should give them burial.
 Esca. 'Twas very strange.
 Hel.   And yet but justice; for though
This king were great, his greatness was no guard
To bar heaven's shaft, but sin had his reward.
 Esca. 'Tis very true.

   Enter two or three Lords.

 First Lord. See, not a man in private conference
Or council has respect with him but he.

94 *address'd.* Dressed.

Pericles (Ian Richardson) and Thaisa (Susan Fleetwood) dance, Royal Shakespeare Co, 1969

'The Knights and Ladies dance'. Illustration by Byam Shaw, *The Chiswick Shakespeare*, 1902

34 *censure.* Judgement.

41 *forbear your suffrages.* Put aside your sufferings.

Sec. Lord. It shall no longer grieve without
   reproof.
Third Lord. And cursed be he that will not
   second it.   20
First Lord. Follow me, then. Lord Helicane,
   a word.
Hel. With me? and welcome: happy day, my
   lords.
First Lord. Know that our griefs are risen to
   the top,
And now at length they overflow their banks.
Hel. Your griefs! for what? wrong not your
   prince you love.
First Lord. Wrong not yourself, then, noble
   Helicane;
But if the prince do live, let us salute him,
Or know what ground's made happy by his breath.
If in the world he live, we'll seek him out;
If in his grave he rest, we'll find him there;   30
And be resolved he lives to govern us,
Or dead, give's cause to mourn his funeral,
And leave us to our free election.
● *Sec. Lord.* Whose death indeed's the strongest
   in our censure:
And knowing this kingdom is without a head,—
Like goodly buildings left without a roof
Soon fall to ruin,—your noble self,
That best know how to rule and how to reign,
We thus submit unto,—our sovereign.
All. Live, noble Helicane!   40
● *Hel.* For honour's cause, forbear your suf-
   frages:
If that you love Prince Pericles, forbear.
Take I your wish, I leap into the seas,
Where's hourly trouble for a minute's ease.
A twelvemonth longer, let me entreat you to
Forbear the absence of your king:
If in which time expired, he not return,
I shall with aged patience bear your yoke.
But if I cannot win you to this love,
Go search like nobles, like noble subjects,   50
And in your search spend your adventurous worth;
Whom if you find, and win unto return,
You shall like diamonds sit about his crown.
First Lord. To wisdom he's a fool that will
   not yield;
And since Lord Helicane enjoineth us,
We with our travels will endeavour us.
Hel. Then you love us, we you, and we'll clasp
   hands:
When peers thus knit, a kingdom ever stands.
                                        [*Exeunt.*

SCENE V. *Pentapolis.   A room in the palace.*

Enter SIMONIDES, *reading a letter, at one door:
   the* Knights *meet him.*

First Knight. Good morrow to the good Si-
   monides.
Sim. Knights, from my daughter this I let
   you know,
That for this twelvemonth she'll not undertake
A married life.
Her reason to herself is only known,
Which yet from her by no means can I get.
Sec. Knight. May we not get access to her,
   my lord?
Sim. 'Faith, by no means; she hath so strictly
   tied

Her to her chamber, that 'tis impossible.
● One twelve moons more she'll wear Diana's
    livery;   10
● This by the eye of Cynthia hath she vow'd,
And on her virgin honour will not break it.
    Third Knight. Loath to bid farewell, we take
    our leaves.   [*Exeunt Knights.*
    Sim. So,
They are well dispatch'd; now to my daughter's
    letter:
She tells me here, she'll wed the stranger knight,
Or never more to view nor day nor light.
'Tis well, mistress; your choice agrees with mine;
I like that well: nay, how absolute she's in't,
Not minding whether I dislike or no!   20
Well, I do commend her choice;
And will no longer have it be delay'd.
Soft! here he comes: I must dissemble it.

         Enter PERICLES.

    Per. All fortune to the good Simonides!
    Sim. To you as much, sir! I am beholding
    to you
For your sweet music this last night: I do
Protest my ears were never better fed
With such delightful pleasing harmony.
    Per. It is your grace's pleasure to commend;
Not my desert.
    Sim.   Sir, you are music's master.   30
    Per. The worst of all her scholars, my good
    lord.
    Sim. Let me ask you one thing:
What do you think of my daughter, sir?
    Per. A most virtuous princess.
    Sim. And she is fair too, is she not?
    Per. As a fair day in summer, wondrous fair.
    Sim. Sir, my daughter thinks very well of you;
Ay, so well, that you must be her master,
And she will be your scholar: therefore look to it.
    Per. I am unworthy for her schoolmaster.   40
    Sim. She thinks not so; peruse this writing
    else.
    Per. [*Aside*] What's here?
A letter, that she loves the knight of Tyre!
'Tis the king's subtilty to have my life.
O, seek not to entrap me, gracious lord,
A stranger and distressed gentleman,
That never aim'd so high to love your daughter,
But bent all offices to honour her.
    Sim. Thou hast bewitch'd my daughter, and
    thou art
A villain.   50
    Per. By the gods, I have not:
Never did thought of mine levy offence;
Nor never did my actions yet commence
A deed might gain her love or your displeasure.
    Sim. Traitor, thou liest.
    Per.   Traitor!
    Sim.   Ay, traitor.
    Per. Even in his throat—unless it be the king—
That calls me traitor, I return the lie.
    Sim. [*Aside*] Now, by the gods, I do applaud
    his courage.
    Per. My actions are as noble as my thoughts,
● That never relish'd of a base descent.   60
I came unto your court for honour's cause,
And not to be a rebel to her state;
And he that otherwise accounts of me,

10 *Diana.* Goddess of chastity.

11 *Cynthia.* i.e. Diana.

Simonides: '... she'll wear Diana's livery; This by the
eye of Cynthia hath she vow'd'. Woodcut of Diana, the
moon goddess, from Vincenzo Cartari's *Imagini delli dei
de gl'antichi*, 1674

60 *relish'd of.* Tainted by.

Susan Fleetwood as Thaisa, Royal Shakespeare Co, 1969

1 *yslaked*. Quietened. *rout*. Revellers.

9 *Hymen*. God of marriage.

13 *eche*. Eke; increase.

15 *dern*. Dreary. *perch*. Distance.

This sword shall prove he's honour's enemy.
  Sim. No?
Here comes my daughter, she can witness it.

             Enter THAISA.

  Per. Then, as you are as virtuous as fair,
Resolve your angry father, if my tongue
Did e'er solicit, or my hand subscribe
To any syllable that made love to you.   70
  Thai. Why, sir, say if you had,
Who takes offence at that would make me glad?
  Sim. Yea, mistress, are you so peremptory?
[*Aside*] I am glad on't with all my heart.—
I'll tame you; I'll bring you in subjection.
Will you, not having my consent,
Bestow your love and your affections
Upon a stranger? [*Aside*] who, for aught I know,
May be, nor can I think the contrary,
As great in blood as I myself.—   80
Therefore hear you, mistress; either frame
Your will to mine,—and you, sir, hear you,
Either be ruled by me, or I will make you—
Man and wife:
Nay, come, your hands and lips must seal it too:
And being join'd, I'll thus your hopes destroy;
And for a further grief,—God give you joy!—
What, are you both pleased?
  Thai.   Yes, if you love me, sir.
  Per. Even as my life my blood that fosters it.
  Sim. What, are you both agreed?   90
  Both. Yes, if it please your majesty.
  Sim. It pleaseth me so well, that I will see
    you wed;
And then with what haste you can get you to
    bed.   [*Exeunt.*

ACT III.

Enter GOWER.

●   *Gow.* Now sleep yslaked hath the rout;
    No din but snores the house about,
    Made louder by the o'er-fed breast
    Of this most pompous marriage-feast.
    The cat, with eyne of burning coal,
    Now couches fore the mouse's hole;
    And crickets sing at the oven's mouth,
    E'er the blither for their drouth.
●   Hymen hath brought the bride to bed,
    Where, by the loss of maidenhead,   10
    A babe is moulded. Be attent,
    And time that is so briefly spent
●   With your fine fancies quaintly eche:
    What's dumb in show I'll plain with speech.

DUMB SHOW.

Enter, PERICLES *and* SIMONIDES, *at one door, with* Attendants; *a* Messenger *meets them, kneels, and gives* PERICLES *a letter:* PERICLES *shows it* SIMONIDES; *the* Lords *kneel to him. Then enter* THAISA *with child, with* LYCHO-RIDA *a nurse. The* KING *shows her the letter; she rejoices: she and* PERICLES *take leave of her father, and depart with* LYCHORIDA *and their* Attendants. *Then exeunt* SIMONIDES *and the rest.*

●   By many a dern and painful perch
    Of Pericles the careful search,

By the four opposing coigns
Which the world together joins,
Is made with all due diligence
That horse and sail and high expense   20
Can stead the quest.   At last from Tyre,
Fame answering the most strange inquire,
To the court of King Simonides
Are letters brought, the tenour these:
Antiochus and his daughter dead;
The men of Tyrus on the head
Of Helicanus would set on
The crown of Tyre, but he will none:
The mutiny he there hastes t' oppress;
Says to 'em, if King Pericles   30
Come not home in twice six moons,
He, obedient to their dooms,
Will take the crown.   The sum of this,
Brought hither to Pentapolis,
Y-ravishèd the regions round,
And every one with claps can sound,
' Our heir-apparent is a king!
Who dream'd, who thought of such a thing?'
Brief, he must hence depart to Tyre:
His queen with child makes her desire—   40
Which who shall cross?—along to go:
Omit we all their dole and woe:
Lychorida, her nurse, she takes,
And so to sea.   Their vessel shakes
On Neptune's billow; half the flood
Hath their keel cut: but fortune's mood
Varies again; the grisled north
Disgorges such a tempest forth,
That, as a duck for life that dives,
So up and down the poor ship drives: 50
The lady shrieks, and well-a-near
Does fall in travail with her fear:
And what ensues in this fell storm
Shall for itself itself perform.
I nill relate, action may
Conveniently the rest convey;
Which might not what by me is told.
In your imagination hold
This stage the ship, upon whose deck   59
The sea-tost Pericles appears to speak. [*Exit.*

SCENE I.

Enter PERICLES, *on shipboard.*

Per. Thou god of this great vast, rebuke
    these surges,
Which wash both heaven and hell; and thou,
    that hast
Upon the winds command, bind them in brass,
Having call'd them from the deep!   O, still
Thy deafening, dreadful thunders; gently quench
Thy nimble, sulphurous flashes!   O, how, Ly-
    chorida,
How does my queen?   Thou stormest venom-
    ously;
Wilt thou spit all thyself?   The seaman's whistle
Is as a whisper in the ears of death,
Unheard.   Lychorida!—Lucina, O   10
Divinest patroness, and midwife gentle
To those that cry by night, convey thy deity
Aboard our dancing boat; make swift the pangs
Of my queen's travails!

Enter LYCHORIDA, *with an Infant.*
           Now, Lychorida!

17 *coigns.* Corners.

32 *dooms.* Sentences.

35 *Y-ravished.* Enraptured.

55 *nill.* Will not.

Edric Connor as Gower, Stratford-upon-Avon, 1958

8 *spit.* Pierce.

16 *conceit.* Understanding.

39 *flaw.* Storm.

43 *bolins.* Bow-lines.

First Sailor: '. . . the wind is loud, and will not lie till the ship be cleared of the dead.' Engraving of Boreas, the blustery North wind, from Gabriele Simeoni's *La vita et Metamorfoses d'Ovidio*, 1559

Lyc.   Here is a thing too young for such a place,
Who, if it had conceit, would die, as I
Am like to do: take in your arms this piece
Of your dead queen.
   Per.   How, how, Lychorida!
   Lyc.   Patience, good sir; do not assist the storm.
Here's all that is left living of your queen,   20
A little daughter: for the sake of it,
Be manly, and take comfort.
   Per.   O you gods!
Why do you make us love your goodly gifts,
And snatch them straight away? We here below
Recall not what we give, and therein may
Use honour with you.
   Lyc.   Patience, good sir,
Even for this charge.
   Per.   Now, mild may be thy life!
For a more blustrous birth had never babe:
Quiet and gentle thy conditions! for
Thou art the rudeliest welcome to this world   30
That ever was prince's child.   Happy what follows!
Thou hast as chiding a nativity
As fire, air, water, earth, and heaven can make,
To herald thee from the womb: even at the first
Thy loss is more than can thy portage quit,
With all thou canst find here.   Now, the good gods
Throw their best eyes upon 't!

Enter two Sailors.

   First Sail. What courage, sir? God save you!
   Per.   Courage enough: I do not fear the flaw;
It hath done to me the worst.   Yet, for the love   40
Of this poor infant, this fresh-new sea-farer,
I would it would be quiet.
   First Sail Slack the bolins there! Thou wilt not, wilt thou?   Blow, and split thyself.
   Sec. Sail.   But sea-room, an the brine and cloudy billow kiss the moon, I care not.
   First Sail.   Sir, your queen must overboard: the sea works high, the wind is loud, and will not lie till the ship be cleared of the dead.
   Per.   That's your superstition.   50
   First Sail.   Pardon us, sir; with us at sea it hath been still observed: and we are strong in custom.   Therefore briefly yield her; for she must overboard straight.
   Per.   As you think meet.   Most wretched queen!
   Lyc.   Here she lies, sir.
   Per.   A terrible childbed hast thou had, my dear;
No light, no fire: the unfriendly elements
Forgot thee utterly: nor have I time
To give thee hallow'd to thy grave, but straight   60
Must cast thee, scarcely coffin'd, in the ooze,
Where, for a monument upon thy bones,
And e'er-remaining lamps, the belching whale
And humming water must o'erwhelm thy corpse,
Lying with simple shells.   O Lychorida,
Bid Nestor bring me spices, ink and paper,
My casket and my jewels; and bid Nicander
Bring me the satin coffer: lay the babe
Upon the pillow: hie thee, whiles I say
A priestly farewell to her: suddenly, woman.   70
   [Exit Lychorida.

Sec. Sail. Sir, we have a chest beneath the
●hatches, caulked and bitumed ready.
    Per. I thank thee.   Mariner, say what coast
    is this?
    Sec. Sail. We are near Tarsus.
    Per. Thither, gentle mariner,
Alter thy course for Tyre.   When canst thou
    reach it?
    Sec. Sail. By break of day, if the wind cease.
    Per. O, make for Tarsus!
There will I visit Cleon, for the babe
Cannot hold out to Tyrus: there I'll leave it 80
At careful nursing.   Go thy ways, good mariner:
I'll bring the body presently.   [*Exeunt.*

SCENE II. *Ephesus.   A room in Cerimon's
house.*

Enter CERIMON, *with a Servant, and some
Persons who have been shipwrecked.*

    Cer. Philemon, ho!

        Enter PHILEMON.

    Phil. Doth my lord call?
    Cer. Get fire and meat for these poor men:
'T has been a turbulent and stormy night.
    Serv. I have been in many; but such a night
    as this,
Till now, I ne'er endured.
    Cer. Your master will be dead ere you return;
There's nothing can be minister'd to nature
That can recover him. [*To Philemon*] Give this
    to the 'pothecary,
And tell me how it works.
        [*Exeunt all but Cerimon.*

    Enter two Gentlemen.

First Gent.   Good morrow.   10
Sec. Gent. Good morrow to your lordship.
Cer.   Gentlemen,
Why do you stir so early?
    First Gent. Sir,
Our lodgings, standing bleak upon the sea,
Shook as the earth did quake;
●The very principals did seem to rend,
And all-to topple: pure surprise and fear
Made me to quit the house.
    Sec. Gent. That is the cause we trouble you
    so early;
'Tis not our husbandry.
    Cer.   O, you say well.   20
    First Gent. But I much marvel that your
    lordship, having
Rich tire about you, should at these early hours
Shake off the golden slumber of repose.
'Tis most strange,
Nature should be so conversant with pain,
Being thereto not compell'd.
    Cer.   I hold it ever,
Virtue and cunning were endowments greater
Than nobleness and riches: careless heirs
May the two latter darken and expend;
But immortality attends the former,   30
Making a man a god.   'Tis known, I ever
Have studied physic, through which secret art,
By turning o'er authorities, I have,
Together with my practice, made familiar
To me and to my aid the blest infusions

72 *caulked*. With the seams sealed. *bitumed*. Tarred.

16 *principals*. Main beams.

Cerimon: ''Tis known, I ever Have studied physic …'
Engraving of an apothecary preparing distillations, 16th
century

63 *corse.* Corpse.

67 *Apollo.* God of medicine. *perfect me.* Let me comprehend fully. *characters.* Writing.

Apollo, Greek god of the arts, prophecy, medicine and light. Engraving from a Roman medal in G. du Choul's *Discours de la Religion des Anciens Romains,* 1567

85 *lien.* Laid.

That dwell in vegetives, in metals, stones;
And I can speak of the disturbances
That nature works, and of her cures; which doth give me
A more content in course of true delight
Than to be thirsty after tottering honour,   40
Or tie my treasure up in silken bags,
To please the fool and death.
    Sec. Gent.   Your honour has through Ephesus pour'd forth
Your charity, and hundreds call themselves
Your creatures, who by you have been restored:
And not your knowledge, your personal pain, but even
Your purse, still open, hath built Lord Cerimon
Such strong renown as time shall ne'er decay.

        Enter two or three Servants *with a chest.*

    First Serv.   So; lift there.
    Cer.   What is that?
    First Serv.   Sir, even now
Did the sea toss upon our shore this chest: 50
'Tis of some wreck.
    Cer.   Set 't down, let's look upon't.
    Sec. Gent.   'Tis like a coffin, sir.
    Cer.   Whate'er it be,
'Tis wondrous heavy.   Wrench it open straight:
If the sea's stomach be o'ercharged with gold,
†'Tis a good constraint of fortune it belches upon us.
    Sec. Gent.   'Tis so, my lord.
    Cer.   How close 'tis caulk'd and bitumed!
Did the sea cast it up?
    First Serv.   I never saw so huge a billow, sir,
As toss'd it upon shore.
    Cer.   Wrench it open;
Soft! it smells most sweetly in my sense.   60
    Sec. Gent.   A delicate odour.
    Cer.   As ever hit my nostril.   So, up with it.
•O you most potent gods! what's here? a corse!
    First Gent.   Most strange!
    Cer.   Shrouded in cloth of state; balm'd and entreasured
With full bags of spices!   A passport too!
•Apollo, perfect me in the characters!
                [*Reads from a scroll.*
    ' Here I give to understand,
        If e'er this coffin drive a-land,
        I, King Pericles, have lost   70
        This queen, worth all our mundane cost.
        Who finds her, give her burying;
        She was the daughter of a king:
        Besides this treasure for a fee,
        The gods requite his charity!'
If thou livest, Pericles, thou hast a heart
That even cracks for woe!   This chanced to-night.
    Sec. Gent.   Most likely, sir.
    Cer.   Nay, certainly to-night;
For look how fresh she looks!   They were too rough   79
That threw her in the sea.   Make a fire within:
Fetch hither all my boxes in my closet.
                [*Exit a Servant.*
Death may usurp on nature many hours,
And yet the fire of life kindle again
The o'erpress'd spirits.   †I heard of an Egyptian
•That had nine hours lien dead,
Who was by good appliance recovered.

Re-enter a Servant, *with boxes, napkins, and fire*

Well said, well said ; the fire and cloths.
The rough and woeful music that we have,
Cause it to sound, beseech you.
●The viol once more : how thou stirr'st, thou
　　　block !   90
The music there !—I pray you, give her air.
Gentlemen,
This queen will live : nature awakes ; a warmth
Breathes out of her : she hath not been entranced
Above five hours : see how she gins to blow
Into life's flower again !
　　　First Gent.　　　　　The heavens,
Through you, increase our wonder and set up
Your fame for ever.
　　　Cer.　　　　　She is alive ; behold,
Her eyelids, cases to those heavenly jewels
Which Pericles hath lost,   100
Begin to part their fringes of bright gold ;
The diamonds of a most praised water
Do appear, to make the world twice rich.   Live,
And make us weep to hear your fate, fair creature,
Rare as you seem to be.　　　　　[*She moves.*
　　　Thai.　　　　　O dear Diana,
Where am I ?   Where's my lord ?   What world
　　　is this ?
　　　Sec. Gent.   Is not this strange ?
　　　First Gent.　　　　　Most rare.
　　　Cer.　　　　　Hush, my gentle neighbours !
Lend me your hands ; to the next chamber bear
　　　her.
Get linen : now this matter must be look'd to,
For her relapse is mortal.   Come, come ;   110
●And Æsculapius guide us !
　　　　　　　[*Exeunt, carrying her away.*

SCENE III.   *Tarsus.   A room in Cleon's house.*

Enter PERICLES, CLEON, DIONYZA, *and* LYCHO-
RIDA *with* MARINA *in her arms.*

　　　Per.   Most honour'd Cleon, I must needs be
　　　gone ;
My twelve months are expired, and Tyrus stands
In a litigious peace.   You, and your lady,
Take from my heart all thankfulness !   The gods
Make up the rest upon you !
　　　Cle.   Your shafts of fortune, though they hurt
　　　you mortally,
Yet glance full wanderingly on us.
　　　Dion.　　　　　O your sweet queen !
That the strict fates had pleased you had brought
　　　her hither,
To have bless'd mine eyes with her !
　　　Per.　　　　　We cannot but obey
The powers above us.   Could I rage and roar 10
As doth the sea she lies in, yet the end
Must be as 'tis.   My gentle babe Marina, whom,
For she was born at sea, I have named so, here
I charge your charity withal, leaving her
The infant of your care ; beseeching you
To give her princely training, that she may be
Manner'd as she is born.
　　　Cle.　　　　　Fear not, my lord, but think
Your grace, that fed my country with your corn,
For which the people's prayers still fall upon you,
Must in your child be thought on.   If neglection
Should therein make me vile, the common body,

90 *block.* Unmoving thing.

Thaisa : 'Where am I ? Where's my lord ? What world is this ?' Thaisa (Stephanie Bidmead) with Cerimon (Anthony Nicholls) Stratford-upon-Avon, 1958

111 *Æsculapius.* God of healing.

Aesculapius. Engraving from Vincenzo Cartari's *Imagini delli dei de gl'antichi*, 1764

Cleon: 'We'll . . . give you up to the mask'd Neptune'.
Engraving of Neptune, god of the sea, from Andrea
Alciati's *Emblemata*, 1577

---

6 *my eaning time.* When I was giving birth.

10 *vestal.* Virginal.

14 *date.* Lifespan.

4 *votaress.* Priestess.

12 *wrack.* Ruin.

By you relieved, would force me to my duty:
But if to that my nature need a spur,
The gods revenge it upon me and mine,
To the end of generation!
  Per.   I believe you;
Your honour and your goodness teach me to't,
Without your vows. Till she be married, madam,
By bright Diana, whom we honour, all
Unscissar'd shall this hair of mine remain,
Though I show ill in't. So I take my leave. 30
Good madam, make me blessed in your care
In bringing up my child.
  Dion.   I have one myself,
Who shall not be more dear to my respect
Than yours, my lord.
  Per. Madam, my thanks and prayers.
  Cle. We'll bring your grace e'en to the edge
o' the shore,
Then give you up to the mask'd Neptune and
The gentlest winds of heaven.
  Per.   I will embrace
Your offer. Come, dearest madam. O, no tears,
Lychorida, no tears:
Look to your little mistress, on whose grace 40
You may depend hereafter. Come, my lord.
          [*Exeunt.*

SCENE IV. *Ephesus. A room in Cerimon's
house.*

Enter CERIMON *and* THAISA.

  Cer. Madam, this letter, and some certain
  jewels,
Lay with you in your coffer: which are now
At your command. Know you the character?
  Thai. It is my lord's.
That I was shipp'd at sea, I well remember,
Even on my eaning time; but whether there
Deliver'd, by the holy gods,
I cannot rightly say. But since King Pericles,
My wedded lord, I ne'er shall see again,
A vestal livery will I take me to, 10
And never more have joy.
  Cer. Madam, if this you purpose as ye speak,
Diana's temple is not distant far,
Where you may abide till your date expire.
Moreover, if you please, a niece of mine
Shall there attend you.
  Thai. My recompense is thanks, that's all;
Yet my good will is great, though the gift small.
          [*Exeunt.*

ACT IV.

Enter GOWER.

  Gow. Imagine Pericles arrived at Tyre,
Welcomed and settled to his own desire.
His woeful queen we leave at Ephesus,
Unto Diana there a votaress.
Now to Marina bend your mind,
Whom our fast-growing scene must find
At Tarsus, and by Cleon train'd
In music, letters; who hath gain'd
Of education all the grace,
Which makes her both the heart and place 10
Of general wonder. But, alack,
That monster envy, oft the wrack
Of earned praise, Marina's life
Seeks to take off by treason's knife.

And in this kind hath our Cleon
One daughter, and a wench full grown,
Even ripe for marriage-rite; this maid
● Hight Philoten: and it is said
For certain in our story, she
Would ever with Marina be: 20
● Be't when she weaved the sleided silk
With fingers long, small, white as milk;
Or when she would with sharp needle wound
● The cambric, which she made more sound
By hurting it; or when to the lute
She sung, and made the night-bird mute,
That still records with moan; or when
She would with rich and constant pen
● Vail to her mistress Dian; still
This Philoten contends in skill   30
With absolute Marina: so
● With the dove of Paphos might the crow
Vie feathers white.   Marina gets
All praises, which are paid as debts,
And not as given.   This so darks
In Philoten all graceful marks,
That Cleon's wife, with envy rare,
A present murderer does prepare
For good Marina, that her daughter
Might stand peerless by this slaughter.   40
The sooner her vile thoughts to stead,
Lychorida, our nurse, is dead:
And cursed Dionyza hath
The pregnant instrument of wrath
● Prest for this blow.   The unborn event
I do commend to your content:
Only I carry winged time
Post on the lame feet of my rhyme;
Which never could I so convey,
Unless your thoughts went on my way.   50
Dionyza does appear,
With Leonine, a murderer.   [*Exit.*

SCENE I.   *Tarsus.   An open place near the
sea-shore.*

Enter DIONYZA *and* LEONINE.

Dion.   Thy oath remember; thou hast sworn
    to do't:
'Tis but a blow, which never shall be known.
Thou canst not do a thing in the world so soon,
To yield thee so much profit.   Let not conscience,
Which is but cold, inflaming love i' thy bosom,
Inflame too nicely; nor let pity, which
Even women have cast off, melt thee, but be
A soldier to thy purpose.
  Leon.   I will do't; but yet she is a goodly
    creature.   9
  Dion.   The fitter, then, the gods should have
her.   †Here she comes weeping for her only mis-
tress' death.   Thou art resolved?
  Leon.   I am resolved.

Enter MARINA, *with a basket of flowers.*

● *Mar.*   No, I will rob Tellus of her weed,
To strew thy green with flowers: the yellows,
    blues,
The purple violets, and marigolds,
Shall as a carpet hang upon thy grave,
While summer-days do last.   Ay me! poor maid,
Born in a tempest, when my mother died,
This world to me is like a lasting storm,   20
Whirring me from my friends.

18 *Hight.* Is called.

21 *sleided.* Sleaved. Fine silk threads made by separating thicker ones.

24 *cambric.* Linen.

29 *Vail.* Pay homage. *Dian.* Diana.

32 *Paphos.* Birthplace of Venus.

45 *Prest.* Prepared.

14 *Tellus.* The Earth. *weed.* Dress.

Tellus, the earth goddess. Engraving from Vincenzo Cartari's *Imagini delli dei de gl'antichi*, 1764

25 *favour.* Appearance.

63 *dropping.* Dripping.

77 *la.* Indeed.

Dion.   How now, Marina! why do you keep
    alone?
How chance my daughter is not with you? Do not
Consume your blood with sorrowing: you have
● A nurse of me. Lord, how your favour's changed
With this unprofitable woe!
Come, give me your flowers, ere the sea mar it.
Walk with Leonine; the air is quick there,
And it pierces and sharpens the stomach. Come,
Leonine, take her by the arm, walk with her.   30
    Mar.   No, I pray you;
I'll not bereave you of your servant.
    Dion.   Come, come;
I love the king your father, and yourself,
With more than foreign heart. We every day
Expect him here: when he shall come and find
Our paragon to all reports thus blasted,
He will repent the breadth of his great voyage;
Blame both my lord and me, that we have taken
No care to your best courses. Go, I pray you,
Walk, and be cheerful once again; reserve   40
That excellent complexion, which did steal
The eyes of young and old. Care not for me;
I can go home alone.
    Mar.   Well, I will go;
But yet I have no desire to it.
    Dion. Come, come, I know 'tis good for you.
Walk half an hour, Leonine, at the least:
Remember what I have said.
    Leon.   I warrant you, madam.
    Dion.   I'll leave you, my sweet lady, for a
    while:
Pray, walk softly, do not heat your blood:
What! I must have a care of you.
    Mar.   My thanks, sweet madam. 50
                    [*Exit Dionyza.*
Is this wind westerly that blows?
    Leon.   South-west.
    Mar. When I was born, the wind was north.
    Leon.   Was't so?
    Mar. My father, as nurse said, did never fear,
But cried 'Good seamen!' to the sailors, galling
His kingly hands, haling ropes;
And, clasping to the mast, endured a sea
That almost burst the deck.
    Leon. When was this?
    Mar. When I was born:
Never was waves nor wind more violent;   60
And from the ladder-tackle washes off
A canvas-climber. 'Ha!' says one, 'wilt out?'
● And with a dropping industry they skip
From stem to stern: the boatswain whistles, and
The master calls, and trebles their confusion.
    Leon. Come, say your prayers.
    Mar. What mean you?
    Leon. If you require a little space for prayer,
I grant it: pray; but be not tedious,
For the gods are quick of ear, and I am sworn 70
To do my work with haste.
    Mar.   Why will you kill me?
    Leon. To satisfy my lady.
    Mar. Why would she have me kill'd?
Now, as I can remember, by my troth,
I never did her hurt in all my life:
I never spake bad word, nor did ill turn
● To any living creature: believe me, la,
I never kill'd a mouse, nor hurt a fly:
I trod upon a worm against my will,
But I wept for it. How have I offended,   80

Wherein my death might yield her any profit,
Or my life imply her any danger?
    Leon.   My commission
Is not to reason of the deed, but do it.
    Mar.   You will not do't for all the world, I
        hope.
You are well favour'd, and your looks foreshow
You have a gentle heart.   I saw you lately,
When you caught hurt in parting two that fought:
Good sooth, it show'd well in you: do so now:
Your lady seeks my life; come you between,   90
And save poor me, the weaker.
    Leon.   I am sworn,
And will dispatch.   [*He seizes her.*

Enter Pirates.

First Pirate.   Hold, villain!
                         [*Leonine runs away.*
Sec. Pirate.   A prize! a prize!
Third Pirate.   Half-part, mates, half-part.
Come, let's have her aboard suddenly.
                  [*Exeunt Pirates with Marina.*

Re-enter LEONINE.

    Leon.   These roguing thieves serve the great
        pirate Valdes;
And they have seized Marina.   Let her go:
There's no hope she will return.   I'll swear she's
        dead,
And thrown into the sea.   But I'll see further: 100
Perhaps they will but please themselves upon her,
Not carry her aboard.   If she remain,
Whom they have ravish'd must by me be slain.
                                [*Exit.*

SCENE II.   *Mytilene.   A room in a brothel.*

Enter PANDAR, Bawd, *and* BOULT.

    Pand.   Boult!
    Boult.   Sir?
    Pand.   Search the market narrowly; Mytilene
is full of gallants.   We lost too much money this
mart by being too wenchless.
    Bawd.   We were never so much out of crea-
tures.   We have but poor three, and they can do no
more than they can do; and they with continual
action are even as good as rotten.   9
    Pand.   Therefore let's have fresh ones, what-
e'er we pay for them.   If there be not a conscience to be used in every trade, we shall never
prosper.
    Bawd.   Thou sayest true: 'tis not our bringing
up of poor bastards,—as, I think, I have brought
up some eleven—
    Boult.   Ay, to eleven; and brought them down
again.   But shall I search the market?
    Bawd.   What else, man?   The stuff we have,
a strong wind will blow it to pieces, they are so
pitifully sodden.   21
    Pand.   Thou sayest true; they're too unwhole-
some, o' conscience.   The poor Transylvanian is
dead, that lay with the little baggage.
● *Boult.*   Ay, she quickly pooped him, she made
him roast-meat for worms.   But I'll go search the
market.   [*Exit.*
● *Pand.*   Three or four thousand chequins were
● as pretty a proportion to live quietly, and so give
over.   30

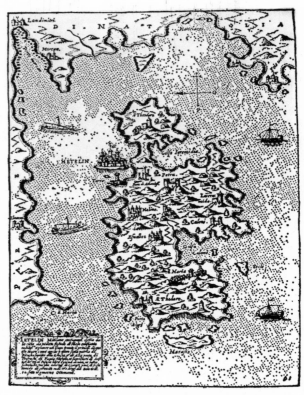

The island of Mytilene (Lesbos), off the coast of Turkey.
Engraving from Giovanni Camocio's *Isole, famosi porti,
fortezze, e terre maritime,* 1574

25 *pooped him.* i.e. gave him venereal disease.

28 *chequins.* Gold coins.

29-30 *proportion.* Fortune. *give over.* Retire.

49 *lost my earnest*. Forfeited my deposit.

55 *bated*. Knocked down below. *doit*. Tiny coin.

77 *light*. Fallen.

Bawd. Why to give over, I pray you? is it a shame to get when we are old?

Pand. O, our credit comes not in like the commodity, nor the commodity wages not with the danger: therefore, if in our youths we could pick up some pretty estate, 'twere not amiss to keep our door hatched. Besides, the sore terms we stand upon with the gods will be strong with us for giving over.   39

Bawd. Come, other sorts offend as well as we.

Pand. As well as we! ay, and better too; we offend worse. Neither is our profession any trade; it's no calling. But here comes Boult.

Re-enter BOULT, *with the* Pirates *and* MARINA.

Boult. [*To Marina*] Come your ways. My masters, you say she's a virgin?

First Pirate. O, sir, we doubt it not.

Boult. Master, I have gone through for this piece, you see: if you like her, so; if not, I have lost my earnest.

Bawd. Boult, has she any qualities?   50

Boult. She has a good face, speaks well, and has excellent good clothes: there's no further necessity of qualities can make her be refused.

Bawd. What's her price, Boult?

Boult. I cannot be bated one doit of a thousand pieces.

Pand. Well, follow me, my masters, you shall have your money presently. Wife, take her in: instruct her what she has to do, that she may not be raw in her entertainment.   60
          [*Exeunt Pandar and Pirates.*

Bawd. Boult, take you the marks of her, the colour of her hair, complexion, height, age, with warrant of her virginity; and cry 'He that will give most shall have her first.' Such a maidenhead were no cheap thing, if men were as they have been. Get this done as I command you.

Boult. Performance shall follow.   [*Exit.*

Mar. Alack that Leonine was so slack, so slow!
He should have struck, not spoke; or that these pirates,
Not enough barbarous, had not o'erboard thrown me   70
For to seek my mother!

Bawd. Why lament you, pretty one?

Mar. That I am pretty.

Bawd. Come, the gods have done their part in you.

Mar. I accuse them not.

Bawd. You are light into my hands, where you are like to live.

Mar. The more my fault
To scape his hands where I was like to die.   80

Bawd. Ay, and you shall live in pleasure.

Mar. No.

Bawd. Yes, indeed shall you, and taste gentlemen of all fashions: you shall fare well; you shall have the difference of all complexions. What! do you stop your ears?

Mar. Are you a woman?

Bawd. What would you have me be, an I be not a woman?

Mar. An honest woman, or not a woman.   90

Bawd. Marry, whip thee, gosling: I think I shall have something to do with you. Come, you're a young foolish sapling, and must be bowed as I would have you.

Mar. The gods defend me!

Bawd. If it please the gods to defend you by men, then men must comfort you, men must feed you, men must stir you up. Boult's returned.

Re-enter BOULT.

Now, sir, hast thou cried her through the market?

Boult. I have cried her almost to the number of her hairs; I have drawn her picture with my voice.

Bawd. And I prithee tell me, how dost thou find the inclination of the people, especially of the younger sort?

Boult. 'Faith, they listened to me as they would have hearkened to their father's testament. There was a Spaniard's mouth so watered, that he went to bed to her very description. 109

Bawd. We shall have him here to-morrow with his best ruff on.

Boult. To-night, to-night. But, mistress, do you know the French knight that cowers i' the hams?

Bawd. Who, Monsieur Veroles?

Boult. Ay, he: he offered to cut a caper at the proclamation; but he made a groan at it, and swore he would see her to-morrow.

Bawd. Well, well; as for him, he brought his disease hither: here he does but repair it. I know he will come in our shadow, to scatter his crowns in the sun.

Boult. Well, if we had of every nation a traveller, we should lodge them with this sign.

Bawd. [*To Mar.*] Pray you, come hither awhile. You have fortunes coming upon you. Mark me: you must seem to do that fearfully which you commit willingly, despise profit where you have most gain. To weep that you live as ye do makes pity in your lovers: seldom but that pity begets you a good opinion, and that opinion a mere profit.

Mar. I understand you not.

Boult. O, take her home, mistress, take her home: these blushes of hers must be quenched with some present practice.

Bawd. Thou sayest true, i' faith, so they must; for your bride goes to that with shame which is her way to go with warrant. 139

Boult. 'Faith, some do, and some do not. But, mistress, if I have bargained for the joint,—

Bawd. Thou mayst cut a morsel off the spit.

Boult. I may so.

Bawd. Who should deny it? Come, young one, I like the manner of your garments well.

Boult. Ay, by my faith, they shall not be changed yet.

Bawd. Boult, spend thou that in the town: report what a sojourner we have; you'll lose nothing by custom. When nature framed this piece, she meant thee a good turn; therefore say what a paragon she is, and thou hast the harvest out of thine own report.

Boult. I warrant you, mistress, thunder shall not so awake the beds of eels as my giving out her beauty stir up the lewdly-inclined. I'll bring home some to-night.

Bawd. Come your ways; follow me.

113–114 *cowers i' the hams.* Totters on his legs.

Bawd: '. . . as for him, he brought his disease hither'. Woodcut of 'The Syphilitic' by Albrecht Dürer (1471–1528)

141 *the joint.* The whole cut.

18 *attribute*. Reputation.

34 *blurted at*. Scorned. *malkin*. Slut.

Mar. If fires be hot, knives sharp, or waters
  deep,
Untied I still my virgin knot will keep.   160
Diana, aid my purpose!
 Bawd. What have we to do with Diana? Pray
you, will you go with us?   [*Exeunt.*

SCENE III. *Tarsus.* *A room in Cleon's house.*

Enter CLEON *and* DIONYZA.

 Dion. Why, are you foolish? Can it be un-
  done?
 Cle. O Dionyza, such a piece of slaughter
The sun and moon ne'er look'd upon!
 Dion.   I think
You'll turn a child again.
 Cle. Were I chief lord of all this spacious
  world,
I'ld give it to undo the deed. O lady,
Much less in blood than virtue, yet a princess
To equal any single crown o' the earth
I' the justice of compare! O villain Leonine!
Whom thou hast poison'd too: 10
If thou hadst drunk to him, 't had been a kindness
Becoming well thy fact: what canst thou say
When noble Pericles shall demand his child?
 Dion. That she is dead. Nurses are not the
  fates,
To foster it, nor ever to preserve.
She died at night; I'll say so. Who can cross it?
Unless you play the pious innocent,
•And for an honest attribute cry out
'She died by foul play.'
 Cle.   O, go to. Well, well,
Of all the faults beneath the heavens, the gods 20
Do like this worst.
 Dion.   Be one of those that think
The petty wrens of Tarsus will fly hence,
And open this to Pericles. I do shame
To think of what a noble strain you are,
And of how coward a spirit.
 Cle.   To such proceeding
Who ever but his approbation added,
Though not his prime consent, he did not flow
From honourable sources.
 Dion.   Be it so, then:
Yet none does know, but you, how she came dead,
Nor none can know, Leonine being gone.   30
She did distain my child, and stood between
Her and her fortunes: none would look on her,
But cast their gazes on Marina's face;
•Whilst ours was blurted at and held a malkin
Not worth the time of day. It pierced me
  thorough;
And though you call my course unnatural,
You not your child well loving, yet I find
It greets me as an enterprise of kindness
Perform'd to your sole daughter.
 Cle.   Heavens forgive it!
 Dion. And as for Pericles,   40
What should he say? We wept after her hearse,
And yet we mourn: her monument
Is almost finish'd, and her epitaphs
In glittering golden characters express
A general praise to her, and care in us
At whose expense 'tis done.
 Cle.   Thou art like the harpy,
Which, to betray, dost, with thine angel's face,
Seize with thine eagle's talons.

Dion. You are like one that superstitiously 49
Doth swear to the gods that winter kills the flies:
But yet I know you'll do as I advise. [*Exeunt.*

SCENE IV.

Enter GOWER, *before the monument of* MARINA
at Tarsus.

Gow. Thus time we waste, and longest
    leagues make short;
Sail seas in cockles, have an wish but for't;
Making, to take your imagination,
• From bourn to bourn, region to region.
By you being pardon'd, we commit no crime
To use one language in each several clime
Where our scenes seem to live.   I do beseech
    you
To learn of me, who stand i' the gaps to teach
    you,
The stages of our story.   Pericles
Is now again thwarting the wayward seas,   10
Attended on by many a lord and knight,
To see his daughter, all his life's delight.
Old Escanes, whom Helicanus late
Advanced in time to great and high estate,
Is left to govern.   Bear you it in mind,
Old Helicanus goes along behind.
Well-sailing ships and bounteous winds have
    brought
This king to Tarsus,—think his pilot thought;
So with his steerage shall your thoughts grow
    on,—   19
To fetch his daughter home, who first is gone.
• Like motes and shadows see them move awhile;
Your ears unto your eyes I'll reconcile.

DUMB SHOW.

Enter PERICLES, *at one door, with all his train;*
CLEON *and* DIONYZA, *at the other.* CLEON
shows PERICLES *the tomb; whereat* PERICLES
*makes lamentation, puts on sackcloth, and in
a mighty passion departs. Then exeunt* CLEON
and DIONYZA.

See how belief may suffer by foul show!
This borrow'd passion stands for true old woe;
And Pericles, in sorrow all devour'd,
With sighs shot through, and biggest tears o'er-
    shower'd,
Leaves Tarsus and again embarks. He swears
Never to wash his face, nor cut his hairs:
He puts on sackcloth, and to sea. He bears
A tempest, which his mortal vessel tears,   30
And yet he rides it out.   Now please you wit
The epitaph is for Marina writ
By wicked Dionyza.
    [*Reads the inscription on Marina's
             monument.*
'The fairest, sweet'st, and best lies here,
Who wither'd in her spring of year.
She was of Tyrus the king's daughter,
On whom foul death hath made this slaughter;
Marina was she call'd; and at her birth,
• Thetis, being proud, swallow'd some part o'
    the earth:
Therefore the earth, fearing to be o'erflow'd,   40
Hath Thetis' birth-child on the heavens be-
    stow'd:

4 *bourn.* Boundary.

21 *motes.* Particles of dust.

Gower before the monument of Marina at Tarsus.
Illustration by Byam Shaw, *The Chiswick Shakespeare,*
1902

39 *Thetis.* Legendary sea nymph.

Thetis. Engraving from Geoffrey Witney's *A Choice of
Emblems,* 1586

42 *stint.* Stop.

Gower: 'Let Pericles ... bear his courses to be ordered By Lady Fortune'. Engraving of Fortune from a Roman medal in G. du Choul's *Discours de la Religion des Anciens Romains*, 1567

49 *well-a-day.* Grief.

7 *vestals.* i.e. virgins.

9 *rutting.* Fornicating.

4 *Priapus.* God of procreation.

14 *green-sickness.* Squeamishness.

19 *lown.* Base type.

28 *wholesome iniquity.* i.e. clean prostitute.

32 *deed of darkness.* Fornication.

Wherefore she does, and swears she'll never
    stint,
Make raging battery upon shores of flint.'
No visor does become black villany
So well as soft and tender flattery.
Let Pericles believe his daughter's dead,
And bear his courses to be ordered
By Lady Fortune; while our scene must play
His daughter's woe and heavy well-a-day
In her unholy service. Patience, then,   50
And think you now are all in Mytilene. [*Exit.*

SCENE V. *Mytilene. A street before the brothel.*

Enter, from the brothel, two Gentlemen.

First Gent. Did you ever hear the like?
Sec. Gent. No, nor never shall do in such a place as this, she being once gone.
First Gent. But to have divinity preached there! did you ever dream of such a thing?
Sec. Gent. No, no. Come, I am for no more bawdy-houses: shall's go hear the vestals sing?
First Gent. I'll do any thing now that is virtuous; but I am out of the road of rutting for ever.   [*Exeunt.* 10

SCENE VI. *The same. A room in the brothel.*

Enter Pandar, Bawd, *and* BOULT.

Pand. Well, I had rather than twice the worth of her she had ne'er come here.
Bawd. Fie, fie upon her! she's able to freeze the god Priapus, and undo a whole generation. We must either get her ravished, or be rid of her. When she should do for clients her fitment, and do me the kindness of our profession, she has me her quirks, her reasons, her master reasons, her prayers, her knees; that she would make a puritan of the devil, if he should cheapen a kiss of her.
Boult. 'Faith, I must ravish her, or she'll disfurnish us of all our cavaliers, and make our swearers priests.
Pand. Now, the pox upon her green-sickness for me!
Bawd. 'Faith, there's no way to be rid on't but by the way to the pox. Here comes the Lord Lysimachus disguised.
Boult. We should have both lord and lown, if the peevish baggage would but give way to customers.   21

Enter LYSIMACHUS.

Lys. How now! How a dozen of virginities?
Bawd. Now, the gods to bless your honour!
Boult. I am glad to see your honour in good health.
Lys. You may so; 'tis the better for you that your resorters stand upon sound legs. How now! wholesome iniquity have you that a man may deal withal, and defy the surgeon?
Bawd. We have here one, sir, if she would— but there never came her like in Mytilene.   31
Lys. If she'ld do the deed of darkness, thou wouldst say.
Bawd. Your honour knows what 'tis to say well enough.
Lys. Well, call forth, call forth.
Boult. For flesh and blood, sir, white and red,

you shall see a rose; and she were a rose indeed,
if she had but—
 Lys. What, prithee?   40
 Boult. O, sir, I can be modest.
 Lys. That dignifies the renown of a bawd, no
less than it gives a good report to a number to be
chaste.   [*Exit Boult.*
 Bawd. Here comes that which grows to the
stalk; never plucked yet, I can assure you.

   Re-enter BOULT *with* MARINA.

Is she not a fair creature?
 Lys. 'Faith, she would serve after a long
voyage at sea. Well, there's for you: leave us.
 Bawd. I beseech your honour, give me leave:
a word, and I'll have done presently. 51
 Lys. I beseech you, do.
 Bawd. [*To Marina*] First, I would have you
note, this is an honourable man.
 Mar. I desire to find him so, that I may
worthily note him.
 Bawd. Next, he's the governor of this coun-
try, and a man whom I am bound to.
 Mar. If he govern the country, you are bound
to him indeed; but how honourable he is in that,
I know not.   61
 Bawd. Pray you, without any more virginal
fencing, will you use him kindly? He will line
your apron with gold.
 Mar. What he will do graciously, I will thank-
fully receive.
 Lys. Ha' you done?
 Bawd. My lord, she's not paced yet: you
must take some pains to work her to your manage.
Come, we will leave his honour and her together.
Go thy ways.
    [*Exeunt Bawd, Pandar, and Boult.*
 Lys. Now, pretty one, how long have you
been at this trade?
 Mar. What trade, sir?
 Lys. Why, I cannot name't but I shall offend.
 Mar. I cannot be offended with my trade.
Please you to name it.
 Lys. How long have you been of this profession?
 Mar. E'er since I can remember.
 Lys Did you go to't so young? Were you a
gamester at five or at seven?   81
 Mar. Earlier too, sir, if now I be one.
 Lys. Why, the house you dwell in proclaims
you to be a creature of sale.
 Mar. Do you know this house to be a place
of such resort, and will come into't? I hear say
you are of honourable parts, and are the governor
of this place.
 Lys. Why, hath your principal made known
unto you who I am?   90
 Mar. Who is my principal?
 Lys. Why, your herb-woman; she that sets
seeds and roots of shame and iniquity. O, you
have heard something of my power, and so stand
aloof for more serious wooing. But I protest to
thee, pretty one, my authority shall not see thee,
or else look friendly upon thee. Come, bring me
to me private place: come, come.
 Mar. If you were born to honour, show it now;
If put upon you, make the judgement good 100
That thought you worthy of it.
 Lys. How's this? how's this? Some more;
 be sage.

132 *cope.* Sky.

Mar.   For me,
That am a maid, though most ungentle fortune
Have placed me in this sty, where, since I came,
Diseases have been sold dearer than physic,
O, that the gods
Would set me free from this unhallow'd place,
Though they did change me to the meanest bird
That flies i' the purer air!
      Lys.   I did not think
Thou couldst have spoke so well; ne'er dream'd
      thou couldst.   110
Had I brought hither a corrupted mind,
Thy speech had alter'd it. Hold, here's gold
      for thee:
Persever in that clear way thou goest,
And the gods strengthen thee!
      Mar.   The good gods preserve you!
      Lys. For me, be you thoughten
That I came with no ill intent; for to me
The very doors and windows savour vilely.
Fare thee well. Thou art a piece of virtue, and
I doubt not but thy training hath been noble.
Hold, here's more gold for thee.   120
A curse upon him, die he like a thief,
That robs thee of thy goodness! If thou dost
Hear from me, it shall be for thy good.

Re-enter BOULT.

Boult. I beseech your honour, one piece for
me.
      Lys. Avaunt, thou damned door-keeper!
Your house, but for this virgin that doth prop it,
Would sink and overwhelm you. Away! [*Exit.*
      Boult. How's this? We must take another
course with you. If your peevish chastity,
which is not worth a breakfast in the cheapest
country under the cope, shall undo a whole
household, let me be gelded like a spaniel.
Come your ways.
      Mar. Whither would you have me?
      Boult. I must have your maidenhead taken
off, or the common hangman shall execute it.
Come your ways. We'll have no more gentlemen driven away. Come your ways, I say.

Re-enter Bawd.

Bawd. How now! what's the matter?   140
      Boult. Worse and worse, mistress; she has
here spoken holy words to the Lord Lysimachus.
      Bawd. O abominable!
      Boult. She makes our profession as it were to
stink afore the face of the gods.
      Bawd. Marry, hang her up for ever!
      Boult. The nobleman would have dealt with
her like a nobleman, and she sent him away as
cold as a snowball; saying his prayers too.   149
      Bawd. Boult, take her away; use her at thy
pleasure: crack the glass of her virginity, and
make the rest malleable.
      Boult. An if she were a thornier piece of
ground than she is, she shall be ploughed.
      Mar. Hark, hark, you gods!
      Bawd. She conjures: away with her! Would
she had never come within my doors! Marry,
hang you! She's born to undo us. Will you
not go the way of women-kind? Marry, come
up, my dish of chastity with rosemary and bays!
                                    [*Exit.*

Boult. Come, mistress ; come your ways with me.

Mar. Whither wilt thou have me?

Boult. To take from you the jewel you hold so dear.

Mar. Prithee, tell me one thing first.

Boult. Come now, your one thing.

Mar. What canst thou wish thine enemy to be?

Boult. Why, I could wish him to be my master, or rather, my mistress.   170

Mar. Neither of these are so bad as thou art,
Since they do better thee in their command.
● Thou hold'st a place, for which the pained'st fiend
Of hell would not in reputation change :
Thou art the damned doorkeeper to every
● Coistrel that comes inquiring for his Tib ;
To the choleric fisting of every rogue
Thy ear is liable ; thy food is such
As hath been belch'd on by infected lungs.   179

Boult. What would you have me do? go to the wars, would you? where a man may serve seven years for the loss of a leg, and have not money enough in the end to buy him a wooden one?

Mar. Do any thing but this thou doest. Empty
● Old receptacles, or common shores, of filth ;
● Serve by indenture to the common hangman :
Any of these ways are yet better than this ;
For what thou professest, a baboon, could he speak,
Would own a name too dear.   O, that the gods
Would safely deliver me from this place !   191
Here, here's gold for thee.
If that thy master would gain by me,
Proclaim that I can sing, weave, sew, and dance,
With other virtues, which I'll keep from boast ;
And I will undertake all these to teach.
I doubt not but this populous city will
Yield many scholars.

Boult. But can you teach all this you speak of?

Mar. Prove that I cannot, take me home again,
And prostitute me to the basest groom   201
That doth frequent your house.

Boult. Well, I will see what I can do for thee : if I can place thee, I will.

Mar. But amongst honest women.

Boult. 'Faith, my acquaintance lies little amongst them.   But since my master and mistress have bought you, there's no going but by their consent: therefore I will make them acquainted with your purpose, and I doubt not but I shall find them tractable enough.   Come, I'll do for thee what I can ; come your ways.

[*Exeunt.*

ACT V.

Enter GOWER.

Gow. Marina thus the brothel 'scapes, and chances
Into an honest house, our story says.
She sings like one immortal, and she dances
As goddess-like to her admired lays ;
● Deep clerks she dumbs ; and with her neeld composes
Nature's own shape, of bud, bird, branch, or berry,
That even her art sisters the natural roses ;
● Her inkle, silk, twin with the rubied cherry :
That pupils lacks she none of noble race,

173 *pained'st fiend.* Most tormented devil.

176 *Coistrel.* Scoundrel. *Tib.* Slut.

186 *common shores.* The banks of rivers, and particularly of tidal rivers between high and low water, were used as tips for sewage.

187 *by indenture.* As apprentice.

Gower: Marina ... sings like one immortal'. Marina's music enchants her listeners. Engraving from *La storia d'Appollonia di Tiro e Tarsia*, 1616

5 *neeld.* Needle.

8 *inkle.* Thread.

1902
BYAM·SHAW

Who pour their bounty on her; and her gain   10
She gives the cursed bawd.   Here we her place:
And to her father turn our thoughts again,
Where we left him, on the sea.   We there him
    lost;
Whence, driven before the winds, he is arrived
Here where his daughter dwells; and on this coast
Suppose him now at anchor.   The city strived
God Neptune's annual feast to keep: from whence
Lysimachus our Tyrian ship espies,
His banners sable, trimm'd with rich expense;
And to him in his barge with fervour hies.   20
In your supposing once more put your sight
Of heavy Pericles; think this his bark:
Where what is done in action, more, if might,
Shall be discover'd; please you, sit and hark.
                                 [Exit.

SCENE I.   *On board Pericles' ship, off Mytilene.*
   A close pavilion on deck, with a curtain before
   it; Pericles within it, reclined on a couch.
   A barge lying beside the Tyrian vessel.

Enter two Sailors, *one belonging to the Tyrian*
   vessel, the other to the barge; to them HELI-
CANUS.

   Tyr. Sail. [*To the Sailor of Mytilene*]
     Where is lord Helicanus? he can resolve you.
O, here he is.
Sir, there's a barge put off from Mytilene,
And in it is Lysimachus the governor,
Who craves to come aboard.   What is your will?
   Hel.   That he have his.   Call up some gentle-
    men.
   Tyr. Sail.   Ho, gentlemen! my lord calls.

   Enter two or three Gentlemen.

   First Gent.   Doth your lordship call?
   Hel.   Gentlemen, there's some of worth would
    come aboard;
I pray ye, greet them fairly.   10
   [*The Gentlemen and the two Sailors descend,*
                 and go on board the barge.

Enter, from thence, LYSIMACHUS *and* Lords;
   with the Gentlemen *and the two* Sailors.

   Tyr. Sail.   Sir,
This is the man that can, in aught you would,
Resolve you
   Lys.   Hail, reverend sir! the gods preserve
    you!
   Hel.   And you, sir, to outlive the age I am,
And die as I would do.
   Lys.   You wish me well.
Being on shore, honouring of Neptune's triumphs,
Seeing this goodly vessel ride before us,
I made to it, to know of whence you are.
   Hel.   First, what is your place?   20
   Lys.   I am the governor of this place you lie
    before.
   Hel.   Sir,
Our vessel is of Tyre, in it the king;
A man who for this three months hath not spoken
To any one, nor taken sustenance
But to prorogue his grief.
   Lys.   Upon what ground is his distemperature?
   Hel.   'Twould be too tedious to repeat;
But the main grief springs from the loss
Of a beloved daughter and a wife.   30

Map showing the area of Pericles' travels. From Herman
Moll's *Geographia Classica*, 1726

9 *some of worth.* Some people of rank.

Opposite : Gower as Chorus. Illustration by Byam Shaw,
The Chiswick Shakespeare, 1902

33 *bootless*. Unavailing.

60 *graff*. Grafted plant.

Lys.   May we not see him?

Hel.   You may;

●But bootless is your sight: he will not speak
To any.

Lys.   Yet let me obtain my wish.

Hel.   Behold him. [*Pericles discovered.*] This
              was a goodly person,
Till the disaster that, one mortal night,
Drove him to this.

Lys.   Sir king, all hail! the gods preserve you!
Hail, royal sir!   40

Hel.   It is in vain; he will not speak to you.

First Lord.   Sir,
We have a maid in Mytilene, I durst wager,
Would win some words of him

Lys.   'Tis well bethought.
She questionless with her sweet harmony
And other chosen attractions, would allure,
And make a battery through his deafen'd parts,
Which now are midway stopp'd:
She is all happy as the fairest of all,
And, with her fellow maids, is now upon   50
The leafy shelter that abuts against
The island's side.

                    [*Whispers a Lord, who goes off in the
                              barge of Lysimachus.*

Hel.   Sure, all's effectless; yet nothing we'll
              omit
That bears recovery's name.   But, since your
              kindness
We have stretch'd thus far, let us beseech you
That for our gold we may provision have,
Wherein we are not destitute for want,
But weary for the staleness.

Lys.   O, sir, a courtesy
Which if we should deny, the most just gods
●For every graff would send a caterpillar,   60
And so afflict our province.   Yet once more
Let me entreat to know at large the cause
Of your king's sorrow.

Hel.   Sit, sir, I will recount it to you:
But, see, I am prevented.

Re-enter, from the barge, Lord, *with* MARINA,
              and a young Lady.

Lys.   O, here is
The lady that I sent for.   Welcome, fair one!
Is't not a goodly presence?

Hel.   She's a gallant lady.

Lys.   She's such a one, that, were I well
              assured
Came of a gentle kind and noble stock,
I'ld wish no better choice, and think me rarely
              wed.
Fair one, all goodness that consists in bounty   70
Expect even here, where is a kingly patient:
If that thy prosperous and artificial feat
Can draw him but to answer thee in aught,
Thy sacred physic shall receive such pay
As thy desires can wish.

Mar.   Sir, I will use
My utmost skill in his recovery,
Provided
That none but I and my companion maid
Be suffer'd to come near him.

Lys.   Come, let us leave her;
And the gods make her prosperous!   80

                    [*Marina sings.*

Lys.   Mark'd he your music?

Mar.   No, nor look'd on us.
Lys. See, she will speak to him.
Mar.   Hail, sir! my lord, lend ear.
Per. Hum, ha!
Mar.   I am a maid,
My lord, that ne'er before invited eyes,
But have been gazed on like a comet: she speaks,
My lord, that, may be, hath endured a grief
Might equal yours, if both were justly weigh'd.
Though wayward fortune did malign my state, 90
My derivation was from ancestors
Who stood equivalent with mighty kings:
But time hath rooted out my parentage,
And to the world and awkward casualties
Bound me in servitude. [*Aside*] I will desist;
But there is something glows upon my cheek,
And whispers in mine ear 'Go not till he speak.'
   Per. My fortunes—parentage—good parent-
           age—
To equal mine!—was it not thus? what say you?
   Mar. I said, my lord, if you did know my
           parentage,   100
You would not do me violence.
   Per. I do think so.   Pray you, turn your eyes
           upon me.
You are like something that— What country-
           woman?
Here of these shores?
   Mar.   No, nor of any shores:
Yet I was mortally brought forth, and am
No other than I appear.
   Per. I am great with woe, and shall deliver
           weeping.
My dearest wife was like this maid, and such
           a one
My daughter might have been: my queen's
           square brows;
Her stature to an inch; as wand-like straight; 110
As silver-voiced; her eyes as jewel-like
And cased as richly; in pace another Juno;
Who starves the ears she feeds, and makes them
           hungry,
The more she gives them speech. Where do
           you live?
   Mar. Where I am but a stranger: from the
           deck
You may discern the place.
   Per.   Where were you bred?
And how achieved you these endowments, which
You make more rich to owe?
   Mar. If I should tell my history, it would
           seem
Like lies disdain'd in the reporting.
   Per.   Prithee, speak: 120
Falseness cannot come from thee; for thou
           look'st
Modest as Justice, and thou seem'st a palace
For the crown'd Truth to dwell in: I will believe
           thee,
And make my senses credit thy relation
To points that seem impossible; for thou look'st
Like one I loved indeed. What were thy friends?
Didst thou not say, when I did push thee back—
Which was when I perceived thee—that thou
           camest
From good descending?
   Mar.   So indeed I did.
   Per. Report thy parentage. I think thou
           said'st   130

Marina: 'Hail, sir! my lord, lend ear'. Marina (Geraldine McEwan) with Pericles (Richard Johnson), Stratford-upon-Avon, 1958

175 *drawn.* Drawn a weapon.

Richard Johnson as Pericles, Stratford-upon-Avon, 1958

Thou hadst been toss'd from wrong to injury,
And that thou thought'st thy griefs might equal
    mine,
If both were open'd.
   Mar.   Some such thing
I said, and said no more but what my thoughts
Did warrant me was likely.
   Per.   Tell thy story;
If thine consider'd prove the thousandth part
Of my endurance, thou art a man, and I
Have suffer'd like a girl: yet thou dost look
Like Patience gazing on kings' graves, and
    smiling
Extremity out of act. What were thy friends? 140
How lost thou them? Thy name, my most kind
    virgin?
Recount, I do beseech thee: come, sit by me.
   Mar. My name is Marina.
   Per.   O, I am mock'd,
And thou by some incensed god sent hither
To make the world to laugh at me.
   Mar.   Patience, good sir,
Or here I 'll cease.
   Per.   Nay, I 'll be patient.
Thou little know'st how thou dost startle me,
To call thyself Marina.
   Mar. The name
Was given me by one that had some power, 150
My father, and a king.
   Per.   How! a king's daughter?
And call'd Marina?
   Mar.   You said you would believe me;
But, not to be a troubler of your peace,
I will end here.
   Per.   But are you flesh and blood?
Have you a working pulse? and are no fairy?
Motion! Well; speak on. Where were you
    born?
And wherefore call'd Marina?
   Mar.   Call'd Marina
For I was born at sea.
   Per.   At sea! what mother?
   Mar. My mother was the daughter of a king;
Who died the minute I was born,   160
As my good nurse Lychorida hath oft
Deliver'd weeping.
   Per.   O, stop there a little!
[*Aside*] This is the rarest dream that e'er dull
    sleep
Did mock sad fools withal: this cannot be:
My daughter's buried. Well: where were you
    bred?
I 'll hear you more, to the bottom of your story,
And never interrupt you.
   Mar. You scorn: believe me, 'twere best I
    did give o'er.
   Per. I will believe you by the syllable
Of what you shall deliver. Yet, give me leave: 170
How came you in these parts? where were you
    bred?
   Mar. The king my father did in Tarsus leave
    me;
Till cruel Cleon, with his wicked wife,
Did seek to murder me: and having woo'd
●A villain to attempt it, who having drawn to do 't,
A crew of pirates came and rescued me;
Brought me to Mytilene. But, good sir,
Whither will you have me? Why do you weep?
    It may be,

You think me an impostor: no, good faith;
I am the daughter to King Pericles,   180
If good King Pericles be.
   Per. Ho, Helicanus!
   Hel. Calls my lord?
   Per. Thou art a grave and noble counsellor,
Most wise in general: tell me, if thou canst,
What this maid is, or what is like to be,
That thus hath made me weep?
   Hel.   I know not; but
Here is the regent, sir, of Mytilene
Speaks nobly of her.
   Lys.   She would never tell
Her parentage; being demanded that,   190
She would sit still and weep.
   Per. O Helicanus, strike me, honour'd sir;
Give me a gash, put me to present pain;
Lest this great sea of joys rushing upon me
O'erbear the shores of my mortality,
And drown me with their sweetness. O, come
    hither,
Thou that beget'st him that did thee beget;
Thou that wast born at sea, buried at Tarsus,
And found at sea again! O Helicanus,
Down on thy knees, thank the holy gods as
    loud   200
As thunder threatens us: this is Marina.
What was thy mother's name? tell me but that,
For truth can never be confirm'd enough,
Though doubts did ever sleep.
   Mar.   First, sir, I pray,
What is your title?
   Per. I am Pericles of Tyre: but tell me now
My drown'd queen's name, as in the rest you
    said
Thou hast been godlike perfect,
†The heir of kingdoms and another like
To Pericles thy father.   210
   Mar. Is it no more to be your daughter than
To say my mother's name was Thaisa?
Thaisa was my mother, who did end
The minute I began.
   Per. Now, blessing on thee! rise; thou art
    my child.
Give me fresh garments. Mine own, Helicanus;
She is not dead at Tarsus, as she should have
    been,
By savage Cleon: she shall tell thee all;
When thou shalt kneel, and justify in knowledge
She is thy very princess. Who is this?   220
   Hel. Sir, 'tis the governor of Mytilene,
Who, hearing of your melancholy state,
Did come to see you.
   Per.   I embrace you.
Give me my robes. I am wild in my be-
    holding.
O heavens bless my girl! But, hark, what
    music?
Tell Helicanus, my Marina, tell him
O'er, point by point, for yet he seems to doubt,
How sure you are my daughter. But, what
    music?
   Hel. My lord, I hear none.
   Per. None!   230
The music of the spheres! List, my Marina.
   Lys. It is not good to cross him; give him
    way.
   Per. Rarest sounds! Do ye not hear?
   Lys.   My lord, I hear. [*Music.*

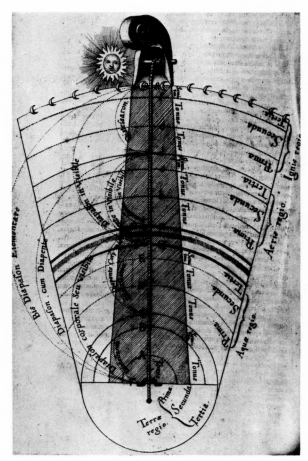

Pericles: 'The music of the spheres!' Representation of
the music of the spheres from Robert Fludd's *Utriusque
Cosmi Metaphysica*, 1617

235 *nips me unto.* Compels me to.

256 *eftsoons.* Before long.

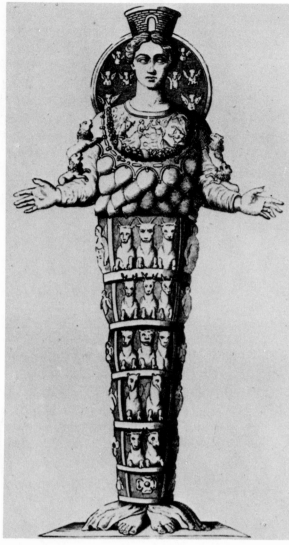

Diana of Ephesus. From 19th century engraving

Per.   Most heavenly music!
●It nips me unto listening, and thick slumber
Hangs upon mine eyes: let me rest.   [*Sleeps.*
Lys.   A pillow for his head:
So, leave him all.   Well, my companion friends,
If this but answer to my just belief,
I'll well remember you.   240
                          [*Exeunt all but Pericles.*

DIANA *appears to* PERICLES *as in a vision.*

Dia.   My temple stands in Ephesus: hie thee
     thither,
And do upon mine altar sacrifice.
There, when my maiden priests are met together,
Before the people all,
Reveal how thou at sea didst lose thy wife:
To mourn thy crosses, with thy daughter's, call
And give them repetition to the life.
Or perform my bidding, or thou livest in woe;
Do it, and happy; by my silver bow!
Awake, and tell thy dream.   [*Disappears.* 250
Per.   Celestial Dian, goddess argentine,
I will obey thee.   Helicanus!

Re-enter HELICANUS, LYSIMACHUS, *and*
     MARINA.

Hel.   Sir?
Per.   My purpose was for Tarsus, there to
     strike
The inhospitable Cleon; but I am
For other service first: toward Ephesus
●Turn our blown sails; eftsoons I'll tell thee why.
[*To Lysimachus*] Shall we refresh us, sir, upon
     your shore,
And give you gold for such provision
As our intents will need?
Lys.   Sir,   260
With all my heart; and, when you come ashore,
I have another suit.
Per.   You shall prevail,
Were it to woo my daughter; for it seems
You have been noble towards her.
Lys.   Sir, lend me your arm.
Per.   Come, my Marina.   [*Exeunt.*

SCENE II.   *Enter* GOWER, *before the temple of*
     DIANA *at Ephesus.*

Gow.   Now our sands are almost run:
More a little, and then dumb.
This, my last boon, give me,
For such kindness must relieve me,
That you aptly will suppose   270
What pageantry, what feats, what shows,
What minstrelsy, and pretty din,
The regent made in Mytilene
To greet the king.   So he thrived,
That he is promised to be wived
To fair Marina; but in no wise
Till he had done his sacrifice,
As Dian bade: whereto being bound,
The interim, pray you, all confound.
In feather'd briefness sails are fill'd,   280
And wishes fall out as they're will'd.
At Ephesus, the temple see,
Our king and all his company.
That he can hither come so soon,
Is by your fancy's thankful doom.   [*Exit.*

SCENE III.   *The temple of Diana at Ephesus;*
THAISA standing near the altar, as high
priestess; a number of Virgins on each side;
CERIMON and other Inhabitants of Ephesus
attending.

Enter PERICLES, with his train; LYSIMACHUS,
HELICANUS, MARINA, *and a* Lady.

Per.   Hail, Dian! to perform thy just com-
        mand,
I here confess myself the king of Tyre;
Who, frighted from my country, did wed
At Pentapolis the fair Thaisa.
At sea in childbed died she, but brought forth
A maid-child call'd Marina; who, O goddess,
● Wears yet thy silver livery.   She at Tarsus
Was nursed with Cleon; who at fourteen years
He sought to murder: but her better stars
Brought her to Mytilene; 'gainst whose shore   10
● Riding, her fortunes brought the maid aboard us,
Where, by her own most clear remembrance, she
Made known herself my daughter.
    Thai.   Voice and favour!
You are, you are—O royal Pericles!   [*Faints.*
    Per.   What means the nun? she dies! help,
        gentlemen!
    Cer.   Noble sir,
If you have told Diana's altar true,
This is your wife.
    Per.   Reverend appearer, no;
I threw her overboard with these very arms.
    Cer.   Upon this coast, I warrant you.
    Per.   'Tis most certain. 20
    Cer.   Look to the lady; O, she's but o'erjoy'd.
Early in blustering morn this lady was
Thrown upon this shore.   I oped the coffin,
Found there rich jewels; recover'd her, and
        placed her
Here in Diana's temple.
    Per.   May we see them?
    Cer.   Great sir, they shall be brought you to
        my house,
Whither I invite you.   Look, Thaisa is
Recovered
    Thai.   O, let me look!
If he be none of mine, my sanctity
Will to my sense bend no licentious ear,   30
But curb it, spite of seeing.   O, my lord,
Are you not Pericles?   Like him you spake,
Like him you are: did you not name a tempest,
A birth, and death?
    Per.   The voice of dead Thaisa!
    Thai.   That Thaisa am I, supposed dead
And drown'd.
    Per.   Immortal Dian!
    Thai.   Now I know you better.
When we with tears parted Pentapolis,
The king my father gave you such a ring.
                            [*Shows a ring.*
    Per.   This, this: no more, you gods! your
        present kindness   40
Makes my past miseries sports: you shall do well,
That on the touching of her lips I may
Melt and no more be seen.   O, come, be buried
A second time within these arms.
    Mar.   My heart
Leaps to be gone into my mother's bosom.
                            [*Kneels to Thaisa.*

Temple of Diana at Ephesus. Engraving from a Roman
medal in G. du Choul's *Discours de la Religion des
Anciens Romains*, 1567

'. . . a number of Virgins on each side.' Engraving from
a Roman medal in G. du Choul's *Discours de la Religion
des Anciens Romains*, 1567

7 *Wears . . . livery.* Is still a virgin.

11 *Riding.* i.e. at anchor.

Pericles: 'Pure Dian, bless thee for thy vision!' Illustration by Byam Shaw, *The Chiswick Shakespeare*, 1902

---

73 *ornament.* i.e. beard.

Per. Look, who kneels here! Flesh of thy
    flesh, Thaisa;
Thy burden at the sea, and call'd Marina
For she was yielded there.
    Thai.   Blest, and mine own!
    Hel. Hail, madam, and my queen!
    Thai.   I know you not.
    Per. You have heard me say, when I did fly
    from Tyre,   50
I left behind an ancient substitute:
Can you remember what I call'd the man?
I have named him oft.
    Thai.   'Twas Helicanus then.
    Per. Still confirmation:
Embrace him, dear Thaisa; this is he.
Now do I long to hear how you were found;
How possibly preserved; and who to thank,
Besides the gods, for this great miracle.
    Thai. Lord Cerimon, my lord; this man,
Through whom the gods have shown their power;
    that can   60
From first to last resolve you.
    Per.   Reverend sir,
The gods can have no mortal officer
More like a god than you. Will you deliver
How this dead queen re-lives?
    Cer.   I will, my lord.
Beseech you, first go with me to my house,
Where shall be shown you all was found with her;
How she came placed here in the temple;
No needful thing omitted.
    Per. Pure Dian, bless thee for thy vision! I
Will offer night-oblations to thee. Thaisa, 70
This prince, the fair-betrothed of your daughter,
Shall marry her at Pentapolis. And now,
This ornament
Makes me look dismal will I clip to form;
And what this fourteen years no razor touch'd,
To grace thy marriage-day, I'll beautify.
    Thai. Lord Cerimon hath letters of good
    credit, sir,
My father's dead.
    Per. Heavens make a star of him! Yet there,
    my queen,
We'll celebrate their nuptials, and ourselves 80
Will in that kingdom spend our following days:
Our son and daughter shall in Tyrus reign.
Lord Cerimon, we do our longing stay
To hear the rest untold: sir, lead's the way.
                          [*Exeunt.*

Enter GOWER.

    Gow. In Antiochus and his daughter you
    have heard
Of monstrous lust the due and just reward:
In Pericles, his queen and daughter, seen,
Although assail'd with fortune fierce and keen,
Virtue preserved from fell destruction's blast,
Led on by heaven, and crown'd with joy at last:
In Helicanus may you well descry   91
A figure of truth, of faith, of loyalty:
In reverend Cerimon there well appears
The worth that learned charity aye wears:
For wicked Cleon and his wife, when fame
Had spread their cursed deed, and honour'd
    name
Of Pericles, to rage the city turn,
That him and his they in his palace burn;

The gods for murder seemed so content
To punish them; although not done, but meant.
So, on your patience evermore attending,   100
New joy wait on you! Here our play has ending.
                              [*Exit.*

Effigy of John Gower from his tomb in St Saviour's
Church, Southwark

Cymbeline

1609

CYMBELINE is a curious play, difficult for us to appreciate and interpret. For one thing it is experimental, in the direction of romance, where there were no satisfactory models, and is an amalgam of diverse elements. For another, its incongruities should be taken comically, as if in inverted commas – Cloten's decapitation and his head brought on as a stage-property, the sudden surprises and sensational improbabilities. When, at the end, Cymbeline's lost sons are presented to him and Imogen is recovered from presumed death, he says,

> O, what am I?
> A mother to the birth of three? –

one cannot but think that Shakespeare was writing with his tongue in his cheek. And at several other points similarly. Of course there are serious elements too – Iachimo's intrusion upon Imogen, which Shakespeare added for himself to the folk-tale love-wager theme, can hardly be regarded as comic. It is a reminiscence from *The Rape of Lucrece* – and the play is full of reminiscences.

Something new was demanded for the public, for the two publics now, of Blackfriars as well as the Globe; so the old master is trying his hand out at a dual-purpose play. In performance one or other of these elements can be – indeed, must be – cut down; the masque-like theophany at the end, with the descent of Jupiter, would have been for Blackfriars with its more elaborate scenic devices. A modern French producer thought it 'sacrilege' to sacrifice a word of Shakespeare's, but this is absurd: he would not have minded cutting, the demands of the stage were all in all, and long plays like *Cymbeline* and *Hamlet* exemplify obvious alternatives.

After the advent of Inigo Jones with his spectacular scenic creations the taste of the sophisticated public moved towards this sort of thing, and there came a revival of old romantic plays, with their episodic, fairyland character.

The Play. These last plays have long and detailed stage-directions: Shakespeare was writing at home in the country. The long closure of the theatres, from July 1608 to

December 1609, gave him plenty of time, and *Cymbeline* is over-long and full of reminders of his own work. The triple recognition at the end is closely similar to that of his recent *Pericles*. He had been re-reading *Venus and Adonis* and *The Rape of Lucrece*. The comic clod, Cloten, had been dressed in Posthumus' clothes, and Imogen, taking his body for that of her husband, cries,

Imogen in the cave. Nineteenth century engraving from a painting by T. Graham (1840–1906)

> O Posthumus, alas,
> Where is thy head? where's that? Ay me! where's that?

All this is, surely, to be taken comically. When asked by the invading Romans for his name, she gives Richard du Champ. It has been suggested that this was for Richard Field, the Stratford printer of the two poems – all the more likely now that Shakespeare had become part-owner of the theatre in Blackfriars, where Field's press (and his French wife) held out.

Many more memories recur throughout this long-winded play. All his life Shakespeare was apt to think of Tarquin – he was a very sexy man himself, and the image must have given him a kick. We have Cleopatra once more in glory on the Cydnus, and the story of Tereus and Philomela which sparked off *Titus Andronicus*. The 'Arabian bird' appears from *Antony and Cleopatra*, and 'the worms of the Nile' (but why does he so

725

often refer to snakes as 'worms'?) Yet another apostrophe to gold and the ill effects of its cult refers back to *Timon*. The charm of innocent country life in the mountains of Wales, lived by old Belarius and Cymbeline's unknown sons, as opposed to the falsity and treacheries of Court life, re-appears from *As You Like It* or even goes right back to *Henry VI*.

Altogether, with leisure on hand at Stratford, he was looking through his own past work. For the elements of his story he had those old stand-bys, Holinshed, *The Mirror for Magistrates* and the *Faerie Queene*. He hardly needed Boccaccio or anything else for the familiar folk-tale of a husband wagering everything on his wife's fidelity. (After his own variegated experiences in London he had come back to a faithful wife of his own at home.) A new element in the play is the character of the Doctor, who instructs the wicked Queen – another dissembling deceitful Tamora – in the use of drugs. His son-in-law could have instructed him about that.

Iachimo – the Italian adventurer who instigated the husband Posthumus to take the wager upon Imogen's fidelity and gets into her bedroom in a chest, to report everything – is another, more light-hearted Iago. Here we have a curious feature in the reflection on Italians:

> What false Italian,
> As poisonous-tongued as -handed, hath prevailed
> On thy too ready hearing?

This accounts for Posthumus' onslaught on womankind:

> Is there no way for men to be, but women
> Must be half-workers?...
>   Could I find out
> The woman's part in me! For there's no motion
> That tends to vice in man but I affirm
> It is the woman's part. Be it lying, note it,
> The woman's; flattering, hers; deceiving, hers;
> Lust and rank thoughts, hers, hers; revenges, hers;
> Ambitions, covetings, changes of pride, disdain,
> Nice longing, slanders, mutability –

we cannot but recognise the experience portrayed in the Sonnets. Posthumus goes on, curiously:

> I'll write against them.

This very year 1609 saw the publication of the Sonnets, and only a year or so after, Emilia Lanier's replication with its attack on men, inserted in prose, before her own long quasi-religious poem. (Certainly ambition had been a consuming passion with her, and all those other characteristics 'noted' were recognisable too.)

We do not need to repeat the complexities, the windings, sudden turns and surprises, the improbabilities, which so offended Dr. Johnson. Once more, the dramatist did not mind improbabilities or incongruities, any more than the audience did, and he was out to give them what they wanted. The play has a double, or even triple, plot and all admit the experienced skill with which so many threads are drawn together at the end. As against the fairy-tale background from remote British history – Cymbeline (Cunobelinus), a Cloton as a supposed Duke of Cornwall, a world beyond the Severn, Wales and Milford Haven, as a port of disembarkation from Italy! – the characters are real and possess veracity.

Cymbeline is a kind of silly Lear, easily taken in by a dissembling wife, real enough; though Posthumus is too credulous, there are such types as he and Iachimo; Imogen has always been found moving, so too the faithful Pisanio.

Style. The language in which the play is written can only be described as extraordinary. Shakespeare had always had a lordly way with words, a fondness for rare and grand, impressive words. Increasingly, he does what he likes with them: he will frequently use nouns as verbs, and sometimes a preposition, 'beneath', for example, as a noun. Instinctively he uses a visual word rather than an abstract one. Posthumus puts aside the thought of another wife:

> give me but this I have,
> And cere up my embracements from a next
> With bonds of death!

The words 'cere up' come to mind for he sees the waxen shroud, and the idea of sealing is behind the thought of wax. He always had been double-minded: hence all the double-talk and punning throughout his work, which Dr. Johnson considered *his* fatal Cleopatra. The habit grew upon him until he expresses himself, not only elliptically, but so obliquely as to be devious – it is often difficult to know what he means. The very first words of the play are:

> You do not meet a man but frowns. Our bloods
> No more obey the heavens than our courtiers
> Still seem as does the King's.

Only Shakespeare would use the word 'bloods' for moods, and the rest is obscure: it implies that the courtiers do not agree with the King's mood (in exiling Posthumus for marrying Imogen).

In Cloten's comic duel, his sword missed its thrust. This is the way it is expressed: 'His steel was in debt. It went o' th' backside the town', i.e. like a debtor, it took a back road. Iachimo praises Imogen to her face, in contrast with others, thus:

> It cannot be i' th' eye, for apes and monkeys,
> 'Twixt two such shes, would chatter this way and
> Contemn with mows the other; nor i' th' judgment,
> For idiots, in this case of favour, would
> Be wisely definite.

We know that he wrote rapidly; evidently his pen could not keep up with his thoughts. We know too that his manuscripts were illegible, and gave both transcribers and printers much trouble.

Here is a thought he puts in concrete, visual terms, because he *sees* it:

> The love I bear him
> Made me to fan you thus; but the gods made you,
> Unlike all others, chaffless.

Iachimo simply means that he was testing Imogen, and she was faultless, but the image behind the word 'fan' is that of winnowing, and she is without chaff. Note, too, that the image is from country life. Even a quite simple thought is thus worded:

> Frame yourself
> To orderly solicits, and be friended
> With aptness of the season;

i.e. make your requests in order and at apt times. For 'give an account' Shakespeare will say 'words him'; for 'tell about', 'story him'. Or what about a passage like this, when Imogen is persuaded that Posthumus has been unfaithful to her away in Italy? –

> To think, when thou shalt be disedged by her
> That now thou tirest on, how thy memory
> Will then be panged by me.

'Disedged' is Shakespeare's coinage, and it has a visual element in it, for it means dulling the edge of sexual desire. 'Tirest' is double-talk, for it suggests both preying on, like a bird of prey, and also tiring of her. 'Panged' is a verb coined from the noun 'pang'. The psychological subtlety behind it is that when she and her husband had been together when first married, Imogen had chastely moderated his pressing desires.

But what a writer! And how difficult for the modern reader! There is much to be said for modernising him.

This is not to say that there are not passages of fine poetry, and others of the most effective simplicity: he can do both, as he chooses. We are given two beautiful songs – Fidele's, the name Imogen takes, is one of the most moving he ever wrote, with its burden of farewell:

> Fear no more the heat o' th' sun,
> Nor the furious winter's rages;
> Thou thy worldly task hast done,
> Home art gone and ta'en thy wages . . .

Age and Time. In this remote fairy-tale world there are few touches of the time. The story is put into the framework of a conflict between Rome and ancient Britain, over the payment of tribute. This gives the cue for a couple of patriotic statements like those of John of Gaunt and Faulconbridge earlier. (How much of the past is taken up into this reminiscent play!)

> Our countrymen
> Are men more ordered than when Julius Caesar
> Smiled at their lack of skill, but found their courage
> Worthy his frowning at.

(Visual again.)

> Their discipline
> Now mingled with their courages, will make known
> To their approvers they are people such
> That mend upon the world.

728

This was true enough, after the long struggle with Spain for a place in the sun, and with the English colonisation of North America now going forward.

Lesser evidences of the time occur in a whole scene devoted to playing bowls, a favourite game with Shakespeare (and rather upper-class then). The stupid Cloten goes on about being free to utter what oaths he likes – a reference to the recent Jacobean statute against Oaths, which made for further difficulties when it came to printing the plays. As for stage-apparel, we hear of 'cloak-bag, doublet, hat, hose' – so the clothes worn were Jacobean. So were the rushes on the floor, and the equipment, of Imogen's bedroom. Here we may note again Shakespeare's interest in the work of his neighbours in Southwark, the sculptors who made so many chimney-pieces for great houses as well as monuments:

> The chimney
> Is south the chamber, and the chimney piece
> Chaste Dian bathing. Never saw I figures
> So likely to report themselves. The cutter
> Was as another nature, dumb; outwent her,
> Motion and breath left out.

In taking the bracelet off the sleeping Imogen, to confirm his false story to Posthumus, Iachimo breathes:

> O sleep, thou ape of death, lie dull upon her.
> And be her sense but as a monument,
> Thus in a chapel lying.

Cymbeline's son, Arviragus, in an exquisite passage strewing flowers on Fidele's body, thinking her dead, says that the robin, bringing moss, shames

> Those rich-left heirs that let their fathers lie
> Without a monument.

This, however, would not happen to him: the faithful family called upon one of the Southwark sculptors for the monument at Stratford.

The Text in the Folio offers no great problem, it is reasonably good, and is thought to have been from a scribe's transcript of Shakespeare's difficult hand.

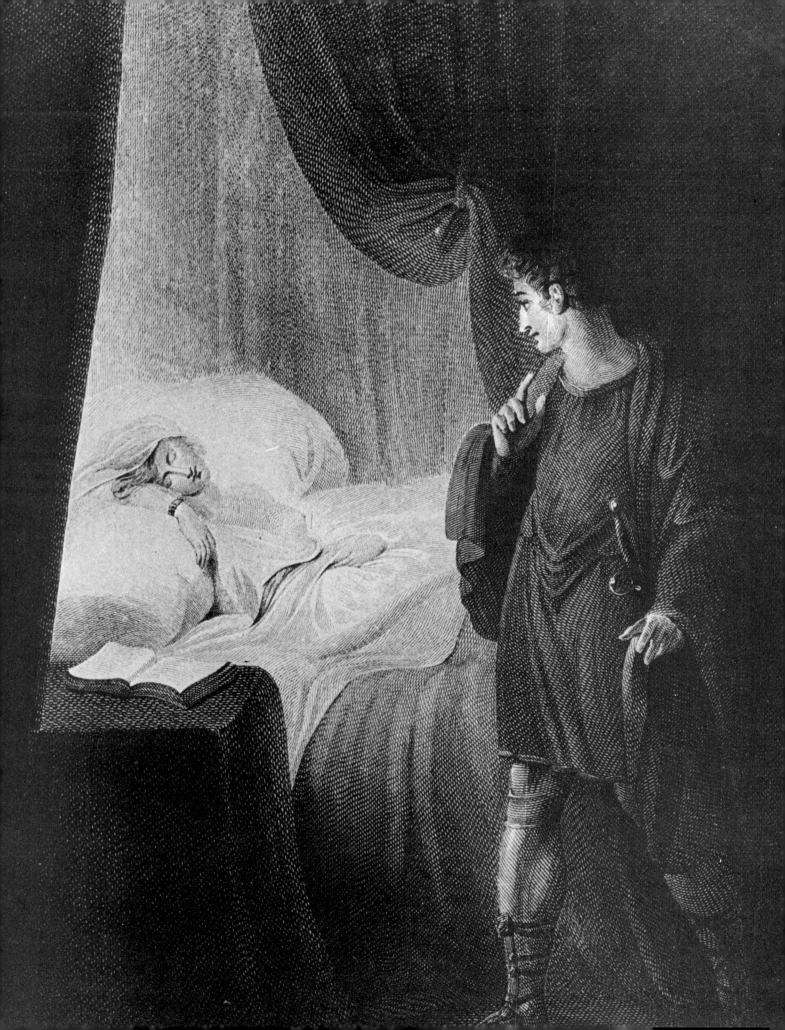

CYMBELINE.

DRAMATIS PERSONÆ.

CYMBELINE, king of Britain.
CLOTEN, son to the Queen by a former husband.
POSTHUMUS LEONATUS, a gentleman, husband to Imogen.
BELARIUS, a banished lord, disguised under the name of Morgan.
GUIDERIUS,
ARVIRAGUS, } sons to Cymbeline, disguised under the names of Polydore and Cadwal, supposed sons to Morgan.
PHILARIO, friend to Posthumus,
IACHIMO, friend to Philario, } Italians.
CAIUS LUCIUS, general of the Roman forces.
PISANIO, servant to Posthumus.
CORNELIUS, a physician.
A Roman Captain.

Two British Captains.
A Frenchman, friend to Philario.
Two Lords of Cymbeline's court.
Two Gentlemen of the same.
Two Gaolers.

Queen, wife to Cymbeline.
IMOGEN, daughter to Cymbeline by a former queen.
HELEN, a lady attending on Imogen.

Lords, Ladies, Roman Senators, Tribunes, a Soothsayer, a Dutchman, a Spaniard, Musicians, Officers, Captains, Soldiers, Messengers, and other attendants.

Apparitions.

SCENE: *Britain; Rome.*

● *A bullet beside a text line indicates an annotation in the opposite column*

ACT I.

SCENE I. *Britain.   The garden of Cymbeline's palace.*

Enter two Gentlemen.

First Gent.   You do not meet a man but frowns: our bloods
No more obey the heavens than our courtiers
Still seem as does the king.
   Sec. Gent.   But what's the matter?
   First Gent.   His daughter, and the heir of 's kingdom, whom
He purposed to his wife's sole son—a widow

Set design by J. Gower Parks, Stratford-upon-Avon, 1937

Opposite: Iachimo gazes upon the sleeping Imogen. Engraving from a painting by Richard Westall (1765–1836)

6 *referr'd herself*. Given herself in marriage.

24 *Endows . . . he*. Belongs to any other man but him.

25 *extend*. Praise.

37 *fond of issue*. Doting on his children.

49 *feated*. Reflected favourably.

●That late he married—hath referr'd herself
Unto a poor but worthy gentleman : she's wedded ;
Her husband banish'd ; she imprison'd : all
Is outward sorrow ; though I think the king
Be touch'd at very heart.
 Sec. Gent.   None but the king? 10
 First Gent. He that hath lost her too ; so is
  the queen,
That most desired the match ; but not a courtier,
Although they wear their faces to the bent
Of the king's looks, hath a heart that is not
Glad at the thing they scowl at.
 Sec. Gent.   And why so?
 First Gent. He that hath miss'd the princess
  is a thing
Too bad for bad report : and he that hath her—
I mean, that married her, alack, good man !
And therefore banish'd—is a creature such
As, to seek through the regions of the earth 20
For one his like, there would be something failing
In him that should compare.   I do not think
So fair an outward and such stuff within
●Endows a man but he.
 Sec. Gent.   You speak him far.
● *First Gent.* I do extend him, sir, within him-
  self,
Crush him together rather than unfold
His measure duly.
 Sec. Gent. What's his name and birth?
 First Gent. I cannot delve him to the root :
  his father
Was called Sicilius, who did join his honour
Against the Romans with Cassibelan, 30
But had his titles by Tenantius whom
He served with glory and admired success,
So gain'd the sur-addition Leonatus ;
And had, besides this gentleman in question,
Two other sons, who in the wars o' the time
Died with their swords in hand ; for which their
  father,
●Then old and fond of issue, took such sorrow
That he quit being, and his gentle lady,
Big of this gentleman our theme, deceased
As he was born.   The king he takes the babe 40
To his protection, calls him Posthumus Leonatus,
Breeds him and makes him of his bed-chamber,
Puts to him all the learnings that his time
Could make him the receiver of ; which he took,
As we do air, fast as 'twas minister'd,
And in 's spring became a harvest, lived in court—
Which rare it is to do—most praised, most loved,
A sample to the more mature
●A glass that feated them, and to the graver
A child that guided dotards ; to his mistress, 50
For whom he now is banish'd, her own price
Proclaims how she esteem'd him and his virtue ;
By her election may be truly read
What kind of man he is.
 Sec. Gent.   I honour him
Even out of your report.   But, pray you, tell me,
Is she sole child to the king?
 First Gent.   His only child.
He had two sons : if this be worth your hearing,
Mark it : the eldest of them at three years old,
I' the swathing-clothes the other, from their nur-
  sery
Were stol'n, and to this hour no guess in know-
  ledge 60
Which way they went.

Sec. Gent.   How long is this ago?
First Gent.   Some twenty years.
Sec. Gent.   That a king's children should be so
    convey'd,
So slackly guarded, and the search so slow,
That could not trace them!
First Gent.   Howsoe'er 'tis strange,
Or that the negligence may well be laugh'd at,
Yet is it true, sir.
Sec. Gent.   I do well believe you.
First Gent.   We must forbear: here comes the
    gentleman,
The queen, and princess.   [*Exeunt.*

Enter the QUEEN, POSTHUMUS, *and* IMOGEN.

Queen.   No, be assured you shall not find me,
    daughter,   70
After the slander of most stepmothers,
Evil-eyed unto you: you're my prisoner, but
Your gaoler shall deliver you the keys
That lock up your restraint. For you, Posthumus,
So soon as I can win the offended king,
I will be known your advocate: marry, yet
The fire of rage is in him, and 'twere good
•You lean'd unto his sentence with what patience
Your wisdom may inform you.
Post.   Please your highness,
I will from hence to-day.
Queen.   You know the peril.   80
I'll fetch a turn about the garden, pitying
The pangs of barr'd affections, though the king
Hath charged you should not speak together.
                                            [*Exit.*
Imo.   O
Dissembling courtesy! How fine this tyrant
Can tickle where she wounds! My dearest hus-
    band,
I something fear my father's wrath; but nothing—
Always reserved my holy duty—what
His rage can do on me: you must be gone;
And I shall here abide the hourly shot
Of angry eyes, not comforted to live,   90
But that there is this jewel in the world
That I may see again.
Post.   My queen! my mistress!
O lady, weep no more, lest I give cause
To be suspected of more tenderness
Than doth become a man. I will remain
The loyal'st husband that did e'er plight troth:
My residence in Rome at one Philario's,
Who to my father was a friend, to me
Known but by letter: thither write, my queen,
And with mine eyes I'll drink the words you send,
Though ink be made of gall.

Re-enter QUEEN.

Queen.   Be brief, I pray you: 101
If the king come, I shall incur I know not
How much of his displeasure. [*Aside*] Yet I'll
    move him
To walk this way: I never do him wrong,
•But he does buy my injuries, to be friends;
Pays dear for my offences.   [*Exit.*
Post.   Should we be taking leave
As long a term as yet we have to live,
The loathness to depart would grow. Adieu!
Imo.   Nay, stay a little:
Were you but riding forth to air yourself,   110
Such parting were too petty. Look here, love;

78 *lean'd unto.* Accepted.

105 *buy my injuries.* Willingly puts himself in the wrong instead of me.

Imogen: 'Nay, stay a little...' Peggy Ashcroft as Imogen and Richard Johnson as Posthumus, Stratford-upon-Avon, 1957

116 *sear up.* Cauterize.

Posthumus: 'for my sake wear this . . .' Engraving from
a painting by William Hamilton (1751–1801)

126 *fraught.* Burden.

140 *puttock.* Buzzard.

149 *neat-herd.* Cattleman.

This diamond was my mother's: take it, heart;
But keep it till you woo another wife,
When Imogen is dead.
   Post.   How, how! another?
You gentle gods, give me but this I have,
And sear up my embracements from a next
With bonds of death! [*Putting on the ring.*]
   Remain, remain thou here
While sense can keep it on. And, sweetest,
   fairest,
As I my poor self did exchange for you,
To your so infinite loss, so in our trifles   120
I still win of you: for my sake wear this;
It is a manacle of love; I'll place it
Upon this fairest prisoner.
          [*Putting a bracelet upon her arm.*
   Imo.   O the gods!
When shall we see again?

     Enter CYMBELINE *and* Lords.

   Post.   Alack, the king!
   Cym.   Thou basest thing, avoid! hence, from
   my sight!
If after this command thou fraught the court
With thy unworthiness, thou diest: away!
Thou'rt poison to my blood.
   Post.   The gods protect you!
And bless the good remainders of the court!
I am gone.   [*Exit.*
   Imo.   There cannot be a pinch in death   130
More sharp than this is.
   Cym.   O disloyal thing,
That shouldst repair my youth, thou heap'st
A year's age on me.
   Imo.   I beseech you, sir,
Harm not yourself with your vexation:
I am senseless of your wrath; a touch more rare
Subdues all pangs, all fears.
   Cym.   Past grace? obedience?
   Imo. Past hope, and in despair; that way, past
   grace.
   Cym.   That mightst have had the sole son of
   my queen!
   Imo. O blest, that I might not! I chose an eagle,
And did avoid a puttock.   140
   Cym.   Thou took'st a beggar; wouldst have
   made my throne
A seat for baseness.
   Imo.   No; I rather added
A lustre to it.
   Cym.   O thou vile one!
   Imo.   Sir,
It is your fault that I have loved Posthumus:
You bred him as my playfellow, and he is
A man worth any woman, overbuys me
Almost the sum he pays.
   Cym.   What, art thou mad?
   Imo. Almost, sir: heaven restore me! Would
   I were
A neat-herd's daughter, and my Leonatus
Our neighbour shepherd's son!
   Cym.   Thou foolish thing! 150

     Re-enter QUEEN.

They were again together: you have done
Not after our command. Away with her,
And pen her up.
   Queen.   Beseech your patience. Peace,
Dear lady daughter, peace! Sweet sovereign,

Leave us to ourselves; and make yourself some
    comfort
Out of your best advice.
Cym.   Nay, let her languish
A drop of blood a day; and, being aged,
Die of this folly! [*Exeunt Cymbeline and Lords.*
Queen.   Fie! you must give way.

             Enter PISANIO.

Here is your servant. How now, sir! What
    news?
    Pis. My lord your son drew on my master.
    Queen.   Ha! 160
No harm, I trust, is done?
    Pis.   There might have been,
But that my master rather play'd than fought
And had no help of anger: they were parted
By gentlemen at hand.
    Queen.   I am very glad on 't.
    Imo. Your son's my father's friend; he takes
    his part.
To draw upon an exile! O brave sir!
• I would they were in Afric both together;
Myself by with a needle, that I might prick
The goer-back. Why came you from your master?
    Pis. On his command: he would not suffer me
To bring him to the haven; left these notes 171
Of what commands I should be subject to,
When 't pleased you to employ me.
    Queen.   This hath been
Your faithful servant: I dare lay mine honour
He will remain so.
    Pis.   I humbly thank your highness.
    Queen. Pray, walk awhile.
    Imo.   About some half-hour hence,
I pray you, speak with me: you shall at least
Go see my lord aboard: for this time leave me.
                            [*Exeunt.*

    SCENE II. *The same. A public place.*

      Enter CLOTEN *and two* Lords.

First Lord. Sir, I would advise you to shift a
shirt; the violence of action hath made you reek
as a sacrifice: where air comes out, air comes in:
there's none abroad so wholesome as that you
vent.
    Clo. If my shirt were bloody, then to shift it.
Have I hurt him?
    Sec. Lord. [*Aside*] No, 'faith; not so much as
his patience.   9
• *First Lord.* Hurt him! his body's a passable
carcass, if he be not hurt: it is a throughfare for
steel, if it be not hurt.
    Sec. Lord. [*Aside*] His steel was in debt; it
went o' the backside the town.
    Clo. The villain would not stand me.
    Sec. Lord. [*Aside*] No; but he fled forward
still, toward your face.
    First Lord. Stand you! You have land enough
of your own: but he added to your having; gave
you some ground.   20
    Sec. Lord. [*Aside*] As many inches as you
have oceans. Puppies!
    Clo. I would they had not come between us.
    Sec. Lord. [*Aside*] So would I, till you had
measured how long a fool you were upon the
ground.

Costume design for the lady-in-waiting to the Queen by
John Napier with Martyn Bainbridge and Sue Jenkinson,
Royal Shakespeare Co, 1974

167 *Afric*. Africa, i.e. the wilderness.

10 *passable*. Penetrable without damage.

32-33 *a good sign.* A good outside.

Ellen Terry as Imogen. Drawing by Sir L. Alma-Tadema, 1906

---

24 *With . . . vantage.* At his earliest opportunity.

32 *encounter . . . orisons.* Join me in prayers.

Clo. And that she should love this fellow and refuse me!

Sec. Lord. [*Aside*] If it be a sin to make a true election, she is damned.   30

First Lord. Sir, as I told you always, her
● beauty and her brain go not together: she's a good sign, but I have seen small reflection of her wit.

Sec. Lord. [*Aside*] She shines not upon fools, lest the reflection should hurt her.

Clo. Come, I'll to my chamber. Would there had been some hurt done!

Sec. Lord. [*Aside*] I wish not so; unless it had been the fall of an ass, which is no great hurt.

Clo. You'll go with us?   40

First Lord. I'll attend your lordship.

Clo. Nay, come, let's go together.

Sec. Lord. Well, my lord.   [*Exeunt.*

SCENE III.   *A room in Cymbeline's palace.*

Enter IMOGEN *and* PISANIO.

Imo. I would thou grew'st unto the shores o' the haven,
And question'dst every sail: if he should write,
And I not have it, 'twere a paper lost,
As offer'd mercy is.   What was the last
That he spake to thee?

Pis.   It was his queen, his queen!

Imo. Then waved his handkerchief?

Pis.   And kiss'd it, madam.

Imo. Senseless linen! happier therein than I!
And that was all?

Pis.   No, madam; for so long
As he could make me with this eye or ear
Distinguish him from others, he did keep   10
The deck, with glove, or hat, or handkerchief,
Still waving, as the fits and stirs of 's mind
Could best express how slow his soul sail'd on,
How swift his ship.

Imo.   Thou shouldst have made him
As little as a crow, or less, ere left
To after-eye him.

Pis.   Madam, so I did.

Imo. I would have broke mine eye-strings; crack'd them, but
To look upon him, till the diminution
Of space had pointed him sharp as my needle,
Nay, follow'd him, till he had melted from   20
The smallness of a gnat to air, and then
Have turn'd mine eye and wept.   But, good Pisanio,
When shall we hear from him?

Pis.   Be assured, madam,
● With his next vantage.

Imo. I did not take my leave of him, but had
Most pretty things to say: ere I could tell him
How I would think on him at certain hours
Such thoughts and such, or I could make him swear
The shes of Italy should not betray
Mine interest and his honour, or have charged him,   30
At the sixth hour of morn, at noon, at midnight,
● To encounter me with orisons, for then
I am in heaven for him; or ere I could
Give him that parting kiss which I had set
Betwixt two charming words, comes in my father
And like the tyrannous breathing of the north
Shakes all our buds from growing

Enter a Lady.

Lady.   The queen, madam,
Desires your highness' company.

Imo.   Those things I bid you do, get them
dispatch'd.
I will attend the queen.

Pis.   Madam, I shall. [*Exeunt.* 40

SCENE IV.   *Rome.   Philario's house.*

Enter PHILARIO, IACHIMO, *a* Frenchman, *a*
Dutchman, *and a* Spaniard.

Iach.   Believe it, sir, I have seen him in Britain:
● he was then of a crescent note, expected to prove
so worthy as since he hath been allowed the name
of; but I could then have looked on him without
the help of admiration, though the catalogue of
his endowments had been tabled by his side and
I to peruse him by items.

Phi.   You speak of him when he was less furnished than now he is with that which makes him
both without and within.   10

French.   I have seen him in France: we had
very many there could behold the sun with as
firm eyes as he.

Iach.   This matter of marrying his king's
daughter, wherein he must be weighed rather by
● her value than his own, words him, I doubt not,
a great deal from the matter.

French.   And then his banishment.

Iach.   Ay, and the approbation of those that
weep this lamentable divorce under her colours
are wonderfully to extend him; be it but to for-
tify her judgement, which else an easy battery
might lay flat, for taking a beggar without less
quality.   But how comes it he is to sojourn with
● you?   How creeps acquaintance?

Phi.   His father and I were soldiers together;
to whom I have been often bound for no less than
my life.   Here comes the Briton: let him be so
entertained amongst you as suits, with gentlemen
of your knowing, to a stranger of his quality.   30

Enter POSTHUMUS.

I beseech you all, be better known to this gentleman, whom I commend to you as a noble
friend of mine: how worthy he is I will leave to
appear hereafter, rather than story him in his
own hearing.

French.   Sir, we have known together in Or-
leans.

Post.   Since when I have been debtor to you
for courtesies, which I will be ever to pay and yet
pay still.   40

French.   Sir, you o'er-rate my poor kindness:
● I was glad I did atone my countryman and you;
it had been pity you should have been put together with so mortal a purpose as then each bore,
upon importance of so slight and trivial a nature.

Post.   By your pardon, sir, I was then a young
traveller; rather shunned to go even with what
I heard than in my every action to be guided by
others' experiences: but upon my mended judgement—if I offend not to say it is mended—my
quarrel was not altogether slight.   51

French.   'Faith, yes, to be put to the arbitrement of swords, and by such two that would by
all likelihood have confounded one the other, or
have fallen both.

2 *of a crescent note.* Of rising reputation.

16 *words him.* Suggests.

25 *How creeps acquaintance?* How can he claim to be
your friend?

42 *atone.* Make peace between.

59-60 *suffer the report.* i.e. be reported without hesitation.

Costume design for Iachimo by Rene Allio, Royal Shakespeare Co, 1962

65 *constant-qualified.* Totally accomplished.

118 *moiety.* Half.

Iach. Can we, with manners, ask what was the difference?

French. Safely, I think: 'twas a contention in public, which may, without contradiction, suffer the report. It was much like an argument that fell out last night, where each of us fell in praise of our country mistresses; this gentleman at that time vouching—and upon warrant of bloody affirmation—his to be more fair, virtuous, wise, chaste, constant-qualified and less attemptable than any the rarest of our ladies in France.

Iach. That lady is not now living, or this gentleman's opinion by this worn out.

Post. She holds her virtue still and I my mind.

Iach. You must not so far prefer her 'fore ours of Italy. 71

Post. Being so far provoked as I was in France, I would abate her nothing, though I profess myself her adorer, not her friend.

Iach. As fair and as good—a kind of hand-in-hand comparison—had been something too fair and too good for any lady in Britain. If she went before others I have seen, as that diamond of yours outlustres many I have beheld, I could not but believe she excelled many: but I have not seen the most precious diamond that is, nor you the lady.

Post. I praised her as I rated her: so do I my stone.

Iach. What do you esteem it at?

Post. More than the world enjoys.

Iach. Either your unparagoned mistress is dead, or she's outprized by a trifle.

Post. You are mistaken: the one may be sold, or given, if there were wealth enough for the purchase, or merit for the gift: the other is not a thing for sale, and only the gift of the gods.

Iach. Which the gods have given you?

Post. Which, by their graces, I will keep.

Iach. You may wear her in title yours: but, you know, strange fowl light upon neighbouring ponds. Your ring may be stolen too: so your brace of unprizable estimations; the one is but frail and the other casual; a cunning thief, or a that way accomplished courtier, would hazard the winning both of first and last.

Post. Your Italy contains none so accomplished a courtier to convince the honour of my mistress, if, in the holding or loss of that, you term her frail. I do nothing doubt you have store of thieves; notwithstanding, I fear not my ring.

Phi. Let us leave here, gentlemen. 109

Post. Sir, with all my heart. This worthy signior, I thank him, makes no stranger of me; we are familiar at first.

Iach. With five times so much conversation, I should get ground of your fair mistress, make her go back, even to the yielding, had I admittance and opportunity to friend.

Post. No, no.

Iach. I dare thereupon pawn the moiety of my estate to your ring; which, in my opinion, o'ervalues it something: but I make my wager rather against your confidence than her reputation: and, to bar your offence herein too, I durst attempt it against any lady in the world.

Post. You are a great deal abused in too bold

a persuasion; and I doubt not you sustain what you're worthy of by your attempt.

Iach. What's that?

Post. A repulse: though your attempt, as you call it, deserve more; a punishment too.   129

Phi. Gentlemen, enough of this: it came in too suddenly; let it die as it was born, and, I pray you, be better acquainted.

Iach. Would I had put my estate and my neighbour's on the approbation of what I have spoke!

Post. What lady would you choose to assail?

Iach. Yours; whom in constancy you think
• stands so safe. I will lay you ten thousand ducats to your ring, that, commend me to the court where your lady is, with no more advantage than the opportunity of a second conference, and I will bring from thence that honour of hers which you imagine so reserved.

Post. I will wage against your gold, gold to it: my ring I hold dear as my finger; 'tis part of it.

Iach. You are afraid, and therein the wiser. If you buy ladies' flesh at a million a dram, you cannot preserve it from tainting: but I see you
• have some religion in you, that you fear.   149

Post. This is but a custom in your tongue; you bear a graver purpose, I hope.

Iach. I am the master of my speeches, and would undergo what's spoken, I swear.

Post. Will you? I shall but lend my diamond till your return: let there be covenants drawn between 's: my mistress exceeds in goodness the hugeness of your unworthy thinking: I dare you to this match: here's my ring.

Phi. I will have it no lay.   159

Iach. By the gods, it is one. If I bring you no sufficient testimony that I have enjoyed the dearest bodily part of your mistress, my ten thousand ducats are yours; so is your diamond too: if I come off, and leave her in such honour as you have trust in, she your jewel, this your jewel, and my gold are yours: provided I have your commendation for my more free entertainment.

Post. I embrace these conditions; let us have articles betwixt us. Only, thus far you shall answer: if you make your voyage upon her and give me directly to understand you have prevailed, I am no further your enemy; she is not worth our debate: if she remain unseduced, you not making it appear otherwise, for your ill opinion and the assault you have made to her chastity you shall answer me with your sword.

Iach. Your hand; a covenant: we will have these things set down by lawful counsel, and straight away for Britain, lest the bargain should catch cold and starve: I will fetch my gold and have our two wagers recorded.   181

Post. Agreed.

[*Exeunt Posthumus and Iachimo.*

French. Will this hold, think you?

Phi. Signior Iachimo will not from it. Pray, let us follow 'em.   [*Exeunt.*

SCENE V. *Britain. A room in Cymbeline's palace.*

Enter QUEEN, Ladies, *and* CORNELIUS.

Queen. Whiles yet the dew's on ground, gather those flowers:

138 *ducat.* Continental coin.

Iachimo: 'If you buy ladies' flesh at a million a dram, you cannot preserve it from tainting.' Donald Wolfit as Iachimo, Stratford-upon-Avon, 1937

149 *religion.* i.e. reservation.

Queen: 'Now, master doctor, have you brought those drugs?' Clare Harris as the Queen, Stratford-upon-Avon, 1937

---

17 *amplify my judgement*. Extend my knowledge.

18 *conclusions*. Experiments.

22 *Allayments*. Antidotes. *act*. Action.

Make haste: who has the note of them?
　First Lady.　　　　　　　　　　　I, madam.
　Queen. Dispatch.　　　　　[*Exeunt Ladies*.
Now, master doctor, have you brought those
　　　drugs?
　Cor.　Pleaseth your highness, ay: here they
　　　are, madam:　　　[*Presenting a small box*.
But I beseech your grace, without offence,—
My conscience bids me ask—wherefore you have
Commanded of me these most poisonous com-
　　　pounds,
Which are the movers of a languishing death;
But though slow, deadly?
　Queen.　　　　　　　I wonder, doctor,　10
Thou ask'st me such a question.　Have I not been
Thy pupil long?　Hast thou not learn'd me how
To make perfumes? distil? preserve? yea, so
That our great king himself doth woo me oft
For my confections? Having thus far proceeded,—
Unless thou think'st me devilish—is't not meet
● That I did amplify my judgement in
● Other conclusions?　I will try the forces
Of these thy compounds on such creatures as
We count not worth the hanging, but none human,
To try the vigour of them and apply　　21
● Allayments to their act, and by them gather
Their several virtues and effects.
　Cor.　　　　　　　　　Your highness
Shall from this practice but make hard your heart:
Besides, the seeing these effects will be
Both noisome and infectious.
　Queen.　　　　　　　O, content thee.

Enter PISANIO.

[*Aside*] Here comes a flattering rascal; upon him
Will I first work: he's for his master,
And enemy to my son.　How now, Pisanio!
Doctor, your service for this time is ended;　30
Take your own way.
　Cor.　[*Aside*] I do suspect you, madam;
But you shall do no harm.
　Queen.　[*To Pisanio*] Hark thee, a word.
　Cor. [*Aside*] I do not like her.　She doth
　　　think she has
Strange lingering poisons: I do know her spirit,
And will not trust one of her malice with
A drug of such damn'd nature.　Those she has
Will stupify and dull the sense awhile;
Which first, perchance, she'll prove on cats and
　　　dogs,
Then afterward up higher: but there is
No danger in what show of death it makes,　40
More than the locking-up the spirits a time,
To be more fresh, reviving.　She is fool'd
With a most false effect; and I the truer,
So to be false with her.
　Queen.　　　　　No further service, doctor,
Until I send for thee.
　Cor.　　　　I humbly take my leave. [*Exit*.
　Queen. Weeps she still, say'st thou?　Dost
　　　thou think in time
She will not quench and let instructions enter
Where folly now possesses?　Do thou work:
When thou shalt bring me word she loves my
　　　son,
I'll tell thee on the instant thou art then　50
As great as is thy master, greater, for
His fortunes all lie speechless and his name
Is at last gasp: return he cannot, nor

Continue where he is: to shift his being
Is to exchange one misery with another,
And every day that comes comes to decay
A day's work in him.   What shalt thou expect,
To be depender on a thing that leans,
Who cannot be new built, nor has no friends,   59
So much as but to prop him? [*The Queen drops the
        box: Pisanio takes it up.*]   Thou takest up
Thou know'st not what; but take it for thy labour:
It is a thing I made, which hath the king
Five times redeem'd from death: I do not know
What is more cordial.   Nay, I prithee, take it;
It is an earnest of a further good
That I mean to thee.   Tell thy mistress how
The case stands with her; do't as from thyself.
Think what a chance thou changest on, but think
Thou hast thy mistress still, to boot, my son,
Who shall take notice of thee: I'll move the king
To any shape of thy preferment such   71
As thou'lt desire; and then myself, I chiefly,
That set thee on to this desert, am bound
To load thy merit richly.   Call my women:
Think on my words.   [*Exit Pisanio.*
        A sly and constant knave,
Not to be shaked; the agent for his master
And the remembrancer of her to hold
The hand-fast to her lord.   I have given him that
Which, if he take, shall quite unpeople her
Of liegers for her sweet, and which she after,   80
Except she bend her humour, shall be assured
To taste of too.

        Re-enter PISANIO *and* Ladies.

        So, so: well done, well done:
The violets, cowslips, and the primroses,
Bear to my closet.   Fare thee well, Pisanio;
Think on my words. [*Exeunt Queen and Ladies.*
    Pis.   And shall do:
But when to my good lord I prove untrue,
I'll choke myself: there's all I'll do for you. [*Exit.*

SCENE VI.   *The same.   Another room in the
                palace.*

        Enter IMOGEN.

Imo.   A father cruel, and a step-dame false;
A foolish suitor to a wedded lady,
That hath her husband banish'd;—O, that hus-
        band!
My supreme crown of grief! and those repeated
Vexations of it!   Had I been thief-stol'n,
As my two brothers, happy! but most miserable
Is the desire that's glorious: blest be those,
How mean soe'er, that have their honest wills,
Which seasons comfort.   Who may this be?   Fie!

        Enter PISANIO *and* IACHIMO.

Pis.   Madam, a noble gentleman of Rome,   10
Comes from my lord with letters.
    Iach.   Change you, madam?
The worthy Leonatus is in safety
And greets your highness dearly.
                [*Presents a letter.*
    Imo.   Thanks, good sir:
You're kindly welcome.
    Iach. [*Aside*] All of her that is out of door
        most rich!
If she be furnish'd with a mind so rare,
She is alone the Arabian bird, and I

80 *liegers.* Followers.

11 *Change you.* Do you change expression.

15 *out of door.* Visible.

17 *Arabian bird.* i.e. legendary phoenix.

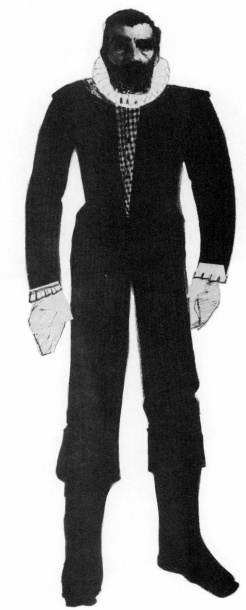

Costume design for Pisanio by John Napier with
Martyn Bainbridge and Sue Jenkinson, Royal Shakespeare Co, 1974

20 *Parthian*. Asian people, skilled archers, who shot behind them as they retreated.

Imogen: 'So far I read aloud . . .' Laura Addison as Imogen, Sadler's Wells Theatre, London, 1847

36 *number'd*. Pebbled.

38 *admiration*. Astonishment.

47 *trow*. I wonder.

51 *raps*. Transports.

66 *Gallian*. French.

Have lost the wager.   Boldness be my friend!
Arm me, audacity, from head to foot!
●Or, like the Parthian, I shall flying fight;   20
Rather, directly fly.
    Imo. [*Reads*] 'He is one of the noblest note,
to whose kindnesses I am most infinitely tied.
Reflect upon him accordingly, as you value your
trust—   LEONATUS.'
So far I read aloud:
But even the very middle of my heart
Is warm'd by the rest, and takes it thankfully.
You are as welcome, worthy sir, as I
Have words to bid you, and shall find it so   30
In all that I can do.
    Iach.   Thanks, fairest lady.
What, are men mad?   Hath nature given them
    eyes
To see this vaulted arch, and the rich crop
Of sea and land, which can distinguish 'twixt
The fiery orbs above and the twinn'd stones
●Upon the number'd beach? and can we not
Partition make with spectacles so precious
●'Twixt fair and foul?
    Imo.   What makes your admiration?
    Iach. It cannot be i' the eye, for apes and
    monkeys
'Twixt two such shes would chatter this way and
Contemn with mows the other; nor i' the judge-
    ment,   41
For idiots in this case of favour would
Be wisely definite; nor i' the appetite;
Sluttery to such neat excellence opposed
Should make desire vomit emptiness,
Not so allured to feed.
●   *Imo.* What is the matter, trow?
    Iach.   The cloyed will,
That satiate yet unsatisfied desire, that tub
Both fill'd and running, ravening first the lamb
Longs after for the garbage.
    Imo.   What, dear sir,   50
●Thus raps you?   Are you well?
    Iach. Thanks, madam; well. [*To Pisanio*]
    Beseech you, sir, desire
My man's abode where I did leave him: he
Is strange and peevish.
    Pis.   I was going, sir,
To give him welcome.   [*Exit.*
    Imo. Continues well my lord?   His health,
    beseech you?
    Iach. Well, madam.
    Imo. Is he disposed to mirth?   I hope he is.
    Iach. Exceeding pleasant; none a stranger
    there
So merry and so gamesome: he is call'd   60
The Briton reveller.
    Imo.   When he was here,
He did incline to sadness, and oft-times
Not knowing why.
    Iach.   I never saw him sad.
There is a Frenchman his companion, one
An eminent monsieur, that, it seems, much loves
●A Gallian girl at home; he furnaces
The thick sighs from him, whiles the jolly
    Briton—
Your lord, I mean—laughs from's free lungs,
    cries 'O,
Can my sides hold, to think that man, who
    knows
By history, report, or his own proof,   70

What woman is, yea, what she cannot choose
But must be, will his free hours languish for,
Assured bondage?'
   Imo.   Will my lord say so?
   Iach.   Ay, madam, with his eyes in flood with
       laughter :
It is a recreation to be by
And hear him mock the Frenchman. But, heavens
       know,
Some men are much to blame.
   Imo.   Not he, I hope.
   Iach.   Not he : but yet heaven's bounty to-
       wards him might
Be used more thankfully.   In himself, 'tis much ;
● In you, which I account his beyond all talents, 80
Whilst I am bound to wonder, I am bound
To pity too.
   Imo.   What do you pity, sir?
   Iach.   Two creatures heartily.
   Imo.   Am I one, sir?
You look on me : what wreck discern you in me
Deserves your pity?
   Iach.   Lamentable ! What,
To hide me from the radiant sun and solace
● I' the dungeon by a snuff?
   Imo.   I pray you, sir,
Deliver with more openness your answers
To my demands.   Why do you pity me?
   Iach.   That others do—   90
I was about to say—enjoy your——But
It is an office of the gods to venge it,
Not mine to speak on't.
   Imo.   You do seem to know
Something of me, or what concerns me : pray
       you,—
Since doubting things go ill often hurts more
Than to be sure they do ; for certainties
Either are past remedies, or, timely knowing,
The remedy then born—discover to me
What both you spur and stop.
   Iach.   Had I this cheek 99
To bathe my lips upon ; this hand, whose touch,
Whose every touch, would force the feeler's soul
To the oath of loyalty ; this object, which
Takes prisoner the wild motion of mine eye,
Fixing it only here ; should I, damn'd then,
Slaver with lips as common as the stairs
That mount the Capitol ; join gripes with hands
Made hard with hourly falsehood—falsehood, as
With labour ; then by-peeping in an eye
Base and unlustrous as the smoky light
That's fed with stinking tallow ; it were fit   110
That all the plagues of hell should at one time
Encounter such revolt.
   Imo.   My lord, I fear,
Has forgot Britain.
   Iach.   And himself.   Not I,
Inclined to this intelligence, pronounce
The beggary of his change ; but 'tis your graces
● That from my mutest conscience to my tongue
Charms this report out.
   Imo.   Let me hear no more.
   Iach.   O dearest soul ! your cause doth strike
       my heart
With pity, that doth make me sick.   A lady
● So fair, and fasten'd to an empery,   120
Would make the great'st king double,—to be
       partner'd
● With tomboys hired with that self exhibition

80 *beyond all talents.* Priceless.

87 *snuff.* Candle stub.

116 *mutest conscience.* Most private thoughts.

120 *empery.* Empire.

122 *tomboys.* Lewd women. *self exhibition.* Same allowance.

Costume design for Imogen by J. Gower Parks, Stratford-upon-Avon, 1937

133 *Diana*. Goddess of chastity.

134 *vaulting variable ramps*. Leaping various whores.

137 *runagate*. Truant from.

Julia Arthur as Imogen, Lyceum Theatre, London, 1896

151 *mart*. Market.

152 *stew*. Brothel.

163 *affiance*. Loyalty.

178 *chaffless*. Faultless.

Which your own coffers yield! with diseased ventures
That play with all infirmities for gold
Which rottenness can lend nature! such boil'd stuff
As well might poison poison!   Be revenged;
Or she that bore you was no queen, and you
Recoil from your great stock.
 Imo.   Revenged!
How should I be revenged?   If this be true,—
As I have such a heart that both mine ears **130**
Must not in haste abuse—if it be true,
How should I be revenged?
 Iach.   Should he make me
•Live, like Diana's priest, betwixt cold sheets,
•Whiles he is vaulting variable ramps,
In your despite, upon your purse?   Revenge it.
I dedicate myself to your sweet pleasure,
•More noble than that runagate to your bed,
And will continue fast to your affection,
Still close as sure.
 Imo.   What, ho, Pisanio!
 Iach. Let me my service tender on your lips.
 Imo. Away!   I do condemn mine ears that have **141**
So long attended thee.   If thou wert honourable,
Thou wouldst have told this tale for virtue, not
For such an end thou seek'st,—as base as strange.
Thou wrong'st a gentleman, who is as far
From thy report as thou from honour, and
Solicit'st here a lady that disdains
Thee and the devil alike.   What ho, Pisanio!
The king my father shall be made acquainted
Of thy assault: if he shall think it fit, **150**
•A saucy stranger in his court to mart
•As in a Romish stew and to expound
His beastly mind to us, he hath a court
He little cares for and a daughter who
He not respects at all.   What, ho, Pisanio!
 Iach. O happy Leonatus! I may say:
The credit that thy lady hath of thee
Deserves thy trust, and thy most perfect goodness
Her assured credit.   Blessed live you long!
A lady to the worthiest sir that ever **160**
Country call'd his! and you his mistress, only
For the most worthiest fit!   Give me your pardon.
•I have spoke this, to know if your affiance
Were deeply rooted; and shall make your lord,
That which he is, new o'er: and he is one
The truest manner'd; such a holy witch
That he enchants societies into him;
Half all men's hearts are his.
 Imo.   You make amends.
 Iach. He sits 'mongst men like a descended god:
He hath a kind of honour sets him off, **170**
More than a mortal seeming.   Be not angry,
Most mighty princess, that I have adventured
To try your taking of a false report; which hath
Honour'd with confirmation your great judgement
In the election of a sir so rare,
Which you know cannot err: the love I bear him
Made me to fan you thus, but the gods made you,
•Unlike all others, chaffless.   Pray, your pardon.
 Imo. All's well, sir: take my power i' the court for yours.
 Iach. My humble thanks.   I had almost forgot
To entreat your grace but in a small request, **181**
And yet of moment too, for it concerns

Your lord; myself and other noble friends
Are partners in the business.

   Imo.   Pray, what is't?

   Iach. Some dozen Romans of us and your
      lord—
The best feather of our wing—have mingled sums
To buy a present for the emperor;
Which I, the factor for the rest, have done
In France: 'tis plate of rare device, and jewels
Of rich and exquisite form; their values great;
And I am something curious, being strange, 191
To have them in safe stowage: may it please you
To take them in protection?

   Imo.   Willingly;
And pawn mine honour for their safety: since
My lord hath interest in them, I will keep them
In my bedchamber.

   Iach.   They are in a trunk,
Attended by my men: I will make bold
To send them to you, only for this night;
I must aboard to-morrow.

   Imo.   O, no, no.

   Iach. Yes, I beseech; or I shall short my word
By lengthening my return. From Gallia   201
I cross'd the seas on purpose and on promise
To see your grace.

   Imo.   I thank you for your pains:
But not away to-morrow!

   Iach.   O, I must, madam:
Therefore I shall beseech you, if you please
To greet your lord with writing, do't to-night:
I have outstood my time; which is material
To the tender of our present.

   Imo.   I will write.
Send your trunk to me; it shall safe be kept, 209
And truly yielded you. You're very welcome.

                               [*Exeunt.*

ACT II.

SCENE I. *Britain. Before Cymbeline's palace.*

Enter CLOTEN *and two* Lords.

   Clo. Was there ever man had such luck! when I kissed the jack, upon an up-cast to be hit away! I had a hundred pound on't: and then a whoreson jackanapes must take me up for swearing; as if I borrowed mine oaths of him and might not spend them at my pleasure.

   First Lord. What got he by that? You have broke his pate with your bowl.

   Sec. Lord. [*Aside*] If his wit had been like him that broke it, it would have run all out.   10

   Clo. When a gentleman is disposed to swear, it is not for any standers-by to curtail his oaths, ha?

   Sec. Lord. No, my lord; [*Aside*] nor crop the ears of them.

   Clo. Whoreson dog! I give him satisfaction? Would he had been one of my rank!

   Sec. Lord. [*Aside*] To have smelt like a fool.

   Clo. I am not vexed more at any thing in the earth: a pox on't! I had rather not be so noble as I am; they dare not fight with me, because of the queen my mother: every Jack-slave hath his bellyful of fighting, and I must go up and down like a cock that nobody can match.

   Sec. Lord. [*Aside*] You are cock and capon too; and you crow, cock, with your comb on.

200 *short.* Break.

201 *Gallia.* France.

Tom Mead as Iachimo in Henry Irving's production at the Lyceum Theatre, London, 1896

8 *pate.* Skull.

29 *undertake*. Take on in a duel.

47 *derogation*. Lowering myself.

60 *for his heart*. For the life of him.

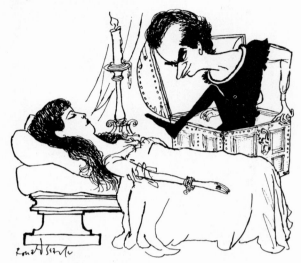

Barbara Jefford as Imogen and Derek Godfrey as Iachimo. A cartoon by Ronald Searle from the 1956 Stratford-upon-Avon production

Clo. Sayest thou?

Sec. Lord. It is not fit your lordship should
undertake every companion that you give offence
to.   30

Clo. No, I know that: but it is fit I should
commit offence to my inferiors.

Sec. Lord. Ay, it is fit for your lordship only.

Clo. Why, so I say.

First Lord. Did you hear of a stranger that's
come to court to-night?

Clo. A stranger, and I not know on't!

Sec. Lord. [*Aside*] He's a strange fellow himself, and knows it not.

First Lord. There's an Italian come; and,
'tis thought, one of Leonatus' friends.   41

Clo. Leonatus! a banished rascal; and he's
another, whatsoever he be. Who told you of
this stranger?

First Lord. One of your lordship's pages.

Clo. Is it fit I went to look upon him? is there
no derogation in't?

Sec. Lord. You cannot derogate, my lord.

Clo. Not easily, I think.   49

Sec. Lord. [*Aside*] You are a fool granted:
therefore your issues, being foolish, do not derogate.

Clo. Come, I'll go see this Italian: what I
have lost to-day at bowls I'll win to-night of him.
Come, go.

Sec. Lord. I'll attend your lordship.
                                          [*Exeunt Cloten and First Lord.*
That such a crafty devil as is his mother
Should yield the world this ass! a woman that
Bears all down with her brain; and this her son
Cannot take two from twenty, for his heart,   60
And leave eighteen. Alas, poor princess,
Thou divine Imogen, what thou endurest,
Betwixt a father by thy step-dame govern'd,
A mother hourly coining plots, a wooer
More hateful than the foul expulsion is
Of thy dear husband, than that horrid act
Of the divorce he'ld make! The heavens hold
                                          firm
The walls of thy dear honour, keep unshaked
That temple, thy fair mind, that thou mayst stand,
To enjoy thy banish'd lord and this great land!
                                                         [*Exit.* 70

SCENE II.   *Imogen's bedchamber in Cymbeline's palace: a trunk in one corner of it.*

IMOGEN *in bed, reading; a* Lady *attending.*

Imo. Who's there? my woman Helen?

Lady.   Please you, madam.

Imo. What hour is it?

Lady.   Almost midnight, madam.

Imo. I have read three hours then: mine eyes
                                          are weak:
Fold down the leaf where I have left: to bed:
Take not away the taper, leave it burning;
And if thou canst awake by four o' the clock,
I prithee, call me. Sleep hath seized me wholly.
                                                         [*Exit Lady.*
To your protection I commend me, gods.
From fairies and the tempters of the night
Guard me, beseech ye.   10
            [*Sleeps. Iachimo comes from the trunk.*
Iach. The crickets sing, and man's o'er-la-
bour'd sense

● Repairs itself by rest.   Our Tarquin thus
Did softly press the rushes, ere he waken'd
● The chastity he wounded.   Cytherea,
How bravely thou becomest thy bed, fresh lily,
And whiter than the sheets!   That I might touch!
But kiss; one kiss!   Rubies unparagon'd,
How dearly they do't!   'Tis her breathing that
Perfumes the chamber thus: the flame o' the
      taper
Bows toward her, and would under-peep her lids,
To see the enclosed lights, now canopied   21
Under these windows, white and azure laced
With blue of heaven's own tinct.   But my design,
To note the chamber: I will write all down:
Such and such pictures; there the window; such
The adornment of her bed; the arras; figures,
Why, such and such; and the contents o' the
      story.
Ah, but some natural notes about her body,
Above ten thousand meaner moveables
Would testify, to enrich mine inventory.   30
O sleep, thou ape of death, lie dull upon her!
And be her sense but as a monument,
Thus in a chapel lying!   Come off, come off:
                    [Taking off her bracelet.
● As slippery as the Gordian knot was hard!
'Tis mine; and this will witness outwardly,
As strongly as the conscience does within,
To the madding of her lord.   On her left breast
● A mole cinque-spotted, like the crimson drops
● I' the bottom of a cowslip: here's a voucher,
Stronger than ever law could make: this secret
Will force him think I have pick'd the lock and
      ta'en   41
The treasure of her honour.   No more.   To
      what end?
Why should I write this down, that's riveted,
Screw'd to my memory?   She hath been read-
      ing late
● The tale of Tereus; here the leaf's turn'd down
Where Philomel gave up.   I have enough:
To the trunk again, and shut the spring of it.
Swift, swift, you dragons of the night, that
      dawning
May bare the raven's eye!   I lodge in fear;
Though this a heavenly angel, hell is here.   50
                          [Clock strikes.
One, two, three: time, time!
            [Goes into the trunk.   The scene closes.

SCENE III.   *An ante-chamber adjoining Imo-*
            gen's apartments.

Enter CLOTEN *and* Lords.

First Lord.   Your lordship is the most patient
man in loss, the most coldest that ever turned up
ace.
   Clo.   It would make any man cold to lose.
   First Lord.   But not every man patient after
the noble temper of your lordship.   You are
most hot and furious when you win.
   Clo.   Winning will put any man into courage.
If I could get this foolish Imogen, I should have
gold enough.   It's almost morning, is't not?   10
   First Lord.   Day, my lord.
   Clo.   I would this music would come: I am
advised to give her music o' mornings; they say
it will penetrate.

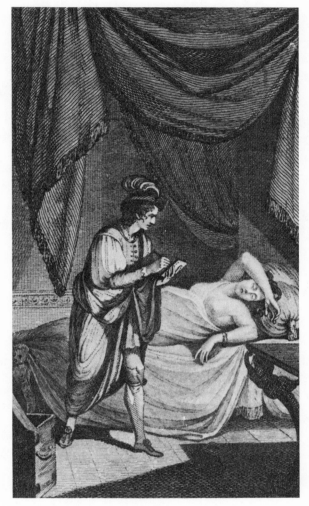

Iachimo: 'I will write all down: Such and such pictures
. . .' Engraving from Bell's edition of Shakespeare's
works, 1773

34 *Gordian knot.* Refers to the legend of the intricate
knot which Alexander cut with his sword.

38 *cinque-spotted.* Made up of five spots.

39 *a voucher.* Evidence.

45 *Tereus.* Legendary king who raped Philomel, his
sister-in-law.

Cloten: 'Come on; tune . . .' Engraving by Kenny Meadows from Barry Cornwall's *The Works of Shakspere*, 1846

22 *Phœbus.* The Sun-god.

24 *chaliced.* Cup-shaped.

25 *winking Mary-buds.* Marigolds.

34 *unpaved.* Castrated.

50 *vantages.* Opportunities.

Enter Musicians.

Come on; tune: if you can penetrate her with your fingering, so; we'll try with tongue too: if none will do, let her remain; but I'll never give o'er. First, a very excellent good-conceited thing; after, a wonderful sweet air, with admirable rich words to it: and then let her consider.   20

SONG.
Hark, hark! the lark at heaven's gate sings,
  And Phœbus 'gins arise,
His steeds to water at those springs
  On chaliced flowers that lies;
And winking Mary-buds begin
  To ope their golden eyes:
With every thing that pretty is,
  My lady sweet, arise:
    Arise, arise.   30

Clo. So, get you gone. If this penetrate, I will consider your music the better: if it do not, it is a vice in her ears, which horse-hairs and calves'-guts, nor the voice of unpaved eunuch to boot, can never amend.   [*Exeunt Musicians.*
Sec. Lord. Here comes the king.
Clo. I am glad I was up so late; for that's the reason I was up so early: he cannot choose but take this service I have done fatherly.

Enter CYMBELINE *and* QUEEN.

Good morrow to your majesty and to my gracious mother.   41
Cym. Attend you here the door of our stern daughter?
Will she not forth?
Clo. I have assailed her with music, but she vouchsafes no notice.
Cym. The exile of her minion is too new;
She hath not yet forgot him: some more time
Must wear the print of his remembrance out,
And then she's yours.
Queen.   You are most bound to the king,
Who lets go by no vantages that may   50
Prefer you to his daughter. Frame yourself
To orderly soliciting, and be friended
With aptness of the season; make denials
Increase your services; so seem as if
You were inspired to do those duties which
You tender to her; that you in all obey her,
Save when command to your dismission tends,
And therein you are senseless.
Clo.   Senseless! not so.

Enter a Messenger.

Mess. So like you, sir, ambassadors from Rome;
The one is Caius Lucius.
Cym.   A worthy fellow,   60
Albeit he comes on angry purpose now;
But that's no fault of his: we must receive him
According to the honour of his sender;
And towards himself, his goodness forespent on us,
We must extend our notice. Our dear son,
When you have given good morning to your mistress,
Attend the queen and us; we shall have need
To employ you towards this Roman. Come, our queen.   [*Exeunt all but Cloten.*
Clo. If she be up, I'll speak with her; if not,

748

Let her lie still and dream. [*Knocks*] By your
    leave, ho!   70
I know her women are about her: what
If I do line one of their hands? 'Tis gold
Which buys admittance; oft it doth; yea, and
    makes
• Diana's rangers false themselves, yield up
Their deer to the stand o' the stealer; and 'tis
    gold
Which makes the true man kill'd and saves the
    thief;
Nay, sometime hangs both thief and true man:
    what
Can it not do and undo? I will make
One of her women lawyer to me, for
I yet not understand the case myself.   80
[*Knocks*] By your leave.

          Enter a Lady.

Lady. Who's there that knocks?
Clo.   A gentleman.
Lady.   No more?
Clo. Yes, and a gentlewoman's son.
Lady.   That's more
Than some, whose tailors are as dear as yours,
Can justly boast of. What's your lordship's
    pleasure?
Clo. Your lady's person: is she ready?
Lady.   Ay,
To keep her chamber.
Clo.   There is gold for you;
Sell me your good report.
    Lady. How! my good name? or to report of
    you
What I shall think is good?—The princess!   90

          Enter IMOGEN.

Clo. Good morrow, fairest: sister, your sweet
    hand.   [*Exit Lady.*
Imo. Good morrow, sir. You lay out too
    much pains
For purchasing but trouble: the thanks I give
Is telling you that I am poor of thanks
And scarce can spare them.
    Clo.   Still, I swear I love you.
• *Imo.* If you but said so, 'twere as deep with
    me:
If you swear still, your recompense is still
That I regard it not.
Clo.   This is no answer.
Imo. But that you shall not say I yield being
    silent,
I would not speak. I pray you, spare me: 'faith,
I shall unfold equal discourtesy   101
To your best kindness: one of your great knowing
Should learn, being taught, forbearance.
    Clo. To leave you in your madness, 'twere
    my sin:
I will not.
    Imo. Fools are not mad folks.
Clo.   Do you call me fool?
    Imo. As I am mad, I do:
If you'll be patient, I'll no more be mad;
That cures us both. I am much sorry, sir,
You put me to forget a lady's manners,   110
By being so verbal: and learn now, for all,
That I, which know my heart, do here pronounce,
By the very truth of it, I care not for you,
And am so near the lack of charity—

74 *Diana's rangers.* Nymphs of chastity.

Costume design for Helen, Imogen's maid, by J. Gower
Parks, Stratford-upon-Avon, 1937

96 *as deep.* The same.

124 *self-figured knot*. Self-arranged marriage.

125 *enlargement*. Freedom.

128 *hilding*. Good-for-nothing.

129 *pantler*. Pantry servant.

130 *Jupiter*. Jove, king of gods.

Jove or Jupiter was king of the Roman gods. From a
19th century engraving

139 *clipp'd*. Covered.

156 *an action*. A matter for the courts.

To accuse myself—I hate you; which I had rather
You felt than make 't my boast.
   Clo.   You sin against
Obedience, which you owe your father.   For
The contract you pretend with that base wretch,
One bred of alms and foster'd with cold dishes,
With scraps o' the court, it is no contract, none:
And though it be allow'd in meaner parties—   121
Yet who than he more mean?—to knit their souls,
On whom there is no more dependency
• But brats and beggary, in self-figured knot;
• Yet you are curb'd from that enlargement by
The consequence o' the crown, and must not soil
The precious note of it with a base slave,
• A hilding for a livery, a squire's cloth,
• A pantler, not so eminent.
   Imo.   Profane fellow!
• Wert thou the son of Jupiter and no more   130
But what thou art besides, thou wert too base
To be his groom: thou wert dignified enough,
Even to the point of envy, if 'twere made
Comparative for your virtues, to be styled
The under-hangman of his kingdom, and hated
For being preferr'd so well.
   Clo.   The south-fog rot him!
   Imo. He never can meet more mischance than
     come
To be but named of thee. His meanest garment,
• That ever hath but clipp'd his body, is dearer
In my respect than all the hairs above thee,   140
Were they all made such men. How now, Pi-
    sanio!

       Enter PISANIO.

   Clo. 'His garment!' Now the devil—
   Imo. To Dorothy my woman hie thee pre-
    sently—
   Clo. 'His garment!'
   Imo.   I am sprited with a fool,
Frighted, and anger'd worse: go bid my woman
Search for a jewel that too casually
Hath left mine arm: it was thy master's:'shrew me,
If I would lose it for a revenue
Of any king's in Europe. I do think
I saw 't this morning: confident I am   150
Last night 'twas on mine arm; I kiss'd it:
I hope it be not gone to tell my lord
That I kiss aught but he.
   Pis.   'Twill not be lost.
   Imo. I hope so: go and search.
                   [*Exit Pisanio.*
   Clo.   You have abused me:
'His meanest garment!'
   Imo.   Ay, I said so, sir:
• If you will make 't an action, call witness to 't.
   Clo. I will inform your father.
   Imo.   Your mother too:
She's my good lady, and will conceive, I hope,
But the worst of me. So, I leave you, sir,
To the worst of discontent.   [*Exit.*
   Clo.   I'll be revenged: 160
'His meanest garment!' Well.   [*Exit.*

    SCENE IV. *Rome. Philario's house.*

    Enter POSTHUMUS *and* PHILARIO.

   Post. Fear it not, sir: I would I were so sure
To win the king as I am bold her honour
Will remain hers.
   Phi.   What means do you make to him?

Post.   Not any, but abide the change of time,
Quake in the present winter's state and wish
That warmer days would come: in these sear'd hopes,
I barely gratify your love; they failing,
I must die much your debtor.
　Phi.   Your very goodness and your company
O'erpays all I can do.   By this, your king   10
Hath heard of great Augustus: Caius Lucius
Will do's commission throughly: and I think
He'll grant the tribute, send the arrearages,
Or look upon our Romans, whose remembrance
Is yet fresh in their grief.
　Post.   　　　　　I do believe,
Statist though I am none, nor like to be,
That this will prove a war; and you shall hear
The legions now in Gallia sooner landed
In our not-fearing Britain than have tidings
Of any penny tribute paid.   Our countrymen   20
Are men more order'd than when Julius Cæsar
Smiled at their lack of skill, but found their courage
Worthy his frowning at: their discipline,
Now mingled with their courages, will make known
To their approvers they are people such
That mend upon the world.

　　　　　Enter IACHIMO.

　Phi.   　　　　　See! Iachimo!
　Post.   The swiftest harts have posted you by land;
And winds of all the corners kiss'd your sails,
To make your vessel nimble.
　Phi.   　　　　　Welcome, sir.
　Post.   I hope the briefness of your answer made
The speediness of your return.
　Iach.   　　　　　Your lady   31
Is one of the fairest that I have look'd upon.
　Post.   And therewithal the best; or let her beauty
Look through a casement to allure false hearts
And be false with them.
　Iach.   　　　　　Here are letters for you.
　Post.   Their tenour good, I trust.
　Iach.   　　　　　'Tis very like.
　Phi.   Was Caius Lucius in the Britain court
When you were there?
　Iach.   　　　　　He was expected then,
But not approach'd.
　Post.   　　　　　All is well yet.
Sparkles this stone as it was wont? or is't not   40
Too dull for your good wearing?
　Iach.   　　　　　If I had lost it,
I should have lost the worth of it in gold.
I'll make a journey twice as far, to enjoy
A second night of such sweet shortness which
Was mine in Britain, for the ring is won.
　Post.   The stone's too hard to come by.
　Iach.   　　　　　Not a whit,
Your lady being so easy.
　Post.   　　　　　Make not, sir,
Your loss your sport: I hope you know that we
Must not continue friends.
　Iach.   　　　　　Good sir, we must,
If you keep covenant.   Had I not brought   50
The knowledge of your mistress home, I grant
We were to question further: but I now
Profess myself the winner of her honour,
Together with your ring; and not the wronger
Of her or you, having proceeded but

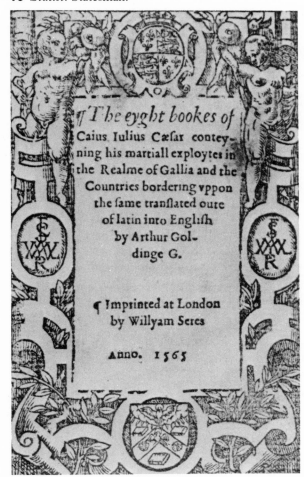

The title-page of Julius Caesar's *Commentaries on the Gallic Wars*, translated into English by Arthur Golding, 1565

25 *their approvers.* Those who test them.

51 *knowledge.* Carnal knowledge.

65 *spare.* Omit.

70 *Roman.* Mark Antony.

71 *Cydnus.* The river Cleopatra sailed up.

76 *the . . . was.* It was so lifelike.

Chaste Diana bathing. From a 16th century woodcut

88 *fretted.* Decorated.

96 *pale.* Calm.

By both your wills.
   Post.   If you can make't apparent
That you have tasted her in bed, my hand
And ring is yours; if not, the foul opinion
You had of her pure honour gains or loses
Your sword or mine, or masterless leaves both   60
To who shall find them.
   Iach.   Sir, my circumstances,
Being so near the truth as I will make them,
Must first induce you to believe: whose strength
I will confirm with oath; which, I doubt not,
●You'll give me leave to spare, when you shall find
You need it not.
   Post.   Proceed.
   Iach.   First, her bedchamber,—
Where, I confess, I slept not, but profess
Had that was well worth watching—it was hang'd
With tapestry of silk and silver; the story
●Proud Cleopatra, when she met her Roman,   70
●And Cydnus swell'd above the banks, or for
The press of boats or pride: a piece of work
So bravely done, so rich, that it did strive
In workmanship and value; which I wonder'd
Could be so rarely and exactly wrought,
●Since the true life on't was—
   Post.   This is true;
And this you might have heard of here, by me,
Or by some other.
   Iach.   More particulars
Must justify my knowledge.
   Post.   So they must,
Or do your honour injury.
   Iach.   The chimney   80
Is south the chamber, and the chimney-piece
Chaste Dian bathing: never saw I figures
So likely to report themselves: the cutter
Was as another nature, dumb; outwent her,
Motion and breath left out.
   Post.   This is a thing
Which you might from relation likewise reap,
Being, as it is, much spoke of.
   Iach.   The roof o' the chamber
●With golden cherubins is fretted: her andirons—
I had forgot them—were two winking Cupids
Of silver, each on one foot standing, nicely   90
Depending on their brands.
   Post.   This is her honour!
Let it be granted you have seen all this—and praise
Be given to your remembrance—the description
Of what is in her chamber nothing saves
The wager you have laid.
   Iach.   Then, if you can,
               [Showing the bracelet.
●Be pale: I beg but leave to air this jewel; see!
And now 'tis up again: it must be married
To that your diamond; I'll keep them.
   Post.   Jove!
Once more let me behold it: is it that
Which I left with her?
   Iach.   Sir—I thank her—that: 100
She stripp'd it from her arm; I see her yet;
Her pretty action did outsell her gift,
And yet enrich'd it too: she gave it me, and said
She prized it once.
   Post.   May be she pluck'd it off
To send it me.
   Iach.   She writes so to you, doth she?
   Post. O, no, no, no! 'tis true. Here, take this
     too;   *[Gives the ring.*

●It is a basilisk unto mine eye,
Kills me to look on't.   Let there be no honour
Where there is beauty; truth, where semblance;
            love,   109
Where there's another man: the vows of women
Of no more bondage be, to where they are made,
Than they are to their virtues; which is nothing.
O, above measure false!
    Phi.   Have patience, sir,
And take your ring again; 'tis not yet won:
●It may be probable she lost it; or
Who knows if one of her women, being corrupted,
Hath stol'n it from her?
    Post.   Very true;
And so, I hope, he came by't.   Back my ring:
Render to me some corporal sign about her,
More evident than this; for this was stolen.   120
    Iach.   By Jupiter, I had it from her arm.
    Post.   Hark you, he swears; by Jupiter he
            swears.
'Tis true:—nay, keep the ring—'tis true: I am sure
She would not lose it: her attendants are
All sworn and honourable:—they induced to steal
            it!
And by a stranger!—No, he hath enjoy'd her:
●The cognizance of her incontinency
Is this: she hath bought the name of whore thus
            dearly.
There, take thy hire; and all the fiends of hell
Divide themselves between you!
    Phi.   Sir, be patient: 130
This is not strong enough to be believed
Of one persuaded well of—
    Post.   Never talk on't;
She hath been colted by him.
    Iach.   If you seek
For further satisfying, under her breast—
Worthy the pressing—lies a mole, right proud
Of that most delicate lodging: by my life,
I kiss'd it; and it gave me present hunger
To feed again, though full.   You do remember
This stain upon her?
    Post.   Ay, and it doth confirm
Another stain, as big as hell can hold,   140
Were there no more but it.
    Iach.   Will you hear more?
    Post.   Spare your arithmetic: never count the
            turns;
Once, and a million!
    Iach.   I'll be sworn—
    Post.   No swearing
If you will swear you have not done't, you lie;
And I will kill thee, if thou dost deny
Thou 'st made me cuckold.
    Iach.   I'll deny nothing.
● *Post.*   O, that I had her here, to tear her limb-
            meal!
I will go there and do't, i' the court, before
Her father.   I'll do something—   [*Exit.*
    Phi.   Quite besides
The government of patience!   You have won: 150
Let's follow him, and pervert the present wrath
He hath against himself.
    Iach.   With all my heart. [*Exeunt.*

SCENE V.   *Another room in Philario's house.*

            Enter POSTHUMUS.

    Post. Is there no way for men to be but women

Posthumus: 'nay, keep the ring- 'tis true: I am sure She
would not lose it.' Engraving by Kenny Meadows from
Barry Cornwall's *The Works of Shakspere*, 1846

107 *basilisk.* Legendary reptile whose glance was fatal.

115 *probable.* Provable.

127 *cognizance.* Evidence.

147 *limbmeal.* Limb by limb.

5 *stamp'd.* i.e. conceived.

11 *pudency.* Modesty.

12 *Saturn.* Cold and gloomy god.

10 *to kill the marvel.* To round off this amazing thing.

A court scene in Cymbeline's palace, Stratford-upon-Avon, 1957

Must be half-workers? We are all bastards;
And that most venerable man which I
Did call my father, was I know not where
● When I was stamp'd; some coiner with his tools
Made me a counterfeit: yet my mother seem'd
The Dian of that time: so doth my wife
The nonpareil of this. O, vengeance, vengeance!
Me of my lawful pleasure she restrain'd
And pray'd me oft forbearance; did it with   10
● A pudency so rosy the sweet view on't
● Might well have warm'd old Saturn; that I
      thought her
As chaste as unsunn'd snow. O, all the devils!
This yellow Iachimo, in an hour,—was't not?—
Or less,—at first?—perchance he spoke not, but,
Like a full-acorn'd boar, a German one,
Cried 'O!' and mounted; found no opposition
But what he look'd for should oppose and she
Should from encounter guard. Could I find out
The woman's part in me! For there's no
      motion   20
That tends to vice in man, but I affirm
It is the woman's part: be it lying, note it,
The woman's; flattering, hers; deceiving, hers;
Lust and rank thoughts, hers, hers; revenges,
      hers;
Ambitions, covetings, change of prides, disdain,
Nice longing, slanders, mutability,
All faults that may be named, nay, that hell
      knows,
Why, hers, in part or all; but rather, all;
For even to vice
They are not constant, but are changing still   30
One vice, but of a minute old, for one
Not half so old as that. I'll write against them,
Detest them, curse them: yet 'tis greater skill
In a true hate, to pray they have their will:
The very devils cannot plague them better.
                                            [*Exit.*

ACT III.

SCENE I. *Britain. A hall in Cymbeline's palace.*

Enter in state, CYMBELINE, QUEEN, CLOTEN, *and* Lords *at one door, and at another,* CAIUS LUCIUS *and* Attendants.

Cym. Now say, what would Augustus Cæsar
      with us?
Luc. When Julius Cæsar, whose remem-
      brance yet
Lives in men's eyes and will to ears and tongues
Be theme and hearing ever, was in this Britain
And conquer'd it, Cassibelan, thine uncle,—
Famous in Cæsar's praises, no whit less
Than in his feats deserving it—for him
And his succession granted Rome a tribute,
Yearly three thousand pounds, which by thee
      lately
● Is left untender'd.
Queen.   And, to kill the marvel,   10
Shall be so ever.
Clo.   There be many Cæsars,
Ere such another Julius. Britain is
A world by itself; and we will nothing pay
For wearing our own noses.
Queen.   That opportunity
Which then they had to take from 's, to resume

We have again.   Remember, sir, my liege,
The kings your ancestors, together with
The natural bravery of your isle, which stands
● As Neptune's park, ribbed and paled in
With rocks unscaleable and roaring waters,   20
With sands that will not bear your enemies'
          boats,
But suck them up to the topmast.   A kind of
          conquest
Cæsar made here; but made not here his brag
Of 'Came' and 'saw' and 'overcame:' with
          shame—
The first that ever touch'd him—he was carried
From off our coast, twice beaten; and his
          shipping—
Poor ignorant baubles!—on our terrible seas,
Like egg-shells moved upon their surges, crack'd
As easily 'gainst our rocks: for joy whereof
The famed Cassibelan, who was once at point—
● O giglot fortune!—to master Cæsar's sword,   31
● Made Lud's town with rejoicing fires bright
And Britons strut with courage.
      Clo.   Come, there's no more tribute to be
paid: our kingdom is stronger than it was at
● that time; and, as I said, there is no moe such
Cæsars: other of them may have crook'd noses,
but to owe such straight arms, none.
      Cym.   Son, let your mother end.   39
● *Clo.*   We have yet many among us can gripe
as hard as Cassibelan: I do not say I am one;
but I have a hand.   Why tribute? why should
we pay tribute?   If Cæsar can hide the sun from
us with a blanket, or put the moon in his pocket,
we will pay him tribute for light; else, sir, no
more tribute, pray you now.
      Cym.   You must know,
Till the injurious Romans did extort
This tribute from us, we were free: Cæsar's am-
          bition,
Which swell'd so much that it did almost
          stretch   50
The sides o' the world, against all colour here
Did put the yoke upon 's; which to shake off
Becomes a warlike people, whom we reckon
Ourselves to be.
      Clo. and Lords.   We do.
      Cym.   Say, then, to Cæsar,
● Our ancestor was that Mulmutius which
Ordain'd our laws, whose use the sword of Cæsar
Hath too much mangled; whose repair and
          franchise
Shall, by the power we hold, be our good deed,
Though Rome be therefore angry: Mulmutius
          made our laws,
Who was the first of Britain which did put   60
His brows within a golden crown and call'd
Himself a king.
      Luc.   I am sorry, Cymbeline,
That I am to pronounce Augustus Cæsar—
Cæsar, that hath more kings his servants than
Thyself domestic officers—thine enemy:
Receive it from me, then: war and confusion
In Cæsar's name pronounce I 'gainst thee: look
For fury not to be resisted.   Thus defied,
I thank thee for myself.
      Cym.   Thou art welcome, Caius.
Thy Cæsar knighted me; my youth I spent   70
Much under him; of him I gather'd honour;
Which he to seek of me again, perforce,

19 *Neptune's park.* i.e. the sea. *ribbed.* Enclosed. *paled.* Fenced.

31 *giglot.* Fickle (compare the modern word 'gigolo').

32 *Lud's town.* London.

Cloten: 'Come, there's no more tribute to be paid.' Paul Scofield as Cloten, Stratford-upon-Avon, 1946

36 *moe.* More.

40 *gripe.* Grapple.

55 *Mulmutius.* Legendary early king.

73 *perfect*. Well aware.

74 *Pannonians and Dalmatians*. Balkan peoples.

Pisanio: 'How! that I should murder her?' Thomas Hull as Pisanio. Engraving from Bell's edition of Shakespeare, 1775

21 *feodary*. Accomplice.

28 *characters*. Handwriting.

36 *locks of counsel*. Seals of secrecy.

●Behoves me keep at utterance.   I am perfect
●That the Pannonians and Dalmatians for
 Their liberties are now in arms; a precedent
 Which not to read would show the Britons cold:
 So Cæsar shall not find them.
   Luc.   Let proof speak.
   Clo.   His majesty bids you welcome.   Make
pastime with us a day or two, or longer: if you
seek us afterwards in other terms, you shall find
us in our salt-water girdle: if you beat us out
of it, it is yours; if you fall in the adventure,
our crows shall fare the better for you; and
there's an end.
   Luc.   So, sir.
   Cym.   I know your master's pleasure and he
   mine:
All the remain is 'Welcome!'   [*Exeunt.*

   SCENE II.   *Another room in the palace.*

   Enter PISANIO, *with a letter.*

   Pis.   How! of adultery?   Wherefore write
   you not
What monster 's her accuser?   Leonatus!
O master! what a strange infection
Is fall'n into thy ear!   What false Italian,
As poisonous-tongued as handed, hath prevail'd
On thy too ready hearing?   Disloyal!   No:
She 's punish'd for her truth, and undergoes,
More goddess-like than wife-like, such assaults
As would take in some virtue.   O my master!
Thy mind to her is now as low as were   10
Thy fortunes.   How! that I should murder her?
Upon the love and truth and vows which I
Have made to thy command? I, her? her blood?
If it be so to do good service, never
Let me be counted serviceable.   How look I,
That I should seem to lack humanity
So much as this fact comes to? [*Reading*] 'Do't:
   the letter
That I have sent her, by her own command
Shall give thee opportunity.'   O damn'd paper!
Black as the ink that's on thee!   Senseless
   bauble,   20
●Art thou a feodary for this act, and look'st
So virgin-like without?   Lo, here she comes.
I am ignorant in what I am commanded.

   Enter IMOGEN.

   Imo.   How now, Pisanio!
   Pis.   Madam, here is a letter from my lord.
   Imo.   Who? thy lord? that is my lord,
   Leonatus!
O, learn'd indeed were that astronomer
●That knew the stars as I his characters;
He'ld lay the future open.   You good gods,
Let what is here contain'd relish of love,   30
Of my lord's health, of his content, yet not
That we two are asunder; let that grieve him:
Some griefs are med'cinable; that is one of
   them,
For it doth physic love: of his content,
All but in that!   Good wax, thy leave.   Blest be
●You bees that make these locks of counsel.
   Lovers
And men in dangerous bonds pray not alike:
Though forfeiters you cast in prison, yet
You clasp young Cupid's tables.   Good news,
   gods!   39

[*Reads*] 'Justice, and your father's wrath, should he take me in his dominion, could not be so cruel to me, as you, O the dearest of creatures, would even renew me with your eyes.
● Take notice that I am in Cambria, at Milford-Haven: what your own love will out of this advise you, follow.   So he wishes you all happiness, that remains loyal to his vow, and your, increasing in love,

LEONATUS POSTHUMUS.'

O, for a horse with wings ! Hear'st thou, Pisanio?
He is at Milford-Haven: read, and tell me   51
How far 'tis thither.   If one of mean affairs
May plod it in a week, why may not I
Glide thither in a day?   Then, true Pisanio,—
Who long'st, like me, to see thy lord; who long'st,—
● O, let me bate,—but not like me—yet long'st,
But in a fainter kind:—O, not like me;
For mine's beyond beyond—say, and speak thick;
Love's counsellor should fill the bores of hearing,
To the smothering of the sense—how far it is 60
To this same blessed Milford: and by the way
Tell me how Wales was made so happy as
To inherit such a haven: but first of all,
How we may steal from hence, and for the gap
That we shall make in time, from our hence-going
And our return, to excuse: but first, how get hence:
Why should excuse be born or e'er begot?
We'll talk of that hereafter.   Prithee, speak,
How many score of miles may we well ride
'Twixt hour and hour?
   Pis.   One score 'twixt sun and sun,
Madam, 's enough for you: [*Aside*] and too much too.   71
   Imo.   Why, one that rode to's execution, man,
Could never go so slow: I have heard of riding wagers,
Where horses have been nimbler than the sands
● That run i' the clock's behalf.   But this is foolery:
Go bid my woman feign a sickness; say
She'll home to her father: and provide me presently
A riding-suit, no costlier than would fit
● A franklin's housewife.
   Pis.   Madam, you're best consider.
   Imo. I see before me, man : nor here, nor here,
Nor what ensues, but have a fog in them,   81
That I cannot look through.   Away, I prithee;
Do as I bid thee : there's no more to say;
Accessible is none but Milford way.   (*Exeunt.*

SCENE III.   Wales: a mountainous country
with a cave.

Enter, from the cave, BELARIUS; GUIDERIUS,
and ARVIRAGUS following.

   Bel. A goodly day not to keep house, with such
Whose roof's as low as ours ! Stoop, boys; this gate
Instructs you how to adore the heavens and bows you
● To a morning's holy office: the gates of monarchs
● Are arch'd so high that giants may jet through
And keep their impious turbans on, without

44 *Cambria*. Wales.

56 *bate*. Restrain.

75 *i' the clock's behalf*. In an hour glass.

79 *franklin's*. Yeoman farmer's.

4 *holy office*. Prayer.

5 *jet*. Swagger.

20 *sharded.* In cow-dung.

22 *check.* Rebuke.

33 *travelling a-bed.* i.e. in imagination.

Costume designs for Arviragus and Belarius by J. Gower Parks, Stratford-upon-Avon, 1937

63 *mellow hangings.* Fruit.

Good morrow to the sun. Hail, thou fair heaven!
We house i' the rock, yet use thee not so hardly
As prouder livers do.
Gui.   Hail, heaven!
Arv.   Hail, heaven!
Bel.   Now for our mountain sport: up to yond
   hill;   10
Your legs are young; I'll tread these flats. Con-
   sider,
When you above perceive me like a crow,
That it is place which lessens and sets off:
And you may then revolve what tales I have
   told you
Of courts, of princes, of the tricks in war:
This service is not service, so being done,
But being so allow'd: to apprehend thus,
Draws us a profit from all things we see;
And often, to our comfort, shall we find
● The sharded beetle in a safer hold   20
Than is the full-wing'd eagle.   O, this life
● Is nobler than attending for a check,
Richer than doing nothing for a bauble,
Prouder than rustling in unpaid-for silk:
Such gain the cap of him that makes 'em fine,
Yet keeps his book uncross'd: no life to ours.
   Gui.   Out of your proof you speak: we, poor
      unfledged,
Have never wing'd from view o' the nest, nor
      know not
What air's from home.   Haply this life is best,
If quiet life be best; sweeter to you   30
That have a sharper known; well corresponding
With your stiff age: but unto us it is
● A cell of ignorance; travelling a-bed;
A prison for a debtor, that not dares
To stride a limit.
   Arv.   What should we speak of
When we are old as you? when we shall hear
The rain and wind beat dark December, how,
In this our pinching cave, shall we discourse
The freezing hours away? We have seen nothing;
We are beastly, subtle as the fox for prey,   40
Like warlike as the wolf for what we eat;
Our valour is to chase what flies; our cage
We make a quire, as doth the prison'd bird,
And sing our bondage freely.
   Bel.   How you speak!
Did you but know the city's usuries
And felt them knowingly; the art o' the court,
As hard to leave as keep; whose top to climb
Is certain falling, or so slippery that
The fear's as bad as falling; the toil o' the war,
A pain that only seems to seek out danger   50
I' the name of fame and honour; which dies i' the
      search,
And hath as oft a slanderous epitaph
As record of fair act; nay, many times,
Doth ill deserve by doing well; what's worse,
Must court'sy at the censure:—O boys, this story
The world may read in me: my body's mark'd
With Roman swords, and my report was once
First with the best of note: Cymbeline loved me,
And when a soldier was the theme, my name
Was not far off: then was I as a tree   60
Whose boughs did bend with fruit: but in one
      night,
A storm or robbery, call it what you will,
● Shook down my mellow hangings, nay, my leaves,
And left me bare to weather.

Gui.   Uncertain favour!
Bel.   My fault being nothing—as I have told
        you oft—
But that two villains, whose false oaths prevail'd
Before my perfect honour, swore to Cymbeline
I was confederate with the Romans: so
Follow'd my banishment, and this twenty years
This rock and these demesnes have been my
        world;   70
Where I have lived at honest freedom, paid
More pious debts to heaven than in all
The fore-end of my time.   But up to the moun-
        tains!
This is not hunters' language: he that strikes
The venison first shall be the lord o' the feast;
To him the other two shall minister;
And we will fear no poison, which attends
In place of greater state.   I'll meet you in the
        valleys. [*Exeunt Guiderius and Arviragus.*
How hard it is to hide the sparks of nature!
These boys know little they are sons to the king;
Nor Cymbeline dreams that they are alive.   81
They think they are mine; and though train'd up
        thus meanly
I' the cave wherein they bow, their thoughts
        do hit
The roofs of palaces, and nature prompts them
In simple and low things to prince it much
Beyond the trick of others.   This Polydore,
The heir of Cymbeline and Britain, who
The king his father call'd Guiderius,—Jove!
When on my three-foot stool I sit and tell
The warlike feats I have done, his spirits fly out
Into my story: say 'Thus mine enemy fell,   91
And thus I set my foot on's neck;' even then
The princely blood flows in his cheek, he sweats,
Strains his young nerves and puts himself in
        posture
That acts my words. The younger brother, Cadwal,
Once Arviragus, in as like a figure,
Strikes life into my speech and shows much more
His own conceiving.—Hark, the game is roused!—
O Cymbeline! heaven and my conscience knows
Thou didst unjustly banish me: whereon,   100
At three and two years old, I stole these babes;
Thinking to bar thee of succession, as
Thou reft'st me of my lands.   Euriphile,
Thou wast their nurse; they took thee for their
        mother,
And every day do honour to her grave:
Myself, Belarius, that am Morgan call'd,
They take for natural father.   The game is up.
                                        [*Exit.*

SCENE IV.   *Country near Milford-Haven.*

Enter PISANIO *and* IMOGEN.

Imo.   Thou told'st me, when we came from
        horse, the place
Was near at hand: ne'er long'd my mother so
To see me first, as I have now.   Pisanio! man!
Where is Posthumus?   What is in thy mind,
That makes thee stare thus?   Wherefore breaks
        that sigh
From the inward of thee? One, but painted thus,
Would be interpreted a thing perplex'd
Beyond self-explication: put thyself
Into a haviour of less fear, ere wildness
Vanquish my staider senses.   What's the matter?

Belarius: '. . . he that strikes The venison first shall be the lord o' the feast.' Woodcut of a hunting scene from George Turberville's *The Noble Art of Venerie or Hunting*, 1611

---

1 *came from horse.* Dismounted.

9 *haviour.* Appearance.

16 *hard point*. Tough spot.

Travelling costume for Imogen by Rene Allio, RSC, 1962

51 *favour*. Appearance. *jay*. Courtesan.

60 *Æneas*. Who deserted Dido.

61 *Sinon*. Who deceived the Trojans into taking in the wooden horse.

Why tender'st thou that paper to me, with   11
A look untender?   If't be summer news,
Smile to't before; if winterly, thou need'st
But keep that countenance still.   My husband's
   hand!
That drug-damn'd Italy hath out-crafted him,
●And he's at some hard point.   Speak, man: thy
   tongue
May take off some extremity, which to read
Would be even mortal to me.
   Pis.   Please you, read;
And you shall find me, wretched man, a thing
The most disdain'd of fortune.   20
   Imo. [*Reads*] 'Thy mistress, Pisanio, hath
played the strumpet in my bed; the testimonies
whereof lie bleeding in me.   I speak not out of
weak surmises, but from proof as strong as my
grief and as certain as I expect my revenge.
That part thou, Pisanio, must act for me, if thy
faith be not tainted with the breach of hers.   Let
thine own hands take away her life: I shall give
thee opportunity at Milford-Haven.   She hath
my letter for the purpose: where, if thou fear to
strike and to make me certain it is done, thou art
the pandar to her dishonour and equally to me
disloyal.'
   Pis.   What shall I need to draw my sword?
   the paper
Hath cut her throat already.   No, 'tis slander,
Whose edge is sharper than the sword, whose
   tongue
Outvenoms all the worms of Nile, whose breath
Rides on the posting winds and doth belie
All corners of the world: kings, queens and
   states,
Maids, matrons, nay, the secrets of the grave 40
This viperous slander enters.   What cheer,
   madam?
   Imo.   False to his bed!   What is it to be false?
To lie in watch there and to think on him?
To weep 'twixt clock and clock? if sleep charge
   nature,
To break it with a fearful dream of him
And cry myself awake? that's false to's bed,
   is it?
   Pis.   Alas, good lady!
   Imo. I false! Thy conscience witness: Iachimo,
Thou didst accuse him of incontinency;
Thou then look'dst like a villain; now methinks
●Thy favour's good enough.   Some jay of Italy 51
†Whose mother was her painting, hath betray'd
   him:
Poor I am stale, a garment out of fashion;
And, for I am richer than to hang by the walls,
I must be ripp'd:—to pieces with me!—O,
Men's vows are women's traitors!   All good
   seeming,
By thy revolt, O husband, shall be thought
Put on for villany; not born where't grows,
But worn a bait for ladies.
   Pis.   Good madam, hear me.
● *Imo.*   True honest men being heard, like false
   Æneas,   60
●Were in his time thought false, and Sinon's
   weeping
Did scandal many a holy tear, took pity
From most true wretchedness: so thou, Posthu-
   mus,
Wilt lay the leaven on all proper men;

Goodly and gallant shall be false and perjured
From thy great fail.   Come, fellow, be thou honest:
Do thou thy master's bidding: when thou see'st
    him,
A little witness my obedience: look!
I draw the sword myself: take it, and hit
The innocent mansion of my love, my heart: 70
Fear not; 'tis empty of all things but grief:
Thy master is not there, who was indeed
The riches of it: do his bidding; strike.
Thou mayst be valiant in a better cause;
But now thou seem'st a coward.
        Pis.   Hence, vile instrument!
Thou shalt not damn my hand.
        Imo.   Why, I must die;
And if I do not by thy hand, thou art
No servant of thy master's.   Against self-slaughter
There is a prohibition so divine
That cravens my weak hand.   Come, here's my
    heart.   80
Something's afore't.   Soft, soft! we'll no defence;
Obedient as the scabbard.   What is here?
The scriptures of the loyal Leonatus,
All turn'd to heresy?   Away, away,
Corrupters of my faith! you shall no more
Be stomachers to my heart.   Thus may poor fools
Believe false teachers: though those that are be-
    tray'd
Do feel the treason sharply, yet the traitor
Stands in worse case of woe.
And thou, Posthumus, thou that didst set up   90
My disobedience 'gainst the king my father
And make me put into contempt the suits
Of princely fellows, shalt hereafter find
• It is no act of common passage, but
A strain of rareness: and I grieve myself
• To think, when thou shalt be disedged by her
• That now thou tirest on, how thy memory
Will then be pang'd by me.   Prithee, dispatch:
The lamb entreats the butcher: where's thy knife?
Thou art too slow to do thy master's bidding,   100
When I desire it too.
        Pis.   O gracious lady,
Since I received command to do this business
I have not slept one wink.
        Imo.   Do't, and to bed then.
        Pis.   I'll wake mine eye-balls blind first.
        Imo.   Wherefore then
Didst undertake it?   Why hast thou abused
So many miles with a pretence? this place?
Mine action and thine own? our horses' labour?
The time inviting thee? the perturb'd court,
For my being absent? whereunto I never
Purpose return.   Why hast thou gone so far,   110
To be unbent when thou hast ta'en thy stand,
The elected deer before thee?
        Pis.   But to win time
To lose so bad employment; in the which
I have consider'd of a course.   Good lady,
Hear me with patience.
        Imo.   Talk thy tongue weary; speak:
I have heard I am a strumpet; and mine ear,
Therein false struck, can take no greater wound,
• Nor tent to bottom that.   But speak.
        Pis.   Then, madam,
I thought you would not back again.
        Imo.   Most like;
Bringing me here to kill me.
        Pis.   Not so, neither: 120

Imogen: 'Come, here's my heart.' Engraving from a
painting by John Hoppner (1759–1810)

94 *act of common passage*. Ordinary action.

96 *disedged*. Satiated.

97 *tirest*. Feed hungrily.

118 *tent*. Probe.

150 *Pretty . . . view.* Ingenious and watchful.

166 *Titan.* Hyperion, the sun.

173 *answer to.* Match. *in their serving.* When you have them on.

Costume design for the Queen by J. Gower Parks, Stratford-upon-Avon, 1937

But if I were as wise as honest, then
My purpose would prove well.   It cannot be
But that my master is abused:
Some villain, ay, and singular in his art,
Hath done you both this cursed injury.
  Imo.   Some Roman courtezan.
  Pis.   No, on my life.
I'll give but notice you are dead and send him
Some bloody sign of it; for 'tis commanded
I should do so: you shall be miss'd at court,
And that will well confirm it.
  Imo.   Why, good fellow, 130
What shall I do the while? where bide? how live?
Or in my life what comfort, when I am
Dead to my husband?
  Pis.   If you'll back to the court—
  Imo.   No court, no father; nor no more ado
†With that harsh, noble, simple nothing,
That Cloten, whose love-suit hath been to me
As fearful as a siege.
  Pis.   If not at court,
Then not in Britain must you bide.
  Imo.   Where then?
Hath Britain all the sun that shines? Day, night,
Are they not but in Britain? I' the world's volume
Our Britain seems as of it, but not in 't;   141
In a great pool a swan's nest: prithee, think
There's livers out of Britain.
  Pis.   I am most glad
You think of other place.   The ambassador,
Lucius the Roman, comes to Milford-Haven
To-morrow: now, if you could wear a mind
Dark as your fortune is, and but disguise
That which, to appear itself, must not yet be
But by self-danger, you should tread a course
●†Pretty and full of view; yea, haply, near   150
The residence of Posthumus; so nigh at least
That though his actions were not visible, yet
Report should render him hourly to your ear
As truly as he moves.
  Imo.   O, for such means!
Though peril to my modesty, not death on't,
I would adventure.
  Pis.   Well, then, here's the point:
You must forget to be a woman; change
Command into obedience: fear and niceness—
The handmaids of all women, or, more truly,
Woman it pretty self—into a waggish courage:
Ready in gibes, quick-answer'd, saucy and   161
As quarrelous as the weasel; nay, you must
Forget that rarest treasure of your cheek,
Exposing it—but, O, the harder heart!
Alack, no remedy!—to the greedy touch
●Of common-kissing Titan, and forget
Your laboursome and dainty trims, wherein
You made great Juno angry.
  Imo.   Nay, be brief:
I see into thy end, and am almost
A man already.
  Pis.   First, make yourself but like one. 170
Fore-thinking this, I have already fit—
'Tis in my cloak-bag—doublet, hat, hose, all
●That answer to them: would you in their serving,
And with what imitation you can borrow
From youth of such a season, 'fore noble Lucius
Present yourself, desire his service, tell him
Wherein you're happy,—which you'll make him
        know,
If that his head have ear in music,—doubtless

With joy he will embrace you, for he's honour-
able
And doubling that, most holy. Your means
abroad,   180
You have me, rich; and I will never fail
Beginning nor supplyment.
   Imo.   Thou art all the comfort
The gods will diet me with.   Prithee, away:
There's more to be consider'd; but we'll even
All that good time will give us: this attempt
I am soldier to, and will abide it with
A prince's courage.   Away, I prithee.
   Pis.   Well, madam, we must take a short fare-
well,
Lest, being miss'd, I be suspected of
Your carriage from the court. My noble mistress,
Here is a box; I had it from the queen: 191
What's in't is precious; if you are sick at sea,
Or stomach-qualm'd at land, a dram of this
Will drive away distemper.   To some shade,
And fit you to your manhood.   May the gods
Direct you to the best!
   Imo. Amen: I thank thee. [*Exeunt, severally.*

SCENE V. *A room in Cymbeline's palace.*

Enter CYMBELINE, QUEEN, CLOTEN, LUCIUS,
        Lords, *and* Attendants.

   Cym.   Thus far; and so farewell.
   Luc.   Thanks, royal sir.
My emperor hath wrote, I must from hence;
And am right sorry that I must report ye
My master's enemy.
   Cym.   Our subjects, sir,
Will not endure his yoke; and for ourself
To show less sovereignty than they, must needs
Appear unkinglike.
   Luc.   So, sir: I desire of you
A conduct over-land to Milford-Haven.
Madam, all joy befal your grace!
   Queen.   And you!
   Cym.   My lords, you are appointed for that
office;   10
The due of honour in no point omit.
So farewell, noble Lucius.
   Luc.   Your hand, my lord.
   Clo.   Receive it friendly; but from this time
forth
I wear it as your enemy.
   Luc.   Sir, the event
Is yet to name the winner: fare you well.
   Cym.   Leave not the worthy Lucius, good my
lords,
Till he have cross'd the Severn.   Happiness!
              [*Exeunt Lucius and Lords.*
   Queen.   He goes hence frowning: but it
honours us
That we have given him cause.
   Clo.   'Tis all the better;
Your valiant Britons have their wishes in it.   20
   Cym.   Lucius hath wrote already to the emperor
How it goes here.   It fits us therefore ripely
Our chariots and our horsemen be in readiness:
The powers that he already hath in Gallia
Will soon be drawn to head, from whence he
moves
His war for Britain.
   Queen.   'Tis not sleepy business;
But must be look'd to speedily and strongly.

Imogen: 'this attempt I am soldier to . . .' Sarah Smith
as Imogen, 1806

___

22 *ripely*. Fully.

Joan Miller as the Queen and Robert Harris as Cymbeline, Stratford-upon-Avon, 1957

---

35 *slight*. Easy. *sufferance*. Allowing it.

51 *to blame*. Faulty.

56 *stand'st so*. Support.

Cym. Our expectation that it would be thus
Hath made us forward.   But, my gentle queen,
Where is our daughter?   She hath not appear'd
Before the Roman, nor to us hath tender'd   31
The duty of the day: she looks us like
A thing more made of malice than of duty:
We have noted it.   Call her before us; for
● We have been too slight in sufferance.
                              [*Exit an Attendant.*
   Queen.   Royal sir,
Since the exile of Posthumus, most retired
Hath her life been; the cure whereof, my lord,
'Tis time must do.   Beseech your majesty,
Forbear sharp speeches to her: she's a lady
So tender of rebukes that words are strokes   40
And strokes death to her.

                    Re-enter Attendant.

   Cym.   Where is she, sir?   How
Can her contempt be answer'd?
   Atten.   Please you, sir,
Her chambers are all lock'd; and there's no answer
That will be given to the loudest noise we make.
   Queen.   My lord, when last I went to visit her,
She pray'd me to excuse her keeping close,
Whereto constrain'd by her infirmity,
She should that duty leave unpaid to you,
Which daily she was bound to proffer: this
She wish'd me to make known; but our great
         court   50
● Made me to blame in memory.
   Cym.   Her doors lock'd?
Not seen of late?   Grant, heavens, that which I fear
Prove false!   [*Exit.*
   Queen.   Son, I say, follow the king.
   Clo.   That man of hers, Pisanio, her old servant,
I have not seen these two days.
   Queen.   Go, look after. [*Exit Cloten.*
● Pisanio, thou that stand'st so for Posthumus!
He hath a drug of mine; I pray his absence
Proceed by swallowing that, for he believes
It is a thing most precious.   But for her,
Where is she gone?   Haply, despair hath seized
         her,   60
Or, wing'd with fervour of her love, she's flown
To her desired Posthumus: gone she is
To death or to dishonour; and my end
Can make good use of either: she being down,
I have the placing of the British crown.

                    Re-enter CLOTEN.

How now, my son!
   Clo.   'Tis certain she is fled.
Go in and cheer the king: he rages; none
Dare come about him.
   Queen.   [*Aside*] All the better: may
This night forestall him of the coming day! [*Exit.*
   Clo.   I love and hate her: for she's fair and
         royal,   70
And that she hath all courtly parts more exquisite
Than lady, ladies, woman; from every one
The best she hath, and she, of all compounded,
Outsells them all; I love her therefore: but
Disdaining me and throwing favours on
The low Posthumus slanders so her judgement
That what's else rare is choked; and in that point
I will conclude to hate her, nay, indeed,
To be revenged upon her.   For when fools   79
Shall—

Enter PISANIO.

Who is here? What, are you packing, sirrah?
Come hither: ah, you precious pandar! Villain,
Where is thy lady? In a word; or else
Thou art straightway with the fiends.
    Pis.   O, good my lord!
    Clo.   Where is thy lady? or, by Jupiter,—
I will not ask again. Close villain,
I'll have this secret from thy heart, or rip
Thy heart to find it. Is she with Posthumus?
From whose so many weights of baseness cannot
A dram of worth be drawn.
    Pis.   Alas, my lord,   89
How can she be with him? When was she miss'd?
He is in Rome.
    Clo.   Where is she, sir? Come nearer;
No further halting: satisfy me home
What is become of her.
    Pis.   O, my all-worthy lord!
    Clo.   All-worthy villain!
Discover where thy mistress is at once,
At the next word: no more of 'worthy lord!'
Speak, or thy silence on the instant is
Thy condemnation and thy death.
    Pis.   Then, sir,
This paper is the history of my knowledge   99
Touching her flight.   *[Presenting a letter.*
    Clo.   Let's see't. I will pursue her
Even to Augustus' throne.
    Pis.   *[Aside]* Or this, or perish.
She's far enough; and what he learns by this
May prove his travel, not her danger.
    Clo.   Hum!
    Pis.   *[Aside]* I'll write to my lord she's dead.
    O Imogen,
Safe mayst thou wander, safe return again!
    Clo.   Sirrah, is this letter true?
    Pis.   Sir, as I think.
    Clo.   It is Posthumus' hand; I know't. Sirrah, if thou wouldst not be a villain, but do me true service, undergo those employments wherein I should have cause to use thee with a serious industry, that is, what villany soe'er I bid thee do, to perform it directly and truly, I would think thee an honest man: thou shouldst neither want my means for thy relief nor my voice for thy preferment.
    Pis.   Well, my good lord.
    Clo.   Wilt thou serve me? for since patiently and constantly thou hast stuck to the bare fortune of that beggar Posthumus, thou canst not, in the course of gratitude, but be a diligent follower of mine: wilt thou serve me?
    Pis.   Sir, I will.
    Clo.   Give me thy hand; here's my purse. Hast any of thy late master's garments in thy possession?
    Pis.   I have, my lord, at my lodging, the same suit he wore when he took leave of my lady and mistress.   129
    Clo.   The first service thou dost me, fetch that suit hither: let it be thy first service; go.
    Pis.   I shall, my lord.   *[Exit.*
    Clo.   Meet thee at Milford-Haven!—I forgot to ask him one thing; I'll remember't anon:— even there, thou villain Posthumus, will I kill thee. I would these garments were come. She said upon a time—the bitterness of it I now belch

Costume design for Cloten by J. Gower Parks, Stratford-upon-Avon, 1937

163 *to my loss.* Injure myself.

168 *labour.* Trouble. *meed.* Reward.

12 *in fulness.* When fully equipped.

13 *sorer.* Worse.

Imogen: 'But what is this? . . . 'tis some savage hold.'
Engraving from a painting by Richard Westall (1765–1836)

from my heart—that she held the very garment of Posthumus in more respect than my noble and natural person, together with the adornment of my qualities.   With that suit upon my back, will I ravish her: first kill him, and in her eyes; there shall she see my valour, which will then be a torment to her contempt.   He on the ground, my speech of insultment ended on his dead body, and when my lust hath dined,—which, as I say, to vex her I will execute in the clothes that she so praised,—to the court I'll knock her back, foot her home again.   She hath despised me rejoicingly, and I'll be merry in my revenge.   150

Re-enter PISANIO, *with the clothes.*

Be those the garments?
  Pis.   Ay, my noble lord.
  Clo.   How long is't since she went to Milford-Haven?
  Pis.   She can scarce be there yet.
  Clo.   Bring this apparel to my chamber; that is the second thing that I have commanded thee: the third is, that thou wilt be a voluntary mute to my design.   Be but duteous, and true preferment shall tender itself to thee.   My revenge is now at Milford: would I had wings to follow it! Come, and be true.   [*Exit.*
• *Pis.*   Thou bid'st me to my loss: for true to thee
Were to prove false, which I will never be,
To him that is most true.   To Milford go,
And find not her whom thou pursuest.   Flow, flow,
You heavenly blessings, on her!   This fool's speed
•Be cross'd with slowness; labour be his meed!
                                        [*Exit.*

SCENE VI.   *Wales.   Before the cave of Belarius.*

Enter IMOGEN, *in boy's clothes.*

  Imo.   I see a man's life is a tedious one:
I have tired myself, and for two nights together
Have made the ground my bed.   I should be sick,
But that my resolution helps me.   Milford,
When from the mountain-top Pisanio show'd thee,
Thou wast within a ken: O Jove!   I think
Foundations fly the wretched; such, I mean,
Where they should be relieved.   Two beggars told me
I could not miss my way: will poor folks lie,
That have afflictions on them, knowing 'tis   10
A punishment or trial?   Yes; no wonder,
•When rich ones scarce tell true.   To lapse in fulness
• Is sorer than to lie for need, and falsehood
Is worse in kings than beggars.   My dear lord!
Thou art one o' the false ones.   Now I think on thee,
My hunger's gone; but even before, I was
At point to sink for food.   But what is this?
Here is a path to't: 'tis some savage hold:
I were best not call; I dare not call: yet famine,
Ere clean it o'erthrow nature, makes it valiant. 20
Plenty and peace breeds cowards: hardness ever
Of hardiness is mother.   Ho! who's here?
If any thing that's civil, speak; if savage,

Take or lend.   Ho! No answer? Then I'll enter.
Best draw my sword; and if mine enemy
But fear the sword like me, he'll scarcely look on't.
Such a foe, good heavens!   [*Exit, to the cave.*

Enter BELARIUS, GUIDERIUS, *and* ARVIRAGUS.

● *Bel.*   You, Polydore, have proved best wood-man and
Are master of the feast: Cadwal and I
Will play the cook and servant; 'tis our match:
The sweat of industry would dry and die,   31
But for the end it works to. Come; our stomachs
Will make what's homely savoury: weariness
Can snore upon the flint, when resty sloth
Finds the down pillow hard. Now peace be here,
●Poor house, that keep'st thyself!
     Gui.   I am throughly weary.
     Arv.   I am weak with toil, yet strong in appe-tite.
● *Gui.*   There is cold meat i' the cave; we'll browse on that,
Whilst what we have kill'd be cook'd.
     Bel. [*Looking into the cave*] Stay; come not in.
But that it eats our victuals, I should think   41
Here were a fairy.
     Gui.   What's the matter, sir?
     Bel.   By Jupiter, an angel! or, if not,
An earthly paragon! Behold divineness
No elder than a boy!

Re-enter IMOGEN.

Imo.   Good masters, harm me not:
Before I enter'd here, I call'd; and thought
To have begg'd or bought what I have took: good troth,
I have stol'n nought, nor would not, though I had found
Gold strew'd i' the floor. Here's money for my meat: 50
I would have left it on the board so soon
As I had made my meal, and parted
With prayers for the provider.
     Gui.   Money, youth?
     Arv.   All gold and silver rather turn to dirt!
As 'tis no better reckon'd, but of those
Who worship dirty gods.
     Imo.   I see you're angry:
Know, if you kill me for my fault, I should
Have died had I not made it.
     Bel.   Whither bound?
     Imo.   To Milford-Haven.
     Bel.   What's your name?   60
● *Imo.*   Fidele, sir. I have a kinsman who
Is bound for Italy; he embark'd at Milford;
To whom being going, almost spent with hunger,
I am fall'n in this offence.
     Bel.   Prithee, fair youth,
Think us no churls, nor measure our good minds
By this rude place we live in. Well encounter'd!
'Tis almost night: you shall have better cheer
Ere you depart; and thanks to stay and eat it.
Boys, bid him welcome.
     Gui.   Were you a woman, youth,
I should woo hard but be your groom. In honesty,   70
I bid for you as I'ld buy.
     Arv.   I'll make't my comfort

28 *woodman.* Hunter.

36 *keep'st thyself.* i.e. empty.

38 *browse.* Nibble.

Belarius: 'By Jupiter, an angel!' Painting by Edward Penny (1714–1791)

61 *Fidele.* i.e. faithful.

77 *prize.* Value, i.e. as heir.

Belarius: 'Fair youth, come in;' Engraving by H. Gravelot from T. Hanmer's edition of Shakespeare's works, 1744

6 *fall'n-off.* Rebellious.

He is a man; I'll love him as my brother:
And such a welcome as I'ld give to him
After long absence, such is yours: most welcome!
Be sprightly, for you fall 'mongst friends.
    Imo.   'Mongst friends,
If brothers. [*Aside*] Would it had been so, that they
Had been my father's sons! then had my **prize**
Been less, and so more equal ballasting
To thee, Posthumus.
    Bel.   He wrings at some distress.
    Gui.   Would I could free't!
    Arv.   Or I, whate'er it be, 80
What pain it cost, what danger.   Gods!
    Bel.   Hark, boys.
                      [*Whispering.*
    Imo. Great men,
That had a court no bigger than this cave,
That did attend themselves and had the virtue
Which their own conscience seal'd them—laying by
That nothing-gift of differing multitudes—
Could not out-peer these twain. Pardon me, gods!
I'ld change my sex to be companion with them,
Since Leonatus's false.
    Bel.   It shall be so.
Boys, we'll go dress our hunt. Fair youth, come in: 90
Discourse is heavy, fasting; when we have supp'd,
We'll mannerly demand thee of thy story,
So far as thou wilt speak it.
    Gui.   Pray, draw near.
    Arv. The night to the owl and morn to the lark less welcome.
    Imo. Thanks, sir.
    Arv. I pray, draw near.   [*Exeunt.*

SCENE VII.   *Rome.   A public place.*

Enter two Senators *and* Tribunes.

    First Sen. This is the tenour of the emperor's writ:
That since the common men are now in action
'Gainst the Pannonians and Dalmatians,
And that the legions now in Gallia are
Full weak to undertake our wars against
The fall'n-off Britons, that we do incite
The gentry to this business.   He creates
Lucius proconsul: and to you the tribunes,
For this immediate levy, he commends
His absolute commission.   Long live Cæsar! 10
    First Tri. Is Lucius general of the forces?
    Sec. Sen.   Ay.
    First Tri. Remaining now in Gallia?
    First Sen.   With those legions
Which I have spoke of, whereunto your levy
Must be supplyant: the words of your commission
Will tie you to the numbers and the time
Of their dispatch.
    First Tri.   We will discharge our duty.
                      [*Exeunt.*

ACT IV.

SCENE I.   *Wales: near the cave of Belarius.*

Enter CLOTEN.

    Clo. I am near to the place where they should meet, if Pisanio have mapped it truly.   How fit his garments serve me ! Why should his mistress, who was made by him that made the tailor, not be fit too? the rather—saving reverence of the ● word—for 'tis said a woman's fitness comes by fits. Therein I must play the workman. I dare speak it to myself—for it is not vain-glory for a man and his glass to confer in his own chamber—I mean, the lines of my body are as well drawn as his ; no less young, more strong, not beneath him in fortunes, beyond him in the advantage of the time, ● above him in birth, alike conversant in general services, and more remarkable in single oppositions : yet this imperceiverant thing loves him in my despite. What mortality is ! Posthumus, thy head, which now is growing upon thy shoulders, shall within this hour be off ; thy mistress enforced ; thy garments cut to pieces before thy face : and all this done, spurn her home to her father ; who may haply be a little angry for my so rough usage ; but my mother, having power of his testiness, shall turn all into my commendations.   My horse is tied up safe : out, sword, and to a sore purpose ! Fortune, put them into my hand ! This is the very description of their meeting-place ; and the fellow dares not deceive me.

[*Exit.*

SCENE II. *Before the cave of Belarius.*

Enter, from the cave, BELARIUS, GUIDERIUS, ARVIRAGUS, *and* IMOGEN.

 Bel. [*To Imogen*] You are not well: remain here in the cave ;
We'll come to you after hunting.
 Arv.   [*To Imogen*] Brother, stay here :
Are we not brothers ?
 Imo.   So man and man should be ;
But clay and clay differs in dignity,
Whose dust is both alike. I am very sick.
 Gui. Go you to hunting ; I'll abide with him.
 Imo. So sick I am not, yet I am not well ;
● But not so citizen a wanton as
To seem to die ere sick : so please you, leave me ;
Stick to your journal course : the breach of custom 10
Is breach of all. I am ill, but your being by me
Cannot amend me ; society is no comfort
To one not sociable : I am not very sick,
Since I can reason of it. Pray you, trust me here :
I'll rob none but myself ; and let me die,
Stealing so poorly.
 Gui.   I love thee ; I have spoke it :
How much the quantity, the weight as much,
As I do love my father.
 Bel.   What ! how ! how !
 Arv. If it be sin to say so, sir, I yoke me
In my good brother's fault : I know not why 20
I love this youth ; and I have heard you say,
Love's reason's without reason : the bier at door,
And a demand who is't shall die, I'ld say
'My father, not this youth.'
 Bel.   [*Aside*] O noble strain !
O worthiness of nature ! breed of greatness !
Cowards father cowards and base things sire base :
Nature hath meal and bran, contempt and grace.
I'm not their father ; yet who this should be,
Doth miracle itself, loved before me.
'Tis the ninth hour o' the morn.
 Arv.   Brother, farewell. 30

6 *fitness.* Amorous inclinations.

13-14 *general services.* Military service.

Belarius: 'You are not well: remain here in the cave ; We'll come to you after hunting.' R. Hatteraff as Arviragus, A. Milroy as Belarius and Nora Lancaster as Imogen, Queen's Theatre, Manchester, 1905

8 *citizen a wanton.* Citified a child.

49 *In characters.* Into letters.

58 *spurs.* Roots.

Costume design for Imogen as a boy by Rene Allio, Royal Shakespeare Co, 1962

Imo. I wish ye sport.
Arv.   You health.   So please you, sir.
Imo. [*Aside*] These are kind creatures. Gods,
   what lies I have heard !
Our courtiers say all's savage but at court :
Experience, O, thou disprovest report !
The imperious seas breed monsters, for the dish
Poor tributary rivers as sweet fish.
I am sick still ; heart-sick.   Pisanio,
I'll now taste of thy drug.   [*Swallows some.*
Gui.   I could not stir him :
He said he was gentle, but unfortunate ;
Dishonestly afflicted, but yet honest.   40
   Arv. Thus did he answer me : yet said, here-
   after
I might know more.
   Bel.   To the field, to the field !
We'll leave you for this time : go in and rest.
   Arv. We'll not be long away.
   Bel.   Pray, be not sick,
For you must be our housewife.
   Imo.   Well or ill,
I am bound to you.
   Bel.   And shalt be ever.
                        [*Exit Imogen, to the cave.*
This youth, howe'er distress'd, appears he hath
   had
Good ancestors.
   Arv.   How angel-like he sings !
   Gui. But his neat cookery ! he cut our roots
•In characters,
And sauced our broths, as Juno had been sick 50
And he her dieter.
   Arv.   Nobly he yokes
A smiling with a sigh, as if the sigh
Was that it was, for not being such a smile ;
The smile mocking the sigh, that it would fly
From so divine a temple, to commix
With winds that sailors rail at.
   Gui.   I do note
That grief and patience, rooted in him both,
•Mingle their spurs together.
   Arv.   Grow, patience !
And let the stinking elder, grief, untwine
His perishing root with the increasing vine ! 60
   Bel. It is great morning. Come, away !—
   Who's there ?

                Enter CLOTEN.

   Clo. I cannot find those runagates ; that villain
Hath mock'd me.   I am faint.
   Bel.   'Those runagates !'
Means he not us ? I partly know him : 'tis
Cloten, the son o' the queen.   I fear some ambush.
I saw him not these many years, and yet
I know 'tis he.   We are held as outlaws : hence !
   Gui. He is but one : you and my brother
   search
What companies are near : pray you, away ;
Let me alone with him.
                [*Exeunt Belarius and Arviragus.*
   Clo.   Soft ! What are you 70
That fly me thus ? some villain mountaineers ?
I have heard of such.   What slave art thou ?
   Gui.   A thing
More slavish did I ne'er than answering
A slave without a knock.
   Clo.   Thou art a robber,
A law-breaker, a villain : yield thee, thief.

Gui.   To who? to thee?   What art thou?
Have not I
An arm as big as thine? a heart as big?
Thy words, I grant, are bigger, for I wear not
My dagger in my mouth.   Say what thou art,
Why I should yield to thee?
Clo.   Thou villain base, 80
Know'st me not by my clothes?
Gui.   No, nor thy tailor, rascal,
Who is thy grandfather: he made those clothes,
Which, as it seems, make thee.
Clo.   Thou precious varlet,
My tailor made them not.
Gui.   Hence, then, and thank
The man that gave them thee.   Thou art some
fool:
I am loath to beat thee.
Clo.   Thou injurious thief,
Hear but my name, and tremble.
Gui.   What's thy name?
Clo.   Cloten, thou villain.
Gui.   Cloten, thou double villain, be thy name,
I cannot tremble at it: were it Toad, or Adder,
Spider,   90
'Twould move me sooner.
Clo.   To thy further fear,
Nay, to thy mere confusion, thou shalt know
I am son to the queen.
Gui.   I am sorry for't; not seeming
So worthy as thy birth.
Clo.   Art not afeard?
Gui.   Those that I reverence those I fear, the
wise:
At fools I laugh, not fear them.
Clo.   Die the death:
When I have slain thee with my proper hand,
I'll follow those that even now fled hence,
And on the gates of Lud's-town set your heads:
Yield, rustic mountaineer. [*Exeunt, fighting.* 100

Re-enter BELARIUS *and* ARVIRAGUS.

Bel.   No companies abroad?
Arv.   None in the world: you did mistake
him, sure.
Bel.   I cannot tell: long is it since I saw him,
• But time hath nothing blurr'd those lines of favour
Which then he wore; the snatches in his voice,
And burst of speaking, were as his: I am absolute
'Twas very Cloten.
Arv.   In this place we left them:
I wish my brother make good time with him,
• You say he is so fell.
Bel.   Being scarce made up,
I mean, to man, he had not apprehension   110
Of roaring terrors; for the effect of judgement
Is oft the cause of fear.   But, see, thy brother.

Re-enter GUIDERIUS, *with* CLOTEN'S *head*.

Gui.   This Cloten was a fool, an empty purse;
There was no money in't: not Hercules
Could have knock'd out his brains, for he had
none:
Yet I not doing this, the fool had borne
My head as I do his.
Bel.   What hast thou done?
• *Gui.*   I am perfect what: cut off one Cloten's
head,
Son to the queen, after his own report;
Who call'd me traitor, mountaineer, and swore 120

104 *lines of favour*. Features.

109 *fell*. Dangerous. *made up*. Mature.

Guiderius with Cloten's head. Jonathan Kent as Guiderius, Royal Shakespeare Co, 1974

118 *perfect*. Fully aware.

121 *take us in.* Conquer us.

139 *make some stronger head.* Gather a larger force.

149 *long forth.* Tedious.

●With his own single hand he 'ld take us in,
Displace our heads where—thank the gods !—they
  grow,
And set them on Lud's-town.
 Bel.   We are all undone.
 Gui. Why, worthy father, what have we to
  lose,
But that he swore to take, our lives ?   The law
Protects not us : then why should we be tender
To let an arrogant piece of flesh threat us,
Play judge and executioner all himself,
For we do fear the law ?   What company
Discover you abroad ?
 Bel.   No single soul   130
Can we set eye on ; but in all safe reason
He must have some attendants.   Though his
  humour
Was nothing but mutation, ay, and that
From one bad thing to worse ; not frenzy, not
Absolute madness could so far have raved
To bring him here alone ; although perhaps
It may be heard at court that such as we
Cave here, hunt here, are outlaws, and in time
●May make some stronger head ; the which he
  hearing—
As it is like him—might break out, and swear 140
He 'ld fetch us in ; yet is 't not probable
To come alone, either he so undertaking,
Or they so suffering : then on good ground we
  fear,
If we do fear this body hath a tail
More perilous than the head.
 Arv.   Let ordinance
Come as the gods foresay it : howsoe'er,
My brother hath done well.
 Bel.   I had no mind
To hunt this day : the boy Fidele's sickness
●Did make my way long forth.
 Gui.   With his own sword,
Which he did wave against my throat, I have
  ta'en   150
His head from him : I 'll throw 't into the creek
Behind our rock ; and let it to the sea,
And tell the fishes he 's the queen's son, Cloten :
That 's all I reck.   [*Exit.*
 Bel.   I fear 'twill be revenged :
Would, Polydore, thou hadst not done 't ! though
  valour
Becomes thee well enough.
 Arv.   Would I had done 't,
So the revenge alone pursued me !   Polydore,
I love thee brotherly, but envy much
Thou hast robb'd me of this deed : I would re-
  venges,
That possible strength might meet, would seek
  us through   160
And put us to our answer.
 Bel.   Well, 'tis done :
We 'll hunt no more to-day, nor seek for danger
Where there 's no profit.   I prithee, to our rock ;
You and Fidele play the cooks : I 'll stay
Till hasty Polydore return, and bring him
To dinner presently.
 Arv.   Poor sick Fidele !
I 'll willingly to him : to gain his colour
I 'ld let a parish of such Clotens blood,
And praise myself for charity.   [*Exit.*
 Bel.   O thou goddess, 169
Thou divine Nature, how thyself thou blazon'st

In these two princely boys! They are as gentle
As zephyrs blowing below the violet,
Not wagging his sweet head; and yet as rough,
●Their royal blood enchafed, as the rudest wind,
That by the top doth take the mountain pine,
And make him stoop to the vale. 'Tis wonder
That an invisible instinct should frame them
To royalty unlearn'd, honour untaught,
Civility not seen from other, valour
That wildly grows in them, but yields a crop 180
As if it had been sow'd. Yet still it's strange
What Cloten's being here to us portends,
Or what his death will bring us.

Re-enter GUIDERIUS.

Gui.   Where's my brother?
●I have sent Cloten's clotpoll down the stream,
In embassy to his mother: his body's hostage
For his return. [*Solemn music.*
Bel.   My ingenious instrument!
Hark, Polydore, it sounds! But what occasion
Hath Cadwal now to give it motion? Hark!
Gui. Is he at home?
Bel.   He went hence even now.
Gui. What does he mean? since death of my
        dear'st mother 190
It did not speak before. All solemn things
Should answer solemn accidents. The matter?
Triumphs for nothing and lamenting toys
Is jollity for apes and grief for boys.
Is Cadwal mad?
Bel   Look, here he comes,
And brings the dire occasion in his arms
Of what we blame him for.

Re-enter ARVIRAGUS, *with* IMOGEN, *as dead,*
bearing her in his arms.

Arv.   The bird is dead
That we have made so much on. I had rather
Have skipp'd from sixteen years of age to sixty,
To have turn'd my leaping-time into a crutch, 200
Than have seen this.
Gui.   O sweetest, fairest lily!
My brother wears thee not the one half so well
As when thou grew'st thyself.
Bel.   O melancholy!
Who ever yet could sound thy bottom? find
●The ooze, to show what coast thy sluggish crare
Might easiliest harbour in? Thou blessed thing!
Jove knows what man thou mightst have made;
        but I,
Thou diedst, a most rare boy, of melancholy.
How found you him?
Arv.   Stark, as you see: 209
Thus smiling, as some fly had tickled slumber,
Not as death's dart, being laugh'd at: his right
        cheek
Reposing on a cushion.
Gui.   Where?
Arv.   O' the floor;
●His arms thus leagued: I thought he slept, and put
●My clouted brogues from off my feet, whose rude-
        ness
Answer'd my steps too loud.
Gui.   Why, he but sleeps:
If he be gone, he'll make his grave a bed;
With female fairies will his tomb be haunted,
And worms will not come to thee.
Arv.   With fairest flowers

174 *enchafed.* Aroused.

184 *clotpoll.* Thick head.

Arviragus: 'The bird is dead That we have made so
much on.' Painting by George Dawe

205 *crare.* Small ship.

213 *leagued.* Crossed.

214 *clouted brogues.* Nailed shoes.

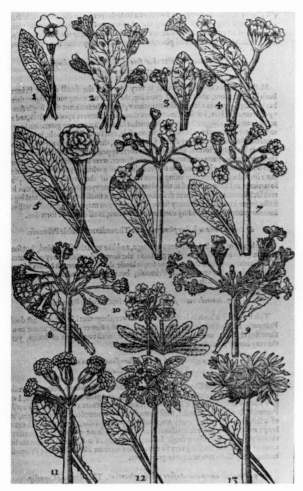

Arviragus: 'thou shalt not lack The flower that's like thy face . . .' Primrose, cowslip and other flowers. Woodcut from John Parkinson's *The Garden of Pleasant Flowers*, 1629

---

223 *eglantine.* Sweet briar.

224 *ruddock.* Robin redbreast.

229 *winter-ground.* Straw.

252 *Thersites.* Cynical Greek. *Ajax.* Valiant Greek (from Homer's *Iliad*).

Whilst summer lasts and I live here, Fidele, 219
I'll sweeten thy sad grave: thou shalt not lack
The flower that's like thy face, pale primrose, nor
The azured harebell, like thy veins, no, nor
● The leaf of eglantine, whom not to slander,
● Out-sweeten'd not thy breath: the ruddock would,
With charitable bill,—O bill, sore-shaming
Those rich-left heirs that let their fathers lie
Without a monument!—bring thee all this;
Yea, and furr'd moss besides, when flowers are none,
● To winter-ground thy corse.
   Gui.   Prithee, have done;
And do not play in wench-like words with that
Which is so serious.   Let us bury him,   231
And not protract with admiration what
Is now due debt.   To the grave!
   Arv.   Say, where shall's lay him?
   Gui.   By good Euriphile, our mother.
   Arv.   Be't so:
And let us, Polydore, though now our voices
Have got the mannish crack, sing him to the ground,
As once our mother; use like note and words,
Save that Euriphile must be Fidele.
   Gui.   Cadwal,
I cannot sing: I'll weep, and word it with thee;
For notes of sorrow out of tune are worse   241
Than priests and fanes that lie.
   Arv.   We'll speak it, then.
   Bel.   Great griefs, I see, medicine the less; for Cloten
Is quite forgot.   He was a queen's son, boys;
And though he came our enemy, remember
He was paid for that: though mean and mighty, rotting
Together, have one dust, yet reverence,
That angel of the world, doth make distinction
Of place 'tween high and low.   Our foe was princely;
And though you took his life, as being our foe,
Yet bury him as a prince.
   Gui.   Pray you, fetch him hither.   251
● Thersites' body is as good as Ajax',
When neither are alive.
   Arv.   If you'll go fetch him,
We'll say our song the whilst.   Brother, begin.
                 [*Exit Belarius.*
   Gui.   Nay, Cadwal, we must lay his head to the east;
My father hath a reason for't.
   Arv.   'Tis true.
   Gui.   Come on then, and remove him.
   Arv.   So.   Begin.

SONG.

   Gui.   Fear no more the heat o' the sun,
      Nor the furious winter's rages;
   Thou thy worldly task hast done,   260
      Home art gone, and ta'en thy wages:
   Golden lads and girls all must,
   As chimney-sweepers, come to dust.

   Arv.   Fear no more the frown o' the great;
      Thou art past the tyrant's stroke;
   Care no more to clothe and eat;
      To thee the reed is as the oak:
   The sceptre, learning, physic, must
   All follow this, and come to dust.

Gui. Fear no more the lightning-flash,   270
Arv.   Nor the all-dreaded thunder-stone;
Gui. Fear not slander, censure rash;
Arv.   Thou hast finish'd joy and moan:
Both. All lovers young, all lovers must
      Consign to thee, and come to dust.

Gui. No exorciser harm thee!
Arv. Nor no witchcraft charm thee!
Gui. Ghost unlaid forbear thee!
Arv. Nothing ill come near thee!
Both. Quiet consummation have;   280
      And renowned be thy grave!

Re-enter BELARIUS, *with the body of* CLOTEN.

Gui. We have done our obsequies: come, lay
    him down.
Bel. Here's a few flowers; but 'bout midnight,
    more:
The herbs that have on them cold dew o' the night
Are strewings fitt'st for graves. Upon their faces.
You were as flowers, now wither'd: even so
These herblets shall, which we upon you strew.
Come on, away: apart upon our knees.
The ground that gave them first has them again:
Their pleasures here are past, so is their pain. 290
    [*Exeunt Belarius, Guiderius, and Arviragus.*
Imo. [*Awaking*] Yes, sir, to Milford-Haven;
    which is the way?—
I thank you.—By yond bush?—Pray, how far
    thither?
●'Ods pittikins! can it be six mile yet?—
I have gone all night. 'Faith, I'll lie down and
    sleep.
But, soft! no bedfellow!—O gods and goddesses!
        [*Seeing the body of Cloten.*
These flowers are like the pleasures of the world;
This bloody man, the care on't. I hope I dream;
For so I thought I was a cave-keeper,
And cook to honest creatures: but 'tis not so;
'Twas but a bolt of nothing, shot at nothing, 300
Which the brain makes of fumes: our very eyes
Are sometimes like our judgements, blind. Good
    faith,
I tremble still with fear: but if there be
Yet left in heaven as small a drop of pity
As a wren's eye, fear'd gods, a part of it!
The dream's here still: even when I wake, it is
Without me, as within me; not imagined, felt.
A headless man! The garments of Posthumus!
I know the shape of's leg: this is his hand;
●His foot Mercurial; his Martial thigh;   310
The brawns of Hercules: but his Jovial face—
Murder in heaven?—How!—'Tis gone. Pisanio,
●All curses madded Hecuba gave the Greeks,
And mine to boot, be darted on thee! Thou,
●Conspired with that irregulous devil, Cloten,
Hast here cut off my lord. To write and read
Be henceforth treacherous! Damn'd Pisanio
Hath with his forged letters,—damn'd Pisanio—
From this most bravest vessel of the world
Struck the main-top! O Posthumus! alas, 320
Where is thy head? where's that? Ay me!
    where's that?
Pisanio might have kill'd thee at the heart,
And left this head on. How should this be?
    Pisanio?
'Tis he and Cloten: malice and lucre in them

293 *'Ods pittikins.* May God have pity.

310 *Mercury.* Messenger of the gods. *Mars.* God of war.

Imogen: 'The brawns of Hercules . . .' Hercules was a Greek demi-god whose name was synonymous with strength. Engraving from a painting by Nicolas Poussin, 1803

313 *Hecuba.* Queen of Troy.

315 *irregulous.* Lawless.

Costume design for Roman soldiers by John Napier with
Martyn Bainbridge and Sue Jenkinson, Royal Shakespeare Co, 1974

325 *pregnant*. Obvious.

337 *confiners*. Inhabitants.

341 *Syenna*. The ruler of Sienna.

•Have laid this woe here.   O, 'tis pregnant, preg-
         nant!
The drug he gave me, which he said was precious
And cordial to me, have I not found it
Murderous to the senses? That confirms it home:
This is Pisanio's deed, and Cloten's: O!
Give colour to my pale cheek with thy blood, 330
That we the horrider may seem to those
Which chance to find us: O, my lord, my lord!
                    [*Falls on the body.*

Enter Lucius, *a* Captain *and other* Officers, *and*
         a Soothsayer.

   Cap. To them the legions garrison'd in Gallia,
After your will, have cross'd the sea, attending
You here at Milford-Haven with your ships:
They are in readiness.
   Luc.   But what from Rome?
• *Cap.*   The senate hath stirr'd up the confiners
And gentlemen of Italy, most willing spirits,
That promise noble service: and they come
Under the conduct of bold Iachimo,   340
•Syenna's brother.
   Luc.   When expect you them?
   Cap. With the next benefit o' the wind.
   Luc.   This forwardness
Makes our hopes fair.   Command our present
         numbers
Be muster'd; bid the captains look to't. Now, sir,
What have you dream'd of late of this war's pur-
         pose?
   Sooth. Last night the very gods show'd me a
         vision—
I fast and pray'd for their intelligence—thus:
I saw Jove's bird, the Roman eagle, wing'd
From the spongy south to this part of the west,
There vanish'd in the sunbeams: which portends—
Unless my sins abuse my divination—
Success to the Roman host.
   Luc.   Dream often so,
And never false.   Soft, ho! what trunk is here
Without his top? The ruin speaks that sometime
It was a worthy building.   How! a page!
Or dead, or sleeping on him? But dead rather;
For nature doth abhor to make his bed
With the defunct, or sleep upon the dead.
Let's see the boy's face.
   Cap.   He's alive, my lord.
   Luc. He'll then instruct us of this body.
         Young one,   360
Inform us of thy fortunes, for it seems
They crave to be demanded.   Who is this
Thou makest thy bloody pillow? Or who was he
That, otherwise than noble nature did,
Hath alter'd that good picture? What's thy in-
         terest
In this sad wreck? How came it? Who is it?
What art thou?
   Imo.   I am nothing: or if not,
Nothing to be were better. This was my master,
A very valiant Briton and a good,
That here by mountaineers lies slain.   Alas! 370
There is no more such masters: I may wander
From east to occident, cry out for service,
Try many, all good, serve truly, never
Find such another master.
   Luc.   'Lack, good youth!
Thou movest no less with thy complaining than

Thy master in bleeding: say his name, good
 friend.
 Imo. Richard du Champ. [*Aside*] If I do lie
 and do
No harm by it, though the gods hear, I hope
They'll pardon it.—Say you, sir?
 Luc.   Thy name?
 Imo.   Fidele, sir.
 Luc. Thou dost approve thyself the very same:
Thy name well fits thy faith, thy faith thy name.
Wilt take thy chance with me? I will not say
Thou shalt be so well master'd, but, be sure,
No less beloved. The Roman emperor's letters,
Sent by a consul to me, should not sooner
● Than thine own worth prefer thee: go with me.
 Imo. I'll follow, sir. But first, an't please
 the gods,
I'll hide my master from the flies, as deep
● As these poor pickaxes can dig; and when
With wild wood-leaves and weeds I ha' strew'd
 his grave,   390
And on it said a century of prayers,
Such as I can, twice o'er, I'll weep and sigh;
And leaving so his service, follow you,
So please you entertain me.
 Luc.   Ay, good youth;
And rather father thee than master thee.
My friends,
The boy hath taught us manly duties: let us
Find out the prettiest daisied plot we can,
● And make him with our pikes and partisans
● A grave: come, arm him. Boy, he is preferr'd
By thee to us, and he shall be interr'd 401
As soldiers can. Be cheerful; wipe thine eyes:
Some falls are means the happier to arise.
             [*Exeunt.*

SCENE III. *A room in Cymbeline's palace.*

Enter CYMBELINE, Lords, PISANIO, *and*
    Attendants.

 Cym. Again; and bring me word how 'tis with
 her.   [*Exit an Attendant.*
A fever with the absence of her son,
A madness, of which her life's in danger. Hea-
 vens,
How deeply you at once do touch me! Imogen,
The great part of my comfort, gone; my queen
Upon a desperate bed, and in a time
When fearful wars point at me; her son gone,
So needful for this present: it strikes me, past
The hope of comfort. But for thee, fellow,
Who needs must know of her departure and 10
Dost seem so ignorant, we'll enforce it from thee
By a sharp torture.
 Pis.   Sir, my life is yours;
I humbly set it at your will; but, for my mistress,
I nothing know where she remains, why gone,
Nor when she purposes return. Beseech your
 highness,
Hold me your loyal servant.
 First Lord.   Good my liege,
The day that she was missing he was here:
I dare be bound he's true and shall perform
All parts of his subjection loyally. For Cloten,
There wants no diligence in seeking him, 20
And will, no doubt, be found.
 Cym.   The time is troublesome.

386 *prefer.* Recommend.

389 *pickaxes.* i.e. fingers and nails.

399 *partisan.* Long-handled pike like a halberd.

400 *arm.* Lift.

Peggy Ashcroft as Imogen. Painting by Anthony Devas,
1957

22 *slip you*. Release you. *jealousy*. Suspicion.

28 *amazed with matter*. Distracted with worries.

Belarius (Tony Church) with Guiderius (Jonathan Kent) and Arviragus (Julian Barnes) Royal Shakespeare Co, 1974

11 *render*. Explanation.

18 *quarter'd*. Camp.

●[*To Pisanio*] We'll slip you for a season; but our jealousy
Does yet depend.
    First Lord.   So please your majesty,
The Roman legions, all from Gallia drawn,
Are landed on your coast, with a supply
Of Roman gentlemen, by the senate sent.
    Cym.   Now for the counsel of my son and queen !
●I am amazed with matter.
    First Lord.   Good my liege,
Your preparation can affront no less
Than what you hear of: come more, for more you're ready :   30
The want is but to put those powers in motion
That long to move.
    Cym.   I thank you.   Let's withdraw ;
And meet the time as it seeks us.   We fear not
What can from Italy annoy us ; but
We grieve at chances here.   Away!
                  [*Exeunt all but Pisanio.*
    Pis.   I heard no letter from my master since
I wrote him Imogen was slain: 'tis strange :
Nor hear I from my mistress, who did promise
To yield me often tidings: neither know I
What is betid to Cloten; but remain   40
Perplex'd in all.   The heavens still must work.
Wherein I am false I am honest; not true, to be true.
These present wars shall find I love my country,
Even to the note o' the king, or I 'll fall in them.
All other doubts, by time let them be clear'd :
Fortune brings in some boats that are not steer'd.
                        [*Exit.*

SCENE IV.   *Wales: before the cave of Belarius.*

Enter BELARIUS, GUIDERIUS, *and* ARVIRAGUS.

    Gui.   The noise is round about us.
    Bel.   Let us from it.
    Arv.   What pleasure, sir, find we in life, to lock it
From action and adventure?
    Gui.   Nay, what hope
Have we in hiding us?   This way, the Romans
Must or for Britons slay us, or receive us
For barbarous and unnatural revolts
During their use, and slay us after.
    Bel.   Sons,
We'll higher to the mountains; there secure us.
To the king's party there's no going: newness
Of Cloten's death—we being not known, not muster'd   10
●Among the bands—may drive us to a render
Where we have lived, and so extort from 's that
Which we have done, whose answer would be death
Drawn on with torture.
    Gui.   This is, sir, a doubt
In such a time nothing becoming you,
Nor satisfying us.
    Arv.   It is not likely
That when they hear the Roman horses neigh,
●Behold their quarter'd fires, have both their eyes
And ears so cloy'd importantly as now,
That they will waste their time upon our note, 20
To know from whence we are.
    Bel.   O, I am known

Of many in the army: many years,
●Though Cloten then but young, you see, not
    wore him
From my remembrance. And, besides, the king
Hath not deserved my service nor your loves;
Who find in my exile the want of breeding,
The certainty of this hard life; aye hopeless
To have the courtesy your cradle promised,
●But to be still hot summer's tanlings and
The shrinking slaves of winter.
    Gui.   Than be so   30
Better to cease to be. Pray, sir, to the army:
I and my brother are not known; yourself
●So out of thought, and thereto so o'ergrown,
Cannot be question'd.
    Arv.   By this sun that shines,
I'll thither: what thing is it that I never
Did see man die! scarce ever look'd on blood,
But that of coward hares, hot goats, and venison!
Never bestrid a horse, save one that had
A rider like myself, who ne'er wore rowel
Nor iron on his heel! I am ashamed   40
To look upon the holy sun, to have
The benefit of his blest beams, remaining
So long a poor unknown.
    Gui.   By heavens, I'll go:
If you will bless me, sir, and give me leave,
I'll take the better care, but if you will not,
The hazard therefore due fall on me by
The hands of Romans!
    Arv.   So say I: amen.
    Bel. No reason I, since of your lives you set
So slight a valuation, should reserve
●My crack'd one to more care. Have with you,
    boys!   50
If in your country wars you chance to die,
That is my bed too, lads, and there I'll lie:
Lead, lead. [*Aside*] The time seems long; their
    blood thinks scorn,
Till it fly out and show them princes born.
                        [*Exeunt.*

ACT V.

Scene I. *Britain. The Roman camp.*

Enter Posthumus, *with a bloody handkerchief.*

    Post. Yea, bloody cloth, I'll keep thee, for I
    wish'd
Thou shouldst be colour'd thus. You married ones,
If each of you should take this course, how many
Must murder wives much better than themselves
●For wrying but a little! O Pisanio!
Every good servant does not all commands:
No bond but to do just ones. Gods! if you
Should have ta'en vengeance on my faults, I never
Had lived to put on this: so had you saved
The noble Imogen to repent, and struck   10
Me, wretch more worth your vengeance. But,
    alack,
You snatch some hence for little faults; that's
    love,
To have them fall no more: you some permit
†To second ills with ills, each elder worse,
And make them dread it, to the doers' thrift.
But Imogen is your own: do your best wills,
And make me blest to obey! I am brought hither
Among the Italian gentry, and to fight
Against my lady's kingdom: 'tis enough

23 *not wore him.* Did not erase him.

29 *tanlings.* Sunburned victims.

33 *o'ergrown.* Grown out of memory.

50 *crack'd.* i.e. with age.

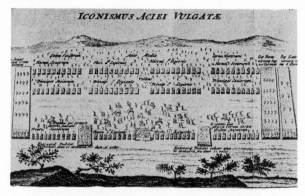

A plan of a Roman camp. Engraving from Basil Kennett's
Romae Antiquae Notitia, 1769

5 *wrying.* Straying.

32 *guise*. Practice.

Iachimo disarmed by Posthumus. Drawing by Robert
Smirke (1752–1845)

---

4 *carl*. Peasant.

17–18 *or betimes Let's*. Let us immediately either.

That, Britain, I have kill'd thy mistress; peace!
I'll give no wound to thee. Therefore, good
    heavens,   21
Hear patiently my purpose: I'll disrobe me
Of these Italian weeds and suit myself
As does a Briton peasant: so I'll fight
Against the part I come with; so I'll die
For thee, O Imogen, even for whom my life
Is every breath a death; and thus, unknown,
Pitied nor hated, to the face of peril
Myself I'll dedicate.   Let me make men know
More valour in me than my habits show.   30
Gods, put the strength o' the Leonati in me!
• To shame the guise o' the world, I will begin
The fashion, less without and more within. [*Exit.*

SCENE II.   *Field of battle between the British
            and Roman camps.*

Enter, from one side, LUCIUS, IACHIMO, *and
    the* Roman Army; *from the other side, the*
    British Army; LEONATUS POSTHUMUS *fol-
    lowing, like a poor soldier.   They march over
    and go out.   Then enter again, in skirmish,*
    IACHIMO *and* POSTHUMUS: *he vanquisheth
    and disarmeth* IACHIMO, *and then leaves him.*

Iach.   The heaviness and guilt within my
    bosom
Takes off my manhood: I have belied a lady,
The princess of this country, and the air on't
• Revengingly enfeebles me; or could this carl,
A very drudge of nature's, have subdued me
In my profession? Knighthoods and honours,
    borne
As I wear mine, are titles but of scorn.
If that thy gentry, Britain, go before
This lout as he exceeds our lords, the odds
Is that we scarce are men and you are gods.   10
                                            [*Exit.*

The battle continues; the Britons *fly;* CYMBE-
    LINE *is taken: then enter, to his rescue,*
    BELARIUS, GUIDERIUS, *and* ARVIRAGUS.

Bel.   Stand, stand! We have the advantage
    of the ground:
The lane is guarded: nothing routs us but
The villany of our fears.
    Gui. }
    Arv. }   Stand, stand, and fight!

Re-enter POSTHUMUS, *and seconds the* Britons:
    they rescue CYMBELINE, *and exeunt.   Then
    re-enter* LUCIUS, *and* IACHIMO, *with* IMOGEN.

Luc.   Away, boy, from the troops, and save
    thyself;
For friends kill friends, and the disorder's such
As war were hoodwink'd.
    Iach.   'Tis their fresh supplies.
• *Luc.*   It is a day turn'd strangely: or betimes
Let's re-inforce, or fly.   [*Exeunt.*

SCENE III.   *Another part of the field.*

Enter POSTHUMUS *and a* British Lord.

Lord.   Camest thou from where they made
    the stand?
Post.   I did:
Though you, it seems, come from the fliers.
    Lord.   I did.

Post. No blame be to you, sir; for all was lost,
But that the heavens fought: the king himself
Of his wings destitute, the army broken,
And but the backs of Britons seen, all flying
Through a strait lane; the enemy full-hearted,
Lolling the tongue with slaughtering, having work
More plentiful than tools to do't, struck down 9
Some mortally, some slightly touch'd, some falling
Merely through fear; that the strait pass was damm'd
With dead men hurt behind, and cowards living
To die with lengthen'd shame.
    Lord. Where was this lane?
    Post. Close by the battle, ditch'd, and wall'd with turf;
Which gave advantage to an ancient soldier,
An honest one, I warrant; who deserved
So long a breeding as his white beard came to,
In doing this for's country: athwart the lane,
He, with two striplings—lads more like to run 19
The country base than to commit such slaughter;
With faces fit for masks, or rather fairer
Than those for preservation cased, or shame,—
Made good the passage; cried to those that fled,
'Our Britain's harts die flying, not our men:
To darkness fleet souls that fly backwards. Stand;
Or we are Romans and will give you that
Like beasts which you shun beastly, and may save,
But to look back in frown: stand, stand.' These three,
Three thousand confident, in act as many—
For three performers are the file when all 30
The rest do nothing—with this word 'Stand, stand,'
Accommodated by the place, more charming
With their own nobleness, which could have turn'd
A distaff to a lance, gilded pale looks,
Part shame, part spirit renew'd; that some, turn'd coward
But by example—O, a sin in war,
Damn'd in the first beginners!—gan to look
The way that they did, and to grin like lions
Upon the pikes o' the hunters. Then began
A stop i' the chaser, a retire, anon 40
A rout, confusion thick; forthwith they fly
Chickens, the way which they stoop'd eagles; slaves,
The strides they victors made: and now our cowards,
Like fragments in hard voyages, became
The life o' the need: having found the back-door open
Of the unguarded hearts, heavens, how they wound!
Some slain before; some dying; some their friends
O'er-borne i' the former wave: ten, chased by one,
Are now each one the slaughter-man of twenty:
Those that would die or ere resist are grown 50
The mortal bugs o' the field.
    Lord. This was strange chance:
A narrow lane, an old man, and two boys.
    Post. Nay, do not wonder at it: you are made
Rather to wonder at the things you hear
Than to work any. Will you rhyme upon't,
And vent it for a mockery? Here is one:
'Two boys, an old man twice a boy, a lane,
Preserved the Britons, was the Romans' bane.'

20 *base.* Safe 'home' in a ball game.

25 *darkness.* Hell.

34 *distaff to a lance.* i.e. a housewife into a soldier.

44 *fragments.* Scraps of food.

45 *The life o' the need.* Essential to life.

79 *answer*. Punishment.

Lord.   Nay, be not angry, sir.
Post.   'Lack, to what end?
Who dares not stand his foe, I'll be his friend;   60
For if he'll do as he is made to do,
I know he'll quickly fly my friendship too.
You have put me into rhyme.
Lord.   Farewell; you're angry.
Post.   Still going? [*Exit Lord.*] This is a
      lord!   O noble misery,
To be i' the field, and ask 'what news?' of me!
To-day how many would have given their honours
To have saved their carcases! took heel to do't,
And yet died too! I, in mine own woe charm'd,
Could not find death where I did hear him groan,
Nor feel him where he struck: being an ugly
      monster,   70
'Tis strange he hides him in fresh cups, soft beds,
Sweet words; or hath more ministers than we
That draw his knives i' the war.   Well, I will
      find him:
For being now a favourer to the Briton,
No more a Briton, I have resumed again
The part I came in: fight I will no more,
But yield me to the veriest hind that shall
Once touch my shoulder.   Great the slaughter is
• Here made by the Roman; great the answer be
Britons must take.   For me, my ransom's death;
On either side I come to spend my breath;   81
Which neither here I'll keep nor bear again,
But end it by some means for Imogen.

Enter two British Captains *and* Soldiers.

First Cap.   Great Jupiter be praised!   Lucius
      is taken.
'Tis thought the old man and his sons were angels.
Sec. Cap.   There was a fourth man, in a silly
      habit,
That gave the affront with them.
First Cap.   So 'tis reported:
But none of 'em can be found.   Stand! who's
      there?
Post.   A Roman,
Who had not now been drooping here, if seconds
Had answer'd him.
Sec. Cap.   Lay hands on him; a dog!   91
A leg of Rome shall not return to tell
What crows have peck'd them here.   He brags
      his service
As if he were of note: bring him to the king.

Enter CYMBELINE, BELARIUS, GUIDERIUS, AR-
      VIRAGUS, PISANIO, Soldiers, Attendants, *and*
      Roman Captives.   *The* Captains *present* POST-
      HUMUS *to* CYMBELINE, *who delivers him over
      to a* Gaoler: *then exeunt omnes.*

SCENE IV.   *A British prison.*

Enter POSTHUMUS *and two* Gaolers.

First Gaol.   You shall not now be stol'n, you
      have locks upon you;
So graze as you find pasture.
Sec. Gaol.   Ay, or a stomach.
                        [*Exeunt Gaolers.*
Post.   Most welcome, bondage! for thou art
      a way,
I think, to liberty: yet am I better
Than one that's sick o' the gout; since he had
      rather

Groan so in perpetuity than be cured
By the sure physician, death, who is the key
To unbar these locks.   My conscience, thou art
    fetter'd
More than my shanks and wrists: you good gods,
    give me
The penitent instrument to pick that bolt,   10
Then, free for ever!   Is't enough I am sorry?
So children temporal fathers do appease;
Gods are more full of mercy.   Must I repent?
• I cannot do it better than in gyves,
Desired more than constrain'd: to satisfy,
If of my freedom 'tis the main part, take
No stricter render of me than my all.
I know you are more clement than vile men,
Who of their broken debtors take a third,
A sixth, a tenth, letting them thrive again   20
On their abatement: that's not my desire:
For Imogen's dear life take mine; and though
'Tis not so dear, yet 'tis a life; you coin'd it:
'Tween man and man they weigh not every stamp;
Though light, take pieces for the figure's sake:
You rather mine, being yours: and so, great
    powers,
If you will take this audit, take this life,
And cancel these cold bonds.   O Imogen!
I'll speak to thee in silence.   [*Sleeps.*

Solemn music.   Enter, as in an apparition,
Sicilius Leonatus, *father to Posthumus, an
old man, attired like a warrior; leading in
his hand an ancient matron, his wife, and
mother to Posthumus, with music before them:
then, after other music, follow the two young*
Leonati, *brothers to Posthumus, with wounds
as they died in the wars.   They circle* Posthumus *round, as he lies sleeping.*

• *Sici.*   No more, thou thunder-master, show   30
      Thy spite on mortal flies:
   With Mars fall out, with Juno chide,
      That thy adulteries
•   Rates and revenges.
   Hath my poor boy done aught but well,
      Whose face I never saw?
   I died whilst in the womb he stay'd
      Attending nature's law:
   Whose father then, as men report
      Thou orphans' father art,   40
   Thou shouldst have been, and shielded him
•   From this earth-vexing smart.

• *Moth.* Lucina lent not me her aid,
•   But took me in my throes;
   That from me was Posthumus ript,
      Came crying 'mongst his foes,
      A thing of pity!

Sici.   Great nature, like his ancestry,
      Moulded the stuff so fair,
   That he deserved the praise o' the world,
      As great Sicilius' heir.   51

First Bro. When once he was mature for man,
      In Britain where was he
   That could stand up his parallel;
      Or fruitful object be
   In eye of Imogen, that best
      Could deem his dignity?

14 *gyves.* Shackles.

Elizabethan representation of a classical warrior. Woodcut from *New and Singular patterns to make divers sorts
of Lace,* 1591

30 *thunder-master.* i.e. Jove, king of the gods.

34 *Rates.* Berates.

42 *earth-vexing smart.* i.e. the stings of life.

43 *Lucina.* Goddess of childbirth.

44 *in my throes.* Childbirth.

60 *Leonati seat*. The home of the Leonati family.

67 *geck*. Dupe.

75 *Like hardiment*. Similar valiant actions.

Costume design for Jupiter by Rene Allio, Royal Shakespeare Co, 1962

97 *Elysium*. Greek paradise.

Moth. With marriage wherefore was he mock'd,
  To be exiled, and thrown
    From Leonati seat, and cast   60
    From her his dearest one,
      Sweet Imogen?

Sici. Why did you suffer Iachimo,
    Slight thing of Italy,
  To taint his nobler heart and brain
    With needless jealousy;
    And to become the geck and scorn
      O' th' other's villany?

Sec. Bro.   For this from stiller seats we came,
    Our parents and us twain,   70
  That striking in our country's cause
    Fell bravely and were slain,
  Our fealty and Tenantius' right
    With honour to maintain.

First Bro.   Like hardiment Posthumus hath
    To Cymbeline perform'd:
  Then, Jupiter, thou king of gods,
    Why hast thou thus adjourn'd
  The graces for his merits due,
    Being all to dolours turn'd?   80

Sici. Thy crystal window ope; look out;
    No longer exercise
  Upon a valiant race thy harsh
    And potent injuries.

Moth. Since, Jupiter, our son is good,
    Take off his miseries.
Sici. Peep through thy marble mansion; help;
    Or we poor ghosts will cry
  To the shining synod of the rest
    Against thy deity.   90

Both Bro. Help, Jupiter; or we appeal,
    And from thy justice fly.

JUPITER *descends in thunder and lightning,
sitting upon an eagle: he throws a thunderbolt. The Ghosts fall on their knees.*

Jup. No more, you petty spirits of region low,
  Offend our hearing; hush! How dare you
    ghosts
Accuse the thunderer, whose bolt, you know,
  Sky-planted batters all rebelling coasts?
Poor shadows of Elysium, hence, and rest
  Upon your never-withering banks of flowers:
Be not with mortal accidents opprest;
  No care of yours it is; you know 'tis ours.   100
Whom best I love I cross; to make my gift,
  The more delay'd, delighted.   Be content;
Your low-laid son our godhead will uplift:
  His comforts thrive, his trials well are spent.
Our Jovial star reign'd at his birth, and in
  Our temple was he married.   Rise, and fade.
He shall be lord of lady Imogen,
  And happier much by his affliction made.
This tablet lay upon his breast, wherein
  Our pleasure his full fortune doth confine: 110
And so, away: no further with your din
  Express impatience, lest you stir up mine.
  Mount, eagle, to my palace crystalline.
                              [*Ascends.*
Sici. He came in thunder; his celestial breath
Was sulphurous to smell: the holy eagle

Stoop'd, as to foot us: his ascension is
More sweet than our blest fields: his royal bird
●Prunes the immortal wing and cloys his beak,
As when his god is pleased.
    All.   Thanks, Jupiter!
    Sici. The marble pavement closes, he is
    enter'd   120
His radiant roof. Away! and, to be blest,
Let us with care perform his great behest.
                       [The Ghosts vanish.
    Post. [Waking] Sleep, thou hast been a grand-
    sire, and begot
A father to me; and thou hast created
A mother and two brothers: but, O scorn!
Gone! they went hence so soon as they were
    born:
And so I am awake. Poor wretches that depend
On greatness' favour dream as I have done,
Wake and find nothing. But, alas, I swerve:
Many dream not to find, neither deserve,   130
And yet are steep'd in favours; so am I,
That have this golden chance and know not why.
What fairies haunt this ground? A book? O
    rare one!
●Be not, as is our fangled world, a garment
Nobler than that it covers: let thy effects
So follow, to be most unlike our courtiers,
As good as promise.
    [Reads] 'When as a lion's whelp shall, to himself
unknown, without seeking find, and be embraced
by a piece of tender air; and when from a stately
cedar shall be lopped branches, which, being
dead many years, shall after revive, be jointed
to the old stock and freshly grow; then shall
Posthumus end his miseries, Britain be fortunate
and flourish in peace and plenty.'
'Tis still a dream, or else such stuff as madmen
Tongue and brain not; either both or nothing;
Or senseless speaking or a speaking such
As sense cannot untie. Be what it is,
The action of my life is like it, which   150
I'll keep, if but for sympathy.

          Re-enter Gaolers.

    First Gaol. Come, sir, are you ready for
death?
    Post. Over-roasted rather; ready long ago.
    First Gaol. Hanging is the word, sir: if you
be ready for that, you are well cooked.
    Post. So, if I prove a good repast to the
spectators, the dish pays the shot.
    First Gaol. A heavy reckoning for you, sir.
But the comfort is, you shall be called to no
more payments, fear no more tavern-bills; which
are often the sadness of parting, as the procuring
of mirth: you come in faint for want of meat,
depart reeling with too much drink; sorry that
you have paid too much, and sorry that you are
●paid too much; purse and brain both empty;
the brain the heavier for being too light, the
purse too light, being drawn of heaviness: of
this contradiction you shall now be quit. O,
the charity of a penny cord! it sums up thousands in a trice: you have no true debitor and
creditor but it; of what's past, is, and to come,
the discharge: your neck, sir, is pen, book and
counters; so the acquittance follows.
    Post. I am merrier to die than thou art
to live.

118 *Prunes.* Preens. *cloys.* Clatters.

Costume design for Leonatus Posthumus by J. Gower
Parks, Stratford-upon-Avon, 1937

134 *fangled.* Fancy.

166 *paid.* Punished.

First Gaoler: 'Unless a man would marry a gallows and beget young gibbets . . .' A gibbet of hanged men. Engraving from F. W. Fairholt from J. O. Halliwell's edition of Shakespeare's works, 1853–1865

---

180 *officer.* Executioner.

5 *targes of proof.* Armoured shields.

First Gaol. Indeed, sir, he that sleeps feels not the tooth-ache : but a man that were to sleep your sleep, and a hangman to help him to bed, ● I think he would change places with his officer; for, look you, sir, you know not which way you shall go.

Post. Yes, indeed do I, fellow.

First Gaol. Your death has eyes in 's head then; I have not seen him so pictured: you must either be directed by some that take upon them to know, or to take upon yourself that which I am sure you do not know, or jump the after inquiry on your own peril: and how you shall speed in your journey's end, I think you'll never return to tell one.   191

Post. I tell thee, fellow, there. are none want eyes to direct them the way I am going, but such as wink and will not use them.

First Gaol. What an infinite mock is this, that a man should have the best use of eyes to see the way of blindness! I am sure hanging's the way of winking.

Enter a Messenger.

Mess. Knock off his manacles; bring your prisoner to the king.   200

Post. Thou bring'st good news; I am called to be made free.

First Gaol. I'll be hang'd then.

Post. Thou shalt be then freer than a gaoler; no bolts for the dead.

                    [*Exeunt all but the First Gaoler.*

First Gaol. Unless a man would marry a gallows and beget young gibbets, I never saw one so prone. Yet, on my conscience, there are verier knaves desire to live, for all he be a Roman: and there be some of them too that die against their wills; so should I, if I were one. I would we were all of one mind, and one mind good; O, there were desolation of gaolers and gallowses! I speak against my present profit, but my wish hath a preferment in 't.   [*Exit.*

SCENE V. *Cymbeline's tent.*

Enter CYMBELINE, BELARIUS, GUIDERIUS, AR-VIRAGUS, PISANIO, Lords, Officers, *and* At-tendants.

Cym.   Stand by my side, you whom the gods have made
Preservers of my throne.   Woe is my heart
That the poor soldier that so richly fought,
Whose rags shamed gilded arms, whose naked breast
● Stepp'd before targes of proof, cannot be found:
He shall be happy that can find him, if
Our grace can make him so.
Bel.   I never saw
Such noble fury in so poor a thing;
Such precious deeds in one that promised nought
But beggary and poor looks.
Cym.   No tidings of him? 10
Pis.   He hath been search'd among the dead and living,
But no trace of him.
Cym.   To my grief, I am
The heir of his reward; [*To Belarius, Guiderius, and Arviragus*] which I will add
To you, the liver, heart and brain of Britain,

By whom I grant she lives.   'Tis now the time
To ask of whence you are.   Report it.
   Bel.   Sir,
In Cambria are we born, and gentlemen:
Further to boast were neither true nor modest,
Unless I add, we are honest.
   Cym.   Bow your knees.
Arise my knights o' the battle: I create you   20
Companions to our person and will fit you
With dignities becoming your estates.

        Enter CORNELIUS *and* Ladies.

There's business in these faces.   Why so sadly
Greet you our victory? you look like Romans,
And not o' the court of Britain.
   Cor.   Hail, great king!
To sour your happiness, I must report
The queen is dead.
   Cym.   Who worse than a physician
Would this report become?   But I consider,
By medicine life may be prolong'd, yet death
Will seize the doctor too.   How ended she?   30
   Cor.   With horror, madly dying, like her life,
Which, being cruel to the world, concluded
Most cruel to herself.   What she confess'd
I will report, so please you: these her women
Can trip me, if I err; who with wet cheeks
Were present when she finish'd.
   Cym.   Prithee, say.
   Cor.   First, she confess'd she never loved you,
     only
Affected greatness got by you, not you:
Married your royalty, was wife to your place;
Abhorr'd your person.
   Cym.   She alone knew this;   40
And, but she spoke it dying, I would not
Believe her lips in opening it.   Proceed.
  ● *Cor.*   Your daughter, whom she bore in hand
     to love
With such integrity, she did confess
Was as a scorpion to her sight; whose life,
But that her flight prevented it, she had
Ta'en off by poison.
   Cym.   O most delicate fiend!
Who is't can read a woman?   Is there more?
   Cor.   More, sir, and worse.   She did confess
     she had
For you a mortal mineral; which, being took, 50
Should by the minute feed on life and lingering
By inches waste you: in which time she pur-
     posed,
By watching, weeping, tendance, kissing, to
O'ercome you with her show, and in time,
When she had fitted you with her craft, to work
Her son into the adoption of the crown:
But, failing of her end by his strange absence,
Grew shameless-desperate; open'd, in despite
Of heaven and men, her purposes; repented
The evils she hatch'd were not effected; so   60
Despairing died.
   Cym.   Heard you all this, her women?
   First Lady.   We did, so please your highness.
   Cym.   Mine eyes
Were not in fault, for she was beautiful;
Mine ears, that heard her flattery; nor my heart,
That thought her like her seeming; it had been
     vicious
To have mistrusted her: yet, O my daughter!

43 *bore in hand.* Pretended.

Costume design for Lucius by John Napier with Martyn Bainbridge and Sue Jenkinson, Royal Shakespeare Co, 1974

87 *occasions.* Needs.

88 *feat.* Dexterous.

93 *favour.* Face.

That it was folly in me, thou mayst say,
And prove it in thy feeling.   Heaven mend all!

Enter LUCIUS, IACHIMO, *the* Soothsayer, *and
other* Roman Prisoners, *guarded;* POSTHUMUS
behind, and IMOGEN.

Thou comest not, Caius, now for tribute; that 69
The Britons have razed out, though with the loss
Of many a bold one; whose kinsmen have made
    suit
That their good souls may be appeased with
    slaughter
Of you their captives, which ourself have granted:
So think of your estate.
    Luc.   Consider, sir, the chance of war: the day
Was yours by accident; had it gone with us,
We should not, when the blood was cool, have
    threaten'd
Our prisoners with the sword.   But since the gods
Will have it thus, that nothing but our lives
May be call'd ransom, let it come: sufficeth 80
A Roman with a Roman's heart can suffer:
Augustus lives to think on't: and so much
For my peculiar care.   This one thing only
I will entreat; my boy, a Briton born,
Let him be ransom'd: never master had
A page so kind, so duteous, diligent,
● So tender over his occasions, true,
● So feat, so nurse-like: let his virtue join
With my request, which I'll make bold your
    highness
Cannot deny; he hath done no Briton harm, 90
Though he have served a Roman: save him, sir,
And spare no blood beside.
    Cym.   I have surely seen him:
● His favour is familiar to me.   Boy,
Thou hast look'd thyself into my grace,
†And art mine own.   I know not why, wherefore,
To say 'live, boy:' ne'er thank thy master; live:
And ask of Cymbeline what boon thou wilt,
Fitting my bounty and thy state, I'll give it;
Yea, though thou do demand a prisoner,
The noblest ta'en.
    Imo.   I humbly thank your highness. 100
    Luc.   I do not bid thee beg my life, good lad;
And yet I know thou wilt.
    Imo.   No, no: alack,
There's other work in hand: I see a thing
Bitter to me as death: your life, good master,
Must shuffle for itself.
    Luc.   The boy disdains me,
He leaves me, scorns me: briefly die their joys
That place them on the truth of girls and boys.
Why stands he so perplex'd?
    Cym.   What wouldst thou, boy?
I love thee more and more: think more and more
What's best to ask.   Know'st him thou look'st
    on? speak,   110
Wilt have him live?   Is he thy kin? thy friend?
    Imo.   He is a Roman; no more kin to me
Than I to your highness; who, being born your
    vassal,
Am something nearer.
    Cym.   Wherefore eyest him so?
    Imo.   I'll tell you, sir, in private, if you please
To give me hearing.
    Cym.   Ay, with all my heart,
And lend my best attention.   What's thy name?
    Imo.   Fidele, sir.

Cym.   Thou'rt my good youth, my page;
I'll be thy master: walk with me; speak freely.
      [*Cymbeline and Imogen converse apart.*
    Bel. Is not this boy revived from death?
    Arv.   One sand another 120
Not more resembles that sweet rosy lad
Who died, and was Fidele.   What think you?
    Gui. The same dead thing alive.
    Bel. Peace, peace! see further; he eyes us
not; forbear;
Creatures may be alike: were't he, I am sure
He would have spoke to us.
    Gui.   But we saw him dead.
    Bel. Be silent; let's see further.
    Pis.   [*Aside*] It is my mistress:
Since she is living, let the time run on
To good or bad.
      [*Cymbeline and Imogen come forward.*
    Cym.   Come, stand thou by our side;
Make thy demand aloud. [*To Iachimo*] Sir,
    step you forth;   130
Give answer to this boy, and do it freely;
Or, by our greatness and the grace of it,
Which is our honour, bitter torture shall
Winnow the truth from falsehood.   On, speak to
    him.
    Imo. My boon is, that this gentleman may
    render
Of whom he had this ring.
    Post.   [*Aside*] What's that to him?
    Cym. That diamond upon your finger, say
How came it yours?
    Iach. Thou'lt torture me to leave unspoken
    that
Which, to be spoke, would torture thee.
    Cym.   How! me? 140
    Iach. I am glad to be constrain'd to utter that
Which torments me to conceal.   By villany
I got this ring: 'twas Leonatus' jewel;
Whom thou didst banish; and—which more may
    grieve thee,
As it doth me—a nobler sir ne'er lived
'Twixt sky and ground.   Wilt thou hear more,
    my lord?
    Cym. All that belongs to this.
    Iach.   That paragon, thy daughter,—
For whom my heart drops blood, and my false
    spirits
Quail to remember— Give me leave; I faint.
    Cym. My daughter! what of her?   Renew
    thy strength: 150
I had rather thou shouldst live while nature will
Than die ere I hear more: strive, man, and speak.
    Iach. Upon a time,—unhappy was the clock
That struck the hour!—it was in Rome,—ac-
    cursed
The mansion where!—'twas at a feast,—O, would
Our viands had been poison'd, or at least
Those which I heaved to head!—the good Post-
    humus—
What should I say? he was too good to be
Where ill men were; and was the best of all
Amongst the rarest of good ones,—sitting sadly,
Hearing us praise our loves of Italy   161
For beauty that made barren the swell'd boast
Of him that best could speak, for feature, laming
The shrine of Venus, or straight-pight Minerva,
Postures beyond brief nature, for condition,
A shop of all the qualities that man

Iachimo: '... laming The shrine of Venus...' Venus the Roman goddess of love. Engraving from a painting by Nicolas Poussin, 1803

185 *In suit.* By courtship.

189 *carbuncle.* Ruby or garnet.

Costume design for Iachimo by J. Gower-Parks
Stratford-upon-Avon, 1937

190 *Of Phœbus' wheel.* From the wheel of the sun-god's chariot.

199 *practice.* Scheming.

200 *simular.* Counterfeit.

Loves woman for, besides that hook of wiving,
Fairness which strikes the eye—
   Cym.   I stand on fire:
Come to the matter.
   Iach.   All too soon I shall,
Unless thou wouldst grieve quickly. This Post-
    humus,   170
Most like a noble lord in love and one
That had a royal lover, took his hint;
And, not dispraising whom we praised,—therein
He was as calm as virtue—he began
His mistress' picture; which by his tongue being
    made,
And then a mind put in't, either our brags
Were crack'd of kitchen-trulls, or his description
Proved us unspeaking sots.
   Cym.   Nay, nay, to the purpose.
   Iach. Your daughter's chastity—there it begins.
He spake of her, as Dian had hot dreams, 180
And she alone were cold: whereat I, wretch,
Made scruple of his praise; and wager'd with him
Pieces of gold 'gainst this which then he wore
Upon his honour'd finger, to attain
• In suit the place of's bed and win this ring
By hers and mine adultery. He, true knight,
No lesser of her honour confident
Than I did truly find her, stakes this ring;
• And would so, had it been a carbuncle 189
• Of Phœbus' wheel, and might so safely, had it
Been all the worth of's car. Away to Britain
Post I in this design: well may you, sir,
Remember me at court; where I was taught
Of your chaste daughter the wide difference
'Twixt amorous and villanous. Being thus
    quench'd
Of hope, not longing, mine Italian brain
'Gan in your duller Britain operate
Most vilely; for my vantage, excellent:
• And, to be brief, my practice so prevail'd,
• That I return'd with simular proof enough 200
To make the noble Leonatus mad,
By wounding his belief in her renown
With tokens thus, and thus; averring notes
Of chamber-hanging, pictures, this her bracelet,—
O cunning, how I got it!—nay, some marks
Of secret on her person, that he could not
But think her bond of chastity quite crack'd,
I having ta'en the forfeit. Whereupon—
Methinks, I see him now—
   Post.   [*Advancing*] Ay, so thou dost,
Italian fiend! Ay me, most credulous fool, 210
Egregious murderer, thief, any thing
That's due to all the villains past, in being,
To come! O, give me cord, or knife, or poison,
Some upright justicer! Thou, king, send out
For torturers ingenious: it is I
That all the abhorred things o' the earth amend
By being worse than they. I am Posthumus,
That kill'd thy daughter:—villain-like, I lie—
That caused a lesser villain than myself,
A sacrilegious thief, to do't: the temple 220
Of virtue was she; yea, and she herself.
Spit, and throw stones, cast mire upon me, set
The dogs o' the street to bay me: every villain
Be call'd Posthumus Leonatus; and
Be villany less than 'twas! O Imogen!
My queen, my life, my wife! O Imogen,
Imogen, Imogen!
   Imo.   Peace, my lord; hear, hear—

Post. Shall's have a play of this? Thou scorn-
  ful page,
There lie thy part.   [*Striking her: she falls.*
  Pis.   O, gentlemen, help!   229
Mine and your mistress! O, my lord Posthumus!
You ne'er kill'd Imogen till now. Help, help!
Mine honour'd lady!
  Cym.   Does the world go round?
  Post. How come these staggers on me?
  Pis.   Wake, my mistress!
  Cym. If this be so, the gods do mean to
    strike me
To death with mortal joy.
  Pis.   How fares my mistress?
  Imo. O, get thee from my sight;
Thou gavest me poison: dangerous fellow, hence!
Breathe not where princes are.
  Cym.   The tune of Imogen!
  Pis. Lady,
The gods throw stones of sulphur on me, if 240
That box I gave you was not thought by me
A precious thing: I had it from the queen.
  Cym. New matter still?
  Imo.   It poison'd me.
  Cor.   O gods!
I left out one thing which the queen confess'd,
Which must approve thee honest: 'If Pisanio
Have' said she 'given his mistress that confection
Which I gave him for cordial, she is served
As I would serve a rat.'
  Cym.   What's this, Cornelius?
  Cor. The queen, sir, very oft importuned me
To temper poisons for her, still pretending 250
The satisfaction of her knowledge only
In killing creatures vile, as cats and dogs,
Of no esteem: I, dreading that her purpose
Was of more danger, did compound for her
A certain stuff, which, being ta'en, would cease
The present power of life, but in short time
All offices of nature should again
Do their due functions. Have you ta'en of it?
  Imo. Most like I did, for I was dead.
  Bel.   My boys,
There was our error.
  Gui.   This is, sure, Fidele. 260
  Imo. Why did you throw your wedded lady
    from you?
Think that you are upon a rock; and now
Throw me again.   [*Embracing him.*
  Post.   Hang there like fruit, my soul,
Till the tree die!
  Cym.   How now, my flesh, my child!
What, makest thou me a dullard in this act?
Wilt thou not speak to me?
  Imo.   [*Kneeling*] Your blessing, sir.
  Bel. [*To Guiderius and Arviragus*] Though
    you did love this youth, I blame ye not;
You had a motive for't.
  Cym.   My tears that fall
Prove holy water on thee! Imogen,
Thy mother's dead.
  Imo.   I am sorry for't, my lord. 270
  Cym. O, she was naught; and long of her it
    was
That we meet here so strangely: but her son
Is gone, we know not how nor where.
  Pis.   My lord,
Now fear is from me, I'll speak troth. Lord
  Cloten,

Imogen embraces Posthumus. Engraving by Kenny
Meadows from Barry Cornwall's *The Works of Shakspere*,
1846

287 *Marry.* By the Virgin Mary. *forfend.* Forbid.

305 *scar for.* Suffered (wounds) for.

Ellen Terry as Imogen, Lyceum Theatre, London, 1896

Upon my lady's missing, came to me
With his sword drawn; foam'd at the mouth, and
    swore,
If I discover'd not which way she was gone,
It was my instant death.   By accident,
I had a feigned letter of my master's
Then in my pocket; which directed him   280
To seek her on the mountains hear to Milford;
Where, in a frenzy, in my master's garments,
Which he enforced from me, away he posts
With unchaste purpose and with oath to violate
My lady's honour: what became of him
I further know not.
    Gui.   Let me end the story:
• I slew him there.
    Cym.   Marry, the gods forfend!
I would not thy good deeds should from my lips
Pluck a hard sentence: prithee, valiant youth,
Deny't again.
    Gui.   I have spoke it, and I did it.   290
    Cym. He was a prince.
    Gui. A most incivil one: the wrongs he did me
Were nothing prince-like; for he did provoke me
With language that would make me spurn the sea,
If it could so roar to me: I cut off's head;
And am right glad he is not standing here
To tell this tale of mine.
    Cym.   I am sorry for thee:
By thine own tongue thou art condemn'd, and
    must
Endure our law: thou'rt dead.
    Imo.   That headless man
I thought had been my lord.
    Cym.   Bind the offender,   300
And take him from our presence.
    Bel.   Stay, sir king:
This man is better than the man he slew,
As well descended as thyself; and hath
More of thee merited than a band of Clotens
• Had ever scar for. [*To the Guard*] Let his arms
    alone;
They were not born for bondage.
    Cym.   Why, old soldier,
Wilt thou undo the worth thou art unpaid for,
By tasting of our wrath?   How of descent
As good as we?
    Arv.   In that he spake too far.
    Cym. And thou shalt die for't.
    Bel.   We will die all three: 310
But I will prove that two on's are as good
As I have given out him.   My sons, I must,
For mine own part, unfold a dangerous speech,
Though, haply, well for you.
    Arv.   Your danger's ours.
    Gui. And our good his.
    Bel.   Have at it then, by leave.
Thou hadst, great king, a subject who
Was call'd Belarius.
    Cym.   What of him? he is
A banish'd traitor.
    Bel.   He it is that hath
Assumed this age; indeed a banish'd man;
I know not how a traitor.
    Cym.   Take him hence: 320
The whole world shall not save him.
    Bel.   Not too hot:
First pay me for the nursing of thy sons;
And let it be confiscate all, so soon
As I have received it.

Cym. Nursing of my sons!
Bel. I am too blunt and saucy: here's my
knee:
Ere I arise, I will prefer my sons;
Then spare not the old father. Mighty sir,
These two young gentlemen, that call me father
And think they are my sons, are none of mine;
They are the issue of your loins, my liege, 330
'And blood of your begetting.
Cym. How! my issue!
Bel. So sure as you your father's. I, old
Morgan,
Am that Belarius whom you sometime banish'd:
● Your pleasure was my mere offence, my punish-
ment
Itself, and all my treason; that I suffer'd
Was all the harm I did. These gentle princes—
For such and so they are—these twenty years
Have I train'd up: those arts they have as I
Could put into them; my breeding was, sir, as 339
Your highness knows. Their nurse, Euriphile,
Whom for the theft I wedded, stole these children
Upon my banishment: I moved her to't,
Having received the punishment before,
For that which I did then: beaten for loyalty
Excited me to treason: their dear loss,
The more of you 'twas felt, the more it shaped
Unto my end of stealing them. But, gracious sir,
Here are your sons again; and I must lose
Two of the sweet'st companions in the world.
The benediction of these covering heavens 350
Fall on their heads like dew! for they are worthy
To inlay heaven with stars.
Cym. Thou weep'st, and speak'st.
The service that you three have done is more
● Unlike than this thou tell'st. I lost my children:
If these be they, I know not how to wish
A pair of worthier sons.
Bel. Be pleased awhile.
This gentleman, whom I call Polydore,
Most worthy prince, as yours, is true Guiderius:
This gentleman, my Cadwal, Arviragus, 359
Your younger princely son; he, sir, was lapp'd
In a most curious mantle, wrought by the hand
Of his queen mother, which for more probation
I can with ease produce.
Cym. Guiderius had
Upon his neck a mole, a sanguine star;
It was a mark of wonder.
Bel. This is he;
Who hath upon him still that natural stamp:
It was wise nature's end in the donation,
To be his evidence now.
Cym. O, what, am I
A mother to the birth of three? Ne'er mother 369
Rejoiced deliverance more. Blest pray you be,
● That, after this strange starting from your orbs,
You may reign in them now! O Imogen,
Thou hast lost by this a kingdom.
Imo. No, my lord;
I have got two worlds by't. O my gentle brothers,
Have we thus met? O, never say hereafter
But I am truest speaker: you call'd me brother,
When I was but your sister; I you brothers,
When ye were so indeed.
Cym. Did you e'er meet?
Arv. Ay, my good lord.
Gui. And at first meeting loved;
Continued so, until we thought he died. 380

334 *mere.* Entire.

354 *Unlike.* Improbable.

371 *starting.* Bursting out. *orbs.* Spheres.

Costume design for Belarius by Rene Allio, Royal
Shakespeare Co, 1962

388 *your three motives.* What brought each of you three.

396 *counterchange.* Interaction.

397 *severally.* In each individual.

409 *in poor beseeming.* Disguised as a poor man. *fitment.* Suitable garment.

428 *spritely shows.* Apparitions of spirits.

430 *label.* Slip of paper.

Cor.   By the **queen's** dram she swallow'd.
Cym.   O rare instinct!
When shall I hear all through? This fierce abridgement
Hath to it circumstantial branches, which
Distinction should be rich in. Where? how lived you?
And when came you to serve our Roman captive?
How parted witn your brothers? how first met them?
Why fled you from the court? and whither? These,
● And your three motives to the battle, with
I know not how much more, should be demanded;
And all the other by-dependencies,   390
From chance to chance: but nor the time nor place
Will serve our long inter'gatories.   See,
Posthumus anchors upon Imogen,
And she, like harmless lightning, throws her eye
On him, her brothers, me, her master, hitting
● Each object with a joy: the counterchange
● Is severally in all.   Let's quit this ground,
And smoke the temple with our sacrifices.
[*To Belarius*] Thou art my brother; so we'll hold thee ever.
  Imo.   You are my father too, and did relieve me,   400
To see this gracious season.
  Cym.   All o'erjoy'd,
Save these in bonds: let them be joyful too,
For they shall taste our comfort.
  Imo.   My good master,
I will yet do you service.
  Luc.   Happy be you!
  Cym. The forlorn soldier, that so nobly fought,
He would have well becomed this place, and graced
The thankings of a king.
  Post.   I am, sir,
The soldier that did company these three
● In poor beseeming; 'twas a fitment for
The purpose I then follow'd. That I was he,   410
Speak, Iachimo: I had you down and might
Have made you finish.
  Iach. [*Kneeling*] I am down again:
But now my heavy conscience sinks my knee,
As then your force did.   Take that life, beseech you,
Which I so often owe: but your ring first;
And here the bracelet of the truest princess
That ever swore her faith.
  Post.   Kneel not to me:
The power that I have on you is to spare you;
The malice towards you to forgive you: live,
And deal with others better.
  Cym.   Nobly doom'd!   420
We'll learn our freeness of a son-in-law;
Pardon's the word to all.
  Arv.   You holp us, sir,
As you did mean indeed to be our brother;
Joy'd are we that you are.
  Post. Your servant, princes.   Good my lord of Rome,
Call forth your soothsayer: as I slept, methought
Great Jupiter, upon his eagle back'd,
● Appear'd to me, with other spritely shows
Of mine own kindred: when I waked, I found
● This label on my bosom; whose containing   430

● Is so from sense in hardness, that I can
● Make no collection of it: let him show
His skill in the construction.
    Luc.   Philarmonus!
    Sooth.   Here, my good lord.
    Luc.   Read, and declare the meaning.
    Sooth. [*Reads*] 'When as a lion's whelp shall,
to himself unknown, without seeking find, and be
embraced by a piece of tender air; and when
from a stately cedar shall be lopped branches,
which, being dead many years, shall after revive,
be jointed to the old stock, and freshly grow;
then shall Posthumus end his miseries, Britain be
fortunate and flourish in peace and plenty.'
Thou, Leonatus, art the lion's whelp;
The fit and apt construction of thy name,
Being Leo-natus, doth import so much.
[*To Cymbeline*] The piece of tender air, thy
      virtuous daughter,
Which we call 'mollis aer;' and 'mollis aer'
We term it 'mulier:' which 'mulier' I divine
Is this most constant wife; who, even now,
Answering the letter of the oracle,   450
● Unknown to you, unsought, were clipp'd about
With this most tender air.
    Cym.   This hath some seeming.
    Sooth.   The lofty cedar, royal Cymbeline,
Personates thee: and thy lopp'd branches point
Thy two sons forth; who, by Belarius stol'n,
For many years thought dead, are now revived,
To the majestic cedar join'd, whose issue
Promises Britain peace and plenty.
    Cym.   Well;
My peace we will begin. And, Caius Lucius,
Although the victor, we submit to Cæsar,   460
And to the Roman empire; promising
To pay our wonted tribute, from the which
We were dissuaded by our wicked queen;
Whom heavens, in justice, both on her and hers,
Have laid most heavy hand.
    Sooth.   The fingers of the powers above do
      tune
The harmony of this peace. The vision
Which I made known to Lucius, ere the stroke
Of this yet scarce-cold battle, at this instant
Is full accomplish'd; for the Roman eagle,   470
From south to west on wing soaring aloft,
Lessen'd herself, and in the beams o' the sun
So vanish'd: which foreshow'd our princely eagle,
The imperial Cæsar, should again unite
His favour with the radiant Cymbeline,
Which shines here in the west.
    Cym.   Laud we the gods;
And let our crooked smokes climb to their
      nostrils
From our blest altars. Publish we this peace
To all our subjects. Set we forward: let
A Roman and a British ensign wave   480
Friendly together: so through Lud's-town march:
And in the temple of great Jupiter
Our peace we'll ratify; seal it with feasts.
Set on there! Never was a war did cease,
Ere bloody hands were wash'd, with such a peace.
                        [*Exeunt.*

Soothsayer: 'for the Roman eagle, From south to west on wing soaring aloft . . .' Roman eagle as a standard. From a 19th century engraving.

---

431 *from sense in hardness.* Hard to understand.

432 *collection.* Conclusion.

451 *clipp'd about.* Embraced.

The Winter's Tale

1610-11

THE WINTER'S TALE is a singularly beautiful, and an inspired play, from beginning to end, where *Cymbeline* gives the impression of having been laboured. The new play is not long, and seems to have been written at Stratford in one onrush in the winter of 1610–11. With this play the dramatist completely mastered the new genre and, with the next, *The Tempest*, produced two masterpieces, for others to follow. John Fletcher, who was to succeed him as dramatist-in-chief to the Company, was already working along these lines with his *Philaster*; much influenced by the old master, he was to make the new genre his own.

Shakespeare had a subject that he knew would appeal, from the success of Robert Greene's romance, *Pandosto*, which provided the story and the ground-work for him. The novel, written in the exciting year 1588, had been recently republished, under a new title, in 1607. It is ironical to think, after what had happened between Greene and Shakespeare at the beginning of his career, that he was now, at the end of it, writing with Greene's work beside him. The dramatist followed the outlines fairly clearly, but filled it with the breath of his own inspiration.

The subject of Leontes' psychotic jealousy of his wife, Hermione, evidently inspired him and immeasurably more is made of it – half the play, in fact. The characters of the Queen's faithful lady, Paulina, and the King's no less trusty Camillo, are portrayed in depth and win our complete sympathy. Autolycus, the enchanting, thieving pedlar, is all Shakespeare's invention, and one of his happiest. The Queen herself is a moving creation and, in her regal dignity in circumstances of injured innocence, has much in common with Catherine of Aragon, in the last play of all, *Henry VIII*. The hearts of the sentimental have always been taken – as probably Shakespeare's was – by his girls, Imogen and Miranda and, in this play, Perdita. There is even an Emilia, but she has only the part of a waiting woman.

The Play. Simon Forman saw it at the Globe on 15 May 1611 and gives us a full account of it. He was particularly interested, as he would be, in Leontes' jealousy and his sending to the Oracle at Delos to know the truth as to his suspicions; in the bringing up of the King's abandoned child by a shepherd and her ultimate discovery; and the character of

Autolycus, who was much in Forman's line. 'Beware of trusting feigned beggars or fawning fellows', he wrote. It was performed at Court on Gunpowder day, 5 November 1611, and again among the entertainments for the marriage of Princess Elizabeth to the Elector Palatine in 1613 (from which the present royal house in Britain descends). Half-a-dozen of the master's plays were presented, by far the foremost dramatist of the time.

For his setting he picked most of his names out of Plutarch or Sidney's *Arcadia*, and Autolycus from the beloved Ovid; oddly enough, a Florizel occurs at Stratford.

Leontes. The character of Leontes dominates the first half of the play, and it is one of the most original and intuitive Shakespeare ever created. In it he intuited the whole nature of schizophrenia, in its modern diagnosis, and portrayed precisely how it works. We have the alternation of perfectly sane with mad speeches – the latter difficult to write, but completely authentic and convincing. The jealousy is the more deep-seated because Leontes and Polixenes had been such close friends in their youth. Under the compulsion of his psychosis – Paulina recognises the symptoms from the first and calls them his 'lunes' – the King's mind works with the formal reasoning and cunning of schizophrenics, cleverly picking up every indication to buttress his complex and corroborate his suspicions.

The first Act, in which all this is developed, is one of the most compelling Shakespeare ever wrote, with an ominous, frightening atmosphere, the foreboding of what is to come. As was usual with him throughout his career, he increased the tension by emphasising former friendship and fondness – not only, as we have seen, for dramatic impact but also for the revelation of the depths in human beings and the extremes they will go to, under stress. Polixenes diagnoses the case:

> This jealousy
> Is for a precious creature: as she's rare,
> Must it be great; and, as his person's mighty,
> Must it be violent; and, as he does conceive
> He is dishonoured by a man which ever
> Professed to him, why, his revenges must
> In that be made more bitter. Fear o'ershades me.

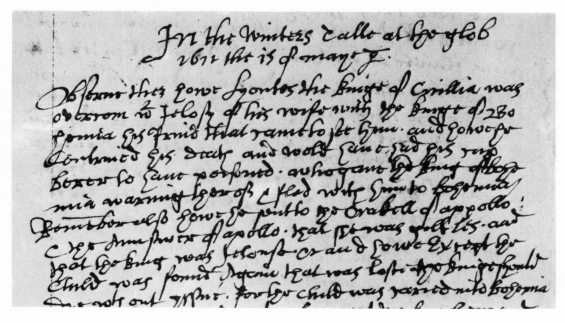

Simon Forman's description of a performance of The Winter's Tale *at the Globe, 15th May 1611. From his* MS. The Bocke of Plaies and Notes thereof ...

797

Elizabeth of Bohemia, daughter of James I. The Winter's Tale *was one of the entertainments for her marriage to the Elector Palatine in 1613. Painting from the studio of van Miereveldt c. 1623*

It is over these extremes that question has been so often raised as to the probability of the action; though that was not to the point with the Elizabethans, Shakespeare's imagination saw more deeply into human nature than any rationalist psychology. And, actually, events in everybody's mind at the time bore him out. Leontes sent his Queen to prison, where she was supposed to have died. Elizabeth I's father, Henry VIII, not only sent her mother and her cousin – Anne Boleyn and Catherine Howard, both his Queens – to the Tower but beheaded them. Leontes lost his wife, and his only son and heir died. This is what happened to Richard III after the murder of the Princes in the Tower: his son, for whose succession it had been done, died and then his Queen. Leontes was hardly more stricken by fate, and by remorse, than Richard.

The Queen is cited before a court of justice, as Catherine and Henry appeared before the court at Blackfriars. Her speeches, in their dignity and sense of outrage, look forward to Catherine: she too was an alien, receiving no sort of justice in the country into which she had married:

> The Emperor of Russia was my father:
> O that he were alive, and here beholding
> His daughter's trial!

At that moment the lords arrive with the declaration of the Oracle that Hermione and Polixenes are blameless, Leontes' suspicions false. He refuses to believe it. Upon the heels of this his sick son dies; the Queen faints and is borne away, Paulina returns to tell him that she has died. These blows confirm the Oracle, and Leontes is struck with remorse and grief.

His conversion is highly sensational; but everybody knows that there are such sudden conversions.

Chorus. Act IV is introduced by Time, a Chorus, as in *Pericles*, to leap over time and tell us the events of the intervening years:

> Impute it not a crime
> To me, or my swift passage, that I slide
> O'er sixteen years . . .
>   since it is in my power
> To o'erthrow law, and in one, self-born hour
> To plant and o'erwhelm custom.

The author makes up to the audience in his usual courteous manner (unlike Ben Jonson):

> Of this allow,
> If ever you have spent time worse ere now;
> If never, yet that Time himself doth say,
> He wishes earnestly you never may.

Pastoral. The pastoral element takes over. The Queen's child, Perdita, born in prison, is carried overseas – like Marina in *Pericles* – where she is brought up by a shepherd, who, from the jewels and trinkets brought with the child, knows something of her story. Here she is, of course, wooed by Florizel, Polixenes' son and heir.

All that is charming enough, but enchantment enters the play with Autolycus, his petty thievings from Clown and shepherds, the way the country folk fall for his wares, his cozening tricks and his songs, the sheep-shearing feast they all attend. Perdita and

The finding of Perdita. Painting by Henry Thomson (1773–1843)

Florizel are watched by Polixenes and Camillo, thus skilfully bringing the two halves of the action together. The poetry is breath-taking, from the moment Autolycus enters, singing:

> When daffodils begin to peer,
> > With heigh! the doxy over the dale,
> Why then comes in the sweet o'the year,
> > For the red blood reigns in the winter's pale.

And Perdita takes up with

> daffodils
> That come before the swallow dares, and take
> The winds of March with beauty; violets, dim,
> But sweeter than the lids of Juno's eyes
> Or Cytherea's breath; pale primroses
> That die unmarried, ere they can behold
> Bright Phoebus in his strength; bold oxlips and
> The crown imperial; lilies of all kinds . . .

Amid the galaxy of flowers from English fields, we should notice how, as through all his work, the classical images and comparisons spring naturally to mind from his early education.

Along with school at Stratford, from the very first – Plautus, Ovid and Seneca, with *The Comedy of Errors* and *Titus Andronicus* – there is the Warwickshire and Cotswold background that comes into several of the plays, from *The Taming of the Shrew* on. Here we have authentic, loving observation: 'Let me see – what am I to buy for our sheep-shearing feast? Three pound of sugar, five pound of currants, rice – what will this sister of mine do with rice? [One throws rice at weddings.] But my father hath made her mistress of the feast, and she lays it on.' She has made nosegays for the shearers, who can all sing the three-men songs of the time – only one Puritan among them, 'and he sings psalms to hornpipes.' This is to suggest that he is a cuckold.

The country fellow doesn't know whether he has got money enough to pay for it all. 'Let me see – every 'leven wether tods – every tod yields pound and odd shilling – fifteen hundred shorn, what comes the wool to? . . . I cannot do't without counters.' How often Shakespeare must have observed that in the country round about or at Stratford market! As in *The Two Gentleman of Verona*, years before, the Whitsun pastorals are recalled:

> Methinks I play as I have seen them do
> In Whitsun pastorals . . .

The girls press around Autolycus for fairings: 'I love a ballad in print, a'life, for then we are sure they are true.' In contrast to the jukeboxes of today, they can all sing: 'We can both sing it. If thou'lt bear a part, thou shalt hear: 'tis in three parts . . . We had the tune on't a month ago.'

It is the authentic voice of traditional rural England, which some of us can still remember.

Personal. Though the play is full of romance and pastoral delights, the passion and pain of jealous emotion, grief and sensational surprise, it never loses touch with the ground of reality. Here is a homely scene:

> when my old wife lived, upon
> This day she was both pantler, butler, cook,
> Both dame and servant; welcomed all, served all;
> Would sing her song and dance her turn; now here
> At upper end o'the table; now i'the middle;
> On his shoulder, and his; her face o'fire
> With labour, and the thing she took to quench it
> She would to each one sip.

Does it represent a home-coming? It sounds like it.

But perhaps here, too, is a no less authentic recollection:

> Besides, you know,
> Prosperity's the very bond of love,
> Whose fresh complexion and whose heart together
> Affliction alters.

We have a passage between Shepherd and Clown on the familiar theme earlier of gentility, and how one becomes a 'gentleman-born'. (The dramatist became a gentleman-born by taking out a coat-of-arms in his father's name, so that he should have been born a gentleman.)

The device of the living statue – the form in which Hermione returns to Leontes – had been used before by Lyly and Marston. One accepts it – and the reconciliation, the forgiveness and renewal, are beyond anything: perhaps equalled only by Lear's eventual recognition of Cordelia. We have noticed Shakespeare's interest in monuments: this is 'a piece many years in doing and now newly performed [i.e. finished] by that rare Italian master, Julio Romano, who – had he himself eternity and could put breath into his work – would beguile Nature of her custom, so perfectly he is her ape.' Once more we observe the aesthetic taste of the time – naturalness, lifelikeness, reality and grace. It is appropriate that Julio Romano should have been the one artist Shakespeare names (as Marlowe was the one poet he virtually names); for Julio, though Raphael's pupil, reacted away from classicism into a highly personal style, extreme, erotic, violent. Evidently a congenial spirit.

The episode of the bear – pursuing Antigonus off the stage, to amuse the groundlings – is thought to have been suggested, along with the dance of the twelve satyrs, from Ben Jonson's masque of Oberon, performed at New Year 1611. The language of the play, though it contains as many rare and *recherché* words as ever, is nothing like so convoluted and difficult as that of *Cymbeline*; it has much more direct and forceful speaking and more poetry: signs that where one was laboured, the other was inspired.

The Text is an excellent one as it appeared in the Folio, it is thought from the transcript made by the Company's experienced scribe, Ralph Crane. Stage-directions were cut, however, and in place we find, exceptionally, act-scene divisions with a list of the characters to appear at the opening of each scene.

THE WINTER'S TALE.

DRAMATIS PERSONÆ.

LEONTES, king of Sicilia.
MAMILLIUS, young prince of Sicilia.
CAMILLO,
ANTIGONUS,
CLEOMENES, } Four Lords of Sicilia.
DION,
POLIXENES, king of Bohemia.
FLORIZEL, prince of Bohemia.
ARCHIDAMUS, a Lord of Bohemia.
Old Shepherd, reputed father of Perdita.
Clown, his son.
AUTOLYCUS, a rogue.
A Mariner.

A Gaoler.

HERMIONE, queen to Leontes.
PERDITA, daughter to Leontes and Hermione.
PAULINA, wife to Antigonus.
EMILIA, a lady attending on Hermione.
MOPSA,
DORCAS, } Shepherdesses.

Other Lords and Gentlemen, Ladies, Officers, and Servants, Shepherds, and Shepherdesses.

Time, as Chorus.

SCENE: *Sicilia, and Bohemia.*

● *A bullet beside a text line indicates an annotation in the opposite column.*

ACT I.

SCENE I. *Antechamber in* LEONTES' *palace.*

Enter CAMILLO *and* ARCHIDAMUS.

Arch. If you shall chance, Camillo, to visit Bohemia, on the like occasion whereon my services are now on foot, you shall see, as I have said, great difference betwixt our Bohemia and your Sicilia.

Cam. I think, this coming summer, the King of Sicilia means to pay Bohemia the visitation which he justly owes him.

Arch. Wherein our entertainment shall shame us we will be justified in our loves; for indeed—

Cam. Beseech you,— 11

Arch. Verily, I speak it in the freedom of

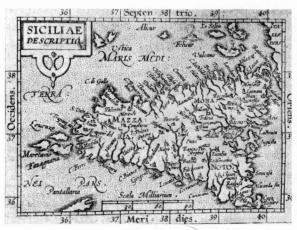

Sicily. Engraving from Abraham Ortelius' *Epitome to the Theatre of the World,* 1598

Opposite : Perdita. Drawing by G. A. Storey (1834–1919)

30 *attorneyed.* Performed by proxy.

43 *physics the subject.* Invigorates the people.

1 *watery star.* i.e. moon.

13 *sneaping.* Biting.

17 *sooth.* Truly.

my knowledge: we cannot with such magnificence—in so rare—I know not what to say.   We will give you sleepy drinks, that your senses, unintelligent of our insufficience, may, though they cannot praise us, as little accuse us.

Cam.   You pay a great deal too dear for what's given freely.   19

Arch.   Believe me, I speak as my understanding instructs me and as mine honesty puts it to utterance.

Cam.   Sicilia cannot show himself over-kind to Bohemia.   They were trained together in their childhoods; and there rooted betwixt them then such an affection, which cannot choose but branch now.   Since their more mature dignities and royal necessities made separation of their society, their encounters, though not personal, ⚫have been royally attorneyed with interchange of gifts, letters, loving embassies; that they have seemed to be together, though absent, shook hands, as over a vast, and embraced, as it were, from the ends of opposed winds.   The heavens continue their loves!

Arch.   I think there is not in the world either malice or matter to alter it.   You have an unspeakable comfort of your young prince Mamillius: it is a gentleman of the greatest promise that ever came into my note.   40

Cam.   I very well agree with you in the hopes of him: it is a gallant child; one that ⚫indeed physics the subject, makes old hearts fresh: they that went on crutches ere he was born desire yet their life to see him a man.

Arch.   Would they else be content to die?

Cam.   Yes; if there were no other excuse why they should desire to live.

Arch.   If the king had no son, they would desire to live on crutches till he had one.   50
                                                      [*Exeunt.*

SCENE II.   *A room of state in the same.*

Enter LEONTES, HERMIONE, MAMILLIUS, POLIXENES, CAMILLO, *and* Attendants.

⚫   *Pol.*   Nine changes of the watery star hath
            been
The shepherd's note since we have left our throne
Without a burthen: time as long again
Would be fill'd up, my brother, with our thanks;
And yet we should, for perpetuity,
Go hence in debt: and therefore, like a cipher,
Yet standing in rich place, I multiply
With one 'We thank you' many thousands moe
That go before it.

Leon.   Stay your thanks a while;
And pay them when you part.

Pol.   Sir, that's to-morrow.   10
I am question'd by my fears, of what may chance
Or breed upon our absence; that may blow
⚫No sneaping winds at home, to make us say
'This is put forth too truly:' besides, I have
            stay'd
To tire your royalty.

Leon.   We are tougher, brother,
Than you can put us to't.

Pol.   No longer stay.

⚫ *Leon.*   One seven-night longer.

Pol.   Very sooth, to-morrow.

Leon. We'll part the time between's then;
  and in that
I'll no gainsaying.
  Pol.   Press me not, beseech you, so.
There is no tongue that moves, none, **none** i'
  the world,   20
So soon as yours could win me: so it should now,
Were there necessity in your request, although
'Twere needful I denied it.   My affairs
Do even drag me homeward: which to hinder
Were in your love a whip to me; my stay
To you a charge and trouble: to save both,
Farewell, our brother.
  Leon.   Tongue-tied our queen? speak you.
  Her. I had thought, sir, to have held my
  peace until
You had drawn oaths from him not to stay.
  You, sir,
Charge him too coldly. Tell him, you are sure 30
All in Bohemia's well; this satisfaction
The by-gone day proclaim'd: say this to him,
● He's beat from his best ward.
  Leon.   Well said, Hermione.
  Her. To tell, he longs to see his son, were
  strong:
But let him say so then, and let him go;
But let him swear so, and he shall not stay,
We'll thwack him hence with distaffs.
Yet of your royal presence I'll adventure
The borrow of a week.   When at Bohemia
You take my lord, I'll give him my com-
  mission   40
● To let him there a month behind the gest
Prefix'd for's parting: yet, good deed, Leontes,
● I love thee not a jar o' the clock behind
What lady-she her lord.   You'll stay?
  Pol.   No, madam.
  Her. Nay, but you will?
  Pol.   I may not, verily.
  Her. Verily!
● You put me off with limber vows; but I,
● Though you would seek to unsphere the stars
  with oaths,
Should yet say 'Sir, no going.' Verily,
You shall not go: a lady's 'Verily''s   50
As potent as a lord's.   Will you go yet?
Force me to keep you as a prisoner,
Not like a guest; so you shall pay your fees
When you depart, and save your thanks.   How
  say you?
My prisoner? or my guest? by your dread
  'Verily,'
One of them you shall be.
  Pol.   Your guest, then, madam:
To be your prisoner should import offending;
Which is for me less easy to commit
Than you to punish.
  Her.   Not your gaoler, then,   59
But your kind hostess.   Come, I'll question you
Of my lord's tricks and yours when you were boys:
You were pretty lordings then?
  Pol.   We were, fair queen,
Two lads that thought there was no more behind
But such a day to-morrow as to-day,
And to be boy eternal.
  Her.   Was not my lord
The verier wag o' the two?
  Pol. We were as twinn'd lambs that did frisk
  i' the sun,

33 *ward.* Defence.

41 *let.* Stay. *gest.* Time.

43 *jar.* Tick.

Hermione (Judi Dench) and Leontes (Barrie Ingham)
with Mamillius, Royal Shakespeare Co, 1969

47 *limber.* Nimble.

Hermione: 'You put me off with limber vows;' Malcolm
Keen as Leontes, Veronica Turleigh as Hermione and
Alistair Sim as Polixenes, Old Vic, 1933

48 *unsphere the stars.* Set the stars from their courses.

74–75 *the . . . ours.* i.e. we would not even have been guilty of original sin.

80 *Grace to boot!* i.e. Gracious, what next!

Hermione: 'Grace to boot!' Marilyn Taylerson as Hermione and John Woodvine as Polixenes, Royal Shakespeare Co, 1976

96 *heat.* Race.

104 *clap thyself.* i.e. clap hands with me in agreement; and a pun on the word 'clepe', meaning 'name'.

110 *tremor cordis.* Palpitations.

And bleat the one at the other: what we changed
Was innocence for innocence; we knew not
The doctrine of ill-doing, nor dream'd   70
That any did.   Had we pursued that life,
And our weak spirits ne'er been higher rear'd
With stronger blood, we should have answer'd heaven
●Boldly 'not guilty;' the imposition clear'd
Hereditary ours.
   Her.   By this we gather
You have tripp'd since.
   Pol.   O my most sacred lady!
Temptations have since then been born to's; for
In those unfledged days was my wife a girl;
Your precious self had then not cross'd the eyes
Of my young play-fellow.
● *Her.*   Grace to boot!   80
Of this make no conclusion, lest you say
Your queen and I are devils: yet go on;
The offences we have made you do we'll answer,
If you first sinn'd with us and that with us
You did continue fault and that you slipp'd not
With any but with us.
   Leon.   Is he won yet?
   Her. He'll stay, my lord.
   Leon.   At my request he would not.
Hermione, my dearest, thou never spokest
To better purpose.
   Her.   Never?
   Leon.   Never, but once.
   Her. What! have I twice said well? when
    was't before?   90
I prithee tell me; cram's with praise, and make's
As fat as tame things: one good deed dying tongueless
Slaughters a thousand waiting upon that.
Our praises are our wages: you may ride's
With one soft kiss a thousand furlongs ere
●With spur we heat an acre.   But to the goal:
My last good deed was to entreat his stay:
What was my first? it has an elder sister,
Or I mistake you: O, would her name were Grace!
But once before I spoke to the purpose: when?
Nay, let me have't; I long.
   Leon.   Why, that was when   101
Three crabbed months had sour'd themselves to death,
Ere I could make thee open thy white hand
●And clap thyself my love: then didst thou utter
'I am yours for ever.'
   Her.   'Tis grace indeed.
Why, lo you now, I have spoke to the purpose twice:
The one for ever earn'd a royal husband;
The other for some while a friend.
   Leon.   [*Aside*] Too hot, too hot!
To mingle friendship far is mingling bloods.
●I have tremor cordis on me: my heart dances;
But not for joy; not joy.   This entertainment   111
May a free face put on, derive a liberty
From heartiness, from bounty, fertile bosom,
And well become the agent; 't may, I grant;
But to be paddling palms and pinching fingers,
As now they are, and making practised smiles,
As in a looking-glass, and then to sigh, as 'twere
The mort o' the deer; O, that is entertainment
My bosom likes not, nor my brows! Mamillius,
Art thou my boy?

● *Mam.*   Ay, my good lord.
 Leon.   I' fecks! 120
● Why, that's my bawcock. What, hast smutch'd
      thy nose?
 They say it is a copy out of mine. Come, cap-
      tain,
 We must be neat; not neat, but cleanly, cap-
      tain:
 And yet the steer, the heifer and the calf
● Are all call'd neat.—Still virginalling
 Upon his palm!—How now, you wanton calf!
 Art thou my calf?
 Mam.   Yes, if you will, my lord.
● *Leon.* Thou want'st a rough pash and the
      shoots that I have,
 To be full like me: yet they say we are
 Almost as like as eggs; women say so,   130
 That will say any thing: but were they false
 As o'er-dyed blacks, as wind, as waters, false
 As dice are to be wish'd by one that fixes
● No bourn 'twixt his and mine, yet were it true
 To say this boy were like me. Come, sir page,
● Look on me with your welkin eye: sweet villain!
● Most dear'st! my collop! Can thy dam?—may't
      be?—
 Affection! thy intention stabs the centre:
 Thou dost make possible things not so held,
 Communicatest with dreams;—how can this be?—
● With what's unreal thou coactive art,   141
 And fellow'st nothing: then 'tis very credent
 Thou mayst co-join with something; and thou
      dost,
 And that beyond commission, and I find it,
 And that to the infection of my brains
 And hardening of my brows.
 Pol.   What means Sicilia?
 Her. He something seems unsettled.
 Pol.   How, my lord!
 What cheer? how is 't with you, best brother?
 Her.   You look
 As if you held a brow of much distraction:
 Are you moved, my lord?
 Leon.   No, in good earnest. 150
 How sometimes nature will betray its folly,
 Its tenderness, and make itself a pastime
 To harder bosoms! Looking on the lines
 Of my boy's face, methoughts I did recoil
 Twenty-three years, and saw myself unbreech'd,
 In my green velvet coat, my dagger muzzled,
 Lest it should bite its master, and so prove,
 As ornaments oft do, too dangerous:
 How like, methought, I then was to this kernel,
● This squash, this gentleman. Mine honest friend,
● Will you take eggs for money?   161
 Mam. No, my lord, I 'll fight.
● *Leon.* You will! why, happy man be's dole!
      My brother,
 Are you so fond of your young prince as we
 Do seem to be of ours?
 Pol.   If at home, sir,
 He's all my exercise, my mirth, my matter,
 Now my sworn friend and then mine enemy,
 My parasite, my soldier, statesman, all:
 He makes a July's day short as December,
 And with his varying childness cures in me 170
 Thoughts that would thick my blood.
 Leon.   So stands this squire
 Officed with me: we two will walk, my lord,
 And leave you to your graver steps. Hermione,

120 *I' fecks!* In faith!

121 *bawcock.* Fine fellow.

125 *virginalling.* Playing the virginals.

Playing the virginals. Engraving from Charles Knight's
Pictorial Edition of the Works of Shakspere, 1839–43

128 *a rough . . . shoots.* A shabby bull's head complete
with horns to be like me.

134 *bourn.* Limit.

136 *welkin.* i.e. sky-blue.

137 *collop.* A delicate piece of meat.

141 *coactive.* Associating.

160 *squash.* Unripe pea-pod.

161 *take eggs for money.* i.e. be fobbed off.

163 *happy . . . dole.* May you be a happy fellow.

183 *neb*. Beak.

202 *predominant*. i.e. in the ascendant.

204 *No barricado*. i.e. there is no barricading the womb.

Leontes: 'No barricado for a belly . . .' Ian McKellan as Leontes and Marilyn Taylerson as Hermione, Royal Shakespeare Co, 1976

Charles Kean as Leontes and Ellen Terry as Mamillius, Princess's Theatre, London, 1856

219 *gust*. Taste.

How thou lovest us, show in our brother's wel-
      come;
Let what is dear in Sicily be cheap:
Next to thyself and my young rover, he's
Apparent to my heart.
    Her.   If you would seek us,
We are yours i' the garden: shall's attend you
      there?
    Leon. To your own bents dispose you: you'll
      be found,
Be you beneath the sky. [*Aside*] I am angling
      now,   180
Though you perceive me not how I give line.
Go to, go to!
●How she holds up the neb, the bill to him!
And arms her with the boldness of a wife
To her allowing husband!
              [*Exeunt Polixenes, Hermione, and
                                    Attendants.*
              Gone already!
Inch-thick, knee-deep, o'er head and ears a fork'd
      one!
Go, play, boy, play: thy mother plays, and I
Play too, but so disgraced a part, whose issue
Will hiss me to my grave: contempt and clamour
Will be my knell. Go, play, boy, play. There
      have been,   190
Or I am much deceived, cuckolds ere now;
And many a man there is, even at this present,
Now while I speak this, holds his wife by the arm,
That little thinks she has been sluiced in's
      absence
And his pond fish'd by his next neighbour, by
Sir Smile, his neighbour: nay, there's comfort in't
Whiles other men have gates and those gates
      open'd,
As mine, against their will. Should all despair
That have revolted wives, the tenth of mankind
Would hang themselves. Physic for't there is
      none;   200
It is a bawdy planet, that will strike
●Where 'tis predominant; and 'tis powerful,
      think it,
From east, west, north and south: be it concluded,
●No barricado for a belly; know't;
It will let in and out the enemy
With bag and baggage: many thousand on's
Have the disease, and feel't not. How now, boy!
    Mam. I am like you, they say.
    Leon.   Why, that's some comfort.
What, Camillo there?
    Cam. Ay, my good lord.   210
    Leon. Go play, Mamillius; thou'rt an honest
      man.   [*Exit Mamillius.*
Camillo, this great sir will yet stay longer.
    Cam. You had much ado to make his anchor
      hold:
When you cast out, it still came home.
    Leon.   Didst note it?
    Cam. He would not stay at your petitions;
      made
His business more material.
    Leon.   Didst perceive it?
[*Aside*] They're here with me already, whisper-
      ing, rounding
'Sicilia is a so-forth:' 'tis far gone,
●When I shall gust it last. How came 't, Camillo,
That he did stay?
    Cam.   At the good queen's entreaty. 220

Leon.   At the queen's be't: 'good' should be
    pertinent;
But, so it is, it is not.   Was this taken
By any understanding pate but thine?
●For thy conceit is soaking, will draw in
●More than the common blocks: not noted, is't,
But of the finer natures? by some severals
●Of head-piece extraordinary? lower messes
●Perchance are to this business purblind? say.
    Cam.   Business, my lord!   I think most un-
    derstand
Bohemia stays here longer.
    Leon.   Ha!
    Cam.   Stays here longer.   230
    Leon.   Ay, but why?
    Cam.   To satisfy your highness and the en-
    treaties
Of our most gracious mistress.
    Leon.   Satisfy!
The entreaties of your mistress! satisfy!
Let that suffice.   I have trusted thee, Camillo,
With all the nearest things to my heart, as well
My chamber-councils, wherein, priest-like, thou
Hast cleansed my bosom, I from thee departed
Thy penitent reform'd: but we have been
Deceived in thy integrity, deceived   240
In that which seems so.
    Cam.   Be it forbid, my lord!
    Leon.   To bide upon't, thou art not honest, or,
If thou inclinest that way, thou art a coward,
●Which hoxes honesty behind, restraining
From course required; or else thou must be
    counted
A servant grafted in my serious trust
And therein negligent; or else a fool
That seest a game play'd home, the rich stake
    drawn,
And takest it all for jest.
    Cam.   My gracious lord,
I may be negligent, foolish and fearful;   250
In every one of these no man is free,
But that his negligence, his folly, fear,
Among the infinite doings of the world,
Sometime puts forth.   In your affairs, my lord,
If ever I were wilful-negligent,
It was my folly; if industriously
I play'd the fool, it was my negligence,
Not weighing well the end; if ever fearful
To do a thing, where I the issue doubted,
Whereof the execution did cry out   260
Against the non-performance, 'twas a fear
Which oft infects the wisest: these, my lord,
Are such allow'd infirmities that honesty
Is never free of.   But, beseech your grace,
Be plainer with me; let me know my trespass
By its own visage: if I then deny it,
'Tis none of mine.
    Leon.   Ha' not you seen, Camillo,—
●But that's past doubt, you have, or your eye-
    glass
Is thicker than a cuckold's horn,—or heard,—
For to a vision so apparent rumour   270
Cannot be mute,—or thought,—for cogitation
Resides not in that man that does not think,—
My wife is slippery?   If thou wilt confess,
Or else be impudently negative,
To have nor eyes nor ears nor thought, then say
●My wife's a hobby-horse, deserves a name
●As rank as any flax-wench that puts to

Set design for Charles Kean's production, Princess's
Theatre, London, 1856

---

224 *conceit.* Understanding. *soaking.* i.e. absorbent.

225 *blocks.* Blockheads.

227 *lower messes.* Inferior people.

228 *purblind.* Completely blind.

244 *hoxes.* Disables; hamstrings.

268 *eye-glass.* Cornea.

276 *hobby-horse.* Promiscuous woman.

277 *flax-wench.* Common woman. *puts to.* i.e. forni-
cates.

291 *pin and web.* Cataract.

306 *The . . . glass.* i.e. one hour.

311 *thrifts.* Advantages.

314 *bench'd.* i.e. given a position of authority.

317 *To give . . . wink.* To close my enemy's eyes for ever.

333 *blench.* Deceive himself.

Before her troth-plight: say't and justify't.
 Cam.   I would not be a stander-by to hear
My sovereign mistress clouded so, without 280
My present vengeance taken: 'shrew my heart,
You never spoke what did become you less
Than this; which to reiterate were sin
As deep as that, though true.
 Leon.   Is whispering nothing?
Is leaning cheek to cheek? is meeting noses?
Kissing with inside lip? stopping the career
Of laughter with a sigh?—a note infallible
Of breaking honesty—horsing foot on foot?
Skulking in corners? wishing clocks more swift?
Hours, minutes? noon, midnight? and all eyes
•Blind with the pin and web but theirs, theirs only,
That would unseen be wicked? is this nothing?
Why, then the world and all that's in't is
  nothing;
The covering sky is nothing; Bohemia nothing;
My wife is nothing; nor nothing have these
  nothings,
If this be nothing.
 Cam.   Good my lord, be cured
Of this diseased opinion, and betimes;
For 'tis most dangerous.
 Leon.   Say it be, 'tis true.
 Cam.   No, no, my lord.
 Leon.   It is; you lie, you lie:
I say thou liest, Camillo, and I hate thee, 300
Pronounce thee a gross lout, a mindless slave,
Or else a hovering temporizer, that
Canst with thine eyes at once see good and evil,
Inclining to them both: were my wife's liver
Infected as her life, she would not live
•The running of one glass.
 Cam.   Who does infect her?
 Leon. Why, he that wears her like her medal,
  hanging
About his neck, Bohemia: who, if I
Had servants true about me, that bare eyes
To see alike mine honour as their profits, 310
•Their own particular thrifts, they would do that
Which should undo more doing: ay, and thou,
His cupbearer,—whom I from meaner form
•Have bench'd and rear'd to worship, who mayst
  see
Plainly as heaven sees earth and earth sees
  heaven,
How I am galled,—mightst bespice a cup,
•To give mine enemy a lasting wink;
Which draught to me were cordial.
 Cam.   Sir, my lord,
I could do this, and that with no rash potion,
But with a lingering dram that should not work
Maliciously like poison: but I cannot 321
Believe this crack to be in my dread mistress,
So sovereignly being honourable.
I have loved thee,—
 Leon.   †Make that thy question, and go rot!
Dost think I am so muddy, so unsettled,
To appoint myself in this vexation, sully
The purity and whiteness of my sheets,
Which to preserve is sleep, which being spotted
Is goads, thorns, nettles, tails of wasps,
Give scandal to the blood o' the prince my son,
Who I do think is mine and love as mine, 331
Without ripe moving to 't? Would I do this?
•Could man so blench?
 Cam.   I must believe you, sir:

●I do; and will fetch off Bohemia for't;
Provided that, when he's removed, your highness
Will take again your queen as yours at first,
Even for your son's sake; and thereby for sealing
The injury of tongues in courts and kingdoms
Known and allied to yours.
  Leon.   Thou dost advise me
Even so as I mine own course have set down: 340
I'll give no blemish to her honour, none.
  Cam. My lord,
Go then; and with a countenance as clear
As friendship wears at feasts, keep with Bohemia
And with your queen: I am his cupbearer:
If from me he have wholesome beverage,
Account me not your servant.
  Leon.   This is all:
Do't and thou hast the one half of my heart;
Do't not, thou split'st thine own.
  Cam.   I'll do't, my lord.
  Leon. I will seem friendly, as thou hast ad-
   vised me.   [*Exit.* 350
  Cam. O miserable lady! But, for me,
What case stand I in? I must be the poisoner
Of good Polixenes; and my ground to do't
Is the obedience to a master, one
Who in rebellion with himself will have
All that are his so too. To do this deed,
Promotion follows. If I could find example
Of thousands that had struck anointed kings
And flourish'd after, I'ld not do't; but since
Nor brass nor stone nor parchment bears not one,
Let villany itself forswear't. I must 361
Forsake the court: to do't, or no, is certain
●To me a break-neck. Happy star reign now!
Here comes Bohemia.

    Re-enter POLIXENES.

  Pol.   This is strange: methinks
My favour here begins to warp. Not speak?
Good day, Camillo.
  Cam.   Hail, most royal sir!
  Pol. What is the news i' the court?
  Cam.   None rare, my lord.
  Pol. The king hath on him such a countenance
As he had lost some province and a region
Loved as he loves himself: even now I met him
With customary compliment; when he, 371
Wafting his eyes to the contrary and falling
A lip of much contempt, speeds from me and
So leaves me to consider what is breeding
That changeth thus his manners.
  Cam. I dare not know, my lord.
  Pol. How! dare not! do not. Do you know,
   and dare not?
Be intelligent to me: 'tis thereabouts;
For, to yourself, what you do know, you must,
And cannot say, you dare not. Good Camillo, 380
Your changed complexions are to me a mirror
Which shows me mine changed too; for I must be
A party in this alteration, finding
Myself thus alter'd with't.
  Cam.   There is a sickness
Which puts some of us in distemper, but
I cannot name the disease; and it is caught
Of you that yet are well.
  Pol.   How! caught of me!
●Make me not sighted like the basilisk:
I have look'd on thousands, who have sped the
   better

334 *fetch off.* i.e. kill (double meaning).

Camillo: 'I . . . will fetch off Bohemia for't;' Paul Scofield as Camillo. Drawing by Dame Laura Knight, 1948

363 *To . . . break-neck.* i.e. to be injurious to me. *Happy.* Fortunate.

388 *basilisk.* Legendary monster whose look was deadly.

Costume design for Polixenes by Jacques Noel, Stratford-upon-Avon, 1960

394 *success.* Succession.

416 *vice.* Force.

419 *the Best.* Jesus Christ.

By my regard, but kill'd none so.   Camillo,—
As you are certainly a gentleman, thereto   391
Clerk-like experienced, which no less adorns
Our gentry than our parents' noble names,
●In whose success we are gentle,—I beseech you,
If you know aught which does behove my know-
        ledge
Thereof to be inform'd, imprison't not
In ignorant concealment.
    Cam.   I may not answer.
    Pol. A sickness caught of me, and yet I well!
I must be answer'd.   Dost thou hear, Camillo?
I conjure thee, by all the parts of man   400
Which honour does acknowledge, whereof the
        least
Is not this suit of mine, that thou declare
What incidency thou dost guess of harm
Is creeping toward me; how far off, how near;
Which way to be prevented, if to be;
If not, how best to bear it.
    Cam.   Sir, I will tell you;
Since I am charged in honour and by him
That I think honourable: therefore mark my
        counsel,
Which must be even as swiftly follow'd as
I mean to utter it, or both yourself and me   410
Cry lost, and so good night!
    Pol.   On, good Camillo.
    Cam. I am appointed him to murder you.
    Pol. By whom, Camillo?
    Cam.   By the king.
    Pol.   For what?
    Cam. He thinks, nay, with all confidence he
        swears,
As he had seen't or been an instrument
●To vice you to't, that you have touch'd his queen
Forbiddenly.
    Pol.   O, then my best blood turn
To an infected jelly and my name
●Be yoked with his that did betray the Best!
Turn then my freshest reputation to   420
A savour that may strike the dullest nostril
Where I arrive, and my approach be shunn'd,
Nay, hated too, worse than the great'st infection
That e'er was heard or read!
    Cam.   Swear his thought over
By each particular star in heaven and
By all their influences, you may as well
Forbid the sea for to obey the moon
As or by oath remove or counsel shake
The fabric of his folly, whose foundation
Is piled upon his faith and will continue   430
The standing of his body.
    Pol.   How should this grow?
    Cam. I know not: but I am sure 'tis safer to
Avoid what's grown than question how 'tis born.
If therefore you dare trust my honesty,
That lies enclosed in this trunk which you
Shall bear along impawn'd, away to-night!
Your followers I will whisper to the business,
And will by twos and threes at several posterns
Clear them o' the city.   For myself, I'll put
My fortunes to your service, which are here   440
By this discovery lost.   Be not uncertain;
For, by the honour of my parents, I
Have utter'd truth: which if you seek to prove,
I dare not stand by; nor shall you be safer
Than one condemn'd by the king's own mouth,
        thereon

His execution sworn.
   Pol.   I do believe thee:
I saw his heart in's face.   Give me thy hand:
Be pilot to me and thy places shall
Still neighbour mine.   My ships are ready and
My people did expect my hence departure   450
Two days ago.   This jealousy
Is for a precious creature: as she's rare,
Must it be great, and as his person's mighty,
Must it be violent, and as he does conceive
He is dishonour'd by a man which ever
•Profess'd to him, why, his revenges must
In that be made more bitter.   Fear o'ershades me:
Good expedition be my friend, and comfort
†The gracious queen, part of his theme, but
    nothing
Of his ill-ta'en suspicion!   Come, Camillo;   460
I will respect thee as a father if
•Thou bear'st my life off hence: let us avoid.
   Cam.   It is in mine authority to command
The keys of all the posterns: please your highness
To take the urgent hour.   Come, sir, away.
                              [*Exeunt.*

ACT II.

Scene I.   *A room in* Leontes' *palace.*

Enter Hermione, Mamillius, *and* Ladies.

   Her.   Take the boy to you: he so troubles me,
'Tis past enduring.
   First Lady.   Come, my gracious lord,
Shall I be your playfellow?
   Mam.   No, I'll none of you.
   First Lady.   Why, my sweet lord?
   Mam.   You'll kiss me hard and speak to
    me as if
I were a baby still.   I love you better.
   Sec. Lady.   And why so, my lord?
   Mam.   Not for because
Your brows are blacker; yet black brows, they say,
Become some women best, so that there be not
Too much hair there, but in a semicircle,   10
Or a half-moon made with a pen.
   Sec. Lady.   Who taught you this?
   Mam.   I learnt it out of women's faces.
    Pray now
What colour are your eyebrows?
   First Lady.   Blue, my lord.
   Mam.   Nay, that's a mock: I have seen a
    lady's nose
That has been blue, but not her eyebrows.
   First Lady.   Hark ye;
The queen your mother rounds apace: we shall
Present our services to a fine new prince
•One of these days; and then you'ld wanton
    with us,
If we would have you.
   Sec. Lady.   She is spread of late
Into a goodly bulk: good time encounter her!   20
   Her.   What wisdom stirs amongst you? Come,
    sir, now
I am for you again: pray you, sit by us,
And tell's a tale.
   Mam.   Merry or sad shall't be?
   Her.   As merry as you will.
   Mam.   A sad tale's best for winter: I have one
Of sprites and goblins.
   Her.   Let's have that, good sir.

Costume design for Camillo by Jacques Noel, Stratford-upon-Avon, 1960

---

456 *Profess'd.* i.e. declared friendship.

462 *avoid.* Leave.

18 *wanton.* Play.

31 *crickets.* i.e. titterers.

35 *scour.* Rush.

38 *Alack . . . knowledge.* i.e. I wish I knew less!

40 *spider.* Spiders were believed to poison any liquid they touched.

51 *pinch'd.* Wretched. *trick.* Toy.

Leontes: 'He has discover'd my design, and I Remain a pinch'd thing;' Henry Ainley as Leontes and Lillah McCarthy as Hermione, Savoy Theatre, London, 1912

69 *without-door form.* Appearance.

72 *out.* Deceived.

Come on. sit down : come on, and do your best
To fright me with your sprites ; you're powerful
    at it.
    Mam.   There was a man—
    Her.   Nay, come, sit down ; then on.
    Mam.   Dwelt by a churchyard : I will tell it
        softly ;   30
●Yond crickets shall not hear it.
    Her.   Come on, then,
And give 't me in mine ear.

    Enter LEONTES, *with* ANTIGONUS, Lords,
            and others.

    Leon.   Was he met there? his train? Camillo
        with him?
    First Lord.   Behind the tuft of pines I met
        them ; never
●Saw I men scour so on their way : I eyed them
Even to their ships.
    Leon.   How blest am I
In my just censure, in my true opinion !
●Alack, for lesser knowledge ! how accursed
In being so blest ! There may be in the cup
●A spider steep'd, and one may drink, depart,   40
And yet partake no venom, for his knowledge
Is not infected : but if one present
The abhorr'd ingredient to his eye, make known
How he hath drunk, he cracks his gorge, his
        sides,
With violent hefts. I have drunk, and seen
        the spider.
Camillo was his help in this, his pandar :
There is a plot against my life, my crown :
All's true that is mistrusted : that false villain
Whom I employ'd was pre-employ'd by him :
He has discover'd my design, and I   50
●Remain a pinch'd thing ; yea, a very trick
For them to play at will. How came the posterns
So easily open?
    First Lord.   By his great authority ;
Which often hath no less prevail'd than so
On your command.
    Leon.   I know 't too well.
Give me the boy : I am glad you did not nurse
        him :
Though he does bear some signs of me, yet you
Have too much blood in him.
    Her.   What is this? sport?
    Leon.   Bear the boy hence ; he shall not come
        about her ;
Away with him ! and let her sport herself   60
With that she's big with ; for 'tis Polixenes
Has made thee swell thus.
    Her.   But I 'ld say he had not,
And I 'll be sworn you would believe my saying,
Howe'er you lean to the nayward.
    Leon.   You, my lords,
Look on her, mark her well ; be but about
To say ' she is a goodly lady,' and
The justice of your hearts will thereto add
'' Tis pity she's not honest, honourable :'
●Praise her but for this her without-door form,
Which on my faith deserves high speech, and
        straight   70
The shrug, the hum or ha, these petty brands
●That calumny doth use—O, I am out—
That mercy does, for calumny will sear
Virtue itself : these shrugs, these hums and ha's,

When you· have said 'she's goodly,' come between
Ere you can say 'she's honest:' but be't known,
From him that has most cause to grieve it should be,
She's an adulteress.

Her.   Should a villain say so,
●The most replenish'd villain in the world,
He were as much more villain: you, my lord, 80
Do but mistake.

Leon.   You have mistook, my lady,
Polixenes for Leontes: O thou thing!
Which I'll not call a creature of thy place,
Lest barbarism, making me the precedent,
Should a like language use to all degrees
And mannerly distinguishment leave out
Betwixt the prince and beggar: I have said
She's an adulteress; I have said with whom:
More, she's a traitor and Camillo is
A federary with her, and one that knows   90
What she should shame to know herself
But with her most vile principal, that she's
●A bed-swerver, even as bad as those
●That vulgars give bold'st titles, ay, and privy
To this their late escape.

Her.   No, by my life,
Privy to none of this. How will this grieve you,
When you shall come to clearer knowledge, that
You thus have publish'd me! Gentle my lord,
You scarce can right me throughly then to say
You did mistake.

Leon.   No; if I mistake   100
In those foundations which I build upon,
●The centre is not big enough to bear
A school-boy's top. Away with her! to prison!
●He who shall speak for her is afar off guilty
●But that he speaks.

Her.   There's some ill planet reigns:
I must be patient till the heavens look
With an aspect more favourable. Good my lords,/
I am not prone to weeping, as our sex
Commonly are; the want of which vain dew
Perchance shall dry your pities: but I have   110
That honourable grief lodged here which burns
Worse than tears drown: beseech you all, my lords,
With thoughts so qualified as your charities
Shall best instruct you, measure me; and so
The king's will be perform'd!

Leon.   Shall I be heard?

Her. Who is't that goes with me? Beseech your highness,
My women may be with me; for you see
My plight requires it. Do not weep, good fools;
There is no cause: when you shall know your mistress
Has deserved prison, then abound in tears   120
As I come out: this action I now go on
Is for my better grace. Adieu, my lord:
I never wish'd to see you sorry; now
I trust I shall. My women, come; you have leave.

Leon. Go, do our bidding; hence!

    [*Exit Queen, guarded; with Ladies.*

First Lord. Beseech your highness, call the queen again.

Ant. Be certain what you do, sir, lest your justice

79 *replenish'd.* Accomplished.

93 *bed-swerver.* Adulteress.

94 *vulgars.* Common folk. *bold'st titles.* Worst names.

102 *centre.* World.

104 *afar off.* Indirectly.

105 *But . . . speaks.* If he so much as says it.

Hermione: '. . . I have That honourable grief lodged here . . .' Judi Dench as Hermione and Barrie Ingham as Leontes, Royal Shakespeare Co, 1969

143 *land-damn.* Thrash, lambaste.

149 *glib.* Castrate.

172 *overture.* Public disclosure.

177 *nought for approbation.* Nothing to prove.

Prove violence; in the which **three great** ones suffer,
Yourself, your queen, your son.
  First Lord.   For her, my lord,
I dare my life lay down and will do't, sir, 130
Please you to accept it, that the queen is spotless
I' the eyes of heaven and to you; I mean,
In this which you accuse her.
  Ant.   If it prove
† She's otherwise, I'll keep my stables where
I lodge my wife; I'll go in couples with her;
Than when I feel and see her no farther trust her;
For every inch of woman in the world,
Ay, every dram of woman's flesh is false,
If she be.
  Leon. Hold your peaces.
  First Lord.   Good my lord,—
  Ant. It is for you we speak, not for ourselves:
You are abused and by some putter-on 141
That will be damn'd for't; would I knew the villain,
● †I would land-damn him. Be she honour-flaw'd,
I have three daughters; the eldest is eleven;
The second and the third, nine, and some five;
If this prove true, they'll pay for't: by mine honour,
I'll geld 'em all; fourteen they shall not see,
To bring false generations: they are co-heirs;
● And I had rather glib myself than they
Should not produce fair issue.
  Leon.   Cease; no more.
You smell this business with a sense as cold 151
As is a dead man's nose: but I do see't and feel't,
As you feel doing thus; and see withal
The instruments that feel.
  Ant.   If it be so,
We need no grave to bury honesty:
There's not a grain of it the face to sweeten
Of the whole dungy earth.
  Leon.   What! lack I credit?
  First Lord. I had rather you did lack than I, my lord,
Upon this ground; and more it would content me
To have her honour true than your suspicion, 160
Be blamed for't how you might.
  Leon.   Why, what need we
Commune with you of this, but rather follow
Our forceful instigation? Our prerogative
Calls not your counsels, but our natural goodness
Imparts this; which if you, or stupified
Or seeming so in skill, cannot or will not
Relish a truth like us, inform yourselves
We need no more of your advice: the matter,
The loss, the gain, the ordering on't, is all
Properly ours.
  Ant. And I wish, my liege, 170
You had only in your silent judgment tried it,
● Without more overture.
  Leon.   How could that be?
Either thou art most ignorant by age,
Or thou wert born a fool. Camillo's flight,
Added to their familiarity,
Which was as gross as ever touch'd conjecture,
● That lack'd sight only, nought for approbation
But only seeing, all other circumstances
Made up to the deed, doth push on this proceeding:
Yet, for a greater confirmation, 180
For in an act of this importance 'twere

Most piteous to be wild, I have dispatch'd in post
●To sacred Delphos, to Apollo's temple,
Cleomenes and Dion, whom you know
●Of stuff'd sufficiency: now from the oracle
They will bring all; whose spiritual counsel had,
Shall stop or spur me.   Have I done well?
   First Lord.   Well done, my lord.
   Leon.   Though I am satisfied and need no
     more
Than what I know, yet shall the oracle   190
Give rest to the minds of others, such as he
Whose ignorant credulity will not
Come up to the truth. So have we thought it good
From our free person she should be confined,
Lest that the treachery of the two fled hence
Be left her to perform.   Come, follow us;
We are to speak in public; for this business
●Will raise us all.
   Ant. [*Aside*] To laughter, as I take it,
If the good truth were known.   [*Exeunt.*

SCENE II. *A prison.*

Enter PAULINA, *a* Gentleman, *and* Attendants.

   Paul.   The keeper of the prison, call to him;
Let him have knowledge who I am. [*Exit Gent.*
                      Good lady,
No court in Europe is too good for thee;
What dost thou then in prison?

Re-enter Gentleman, *with the* Gaoler.

                    Now, good sir,
You know me, do you not?
   Gaol.   For a worthy lady
And one whom much I honour.
   Paul.   Pray you then,
Conduct me to the queen.
   Gaol.   I may not, madam:
To the contrary I have express commandment.
   Paul.   Here's ado,
To lock up honesty and honour from   10
The access of gentle visitors! Is't lawful, pray
     you,
To see her women? any of them? Emilia?
   Gaol.   So please you, madam,
To put apart these your attendants, I
Shall bring Emilia forth.
   Paul.   I pray now, call her.
Withdraw yourselves.
         [*Exeunt Gentleman and Attendants.*
   Gaol.   And, madam,
I must be present at your conference.
   Paul.   Well, be't so, prithee. [*Exit Gaoler.*
Here's such ado to make no stain a stain
As passes colouring.

Re-enter Gaoler, *with* EMILIA.

          Dear gentlewoman,   20
How fares our gracious lady?
   Emil.   As well as one so great and so forlorn
May hold together: on her frights and griefs,
Which never tender lady hath borne greater,
She is something before her time deliver'd.
   Paul.   A boy?
   Emil.   A daughter, and a goodly babe,
Lusty and like to live: the queen receives
Much comfort in't; says 'My poor prisoner,
I am innocent as you.'
   Paul.   I dare be sworn:

183 *Delphos.* i.e. Delos, the legendary island birthplace
of Apollo.

Avenue leading to the Temple of Apollo on the island
of Delos

---

185 *stuff'd sufficiency.* Adequate ability.

198 *raise.* Rouse.

30 *lunes*. Fits of lunacy.

Costume design for Paulina by Jacques Noel, Stratford-upon-Avon, 1960

57 *to pass it*. When I do it.

5 *blank*. Centre of the target.

8 *moiety*. Part.

●These dangerous unsafe lunes i' the king, be-
      shrew them!   30
He must be told on't, and he shall: the office
Becomes a woman best; I'll take't upon me:
If I prove honey-mouth'd, let my tongue blister
And never to my red-look'd anger be
The trumpet any more.   Pray you, Emilia,
Commend my best obedience to the queen:
If she dares trust me with her little babe,
I'll show't the king and undertake to be
Her advocate to the loud'st.   We do not know
How he may soften at the sight o' the child: 40
The silence often of pure innocence
Persuades when speaking fails.
      Emil.   Most worthy madam,
Your honour and your goodness is so evident
That your free undertaking cannot miss
A thriving issue: there is no lady living
So meet for this great errand.   Please your lady-
      ship
To visit the next room, I'll presently
Acquaint the queen of your most noble offer;
Who but to-day hammer'd of this design,
But durst not tempt a minister of honour,   50
Lest she should be denied.
      Paul.   Tell her, Emilia,
I'll use that tongue I have: if wit flow from't
As boldness from my bosom, let't not be doubted
I shall do good.
      Emil.   Now be you blest for it!
I'll to the queen: please you, come something
      nearer.
      Gaol.   Madam, if't please the queen to send
      the babe,
●I know not what I shall incur to pass it,
Having no warrant.
      Paul.   You need not fear it, sir:
This child was prisoner to the womb and is
By law and process of great nature thence   60
Freed and enfranchised, not a party to
The anger of the king nor guilty of,
If any be, the trespass of the queen.
      Gaol.   I do believe it.
      Paul.   Do not you fear: upon mine honour, I
Will stand betwixt you and danger.   [*Exeunt.*

SCENE III.   *A room in* LEONTES' *palace.*

Enter LEONTES, ANTIGONUS, Lords, *and*
      Servants.

      Leon.   Nor night nor day no rest: it is but
      weakness
To bear the matter thus; mere weakness.   If
The cause were not in being,—part o' the cause,
She the adulteress; for the harlot king
●Is quite beyond mine arm, out of the blank
And level of my brain, plot-proof; but she
I can hook to me: say that she were gone,
●Given to the fire, a moiety of my rest
Might come to me again.   Who's there?
      First Serv.   My lord?
      Leon.   How does the boy?
      First Serv.   He took good rest to-night;   10
'Tis hoped his sickness is discharged.
      Leon.   To see his nobleness!
Conceiving the dishonour of his mother,
He straight declined, droop'd, took it deeply,
Fasten'd and fix'd the shame on't in himself,
Threw off his spirit, his appetite, his sleep,

And downright languish'd. Leave me solely: go,
See how he fares. [*Exit Serv.*] Fie, fie! no
    thought of him:
The very thought of my revenges that way
Recoil upon me: in himself too mighty,   20
And in his parties, his alliance; let him be
Until a time may serve: for present vengeance,
Take it on her. Camillo and Polixenes
Laugh at me, make their pastime at my sorrow:
They should not laugh if I could reach them, nor
Shall she within my power.

        Enter PAULINA, *with a child.*

  First Lord.   You must not enter.
  Paul. Nay, rather, good my lords, be second
    to me:
Fear you his tyrannous passion more, alas,
Than the queen's life? a gracious innocent soul,
More free than he is jealous.
  Ant.   That's enough.   30
  Sec. Serv. Madam, he hath not slept to-night;
    commanded
None should come at him.
  Paul.   Not so hot, good sir:
I come to bring him sleep. 'Tis such as you,
That creep like shadows by him and do sigh
At each his needless heavings, such as you
Nourish the cause of his awaking: I
Do come with words as medicinal as true,
Honest as either, to purge him of that humour
That presses him from sleep.
  Leon.   What noise there, ho?
  Paul. No noise, my lord; but needful confer-
    ence   40
About some gossips for your highness.
  Leon.   How!
Away with that audacious lady! Antigonus,
I charged thee that she should not come about me:
I knew she would.
  Ant.   I told her so, my lord,
On your displeasure's peril and on mine,
She should not visit you.
  Leon.   What, canst not rule her?
  Paul. From all dishonesty he can: in this,
Unless he take the course that you have done,
Commit me for committing honour, trust it,
He shall not rule me.
  Ant.   La you now, you hear: 50
When she will take the rein I let her run;
But she'll not stumble.
  Paul.   Good my liege, I come;
And, I beseech you, hear me, who profess
Myself your loyal servant, your physician,
Your most obedient counsellor, yet that dare
Less appear so in comforting your evils,
Than such as most seem yours: I say, I come
From your good queen.
  Leon.   Good queen!
  Paul.   Good queen, my lord,
Good queen; I say good queen;
And would by combat make her good, so were I
A man, the worst about you.   61
  Leon.   Force her hence.
  Paul. Let him that makes but trifles of his eyes
First hand me: on mine own accord I'll off;
But first I'll do my errand. The good queen,
For she is good, hath brought you forth a daughter;
Here 'tis; commends it to your blessing.
               [*Laying down the child.*

First Lord: 'You must not enter.' Scene design by
Motley, Stratford-upon-Avon, 1948

---

49 *Commit.* Imprison.

Paulina: 'I am . . . no less honest Than you are mad;'
Drawing by Robert Smirke (1752–1845)

---

74 *woman-tired*. Nagged.

75 *dame Partlet*. i.e. shrill hen.

90 *callet*. Scold.

Leontes: 'This brat is none of mine;' Peggy Ashcroft as Paulina and Eric Porter as Leontes, Stratford-upon-Avon, 1960

---

109 *lozel*. Worthless, profligate.

Leon.   Out!
A mankind witch! Hence with her, out o' door:
A most intelligencing bawd!
   Paul.   Not so:
I am as ignorant in that as you
In so entitling me, and no less honest   70
Than you are mad; which is enough, I'll warrant,
As this world goes, to pass for honest.
   Leon.   Traitors!
Will you not push her out? Give her the bastard.
●Thou dotard! thou art woman-tired, unroosted
●By thy dame Partlet here. Take up the bastard;
Take't up, I say; give't to thy crone.
   Paul.   For ever
Unvenerable be thy hands, if thou
Takest up the princess by that forced baseness
Which he has put upon't!
   Leon.   He dreads his wife.
   Paul. So I would you did; then 'twere past
      all doubt   80
You'ld call your children yours.
   Leon.   A nest of traitors!
   Ant. I am none, by this good light.
   Paul.   Nor I, nor any
But one that's here, and that's himself, for he
The sacred honour of himself, his queen's,
His hopeful son's, his babe's, betrays to slander,
Whose sting is sharper than the sword's; and
      will not—
For, as the case now stands, it is a curse
He cannot be compell'd to't—once remove
The root of his opinion, which is rotten
●As ever oak or stone was sound.
   Leon.   A callet   90
Of boundless tongue, who late hath beat her
      husband
And now baits me! This brat is none of mine;
It is the issue of Polixenes:
Hence with it, and together with the dam
Commit them to the fire!
   Paul.   It is yours;
And, might we lay the old proverb to your charge,
So like you, 'tis the worse. Behold, my lords,
Although the print be little, the whole matter
And copy of the father, eye, nose, lip,
The trick of's frown, his forehead, nay, the valley,
The pretty dimples of his chin and cheek,   101
His smiles,
The very mould and frame of hand, nail, finger:
And thou, good goddess Nature, which hast
      made it
So like to him that got it, if thou hast
The ordering of the mind too, 'mongst all colours
No yellow in't, lest she suspect, as he does,
Her children not her husband's!
   Leon.   A gross hag!
●And, lozel, thou art worthy to be hang'd,
That wilt not stay her tongue.
   Ant.   Hang all the husbands   110
That cannot do that feat, you'll leave yourself
Hardly one subject.
   Leon.   Once more, take her hence.
   Paul. A most unworthy and unnatural lord
Can do no more.
   Leon.   I'll ha' thee burnt.
   Paul.   I care not:
It is an heretic that makes the fire,
Not she which burns in't. I'll not call you tyrant;
But this most cruel usage of your queen,

Not able to produce more accusation
Than your own weak-hinged fancy, something
        savours
Of tyranny and will ignoble make you,   120
Yea, scandalous to the world.
    Leon.   On your allegiance,
Out of the chamber with her ! Were I a tyrant,
Where were her life ? she durst not call me so,
If she did know me one.   Away with her !
    Paul. I pray you, do not push me ; I'll be gone.
Look to your babe, my lord ; 'tis yours : Jove
        send her
A better guiding spirit ! What needs these hands ?
You, that are thus so tender o'er his follies,
Will never do him good, not one of you.
So, so : farewell ; we are gone.   [*Exit.* 130
    Leon. Thou, traitor, hast set on thy wife to
        this.
My child ? away with 't ! Even thou, that hast
A heart so tender o'er it, take it hence
And see it instantly consumed with fire ;
Even thou and none but thou.   Take it up straight :
Within this hour bring me word 'tis done,
And by good testimony, or I 'll seize thy life,
With what thou else call'st thine.   If thou refuse
And wilt encounter with my wrath, say so ;
The bastard brains with these my proper hands
Shall I dash out.   Go, take it to the fire ;   140
For thou set'st on thy wife.
    Ant.   I did not, sir :
These lords, my noble fellows, if they please,
Can clear me in 't.
    Lords.   We can : my royal liege,
He is not guilty of her coming hither.
    Leon. You 're liars all.
    First Lord. Beseech your highness, give us
        better credit :
We have always truly served you, and beseech you
So to esteem of us, and on our knees we beg,
As recompense of our dear services   150
Past and to come, that you do change this purpose,
Which being so horrible, so bloody, must
Lead on to some foul issue : we all kneel.
    Leon. I am a feather for each wind that blows :
Shall I live on to see this bastard kneel
And call me father ? better burn it now
Than curse it then.   But be it ; let it live.
It shall not neither.   You, sir, come you hither ;
You that have been so tenderly officious
⦁With Lady Margery, your midwife there,   160
To save this bastard's life,—for 'tis a bastard,
So sure as this beard's grey,—what will you ad-
        venture
To save this brat's life ?
    Ant.   Any thing, my lord,
That my ability may undergo
And nobleness impose : at least thus much :
I 'll pawn the little blood which I have left
To save the innocent : any thing possible.
    Leon. It shall be possible.   Swear by this
        sword
Thou wilt perform my bidding.
    Ant.   I will, my lord.
    Leon. Mark and perform it, see'st thou ! for
        the fail   170
Of any point in 't shall not only be
Death to thyself but to thy lewd-tongued wife,
Whom for this time we pardon.   We enjoin thee,
As thou art liege-man to us, that thou carry

160 *Lady Margery.* Hen.

Antigonus: 'Some powerful spirit instruct the kites and ravens To be thy nurses!' Raven, from 12th century Latin bestiary

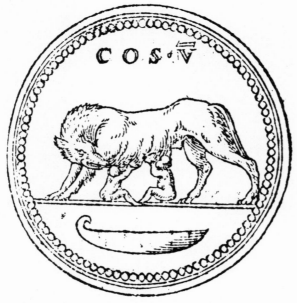

Antigonus: 'Wolves and bears ... Casting their savageness aside ...' Engraving of Romulus and Remus nursed by a wolf, from G. du Choul's *Discours de la Religion des Anciens Romains*, 1567

This female bastard hence and that thou bear it
To some remote and desert place quite out
Of our dominions, and that there thou leave it,
Without more mercy, to it own protection
And favour of the climate.   As by strange fortune
It came to us, I do in justice charge thee,   180
On thy soul's peril and thy body's torture,
That thou commend it strangely to some place
Where chance may nurse or end it.   Take it up.
   Ant.   I swear to do this, though a present
      death
Had been more merciful.   Come on, poor babe:
Some powerful spirit instruct the kites and ravens
To be thy nurses!   Wolves and bears, they say,
Casting their savageness aside have done
Like offices of pity.   Sir, be prosperous
In more than this deed does require!   And blessing
Against this cruelty fight on thy side,   191
Poor thing, condemn'd to loss!
                              [*Exit with the child*.
   Leon.   No, I'll not rear
Another's issue.

                  Enter a Servant.

   Serv.   Please your highness, posts
From those you sent to the oracle are come
An hour since: Cleomenes and Dion,
Being well arrived from Delphos, are both landed,
Hasting to the court.
   First Lord.   So please you, sir, their speed
Hath been beyond account.
   Leon.   Twenty three days
They have been absent: 'tis good speed; foretells
The great Apollo suddenly will have   200
The truth of this appear.   Prepare you, lords;
Summon a session, that we may arraign
Our most disloyal lady, for, as she hath
Been publicly accused, so shall she have
A just and open trial.   While she lives
My heart will be a burthen to me.   Leave me,
And think upon my bidding.   [*Exeunt*.

                     ACT III.

         SCENE I.   *A sea-port in Sicilia*.

            Enter CLEOMENES *and* DION.

   Cleo.   The climate's delicate, the air most
         sweet,
Fertile the isle, the temple much surpassing
The common praise it bears.
   Dion.   I shall report,
For most it caught me, the celestial habits,
Methinks I so should term them, and the rever-
      ence
Of the grave wearers.   O, the sacrifice!
How ceremonious, solemn and unearthly
It was i' the offering!
   Cleo.   But of all, the burst
And the ear-deafening voice o' the oracle,
Kin to Jove's thunder, so surprised my sense,   10
That I was nothing.
   Dion.   If the event o' the journey
Prove as successful to the queen,—O be't so!—
As it hath been to us rare, pleasant, speedy,
The time is worth the use on't.
   Cleo.   Great Apollo
Turn all to the best!   These proclamations,
So forcing faults upon Hermione,

I little like.
   Dion.   The violent carriage of it
Will clear or end the business: when the oracle,
Thus by Apollo's great divine seal'd up,
Shall the contents discover, something rare   20
Even then will rush to knowledge. Go: fresh
   horses!
And gracious be the issue!   [*Exeunt.*

SCENE II.   *A court of Justice.*

Enter LEONTES, Lords, *and* Officers.

● *Leon.*   This sessions, to our great grief we
   pronounce,
Even pushes 'gainst our heart: the party tried
The daughter of a king, our wife, and one
Of us too much beloved.   Let us be clear'd
Of being tyrannous, since we so openly
Proceed in justice, which shall have due course,
Even to the guilt or the purgation.
Produce the prisoner.
   Off.   It is his highness' pleasure that the queen
Appear in person here in court. Silence!   10

Enter HERMIONE *guarded;* PAULINA *and*
Ladies *attending.*

   Leon.   Read the indictment.
   Off.   [*Reads*] Hermione, queen to the worthy
Leontes, king of Sicilia, thou art here accused
and arraigned of high treason, in committing
adultery with Polixenes, king of Bohemia, and
conspiring with Camillo to take away the life of
our sovereign lord the king, thy royal husband:
the pretence whereof being by circumstances
partly laid open, thou, Hermione, contrary to the
faith and allegiance of a true subject, didst coun-
sel and aid them, for their better safety, to fly
away by night.
   Her.   Since what I am to say must be but
   that
Which contradicts my accusation and
The testimony on my part no other
● But what comes from myself, it shall scarce boot
   me
To say 'not guilty:' mine integrity
Being counted falsehood, shall, as I express it,
Be so received.   But thus: if powers divine
Behold our human actions, as they do,   30
I doubt not then but innocence shall make
False accusation blush and tyranny
Tremble at patience. You, my lord, best know,
Who least will seem to do so, my past life
Hath been as continent, as chaste, as true,
As I am now unhappy; which is more
Than history can pattern, though devised
And play'd to take spectators. For behold me
● A fellow of the royal bed, which owe
A moiety of the throne, a great king's daughter,
The mother to a hopeful prince, here standing 41
To prate and talk for life and honour 'fore
Who please to come and hear. For life, I prize it
As I weigh grief, which I would spare: for
   honour,
'Tis a derivative from me to mine,
And only that I stand for. I appeal
To your own conscience, sir, before Polixenes
Came to your court, how I was in your grace,
How merited to be so; since he came,
With what encounter so uncurrent I   50

1 *sessions.* Trial.

26 *boot.* Profit.

39 *owe.* Own.

Mary Anderson as Hermione, Lyceum Theatre, London,
1887

Ian McKellen as Leontes, Royal Shakespeare Co, 1976

77 *Wotting.* Knowing.

102 *Haled.* Dragged.

105 *fashion.* Kind.

107 *of limit.* Limited.

Have strain'd to appear thus: if one jot beyond
The bound of honour, or in act or will
That way inclining, harden'd be the hearts
Of all that hear me, and my near'st of kin
Cry fie upon my grave!
    Leon.   I ne'er heard yet
That any of these bolder vices wanted
Less impudence to gainsay what they did
Than to perform it first.
    Her.   That's true enough;
Though 'tis a saying, sir, not due to me.
    Leon. You will not own it.
    Her.   †More than mistress of 60
Which comes to me in name of fault, I must not
At all acknowledge.   For Polixenes,
With whom I am accused, I do confess
I loved him as in honour he required,
With such a kind of love as might become
A lady like me, with a love even such,
So and no other, as yourself commanded:
Which not to have done I think had been in me
Both disobedience and ingratitude
To you and toward your friend, whose love had
      spoke,   70
Even since it could speak, from an infant, freely
That it was yours.   Now, for conspiracy,
I know not how it tastes;. though it be dish'd
For me to try how: all I know of it
Is that Camillo was an honest man;
And why he left your court, the gods themselves,
•Wotting no more than I, are ignorant.
    Leon. You knew of his departure, as you know
What you have underta'en to do in's absence.
    Her. Sir,   80
You speak a language that I understand not:
My life stands in the level of your dreams,
Which I'll lay down.
    Leon.   Your actions are my dreams;
You had a bastard by Polixenes,
And I but dream'd it.   As you were past all
      shame,—
Those of your fact are so—so past all truth:
Which to deny concerns more than avails; for as
Thy brat hath been cast out, like to itself,
No father owning it,—which is, indeed,
More criminal in thee than it,—so thou   90
Shalt feel our justice, in whose easiest passage
Look for no less than death.
    Her.   Sir, spare your threats:
The bug which you would fright me with I seek.
To me can life be no commodity:
The crown and comfort of my life, your favour,
I do give lost; for I do feel it gone,
But know not how it went.   My second joy
And first-fruits of my body, from his presence
I am barr'd, like one infectious.   My third com-
    fort,
Starr'd most unluckily, is from my breast,   100
The innocent milk in it most innocent mouth,
•Haled out to murder: myself on every post
Proclaim'd a strumpet: with immodest hatred
The child-bed privilege denied, which 'longs
•To women of all fashion; lastly, hurried
Here to this place, i' the open air, before
•I have got strength of limit.   Now, my liege,
Tell me what blessings I have here alive,
That I should fear to die?   Therefore proceed.
But yet hear this; mistake me not; no life, 110
I prize it not a straw, but for mine honour,

Which I would free, if I shall be condemn'd
Upon surmises, all proofs sleeping else
But what your jealousies awake, I tell you
'Tis rigour and not law.   Your honours all,
I do refer me to the oracle:
Apollo be my judge!
 First Lord. This your request
Is altogether just: therefore bring forth,
And in Apollo's name, his oracle.
       [*Exeunt certain Officers.*
 Her.   The Emperor of Russia was my father:
O that he were alive, and here beholding 121
His daughter's trial! that he did but see
•The flatness of my misery, yet with eyes
Of pity, not revenge!

 Re-enter Officers, *with* CLEOMENES *and* DION.

 Off.   You here shall swear upon this sword of
  justice,
That you, Cleomenes and Dion, have
Been both at Delphos, and from thence have
  brought
This seal'd-up oracle, by the hand deliver'd
Of great Apollo's priest and that since then
You have not dared to break the holy seal 130
Nor read the secrets in't.
 Cleo. Dion. All this we swear.
 Leon.   Break up the seals and read.
 Off.   [*Reads*] Hermione is chaste; Polixenes
blameless; Camillo a true subject; Leontes a
jealous tyrant; his innocent babe truly begotten;
and the king shall live without an heir, if that
which is lost be not found.
 Lords.   Now blessed be the great Apollo!
 Her.   Praised!
 Leon.   Hast thou read truth?
 Off.   Ay, my lord; even so
As it is here set down. 140
 Leon.   There is no truth at all i' the oracle:
The sessions shall proceed: this is mere falsehood.

    Enter Servant.

 Serv.   My lord the king, the king!
 Leon.   What is the business?
 Serv.   O sir, I shall be hated to report it!
•The prince your son, with mere conceit and fear
Of the queen's speed, is gone.
 Leon.   How! gone!
 Serv.   Is dead.
 Leon.   Apollo's angry; and the heavens them-
  selves
Do strike at my injustice.   [*Hermione swoons.*]
  How now there!
 Paul.   This news is mortal to the queen: look
  down
And see what death is doing.
 Leon.   Take her hence: 150
Her heart is but o'ercharged; she will recover:
I have too much believed mine own suspicion:
Beseech you, tenderly apply to her
Some remedies for life.
[*Exeunt Paulina and Ladies, with Hermione.*
      Apollo, pardon
My great profaneness 'gainst thine oracle!
I'll reconcile me to Polixenes,
New woo my queen, recall the good Camillo,
Whom I proclaim a man of truth, of mercy;
For, being transported by my jealousies
To bloody thoughts and to revenge, I chose 160

123 *flatness.* Depth.

145–146 *with mere . . . speed.* With no more than thought
and fear of the Queen's fate.

Paulina: '. . . look down And see what death is doing.'
The Victorian actors Miss Lovell as Paulina, John
Ryder as Leontes and Eleanor Buffon as Hermione.

168 *Unclasp'd.* Revealed. *practice.* Plot.

174 *lace.* i.e. the laces of my bodice.

185 *spices.* Samples.

210 *stir.* Move.

Leontes: 'I have deserved All tongues to talk their
bitterest.' William Devlin as Leontes and Dorothy Green
as Paulina, Old Vic Theatre, London, 1936

Camillo for the minister to poison
My friend Polixenes: which had been done,
But that the good mind of Camillo tardied
My swift command, though I with death and with
Reward did threaten and encourage him,
Not doing 't and being done: he, most humane
And fill'd with honour, to my kingly guest
● Unclasp'd my practice, quit his fortunes here,
Which you knew great, and to the hazard
Of all incertainties himself commended,   170
No richer than his honour: how he glisters
Thorough my rust! and how his piety
Does my deeds make the blacker!

Re-enter PAULINA.

Paul.   Woe the while!
● O, cut my lace, lest my heart, cracking it,
Break too!
   First Lord.   What fit is this, good lady?
   Paul.   What studied torments, tyrant, hast
        for me?
What wheels? racks? fires? what flaying? boiling?
In leads or oils? what old or newer torture
Must I receive, whose every word deserves
To taste of thy most worst? Thy tyranny   180
Together working with thy jealousies,
Fancies too weak for boys, too green and idle
For girls of nine, O, think what they have done
And then run mad indeed, stark mad! for all
● Thy by-gone fooleries were but spices of it.
That thou betray'dst Polixenes, 'twas nothing;
That did but show thee, of a fool, inconstant
And damnable ingrateful: nor was 't much,
Thou wouldst have poison'd good Camillo's honour,
To have him kill a king; poor trespasses,   190
More monstrous standing by: whereof I reckon
The casting forth to crows thy baby-daughter
To be or none or little; though a devil
Would have shed water out of fire ere done 't:
Nor is 't directly laid to thee, the death
Of the young prince, whose honourable thoughts,
Thoughts high for one so tender, cleft the heart
That could conceive a gross and foolish sire
Blemish'd his gracious dam: this is not, no,
Laid to thy answer: but the last.—O lords,   200
When I have said, cry 'woe!'—the queen, the
        queen,
The sweet'st, dear'st creature's dead, and ven-
        geance for 't
Not dropp'd down yet.
   First Lord.   The higher powers forbid!
   Paul. I say she's dead; I'll swear 't.   If
        word nor oath
Prevail not, go and see: if you can bring
Tincture or lustre in her lip, her eye,
Heat outwardly or breath within, I'll serve you
As I would do the gods.   But, O thou tyrant!
Do not repent these things, for they are heavier
● Than all thy woes can stir: therefore betake thee
To nothing but despair.   A thousand knees   211
Ten thousand years together, naked, fasting,
Upon a barren mountain, and still winter
In storm perpetual, could not move the gods
To look that way thou wert.
   Leon.   Go on, go on:
Thou canst not speak too much; I have deserved
All tongues to talk their bitterest.
   First Lord.   Say no more:
Howe'er the business goes, you have made fault

I' the boldness of your speech.
    Paul.   I am sorry for't:
All faults I make, when I shall come to know them,
I do repent.   Alas! I have show'd too much   221
The rashness of a woman : he is touch'd
To the noble heart.   What's gone and what's
        past help
Should be past grief: do not receive affliction
At my petition ; I beseech you, rather
Let me be punish'd, that have minded you
Of what you should forget.   Now, good my liege,
Sir, royal sir, forgive a foolish woman :
The love I bore your queen—lo, fool again !—
I 'll speak of her no more, nor of your children ;
I 'll not remember you of my own lord,   231
Who is lost too : take your patience to you,
And I 'll say nothing.
    Leon.   Thou didst speak but well
When most the truth ; which I receive much better
Than to be pitied of thee.   Prithee, bring me
To the dead bodies of my queen and son :
One grave shall be for both : upon them shall
The causes of their death appear, unto
Our shame perpetual.   Once a day I 'll visit
The chapel where they lie, and tears shed there
Shall be my recreation : so long as nature   241
Will bear up with this exercise, so long
I daily vow to use it.   Come and lead me
Unto these sorrows.   [*Exeunt.*

SCENE III.   *Bohemia.   A desert country near
          the sea.*

Enter ANTIGONUS *with a Child, and a* Mariner.

    Ant.   Thou art perfect then, our ship hath
        touch'd upon
The deserts of Bohemia?
    Mar.   Ay, my lord : and fear
We have landed in ill time : the skies look grimly
And threaten present blusters.   In my conscience,
The heavens with that we have in hand are angry
And frown upon 's.
    Ant.   Their sacred wills be done! Go, get
        aboard ;
Look to thy bark : I 'll not be long before
I call upon thee.
    Mar.   Make your best haste, and go not   10
Too far i' the land : 'tis like to be loud weather ;
Besides, this place is famous for the creatures
● Of prey that keep upon 't.
    Ant.   Go thou away :
I 'll follow instantly.
    Mar.   I am glad at heart
To be so rid o' the business.   [*Exit.*
    Ant.   Come, poor babe :
I have heard, but not believed, the spirits o' the
        dead
May walk again : if such thing be, thy mother
Appear'd to me last night, for ne'er was dream
So like a waking.   To me comes a creature,
Sometimes her head on one side, some another ;
I never saw a vessel of like sorrow,   21
So fill'd and so becoming : in pure white robes,
Like very sanctity, she did approach
My cabin where I lay ; thrice bow'd before me,
And gasping to begin some speech, her eyes
● Became two spouts : the fury spent, anon
Did this break from her : 'Good Antigonus,
Since fate, against thy better disposition,

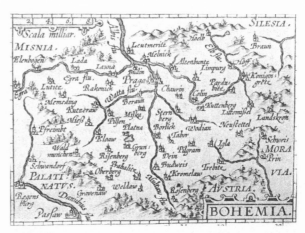

Bohemia. Engraving from Abraham Ortelius' *Epitome
to the Theatre of the World,* 1598

13 *keep.* Live.

26 *anon.* Soon.

Costume design for Antigonus by Jacques Noel,
Stratford-upon-Avon, 1960

33 *Perdita*. i.e. lost one.

41 *squared*. Influenced.

63 *ancientry*. Old people.

70 *barne*. Child.

71 *child*. Girl.

73 *'scape*. Escapade.

76 *got*. Begot.

Shepherd: 'I'll take it up for pity.' Engraving by Henry Fuseli (1741–1825)

Hath made thy person for the thrower-out
Of my poor babe, according to thine oath, 30
Places remote enough are in Bohemia,
There weep and leave it crying; and, for the babe
● Is counted lost for ever, Perdita,
I prithee, call't.   For this ungentle business,
Put on thee by my lord, thou ne'er shalt see
Thy wife Paulina more.'   And so, with shrieks,
She melted into air.   Affrighted much,
I did in time collect myself and thought
This was so and no slumber.   Dreams are toys:
Yet for this once, yea, superstitiously, 40
● I will be squared by this.   I do believe
Hermione hath suffer'd death, and that
Apollo would, this being indeed the issue
Of King Polixenes, it should here be laid,
Either for life or death, upon the earth
Of its right father.   Blossom, speed thee well!
There lie, and there thy character: there these;
Which may, if fortune please, both breed thee, pretty,
And still rest thine.   The storm begins: poor wretch,
That for thy mother's fault art thus exposed 50
To loss and what may follow!   Weep I cannot,
But my heart bleeds; and most accursed am I
To be by oath enjoin'd to this.   Farewell!
The day frowns more and more: thou'rt like to have
A lullaby too rough: I never saw
The heavens so dim by day.   A savage clamour!
Well may I get aboard!   This is the chase:
I am gone for ever.   [*Exit, pursued by a bear.*
Enter a Shepherd.
Shep. I would there were no age between
sixteen and three-and-twenty, or that youth would
sleep out the rest; for there is nothing in the
between but getting wenches with child, wrong-
● ing the ancientry, stealing, fighting—Hark you
now!   Would any but these boiled brains of
nineteen and two-and-twenty hunt this weather?
They have scared away two of my best sheep,
which I fear the wolf will sooner find than the
master: if any where I have them, 'tis by the sea-
side, browsing of ivy.   Good luck, an't be thy
● will! what have we here?   Mercy on's, a barne;
● a very pretty barne!   A boy or a child, I wonder?
A pretty one; a very pretty one: sure, some
● 'scape: though I am not bookish, yet I can read
waiting-gentlewoman in the 'scape.   This has
been some stair-work, some trunk-work, some
● behind-door-work: they were warmer that got
this than the poor thing is here.   I'll take it up
for pity: yet I'll tarry till my son come; he hal-
looed but even now.   Whoa, ho, hoa!

Enter Clown.

Clo. Hilloa, loa! 80
Shep. What, art so near?   If thou'lt see a
thing to talk on when thou art dead and rotten,
come hither.   What ailest thou, man?
Clo. I have seen two such sights, by sea and
by land! but I am not to say it is a sea, for it is
now the sky: betwixt the firmament and it you
cannot thrust a bodkin's point.
Shep. Why, boy, how is it?
Clo. I would you did but see how it chafes,
how it rages, how it takes up the shore! but
that's not to the point.   O, the most piteous cry

of the poor souls! sometimes to see 'em, and not to see 'em; now the ship boring the moon with her main-mast, and anon swallowed with yest and froth, as you'ld thrust a cork into a hogshead. And then for the land-service, to see how the bear tore out his shoulder-bone; how he cried to me for help and said his name was Antigonus, a nobleman. But to make an end of the ship, to see how the sea flap-dragoned it: but, first, how the poor souls roared, and the sea mocked them; and how the poor gentleman roared and the bear mocked him, both roaring louder than the sea or weather.

Shep. Name of mercy, when was this, boy?

Clo. Now, now: I have not winked since I saw these sights: the men are not yet cold under water, nor the bear half dined on the gentleman: he's at it now.

Shep. Would I had been by, to have helped the old man! III

Clo. I would you had been by the ship side, to have helped her: there your charity would have lacked footing.

Shep. Heavy matters! heavy matters! but look thee here, boy. Now bless thyself: thou mettest with things dying, I with things new-born. Here's a sight for thee; look thee, a bearing-cloth for a squire's child! look thee here; take up, take up, boy; open't. So, let's see: it was told me I should be rich by the fairies. This is some changeling: open't. What's within, boy?

Clo. You're a made old man: if the sins of your youth are forgiven you, you're well to live. Gold! all gold!

Shep. This is fairy gold, boy, and 'twill prove so: up with't, keep it close: home, home, the next way. We are lucky, boy; and to be so still requires nothing but secrecy. Let my sheep go: come, good boy, the next way home.

Clo. Go you the next way with your findings. I'll go see if the bear be gone from the gentleman and how much he hath eaten: they are never curst but when they are hungry: if there be any of him left, I'll bury it.

Shep. That's a good deed. If thou mayest discern by that which is left of him what he is, fetch me to the sight of him.

Clo. Marry, will I; and you shall help to put him i' the ground. 141

Shep. 'Tis a lucky day, boy, and we'll do good deeds on't. [*Exeunt.*

ACT IV. Scene I.

Enter Time, *the* Chorus.

Time. I, that please some, try all, both joy and terror
Of good and bad, that makes and unfolds error,
Now take upon me, in the name of Time,
To use my wings. Impute it not a crime
To me or my swift passage, that I slide
O'er sixteen years and leave the growth untried
Of that wide gap, since it is in my power
To o'erthrow law and in one self-born hour
To plant and o'erwhelm custom. Let me pass
The same I am, ere ancient'st order was 10
Or what is now received: I witness to

A storm with a shipwreck. Detail from a painting by Claude Joseph Vernet (1714–1789)

Clown: '. . . the bear tore out his shoulder-bone;' Bear, from 12th century Latin bestiary

100 *flap-dragoned.* Gulped up.

119 *bearing-cloth.* Christening robe.

6 *growth untried.* Events untold.

18 *fond*. Foolish.

26 *list not*. Do not wish to.

Costume design for Time, by Jacques Noel, Stratford-upon-Avon, 1960

The times that brought them in; so shall I do
To the freshest things now reigning and make stale
The glistering of this present, as my tale
Now seems to it.   Your patience this allowing,
I turn my glass and give my scene such growing
As you had slept between : Leontes leaving,
● The effects of his fond jealousies so grieving
That he shuts up himself, imagine me,
Gentle spectators, that I now may be   20
In fair Bohemia; and remember well,
I mentioned a son o' the king's, which Florizel
I now name to you; and with speed so pace
To speak of Perdita, now grown in grace
Equal with wondering: what of her ensues
● I list not prophesy; but let Time's news
Be known when 'tis brought forth.   A shepherd's daughter,
And what to her adheres, which follows after,
Is the argument of Time.   Of this allow,
If ever you have spent time worse ere now;   30
If never, yet that Time himself doth say
He wishes earnestly you never may.   [*Exit*.

SCENE II. *Bohemia.   The palace of* POLIXENES.

Enter POLIXENES *and* CAMILLO.

Pol.   I pray thee, good Camillo, be no more importunate : 'tis a sickness denying thee any thing; a death to grant this.

Cam.   It is fifteen years since I saw my country : though I have for the most part been aired abroad, I desire to lay my bones there. Besides, the penitent king, my master, hath sent for me; to whose feeling sorrows I might be some allay, or I o'erween to think so, which is another spur to my departure.   10

Pol.   As thou lovest me, Camillo, wipe not out the rest of thy services by leaving me now: the need I have of thee thine own goodness hath made; better not to have had thee than thus to want thee : thou, having made me businesses which none without thee can sufficiently manage, must either stay to execute them thyself or take away with thee the very services thou hast done; which if I have not enough considered, as too much I cannot, to be more thankful to thee shall be my study, and my profit therein the heaping friendships.   Of that fatal country, Sicilia, prithee speak no more; whose very naming punishes me with the remembrance of that penitent, as thou callest him, and reconciled king, my brother; whose loss of his most precious queen and children are even now to be afresh lamented.   Say to me, when sawest thou the Prince Florizel, my son?   Kings are no less unhappy, their issue not being gracious, than they are in losing them when they have approved their virtues.

Cam.   Sir, it is three days since I saw the prince.   What his happier affairs may be, are to me unknown : but I have missingly noted, he is of late much retired from court and is less frequent to his princely exercises than formerly he hath appeared.

Pol.   I have considered so much, Camillo, and with some care; so far that I have eyes under my service which look upon his removedness; from whom I have this intelligence, that he is seldom from the house of a most homely shepherd; a man, they say, that from very nothing, and beyond the imagination of his neighbours, is grown into an unspeakable estate.

Cam. I have heard, sir, of such a man, who hath a daughter of most rare note: the report of her is extended more than can be thought to begin from such a cottage.   50

Pol. That's likewise part of my intelligence; but, I fear, the angle that plucks our son thither. Thou shalt accompany us to the place; where we will, not appearing what we are, have some question with the shepherd; from whose simplicity I think it not uneasy to get the cause of my son's resort thither. Prithee, be my present partner in this business, and lay aside the thoughts of Sicilia.

Cam. I willingly obey your command.

Pol. My best Camillo! We must disguise ourselves.   [*Exeunt.*

SCENE III. *A road near the* Shepherd's *cottage.*

Enter AUTOLYCUS, *singing.*

When daffodils begin to peer,
With heigh! the doxy over the dale,
Why, then comes in the sweet o' the year;
For the red blood reigns in the winter's pale.

The white sheet bleaching on the hedge,
With heigh! the sweet birds, O, how they sing!
Doth set my pugging tooth on edge;
For a quart of ale is a dish for a king.

The lark, that tirra-lyra chants,
With heigh! with heigh! the thrush and the jay,
Are summer songs for me and my aunts,   11
While we lie tumbling in the hay.

I have served Prince Florizel and in my time wore three-pile; but now I am out of service:

But shall I go mourn for that, my dear?
The pale moon shines by night:
And when I wander here and there,
I then do most go right.

If tinkers may have leave to live,
And bear the sow-skin budget,   20
Then my account I well may give,
And in the stocks avouch it.

My traffic is sheets; when the kite builds, look to lesser linen. My father named me Autolycus: who being, as I am, littered under Mercury, was likewise a snapper-up of unconsidered trifles. With die and drab I purchased this caparison, and my revenue is the silly cheat. Gallows and knock are too powerful on the highway: beating and hanging are terrors to me: for the life to come, I sleep out the thought of it. A prize! a prize!

Enter Clown.

Clo. Let me see: every 'leven wether tods; every tod yields pound and odd shilling; fifteen hundred shorn, what comes the wool to?

Aut. [*Aside*] If the springe hold, the cock's mine.

Clo. I cannot do't without counters. Let me see; what am I to buy for our sheep-shearing

52 *angle.* Hook.

2 *doxy.* Beggar's woman.

7 *pugging tooth.* Taste for thieving.

11 *aunts.* Whores.

14 *three-pile.* Fine velvet.

Autolycus: 'I have served Prince Florizel and in my time wore three-pile.' John Fawcett as Autolycus, Covent Garden Theatre, London, 1827. Painting by T. Wagmas (1787–1863)

20 *budget.* Bag.

27 *die.* Dice. *drab.* Pimping. *caparison.* Attire.

28–29 *Silly cheat.* Cheating the foolish. *Gallows and knock.* Punishment for robbery was beating and hanging.

33 *'leven wether.* Eleven sheep. *tod.* A unit of measure of wool.

44–45 *three-man-song-men.* Singers in three parts.

46 *means.* Tenors.

48 *warden.* Stewed pear.

50 *race.* Root.

60 *stripes.* Beatings.

92 *troll-my-dames.* i.e. 'a game of hoops' and 'a bunch of whores'.

101 *ape-bearer.* Travelling showman.

102–103 *compassed a motion.* Acquired a puppet show.

feast? Three pound of sugar, five pound of currants, rice,—what will this sister of mine do with rice? But my father hath made her mistress of the feast, and she lays it on. She hath made me four and twenty nosegays for the shearers, three-man-song-men all, and very good ones; but they are most of them means and bases; but one puritan amongst them, and he sings psalms to hornpipes. I must have saffron to colour the warden pies; mace; dates?—none, that's out of my note; nutmegs, seven; a race or two of ginger, but that I may beg; four pound of prunes, and as many of raisins o' the sun.

Aut. O that ever I was born!
  [*Grovelling on the ground.*

Clo. I' the name of me—

Aut. O, help me, help me! pluck but off these rags; and then, death, death!

Clo. Alack, poor soul! thou hast need of more rags to lay on thee, rather than have these off.

Aut. O sir, the loathsomeness of them offends me more than the stripes I have received, which are mighty ones and millions.   61

Clo. Alas, poor man! a million of beating may come to a great matter.

Aut. I am robbed, sir, and beaten; my money and apparel ta'en from me, and these detestable things put upon me.

Clo. What, by a horseman, or a footman?

Aut. A footman, sweet sir, a footman.

Clo. Indeed, he should be a footman by the garments he has left with thee: if this be a horseman's coat, it hath seen very hot service. Lend me thy hand, I'll help thee: come, lend me thy hand.

Aut. O, good sir, tenderly, O!

Clo. Alas, poor soul!

Aut. O, good sir, softly, good sir! I fear, sir, my shoulder-blade is out.

Clo. How now! canst stand?

Aut. [*Picking his pocket*] Softly, dear sir; good sir, softly. You ha' done me a charitable office.   81

Clo. Dost lack any money? I have a little money for thee.

Aut. No, good sweet sir; no, I beseech you, sir: I have a kinsman not past three quarters of a mile hence, unto whom I was going; I shall there have money, or any thing I want: offer me no money, I pray you; that kills my heart.

Clo. What manner of fellow was he that robbed you?   90

Aut. A fellow, sir, that I have known to go about with troll-my-dames: I knew him once a servant of the prince: I cannot tell, good sir, for which of his virtues it was, but he was certainly whipped out of the court.

Clo. His vices, you would say; there's no virtue whipped out of the court: they cherish it to make it stay there; and yet it will no more but abide.   99

Aut. Vices, I would say, sir. I know this man well: he hath been since an ape-bearer; then a process-server, a bailiff; then he compassed a motion of the Prodigal Son, and married a tinker's wife within a mile where my land and living lies; and, having flown over many knavish professions, he settled only in rogue: some call him Autolycus.

Clo. Out upon him! prig, for my life, prig:
he haunts wakes, fairs and bear-baitings.

Aut. Very true, sir; he, sir, he; that's the
rogue that put me into this apparel.   III

Clo. Not a more cowardly rogue in all Bohemia: if you had but looked big and spit at him,
he'ld have run.

Aut. I must confess to you, sir, I am no
fighter: I am false of heart that way; and that
he knew, I warrant him.

Clo. How do you now?

Aut. Sweet sir, much better than I was; I
can stand and walk: I will even take my leave
of you, and pace softly towards my kinsman's.

Clo. Shall I bring thee on the way?

Aut. No, good-faced sir; no, sweet sir.

Clo. Then fare thee well: I must go buy
spices for our sheep-shearing.

Aut. Prosper you, sweet sir! [*Exit Clown.*]
Your purse is not hot enough to purchase your
spice. I'll be with you at your sheep-shearing
too: if I make not this cheat bring out another
and the shearers prove sheep, let me be unrolled
and my name put in the book of virtue!   131

[*Sings*] Jog on, jog on, the foot-path way,
    And merrily hent the stile-a:
A merry heart goes all the day,
    Your sad tires in a mile-a.   [*Exit.*

SCENE IV. *The* Shepherd's *cottage.*

Enter FLORIZEL *and* PERDITA.

Flo. These your unusual weeds to each part
    of you
Do give a life: no shepherdess, but Flora
Peering in April's front. This your sheep-shearing
Is as a meeting of the petty gods,
And you the queen on 't.

Per.   Sir, my gracious lord,
To chide at your extremes it not becomes me:
O, pardon, that I name them! Your high self,
The gracious mark o' the land, you have obscured
With a swain's wearing, and me, poor lowly maid,
Most goddess-like prank'd up: but that our feasts
In every mess have folly and the feeders   11
Digest it with a custom, I should blush
To see you so attired, sworn, I think,
To show myself a glass.

Flo.   I bless the time
When my good falcon made her flight across
Thy father's ground.

Per.   Now Jove afford you cause!
To me the difference forges dread; your greatness
Hath not been used to fear. Even now I tremble
To think your father, by some accident,
Should pass this way as you did: O, the Fates!   20
How would he look, to see his work so noble
Vilely bound up? What would he say? Or how
Should I, in these my borrow'd flaunts, behold
The sternness of his presence?

Flo.   Apprehend
Nothing but jollity. The gods themselves,
Humbling their deities to love, have taken
The shapes of beasts upon them: Jupiter
Became a bull, and bellow'd; the green Neptune
A ram, and bleated; and the fire-robed god,
Golden Apollo, a poor humble swain,   30
As I seem now. Their transformations
Were never for a piece of beauty rarer,

108 *prig.* Thief.

116 *false.* i.e. weak.

130 *unrolled.* Struck off the roll.

133 *hent.* i.e. jump right over.

2 *Flora.* Goddess of flowers.

Mary Robinson (1758–1800) as Perdita. Painting by
Thomas Gainsborough, 1781

Florizel: 'Thou dearest Perdita . . .' The Victorian
actors Jenny Marston as Perdita and Frederick Robinson
as Florizel.

56 *pantler.* Pantry servant.

82 *streak'd gillyvors.* Striped pinks.

Nor in a way so chaste, since my desires
Run not before mine honour, nor my lusts
Burn hotter than my faith.
 Per.   O, but, sir,
Your resolution cannot hold, when 'tis
Opposed, as it must be, by the power of the king:
One of these two must be necessities,
Which then will speak, that you must change
   this purpose,
Or I my life.
 Flo. Thou dearest Perdita,   40
With these forced thoughts, I prithee, darken not
The mirth o' the feast.   Or I'll be thine, my fair,
Or not my father's.   For I cannot be
Mine own, nor any thing to any, if
I be not thine.   To this I am most constant,
Though destiny say no.   Be merry, gentle;
Strangle such thoughts as these with any thing
That you behold the while.   Your guests are
   coming:
Lift up your countenance, as it were the day
Of celebration of that nuptial which   50
We two have sworn shall come.
 Per.   O lady Fortune,
Stand you auspicious!
 Flo.   See, your guests approach:
Address yourself to entertain them sprightly,
And let's be red with mirth.

Enter Shepherd, Clown, Mopsa, Dorcas, *and
 others, with* Polixenes *and* Camillo *disguised.*

 Shep. Fie, daughter! when my old wife
   lived, upon
●This day she was both pantler, butler, cook,
Both dame and servant; welcomed all, served all;
Would sing her song and dance her turn; now
   here,
At upper end o' the table, now i' the middle;
On his shoulder, and his; her face o' fire 60
With labour and the thing she took to quench it,
She would to each one sip.   You are retired,
As if you were a feasted one and not
The hostess of the meeting: pray you, bid
These unknown friends to's welcome; for it is
A way to make us better friends, more known.
Come, quench your blushes and present yourself
That which you are, mistress o' the feast:
   come on,
And bid us welcome to your sheep-shearing,
As your good flock shall prosper.
 Per.   [*To Pol.*] Sir, welcome: 70
It is my father's will I should take on me
The hostess-ship o' the day.   [*To Cam.*] You're
   welcome, sir.
Give me those flowers there, Dorcas.   Reverend
   sirs,
For you there's rosemary and rue; these keep
Seeming and savour all the winter long:
Grace and remembrance be to you both,
And welcome to our shearing!
 Pol.   Shepherdess,—
A fair one are you—well you fit our ages
With flowers of winter.
 Per.   Sir, the year growing ancient,
Not yet on summer's death, nor on the birth 80
Of trembling winter, the fairest flowers o' the
   season
●Are our carnations and streak'd gillyvors,

Which some call nature's bastards : of that kind
Our rustic garden's barren ; and I care not
● To get slips of them.
    Pol.   Wherefore, gentle maiden,
Do you neglect them?
    Per.   For I have heard it said
● There is an art which in their piedness shares
With great creating nature.
    Pol.   Say there be ;
Yet nature is made better by no mean
But nature makes that mean : so, over that art 90
Which you say adds to nature, is an art
That nature makes. You see, sweet maid, we
    marry
● A gentler scion to the wildest stock,
And make conceive a bark of baser kind
By bud of nobler race : this is an art
Which does mend nature, change it rather, but
The art itself is nature.
    Per.   So it is.
    Pol. Then make your garden rich in gillyvors,
And do not call them bastards.
    Per.   I'll not put
● The dibble in earth to set one slip of them ; 100
No more than were I painted I would wish
This youth should say 'twere well and only
    therefore
Desire to breed by me. Here's flowers for you ;
Hot lavender, mints, savory, marjoram ;
The marigold, that goes to bed wi' the sun
And with him rises weeping : these are flowers
Of middle summer, and I think they are given
To men of middle age. You're very welcome.
    Cam. I should leave grazing, were I of your
    flock,
And only live by gazing.
    Per.   Out, alas ! 110
You'ld be so lean, that blasts of January
Would blow you through and through. Now,
    my fair'st friend,
I would I had some flowers o' the spring that
    might
Become your time of day ; and yours, and yours,
That wear upon your virgin branches yet
● Your maidenheads growing : O Proserpina,
For the flowers now, that frighted thou let'st fall
● From Dis's waggon ! daffodils,
That come before the swallow dares, and take
The winds of March with beauty ; violets dim,
But sweeter than the lids of Juno's eyes 121
● Or Cytherea's breath ; pale primroses,
That die unmarried, ere they can behold
● Bright Phœbus in his strength—a malady
Most incident to maids ; bold oxlips and
The crown imperial ; lilies of all kinds,
● The flower-de-luce being one ! O, these I lack,
To make you garlands of, and my sweet friend,
To strew him o'er and o'er !
    Flo.   What, like a corse?
    Per. No, like a bank for love to lie and play on ;
Not like a corse ; or if, not to be buried, 131
But quick and in mine arms. Come, take your
    flowers :
Methinks I play as I have seen them do
In Whitsun pastorals : sure this robe of mine
Does change my disposition.
    Flo.   What you do
Still betters what is done. When you speak,
    sweet,

85 *slips.* Carnations and pinks are propagated by cuttings. For the next few lines there are several puns on gardeners' terms.

87 *piedness.* Particoloration.

93 *scion.* Cutting.

Polixenes : '... we marry A gentler scion to the wildest stock ...' Perdita, Florizel and Polixenes. Detail from a painting by Francis Wheatley (1749–1801)

100 *dibble.* Gardening tool.

116 *Proserpina.* Goddess of spring.

118 *Dis.* Pluto, god of the Underworld.

122 *Cytherea.* Venus.

124 *Phœbus.* Sun-god.

127 *flower-de-luce.* Fleur-de-lis, iris.

Rural dance. Engraving from Chapter House Treaties,
1527

169 *a worthy feeding.* Good pasture.

171 *like sooth.* i.e. as if it is true.

176 *featly.* Nimbly.

I'ld have you do it ever: when you sing,
I'ld have you buy and sell so, so give alms,
Pray so; and, for the ordering your affairs,
To sing them too: when you do dance, I wish you
A wave o' the sea, that you might ever do   141
Nothing but that; move still, still so,
And own no other function: each your doing,
So singular in each particular,
Crowns what you are doing in the present deed,
That all your acts are queens.
   Per.   O Doricles,
Your praises are too large: but that your youth,
And the true blood which peepeth fairly through't,
Do plainly give you out an unstain'd shepherd,
With wisdom I might fear, my Doricles,   150
You woo'd me the false way.
   Flo.   I think you have
As little skill to fear as I have purpose
To put you to't.   But come; our dance, I pray:
Your hand, my Perdita: so turtles pair,
That never mean to part.
   Per.   I'll swear for 'em.
   Pol.   This is the prettiest low-born lass that
     ever
Ran on the green-sward: nothing she does or
     seems
But smacks of something greater than herself,
Too noble for this place.
   Cam.   He tells her something
That makes her blood look out: good sooth, she is
The queen of curds and cream.   161
   Clo.   Come on, strike up!
   Dor.   Mopsa must be your mistress: marry,
     garlic,
To mend her kissing with!
   Mop.   Now, in good time!
   Clo.   Not a word, a word; we stand upon our
     manners.
Come, strike up!
     [*Music. Here a dance of Shepherds and*
                   Shepherdesses.
   Pol.   Pray, good shepherd, what fair swain is
     this
Which dances with your daughter?
   Shep.   They call him Doricles; and boasts
     himself
● To have a worthy feeding: but I have it
Upon his own report and I believe it;   170
● He looks like sooth.   He says he loves my
     daughter:
I think so too; for never gazed the moon
Upon the water as he'll stand and read
As 'twere my daughter's eyes: and, to be plain,
I think there is not half a kiss to choose
● Who loves another best.
   Pol.   She dances featly.
   Shep.   So she does any thing; though I re-
     port it,
That should be silent: if young Doricles
Do light upon her, she shall bring him that
Which he not dreams of.   180

Enter Servant.

   Serv.   O master, if you did but hear the pedlar at the door, you would never dance again
after a tabor and pipe; no, the bagpipe could not
move you: he sings several tunes faster than
you'll tell money; he utters them as he had eaten
ballads and all men's ears grew to his tunes.

Clo. He could never come better; he shall come in. I love a ballad but even too well, if it be doleful matter merrily set down, or a very pleasant thing indeed and sung lamentably.   190

Serv. He hath songs for man or woman, of all sizes; no milliner can so fit his customers with gloves: he has the prettiest love-songs for maids; so without bawdry, which is strange; with such delicate burthens of dildos and fadings, 'jump her and thump her;' and where some stretch-mouthed rascal would, as it were, mean mischief and break a foul gap into the matter, he makes the maid to answer 'Whoop, do me no harm, good man;' puts him off, slights him, with 'Whoop, do me no harm, good man.'   201

Pol. This is a brave fellow.

Clo. Believe me, thou talkest of an admirable conceited fellow. Has he any unbraided wares?

Serv. He hath ribbons of all the colours i' the rainbow; points more than all the lawyers in Bohemia can learnedly handle, though they come to him by the gross: inkles, caddisses, cambrics, lawns: why, he sings 'em over as they were gods or goddesses; you would think a smock were a she-angel, he so chants to the sleeve-hand and the work about the square on 't.

Clo. Prithee bring him in; and let him approach singing.

Per. Forewarn him that he use no scurrilous words in 's tunes.   [*Exit Servant.*

Clo. You have of these pedlars, that have more in them than you'ld think, sister.

Per. Ay, good brother, or go about to think.

Enter AUTOLYCUS, *singing.*

Lawn as white as driven snow;   220
Cyprus black as e'er was crow;
Gloves as sweet as damask roses;
Masks for faces and for noses;
Bugle bracelet, necklace amber,
Perfume for a lady's chamber;
Golden quoifs and stomachers,
For my lads to give their dears:
Pins and poking-sticks of steel,
What maids lack from head to heel:
Come buy of me, come; come buy, come buy;
Buy, lads, or else your lasses cry: 231
Come buy.

Clo. If I were not in love with Mopsa, thou shouldst take no money of me; but being enthralled as I am, it will also be the bondage of certain ribbons and gloves.

Mop. I was promised them against the feast; but they come not too late now.

Dor. He hath promised you more than that, or there be liars.   240

Mop. He hath paid you all he promised you: may be, he has paid you more, which will shame you to give him again.

Clo. Is there no manners left among maids? will they wear their plackets where they should bear their faces? Is there not milking-time, when you are going to bed, or kiln-hole, to whistle off these secrets, but you must be tittle-tattling before all our guests? 'tis well they are whispering: clamour your tongues, and not a word more.   251

Mop. I have done. Come, you promised me a tawdry-lace and a pair of sweet gloves.

195 *burthens.* Tunes. *dildo.* Phallus. *fadings.* Fadings out (with bawdy suggestion).

198 *break a foul gap into.* Rudely interrupt.

204 *conceited.* Witty. *unbraided.* New.

206 *points.* i.e. 'laces' and 'legal points'.

208 *inkles.* Linen tapes. *caddisses.* Garter tape.

211 *sleeve-hand.* Cuff.

212 *square.* Breast piece.

221 *Cyprus.* Crepe.

224 *Bugle.* Black glass beads.

226 *quoifs.* Tight fitting caps.

228 *poking-sticks.* Stiffening iron.

235 *bondage.* Making up a parcel.

245 *placket.* i.e. 'slit in petticoat' and 'private parts'.

248 *whistle off.* Speak secretly of.

261 *parcels of charge.* Items of value.

Autolycus: 'Here's one to a very doleful tune ...'
Painting by C. R. Leslie (1794–1859)

268 *carbonadoed.* Broiled.

Clo. Have I not told thee how I was cozened by the way and lost all my money?

Aut. And indeed, sir, there are cozeners abroad; therefore it behoves men to be wary.

Clo. Fear not thou, man, thou shalt lose nothing here.

Aut. I hope so, sir; for I have about me many parcels of charge.   261

Clo. What hast here? ballads?

Mop. Pray now, buy some: I love a ballad in print o' life, for then we are sure they are true.

Aut. Here's one to a very doleful tune, how a usurer's wife was brought to bed of twenty money-bags at a burthen and how she longed to eat adders' heads and toads carbonadoed.

Mop. Is it true, think you?

Aut. Very true, and but a month old.   270

Dor. Bless me from marrying a usurer!

Aut. Here's the midwife's name to't, one Mistress Tale-porter, and five or six honest wives that were present. Why should I carry lies abroad?

Mop. Pray you now, buy it.

Clo. Come on, lay it by: and let's first see moe ballads; we'll buy the other things anon.

Aut. Here's another ballad of a fish, that appeared upon the coast on Wednesday the fourscore of April, forty thousand fathom above water, and sung this ballad against the hard hearts of maids: it was thought she was a woman and was turned into a cold fish for she would not exchange flesh with one that loved her: the ballad is very pitiful and as true.

Dor. Is it true too, think you?

Aut. Five justices' hands at it, and witnesses more than my pack will hold.

Clo. Lay it by too: another.   290

Aut. This is a merry ballad, but a very pretty one.

Mop. Let's have some merry ones.

Aut. Why, this is a passing merry one and goes to the tune of 'Two maids wooing a man:' there's scarce a maid westward but she sings it; 'tis in request, I can tell you.

Mop. We can both sing it: if thou'lt bear a part, thou shalt hear; 'tis in three parts.

Dor. We had the tune on't a month ago.   300

Aut. I can bear my part; you must know 'tis my occupation; have at it with you.

SONG.

A. Get you hence, for I must go
    Where it fits not you to know.
        D. Whither? *M.* O, whither? *D.* Whither?
    M. It becomes thy oath full well,
        Thou to me thy secrets tell.
            D. Me too, let me go thither.
    M. Or thou goest to the grange or mill.
    D. If to either, thou dost ill.   310
A. Neither. *D.* What, neither? *A.* Neither.
    D. Thou hast sworn my love to be.
    M. Thou hast sworn it more to me:
        Then whither goest? say, whither?

Clo. We'll have this song out anon by ourselves: my father and the gentlemen are in sad talk, and we'll not trouble them. Come, bring away thy pack after me. Wenches, I'll buy for you both. Pedlar, let's have the first choice. Follow me, girls. [*Exit with Dorcas and Mopsa.*

Aut. And you shall pay well for 'em.
[*Follows singing.*
> Will you buy any tape,
> Or lace for your cape,
> My dainty duck, my dear-a?
> Any silk, any thread,
> Any toys for your head,
> Of the new'st and finest, finest wear-a?
> Come to the pedlar;
> Money 's a medler,
> That doth utter all men's ware-a. [*Exit.* 330

Re-enter Servant.

Serv. Master, there is three carters, three shepherds, three neat-herds, three swine-herds, that have made themselves all men of hair, they call themselves Saltiers, and they have a dance which the wenches say is a gallimaufry of gambols, because they are not in 't; but they themselves are o' the mind, if it be not too rough for some that know little but bowling, it will please plentifully. 339
Shep. Away! we'll none on 't: here has been too much homely foolery already. I know, sir, we weary you.
Pol. You weary those that refresh us: pray, let's see these four threes of herdsmen.
Serv. One three of them, by their own report, sir, hath danced before the king; and not the worst of the three but jumps twelve foot and a half by the squier.
Shep. Leave your prating: since these good men are pleased, let them come in; but quickly now. 351
Serv. Why, they stay at door, sir. [*Exit.*

Here a dance of twelve Satyrs.

Pol. O, father, you'll know more of that hereafter.
[*To Cam.*] Is it not too far gone? 'Tis time to part them.
He's simple and tells much. [*To Flor.*] How now, fair shepherd!
Your heart is full of something that does take
Your mind from feasting. Sooth, when I was young
And handed love as you do, I was wont
To load my she with knacks: I would have ransack'd 359
The pedlar's silken treasury and have pour'd it
To her acceptance; you have let him go
And nothing marted with him. If your lass
Interpretation should abuse and call this
Your lack of love or bounty, you were straited
For a reply, at least if you make a care
Of happy holding her.
Flo.   Old sir, I know
She prizes not such trifles as these are:
The gifts she looks from me are pack'd and lock'd
Up in my heart; which I have given already, 369
But not deliver'd. O, hear me breathe my life
Before this ancient sir, who, it should seem,
Hath sometime loved! I take thy hand, this hand,
As soft as dove's down and as white as it,
Or Ethiopian's tooth, or the fann'd snow that's bolted
By the northern blasts twice o'er.
Pol.   What follows this?

330 *utter.* Concern.

332 *neat-herds.* Cow herds.

333 *of hair.* i.e. covered with skins.

335 *gallimaufry.* Medley.

348 *by the squier.* By the rule.

362 *nothing marted.* Made no business.

364 *straited.* At a loss.

Florizel: 'I take thy hand . . .' Peggy Ashcroft as Perdita and William Fox as Florizel, Old Vic Theatre, London, 1932

374 *bolted.* Sifted.

Florizel, Perdita and Polixenes and Camillo in disguise.
Engraving from a design by F. Hayman (1708–1776)

409 *altering rheums.* Serious catarrh.

How prettily the young swain seems to wash
The hand was fair before!   I have put you out:
But to your protestation; let me hear
What you profess.
 Flo.   Do, and be witness to 't. 379
 Pol. And this my neighbour too?
 Flo.   And he, and more
Than he, and men, the earth, the heavens, and all:
That, were I crown'd the most imperial monarch,
Thereof most worthy, were I the fairest youth
That ever made eye swerve, had force and know-
   ledge
More than was ever man's, I would not prize them
Without her love; for her employ them all;
Commend them and condemn them to her service
Or to their own perdition.
 Pol.   Fairly offer'd.
 Cam. This shows a sound affection.
 Shep.   But, my daughter,
Say you the like to him?
 Per.   I cannot speak 390
So well, nothing so well; no, nor mean better:
By the pattern of mine own thoughts I cut out
The purity of his.
 Shep.   Take hands, a bargain!
And, friends unknown, you shall bear witness
   to 't:
I give my daughter to him, and will make
Her portion equal his.
 Flo.   O, that must be
I' the virtue of your daughter: one being dead,
I shall have more than you can dream of yet;
Enough then for your wonder. But, come on, 399
Contract us 'fore these witnesses.
 Shep.   Come, your hand;
And, daughter, yours.
 Pol.   Soft, swain, awhile, beseech you;
Have you a father?
 Flo.   I have: but what of him?
 Pol. Knows he of this?
 Flo.   He neither does nor shall.
 Pol. Methinks a father
Is at the nuptial of his son a guest
That best becomes the table. Pray you once more,
Is not your father grown incapable
Of reasonable affairs? is he not stupid
• With age and altering rheums? can he speak?
  hear?   409
Know man from man? dispute his own estate?
Lies he not bed-rid? and again does nothing
But what he did being childish?
 Flo.   No, good sir;
He has his health and ampler strength indeed
Than most have of his age.
 Pol.   By my white beard,
You offer him, if this be so, a wrong
Something unfilial: reason my son
Should choose himself a wife, but as good reason
The father, all whose joy is nothing else
But fair posterity, should hold some counsel
In such a business.
 Flo.   I yield all this; 420
But for some other reasons, my grave sir,
Which 'tis not fit you know, I not acquaint
My father of this business.
 Pol.   Let him know 't.
 Flo. He shall not.
 Pol.   Prithee, let him.
 Flo.   No, he must not.

Shep.   Let him, my son: he shall not need to grieve
At knowing of thy choice.
Flo.   Come, come, he must not.
Mark our contract.
Pol.   Mark your divorce, young sir,
                           [*Discovering himself.*
Whom son I dare not call; thou art too base
To be acknowledged: thou a sceptre's heir,   429
That thus affect'st a sheep-hook! Thou old traitor,
I am sorry that by hanging thee I can
But shorten thy life one week.   And thou, fresh piece
Of excellent witchcraft, who of force must know
The royal fool thou copest with,—
Shep.   O, my heart!
Pol. I'll have thy beauty scratch'd with briers, and made
●More homely than thy state.   For thee, fond boy,
If I may ever know thou dost but sigh
That thou no more shalt see this knack, as never
I mean thou shalt, we'll bar thee from succession:
Not hold thee of our blood, no, not our kin,   440
●Far than Deucalion off: mark thou my words:
Follow us to the court.   Thou churl, for this time,
Though full of our displeasure, yet we free thee
From the dead blow of it.   And you, enchantment,—
Worthy enough a herdsman; yea, him too,
That makes himself, but for our honour therein,
Unworthy thee,—if ever henceforth thou
These rural latches to his entrance open,
Or hoop his body more with thy embraces,
I will devise a death as cruel for thee   450
As thou art tender to 't.   [*Exit.*
Per.   Even here undone!
I was not much afeard; for once or twice
I was about to speak and tell him plainly,
The selfsame sun that shines upon his court
Hides not his visage from our cottage but
Looks on alike.   Will 't please you, sir, be gone?
I told you what would come of this: beseech you,
Of your own state take care: this dream of mine,—
●Being now awake, I'll queen it no inch farther,
But milk my ewes and weep.   460
Cam.   Why, how now, father!
Speak ere thou diest.
Shep.   I cannot speak, nor think,
Nor dare to know that which I know.   O sir!
You have undone a man of fourscore three,
That thought to fill his grave in quiet, yea,
To die upon the bed my father died,
To lie close by his honest bones: but now
Some hangman must put on my shroud and lay me
●Where no priest shovels in dust.   O cursed wretch,
That knew'st this was the prince, and wouldst adventure   471
To mingle faith with him!   Undone! undone!
If I might die within this hour, I have lived
To die when I desire.   [*Exit.*
Flo.   Why look you so upon me?
I am but sorry, not afeard; delay'd,
But nothing alter'd: what I was, I am:
More straining on for plucking back, not following
My leash unwillingly.
Cam.   Gracious my lord,
You know your father's temper: at this time
He will allow no speech, which I do guess

436 *homely.* Rustic.

441 *Deucalion.* Legendary Noah.

459 *I'll . . . farther.* i.e. I will not continue to be hostess of this party.

470 *Where . . . dust.* i.e. in unhallowed ground.

492 *fancy.* Love.

Florizel: 'Hark, Perdita. I'll hear you by and by.' Emily Fowler as Perdita and Edward Compton as Florizel, Theatre Royal, Drury Lane, London, 1878

524 *curious.* Anxious.

You do not purpose to him; and as hardly
Will he endure your sight as yet, I fear: 480
Then, till the fury of his highness settle,
Come not before him.
 Flo.   I not purpose it.
I think, Camillo?
 Cam.   Even he, my lord.
 Per. How often have I told you 'twould be
  thus!
How often said, my dignity would last
But till 'twere known!
 Flo.   It cannot fail but by
The violation of my faith; and then
Let nature crush the sides o' the earth together
And mar the seeds within! Lift up thy looks:
From my succession wipe me, father; I   490
Am heir to my affection.
 Cam.   Be advised.
 ● *Flo.* I am, and by my fancy: if my reason
Will thereto be obedient, I have reason;
If not, my senses, better pleased with madness,
Do bid it welcome.
 Cam.   This is desperate, sir.
 Flo. So call it: but it does fulfil my vow;
I needs must think it honesty. Camillo,
Not for Bohemia, nor the pomp that may
Be thereat glean'd, for all the sun sees or   499
The close earth wombs or the profound seas hide
In unknown fathoms, will I break my oath
To this my fair beloved: therefore, I pray you,
As you have ever been my father's honour'd
  friend,
When he shall miss me,—as, in faith, I mean not
To see him any more,—cast your good counsels
Upon his passion: let myself and fortune
Tug for the time to come. This you may know
And so deliver, I am put to sea
With her whom here I cannot hold on shore:
And most opportune to our need I have   510
A vessel rides fast by, but not prepared
For this design. What course I mean to hold
Shall nothing benefit your knowledge, nor
Concern me the reporting.
 Cam.   O my lord!
I would your spirit were easier for advice,
Or stronger for your need.
 Flo. Hark, Perdita.[*Drawing her aside.*
I'll hear you by and by.
 Cam.   He's irremoveable,
Resolved for flight. Now were I happy, if
His going I could frame to serve my turn,   519
Save him from danger, do him love and honour,
Purchase the sight again of dear Sicilia
And that unhappy king, my master, whom
I so much thirst to see.
 Flo.   Now, good Camillo;
 ● I am so fraught with curious business that
I leave out ceremony.
 Cam.   Sir, I think
You have heard of my poor services, i' the love
That I have borne your father?
 Flo.   Very nobly
Have you deserved: it is my father's music
To speak your deeds, not little of his care   529
To have them recompensed as thought on.
 Cam.   Well, my lord,
If you may please to think I love the king
And through him what is nearest to him, which is
Your gracious self, embrace but my direction:

If your more ponderous and settled project
May suffer alteration, on mine honour,
I'll point you where you shall have such receiving
As shall become your highness; where you may
Enjoy your mistress, from the whom, I see,
There's no disjunction to be made, but by— 539
As heavens forfend !—your ruin; marry her,
And, with my best endeavours in your absence,
Your discontenting father strive to qualify
And bring him up to liking.
   Flo. How, Camillo,
May this, almost a miracle, be done?
That I may call thee something more than man
And after that trust to thee.
   Cam. Have you thought on
A place whereto you'll go?
   Flo. Not any yet:
But as the unthought-on accident is guilty
To what we wildly do, so we profess
Ourselves to be the slaves of chance and flies 550
Of every wind that blows.
   Cam. Then list to me:
This follows, if you will not change your purpose
But undergo this flight, make for Sicilia,
And there present yourself and your fair princess,
For so I see she must be, 'fore Leontes:
She shall be habited as it becomes
The partner of your bed.   Methinks I see
Leontes opening his free arms and weeping 558
His welcomes forth; asks thee the son forgiveness,
As 'twere i' the father's person; kisses the hands
Of your fresh princess; o'er and o'er divides him
'Twixt his unkindness and his kindness; the one
He chides to hell and bids the other grow
Faster than thought or time.
   Flo. Worthy Camillo,
What colour for my visitation shall I
Hold up before him?
   Cam. Sent by the king your father
To greet him and to give him comforts.   Sir,
The manner of your bearing towards him, with
What you as from your father shall deliver,
Things known betwixt us three, I'll write you
     down: 570
The which shall point you forth at every sitting
What you must say; that he shall not perceive
But that you have your father's bosom there
And speak his very heart.
   Flo. I am bound to you:
There is some sap in this.
   Cam. A course more promising
Than a wild dedication of yourselves
To unpath'd waters, undream'd shores, most cer-
     tain
To miseries enough; no hope to help you,
But as you shake off one to take another:
Nothing so certain as your anchors, who 580
Do their best office, if they can but stay you
Where you'll be loath to be: besides you know
Prosperity's the very bond of love,
Whose fresh complexion and whose heart together
Affliction alters.
   Per. One of these is true:
I think affliction may subdue the cheek,
But not take in the mind.
   Cam. Yea, say you so?
There shall not at your father's house these seven
     years
Be born another such.

591 *She . . . birth.* i.e. she is lowly born.

608 *pomander.* Ball of spices carried as protection against infection; often an orange stuck with cloves.

609 *table-book.* Pocket notebook.

618 *pettitoes.* Pigs' trotters.

621 *senseless.* Numb.

628 *whoo-bub.* Hubbub.

629 *Choughs from the chaff.* Crows from the husks of corn.

Flo.   My good Camillo,
She is as forward of her breeding as   590
●†She is i' the rear our birth.
    Cam.   I cannot say 'tis pity
She lacks instructions, for she seems a mistress
To most that teach.
    Per.   Your pardon, sir; for this
I'll blush you thanks.
    Flo.   My prettiest Perdita!
But O, the thorns we stand upon! Camillo,
Preserver of my father, now of me,
The medicine of our house, how shall we do?
We are not furnish'd like Bohemia's son,
Nor shall appear in Sicilia.
    Cam.   My lord,
Fear none of this: I think you know my fortunes
Do all lie there: it shall be so my care   601
To have you royally appointed as if
The scene you play were mine. For instance, sir,
That you may know you shall not want, one word.
                              [*They talk aside.*

          Re-enter AUTOLYCUS.

    Aut. Ha, ha! what a fool Honesty is! and Trust, his sworn brother, a very simple gentleman! I have sold all my trumpery; not a coun-
●terfeit stone, not a ribbon, glass, pomander,
●brooch, table-book, ballad, knife, tape, glove, shoe-tie, bracelet, horn-ring, to keep my pack from fasting: they throng who should buy first, as if my trinkets had been hallowed and brought a benediction to the buyer: by which means I saw whose purse was best in picture; and what I saw, to my good use I remembered. My clown, who wants but something to be a reasonable man, grew so in love with the wenches' song, that he
●would not stir his pettitoes till he had both tune and words; which so drew the rest of the herd to me that all their other senses stuck in ears: you
●might have pinched a placket, it was senseless; 'twas nothing to geld a codpiece of a purse; I could have filed keys off that hung in chains: no hearing, no feeling, but my sir's song, and admiring the nothing of it. So that in this time of lethargy I picked and cut most of their festival purses; and had not the old man come in with a
●whoo-bub against his daughter and the king's
●son and scared my choughs from the chaff, I had not left a purse alive in the whole army.   630
[*Camillo, Florizel, and Perdita come forward.*
    Cam. Nay, but my letters, by this means being there
So soon as you arrive, shall clear that doubt.
    Flo. And those that you'll procure from King Leontes—
    Cam. Shall satisfy your father.
    Per.   Happy be you!
All that you speak shows fair.
    Cam.   Who have we here?
                              [*Seeing Autolycus.*
We'll make an instrument of this, omit Nothing may give us aid.
    Aut. If they have overheard me now, why, hanging.   639
    Cam. How now, good fellow! why shakest thou so? Fear not, man; here's no harm intended to thee.
    Aut. I am a poor fellow, sir.
    Cam. Why, be so still; here's nobody will

steal that from thee: yet for the outside of thy poverty we must make an exchange; therefore discase thee instantly,—thou must think there's a necessity in't,—and change garments with this gentleman: though the pennyworth on his side
● be the worst, yet hold thee, there's some boot.

Aut. I am a poor fellow, sir. [*Aside*] I know ye well enough.

Cam. Nay, prithee, dispatch: the gentleman is half flayed already.

Aut. Are you in earnest, sir? [*Aside*] I smell the trick on't.

Flo. Dispatch, I prithee.

Aut. Indeed, I have had earnest; but I cannot with conscience take it.

Cam. Unbuckle, unbuckle.   660

[*Florizel and Autolycus exchange garments.*]

Fortunate mistress,—let my prophecy
Come home to ye!—you must retire yourself
Into some covert: take your sweetheart's hat
And pluck it o'er your brows, muffle your face,
● Dismantle you, and, as you can, disliken
The truth of your own seeming; that you may—
● For I do fear eyes over—to shipboard
Get undescried.

Per.   I see the play so lies
That I must bear a part.

Cam.   No remedy.   669
Have you done there?

Flo.   Should I now meet my father,
He would not call me son.

Cam.   Nay, you shall have no hat.
[*Giving it to Perdita.*]
Come, lady, come. Farewell, my friend.

Aut.   Adieu, sir.

Flo. O Perdita, what have we twain forgot!
Pray you, a word.

Cam. [*Aside*] What I do next, shall be to
          tell the king
Of this escape and whither they are bound;
Wherein my hope is I shall so prevail
To force him after: in whose company
I shall review Sicilia, for whose sight
I have a woman's longing.

Flo.   Fortune speed us!   680
Thus we set on, Camillo, to the sea-side.

Cam. The swifter speed the better.

[*Exeunt Florizel, Perdita, and Camillo.*]

Aut. I understand the business, I hear it: to have an open ear, a quick eye, and a nimble hand, is necessary for a cut-purse; a good nose is requisite also, to smell out work for the other senses. I see this is the time that the unjust man doth thrive. What an exchange had this been without boot! What a boot is here with this exchange! Sure the gods do this year connive at us, and we may do any thing extempore. The prince himself is about a piece of iniquity, stealing away from his father with
● his clog at his heels: if I thought it were a piece of honesty to acquaint the king withal, I would not do't: I hold it the more knavery to conceal it; and therein am I constant to my profession.

Re-enter Clown *and* Shepherd.

Aside, aside; here is more matter for a hot brain: every lane's end, every shop, church, session, hanging, yields a careful man work. 701

Camillo: '... change garments with this gentleman.' Michael Williams as Autolycus, Royal Shakespeare Co, 1976

---

650 *boot.* Profit.

665 *disliken.* Disguise.

667 *over.* Overlook us.

694 *his clog.* i.e. Perdita.

727 *fardel.* Bundle.

Shepherd: '... there is that in this fardel will make him scratch his beard.' Scene from Harley Granville-Barker's production, Savoy Theatre, London, 1912

733 *excrement.* Growth of hair.

738 *condition.* Contents.

756 *measure.* Bearing.

759 *toaze.* Tease.

760 *cap-a-pe.* Head to foot.

Clo. See, see; what a man you are now! There is no other way but to tell the king she's a changeling and none of your flesh and blood.

Shep. Nay, but hear me.

Clo. Nay, but hear me.

Shep. Go to, then.   708

Clo. She being none of your flesh and blood, your flesh and blood has not offended the king; and so your flesh and blood is not to be punished by him. Show those things you found about her, those secret things, all but what she has with her: this being done, let the law go whistle: I warrant you.

Shep. I will tell the king all, every word, yea, and his son's pranks too; who, I may say, is no honest man, neither to his father nor to me, to go about to make me the king's brother-in-law.   720

Clo. Indeed, brother-in-law was the farthest off you could have been to him and then your blood had been the dearer by I know how much an ounce.

Aut. [*Aside*] Very wisely, puppies!

Shep. Well, let us to the king: there is that in this fardel will make him scratch his beard.

Aut. [*Aside*] I know not what impediment this complaint may be to the flight of my master.

Clo. Pray heartily he be at palace.   730

Aut. [*Aside*] Though I am not naturally honest, I am so sometimes by chance: let me pocket up my pedlar's excrement. [*Takes off his false beard.*] How now, rustics! whither are you bound?

Shep. To the palace, an it like your worship.

Aut. Your affairs there, what, with whom, the condition of that fardel, the place of your dwelling, your names, your ages, of what having, breeding, and any thing that is fitting to be known, discover.

Clo. We are but plain fellows, sir.

Aut. A lie; you are rough and hairy. Let me have no lying: it becomes none but tradesmen, and they often give us soldiers the lie: but we pay them for it with stamped coin, not stabbing steel; therefore they do not give us the lie.

Clo. Your worship had like to have given us one, if you had not taken yourself with the manner.

Shep. Are you a courtier, an't like you, sir?

Aut. Whether it like me or no, I am a courtier. Seest thou not the air of the court in these enfoldings? hath not my gait in it the measure of the court? receives not thy nose court-odour from me? reflect I not on thy baseness court-contempt? Thinkest thou, for that I insinuate, or †toaze from thee thy business, I am therefore no courtier? I am courtier cap-a-pe; and one that will either push on or pluck back thy business there: whereupon I command thee to open thy affair.

Shep. My business, sir, is to the king.

Aut. What advocate hast thou to him?

Shep. I know not, an't like you.

Clo. Advocate's the court-word for a pheasant: say you have none.

Shep. None, sir; I have no pheasant, cock nor hen.   770

Aut. How blessed are we that are not simple men!

Yet nature might have made me as these are,
Therefore I will not disdain.

Clo. This cannot be but a great courtier.

Shep. His garments are rich, but he wears them not handsomely.

Clo. He seems to be the more noble in being fantastical: a great man, I'll warrant; I know by the picking on's teeth.

Aut. The fardel there? what's i' the fardel? Wherefore that box? 781

Shep. Sir, there lies such secrets in this fardel and box, which none must know but the king; and which he shall know within this hour, if I may come to the speech of him.

Aut. Age, thou hast lost thy labour.

Shep. Why, sir?

Aut. The king is not at the palace; he is gone aboard a new ship to purge melancholy and air himself: for, if thou beest capable of things serious, thou must know the king is full of grief.

Shep. So 'tis said, sir; about his son, that should have married a shepherd's daughter.

Aut. If that shepherd be not in hand-fast, let him fly: the curses he shall have, the tortures he shall feel, will break the back of man, the heart of monster.

Clo. Think you so, sir? 798

Aut. Not he alone shall suffer what wit can make heavy and vengeance bitter; but those that are germane to him, though removed fifty times, shall all come under the hangman: which though it be great pity, yet it is necessary. An old sheep-whistling rogue, a ram-tender, to offer to have his daughter come into grace! Some say he shall be stoned; but that death is too soft for him, say I: draw our throne into a sheep-cote! all deaths are too few, the sharpest too easy.

Clo. Has the old man e'er a son, sir, do you hear, an't like you, sir? 810

Aut. He has a son, who shall be flayed alive; then 'nointed over with honey, set on the head of a wasp's nest; then stand till he be three quarters and a dram dead; then recovered again with aqua-vitæ or some other hot infusion; then, raw as he is, and in the hottest day prognostication proclaims, shall he be set against a brick-wall, the sun looking with a southward eye upon him, where he is to behold him with flies blown to death. But what talk we of these traitorly rascals, whose miseries are to be smiled at, their offences being so capital? Tell me, for you seem to be honest plain men, what you have to the king: being something gently considered, I'll bring you where he is aboard, tender your persons to his presence, whisper him in your behalfs; and if it be in man besides the king to effect your suits, here is man shall do it. 828

Clo. He seems to be of great authority: close with him, give him gold; and though authority be a stubborn bear, yet he is oft led by the nose with gold: show the inside of your purse to the outside of his hand, and no more ado. Remember 'stoned,' and 'flayed alive.'

Shep. An't please you, sir, to undertake the business for us, here is that gold I have: I'll make it as much more and leave this young man in pawn till I bring it you.

816 *prognostication.* The almanac.

Leontes: 'Whilst I remember Her and her virtues . . .'
The English Edwardian actor Charles Fry as Leontes.

Aut. After I have done what I promised?
Shep. Ay, sir.   840
Aut. Well, give me the moiety. Are you a party in this business?
Clo. In some sort, sir: but though my case be a pitiful one, I hope I shall not be flayed out of it.
Aut. O, that's the case of the shepherd's son: hang him, he'll be made an example.
Clo. Comfort, good comfort! We must to the king and show our strange sights: he must know 'tis none of your daughter nor my sister; we are gone else. Sir, I will give you as much as this old man does when the business is performed, and remain, as he says, your pawn till it be brought you.
Aut. I will trust you. Walk before toward the sea-side; go on the right hand: I will but look upon the hedge and follow you.
Clo. We are blest in this man, as I may say, even blest.
Shep. Let's before as he bids us: he was provided to do us good.   860
    [*Exeunt Shepherd and Clown.*
Aut. If I had a mind to be honest, I see Fortune would not suffer me: she drops booties in my mouth. I am courted now with a double occasion, gold and a means to do the prince my master good; which who knows how that may turn back to my advancement? I will bring these two moles, these blind ones, aboard him: if he think it fit to shore them again and that the complaint they have to the king concerns him nothing, let him call me rogue for being so far officious; for I am proof against that title and what shame else belongs to't. To him will I present them: there may be matter in it.   [*Exit.*

ACT V.

SCENE I. *A room in* LEONTES' *palace.*

Enter LEONTES, CLEOMENES, DION, PAULINA,
        and Servants.

Cleo. Sir, you have done enough, and have perform'd
A saint-like sorrow: no fault could you make,
Which you have not redeem'd; indeed, paid down
More penitence than done trespass: at the last,
Do as the heavens have done, forget your evil;
With them forgive yourself.
Leon.   Whilst I remember
Her and her virtues, I cannot forget
My blemishes in them, and so still think of
The wrong I did myself; which was so much,   10
That heirless it hath made my kingdom and
Destroy'd the sweet'st companion that e'er man
Bred his hopes out of.
Paul.   True, too true, my lord:
If, one by one, you wedded all the world,
Or from the all that are took something good,
To make a perfect woman, she you kill'd
Would be unparallel'd.
Leon.   I think so. Kill'd!
She I kill'd! I did so: but thou strikest me
Sorely, to say I did; it is as bitter
Upon thy tongue as in my thought: now, good now,
Say so but seldom.
Cleo.   Not at all, good lady: 20

You might have spoken a thousand things that
      would
Have done the time more benefit and graced
Your kindness better.
 Paul.   You are one of those
Would have him wed again.
 Dion.   If you would not so,
You pity not the state, nor the remembrance
Of his most sovereign name; consider little
What dangers, by his highness' fail of issue,
May drop upon his kingdom and devour
Incertain lookers on. What were more holy
Than to rejoice the former queen is well? 30
What holier than, for royalty's repair,
For present comfort and for future good,
To bless the bed of majesty again
With a sweet fellow to't?
 Paul.   There is none worthy,
Respecting her that's gone. Besides, the gods
Will have fulfill'd their secret purposes;
For has not the divine Apollo said,
Is't not the tenour of his oracle,
That King Leontes shall not have an heir
Till his lost child be found? which that it shall,
Is all as monstrous to our human reason 41
As my Antigonus to break his grave
And come again to me; who, on my life,
Did perish with the infant. 'Tis your counsel
My lord should to the heavens be contrary,
Oppose against their wills. [*To Leontes.*] Care
      not for issue;
The crown will find an heir: great Alexander
Left his to the worthiest; so his successor
Was like to be the best.
 Leon.   Good Paulina,
Who hast the memory of Hermione, 50
I know, in honour, O, that ever I
Had squared me to thy counsel! then, even now,
I might have look'd upon my queen's full eyes,
Have taken treasure from her lips—
 Paul.   And left them
More rich for what they yielded.
 Leon.   Thou speak'st truth.
No more such wives; therefore, no wife: one
      worse,
And better used, would make her sainted spirit
Again possess her corpse, and on this stage,
Where we're offenders now, appear soul-vex'd,
†And begin, 'Why to me?'
 Paul.   Had she such power, 60
She had just cause.
 Leon. She had; and would incense me
To murder her I married.
 Paul.   I should so.
Were I the ghost that walk'd, I'ld bid you mark
Her eye, and tell me for what dull part in't
You chose her; then I'ld shriek, that even your
      ears
Should rift to hear me; and the words that fol-
      low'd
Should be 'Remember mine.'
 Leon.   Stars, stars,
And all eyes else dead coals! Fear thou no wife;
I'll have no wife, Paulina.
 Paul.   Will you swear
Never to marry but by my free leave? 70
 Leon. Never, Paulina; so be blest my spirit!
 Paul. Then, good my lords, bear witness to
      his oath.

90 *out of circumstance.* Without ceremony.

Cleo. You tempt him over-much.
Paul.   Unless another,
As like Hermione as is her picture,
Affront his eye.
    Cleo.   Good madam,—
    Paul.   I have done.
Yet, if my lord will marry,—if you will, sir,
No remedy, but you will,—give me the office
To choose you a queen: she shall not be so
        young
As was your former; but she shall be such
As, walk'd your first queen's ghost, it should take
        joy   80
To see her in your arms.
    Leon.   My true Paulina,
We shall not marry till thou bid'st us.
    Paul.   That
Shall be when your first queen's again in breath;
Never till then.

            Enter a Gentleman.

    Gent. One that gives out himself Prince
        Florizel,
Son of Polixenes, with his princess, she
The fairest I have yet beheld, desires access
To your high presence.
    Leon.   What with him? he comes not
Like to his father's greatness: his approach,
● So out of circumstance and sudden, tells us   90
'Tis not a visitation framed, but forced
By need and accident. What train?
    Gent.   But few,
And those but mean.
    Leon.   His princess, say you, with him?
    Gent. Ay, the most peerless piece of earth, I
        think,
That e'er the sun shone bright on.
    Paul.   O Hermione,
As every present time doth boast itself
Above a better gone, so must thy grave
Give way to what's seen now! Sir, you yourself
Have said and writ so, but your writing now
Is colder than that theme, 'She had not been, 100
Nor was not to be equall'd;'—thus your verse
Flow'd with her beauty once: 'tis shrewdly ebb'd,
To say you have seen a better.
    Gent.   Pardon, madam:
The one I have almost forgot,—your pardon,—
The other, when she has obtain'd your eye,
Will have your tongue too. This is a creature,
Would she begin a sect, might quench the zeal
Of all professors else, make proselytes
Of who she but bid follow.
    Paul.   How! not women?
    Gent. Women will love her, that she is a
        woman   110
More worth than any man; men, that she is
The rarest of all women.
    Leon.   Go, Cleomenes;
Yourself, assisted with your honour'd friends,
Bring them to our embracement. Still, 'tis strange
                [Exeunt Cleomenes and others.
He thus should steal upon us.
    Paul.   Had our prince,
Jewel of children, seen this hour, he had pair'd
Well with this lord: there was not full a month
Between their births.
    Leon. Prithee, no more; cease; thou know'st
He dies to me again when talk'd of: sure,   120

When I shall see this gentleman, thy speeches
Will bring me to consider that which may
Unfurnish me of reason.   They are come.

Re-enter CLEOMENES *and others, with*
FLORIZEL *and* PERDITA.

Your mother was most true to wedlock, prince;
For she did print your royal father off,
Conceiving you: were I but twenty one,
Your father's image is so hit in you,
His very air, that I should call you brother,
As I did him, and speak of something wildly
By us perform'd before.   Most dearly welcome!
And your fair princess,—goddess!—O, alas! 131
I lost a couple, that 'twixt heaven and earth
Might thus have stood begetting wonder as
You, gracious couple, do: and then I lost—
All mine own folly—the society,
Amity too, of your brave father, whom,
Though bearing misery, I desire my life
Once more to look on him.
    Flo.   By his command
Have I here touch'd Sicilia and from him
• Give you all greetings that a king, at friend, 140
Can send his brother: and, but infirmity
Which waits upon worn times hath something
    seized
His wish'd ability, he had himself
The lands and waters 'twixt your throne and his
Measured to look upon you; whom he loves—
He bade me say so—more than all the sceptres
And those that bear them living.
    Leon.   O my brother,
Good gentleman! the wrongs I have done thee
    stir
Afresh within me, and these thy offices,
So rarely kind, are as interpreters   150
Of my behind-hand slackness.   Welcome hither,
As is the spring to the earth.   And hath he too
Exposed this paragon to the fearful usage,
At least ungentle, of the dreadful Neptune,
To greet a man not worth her pains, much less
The adventure of her person?
    Flo.   Good my lord,
• She came from Libya.
    Leon.   Where the warlike Smalus,
That noble honour'd lord, is fear'd and loved?
    Flo. Most royal sir, from thence; from him,
    whose daughter
His tears proclaim'd his, parting with her: thence,
A prosperous south-wind friendly, we have
    cross'd,   161
To execute the charge my father gave me
For visiting your highness: my best train
I have from your Sicilian shores dismiss'd;
Who for Bohemia bend, to signify
Not only my success in Libya, sir,
But my arrival and my wife's in safety
Here where we are.
    Leon.   The blessed gods
Purge all infection from our air whilst you
Do climate here! You have a holy father, 170
A graceful gentleman; against whose person,
So sacred as it is, I have done sin:
For which the heavens, taking angry note,
Have left me issueless; and your father's blest,
As he from heaven merits it, with you
Worthy his goodness.   What might I have been,

Leontes: 'Exposed this paragon to ... the dreadful Neptune.' Engraving from a Roman medal in G. du Choul's *Discours de la Religion de les Anciens Romains,* 1567

157 *Smalus.* Legendary sea-captain.

Caroline Heath as Florizel and Carlotta Leclercq as
Perdita, Princess's Theatre, London, 1856

---

210 *speed.* i.e. encouragement.

Might I a son and daughter now have look'd on,
Such goodly things as you!

Enter a Lord.

Lord.   Most noble sir,
That which I shall report will bear no credit,
Were not the proof so nigh. Please you, great sir,
Bohemia greets you from himself by me;   181
Desires you to attach his son, who has—
His dignity and duty both cast off—
Fled from his father, from his hopes, and with
A shepherd's daughter.
    Leon.   Where's Bohemia? speak.
    Lord. Here in your city; I now came from
        him:
I speak amazedly; and it becomes
My marvel and my message. To your court
Whiles he was hastening, in the chase, it seems,
Of this fair couple, meets he on the way   190
The father of this seeming lady and
Her brother, having both their country quitted
With this young prince.
    Flo.   Camillo has betray'd me;
Whose honour and whose honesty till now
Endured all weathers.
    Lord.   Lay't so to his charge:
He's with the king your father.
    Leon.   Who? Camillo?
    Lord. Camillo, sir; I spake with him; who now
Has these poor men in question. Never saw I
Wretches so quake: they kneel, they kiss the
        earth;
Forswear themselves as often as they speak: 200
Bohemia stops his ears, and threatens them
With divers deaths in death.
    Per.   O my poor father!
The heaven sets spies upon us, will not have
Our contract celebrated.
    Leon.   You are married?
    Flo. We are not, sir, nor are we like to be;
The stars, I see, will kiss the valleys first:
The odds for high and low's alike.
    Leon.   My lord,
Is this the daughter of a king?
    Flo.   She is,
When once she is my wife.
● *Leon.* That 'once,' I see by your good father's
        speed,   210
Will come on very slowly. I am sorry,
Most sorry, you have broken from his liking
Where you were tied in duty, and as sorry
Your choice is not so rich in worth as beauty,
That you might well enjoy her.
    Flo.   Dear, look up:
Though Fortune, visible an enemy,
Should chase us with my father, power no jot
Hath she to change our loves. Beseech you, sir,
Remember since you owed no more to time
Than I do now: with thought of such affections,
Step forth mine advocate; at your request   221
My father will grant precious things as trifles.
    Leon. Would he do so, I'ld beg your precious
        mistress,
Which he counts but a trifle.
    Paul.   Sir, my liege,
Your eye hath too much youth in't: not a month
'Fore your queen died, she was more worth such
        gazes
Than what you look on now.

Leon.   I thought of her,
Even in these looks I made. [*To Florizel.*] But
    your petition
Is yet unanswer'd.   I will to your father:
Your honour not o'erthrown by your desires, 230
I am friend to them and you: upon which errand
I now go toward him; therefore follow me
And mark what way I make: come, good my
    lord.   [*Exeunt.*

SCENE II.   *Before* LEONTES' *palace.*

Enter AUTOLYCUS *and a* Gentleman.

Aut.   Beseech you, sir, were you present at
this relation?

First Gent.   I was by at the opening of the
fardel, heard the old shepherd deliver the manner
how he found it: whereupon, after a little amazed-
ness, we were all commanded out of the chamber;
only this methought I heard the shepherd say, he
found the child.

Aut.   I would most gladly know the issue of it.

First Gent.   I make a broken delivery of the
business; but the changes I perceived in the king
and Camillo were very notes of admiration: they
seemed almost, with staring on one another, to
tear the cases of their eyes; there was speech in
their dumbness, language in their very gesture;
they looked as they had heard of a world ransomed,
or one destroyed: a notable passion of wonder
appeared in them; but the wisest beholder, that
knew no more but seeing, could not say if the
importance were joy or sorrow; but in the extremity of the one, it must needs be.

Enter another Gentleman.

Here comes a gentleman that haply knows more.
The news, Rogero?

Sec. Gent.   Nothing but bonfires: the oracle is
fulfilled; the king's daughter is found: such a
deal of wonder is broken out within this hour that
ballad-makers cannot be able to express it.

Enter a third Gentleman.

Here comes the Lady Paulina's steward: he can
deliver you more.   How goes it now, sir? this
news which is called true is so like an old tale,
that the verity of it is in strong suspicion: has
the king found his heir?

Third Gent.   Most true, if ever truth were
• pregnant by circumstance: that which you hear
you'll swear you see, there is such unity in the
proofs.   The mantle of Queen Hermione's, her
jewel about the neck of it, the letters of Antigonus
• found with it which they know to be his character,
the majesty of the creature in resemblance of the
mother, the affection of nobleness which nature
shows above her breeding, and many other evidences proclaim her with all certainty to be the
king's daughter.   Did you see the meeting of the
two kings?

Sec. Gent.   No.

Third Gent.   Then have you lost a sight, which
was to be seen, cannot be spoken of.   There might
you have beheld one joy crown another, so and
in such manner that it seemed sorrow wept to take
leave of them, for their joy waded in tears   There
was casting up of eyes, holding up of hands, with
countenance of such distraction that they were to
• be known by garment, not by favour.   Our king,

Costume design for Leontes by Jacques Noel, Stratford-
upon-Avon, 1960

---

34 *pregnant.* Obvious.

38 *character.* Handwriting.

53 *favour.* Face.

106 *Julio Romano.* Italian painter. See introduction.

Julio Romano (1492 or 1499–1546) Engraving after a self portrait

being ready to leap out of himself for joy of his found daughter, as if that joy were now become a loss, cries 'O, thy mother, thy mother!' then asks Bohemia forgiveness; then embraces his son-in-law; then again worries he his daughter with clipping her; now he thanks the old shepherd, which stands by like a weather-bitten conduit of many kings' reigns. I never heard of such another encounter, which lames report to follow it and undoes description to do it.

Sec. Gent. What, pray you, became of Antigonus, that carried hence the child?

Third Gent. Like an old tale still, which will have matter to rehearse, though credit be asleep and not an ear open. He was torn to pieces with a bear: this avouches the shepherd's son; who has not only his innocence, which seems much, to justify him, but a handkerchief and rings of his that Paulina knows.

First Gent. What became of his bark and his followers?

Third Gent. Wrecked the same instant of their master's death and in the view of the shepherd: so that all the instruments which aided to expose the child were even then lost when it was found. But O, the noble combat that 'twixt joy and sorrow was fought in Paulina! She had one eye declined for the loss of her husband, another elevated that the oracle was fulfilled: she lifted the princess from the earth, and so locks her in embracing, as if she would pin her to her heart that she might no more be in danger of losing.

First Gent. The dignity of this act was worth the audience of kings and princes; for by such was it acted.

Third Gent. One of the prettiest touches of all and that which angled for mine eyes, caught the water though not the fish, was when, at the relation of the queen's death, with the manner how she came to 't bravely confessed and lamented by the king, how attentiveness wounded his daughter; till, from one sign of dolour to another, she did, with an 'Alas,' I would fain say, bleed tears, for I am sure my heart wept blood. Who was most marble there changed colour; some swooned, all sorrowed: if all the world could have seen 't, the woe had been universal.   100

First Gent. Are they returned to the court?

Third Gent. No: the princess hearing of her mother's statue, which is in the keeping of Paulina,—a piece many years in doing and now newly performed by that rare Italian master, Julio Romano, who, had he himself eternity and could put breath into his work, would beguile Nature of her custom, so perfectly he is her ape: he so near to Hermione hath done Hermione that they say one would speak to her and stand in hope of answer: thither with all greediness of affection are they gone, and there they intend to sup.

Sec. Gent. I thought she had some great matter there in hand; for she hath privately twice or thrice a day, ever since the death of Hermione, visited that removed house. Shall we thither and with our company piece the rejoicing?

First Gent. Who would be thence that has the benefit of access? every wink of an eye some new grace will be born: our absence makes us unthrifty to our knowledge.   Let's along.   121
[*Exeunt Gentlemen.*

Aut. Now, had I not the dash of my former life in me, would preferment drop on my head. I brought the old man and his son aboard the prince; told him I heard them talk of a fardel and I know not what: but he at that time, over-fond of the shepherd's daughter, so he then took her to be, who began to be much sea-sick, and himself little better, extremity of weather continuing, this mystery remained undiscovered. But 'tis all one to me; for had I been the finder out of this secret, it would not have relished among my other discredits.

Enter Shepherd *and* Clown.

Here come those I have done good to against my will, and already appearing in the blossoms of their fortune.

- *Shep.* Come, boy; I am past moe children, but thy sons and daughters will be all gentlemen born.

Clo. You are well met, sir. You denied to fight with me this other day, because I was no gentleman born. See you these clothes? say you see them not and think me still no gentleman born: you were best say these robes are not gentlemen born: give me the lie, do, and try whether I am not now a gentleman born.

Aut. I know you are now, sir, a gentleman born.

Clo. Ay, and have been so any time these four hours.

Shep. And so have I, boy.   149

Clo. So you have: but I was a gentleman born before my father; for the king's son took me by the hand, and called me brother; and then the two kings called my father brother; and then the prince my brother and the princess my sister called my father father; and so we wept, and there was the first gentleman-like tears that ever we shed.

Shep. We may live, son, to shed many more.

Clo. Ay; or else 'twere hard luck, being in so preposterous estate as we are.   159

Aut. I humbly beseech you, sir, to pardon me all the faults I have committed to your worship and to give me your good report to the prince my master.

Shep. Prithee, son, do; for we must be gentle, now we are gentlemen.

Clo. Thou wilt amend thy life?

Aut. Ay, an it like your good worship.

Clo. Give me thy hand: I will swear to the prince thou art as honest a true fellow as any is in Bohemia.   170

Shep. You may say it, but not swear it.

Clo. Not swear it, now I am a gentleman?
- Let boors and franklins say it, I'll swear it.

Shep. How if it be false, son?

Clo. If it be ne'er so false, a true gentleman may swear it in the behalf of his friend: and I'll swear to the prince thou art a tall fellow of thy hands and that thou wilt not be drunk; but I know thou art no tall fellow of thy hands and that thou wilt be drunk: but I'll swear it, and I would thou wouldst be a tall fellow of thy hands.

Aut. I will prove so, sir, to my power.

Clo. Ay, by any means prove a tall fellow: if I do not wonder how thou darest venture to be drunk, not being a tall fellow, trust me not. Hark! the kings and the princes, our kindred, are going to see the queen's picture. Come, follow us: we'll be thy good masters. [*Exeunt.*

137 *moe.* More.

173 *boors.* Peasants. *franklins.* Yeomen.

19 *mock'd.* Copied.

Paulina: '... prepare To see the life as lively mock'd as ever ...' Mary Anderson as Hermione, Lyceum Theatre, London, 1887

Opposite: Mrs Charles Kean as Hermione, Princess's Theatre, London, Painting by C. R. Leslie (1794–1859)

SCENE III.   *A chapel in* PAULINA'S *house.*

Enter LEONTES, POLIXENES, FLORIZEL, PER-
    DITA, CAMILLO, PAULINA, Lords, *and* At-
    tendants.

 Leon.   O grave and good Paulina, the great
  comfort
That I have had of thee!
 Paul.   What, sovereign sir,
I did not well I meant well.   All my services
You have paid home: but that you have vouch-
  safed,
With your crown'd brother and these your con-
  tracted
Heirs of your kingdoms, my poor house to visit,
It is a surplus of your grace, which never
My life may last to answer.
 Leon.   O Paulina,
We honour you with trouble: but we came
To see the statue of our queen: your gallery 10
Have we pass'd through, not without much con-
  tent
In many singularities; but we saw not
That which my daughter came to look upon,
The statue of her mother.
 Paul.   As she lived peerless,
So her dead likeness, I do well believe,
Excels whatever yet you look'd upon
Or hand of man hath done; therefore I keep it
Lonely, apart.   But here it is: prepare
● To see the life as lively mock'd as ever   19
Still sleep mock'd death: behold, and say 'tis well.
  [*Paulina draws a curtain, and discovers*
    Hermione standing like a statue.
I like your silence, it the more shows off
Your wonder: but yet speak; first, you, my liege.
Comes it not something near?
 Leon.   Her natural posture!
Chide me, dear stone, that I may say indeed
Thou art Hermione; or rather, thou art she
In thy not chiding, for she was as tender
As infancy and grace.   But yet, Paulina,
Hermione was not so much wrinkled, nothing
So aged as this seems.
 Pol.   O, not by much.
 Paul.   So much the more our carver's excel-
  lence;   30
Which lets go by some sixteen years and makes
  her
As she lived now.
 Leon.   As now she might have done,
So much to my good comfort, as it is
Now piercing to my soul.   O, thus she stood,
Even with such life of majesty, warm life,
As now it coldly stands, when first I woo'd her!
I am ashamed: does not the stone rebuke me
For being more stone than it?   O royal piece,
There's magic in thy majesty, which has
My evils conjured to remembrance and   40
From thy admiring daughter took the spirits,
Standing like stone with thee.
 Per.   And give me leave,
And do not say 'tis superstition, that
I kneel and then implore her blessing.   Lady,
Dear queen, that ended when I but began,
Give me that hand of yours to kiss.
 Paul.   O, patience!
The statue is but newly fix'd, the colour's
Not dry.

56 *piece up*. Add to.

67 *fixture*. Colouring.

Paulina: 'Music, awake her; strike!' Engraving from a painting by William Hamilton (1751–1801)

Cam. My lord, your sorrow was too sore laid on,
Which sixteen winters cannot blow away,   50
So many summers dry: scarce any joy
Did ever so long live; no sorrow
But kill'd itself much sooner.
   Pol.   Dear my brother,
Let him that was the cause of this have power
To take off so much grief from you as he
● Will piece up in himself.
   Paul.   Indeed, my lord,
If I had thought the sight of my poor image
Would thus have wrought you,—for the stone is
      mine—
I'ld not have show'd it.
   Leon.   Do not draw the curtain.
   Paul. No longer shall you gaze on't, lest
      your fancy   60
May think anon it moves.
   Leon.   Let be, let be.
Would I were dead, but that, methinks, already—
What was he that did make it? See, my lord,
Would you not deem it breathed? and that those
      veins
Did verily bear blood?
   Pol.   Masterly done:
The very life seems warm upon her lip.
● *Leon.* The fixure of her eye has motion in't,
As we are mock'd with art.
   Paul.   I'll draw the curtain:
My lord's almost so far transported that
He'll think anon it lives.
   Leon.   O sweet Paulina,   70
Make me to think so twenty years together!
No settled senses of the world can match
The pleasure of that madness. Let't alone.
   Paul. I am sorry, sir, I have thus far stirr'd
      you: but
I could afflict you farther.
   Leon.   Do, Paulina;
For this affliction has a taste as sweet
As any cordial comfort. Still, methinks,
There is an air comes from her: what fine chisel
Could ever yet cut breath? Let no man mock me,
For I will kiss her.
   Paul.   Good my lord, forbear: 80
The ruddiness upon her lip is wet;
You'll mar it if you kiss it, stain your own
With oily painting. Shall I draw the curtain?
   Leon. No, not these twenty years.
   Per.   So long could I
Stand by, a looker on.
   Paul.   Either forbear,
Quit presently the chapel, or resolve you
For more amazement. If you can behold it,
I'll make the statue move indeed, descend
And take you by the hand: but then you'll think—
Which I protest against—I am assisted   90
By wicked powers.
   Leon.   What you can make her do,
I am content to look on: what to speak,
I am content to hear; for 'tis as easy
To make her speak as move.
   Paul.   It is required
You do awake your faith. Then all stand still;
On: those that think it is unlawful business
I am about, let them depart.
   Leon.   Proceed:
No foot shall stir.
   Paul.   Music, awake her; strike! [*Music.*

'Tis time; descend; be stone no more; approach:
Strike all that look upon with marvel.   Come, 100
I 'll fill your grave up: stir, nay, come away,
Bequeath to death your numbness, for from him
Dear life redeems you.   You perceive she stirs:
      [*Hermione comes down.*
Start not; her actions shall be holy as
You hear my spell is lawful: do not shun her
Until you see her die again; for then
You kill her double.   Nay, present your hand:
When she was young you woo'd her; now in age
Is she become the suitor?
  Leon.   O, she's warm!
If this be magic, let it be an art   110
Lawful as eating.
  Pol.   She embraces him.
  Cam. She hangs about his neck:
If she pertain to life let her speak too.
  Pol. Ay, and make 't manifest where she has
   lived,
Or how stolen from the dead.
  Paul.   That she is living,
Were it but told you, should be hooted at
Like an old tale: but it appears she lives,
Though yet she speak not.   Mark a little while.
Please you to interpose, fair madam: kneel
And pray your mother's blessing.   Turn, good
  lady;   120
Our Perdita is found.
  Her.   You gods, look down
And from your sacred vials pour your graces
Upon my daughter's head!   Tell me, mine own,
Where hast thou been preserved? where lived?
  how found
Thy father's court? for thou shalt hear that I,
Knowing by Paulina that the oracle
Gave hope thou wast in being, have preserved
Myself to see the issue.
  Paul.   There's time enough for that;
● Lest they desire upon this push to trouble
● Your joys with like relation.   Go together, 130
You precious winners all; your exultation
Partake to every one.   I, an old turtle,
Will wing me to some wither'd bough and there
My mate, that's never to be found again,
● Lament till I am lost.
  Leon.   O, peace, Paulina!
Thou shouldst a husband take by my consent,
As I by thine a wife: this is a match,
And made between 's by vows.   Thou hast found
  mine;
But how, is to be question'd; for I saw her,
As I thought, dead, and have in vain said many 140
A prayer upon her grave.   I 'll not seek far—
For him, I partly know his mind—to find thee
An honourable husband.   Come, Camillo,
And take her by the hand, whose worth and
  honesty
Is richly noted and here justified
By us, a pair of kings.   Let's from this place.
What! look upon my brother: both your pardons,
That e'er I put between your holy looks
My ill suspicion.   This is your son-in-law
And son unto the king, who, heavens directing, 150
● Is troth-plight to your daughter.   Good Paulina,
Lead us from hence, where we may leisurely
Each one demand and answer to his part
Perform'd in this wide gap of time since first
We were dissever'd: hastily lead away. [*Exeunt.*

Hermione: 'You gods . . . pour your graces Upon my daughter's head!' Drawing by Thomas Stothard (1755–1834)

129 *upon this push.* At this time of stress.

130 *relation.* Retelling.

135 *lost.* Dead.

151 *troth-plight.* Betrothed.

The Tempest

1611

The Winter's Tale was followed by an exquisite masterpiece, *The Tempest*, which was played later the same year on Hallowmas night (1 November) before the King at Whitehall. It has not the power and drama generated by the theme of the former; but its poetry is no less, and its interest even richer and more diverse, particularly in what relates to the New World.

For, with the formation of the Virginia Company, the foundation of Jamestown, the voyages going out to the American coast, there was mounting national interest in these ventures. Shakespeare had a considerable number of friends actively involved; he read the Voyages and Travels, as he had read Hakluyt, along with the news pamphlets. In 1609 the flagship of the small fleet going out with reinforcements for Virginia, the *Sea Venture*, met with a tornado off Bermuda, ran in on the rocks a wreck and yet, miraculously, not a life was lost. Jourdan's pamphlet, *A Discovery of the Bermudas, otherwise called the Isle of Devils*, alerted Shakespeare to the subject when it was published in 1610.

His full knowledge of the event, in circumstantial detail, came from William Strachey's manuscript account of the wreck, and its redemption, which came back to Blackfriars, dedicated to some 'Noble Lady' Shakespeare would have known. Strachey himself was more interesting: a literary man who had contributed a sonnet for Ben Jonson's *Sejanus* (in which Shakespeare had acted), was a shareholder in the Boys' Company, the Children of the Revels, and frequently in and out of Blackfriars. The details of the tempest conjured up by Prospero's arts for his purposes closely follow those given by Strachey, to the St. Elmo's fire-ball running down the rigging. Events that follow in the play are sparked off by those that happened in the island, and other suggestions come from Shakespeare's reading. Dr. Johnson noticed that he was a 'diligent reader'.

Contemporaries thought that the uninhabited island, 'the still-vexed Bermoothes' – the constantly storm-vexed – was given over to devils, as Jourdan's pamphlet shows, and to enchantment. Thus the first, and dominant, theme of the play is magic – fascinating to a world in which 'Dr' Dee and 'Dr' Forman were notorious, but in the nature of things not so dramatic as that of human conflict. For Prospero's magic has determined

IOHANNES DEE.
Londinenſis,

Far left:
*Doctor and
astrologer, Simon
Forman. Engrav-
ing reproduced for
Francis Grose and
Thomas Astle,*
The Antiquarian
Repertory, *1808*

Left: *Mathema-
tician and
astrologer, John
Dee*

the outcome beforehand and at every juncture he controls the action through the operations of his sprite, Ariel. (Just as Dr. Dee needed his medium, Kelly, in order to operate.)

The island is several times described, with its qualities. Even Caliban, who was its possessor before Prospero came and enslaved him, is moved to poetry:

> the isle is full of noises,
> Sounds and sweet airs, that give delight and hurt not.
> Sometimes a thousand twangling instruments
> Will hum about mine ears; and sometime voices
> That, if I then had waked after long sleep,
> Will make me sleep again.

Caliban is the most original creation in the play, one of Shakespeare's most remarkable, and is the upshot of reading and reflexion. He is based on the various accounts of the American Indians coming home from the New World.

> When thou cam'st first
> Thou strok'st me and made much of me; wouldst give me
> Water with berries in't; and teach me how
> To name the bigger light, and how the less,
> That burn by day and night.

This is entirely in keeping with the *True Report* of the new-found land of Virginia by Ralegh's agent, Thomas Hariot, who had shown the Indians the stars and planets through his perspective glass.

> And then I loved thee,
> And showed thee all the qualities o'the isle,
> The fresh springs, brine-pits, barren place and fertile.

861

The primitive possessor of the land had been ready to worship the newcomer; and when the baser elements of the ship's company come a-land, Caliban is pathetically ready to venerate and serve them, a jester and a drunken butler:

> I prithee, let me bring thee where crabs grow;
> And I with my long nails will dig thee pig-nuts;
> Show thee a jay's nest, and instruct thee how
> To snare the nimble marmoset; I'll bring thee
> To clustering filberts, and sometimes I'll get thee
> Young scammels [sea-mews] from the rocks.

The rascally Stephano and Trinculo respond by making the poor primitive drunk – and fire-water proved the ruin of the American Indian. Caliban, however, led them on to make an attempt on Prospero's life.

Conspiracy. More important than this mutiny is the conspiracy in which Antonio, who had usurped Prospero's place as Duke of Milan, tries to inveigle Sebastian into killing his brother Alonso, the King of Naples. These grandees had been on board the ship which, approaching too near the island, had foundered in the storm raised by Prospero, though he had brought them safe to land for his purposes.

In historic fact there had been a mutiny against the governor during that winter on Bermuda, the leader of which had been hanged on a tree – and the tree occurs in the play. And a dangerous conspiracy blew up during the starving time in Virginia, led by two Germans, who received their come-uppance.

Primitive Communism. It is given to Gonzalo, 'an honest old councillor', to put forward the ideal of blissful communism, which Shakespeare had read about in Florio's *Montaigne*; and he leaves us in no doubt what he thought of it.

> I'the commonwealth I would by contraries
> Execute all things; for no kind of traffic [commerce]
> Would I admit; no name of magistrate;
> Letters should not be known –

one is reminded of Jack Cade years earlier –

>   riches, poverty,
> And use of service, none; contract, succession,
> Bourn, bound of land, tilth, vineyard, none;
> No use of metal, corn, or wine, or oil;
> No occupation; all men idle, all.

The women were all to be innocent and pure. Yet

> All things in common Nature should produce
> Without sweat or endeavour: treason, felony,
> Sword, pike, knife, gun, or need of any engine,
> Would I not have. But Nature should bring forth,
> Of its own kind, all foison [harvest], all abundance,
> To feed my innocent people.

One cynical hearer of this nonsense inquires:

>   No marrying 'mong his subjects?

Another concludes:

>   None, man, all idle: whores and knaves.

So much for Montaigne's illusions about primitive man; Shakespeare depicts the 'man in a state of nature' of the political philosophers as a Caliban. At no time in his career had he any use for illusions about life and the human condition, and no-one has ever had deeper insight into it.

This is not to say that his view was a cynical one: the purpose of Prospero's bringing these men to the island was their redemption, his forgiveness, and reconciliation. Shakespeare knew the truth about human nature, both sides to it; we cannot doubt that Prospero speaks for him:

>   the rarer action is
>   In virtue than in vengeance.

Magic was much in the air at this time, with a king on the throne who was an authority on demonology, and Prospero is a properly mysterious character: a Magus, or *mage*. His power depends on his books – and we remember the magical importance that both Dee and Forman attached to their books. Caliban alerts Stephano and Trinculo:

> First to possess his books; for without them
> He's but a sot, as I am, nor hath not
> One spirit to command . . .
> Burn but his books.

Instead, Prospero raises up hunters and hounds, and, with Ariel, sets them on this nasty crew. They call the hounds by their names: 'Hey, Mountain, hey!' 'Silver! there it goes, Silver.' 'Fury, Fury! there, Tyrant, there! hark, hark!' 'Hark, they roar!'

> Let them be hunted soundly. At this hour
> Lies at my mercy all mine enemies:
> Shortly shall all my labours end, and thou
> Shalt have the air at freedom. For a little
> Follow and do me service.

To do this scene, and several others, justice – perhaps to realise this play as a whole – one needs the resources of film. Here we are reminded of Shakespeare's enthusiasm for the hunt, from the very beginning.

He may have intuited his own farewell to his art in Prospero's renunciation of his:

> I'll break my staff,
> Bury it certain fathoms in the earth,
> And deeper than did ever plummet sound
> I'll drown my book.

This comes at the end of the marvellous speech:

> Ye elves of hills, brooks, standing lakes, and groves . . .
>   You demi-puppets that
> By moonshine do the green sour ringlets make,
> Whereof the ewe not bites; and you whose pastime
> Is to make midnight mushrooms, that rejoice
> To hear the solemn curfew . . .

All that goes back to the country lore he loved, of Mercutio's evocation and *A Midsummer Night's Dream*.

The youthful love of Ferdinand and Miranda – that went to Victorian hearts and filled so much of their commentary – we may take for granted: it is charmingly rendered, as was that of Florizel and Perdita. Of more special interest is that the reason for Caliban's subjection and servitude was his attempt to rape Miranda. Contemporary travellers, not having had a course in anthropology, were shocked by the laxity of morals in the New World. (The Puritans would put that right – by decimating the Indians.)

We take for granted, too, a complete scene given up to the master's old habit of verbal play and punning. It should have been obvious to Dr. Johnson that, even apart from its appeal to the contemporary audience, it was necessary to fill up the interstices of the action. We should observe that the language of the play, filled with beauty, is perhaps simpler again than *The Winter's Tale*, and far more so than the laboured contortions of *Cymbeline*. The play is, as the island was, full of music, and the marriage of the lovers is adorned with a formal masque, which must have appealed at Blackfriars. Goddesses descend to bless them; more endearing are the country reapers who dance:

> You sunburned sicklemen, of August weary

(was he writing that August, one wonders?)

> Come hither from the furrow, and be merry;
> Make holiday, your rye-straw hats put on.
> And these fresh nymphs encounter every one
> In country footing.

The songs are exquisite, as ever. 'Full fathom five' – the 'five-fathom' goes back to *Romeo and Juliet*; in 'Come unto these yellow sands . . .' the phrase 'the wild waves whist' goes right back – after all these years and all the work between – to Marlowe. (And what might not *he* have achieved, too, if only he had lived!)

It is all as if Shakespeare were rounding things up.

In the Epilogue, speaking in the person of Prospero, he is speaking doubly, as so often, partly for himself:

> Now my charms are all o'erthrown,
> And what strength I have's mine own,
> Which is most faint . . .

Then, propitiating the audience, as all along:

> Gentle breath of yours my sails
> Must fill, or else my project fails,
> Which was to please.

The Text in the Folio is an excellent one, with more elaborate stage-directions than for any other play, for evidently he was writing away at home in the country. One wonders whether the passage describing Caliban as a 'mooncalf' suggested the remarkable satiric poem of that title to Shakespeare's prolific countryman, Drayton, who certainly was inspired by *A Midsummer Night's Dream* for his delightful 'Nymphidia'.

Ben Jonson observed of Caliban, 'if there be never a "Servant-monster" in the fair – who can help it? he (the author) says; nor a nest of antics [fantastics]. He is loth to make Nature afraid in his plays, like those that beget *Tales*, *Tempests*, and such-like drolleries.' This is grumpy, rather than really bad-tempered, and Ben more than made up for his quips by the magnificent generosity of his tributes to the Master in, and his help over, the Folio edition of his plays.

THE TEMPEST.

DRAMATIS PERSONÆ.

ALONSO, King of Naples.
SEBASTIAN, his brother.
PROSPERO, the right Duke of Milan.
ANTONIO, his brother, the usurping Duke of Milan.
FERDINAND, son to the King of Naples.
GONZALO, an honest old Counsellor.
ADRIAN,
FRANCISCO, } Lords.
CALIBAN, a savage and deformed Slave.
TRINCULO, a Jester.
STEPHANO, a drunken Butler.
Master of a Ship.

Boatswain.
Mariners.
MIRANDA, daughter to Prospero.
ARIEL, an airy Spirit.
IRIS,
CERES,
JUNO, } presented by Spirits.
Nymphs,
Reapers,

Other Spirits attending on Prospero.
SCENE—*A ship at Sea: an island.*

● *A bullet beside a text line indicates an annotation in the opposite column*

ACT I.

SCENE I. *On a ship at sea: a tempestuous noise of thunder and lightning heard.*

Enter a Ship-Master *and* a Boatswain.

Mast. Boatswain!
Boats. Here, master: what cheer?
Mast. Good, speak to the mariners: fall to't,
● yarely, or we run ourselves aground: bestir, bestir. [*Exit.*

Enter Mariners.

Boats. Heigh, my hearts! cheerly, cheerly, my hearts! yare, yare! Take in the topsail. Tend to the master's whistle. Blow, till thou burst thy wind, if room enough!

Enter ALONSO, SEBASTIAN, ANTONIO, FERDINAND, GONZALO, *and others.*

Alon. Good boatswain, have care. Where's
● the master? Play the men. 11
Boats. I pray now, keep below.

The storm at sea. Scene painting by Thanas Grieve, Princess's Theatre, London, 1857

4 *yarely.* Briskly.

11 *Play.* Ply.

Opposite: Prospero and Miranda. Painting by William Hamilton (1751–1801)

18 *roarers.* i.e. 'waves' and 'bullies'.

46 *whoreson.* Bastard.

51 *unstanched.* Loose.

60 *wide-chapp'd.* Wide jawed.

A galley of the 16th century. Engraving from a contemporary German woodcut by F. W. Fairholt from J. O. Halliwell's edition of Shakespeare's works, 1853–65

Ant. Where is the master, boatswain?

Boats. Do you not hear him? You mar our labour: keep your cabins: you do assist the storm.

Gon. Nay, good, be patient.

Boats. When the sea is. Hence! What cares these roarers for the name of king? To cabin: silence! trouble us not.

Gon. Good, yet remember whom thou hast aboard.   21

Boats. None that I more love than myself. You are a counsellor; if you can command these elements to silence, and work the peace of the present, we will not hand a rope more; use your authority: if you cannot, give thanks you have lived so long, and make yourself ready in your cabin for the mischance of the hour, if it so hap. Cheerly, good hearts! Out of our way, I say.   [*Exit.*

Gon. I have great comfort from this fellow: methinks he hath no drowning mark upon him; his complexion is perfect gallows. Stand fast, good Fate, to his hanging: make the rope of his destiny our cable, for our own doth little advantage. If he be not born to be hanged, our case is miserable.   [*Exeunt.*

Re-enter Boatswain.

Boats. Down with the topmast! yare! lower, lower! Bring her to try with main-course. [*A cry within.*] A plague upon this howling! they are louder than the weather or our office.   40

Re-enter SEBASTIAN, ANTONIO, *and* GONZALO.

Yet again! what do you here? Shall we give o'er and drown? Have you a mind to sink?

Seb. A pox o' your throat, you bawling, blasphemous, incharitable dog!

Boats. Work you then.

Ant. Hang, cur! hang, you whoreson, insolent noisemaker! We are less afraid to be drowned than thou art.

Gon. I'll warrant him for drowning; though the ship were no stronger than a nutshell and as leaky as an unstanched wench.

Boats. Lay her a-hold, a-hold! set her two courses off to sea again; lay her off.

Enter Mariners *wet.*

Mariners. All lost! to prayers, to prayers! all lost!

Boats. What, must our mouths be cold?

Gon. The king and prince at prayers! let's assist them,
For our case is as theirs.

Seb.   I'm out of patience.

Ant. We are merely cheated of our lives by drunkards:
This wide-chapp'd rascal—would thou mightst lie drowning   60
The washing of ten tides!

Gon.   He'll be hang'd yet,
Though every drop of water swear against it
And gape at widest to glut him.

[*A confused noise within:* ' Mercy on us!—
'We split, we split!'—'Farewell my wife and children!'—
'Farewell, brother!'—'We split, we split, we split!']

Ant. Let's all sink with the king.

Seb.   Let's take leave of him.
                    [*Exeunt Ant. and Seb.*
Gon.   Now would I give a thousand furlongs
of sea for an acre of barren ground, long heath,
brown furze, any thing.   The wills above be
● done! but I would fain die a dry death. [*Exeunt.*

SCENE II. *The island.   Before* PROSPERO'S *cell.*

Enter PROSPERO *and* MIRANDA.

Mir.   If by your art, my dearest father, you have
Put the wild waters in this roar, allay them.
The sky, it seems, would pour down stinking pitch,
● But that the sea, mounting to the welkin's cheek,
Dashes the fire out.   O, I have suffer'd
With those that I saw suffer : a brave vessel,
Who had, no doubt, some noble creature in her,
Dash'd all to pieces.   O, the cry did knock
Against my very heart.   Poor souls, they perish'd.
Had I been any god of power, I would   10
Have sunk the sea within the earth or ere
It should the good ship so have swallow'd and
● The fraughting souls within her.
     Pros.   Be collected :
No more amazement : tell your piteous heart
There's no harm done.
     Mir.   O, woe the day!
     Pros.   No harm.
I have done nothing but in care of thee,
Of thee, my dear one, thee, my daughter, who
Art ignorant of what thou art, nought knowing
Of whence I am, nor that I am more better
Than Prospero, master of a full poor cell,   20
And thy no greater father.
     Mir.   More to know
Did never meddle with my thoughts.
     Pros.   'Tis time
I should inform thee farther.   Lend thy hand,
And pluck my magic garment from me.   So :
                    [*Lays down his mantle.*
Lie there, my art.   Wipe thou thine eyes ; have
     comfort.
The direful spectacle of the wreck, which touch'd
The very virtue of compassion in thee,
I have with such provision in mine art
So safely ordered that there is no soul—
● No, not so much perdition as an hair   30
Betid to any creature in the vessel
Which thou heard'st cry, which thou saw'st sink.
     Sit down ;
For thou must now know farther.
     Mir.   You have often
Begun to tell me what I am, but stopp'd
● And left me to a bootless inquisition,
Concluding ' Stay : not yet.'
     Pros.   The hour's now come ;
The very minute bids thee ope thine ear ;
Obey and be attentive.   Canst thou remember
A time before we came unto this cell ?
I do not think thou canst, for then thou wast not 40
Out three years old.
     Mir.   Certainly, sir, I can.
     Pros. By what ? by any other house or person ?
Of any thing the image tell me that
Hath kept with thy remembrance.
     Mir.   'Tis far off
And rather like a dream than an assurance
That my remembrance warrants.   Had I not
Four or five women once that tended me ?

71 *fain.* Rather.

4 *welkin's cheek.* The face of the sky.

Miranda : 'a brave vessel . . . Dash'd all to pieces.'
Miranda and Prospero viewing the tempest. Drawing by
P. J. de Loutherbourg (1740–1812)

13 *fraughting souls.* i.e. the people carried as freight.

30-31 *perdition . . . Betid.* i.e. as a hair shall be lost.

35 *bootless inquisition.* Profitless inquiry.

63 *holp.* Helped.

64 *teen.* Anxiety.

71 *signories.* Italian states.

81 *trash.* Discard. *over-topping.* Exceeding their authority.

87 *verdure.* Sap, that is power.

97 *sans.* Without.

Prospero and Miranda. Drawing by J. M. Wright (1777–1866)

Pros. Thou hadst, and more, Miranda. But how is it
That this lives in thy mind? What seest thou else
In the dark backward and abysm of time? 50
If thou remember'st aught ere thou camest here,
How thou camest here thou mayst.
  Mir.   But that I do not.
  Pros. Twelve year since, Miranda, twelve year since,
Thy father was the Duke of Milan and
A prince of power.
  Mir.   Sir, are not you my father?
  Pros. Thy mother was a piece of virtue, and
She said thou wast my daughter; and thy father
Was Duke of Milan; and thou his only heir
And princess no worse issued.
  Mir.   O the heavens!
What foul play had we, that we came from thence?
Or blessed was't we did?
  Pros.   Both, both, my girl: 61
By foul play, as thou say'st, were we heaved thence,
● But blessedly holp hither.
  Mir.   O, my heart bleeds
● To think o' the teen that I have turn'd you to,
Which is from my remembrance! Please you, farther.
  Pr. My brother and thy uncle, call'd Antonio—
I pray thee, mark me—that a brother should
Be so perfidious!—he whom next thyself
Of all the world I loved and to him put
The manage of my state; as at that time 70
● Through all the signories it was the first
And Prospero the prime duke, being so reputed
In dignity, and for the liberal arts
Without a parallel; those being all my study,
The government I cast upon my brother
And to my state grew stranger, being transported
And rapt in secret studies. Thy false uncle—
Dost thou attend me?
  Mir.   Sir, most heedfully.
  Pros. Being once perfected how to grant suits,
How to deny them, who to advance and who 80
● To trash for over-topping, new created
The creatures that were mine, I say, or changed 'em,
Or else new form'd 'em; having both the key
Of officer and office, set all hearts i' the state
To what tune pleased his ear; that now he was
The ivy which had hid my princely trunk,
● And suck'd my verdure out on't. Thou attend'st not.
  Mir. O, good sir, I do.
  Pros.   I pray thee, mark me.
I, thus neglecting worldly ends, all dedicated
To closeness and the bettering of my mind 90
With that which, but by being so retired,
O'er-prized all popular rate, in my false brother
Awaked an evil nature; and my trust,
Like a good parent, did beget of him
A falsehood in its contrary as great
As my trust was; which had indeed no limit,
● A confidence sans bound. He being thus lorded,
Not only with what my revenue yielded,
But what my power might else exact, like one
† Who having into truth, by telling of it, 100
Made such a sinner of his memory,
To credit his own lie, he did believe
He was indeed the duke; out o' the substitution

And executing the outward face of royalty,
With all prerogative: hence his ambition grow-
  ing—
Dost thou hear?
    Mir.   Your tale, sir, would cure deafness.
    Pros.   To have no screen between this part he
      play'd
And him he play'd it for, he needs will be
Absolute Milan.   Me, poor man, my library
Was dukedom large enough: of temporal royal-
  ties   110
He thinks me now incapable; confederates—
So dry he was for sway—wi' the King of Naples
To give him annual tribute, do him homage,
Subject his coronet to his crown and bend
The dukedom yet unbow'd—alas, poor Milan!—
To most ignoble stooping.
    Mir.   O the heavens!
    Pros.   Mark his condition and the event; then
      tell me
If this might be a brother.
    Mir.   I should sin
To think but nobly of my grandmother:
Good wombs have borne bad sons.
    Pros.   Now the condition. 120
This King of Naples, being an enemy
To me inveterate, hearkens my brother's suit;
Which was, that he, in lieu o' the premises
Of homage and I know not how much tribute,
Should presently extirpate me and mine
Out of the dukedom and confer fair Milan
With all the honours on my brother: whereon,
A treacherous army levied, one midnight
Fated to the purpose did Antonio open
The gates of Milan, and, i' the dead of dark-
  ness,   130
The ministers for the purpose hurried thence
Me and thy crying self.
    Mir.   Alack, for pity!
I, not remembering how I cried out then,
Will cry it o'er again: it is a hint
That wrings mine eyes to't.
    Pros.   Hear a little further
And then I'll bring thee to the present business
Which now's upon's; without the which this story
Were most impertinent.
    Mir.   Wherefore did they not
That hour destroy us?
    Pros.   Well demanded, wench:
My tale provokes that question.   Dear, they
      durst not,   140
So dear the love my people bore me, nor set
A mark so bloody on the business, but
With colours fairer painted their foul ends.
In few, they hurried us aboard a bark,
Bore us some leagues to sea; where they prepared
A rotten carcass of a boat, not rigg'd,
Nor tackle, sail, nor mast; the very rats
Instinctively have quit it: there they hoist us,
To cry to the sea that roar'd to us, to sigh
To the winds whose pity, sighing back again, 150
Did us but loving wrong.
    Mir.   Alack, what trouble
Was I then to you!
    Pros.   O, a cherubin
Thou wast that did preserve me.   Thou didst
      smile,
Infused with a fortitude from heaven,
When I have deck'd the sea with drops full salt,

Miranda: 'Your tale, sir, would cure deafness'. Miranda
(Peggy Ashcroft) and Prospero (Harcourt Williams),
Old Vic Theatre, London, 1933

157 *undergoing stomach.* Spirit of endurance.

Ariel: 'All hail, great master!' Drawing by W. Hamilton
for A. J. Valpy's *Plays and Poems of Shakespeare,* 1842

196 *beak.* Bow.

201 *Jove.* Legendary god of heaven.

204 *Neptune.* Legendary god of the sea.

207 *coil.* Confusion.

Under my burthen groan'd; which raised in me
● An undergoing stomach, to bear up
Against what should ensue.
    Mir.   How came we ashore?
    Pros. By Providence divine.
Some food we had and some fresh water that 160
A noble Neapolitan, Gonzalo,
Out of his charity, who being then appointed
Master of this design, did give us, with
Rich garments, linens, stuffs and necessaries,
Which since have steaded much; so, of his gen-
        tleness,
Knowing I loved my books, he furnish'd me
From mine own library with volumes that
I prize above my dukedom.
    Mir.   Would I might
But ever see that man!
    Pros.   Now I arise: [*Resumes his mantle.*
Sit still, and hear the last of our sea-sorrow.   170
Here in this island we arrived; and here
Have I, thy schoolmaster, made thee more profit
Than other princesses can that have more time
For vainer hours and tutors not so careful.
    Mir. Heavens thank you for't! And now, I
        pray you, sir,
For still 'tis beating in my mind, your reason
For raising this sea-storm?
    Pros.   Know thus far forth.
By accident most strange, bountiful Fortune,
Now my dear lady, hath mine enemies
Brought to this shore; and by my prescience 180
I find my zenith doth depend upon
A most auspicious star, whose influence
If now I court not but omit, my fortunes
Will ever after droop. Here cease more questions:
Thou art inclined to sleep; 'tis a good dulness,
And give it way: I know thou canst not choose.
                      [*Miranda sleeps.*
Come away, servant, come. I am ready now.
Approach, my Ariel, come.
            Enter ARIEL.
    Ari. All hail, great master! grave sir, hail!
        I come
To answer thy best pleasure; be't to fly,   190
To swim, to dive into the fire, to ride
On the curl'd clouds, to thy strong bidding task
Ariel and all his quality.
    Pros.   Hast thou, spirit,
Perform'd to point the tempest that I bade thee?
    Ari. To every article.
● I boarded the king's ship; now on the beak,
Now in the waist, the deck, in every cabin,
I flamed amazement: sometime I'ld divide,
And burn in many places; on the topmast,
The yards and bowsprit, would I flame distinctly,
● Then meet and join. Jove's lightnings, the pre-
        cursors   201
O' the dreadful thunder-claps, more momentary
And sight-outrunning were not; the fire and cracks
● Of sulphurous roaring the most mighty Neptune
Seem to besiege and make his bold waves tremble,
Yea, his dread trident shake.
    Pros.   My brave spirit!
● Who was so firm, so constant, that this coil
Would not infect his reason?
    Ari.   Not a soul
But felt a fever of the mad and play'd
Some tricks of desperation. All but mariners 210
Plunged in the foaming brine and quit the vessel,

Then all afire with me : the king's son, Ferdinand,
With hair up-staring,—then like reeds, not hair,—
Was the first man that leap'd; cried, 'Hell is empty,
And all the devils are here.'
   Pros.   Why, that's my spirit !
But was not this nigh shore ?
   Ari.   Close by, my master.
   Pros.   But are they, Ariel, safe ?
   Ari.   Not a hair perish'd ;
On their sustaining garments not a blemish,
But fresher than before : and, as thou badest me,
In troops I have dispersed them 'bout the isle. 220
The king's son have I landed by himself ;
Whom I left cooling of the air with sighs
In an odd angle of the isle and sitting,
His arms in this sad knot.
   Pros.   Of the king's ship
The mariners say how thou hast disposed
And all the rest o' the fleet.
   Ari.   Safely in harbour
Is the king's ship; in the deep nook, where once
Thou call'dst me up at midnight to fetch dew
● From the still-vex'd Bermoothes, there she's hid :
The mariners all under hatches stow'd ;   230
Who, with a charm join'd to their suffer'd labour,
I have left asleep : and for the rest o' the fleet
Which I dispersed, they all have met again
● And are upon the Mediterranean flote,
Bound sadly home for Naples,
Supposing that they saw the king's ship wreck'd
And his great person perish.
   Pros.   Ariel, thy charge
Exactly is perform'd : but there's more work.
What is the time o' the day ?
   Ari.   Past the mid season.
●   *Pros.* At least two glasses. The time 'twixt
     six and now   240
Must by us both be spent most preciously.
   Ari. Is there more toil ? Since thou dost give me pains,
Let me remember thee what thou hast promised,
Which is not yet perform'd me.
   Pros.   How now? moody?
What is't thou canst demand ?
   Ari.   My liberty.
   Pros.   Before the time be out? no more !
   Ari.   I prithee,
Remember I have done thee worthy service ;
Told thee no lies, made thee no mistakings, served
Without or grudge or grumblings : thou didst promise
● To bate me a full year.
   Pros.   Dost thou forget   250
From what a torment I did free thee ?
   Ari.   No.
   Pros. Thou dost, and think'st it much to tread the ooze
Of the salt deep,
To run upon the sharp wind of the north,
To do me business in the veins o' the earth
When it is baked with frost.
   Ari.   I do not, sir.
   Pros. Thou liest, malignant thing ! Hast thou forgot
The foul witch Sycorax, who with age and envy
Was grown into a hoop? hast thou forgot her ?
   Ari. No, sir.

The shipwreck as related by Ariel. Engraving from a painting by George Romney (1734–1802)

229 *Bermoothes.* The Bermudas.

234 *flote.* Flood, sea.

240 *two glasses.* Two hours.

250 *bate me.* Let me off.

261 *Argier*. Algiers.

274 *hests*. Behests.

Prospero: 'Go make thyself like a nymph o' the sea'.
Drawing of Miranda, Prospero and Ariel by Richard
Parkes Bonington (1802–1828)

Pros.   Thou hast. Where was she born?
   speak ; tell me.   260
 Ari.   Sir, in Argier.
 Pros.   O, was she so? I must
Once in a month recount what thou hast been,
Which thou forget'st. This damn'd witch Sycorax,
For mischiefs manifold and sorceries terrible
To enter human hearing, from Argier,
Thou know'st, was banish'd : for one thing she did
They would not take her life. Is not this true?
 Ari.   Ay, sir.
 Pros.   This blue-eyed hag was hither brought
   with child
And here was left by the sailors. Thou, my slave,
As thou report'st thyself, wast then her servant ;
And, for thou wast a spirit too delicate
To act her earthy and abhorr'd commands,
Refusing her grand hests, she did confine thee,
By help of her more potent ministers
And in her most unmitigable rage,
Into a cloven pine ; within which rift
Imprison'd thou didst painfully remain
A dozen years ; within which space she died
And left thee there ; where thou didst vent thy
   groans   280
As fast as mill-wheels strike. Then was this
   island—
Save for the son that she did litter here,
A freckled whelp hag-born—not honour'd with
A human shape.
 Ari.   Yes, Caliban her son.
 Pros.   Dull thing, I say so ; he, that Caliban
Whom now I keep in service. Thou best know'st
What torment I did find thee in ; thy groans
Did make wolves howl and penetrate the breasts
Of ever angry bears : it was a torment
To lay upon the damn'd, which Sycorax   290
Could not again undo : it was mine art,
When I arrived and heard thee, that made gape
The pine and let thee out.
 Ari.   I thank thee, master.
 Pr.   If thou more murmur'st, I will rend an oak
And peg thee in his knotty entrails till
Thou hast howl'd away twelve winters.
 Ari.   Pardon, master ;
I will be correspondent to command
And do my spiriting gently.
 Pros.   Do so, and after two days
I will discharge thee.
 Ari.   That's my noble master !
What shall I do? say what ; what shall I do? 300
 Pros.   Go make thyself like a nymph o' the sea :
   be subject
To no sight but thine and mine, invisible
To every eyeball else. Go take this shape
And hither come in't : go, hence with diligence !
                              [*Exit Ariel.*
Awake, dear heart, awake ! thou hast slept well ;
Awake !
 Mir.   The strangeness of your story put
Heaviness in me.
 Pros.   Shake it off. Come on ;
We'll visit Caliban my slave, who never
Yields us kind answer.
 Mir.   'Tis a villain, sir,
I do not love to look on.
 Pros.   But, as 'tis,   310
We cannot miss him : he does make our fire,
Fetch in our wood and serves in offices

That profit us.   What, ho! slave! Caliban!
Thou earth, thou! speak.
   Cal. [*Within*] There's wood enough within.
   Pros.   Come forth, I say! there's other busi-
      ness for thee:
Come, thou tortoise! when?

     Re-enter ARIEL *like a water-nymph.*

Fine apparition!   My quaint Ariel,
Hark in thine ear.
   Ari.   My lord, it shall be done. [*Exit.*
   Pros.   Thou poisonous slave, got by the devil
      himself
Upon thy wicked dam, come forth!   320

     Enter CALIBAN.

   Cal. As wicked dew as e'er my mother brush'd
With raven's feather from unwholesome fen
Drop on you both! a south-west blow on ye
And blister you all o'er!
   Pros.   For this, be sure, to-night thou shalt
      have cramps,
•Side-stitches that shall pen thy breath up; urchins
Shall, for that vast of night that they may work,
All exercise on thee; thou shalt be pinch'd
As thick as honeycomb, each pinch more stinging
Than bees that made 'em.
   Cal.   I must eat my dinner. 330
This island's mine, by Sycorax my mother,
Which thou takest from me.   When thou camest
     first,
Thou strokedst me and madest much of me,
     wouldst give me
Water with berries in't, and teach me how
To name the bigger light, and how the less,
That burn by day and night: and then I loved
     thee
And show'd thee all the qualities o' the isle,
The fresh springs, brine-pits, barren place and
     fertile:
Cursed be I that did so!   All the charms
Of Sycorax, toads, beetles, bats, light on you!
For I am all the subjects that you have,   341
Which first was mine own king: and here you
     sty me
In this hard rock, whiles you do keep from me
The rest o' the island.
   Pros.   Thou most lying slave,
Whom stripes may move, not kindness! I have
     used thee,
Filth as thou art, with human care, and lodged
     thee
In mine own cell, till thou didst seek to violate
The honour of my child.
   Cal.   O ho, O ho! would't had been done!
Thou didst prevent me; I had peopled else   350
This isle with Calibans.
   Pros.   Abhorred slave,
Which any print of goodness wilt not take,
Being capable of all ill!   I pitied thee,
Took pains to make thee speak, taught thee each
     hour
One thing or other: when thou didst not, savage,
Know thine own meaning, but wouldst gabble like
A thing most brutish, I endow'd thy purposes
With words that made them known.   But thy vile
     race,
**Though thou didst learn, had that in't which
     good natures**

Prospero: 'For this, be sure, to-night thou shalt have cramps . . .' Miranda, Prospero and Caliban. Engraving from a painting by H. Fuseli (1741–1825)

326 *urchins.* Hedgehogs.

364 *rid.* Destroy.

373 *Setebos.* Patagonian god, referred to in Robert Eden's *History of Travaile,* 1577

379 *whist.* Silent.

380 *featly.* Nimbly.

381 *burthen bear.* Sing the melody.

407 *owes.* Owns.

Miranda: 'Believe me, sir, It carries a brave form.' Miranda and Prospero approach Ferdinand. Engraving by H. Gravelot from a design by T. Hayman. From Hanmer's edition of Shakespeare's works, 1744

Could not abide to be with; therefore wast thou
Deservedly confined into this rock,   361
Who hadst deserved more than a prison.
  Cal. You taught me language; and my profit on't
●Is, I know how to curse. The red plague rid you
For learning me your language!
  Pros.   Hag-seed, hence!
Fetch us in fuel; and be quick, thou'rt best,
To answer other business. Shrug'st thou, malice?
If thou negle&ct'st or dost unwillingly
What I command, I'll rack thee with old cramps,
Fill all thy bones with aches, make thee roar   370
That beasts shall tremble at thy din.
  Cal.   No, pray thee.
[*Aside*] I must obey: his art is of such power,
●It would control my dam's god, Setebos,
And make a vassal of him.
  Pros.   So, slave; hence! [*Exit Caliban.*

Re-enter ARIEL, *invisible, playing and singing;*
      FERDINAND *following.*

ARIEL'S *song.*

  Come unto these yellow sands,
      And then take hands:
  Courtsied when you have and kiss'd
●   The wild waves whist,
●   Foot it featly here and there;   380
●   And, sweet sprites, the burthen bear.
Burthen [*dispersedly*]. Hark, hark!
                          Bow-wow.
      The watch-dogs bark:
                          Bow-wow.
  Ari. Hark, hark! I hear
      The strain of strutting chanticleer
      Cry, Cock-a-diddle-dow.

  Fer. Where should this music be? i' the air or
      the earth?
It sounds no more: and, sure, it waits upon
Some god o' the island.   Sitting on a bank,
Weeping again the king my father's wreck,   390
This music crept by me upon the waters,
Allaying both their fury and my passion
With its sweet air: thence I have follow'd it,
Or it hath drawn me rather.   But 'tis gone.
No, it begins again.

ARIEL *sings.*

  Full fathom five thy father lies;
      Of his bones are coral made;
  Those are pearls that were his eyes:
      Nothing of him that doth fade
  But doth suffer a sea-change   400
  Into something rich and strange.
  Sea-nymphs hourly ring his knell:
                    Burthen. Ding-dong.
  Ari. Hark! now I hear them,—Ding-dong, bell.

  Fer. The ditty does remember my drown'd
      father.
This is no mortal business, nor no sound
●That the earth owes. I hear it now above me.
  Pros. The fringed curtains of thine eye advance
And say what thou seest yond.
  Mir.   What is't? a spirit?
Lord, how it looks about! Believe me, sir,   410
It carries a brave form.   But 'tis a spirit.

Pros. No, wench; it eats and sleeps and hath such senses
As we have, such. This gallant which thou seest
Was in the wreck; and, but he's something stain'd
● With grief that's beauty's canker, thou mightst call him
A goodly person: he hath lost his fellows
And strays about to find 'em.
    Mir.   I might call him
A thing divine, for nothing natural
I ever saw so noble.
    Pros.   [*Aside*] It goes on, I see,
As my soul prompts it. Spirit, fine spirit! I'll free thee   420
Within two days for this.
    Fer.   Most sure, the goddess
On whom these airs attend! Vouchsafe my prayer
May know if you remain upon this island;
And that you will some good instruction give
How I may bear me here: my prime request,
Which I do last pronounce, is, O you wonder!
If you be maid or no?
    Mir.   No wonder, sir;
But certainly a maid.
    Fer.   My language! heavens!
I am the best of them that speak this speech,
Were I but where 'tis spoken.
    Pros.   How? the best? 430
What wert thou, if the King of Naples heard thee?
    Fer. A single thing, as I am now, that wonders
To hear thee speak of Naples. He does hear me;
And that he does I weep: myself am Naples,
Who with mine eyes, never since at ebb, beheld
The king my father wreck'd.
    Mir.   Alack, for mercy!
    Fer. Yes, faith, and all his lords; the Duke of Milan
And his brave son being twain.
    Pros.   [*Aside*] The Duke of Milan
And his more braver daughter could control thee,
If now 'twere fit to do't. At the first sight 440
● They have changed eyes. Delicate Ariel,
I'll set thee free for this. [*To Fer.*] A word, good sir;
I fear you have done yourself some wrong: a word.
    Mir. Why speaks my father so ungently? This
Is the third man that e'er I saw, the first
That e'er I sigh'd for: pity move my father
To be inclined my way!
    Fer.   O, if a virgin,
● And your affection not gone forth, I'll make you
The queen of Naples.
    Pros.   Soft, sir! one word more.
[*Aside*] They are both in either's powers; but this swift business 450
I must uneasy make, lest too light winning
Make the prize light. [*To Fer.*] One word more;
    I charge thee
That thou attend me: thou dost here usurp
The name thou owest not; and hast put thyself
Upon this island as a spy, to win it
From me, the lord on't.
    Fer.   No, as I am a man.
    Mir. There's nothing ill can dwell in such a temple:
If the ill spirit have so fair a house,
Good things will strive to dwell with't.
    Pros.   Follow me.
Speak not you for him; he's a traitor. Come;

415 *canker.* A malignant disease.

Ferdinand: 'To hear thee speak of Naples'. View of Naples from the sea. Engraving from Charles Knight's *Pictorial Edition of the Works of Shakspere*, 1839–43

441 *changed eyes.* Exchanged glances.

448 *gone forth.* Pledged.

471 *ward*. Threatening stance.

Prospero: '. . . come from thy ward, For I can here disarm thee with this stick.' Engraving from Bellamy's edition, . . . 1791

I'll manacle thy neck and feet together: 461
Sea-water shalt thou drink; thy food shall be
The fresh-brook muscles, wither'd roots and
      husks
Wherein the acorn cradled.   Follow.
 Fer.   No;
I will resist such entertainment till
Mine enemy has more power.
   [*Draws, and is charmed from moving.*
 Mir.   O dear father,
Make not too rash a trial of him, for
He's gentle and not fearful.
 Pros.   What? I say,
My foot my tutor?   Put thy sword up, traitor;
Who makest a show but darest not strike, thy
      conscience   470
Is so possess'd with guilt: come from thy ward,
For I can here disarm thee with this stick
And make thy weapon drop.
 Mir.   Beseech you, father.
 Pros.   Hence! hang not on my garments.
 Mir.   Sir, have pity;
I'll be his surety.
 Pros.   Silence! one word more
Shall make me chide thee, if not hate thee. What!
An advocate for an impostor! hush!
Thou think'st there is no more such shapes as he,
Having seen but him and Caliban: foolish wench!
To the most of men this is a Caliban   480
And they to him are angels.
 Mir.   My affections
Are then most humble; I have no ambition
To see a goodlier man.
 Pros.   Come on; obey:
Thy nerves are in their infancy again
And have no vigour in them.
 Fer.   So they are;
My spirits, as in a dream, are all bound up.
My father's loss, the weakness which I feel,
The wreck of all my friends, nor this man's
      threats,
To whom I am subdued, are but light to me,
Might I but through my prison once a day   490
Behold this maid: all corners else o' the earth
Let liberty make use of; space enough
Have I in such a prison.
 Pros. [*Aside*] It works. [*To Fer.*] Come on.
Thou hast done well, fine Ariel! [*To Fer.*] Fol-
  low me.
[*To Ari.*] Hark what thou else shalt do me.
 Mir.   Be of comfort;
My father's of a better nature, sir,
Than he appears by speech: this is unwonted
Which now came from him.
 Pros.   Thou shalt be as free
As mountain winds: but then exactly do
All points of my command.
 Ari.   To the syllable.   500
 Pros.   Come, follow.   Speak not for him.
         [*Exeunt.*

ACT II.

SCENE I.   *Another part of the island.*

Enter ALONSO, SEBASTIAN, ANTONIO, GONZALO,
 ADRIAN, FRANCISCO, *and others.*

 Gon.   Beseech you, sir, be merry; you have
 cause,

So have we all, of joy; for our escape
Is much beyond our loss.   Our hint of woe
Is common; every day some sailor's wife,
The masters of some merchant and the merchant
Have just our theme of woe; but for the miracle,
I mean our preservation, few in millions
Can speak like us: then wisely, good sir, weigh
Our sorrow with our comfort.
 Alon.   Prithee, peace.
 Seb. He receives comfort like cold porridge.
 Ant. The visitor will not give him o'er so. 11
 Seb. Look, he's winding up the watch of his
wit; by and by it will strike.
 Gon. Sir,—
 Seb. One: tell.
 Gon. When every grief is entertain'd that's
  offer'd,
Comes to the entertainer—
 Seb. A dollar.
 Gon. Dolour comes to him, indeed: you have
spoken truer than you purposed. 20
 Seb. You have taken it wiselier than I meant
you should.
 Gon. Therefore, my lord,—
 Ant. Fie, what a spendthrift is he of his
  tongue!
 Alon. I prithee, spare.
 Gon. Well, I have done: but yet,—
 Seb. He will be talking.
 Ant. Which, of he or Adrian, for a good wager,
first begins to crow?
 Seb. The old cock. 30
 Ant. The cockerel.
 Seb. Done.   The wager?
 Ant. A laughter.
 Seb. A match!
 Adr. Though this island seem to be desert,—
 Seb. Ha, ha, ha!   So, you're paid.
 Adr. Uninhabitable and almost inaccessible,—
 Seb. Yet,—
 Adr. Yet,—
 Ant. He could not miss't. 40
 Adr. It must needs be of subtle, tender and
delicate temperance.
 Ant. Temperance was a delicate wench.
 Seb. Ay, and a subtle; as he most learnedly
delivered.
 Adr. The air breathes upon us here most
  sweetly.
 Seb. As if it had lungs and rotten ones.
 Ant. Or as 'twere perfumed by a fen.
 Gon. Here is every thing advantageous to life.
 Ant. True; save means to live. 50
 Seb. Of that there's none, or little.
 Gon. How lush and lusty the grass looks! how
green!
 Ant. The ground indeed is tawny.
 Seb. With an eye of green in't.
 Ant. He misses not much.
 Seb. No; he doth but mistake the truth totally.
 Gon. But the rarity of it is,—which is indeed
almost beyond credit,—
 Seb. As many vouched rarities are.
 Gon. That our garments, being, as they were,
drenched in the sea, hold notwithstanding their
freshness and glosses, being rather new-dyed
than stained with salt water.
 Ant. If but one of his pockets could speak,
would it not say he lies?

Costume design for Antonio, Duke of Milan, by J.
Gower Parks, Stratford-upon-Avon, 1938

76 *Dido.* Legendary Dido, who fell in love with Aeneas.

100 *Bate.* Except.

Seb.   Ay, or very falsely pocket up his report.

Gon.   Methinks our garments are now as fresh as when we put them on first in Afric, at the marriage of the king's fair daughter Claribel to the King of Tunis.   **71**

Seb.   'Twas a sweet marriage, and we prosper well in our return.

Adr.   Tunis was never graced before with such a paragon to their queen.

● *Gon.*   Not since widow Dido's time.

Ant.   Widow! a pox o' that! How came that widow in? widow Dido!

Seb.   What if he had said 'widower Æneas' too?   Good Lord, how you take it!

Adr.   'Widow Dido' said you? you make me study of that: she was of Carthage, not of Tunis.

Gon.   This Tunis, sir, was Carthage.

Adr.   Carthage?

Gon.   I assure you, Carthage.

Seb.   His word is more than the miraculous harp; he hath raised the wall and houses too.

Ant.   What impossible matter will he make easy next?

Seb.   I think he will carry this island home in his pocket and give it his son for an apple.   91

Ant.   And, sowing the kernels of it in the sea, bring forth more islands.

Gon.   Ay.

Ant.   Why, in good time.

Gon.   Sir, we were talking that our garments seem now as fresh as when we were at Tunis at the marriage of your daughter, who is now queen.

Ant.   And the rarest that e'er came there.

● *Seb.*   Bate, I beseech you, widow Dido.   **100**

Ant.   O, widow Dido! ay, widow Dido.

Gon.   Is not, sir, my doublet as fresh as the first day I wore it?   I mean, in a sort.

Ant.   That sort was well fished for.

Gon.   When I wore it at your daughter's marriage?

Alon.   You cram these words into mine ears against

The stomach of my sense.   Would I had never

Married my daughter there! for, coming thence,

My son is lost and, in my rate, she too,

Who is so far from Italy removed   110

I ne'er again shall see her.   O thou mine heir

Of Naples and of Milan, what strange fish

Hath made his meal on thee?

Fran.   Sir, he may live:

I saw him beat the surges under him,

And ride upon their backs; he trod the water,

Whose enmity he flung aside, and breasted

The surge most swoln that met him; his bold head

'Bove the contentious waves he kept, and oar'd

Himself with his good arms in lusty stroke

To the shore, that o'er his wave-worn basis bow'd,

As stooping to relieve him: I not doubt   121

He came alive to land.

Alon.   No, no, he's gone.

Seb.   Sir, you may thank yourself for this great loss,

That would not bless our Europe with your daughter,

But rather lose her to an African;

Where she at least is banish'd from your eye,

Who hath cause to wet the grief on 't.

Alon.   Prithee, peace.

Seb. You were kneel'd to and importuned
otherwise
By all of us, and the fair soul herself
Weigh'd between loathness and obedience, at 130
Which end o' the beam should bow. We have
lost your son,
I fear, for ever: Milan and Naples have
●Moe widows in them of this business' making
Than we bring men to comfort them:
The fault's your own.
   Alon.   So is the dear'st o' the loss.
   Gon. My lord Sebastian,
The truth you speak doth lack some gentleness
And time to speak it in: you rub the sore,
When you should bring the plaster.
   Seb.   Very well.
   Ant. And most chirurgeonly.   140
   Gon. It is foul weather in us all, good sir,
When you are cloudy.
   Seb.   Foul weather?
   Ant.   Very foul.
   Gon. Had I plantation of this isle, my lord,—
   Ant. He'ld sow't with nettle-seed.
   Seb.   Or docks, or mallows.
   Gon. And were the king on't, what would I do?
   Seb. 'Scape being drunk for want of wine.
   Gon. I' the commonwealth I would by con-
traries
●Execute all things; for no kind of traffic
Would I admit; no name of magistrate;
Letters should not be known; riches, poverty,
And use of service, none; contract, succession,
●Bourn, bound of land, tilth, vineyard, none;
No use of metal, corn, or wine, or oil;
No occupation; all men idle, all;
And women too, but innocent and pure;
No sovereignty;—
   Seb.   Yet he would be king on't.
   Ant. The latter end of his commonwealth for-
gets the beginning.
   Gon. All things in common nature should pro-
duce
Without sweat or endeavour: treason, felony, 160
Sword, pike, knife, gun, or need of any engine,
Would I not have; but nature should bring forth,
●Of it own kind, all foison, all abundance,
To feed my innocent people.
   Seb. No marrying 'mong his subjects?
   Ant. None, man; all idle: whores and knaves.
   Gon. I would with such perfection govern, sir,
To excel the golden age.
   Seb.   God save his majesty!
   Ant. Long live Gonzalo!
   Gon.   And,—do you mark me, sir?
   Alon. Prithee, no more: thou dost talk no-
thing to me.   171
   Gon. I do well believe your highness; and
did it to minister occasion to these gentlemen,
who are of such sensible and nimble lungs that
they always use to laugh at nothing.
   Ant. 'Twas you we laughed at.
   Gon. Who in this kind of merry fooling am
nothing to you: so you may continue and laugh
at nothing still.
   Ant. What a blow was there given!   180
● *Seb.* An it had not fallen flat-long.
   Gon. You are gentlemen of brave mettle; you
would lift the moon out of her sphere, if she
would continue in it five weeks without changing.

133 *Moe.* More.

148 *traffic.* Trade.

152 *Bourn.* Limits of property. *tilth.* Cultivation of land.

163 *foison.* Plenty.

181 *An.* If. *flat-long.* With the flat of the blade.

Costume design for Gonzalo by Percy Anderson, 1904

Priscilla Horton as Ariel, Covent Garden Theatre, 1838
Painting by Daniel Maclise (1806–1870)

---

185 *bat-fowling*. Bird-catching with a light.

188 *discretion*. Reputation.

231 *throes*. Costs. *yield*. Offer.

Enter ARIEL, *invisible, playing solemn music.*
- *Seb.*   We would so, and then go a bat-fowling.
   Ant.   Nay, good my lord, be not angry.
   Gon.   No, I warrant you; I will not adventure
- my discretion so weakly.   Will you laugh me
asleep, for I am very heavy?
   Ant.   Go sleep, and hear us.   190
            [*All sleep except Alon., Seb., and Ant.*
   Alon.   What, all so soon asleep!   I wish mine
      eyes
Would, with themselves, shut up my thoughts: I
   find
They are inclined to do so.
   Seb.   Please you, sir,
Do not omit the heavy offer of it:
It seldom visits sorrow; when it doth,
It is a comforter.
   Ant.   We two, my lord,
Will guard your person while you take your rest,
And watch your safety.
   Alon.   Thank you.   Wondrous heavy.
            [*Alonso sleeps.   Exit Ariel.*
   Seb.   What a strange drowsiness possesses them!
   Ant.   It is the quality o' the climate.
   Seb.   Why 200
Doth it not then our eyelids sink?   I find not
Myself disposed to sleep.
   Ant.   Nor I; my spirits are nimble.
They fell together all, as by consent;
They dropp'd, as by a thunder-stroke.   What
   might,
Worthy Sebastian?   O, what might?—No more:—
And yet methinks I see it in thy face,
What thou shouldst be: the occasion speaks thee,
   and
My strong imagination sees a crown
Dropping upon thy head.
   Seb.   What, art thou waking?
   Ant.   Do you not hear me speak?
   Seb.   I do; and surely
It is a sleepy language and thou speak'st   211
Out of thy sleep.   What is it thou didst say?
This is a strange repose, to be asleep
With eyes wide open; standing, speaking, moving,
And yet so fast asleep.
   Ant.   Noble Sebastian,
Thou let'st thy fortune sleep—die, rather; wink'st
Whiles thou art waking.
   Seb.   Thou dost snore distinctly;
There's meaning in thy snores.
   Ant.   I am more serious than my custom: you
Must be so too, if heed me; which to do   220
Trebles thee o'er.
   Seb.   Well, I am standing water.
   Ant.   I'll teach you how to flow.
   Seb.   Do so: to ebb
Hereditary sloth instructs me.
   Ant.   O,
If you but knew how you the purpose cherish
Whiles thus you mock it! how, in stripping it,
You more invest it!   Ebbing men, indeed,
Most often do so near the bottom run
By their own fear or sloth.
   Seb.   Prithee, say on:
The setting of thine eye and cheek proclaim
A matter from thee, and a birth indeed   230
- Which throes thee much to yield.
   Ant.   Thus, sir:
Although this lord of weak remembrance, this,

Who shall be of as little memory
When he is earth'd, hath here almost persuaded,—
For he's a spirit of persuasion, only
Professes to persuade,—the king his son's alive,
'Tis as impossible that he's undrown'd
As he that sleeps here swims.
  Seb.   I have no hope
That he's undrown'd.
  Ant.   O, out of that 'no hope'
What great hope have you! no hope that way is
Another way so high a hope that even 241
Ambition cannot pierce a wink beyond,
But doubt discovery there. Will you grant with me
That Ferdinand is drown'd?
  Seb.   He's gone.
  Ant.   Then, tell me,
Who's the next heir of Naples?
  Seb.   Claribel.
  Ant. She that is queen of Tunis; she that
  dwells
Ten leagues beyond man's life; she that from
  Naples
Can have no note, unless the sun were post—
The man i' the moon's too slow—till new-born chins
Be rough and razorable; she that—from whom?
We all were sea-swallow'd, though some cast
  again, 251
And by that destiny to perform an act
Whereof what's past is prologue, what to come
In yours and my discharge.
  Seb.   What stuff is this! how say you?
'Tis true, my brother's daughter's queen of Tunis;
So is she heir of Naples; 'twixt which regions
There is some space.
  Ant.   A space whose every cubit
Seems to cry out, 'How shall that Claribel
Measure us back to Naples? Keep in Tunis,
And let Sebastian wake.' Say, this were death
That now hath seized them; why, they were no
  worse 261
Than now they are. There be that can rule Naples
As well as he that sleeps; lords that can prate
As amply and unnecessarily
As this Gonzalo; I myself could make
A chough of as deep chat. O, that you bore
The mind that I do! what a sleep were this
For your advancement! Do you understand me?
  Seb. Methinks I do.
  Ant.   And how does your content
• Tender your own good fortune?
  Seb.   I remember 270
You did supplant your brother Prospero.
  Ant.   True:
And look how well my garments sit upon me;
• Much feater than before: my brother's servants
Were then my fellows; now they are my men.
  Seb. But, for your conscience?
• *Ant.* Ay, sir; where lies that? if 'twere a kibe,
'Twould put me to my slipper: but I feel not
This deity in my bosom: twenty consciences,
• That stand 'twixt me and Milan, candied be they
And melt ere they molest! Here lies your brother,
No better than the earth he lies upon, 281
If he were that which now he's like, that's dead;
Whom I, with this obedient steel, three inches of it,
Can lay to bed for ever; whiles you, doing thus,
To the perpetual wink for aye might put
This ancient morsel, this Sir Prudence, who
Should not upbraid our course. For all the rest,

270 *Tender.* Regard.

273 *feater.* More gracefully.

276 *kibe.* Sore heel.

279 *candied.* Frozen.

Costume design for Antonio by Percy Anderson, 1904

289 *tell the clock.* Agree.

3 *By inch-meal.* Inch by inch.

Costume design for Ariel by Paul Shelving, Stratford-upon-Avon, 1946

They'll take suggestion as a cat laps milk;
●They'll tell the clock to any business that
We say befits the hour.
 Seb.   Thy case, dear friend, 290
Shall be my precedent; as thou got'st Milan,
I'll come by Naples. Draw thy sword: one stroke
Shall free thee from the tribute which thou payest:
And I the king shall love thee.
 Ant.   Draw together;
And when I rear my hand, do you the like,
To fall it on Gonzalo.
 Seb. O, but one word. [*They talk apart.*

    Re-enter ARIEL, *invisible.*

 Ari. My master through his art foresees the
  danger
That you, his friend, are in; and sends me forth—
For else his project dies—to keep them living.
      [*Sings in Gonzalo's ear.*

  While you here do snoring lie, 300
  Open-eyed conspiracy
   His time doth take.
  If of life you keep a care,
  Shake off slumber, and beware:
   Awake, awake!

 Ant. Then let us both be sudden.
 Gon.   Now, good angels
Preserve the king.   [*They wake.*
 Alon. Why, how now? ho, awake! Why are
  you drawn?
Wherefore this ghastly looking?
 Gon.   What's the matter?
 Seb. Whiles we stood here securing your repose,
Even now, we heard a hollow burst of bellowing
Like bulls, or rather lions: did't not wake you?
It struck mine ear most terribly.
 Alon.   I heard nothing.
 Ant. O, 'twas a din to fright a monster's ear,
To make an earthquake! sure, it was the roar
Of a whole herd of lions.
 Alon.   Heard you this, Gonzalo?
 Gon. Upon mine honour, sir, I heard a hum-
  ming,
And that a strange one too, which did awake me:
I shaked you, sir, and cried: as mine eyes open'd,
I saw their weapons drawn: there was a noise, 320
That's verily. 'Tis best we stand upon our guard,
Or that we quit this place: let's draw our weapons.
 Alon. Lead off this ground; and let's make
  further search
For my poor son.
 Gon. Heavens keep him from these beasts!
For he is, sure, i' the island.
 Alon.   Lead away.
 Ari. Prospero my lord shall know what I have
  done:
So, king, go safely on to seek thy son. [*Exeunt.*

   SCENE II. *Another part of the island.*

 Enter CALIBAN *with a burden of wood. A
   noise of thunder heard.*

 Cal. All the infections that the sun sucks up
From bogs, fens, flats, on Prosper fall and make
  him
●By inch-meal a disease! His spirits hear me
And yet I needs must curse. But they'll nor pinch,

● Fright me with urchin-shows, pitch me i' the mire,
Nor lead me, like a firebrand, in the dark
Out of my way, unless he bid 'em; but
For every trifle are they set upon me;
Sometime like apes that mow and chatter at me
And after bite me, then like hedgehogs which 10
Lie tumbling in my barefoot way and mount
Their pricks at my footfall; sometime am I
All wound with adders who with cloven tongues
Do hiss me into madness.

Enter TRINCULO.
　　　　　　　　　Lo, now, lo!
Here comes a spirit of his, and to torment me
For bringing wood in slowly. I'll fall flat;
Perchance he will not mind me.
Trin. Here's neither bush nor shrub, to bear
off any weather at all, and another storm brewing;
I hear it sing i' the wind: yond same black cloud,
● yond huge one, looks like a foul bombard that
would shed his liquor. If it should thunder as it
did before, I know not where to hide my head:
yond same cloud cannot choose but fall by pail-
fuls. What have we here? a man or a fish? dead
or alive? A fish: he smells like a fish; a very
ancient and fish-like smell; a kind of not of the
● newest Poor-John. A strange fish! Were I in
England now, as once I was, and had but this fish
painted, not a holiday fool there but would give
a piece of silver: there would this monster make
a man; any strange beast there makes a man:
● when they will not give a doit to relieve a lame
beggar, they will lay out ten to see a dead Indian.
Legged like a man! and his fins like arms! Warm
o' my troth! I do now let loose my opinion; hold
it no longer: this is no fish, but an islander, that
hath lately suffered by a thunderbolt. [*Thunder.*]
Alas, the storm is come again! my best way is to
● creep under his gaberdine; there is no other shelter
hereabout: misery acquaints a man with strange
bed-fellows. I will here shroud till the dregs of
the storm be past.

Enter STEPHANO, *singing: a bottle in his hand.*

Ste. I shall no more to sea, to sea,
　　　　Here shall I die ashore—

This is a very scurvy tune to sing at a man's
funeral: well, here's my comfort.　　[*Drinks.*
[*Sings.*
　The master, the swabber, the boatswain and I,
　　　　The gunner and his mate
　Loved Mall, Meg and Marian and Margery, 50
　　　But none of us cared for Kate;
　　　For she had a tongue with a tang,
　　　Would cry to a sailor, Go hang!
　She loved not the savour of tar nor of pitch,
　Yet a tailor might scratch her where'er she
　　　　did itch:
　　　Then to sea, boys, and let her go hang!

This is a scurvy tune too: but here's my comfort.
　　　　　　　　　　　　　[*Drinks.*
Cal. Do not torment me: Oh!
Ste. What's the matter? Have we devils
here? Do you put tricks upon's with savages and
● men of Ind, ha? I have not 'scaped drowning to
be afeard now of your four legs; for it hath been
said, As proper a man as ever went on four legs

5 *urchin-shows.* Goblins.

21 *bombard.* Leather bottle.

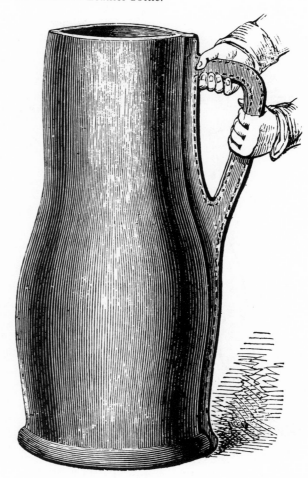

A bombard, which held 8 gallons of liquid. Engraving
by F. W. Fairholt from J. O. Halliwell's *Complete Works
of Shakespeare*, 1853–65

28 *Poor-John.* Dried hake.

33 *doit.* Small coin.

40 *gaberdine.* Cloak of smooth, twill-woven cloth.

61 *Ind.* India.

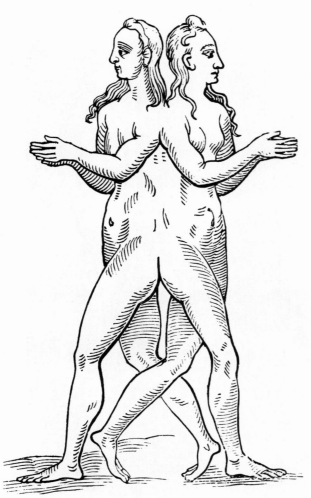

Stephano: 'There is some monster of the isle with four legs . . .' Engraving from a contemporary woodcut by F. W. Fairholt from J. O. Halliwell's *Complete Works of Shakespeare*, 1853–65

73 *neat's-leather*. Cowhide.

89 *chaps*. Mouth.

110 *siege*. Excrement.

111 *moon-calf*. Monster.

cannot make him give ground; and it shall be said so again while Stephano breathes at nostrils.

Cal.   The spirit torments me; Oh!

Ste.   This is some monster of the isle with four legs, who hath got, as I take it, an ague. Where the devil should he learn our language? I will give him some relief, if it be but for that. If I can recover him and keep him tame and get to Naples with him, he's a present for any emperor that ever trod on neat's-leather.

Cal.   Do not torment me, prithee; I'll bring my wood home faster.

Ste.   He's in his fit now and does not talk after the wisest.   He shall taste of my bottle: if he have never drunk wine afore, it will go near to remove his fit.   If I can recover him and keep him tame, I will not take too much for him; he shall pay for him that hath him, and that soundly.

Cal.   Thou dost me yet but little hurt; thou wilt anon, I know it by thy trembling: now Prosper works upon thee.

Ste.   Come on your ways; open your mouth; here is that which will give language to you, cat: open your mouth; this will shake your shaking, I can tell you, and that soundly: you cannot tell who's your friend: open your chaps again.

Trin.   I should know that voice: it should be —but he is drowned; and these are devils: O defend me!

Ste.   Four legs and two voices: a most delicate monster!   His forward voice now is to speak well of his friend; his backward voice is to utter foul speeches and to detract.   If all the wine in my bottle will recover him, I will help his ague. Come.   Amen!   I will pour some in thy other mouth.

Trin.   Stephano!   100

Ste.   Doth thy other mouth call me?   Mercy, mercy!   This is a devil, and no monster: I will leave him; I have no long spoon.

Trin.   Stephano!   If thou beest Stephano, touch me and speak to me; for I am Trinculo— be not afeard—thy good friend Trinculo.

Ste.   If thou beest Trinculo, come forth: I'll pull thee by the lesser legs: if any be Trinculo's legs, these are they.   Thou art very Trinculo indeed!   How camest thou to be the siege of this moon-calf? can he vent Trinculos?

Trin.   I took him to be killed with a thunderstroke.   But art thou not drowned, Stephano?   I hope now thou art not drowned.   Is the storm overblown?   I hid me under the dead moon-calf's gaberdine for fear of the storm.   And art thou living, Stephano?   O Stephano, two Neapolitans 'scaped!

Ste.   Prithee, do not turn me about; my stomach is not constant.

Cal.   [*Aside*] These be fine things, an if they be not sprites.   120
That's a brave god and bears celestial liquor. I will kneel to him.

Ste.   How didst thou 'scape?   How camest thou hither? swear by this bottle how thou camest hither.   I escaped upon a butt of sack which the sailors heaved o'erboard, by this bottle! which I made of the bark of a tree with mine own hands since I was cast ashore.

Cal.   I'll swear upon that bottle to be thy true subject; for the liquor is not earthly.   130

Ste.   Here; swear then how thou escapedst.

Trin. Swum ashore, man, like a duck: I can swim like a duck, I'll be sworn.

Ste. Here, kiss the book. Though thou canst swim like a duck, thou art made like a goose.

Trin. O Stephano, hast any more of this?

Ste. The whole butt, man: my cellar is in a rock by the sea-side where my wine is hid. How now, moon-calf! how does thine ague?

Cal. Hast thou not dropp'd from heaven? 140

Ste. Out o' the moon, I do assure thee: I was the man i' the moon when time was.

Cal. I have seen thee in her and I do adore thee: My mistress show'd me thee and thy dog and thy bush.

Ste. Come, swear to that; kiss the book: I will furnish it anon with new contents: swear.

Trin. By this good light, this is a very shallow monster! I afeard of him! A very weak monster! The man i' the moon! A most poor credulous monster! Well drawn, monster, in good sooth!

Cal. I'll show thee every fertile inch o' th' island;
And I will kiss thy foot: I prithee, be my god.

Trin. By this light, a most perfidious and drunken monster! when's god's asleep, he'll rob his bottle.

Cal. I'll kiss thy foot; I'll swear myself thy subject.

Ste. Come on then; down, and swear.

Trin. I shall laugh myself to death at this puppy-headed monster. A most scurvy monster! I could find in my heart to beat him,— 160

Ste. Come, kiss.

Trin. But that the poor monster's in drink: an abominable monster!

Cal. I'll show thee the best springs; I'll pluck thee berries;
I'll fish for thee and get thee wood enough.
A plague upon the tyrant that I serve!
I'll bear him no more sticks, but follow thee,
Thou wondrous man.

Trin. A most ridiculous monster, to make a wonder of a poor drunkard! 170

Cal. I prithee, let me bring thee where crabs grow;
●And I with my long nails will dig thee pig-nuts;
Show thee a jay's nest and instruct thee how
To snare the nimble marmoset; I'll bring thee
To clustering filberts and sometimes I'll get thee
●Young scamels from the rock. Wilt thou go with me?

Ste. I prithee now, lead the way without any more talking. Trinculo, the king and all our company else being drowned, we will inherit here: here; bear my bottle: fellow Trinculo, we'll fill him by and by again.

Cal. [*Sings drunkenly*]
  Farewell, master; farewell, farewell!

Trin. A howling monster; a drunken monster!

Cal. No more dams I'll make for fish;
    Nor fetch in firing
    At requiring;
  Nor scrape trencher, nor wash dish:
    'Ban, 'Ban, Cacaliban
    Has a new master: get a new man.

Freedom, hey-day! hey-day, freedom! freedom, hey-day, freedom! 191

Ste. O brave monster! Lead the way. [*Exeunt.*

172 *pig-nuts.* Peanuts.

F. R. Benson, the Edwardian actor, as Caliban, Lyceum Theatre, London, 1900

176 *scamels.* Small sea-birds.

11 *sore.* Harsh.

15 *Most busy lest.* i.e. least aware of being busy.

Miranda: 'Work not so hard . . .' Drawing of Ferdinand and Miranda with Prospero at a distance by H. Gravelot (1699–1773)

46 *put it to the foil.* i.e. set it off by comparison; also set about getting rid of it.

ACT III.

SCENE I. *Before* PROSPERO'S *cell.*

Enter FERDINAND, *bearing a log.*

Fer.   There be some sports are painful, and their labour
Delight in them sets off: some kinds of baseness
Are nobly undergone and most poor matters
Point to rich ends.   This my mean task
Would be as heavy to me as odious, but
The mistress which I serve quickens what's dead
And makes my labours pleasures: O, she is
Ten times more gentle than her father's crabbed,
And he's composed of harshness.   I must remove
Some thousands of these logs and pile them up,
● Upon a sore injunction: my sweet mistress
Weeps when she sees me work, and says, such baseness
Had never like executor.   I forget:
But these sweet thoughts do even refresh my labours,
●† Most busy lest, when I do it.

Enter MIRANDA; *and* PROSPERO *at a distance, unseen.*

Mir.   Alas, now, pray you,
Work not so hard: I would the lightning had
Burnt up those logs that you are enjoin'd to pile!
Pray, set it down and rest you: when this burns,
'Twill weep for having wearied you.   My father
Is hard at study; pray now, rest yourself;   20
He's safe for these three hours.
Fer.   O most dear mistress,
The sun will set before I shall discharge
What I must strive to do.
Mir.   If you'll sit down,
I'll bear your logs the while: pray, give me that;
I'll carry it to the pile.
Fer.   No, precious creature;
I had rather crack my sinews, break my back,
Than you should such dishonour undergo,
While I sit lazy by.
Mir.   It would become me
As well as it does you: and I should do it
With much more ease; for my good will is to it,
And yours it is against.
Pros.   Poor worm, thou art infected!
This visitation shows it.
Mir.   You look wearily.
Fer.   No, noble mistress; 'tis fresh morning with me
When you are by at night.   I do beseech you—
Chiefly that I might set it in my prayers—
What is your name?
Mir.   Miranda.—O my father,
I have broke your hest to say so!
Fer.   Admired Miranda!
Indeed the top of admiration! worth
What's dearest to the world!   Full many a lady
I have eyed with best regard and many a time   40
The harmony of their tongues hath into bondage
Brought my too diligent ear: for several virtues
Have I liked several women; never any
With so full soul, but some defect in her
Did quarrel with the noblest grace she owed
● And put it to the foil: but you, O you,
So perfect and so peerless, are created
Of every creature's best!

Mir.   I do not know
One of my sex; no woman's face remember,
Save, from my glass, mine own; nor have I seen
More that I may call men than you, good friend,
And my dear father: how features are abroad,
•I am skilless of; but, by my modesty,
The jewel in my dower, I would not wish
Any companion in the world but you,
Nor can imagination form a shape,
Besides yourself, to like of.   But I prattle
Something too wildly and my father's precepts
I therein do forget.
    Fer.   I am in my condition
A prince, Miranda; I do think, a king;   60
I would, not so!—and would no more endure
This wooden slavery than to suffer
The flesh-fly blow my mouth.   Hear my soul
          speak:
The very instant that I saw you, did
My heart fly to your service; there resides,
To make me slave to it; and for your sake
Am I this patient log-man.
    Mir.   Do you love me?
    Fer. O heaven, O earth, bear witness to this
          sound
And crown what I profess with kind event
If I speak true! if hollowly, invert   70
What best is boded me to mischief!   I
Beyond all limit of what else i' the world
Do love, prize, honour you.
    Mir.   I am a fool
To weep at what I am glad of.
    Pros.   Fair encounter
Of two most rare affections!   Heavens rain grace
On that which breeds between 'em!
    Fer.   Wherefore weep you?
    Mir. At mine unworthiness that dare not offer
What I desire to give, and much less take
What I shall die to want.   But this is trifling;
And all the more it seeks to hide itself,   80
The bigger bulk it shows.   Hence, bashful cunning!
And prompt me, plain and holy innocence!
I am your wife, if you will marry me;
If not, I'll die your maid: to be your fellow
You may deny me; but I'll be your servant,
Whether you will or no.
    Fer.   My mistress, dearest;
And I thus humble ever.
    Mir.   My husband, then?
    Fer. Ay, with a heart as willing
As bondage e'er of freedom: here's my hand.
    Mir. And mine, with my heart in't: and now
          farewell   90
Till half an hour hence.
    Fer.   A thousand thousand!
          [*Exeunt Fer. and Mir. severally.*
    Pros. So glad of this as they I cannot be,
Who are surprised withal; but my rejoicing
At nothing can be more.   I'll to my book,
For yet ere supper-time must I perform
Much business appertaining.   [*Exit.*

SCENE II. *Another part of the island.*

Enter CALIBAN, STEPHANO, *and* TRINCULO.

    Ste. Tell not me; when the butt is out, we
will drink water; not a drop before: therefore
•bear up, and board 'em.   Servant-monster, drink
to me.

53 *skilless.* Lacking knowledge.

Miranda and Ferdinand. Engraving from a drawing by William Nelson Gardiner for E. Harding's *Plays of Shakespeare*, 1798–1800

3 *bear . . . 'em.* Maritime exhortation, a manoeuvre in sea-fighting; i.e. drink up.

Stephano: 'Drink, servant-monster, when I bid thee...'
Trinculo, Stephano and Caliban. Engraving from Bell's
edition of *Shakespeare*, 1773

18-20 *standard*. Standard-bearer; and upright flag-pole.

29-30 *in case*. In a state. *deboshed*. Debauched.

Trin. Servant-monster! the folly of this island! They say there's but five upon this isle: we are three of them; if th' other two be brained like us, the state totters.

Ste. Drink, servant-monster, when I bid thee: thy eyes are almost set in thy head.   10

Trin. Where should they be set else? he were a brave monster indeed, if they were set in his tail.

Ste. My man-monster hath drown'd his tongue in sack: for my part, the sea cannot drown me; I swam, ere I could recover the shore, five and thirty leagues off and on. By this light, thou ●shalt be my lieutenant, monster, or my standard.

Trin. Your lieutenant, if you list; he's no standard.   20

Ste. We'll not run, Monsieur Monster.

Trin. Nor go neither; but you'll lie like dogs and yet say nothing neither.

Ste. Moon-calf, speak once in thy life, if thou beest a good moon-calf.

Cal. How does thy honour? Let me lick thy shoe.
I'll not serve him; he is not valiant.

Trin. Thou liest, most ignorant monster: I ●am in case to justle a constable. Why, thou deboshed fish, thou, was there ever man a coward that hath drunk so much sack as I to-day? Wilt thou tell a monstrous lie, being but half a fish and half a monster?

Cal. Lo, how he mocks me! wilt thou let him, my lord?

Trin. 'Lord' quoth he! That a monster should be such a natural!

Cal. Lo, lo, again! bite him to death, I prithee.

Ste. Trinculo, keep a good tongue in your head: if you prove a mutineer,—the next tree! The poor monster's my subject and he shall not suffer indignity.

Cal. I thank my noble lord. Wilt thou be pleased to hearken once again to the suit I made to thee?

Ste. Marry, will I: kneel and repeat it; I will stand, and so shall Trinculo.

Enter ARIEL, *invisible*.

Cal. As I told thee before, I am subject to a tyrant, a sorcerer, that by his cunning hath cheated me of the island.   50

Ari. Thou liest.

Cal. Thou liest, thou jesting monkey, thou: I would my valiant master would destroy thee! I do not lie.

Ste. Trinculo, if you trouble him any more in's tale, by this hand, I will supplant some of your teeth.

Trin. Why, I said nothing.

Ste. Mum, then, and no more. Proceed.

Cal. I say, by sorcery he got this isle;   60
From me he got it. If thy greatness will
Revenge it on him,—for I know thou darest,
But this thing dare not,—

Ste. That's most certain.

Cal. Thou shalt be lord of it and I'll serve thee.

Ste. How now shall this be compassed? Canst thou bring me to the party?

Cal. Yea, yea, my lord: I'll yield him thee asleep,

Where thou mayst knock a nail into his head.
   Ari.   Thou liest; thou canst not.   70
   Cal.   What a pied ninny's this! Thou scurvy
     patch!
I do beseech thy greatness, give him blows
And take his bottle from him: when that's gone
He shall drink nought but brine; for I'll not
     show him
• Where the quick freshes are.
   Ste.   Trinculo, run into no further danger:
interrupt the monster one word further, and, by
this hand, I'll turn my mercy out o' doors and
make a stock-fish of thee.
   Trin.   Why, what did I? I did nothing. I'll
go farther off.   81
   Ste.   Didst thou not say he lied?
   Ari.   Thou liest.
   Ste.   Do I so? take thou that. [*Beats Trin.*]
As you like this, give me the lie another time.
   Trin.   I did not give the lie. Out o' your wits
and hearing too? A pox o' your bottle! this can
sack and drinking do. A murrain on your mon-
ster, and the devil take your fingers!
   Cal.   Ha, ha, ha!   90
   Ste.   Now, forward with your tale. Prithee,
stand farther off.
   Cal.   Beat him enough: after a little time
I'll beat him too.
   Ste.   Stand farther.   Come, proceed.
   Cal.   Why, as I told thee, 'tis a custom with
     him,
I' th' afternoon to sleep: there thou mayst brain
     him,
Having first seized his books, or with a log
Batter his skull, or paunch him with a stake,
• Or cut his wezand with thy knife.   Remember
First to possess his books; for without them 100
He's but a sot, as I am, nor hath not
One spirit to command: they all do hate him
As rootedly as I.   Burn but his books.
He has brave utensils,—for so he calls them,—
Which, when he has a house, he'll deck withal.
And that most deeply to consider is
The beauty of his daughter; he himself
Calls her a nonpareil: I never saw a woman,
But only Sycorax my dam and she;
But she as far surpasseth Sycorax   110
As great'st does least.
   Ste.   Is it so brave a lass?
   Cal.   Ay, lord; she will become thy bed, I warrant.
And bring thee forth brave brood.
   Ste.   Monster, I will kill this man: his daughter
and I will be king and queen,—save our graces!—
and Trinculo and thyself shall be viceroys.   Dost
thou like the plot, Trinculo?
   Trin.   Excellent.
   Ste.   Give me thy hand: I am sorry I beat
thee; but, while thou livest, keep a good tongue
in thy head.   121
   Cal.   Within this half hour will he be asleep:
Wilt thou destroy him then?
   Ste.   Ay, on mine honour.
   Ari.   This will I tell my master.
   Cal.   Thou makest me merry; I am full of
     pleasure:
Let us be jocund: will you troll the catch
You taught me but while-ere?
   Ste.   At thy request, monster, I will do reason,
any reason. Come on, Trinculo, let us sing. [*Sings.*

75 *quick freshes.* Fresh running streams.

99 *wezand.* Wind-pipe.

Trinculo, Stephano, Caliban and Ariel. Drawing by
J. M. Wright (1777–1866)

136 *Nobody.* i.e. a monster.

Nobody monster from the title page of a comedy called *No-body and Some-body*, 1606. Engraving from Charles Knight's *Pictorial Edition of the Works of Shakspere*, 1839–43

1 *By'r lakin.* By Our Lady.

3 *forth-rights and meanders.* Straight and crooked paths.

Flout 'em and scout 'em   **130**
And scout 'em and flout 'em;
    Thought is free.
  Cal.   That's not the tune.
    [*Ariel plays the tune on a tabor and pipe.*
  Ste.   What is this same?
  Trin.   This is the tune of our catch, played
by the picture of Nobody.
  Ste.   If thou beest a man, show thyself in thy
likeness: if thou beest a devil, take't as thou list.
  Trin.   O, forgive me my sins!
  Ste.   He that dies pays all debts: I defy thee.
Mercy upon us!   **141**
  Cal.   Art thou afeard?
  Ste.   No, monster, not I.
  Cal.   Be not afeard; the isle is full of noises,
Sounds and sweet airs, that give delight and hurt
    not.
Sometimes a thousand twangling instruments
Will hum about mine ears, and sometime voices
That, if I then had waked after long sleep,
Will make me sleep again: and then, in dreaming,
The clouds methought would open and show
    riches   **150**
Ready to drop upon me, that, when I waked,
I cried to dream again.
  Ste.   This will prove a brave kingdom to me,
where I shall have my music for nothing.
  Cal.   When Prospero is destroyed.
  Ste.   That shall be by and by: I remember
the story.
  Trin.   The sound is going away; let's follow
it, and after do our work.
  Ste.   Lead, monster; we'll follow.   I would I
could see this taborer; he lays it on.   **161**
  Trin.   Wilt come?   I'll follow, Stephano.
    [*Exeunt.*

SCENE III.   *Another part of the island.*

Enter ALONSO, SEBASTIAN, ANTONIO, GONZALO,
    ADRIAN, FRANCISCO, *and others.*

  Gon.   By'r lakin, I can go no further, sir;
My old bones ache: here's a maze trod indeed
Through forth-rights and meanders!   By your
    patience,
I needs must rest me.
  Alon.   Old lord, I cannot blame thee,
Who am myself attach'd with weariness,
To the dulling of my spirits: sit down, and rest.
Even here I will put off my hope and keep it
No longer for my flatterer: he is drown'd
Whom thus we stray to find, and the sea mocks
Our frustrate search on land.   Well, let him go.   10
  Ant.   [*Aside to Seb.*]   I am right glad that he's
    so out of hope.
Do not, for one repulse, forego the purpose
That you resolved to effect.
  Seb.   [*Aside to Ant.*]   The next advantage
Will we take throughly.
  Ant. [*Aside to Seb.*]   Let it be to-night;
For, now they are oppress'd with travel, they
Will not, nor cannot, use such vigilance
As when they are fresh.
  Seb [*Aside to Ant.*]   I say, to-night: no more.
    [*Solemn and strange music.*
  Alon.   What harmony is this?   My good
    friends, hark!
  Gon.   Marvellous sweet music!

Enter PROSPERO *above, invisible. Enter several strange Shapes, bringing in a banquet; they dance about it with gentle actions of salutation; and, inviting the King, &c. to eat, they depart.*

- *Alon.*   Give us kind keepers, heavens!   What were these?   20
- *Seb.*   A living drollery.   Now I will believe
That there are unicorns, that in Arabia
There is one tree, the phœnix' throne, one phœnix
At this hour reigning there.
     Ant.   I 'll believe both;
And what does else want credit, come to me,
And I 'll be sworn 'tis true: travellers ne'er did lie,
Though fools at home condemn 'em.
     Gon.   If in Naples
I should report this now, would they believe me?
If I should say, I saw such islanders—
- For, certes, these are people of the island—   30
Who, though they are of monstrous shape, yet, note,
Their manners are more gentle-kind than of
Our human generation you shall find
Many, nay, almost any.
     Pros.   [*Aside*] Honest lord,
Thou hast said well; for some of you there present
Are worse than devils.
     Alon.   I cannot too much muse
Such shapes, such gesture and such sound, expressing,
Although they want the use of tongue, a kind
Of excellent dumb discourse.
     Pros.   [*Aside*] Praise in departing.
     Fran.   They vanish'd strangely.
     Seb.   No matter, since   40
They have left their viands behind; for we have stomachs.
Will 't please you taste of what is here?
     Alon.   Not I.
     Gon.   Faith, sir, you need not fear.   When we were boys,
Who would believe that there were mountaineers
- Dew-lapp'd like bulls, whose throats had hanging at 'em
Wallets of flesh? or that there were such men
Whose heads stood in their breasts? which now we find
- Each putter-out of five for one will bring us
Good warrant of.
     Alon.   I will stand to and feed,
Although my last: no matter, since I feel   50
The best is past.   Brother, my lord the duke,
Stand to and do as we.

Thunder and lightning. Enter ARIEL, *like a harpy; claps his wings upon the table; and, with a quaint device, the banquet vanishes.*

     Ari.   You are three men of sin, whom Destiny,
That hath to instrument this lower world
And what is in 't, the never-surfeited sea
Hath caused to belch up you; and on this island
Where man doth not inhabit; you 'mongst men
Being most unfit to live.   I have made you mad;
And even with such-like valour men hang and drown
Their proper selves.
          [*Alon., Seb. &c. draw their swords.*
               You fools! I and my fellows   60
Are ministers of Fate: the elements,

---

20 *kind keepers.* Guardian angels.

21 *living drollery.* A puppet-show using real people.

30 *certes.* Certainly.

45 *Dew-lapp'd.* Hung with fleshy throats.

48 *putter-out.* Lender.

'Enter ARIEL, like a harpy'. Engraving of a harpy from Charles Knight's *Pictorial Edition of the Works of Shakspere*, 1839–43

64 *still.* Constantly.

65 *dowle.* Small feather.

71 *requit.* Repaid.

Costume design of Ariel as a harpy by J. Gower Parks, Stratford-upon-Avon, 1938

---

99 *did bass my trespass.* Did make my crime resound.

108 *ecstasy.* Madness.

Of whom your swords are temper'd, may as well
Wound the loud winds, or with bemock'd-at stabs
● Kill the still-closing waters, as diminish
● One dowle that's in my plume: my fellow-ministers
Are like invulnerable.   If you could hurt,
Your swords are now too massy for your strengths
And will not be uplifted.   But remember—
For that's my business to you—that you three
From Milan did supplant good Prospero;   70
● Exposed unto the sea, which hath requit it,
Him and his innocent child: for which foul deed
The powers, delaying, not forgetting, have
Incensed the seas and shores, yea, all the crea-
    tures,
Against your peace.   Thee of thy son, Alonso,
They have bereft; and do pronounce by me
Lingering perdition, worse than any death
Can be at once, shall step by step attend
You and your ways; whose wraths to guard you
    from—
Which here, in this most desolate isle, else falls
Upon your heads—is nothing but heart-sorrow 81
And a clear life ensuing.

*He vanishes in thunder; then, to soft music,
enter the Shapes again, and dance, with mocks
and mows, and carrying out the table.*

Pros.   Bravely the figure of this harpy hast thou
Perform'd, my Ariel; a grace it had, devouring:
Of my instruction hast thou nothing bated
In what thou hadst to say: so, with good life
And observation strange, my meaner ministers
Their several kinds have done.   My high charms
    work
And these mine enemies are all knit up
In their distractions; they now are in my power;
And in these fits I leave them, while I visit   91
Young Ferdinand, whom they suppose is drown'd,
And his and mine loved darling.   [*Exit above.*
Gon.   I' the name of something holy, sir, why
    stand you
In this strange stare?
Alon.   O, it is monstrous, monstrous!
Methought the billows spoke and told me of it;
The winds did sing it to me, and the thunder,
That deep and dreadful organ-pipe, pronounced
● The name of Prosper: it did bass my trespass.
Therefore my son i' the ooze is bedded, and   100
I'll seek him deeper than e'er plummet sounded
And with him there lie mudded.   [*Exit.*
Seb.   But one fiend at a time,
I'll fight their legions o'er.
Ant.   I'll be thy second.
    [*Exeunt Seb. and Ant.*
Gon.   All three of them are desperate: their
    great guilt,
Like poison given to work a great time after,
Now 'gins to bite the spirits.   I do beseech you
That are of suppler joints, follow them swiftly
● And hinder them from what this ecstasy
May now provoke them to.
Adr.   Follow, I pray you.   [*Exeunt.*

ACT IV.

SCENE I.   *Before* PROSPERO'S *cell.*

Enter PROSPERO, FERDINAND, *and* MIRANDA.

Pros.   If I have too austerely punish'd you,
Your compensation makes amends, for I

● Have given you here a thrid of mine own life,
Or that for which I live; who once again
I tender to thy hand: all thy vexations
Were but my trials of thy love, and thou
Hast strangely stood the test: here, afore Heaven,
I ratify this my rich gift.   O Ferdinand,
Do not smile at me that I boast her off,
For thou shalt find she will outstrip all praise 10
And make it halt behind her.
    Fer.   I do believe it
Against an oracle.
    Pros. Then, as my gift and thine own acquisition
Worthily purchased, take my daughter: but
If thou dost break her virgin-knot before
All sanctimonious ceremonies may
With full and holy rite be minister'd,
● No sweet aspersion shall the heavens let fall
To make this contract grow; but barren hate,
Sour-eyed disdain and discord shall bestrew 20
The union of your bed with weeds so loathly
That you shall hate it both: therefore take heed,
● As Hymen's lamps shall light you.
    Fer.   As I hope
For quiet days, fair issue and long life,
With such love as 'tis now, the murkiest den,
The most opportune place, the strong'st suggestion
Our worser genius can, shall never melt
Mine honour into lust, to take away
The edge of that day's celebration
● When I shall think, or Phœbus' steeds are found-
    er'd,   30
Or Night kept chain'd below.
    Pros.   Fairly spoke.
Sit then and talk with her; she is thine own.
What, Ariel! my industrious servant, Ariel!

Enter ARIEL.

    Ari. What would my potent master? here I am.
    Pros. Thou and thy meaner fellows your last
    service
Did worthily perform; and I must use you
In such another trick.   Go bring the rabble,
O'er whom I give thee power, here to this place:
Incite them to quick motion; for I must
Bestow upon the eyes of this young couple 40
Some vanity of mine art: it is my promise,
● And they expect it from me.
    Ari.   Presently?
    Pros. Ay, with a twink.
    Ari. Before you can say 'come' and 'go,'
           And breathe twice and cry 'so, so,'
           Each one, tripping on his toe,
           Will be here with mop and mow.
           Do you love me, master? no?
    Pros. Dearly, my delicate Ariel.   Do not ap-
    proach
Till thou dost hear me call.
    Ari.   Well, I conceive. [*Exit.* 50
    Pros. Look thou be true; do not give dalliance
Too much the rein: the strongest oaths are straw
To the fire i' the blood: be more abstemious,
Or else, good night your vow!
    Fer.   I warrant you, sir;
The white cold virgin snow upon my heart
Abates the ardour of my liver.
    Pros.   Well.
● Now come, my Ariel! bring a corollary,
● Rather than want a spirit: appear, and pertly!
No tongue! all eyes! be silent.   [*Soft music.*

3 *thrid*. Third.

Prospero: O Ferdinand, Do not smile at me that I boast her off...' Prospero, Miranda and Ferdinand. Engraving from a design by Thomas Stothard from E. Harding's *Plays of Shakespeare*, 1798–1800

---

18 *aspersion*. Blessing.

23 *Hymen*. God of marriage.

30 *Phœbus*. Sun-god.

42 *Presently*. Straight away.

57 *corollary*. i.e. extra.

58 *want*. Lack.

60 *Ceres*. Goddess of fertility.

63 *stover*. Winter food for cattle.

64 *pioned*. Dug out. *twilled*. Reinforced.

68 *pole-clipt*. i.e. pruned.

69 *marge*. Shore.

77 *wife of Jupiter*. i.e. Juno.

81 *bosky*. Wooded.

89 *Dis*. King of the underworld.

90 *blind boy*. i.e. Cupid.

93 *Paphos*. Haunt of Venus.

98 *Mars*. God of war. *minion*. i.e. Venus.

99 *waspish-headed son*. i.e. Cupid.

110 *foison*. Abundance.

Enter IRIS.

Iris. Ceres, most bounteous lady, thy rich leas
Of wheat, rye, barley, vetches, oats and pease;
Thy turfy mountains, where live nibbling sheep,
And flat meads thatch'd with stover, them to keep;
Thy banks with pioned and twilled brims,
Which spongy April at thy hest betrims,
To make cold nymphs chaste crowns: and thy
        broom-groves,
Whose shadow the dismissed bachelor loves,
Being lass-lorn; thy pole-clipt vineyard;
And thy sea-marge, sterile and rocky-hard,
Where thou thyself dost air;—the queen o' the sky,
Whose watery arch and messenger am I,   71
Bids thee leave these, and with her sovereign
        grace,
Here on this grass-plot, in this very place,
To come and sport: her peacocks fly amain:
Approach, rich Ceres, her to entertain.

Enter CERES.

Cer. Hail, many-colour'd messenger, that ne'er
Dost disobey the wife of Jupiter;
Who with thy saffron wings upon my flowers
Diffusest honey-drops, refreshing showers,
And with each end of thy blue bow dost crown 80
My bosky acres and my unshrubb'd down,
Rich scarf to my proud earth; why hath thy queen
Summon'd me hither, to this short-grass'd green?
Iris. A contract of true love to celebrate;
And some donation freely to estate
On the blest lovers.
Cer.   Tell me, heavenly bow,
If Venus or her son, as thou dost know,
Do now attend the queen? Since they did plot
The means that dusky Dis my daughter got,
Her and her blind boy's scandal'd company   90
I have forsworn.
Iris.   Of her society
Be not afraid: I met her deity
Cutting the clouds towards Paphos and her son
Dove-drawn with her. Here thought they to have
        done
Some wanton charm upon this man and maid,
Whose vows are, that no bed-right shall be paid
Till Hymen's torch be lighted: but in vain;
Mars's hot minion is return'd again;
Her waspish-headed son has broke his arrows,
Swears he will shoot no more but play with spar-
        rows   100
And be a boy right out.
Cer.   High'st queen of state,
Great Juno, comes; I know her by her gait.

Enter JUNO.

Juno. How does my bounteous sister? Go
        with me
To bless this twain, that they may prosperous be
And honour'd in their issue.   [*They sing:*

Juno. Honour, riches, marriage-blessing,
        Long continuance, and increasing,
        Hourly joys be still upon you!
        Juno sings her blessings on you.

Cer. Earth's increase, foison plenty,   110
        Barns and garners never empty,
        Vines with clustering bunches growing,
        Plants with goodly burthen bowing;

Spring come to you at the farthest
In the very end of harvest!
Scarcity and want shall shun you;
Ceres' blessing so is on you.
Fer.   This is a most majestic vision, and
Harmonious charmingly.   May I be bold
To think these spirits?
Pros.   Spirits, which by mine art   120
I have from their confines call'd to enact
My present fancies.
Fer.   Let me live here ever;
So rare a wonder'd father and a wife
Makes this place Paradise.
                    [*Juno and Ceres whisper, and send
                         Iris on employment.*
Pros.   Sweet, now, silence!
Juno and Ceres whisper seriously;
There's something else to do: hush, and be mute,
Or else our spell is marr'd.
Iris.   You nymphs, call'd Naiads, of the wind-
         ring brooks,
With your sedged crowns and ever-harmless looks,
Leave your crisp channels and on this green land
Answer your summons; Juno does command:
Come, temperate nymphs, and help to celebrate
A contract of true love; be not too late.

Enter certain Nymphs.

You sunburnt sicklemen, of August weary,
Come hither from the furrow and be merry:
Make holiday; your rye-straw hats put on
And these fresh nymphs encounter every one
In country footing.

*Enter certain Reapers, properly habited: they
   join with the Nymphs in a graceful dance;
   towards the end whereof* PROSPERO *starts suddenly, and speaks; after which, to a strange,
   hollow, and confused noise, they heavily vanish.*

Pros. [*Aside*] I had forgot that foul conspiracy
Of the beast Caliban and his confederates   140
Against my life: the minute of their plot
●Is almost come. [*To the Spirits.*]   Well done!
         avoid; no more!
Fer.   This is strange: your father's in some
         passion
That works him strongly.
Mir.   Never till this day
Saw I him touch'd with anger so distemper'd.
Pros.   You do look, my son, in a moved sort,
As if you were dismay'd: be cheerful, sir.
Our revels now are ended.   These our actors,
As I foretold you, were all spirits and
Are melted into air, into thin air: 150
And, like the baseless fabric of this vision,
The cloud-capp'd towers, the gorgeous palaces,
The solemn temples, the great globe itself,
Yea, all which it inherit, shall dissolve
And, like this insubstantial pageant faded,
●Leave not a rack behind.   We are such stuff
As dreams are made on, and our little life
Is rounded with a sleep.   Sir, I am vex'd;
Bear with my weakness; my old brain is troubled:
Be not disturb'd with my infirmity: 160
If you be pleased, retire into my cell
And there repose: a turn or two I'll walk,
To still my beating mind.
Fer. Mir.   We wish your peace. [*Exeunt.*

142 *avoid*. Be gone.

Prospero: You do look, my son, in a moved sort . . .'
Ferdinand, Miranda and Prospero. Engraving from a
painting by Joseph Wright of Derby (1734–97)

156 *rack*. Shred of a cloud.

Pros. Come with a thought.   I thank thee,
Ariel: come.

Enter ARIEL.

Ari. Thy thoughts I cleave to.   What's thy
   pleasure?
Pros.   Spirit,
We must prepare to meet with Caliban.
   Ari. Ay, my commander: when I presented
      Ceres,
I thought to have told thee of it, but I fear'd
Lest I might anger thee.
   Pros.   Say again, where didst thou leave these
      varlets?   170
   Ari. I told you, sir, they were red-hot with
      drinking;
So full of valour that they smote the air
For breathing in their faces; beat the ground
For kissing of their feet; yet always bending
Towards their project.   Then I beat my tabor;
At which, like unback'd colts, they prick'd their
   ears,
Advanced their eyelids, lifted up their noses
As they smelt music: so I charm'd their ears
That calf-like they my lowing follow'd through
● Tooth'd briers, sharp furzes, pricking goss and
      thorns,   180
Which enter'd their frail shins: at last I left them
● I' the filthy-mantled pool beyond your cell,
There dancing up to the chins, that the foul lake
O'erstunk their feet.
   Pros.   This was well done, my bird.
Thy shape invisible retain thou still:
The trumpery in my house, go bring it hither,
● For stale to catch these thieves.
   Ari.   I go, I go. [*Exit.*
   Pros. A devil, a born devil, on whose nature
Nurture can never stick; on whom my pains,
Humanely taken, all, all lost, quite lost;   190
And as with age his body uglier grows,
So his mind cankers.   I will plague them all,
Even to roaring.

Re-enter ARIEL, *loaden with glistering apparel, &c.*

Come, hang them on this line.

PROSPERO *and* ARIEL *remain, invisible.   Enter*
CALIBAN, STEPHANO, *and* TRINCULO, *all wet.*

   Cal. Pray you, tread softly, that the blind
      mole may not
Hear a foot fall: we now are near his cell.
   Ste. Monster, your fairy, which you say is a
harmless fairy, has done little better than played
the Jack with us.
   Trin. Monster, I do smell all horse-piss; at
which my nose is in great indignation.   200
   Ste. So is mine.   Do you hear, monster?   If
I should take a displeasure against you, look you,—
   Trin. Thou wert but a lost monster.
   Cal. Good my lord, give me thy favour still.
Be patient, for the prize I'll bring thee to
Shall hoodwink this mischance: therefore speak
      softly.
All's hush'd as midnight yet.
   Trin. Ay, but to lose our bottles in the pool,—
   Ste. There is not only disgrace and dishonour
in that, monster, but an infinite loss.   210

Ariel: 'I told you, sir, they were red-hot with drinking . . .' Ariel (Brian Bedford) and Prospero (John
Gielgud), Stratford-upon-Avon, 1957

180 *goss.* Gorse.

182 *filthy-mantled.* Scum covered.

187 *stale.* Decoys.

Opposite : Prospero with Ariel. Drawing by J. M. Wright
(1777–1866)

Stephano: 'I will fetch off my bottle, though I be o'er ears for my labour'. Drawing of Trinculo, Stephano and Caliban by Robert Smirke (1752–1845)

---

239 *line and level.* According to rule.

244 *pass of pate.* Thrust of wit.

246 *lime.* Bird lime.

262 *pard.* Leopard. *cat o' mountain.* Panther.

Trin. That's more to me than my wetting: yet this is your harmless fairy, monster.

Ste. I will fetch off my bottle, though I be o'er ears for my labour.

Cal. Prithee, my king, be quiet. See'st thou here,
This is the mouth o' the cell: no noise, and enter.
Do that good mischief which may make this island
Thine own for ever, and I, thy Caliban,
For aye thy foot-licker.

Ste. Give me thy hand. I do begin to have bloody thoughts.   221

Trin. O king Stephano! O peer! O worthy Stephano! look what a wardrobe here is for thee!

Cal. Let it alone, thou fool; it is but trash.

Trin. O, ho, monster! we know what belongs to a frippery. O king Stephano!

Ste. Put off that gown, Trinculo; by this hand, I'll have that gown.

Trin. Thy grace shall have it.

Cal. The dropsy drown this fool! what do you mean   230
To dote thus on such luggage? Let's alone
And do the murder first: if he awake,
From toe to crown he'll fill our skins with pinches,
Make us strange stuff.

Ste. Be you quiet, monster. Mistress line, is not this my jerkin? Now is the jerkin under the line: now, jerkin, you are like to lose your hair and prove a bald jerkin.

Trin. Do, do: we steal by line and level, an't like your grace.   240

Ste. I thank thee for that jest; here's a garment for't: wit shall not go unrewarded while I am king of this country. 'Steal by line and level' is an excellent pass of pate; there's another garment for't.

Trin. Monster, come, put some lime upon your fingers, and away with the rest.

Cal. I will have none on't: we shall lose our time,
And all be turn'd to barnacles, or to apes
With foreheads villanous low.   250

Ste. Monster, lay-to your fingers: help to bear this away where my hogshead of wine is, or I'll turn you out of my kingdom: go to, carry this.

Trin. And this.

Ste. Ay, and this.

A noise of hunters heard. Enter divers Spirits, in shape of dogs and hounds, and hunt them about, PROSPERO *and* ARIEL *setting them on.*

Pros. Hey, Mountain, hey!

Ari. Silver! there it goes, Silver!

Pros. Fury, Fury! there, Tyrant, there! hark! hark! [*Cal., Ste., and Trin. are driven out.*
Go charge my goblins that they grind their joints
With dry convulsions, shorten up their sinews
With aged cramps, and more pinch-spotted make them
Than pard or cat o' mountain.

Ari.   Hark, they roar!

Pros. Let them be hunted soundly. At this hour
Lie at my mercy all mine enemies:
Shortly shall all my labours end, and thou
Shalt have the air at freedom: for a little
Follow, and do me service.   [*Exeunt.*

ACT V.

SCENE I. *Before* PROSPERO'S *cell.*

Enter PROSPERO *in his magic robes, and* ARIEL.

Pros. ·Now does my project gather to a head:
My charms crack not; my spirits obey; and time
Goes upright with his carriage.   How's the day?
  Ar. On the sixth hour; at which time, my lord,
You said our work should cease.
  Pros.   I did say so,
When first I raised the tempest.   Say, my spirit,
How fares the king and's followers?
  Ari.   Confined together
In the same fashion as you gave in charge,
Just as you left them; all prisoners, sir,
● In the line-grove which weather-fends your cell:
They cannot budge till your release.   The king,
His brother and yours, abide all three distracted
And the remainder mourning over them,
Brimful of sorrow and dismay; but chiefly
Him that you term'd, sir, 'The good old lord,
        Gonzalo;'
His tears run down his beard, like winter's drops
From eaves of reeds.   Your charm so strongly
        works 'em
That if you now beheld them, your affections
Would become tender.
  Pros.   Dost thou think so, spirit?
  Ari.   Mine would, sir, were I human.
  Pros.   And mine shall.   20
Hast thou, which art but air, a touch, a feeling
Of their afflictions, and shall not myself,
One of their kind, that relish all as sharply,
Passion as they, be kindlier moved than thou art?
Though with their high wrongs I am struck to
        the quick,
Yet with my nobler reason 'gainst my fury
Do I take part: the rarer action is
In virtue than in vengeance: they being penitent,
The sole drift of my purpose doth extend
Not a frown further.   Go release them, Ariel: 30
My charms I'll break, their senses I'll restore,
And they shall be themselves.
  Ari.   I'll fetch them, sir.   [*Exit.*
  Pros.   Ye elves of hills, brooks, standing lakes
        and groves,
And ye that on the sands with printless foot
Do chase the ebbing Neptune and do fly him
When he comes back; you demi-puppets that
By moonshine do the green sour ringlets make,
Whereof the ewe not bites, and you whose pastime
Is to make midnight mushrooms, that rejoice
To hear the solemn curfew; by whose aid,   40
Weak masters though ye be, I have bedimm'd
The noontide sun, call'd forth the mutinous winds,
And 'twixt the green sea and the azured vault
Set roaring war: to the dread rattling thunder
Have I given fire and rifted Jove's stout oak
With his own bolt; the strong-based promontory
● Have I made shake and by the spurs pluck'd up
The pine and cedar: graves at my command
Have waked their sleepers, oped, and let 'em forth
By my so potent art.   But this rough magic   50
I here abjure, and, when I have required
Some heavenly music, which even now I do,
To work mine end upon their senses that
This airy charm is for, I'll break my staff,
Bury it certain fathoms in the earth,

10 *weather-fends.* Protects from the weather.

47 *spurs.* Roots.

Prospero (Tom Fleming) and Ariel (Ian Holm), Royal
Shakespeare Co, 1963

A charmed circle. Engraving from a 14th century manuscript

---

63 *sociable.* Sympathetic.

64 *Fall fellowly drops.* Weep like yours.

85 *discase me.* i.e. remove my robe.

Ariel helps to attire Prospero. Engraving by T. Stothard from E. Harding's *Plays of Shakespeare*, 1798–1800

And deeper than did ever plummet sound
I'll drown my book.   [*Solemn music.*

Re-enter ARIEL *before: then* ALONSO, *with a frantic gesture, attended by* GONZALO; SE-BASTIAN *and* ANTONIO *in like manner, attended by* ADRIAN *and* FRANCISCO: *they all enter the circle which* PROSPERO *had made, and there stand charmed; which* PROSPERO *observing, speaks:*

A solemn air and the best comforter
To an unsettled fancy cure thy brains,
Now useless, boil'd within thy skull! There stand,
For you are spell-stopp'd.
Holy Gonzalo, honourable man,
● Mine eyes, even sociable to the show of thine,
● Fall fellowly drops.   The charm dissolves apace,
And as the morning steals upon the night,
Melting the darkness, so their rising senses
Begin to chase the ignorant fumes that mantle
Their clearer reason.   O good Gonzalo,
My true preserver, and a loyal sir
To him thou follow'st! I will pay thy graces   70
Home both in word and deed.   Most cruelly
Didst thou, Alonso, use me and my daughter:
Thy brother was a furtherer in the act.
Thou art pinch'd for't now, Sebastian.   Flesh
   and blood,
You, brother mine, that entertain'd ambition,
Expell'd remorse and nature; who, with Se-
   bastian,
Whose inward pinches therefore are most strong,
Would here have kill'd your king; I do forgive
   thee,
Unnatural though thou art.   Their understanding
Begins to swell, and the approaching tide   80
Will shortly fill the reasonable shore
That now lies foul and muddy.   Not one of them
That yet looks on me, or would know me: Ariel,
Fetch me the hat and rapier in my cell:
● I will discase me, and myself present
As I was sometime Milan: quickly, spirit;
Thou shalt ere long be free.

　　　ARIEL *sings and helps to attire him.*
　　Where the bee sucks, there suck I:
　　In a cowslip's bell I lie;
　　There I couch when owls do cry.   90
　　On the bat's back I do fly
　　After summer merrily.
　Merrily, merrily shall I live now
　Under the blossom that hangs on the bough.

Pros.   Why, that's my dainty Ariel! I shall
   miss thee;
But yet thou shalt have freedom: so, so, so.
To the king's ship, invisible as thou art:
There shalt thou find the mariners asleep
Under the hatches; the master and the boatswain
Being awake, enforce them to this place,   100
And presently, I prithee.
　Ari.   I drink the air before me, and return
Or ere your pulse twice beat.   [*Exit.*
　Gon.   All torment, trouble, wonder and amaze-
   ment
Inhabits here: some heavenly power guide us
Out of this fearful country!
　Pros.   Behold, sir king,
The wronged Duke of Milan, Prospero:

For more assurance that a living prince
Does now speak to thee, I embrace thy body;
And to thee and thy company I bid   110
A hearty welcome.
   Alon.   Whether thou be'st he or no,
Or some enchanted trifle to abuse me,
As late I have been, I not know: thy pulse
Beats as of flesh and blood; and, since I saw
   thee,
The affliction of my mind amends, with which,
I fear, a madness held me: this must crave,
An if this be at all, a most strange story.
Thy dukedom I resign and do entreat
Thou pardon me my wrongs.   But how should
   Prospero
Be living and be here?
   Pros.   First, noble friend,   120
Let me embrace thine age, whose honour cannot
Be measured or confined.
   Gon.   Whether this be
Or be not, I'll not swear.
   Pros.   You do yet taste
Some subtilties o' the isle, that will not let you
Believe things certain.   Welcome, my friends all!
[*Aside to Seb. and Ant.*] But you, my brace of
   lords, were I so minded,
I here could pluck his highness' frown upon you
And justify you traitors: at this time
I will tell no tales.
   Seb.   [*Aside*] The devil speaks in him.
   Pros.   No.
For you, most wicked sir, whom to call brother
Would even infect my mouth, I do forgive
Thy rankest fault; all of them; and require
My dukedom of thee, which perforce, I know,
Thou must restore.
   Alon.   If thou be'st Prospero,
Give us particulars of thy preservation;
How thou hast met us here, who three hours since
Were wreck'd upon this shore; where I have lost—
How sharp the point of this remembrance is!—
My dear son Ferdinand.
   Pros.   I am woe for't, sir.
   Alon. Irreparable is the loss, and patience 140
Says it is past her cure.
   Pros.   I rather think
You have not sought her help, of whose soft grace
For the like loss I have her sovereign aid
And rest myself content.
   Alon.   You the like loss!
   Pros. As great to me as late; and, supportable
To make the dear loss, have I means much weaker
Than you may call to comfort you, for I
Have lost my daughter.
   Alon.   A daughter?
O heavens, that they were living both in Naples,
The king and queen there! that they were, I wish
Myself were mudded in that oozy bed
Where my son lies.   When did you lose your
   daughter?
   Pros. In this last tempest. I perceive, these lords
At this encounter do so much admire
That they devour their reason and scarce think
Their eyes do offices of truth, their words
Are natural breath: but, howsoe'er you have
Been justled from your senses, know for certain
That I am Prospero and that very duke
Which was thrust forth of Milan, who most
   strangely   160

Costume design for Prospero by Loudon Sainthill,
Stratford-upon-Avon, 1952

Ferdinand and Miranda playing chess. Drawing by Francis Wheatley (1749–1801)

---

167 *abroad*. Apart from me.

Upon this shore, where you were wreck'd, was
    landed,
To be the lord on't.   No more yet of this;
For 'tis a chronicle of day by day,
Not a relation for a breakfast nor
Befitting this first meeting.   Welcome, sir;
This cell's my court: here have I few attendants
And subjects none abroad: pray you, look in.
My dukedom since you have given me again,
I will requite you with as good a thing;
At least bring forth a wonder, to content ye   170
As much as me my dukedom.

Here Prospero discovers FERDINAND *and* MI-
    RANDA *playing at chess.*

Mir.   Sweet lord, you play me false.
Fer.   No, my dear'st love,
I would not for the world.
Mir.   Yes, for a score of kingdoms you should
    wrangle,
And I would call it fair play.
Alon.   If this prove
A vision of the Island, one dear son
Shall I twice lose.
Seb.   A most high miracle!
Fer.   Though the seas threaten, they are
    merciful;
I have cursed them without cause.   [*Kneels.*
Alon.   Now all the blessings
Of a glad father compass thee about!   180
Arise, and say how thou camest here.
Mir.   O, wonder!
How many goodly creatures are there here!
How beauteous mankind is! O brave new world,
That has such people in't!
Pros.   'Tis new to thee.
Alon.   What is this maid with whom thou
    wast at play?
Your eld'st acquaintance cannot be three hours:
Is she the goddess that hath sever'd us,
And brought us thus together?
Fer.   Sir, she is mortal;
But by immortal Providence she's mine:
I chose her when I could not ask my father   190
For his advice, nor thought I had one.   She
Is daughter to this famous Duke of Milan,
Of whom so often I have heard renown,
But never saw before; of whom I have
Received a second life; and second father
This lady makes him to me.
Alon.   I am hers:
But, O, how oddly will it sound that I
Must ask my child forgiveness!
Pros.   There, sir, stop:
Let us not burthen our remembrance with
A heaviness that's gone.
Gon.   I have inly wept,   200
Or should have spoke ere this.   Look down, you
    gods,
And on this couple drop a blessed crown!
For it is you that have chalk'd forth the way
Which brought us hither.
Alon.   I say, Amen, Gonzalo!
Gon.   Was Milan thrust from Milan, that his
    issue
Should become kings of Naples? O, rejoice
Beyond a common joy, and set it down
With gold on lasting pillars: In one voyage
Did Claribel her husband find at Tunis

And Ferdinand, her brother, found a wife   210
Where he himself was lost, Prospero his dukedom
In a poor isle and all of us ourselves
When no man was his own.
    Alon. [*To Fer. and Mir.*] Give me your hands:
Let grief and sorrow still embrace his heart
That doth not wish you joy!
    Gon.   Be it so! Amen!

Re-enter ARIEL, *with the* Master *and* Boatswain
amazedly following.

O, look, sir, look, sir! here is more of us:
I prophesied, if a gallows were on land,
This fellow could not drown.   Now, blasphemy,
That swear'st grace o'erboard, not an oath on shore?
Hast thou no mouth by land?   What is the news?
    Boats.   The best news is, that we have safely
        found   221
Our king and company; the next, our ship—
Which, but three glasses since, we gave out split—
• Is tight and yare and bravely rigg'd as when
We first put out to sea.
    Ari. [*Aside to Pros.*] Sir, all this service
Have I done since I went.
    Pros. [*Aside to Ari.*] My tricksy spirit!
    Alon.   These are not natural events; they
        strengthen
From strange to stranger.   Say, how came you
        hither?
    Boats.   If I did think, sir, I were well awake,
I'ld strive to tell you.   We were dead of sleep,
And—how we know not—all clapp'd under hatches;
Where but even now with strange and several
        noises
Of roaring, shrieking, howling, jingling chains,
And moe diversity of sounds, all horrible,
We were awaked; straightway, at liberty;
Where we, in all her trim, freshly beheld
Our royal, good and gallant ship, our master
Capering to eye her: on a trice, so please you,
Even in a dream, were we divided from them
And were brought moping hither.
    Ari.   [*Aside to Pros.*] Was't well done? 240
    Pros. [*Aside to Ari.*] Bravely, my diligence.
Thou shalt be free.
    Alon.   This is as strange a maze as e'er men
        trod:
And there is in this business more than nature
Was ever conduct of: some oracle
Must rectify our knowledge.
    Pros.   Sir, my liege,
• Do not infest your mind with beating on
The strangeness of this business; at pick'd leisure
• Which shall be shortly, single I'll resolve you,
Which to you shall seem probable, of every
These happen'd accidents; till when, be cheerful
And think of each thing well. [*Aside to Ari.*]
    Come hither, spirit: 251
Set Caliban and his companions free;
Untie the spell. [*Exit Ariel.*]   How fares my
    gracious sir?
There are yet missing of your company
Some few odd lads that you remember not.

Re-enter ARIEL, *driving in* CALIBAN, STEPHANO
and TRINCULO, *in their stolen apparel.*

    Ste.   Every man shift for all the rest, and let
no man take care for himself; for all is but fortune.   Coragio, bully-monster, coragio!

Costume design for Stephano and Trinculo by J. Gower
Parks, Stratford-upon-Avon, 1938

---

224 *yare*. Ready.

246 *beating on*. Trying to explain.

248 *single*. One by one.

280 *gilded.* i.e. flushed.

Prospero: 'He is as disproportion'd in his manners . . .'
Prospero (John Gielgud) and Caliban (Alec Clunes),
Stratford-upon-Avon, 1957

Trin.   If these be true spies which I wear in
my head, here's a goodly sight.   260
Cal.   O Setebos, these be brave spirits indeed!
How fine my master is!   I am afraid
He will chastise me.
Seb.   Ha, ha!
What things are these, my lord Antonio?
Will money buy 'em?
Ant.   Very like; one of them
Is a plain fish, and, no doubt, marketable.
Pros.   Mark but the badges of these men, my
lords,
Then say if they be true.   This mis-shapen knave,
His mother was a witch, and one so strong
That could control the moon, make flows and ebbs,
And deal in her command without her power. 271
These three have robb'd me; and this demi-devil—
For he's a bastard one—had plotted with them
To take my life.   Two of these fellows you
Must know and own; this thing of darkness I
Acknowledge mine.
Cal.   I shall be pinch'd to death.
Alon.   Is not this Stephano, my drunken butler?
Seb.   He is drunk now: where had he wine?
Alon.   And Trinculo is reeling ripe: where
should they
•Find this grand liquor that hath gilded 'em? 280
How camest thou in this pickle?
Trin.   I have been in such a pickle since I
saw you last that, I fear me, will never out of
my bones: I shall not fear fly-blowing.
Seb.   Why, how now, Stephano!
Ste.   O, touch me not;   I am not Stephano,
but a cramp.
Pros.   You'ld be king o' the isle, sirrah?
Ste.   I should have been a sore one then.
Alon.   This is a strange thing as e'er I look'd
on.   [*Pointing to Caliban.*
Pros.   He is as disproportion'd in his manners
As in his shape.   Go, sirrah, to my cell;   291
Take with you your companions; as you look
To have my pardon, trim it handsomely.
Cal.   Ay, that I will; and I'll be wise hereafter
And seek for grace.   What a thrice-double ass
Was I, to take this drunkard for a god
And worship this dull fool!
Pros.   Go to; away!
Alon.   Hence, and bestow your luggage where
you found it.
Seb.   Or stole it, rather.   300
                [*Exeunt Cal., Ste., and Trin.*
Pros.   Sir, I invite your highness and your
train   300
To my poor cell, where you shall take your rest
For this one night; which, part of it, I'll waste
With such discourse as, I not doubt, shall make it
Go quick away; the story of my life
And the particular accidents gone by
Since I came to this isle: and in the morn
I'll bring you to your ship and so to Naples,
Where I have hope to see the nuptial
Of these our dear-beloved solemnized;
And thence retire me to my Milan, where   310
Every third thought shall be my grave.
Alon.   I long
To hear the story of your life, which must
Take the ear strangely.
Pros.   I'll deliver all;
And promise you calm seas, auspicious gales

And sail so expeditious that shall catch
Your royal fleet far off. [*Aside to Ari.*] My Ariel,
    chick,
That is thy charge: then to the elements
Be free, and fare thou well!   Please you, draw
    near.   [*Exeunt.*

EPILOGUE.

SPOKEN BY PROSPERO.

Now my charms are all o'erthrown,
And what strength I have's mine own,
Which is most faint: now, 'tis true,
I must be here confined by you,
Or sent to Naples.   Let me not,
Since I have my dukedom got
And pardon'd the deceiver, dwell
In this bare island by your spell;
But release me from my bands
With the help of your good hands: 10
Gentle breath of yours my sails
Must fill, or else my project fails,
Which was to please.   Now I want
Spirits to enforce, art to enchant,
And my ending is despair,
Unless I be relieved by prayer,
Which pierces so that it assaults
Mercy itself and frees all faults.
As you from crimes would pardon'd be,
Let your indulgence set me free.   20

Michael Redgrave as Prospero, Stratford-upon-Avon, 1951

Further Reading

The following bibliography has been selected from an enormous literature on the subject, and is intended as a guide for the general reader.

EDITIONS

Recommended editions of Shakespeare in one volume are: The Complete Works edited by Peter Alexander, 1951; the Riverside Shakespeare edited by G. Blakemore Evans; and the Complete Works edited by Charles J. Sisson, 1954.
The most useful editions of the plays in separate volumes are the New Arden Shakespeare (general editors, Harold F. Brooks and Harold Jenkins), which cover textual problems and include commentary on the text; the New Penguin Shakespeare (general editor T. J. B. Spencer); and the Pelican Shakespeare (general editor Alfred Harbage). The New Cambridge Shakespeare edited by Arthur Quiller-Couch and John Dover Wilson is stimulating for its introductions and (not always reliable) suggestions. The most detailed textual commentary including stage history up to its date of publication (1888) is in the New Variorum Shakespeare edited by Horace H. Furness. (Paperback edition by Dover Publications, New York.)

GENERAL REFERENCE

Abbott, E. A. *A Shakespeare Grammar*, 1870
Bartlett, John *A New and Complete Concordance . . . to . . . Shakespeare*, 1962
Bullough, Geoffrey *Narrative and Dramatic Sources of Shakespeare*, 1957–73
Greg, W. W. *The Editorial Problem in Shakespeare*, 1942
Greg, W. W. *The Shakespeare First Folio*, 1955
Hinman, Charlton *The Printing and Proof-Reading of the First Folio of Shakespeare*, 1963
Kökeritz, Helge *Shakespeare's Pronunciation*, 1953
Muir, Kenneth *Shakespeare's Sources*, 1961
Munro, J. (ed.) *The Shakespeare Allusion-Book*, 1932
Onions, Charles T. *A Shakespeare Glossary* (revised ed.), 1953
Partridge, Eric *Shakespeare's Bawdy*, 1948
Sisson, C. J. *New Readings in Shakespeare*, 1956
Thomson, J. A. K. *Shakespeare and the Classics*, 1952
Whitaker, V. K. *Shakespeare's Use of Learning*, 1953

SHAKESPEARE'S LIFE

Alexander, Peter *Shakespeare's Life and Art*, 1964
Bentley, G. E. *Shakespeare. A Biographical Handbook*, 1961
Brinkworth, E. R. C. *Shakespeare and the Bawdy Court of Stratford*, 1972
Chambers, E. K. *Shakespeare: A Survey*, 1925
Chambers, E. K. *Sources for a Biography of Shakespeare*, 1946
Chambers, E. K. *William Shakespeare. A Study of Facts and Problems*, 2 vols. 1930
Eccles, Mark *Shakespeare in Warwickshire*, 1961
Fripp, E. I. *Shakespeare, Man and Artist*, 2 vols. 1938
Fripp, E. I. *Shakespeare Studies, Biographical and Literary*, 1930

Fripp, E. I. *Shakespeare's Haunts near Stratford*, 1929
Joseph, Harriet *John Hall, Man and Physician*, 1964
Rowse, A. L. *Shakespeare the Man*, 1973
Rowse, A. L. *Shakespeare's Southampton, Patron of Virginia*, 1965
Rowse, A. L. *Simon Forman. Sex and Society in Shakespeare's Age*, 1974
Rowse, A. L. *William Shakespeare: A Biography*, 1963
Schoenbaum, S. *William Shakespeare: A Documentary Life* (2nd ed. revised with corrections), 1977
Speaight, Robert *Shakespeare. The Man and his Achievement*, 1977

SHAKESPEARE'S CONTEMPORARIES

Aubrey, J. *Brief Lives* edited by Andrew Clark, 2 vols. 1898
Bald, R. C. *John Donne: A Life*, 1970
Barker, Richard H. *Thomas Middleton*, 1958
Beaumont, F. and Fletcher, J. *Dramatic Works* edited by Fredson Bowers, 1966–76
Boas, F. S. *Christopher Marlowe: A Biographical and Critical Study*, 1940
Chambers, E. K. *Sir Henry Lee*, 1936
Chapman, George *Plays and Poems* edited by T. Parrott, 1910–1914
Dekker, Thomas *The Dramatic Works* edited by Fredson Bowers, 1953–61
Gerrard, Earnest A. *Elizabethan Drama and Dramatists, 1583–1603*, 1928
Greene, Robert *Life and Complete Works* edited by A. B. Grosart, 1881–86
Harrison, G. B. *The Life and Death of Robert Devereux, Earl of Essex*, 1937
Harvey, Gabriel *Complete Works* edited by A. B. Grosart, 1884
Gabriel Harvey's Marginalia edited by G. C. Moore Smith, 1913
Heywood, John *Works* edited by B. A. Milligan, 1956
Heywood, Thomas *Dramatic Works* edited by R. H. Shepherd, 1874
Horne, D. H. *The Life and Minor Works of George Peele*, 1952
Hosking, G. L. *The Life and Times of Edward Alleyn*, 1952
Hunter, G. K. *John Lyly. The Humanist as Courtier*, 1962
Jenkins, Elizabeth *Elizabeth and Leicester*, 1961
Jones, H. S. V. *A Spenser Handbook*, 1930
Jonson, Ben *Works* edited by C. H. Herford, Percy and Evelyn Simpson, 1925–50
Judson, A. C. *The Life of Edmund Spenser*, 1945
Kyd, Thomas *Works* edited by F. S. Boas, 1901
Leishman, J. B. (ed.) *The Three Parnassus Plays, 1598–1601*, 1949
Lyly, John *Complete Works* edited by R. W. Bond, 1902
Marlowe, Christopher *Complete Works* edited by Fredson Bowers, 2 vols. 1973
Marston, John *Works* edited by H. Harvey Wood, 3 vols. 1934
Maurier, Daphne du *Golden Lads. A Study of Anthony Bacon, Francis and their Friends*, 1975
Middleton, Thomas *Works* edited by A. H. Bullen, 1885–86
Mirror for Magistrates edited by Lily B. Campbell, 1938
Nashe, Thomas *Works* edited by R. B. McKerrow and F. P. Wilson, 1958

Prouty, C. T. *George Gascoigne*, 1942
Rees, Joan *Samuel Daniel : A Critical and Biographical Study*, 1964
Rees, Joan *Fulke Greville, Lord Brooke, 1554–1628*, 1971
Rowse, A. L. *Christopher Marlowe : A Biography*, 1964
Sidney, Sir Philip *Arcadia* edited by Maurice Evans, 1977
Sidney, Sir Philip *The Poems* edited by William A. Ringler, 1962
Sisson, C. J. (ed.) *Thomas Lodge and other Elizabethans*, 1933
Stopes, Charlotte C. *The Life of Henry, Third Earl of Southampton, Shakespeare's Patron*, 1922
Stopes, Charlotte C. *Shakespeare's Warwickshire Contemporaries*, 1907
Strachey, Lytton *Elizabeth and Essex*, 1928
Ward, B. M. *The Seventeenth Earl of Oxford, 1550–1604*, 1928
Webster, John *Complete Works* edited by F. L. Lucas, 1927
Yates, Francis A. *John Florio*, 1934

SHAKESPEARE'S ENGLAND

Black, J. B. *The Reign of Elizabeth, 1558–1603*, 1936
Byrne, M. St Clare *Elizabethan Life in Town and Country* (revised ed.), 1961
Byrne, M. St Clare *The Elizabethan Home*, 1930
Davies, Godfrey *The Early Stuarts, 1603–1660*, 1938
Elton, G. R. *England under the Tudors*, 1956
Harrison, G. B. *England in Shakespeare's Day*, 1928
Harrison, G. B. *The Elizabethan Journals, 1591–1603*, 1938
Harrison, G. B. *A Jacobean Journal, 1603–1606*, 1941
Harrison, G. B. *A Second Jacobean Journal, 1607–1610*, 1958
Jones, Richard F. *Ancients and Moderns*, 1965
Judges, A. V. (ed.) *The Elizabethan Underworld*, 1930
Neale, J. E. *Queen Elizabeth*, 1934
Nicoll, Allardyce *The Elizabethans*, 1957
Rowse, A. L. *The Elizabethans and America*, 1959
Rowse, A. L. *The Elizabethan Renaissance :* vol 1, The Life of the Society, 1971 ; vol 2, The Cultural Achievement, 1972
Rowse, A. L. *The England of Elizabeth*, 1950
Rowse, A. L. *The Expansion of Elizabethan England*, 1955
Shakespeare's England : An Account of the Life and Manners of his Age, 2 vols. 1916–17
Stow's Survey of London edited by C. L. Kingsford, 2 vols. 1908
Strong, Roy *The English Icon : Elizabethan and Jacobean Portraiture*, 1969
Strong, Roy *The Portraits of Queen Elizabeth I*, 1963
Tillyard, E. M. W. *The Elizabethan World Picture*, 1943
Wilson, F. P. *The Plague in Shakespeare's London*, 1927
Wilson, John Dover *Life in Shakespeare's England*, 1911

SHAKESPEARE CRITICISM

Bamborough, J. B. *The Little World of Man*, 1952
Bradby, Anne (ed.) *Shakespearian Criticism, 1919–1935*, 1936
Bush, Douglas *English Literature in the Earlier Seventeenth Century*, 1945
Buxton, John *Elizabethan Taste*, 1965
Clemens, W. H. *The Development of Shakespeare's Imagery*, 1951
Coleridge, S. T. *Notes and Lectures upon Shakespeare*, 1849
Coleridge, S. T. *Shakespearean Criticism* edited by T. M. Raysor, 2 vols. 1930
Eastman, Arthur M. *A Short History of Shakespeare Criticism*, 1968
Eliot, T. S. *Selected Essays*, 1932
Granville-Barker, H. and Harrison, G. B. (eds.) *A Companion to Shakespeare Studies*, 1934
Hazlitt, William *The Characters of Shakespeare's Plays*, 1805
Johnson on Shakespeare edited by Sir Walter Raleigh, 1925
Knights, L. C. *Some Shakespearean Themes*, 1959
Lewis, C. S. *English Literature in the Sixteenth Century*, 1954
Mahood, M. M. *Shakespeare's Wordplay*, 1957
Muir, K. and Schoenbaum, S. *A New Companion to Shakespeare Studies*, 1971
Murry, John Middleton *Shakespeare*, 1936
Ralli, Augustus *A History of Shakespearian Criticism*, 2 vols. 1932
Shakespeare Quarterly edited by J. G. McManaway (periodical)
Shakespeare Survey edited by Kenneth Muir (annual periodical)
Smith, David Nichol (ed.) *Shakespeare Criticism*, 1949
Smith, Gregory *Elizabethan Critical Essays*, 2 vols. 1904
Smith, Logan P. *On Reading Shakespeare*, 1933
Spencer, Theodore *Shakespeare and the Nature of Man*, 1943
Spurgeon, Caroline *Shakespeare's Imagery and What It Tells Us*, 1935
Stewart, J. I. M. *Character and Motive in Shakespeare*, 1951
Wilson, F. P. *Elizabethan and Jacobean*, 1945
Wilson, F. P. *Marlowe and the Early Shakespeare*, 1953

SHAKESPEARE AND THE STAGE

Adams, Joseph Q. *Shakespearean Playhouses*, 1917
Baldwin, T. W. *Organization and Personnel of the Shakespearean Company*, 1927
Banke, C. de *Shakespeare Stage Productions, Then and Now*, 1953
Beckerman, Bernard *Shakespeare at the Globe*, 1962
Bentley, G. E. *The Jacobean and Caroline Stage*, 4 vols. 1941
Bentley, G. E. *The Profession of Dramatist in Shakespeare's Time, 1590–1642*, 1971
Bentley, G. E. *Shakespeare and his Theatre*, 1964
Bethell, S. L. *Shakespeare and the Popular Dramatic Tradition*, 1944
Bradbrook, M. C. *Elizabethan Stage Conditions*, 1932
Bradbrook, M. C. *The Rise of the Common Player*, 1962
Brown, Ivor *Shakespeare and the Actors*, 1970
Chambers, E. K. *The Elizabethan Stage*, 4 vols. 1924
Coghill, Neville *Shakespeare's Professional Skills*, 1964
Gildersleeve, V. C. *Government Regulation of the Elizabethan Drama*, 1908
Greg, W. W. *Henslowe's Papers*, 3 vols. 1904–1908
Greg, W. W. *Dramatic Documents from the Elizabethan Playhouses*, 2 vols. 1931
Harbage, Alfred *As They Liked It*, 1947
Harbage, Alfred *Shakespeare and the Rival Traditions*, 1952
Harbage, Alfred *Shakespeare's Audience*, 1941
Harbage, Alfred *Theatre for Shakespeare*, 1955
Harrison, G. B. *Elizabethan Plays and Players*, 1940
Henslowe's Diary, edited by R. A. Foakes and R. T. Rickert, 1961
Hodges, C. W. *The Globe Restored*, 1953
Holmes, M. *Shakespeare and his Players*, 1973
Holmes, M. *Shakespeare's Public*, 1960
Joseph, Bertram *Acting Shakespeare*, 1960
Knights, L. C. *Drama and Society in the Age of Jonson*, 1937
Lawrence, W. J. *The Physical Conditions of the Elizabethan Public Playhouses*, 1927
Leech, Clifford *The John Fletcher Plays*, 1962
Mehl, Dieter *The Elizabethan Dumb Show*, 1964
Nagler, A. M. *Shakespeare's Stage*, 1958
Poel, William *Shakespeare in the Theatre*, 1913
Purdom, C. B. *Producing Shakespeare*, 1950
Smith, D. Nichol *Shakespeare in the Eighteenth Century*, 1928
Smith, Irwin *Shakespeare's Blackfriars Playhouse*, 1964
Smith, Irwin *Shakespeare's Globe Playhouse*, 1956

TO THE READER

An obelisk (†) indicates a probable corruption of the original text for which there is no satisfactory or generally acceptable emendation.

Index

This index is limited to proper names excluding Shakespeare and the characters in his plays and poems. Page numbers in *italics* refer to illustrations.

ACKNOWLEDGEMENTS

With special thanks to:
Ben and John Freeman
Geoff Goode Photographics
Dermot Hayes
Maire Nic Suibhne

Ashmolean Museum, Oxford
William Barnard
Marquis of Bath, Longleat
Birmingham Public Libraries
The Bodleian Library, Oxford
British Film Institute
The British Library
The British Museum
The Duke of Buccleuch and Queensberry
Joe Cocks Studio
A. C. Cooper Ltd.
Corpus Christi College, Cambridge
County Archives, Essex Records Office
Courtauld Institute of Art
Crawford Films Ltd
The Governors of Dulwich College Picture Gallery
Mary Evans Picture Library
John R. Freeman Ltd.

John Napier
Charlotte Parry-Crooke
Marian Pringle and the staff at the Shakespeare Birthplace Trust

The Fine Arts Society Ltd., London
Fitzwilliam Museum, Cambridge
Gilling Castle
Goodwood House
Guildhall Library
Harvard Theatre Collection
William Heinemann Ltd.
Holte Photographics Ltd.
Henry E. Huntington Library
By Gracious Permission of Her Majesty the Queen
Alix Jeffry
George E. Joseph
Kunthaus, Zurich
The Museum of London
Liverpool Art Gallery
Magdalene College, Cambridge
Manchester Art Gallery

Sally Rousham
Patrick Rudd
Tantraline Ltd
Robert R. Wark, Huntington Library, California

Mander and Mitchenson
Mansell Collection
Mappin Art Gallery
Maudsley Hospital, London
National Galleries of Scotland
National Gallery, London
National Portrait Gallery, London
National Maritime Museum, London
Newport Museum of Art Gallery
National Trust
University College of North Wales
Queen's College, Cambridge
Preston Art Gallery
Duchess of Portland
Earl of Pembroke
Oliver Robinson (Estate of W. Heath Robinson)
Royal Academy of Art

Rita Wuethrich
Sarah Woodcock, Theatre Collection, Victoria and Albert Museum
Beno Zeiner

Royal Holloway College
Royal Shakespeare Theatre
St. Faith's Church, King's Lynn
The Shakespeare Birthplace Trust
Sheffield City Art Galleries
Mr Simon Wingfield Digby, Sherborne Castle
V. Siviter Smith & Co. Ltd.
The Tate Gallery
Arthur Tooth & Sons
United Artists
Victoria and Albert Museum
Wadsworth Atheneum, Hartford
Walker Art Gallery, Liverpool
Warburg Institute, University of London
Weidenfeld and Nicolson
Wolverhampton Art Galleries and Museums